THE BOOK OF MORMON

ANOTHER TESTAMENT OF JESUS CHRIST

Journal Edition

SALT LAKE CITY, UTAH

First English edition published in Palmyra, New York, in 1830.

ISBN 978-1-62972-975-6 (3-pc hardbound)

Printed in China
RR Donnelley, Shenzhen, China

10 9 8 7 6 5 4 3 2 1

THE

BOOK OF MORMON

AN ACCOUNT WRITTEN BY

THE HAND OF MORMON

UPON PLATES

TAKEN FROM THE PLATES OF NEPHI

Wherefore, it is an abridgment of the record of the people of Nephi, and also of the Lamanites—Written to the Lamanites, who are a remnant of the house of Israel; and also to Jew and Gentile—Written by way of commandment, and also by the spirit of prophecy and of revelation—Written and sealed up, and hid up unto the Lord, that they might not be destroyed—To come forth by the gift and power of God unto the interpretation thereof—Sealed by the hand of Moroni, and hid up unto the Lord, to come forth in due time by way of the Gentile—The interpretation thereof by the gift of God.

An abridgment taken from the Book of Ether also, which is a record of the people of Jared, who were scattered at the time the Lord confounded the language of the people, when they were building a tower to get to heaven—Which is to show unto the remnant of the house of Israel what great things the Lord hath done for their fathers; and that they may know the covenants of the Lord, that they are not cast off forever—And also to the convincing of the Jew and Gentile that JESUS is the CHRIST, the ETERNAL GOD, manifesting himself unto all nations—And now, if there are faults they are the mistakes of men; wherefore, condemn not the things of God, that ye may be found spotless at the judgment-seat of Christ.

TRANSLATED BY JOSEPH SMITH, JUN.

ABBREVIATIONS

Old Testament

Gen.	Genesis
Ex.	Exodus
Lev.	Leviticus
Num.	Numbers
Deut.	Deuteronomy
Josh.	Joshua
Judg.	Judges
Ruth	Ruth
1 Sam.	1 Samuel
2 Sam.	2 Samuel
1 Kgs.	1 Kings
2 Kgs.	2 Kings
1 Chr.	1 Chronicles
2 Chr.	2 Chronicles
Ezra	Ezra
Neh.	Nehemiah
Esth.	Esther
Job	Job
Ps.	Psalms
Prov.	Proverbs
Eccl.	Ecclesiastes
Song	Song of Solomon
Isa.	Isaiah
Jer.	Jeremiah
Lam.	Lamentations
Ezek.	Ezekiel
Dan.	Daniel
Hosea	Hosea
Joel	Joel
Amos	Amos
Obad.	Obadiah
Jonah	Jonah
Micah	Micah
Nahum	Nahum
Hab.	Habakkuk
Zeph.	Zephaniah
Hag.	Haggai
Zech.	Zechariah
Mal.	Malachi

New Testament

Matt.	Matthew
Mark	Mark
Luke	Luke
John	John
Acts	Acts
Rom.	Romans
1 Cor.	1 Corinthians
2 Cor.	2 Corinthians
Gal.	Galatians
Eph.	Ephesians
Philip.	Philippians
Col.	Colossians
1 Thes.	1 Thessalonians
2 Thes.	2 Thessalonians
1 Tim.	1 Timothy
2 Tim.	2 Timothy
Titus	Titus
Philem.	Philemon
Heb.	Hebrews
James	James
1 Pet.	1 Peter
2 Pet.	2 Peter
1 Jn.	1 John
2 Jn.	2 John
3 Jn.	3 John
Jude	Jude
Rev.	Revelation

Book of Mormon

1 Ne.	1 Nephi
2 Ne.	2 Nephi
Jacob	Jacob
Enos	Enos
Jarom	Jarom
Omni	Omni
W of M	Words of Mormon
Mosiah	Mosiah
Alma	Alma
Hel.	Helaman
3 Ne.	3 Nephi
4 Ne.	4 Nephi
Morm.	Mormon
Ether	Ether
Moro.	Moroni

Doctrine and Covenants

D&C	Doctrine and Covenants
OD	Official Declaration

Pearl of Great Price

Moses	Moses
Abr.	Abraham
JS—M	Joseph Smith—Matthew
JS—H	Joseph Smith—History
A of F	Articles of Faith

Other Abbreviations and Explanations

JST	Joseph Smith Translation
TG	Topical Guide
BD	Bible Dictionary
HEB	An alternate translation from the Hebrew
GR	An alternate translation from the Greek
IE	An explanation of idioms and difficult wording
OR	Alternate words that clarify the meaning of an archaic expression

CONTENTS

INTRODUCTION

The Book of Mormon is a volume of holy scripture comparable to the Bible. It is a record of God's dealings with ancient inhabitants of the Americas and contains the fulness of the everlasting gospel.

The book was written by many ancient prophets by the spirit of prophecy and revelation. Their words, written on gold plates, were quoted and abridged by a prophet-historian named Mormon. The record gives an account of two great civilizations. One came from Jerusalem in 600 B.C. and afterward separated into two nations, known as the Nephites and the Lamanites. The other came much earlier when the Lord confounded the tongues at the Tower of Babel. This group is known as the Jaredites. After thousands of years, all were destroyed except the Lamanites, and they are among the ancestors of the American Indians.

The crowning event recorded in the Book of Mormon is the personal ministry of the Lord Jesus Christ among the Nephites soon after His resurrection. It puts forth the doctrines of the gospel, outlines the plan of salvation, and tells men what they must do to gain peace in this life and eternal salvation in the life to come.

After Mormon completed his writings, he delivered the account to his son Moroni, who added a few words of his own and hid up the plates in the Hill Cumorah. On September 21, 1823, the same Moroni, then a glorified, resurrected being, appeared to the Prophet Joseph Smith and instructed him relative to the ancient record and its destined translation into the English language.

In due course the plates were delivered to Joseph Smith, who translated them by the gift and power of God. The record is now published in many languages as a new and additional witness that Jesus Christ is the Son of the living God and that all who will come unto Him and obey the laws and ordinances of His gospel may be saved.

Concerning this record the Prophet Joseph Smith said: "I told the brethren that the Book of Mormon was the most correct of any book on earth, and the keystone of our religion, and a man would get nearer to God by abiding by its precepts, than by any other book."

In addition to Joseph Smith, the Lord provided for eleven others to see the gold plates for themselves and to be special witnesses of the truth and divinity of the Book of Mormon. Their written testimonies are included herewith as "The Testimony of Three Witnesses" and "The Testimony of Eight Witnesses."

We invite all men everywhere to read the Book of Mormon, to ponder in their hearts the message it contains, and then to ask God, the Eternal Father, in the name of Christ if the book is true. Those who pursue this course and ask in faith will gain a testimony of its truth and divinity by the power of the Holy Ghost. (See Moroni 10:3–5.)

Those who gain this divine witness from the Holy Spirit will also come to know by the same power that Jesus Christ is the Savior of the world, that Joseph Smith is His revelator and prophet in these last days, and that The Church of Jesus Christ of Latter-day Saints is the Lord's kingdom once again established on the earth, preparatory to the Second Coming of the Messiah.

THE TESTIMONY OF THREE WITNESSES

Be it known unto all nations, kindreds, tongues, and people, unto whom this work shall come: That we, through the grace of God the Father, and our Lord Jesus Christ, have seen the plates which contain this record, which is a record of the people of Nephi, and also of the Lamanites, their brethren, and also of the people of Jared, who came from the tower of which hath been spoken. And we also know that they have been translated by the gift and power of God, for his voice hath declared it unto us; wherefore we know of a surety that the work is true. And we also testify that we have seen the engravings which are upon the plates; and they have been shown unto us by the power of God, and not of man. And we declare with words of soberness, that an angel of God came down from heaven, and he brought and laid before our eyes, that we beheld and saw the plates, and the engravings thereon; and we know that it is by the grace of God the Father, and our Lord Jesus Christ, that we beheld and bear record that these things are true. And it is marvelous in our eyes. Nevertheless, the voice of the Lord commanded us that we should bear record of it; wherefore, to be obedient unto the commandments of God, we bear testimony of these things. And we know that if we are faithful in Christ, we shall rid our garments of the blood of all men, and be found spotless before the judgment-seat of Christ, and shall dwell with him eternally in the heavens. And the honor be to the Father, and to the Son, and to the Holy Ghost, which is one God. Amen.

Oliver Cowdery
David Whitmer
Martin Harris

THE TESTIMONY OF EIGHT WITNESSES

Be it known unto all nations, kindreds, tongues, and people, unto whom this work shall come: That Joseph Smith, Jun., the translator of this work, has shown unto us the plates of which hath been spoken, which have the appearance of gold; and as many of the leaves as the said Smith has translated we did handle with our hands; and we also saw the engravings thereon, all of which has the appearance of ancient work, and of curious workmanship. And this we bear record with words of soberness, that the said Smith has shown unto us, for we have seen and hefted, and know of a surety that the said Smith has got the plates of which we have spoken. And we give our names unto the world, to witness unto the world that which we have seen. And we lie not, God bearing witness of it.

Christian Whitmer
Jacob Whitmer
Peter Whitmer, Jun.
John Whitmer
Hiram Page
Joseph Smith, Sen.
Hyrum Smith
Samuel H. Smith

THE TESTIMONY OF THE PROPHET JOSEPH SMITH

The Prophet Joseph Smith's own words about the coming forth of the Book of Mormon are:

"On the evening of the . . . twenty-first of September [1823] . . . I betook myself to prayer and supplication to Almighty God. . . .

"While I was thus in the act of calling upon God, I discovered a light appearing in my room, which continued to increase until the room was lighter than at noonday, when immediately a personage appeared at my bedside, standing in the air, for his feet did not touch the floor.

"He had on a loose robe of most exquisite whiteness. It was a whiteness beyond anything earthly I had ever seen; nor do I believe that any earthly thing could be made to appear so exceedingly white and brilliant. His hands were naked, and his arms also, a little above the wrist; so, also, were his feet naked, as were his legs, a little above the ankles. His head and neck were also bare. I could discover that he had no other clothing on but this robe, as it was open, so that I could see into his bosom.

"Not only was his robe exceedingly white, but his whole person was glorious beyond description, and his countenance truly like lightning. The room was exceedingly light, but not so very bright as immediately around his person. When I first looked upon him, I was afraid; but the fear soon left me.

"He called me by name, and said unto me that he was a messenger sent from the presence of God to me, and that his name was Moroni; that God had a work for me to do; and that my name should be had for good and evil among all nations, kindreds, and tongues, or that it should be both good and evil spoken of among all people.

"He said there was a book deposited, written upon gold plates, giving an account of the former inhabitants of this continent, and the source from whence they sprang. He also said that the fulness of the everlasting Gospel was contained in it, as delivered by the Savior to the ancient inhabitants;

"Also, that there were two stones in silver bows—and these stones, fastened to a breastplate, constituted what is called the Urim and Thummim—deposited with the plates; and the possession and use of these stones were what constituted 'seers' in ancient or former times; and that God had prepared them for the purpose of translating the book. . . .

"Again, he told me, that when I got those plates of which he had spoken—for the time that they should be obtained was not yet fulfilled—I should not show them to any person; neither the breastplate with the Urim and Thummim; only to those to whom I should be commanded to show them; if I did I should be destroyed. While he was conversing with me about the plates, the vision was opened to my mind that I could see the place where the plates were deposited, and that so clearly and distinctly that I knew the place again when I visited it.

"After this communication, I saw the light in the room begin to gather immediately around the person of him who had been speaking to me, and it continued to do so until the room was again left dark, except just around him; when, instantly I saw, as it were, a conduit open right up into heaven, and he ascended till he entirely disappeared, and the room was left as it had been before this heavenly light had made its appearance.

"I lay musing on the singularity of the scene, and marveling greatly at what had been told to me by this extraordinary messenger; when, in the midst of my meditation, I suddenly discovered that my room was again beginning to get lighted, and in an instant, as it were, the same heavenly messenger was again by my bedside.

"He commenced, and again related the very same things which he had done at his first visit, without the least variation; which having done, he informed me of great judgments which were coming upon the earth, with great desolations by famine, sword, and pestilence; and that these grievous judgments would come on the earth in this generation. Having related these things, he again ascended as he had done before.

"By this time, so deep were the impressions made on my mind, that sleep had fled from my eyes, and I lay overwhelmed in astonishment at what I had both seen and heard. But what was my surprise when again I beheld the same messenger at my bedside, and heard him rehearse or repeat over again to me the same things as before; and added a caution to me, telling me that Satan would try to tempt me (in consequence of the indigent circumstances of my father's family), to get the plates for the purpose of getting rich. This he forbade me, saying that I must have no other object in view in getting the plates but to glorify God, and must not be influenced by any other motive than that of building his kingdom; otherwise I could not get them.

"After this third visit, he again ascended into heaven as before, and I was again left to ponder on the strangeness of what I had just experienced; when almost immediately after the heavenly messenger had ascended from me for the third time, the cock crowed, and I found that day was approaching, so that our interviews must have occupied the whole of that night.

"I shortly after arose from my bed, and, as usual, went to the necessary labors of the day; but, in attempting to work as at other times, I found my strength so exhausted as to render me entirely unable. My father, who was laboring along with me, discovered something to be wrong with me, and told me to go home. I started with the intention of going to the house; but, in attempting to cross the fence out of the field where we were, my strength entirely failed me, and I fell helpless on the ground, and for a time was quite unconscious of anything.

"The first thing that I can recollect was a voice speaking unto me, calling me by name. I looked up, and beheld the same messenger standing over my head, surrounded by light as before. He then again related unto me all that he had related to me the previous night, and commanded me to go to my father and tell him of the vision and commandments which I had received.

"I obeyed; I returned to my father in the field, and rehearsed the whole matter to him. He replied to me that it was of God, and told me to go and do as commanded by the messenger. I left the field, and went to the place where the messenger had told me the plates were deposited; and owing to the distinctness of the vision which I had had concerning it, I knew the place the instant that I arrived there.

"Convenient to the village of Manchester, Ontario county, New York, stands a hill of considerable size, and the most elevated of any in the neighborhood. On the west side of this hill, not far from the top, under a stone of considerable size, lay the plates, deposited in a stone box. This stone was thick and rounding in the middle on the upper side, and thinner towards the edges, so that the middle part of it was visible above the ground, but the edge all around was covered with earth.

"Having removed the earth, I obtained a lever, which I got fixed under the edge of the stone, and with a little exertion raised it up. I looked in, and there indeed did I behold the plates, the Urim and Thummim, and the breastplate, as stated by the messenger. The box in which they lay was formed by laying stones together in some kind of cement. In the bottom of the box were laid two stones crossways of the box, and on these stones lay the plates and the other things with them.

"I made an attempt to take them out, but was forbidden by the messenger, and was again informed that the time for bringing them forth had not yet arrived, neither would it, until four years from that time; but he told me that I should come to that place precisely in one year from that time, and that he would there meet with me, and that I should continue to do so until the time should come for obtaining the plates.

"Accordingly, as I had been commanded, I went at the end of each year, and at each time I found the same messenger there, and received instruction and intelligence from him at each of our interviews, respecting what the Lord was going to do, and how and in what manner his kingdom was to be conducted in the last days. . . .

"At length the time arrived for obtaining the plates, the Urim and Thummim, and the breastplate. On the twenty-second day of September, one thousand eight hundred and twenty-seven, having gone as usual at the end of another year to the place where they were deposited, the same heavenly messenger delivered them up to me with this charge: that I should be responsible for them; that if I should let them go carelessly, or through any neglect of mine, I should be cut off; but that if I would use all my endeavors to preserve them, until he, the messenger, should call for them, they should be protected.

"I soon found out the reason why I had received such strict charges to keep them safe, and why it was that the messenger had said that when I had done what was required at my hand, he would call for them. For no sooner was it known that I had them, than the most strenuous exertions were used to get them from me. Every stratagem that could be invented was resorted to for that purpose. The persecution became more bitter and severe than before, and multitudes were on the alert continually to get them from me if possible. But by the wisdom of God, they remained safe in my hands, until I had accomplished by them what was required at my hand. When, according to arrangements, the messenger called for them, I delivered them up to him; and he has them in his charge until this day, being the second day of May, one thousand eight hundred and thirty-eight."

For a more complete account, see Joseph Smith—History in the Pearl of Great Price.

The ancient record thus brought forth from the earth as the voice of a people speaking from the dust, and translated into modern speech by the gift and power of God as attested by Divine affirmation, was first published to the world in the year 1830 as THE BOOK OF MORMON.

A BRIEF EXPLANATION ABOUT THE BOOK OF MORMON

The Book of Mormon is a sacred record of peoples in ancient America and was engraved upon metal plates. Sources from which this record was compiled include the following:

1. *The Plates of Nephi,* which were of two kinds: the small plates and the large plates. The former were more particularly devoted to spiritual matters and the ministry and teachings of the prophets, while the latter were occupied mostly by a secular history of the peoples concerned (1 Nephi 9:2–4). From the time of Mosiah, however, the large plates also included items of major spiritual importance.
2. *The Plates of Mormon,* which consist of an abridgment by Mormon from the large plates of Nephi, with many commentaries. These plates also contained a continuation of the history by Mormon and additions by his son Moroni.
3. *The Plates of Ether,* which present a history of the Jaredites. This record was abridged by Moroni, who inserted comments of his own and incorporated the record with the general history under the title "Book of Ether."
4. *The Plates of Brass* brought by the people of Lehi from Jerusalem in 600 B.C. These contained "the five books of Moses, . . . and also a record of the Jews from the beginning, . . . down to the commencement of the reign of Zedekiah, king of Judah; and also the prophecies of the holy prophets" (1 Nephi 5:11–13). Many quotations from these plates, citing Isaiah and other biblical and nonbiblical prophets, appear in the Book of Mormon.

The Book of Mormon comprises fifteen main parts or divisions, known, with one exception, as books, usually designated by the name of their principal author. The first portion (the first six books, ending with Omni) is a translation from the small plates of Nephi. Between the books of Omni and Mosiah is an insert called the Words of Mormon. This insert connects the record engraved on the small plates with Mormon's abridgment of the large plates.

The longest portion, from Mosiah through Mormon chapter 7, is a translation of Mormon's abridgment of the large plates of Nephi. The concluding portion, from Mormon chapter 8 to the end of the volume, was engraved by Mormon's son Moroni, who, after finishing the record of his father's life, made an abridgment of the Jaredite record (as the book of Ether) and later added the parts known as the book of Moroni.

In or about the year A.D. 421, Moroni, the last of the Nephite prophet-historians, sealed the sacred record and hid it up unto the Lord, to be brought forth in the latter days, as predicted by the voice of God through His ancient prophets. In A.D. 1823, this same Moroni, then a resurrected personage, visited the Prophet Joseph Smith and subsequently delivered the engraved plates to him.

About this edition: The original title page, immediately preceding the contents page, is taken from the plates and is part of the sacred text. Introductions in a non-italic typeface, such as in 1 Nephi and immediately preceding Mosiah chapter 9, are also part of the sacred text. Introductions in italics, such as in chapter headings, are not original to the text but are study helps included for convenience in reading.

Some minor errors in the text have been perpetuated in past editions of the Book of Mormon. This edition contains corrections that seem appropriate to bring the material into conformity with prepublication manuscripts and early editions edited by the Prophet Joseph Smith.

THE FIRST BOOK OF NEPHI

HIS REIGN AND MINISTRY

An account of Lehi and his wife Sariah, and his four sons, being called, (beginning at the eldest) Laman, Lemuel, Sam, and Nephi. The Lord warns Lehi to depart out of the land of Jerusalem, because he prophesieth unto the people concerning their iniquity and they seek to destroy his life. He taketh three days' journey into the wilderness with his family. Nephi taketh his brethren and returneth to the land of Jerusalem after the record of the Jews. The account of their sufferings. They take the daughters of Ishmael to wife. They take their families and depart into the wilderness. Their sufferings and afflictions in the wilderness. The course of their travels. They come to the large waters. Nephi's brethren rebel against him. He confoundeth them, and buildeth a ship. They call the name of the place Bountiful. They cross the large waters into the promised land, and so forth. This is according to the account of Nephi; or in other words, I, Nephi, wrote this record.

CHAPTER 1

Nephi begins the record of his people—Lehi sees in vision a pillar of fire and reads from a book of prophecy—He praises God, foretells the coming of the Messiah, and prophesies the destruction of Jerusalem—He is persecuted by the Jews. About 600 B.C.

I, NEPHI, having been [a]born
of [b]goodly [c]parents, therefore I
was [d]taught somewhat in all the
learning of my father; and having
seen many [e]afflictions in the course
of my days, nevertheless, having
been highly favored of the Lord in all
my days; yea, having had a great
knowledge of the goodness and
the mysteries of God, therefore I
make a [f]record of my proceedings
in my days.

2 Yea, I make a record in the [a]lan-
guage of my father, which consists
of the learning of the Jews and the
language of the Egyptians.

3 And I know that the record which
I make is [a]true; and I make it with
mine own hand; and I make it according to my knowledge.

4 For it came to pass in the commencement of the [a]first year of the
reign of [b]Zedekiah, king of Judah,
(my father, Lehi, having dwelt at
[c]Jerusalem in all his days); and in
that same year there came many
[d]prophets, prophesying unto the
people that they must [e]repent, or
the great city [f]Jerusalem must be
destroyed.

5 Wherefore it came to pass that
my father, Lehi, as he went forth
prayed unto the Lord, yea, even

---

1 1*a* TG Birthright.
b Prov. 22:1.
c Mosiah 1:2 (2–3); D&C 68:25 (25, 28). TG Honoring Father and Mother.
d Enos 1:1. TG Education; Family, Children, Responsibilities toward; Family, Love within.
e TG Affliction; Blessing; God, Gifts of.
f TG Record Keeping; Scriptures, Writing of.
2*a* Mosiah 1:4; Morm. 9:32 (32–33).
3*a* 1 Ne. 14:30; 2 Ne. 25:20; Mosiah 1:6; Alma 3:12; Ether 5:3 (1–3).
4*a* 1 Ne. 2:4; Mosiah 6:4.
b 2 Kgs. 24:18; 2 Chr. 36:10; Jer. 37:1; 44:30; 49:34; 52:3 (3–5); Omni 1:15.
c 1 Chr. 9:3; 2 Chr. 15:9; Alma 7:10.
d 2 Kgs. 17:13 (13–15); 2 Chr. 36:15 (15–16); Jer. 7:25; 26:20. TG Prophets, Mission of.
e TG Repent.
f Jer. 26:18 (17–19); 2 Ne. 1:4; Hel. 8:20. TG Israel, Bondage of, in Other Lands; Jerusalem.

with all his [a]heart, in behalf of his
people.
6 And it came to pass as he prayed
unto the Lord, there came a [a]pillar
of fire and dwelt upon a rock before
him; and he saw and heard much;
and because of the things which he
saw and heard he did [b]quake and
tremble exceedingly.
7 And it came to pass that he returned to his own house at Jerusalem; and he cast himself upon
his bed, being [a]overcome with the
Spirit and the things which he had
seen.
8 And being thus overcome with
the Spirit, he was carried away
in a [a]vision, even that he saw the
[b]heavens open, and he thought he
[c]saw God sitting upon his throne,
surrounded with numberless concourses of angels in the attitude
of singing and praising their God.
9 And it came to pass that he saw
One descending out of the midst
of heaven, and he beheld that his
[a]luster was above that of the sun
at noon-day.
10 And he also saw [a]twelve others
following him, and their brightness
did exceed that of the stars in the
firmament.
11 And they came down and went
forth upon the face of the earth; and
the first came and [a]stood before my
father, and gave unto him a [b]book,
and bade him that he should read.
12 And it came to pass that as he
read, he was filled with the [a]Spirit
of the Lord.
13 And he read, saying: Wo, wo,
unto Jerusalem, for I have seen
thine [a]abominations! Yea, and many
things did my father read concerning [b]Jerusalem—that it should be
destroyed, and the inhabitants
thereof; many should perish by the
sword, and many should be [c]carried
away captive into Babylon.
14 And it came to pass that when
my father had read and seen many
great and marvelous things, he did
exclaim many things unto the Lord;
such as: Great and marvelous are
thy works, O Lord God Almighty!
Thy throne is high in the heavens,
and thy [a]power, and goodness, and
mercy are over all the inhabitants
of the earth; and, because thou art
merciful, thou wilt not suffer those
who [b]come unto thee that they shall
perish!
15 And after this manner was
the language of my father in the
praising of his God; for his soul did
rejoice, and his whole heart was
filled, because of the things which
he had seen, yea, which the Lord
had shown unto him.
16 And now I, Nephi, do not make
a full account of the things which
my father hath written, for he hath
written many things which he saw
in [a]visions and in [b]dreams; and
he also hath written many things
which he [c]prophesied and spake

5*a* Jer. 29:13;
James 5:16;
2 Ne. 4:24 (23–25).
6*a* Ex. 13:21;
Hel. 5:24 (24, 43);
D&C 29:12;
JS—H 1:16, 30.
b Isa. 6:5 (1–5).
7*a* Dan. 8:27 (26–27);
10:8 (8–12);
1 Ne. 17:47;
Alma 27:17;
Moses 1:10 (9–10).
8*a* 1 Ne. 3:18 (17–18); 5:4.
TG Vision.
b Ezek. 1:1;
Acts 7:56 (55–56);
1 Ne. 11:14;
Alma 36:22;
Hel. 5:48 (45–49);
D&C 137:1.
c TG God, Manifestations of;
God, Privilege of Seeing.
9*a* JS—H 1:17 (16–17),
30 (30–32).
10*a* TG Apostles.
11*a* 1 Sam. 3:10;
D&C 110:2 (2–3).
b Ezek. 2:9 (9–10);
Rev. 10:9 (2–11).
12*a* Gen. 41:38;
Mosiah 27:24;
Alma 18:16.
13*a* 2 Kgs. 24:19;
2 Chr. 36:14;
Jer. 13:27.
b 2 Kgs. 23:27; 24:2;
Jer. 13:14;
Ezek. 15:6 (6–8);
1 Ne. 2:13; 3:17.
c 2 Kgs. 20:17 (17–18);
Jer. 52:15 (3–15);
2 Ne. 25:10;
Omni 1:15.
TG Babylon.
14*a* TG God, Power of.
b 2 Ne. 26:25 (24–28);
Alma 5:34 (33–36);
3 Ne. 9:14 (13–14).
16*a* Ezek. 1:1;
JS—H 1:24 (21–25).
b 1 Ne. 8:2 (2–38).
c 1 Ne. 7:1.

unto his children, of which I shall not make a full account.

17 But I shall make an account of my proceedings in my days. Behold, I make an [a]abridgment of the record of my [b]father, upon [c]plates which I have made with mine own hands; wherefore, after I have abridged the record of my [d]father then will I make an account of mine own life.

18 Therefore, I would that ye should know, that after the Lord had shown so many marvelous things unto my father, Lehi, yea, concerning the [a]destruction of Jerusalem, behold he went forth among the people, and began to [b]prophesy and to declare unto them concerning the things which he had both seen and heard.

19 And it came to pass that the [a]Jews did [b]mock him because of the things which he testified of them; for he truly testified of their [c]wickedness and their abominations; and he testified that the things which he saw and heard, and also the things which he read in the book, manifested plainly of the coming of a [d]Messiah, and also the redemption of the world.

20 And when the Jews heard these things they were angry with him; yea, even as with the prophets of old, whom they had [a]cast out, and stoned, and slain; and they also [b]sought his life, that they might take it away. But behold, I, Nephi, will show unto you that the tender [c]mercies of the Lord are over all those whom he hath chosen, because of their faith, to make them mighty even unto the power of [d]deliverance.

CHAPTER 2

Lehi takes his family into the wilderness by the Red Sea—They leave their property—Lehi offers a sacrifice to the Lord and teaches his sons to keep the commandments—Laman and Lemuel murmur against their father—Nephi is obedient and prays in faith; the Lord speaks to him, and he is chosen to rule over his brethren. About 600 B.C.

FOR behold, it came to pass that the Lord spake unto my father, yea, even in a dream, and said unto him: Blessed art thou Lehi, because of the things which thou hast done; and because thou hast been faithful and declared unto this people the things which I commanded thee, behold, they seek to [a]take away thy [b]life.

2 And it came to pass that the Lord [a]commanded my father, even in a [b]dream, that he should [c]take his family and depart into the wilderness.

3 And it came to pass that he was [a]obedient unto the word of the Lord, wherefore he did as the Lord commanded him.

4 And it came to pass that he departed into the wilderness. And he left his house, and the land of his inheritance, and his gold, and his silver, and his precious things, and took nothing with him, save it

---

17*a* 1 Ne. 9:2 (2–5); Enos 1:13 (13, 15–18). TG Scriptures, Writing of.
b 1 Ne. 6:1 (1–3); 8:29 (29–30); 19:1 (1–6).
c 1 Ne. 10:15.
d 2 Ne. 4:14; 5:33 (29–33); D&C 10:42.
18*a* 2 Ne. 25:9; D&C 5:20.
b TG Prophets, Mission of; Prophets, Rejection of.
19*a* TG Apostasy of Israel.
b 2 Chr. 36:16; Jer. 25:4 (1–4); Ezek. 5:6; 1 Ne. 2:13; 7:14.
c 1 Ne. 17:22.
d TG Jesus Christ, Prophecies about.
20*a* Jer. 13:11; Hel. 13:24 (24–28).
b Jer. 11:19; 1 Ne. 2:2 (1–4). TG Prophets, Rejection of.
c Gen. 32:10; Alma 34:38; D&C 46:15.
d TG Deliver.
2 1*a* TG Persecution.
b 1 Ne. 7:14.
2*a* 1 Ne. 3:16; 4:34; 5:8; 17:44; Mosiah 7:20; Alma 9:9. TG Called of God.
b TG Dream.
c Gen. 12:1; 19:12; 1 Ne. 1:20 (18–20); 2 Ne. 10:20; Ether 1:42; Abr. 2:3. TG Protection, Divine.
3*a* TG Commitment.

were his family, and provisions, and tents, and [a]departed into the wilderness.
5 And he came down by the borders near the shore of the [a]Red Sea; and he traveled in the wilderness in the borders which are nearer the Red Sea; and he did travel in the wilderness with his family, which consisted of my mother, Sariah, and my elder brothers, who were Laman, Lemuel, and Sam.
6 And it came to pass that when he had traveled three days in the wilderness, he pitched his tent in a [a]valley by the side of a [b]river of water.
7 And it came to pass that he built an [a]altar of [b]stones, and made an [c]offering unto the Lord, and gave [d]thanks unto the Lord our God.
8 And it came to pass that he called the name of the river, Laman, and it emptied into the Red Sea; and the valley was in the borders near the mouth thereof.
9 And when my father saw that the waters of the river emptied into the [a]fountain of the Red Sea, he spake unto Laman, saying: O that thou mightest be like unto this river, continually running into the fountain of all righteousness!
10 And he also spake unto Lemuel: O that thou mightest be like unto this valley, [a]firm and [b]steadfast, and immovable in keeping the commandments of the Lord!
11 Now this he spake because of the [a]stiffneckedness of Laman and Lemuel; for behold they did [b]murmur in many things against their [c]father, because he was a [d]visionary man, and had led them out of the land of Jerusalem, to leave the land of their inheritance, and their gold, and their silver, and their precious things, to perish in the wilderness. And this they said he had done because of the foolish imaginations of his heart.
12 And thus Laman and Lemuel, being the eldest, did murmur against their [a]father. And they did [b]murmur because they [c]knew not the dealings of that God who had [d]created them.
13 Neither did they [a]believe that Jerusalem, that great city, could be [b]destroyed according to the words of the prophets. And they were like unto the Jews who were at Jerusalem, who sought to take away the life of my father.
14 And it came to pass that my father did speak unto them in the [a]valley of Lemuel, with [b]power, being filled with the Spirit, until their frames did [c]shake before him. And he did confound them, that they durst not utter against him; wherefore, they did as he commanded them.
15 And my father dwelt in a [a]tent.
16 And it came to pass that I, Nephi, being exceedingly young, nevertheless being large in stature, and also having great desires to know of the [a]mysteries of God,

4*a* 1 Ne. 10:4; 19:8.
5*a* 1 Ne. 16:14; D&C 17:1.
6*a* 1 Ne. 9:1.
b Joel 1:20.
7*a* Gen. 12:7 (7–8); 26:25; Ex. 24:4; Abr. 2:17.
b Ex. 20:25; Deut. 27:5 (5–6); Josh. 8:31 (30–31).
c TG Sacrifice.
d TG Thanksgiving.
9*a* IE fount, or source, like the Gulf of Akaba, which empties into the Red Sea.
10*a* IE like Ezion-geber, the Hebrew roots of which denote firmness and strength, or might of a man.
b TG Dependability.
11*a* TG Stiffnecked.
b 1 Ne. 17:17. TG Murmuring.
c Prov. 20:20.
d 1 Ne. 5:4 (2–4); 17:20.
12*a* Lam. 4:16 (16–17).
b 1 Sam. 3:13; Mosiah 27:8 (7–37); Moses 5:16.
c Moses 4:6.
d Deut. 32:6; D&C 43:23. TG Man, Physical Creation of.
13*a* Ezek. 5:6; 1 Ne. 1:19 (18–20).
b Jer. 13:14; 1 Ne. 1:13 (4–13).
14*a* 1 Ne. 9:1; 16:6 (6, 12).
b TG Priesthood, Power of.
c 1 Ne. 17:45.
15*a* Gen. 12:8; 26:17 (17, 25); 31:25 (25, 33); 1 Ne. 4:38; 10:16.
16*a* TG Mysteries of Godliness.

wherefore, I did cry unto the Lord;
and behold he did [b]visit me, and
did [c]soften my heart that I did [d]be-
lieve all the words which had been
spoken by my [e]father; wherefore, I
did not [f]rebel against him like unto
my brothers.
17 And I spake unto Sam, making
known unto him the things which
the Lord had manifested unto me
by his Holy Spirit. And it came to
pass that he believed in my words.
18 But, behold, Laman and Lemuel
would not hearken unto my words;
and being [a]grieved because of the
hardness of their hearts I cried unto
the Lord for them.
19 And it came to pass that the
Lord spake unto me, saying: Blessed
art thou, Nephi, because of thy
[a]faith, for thou hast sought me
diligently, with lowliness of heart.
20 And inasmuch as ye shall keep
my commandments, ye shall [a]pros-
per, and shall be led to a [b]land of
promise; yea, even a land which I
have prepared for you; yea, a land
which is choice above all other
lands.
21 And inasmuch as thy brethren
shall rebel against thee, they shall
be [a]cut off from the presence of
the Lord.
22 And inasmuch as thou shalt
keep my commandments, thou
shalt be made a [a]ruler and a teacher
over thy brethren.
23 For behold, in that day that
they shall [a]rebel against me, I will
[b]curse them even with a sore curse,
and they shall have no power over
thy seed except they shall [c]rebel
against me also.
24 And if it so be that they rebel
against me, they shall be a [a]scourge
unto thy seed, to [b]stir them up in
the ways of remembrance.

CHAPTER 3

Lehi's sons return to Jerusalem to obtain the plates of brass—Laban refuses to give the plates up—Nephi exhorts and encourages his brethren—Laban steals their property and attempts to slay them—Laman and Lemuel smite Nephi and Sam and are reproved by an angel. About 600–592 B.C.

AND it came to pass that I, Nephi,
returned from [a]speaking with the
Lord, to the tent of my father.
2 And it came to pass that he spake
unto me, saying: Behold I have
dreamed a [a]dream, in the which
the Lord hath commanded me that
thou and thy brethren shall [b]return
to Jerusalem.
3 For behold, Laban hath the
record of the Jews and also a [a]ge-
nealogy of my forefathers, and
they are [b]engraven upon plates of
brass.
4 Wherefore, the Lord hath commanded me that thou and thy
brothers should go unto the house
of Laban, and seek the records, and
bring them down hither into the
wilderness.
5 And now, behold thy brothers
murmur, saying it is a hard thing
which I have required of them; but
behold I have not required it of

16*b* Ps. 8:4; 1 Ne. 3:1; 19:11; Alma 17:10; D&C 5:16. TG Guidance, Divine.
c 1 Kgs. 18:37; Alma 5:7.
d 1 Ne. 11:5.
e TG Honoring Father and Mother.
f TG Family, Love within.
18*a* Alma 31:24; 3 Ne. 7:16.
19*a* 1 Ne. 7:12 (9–13); 15:11.
20*a* Josh. 1:7; 1 Ne. 4:14; Mosiah 1:7.
b Deut. 33:13 (13–16); 1 Chr. 28:8 (7–8); 1 Ne. 5:5 (5, 22); 7:13; Moses 7:17 (17–18). TG Promised Lands.
21*a* Josh. 23:13; 2 Ne. 5:20 (20–24); Alma 9:14 (13–15); 38:1.
22*a* Gen. 37:8 (8–11); 1 Ne. 3:29. TG Authority.
23*a* Job 24:13.
b Deut. 11:28; 1 Ne. 12:22 (22–23); D&C 41:1. TG Curse.
c Josh. 22:16; Mosiah 15:26.
24*a* Josh. 23:13; Judg. 2:22 (22–23).
b 2 Ne. 5:25.
3 1*a* 1 Ne. 2:16.
2*a* TG Dream.
b 1 Ne. 2:4 (1–5); 7:3.
3*a* 1 Ne. 3:12; 5:14.
b Jer. 17:1; 1 Ne. 3:24 (12, 19–24).

them, but it is a commandment of
the Lord.
6 Therefore go, my son, and thou
shalt be favored of the Lord, because
thou hast [a]not [b]murmured.
7 And it came to pass that I, Nephi,
said unto my father: I [a]will go and
do the things which the Lord hath
commanded, for I know that the
Lord giveth no [b]commandments
unto the children of men, save he
shall [c]prepare a way for them that
they may accomplish the thing
which he commandeth them.
8 And it came to pass that when
my father had heard these words he
was exceedingly glad, for he knew
that I had been blessed of the Lord.
9 And I, Nephi, and my brethren
took our journey in the wilderness,
with our tents, to go up to the land
of Jerusalem.
10 And it came to pass that when
we had gone up to the land of Jerusalem, I and my brethren did
consult one with another.
11 And we [a]cast lots—who of us
should go in unto the house of Laban.
And it came to pass that the lot fell
upon Laman; and Laman went in
unto the house of Laban, and he
talked with him as he sat in his
house.
12 And he desired of Laban the
records which were engraven upon
the plates of brass, which contained
the [a]genealogy of my father.
13 And behold, it came to pass
that Laban was angry, and thrust
him out from his presence; and he
would not that he should have the
records. Wherefore, he said unto
him: Behold thou art a robber, and
I will slay thee.
14 But Laman fled out of his presence, and told the things which Laban had done, unto us. And we began
to be exceedingly sorrowful, and
my brethren were about to return
unto my father in the wilderness.
15 But behold I said unto them
that: [a]As the Lord liveth, and as we
live, we will not go down unto our
father in the wilderness until we
have [b]accomplished the thing which
the Lord hath commanded us.
16 Wherefore, let us be faithful
in keeping the commandments of
the Lord; therefore let us go down
to the land of our father's [a]inheri-
tance, for behold he left gold and
silver, and all manner of riches.
And all this he hath done because
of the [b]commandments of the Lord.
17 For he knew that Jerusalem
must be [a]destroyed, because of the
wickedness of the people.
18 For behold, they have [a]rejected
the words of the prophets. Wherefore, if my father should dwell in the
land after he hath been [b]commanded
to flee out of the land, behold, he
would also perish. Wherefore, it
must needs be that he flee out of
the land.
19 And behold, it is wisdom in
God that we should obtain these
[a]records, that we may preserve
unto our children the language of
our fathers;
20 And also that we may [a]preserve
unto them the words which have
been spoken by the mouth of all
the holy [b]prophets, which have
been delivered unto them by the
Spirit and power of God, since the
world began, even down unto this
present time.

6a TG Sustaining Church Leaders.
b TG Murmuring.
7a 1 Sam. 17:32; 1 Kgs. 17:15 (11–15). TG Faith; Loyalty; Obedience.
b TG Commandments of God.
c Gen. 18:14; Philip. 4:13; 1 Ne. 17:3, 50; D&C 5:34.
11a Neh. 10:34; Acts 1:26.
12a 1 Ne. 3:3; 5:14; Jarom 1:1.
15a TG Oath; Promise.
b TG Commitment; Dedication.
16a 1 Ne. 2:4.
b 1 Ne. 2:2; 4:34.
17a 2 Chr. 36:20 (16–20); Jer. 39:9 (1–9); 1 Ne. 1:13.
18a Jer. 26:23 (21–24). TG Prophets, Rejection of.
b 1 Ne. 5:21; 7:2; 16:8.
19a Omni 1:17; Mosiah 1:3 (2–6). TG Record Keeping.
20a TG Scriptures, Preservation of.
b Zech. 7:12; Matt. 11:13; Mosiah 15:13.

21 And it came to pass that after this manner of language did I [a]persuade my brethren, that they might be faithful in keeping the commandments of God.

22 And it came to pass that we went down to the land of our inheritance, and we did gather together our [a]gold, and our silver, and our precious things.

23 And after we had gathered these things together, we went up again unto the house of Laban.

24 And it came to pass that we went in unto Laban, and desired him that he would give unto us the records which were engraven upon the [a]plates of brass, for which we would give unto him our gold, and our silver, and all our precious things.

25 And it came to pass that when Laban saw our property, and that it was exceedingly great, he did [a]lust after it, insomuch that he thrust us out, and sent his servants to slay us, that he might obtain our property.

26 And [a]it came to pass that we did flee before the servants of Laban, and we were obliged to leave behind our property, and it fell into the hands of Laban.

27 And it came to pass that we fled into the wilderness, and the servants of Laban did not overtake us, and we [a]hid ourselves in the cavity of a rock.

28 And it came to pass that Laman was angry with me, and also with my father; and also was Lemuel, for he hearkened unto the words of Laman. Wherefore Laman and Lemuel did speak many [a]hard words unto us, their younger brothers, and they did smite us even with a rod.

29 And it came to pass as they smote us with a rod, behold, an [a]angel of the Lord came and stood before them, and he spake unto them, saying: Why do ye smite your younger brother with a rod? Know ye not that the Lord hath chosen him to be a [b]ruler over you, and this because of your iniquities? Behold ye shall go up to Jerusalem again, and the Lord will [c]deliver Laban into your hands.

30 And after the [a]angel had spoken unto us, he departed.

31 And after the angel had departed, Laman and Lemuel again began to [a]murmur, saying: How is it possible that the Lord will deliver Laban into our hands? Behold, he is a mighty man, and he can command fifty, yea, even he can slay fifty; then why not us?

CHAPTER 4

Nephi slays Laban at the Lord's command and then secures the plates of brass by stratagem—Zoram chooses to join Lehi's family in the wilderness. About 600–592 B.C.

AND it came to pass that I spake unto my brethren, saying: Let us go up again unto Jerusalem, and let us be [a]faithful in keeping the commandments of the Lord; for behold he is mightier than all the earth, then why not [b]mightier than Laban and his fifty, yea, or even than his tens of thousands?

2 Therefore let us go up; let us be [a]strong like unto Moses; for he truly spake unto the waters of the [b]Red Sea and they divided hither and thither, and our fathers came through, out of captivity, on dry ground, and the armies of Pharaoh

---

21*a* TG Family, Love within; Persuade.
22*a* 1 Ne. 2:4.
24*a* 1 Ne. 3:3; 4:24 (24, 38).
25*a* TG Covet.
26*a* 1 Ne. 4:11.
27*a* Josh. 10:16 (16–17); 1 Sam. 13:6; Jer. 36:26; Ether 13:13 (13, 22).
28*a* 1 Ne. 17:18.
29*a* 1 Ne. 4:3; 7:10. TG Angels.
b Gen. 41:43 (41–43); 1 Ne. 2:22.
c 2 Kgs. 3:18; 3 Ne. 3:21.
30*a* 1 Ne. 4:3; 16:38.
31*a* TG Murmuring.
4 1*a* TG Courage; Dependability; Faithful.
b 1 Ne. 7:11. TG God, Power of.
2*a* Deut. 11:8; Prov. 24:10 (10–12).
b Ex. 14:21 (18–30); Josh. 2:10; 1 Ne. 17:26; Mosiah 7:19.

did follow and were drowned in the waters of the Red Sea.

3 Now behold ye know that this is true; and ye also know that an [a]angel hath spoken unto you; wherefore can ye [b]doubt? Let us go up; the Lord is able to [c]deliver us, even as our fathers, and to destroy Laban, even as the Egyptians.

4 Now when I had spoken these words, they were yet wroth, and did still continue to murmur; nevertheless they did follow me up until we came without the walls of Jerusalem.

5 And it was by night; and I caused that they should hide themselves without the walls. And after they had hid themselves, I, Nephi, crept into the city and went forth towards the house of Laban.

6 And I was [a]led by the Spirit, not [b]knowing beforehand the things which I should do.

7 Nevertheless I went forth, and as I came near unto the house of Laban I beheld a man, and he had fallen to the earth before me, for he was [a]drunken with wine.

8 And when I came to him I found that it was Laban.

9 And I beheld his [a]sword, and I drew it forth from the sheath thereof; and the hilt thereof was of pure gold, and the workmanship thereof was exceedingly fine, and I saw that the blade thereof was of the most precious steel.

10 And it came to pass that I was [a]constrained by the Spirit that I should kill Laban; but I said in my heart: Never at any time have I shed the blood of man. And I shrunk and would that I might not slay him.

11 And the Spirit said unto me again: Behold the [a]Lord hath [b]delivered him into thy hands. Yea, and I also knew that he had sought to take away mine own life; yea, and he would not hearken unto the commandments of the Lord; and he also had [c]taken away our property.

12 And it came to pass that the Spirit said unto me again: Slay him, for the Lord hath delivered him into thy hands;

13 Behold the Lord [a]slayeth the [b]wicked to bring forth his righteous purposes. It is [c]better that one man should perish than that a nation should dwindle and perish in [d]unbelief.

14 And now, when I, Nephi, had heard these words, I remembered the words of the Lord which he spake unto me in the wilderness, saying that: [a]Inasmuch as thy seed shall keep my [b]commandments, they shall [c]prosper in the [d]land of promise.

15 Yea, and I also thought that they could not keep the commandments of the Lord according to the [a]law of Moses, save they should have the law.

16 And I also knew that the [a]law was engraven upon the plates of brass.

17 And again, I knew that the Lord had delivered Laban into my hands for this cause—that I might obtain the records according to his commandments.

18 Therefore I did obey the voice of the Spirit, and took Laban by the hair of the head, and I smote off his head with his own [a]sword.

19 And after I had smitten off his

3*a* 1 Ne. 3:30 (29–31); 7:10.
b TG Doubt.
c TG Deliver.
6*a* TG Guidance, Divine; Holy Ghost, Gifts of; Inspiration.
b Heb. 11:8.
7*a* TG Drunkenness.
9*a* 2 Ne. 5:14; D&C 17:1.
10*a* 1 Sam. 15:3 (3–33).
11*a* Deut. 3:3; 1 Sam. 17:46 (41–49).
b 1 Ne. 7:11.
c 1 Ne. 3:26.
13*a* Num. 25:17; Deut. 12:29; Ps. 139:19; 1 Ne. 17:37 (33–38); D&C 98:32 (31–32).
b TG Justice; Punish; Wickedness.
c Alma 30:47. TG Life, Sanctity of.
d TG Unbelief.
14*a* Omni 1:6; Mosiah 2:22; Ether 2:7 (7–12).
b TG Commandments of God.
c 1 Ne. 2:20.
d 1 Ne. 17:13 (13–14); Jacob 2:12.
15*a* Mosiah 1:5 (1–6).
16*a* Josh. 1:8. TG Law of Moses.
18*a* 1 Sam. 17:51.

head with his own sword, I took the
garments of Laban and put them
upon mine own body; yea, even
every whit; and I did gird on his
armor about my loins.
20 And after I had done this, I went
forth unto the treasury of Laban.
And as I went forth towards the
treasury of Laban, behold, I saw the
[a]servant of Laban who had the keys
of the treasury. And I commanded
him in the voice of Laban, that he
should go with me into the treasury.
21 And he supposed me to be his
master, Laban, for he beheld the
garments and also the sword girded
about my loins.
22 And he spake unto me concerning the [a]elders of the Jews, he
knowing that his master, Laban,
had been out by night among them.
23 And I spake unto him as if it
had been Laban.
24 And I also spake unto him that I
should carry the engravings, which
were upon the [a]plates of brass, to
my elder brethren, who were without the walls.
25 And I also bade him that he
should follow me.
26 And he, supposing that I spake
of the [a]brethren of the [b]church, and
that I was truly that Laban whom
I had slain, wherefore he did follow me.
27 And he spake unto me many
times concerning the elders of the
Jews, as I went forth unto my brethren, who were without the walls.
28 And it came to pass that when
Laman saw me he was exceedingly
frightened, and also Lemuel and
Sam. And they fled from before
my presence; for they supposed it
was Laban, and that he had slain
me and had sought to take away
their lives also.
29 And it came to pass that I called
after them, and they did hear me;
wherefore they did cease to flee
from my presence.
30 And it came to pass that when
the servant of Laban beheld my
brethren he began to tremble, and
was about to flee from before me
and return to the city of Jerusalem.
31 And now I, Nephi, being a man
large in stature, and also having received much [a]strength of the Lord,
therefore I did seize upon the servant of Laban, and held him, that
he should not flee.
32 And it came to pass that I spake
with him, that if he would hearken
unto my words, as the Lord liveth,
and as I live, even so that if he would
hearken unto our words, we would
spare his life.
33 And I spake unto him, even
with an [a]oath, that he need not fear;
that he should be a [b]free man like
unto us if he would go down in the
wilderness with us.
34 And I also spake unto him,
saying: Surely the Lord hath [a]com-
manded us to do this thing; and shall
we not be diligent in keeping the
commandments of the Lord? Therefore, if thou wilt go down into the
wilderness to my father thou shalt
have place with us.
35 And it came to pass that [a]Zoram
did take courage at the words which
I spake. Now Zoram was the name of
the servant; and he promised that he
would go down into the wilderness
unto our father. Yea, and he also
made an oath unto us that he would
tarry with us from that time forth.
36 Now we were desirous that he
should tarry with us for this cause,
that the Jews might not know concerning our flight into the wilderness, lest they should pursue us and
destroy us.
37 And it came to pass that when

20*a* 2 Ne. 1:30.
22*a* 2 Sam. 17:15; Ezek. 8:1; Acts 25:15.
24*a* 1 Ne. 3:24 (12, 19–24); 5:10 (10–22).
26*a* Ex. 2:11; Num. 18:6; 2 Sam. 19:41.
b TG Church Organization.
31*a* TG Strength; Strengthen.
33*a* 2 Sam. 21:7. TG Oath.
b TG Free.
34*a* 1 Ne. 2:2; 3:16.
35*a* 1 Ne. 16:7; 2 Ne. 5:6 (5–6); Jacob 1:13; Alma 54:23; 4 Ne. 1:36 (36–37).

Zoram had made an [a]oath unto us,
our [b]fears did cease concerning him.
38 And it came to pass that we
took the plates of brass and the servant of Laban, and departed into
the wilderness, and journeyed unto
the [a]tent of our father.

CHAPTER 5

Sariah complains against Lehi—Both rejoice over the return of their sons—They offer sacrifices—The plates of brass contain writings of Moses and the prophets—The plates identify Lehi as a descendant of Joseph—Lehi prophesies concerning his seed and the preservation of the plates. About 600–592 B.C.

AND it came to pass that after we
had come down into the wilderness
unto our father, behold, he was filled
with joy, and also my mother, Sariah, was exceedingly glad, for she
truly had mourned because of us.
2 For she had supposed that we
had perished in the wilderness; and
she also had [a]complained against
my father, telling him that he was
a [b]visionary man; saying: Behold
thou hast led us forth from the land
of our inheritance, and my sons
are no more, and we perish in the
wilderness.
3 And after this manner of language had my mother complained
against my father.
4 And it had come to pass that
my father spake unto her, saying:
I know that I am a [a]visionary man;
for if I had not seen the things of
God in a [b]vision I should not have
known the goodness of God, but
had tarried at Jerusalem, and had
perished with my brethren.
5 But behold, I have [a]obtained a
[b]land of promise, in the which things
I do rejoice; yea, and I [c]know that
the Lord will deliver my sons out of
the hands of Laban, and bring them
down again unto us in the wilderness.
6 And after this manner of language did my father, Lehi, [a]comfort
my mother, Sariah, concerning us,
while we journeyed in the wilderness up to the land of Jerusalem,
to obtain the record of the Jews.
7 And when we had returned to
the tent of my father, behold their
joy was full, and my mother was
comforted.
8 And she spake, saying: Now I
know of a surety that the Lord hath
[a]commanded my husband to [b]flee
into the wilderness; yea, and I also
know of a surety that the Lord hath
protected my sons, and delivered
them out of the hands of Laban,
and given them power whereby
they could [c]accomplish the thing
which the Lord hath commanded
them. And after this manner of
language did she speak.
9 And it came to pass that they did
rejoice exceedingly, and did offer
[a]sacrifice and burnt offerings unto
the Lord; and they gave [b]thanks
unto the God of Israel.
10 And after they had given thanks
unto the God of Israel, my father,
Lehi, took the records which were
engraven upon the [a]plates of brass,
and he did search them from the
beginning.
11 And he beheld that they did
contain the five [a]books of Moses,
which gave an account of the creation of the world, and also of Adam
and Eve, who were our first parents;

37*a* Ex. 22:11 (10–11); Josh. 9:19 (1–21). TG Oath; Vow.
b TG Trustworthiness.
38*a* 1 Ne. 2:15.
5 2*a* TG Murmuring.
b Gen. 37:19 (8, 19).
4*a* 1 Ne. 2:11; 17:20.
b 1 Ne. 1:8 (8–13); 3:18 (17–18). TG Vision.
5*a* Eph. 1:11; Heb. 6:15 (13–15).
b 1 Ne. 2:20; 18:8 (8, 22–23). TG Promised Lands.
c TG Faith; Trust in God.
6*a* TG Comfort; Family, Love within.
8*a* 1 Ne. 2:2.
b Gen. 19:14.
c 1 Ne. 3:7.
9*a* 1 Ne. 7:22; Mosiah 2:3; 3 Ne. 9:19. TG Law of Moses.
b TG Thanksgiving.
10*a* 1 Ne. 4:24 (24, 38); 13:23.
11*a* Ex. 17:14; Deut. 31:9; Luke 16:29; 24:27; 1 Ne. 19:23; Moses 1:41 (40–41).

12 And also a [a]record of the Jews from the beginning, even down to the commencement of the reign of Zedekiah, king of Judah;

13 And also the prophecies of the holy prophets, from the beginning, even down to the commencement of the reign of [a]Zedekiah; and also many prophecies which have been spoken by the mouth of [b]Jeremiah.

14 And it came to pass that my father, Lehi, also found upon the [a]plates of brass a [b]genealogy of his [c]fathers; wherefore he knew that he was a descendant of [d]Joseph; yea, even that Joseph who was the son of [e]Jacob, who was [f]sold into Egypt, and who was [g]preserved by the hand of the Lord, that he might preserve his father, Jacob, and all his household from perishing with famine.

15 And they were also [a]led out of captivity and out of the land of Egypt, by that same God who had preserved them.

16 And thus my father, Lehi, did discover the genealogy of his fathers. And Laban also was a descendant of [a]Joseph, wherefore he and his fathers had kept the [b]records.

17 And now when my father saw all these things, he was filled with the Spirit, and began to prophesy concerning his seed—

18 That these [a]plates of brass should go forth unto all [b]nations, kindreds, tongues, and people who were of his seed.

19 Wherefore, he said that these plates of brass should [a]never perish; neither should they be dimmed any more by time. And he prophesied many things concerning his seed.

20 And it came to pass that thus far I and my father had kept the commandments wherewith the Lord had commanded us.

21 And we had obtained the records which the Lord had commanded us, and searched them and found that they were desirable; yea, even of great [a]worth unto us, insomuch that we could [b]preserve the commandments of the Lord unto our children.

22 Wherefore, it was wisdom in the Lord that we should carry them with us, as we journeyed in the wilderness towards the land of promise.

CHAPTER 6

Nephi writes of the things of God—Nephi's purpose is to persuade men to come unto the God of Abraham and be saved. About 600–592 B.C.

AND now I, Nephi, do not give the genealogy of my fathers in [a]this part of my record; neither at any time shall I give it after upon these [b]plates which I am [c]writing; for it is given in the record which has been kept by my [d]father; wherefore, I do not write it in this work.

2 For it sufficeth me to say that we are descendants of [a]Joseph.

3 And it mattereth not to me that I am particular to give a full account of all the things of my father, for they cannot be written upon [a]these

12*a* 1 Chr. 9:1. TG Scriptures, Writing of.
13*a* 2 Kgs. 24:18; Jer. 37:1.
b Ezra 1:1; Jer. 36:32 (17–32); 1 Ne. 7:14; Hel. 8:20.
14*a* Mosiah 2:34.
b 1 Ne. 3:3, 12; Jarom 1:1. TG Book of Remembrance.
c TG Israel, Origins of.
d 2 Ne. 3:4; Alma 10:3. TG Israel, Joseph, People of.
e Gen. 25:26; 2 Ne. 20:21; Alma 7:25; D&C 27:10.
f Gen. 37:36 (29–36).
g TG Protection, Divine.
15*a* Gen. 15:14 (13–14); Ex. 15:13; Amos 3:1 (1–2); 1 Ne. 17:31 (23–31); 19:10; D&C 103:16 (16–18); 136:22.
16*a* 2 Chr. 15:9; 1 Ne. 6:2. TG Israel, Joseph, People of.
b TG Record Keeping.
18*a* Alma 22:12.
b JS—H 1:33.
19*a* Alma 37:4.
21*a* TG Scriptures, Value of.
b TG Scriptures, Preservation of.
6 1*a* 2 Ne. 4:15.
b 1 Ne. 9:2.
c TG Scriptures, Writing of.
d 1 Ne. 1:17 (16–17); 19:1 (1–6).
2*a* 1 Ne. 5:16 (14–16).
3*a* Jacob 7:27; Jarom 1:2 (2, 14); Omni 1:1, 30.

plates, for I desire the room that I may write of the things of God.

4 For the fulness of mine intent is that I may [a]persuade men to [b]come unto the God of Abraham, and the God of Isaac, and the God of Jacob, and be saved.

5 Wherefore, the things which are [a]pleasing unto the world I do not write, but the things which are pleasing unto God and unto those who are not of the world.

6 Wherefore, I shall give commandment unto my seed, that they shall not occupy these plates with things which are not of worth unto the children of men.

CHAPTER 7

Lehi's sons return to Jerusalem and invite Ishmael and his household to join them in their journey—Laman and others rebel—Nephi exhorts his brethren to have faith in the Lord—They bind him with cords and plan his destruction—He is freed by the power of faith—His brethren ask forgiveness—Lehi and his company offer sacrifice and burnt offerings. About 600–592 B.C.

AND now I would that ye might know, that after my father, Lehi, had made an end of [a]prophesying concerning his seed, it came to pass that the Lord spake unto him again, saying that it was not meet for him, Lehi, that he should take his family into the wilderness alone; but that his sons should take [b]daughters to [c]wife, that they might raise up [d]seed unto the Lord in the land of promise.

2 And it came to pass that the Lord [a]commanded him that I, Nephi, and my brethren, should again return unto the land of Jerusalem, and bring down Ishmael and his family into the wilderness.

3 And it came to pass that I, Nephi, did [a]again, with my brethren, go forth into the wilderness to go up to Jerusalem.

4 And it came to pass that we went up unto the house of Ishmael, and we did gain favor in the sight of Ishmael, insomuch that we did speak unto him the words of the Lord.

5 And it came to pass that the [a]Lord did soften the heart of Ishmael, and also his household, insomuch that they took their journey with us down into the wilderness to the tent of our father.

6 And it came to pass that as we journeyed in the wilderness, behold Laman and Lemuel, and two of the [a]daughters of Ishmael, and the two [b]sons of Ishmael and their families, did [c]rebel against us; yea, against me, Nephi, and Sam, and their father, Ishmael, and his wife, and his three other daughters.

7 And it came to pass in the which rebellion, they were desirous to return unto the land of Jerusalem.

8 And now I, Nephi, being [a]grieved for the hardness of their hearts, therefore I spake unto them, saying, yea, even unto Laman and unto Lemuel: Behold ye are mine elder brethren, and how is it that ye are so hard in your hearts, and so blind in your minds, that ye have need that I, your [b]younger brother, should speak unto you, yea, and set an [c]example for you?

9 How is it that ye have not hearkened unto the word of the Lord?

10 How is it that ye have [a]forgotten that ye have seen an angel of the Lord?

4*a* Luke 1:4 (3–4);
John 20:31 (30–31).
b 2 Ne. 9:41 (41, 45, 51).
5*a* Gal. 1:10;
1 Thes. 2:4;
Heb. 13:21;
W of M 1:4.
7 1*a* 1 Ne. 1:16.
b 1 Ne. 16:7.
c TG Marriage, Marry.
d Ps. 127:3.
2*a* 1 Ne. 16:8.
3*a* 1 Ne. 3:2.
5*a* TG Guidance, Divine.
6*a* 1 Ne. 16:7 (7, 27).
b 2 Ne. 4:10.
c 1 Ne. 17:18 (17–55).
8*a* Mosiah 28:3;
Alma 31:2;
3 Ne. 17:14;
Moses 7:41.
b 1 Chr. 29:1;
D&C 1:19 (19, 23).
c TG Example.
10*a* Deut. 4:9 (9–13);
1 Ne. 4:3.

11 Yea, and how is it that ye have
forgotten what great things the
Lord hath done for us, in [a]delivering
us out of the hands of Laban, and
also that we should obtain the
record?
12 Yea, and how is it that ye have
forgotten that the Lord is able to
do all [a]things according to his will,
for the children of men, if it so be
that they exercise [b]faith in him?
Wherefore, let us be faithful to him.
13 And if it so be that we are faithful to him, we shall obtain the [a]land
of promise; and ye shall know at
some future period that the word of
the Lord shall be fulfilled concerning the [b]destruction of [c]Jerusalem;
for all things which the Lord hath
spoken concerning the destruction
of Jerusalem must be fulfilled.
14 For behold, the [a]Spirit of the
Lord [b]ceaseth soon to strive with
them; for behold, they have [c]re-
jected the prophets, and [d]Jeremiah
have they cast into prison. And they
have sought to take away the [e]life
of my father, insomuch that they
have driven him out of the land.
15 Now behold, I say unto you that
if ye will return unto Jerusalem ye
shall also perish with them. And
now, if ye have choice, go up to
the land, and remember the words
which I speak unto you, that if ye
go ye will also perish; for thus the
Spirit of the Lord constraineth me
that I should speak.
16 And it came to pass that when
I, Nephi, had spoken these words
unto my brethren, they were angry
with me. And it came to pass that
they did lay their hands upon me,
for behold, they were exceedingly
wroth, and they did [a]bind me with
cords, for they sought to take away
my life, that they might leave me
in the wilderness to be devoured
by wild beasts.
17 But it came to pass that I prayed
unto the Lord, saying: O Lord, according to my faith which is in thee,
wilt thou deliver me from the hands
of my brethren; yea, even give me
[a]strength that I may [b]burst these
bands with which I am bound.
18 And it came to pass that when
I had said these words, behold, the
bands were loosed from off my
hands and feet, and I stood before
my brethren, and I spake unto them
again.
19 And it came to pass that they
were angry with me again, and
sought to lay hands upon me; but
behold, one of the [a]daughters of
Ishmael, yea, and also her mother,
and one of the sons of Ishmael, did
plead with my brethren, insomuch
that they did soften their hearts;
and they did cease striving to take
away my life.
20 And it came to pass that they
were sorrowful, because of their
wickedness, insomuch that they
did bow down before me, and did
plead with me that I would [a]forgive
them of the thing that they had
done against me.
21 And it came to pass that I did
frankly [a]forgive them all that they
had done, and I did exhort them
that they would pray unto the Lord
their God for [b]forgiveness. And it
came to pass that they did so. And
after they had done praying unto
the Lord we did again travel on
our journey towards the tent of our
father.
22 And it came to pass that we did

11*a* 1 Ne. 4:1 (1–38).
12*a* Ps. 18:32 (32–40); 1 Ne. 17:50; Alma 26:12.
b 1 Ne. 2:19 (18–21); 15:11.
13*a* 1 Ne. 2:20. TG Promised Lands.
b 2 Kgs. 25:4 (1–21).
c 2 Ne. 6:8; 25:10; Omni 1:15; Hel. 8:21 (20–21).
14*a* TG God, Spirit of.
b Ezek. 5:6; 1 Ne. 1:19 (18–20); 2:13.
c TG Prophets, Rejection of.
d Jer. 37:15 (15–21).
e 1 Ne. 2:1.
16*a* 1 Ne. 18:11 (11–15).
17*a* Judg. 14:6.
b Jacob 4:6; Alma 14:28 (26–28); 3 Ne. 28:20 (19–22).
19*a* 1 Ne. 16:7; 18:19 (19–20).
20*a* TG Repent.
21*a* TG Family, Love within.
b TG Forgive.

come down unto the tent of our
father. And after I and my brethren
and all the house of Ishmael had come
down unto the tent of my father, they
did give [a]thanks unto the Lord their
God; and they did offer [b]sacrifice
and burnt offerings unto him.

CHAPTER 8

Lehi sees a vision of the tree of life—He partakes of its fruit and desires his family to do likewise—He sees a rod of iron, a strait and narrow path, and the mists of darkness that enshroud men—Sariah, Nephi, and Sam partake of the fruit, but Laman and Lemuel refuse. About 600–592 B.C.

AND it came to pass that we had
gathered together all manner of
[a]seeds of every kind, both of grain
of every kind, and also of the seeds
of fruit of every kind.
2 And it came to pass that while
my father tarried in the wilderness
he spake unto us, saying: Behold, I
have [a]dreamed a dream; or, in other
words, I have [b]seen a [c]vision.
3 And behold, because of the thing
which I have seen, I have reason to
rejoice in the Lord because of [a]Nephi
and also of Sam; for I have reason
to suppose that they, and also many
of their seed, will be saved.
4 But behold, [a]Laman and Lemuel,
I fear exceedingly because of you;
for behold, methought I saw in my
dream, a dark and dreary wilderness.
5 And it came to pass that I saw
a [a]man, and he was dressed in a
white [b]robe; and he came and stood
before me.
6 And it came to pass that he spake
unto me, and bade me follow him.
7 And it came to pass that as I
followed him I beheld myself that
I was in a dark and dreary waste.
8 And after I had traveled for the
space of many hours in darkness, I
began to pray unto the Lord that he
would have [a]mercy on me, according
to the multitude of his tender
mercies.
9 And it came to pass after I had
prayed unto the Lord I beheld a
large and spacious [a]field.
10 And it came to pass that I beheld
a [a]tree, whose [b]fruit was desirable
to make one [c]happy.
11 And it came to pass that I did
go forth and partake of the [a]fruit
thereof; and I beheld that it was most
sweet, above all that I ever before
tasted. Yea, and I beheld that the
fruit thereof was white, to exceed
all the [b]whiteness that I had ever
seen.
12 And as I partook of the fruit
thereof it filled my soul with exceedingly
great [a]joy; wherefore, I
began to be [b]desirous that my family
should partake of it also; for I knew
that it was [c]desirable above all other
fruit.
13 And as I cast my eyes round
about, that perhaps I might discover
my family also, I beheld a [a]river of
water; and it ran along, and it was
near the tree of which I was partaking
the fruit.
14 And I looked to behold from
whence it came; and I saw the head
thereof a little way off; and at the
head thereof I beheld your mother
Sariah, and Sam, and [a]Nephi; and
they stood as if they knew not
whither they should go.
15 And it came to pass that I

22*a* TG Thanksgiving.
b 1 Ne. 5:9.
8 1*a* 1 Ne. 16:11.
2*a* 1 Ne. 1:16; 10:2. TG Dream; Revelation; Vision.
b 1 Ne. 14:29.
c 1 Ne. 10:17.
3*a* 1 Ne. 8:14 (14–18).
4*a* 1 Ne. 8:35.
5*a* Dan. 10:5 (2–12).
b JS—H 1:31 (30–32).
8*a* TG God, Mercy of.
9*a* Matt. 13:38.
10*a* Gen. 2:9; Rev. 2:7 (1–7); 22:2 (1–16); 1 Ne. 11:4, 8 (8–25).
b 1 Ne. 8:24 (15, 20, 24); Alma 32:42 (41–43).
c TG Happiness.
11*a* 1 Ne. 15:36; Alma 5:34.
b 1 Ne. 11:8.
12*a* TG Joy.
b Enos 1:9; Alma 36:24. TG Family, Love within.
c Gen. 3:6; 1 Ne. 15:36.
13*a* 1 Ne. 12:16 (16–18); 15:26–27 (26–29).
14*a* 1 Ne. 8:3 (3–4).

beckoned unto them; and I also did
say unto them with a loud voice
that they should come unto me, and
partake of the fruit, which was desirable above all other fruit.
16 And it came to pass that they
did come unto me and partake of
the fruit also.
17 And it came to pass that I was
desirous that Laman and Lemuel
should come and partake of the
fruit also; wherefore, I cast mine
eyes towards the head of the river,
that perhaps I might see them.
18 And it came to pass that I saw
them, but they would [a]not come
unto me and partake of the fruit.
19 And I beheld a [a]rod of iron, and
it extended along the bank of the
river, and led to the tree by which
I stood.
20 And I also beheld a [a]strait and
narrow path, which came along by
the rod of iron, even to the tree by
which I stood; and it also led by the
head of the fountain, unto a large
and spacious field, as if it had been
a [b]world.
21 And I saw numberless concourses of people, many of whom
were [a]pressing forward, that they
might obtain the [b]path which led
unto the tree by which I stood.
22 And it came to pass that they
did come forth, and commence in
the path which led to the tree.
23 And it came to pass that there
arose a [a]mist of darkness; yea, even
an exceedingly great mist of darkness, insomuch that they who had
commenced in the path did lose their
way, that they wandered off and
were [b]lost.
24 And it came to pass that I beheld others pressing forward, and
they came forth and caught hold of
the end of the rod of iron; and they
did press forward through the mist
of darkness, [a]clinging to the rod of
iron, even until they did come forth
and partake of the [b]fruit of the tree.
25 And after they had partaken of
the fruit of the tree they did cast
their eyes about as if they were
[a]ashamed.
26 And I also cast my eyes round
about, and beheld, on the [a]other
side of the river of water, a great
and [b]spacious building; and it stood
as it were in the [c]air, high above
the earth.
27 And it was filled with people,
both old and young, both male and
female; and their manner of dress
was exceedingly fine; and they
were in the [a]attitude of [b]mocking
and pointing their fingers towards
those who had come at and were
partaking of the fruit.
28 And after they had [a]tasted of
the fruit they were [b]ashamed, because of those that were [c]scoffing
at them; and they [d]fell away into
forbidden paths and were lost.
29 And now I, Nephi, do not speak
[a]all the words of my father.
30 But, to be short in writing,
behold, he saw other multitudes
pressing forward; and they came
and caught hold of the end of the
[a]rod of iron; and they did press their
way forward, continually holding

18*a* 2 Ne. 5:20 (20–25).
19*a* Ps. 2:9; Rev. 2:27; 12:5; 19:15; JST Rev. 19:15 (Rev. 19:15 note *a*); 1 Ne. 8:30; 11:25; 15:23 (23–24).
20*a* Matt. 7:14; 2 Ne. 31:18 (17–20).
b Matt. 13:38.
21*a* D&C 123:12.
b TG Objectives; Path; Way.
23*a* Matt. 13:19 (18–19); 2 Pet. 2:17; 1 Ne. 12:17; 15:24 (23–24).
b TG Apostasy of Individuals.
24*a* TG Diligence; Perseverance.
b 1 Ne. 8:10.
25*a* Rom. 1:16; 2 Tim. 1:8; Alma 46:21; Morm. 8:38.
26*a* Luke 16:26.
b 1 Ne. 11:35 (35–36); 12:18.
c Eph. 2:2 (1–3).
27*a* TG Haughtiness; Pride.
b Matt. 9:24 (20–26). TG Mocking.
28*a* 2 Pet. 2:20 (19–22).
b Mark 4:17 (14–20); 8:38; Luke 8:13 (11–15); John 12:43 (42–43); Rom. 3:3. TG Courage; Fearful.
c TG Peer Influence.
d TG Apostasy of Individuals.
29*a* 1 Ne. 1:17 (16–17).
30*a* 1 Ne. 8:19; 15:24 (23–24).

fast to the rod of iron, until they
came forth and fell down and partook of the fruit of the tree.
31 And he also saw other [a]mul-
titudes feeling their way towards
that great and spacious building.
32 And it came to pass that many
were drowned in the [a]depths of
the [b]fountain; and many were lost
from his view, wandering in strange
roads.
33 And great was the multitude
that did enter into that strange
building. And after they did enter
into that building they did point
the finger of [a]scorn at me and
those that were partaking of the
fruit also; but we heeded them not.
34 These are the words of my
father: For as many as [a]heeded
them, had fallen away.
35 And [a]Laman and Lemuel partook not of the fruit, said my
father.
36 And it came to pass after my
father had spoken all the words of
his dream or vision, which were
many, he said unto us, because
of these things which he saw in a
vision, he exceedingly feared for
Laman and Lemuel; yea, he feared
lest they should be cast off from
the presence of the Lord.
37 And he did [a]exhort them then
with all the feeling of a tender parent, that they would hearken to his
words, that perhaps the Lord would
be merciful to them, and not cast
them off; yea, my father did preach
unto them.
38 And after he had preached
unto them, and also prophesied unto
them of many things, he bade them
to keep the commandments of the
Lord; and he did cease speaking
unto them.

CHAPTER 9

Nephi makes two sets of records—Each is called the plates of Nephi—The larger plates contain a secular history; the smaller ones deal primarily with sacred things. About 600–592 B.C.

AND all these things did my father
see, and hear, and speak, as he dwelt
in a tent, in the [a]valley of Lemuel,
and also a great many more things,
which cannot be written upon these
plates.
2 And now, as I have spoken concerning these plates, behold they
are not the plates upon which I
make a full account of the history
of my people; for the [a]plates upon
which I make a full account of my
people I have given the name of
Nephi; wherefore, they are called
the plates of Nephi, after mine own
name; and these plates also are
called the plates of Nephi.
3 Nevertheless, I have received a
commandment of the Lord that I
should make these plates, for the
special [a]purpose that there should
be an account engraven of the [b]min-
istry of my people.
4 Upon the other plates should be
engraven an account of the reign
of the kings, and the wars and contentions of my people; wherefore
these plates are for the more part of
the ministry; and the [a]other plates
are for the more part of the reign
of the kings and the wars and contentions of my people.

31 *a* Matt. 7:13.
32 *a* 1 Ne. 15:29 (26–29).
b 1 Ne. 8:14 (13–14).
33 *a* Neh. 2:19; Alma 26:23. TG Persecution; Scorn; Scorner.
34 *a* Ex. 23:2; Prov. 19:27; Mosiah 2:37 (33, 37).
35 *a* 1 Ne. 8:4 (4, 17–18); 2 Ne. 5:20 (19–24).
37 *a* TG Family, Children, Responsibilities toward.
9 1 *a* 1 Ne. 2:6 (4–6, 8, 14–15); 16:6 (6, 12).
2 *a* IE the full account is on larger plates; the special account of his ministry is on the smaller plates of Nephi. See Jacob 3:13–14. See also 1 Ne. 1:17 (16–17); 6:1; 10:1; 19:2, 4; Omni 1:1; W of M 1:3 (2–11); D&C 10:38 (38–40).
3 *a* D&C 3:19.
b 1 Ne. 6:3.
4 *a* 2 Ne. 4:14; 5:33 (29–33); Jacob 1:3 (2–4); Jarom 1:14; Omni 1:18; W of M 1:10.

5 Wherefore, the Lord hath commanded me to make these plates
for a [a]wise purpose in him, which
purpose I know not.
6 But the Lord [a]knoweth all things
from the beginning; wherefore, he
prepareth a way to accomplish all
his works among the children of
men; for behold, he hath all [b]power
unto the fulfilling of all his words.
And thus it is. Amen.

CHAPTER 10

Lehi predicts that the Jews will be taken captive by the Babylonians—He tells of the coming among the Jews of a Messiah, a Savior, a Redeemer—Lehi tells also of the coming of the one who should baptize the Lamb of God—Lehi tells of the death and resurrection of the Messiah—He compares the scattering and gathering of Israel to an olive tree—Nephi speaks of the Son of God, of the gift of the Holy Ghost, and of the need for righteousness. About 600–592 B.C.

AND now I, Nephi, proceed to give
an account upon [a]these plates of
my proceedings, and my reign and
ministry; wherefore, to proceed with
mine account, I must speak somewhat of the things of my father,
and also of my brethren.
2 For behold, it came to pass after my father had made an end of
speaking the words of his [a]dream,
and also of exhorting them to all
diligence, he spake unto them concerning the Jews—
3 That after they should be destroyed, even that great city [a]Jeru-
salem, and many be [b]carried away
captive into [c]Babylon, according to
the own due time of the Lord, they
should [d]return again, yea, even be
brought back out of captivity; and
after they should be brought back
out of captivity they should possess
again the land of their inheritance.
4 Yea, even [a]six hundred years
from the time that my father left
Jerusalem, a [b]prophet would the
Lord God raise up among the [c]Jews—
even a [d]Messiah, or, in other words,
a Savior of the world.
5 And he also spake concerning the
prophets, how great a number had
[a]testified of these things, concerning
this Messiah, of whom he had spoken, or this Redeemer of the world.
6 Wherefore, all mankind were in a
[a]lost and in a [b]fallen state, and ever
would be save they should rely on
this Redeemer.
7 And he spake also concerning a
[a]prophet who should come before
the Messiah, to prepare the way of
the Lord—
8 Yea, even he should go forth and
cry in the wilderness: [a]Prepare ye
the way of the Lord, and make his
paths straight; for there standeth
one among you whom ye know not;
and he is mightier than I, whose
shoe's latchet I am not worthy to
unloose. And much spake my father
concerning this thing.
9 And my father said he should

5*a* 1 Ne. 19:3; W of M 1:7; Alma 37:14 (2, 12, 14).
6*a* Isa. 48:3 (3–7); Moses 1:6, 35. TG God, Foreknowledge of; God, Intelligence of; God, Omniscience of.
b Matt. 28:18.
10 1*a* 1 Ne. 9:2 (1–5); 19:3 (1–6).
2*a* 1 Ne. 8:2 (2–36).
3*a* Esth. 2:6; 2 Ne. 6:8; Hel. 8:20 (20–21).
b Ezek. 36:12 (8–15); 2 Ne. 25:10. TG Israel, Bondage of, in Other Lands; Israel, Scattering of.
c Ezek. 24:2; 1 Ne. 1:13; Omni 1:15. TG Babylon.
d Neh. 12:1; Jer. 29:10 (9–10); 2 Ne. 6:9 (8–9); Abr. 2:6.
4*a* 1 Ne. 19:8 (8–14); 2 Ne. 25:19; Alma 13:25; 3 Ne. 1:1.
b 1 Ne. 22:21 (20–21).
c TG Israel, Judah, People of.
d Jacob 1:6. TG Jesus Christ, Birth of; Jesus Christ, Messiah.
5*a* Jacob 7:11; Mosiah 13:33; Hel. 8:24 (19–24); 3 Ne. 20:24 (23–24). TG Jesus Christ, Prophecies about.
6*a* Rom. 3:23; 2 Ne. 2:5 (5–8).
b TG Death, Spiritual, First.
7*a* 1 Ne. 11:27; 2 Ne. 31:4 (4–18). TG Foreordination.
8*a* Isa. 40:3; Matt. 3:3 (1–3); D&C 84:26.

baptize in [a]Bethabara, beyond
Jordan; and he also said he should
[b]baptize with water; even that he
should baptize the Messiah with
water.
10 And after he had baptized the
Messiah with water, he should behold and bear record that he had
baptized the [a]Lamb of God, who
should take away the sins of the
world.
11 And it came to pass after my
father had spoken these words he
spake unto my brethren concerning the gospel which should be
preached among the Jews, and also
concerning the [a]dwindling of the
Jews in [b]unbelief. And after they
had [c]slain the Messiah, who should
come, and after he had been slain
he should [d]rise from the dead, and
should make himself [e]manifest, by
the Holy Ghost, unto the Gentiles.
12 Yea, even my father spake much
concerning the Gentiles, and also
concerning the house of Israel, that
they should be compared like unto
an [a]olive tree, whose [b]branches
should be broken off and should
be [c]scattered upon all the face of
the earth.
13 Wherefore, he said it must needs
be that we should be led with one
accord into the [a]land of promise,
unto the fulfilling of the word of
the Lord, that we should be scattered upon all the face of the earth.
14 And after the house of [a]Israel
should be scattered they should be
[b]gathered together again; or, in fine,
after the [c]Gentiles had received the
fulness of the [d]Gospel, the natural
branches of the [e]olive tree, or the
[f]remnants of the house of [g]Israel,
should be grafted in, or [h]come to the
knowledge of the true Messiah, their
Lord and their Redeemer.
15 And after this manner of language did my father prophesy
and speak unto my brethren, and
also many more things which I do
not write in this book; for I have
written as many of them as were
expedient for me in mine [a]other
book.
16 And all these things, of which
I have spoken, were done as my
father dwelt in a [a]tent, in the valley of Lemuel.
17 And it came to pass after I,
Nephi, having heard all the [a]words
of my father, concerning the things
which he saw in a [b]vision, and also
the things which he spake by the
power of the Holy Ghost, which
power he received by faith on the
Son of God—and the Son of God was
the [c]Messiah who should come—I,
Nephi, was [d]desirous also that I
might see, and hear, and know of
these things, by the power of the
[e]Holy Ghost, which is the [f]gift of
God unto [g]all those who diligently
seek him, as well in times of [h]old

9*a* John 1:28.
b TG Jesus Christ, Baptism of.
10*a* TG Jesus Christ, Lamb of God.
11*a* Rom. 11:1 (1–36); Jacob 4:15 (14–18).
b Morm. 5:14 (14–20). TG Unbelief.
c TG Jesus Christ, Crucifixion of; Jesus Christ, Prophecies about.
d TG Jesus Christ, Resurrection.
e 3 Ne. 15:23 (21–24). TG Holy Ghost, Mission of.
12*a* Gen. 49:22 (22–26); 1 Ne. 15:12; 2 Ne. 3:5 (4–5); Jacob 5:3 (3–77); 6:1 (1–7). TG Vineyard of the Lord.
b TG Israel, Bondage of, in Other Lands.
c Deut. 32:26; 1 Ne. 22:3 (3–8). TG Israel, Scattering of.
13*a* 1 Ne. 2:20. TG Promised Lands.
14*a* TG Israel, Ten Lost Tribes of.
b TG Israel, Gathering of.
c 1 Ne. 13:42; D&C 14:10.
d TG Gospel.
e 1 Ne. 15:7.
f TG Israel, Remnant of.
g TG Israel, Twelve Tribes of.
h 1 Ne. 19:15 (14–17).
15*a* 1 Ne. 1:17 (16–18).
16*a* 1 Ne. 2:15 (15–16).
17*a* Enos 1:3; Alma 36:17 (17–18).
b 1 Ne. 8:2.
c TG Jesus Christ, Messiah.
d 2 Ne. 4:24.
e 2 Pet. 1:21.
f TG God, Gifts of; Holy Ghost, Gift of.
g Moro. 7:36; 10:7 (4–5, 7, 19).
h D&C 20:26.

as in the time that he should manifest himself unto the children of men.
18 For he is the [a]same yesterday, today, and forever; and the way is prepared for all men from the foundation of the world, if it so be that they repent and come unto him.
19 For he that diligently [a]seeketh shall find; and the [b]mysteries of God shall be unfolded unto them, by the power of the [c]Holy Ghost, as well in these times as in times of old, and as well in times of old as in times to come; wherefore, the [d]course of the Lord is one eternal round.
20 Therefore remember, O man, for all thy doings thou shalt be brought into [a]judgment.
21 Wherefore, if ye have sought to do [a]wickedly in the days of your [b]probation, then ye are found [c]unclean before the judgment-seat of God; and no unclean thing can dwell with God; wherefore, ye must be cast off forever.
22 And the Holy Ghost giveth [a]authority that I should speak these things, and deny them not.

CHAPTER 11

Nephi sees the Spirit of the Lord and is shown in vision the tree of life—He sees the mother of the Son of God and learns of the condescension of God—He sees the baptism, ministry, and crucifixion of the Lamb of God—He sees also the call and ministry of the Twelve Apostles of the Lamb. About 600–592 B.C.

For it came to pass after I had desired to know the things that my father had seen, and believing that the Lord was able to make them known unto me, as I sat [a]pondering in mine heart I was [b]caught away in the Spirit of the Lord, yea, into an exceedingly high [c]mountain, which I never had before seen, and upon which I never had before set my foot.
2 And the Spirit said unto me: Behold, what [a]desirest thou?
3 And I said: I desire to behold the things which my father [a]saw.
4 And the Spirit said unto me: [a]Believest thou that thy father saw the [b]tree of which he hath spoken?
5 And I said: Yea, thou knowest that I [a]believe all the words of my father.
6 And when I had spoken these words, the Spirit cried with a loud voice, saying: Hosanna to the Lord, the most high God; for he is God over all the [a]earth, yea, even above all. And blessed art thou, Nephi, because thou [b]believest in the Son of the most high God; wherefore, thou shalt behold the things which thou hast desired.
7 And behold this thing shall be given unto thee for a [a]sign, that after thou hast beheld the tree which bore the fruit which thy father tasted, thou shalt also behold a man descending out of heaven, and him shall ye witness; and after ye have witnessed him ye shall [b]bear record that it is the Son of God.
8 And it came to pass that the Spirit said unto me: Look! And I

18a Heb. 13:8; Morm. 9:9 (9–11); D&C 20:12. TG God, Perfection of.
19a TG Objectives.
b TG Mysteries of Godliness.
c TG Holy Ghost, Source of Testimony.
d Alma 7:20; 37:12; D&C 3:2; 35:1. TG God, Eternal Nature of.
20a Eccl. 12:14; Ezek. 33:20. TG Judgment, the Last.
21a Ezek. 33:9.
b TG Probation.
c 1 Cor. 6:9 (9–10); Morm. 7:7; D&C 76:62 (50–62); 138:20, 37; Moses 6:57.
22a TG Holy Ghost, Mission of.
11 1a D&C 76:19. TG Meditation.
b Dan. 8:2; 2 Cor. 12:2 (1–4); Rev. 21:10; 2 Ne. 4:25; Moses 1:1.
c Ex. 24:13 (12–13); Deut. 10:1; Ether 3:1.
2a Zech. 4:2 (1–6).
3a 1 Ne. 8:2.
4a Mosiah 5:1 (1–2).
b 1 Ne. 8:10 (10–12); 15:22 (21–22).
5a 1 Ne. 2:16.
6a Ex. 9:29; Deut. 10:14; 2 Ne. 29:7; 3 Ne. 11:14; D&C 55:1; Moses 6:44.
b TG Believe.
7a TG Signs.
b TG Testimony; Witness.

looked and beheld a tree; and it was
like unto the [a]tree which my father
had seen; and the [b]beauty thereof
was far beyond, yea, exceeding
of all beauty; and the [c]whiteness
thereof did exceed the whiteness
of the driven snow.
9 And it came to pass after I had
seen the tree, I said unto the Spirit:
I behold thou hast shown unto me
the tree which is [a]precious above all.
10 And he said unto me: What
desirest thou?
11 And I said unto him: To know
the [a]interpretation thereof—for I
spake unto him as a man speaketh; for I beheld that he was in the
[b]form of a man; yet nevertheless, I
knew that it was the Spirit of the
Lord; and he spake unto me as a
man speaketh with another.
12 And it came to pass that he said
unto me: Look! And I looked as if to
look upon him, and I saw him not; for
he had gone from before my presence.
13 And it came to pass that I
looked and beheld the great city of
Jerusalem, and also other cities. And
I beheld the city of Nazareth; and
in the city of [a]Nazareth I beheld a
[b]virgin, and she was exceedingly
fair and white.
14 And it came to pass that I saw
the [a]heavens open; and an angel
came down and stood before me;
and he said unto me: Nephi, what
beholdest thou?
15 And I said unto him: A virgin,
most beautiful and fair above all
other virgins.
16 And he said unto me: Knowest
thou the [a]condescension of God?
17 And I said unto him: I know
that he loveth his children; nevertheless, I do not know the meaning
of all things.
18 And he said unto me: Behold,
the [a]virgin whom thou seest is the
[b]mother of the Son of God, after the
manner of the flesh.
19 And it came to pass that I beheld that she was carried away in
the Spirit; and after she had been
carried away in the [a]Spirit for the
space of a time the angel spake unto
me, saying: Look!
20 And I looked and beheld the
virgin again, bearing a [a]child in
her arms.
21 And the angel said unto me:
Behold the [a]Lamb of God, yea, even
the [b]Son of the Eternal [c]Father!
Knowest thou the meaning of the
[d]tree which thy father saw?
22 And I answered him, saying:
Yea, it is the [a]love of God, which
[b]sheddeth itself abroad in the hearts
of the children of men; wherefore,
it is the [c]most desirable above all
things.
23 And he spake unto me, saying:
Yea, and the most [a]joyous to the
soul.
24 And after he had said these
words, he said unto me: Look! And I
looked, and I beheld the Son of God
[a]going forth among the children of
men; and I saw many fall down at
his feet and worship him.
25 And it came to pass that I beheld
that the [a]rod of iron, which my
father had seen, was the [b]word of
God, which [c]led to the fountain of
[d]living waters, or to the [e]tree of life;

8*a* 1 Ne. 8:10.
b TG Beauty.
c 1 Ne. 8:11.
9*a* 1 Ne. 11:22 (22–25).
11*a* Gen. 40:8.
b TG Spirit Body.
13*a* Matt. 2:23.
b Luke 1:27 (26–27); Alma 7:10.
14*a* Ezek. 1:1; 1 Ne. 1:8 (6–11).
16*a* 1 Ne. 11:26. TG Jesus Christ, Condescension of.
18*a* Luke 1:34 (34–35). TG Foreordination; Jesus Christ, Prophecies about.
b Matt. 1:16; Mosiah 3:8; Alma 19:13. TG Jesus Christ, Birth of.
19*a* Matt. 1:20.
20*a* Luke 2:16.
21*a* TG Jesus Christ, Lamb of God.
b TG Jesus Christ, Divine Sonship.
c TG God the Father, Elohim.
d 1 Ne. 8:10; Alma 5:62.
22*a* TG God, Love of.
b Moro. 8:26.
c 1 Ne. 11:9.
23*a* TG Joy.
24*a* Luke 4:14 (14–21).
25*a* Rev. 2:27; JST Rev. 2:27 (Bible Appendix).
b 1 Ne. 8:19.
c TG Guidance, Divine.
d TG Living Water.
e Gen. 2:9; Prov. 11:30 (22–30); Moses 4:28 (28, 31).

which waters are a representation
of the love of God; and I also beheld
that the tree of life was a representation of the love of God.
26 And the angel said unto me
again: Look and behold the [a]con-
descension of God!
27 And I looked and [a]beheld the
Redeemer of the world, of whom
my father had spoken; and I also
beheld the [b]prophet who should
prepare the way before him. And
the Lamb of God went forth and
was [c]baptized of him; and after
he was baptized, I beheld the heavens open, and the Holy Ghost come
down out of heaven and abide upon
him in the form of a [d]dove.
28 And I beheld that he went
forth ministering unto the people,
in [a]power and great glory; and the
multitudes were gathered together
to hear him; and I beheld that they
cast him out from among them.
29 And I also beheld [a]twelve others following him. And it came to
pass that they were [b]carried away
in the Spirit from before my face,
and I saw them not.
30 And it came to pass that the
angel spake unto me again, saying:
Look! And I looked, and I beheld
the heavens open again, and I saw
[a]angels descending upon the children of men; and they did minister
unto them.
31 And he spake unto me again,
saying: Look! And I looked, and I
beheld the Lamb of God going forth
among the children of men. And I
beheld multitudes of people who
were [a]sick, and who were afflicted
with all manner of diseases, and
with [b]devils and [c]unclean spirits;
and the angel spake and showed
all these things unto me. And they
were [d]healed by the power of the
Lamb of God; and the devils and
the unclean spirits were cast out.
32 And it came to pass that the
angel spake unto me again, saying:
Look! And I looked and beheld the
Lamb of God, that he was [a]taken
by the people; yea, the Son of the
everlasting God was [b]judged of the
world; and I saw and bear record.
33 And I, Nephi, saw that he was
[a]lifted up upon the cross and [b]slain
for the sins of the world.
34 And after he was slain I saw the
multitudes of the earth, that they
were gathered together to [a]fight
against the apostles of the Lamb;
for thus were the twelve called by
the angel of the Lord.
35 And the multitude of the earth
was gathered together; and I beheld that they were in a large and
spacious [a]building, like unto the
building which my father saw. And
the angel of the Lord spake unto
me again, saying: Behold the world
and the wisdom thereof; yea, behold
the house of Israel hath gathered
together to [b]fight against the twelve
apostles of the Lamb.
36 And it came to pass that I saw
and bear record, that the great and
spacious building was the [a]pride of
the world; and it [b]fell, and the fall
thereof was exceedingly great. And
the angel of the Lord spake unto me

26*a* 1 Ne. 11:16.
TG Jesus Christ, Condescension of.
27*a* 2 Ne. 25:13.
b Mal. 3:1; Matt. 11:10; John 1:6 (6–7); 1 Ne. 10:7 (7–10); 2 Ne. 31:4 (4–18); D&C 35:4.
c TG Jesus Christ, Baptism of.
d TG Holy Ghost, Dove, Sign of.
28*a* D&C 138:26.
29*a* 1 Ne. 12:9; 13:40 (24–26, 40).
TG Apostles.
b 1 Ne. 14:30.
30*a* TG Angels.
31*a* TG Sickness.
b Mark 5:15 (15–20); 7:30; Mosiah 3:6 (5–7); Morm. 9:24.
c TG Spirits, Evil or Unclean.
d TG Heal.
32*a* TG Jesus Christ, Betrayal of.
b Mark 15:19 (17–20); Luke 9:44 (44–45).
33*a* Luke 18:31; 2 Ne. 10:3; Mosiah 3:9 (9–10); 3 Ne. 27:14.
b TG Jesus Christ, Atonement through; Jesus Christ, Death of.
34*a* Mark 13:13; 1 Cor. 4:9 (6–13).
35*a* 1 Ne. 8:26; 12:18.
b Micah 3:5; D&C 121:38.
36*a* TG Pride.
b TG Earth, Cleansing of; World, End of.

again, saying: Thus shall be the destruction of all nations, kindreds,
tongues, and people, that shall
fight against the twelve apostles
of the Lamb.

CHAPTER 12

Nephi sees in vision the land of promise; the righteousness, iniquity, and downfall of its inhabitants; the coming of the Lamb of God among them; how the Twelve Disciples and the Twelve Apostles will judge Israel; and the loathsome and filthy state of those who dwindle in unbelief. About 600–592 B.C.

AND it came to pass that the angel
said unto me: Look, and behold
thy seed, and also the seed of thy
brethren. And I looked and beheld
the [a]land of promise; and I beheld
multitudes of people, yea, even as
it were in number as many as the
[b]sand of the sea.
2 And it came to pass that I beheld
multitudes gathered together to
battle, one against the other; and I
beheld [a]wars, and rumors of wars,
and great slaughters with the sword
among my people.
3 And it came to pass that I beheld many generations pass away,
after the manner of wars and contentions in the land; and I beheld
many cities, yea, even that I did not
number them.
4 And it came to pass that I saw
a [a]mist of [b]darkness on the face
of the land of promise; and I saw
lightnings, and I heard thunderings,
and earthquakes, and all manner of
tumultuous noises; and I saw the
earth and the rocks, that they rent;
and I saw mountains tumbling into
pieces; and I saw the plains of the
earth, that they were [c]broken up;
and I saw many cities that they were
[d]sunk; and I saw many that they
were burned with fire; and I saw
many that did tumble to the earth,
because of the quaking thereof.
5 And it came to pass after I saw
these things, I saw the [a]vapor of
darkness, that it passed from off
the face of the earth; and behold, I
saw multitudes who had not fallen
because of the great and terrible
judgments of the Lord.
6 And I saw the heavens open, and
the [a]Lamb of God descending out
of heaven; and he came down and
[b]showed himself unto them.
7 And I also saw and bear record
that the Holy Ghost fell upon [a]twelve
others; and they were ordained of
God, and chosen.
8 And the angel spake unto me,
saying: Behold the twelve disciples of the Lamb, who are chosen
to minister unto thy seed.
9 And he said unto me: Thou
rememberest the [a]twelve apostles
of the Lamb? Behold they are they
who shall [b]judge the twelve tribes
of Israel; wherefore, the twelve
ministers of thy seed shall be judged
of them; for ye are of the house of
Israel.
10 And these [a]twelve ministers
whom thou beholdest shall judge
thy seed. And, behold, they are
righteous forever; for because of
their faith in the Lamb of God their
[b]garments are made white in his
blood.
11 And the angel said unto me:
Look! And I looked, and beheld
[a]three generations pass away in

12 1*a* TG Promised Lands.
b Gen. 22:17 (17–18); 1 Kgs. 4:20.
2*a* Enos 1:24; Morm. 8:7 (7–8). TG War.
4*a* 1 Ne. 19:12; Hel. 14:28 (20–28); 3 Ne. 10:11.
b 1 Ne. 19:10; 2 Ne. 26:3.
c Gen. 7:11.
d 3 Ne. 8:14.
5*a* 3 Ne. 8:20.
6*a* 2 Ne. 26:1 (1, 9); 3 Ne. 11:8 (3–17).
b 2 Ne. 32:6; Alma 7:8; 16:20.
7*a* 3 Ne. 11:22; 12:1.
9*a* Matt. 10:1; Luke 6:13; John 6:70; 1 Ne. 11:29; 13:40 (24–26, 40).
b Matt. 19:28; D&C 29:12. TG Judgment, the Last.
10*a* 3 Ne. 27:27; Morm. 3:18–19.
b Rev. 7:14; 19:8; Alma 5:21 (21–27); 13:11 (11–13); 3 Ne. 27:19 (19–20); D&C 88:85.
11*a* 2 Ne. 26:9 (9–10); 3 Ne. 27:32 (30–32).

righteousness; and their garments
were white even like unto the Lamb
of God. And the angel said unto me:
These are made white in the blood
of the Lamb, because of their faith
in him.
12 And I, Nephi, also saw many of
the [a]fourth generation who passed
away in righteousness.
13 And it came to pass that I saw
the multitudes of the earth gathered together.
14 And the angel said unto me:
Behold thy seed, and also the seed
of thy brethren.
15 And it came to pass that I looked
and beheld the people of my seed
gathered together in multitudes
[a]against the seed of my brethren;
and they were gathered together
to battle.
16 And the angel spake unto me,
saying: Behold the fountain of
[a]filthy water which thy father saw;
yea, even the [b]river of which he
spake; and the depths thereof are
the depths of [c]hell.
17 And the [a]mists of darkness are
the temptations of the devil, which
[b]blindeth the eyes, and hardeneth
the hearts of the children of men,
and leadeth them away into [c]broad
roads, that they perish and are lost.
18 And the large and spacious
[a]building, which thy father saw, is
vain [b]imaginations and the [c]pride
of the children of men. And a great
and a terrible [d]gulf divideth them;
yea, even the word of the [e]justice of
the Eternal God, and the Messiah
who is the Lamb of God, of whom
the Holy Ghost beareth record,
from the beginning of the world
until this time, and from this time
henceforth and forever.
19 And while the angel spake
these words, I beheld and saw that
the seed of my brethren did contend against my seed, according to
the word of the angel; and because
of the pride of my seed, and the
[a]temptations of the devil, I beheld
that the seed of my brethren did
[b]overpower the people of my seed.
20 And it came to pass that I beheld, and saw the people of the
seed of my brethren that they had
overcome my seed; and they went
forth in multitudes upon the face
of the land.
21 And I saw them gathered together in multitudes; and I saw [a]wars
and rumors of wars among them;
and in wars and rumors of wars I
saw [b]many generations pass away.
22 And the angel said unto me:
Behold these shall [a]dwindle in
unbelief.
23 And it came to pass that I beheld, after they had dwindled in
unbelief they became a [a]dark, and
loathsome, and a [b]filthy people,
full of [c]idleness and all manner of
abominations.

CHAPTER 13

Nephi sees in vision the church of the devil set up among the Gentiles, the discovery and colonizing of America, the loss of many plain and precious parts of the Bible, the resultant state of gentile apostasy, the restoration of the gospel, the coming forth of latter-day scripture, and the building up of Zion. About 600–592 B.C.

12*a* 2 Ne. 26:9; Alma 45:12 (10–12); Hel. 13:10 (5, 9–10); 3 Ne. 27:32; 4 Ne. 1:14 (14–41).
15*a* Morm. 6:7 (1–22).
16*a* TG Filthiness.
b 1 Ne. 8:13 (13–14); 15:27 (26–29).
c TG Hell.
17*a* 2 Pet. 2:17; 1 Ne. 8:23; 15:24 (23–24).
b TG Apostasy of Individuals.
c Prov. 4:14; Luke 13:24.
18*a* 1 Ne. 8:26; 11:35 (35–36).
b Jer. 7:24; 9:14.
c TG Haughtiness; Pride.
d Luke 16:26; 1 Ne. 15:28 (28–30).
e TG God, Justice of.
19*a* TG Temptation.
b Jarom 1:10; W of M 1:2 (1–2).
21*a* Morm. 8:8; Moro. 1:2.
b 2 Ne. 1:18.
22*a* 1 Ne. 15:13; 2 Ne. 26:15.
23*a* 2 Ne. 26:33.
b 2 Ne. 5:22 (20–25). TG Filthiness.
c TG Idleness.

AND it came to pass that the angel
spake unto me, saying: Look! And
I looked and beheld many nations
and kingdoms.
2 And the angel said unto me: What
beholdest thou? And I said: I behold
many [a]nations and kingdoms.
3 And he said unto me: These are
the nations and kingdoms of the
Gentiles.
4 And it came to pass that I saw
among the nations of the [a]Gentiles
the formation of a [b]great church.
5 And the angel said unto me:
Behold the formation of a [a]church
which is most abominable above
all other churches, which [b]slayeth
the saints of God, yea, and tortureth
them and bindeth them down, and
yoketh them with a [c]yoke of iron, and
bringeth them down into captivity.
6 And it came to pass that I beheld
this [a]great and [b]abominable church;
and I saw the [c]devil that he was the
founder of it.
7 And I also saw [a]gold, and silver,
and silks, and scarlets, and fine-
twined [b]linen, and all manner of
precious clothing; and I saw many
harlots.
8 And the angel spake unto me,
saying: Behold the gold, and the
silver, and the silks, and the scarlets,
and the fine-twined linen, and the
precious clothing, and the harlots,
are the [a]desires of this great and
abominable church.
9 And also for the [a]praise of the
world do they [b]destroy the saints
of God, and bring them down into
captivity.
10 And it came to pass that I looked
and beheld many waters; and they
divided the Gentiles from the seed
of my brethren.
11 And it came to pass that the
angel said unto me: Behold the
wrath of God is upon the seed of
thy brethren.
12 And I looked and beheld a man
among the Gentiles, who was separated from the seed of my brethren
by the many waters; and I beheld
the Spirit of God, that it came down
and [a]wrought upon the man; and he
went forth upon the many waters,
even unto the seed of my brethren,
who were in the promised land.
13 And it came to pass that I beheld
the Spirit of God, that it wrought
upon other Gentiles; and they went
forth out of captivity, upon the
many waters.
14 And it came to pass that I beheld
many [a]multitudes of the Gentiles
upon the [b]land of promise; and I
beheld the wrath of God, that it
was upon the seed of my brethren;
and they were [c]scattered before the
Gentiles and were smitten.
15 And I beheld the Spirit of the
Lord, that it was upon the Gentiles,
and they did prosper and [a]obtain
the [b]land for their inheritance; and
I beheld that they were white, and
exceedingly fair and [c]beautiful,
like unto my people before they
were [d]slain.
16 And it came to pass that I,
Nephi, beheld that the Gentiles
who had gone forth out of captivity did humble themselves before
the Lord; and the power of the Lord
was [a]with them.
17 And I beheld that their mother
Gentiles were gathered together

---

13 2*a* TG Kings, Earthly; Nations.
4*a* TG Gentiles.
b 1 Ne. 13:26 (26, 34); 14:10 (3, 9–17).
5*a* 2 Ne. 10:16.
b Rev. 17:6 (3–6); 18:24; 1 Ne. 14:13.
c Jer. 28:14 (10–14). TG Bondage, Spiritual.
6*a* D&C 88:94.
b TG Devil, Church of.
c 1 Ne. 22:23 (22–23). TG Devil.
7*a* Morm. 8:37 (36–38).
b Ether 10:24.
8*a* Rev. 18:19 (10–24); Morm. 8:37 (36–41).
9*a* Morm. 8:38.
b Rev. 13:7 (4–7).
12*a* TG Guidance, Divine.
14*a* 2 Ne. 1:11; Morm. 5:19 (19–20).
b TG Promised Lands.
c 1 Ne. 22:7. TG Israel, Scattering of.
15*a* Morm. 5:19.
b 2 Ne. 10:19.
c 2 Ne. 5:21; 4 Ne. 1:10; Morm. 9:6.
d Morm. 6:19 (17–22).
16*a* D&C 101:80.

upon the waters, and upon the land
also, to battle against them.
18 And I beheld that the power
of God was with them, and also
that the wrath of God was upon all
those that were gathered together
[a]against them to battle.
19 And I, Nephi, beheld that the
Gentiles that had gone out of captivity were [a]delivered by the power
of God out of the hands of all other
nations.
20 And it came to pass that I, Nephi,
beheld that they did prosper in
the land; and I beheld a [a]book, and
it was carried forth among them.
21 And the angel said unto me:
Knowest thou the meaning of the
book?
22 And I said unto him: I know not.
23 And he said: Behold it pro-
ceedeth out of the mouth of a Jew.
And I, Nephi, beheld it; and he
said unto me: The [a]book that thou
beholdest is a [b]record of the [c]Jews,
which contains the covenants of
the Lord, which he hath made unto
the house of Israel; and it also con-
taineth many of the prophecies of
the holy prophets; and it is a record
like unto the engravings which are
upon the [d]plates of brass, save there
are not so many; nevertheless, they
contain the covenants of the Lord,
which he hath made unto the house
of Israel; wherefore, they are of great
worth unto the Gentiles.
24 And the angel of the Lord said
unto me: Thou hast beheld that the
[a]book proceeded forth from the
mouth of a Jew; and when it proceeded forth from the mouth of a Jew
it contained the fulness of the gospel
of the Lord, of whom the twelve
apostles bear record; and they bear
record according to the truth which
is in the Lamb of God.
25 Wherefore, these things go forth
from the [a]Jews in purity unto the
[b]Gentiles, according to the truth
which is in God.
26 And after they go forth by the
[a]hand of the twelve apostles of
the Lamb, from the Jews [b]unto the
Gentiles, thou seest the formation of
that [c]great and abominable [d]church,
which is most abominable above
all other churches; for behold, they
have [e]taken away from the gospel
of the Lamb many parts which are
[f]plain and most precious; and also
many covenants of the Lord have
they taken away.
27 And all this have they done that
they might pervert the right ways
of the Lord, that they might blind
the eyes and harden the hearts of
the children of men.
28 Wherefore, thou seest that after
the book hath gone forth through
the hands of the great and abominable church, that there are many
plain and [a]precious things taken
away from the book, which is the
book of the Lamb of God.
29 And after these plain and precious things were [a]taken away it
goeth forth unto all the nations of
the Gentiles; and after it goeth forth
unto all the nations of the Gentiles,
yea, even across the many waters
which thou hast seen with the Gentiles which have gone forth out of
captivity, thou seest—because of
the many plain and precious things
which have been taken out of the

18*a* 1 Ne. 17:35.
19*a* 2 Ne. 10:10 (10–14); 3 Ne. 21:4; Ether 2:12.
20*a* 1 Ne. 13:41 (3–41); 14:23.
23*a* 1 Ne. 13:38; 2 Ne. 29:6 (4–12).
b TG Scriptures, Preservation of.
c 2 Ne. 3:12.
d 1 Ne. 5:10 (10–22); 19:22.
24*a* 2 Ne. 29:3.
25*a* 2 Ne. 29:4 (4–6); D&C 3:16. TG Israel, Judah, People of.
b TG Gentiles.
26*a* Luke 1:1 (1–4); 2 Tim. 4:13.
b Matt. 21:43.
c 1 Ne. 13:4 (4–6); 14:10 (3, 9–17).
d TG Apostasy of the Early Christian Church.
e Morm. 8:33; Moses 1:41. TG False Doctrine; Scriptures, Lost.
f 1 Ne. 14:21 (20–26); A of F 1:8.
28*a* 1 Ne. 14:23.
29*a* 2 Pet. 3:16.

book, which were plain unto the understanding of the children of men,
according to the plainness which
is in the Lamb of God—because of
these things which are taken away
out of the gospel of the Lamb, an
exceedingly great many do stumble, yea, insomuch that Satan hath
great power over them.
30 Nevertheless, thou beholdest
that the Gentiles who have gone
forth out of captivity, and have been
lifted up by the power of God above
all other nations, upon the face of
the land which is choice above all
other lands, which is the land that
the Lord God hath covenanted with
thy father that his seed should have
for the [a]land of their inheritance;
wherefore, thou seest that the Lord
God will not suffer that the Gentiles
will utterly destroy the [b]mixture
of thy [c]seed, which are among thy
brethren.
31 Neither will he suffer that the
Gentiles shall [a]destroy the seed of
thy brethren.
32 Neither will the Lord God suffer that the Gentiles shall forever
remain in that awful state of blindness, which thou beholdest they are
in, because of the plain and most
precious parts of the gospel of the
Lamb which have been kept back
by that [a]abominable church, whose
formation thou hast seen.
33 Wherefore saith the Lamb of
God: I will be [a]merciful unto the
Gentiles, unto the visiting of the
remnant of the house of Israel in
great judgment.
34 And it came to pass that the
angel of the Lord spake unto me,
saying: Behold, saith the Lamb of
God, after I have [a]visited the [b]rem-
nant of the house of Israel—and
this remnant of whom I speak is the
seed of thy father—wherefore, after
I have visited them in judgment,
and smitten them by the hand of
the Gentiles, and after the Gentiles
do [c]stumble exceedingly, because
of the most plain and precious
parts of the [d]gospel of the Lamb
which have been kept back by that
abominable church, which is the
mother of harlots, saith the Lamb—I
will be merciful unto the [e]Gentiles
in that day, insomuch that I will
[f]bring forth unto them, in mine own
power, much of my [g]gospel, which
shall be plain and precious, saith
the Lamb.
35 For, behold, saith the Lamb: I
will manifest myself unto thy seed,
that they shall write many things
which I shall minister unto them,
which shall be plain and precious;
and after thy seed shall be destroyed, and dwindle in unbelief,
and also the seed of thy brethren,
behold, [a]these things shall be hid
up, to come forth unto the Gentiles,
by the gift and power of the Lamb.
36 And in them shall be written
my [a]gospel, saith the Lamb, and my
[b]rock and my salvation.
37 And [a]blessed are they who shall
seek to bring forth my [b]Zion at that
day, for they shall have the [c]gift and
the [d]power of the Holy Ghost; and
if they [e]endure unto the end they

30*a* TG Lands of Inheritance; Promised Lands.
b 2 Ne. 29:12 (12–13); Alma 45:14 (10–14); D&C 3:17.
c 2 Ne. 3:3.
31*a* 2 Ne. 4:7; 10:18 (18–19); Jacob 3:6 (5–9); Hel. 15:12 (10–17); 3 Ne. 16:8 (4–13); Morm. 5:20 (20–21).
32*a* TG Devil, Church of.
33*a* Isa. 42:1 (1, 3–4).
34*a* D&C 124:8; Abr. 1:17.
b TG Israel, Joseph, People of.
c 1 Ne. 14:1 (1–3); 2 Ne. 26:20.
d TG Gospel.
e TG Millennium, Preparing a People for.
f TG Scriptures, Lost.
g D&C 10:62. TG Restoration of the Gospel.
35*a* 1 Ne. 14:7; 22:8; 2 Ne. 27:26 (6–26); 29:1 (1–2). TG Book of Mormon.
36*a* 3 Ne. 27:21.
b 3 Ne. 11:39 (38–39). TG Rock.
37*a* Jacob 5:75 (70–76); D&C 21:9. TG Israel, Mission of; Mission of Latter-day Saints.
b TG Zion.
c TG Holy Ghost, Gift of.
d Luke 24:49; 1 Ne. 14:14; D&C 38:38 (32–38).
e 3 Ne. 27:16. TG Endure; Perseverance; Steadfastness.

shall be [f]lifted up at the last day, and shall be saved in the everlasting [g]kingdom of the Lamb; and whoso shall [h]publish peace, yea, tidings of great joy, how beautiful upon the mountains shall they be.

38 And it came to pass that I beheld the remnant of the seed of my brethren, and also the [a]book of the Lamb of God, which had proceeded forth from the mouth of the Jew, that it came forth from the Gentiles [b]unto the remnant of the seed of my brethren.

39 And after it had come forth unto them I beheld [a]other [b]books, which came forth by the power of the Lamb, from the Gentiles unto them, unto the [c]convincing of the Gentiles and the remnant of the seed of my brethren, and also the Jews who were scattered upon all the face of the earth, that the records of the prophets and of the twelve apostles of the Lamb are [d]true.

40 And the angel spake unto me, saying: These [a]last records, which thou hast seen among the Gentiles, shall [b]establish the truth of the [c]first, which are of the [d]twelve apostles of the Lamb, and shall make known the plain and precious things which have been taken away from them; and shall make known to all kindreds, tongues, and people, that the Lamb of God is the Son of the Eternal Father, and the [e]Savior of the world; and that all men must come unto him, or they cannot be saved.

41 And they must come according to the words which shall be established by the mouth of the Lamb; and the words of the Lamb shall be made known in the records of thy seed, as well as in the [a]records of the twelve apostles of the Lamb; wherefore they both shall be established in [b]one; for there is [c]one God and one [d]Shepherd over all the earth.

42 And the time cometh that he shall manifest himself unto all nations, both unto the [a]Jews and also unto the Gentiles; and after he has manifested himself unto the Jews and also unto the Gentiles, then he shall manifest himself unto the Gentiles and also unto the Jews, and the [b]last shall be first, and the [c]first shall be last.

CHAPTER 14

An angel tells Nephi of the blessings and cursings to fall upon the Gentiles—There are only two churches: the Church of the Lamb of God and the church of the devil—The Saints of God in all nations are persecuted by the great and abominable church—The Apostle John will write concerning the end of the world. About 600–592 B.C.

AND it shall come to pass, that if the [a]Gentiles shall hearken unto the Lamb of God in that day that he shall manifest himself unto them in word, and also in [b]power, in very deed, unto the [c]taking away of their [d]stumbling blocks—

2 And harden not their hearts

37*f* James 4:10.
g TG Kingdom of God, in Heaven.
h Isa. 52:7 (7–10); Mark 13:10; 3 Ne. 20:40.
38*a* 1 Ne. 13:23; 2 Ne. 29:6 (4–6).
b Morm. 5:15; 7:8 (8–9).
39*a* D&C 9:2.
b TG Scriptures to Come Forth.
c Ezek. 37:17 (15–20); 1 Ne. 14:2 (1–5).
d 1 Ne. 14:30.
40*a* 2 Ne. 26:17 (16–17); 27:6 (6–26); 29:12. TG Book of Mormon.
b TG Scriptures, Value of.
c See the title page of the Book of Mormon. TG Bible.
d 1 Ne. 11:29; 12:9.
e Moses 1:6.
41*a* 1 Ne. 13:20 (20–28).
b Ezek. 37:17.
c Deut. 6:4; 2 Ne. 31:21.
d TG Jesus Christ, Good Shepherd.
42*a* D&C 18:6, 26; 19:27; 21:12; 90:9 (8–9); 107:33; 112:4.
b Jacob 5:63; Ether 13:12.
c Luke 13:30; 1 Ne. 10:14; 15:13 (13–20); D&C 14:10.
14 1*a* 1 Ne. 22:9 (8–9); 2 Ne. 30:3; 3 Ne. 16:6 (6–13). TG Gentiles.
b 1 Thes. 1:5; 1 Ne. 14:14; Jacob 6:2 (2–3).
c Ether 12:27.
d Isa. 57:14; Ezek. 7:19; 1 Cor. 1:23; 1 Ne. 13:34 (29, 34); 2 Ne. 26:20.

against the Lamb of God, they shall
be numbered among the seed of thy
father; yea, they shall be [a]numbered
among the house of Israel; and they
shall be a [b]blessed people upon the
[c]promised land forever; they shall
be no more brought down into captivity; and the house of Israel shall
no more be confounded.
3 And that great [a]pit, which hath
been digged for them by that great
and abominable church, which
was founded by the devil and his
children, that he might lead away
the souls of men down to hell—
yea, that great pit which hath been
digged for the destruction of men
shall be filled by those who digged
it, unto their utter destruction,
saith the Lamb of God; not the destruction of the soul, save it be the
casting of it into that [b]hell which
hath no end.
4 For behold, this is according to
the [a]captivity of the devil, and also
according to the justice of God, upon
all those who will work wickedness
and abomination before him.
5 And it came to pass that the angel spake unto me, Nephi, saying:
Thou hast beheld that if the Gentiles
repent it shall be [a]well with them;
and thou also knowest concerning
the covenants of the Lord unto the
house of Israel; and thou also hast
heard that whoso [b]repenteth not
must perish.
6 Therefore, [a]wo be unto the
Gentiles if it so be that they harden
their hearts against the Lamb of
God.
7 For the time cometh, saith the
Lamb of God, that I will work a
great and a [a]marvelous work among
the children of men; a [b]work which
shall be everlasting, either on the
one hand or on the other—either
to the convincing of them unto
[c]peace and [d]life eternal, or unto the
deliverance of them to the hardness
of their hearts and the blindness of
their minds unto their being brought
down into captivity, and also into
destruction, both temporally and
spiritually, according to the [e]cap-
tivity of the devil, of which I have
spoken.
8 And it came to pass that when
the angel had spoken these words,
he said unto me: Rememberest thou
the [a]covenants of the Father unto the
house of Israel? I said unto him, Yea.
9 And it came to pass that he said
unto me: Look, and behold that great
and abominable church, which is
the mother of abominations, whose
founder is the [a]devil.
10 And he said unto me: Behold
there are save [a]two churches only;
the one is the church of the Lamb
of God, and the [b]other is the church
of the [c]devil; wherefore, [d]whoso
belongeth not to the church of the
Lamb of God belongeth to that
great church, which is the mother
of abominations; and she is the
[e]whore of all the earth.
11 And it came to pass that I

2*a* Gal. 3:7 (7, 29); 2 Ne. 10:18 (18–19); 3 Ne. 16:13; 21:6 (6, 22); Abr. 2:10 (9–11).
b 2 Ne. 6:12; 10:10 (8–14); 3 Ne. 16:6 (6–7); 20:27; Morm. 5:19.
c TG Israel, Deliverance of; Israel, Restoration of; Lands of Inheritance.
3*a* Ps. 57:6; Matt. 7:2 (1–2); 1 Ne. 22:14 (13–14); D&C 10:26 (25–27); 109:25.
b Alma 19:29. TG Damnation; Hell.
4*a* TG Bondage, Spiritual.
5*a* 1 Ne. 13:39 (34–42); 22:9.
b TG Repent.
6*a* 2 Ne. 28:32.
7*a* Isa. 29:14; 1 Ne. 13:35; 22:8; 2 Ne. 27:26; 29:1 (1–2); D&C 4:1. TG Restoration of the Gospel.
b TG God, Works of.
c TG Peace; Peace of God.
d Jer. 21:8. TG Eternal Life.
e 2 Ne. 2:29 (26–29); Alma 12:11 (9–11).
8*a* TG Abrahamic Covenant; Israel, Mission of.
9*a* 1 Ne. 15:35; D&C 1:35. TG Devil, Church of.
10*a* 1 Ne. 22:23; 2 Ne. 26:20; Morm. 8:28 (25–41). TG Church.
b 1 Ne. 13:4 (4–6), 26 (26, 34).
c TG Devil, Church of; False Prophets.
d 2 Ne. 10:16.
e Rev. 17:15 (5, 15).

looked and beheld the whore of all
the earth, and she sat upon many
[a]waters; and she had dominion over
[b]all the earth, among all nations,
kindreds, tongues, and people.
12 And it came to pass that I beheld
the church of the Lamb of God, and
its numbers were [a]few, because of
the wickedness and abominations
of the whore who sat upon many
waters; nevertheless, I beheld that
the church of the Lamb, who were
the saints of God, were also upon
[b]all the face of the earth; and their
dominions upon the face of the earth
were small, because of the wickedness of the great whore whom I saw.
13 And it came to pass that I beheld
that the great mother of abominations did gather together multitudes
upon the face of all the earth, among
all the nations of the Gentiles, to
[a]fight against the Lamb of God.
14 And it came to pass that I,
Nephi, beheld the power of the
Lamb of God, that it descended upon
the saints of the church of the Lamb,
and upon the covenant people of
the Lord, who were scattered upon
all the face of the earth; and they
were [a]armed with [b]righteousness
and with the [c]power of God in great
glory.
15 And it came to pass that I beheld
that the wrath of God was [a]poured
out upon that great and abominable
church, insomuch that there were
wars and rumors of wars among
all the [b]nations and kindreds of
the earth.
16 And as there began to be [a]wars
and rumors of wars among all the
nations which belonged to the
mother of abominations, the angel
spake unto me, saying: Behold, the
wrath of God is upon the mother
of harlots; and behold, thou seest
all these things—
17 And when the [a]day cometh
that the [b]wrath of God is poured
out upon the mother of harlots,
which is the great and abominable church of all the earth, whose
founder is the devil, then, at that
day, the [c]work of the Father shall
commence, in preparing the way
for the fulfilling of his [d]covenants,
which he hath made to his people
who are of the house of Israel.
18 And it came to pass that the
angel spake unto me, saying: Look!
19 And I looked and beheld a man,
and he was dressed in a white robe.
20 And the angel said unto me:
Behold [a]one of the twelve apostles
of the Lamb.
21 Behold, he shall [a]see and [b]write
the [c]remainder of these things; yea,
and also many things which have
been.
22 And he shall also write concerning the end of the world.
23 Wherefore, the things which
he shall write are just and true;
and behold they are written in the
[a]book which thou beheld proceed-
ing out of the mouth of the Jew;
and at the time they proceeded out
of the mouth of the Jew, or, at the
time the book proceeded out of the
mouth of the Jew, the things which
were written were plain and pure,
and most [b]precious and easy to the
understanding of all men.

11*a* Jer. 51:13 (12–14).
b D&C 35:11.
12*a* Matt. 7:14;
Jacob 5:70;
3 Ne. 14:14;
D&C 138:26.
b D&C 90:11.
13*a* Rev. 17:6 (1–6); 18:24;
1 Ne. 13:5.
14*a* TG Mission of Latter-day Saints.
b TG Deliver; Protection, Divine.
c Luke 24:49;
1 Ne. 13:37; 14:1;
Jacob 6:2 (2–3);
D&C 38:38 (32–38).
15*a* D&C 115:6 (5–6).
b Mark 13:8;
D&C 87:6.
16*a* 1 Ne. 22:13 (13–14);
Morm. 8:30.
TG War.
17*a* TG Last Days.
b 1 Ne. 21:26;
22:16 (15–16);
3 Ne. 20:20 (19–21).
c 3 Ne. 21:26 (7, 20–29).
TG Israel, Restoration of.
d Morm. 8:21 (21, 41).
TG Abrahamic Covenant.
20*a* Rev. 1:1 (1–3);
1 Ne. 14:27.
21*a* Rev. 1:1.
b 1 Ne. 13:24 (20–40);
A of F 1:8.
c Rev. 4:1.
23*a* 1 Ne. 13:20 (20–24);
Morm. 8:33;
Ether 4:16.
b 1 Ne. 13:28 (28–32).

24 And behold, the things which
this [a]apostle of the Lamb shall write
are many things which thou hast
seen; and behold, the remainder
shalt thou see.
25 But the things which thou shalt
see hereafter thou shalt not write;
for the Lord God hath ordained the
apostle of the Lamb of God that he
should [a]write them.
26 And also others who have been,
to them hath he shown all things,
and they have [a]written them; and
they are [b]sealed up to come forth in
their purity, according to the truth
which is in the Lamb, in the own
due time of the Lord, unto the house
of Israel.
27 And I, Nephi, heard and bear
record, that the name of the apostle
of the Lamb was [a]John, according
to the word of the angel.
28 And behold, I, Nephi, am forbidden that I should write the remainder of the things which I saw
and heard; wherefore the things
which I have written sufficeth me;
and I have written but a small part
of the things which I saw.
29 And I bear record that I saw
the things which my [a]father saw,
and the angel of the Lord did make
them known unto me.
30 And now I make an end of
speaking concerning the things
which I saw while I was [a]carried
away in the Spirit; and if all the
things which I saw are not written,
the things which I have written are
[b]true. And thus it is. Amen.

CHAPTER 15

Lehi's seed are to receive the gospel from the Gentiles in the latter days—The gathering of Israel is likened unto an olive tree whose natural branches will be grafted in again—Nephi interprets the vision of the tree of life and speaks of the justice of God in dividing the wicked from the righteous. About 600–592 B.C.

AND it came to pass that after I,
Nephi, had been carried away in
the Spirit, and seen all these things,
I returned to the tent of my father.
2 And it came to pass that I beheld
my brethren, and they were disputing one with another concerning
the things which my father had
spoken unto them.
3 For he truly spake many great
things unto them, which were hard
to be [a]understood, save a man should
inquire of the Lord; and they being hard in their hearts, therefore
they did not look unto the Lord as
they ought.
4 And now I, Nephi, was grieved
because of the hardness of their
hearts, and also, because of the
things which I had seen, and knew
they must unavoidably come to
pass because of the great wickedness of the children of men.
5 And it came to pass that I was
overcome because of my afflictions,
for I considered that mine [a]afflictions were great above all, because
of the [b]destruction of my people,
for I had beheld their fall.
6 And it came to pass that after I
had received [a]strength I spake unto
my brethren, desiring to know of
them the cause of their disputations.
7 And they said: Behold, we cannot
understand the words which our
father hath spoken concerning the
natural branches of the [a]olive tree,
and also concerning the Gentiles.
8 And I said unto them: Have ye
[a]inquired of the Lord?

24*a* Ether 4:16.
25*a* John 20:30 (30–31); 21:25; Rev. 1:19.
26*a* TG Scriptures, Writing of.
b Dan. 12:9; 2 Ne. 27:10 (6–23); 30:17; Ether 3:21 (21–27); 4:5 (4–7); 12:21; D&C 35:18; JS—H 1:65.
27*a* Rev. 1:1 (1–3).
29*a* 1 Ne. 8:2 (2–35).
30*a* 1 Kgs. 18:12; 1 Ne. 11:29 (19, 29).
b 1 Ne. 13:39; 2 Ne. 25:20.
15 3*a* 1 Cor. 2:11 (10–12). TG Hardheartedness; Understanding.
5*a* Moses 7:44 (41–44).
b Enos 1:13; Morm. 6:1.
6*a* Moses 1:10; JS—H 1:20, 48.
7*a* 1 Ne. 10:14 (2–15).
8*a* 2 Ne. 1:25 (24–27); Mosiah 10:14. TG Problem-Solving.

9 And they said unto me: [a]We have
not; for the Lord maketh no such
thing known unto us.
10 Behold, I said unto them: How
is it that ye do not keep the commandments of the Lord? How is it
that ye will [a]perish, because of the
hardness of your hearts?
11 Do ye not remember the things
which the Lord hath said?—If ye
will not harden your hearts, and
[a]ask me in [b]faith, believing that
ye shall receive, with diligence in
keeping my commandments, surely
these things shall be made known
unto you.
12 Behold, I say unto you, that the
house of Israel was compared unto
an olive tree, by the Spirit of the
Lord which was in our father; and
behold are we not broken off from
the house of Israel, and are we not
a [a]branch of the house of Israel?
13 And now, the thing which our
father meaneth concerning the
grafting in of the natural branches
through the fulness of the Gentiles,
is, that in the latter days, when our
seed shall have [a]dwindled in unbelief, yea, for the space of many
years, and many generations after
the [b]Messiah shall be manifested
in body unto the children of men,
then shall the fulness of the [c]gospel
of the Messiah come unto the Gentiles, and from the [d]Gentiles unto
the remnant of our seed—
14 And at that day shall the remnant of our [a]seed [b]know that they
are of the house of Israel, and that
they are the [c]covenant people of the
Lord; and then shall they know and
[d]come to the [e]knowledge of their
forefathers, and also to the knowledge of the gospel of their Redeemer,
which was ministered unto their
fathers by him; wherefore, they shall
come to the knowledge of their Redeemer and the very points of his
doctrine, that they may know how
to come unto him and be saved.
15 And then at that day will they
not rejoice and give praise unto
their everlasting God, their [a]rock
and their salvation? Yea, at that day,
will they not receive the strength
and nourishment from the true
[b]vine? Yea, will they not come unto
the true fold of God?
16 Behold, I say unto you, Yea;
they shall be remembered again
among the house of Israel; they
shall be [a]grafted in, being a natural branch of the olive tree, into
the true olive tree.
17 And this is what our father
meaneth; and he meaneth that it
will not come to pass until after
they are scattered by the Gentiles;
and he meaneth that it shall come
by way of the Gentiles, that the
Lord may show his power unto the
Gentiles, for the very cause that he
shall be [a]rejected of the Jews, or of
the house of Israel.
18 Wherefore, our father hath not
spoken of our seed alone, but also
of all the house of Israel, pointing
to the covenant which should be
fulfilled in the latter days; which
covenant the Lord made to our
father Abraham, saying: In thy [a]seed
shall all the kindreds of the earth
be [b]blessed.

9*a* D&C 58:33.
10*a* TG Apostasy of Individuals.
11*a* James 1:5 (5–6). TG Prayer.
b 1 Ne. 2:19 (18–21); 7:12 (9–13).
12*a* Gen. 49:22 (22–26); 1 Ne. 10:12 (12–14); 19:24. TG Israel, Joseph, People of.
13*a* 1 Ne. 12:22 (22–23); 2 Ne. 26:15.
b TG Jesus Christ, Messiah.
c TG Gospel; Mission of Latter-day Saints.
d 1 Ne. 13:42; 22:9 (5–10); D&C 14:10. TG Gentiles.
14*a* 2 Ne. 10:2; 3 Ne. 5:23 (21–26); 21:7 (4–29).
b 2 Ne. 3:12; 30:5; Morm. 7:9 (1, 9–10).
c TG Abrahamic Covenant.
d Jacob 3:6.
e D&C 3:18 (16–20). See also title page of the Book of Mormon.
15*a* TG Rock.
b Gen. 49:11; John 15:1.
16*a* Jacob 5:54 (1–77).
17*a* TG Jesus Christ, Betrayal of; Jesus Christ, Crucifixion of.
18*a* Gen. 12:3 (1–3); Abr. 2:11 (6–11). TG Seed of Abraham.
b TG Israel, Mission of.

19 And it came to pass that I,
Nephi, spake much unto them concerning these things; yea, I spake
unto them concerning the [a]restora-
tion of the Jews in the latter days.
20 And I did rehearse unto them
the words of [a]Isaiah, who spake
[b]concerning the [c]restoration of the
Jews, or of the house of Israel; and
after they were restored they should
no more be confounded, neither
should they be scattered again.
And it came to pass that I did speak
many words unto my brethren, that
they were pacified and did [d]humble
themselves before the Lord.
21 And it came to pass that they
did speak unto me again, saying:
What meaneth this thing which
our father saw in a dream? What
meaneth the [a]tree which he saw?
22 And I said unto them: It was a
representation of the [a]tree of life.
23 And they said unto me: What
meaneth the [a]rod of iron which
our father saw, that led to the tree?
24 And I said unto them that it
was the [a]word of God; and whoso
would hearken unto the word of
God, and would [b]hold fast unto it,
they would never perish; neither
could the [c]temptations and the
fiery [d]darts of the [e]adversary overpower them unto blindness, to lead
them away to destruction.
25 Wherefore, I, Nephi, did exhort
them to give [a]heed unto the word
of the Lord; yea, I did exhort them
with all the energies of my soul, and
with all the [b]faculty which I possessed, that they would give heed
to the word of God and remember
to keep his commandments always
in all things.
26 And they said unto me: What
meaneth the [a]river of water which
our father saw?
27 And I said unto them that the
[a]water which my father saw was
[b]filthiness; and so much was his
mind swallowed up in other things
that he beheld not the filthiness of
the water.
28 And I said unto them that it was
an awful [a]gulf, which separated the
wicked from the tree of life, and
also from the saints of God.
29 And I said unto them that it
was a representation of that awful
[a]hell, which the angel said unto me
was prepared for the wicked.
30 And I said unto them that
our father also saw that the [a]justice
of God did also divide the wicked
from the righteous; and the brightness thereof was like unto the
brightness of a flaming [b]fire, which
ascendeth up unto God forever and
ever, and hath no end.
31 And they said unto me: Doth
this thing mean the torment of the
body in the days of [a]probation, or
doth it mean the final state of the
soul after the [b]death of the temporal
body, or doth it speak of the things
which are temporal?
32 And it came to pass that I said
unto them that it was a representation of things both temporal and
spiritual; for the day should come
that they must be judged of their
[a]works, yea, even the works which
were done by the temporal body in
their days of [b]probation.

19*a* Isa. 42:22 (22–23); 1 Ne. 19:15. TG Israel, Gathering of; Israel, Judah, People of.
20*a* 1 Ne. 19:23.
b Isa. 40:9.
c TG Israel, Restoration of.
d 1 Ne. 16:5 (5, 24, 39).
21*a* 1 Ne. 8:10 (10–12).
22*a* 1 Ne. 11:4; Moses 3:9.
23*a* 1 Ne. 8:19 (19–24).
24*a* 1 Ne. 8:19. TG Gospel.
b Prov. 4:13.
c 1 Ne. 8:23. TG Temptation.
d Eph. 6:16; D&C 3:8; 27:17.
e TG Devil.
25*a* D&C 11:2; 32:4; 84:43 (43–44). TG Scriptures, Study of.
b W of M 1:18.
26*a* 1 Ne. 8:13.
27*a* 1 Ne. 12:16 (16–18).
b TG Filthiness.
28*a* Luke 16:26; 1 Ne. 12:18; 2 Ne. 1:13.
29*a* 1 Ne. 8:32 (13–14, 32). TG Hell.
30*a* TG God, Justice of; Justice.
b Num. 11:1 (1, 10); 2 Ne. 26:6.
31*a* TG Probation.
b Alma 40:11 (6–26).
32*a* TG Good Works.
b TG Probation.

33 Wherefore, if they should [a]die
in their wickedness they must be
[b]cast off also, as to the things which
are spiritual, which are pertaining
to righteousness; wherefore, they
must be brought to stand before
God, to be [c]judged of their [d]works;
and if their works have been filthiness they must needs be [e]filthy; and
if they be filthy it must needs be
that they cannot [f]dwell in the kingdom of God; if so, the kingdom of
God must be filthy also.
34 But behold, I say unto you, the
kingdom of God is not filthy, and
there cannot any unclean thing
enter into the kingdom of God;
wherefore there must needs be a
place of [a]filthiness prepared for
that which is filthy.
35 And there is a place prepared,
yea, even that [a]awful [b]hell of which
I have spoken, and the [c]devil is the
preparator of it; wherefore the final state of the souls of men is to
dwell in the kingdom of God, or to
be cast out because of that [d]justice
of which I have spoken.
36 Wherefore, the wicked are rejected from the righteous, and also
from that [a]tree of life, whose fruit is
most precious and most [b]desirable
above all other fruits; yea, and it is
the [c]greatest of all the [d]gifts of God.
And thus I spake unto my brethren.
Amen.

CHAPTER 16

The wicked take the truth to be hard—Lehi's sons marry the daughters of Ishmael—The Liahona guides their course in the wilderness—Messages from the Lord are written on the Liahona from time to time—Ishmael dies; his family murmurs because of afflictions. About 600–592 B.C.

AND now it came to pass that after I,
Nephi, had made an end of speaking
to my brethren, behold they said
unto me: Thou hast declared unto
us hard things, more than we are
able to bear.
2 And it came to pass that I said
unto them that I knew that I had
spoken [a]hard things against the
wicked, according to the truth;
and the righteous have I justified,
and testified that they should be
lifted up at the last day; wherefore, the [b]guilty taketh the [c]truth
to be hard, for it [d]cutteth them to
the very center.
3 And now my brethren, if ye
were righteous and were willing to
hearken to the truth, and give heed
unto it, that ye might [a]walk uprightly before God, then ye would
not murmur because of the truth,
and say: Thou speakest hard things
against us.
4 And it came to pass that I, Nephi,
did exhort my brethren, with all
diligence, to keep the commandments of the Lord.
5 And it came to pass that they
did [a]humble themselves before the
Lord; insomuch that I had joy and
great hopes of them, that they would
walk in the paths of righteousness.
6 Now, all these things were said

33*a* Ezek. 18:26; Mosiah 15:26; Moro. 10:26.
b Alma 12:16; 40:26.
c TG Jesus Christ, Judge; Judgment, the Last.
d Ps. 33:15 (13–15); 3 Ne. 27:25 (23–27).
e 2 Ne. 9:16; D&C 88:35.
f Ps. 15:1 (1–5); 24:3 (3–4); Mosiah 15:23; Alma 11:37; D&C 76:62 (50–70); Moses 6:57 (55–59).
34*a* TG Filthiness.
35*a* 2 Ne. 9:19; Mosiah 26:27.
b TG Hell.
c 1 Ne. 14:9; D&C 1:35.
d TG Justice.
36*a* Gen. 2:9; 1 Ne. 8:11; 2 Ne. 2:15.
b 1 Ne. 8:12.
c Hel. 5:8.
d D&C 14:7. TG God, Gifts of.
16 2*a* Acts 7:54; 2 Ne. 33:5; Enos 1:23; W of M 1:17. TG Chastening.
b John 3:20 (19–21); 7:7; Hel. 13:24 (24–27).
c Prov. 15:10; 2 Ne. 1:26; 9:40.
d Acts 5:33; Mosiah 13:7; Moses 6:37.
3*a* D&C 5:21. TG Walking with God.
5*a* 1 Ne. 15:20; 16:24 (24, 39); 18:4.

and done as my father dwelt in a
tent in the [a]valley which he called
Lemuel.
7 And it came to pass that I,
Nephi, took one of the [a]daughters of
Ishmael to [b]wife; and also, my
brethren took of the [c]daughters of
Ishmael to wife; and also [d]Zoram
took the eldest daughter of Ishmael
to wife.
8 And thus my father had fulfilled
all the [a]commandments of the Lord
which had been given unto him.
And also, I, Nephi, had been blessed
of the Lord exceedingly.
9 And it came to pass that the voice
of the Lord spake unto my father
by night, and commanded him that
on the morrow he should take his
[a]journey into the wilderness.
10 And it came to pass that as my
father arose in the morning, and
went forth to the tent door, to his
great astonishment he beheld upon
the ground a round [a]ball of curious
workmanship; and it was of fine
brass. And within the ball were two
spindles; and the one [b]pointed the
way whither we should go into the
wilderness.
11 And it came to pass that we did
gather together whatsoever things
we should carry into the wilderness,
and all the remainder of our provisions which the Lord had given
unto us; and we did take [a]seed of
every kind that we might carry into
the wilderness.
12 And it came to pass that we did
take our tents and depart into the
wilderness, across the river Laman.
13 And it came to pass that we
traveled for the space of four days,
nearly a south-southeast direction,
and we did pitch our tents again; and
we did call the name of the place
[a]Shazer.
14 And it came to pass that we did
take our bows and our arrows, and
go forth into the wilderness to slay
food for our families; and after we
had slain food for our families we
did return again to our families
in the wilderness, to the place of
Shazer. And we did go forth again
in the wilderness, following the
same direction, keeping in the
most fertile parts of the wilderness,
which were in the borders near the
[a]Red Sea.
15 And it came to pass that we did
travel for the space of many days,
[a]slaying food by the way, with our
bows and our arrows and our stones
and our slings.
16 And we did follow the [a]direc-
tions of the ball, which led us in the
more fertile parts of the wilderness.
17 And after we had traveled for
the space of many days, we did pitch
our tents for the space of a time,
that we might again rest ourselves
and obtain food for our families.
18 And it came to pass that as I,
Nephi, went forth to slay food, behold, I did break my bow, which
was made of fine [a]steel; and after
I did break my bow, behold, my
brethren were angry with me because of the loss of my bow, for we
did obtain no food.
19 And it came to pass that we did
return without food to our families,
and being much fatigued, because
of their journeying, they did suffer
much for the want of food.
20 And it came to pass that Laman
and Lemuel and the sons of Ishmael
did begin to murmur exceedingly,
because of their sufferings and
afflictions in the wilderness; and
also my father began to murmur
against the Lord his God; yea, and
they were all exceedingly sorrowful,

6a 1 Ne. 2:14 (8, 14); 9:1.
7a 1 Ne. 7:1 (1, 19); 18:19 (19–20).
b TG Marriage, Marry.
c 1 Ne. 7:6.
d 1 Ne. 4:35; 2 Ne. 5:6 (5–6).
8a 1 Ne. 3:18; 5:21; 7:2.
9a Omni 1:16.
10a 1 Ne. 16:16; Alma 37:38 (38–47).
b Ex. 13:21.
11a 1 Ne. 8:1; 18:6; Ether 1:41; 2:3.
13a HEB twisting, intertwining.
14a 1 Ne. 2:5; D&C 17:1.
15a Alma 17:7.
16a 1 Ne. 16:10 (10, 16, 26); 18:12 (12, 21); 2 Ne. 5:12; Alma 37:38 (38–47); D&C 17:1.
18a 2 Sam. 22:35; Ps. 18:34.

even that they did [a]murmur against
the Lord.
21 Now it came to pass that I,
Nephi, having been afflicted with
my brethren because of the loss of
my bow, and their bows having lost
their [a]springs, it began to be exceedingly difficult, yea, insomuch that
we could obtain no food.
22 And it came to pass that I, Nephi,
did speak much unto my brethren, because they had hardened
their hearts again, even unto [a]com-
plaining against the Lord their God.
23 And it came to pass that I,
Nephi, did [a]make out of wood a
bow, and out of a straight stick, an
arrow; wherefore, I did arm myself
with a bow and an arrow, with a
sling and with stones. And I said
unto my [b]father: Whither shall I go
to obtain food?
24 And it came to pass that he did
[a]inquire of the Lord, for they had
[b]humbled themselves because of
my words; for I did say many things
unto them in the energy of my soul.
25 And it came to pass that the
voice of the Lord came unto my
father; and he was truly [a]chastened
because of his murmuring against
the Lord, insomuch that he was
brought down into the depths of
sorrow.
26 And it came to pass that the
voice of the Lord said unto him:
Look upon the ball, and behold the
things which are written.
27 And it came to pass that when
my father beheld the things which
were [a]written upon the ball, he did
fear and tremble exceedingly, and
also my brethren and the sons of
Ishmael and our wives.
28 And it came to pass that I, Nephi,
beheld the pointers which were in
the ball, that they did work according to the [a]faith and diligence and
heed which we did give unto them.
29 And there was also written
upon them a new writing, which
was plain to be read, which did give
us [a]understanding concerning the
ways of the Lord; and it was written and changed from time to time,
according to the faith and diligence
which we gave unto it. And thus we
see that by [b]small means the Lord
can bring about great things.
30 And it came to pass that I,
Nephi, did go forth up into the top
of the mountain, according to the
[a]directions which were given upon
the ball.
31 And it came to pass that I did
slay wild [a]beasts, insomuch that I
did obtain food for our families.
32 And it came to pass that I did
return to our tents, bearing the
beasts which I had slain; and now
when they beheld that I had obtained [a]food, how great was their
joy! And it came to pass that they
did humble themselves before the
Lord, and did give thanks unto him.
33 And it came to pass that we did
again take our journey, traveling
nearly the same course as in the
beginning; and after we had traveled for the space of many days we
did pitch our tents again, that we
might tarry for the space of a time.
34 And it came to pass that [a]Ish-
mael died, and was buried in the
place which was called [b]Nahom.
35 And it came to pass that the
daughters of Ishmael did [a]mourn
exceedingly, because of the loss of

20*a* TG Murmuring.
21*a* Gen. 49:24.
22*a* Ex. 16:8; Num. 11:1 (1–2); D&C 29:19.
23*a* TG Initiative.
b TG Honoring Father and Mother.
24*a* TG Guidance, Divine; Prayer.
b 1 Ne. 15:20; 16:5.
25*a* Ether 2:14. TG Chastening; Repent.
27*a* TG Warn.
28*a* Alma 37:40. TG Faith.
29*a* TG Understanding.
b 2 Kgs. 5:13; James 3:4; Alma 37:6 (6–8, 41); D&C 123:16.
30*a* TG Guidance, Divine.
31*a* Gen. 9:3.
32*a* 2 Ne. 1:24. TG Food; Thanksgiving.
34*a* 1 Ne. 7:2 (2–6, 19).
b HEB probably "consolation," from verb *naham*, "be sorry, console oneself."
35*a* TG Mourning.

their father, and because of their
[b]afflictions in the wilderness; and
they did [c]murmur against my father,
because he had brought them out of
the land of Jerusalem, saying: Our
father is dead; yea, and we have wandered much in the wilderness, and
we have suffered much affliction,
hunger, thirst, and fatigue; and after
all these sufferings we must perish
in the wilderness with hunger.
36 And thus they did murmur
against my father, and also against
me; and they were desirous to [a]re-
turn again to Jerusalem.
37 And Laman said unto Lemuel
and also unto the sons of Ishmael:
Behold, let us [a]slay our father, and
also our brother Nephi, who has
taken it upon him to be our [b]ruler
and our teacher, who are his elder
brethren.
38 Now, he says that the Lord has
talked with him, and also that [a]an-
gels have ministered unto him. But
behold, we know that he lies unto
us; and he tells us these things, and
he worketh many things by his
cunning arts, that he may deceive
our eyes, thinking, perhaps, that he
may lead us away into some strange
wilderness; and after he has led
us away, he has thought to make
himself a king and a ruler over us,
that he may do with us according
to his will and pleasure. And after
this manner did my brother Laman
[b]stir up their hearts to [c]anger.
39 And it came to pass that the Lord
was with us, yea, even the voice of
the Lord came and did speak many
words unto them, and did [a]chas-
ten them exceedingly; and after
they were chastened by the voice of
the Lord they did turn away their
anger, and did repent of their sins,
insomuch that the Lord did bless
us again with food, that we did not
perish.

CHAPTER 17

Nephi is commanded to build a ship—His brethren oppose him—He exhorts them by recounting the history of God's dealings with Israel—Nephi is filled with the power of God—His brethren are forbidden to touch him, lest they wither as a dried reed. About 592–591 B.C.

AND it came to pass that we did
again take our journey in the wilderness; and we did travel nearly
eastward from that time forth. And
we did travel and [a]wade through
much affliction in the wilderness;
and our [b]women did bear children
in the wilderness.
2 And so great were the [a]blessings
of the Lord upon us, that while we
did live upon [b]raw [c]meat in the wilderness, our women did give plenty
of suck for their children, and were
strong, yea, even like unto the men;
and they began to bear their journeyings without murmurings.
3 And thus we see that the commandments of God must be fulfilled.
And if it so be that the children
of men keep the commandments
of God he doth nourish them, and
[a]strengthen them, and provide
means whereby they can accomplish the thing which he has commanded them; wherefore, he did
[b]provide means for us while we did
sojourn in the wilderness.
4 And we did sojourn for the space
of many years, yea, even eight years
in the wilderness.
5 And we did come to the land
which we called [a]Bountiful, because

35*b* TG Affliction.
c TG Murmuring.
36*a* Num. 14:4 (1–5).
37*a* 1 Ne. 17:44; 2 Ne. 1:24. TG Murder.
b Gen. 37:10 (9–11); Num. 16:13; 1 Ne. 2:22; 18:10.
38*a* 1 Ne. 3:30 (30–31); 4:3.
b TG Provoking.
c TG Anger.
39*a* TG Chastening.
17 1*a* Ps. 69:2 (1–2, 14).
b TG Woman.
2*a* TG Blessing.
b 1 Ne. 17:12.
c Ex. 16:13 (12–13); 1 Ne. 18:6. TG Meat.
3*a* Ex. 1:19; Ezra 8:22 (22–23); Isa. 45:24; Mosiah 2:41; Alma 26:12. TG Strength.
b Gen. 18:14; 1 Ne. 3:7.
5*a* Alma 22:29 (29–33).

of its much fruit and also wild honey;
and all these things were prepared
of the Lord that we might not perish. And we beheld the sea, which
we called Irreantum, which, being
interpreted, is many waters.
6 And it came to pass that we did
pitch our tents by the seashore;
and notwithstanding we had suffered many [a]afflictions and much
difficulty, yea, even so much that
we cannot write them all, we were
exceedingly rejoiced when we came
to the seashore; and we called the
place Bountiful, because of its much
fruit.
7 And it came to pass that after I,
Nephi, had been in the land of Bountiful for the space of many days,
the voice of the Lord came unto
me, saying: [a]Arise, and get thee into
the mountain. And it came to pass
that I arose and went up into the
mountain, and cried unto the Lord.
8 And it came to pass that the Lord
spake unto me, saying: Thou shalt
[a]construct a ship, after the [b]man-
ner which I shall show thee, that I
may carry thy people across these
waters.
9 And I said: Lord, whither shall
I go that I may find ore to molten,
that I may make [a]tools to construct
the ship after the manner which
thou hast shown unto me?
10 And it came to pass that the
Lord told me whither I should go
to find ore, that I might make tools.
11 And it came to pass that I, Nephi,
did make a bellows wherewith to
[a]blow the fire, of the skins of beasts;
and after I had made a bellows, that
I might have wherewith to blow the
fire, I did smite two stones together
that I might make fire.
12 For the Lord had not hitherto
suffered that we should make much
fire, as we journeyed in the wilderness; for he said: I will make thy
food become sweet, that ye [a]cook
it not;
13 And I will also be your [a]light in
the wilderness; and I will prepare
the way before you, if it so be that
ye shall keep my commandments;
wherefore, inasmuch as ye shall
keep my commandments ye shall
be led towards the [b]promised land;
and ye shall [c]know that it is by me
that ye are led.
14 Yea, and the Lord said also that:
After ye have arrived in the promised land, ye shall [a]know that I, the
Lord, am [b]God; and that I, the Lord,
did [c]deliver you from destruction;
yea, that I did bring you out of the
land of Jerusalem.
15 Wherefore, I, Nephi, did strive
to keep the [a]commandments of the
Lord, and I did [b]exhort my brethren to faithfulness and diligence.
16 And it came to pass that I
did [a]make tools of the ore which
I did molten out of the rock.
17 And when my brethren saw
that I was about to [a]build a ship,
they began to [b]murmur against me,
saying: Our brother is a fool, for he
thinketh that he can build a ship;
yea, and he also thinketh that he
can cross these great waters.
18 And thus my brethren did
[a]complain against me, and were
desirous that they might not labor,
for they did not [b]believe that I could
build a ship; neither would they

6*a* 2 Ne. 4:20.
7*a* Ezek. 3:22 (22–27).
8*a* Gen. 6:14 (14–16).
b Ex. 25:40; 1 Chr. 28:12 (11–12, 19); 1 Ne. 18:2.
9*a* Deut. 8:9; 1 Kgs. 6:7; 1 Chr. 22:3 (3, 14); Job 28:2; Isa. 44:12.
11*a* Isa. 54:16.
12*a* 1 Ne. 17:2.
13*a* Alma 5:37 (37–38); D&C 88:66.
b 1 Ne. 2:20; 4:14; Jacob 2:12.
c Ex. 6:7; 13:21. TG Guidance, Divine.
14*a* 2 Ne. 1:4. TG God, Knowledge about; Testimony.
b D&C 5:2.
c TG Deliver.
15*a* 1 Kgs. 2:3; Prov. 7:2.
b Acts 14:22; Titus 2:15; Heb. 3:13.
16*a* TG Skill.
17*a* 1 Ne. 17:49 (8, 49–51); 18:1 (1–6).
b TG Murmuring.
18*a* 1 Ne. 3:28; 7:6 (6–19); 18:10 (9–22).
b TG Unbelief.

believe that I was instructed of
the Lord.
19 And now it came to pass that I,
Nephi, was exceedingly sorrowful
because of the hardness of their
hearts; and now when they saw that
I began to be sorrowful they were
glad in their hearts, insomuch that
they did [a]rejoice over me, saying:
We knew that ye could not construct a ship, for we knew that ye
were lacking in judgment; wherefore, thou canst not accomplish so
great a work.
20 And thou art like unto our
father, led away by the foolish
[a]imaginations of his heart; yea,
he hath led us out of the land of
Jerusalem, and we have wandered
in the wilderness for these many
years; and our women have toiled,
being big with child; and they have
borne children in the wilderness
and suffered all things, save it
were death; and it would have been
better that they had died before
they came out of Jerusalem than
to have suffered these afflictions.
21 Behold, these many years we
have suffered in the wilderness,
which time we might have enjoyed
our possessions and the land of our
inheritance; yea, and we might have
been happy.
22 And we know that the people
who were in the land of Jerusalem
were a [a]righteous people; for they
kept the statutes and judgments
of the Lord, and all his commandments, according to the law of
Moses; wherefore, we know that
they are a righteous people; and our
father hath judged them, and hath
led us away because we would
hearken unto his words; yea, and
our brother is like unto him. And
after this manner of language did
my brethren murmur and complain
against us.
23 And it came to pass that I,
Nephi, spake unto them, saying: Do
ye believe that our fathers, who were
the children of Israel, would have
been led away out of the hands of
the [a]Egyptians if they had not hearkened unto the words of the Lord?
24 Yea, do ye suppose that they
would have been led out of bondage, if the Lord had not commanded
Moses that he should [a]lead them
out of bondage?
25 Now ye know that the children
of Israel were in [a]bondage; and
ye know that they were laden with
[b]tasks, which were grievous to be
borne; wherefore, ye know that it
must needs be a good thing for
them, that they should be [c]brought
out of bondage.
26 Now ye know that [a]Moses was
commanded of the Lord to do that
great work; and ye know that by
his [b]word the waters of the Red Sea
were divided hither and thither, and
they passed through on dry ground.
27 But ye know that the Egyptians
were [a]drowned in the Red Sea, who
were the armies of Pharaoh.
28 And ye also know that they were
fed with [a]manna in the wilderness.
29 Yea, and ye also know that
Moses, by his word according to the
power of God which was in him,
[a]smote the rock, and there came

19*a* TG Mocking; Persecution.
20*a* 1 Ne. 2:11; 5:4 (2–4).
22*a* 1 Ne. 1:19 (4, 13, 18–20).
23*a* Ex. 20:2; Ps. 80:8; Moses 1:26.
24*a* Ex. 3:10 (2–10); Hosea 12:13 (12–14); 1 Ne. 19:10; 2 Ne. 3:9; 25:20.
25*a* Gen. 15:13 (13–14); Mosiah 11:21; D&C 101:79. TG Israel, Bondage of, in Egypt.
b Ex. 1:11 (10–11); 2:11; 1 Ne. 20:10.
c Ex. 5:1.
26*a* Josh. 24:6; Jer. 2:2; Acts 7:27 (22–39).
b Ex. 14:21 (19–31); Josh. 2:10; Neh. 9:11; 1 Ne. 4:2; Mosiah 7:19; Hel. 8:11; D&C 8:3; Moses 1:25. TG Israel, Deliverance of.
27*a* Josh. 24:6.
28*a* Ex. 16:15 (4, 14–15, 35); Num. 11:7 (7–8); Deut. 8:3; Neh. 9:20; Hosea 13:6 (5–8); John 6:49; Mosiah 7:19.
29*a* Ex. 17:6; Num. 20:11; Deut. 8:15; Neh. 9:15; 1 Ne. 20:21; 2 Ne. 25:20.

forth water, that the children of
Israel might quench their thirst.
30 And notwithstanding they
being led, the Lord their God, their
Redeemer, going before them, [a]lead-
ing them by day and giving light
unto them by night, and doing all
things for them which were [b]expe-
dient for man to receive, they hardened their hearts and blinded their
minds, and [c]reviled against Moses
and against the true and living God.
31 And it came to pass that according to his word he did [a]destroy
them; and according to his word he
did [b]lead them; and according to his
word he did do all things for them;
and there was not any thing done
save it were by his word.
32 And after they had crossed
the river Jordan he did make them
mighty unto the [a]driving out of the
children of the land, yea, unto the
scattering them to destruction.
33 And now, do ye suppose that
the children of this land, who were
in the land of promise, who were
driven out by our fathers, do ye
suppose that they were righteous?
Behold, I say unto you, Nay.
34 Do ye suppose that our fathers
would have been more choice than
they if they had been righteous? I
say unto you, Nay.
35 Behold, the Lord esteemeth all
[a]flesh in one; he that is [b]righteous
is [c]favored of God. But behold, this
[d]people had rejected every word of
God, and they were ripe in iniquity;
and the fulness of the wrath of
God was upon them; and the Lord
did curse the land against them,
and bless it unto our fathers; yea,
he did curse it against them unto
their destruction, and he did bless
it unto our fathers unto their obtaining power over it.
36 Behold, the Lord hath created
the [a]earth that it should be [b]inhab-
ited; and he hath created his children that they should possess it.
37 And he [a]raiseth up a righteous
nation, and destroyeth the nations
of the wicked.
38 And he leadeth away the righteous into precious [a]lands, and the
wicked he [b]destroyeth, and curseth
the land unto them for their sakes.
39 He ruleth high in the heavens,
for it is his throne, and this earth
is his [a]footstool.
40 And he loveth those who will
have him to be their God. Behold,
he loved our [a]fathers, and he
[b]covenanted with them, yea, even
Abraham, [c]Isaac, and [d]Jacob; and he
remembered the covenants which
he had made; wherefore, he did
bring them out of the land of [e]Egypt.
41 And he did straiten them in the
wilderness with his rod; for they
[a]hardened their hearts, even as ye
have; and the Lord straitened them
because of their iniquity. He sent

30*a* Ex. 13:18 (18, 20).
b D&C 18:18; 88:64 (64–65).
c Ex. 32:8; Num. 14:11 (11–12); Ezek. 20:13 (13–16); D&C 84:24 (23–25).
31*a* Num. 26:65.
b Ex. 15:13; 1 Ne. 5:15; D&C 103:16 (16–18).
32*a* Ex. 34:11; Num. 33:52 (52–53); Josh. 11:6; 24:8.
35*a* Acts 10:15 (15, 34); Rom. 2:11; 2 Ne. 26:33 (23–33).
b Ps. 55:22; John 15:10; 1 Ne. 22:17.
c 1 Sam. 2:30; 1 Kgs. 2:3; Ps. 97:10; 145:20 (1–21); Alma 13:4; 28:13; D&C 82:10 (8–10).
d Gen. 15:16; Ex. 23:31 (28–31); Deut. 7:10; Josh. 2:24.
36*a* Gen. 1:28 (26–28); Jer. 27:5; Moses 1:29. TG Earth, Purpose of; Man, a Spirit Child of Heavenly Father; Man, Physical Creation of.
b Isa. 45:18.
37*a* Ps. 1:6; Prov. 14:34; Isa. 45:1 (1–3); 1 Ne. 4:13; Ether 2:10; D&C 98:32 (31–32); 117:6.
38*a* TG Lands of Inheritance.
b Lev. 20:22.
39*a* Isa. 66:1; Lam. 2:1; D&C 38:17; Abr. 2:7.
40*a* TG Israel, Origins of.
b TG Abrahamic Covenant.
c Gen. 21:12; D&C 27:10.
d Gen. 28:4 (1–5).
e Deut. 4:37 (37–38).
41*a* 2 Kgs. 17:7 (7–23).

fiery flying [b]serpents among them;
and after they were bitten he prepared a way that they might be
[c]healed; and the labor which they
had to perform was to look; and
because of the [d]simpleness of the
way, or the easiness of it, there were
many who perished.
42 And they did harden their hearts
from time to time, and they did [a]re-
vile against [b]Moses, and also against
God; nevertheless, ye know that
they were led forth by his matchless
power into the land of promise.
43 And now, after all these things,
the time has come that they have
become wicked, yea, nearly unto
ripeness; and I know not but they are
at this day about to be [a]destroyed;
for I know that the day must surely
come that they must be destroyed,
save a few only, who shall be led
away into captivity.
44 Wherefore, the Lord [a]com-
manded my father that he should
depart into the wilderness; and the
Jews also sought to take away his
life; yea, and [b]ye also have sought
to take away his life; wherefore, ye
are murderers in your hearts and
ye are like unto them.
45 Ye are [a]swift to do iniquity but
slow to remember the Lord your
God. Ye have seen an [b]angel, and he
spake unto you; yea, ye have heard
his voice from time to time; and he
hath spoken unto you in a still small
voice, but ye were [c]past feeling, that
ye could not feel his words; wherefore, he has spoken unto you like
unto the voice of thunder, which
did cause the earth to shake as if
it were to divide asunder.
46 And ye also know that by the
[a]power of his almighty word he can
cause the earth that it shall pass
away; yea, and ye know that by his
word he can cause the rough places to
be made smooth, and smooth places
shall be broken up. O, then, why is it,
that ye can be so hard in your hearts?
47 Behold, my soul is rent with
anguish because of you, and my
heart is pained; I fear lest ye shall
be cast off forever. Behold, I am [a]full
of the Spirit of God, insomuch that
my frame has [b]no strength.
48 And now it came to pass that
when I had spoken these words they
were angry with me, and were desirous to throw me into the depths of
the sea; and as they came forth to lay
their hands upon me I spake unto
them, saying: In the name of the
Almighty God, I command you that
ye [a]touch me not, for I am filled with
the [b]power of God, even unto the
consuming of my flesh; and whoso
shall lay his hands upon me shall
[c]wither even as a dried reed; and he
shall be as naught before the power
of God, for God shall smite him.
49 And it came to pass that I,
Nephi, said unto them that they
should murmur no more against
their father; neither should they
withhold their labor from me, for
God had commanded me that I
should [a]build a ship.
50 And I said unto them: [a]If God
had commanded me to do all things
I could do them. If he should command me that I should say unto
this water, be thou earth, it should
be earth; and if I should say it, it
would be done.
51 And now, if the Lord has such
great power, and has wrought so

41*b* Num. 21:6 (4–9); Deut. 8:15; Alma 33:19 (18–22).
c Hosea 11:3; John 3:14; 2 Ne. 25:20.
d Alma 37:46 (44–47); Hel. 8:15.
42*a* Ex. 32:23; Num. 14:2 (1–12). TG Reviling.
b D&C 84:23.
43*a* Hosea 7:13. TG Israel, Scattering of.
44*a* 1 Ne. 2:2 (1–2).
b 1 Ne. 16:37.
45*a* Mosiah 13:29.
b 1 Ne. 4:3.
c Acts 17:27; Eph. 4:19; 1 Ne. 2:14.
46*a* Hel. 12:10 (6–18).
47*a* Micah 3:8.
b Dan. 10:8 (8, 17); 1 Ne. 1:7; 19:20.
48*a* Mosiah 13:3.
b 2 Ne. 1:27 (26–27). TG God, Power of; Priesthood, Power of.
c 1 Kgs. 13:4 (4–7); Moses 1:11; 6:47.
49*a* 1 Ne. 17:17; 18:1 (1–6).
50*a* Philip. 4:13; 1 Ne. 3:7; D&C 24:13.

many miracles among the children
of men, how is it that he cannot [a]in-
struct me, that I should build a ship?
52 And it came to pass that I,
Nephi, said many things unto my
brethren, insomuch that they were
[a]confounded and could not contend
against me; neither durst they lay
their hands upon me nor touch
me with their fingers, even for
the space of many days. Now they
durst not do this lest they should
wither before me, so powerful was
the [b]Spirit of God; and thus it had
wrought upon them.
53 And it came to pass that the
Lord said unto me: Stretch forth
thine hand again unto thy brethren, and they shall not wither before thee, but I will [a]shock them,
saith the Lord, and this will I do,
that they may know that I am the
Lord their God.
54 And it came to pass that I
stretched forth my hand unto my
brethren, and they did not wither
before me; but the Lord did shake
them, even according to the word
which he had spoken.
55 And now, they said: We know
of a surety that the Lord is [a]with
thee, for we know that it is the
power of the Lord that has shaken
us. And they fell down before me,
and were about to [b]worship me, but
I would not suffer them, saying: I am
thy brother, yea, even thy younger
brother; wherefore, worship the
Lord thy God, and honor thy father
and thy mother, that thy [c]days may
be long in the land which the Lord
thy God shall give thee.

CHAPTER 18

The ship is finished—The births of Jacob and Joseph are mentioned—The company embarks for the promised land—The sons of Ishmael and their wives join in revelry and rebellion—Nephi is bound, and the ship is driven back by a terrible tempest—Nephi is freed, and by his prayer the storm ceases—The people arrive in the promised land. About 591–589 B.C.

AND it came to pass that they did
[a]worship the Lord, and did go forth
with me; and we did work timbers
of curious [b]workmanship. And the
Lord did show me from time to time
after what manner I should work
the timbers of the [c]ship.
2 Now I, Nephi, did not work the
timbers after the manner which
was learned by men, neither did
I build the ship after the manner
of men; but I did build it after the
manner which the Lord had shown
unto me; wherefore, it was not after
the manner of men.
3 And I, Nephi, did go into the
mount oft, and I did [a]pray oft unto
the Lord; wherefore the Lord [b]showed
unto me [c]great things.
4 And it came to pass that after I had
finished the ship, according to the
word of the Lord, my brethren beheld
that it was good, and that the workmanship thereof was exceedingly
fine; wherefore, they did [a]humble
themselves again before the Lord.
5 And it came to pass that the voice
of the Lord came unto my father,
that we should arise and go down
into the ship.
6 And it came to pass that on the
morrow, after we had prepared all
things, much fruits and [a]meat from
the wilderness, and honey in abundance, and provisions according
to that which the Lord had commanded us, we did go down into the
ship, with all our loading and our

51 *a* Gen. 6:14 (14–16); 1 Ne. 18:1.
52 *a* IE ashamed, overawed.
b TG God, Spirit of.
53 *a* IE cause to shake or tremble; see vv. 54–55.
55 *a* Ex. 3:12; Alma 38:4.
b Dan. 2:46; Acts 14:15 (11–15).
c Ex. 20:12; Prov. 9:11; Mosiah 14:10; Hel. 7:24; D&C 5:33.
18 1 *a* 1 Ne. 17:55.
b TG Art.
c 1 Ne. 17:49 (8, 17, 49–51).
3 *a* Jer. 33:3.
b TG Guidance, Divine.
c 2 Ne. 1:24.
4 *a* 1 Ne. 16:5.
6 *a* 1 Ne. 17:2.

[b]seeds, and whatsoever thing we had brought with us, every one according to his age; wherefore, we did all go down into the [c]ship, with our wives and our children.

7 And now, my father had begat two sons in the wilderness; the elder was called [a]Jacob and the younger [b]Joseph.

8 And it came to pass after we had all gone down into the ship, and had taken with us our provisions and things which had been commanded us, we did put forth into the [a]sea and were driven forth before the wind towards the [b]promised land.

9 And after we had been [a]driven forth before the wind for the space of many days, behold, my brethren and the sons of Ishmael and also their wives began to make themselves merry, insomuch that they began to dance, and to sing, and to speak with much [b]rudeness, yea, even that they did forget by what power they had been brought thither; yea, they were lifted up unto exceeding rudeness.

10 And I, Nephi, began to fear exceedingly lest the Lord should be angry with us, and smite us because of our iniquity, that we should be swallowed up in the depths of the sea; wherefore, I, Nephi, began to speak to them with much soberness; but behold they were [a]angry with me, saying: We will not that our younger brother shall be a [b]ruler over us.

11 And it came to pass that Laman and Lemuel did take me and [a]bind me with cords, and they did treat me with much harshness; nevertheless, the Lord did suffer it that he might show forth his power, unto the fulfilling of his word which he had [b]spoken concerning the wicked.

12 And it came to pass that after they had bound me insomuch that I could not move, the [a]compass, which had been prepared of the Lord, did cease to work.

13 Wherefore, they knew not whither they should steer the ship, insomuch that there arose a great [a]storm, yea, a great and terrible tempest, and we were [b]driven back upon the waters for the space of three days; and they began to be frightened exceedingly lest they should be drowned in the sea; nevertheless they did not loose me.

14 And on the fourth day, which we had been driven back, the tempest began to be exceedingly sore.

15 And it came to pass that we were about to be swallowed up in the depths of the sea. And after we had been driven back upon the waters for the space of four days, my brethren began to [a]see that the judgments of God were upon them, and that they must perish save that they should repent of their iniquities; wherefore, they came unto me, and loosed the bands which were upon my wrists, and behold they had swollen exceedingly; and also mine ankles were much swollen, and great was the soreness thereof.

16 Nevertheless, I did look unto my God, and I did [a]praise him all the day long; and I did not murmur against the Lord because of mine afflictions.

17 Now my father, Lehi, had said many things unto them, and also unto the sons of [a]Ishmael; but, behold, they did breathe out much

6*b* 1 Ne. 8:1; 16:11.
c Gen. 7:7.
7*a* 2 Ne. 2:1.
b 2 Ne. 3:1.
8*a* Ps. 8:8; 2 Ne. 10:20.
b 1 Ne. 2:20; 5:5 (5, 22). TG Promised Lands.
9*a* Ether 6:5.
b 2 Ne. 1:2. TG Rioting and Reveling.
10*a* 1 Ne. 17:18 (17–55); 2 Ne. 4:13 (13–14).
b Gen. 37:10 (9–11); 1 Ne. 16:37 (37–38); 2 Ne. 1:25 (25–27).
11*a* 1 Ne. 7:16 (16–20).
b Ex. 23:7; Ps. 37:9 (8–13); Alma 14:11.
12*a* 1 Ne. 16:16 (10, 16, 26); 2 Ne. 5:12; Alma 37:38 (38–47); D&C 17:1.
13*a* Jonah 1:4; Matt. 8:24.
b Mosiah 1:17.
15*a* Hel. 12:3.
16*a* Ezra 3:11 (11–13); 2 Ne. 9:49; Mosiah 2:20 (20–21); Alma 36:28; D&C 136:28.
17*a* 1 Ne. 7:4 (4–20).

threatenings against anyone that
should speak for me; and my parents
being [b]stricken in years, and having
[c]suffered much grief because of their
[d]children, they were brought down,
yea, even upon their sick-beds.
18 Because of their grief and much
sorrow, and the iniquity of my
brethren, they were brought near
even to be carried out of this time
to meet their God; yea, their [a]grey
hairs were about to be brought down
to lie low in the dust; yea, even they
were near to be cast with sorrow
into a watery grave.
19 And Jacob and Joseph also, being young, having need of much
nourishment, were grieved because
of the afflictions of their mother;
and also [a]my wife with her tears and
prayers, and also my children, did
not soften the hearts of my brethren that they would loose me.
20 And there was nothing save
it were the power of God, which
threatened them with destruction,
could soften their [a]hearts; wherefore, when they saw that they were
about to be swallowed up in the
depths of the sea they repented of
the thing which they had done, insomuch that they loosed me.
21 And it came to pass after they
had loosed me, behold, I took the
compass, and it did work whither I
desired it. And it came to pass that
I [a]prayed unto the Lord; and after
I had prayed the winds did cease,
and the storm did cease, and there
was a great calm.
22 And it came to pass that I,
Nephi, did guide the ship, that we
sailed again towards the promised
land.
23 And it came to pass that after
we had sailed for the space of many
days we did arrive at the [a]promised
land; and we went forth upon the
land, and did pitch our tents; and
we did call it the promised land.
24 And it came to pass that we did
begin to till the earth, and we began to plant seeds; yea, we did put
all our [a]seeds into the earth, which
we had brought from the land of
Jerusalem. And it came to pass that
they did grow exceedingly; wherefore, we were blessed in abundance.
25 And it came to pass that we did
find upon the land of promise, as
we journeyed in the wilderness, that
there were [a]beasts in the forests of
every kind, both the cow and the
ox, and the ass and the horse, and
the goat and the wild goat, and all
manner of wild animals, which
were for the use of men. And we
did find all manner of [b]ore, both of
[c]gold, and of silver, and of copper.

CHAPTER 19

Nephi makes plates of ore and records the history of his people—The God of Israel will come six hundred years from the time Lehi left Jerusalem—Nephi tells of His sufferings and crucifixion—The Jews will be despised and scattered until the latter days, when they will return unto the Lord. About 588–570 B.C.

AND it came to pass that the Lord
commanded me, wherefore I did
make plates of ore that I might
engraven upon them the [a]record
of my people. And upon the plates
which I made I did [b]engraven the
record of my [c]father, and also our
journeyings in the wilderness, and
the prophecies of my father; and
also many of mine own prophecies
have I engraven upon them.
2 And I knew not at the time
when I made them that I should be

17*b* Gen. 24:1.
c TG Suffering.
d TG Family, Children, Duties of; Honoring Father and Mother.
18*a* Gen. 42:38.
19*a* 1 Ne. 7:19; 16:7.
20*a* TG Hardheartedness.
21*a* Jonah 1:6.
23*a* Mosiah 10:13. TG Promised Lands.
24*a* 1 Ne. 8:1.
25*a* Enos 1:21.
b 2 Ne. 5:15 (14–16).
c Deut. 33:16 (13–17).
19 1*a* TG Plate; Record Keeping.
b TG Scribe.
c 1 Ne. 1:17 (16–17); 6:1 (1–3); Jacob 7:26 (26–27).

commanded of the Lord to make [a]these plates; wherefore, the record of my father, and the genealogy of his fathers, and the more part of all our proceedings in the wilderness are engraven upon those first plates of which I have spoken; wherefore, the things which transpired before I made [b]these plates are, of a truth, more particularly made mention upon the first plates.
3 And after I had made these plates
by way of commandment, I, Nephi, received a commandment that the ministry and the prophecies, the more plain and precious parts of them, should be written upon [a]these plates; and that the things which were written should be kept for the instruction of my people, who should possess the land, and also for other [b]wise purposes, which purposes are known unto the Lord.
4 Wherefore, I, Nephi, did make
a record upon the [a]other plates, which gives an account, or which gives a greater account of the wars and contentions and destructions of my people. And this have I done, and commanded my people what they should do after I was gone; and that these plates should be handed down from one generation to another, or from one prophet to another, until further commandments of the Lord.
5 And an account of my [a]making
these plates shall be given hereafter; and then, behold, I proceed according to that which I have spoken; and this I do that the more sacred things may be [b]kept for the knowledge of my people.
6 Nevertheless, I do not [a]write any-
thing upon plates save it be that I think it be [b]sacred. And now, if I do err, even did they err of old; not that I would excuse myself because of other men, but because of the [c]weakness which is in me, according to the flesh, I would excuse myself.
7 For the things which some men
esteem to be of great worth, both to the body and soul, others set at [a]naught and trample under their feet. Yea, even the very God of Israel do men [b]trample under their feet; I say, trample under their feet but I would speak in other words—they set him at naught, and [c]hearken not to the voice of his counsels.
8 And behold he [a]cometh, accord-
ing to the words of the angel, in [b]six hundred years from the time my father left Jerusalem.
9 And the world, because of their
iniquity, shall judge him to be a thing of naught; wherefore they scourge him, and he suffereth it; and they smite him, and he suffereth it. Yea, they [a]spit upon him, and he suffereth it, because of his loving [b]kindness and his [c]long-suffering towards the children of men.
10 And the [a]God of our fathers,
who were [b]led out of Egypt, out of bondage, and also were preserved in the wilderness by him, yea, the

2*a* 2 Ne. 5:30; Jacob 3:14.
b 1 Ne. 9:2 (1–5); Omni 1:1.
3*a* 1 Ne. 10:1; Jacob 1:1 (1–4); 3:13 (13–14); 4:1 (1–4).
b 1 Ne. 9:5 (4–5); W of M 1:7; D&C 3:19 (19–20); 10:38 (1–51).
4*a* 1 Ne. 9:4 (2–5); 2 Ne. 5:33.
5*a* 2 Ne. 5:30 (28–33).
b TG Scriptures, Preservation of.
6*a* TG Scriptures, Writing of.
b See title page of the Book of Mormon. TG Sacred.
c Morm. 8:17 (13–17); Ether 12:23 (23–28).
7*a* Num. 15:31 (30–31); 2 Ne. 33:2; Jacob 4:14; D&C 3:7 (4–13).
b Ezek. 34:19; D&C 76:35. TG Blaspheme; Sacrilege.
c TG Disobedience; Prophets, Rejection of.
8*a* TG Jesus Christ, Betrayal of; Jesus Christ, Birth of; Jesus Christ, Prophecies about.
b 1 Ne. 2:4; 10:4 (4–11); 2 Ne. 25:19.
9*a* Isa. 50:6 (5–6); Matt. 27:30.
b TG Kindness.
c TG Forbear.
10*a* 2 Ne. 10:3; 26:12; Mosiah 7:27; 27:31 (30–31); Alma 11:39 (38–39); 3 Ne. 11:14 (14–15).
b Gen. 15:14 (13–14); Ex. 3:10 (2–10); 6:6; 1 Ne. 5:15; 17:24 (24, 31, 40); 2 Ne. 25:20; D&C 136:22.

[c]God of Abraham, and of Isaac, and
the God of Jacob, [d]yieldeth himself,
according to the words of the angel,
as a man, into the hands of [e]wicked
men, to be [f]lifted up, according to
the words of [g]Zenock, and to be
[h]crucified, according to the words
of Neum, and to be buried in a [i]sep-
ulchre, according to the words of
[j]Zenos, which he spake concerning
the three days of [k]darkness, which
should be a sign given of his death
unto those who should inhabit the
isles of the sea, more especially
given unto those who are of the
[l]house of Israel.
11 For thus spake the prophet: The
Lord God surely shall [a]visit all the
house of Israel at that day, some
with his [b]voice, because of their
righteousness, unto their great joy
and salvation, and others with the
[c]thunderings and the lightnings of
his power, by tempest, by fire, and
by [d]smoke, and [e]vapor of [f]darkness,
and by the opening of the [g]earth,
and by [h]mountains which shall be
carried up.
12 And [a]all these things must
surely come, saith the prophet [b]Ze-
nos. And the [c]rocks of the earth must
rend; and because of the [d]groanings
of the earth, many of the kings of
the isles of the sea shall be wrought
upon by the Spirit of God, to exclaim: The God of nature suffers.
13 And as for those who are at
Jerusalem, saith the prophet, they
shall be [a]scourged by all people,
because they crucify the God of
Israel, and turn their hearts aside,
rejecting signs and wonders, and
the power and glory of the God of
Israel.
14 And because they turn their
hearts aside, saith the prophet, and
have [a]despised the Holy One of Israel, they shall wander in the flesh,
and perish, and become a [b]hiss and
a [c]byword, and be [d]hated among
all nations.
15 Nevertheless, when that day
cometh, saith the prophet, that they
[a]no more [b]turn aside their hearts
against the Holy One of Israel, then
will he remember the [c]covenants
which he made to their fathers.
16 Yea, then will he remember
the [a]isles of the sea; yea, and all
the people who are of the house of
Israel, will I [b]gather in, saith the Lord,
according to the words of the prophet
Zenos, from the four quarters of
the earth.
17 Yea, and all the earth shall [a]see
the salvation of the Lord, saith the

10*c* Gen. 32:9; Matt. 22:32; Mosiah 7:19; D&C 136:21. TG Jesus Christ, Jehovah.
d TG Jesus Christ, Condescension of.
e TG Jesus Christ, Betrayal of.
f 3 Ne. 27:14; 28:6.
g BD Lost books. See also Alma 33:15; 34:7; Hel. 8:20 (19–20); 3 Ne. 10:16 (15–16).
h 2 Ne. 6:9; Mosiah 3:9. TG Jesus Christ, Crucifixion of.
i Matt. 27:60; Luke 23:53; 2 Ne. 25:13.
j Jacob 5:1; 6:1; Hel. 15:11.
k 1 Ne. 12:4 (4–5); Hel. 14:27 (20, 27); 3 Ne. 8:19 (3, 19–23); 10:9.
l 3 Ne. 16:1 (1–4).
11*a* D&C 5:16.
b 3 Ne. 9:1 (1–22).
c Hel. 14:21 (20–27); 3 Ne. 8:6 (5–23).
d Gen. 19:28; Ex. 19:18; Morm. 8:29 (29–30); D&C 45:41 (40–41).
e 1 Ne. 12:5.
f Luke 23:44 (44–45). TG Darkness, Physical.
g Num. 16:32; 2 Ne. 26:5.
h 3 Ne. 10:13 (13–14).
12*a* Hel. 14:28 (20–28); 3 Ne. 10:11.
b Jacob 5:1.
c Matt. 27:51 (51–54).
d Moses 7:56 (48–56).
13*a* Matt. 23:38 (37–39); Luke 23:28 (27–30).
14*a* Ps. 22:6; Mosiah 14:3 (3–6).
b Jer. 24:9; 3 Ne. 29:8 (8–9). TG Israel, Bondage of, in Other Lands.
c Deut. 28:37; 1 Kgs. 9:7 (6–7); Joel 2:17; 3 Ne. 16:9 (8–9).
d 2 Ne. 10:6; 25:15. TG Hate.
15*a* 1 Ne. 15:19; 22:12 (11–12).
b TG Israel, Restoration of.
c TG Abrahamic Covenant.
16*a* 1 Ne. 22:4; 2 Ne. 10:21.
b Isa. 49:22 (20–22); 60:4. TG Israel, Gathering of.
17*a* Isa. 40:5 (4–5).

prophet; every nation, kindred,
tongue and people shall be blessed.
18 And I, Nephi, have written these
things unto my people, that perhaps
I might persuade them that they
would [a]remember the Lord their
Redeemer.
19 Wherefore, I speak unto all the
house of Israel, if it so be that they
should obtain [a]these things.
20 For behold, I have workings in
the spirit, which doth [a]weary me
even that all my joints are weak,
for those who are at Jerusalem; for
had not the Lord been merciful, to
show unto me concerning them,
even as he had prophets of old, I
should have perished also.
21 And he surely did show unto
the [a]prophets of old all things [b]con-
cerning them; and also he did show
unto many concerning us; wherefore, it must needs be that we know
concerning them for they are written upon the plates of brass.
22 Now it came to pass that I,
Nephi, did teach my brethren these
things; and it came to pass that I did
read many things to them, which
were engraven upon the [a]plates of
brass, that they might know concerning the doings of the Lord in
other lands, among people of old.
23 And I did read many things
unto them which were written
in the [a]books of Moses; but that I
might more fully persuade them to
believe in the Lord their Redeemer
I did read unto them that which
was written by the prophet [b]Isaiah;
for I did [c]liken all scriptures unto
us, that it might be for our [d]profit
and learning.
24 Wherefore I spake unto them,
saying: Hear ye the words of the
prophet, ye who are a [a]remnant of
the house of Israel, a [b]branch who
have been broken off; [c]hear ye the
words of the prophet, which were
written unto all the house of Israel,
and liken them unto yourselves, that
ye may have hope as well as your
brethren from whom ye have been
broken off; for after this manner
has the prophet written.

CHAPTER 20

The Lord reveals His purposes to Israel—Israel has been chosen in the furnace of affliction and is to go forth from Babylon—Compare Isaiah 48. About 588–570 B.C.

[a]HEARKEN and hear this, O house of
Jacob, who are called by the name of
Israel, and are come forth out of the
waters of Judah, or out of the waters of [b]baptism, who [c]swear by the
name of the Lord, and make mention
of the God of Israel, yet they swear
[d]not in truth nor in righteousness.
2 Nevertheless, they call themselves of the [a]holy city, but they do
[b]not stay themselves upon the God
of Israel, who is the Lord of Hosts;
yea, the Lord of Hosts is his name.
3 Behold, I have declared the [a]for-
mer things from the beginning; and
they went forth out of my mouth,
and I showed them. I did show them
suddenly.
4 And I did it because I knew that
thou art obstinate, and thy [a]neck is
an iron sinew, and thy brow brass;
5 And I have even from the beginning declared to thee; before it came

18*a* Mosiah 13:29.
19*a* Enos 1:16; Morm. 5:12; 7:9 (9–10). TG Israel, Restoration of.
20*a* Dan. 10:8 (8–12); 1 Ne. 1:7; Alma 27:17; Moses 1:10 (9–10).
21*a* 2 Kgs. 17:13; Amos 3:7. TG Prophets, Mission of.
b 3 Ne. 10:16 (16–17).
22*a* 1 Ne. 13:23; 22:1.
23*a* Ex. 17:14; 1 Ne. 5:11; Moses 1:41 (40–41).
b Isa. 1:1; 1 Ne. 15:20; 2 Ne. 25:5 (2–6); 3 Ne. 23:1.
c TG Scriptures, Value of.
d 2 Ne. 4:15.
24*a* 2 Kgs. 19:31.
b Gen. 49:22 (22–26); 1 Ne. 15:12 (12, 16); 2 Ne. 3:5 (4–5).
c TG Scriptures, Study of.
20 1*a* Isa. 48:1 (1–22).
b TG Baptism; Conversion.
c Deut. 6:13.
d Jer. 4:2; 5:2.
2*a* Isa. 52:1. TG Jerusalem.
b TG Hypocrisy; Prophets, Rejection of.
3*a* Isa. 42:9; 46:10 (9–10). TG God, Foreknowledge of.
4*a* TG Stiffnecked.

to pass I [a]showed them thee; and I showed them for fear lest thou shouldst say—Mine idol hath done them, and my graven image, and my molten image hath commanded them.
6 Thou hast seen and heard all this; and will ye [a]not declare them? And that I have showed thee new things from this time, even hidden things, and thou didst not know them.
7 They are created now, and not from the beginning, even before the day when thou heardest them not they were declared unto thee, lest thou shouldst say—Behold I knew them.
8 Yea, and thou heardest not; yea, thou knewest not; yea, from that time thine ear was not opened; for I knew that thou wouldst deal very treacherously, and wast called a [a]transgressor from the womb.
9 Nevertheless, for my [a]name's sake will I defer mine anger, and for my praise will I refrain from thee, that I cut thee not off.
10 For, behold, I have refined thee, I have chosen thee in the furnace of [a]affliction.
11 For mine own sake, yea, for mine own sake will I do this, for I will not suffer my [a]name to be polluted, and I will [b]not give my glory unto another.
12 Hearken unto me, O Jacob, and Israel my called, for I am he; I am the [a]first, and I am also the last.
13 Mine hand hath also [a]laid the foundation of the earth, and my right hand hath spanned the heavens. I [b]call unto them and they stand up together.
14 All ye, assemble yourselves, and hear; who among them hath declared these things unto them? The Lord hath loved him; yea, and he will [a]fulfil his word which he hath declared by them; and he will do his pleasure on [b]Babylon, and his arm shall come upon the Chaldeans.
15 Also, saith the Lord; I the Lord, yea, I have spoken; yea, I have called [a]him to declare, I have brought him, and he shall make his way prosperous.
16 Come ye near unto me; I have not spoken in [a]secret; from the beginning, from the time that it was declared have I spoken; and the Lord God, and his [b]Spirit, hath sent me.
17 And thus saith the Lord, thy [a]Redeemer, the Holy One of Israel; I have sent him, the Lord thy God who teacheth thee to profit, who [b]leadeth thee by the way thou shouldst go, hath done it.
18 O that thou hadst hearkened to my [a]commandments—then had thy [b]peace been as a river, and thy righteousness as the waves of the sea.
19 Thy [a]seed also had been as the sand; the offspring of thy bowels like the gravel thereof; his name should not have been cut off nor destroyed from before me.
20 [a]Go ye forth of Babylon, flee ye from the [b]Chaldeans, with a voice of singing declare ye, tell this, utter to the end of the earth; say ye: The

5*a* TG God, Omniscience of; Idolatry.
6*a* 1 Cor. 9:16.
8*a* Ps. 58:3.
9*a* 1 Sam. 12:22; Ps. 23:3; 1 Jn. 2:12.
10*a* Ex. 1:11 (10–11); 1 Ne. 17:25. TG Affliction.
11*a* Jer. 44:26.
b Isa. 42:8; Moses 4:1 (1–4).
12*a* Rev. 1:17; 22:13. TG Jesus Christ, Firstborn; Jesus Christ, Jehovah.
13*a* Ps. 102:25. TG God the Father, Jehovah; Jesus Christ, Creator.
b Ps. 148:8 (5–10).
14*a* 1 Kgs. 8:56; D&C 64:31; 76:3.
b TG Babylon.
15*a* Isa. 45:1 (1–4).
16*a* Isa. 45:19.
b TG God, Spirit of.
17*a* TG Jesus Christ, Jehovah.
b TG Guidance, Divine.
18*a* Eccl. 8:5.
b TG Israel, Blessings of; Peace of God.
19*a* Gen. 22:17 (15–19); Isa. 48:19 (18–22); Hosea 1:10.
20*a* Jer. 51:6 (6, 44–45); D&C 133:5 (5–14).
b TG Israel, Bondage of, in Other Lands.

Lord hath redeemed his [c]servant Jacob.

21 And they [a]thirsted not; he led them through the deserts; he caused the waters to flow out of the [b]rock for them; he clave the rock also and the waters gushed out.

22 And notwithstanding he hath done all this, and greater also, there is no [a]peace, saith the Lord, unto the wicked.

CHAPTER 21

The Messiah will be a light to the Gentiles and will free the prisoners—Israel will be gathered with power in the last days—Kings will be their nursing fathers—Compare Isaiah 49. About 588–570 B.C.

[a]AND again: Hearken, O ye house of Israel, all ye that are broken off and are driven out because of the wickedness of the pastors of my people; yea, all ye that are broken off, that are scattered abroad, who are of my people, O house of Israel. Listen, O [b]isles, unto me, and hearken ye people from [c]far; the Lord hath called me from the womb; from the bowels of my mother hath he made mention of my name.

2 And he hath made my mouth like a sharp sword; in the shadow of his hand hath he hid me, and made me a polished shaft; in his quiver hath he hid me;

3 And said unto me: Thou art my [a]servant, O Israel, in whom I will be glorified.

4 Then I said, I have labored in [a]vain, I have spent my strength for naught and in vain; surely my judgment is with the Lord, and my work with my God.

5 And now, saith the Lord—that [a]formed me from the womb that I should be his servant, to bring Jacob again to him—though Israel be not gathered, yet shall I be glorious in the eyes of the Lord, and my God shall be my [b]strength.

6 And he said: It is a light thing that thou shouldst be my servant to raise up the [a]tribes of Jacob, and to restore the preserved of Israel. I will also give thee for a [b]light to the [c]Gentiles, that thou mayest be my salvation unto the ends of the earth.

7 Thus saith the Lord, the Redeemer of Israel, his Holy One, to him whom man despiseth, to him whom the nations abhorreth, to servant of rulers: Kings shall see and arise, princes also shall worship, because of the Lord that is faithful.

8 Thus saith the Lord: In an acceptable time have I heard thee, O isles of the sea, and in a day of salvation have I helped thee; and I will preserve thee, and give thee [a]my servant for a covenant of the people, to establish the earth, to cause to inherit the desolate heritages;

9 That thou mayest say to the [a]prisoners: Go forth; to them that sit in [b]darkness: Show yourselves. They shall feed in the ways, and their [c]pastures shall be in all high places.

10 They shall not hunger nor thirst, neither shall the heat nor the sun smite them; for he that hath mercy on them shall lead them, even by the springs of water shall he guide them.

11 And I will make all my mountains a way, and my [a]highways shall be exalted.

20*c* Isa. 44:1 (1–2, 21); 45:4.
21*a* Ps. 107:33 (33–37); Isa. 41:18 (17–20).
b Ex. 17:6; Num. 20:11; 1 Ne. 17:29; 2 Ne. 25:20; D&C 133:26 (26–30).
22*a* Rom. 3:17. TG Peace of God.
21 1*a* Isa. 49:1 (1–26).
b 1 Ne. 22:4; 2 Ne. 10:21 (20–22).
c D&C 1:1.
3*a* Lev. 25:55; Isa. 41:8; D&C 93:46 (45–46).
4*a* Isa. 55:2 (1–2).
5*a* Isa. 44:24.
b TG Strength.
6*a* TG Israel, Twelve Tribes of.
b Ezek. 5:5; D&C 103:9 (8–9); Abr. 2:11 (6–11).
c 3 Ne. 21:11. TG Israel, Mission of.
8*a* 2 Ne. 3:11 (6–15); 3 Ne. 21:11 (8–11); Morm. 8:16 (16, 25).
9*a* TG Salvation for the Dead; Spirits in Prison.
b 2 Ne. 3:5.
c Ezek. 34:14; 1 Ne. 22:25.
11*a* Isa. 62:10; D&C 133:27 (23–32). TG Jesus Christ, Second Coming.

12 And then, O house of Israel, behold, [a]these shall come from far; and lo, these from the north and from the west; and these from the land of Sinim.

13 [a]Sing, O heavens; and be joyful, O earth; for the feet of those who are in the east shall be established; and [b]break forth into singing, O mountains; for they shall be smitten no more; for the Lord hath comforted his people, and will have mercy upon his [c]afflicted.

14 But, behold, Zion hath said: The Lord hath forsaken me, and my Lord hath forgotten me—but he will show that he hath not.

15 For can a [a]woman forget her sucking child, that she should not have [b]compassion on the son of her womb? Yea, they may [c]forget, yet will I not forget thee, O house of Israel.

16 Behold, I have graven thee upon the [a]palms of my hands; thy walls are continually before me.

17 Thy children shall make haste against thy destroyers; and they that made thee [a]waste shall go forth of thee.

18 Lift up thine eyes round about and behold; all these [a]gather themselves together, and they shall come to thee. And as I live, saith the Lord, thou shalt surely clothe thee with them all, as with an ornament, and bind them on even as a bride.

19 For thy waste and thy desolate places, and the land of thy destruction, shall even now be too narrow by reason of the inhabitants; and they that swallowed thee up shall be far away.

20 The children whom thou shalt have, after thou hast lost the first, shall [a]again in thine ears say: The place is too strait for me; give place to me that I may dwell.

21 Then shalt thou say in thine heart: Who hath begotten me these, seeing I have lost my children, and am [a]desolate, a captive, and removing to and fro? And who hath brought up these? Behold, I was left alone; these, where have they been?

22 Thus saith the Lord God: Behold, I will lift up mine hand to the [a]Gentiles, and set up my [b]standard to the people; and they shall bring thy sons in their [c]arms, and thy daughters shall be carried upon their shoulders.

23 And [a]kings shall be thy [b]nursing fathers, and their queens thy nursing mothers; they shall bow down to thee with their face towards the earth, and lick up the dust of thy feet; and thou shalt know that I am the Lord; for they shall not be ashamed that [c]wait for me.

24 For shall the prey be taken from the mighty, or the [a]lawful captives delivered?

25 But thus saith the Lord, even the captives of the mighty shall be taken away, and the prey of the terrible shall be delivered; for I will contend with him that contendeth with thee, and I will save thy children.

26 And I will [a]feed them that

12*a* Isa. 43:5 (5–7).
13*a* Isa. 44:23.
b TG Earth, Renewal of.
c 2 Sam. 22:28; Ps. 18:27; Isa. 49:13.
15*a* TG Woman.
b Ps. 103:13.
c 2 Kgs. 17:38; Isa. 41:17 (15–17); Alma 46:8; D&C 61:36; 133:2.
16*a* Zech. 13:6.
17*a* 3 Ne. 21:13 (12–20).
18*a* Micah 4:11 (11–13).
20*a* TG Israel, Gathering of.
21*a* Isa. 54:1; Gal. 4:27.
22*a* Isa. 66:19 (18–20). TG Israel, Mission of.
b Isa. 11:12 (10–12); 18:3; Zech. 9:16.
c 1 Ne. 22:8; 2 Ne. 10:8 (8–9).
23*a* Isa. 60:16 (14–16).
b 1 Ne. 22:6.
c Gen. 49:18; Prov. 27:18; 2 Ne. 6:13; D&C 98:2; 133:11 (10–11, 45).
24*a* IE the covenant people of the Lord. See also v. 25. JST Isa. 49:25 reads: "But thus saith the Lord; even the captives of the mighty shall be taken away, and the prey of the terrible shall be delivered; *for the mighty God shall deliver his covenant people . . .*"
26*a* 1 Ne. 14:17 (15–17); 22:13 (13–14); 2 Ne. 6:14 (14–18).

oppress thee with their own flesh; they shall be drunken with their own blood as with sweet wine; and all flesh shall [b]know that I, the Lord, am thy [c]Savior and thy Redeemer, the [d]Mighty One of Jacob.

CHAPTER 22

Israel will be scattered upon all the face of the earth—The Gentiles will nurse and nourish Israel with the gospel in the last days—Israel will be gathered and saved, and the wicked will burn as stubble—The kingdom of the devil will be destroyed, and Satan will be bound. About 588–570 B.C.

AND now it came to pass that after I, Nephi, had read these things which were engraven upon the [a]plates of brass, my brethren came unto me and said unto me: What [b]meaneth these things which ye have read? Behold, are they to be understood according to things which are [c]spiritual, which shall come to pass according to the spirit and not the flesh?

2 And I, Nephi, said unto them: Behold they were [a]manifest unto the prophet by the voice of the [b]Spirit; for by the Spirit are all things made known unto the [c]prophets, which shall come upon the children of men according to the flesh.

3 Wherefore, the things of which I have read are things pertaining to things both [a]temporal and spiritual; for it appears that the house of Israel, sooner or later, will be [b]scattered upon all the face of the earth, and also [c]among all nations.

4 And behold, there are many who are already lost from the knowledge of those who are at Jerusalem. Yea, the more part of all the [a]tribes have been [b]led away; and they are [c]scattered to and fro upon the [d]isles of the sea; and whither they are none of us knoweth, save that we know that they have been led away.

5 And since they have been led away, these things have been prophesied concerning them, and also concerning all those who shall hereafter be scattered and be confounded, because of the Holy One of Israel; for against him will they [a]harden their hearts; wherefore, they shall be scattered among all nations and shall be [b]hated of all men.

6 Nevertheless, after they shall be [a]nursed by the [b]Gentiles, and the Lord has lifted up his hand upon the Gentiles and set them up for a standard, and their [c]children have been carried in their arms, and their daughters have been carried upon their shoulders, behold these things of which are spoken are temporal; for thus are the covenants of the Lord with our fathers; and it meaneth us in the days to come, and also all our brethren who are of the house of Israel.

7 And it meaneth that the time cometh that after all the house of Israel have been scattered and confounded, that the Lord God will raise up a mighty nation among the [a]Gentiles, yea, even upon the face of this land; and by them shall our seed be [b]scattered.

8 And after our seed is scattered the

26*b* Ezek. 26:6; Mosiah 11:22 (20–22).
c TG Jesus Christ, Savior.
d TG Jesus Christ, Jehovah.

22 1*a* 1 Ne. 19:22; 2 Ne. 4:2.
b TG Interpretation.
c TG Spiritual.
2*a* 2 Pet. 1:21 (19–21).
b TG God, Spirit of.
c TG Prophecy.
3*a* D&C 29:34 (31–34).
b 1 Ne. 10:12 (12–14); 2 Ne. 25:15 (14–16). TG Israel, Scattering of.
c TG Inspiration.
4*a* TG Israel, Ten Lost Tribes of.
b 2 Ne. 10:22.
c Ps. 107:4; Zech. 2:6.
d Isa. 51:5; 1 Ne. 21:1; 2 Ne. 10:8 (8, 20).
5*a* TG Hardheartedness.
b Luke 23:28–31; 1 Ne. 19:14.
6*a* 1 Ne. 21:23.
b TG Gentiles.
c 1 Ne. 15:13; 2 Ne. 30:3 (1–7).
7*a* 3 Ne. 20:27.
b Isa. 18:7; 1 Ne. 13:14 (12–14); 2 Ne. 1:11.

Lord God will proceed to do a [a]mar-
velous work among the [b]Gentiles,
which shall be of great [c]worth unto
our seed; wherefore, it is likened
unto their being nourished by the
[d]Gentiles and being carried in their
arms and upon their shoulders.
9 And it shall also be of [a]worth
unto the Gentiles; and not only unto
the Gentiles but [b]unto all the [c]house
of Israel, unto the making known
of the [d]covenants of the Father of
heaven unto Abraham, saying: In
thy [e]seed shall all the kindreds of
the earth be [f]blessed.
10 And I would, my brethren, that
ye should know that all the kindreds
of the earth cannot be blessed unless he shall make [a]bare his arm in
the eyes of the nations.
11 Wherefore, the Lord God will
proceed to make bare his arm in the
eyes of all the [a]nations, in bringing
about his covenants and his gospel
unto those who are of the house
of Israel.
12 Wherefore, he will [a]bring them
again out of [b]captivity, and they
shall be [c]gathered together to the
lands of their [d]inheritance; and
they shall be [e]brought out of obscurity and out of [f]darkness; and
they shall know that the [g]Lord is
their [h]Savior and their Redeemer,
the [i]Mighty One of Israel.
13 And the blood of that great and
[a]abominable church, which is the
whore of all the earth, shall turn
upon their own heads; for they shall
[b]war among themselves, and the
sword of their [c]own hands shall fall
upon their own heads, and they shall
be drunken with their own blood.
14 And every [a]nation which shall
war against thee, O house of Israel,
shall be turned one against another, and they shall [b]fall into the
pit which they digged to ensnare
the people of the Lord. And all that
[c]fight against Zion shall be destroyed, and that great whore, who
hath perverted the right ways of
the Lord, yea, that great and abominable church, shall tumble to the
[d]dust and great shall be the fall of it.
15 For behold, saith the prophet,
the time cometh speedily that Satan shall have no more power over
the hearts of the children of men;
for the day soon cometh that all the
proud and they who do wickedly
shall be as [a]stubble; and the day
cometh that they must be [b]burned.
16 For the time soon cometh that
the fulness of the [a]wrath of God shall
be poured out upon all the children

8*a* Isa. 29:14;
1 Ne. 14:7;
2 Ne. 27:26.
TG Restoration of the Gospel.
b 2 Ne. 10:10;
3 Ne. 16:6 (4–7);
Morm. 5:19.
c 1 Ne. 15:14 (13–18);
Jacob 3:6;
3 Ne. 5:23 (21–26);
21:7 (4–29).
d TG Mission of Latter-day Saints.
9*a* 1 Ne. 14:5 (1–5);
2 Ne. 28:2.
b 1 Ne. 15:13 (13–17);
2 Ne. 30:3 (1–7).
c 2 Ne. 29:14 (13–14).
d Deut. 4:31.
e TG Abrahamic Covenant; Seed of Abraham.
f Gen. 12:2;
3 Ne. 20:25 (25, 27).
10*a* Isa. 52:10.
11*a* TG Israel, Mission of.
12*a* Ps. 80:19 (17–19);
D&C 35:25.
b 1 Ne. 21:25 (24–25).
c TG Israel, Gathering of.
d TG Lands of Inheritance.
e TG Israel, Restoration of.
f TG Darkness, Spiritual.
g 1 Ne. 19:15;
2 Ne. 6:11 (10–15).
h TG Jesus Christ, Prophecies about; Jesus Christ, Savior.
i TG Jesus Christ, Jehovah.
13*a* Rev. 17:16 (16–17).
TG Devil, Church of.
b 1 Ne. 14:16 (3, 15–17);
2 Ne. 6:15.
TG War.
c 1 Ne. 21:26 (24–26).
14*a* Luke 21:10.
b Ps. 7:15;
Prov. 26:27; 28:10;
Isa. 60:12;
Zech. 12:9;
1 Ne. 14:3;
2 Ne. 28:8;
D&C 109:25.
c 2 Ne. 10:13; 27:3 (2–3);
Morm. 8:41 (40–41);
D&C 136:36.
TG Protection, Divine.
d Isa. 25:12.
15*a* Isa. 5:23–24;
Nahum 1:10;
Mal. 4:1;
2 Ne. 15:24; 26:6 (4–6);
D&C 64:24 (23–24);
133:64.
b Ps. 21:9 (8–10);
3 Ne. 25:1;
D&C 29:9.
TG Earth, Cleansing of.
16*a* 1 Ne. 14:17;
3 Ne. 20:20 (19–21).

of men; for he will not suffer that the
wicked shall destroy the righteous.
17 Wherefore, he will [a]preserve the
[b]righteous by his power, even if it
so be that the fulness of his wrath
must come, and the righteous be
preserved, even unto the destruction
of their enemies by fire. Wherefore,
the righteous need not fear; for
thus saith the prophet, they shall
be saved, even if it so be as by fire.
18 Behold, my brethren, I say unto
you, that these things must shortly
come; yea, even blood, and fire, and
vapor of smoke must come; and it
must needs be upon the face of this
earth; and it cometh unto men according to the flesh if it so be that
they will harden their hearts against
the Holy One of Israel.
19 For behold, the righteous shall
not perish; for the time surely must
come that all they who fight against
Zion shall be cut off.
20 And the Lord will surely [a]pre-
pare a way for his people, unto the
fulfilling of the words of Moses,
which he spake, saying: A [b]prophet
shall the Lord your God raise up
unto you, like unto me; him shall
ye hear in all things whatsoever
he shall say unto you. And it shall
come to pass that all those who will
not hear that prophet shall be [c]cut
off from among the people.
21 And now I, Nephi, declare unto
you, that this [a]prophet of whom
Moses spake was the Holy One of
Israel; wherefore, he shall execute
[b]judgment in righteousness.
22 And the righteous need not fear,
for they are those who shall not be
confounded. But it is the kingdom
of the devil, which shall be built up
among the children of men, which
kingdom is established among them
which are in the flesh—
23 For the time speedily shall come
that all [a]churches which are built
up to get gain, and all those who
are built up to get power over the
flesh, and those who are built up
to become [b]popular in the eyes of
the world, and those who seek the
lusts of the flesh and the things of
the world, and to do all manner of
iniquity; yea, in fine, all those who
belong to the kingdom of the [c]devil
are they who need fear, and tremble,
and [d]quake; they are those who must
be brought low in the dust; they
are those who must be [e]consumed
as stubble; and this is according to
the words of the prophet.
24 And the time cometh speedily that the righteous must be led
up as [a]calves of the stall, and the
Holy One of Israel must reign in
dominion, and might, and power,
and great [b]glory.
25 And he [a]gathereth his children
from the four quarters of the earth;
and he numbereth his [b]sheep, and
they know him; and there shall be
one fold and one shepherd; and he
shall feed his sheep, and in him
they shall find [c]pasture.
26 And because of the [a]righteous-
ness of his people, [b]Satan has no
power; wherefore, he cannot be
loosed for the space of [c]many years;
for he hath no power over the hearts

17 *a* 2 Ne. 30:10; 3 Ne. 22:13 (13–17); Moses 7:61. TG Protection, Divine.
b Ps. 55:22; 1 Ne. 17:35 (33–38).
20 *a* TG Millennium, Preparing a People for.
b John 4:19; 7:40.
c D&C 133:63.
21 *a* Deut. 18:15 (15–19); Acts 3:22 (20–23); 1 Ne. 10:4; 3 Ne. 20:23; Moses 1:6. TG Jesus Christ, Prophecies about.
b Ps. 98:9; Moses 6:57. TG Jesus Christ, Judge.
23 *a* 1 Ne. 14:10 (9–10); 2 Ne. 26:20. TG Covet; Priestcraft.
b Luke 6:26; Alma 1:3.
c 1 Ne. 13:6.
d 2 Ne. 28:19.
e Zeph. 1:2 (2–3); 2 Ne. 26:6.
24 *a* Amos 6:4; Mal. 4:2; 3 Ne. 25:2.
b TG Jesus Christ, Glory of.
25 *a* Isa. 43:6 (5–7); Eph. 1:10. TG Israel, Gathering of.
b TG Jesus Christ, Good Shepherd; Sheep; Shepherd.
c 1 Ne. 21:9.
26 *a* TG Millennium; Righteousness.
b Rev. 20:2; Alma 48:17 (16–17); D&C 43:31; 45:55; 88:110; 101:28. TG Devil.
c Jacob 5:76.

of the people, for they dwell in
righteousness, and the Holy One
of Israel [d]reigneth.
27 And now behold, I, Nephi, say
unto you that all these [a]things must
come according to the flesh.
28 But, behold, all nations, kindreds, tongues, and people shall
dwell safely in the Holy One of Israel if it so be that they will [a]repent.
29 And now I, Nephi, make an end;
for I durst not speak further as yet
concerning these things.
30 Wherefore, my brethren, I
would that ye should consider that
the things which have been written
upon the [a]plates of brass are true;
and they testify that a man must
be obedient to the commandments
of God.
31 Wherefore, ye need not suppose that I and my father are the
only ones that have testified, and
also taught them. Wherefore, if ye
shall be obedient to the [a]command-
ments, and endure to the end, ye
shall be saved at the last day. And
thus it is. Amen.

THE SECOND BOOK OF NEPHI

An account of the death of Lehi. Nephi's brethren rebel against him. The Lord warns Nephi to depart into the wilderness. His journeyings in the wilderness, and so forth.

CHAPTER 1

Lehi prophesies of a land of liberty—His seed will be scattered and smitten if they reject the Holy One of Israel—He exhorts his sons to put on the armor of righteousness. About 588–570 B.C.

AND now it came to pass that
after I, Nephi, had made an
end of teaching my brethren,
our [a]father, Lehi, also spake many
things unto them, and rehearsed
unto them, how great things the
Lord had done for them in bringing
them out of the land of Jerusalem.
2 And he spake unto them concerning their [a]rebellions upon the
waters, and the mercies of God in
sparing their lives, that they were
not swallowed up in the sea.
3 And he also spake unto them concerning the land of promise, which
they had obtained—how [a]merciful
the Lord had been in [b]warning us
that we should flee out of the land
of Jerusalem.
4 For, behold, said he, I have [a]seen
a [b]vision, in which I know that
[c]Jerusalem is [d]destroyed; and had we
remained in Jerusalem we should
also have [e]perished.
5 But, said he, notwithstanding
our afflictions, we have obtained
a [a]land of promise, a land which is
[b]choice above all other lands; a land
which the Lord God hath [c]covenanted

26*d* TG Jesus Christ, Millennial Reign.
27*a* IE these things pertain to this mortal world.
28*a* TG Forgive; Repent.
30*a* 1 Ne. 19:22; 2 Ne. 4:2.
31*a* Matt. 19:17. TG Commandments of God.

[2 NEPHI]

1 1*a* TG Patriarch.
2*a* Isa. 65:2 (1–5); 1 Ne. 18:9 (9–20); Alma 18:38.
3*a* Gen. 19:16.
b TG Warn.
4*a* 1 Ne. 17:14.
b TG Vision.
c Jer. 26:18 (17–19); 1 Ne. 1:4 (4–18); Hel. 8:20. TG Jerusalem.
d Jer. 44:2.
e Alma 9:22.
5*a* TG Promised Lands.
b Ether 2:10 (7–12).
c TG Vow.

with me should be a land for the
inheritance of my seed. Yea, the
Lord hath [d]covenanted this land
unto me, and to my children forever, and also all those who should
be [e]led out of other countries by the
hand of the Lord.
6 Wherefore, I, Lehi, prophesy
according to the workings of the
Spirit which is in me, that there
shall [a]none come into this land save
they shall be brought by the hand
of the Lord.
7 Wherefore, this [a]land is consecrated unto him whom he shall
bring. And if it so be that they shall
serve him according to the commandments which he hath given,
it shall be a land of [b]liberty unto
them; wherefore, they shall never
be brought down into captivity; if
so, it shall be because of iniquity;
for if iniquity shall abound [c]cursed
shall be the land for their sakes,
but unto the righteous it shall be
blessed forever.
8 And behold, it is wisdom that
this land should be [a]kept as yet from
the knowledge of other [b]nations; for
behold, many nations would overrun the land, that there would be
no place for an inheritance.
9 Wherefore, I, Lehi, have obtained
a [a]promise, that [b]inasmuch as those
whom the Lord God shall bring out
of the land of Jerusalem shall keep
his commandments, they shall [c]pros-
per upon the face of this land; and
they shall be kept from all other
nations, that they may possess this
land unto themselves. And if it so be
that they shall [d]keep his commandments they shall be blessed upon
the face of this land, and there shall
be none to molest them, nor to take
away the land of their [e]inheritance;
and they shall dwell safely forever.
10 But behold, when the time
cometh that they shall dwindle in
[a]unbelief, after they have received
so great blessings from the hand of
the Lord—having a knowledge of
the creation of the earth, and all
men, knowing the great and marvelous works of the Lord from the
creation of the world; having power
given them to do all things by faith;
having all the commandments from
the beginning, and having been
brought by his infinite goodness
into this precious land of promise—
behold, I say, if the day shall come
that they will reject the Holy One
of Israel, the true [b]Messiah, their
Redeemer and their God, behold,
the judgments of him that is [c]just
shall rest upon them.
11 Yea, he will bring [a]other nations unto them, and he will give
unto them power, and he will take
away from them the lands of their
possessions, and he will cause them
to be [b]scattered and smitten.
12 Yea, as one generation passeth
to another there shall be [a]blood-
sheds, and great visitations among
them; wherefore, my sons, I would
that ye would remember; yea, I
would that ye would hearken unto
my words.
13 O that ye would awake; awake
from a deep [a]sleep, yea, even from
the sleep of [b]hell, and shake off
the awful [c]chains by which ye are
bound, which are the chains which
bind the children of men, that they
are carried away captive down to the
eternal [d]gulf of misery and woe.

5*d* TG Covenants.
e Ezra 8:22.
6*a* 2 Ne. 10:22.
7*a* Mosiah 29:32; Alma 46:10 (10–28, 34).
b 2 Ne. 10:11. TG Liberty.
c Alma 45:16 (10–14, 16); Morm. 1:17; Ether 2:11 (8–12).
8*a* 3 Ne. 5:20.
b TG Nations.
9*a* Jacob 1:5.
b 2 Ne. 4:4; Alma 9:13.
c Deut. 29:9; 30:9.
d TG Obedience.
e TG Inheritance.
10*a* TG Unbelief.
b TG Jesus Christ, Messiah.
c TG Justice.
11*a* 1 Ne. 13:14 (12–20); Morm. 5:19 (19–20).
b 1 Ne. 22:7.
12*a* Morm. 1:11 (11–19); 4:1 (1–23); D&C 87:6 (1–6).
13*a* TG Sleep.
b TG Damnation.
c Isa. 58:6; Alma 12:11 (9–11). TG Bondage, Spiritual.
d 1 Ne. 12:18; 15:28 (28–30); Alma 26:20 (19–20); Hel. 3:29.

14 Awake! and arise from the dust,
and hear the words of a trembling
[a]parent, whose limbs ye must soon
lay down in the cold and silent
[b]grave, from whence no traveler
can [c]return; a few more [d]days and
I go the [e]way of all the earth.
15 But behold, the Lord hath [a]re-
deemed my soul from hell; I have
beheld his [b]glory, and I am encircled
about eternally in the [c]arms of his
[d]love.
16 And I desire that ye should remember to observe the [a]statutes and
the judgments of the Lord; behold,
this hath been the anxiety of my
soul from the beginning.
17 My heart hath been weighed
down with sorrow from time to
time, for I have feared, lest for the
hardness of your hearts the Lord
your God should come out in the
fulness of his [a]wrath upon you, that
ye be [b]cut off and destroyed forever;
18 Or, that a [a]cursing should come
upon you for the space of [b]many
generations; and ye are visited by
sword, and by famine, and are hated,
and are led according to the will
and captivity of the [c]devil.
19 O my sons, that these things
might not come upon you, but that
ye might be a choice and a [a]favored
people of the Lord. But behold, his
will be done; for his [b]ways are righteousness forever.
20 And he hath said that: [a]Inas-
much as ye shall keep my [b]com-
mandments ye shall [c]prosper in the
land; but inasmuch as ye will not
keep my commandments ye shall
be cut off from my presence.
21 And now that my soul might
have joy in you, and that my heart
might leave this world with gladness because of you, that I might
not be brought down with grief and
sorrow to the grave, arise from the
dust, my sons, and be [a]men, and be
determined in [b]one mind and in one
heart, united in all things, that ye
may not come down into captivity;
22 That ye may not be [a]cursed with
a sore cursing; and also, that ye may
not incur the displeasure of a [b]just
God upon you, unto the destruction,
yea, the eternal destruction of both
soul and body.
23 Awake, my sons; put on the armor of [a]righteousness. Shake off the
[b]chains with which ye are bound,
and come forth out of obscurity,
and arise from the dust.
24 Rebel no more against your
brother, whose views have been
[a]glorious, and who hath kept the
commandments from the time that
we left Jerusalem; and who hath
been an instrument in the hands of
God, in bringing us forth into the
land of promise; for were it not for
him, we must have perished with
[b]hunger in the wilderness; nevertheless, ye sought to [c]take away his

14*a* TG Family, Love within.
b TG Death.
c Job 10:21.
d Gen. 47:29 (28–29); Jacob 1:9.
e Josh. 23:14; 1 Kgs. 2:2.
15*a* Alma 36:28. TG Jesus Christ, Atonement through.
b Ex. 24:16; Lev. 9:6 (6, 23); Ether 12:6 (6–18). TG Jesus Christ, Glory of.
c Isa. 59:16; Jacob 6:5; Alma 5:33; 3 Ne. 9:14.
d Rom. 8:39. TG God, Love of.
16*a* Deut. 4:6 (5–8); Ezek. 20:11; 2 Ne. 5:10 (10–11).
17*a* 1 Ne. 2:23; 2 Ne. 5:21 (21–24); Alma 3:6 (6–19). TG God, Indignation of.
b Gen. 6:13; 1 Ne. 17:31; Mosiah 12:8; 3 Ne. 9:9.
18*a* TG Curse.
b 1 Ne. 12:21 (20–23).
c Rev. 12:9 (7–9); Moses 1:12. TG Devil.
19*a* TG Peculiar People.
b Hosea 14:9.
20*a* Jarom 1:9; Omni 1:6; Mosiah 1:7; Alma 9:13 (13–14); 36:30; 37:13; 3 Ne. 5:22.
b Lev. 26:3 (3–14); Joel 2:25 (23–26); Amos 5:4 (4–8); Mosiah 26:30.
c Ps. 67:6; Prov. 22:4 (4–5); Mosiah 2:24 (21–25).
21*a* 1 Sam. 4:9; 1 Kgs. 2:2.
b Moses 7:18.
22*a* TG Curse.
b D&C 3:4. TG Justice.
23*a* TG Righteousness.
b TG Bondage, Spiritual.
24*a* 1 Ne. 18:3.
b 1 Ne. 16:32.
c 1 Ne. 16:37.

life; yea, and he hath suffered much sorrow because of you.

25 And I exceedingly fear and tremble because of you, lest he shall suffer again; for behold, ye have [a]accused him that he sought power and [b]authority over you; but I know that he hath not sought for power nor authority over you, but he hath sought the glory of God, and your own eternal welfare.

26 And ye have murmured because he hath been plain unto you. Ye say that he hath used [a]sharpness; ye say that he hath been angry with you; but behold, his [b]sharpness was the sharpness of the power of the word of God, which was in him; and that which ye call anger was the truth, according to that which is in God, which he could not restrain, manifesting boldly concerning your iniquities.

27 And it must needs be that the [a]power of God must be with him, even unto his commanding you that ye must obey. But behold, it was not he, but it was the [b]Spirit of the Lord which was in him, which [c]opened his mouth to utterance that he could not shut it.

28 And now my son, Laman, and also Lemuel and Sam, and also my sons who are the sons of Ishmael, behold, if ye will hearken unto the voice of Nephi ye shall not perish. And if ye will hearken unto him I leave unto you a [a]blessing, yea, even my first blessing.

29 But if ye will not hearken unto him I take away my [a]first blessing, yea, even my blessing, and it shall rest upon him.

30 And now, Zoram, I speak unto you: Behold, thou art the [a]servant of Laban; nevertheless, thou hast been brought out of the land of Jerusalem, and I know that thou art a true [b]friend unto my son, Nephi, forever.

31 Wherefore, because thou hast been faithful thy seed shall be blessed [a]with his seed, that they dwell in prosperity long upon the face of this land; and nothing, save it shall be iniquity among them, shall harm or disturb their prosperity upon the face of this land forever.

32 Wherefore, if ye shall keep the commandments of the Lord, the Lord hath consecrated this land for the security of thy seed with the seed of my son.

CHAPTER 2

Redemption comes through the Holy Messiah—Freedom of choice (agency) is essential to existence and progression—Adam fell that men might be—Men are free to choose liberty and eternal life. About 588–570 B.C.

AND now, Jacob, I speak unto you: Thou art my [a]firstborn in the days of my tribulation in the wilderness. And behold, in thy childhood thou hast suffered afflictions and much sorrow, because of the rudeness of thy brethren.

2 Nevertheless, Jacob, my firstborn in the wilderness, thou knowest the greatness of God; and he shall consecrate thine [a]afflictions for thy gain.

3 Wherefore, thy soul shall be blessed, and thou shalt dwell safely with thy brother, Nephi; and thy days shall be [a]spent in the service of thy God. Wherefore, I know that thou art redeemed, because of the righteousness of thy Redeemer; for thou hast [b]beheld that in the [c]fulness

25*a* 1 Ne. 15:8 (8–11); Mosiah 10:14.
b Gen. 37:10 (9–11); 1 Ne. 2:22.
26*a* Prov. 15:10; 1 Ne. 16:2.
b W of M 1:17; Moro. 9:4; D&C 121:43 (41–43).
27*a* 1 Ne. 17:48.
b D&C 121:43.
c D&C 33:8.
28*a* TG Birthright.
29*a* Gen. 49:3 (3–4); D&C 68:17; Abr. 1:3.
30*a* 1 Ne. 4:20 (20, 35).
b TG Friendship.
31*a* 2 Ne. 5:6.
2 1*a* 1 Ne. 18:7 (7, 19).
2*a* Micah 4:13; 2 Ne. 32:9. TG Affliction.
3*a* Enos 1:1.
b 2 Ne. 11:3.
c TG Fulness.

of time he cometh to bring salvation
unto men.
4 And thou hast [a]beheld in thy
youth his glory; wherefore, thou
art blessed even as they unto whom
he shall minister in the flesh; for
the Spirit is the same, yesterday,
today, and forever. And the way is
prepared from the fall of man, and
[b]salvation is [c]free.
5 And men are instructed sufficiently that they [a]know good from
evil. And the [b]law is given unto men.
And by the law no flesh is [c]justi-
fied; or, by the law men are [d]cut off.
Yea, by the temporal law they were
cut off; and also, by the spiritual
law they perish from that which
is good, and become miserable
forever.
6 Wherefore, [a]redemption cometh
in and through the [b]Holy [c]Messiah;
for he is full of [d]grace and truth.
7 Behold, he offereth himself a
[a]sacrifice for sin, to answer the ends
of the law, unto all those who have
a broken heart and a contrite spirit;
and unto [b]none else can the [c]ends
of the law be answered.
8 Wherefore, how great the importance to make these things known
unto the inhabitants of the earth,
that they may know that there
is no flesh that can dwell in the
presence of God, [a]save it be through
the merits, and mercy, and grace of
the Holy Messiah, who [b]layeth down
his life according to the flesh, and
taketh it again by the power of the
Spirit, that he may bring to pass
the [c]resurrection of the dead, being
the first that should rise.
9 Wherefore, he is the firstfruits
unto God, inasmuch as he shall
make [a]intercession for all the children of men; and they that believe
in him shall be saved.
10 And because of the intercession for [a]all, all men come unto
God; wherefore, they stand in the
presence of him, to be [b]judged of
him according to the truth and [c]ho-
liness which is in him. Wherefore,
the ends of the law which the Holy
One hath given, unto the inflicting
of the [d]punishment which is affixed,
which punishment that is affixed
is in opposition to that of the happiness which is affixed, to answer
the ends of the [e]atonement—
11 For it must needs be, that there
is an [a]opposition in all things. If not
so, my firstborn in the wilderness,
righteousness could not be brought
to pass, neither wickedness, neither holiness nor misery, neither
good nor bad. Wherefore, all things
must needs be a compound in one;

4*a* 2 Ne. 11:3; Jacob 7:5. TG Jesus Christ, Appearances, Antemortal.
b Jude 1:3.
c TG Grace.
5*a* Moro. 7:16.
b Gal. 2:16; 3:2; Mosiah 13:28 (27–28).
c Rom. 3:20 (20–24); 7:5; 2 Ne. 25:23; Alma 42:14 (12–16). TG Justification.
d Lev. 7:20 (20–21); 1 Ne. 10:6; 2 Ne. 9:6 (6–38); Alma 11:42 (40–45); 12:16 (16, 24, 36); 42:7 (6–11); Hel. 14:16 (15–18).
6*a* 1 Ne. 10:6; 2 Ne. 25:20; Mosiah 16:5 (4–5); Alma 12:22 (22–25). TG Jesus Christ, Redeemer; Redemption.
b TG Holiness.
c TG Jesus Christ, Messiah.
d John 1:17 (14, 17); Alma 13:9; Moses 1:6. TG Grace.
7*a* TG Jesus Christ, Atonement through; Sacrifice; Self-Sacrifice.
b 1 Sam. 2:2 (1–10).
c Rom. 10:4.
8*a* 2 Ne. 25:20; 31:21; Mosiah 4:8; 5:8; Alma 21:9; 38:9.
b TG Jesus Christ, Prophecies about.
c 1 Cor. 15:20; Mosiah 13:35; Alma 7:12; 12:25 (24–25); 42:23. TG Jesus Christ, Resurrection.
9*a* Isa. 53:12 (1–12); Mosiah 14:12; 15:8; Moro. 7:28 (27–28). TG Jesus Christ, Mission of.
10*a* Ps. 65:2. TG Jesus Christ, Redeemer.
b TG Jesus Christ, Judge.
c TG Holiness.
d TG Punish.
e 2 Ne. 9:26 (7, 21–22, 26); Alma 22:14; 33:22; 34:9 (8–16). TG Jesus Christ, Atonement through.
11*a* Job 2:10; Matt. 5:45; D&C 29:39; 122:7 (5–9); Moses 6:55. TG Adversity; Agency; Mortality; Opposition.

wherefore, if it should be one body it must needs remain as dead, having no life neither death, nor corruption nor incorruption, happiness nor misery, neither sense nor insensibility.

12 Wherefore, it must needs have been created for a thing of naught; wherefore there would have been no [a]purpose in the end of its creation. Wherefore, this thing must needs destroy the wisdom of God and his eternal purposes, and also the power, and the mercy, and the [b]justice of God.

13 And if ye shall say there is [a]no law, ye shall also say there is no sin. If ye shall say there is no sin, ye shall also say there is no righteousness. And if there be no righteousness there be no happiness. And if there be no righteousness nor happiness there be no punishment nor misery. And if these things are not [b]there is no God. And if there is no God we are not, neither the earth; for there could have been no creation of things, neither to act nor to be acted upon; wherefore, all things must have vanished away.

14 And now, my sons, I speak unto you these things for your profit and [a]learning; for there is a God, and he hath [b]created all things, both the heavens and the earth, and all things that in them are, both things to act and things to be [c]acted upon.

15 And to bring about his eternal [a]purposes in the end of man, after he had [b]created our first parents, and the beasts of the field and the [c]fowls of the air, and in fine, all things which are created, it must needs be that there was an opposition; even the [d]forbidden [e]fruit in [f]opposition to the [g]tree of life; the one being sweet and the other bitter.

16 Wherefore, the Lord God gave unto man that he should [a]act for himself. Wherefore, man could not [b]act for himself save it should be that he was [c]enticed by the one or the other.

17 And I, Lehi, according to the things which I have read, must needs suppose that an [a]angel of God, according to that which is written, had [b]fallen from heaven; wherefore, he became a [c]devil, having sought that which was evil before God.

18 And because he had fallen from heaven, and had become miserable forever, he [a]sought also the misery of all mankind. Wherefore, he said unto Eve, yea, even that old serpent, who is the devil, who is the father of all [b]lies, wherefore he said: Partake of the forbidden fruit, and ye shall not die, but ye shall be as God, [c]knowing good and evil.

19 And after Adam and Eve had [a]partaken of the forbidden fruit they were driven out of the garden of [b]Eden, to till the earth.

20 And they have brought forth

12*a* D&C 88:25.
TG Earth, Purpose of.
b TG God, Justice of.
13*a* Rom. 4:15; 5:13;
2 Ne. 9:25; 11:7.
b Alma 42:13.
14*a* TG Learn.
b TG Creation;
God, Creator;
Jesus Christ, Creator.
c D&C 93:30.
15*a* Isa. 45:18 (17–18);
Matt. 5:48;
Rom. 8:17 (14–21);
Eph. 3:11 (7–12);
Alma 42:26;
D&C 29:43 (42–44);
Moses 1:31, 39.
TG Earth, Purpose of.
b TG Man, Physical
Creation of.
c Gen. 1:20.
d Gen. 2:17 (16–17);
Moses 3:17.
e Gen. 3:6;
Mosiah 3:26;
Alma 12:22 (21–23).
f TG Opposition.
g Gen. 2:9;
1 Ne. 15:36 (22, 28, 36);
Alma 12:26 (21, 23, 26);
32:40.
16*a* Alma 12:31.
TG Initiative.
b 2 Ne. 10:23.
TG Agency.
c D&C 29:39 (39–40).
17*a* TG Council in Heaven.
b Isa. 14:12;
2 Ne. 9:8;
Moses 4:3 (3–4);
Abr. 3:28 (27–28).
TG Sons of Perdition.
c TG Adversary; Devil;
Lucifer; Satan.
18*a* Luke 22:31;
Rev. 13:7;
2 Ne. 28:20 (19–23);
3 Ne. 18:18;
D&C 10:22 (22–27);
50:3; 76:29.
b 2 Ne. 28:8; Moses 4:4.
c Gen. 3:5;
Mosiah 16:3;
Alma 29:5;
Moro. 7:16 (15–19).
19*a* Gen. 2:17 (16–17);
Alma 12:31.
TG Fall of Man.
b TG Eden.

children; yea, even the [a]family of
all the earth.
21 And the days of the children
of [a]men were prolonged, according to the [b]will of God, that they
might [c]repent while in the flesh;
wherefore, their state became a
state of [d]probation, and their time
was lengthened, according to the
commandments which the Lord God
gave unto the children of men. For
he gave commandment that all men
must repent; for he showed unto all
men that they were [e]lost, because of
the transgression of their parents.
22 And now, behold, if Adam
had not transgressed he would not
have fallen, but he would have
remained in the garden of Eden.
And all things which were created
must have remained in the same
state in which they were after they
were created; and they must have
remained forever, and had no end.
23 And they would have had no
[a]children; wherefore they would
have remained in a state of inno-
cence, having no [b]joy, for they knew
no misery; doing no good, for they
knew no [c]sin.
24 But behold, all things have
been done in the wisdom of him
who [a]knoweth all things.
25 [a]Adam [b]fell that men might
be; and men [c]are, that they might
have [d]joy.
26 And the [a]Messiah cometh in
the fulness of time, that he may
[b]redeem the children of men from
the fall. And because that they are
[c]redeemed from the fall they have
become [d]free forever, knowing good
from evil; to act for themselves
and not to be acted upon, save it
be by the punishment of the [e]law
at the great and last day, according
to the commandments which God
hath given.
27 Wherefore, men are [a]free according to the [b]flesh; and [c]all things
are [d]given them which are expedient unto man. And they are free to
[e]choose [f]liberty and eternal [g]life,
through the great Mediator of all
men, or to choose captivity and
death, according to the captivity and
power of the devil; for he seeketh
that all men might be [h]miserable
like unto himself.
28 And now, my sons, I would
that ye should look to the great
[a]Mediator, and hearken unto his
great commandments; and be faithful unto his words, and choose eternal life, according to the will of his
Holy Spirit;
29 And not choose eternal death,
according to the will of the flesh
and the [a]evil which is therein, which
giveth the spirit of the devil power
to [b]captivate, to bring you down to
[c]hell, that he may reign over you in
his own kingdom.
30 I have spoken these few words
unto you all, my sons, in the last
days of my probation; and I have

20*a* 1 Cor. 15:45 (45–48); D&C 27:11; 138:38; Moses 1:34. TG Adam.
21*a* Job 14:1; Alma 12:24; Moses 4:23 (22–25).
b TG God, Will of.
c Alma 34:32. TG Repent.
d TG Mortality; Probation.
e Jacob 7:12.
23*a* Gen. 3:16; Moses 5:11. TG Family; Marriage, Motherhood.
b TG Joy.
c TG Sin.
24*a* TG God, Foreknowledge of; God, Intelligence of; God, Omniscience of.
25*a* TG Adam.
b Moses 6:48. TG Fall of Man.
c TG Mortality.
d Moses 5:10. TG Joy; Man, Potential to Become like Heavenly Father.
26*a* TG Jesus Christ, Messiah.
b TG Salvation, Plan of.
c TG Redemption.
d Gal. 5:1; Alma 41:7; 42:27; Hel. 14:30.
e TG God, Law of.
27*a* Gal. 5:1; Hel. 14:30 (29–30); Moses 6:56.
b TG Mortality.
c 2 Ne. 26:24; Jacob 5:41; Alma 26:37.
d Alma 29:8. TG Talents.
e TG Initiative; Opposition.
f TG Liberty.
g Deut. 30:15.
h D&C 10:22.
28*a* TG Jesus Christ, Mediator.
29*a* TG Evil; Sin.
b Rom. 6:14 (14–18); 1 Ne. 14:7; Alma 12:11 (9–11). TG Bondage, Spiritual.
c TG Hell.

chosen the good part, according
to the words of the prophet. And I
have none other object save it be the
everlasting [a]welfare of your souls.
Amen.

CHAPTER 3

Joseph in Egypt saw the Nephites in vision—He prophesied of Joseph Smith, the latter-day seer; of Moses, who would deliver Israel; and of the coming forth of the Book of Mormon. About 588–570 B.C.

AND now I speak unto you, Joseph,
my [a]last-born. Thou wast born in
the wilderness of mine afflictions;
yea, in the days of my greatest sorrow did thy mother bear thee.
2 And may the Lord consecrate
also unto thee this [a]land, which is
a most precious land, for thine inheritance and the inheritance of
thy seed with thy brethren, for thy
security forever, if it so be that ye
shall keep the commandments of
the Holy One of Israel.
3 And now, Joseph, my last-born,
whom I have brought out of the
wilderness of mine afflictions, may
the Lord bless thee forever, for thy
[a]seed shall not utterly be [b]destroyed.
4 For behold, thou art the fruit of
my loins; and I am a descendant of
[a]Joseph who was carried [b]captive
into Egypt. And great were the [c]cov-
enants of the Lord which he made
unto Joseph.
5 Wherefore, Joseph truly [a]saw our
day. And he obtained a [b]promise
of the Lord, that out of the fruit of
his loins the Lord God would raise
up a [c]righteous [d]branch unto the
house of Israel; not the Messiah, but
a branch which was to be broken
off, nevertheless, to be remembered
in the covenants of the Lord that
the Messiah should be made [e]mani-
fest unto them in the latter days, in
the spirit of power, unto the bringing of them out of [f]darkness unto
light—yea, out of hidden darkness
and out of captivity unto freedom.
6 For Joseph truly testified, saying: A [a]seer shall the Lord my God
raise up, who shall be a choice seer
unto the fruit of my [b]loins.
7 Yea, Joseph truly said: Thus saith
the Lord unto me: A choice [a]seer
will I [b]raise up out of the fruit of
thy loins; and he shall be esteemed
highly among the fruit of thy loins.
And unto him will I give commandment that he shall do a work for
the fruit of thy loins, his brethren,
which shall be of great worth unto
them, even to the bringing of them
to the [c]knowledge of the covenants
which I have made with thy fathers.
8 And I will give unto him a commandment that he shall do [a]none
other work, save the work which
I shall command him. And I will
make him great in mine eyes; for
he shall do my work.
9 And he shall be great like unto
[a]Moses, whom I have said I would
raise up unto you, to [b]deliver my
[c]people, O house of Israel.
10 And [a]Moses will I raise up, to
deliver thy people out of the land of
Egypt.
11 But a [a]seer will I raise up out

30*a* TG Family, Children, Responsibilities toward.
3 1*a* 1 Ne. 18:7 (7, 19).
2*a* 1 Ne. 2:20. TG Promised Lands.
3*a* Gen. 45:7; 1 Ne. 13:30.
b Amos 9:8; 2 Ne. 9:53; 25:21.
4*a* Gen. 39:2; 45:4; 49:22 (22–26); Ps. 77:15; 1 Ne. 5:14 (14–16).
b Gen. 37:36 (29–36).
c Amos 5:15.
5*a* JST Gen. 50:24–38 (Bible Appendix); 2 Ne. 3:22; 4:2 (1–32).
b TG Promise.
c Jacob 2:25.
d Gen. 45:7 (5–7); 49:22 (22–26); 1 Ne. 15:12 (12, 16); 19:24; 2 Ne. 14:2. TG Vineyard of the Lord.
e 2 Ne. 6:14; D&C 3:18 (16–20).
f Isa. 42:16; 1 Jn. 2:8; 1 Ne. 21:9.
6*a* 3 Ne. 21:11 (8–11); Morm. 8:16 (16, 25); Ether 3:28 (21–28). TG Seer.
b D&C 132:30.
7*a* TG Joseph Smith.
b TG Millennium, Preparing a People for.
c TG Book of Mormon.
8*a* D&C 24:9 (8–9).
9*a* Moses 1:41.
b Ex. 3:10 (7–10); 1 Ne. 17:24.
c 2 Ne. 29:14.
10*a* TG Foreordination.
11*a* 1 Ne. 21:8; 3 Ne. 21:11 (8–11); Morm. 8:16 (16, 25). TG Prophets, Mission of.

of the fruit of thy loins; and unto
him will I give [b]power to [c]bring
forth my word unto the seed of thy
loins—and not to the bringing forth
my word only, saith the Lord, but
to the convincing them of my word,
which shall have already gone forth
among them.
12 Wherefore, the fruit of thy loins
shall [a]write; and the fruit of the
loins of [b]Judah shall [c]write; and that
which shall be written by the fruit of
thy loins, and also that which shall
be written by the fruit of the loins
of Judah, shall grow together, unto
the [d]confounding of [e]false doctrines
and laying down of contentions, and
establishing [f]peace among the fruit
of thy loins, and [g]bringing them
to the [h]knowledge of their fathers
in the latter days, and also to the
knowledge of my covenants, saith
the Lord.
13 And out of weakness he shall
be made strong, in that day when
my work shall commence among all
my people, unto the restoring thee,
O house of Israel, saith the Lord.
14 And thus prophesied Joseph,
saying: Behold, that seer will the
Lord bless; and they that seek to
destroy him shall be confounded;
for this promise, which I have obtained of the Lord, of the fruit of
my loins, shall be fulfilled. Behold,
I am sure of the fulfilling of this
promise;
15 And his [a]name shall be called after me; and it shall be after the [b]name
of his father. And he shall be [c]like
unto me; for the thing, which the
Lord shall bring forth by his hand,
by the power of the Lord shall bring
[d]my people unto [e]salvation.
16 Yea, thus prophesied Joseph: I
am sure of this thing, even as I am
sure of the promise of Moses; for
the Lord hath said unto me, I will
[a]preserve thy seed forever.
17 And the Lord hath said: I will
raise up a Moses; and I will give
power unto him in a rod; and I will
give judgment unto him in writing.
Yet I will not loose his tongue, that
he shall speak much, for I will not
make him mighty in speaking. But
I will [a]write unto him my law, by
the finger of mine own hand; and
I will make a [b]spokesman for him.
18 And the Lord said unto me
also: I will raise up unto the fruit of
thy loins; and I will make for him
a spokesman. And I, behold, I will
give unto him that he shall write
the writing of the fruit of thy loins,
unto the fruit of thy loins; and the
spokesman of thy loins shall declare it.
19 And the words which he shall
write shall be the words which are
expedient in my wisdom should go
forth unto the [a]fruit of thy loins.
And it shall be as if the fruit of thy
loins had cried unto them [b]from the
dust; for I know their faith.
20 And they shall [a]cry from the
[b]dust; yea, even repentance unto
their brethren, even after many
generations have gone by them.
And it shall come to pass that their
cry shall go, even according to the
simpleness of their words.
21 Because of their faith their
[a]words shall proceed forth out of

11*b* D&C 5:4 (3–4).
c TG Scriptures to Come Forth.
12*a* TG Book of Mormon.
b 1 Ne. 13:23 (23–29); 2 Ne. 29:12.
c TG Scriptures, Preservation of; Scriptures, Writing of.
d Ezek. 37:17 (15–20); 1 Ne. 13:39 (38–41); 2 Ne. 29:8; 33:10 (10–11).
e TG False Doctrine.
f TG Peacemakers.
g Moro. 1:4.
h 1 Ne. 15:14; 2 Ne. 30:5; 3 Ne. 5:23; Morm. 7:9 (1, 5, 9–10).
15*a* D&C 18:8.
b JS—H 1:3.
c D&C 28:2.
d Enos 1:13 (12–18); Alma 37:19 (1–20).
e TG Scriptures, Value of.
16*a* Gen. 45:7 (1–8); D&C 107:42.
17*a* Deut. 10:2 (2, 4); Moses 2:1. TG Scriptures, Writing of.
b Ex. 4:16 (14–16).
19*a* D&C 28:8.
b Isa. 29:4; 2 Ne. 27:13; 33:13 (13–15); Morm. 9:30; Moro. 10:27.
20*a* 2 Ne. 26:16; Morm. 8:23 (23, 26).
b TG Book of Mormon.
21*a* 2 Ne. 29:2.

my mouth unto their brethren who
are the fruit of thy loins; and the
weakness of their words will I make
strong in their faith, unto the remembering of my covenant which
I made unto thy fathers.
22 And now, behold, my son Joseph, after this manner did my
father of old [a]prophesy.
23 Wherefore, because of this covenant thou art [a]blessed; for thy seed
shall not be destroyed, for they shall
[b]hearken unto the words of the book.
24 And there shall rise up [a]one
mighty among them, who shall do
much good, both in word and in
deed, being an instrument in the
hands of God, with exceeding faith,
to work mighty wonders, and do
that thing which is great in the sight
of God, unto the bringing to pass
much [b]restoration unto the house
of Israel, and unto the seed of thy
brethren.
25 And now, blessed art thou,
Joseph. Behold, thou art little;
wherefore hearken unto the words
of thy brother, Nephi, and it shall
be done unto thee even according
to the words which I have spoken.
Remember the words of thy dying
father. Amen.

CHAPTER 4

Lehi counsels and blesses his posterity—He dies and is buried—Nephi glories in the goodness of God—Nephi puts his trust in the Lord forever. About 588–570 B.C.

AND now, I, Nephi, speak concerning
the prophecies of which my father
hath spoken, concerning [a]Joseph,
who was carried into Egypt.
2 For behold, he truly prophesied concerning all his seed. And
the [a]prophecies which he wrote,
there are not many greater. And he
prophesied concerning us, and our
future generations; and they are
written upon the [b]plates of brass.
3 Wherefore, after my father had
made an end of speaking concerning
the prophecies of Joseph, he called
the children of Laman, his sons, and
his daughters, and said unto them:
Behold, my sons, and my daughters,
who are the sons and the daughters of my [a]firstborn, I would that
ye should give ear unto my words.
4 For the Lord God hath said that:
[a]Inasmuch as ye shall keep my commandments ye shall prosper in the
land; and inasmuch as ye will not
keep my commandments ye shall
be cut off from my presence.
5 But behold, my sons and my
daughters, I cannot go down to my
grave save I should leave a [a]blessing
upon you; for behold, I know that
if ye are [b]brought up in the [c]way ye
should go ye will not depart from it.
6 Wherefore, if ye are [a]cursed,
behold, I leave my blessing upon
you, that the [b]cursing may be taken
from you and be answered upon
the [c]heads of your parents.
7 Wherefore, because of my blessing the Lord God will [a]not suffer
that ye shall perish; wherefore, he
will be [b]merciful unto you and unto
your seed forever.
8 And it came to pass that after my
father had made an end of speaking
to the sons and daughters of Laman,
he caused the sons and daughters of
Lemuel to be brought before him.
9 And he spake unto them, saying:

22*a* 2 Ne. 3:5.
23*a* TG Birthright.
b TG Obedience.
24*a* TG Joseph Smith.
b TG Dispensations; Israel, Restoration of; Restoration of the Gospel.
4 1*a* Gen. 39:2.
2*a* 2 Ne. 3:5.
b 1 Ne. 22:30; 2 Ne. 5:12.
3*a* TG Firstborn.
4*a* 2 Ne. 1:9; Alma 9:13.
5*a* TG Family, Patriarchal; Patriarchal Blessings.
b TG Family, Children, Responsibilities toward.
c Prov. 22:6.
6*a* 1 Ne. 2:23.
b TG Curse.
c D&C 68:25 (25–29).
7*a* 1 Ne. 22:7 (7–8); 2 Ne. 30:3 (3–6); Jacob 1:5. TG Book of Mormon.
b 1 Ne. 13:31; 2 Ne. 10:18 (18–19); Jacob 3:6 (5–9); Hel. 15:12 (10–17); Morm. 5:20 (20–21).

Behold, my sons and my daughters,
who are the sons and the daughters
of my second son; behold I leave
unto you the same blessing which
I left unto the sons and daughters
of Laman; wherefore, thou shalt not
utterly be destroyed; but in the end
thy seed shall be blessed.
10 And it came to pass that when
my father had made an end of speaking unto them, behold, he spake
unto the sons of [a]Ishmael, yea, and
even all his household.
11 And after he had made an end
of speaking unto them, he spake
unto Sam, saying: Blessed art thou,
and thy [a]seed; for thou shalt inherit the land like unto thy brother
Nephi. And thy seed shall be numbered with his seed; and thou shalt
be even like unto thy brother, and
thy seed like unto his seed; and
thou shalt be blessed in all thy
days.
12 And it came to pass after my
father, Lehi, had [a]spoken unto all
his household, according to the
feelings of his heart and the Spirit
of the Lord which was in him, he
waxed [b]old. And it came to pass that
he died, and was buried.
13 And it came to pass that not
many days after his death, Laman
and Lemuel and the sons of Ishmael
were [a]angry with me because of the
admonitions of the Lord.
14 For I, Nephi, was constrained to
speak unto them, according to his
word; for I had spoken many things
unto them, and also my father, before his death; many of which sayings are written upon mine [a]other
plates; for a more history part are
written upon mine other plates.
15 And upon [a]these I [b]write the
things of my soul, and many of
the scriptures which are engraven
upon the plates of brass. For my
soul [c]delighteth in the scriptures,
and my heart [d]pondereth them, and
writeth them for the [e]learning and
the profit of my children.
16 Behold, my [a]soul delighteth
in the things of the Lord; and my
[b]heart pondereth continually upon
the things which I have seen and
heard.
17 Nevertheless, notwithstanding
the great [a]goodness of the Lord, in
showing me his great and marvelous works, my heart exclaimeth:
O [b]wretched man that I am! Yea,
my heart [c]sorroweth because of my
flesh; my soul grieveth because of
mine iniquities.
18 I am encompassed about, because of the temptations and the
sins which do so easily [a]beset me.
19 And when I desire to rejoice,
my heart groaneth because of my
sins; nevertheless, I know in whom
I have [a]trusted.
20 My God hath been my [a]support;
he hath led me through mine [b]af-
flictions in the wilderness; and he
hath preserved me upon the waters
of the great deep.
21 He hath filled me with his
[a]love, even unto the [b]consuming
of my flesh.
22 He hath confounded mine [a]en-
emies, unto the causing of them to
quake before me.
23 Behold, he hath heard my cry by

10*a* 1 Ne. 7:6.
11*a* Jacob 1:14 (12–14).
12*a* Gen. 49:1 (1–27).
b TG Old Age.
13*a* 1 Ne. 7:6 (6–19); 17:18 (17–55); 18:10 (9–22); 2 Ne. 5:2 (1–25). TG Anger.
14*a* 1 Ne. 1:17 (16–17); 9:4; 2 Ne. 5:33 (29–33); D&C 10:42.
15*a* 1 Ne. 6:1 (1–6).
b TG Scriptures, Writing of.
c Ps. 119:24; Moses 6:59.
d TG Meditation; Scriptures, Study of.
e 1 Ne. 19:23. TG Scriptures, Value of.
16*a* TG Spirituality; Thanksgiving.
b TG Heart.
17*a* Ex. 34:6 (5–7); 2 Ne. 9:10; D&C 86:11.
b Rom. 7:24.
c TG Poor in Spirit; Repent; Sorrow.
18*a* Rom. 7:21 (15–25); Heb. 12:1; Alma 7:15.
19*a* TG Trust in God.
20*a* 2 Cor. 4:16.
b 1 Ne. 17:6. TG Affliction; Comfort.
21*a* TG God, Love of.
b D&C 84:33.
22*a* Ps. 3:7 (7–8).

day, and he hath given me [a]knowl-
edge by [b]visions in the night-time.
24 And by day have I waxed bold
in mighty [a]prayer before him; yea,
my voice have I sent up on high;
and angels came down and ministered unto me.
25 And upon the wings of his Spirit
hath my body been [a]carried away
upon exceedingly high mountains.
And mine eyes have beheld great
things, yea, even too great for man;
therefore I was bidden that I should
not write them.
26 O then, if I have seen so great
things, if the Lord in his condescension unto the children of men hath
[a]visited men in so much [b]mercy,
[c]why should my [d]heart weep and my
soul linger in the valley of sorrow,
and my flesh waste away, and my
strength slacken, because of mine
afflictions?
27 And why should I [a]yield to
sin, because of my flesh? Yea, why
should I give way to [b]temptations,
that the evil one have place in my
heart to destroy my [c]peace and afflict my soul? Why am I [d]angry because of mine enemy?
28 Awake, my soul! No longer
[a]droop in sin. Rejoice, O my heart,
and give place no more for the [b]en-
emy of my soul.
29 Do not [a]anger again because of
mine enemies. Do not slacken my
strength because of mine afflictions.
30 Rejoice, O my [a]heart, and cry
unto the Lord, and say: O Lord, I
will praise thee forever; yea, my
soul will rejoice in thee, my God,
and the [b]rock of my salvation.
31 O Lord, wilt thou [a]redeem my
soul? Wilt thou deliver me out of
the hands of mine enemies? Wilt
thou make me that I may shake at
the appearance of [b]sin?
32 May the gates of hell be shut
continually before me, because that
my [a]heart is broken and my spirit
is contrite! O Lord, wilt thou not
shut the gates of thy righteousness
before me, that I may [b]walk in the
path of the low valley, that I may
be strict in the plain road!
33 O Lord, wilt thou encircle me
around in the robe of thy [a]righ-
teousness! O Lord, wilt thou make
a way for mine escape before mine
[b]enemies! Wilt thou make my path
straight before me! Wilt thou not
place a stumbling block in my way—
but that thou wouldst clear my way
before me, and hedge not up my
way, but the ways of mine enemy.
34 O Lord, I have [a]trusted in thee,
and I will [b]trust in thee forever. I
will not put my [c]trust in the arm
of flesh; for I know that cursed is
he that putteth his [d]trust in the
arm of flesh. Yea, cursed is he that
putteth his trust in man or maketh
flesh his arm.
35 Yea, I know that God will give
[a]liberally to him that asketh. Yea,
my God will give me, if I [b]ask [c]not
amiss; therefore I will lift up my
voice unto thee; yea, I will cry
unto thee, my God, the [d]rock of my
[e]righteousness. Behold, my voice

23*a* TG Knowledge.
b 2 Chr. 26:5.
TG Dream; Vision.
24*a* James 5:16;
1 Ne. 1:5 (5–8); 10:17.
25*a* 2 Cor. 12:2 (1–4);
1 Ne. 11:1 (1–36);
Moses 1:1.
26*a* Ex. 3:16; Alma 9:21;
Morm. 1:15.
b TG Compassion;
God, Mercy of.
c Ps. 43:5.
d TG Heart.
27*a* Rom. 6:13 (10–16).
b TG Temptation.
c TG Contentment; Peace;
Peace of God.
d TG Self-Mastery.
28*a* Ps. 42:11.
b TG Adversary;
Enemies.
29*a* TG Anger.
30*a* TG Heart.
b 1 Cor. 3:11 (9–13).
TG Rock.
31*a* Ps. 16:10.
b Rom. 12:9;
Alma 13:12; 37:32.
TG Sin.
32*a* TG Contrite Heart.
b TG Walking with God.
33*a* TG Righteousness.
b Lev. 26:7 (1–13);
D&C 44:5.
34*a* TG Trustworthiness.
b TG Trust in God.
c Ps. 33:16; 44:6 (6–8).
TG Trust Not in the Arm
of Flesh.
d Prov. 14:16; Jer. 17:5;
Morm. 3:9; 4:8.
35*a* James 1:5.
TG Abundant Life.
b TG Prayer.
c Hel. 10:5.
d Deut. 32:4.
e Ps. 4:1.

shall forever ascend up unto thee,
my rock and mine everlasting God.
Amen.

CHAPTER 5

The Nephites separate themselves from the Lamanites, keep the law of Moses, and build a temple—Because of their unbelief, the Lamanites are cut off from the presence of the Lord, are cursed, and become a scourge unto the Nephites. About 588–559 B.C.

BEHOLD, it came to pass that I,
Nephi, did cry much unto the Lord
my God, because of the [a]anger of
my brethren.
2 But behold, their [a]anger did increase against me, insomuch that
they did seek to take away my life.
3 Yea, they did murmur against me,
saying: Our younger brother thinks
to [a]rule over us; and we have had
much trial because of him; wherefore, now let us slay him, that we
may not be afflicted more because
of his words. For behold, we will
not have him to be our ruler; for it
belongs unto us, who are the elder
brethren, to [b]rule over this people.
4 Now I do not write upon these
plates all the words which they
murmured against me. But it sufficeth me to say, that they did seek
to take away my life.
5 And it came to pass that the
Lord did [a]warn me, that I, [b]Nephi,
should depart from them and flee
into the wilderness, and all those
who would go with me.
6 Wherefore, it came to pass that
I, Nephi, did take my family, and
also [a]Zoram and his family, and Sam,
mine elder brother and his family,
and Jacob and Joseph, my younger
brethren, and also my sisters, and
all those who would go with me.
And all those who would go with
me were those who believed in the
[b]warnings and the revelations of
God; wherefore, they did hearken
unto my words.
7 And we did take our tents and
whatsoever things were possible for
us, and did journey in the wilderness
for the space of many days. And after we had journeyed for the space
of many days we did pitch our tents.
8 And my people would that we
should call the name of the place
[a]Nephi; wherefore, we did call it
Nephi.
9 And all those who were with me
did take upon them to call themselves the [a]people of Nephi.
10 And we did observe to keep the
judgments, and the [a]statutes, and
the commandments of the Lord in
all things, according to the [b]law
of Moses.
11 And the Lord was with us; and
we did [a]prosper exceedingly; for we
did sow seed, and we did reap again
in abundance. And we began to raise
flocks, and herds, and animals of
every kind.
12 And I, Nephi, had also brought
the records which were engraven
upon the [a]plates of brass; and also
the [b]ball, or [c]compass, which was
prepared for my father by the hand
of the Lord, according to that which
is written.
13 And it came to pass that we
began to prosper exceedingly, and
to multiply in the land.
14 And I, Nephi, did take the [a]sword
of Laban, and after the manner

5 1*a* 2 Ne. 4:13; Jacob 7:24; Enos 1:20; Mosiah 10:12, 15.
2*a* 1 Ne. 7:6 (6–19); 17:18 (17–55); 18:10 (9–22); 2 Ne. 4:13 (13–14).
3*a* Num. 16:13; 1 Ne. 16:37 (37–38); Mosiah 10:15.
b Alma 54:17.
5*a* TG Guidance, Divine.
b Mosiah 10:13.
6*a* 1 Ne. 4:35; 16:7; 2 Ne. 1:31 (30–32).
b TG Warn.
8*a* Omni 1:12 (12, 27); Mosiah 7:1 (1–7, 21); 9:1 (1–6, 14); 28:1 (1, 5); Alma 2:24; 20:1; 50:8 (8, 11).
9*a* Jacob 1:14.
10*a* Ezek. 20:11; 2 Ne. 1:16 (16–17).
b 2 Ne. 11:4. TG Law of Moses.
11*a* Matt. 6:33.
12*a* 2 Ne. 4:2; Mosiah 1:3 (3–4).
b Mosiah 1:16.
c 1 Ne. 16:16 (10, 16, 26); 18:12 (12, 21); Alma 37:38 (38–47); D&C 17:1.
14*a* 1 Ne. 4:9; Jacob 1:10; W of M 1:13; Mosiah 1:16; D&C 17:1.

of it did make many [b]swords, lest by any means the people who were now called Lamanites should come upon us and destroy us; for I knew their [c]hatred towards me and my children and those who were called my people.

15 And I did teach my people to [a]build buildings, and to [b]work in all [c]manner of wood, and of [d]iron, and of copper, and of [e]brass, and of steel, and of [f]gold, and of silver, and of precious ores, which were in great abundance.

16 And I, Nephi, did [a]build a [b]temple; and I did construct it after the manner of the temple of [c]Solomon save it were not built of so many [d]precious things; for they were not to be found upon the land, wherefore, it could not be built like unto Solomon's [e]temple. But the manner of the construction was like unto the temple of [f]Solomon; and the workmanship thereof was exceedingly fine.

17 And it came to pass that I, Nephi, did cause my people to be [a]industrious, and to [b]labor with their [c]hands.

18 And it came to pass that they would that I should be their [a]king. But I, Nephi, was desirous that they should have no king; nevertheless, I did for them according to that which was in my power.

19 And behold, the words of the Lord had been fulfilled unto my brethren, which he spake concerning them, that I should be their [a]ruler and their teacher. Wherefore, I had been their ruler and their [b]teacher, according to the commandments of the Lord, until the time they sought to take away my life.

20 Wherefore, the word of the Lord was fulfilled which he spake unto me, saying that: Inasmuch as they will [a]not hearken unto thy words they shall be [b]cut off from the presence of the Lord. And behold, they were [c]cut off from his presence.

21 And he had caused the [a]cursing to come upon them, yea, even a sore cursing, because of their iniquity. For behold, they had hardened their hearts against him, that they had become like unto a flint; wherefore, as they were white, and exceedingly fair and [b]delightsome, that they might not be [c]enticing unto my people the Lord God did cause a [d]skin of [e]blackness to come upon them.

22 And thus saith the Lord God: I will cause that they shall be [a]loathsome unto thy people, save they shall repent of their iniquities.

23 And cursed shall be the seed of him that [a]mixeth with their seed; for they shall be cursed even with the same cursing. And the Lord spake it, and it was done.

24 And because of their [a]cursing which was upon them they did become an [b]idle people, full of

---

14*b* Jarom 1:8; Mosiah 10:8; Alma 2:12; Hel. 1:14; 3 Ne. 3:26.
c TG Hate.
15*a* TG Skill.
b TG Art.
c Jarom 1:8.
d Josh. 8:31; 1 Ne. 18:25; Jacob 2:12 (12–13); Hel. 6:9 (9–11); Ether 9:17; 10:23 (12, 23); Moses 5:46.
e Gen. 4:22.
f Ex. 31:4 (4–5); 1 Kgs. 6:21 (21–22); D&C 124:26 (26–27).
16*a* 2 Chr. 3:1 (1–17); D&C 84:5 (5, 31); 124:31 (25–55).
b 1 Kgs. 5:5; Jacob 1:17; Mosiah 1:18; 7:17; 11:10; Alma 16:13; Hel. 3:14 (9, 14); 3 Ne. 11:1. TG Temple.
c 1 Kgs. 6:2.
d 1 Kgs. 5:17.
e 1 Kgs. 9:1.
f 1 Chr. 18:8.
17*a* TG Industry; Work, Value of.
b TG Labor.
c Prov. 31:13.
18*a* 2 Ne. 6:2; Jacob 1:9 (9, 11, 15); Jarom 1:7 (7, 14); Mosiah 1:10.
19*a* 2 Ne. 1:25 (25–27).
b TG Teacher.
20*a* 1 Ne. 8:18.
b 1 Ne. 8:35 (35–36).
c 1 Ne. 2:21; Alma 9:14 (13–15); 38:1.
21*a* TG Curse.
b Gen. 24:16; 1 Ne. 13:15; 4 Ne. 1:10; Morm. 9:6.
c TG Marriage, Temporal.
d 2 Ne. 30:6; 3 Ne. 2:15 (14–16).
e 2 Ne. 26:33; Moses 7:8.
22*a* 1 Ne. 12:23.
23*a* TG Marriage, Interfaith.
24*a* TG Curse.
b Alma 22:28. TG Idleness.

mischief and subtlety, and did seek
in the wilderness for beasts of prey.
25 And the Lord God said unto
me: They shall be a scourge unto
thy seed, to [a]stir them up in remembrance of me; and inasmuch as they
will not remember me, and hearken
unto my words, they shall scourge
them even unto destruction.
26 And it came to pass that I, Nephi,
did [a]consecrate Jacob and Joseph,
that they should be [b]priests and
[c]teachers over the land of my people.
27 And it came to pass that we lived
after the manner of [a]happiness.
28 And thirty years had passed
away from the time we left Jerusalem.
29 And I, Nephi, had kept the
[a]records upon my plates, which I
had made, of my people thus far.
30 And it came to pass that the
Lord God said unto me: [a]Make other
plates; and thou shalt engraven
many things upon them which are
good in my sight, for the profit of
thy people.
31 Wherefore, I, Nephi, to be obedient to the commandments of the
Lord, went and made [a]these plates
upon which I have engraven these
things.
32 And I engraved that which
is pleasing unto God. And if my
people are pleased with the things
of God they will be pleased with
mine engravings which are upon
these plates.
33 And if my people desire to
know the more particular part of
the history of my people they must
search mine [a]other [b]plates.
34 And it sufficeth me to say that
forty years had passed away, and
we had already had wars and contentions with our brethren.

CHAPTER 6

Jacob recounts Jewish history: The Babylonian captivity and return; the ministry and crucifixion of the Holy One of Israel; the help received from the Gentiles; and the Jews' latter-day restoration when they believe in the Messiah. About 559–545 B.C.

THE [a]words of Jacob, the brother
of Nephi, which he spake unto the
people of Nephi:
2 Behold, my beloved brethren, I,
Jacob, having been called of God,
and ordained after the manner of
his holy [a]order, and having been
consecrated by my brother Nephi,
unto whom ye look as a [b]king or a
protector, and on whom ye depend
for safety, behold ye know that I
have spoken unto you exceedingly
many things.
3 Nevertheless, I speak unto you
again; for I am desirous for the [a]wel-
fare of your souls. Yea, mine anxiety
is great for you; and ye yourselves
know that it ever has been. For I
have exhorted you with all diligence;
and I have taught you the words of
my father; and I have spoken unto
you concerning all things which
are [b]written, from the creation of
the world.
4 And now, behold, I would speak
unto you concerning things which
are, and which are to come; wherefore, I will read you the words of
[a]Isaiah. And they are the words
which my brother has desired that I
should speak unto you. And I speak
unto you for your sakes, that ye
may learn and glorify the name of
your God.
5 And now, the words which I shall
read are they which Isaiah spake
concerning all the house of Israel;

25*a* 1 Ne. 2:24.
26*a* Lev. 16:32; Jacob 1:18 (18–19); Mosiah 23:17. TG Priesthood, Authority.
b TG Priest, Melchizedek Priesthood.
c TG Teacher.
27*a* Alma 50:23.
29*a* TG Record Keeping.
30*a* 1 Ne. 19:5 (1–6); Jacob 3:14.
31*a* 1 Ne. 19:3; Jacob 1:1.
33*a* 1 Ne. 1:17 (16–17); 2 Ne. 4:14; D&C 10:42.
b 1 Ne. 19:4; Jacob 1:3.
6 1*a* 2 Ne. 11:1; Jacob 2:1.
2*a* TG Priesthood, Melchizedek.
b 2 Ne. 5:18; Jacob 1:9 (9, 11, 15); Jarom 1:7 (7, 14); Mosiah 1:10.
3*a* Jacob 2:3; Mosiah 25:11.
b TG Scriptures, Value of.
4*a* 3 Ne. 23:1 (1–3).

wherefore, they may be [a]likened
unto you, for ye are of the house of
Israel. And there are many things
which have been spoken by Isaiah
which may be likened unto you, because ye are of the house of Israel.
6 And now, these are the words:
[a]Thus saith the Lord God: Behold,
I will lift up mine hand to the
Gentiles, and set up my [b]standard
to the people; and they shall bring
thy sons in their arms, and thy
daughters shall be carried upon their
shoulders.
7 And [a]kings shall be thy nursing
fathers, and their queens thy nursing mothers; they shall bow down
to thee with their faces towards the
earth, and lick up the dust of thy
feet; and thou shalt know that [b]I
am the Lord; for they shall not be
ashamed that [c]wait for me.
8 And now I, Jacob, would speak
somewhat concerning these words.
For behold, the Lord has shown me
that those who were at [a]Jerusalem,
from whence we came, have been
[b]slain and [c]carried away captive.
9 Nevertheless, the Lord has shown
unto me that they should [a]return
again. And he also has shown unto
me that the Lord God, the Holy One
of Israel, should manifest himself
unto them in the flesh; and after
he should manifest himself they
should [b]scourge him and [c]crucify
him, according to the words of the
angel who spake it unto me.
10 And after they have [a]hardened
their hearts and [b]stiffened their
necks against the Holy One of Israel,
behold, the [c]judgments of the Holy
One of Israel shall come upon them.
And the day cometh that they shall
be smitten and afflicted.
11 Wherefore, after they are driven
to and fro, for thus saith the angel,
many shall be afflicted in the flesh,
and shall not be suffered to [a]per-
ish, because of the prayers of the
faithful; they shall be scattered, and
smitten, and hated; nevertheless, the
Lord will be merciful unto them,
that [b]when they shall come to the
[c]knowledge of their Redeemer, they
shall be [d]gathered together again
to the [e]lands of their inheritance.
12 And blessed are the [a]Gentiles,
they of whom the prophet has written; for behold, if it so be that they
shall repent and fight not against
Zion, and do not unite themselves to
that great and [b]abominable church,
they shall be saved; for the Lord God
will fulfil his [c]covenants which he
has made unto his children; and for
this cause the prophet has written
these things.
13 Wherefore, they that fight
against Zion and the covenant people of the Lord shall lick up the
dust of their feet; and the people
of the Lord shall not be [a]ashamed.
For the people of the Lord are they
who [b]wait for him; for they still
wait for the coming of the Messiah.

5*a* IE applied.
6*a* Isa. 49:22 (22 23); 2 Ne. 10:9.
b TG Ensign.
7*a* Isa. 60:16.
b Isa. 44:8; 45:5 (5–22); 46:9; 3 Ne. 24:6; Moses 1:6.
c Lam. 3:25 (25–26); D&C 133:45.
8*a* Esth. 2:6; 1 Ne. 7:13; 10:3; 2 Ne. 25:6, 10; Omni 1:15; Hel. 8:20 (20–21).
b Ezek. 23:25 (24–29).
c 2 Kgs. 24:14 (10–16); 25:11 (1–12); Jer. 13:19 (19, 24). TG Israel, Bondage of, in Other Lands.
9*a* Jer. 29:10 (9–10); 1 Ne. 10:3.
b TG Jesus Christ, Betrayal of.
c 1 Ne. 19:10 (10, 13); Mosiah 3:9; 3 Ne. 11:14 (14–15). TG Jesus Christ, Crucifixion of.
10*a* TG Hardheartedness.
b TG Stiffnecked.
c Matt. 27:25 (24–25).
11*a* Amos 9:8 (8–9); 2 Ne. 20:20 (20–21).
b 1 Ne. 22:12 (11–12); 2 Ne. 9:2 (1–2).
c Hosea 3:5; D&C 113:10. TG Israel, Restoration of.
d TG Israel, Gathering of.
e TG Lands of Inheritance.
12*a* 1 Ne. 14:2 (1–5); 2 Ne. 10:10 (8–14, 18).
b TG Devil, Church of.
c TG Abrahamic Covenant.
13*a* Joel 2:26 (26–27); 3 Ne. 22:4; D&C 90:17.
b Gen. 49:18; Ps. 25:5; Prov. 20:22; 27:18; Isa. 40:31; 1 Ne. 21:23; D&C 98:2; 133:11, 45.

14 And behold, according to the
words of the prophet, the Messiah
will set himself again the [a]second
time to recover them; wherefore, he
will [b]manifest himself unto them
in power and great glory, unto the
[c]destruction of their enemies, when
that day cometh when they shall
believe in him; and none will he
destroy that believe in him.
15 And they that believe not in
him shall be [a]destroyed, both by
[b]fire, and by tempest, and by earthquakes, and by [c]bloodsheds, and by
[d]pestilence, and by [e]famine. And
they shall know that the Lord is
God, the Holy One of Israel.
16 [a]For shall the prey be taken
from the mighty, or the [b]lawful
captive delivered?
17 But thus saith the Lord: Even
the captives of the mighty shall be
taken away, and the prey of the
terrible shall be delivered; [a]for the
[b]Mighty God shall [c]deliver his covenant people. For thus saith the
Lord: I will contend with them that
contendeth with thee—
18 And I will feed them that
oppress thee, with their own flesh;
and they shall be drunken with
their own blood as with sweet
wine; and all flesh shall know that
I the Lord am thy Savior and thy
[a]Redeemer, the [b]Mighty One of
Jacob.

CHAPTER 7

Jacob continues reading from Isaiah: Isaiah speaks messianically—The Messiah will have the tongue of the learned—He will give His back to the smiters—He will not be confounded—Compare Isaiah 50. About 559–545 B.C.

[a]YEA, for thus saith the Lord: Have
I put thee away, or have I cast thee
off forever? For thus saith the Lord:
Where is the [b]bill of your mother's
[c]divorcement? To whom have I put
thee away, or to which of my [d]credi-
tors have I [e]sold you? Yea, to whom
have I sold you? Behold, for your
iniquities have ye sold yourselves,
and for your transgressions is your
mother put away.
2 Wherefore, when I came, there
was no man; when I [a]called, yea,
there was none to answer. O house of
Israel, is my hand shortened at all
that it cannot redeem, or have I no
power to deliver? Behold, at my rebuke I [b]dry up the [c]sea, I make their
[d]rivers a wilderness and their [e]fish
to stink because the waters are dried
up, and they die because of thirst.
3 I clothe the heavens with [a]black-
ness, and I make [b]sackcloth their
covering.
4 The Lord God hath given me the
[a]tongue of the learned, that I should
know how to speak a word in season
unto thee, O house of Israel. When

14*a* 2 Ne. 21:11; 25:17; 29:1.
b 2 Ne. 3:5; D&C 3:18 (16–20).
c 1 Ne. 21:26 (24–26); 22:13 (13–14).
15*a* 1 Ne. 22:13 (13–23); 2 Ne. 10:16 (15–16); 28:15 (15–32); 3 Ne. 16:8 (8–15); Ether 2:9 (8–11). TG Last Days.
b Joel 1:19 (19–20); Jacob 5:77; 6:3.
c TG Blood, Shedding of.
d Luke 21:11 (10–13); Mosiah 12:4; D&C 97:26 (22–26). TG Plague.
e TG Drought.
16*a* Isa. 49:24 (24–26); 2 Ne. 11:2.
b HEB righteous captive; i.e., the covenant people of the Lord, as stated in v. 17.
17*a* 1 Ne. 21:25.
b TG Jesus Christ, Jehovah.
c 2 Kgs. 17:39; D&C 105:8. TG Jesus Christ, Prophecies about; Jesus Christ, Savior.
18*a* TG Jesus Christ, Redeemer.
b Gen. 49:24; Ps. 132:2; Isa. 1:24; 60:16.
7 1*a* Isa. 50:1 (1–11); 2 Ne. 8:1.
b Jer. 3:8.
c TG Divorce.
d 2 Kgs. 4:1; Matt. 18:25.
e Judg. 4:2; Isa. 52:3. TG Apostasy of Israel.
2*a* Prov. 1:24 (24–27); Isa. 65:12; Alma 5:37.
b Nahum 1:4.
c Ex. 14:21 (1–31); Ps. 106:9; D&C 133:68.
d Josh. 3:16 (15–16).
e Ex. 7:21 (17–21).
3*a* Ex. 10:21.
b Rev. 6:12.
4*a* Luke 21:15.

ye are weary he waketh morning
by morning. He waketh mine ear
to hear as the learned.
5 The Lord God hath opened mine
[a]ear, and I was not rebellious, neither turned away back.
6 I gave my back to the [a]smiter,
and my cheeks to them that plucked
off the hair. I hid not my face from
[b]shame and spitting.
7 For the Lord God will help me,
therefore shall I not be confounded.
Therefore have I set my face like
a flint, and I know that I shall not
be [a]ashamed.
8 And the Lord is near, and he [a]justifieth me. Who will contend with
me? Let us stand together. Who is
mine adversary? Let him come near
me, and I will [b]smite him with the
strength of my mouth.
9 For the Lord God will help me.
And all they who shall [a]condemn
me, behold, all they shall [b]wax old
as a garment, and the moth shall
eat them up.
10 Who is among you that feareth
the Lord, that obeyeth the [a]voice of
his servant, that [b]walketh in darkness and hath no light?
11 Behold all ye that kindle fire,
that compass yourselves about with
sparks, walk in the light of [a]your
fire and in the sparks which ye have
kindled. [b]This shall ye have of mine
hand—ye shall lie down in sorrow.

CHAPTER 8

Jacob continues reading from Isaiah: In the last days, the Lord will comfort Zion and gather Israel—The redeemed will come to Zion amid great joy—Compare Isaiah 51 and 52:1–2. About 559–545 B.C.

[a]HEARKEN unto me, ye that follow
after righteousness. Look unto the
[b]rock from whence ye are hewn, and
to the hole of the pit from whence
ye are digged.
2 Look unto Abraham, your [a]father,
and unto [b]Sarah, she that bare you;
for I called him alone, and blessed
him.
3 For the Lord shall [a]comfort [b]Zion,
he will comfort all her waste places;
and he will make her [c]wilderness
like [d]Eden, and her desert like the
garden of the Lord. Joy and gladness
shall be found therein, thanksgiving and the voice of melody.
4 Hearken unto me, my people; and
give ear unto me, O my nation; for
a [a]law shall proceed from me, and
I will make my judgment to rest
for a [b]light for the people.
5 My righteousness is near; my
[a]salvation is gone forth, and mine
arm shall [b]judge the people. The
[c]isles shall wait upon me, and on
mine arm shall they trust.
6 Lift up your eyes to the [a]heavens,
and look upon the earth beneath;
for the heavens shall [b]vanish away
like smoke, and the earth shall
[c]wax old like a garment; and they
that dwell therein shall die in like
manner. But my salvation shall be
forever, and my righteousness shall
not be abolished.
7 Hearken unto me, ye that know
righteousness, the people in whose
heart I have written my law, [a]fear

5*a* D&C 58:1.
6*a* Isa. 53:4; Matt. 27:26; 2 Ne. 9:5 (4–7).
b TG Shame.
7*a* Rom. 9:33.
8*a* Rom. 8:33 (32–34).
b Isa. 11:4.
9*a* Rom. 8:31.
b Ps. 102:26.
10*a* D&C 1:38.
b TG Walking in Darkness.
11*a* Deut. 12:8; Judg. 17:6.
b D&C 133:70.

8 1*a* Isa. 51:1 (1–23); 2 Ne. 7:1.
b IE Abraham and Sarah; see v. 2. TG Rock.
2*a* Gen. 17:4 (1–8); D&C 109:64; 132:49.
b Gen. 24:36.
3*a* TG Israel, Restoration of.
b TG Zion.
c Isa. 35:2 (1–2, 6–7). TG Israel, Blessings of.
d TG Earth, Renewal of; Eden.
4*a* Isa. 2:3. TG God, Law of.
b TG Light [noun].
5*a* TG Jesus Christ, Savior; Salvation.
b TG Jesus Christ, Judge.
c 2 Ne. 10:20.
6*a* 2 Pet. 3:10.
b Isa. 13:13.
c Ps. 102:26 (25–28).
7*a* Deut. 1:17; Ps. 56:4 (4, 11); 118:6; D&C 122:9. TG Peer Influence.

ye not the [b]reproach of men, neither be ye afraid of their [c]revilings.
8 For the [a]moth shall eat them
up like a garment, and the worm
shall eat them like wool. But my
righteousness shall be forever, and
my salvation from generation to
generation.
9 [a]Awake, awake! Put on [b]strength,
O arm of the Lord; awake as in the
ancient days. Art thou not he that
hath cut [c]Rahab, and wounded the
[d]dragon?
10 Art thou not he who hath dried
the sea, the waters of the great deep;
that hath made the depths of the
sea a [a]way for the ransomed to pass
over?
11 Therefore, the [a]redeemed of the
Lord shall [b]return, and come with
[c]singing unto Zion; and everlasting
joy and holiness shall be upon their
heads; and they shall obtain gladness and joy; sorrow and [d]mourning
shall flee away.
12 [a]I am he; yea, I am he that com-
forteth you. Behold, who art thou,
that thou shouldst be [b]afraid of
man, who shall die, and of the son
of man, who shall be made like unto
[c]grass?
13 And [a]forgettest the Lord thy
maker, that hath [b]stretched forth
the heavens, and laid the foundations of the earth, and hast feared
continually every day, because of
the fury of the [c]oppressor, as if he
were ready to destroy? And where
is the fury of the oppressor?
14 The [a]captive exile hasteneth,
that he may be loosed, and that he
should not die in the pit, nor that
his bread should fail.
15 But I am the Lord thy God,
whose [a]waves roared; the Lord of
Hosts is my name.
16 And I have [a]put my words in
thy mouth, and have covered thee
in the shadow of mine hand, that
I may plant the heavens and lay
the foundations of the earth, and
say unto Zion: Behold, thou art my
[b]people.
17 Awake, awake, stand up, O Jerusalem, which hast drunk at the
hand of the Lord the [a]cup of his
[b]fury—thou hast drunken the dregs
of the cup of trembling wrung out—
18 And none to guide her among
all the sons she hath brought forth;
neither that taketh her by the hand,
of all the sons she hath brought up.
19 These two [a]sons are come unto
thee, who shall be sorry for thee—
thy desolation and destruction, and
the famine and the sword—and by
whom shall I comfort thee?
20 Thy sons have fainted, save
these two; they lie at the head of
all the streets; as a wild bull in a
net, they are full of the fury of the
Lord, the rebuke of thy God.
21 Therefore hear now this, thou
afflicted, and [a]drunken, and not
with wine:
22 Thus saith thy Lord, the Lord
and thy God [a]pleadeth the cause of
his people; behold, I have taken out
of thine hand the cup of trembling,
the dregs of the cup of my fury;
thou shalt no more drink it again.
23 But [a]I will put it into the hand

7*b* TG Reproach.
c TG Hate.
8*a* Isa. 50:9.
9*a* Isa. 52:1.
b D&C 113:8 (7–8).
TG Israel, Restoration of.
c Ps. 89:10;
Isa. 27:1.
d Ezek. 29:3.
10*a* Isa. 35:8 (8–10).
11*a* TG Israel, Restoration of.
b TG Israel, Gathering of.
c Isa. 35:10;
Jer. 31:12 (12–13).
d Rev. 21:4 (2–5).
12*a* D&C 133:47; 136:22.
b Jer. 1:8 (7–8).
c Isa. 40:6 (6–8);
1 Pet. 1:24 (24–25).
13*a* Jer. 23:27 (27–39).
b Job 9:8.
c IE Israel's captors, typifying evil rulers who oppress the righteous; see v. 14.
TG Oppression.
14*a* Isa. 52:2.
15*a* 1 Ne. 4:2.
16*a* TG Israel, Mission of;
Prophets, Mission of.
b 1 Kgs. 8:51;
2 Ne. 3:9; 29:14.
17*a* Jer. 25:15.
b Luke 21:24 (22–24).
19*a* Rev. 11:3 (3–12).
21*a* 2 Ne. 27:4.
22*a* Jer. 50:34.
23*a* Joel 3:16 (9–16);
Zech. 12:9 (2–3, 8–9);
14:12 (3, 12–15).

of them that afflict thee; who have said to thy soul: Bow down, that we may go over—and thou hast laid thy body as the ground and as the street to them that went over.

24 [a]Awake, awake, put on thy [b]strength, O [c]Zion; put on thy beautiful garments, O Jerusalem, the holy city; for henceforth there shall [d]no more come into thee the uncircumcised and the unclean.

25 Shake thyself from the dust; arise, sit down, O Jerusalem; loose thyself from the [a]bands of thy neck, O captive daughter of Zion.

CHAPTER 9

Jacob explains that the Jews will be gathered in all their lands of promise—The Atonement ransoms man from the Fall—The bodies of the dead will come forth from the grave, and their spirits from hell and from paradise—They will be judged—The Atonement saves from death, hell, the devil, and endless torment—The righteous are to be saved in the kingdom of God—Penalties for sins are set forth—The Holy One of Israel is the keeper of the gate. About 559–545 B.C.

AND now, my beloved brethren, I have read these things that ye might know concerning the [a]covenants of the Lord that he has covenanted with all the house of Israel—

2 That he has spoken unto the Jews, by the mouth of his holy prophets, even from the beginning down, from generation to generation, until the time comes that they shall be [a]restored to the true church and fold of God; when they shall be [b]gathered home to the [c]lands of their inheritance, and shall be established in all their lands of promise.

3 Behold, my beloved brethren, I speak unto you these things that ye may rejoice, and [a]lift up your heads forever, because of the blessings which the Lord God shall bestow upon your children.

4 For I know that ye have searched much, many of you, to know of things to come; wherefore I know that ye know that our [a]flesh must waste away and die; nevertheless, in our [b]bodies we shall see God.

5 Yea, I know that ye know that in the body he shall show himself unto those at Jerusalem, from whence we came; for it is expedient that it should be among them; for it behooveth the great [a]Creator that he [b]suffereth himself to become [c]subject unto man in the flesh, and [d]die for [e]all men, that all men might become subject unto him.

6 For as [a]death hath passed upon all men, to fulfil the merciful [b]plan of the great Creator, there must needs be a power of [c]resurrection, and the resurrection must needs come unto man by reason of the [d]fall; and the fall came by reason of [e]transgression; and because man became fallen they were [f]cut off from the [g]presence of the Lord.

7 Wherefore, it must needs be an [a]infinite [b]atonement—save it should be an infinite atonement this

---

24*a* Isa. 52:1 (1–2).
b D&C 113:8 (7–8). TG Strength.
c TG Zion.
d Joel 3:17; Zech. 14:21.
25*a* D&C 113:10 (9–10).
9 1*a* TG Abrahamic Covenant; Israel, Mission of.
2*a* 2 Ne. 6:11 (10–15); 10:7 (5–9). TG Israel, Restoration of; Restoration of the Gospel.
b TG Israel, Gathering of; Mission of Latter-day Saints.
c TG Lands of Inheritance.
3*a* Ps. 24:7 (7–10).
4*a* Gen. 6:3; Moses 8:17.
b Job 19:26; Alma 11:41 (41–45); 42:23; Hel. 14:15 (15–18); Morm. 9:13. TG Body, Sanctity of.
5*a* TG Jesus Christ, Creator.
b 2 Ne. 7:6 (4–9).
c Mark 10:44 (43–44).
d TG Jesus Christ, Death of; Jesus Christ, Mission of.
e John 12:32; 2 Ne. 26:24; 3 Ne. 27:14 (14–15).
6*a* Eccl. 8:8 (6–8).
b TG Salvation, Plan of.
c TG Jesus Christ, Resurrection.
d TG Fall of Man.
e TG Transgress.
f 2 Ne. 2:5 (5–8); Alma 11:42 (40–45).
g TG God, Presence of.
7*a* Alma 34:10.
b Matt. 26:54 (52–56). TG Jesus Christ, Atonement through.

corruption could not put on incorruption. Wherefore, the [c]first judgment which came upon man must
needs have [d]remained to an endless
duration. And if so, this flesh must
have laid down to rot and to crumble
to its mother earth, to rise no more.
8 O the [a]wisdom of God, his [b]mercy
and [c]grace! For behold, if the [d]flesh
should rise no more our spirits must
become subject to that angel who
[e]fell from before the presence of
the Eternal God, and became the
[f]devil, to rise no more.
9 And our spirits must have
become [a]like unto him, and we become devils, [b]angels to a [c]devil, to
be [d]shut out from the presence of
our God, and to remain with the
father of [e]lies, in misery, like unto
himself; yea, to that being who
[f]beguiled our first parents, who
[g]transformeth himself nigh unto an
[h]angel of light, and [i]stirreth up the
children of men unto [j]secret combinations of murder and all manner
of secret works of darkness.
10 O how great the [a]goodness of
our God, who prepareth a way for
our [b]escape from the grasp of this
awful monster; yea, that monster,
[c]death and [d]hell, which I call the
death of the body, and also the death
of the spirit.
11 And because of the way of
[a]deliverance of our God, the Holy
One of Israel, this [b]death, of which
I have spoken, which is the temporal, shall deliver up its dead; which
death is the grave.
12 And this [a]death of which I have
spoken, which is the spiritual death,
shall deliver up its dead; which
spiritual death is [b]hell; wherefore,
death and hell must [c]deliver up their
dead, and hell must deliver up its
[d]captive [e]spirits, and the grave must
deliver up its captive [f]bodies, and
the bodies and the [g]spirits of men
will be [h]restored one to the other;
and it is by the power of the resurrection of the Holy One of Israel.
13 O how great the [a]plan of our God!
For on the other hand, the [b]paradise
of God must deliver up the spirits of
the righteous, and the grave deliver
up the body of the righteous; and
the spirit and the body is [c]restored
to itself again, and all men become
incorruptible, and [d]immortal, and
they are living souls, having a [e]per-
fect [f]knowledge like unto us in the
flesh, save it be that our knowledge
shall be perfect.
14 Wherefore, we shall have a [a]per-
fect [b]knowledge of all our [c]guilt,
and our [d]uncleanness, and our [e]na-
kedness; and the righteous shall

7*c* Mosiah 16:4 (4–7); Alma 11:45; 12:36; 42:6 (6, 9, 14).
d Mosiah 15:19.
8*a* Job 12:13 (7–25); Abr. 3:21. TG God, Wisdom of.
b TG God, Mercy of.
c TG Grace.
d D&C 93:34.
e Isa. 14:12; 2 Ne. 2:17; Moses 4:3 (3–4); Abr. 3:28 (27–28).
f TG Devil.
9*a* 3 Ne. 29:7.
b Jacob 3:11; Alma 5:25, 39; Moro. 9:13.
c 2 Cor. 11:14 (13–15).
d Rev. 12:9 (7–9).
e TG Lying.
f Gen. 3:13 (1–13); Mosiah 16:3; Ether 8:25; Moses 4:19 (5–19).
g Rev. 16:14 (13–14); Alma 30:53.
h D&C 129:8.
i TG Motivations.
j TG Secret Combinations.
10*a* Ex. 34:6 (5–7); 2 Ne. 4:17; D&C 86:11.
b TG Death, Power over.
c Mosiah 16:8 (7–8); Alma 42:15 (6–15).
d TG Hell.
11*a* TG Deliver.
b TG Death.
12*a* TG Death, Spiritual, First.
b D&C 76:84.
c D&C 138:18.
d TG Bondage, Spiritual; Spirits in Prison.
e TG Spirits, Disembodied.
f TG Body, Sanctity of.
g TG Spirit Body.
h TG Resurrection.
13*a* TG Salvation, Plan of.
b D&C 138:19. TG Paradise.
c Alma 11:43; 40:23; 41:4 (3–5); D&C 138:17.
d TG Immortality.
e TG Perfection.
f Eccl. 9:10; D&C 130:18.
14*a* Mosiah 3:25.
b Isa. 59:12; Alma 5:18; 11:43.
c TG Guilt.
d TG Uncleanness.
e Gen. 2:25; Ex. 32:25; Moses 4:13 (13, 16–17).

have a perfect knowledge of their
enjoyment, and their [f]righteousness,
being [g]clothed with [h]purity, yea,
even with the [i]robe of righteousness.
15 And it shall come to pass that
when all men shall have passed from
this first death unto life, insomuch
as they have become immortal, they
must appear before the [a]judgment-
seat of the Holy One of Israel; and
then cometh the [b]judgment, and
then must they be judged according
to the holy judgment of God.
16 And assuredly, as the Lord liveth,
for the Lord God hath spoken it, and
it is his eternal [a]word, which cannot
[b]pass away, that they who are righteous shall be righteous still, and
they who are [c]filthy shall be [d]filthy
still; wherefore, they who are filthy
are the [e]devil and his angels; and
they shall go away into [f]everlasting
fire, prepared for them; and their
[g]torment is as a [h]lake of fire and
brimstone, whose flame ascendeth
up forever and ever and has no end.
17 O the greatness and the [a]justice
of our God! For he executeth all his
words, and they have gone forth
out of his mouth, and his law must
be [b]fulfilled.
18 But, behold, the [a]righteous,
the [b]saints of the Holy One of Israel, they who have believed in the
Holy One of Israel, they who have
endured the [c]crosses of the world,
and despised the shame of it, they
shall [d]inherit the [e]kingdom of God,
which was prepared for them [f]from
the foundation of the world, and
their [g]joy shall be full [h]forever.
19 O the greatness of the mercy
of our God, the Holy One of Israel!
For he [a]delivereth his saints from
that [b]awful monster the devil, and
death, and [c]hell, and that lake of
fire and brimstone, which is endless torment.
20 O how great the [a]holiness of our
God! For he [b]knoweth [c]all things,
and there is not anything save he
knows it.
21 And he cometh into the world
that he may [a]save all men if they
will hearken unto his voice; for behold, he suffereth the pains of all
men, yea, the [b]pains of every living
creature, both men, women, and
children, who belong to the family of [c]Adam.
22 And he suffereth this that the
resurrection might pass upon all
men, that all might stand before
him at the great and judgment day.
23 And he commandeth all men
that they must [a]repent, and be
[b]baptized in his name, having
perfect [c]faith in the Holy One of
Israel, or they cannot be saved in the
kingdom of God.

14*f* TG Righteousness.
g Prov. 31:25.
h TG Purity.
i D&C 109:76.
15*a* TG Judgment, the Last.
b Job 34:12; Ps. 19:9; 2 Ne. 30:9.
16*a* 1 Kgs. 8:56; Ps. 33:11; D&C 1:38 (37–39); Moses 1:4.
b D&C 56:11.
c Prov. 22:8. TG Filthiness.
d 1 Ne. 15:33 (33–35); Alma 7:21; Morm. 9:14; D&C 88:35.
e TG Devil.
f Mosiah 27:28.
g TG Punish.
h Rev. 19:20; 21:8; 2 Ne. 28:23; D&C 63:17; 76:36.
17*a* TG God, Justice of; Justice.
b Ezek. 24:14.
18*a* Ps. 5:12. TG Righteousness.
b TG Saints.
c Luke 14:27.
d Col. 1:12; D&C 45:58 (57–58); 84:38 (33–38).
e TG Exaltation.
f Alma 13:3 (3, 5, 7–9).
g Matt. 5:12 (11–12).
h TG Eternal Life.
19*a* Job 23:7; D&C 108:8.
b 1 Ne. 15:35.
c TG Hell.
20*a* TG Holiness.
b Mosiah 24:12; Alma 26:35. TG God, Foreknowledge of; God, Intelligence of; God, Omniscience of.
c Prov. 5:21; D&C 38:2 (1–2).
21*a* TG Salvation.
b D&C 18:11; 19:18 (15–18). TG Jesus Christ, Trials of.
c D&C 107:54 (53–56); 128:21. TG Adam.
23*a* TG Repent.
b Mosiah 26:22; D&C 76:52 (50–52); 84:74; 137:6. TG Baptism, Essential.
c TG Baptism, Qualifications for; Faith.

24 And if they will not repent
and believe in his [a]name, and be
baptized in his name, and [b]endure
to the end, they must be [c]damned;
for the Lord God, the Holy One of
Israel, has spoken it.
25 Wherefore, he has given a
[a]law; and where there is [b]no [c]law
given there is no [d]punishment; and
where there is no punishment there
is no condemnation; and where
there is no condemnation the mercies of the Holy One of Israel have
claim upon them, because of the
atonement; for they are delivered
by the power of him.
26 For the [a]atonement satisfieth
the demands of his [b]justice upon all
those who [c]have not the [d]law given
to them, that they are [e]delivered
from that awful monster, death and
[f]hell, and the devil, and the lake of
fire and brimstone, which is endless torment; and they are restored
to that God who gave them [g]breath,
which is the Holy One of Israel.
27 But wo unto him that has the
[a]law given, yea, that has all the
commandments of God, like unto us,
and that [b]transgresseth them, and
that [c]wasteth the days of his [d]pro-
bation, for awful is his state!
28 O that cunning [a]plan of the evil
one! O the [b]vainness, and the frail-
ties, and the [c]foolishness of men!
When they are [d]learned they think
they are [e]wise, and they [f]hearken not
unto the [g]counsel of God, for they
set it aside, supposing they know of
themselves, wherefore, their [h]wis-
dom is foolishness and it profiteth
them not. And they shall perish.
29 But to be [a]learned is good if
they [b]hearken unto the [c]counsels of
God.
30 But wo unto the [a]rich, who are
[b]rich as to the things of the [c]world.
For because they are rich they despise the [d]poor, and they persecute
the meek, and their [e]hearts are upon
their treasures; wherefore, their
[f]treasure is their god. And behold,
their [g]treasure shall perish with
them also.
31 And wo unto the deaf that will
not [a]hear; for they shall perish.
32 Wo unto the [a]blind that will
not see; for they shall perish also.
33 Wo unto the [a]uncircumcised
of heart, for a knowledge of their

24*a* TG Jesus Christ, Taking the Name of.
b TG Perseverance.
c TG Damnation.
25*a* TG God, Law of.
b Rom. 4:15; 5:13; 2 Ne. 2:13.
c John 15:22 (22–24); Acts 17:30; Rom. 5:13; James 4:17; Alma 42:17 (12–24). TG Accountability.
d TG Punish.
26*a* Lev. 4:20; Neh. 10:33; 2 Ne. 2:10. TG Jesus Christ, Atonement through.
b TG God, Justice of; Justice.
c Mosiah 3:11; Alma 9:16 (15–16); 42:21.
d Mosiah 15:24; D&C 137:7. TG Ignorance.
e TG Death, Power over.
f TG Spirits in Prison.
g Gen. 2:7; 6:17; Mosiah 2:21; D&C 77:2; 93:33; Abr. 5:7 (7–8).
27*a* Luke 12:47 (47–48). TG God, Law of.
b TG Disobedience.
c TG Idleness; Procrastination; Waste.
d TG Probation.
28*a* Alma 28:13.
b Job 11:12 (11–12); Isa. 9:9 (9–10). TG Vanity.
c Eccl. 4:5; 10:12 (1–3, 12); 2 Ne. 19:17; D&C 35:7. TG Foolishness.
d Luke 16:15; 2 Ne. 26:20; 28:4 (4, 15). TG Education; Worldliness.
e Prov. 14:6; Jer. 8:8 (8–9); Rom. 1:22. TG Pride; Wisdom.
f TG Walking in Darkness.
g Prov. 15:22; Jacob 4:10; Alma 37:12. TG Counsel.
h Prov. 23:4; Eccl. 8:17 (16–17); Ezek. 28:5 (4–5); D&C 76:9. TG Knowledge.
29*a* D&C 67:6. TG Learn.
b 2 Ne. 28:26. TG Submissiveness.
c Jacob 4:10. TG Counsel.
30*a* Jer. 17:11; Luke 12:34; D&C 56:16.
b Matt. 19:23.
c TG World.
d TG Poor.
e TG Hardheartedness.
f TG Treasure.
g Prov. 27:24.
31*a* Ezek. 33:31 (30–33); Matt. 11:15; 13:14; Heb. 5:11 (11–14); Mosiah 26:28; D&C 1:14 (2, 11, 14); Moses 6:27.
32*a* TG Apathy; Spiritual Blindness.
33*a* Rom. 2:29 (27–29).

iniquities shall smite them at the last day.

34 Wo unto the [a]liar, for he shall be thrust down to [b]hell.

35 Wo unto the [a]murderer who deliberately [b]killeth, for he shall [c]die.

36 Wo unto them who commit [a]whoredoms, for they shall be thrust down to hell.

37 Yea, wo unto those that [a]worship idols, for the devil of all devils delighteth in them.

38 And, in fine, wo unto all those who die in their [a]sins; for they shall [b]return to God, and behold his face, and remain in their sins.

39 O, my beloved brethren, remember the awfulness in [a]transgressing against that Holy God, and also the awfulness of yielding to the enticings of that [b]cunning one. Remember, to be [c]carnally-minded is [d]death, and to be [e]spiritually-minded is [f]life [g]eternal.

40 O, my beloved brethren, give ear to my words. Remember the greatness of the Holy One of Israel. Do not say that I have spoken hard things against you; for if ye do, ye will [a]revile against the [b]truth; for I have spoken the words of your Maker. I know that the words of truth are [c]hard against all [d]uncleanness; but the [e]righteous fear them not, for they love the truth and are not shaken.

41 O then, my beloved brethren, [a]come unto the Lord, the Holy One. Remember that his paths are righteous. Behold, the [b]way for man is [c]narrow, but it lieth in a straight course before him, and the keeper of the [d]gate is the Holy One of Israel; and he employeth no servant there; and there is none other way save it be by the gate; for he cannot be deceived, for the Lord God is his name.

42 And whoso [a]knocketh, to him will he open; and the [b]wise, and the learned, and they that are rich, who are puffed up because of their [c]learning, and their [d]wisdom, and their riches—yea, they are they whom he despiseth; and save they shall cast these things away, and consider themselves [e]fools before God, and come down in the depths of [f]humility, he will not open unto them.

43 But the things of the wise and the [a]prudent shall be [b]hid from them forever—yea, that happiness which is prepared for the saints.

44 O, my beloved brethren, remember my words. Behold, I take off my garments, and I shake them before you; I pray the God of my salvation that he view me with his

---

34*a* Prov. 19:9. TG Gossip; Honesty; Lying.
b TG Hell.
35*a* Num. 35:16 (16–25).
b Deut. 19:11; 2 Sam. 12:9; Mosiah 13:21.
c TG Capital Punishment.
36*a* 3 Ne. 12:27 (27–32). TG Chastity; Whore.
37*a* Isa. 41:24 (21–24). TG Idolatry.
38*a* Ezek. 18:24. TG Sin.
b Alma 40:11.
39*a* TG Transgress.
b 2 Ne. 28:21 (20–22); 32:8; Mosiah 2:32; 4:14; Alma 30:42 (42, 53).
c Rom. 8:6. TG Carnal Mind.
d TG Death; Death, Spiritual, First; Hell.
e Prov. 15:24. TG Spirituality.
f Prov. 11:19.
g TG Eternal Life.
40*a* TG Reviling.
b Prov. 15:10; Mosiah 13:7. TG Truth.
c 1 Ne. 16:2; 2 Ne. 28:28; 33:5.
d TG Uncleanness.
e Prov. 28:1.
41*a* 1 Ne. 6:4; Jacob 1:7; Omni 1:26 (25–26); Alma 29:2; 3 Ne. 21:20; Morm. 9:27; Ether 5:5; Moro. 10:30 (30–32).
b Ex. 33:13 (12–13); 2 Ne. 31:21 (17–21); Alma 37:46; D&C 132:22 (22, 25).
c Luke 13:24; 2 Ne. 33:9; Jacob 6:11; Hel. 3:29 (29–30).
d 2 Ne. 31:9 (9, 17–18); 3 Ne. 14:14 (13–14); D&C 22:4; 43:7; 137:2.
42*a* TG Objectives; Study.
b Matt. 11:25. TG Wisdom.
c TG Knowledge; Learn; Worldliness.
d Ezek. 28:5 (4–5).
e 1 Cor. 3:18 (18–21).
f TG Humility; Teachable.
43*a* TG Prudence.
b 1 Cor. 2:14 (9–16).

[a]all-searching eye; wherefore, ye shall know at the last day, when all men shall be judged of their works, that the God of Israel did witness that I [b]shook your iniquities from my soul, and that I stand with brightness before him, and am [c]rid of your blood.
45 O, my beloved brethren, turn away from your sins; shake off the [a]chains of him that would bind you fast; come unto that God who is the [b]rock of your salvation.
46 Prepare your souls for that glorious day when [a]justice shall be administered unto the righteous, even the day of [b]judgment, that ye may not shrink with awful fear; that ye may not remember your awful [c]guilt in perfectness, and be constrained to exclaim: Holy, holy are thy judgments, O Lord God [d]Almighty—but I know my guilt; I transgressed thy law, and my transgressions are mine; and the devil hath [e]obtained me, that I am a prey to his awful misery.
47 But behold, my brethren, is it expedient that I should awake you to an awful reality of these things? Would I harrow up your souls if your minds were pure? Would I be plain unto you according to the plainness of the truth if ye were freed from sin?
48 Behold, if ye were holy I would speak unto you of holiness; but as ye are not holy, and ye look upon me as a [a]teacher, it must needs be expedient that I [b]teach you the consequences of sin.
49 Behold, my soul abhorreth sin, and my heart [a]delighteth in righteousness; and I will [b]praise the holy name of my God.
50 Come, my brethren, every one that [a]thirsteth, come ye to the [b]waters; and he that hath no [c]money, come buy and eat; yea, come buy wine and milk without money and without price.
51 Wherefore, do not spend money for that which is of no worth, nor your [a]labor for that which cannot [b]satisfy. Hearken diligently unto me, and remember the words which I have spoken; and come unto the Holy One of Israel, and [c]feast upon that which perisheth not, neither can be corrupted, and let your soul delight in fatness.
52 Behold, my beloved brethren, remember the words of your God; pray unto him continually by day, and give [a]thanks unto his holy name by night. Let your hearts [b]rejoice.
53 And behold how great the [a]covenants of the Lord, and how great his [b]condescensions unto the children of men; and because of his greatness, and his [c]grace and [d]mercy, he has promised unto us that our seed shall not utterly be destroyed, according to the flesh, but that he would [e]preserve them; and in future generations they shall become a righteous [f]branch unto the house of Israel.
54 And now, my brethren, I would speak unto you more; but on the morrow I will declare unto you the remainder of my words. Amen.

44*a* Jacob 2:10.
b Jacob 1:19.
c Jacob 2:2 (2, 16); Mosiah 2:28; D&C 61:34.
45*a* 2 Ne. 28:22; Alma 36:18.
b TG Rock.
46*a* TG God, Justice of.
b TG Judgment, the Last.
c Mosiah 3:25.
d Gen. 48:3; 1 Ne. 1:14; 3 Ne. 4:32; Moses 2:1.
e TG Apostasy of Individuals.
48*a* 2 Ne. 5:26. TG Teacher; Teaching.
b Deut. 33:10; 2 Chr. 15:3 (1–4); 17:9. TG Prophets, Mission of.
49*a* TG Desire; Motivations.
b Ezra 3:11 (11–13); 1 Ne. 18:16; Alma 36:28.
50*a* Isa. 44:3; 55:1 (1–2).
b TG Living Water.
c Alma 5:34; 42:27.
51*a* Isa. 55:2. TG Work, Value of.
b Eccl. 1:3.
c Prov. 13:25; Enos 1:4; 3 Ne. 12:6.
52*a* TG Thanksgiving.
b Deut. 26:11.
53*a* TG Covenants.
b TG Jesus Christ, Condescension of.
c TG Grace.
d TG Compassion; God, Mercy of.
e TG Protection, Divine.
f TG Vineyard of the Lord.

CHAPTER 10

Jacob explains that the Jews will crucify their God—They will be scattered until they begin to believe in Him—America will be a land of liberty where no king will rule—Reconcile yourselves to God and gain salvation through His grace. About 559–545 B.C.

AND now I, Jacob, speak unto you again, my beloved brethren, concerning this righteous [a]branch of which I have spoken.

2 For behold, the [a]promises which we have obtained are promises unto us according to the flesh; wherefore, as it has been shown unto me that many of our children shall perish in the flesh because of [b]unbelief, nevertheless, God will be merciful unto many; and our children shall be [c]restored, that they may come to that which will give them the true knowledge of their Redeemer.

3 Wherefore, as I said unto you, it must needs be expedient that Christ—for in the last night the [a]angel spake unto me that this should be his name—should [b]come among the [c]Jews, among those who are the more wicked part of the world; and they shall [d]crucify him—for thus it behooveth our God, and there is none other nation on earth that would [e]crucify their [f]God.

4 For should the mighty [a]miracles be wrought among other nations they would repent, and know that he be their God.

5 But because of [a]priestcrafts and iniquities, they at Jerusalem will [b]stiffen their necks against him, that he be [c]crucified.

6 Wherefore, because of their iniquities, destructions, famines, [a]pestilences, and bloodshed shall come upon them; and they who shall not be destroyed shall be [b]scattered among all nations.

7 But behold, thus saith the [a]Lord God: [b]When the day cometh that they shall believe in me, that I am Christ, then have I covenanted with their fathers that they shall be [c]restored in the flesh, upon the earth, unto the [d]lands of their inheritance.

8 And it shall come to pass that they shall be [a]gathered in from their long dispersion, from the [b]isles of the sea, and from the four parts of the earth; and the nations of the Gentiles shall be great in the eyes of me, saith God, in [c]carrying them forth to the lands of their inheritance.

9 [a]Yea, the kings of the Gentiles shall be nursing fathers unto them, and their queens shall become nursing mothers; wherefore, the [b]promises of the Lord are great unto the Gentiles, for he hath spoken it, and who can dispute?

10 But behold, this land, said God, shall be a land of thine inheritance, and the [a]Gentiles shall be blessed upon the land.

11 And this land shall be a land of

---

10 1*a* 1 Ne. 15:12 (12–20); 2 Ne. 3:5; Jacob 5:45 (43–45); Alma 46:24 (24–25).
2*a* 1 Ne. 22:8 (8–12); 3 Ne. 5:23 (21–26); 21:7 (4–29). TG Promise.
b TG Doubt.
c TG Restoration of the Gospel.
3*a* 2 Ne. 2:4; 11:3; 25:19; Jacob 7:5; Moro. 7:22.
b TG Jesus Christ, Prophecies about.
c TG Israel, Judah, People of.
d Luke 18:31; 1 Ne. 11:33; Mosiah 3:9 (9–10).
e Matt. 27:22; Luke 22:2; 23:23 (20–24).
f 1 Ne. 19:10 (7, 10); 2 Ne. 26:12.
4*a* TG Miracle.
5*a* Matt. 27:20 (11–26); Luke 22:2; John 11:47 (47–53). TG Apostasy of Israel; Priestcraft.
b TG Stiffnecked.
c TG Jesus Christ, Crucifixion of.
6*a* TG Plague.
b 1 Ne. 19:14 (13–14); 2 Ne. 25:15. TG Israel, Bondage of, in Other Lands.
7*a* TG Jesus Christ, Lord.
b 2 Ne. 9:2 (1–2); 25:16 (16–17).
c Gen. 49:10. TG Israel, Restoration of.
d TG Lands of Inheritance.
8*a* TG Israel, Gathering of.
b Isa. 51:5; 1 Ne. 22:4; 2 Ne. 29:7; D&C 133:8.
c Isa. 11:14; 1 Ne. 21:22; 22:8.
9*a* Isa. 49:22 (22–23); 2 Ne. 6:6.
b 1 Ne. 22:8 (1–9); Alma 9:24; D&C 3:20.
10*a* 2 Ne. 6:12; 3 Ne. 16:6 (4–7).

[a]liberty unto the Gentiles, and there shall be no [b]kings upon the land, who shall raise up unto the Gentiles.
12 And I will fortify this land
[a]against all other nations.
13 And he that [a]fighteth against
Zion shall [b]perish, saith God.
14 For he that raiseth up a [a]king
against me shall perish, for I, the Lord, the [b]king of heaven, will be their king, and I will be a [c]light unto them forever, that hear my words.
15 Wherefore, for this cause, that
my [a]covenants may be fulfilled which I have made unto the children of men, that I will do unto them while they are in the flesh, I must needs destroy the [b]secret works of [c]darkness, and of murders, and of abominations.
16 Wherefore, he that [a]fighteth
against [b]Zion, both Jew and Gentile, both bond and free, both male and female, [c]shall perish; for [d]they are they who are the [e]whore of all the earth; for [f]they who are [g]not for me are [h]against me, saith our God.
17 For I will [a]fulfil my [b]promises
which I have made unto the children of men, that I will do unto them while they are in the flesh—
18 Wherefore, my beloved breth-
ren, thus saith our God: I will afflict thy seed by the hand of the Gentiles; nevertheless, I will [a]soften the hearts of the [b]Gentiles, that they shall be like unto a father to them; wherefore, the Gentiles shall be [c]blessed and [d]numbered among the house of Israel.
19 Wherefore, I will [a]consecrate
this land unto thy seed, and them who shall be numbered among thy seed, forever, for the land of their inheritance; for it is a choice land, saith God unto me, above all other lands, wherefore I will have all men that dwell thereon that they shall worship me, saith God.
20 And now, my beloved brethren,
seeing that our merciful God has given us so great knowledge concerning these things, let us remember him, and lay aside our sins, and not hang down our heads, for we are not cast off; nevertheless, we have been [a]driven out of the land of our inheritance; but we have been led to a [b]better land, for the Lord has made the sea our [c]path, and we are upon an [d]isle of the sea.
21 But great are the promises of
the Lord unto them who are upon the [a]isles of the sea; wherefore as it says isles, there must needs be more than this, and they are inhabited also by our brethren.
22 For behold, the Lord God has

11*a* TG Liberty.
b 2 Ne. 1:7; Mosiah 29:32.
12*a* 1 Ne. 13:19.
13*a* 1 Ne. 22:14 (14, 19).
b Isa. 60:12.
14*a* TG Kings, Earthly.
b Josh. 2:11; Ps. 44:4; Matt. 2:2; Alma 5:50; D&C 20:17; 38:21 (21–22); 128:22 (22–23); Moses 7:53.
c TG Jesus Christ, Light of the World.
15*a* TG Abrahamic Covenant; Covenants.
b Lev. 19:26; Hel. 3:23; 7:25 (4–5, 21, 25). TG Secret Combinations.
c TG Darkness, Spiritual.
16*a* TG Protection, Divine.
b TG Zion.
c Isa. 41:11 (11–12).
d 1 Ne. 13:5.
e TG Devil, Church of; Whore.
f 1 Ne. 14:10.
g 1 Ne. 22:13 (13–23); 2 Ne. 6:15; 28:15 (15–32); 3 Ne. 16:8 (8–15); Ether 2:9 (8–11).
h Matt. 12:30.
17*a* 1 Kgs. 8:56; D&C 1:38; 101:64.
b TG Promise.
18*a* 1 Ne. 13:31; 2 Ne. 4:7; Jacob 3:6 (5–9); Hel. 15:12 (10–17); Morm. 5:20 (20–21).
b Matt. 8:11 (11–12); 12:21; Luke 13:29 (28–30); Acts 10:45; D&C 45:9 (7–30).
c Eph. 3:6 (1–7); 2 Ne. 33:9; 3 Ne. 21:14.
d Gal. 3:7 (7, 29); 1 Ne. 14:2; 3 Ne. 16:13; 21:6 (6, 22, 25); 30:2; Abr. 2:10 (9–11).
19*a* 1 Ne. 13:15.
20*a* 1 Ne. 1:20 (18–20); 2:2 (1–4).
b 1 Ne. 2:20. TG Promised Lands.
c Ps. 8:8; 1 Ne. 18:8 (5–23).
d Isa. 11:11 (11–12); 42:4; 51:5; Ezek. 26:15 (3, 6–7, 15); 39:6; 2 Ne. 8:5.
21*a* Isa. 49:1; 1 Ne. 19:16; 21:1; 22:4.

[a]led away from time to time from
the house of Israel, according to his
will and pleasure. And now behold,
the Lord remembereth all them who
have been broken off, wherefore he
remembereth us also.
23 Therefore, [a]cheer up your hearts,
and remember that ye are [b]free to
[c]act for yourselves—to [d]choose the
way of everlasting death or the way
of eternal life.
24 Wherefore, my beloved brethren, [a]reconcile yourselves to the
[b]will of God, and not to the will of
the devil and the flesh; and remember, after ye are reconciled unto
God, that it is only in and through
the [c]grace of God that ye are [d]saved.
25 Wherefore, may God [a]raise you
from death by the power of the resurrection, and also from everlasting
death by the power of the [b]atone-
ment, that ye may be received into
the [c]eternal kingdom of God, that
ye may praise him through grace
divine. Amen.

CHAPTER 11

Jacob saw his Redeemer—The law of Moses typifies Christ and proves He will come. About 559–545 B.C.

AND now, [a]Jacob spake many more
things to my people at that time;
nevertheless only these things have I
caused to be [b]written, for the things
which I have written sufficeth me.
2 And now I, Nephi, write [a]more
of the words of [b]Isaiah, for my soul
delighteth in his words. For I will
liken his words unto my people,
and I will send them forth unto
all my children, for he verily [c]saw
my [d]Redeemer, even as I have seen
him.
3 And my brother, Jacob, also
has [a]seen him as I have seen him;
wherefore, I will send their words
forth unto my children to prove
unto them that my words are true.
Wherefore, by the words of [b]three,
God hath said, I will establish my
word. Nevertheless, God sendeth
more [c]witnesses, and he proveth
all his words.
4 Behold, my soul delighteth in
[a]proving unto my people the truth
of the [b]coming of Christ; for, for
this end hath the [c]law of Moses
been given; and all things which
have been given of God from the
beginning of the world, unto man,
are the [d]typifying of him.
5 And also my soul delighteth in
the [a]covenants of the Lord which
he hath made to our fathers; yea,
my soul delighteth in his [b]grace,
and in his justice, and power, and
mercy in the great and eternal plan
of [c]deliverance from death.
6 And my soul delighteth in prov-
ing unto my people that [a]save Christ
should come all men must perish.
7 For if there be [a]no Christ there be
no God; and if there be no God we

22*a* 1 Ne. 22:4 (4–5); 2 Ne. 1:6. TG Israel, Scattering of; Israel, Ten Lost Tribes of.
23*a* TG Cheerful.
b TG Agency.
c 2 Ne. 2:16.
d Deut. 30:19 (15, 19).
24*a* TG Reconciliation.
b TG God, Will of.
c TG Grace.
d TG Salvation; Salvation, Plan of.
25*a* TG Death, Power over; Resurrection.
b TG Jesus Christ, Atonement through.
c TG Eternity.
11 1*a* 2 Ne. 6:1 (1–10).
b 2 Ne. 31:1.
2*a* 2 Ne. 6:16 (16–18).
b 3 Ne. 23:1.
c 2 Ne. 16:1. TG Jesus Christ, Appearances, Antemortal.
d TG Jesus Christ, Jehovah.
3*a* 2 Ne. 2:3 (3–4); 10:3; Jacob 7:5. TG God, Privilege of Seeing.
b 2 Ne. 27:12 (12–14); Ether 5:3 (2–4); D&C 5:11 (11, 15).
c TG Book of Mormon; Witness.
4*a* 2 Ne. 31:2.
b Jacob 4:5; Jarom 1:11; Alma 25:16 (15–16); Ether 12:19 (18–19).
c 2 Ne. 5:10.
d TG Jesus Christ, Types of, in Anticipation; Law of Moses.
5*a* TG Abrahamic Covenant.
b TG Benevolence; Grace.
c TG Deliver; Jesus Christ, Atonement through.
6*a* Mosiah 3:15.
7*a* 2 Ne. 2:13 (13–14).

are not, for there could have been
no [b]creation. But there is a God, and
[c]he is Christ, and he cometh in the
fulness of his own time.
8 And now I write [a]some of the
words of Isaiah, that whoso of my
people shall see these words may
lift up their hearts and rejoice for
all men. Now these are the words,
and ye may liken them unto you
and unto all men.

CHAPTER 12

Isaiah sees the latter-day temple, gathering of Israel, and millennial judgment and peace—The proud and wicked will be brought low at the Second Coming—Compare Isaiah 2. About 559–545 B.C.

1 [a]THE word that Isaiah, the son of
Amoz, saw concerning Judah and
Jerusalem:
2 And it shall come to pass in the
last days, [a]when the [b]mountain of
the Lord's [c]house shall be established
in the top of the [d]mountains,
and shall be exalted above the hills,
and all nations shall flow unto it.
3 And many [a]people shall go and
say, Come ye, and let us go up to
the [b]mountain of the Lord, to the
[c]house of the God of Jacob; and he
will teach us of his ways, and we
will [d]walk in his paths; for out of
Zion shall go forth the law, and the
word of the Lord from Jerusalem.
4 And he shall [a]judge among the
nations, and shall rebuke many
people: and they shall beat their
swords into plow-shares, and their
spears into pruning-hooks—nation
shall not lift up sword against nation,
neither shall they learn war
any more.
5 O house of Jacob, come ye and let
us walk in the light of the Lord; yea,
come, for ye have all [a]gone astray,
every one to his [b]wicked ways.
6 Therefore, O Lord, thou hast
forsaken thy people, the house of
Jacob, because they be replenished
from the east, and hearken unto
[a]soothsayers like the [b]Philistines,
and they please themselves in the
children of strangers.
7 Their land also is full of silver
and gold, neither is there any end
of their [a]treasures; their land is also
full of horses, neither is there any
end of their chariots.
8 Their land is also full of [a]idols;
they worship the work of their own
hands, that which their own fingers
have made.
9 And the mean man [a]boweth [b]not
down, and the great man humbleth
himself not, therefore, forgive him
not.
10 O ye wicked ones, enter into the
rock, and [a]hide thee in the dust, for
the fear of the Lord and the glory
of his majesty shall smite thee.
11 And it shall come to pass that
the [a]lofty looks of man shall be humbled,
and the haughtiness of men
shall be bowed down, and the Lord
alone shall be exalted in that day.
12 For the [a]day of the Lord of

7 *b* Heb. 3:4 (3–4). TG Creation; God, Creator.
c TG Jesus Christ, Jehovah.
8 *a* See the Latter-day Saint edition of the King James Version of the Bible for other notes and cross-references on these chapters from Isaiah.

12 1 *a* Isa. 2:1 (1–22).
2 *a* Comparison with the King James Bible in English shows that there are differences in more than half of the 433 verses of Isaiah quoted in the Book of Mormon, while about 200 verses have the same wording as KJV.
b TG Zion.
c 3 Ne. 24:1.
d Gen. 49:26; D&C 49:25; 109:61; 133:31 (29–31).
3 *a* Zech. 8:22.
b Joel 2:1; 2 Ne. 30:15 (12–18); D&C 133:13.
c Ps. 122:1.
d TG Walking with God.
4 *a* 2 Ne. 21:3 (2–5, 9).
5 *a* 2 Ne. 28:14; Mosiah 14:6; Alma 5:37.
b Isa. 53:6.
6 *a* TG Sorcery.
b Gen. 10:14.
7 *a* TG Treasure.
8 *a* Jer. 2:28. TG Idolatry.
9 *a* Ex. 34:8; Isa. 2:9.
b IE unto God; he worships idols instead.
10 *a* Amos 9:3; Rev. 6:15 (15–16); Alma 12:14.
11 *a* 2 Ne. 15:15 (15–16).
12 *a* TG Day of the Lord.

Hosts soon cometh upon all nations,
yea, upon every one; yea, upon the
[b]proud and lofty, and upon every
one who is lifted up, and he shall
be brought low.
13 Yea, and the day of the Lord
shall come upon all the [a]cedars
of Lebanon, for they are high and
lifted up; and upon all the oaks of
Bashan;
14 And upon all the [a]high mountains, and upon all the hills, and
upon all the nations which are lifted
up, and upon every people;
15 And upon every [a]high tower,
and upon every fenced wall;
16 And upon all the ships of the [a]sea,
and upon all the ships of Tarshish,
and upon all pleasant pictures.
17 And the loftiness of man shall
be bowed down, and the [a]haughti-
ness of men shall be made low; and
the Lord alone shall be exalted in
[b]that day.
18 And the idols he shall utterly
abolish.
19 And they shall go into the holes
of the rocks, and into the caves of the
earth, for the fear of the Lord shall
come upon them and the [a]glory of his
majesty shall smite them, when he
ariseth to shake terribly the earth.
20 In that day a man shall cast
his idols of silver, and his idols of
gold, which he hath made for himself to worship, to the moles and to
the bats;
21 To go into the clefts of the rocks,
and into the tops of the ragged rocks,
for the fear of the Lord shall come
upon them and the majesty of his
glory shall smite them, when he
ariseth to shake terribly the earth.
22 Cease ye from man, whose
breath is in his nostrils; for wherein
is he to be accounted of?

CHAPTER 13

Judah and Jerusalem will be punished for their disobedience—The Lord pleads for and judges His people—The daughters of Zion are cursed and tormented for their worldliness—Compare Isaiah 3. About 559–545 B.C.

[a]FOR behold, the Lord, the Lord of
Hosts, doth take away from Jerusalem, and from Judah, the stay and
the staff, the whole staff of bread,
and the whole stay of water—
2 The [a]mighty man, and the man
of [b]war, the judge, and the prophet,
and the [c]prudent, and the ancient;
3 The captain of fifty, and the
honorable man, and the counselor,
and the cunning artificer, and the
eloquent orator.
4 And I will give children unto
them to be their princes, and babes
shall rule over them.
5 And the people shall be [a]op-
pressed, every one by another,
and every one by his neighbor; the
child shall behave himself [b]proudly
against the ancient, and the base
against the honorable.
6 When a man shall take hold of his
brother of the house of his father,
and shall say: Thou hast clothing,
be thou our ruler, and let not this
[a]ruin come under thy hand—
7 In that day shall he swear, saying: I will not be a healer; for in my
house there is neither bread nor
clothing; make me not a ruler of the
people.
8 For Jerusalem is [a]ruined, and
Judah is [b]fallen, because their

12*b* Job 40:11; Mal. 4:1; 2 Ne. 23:11; D&C 64:24.
13*a* Isa. 37:24; Ezek. 31:3; Zech. 11:1 (1–2).
14*a* Isa. 30:25.
15*a* 3 Ne. 21:15 (15, 18).
16*a* The Greek (Septuagint) has "ships of the sea." The Hebrew has "ships of Tarshish." The Book of Mormon has both, showing that the brass plates had lost neither phrase.
17*a* TG Haughtiness.
b IE the day of the Lord's coming in glory; see vv. 17–21.
19*a* TG Jesus Christ, Glory of.

13 1*a* Isa. 3:1 (1–26).
2*a* 2 Kgs. 24:14.
b 1 Chr. 28:3.
c TG Prudence.
5*a* TG Oppression.
b TG Haughtiness.
6*a* Isa. 3:6.
8*a* Isa. 1:7; Jer. 9:11; Ezek. 36:17 (16–20).
b Lam. 1:3 (1–3).

[c]tongues and their doings have
been against the Lord, to [d]provoke
the eyes of his glory.
9 The show of their countenance
doth witness against them, and
doth declare their [a]sin to be even
as [b]Sodom, and they cannot hide it.
Wo unto their souls, for they have
rewarded evil unto themselves!
10 Say unto the righteous that it is
[a]well with them; for they shall [b]eat
the fruit of their doings.
11 Wo unto the wicked, for they
shall perish; for the reward of their
hands shall be upon them!
12 And my people, children are
their oppressors, and women rule
over them. O my people, they who
[a]lead thee cause thee to err and destroy the way of thy paths.
13 The Lord standeth up to [a]plead,
and standeth to judge the people.
14 The Lord will enter into [a]judg-
ment with the ancients of his people and the princes thereof; for ye
have eaten up the [b]vineyard and the
spoil of the [c]poor in your houses.
15 What mean ye? Ye [a]beat my
people to pieces, and grind the
faces of the poor, saith the Lord
God of Hosts.
16 Moreover, the Lord saith: Because the daughters of Zion are
[a]haughty, and [b]walk with stretched-
forth necks and wanton eyes, walking and mincing as they go, and
making a tinkling with their feet—
17 Therefore the Lord will smite
with a [a]scab the crown of the head
of the daughters of Zion, and the
Lord will [b]discover their secret
parts.
18 In that [a]day the Lord will take
away the bravery of their tinkling
ornaments, and cauls, and round
tires like the moon;
19 The chains and the bracelets,
and the mufflers;
20 The bonnets, and the ornaments
of the legs, and the headbands, and
the tablets, and the ear-rings;
21 The rings, and nose jewels;
22 The changeable suits of apparel,
and the mantles, and the wimples,
and the crisping-pins;
23 The glasses, and the fine linen,
and hoods, and the veils.
24 And it shall come to pass, instead of sweet smell there shall be
stink; and instead of a girdle, a rent;
and instead of well set hair, [a]bald-
ness; and instead of a stomacher, a
girding of sackcloth; [b]burning instead of [c]beauty.
25 Thy men shall fall by the sword
and thy mighty in the war.
26 And her [a]gates shall lament and
[b]mourn; and she shall be desolate,
and shall [c]sit upon the ground.

CHAPTER 14

Zion and her daughters will be redeemed and cleansed in the millennial day—Compare Isaiah 4. About 559–545 B.C.

[a]AND in that day, seven women shall
take hold of one man, saying: We
will eat our own bread, and wear
our own apparel; only let us be
called by thy name to take away
our [b]reproach.
2 In that day shall the [a]branch of
the Lord be beautiful and glorious;
the fruit of the earth excellent and

8*c* Ps. 52:2.
d TG Provoking.
9*a* TG Apostasy of Israel.
b Gen. 18:20 (20–21); 19:5, 24 (24–25); 2 Ne. 23:19. TG Homosexual Behavior.
10*a* Deut. 12:28.
b Ps. 128:2.
12*a* Isa. 9:16. TG Leadership.
13*a* Micah 6:2.
14*a* TG Jesus Christ, Judge.
b Isa. 5:7.
c Ezek. 18:12; 2 Ne. 28:13 (12–13); Hel. 4:12 (11–13).
15*a* Micah 3:3 (2–3); 2 Ne. 26:20.
16*a* TG Haughtiness.
b TG Walking in Darkness.
17*a* Deut. 28:27.
b Jer. 13:22; Nahum 3:5.
18*a* TG Day of the Lord.
24*a* Isa. 22:12; Micah 1:16.
b 2 Ne. 14:4.
c Lam. 1:6 (4–6).
26*a* Jer. 14:2.
b Lam. 1:4 (4–6).
c Lam. 2:10.
14 1*a* Isa. 4:1 (1–6).
b TG Reproach.
2*a* Isa. 60:21; 61:3; 2 Ne. 3:5; Jacob 2:25.

comely to them that are escaped of Israel.

3 And it shall come to pass, they that are [a]left in Zion and remain in Jerusalem shall be called holy, every one that is written among the living in Jerusalem—

4 When the Lord shall have [a]washed away the filth of the daughters of Zion, and shall have purged the blood of Jerusalem from the midst thereof by the spirit of judgment and by the spirit of [b]burning.

5 And the [a]Lord will create upon every dwelling-place of mount Zion, and upon her assemblies, a [b]cloud and smoke by day and the shining of a flaming fire by night; for upon all the glory of Zion shall be a defence.

6 And there shall be a tabernacle for a shadow in the daytime from the heat, and for a place of [a]refuge, and a covert from storm and from rain.

CHAPTER 15

The Lord's vineyard (Israel) will become desolate, and His people will be scattered—Woes will come upon them in their apostate and scattered state—The Lord will lift an ensign and gather Israel—Compare Isaiah 5. About 559–545 B.C.

[a]AND then will I sing to my well-beloved a song of my beloved, touching his [b]vineyard. My well-beloved hath a vineyard in a very fruitful hill.

2 And he fenced it, and gathered out the stones thereof, and planted it with the choicest [a]vine, and built a tower in the midst of it, and also made a wine-press therein; and he looked that it should bring forth grapes, and it brought forth wild grapes.

3 And now, O inhabitants of Jerusalem, and men of Judah, judge, I pray you, betwixt me and my vineyard.

4 What could have been done more to my vineyard that I have not done in it? Wherefore, when I looked that it should bring forth grapes it brought forth wild grapes.

5 And now go to; I will tell you what I will do to my vineyard—I will [a]take away the hedge thereof, and it shall be eaten up; and I will break down the wall thereof, and it shall be trodden down;

6 And I will lay it waste; it shall not be pruned nor digged; but there shall come up [a]briers and thorns; I will also command the clouds that they [b]rain no rain upon it.

7 For the [a]vineyard of the Lord of Hosts is the house of Israel, and the men of Judah his pleasant plant; and he looked for [b]judgment, and behold, [c]oppression; for righteousness, but behold, a cry.

8 Wo unto them that join [a]house to house, till there can be no place, that they may be placed alone in the midst of the earth!

9 In mine ears, said the Lord of Hosts, of a truth many houses shall be desolate, and great and fair cities without inhabitant.

10 Yea, ten acres of vineyard shall yield one [a]bath, and the seed of a homer shall yield an ephah.

11 Wo unto them that rise up early in the morning, that they may [a]follow strong drink, that continue until night, and [b]wine inflame them!

12 And the harp, and the [a]viol, the tabret, and pipe, and wine are in their feasts; but they [b]regard not

---

3*a* Matt. 13:43 (41–43).
4*a* 2 Ne. 13:24 (16–26). TG Wash.
b Mal. 3:2; 4:1.
5*a* Isa. 60:20 (1–3, 19–21). TG God, Presence of.
b Ex. 13:21; Zech. 2:5.
6*a* Isa. 25:4. TG Refuge.

15 1*a* Isa. 5:1 (1–30).
b TG Vineyard of the Lord.
2*a* Jer. 2:21.
5*a* Ps. 80:12 (8–15).
6*a* Isa. 7:23 (23–24); 32:13.
b Lev. 26:4; Jer. 3:3.
7*a* TG Vineyard of the Lord.
b Amos 5:24.
c TG Oppression.

8*a* Micah 2:2.
10*a* BD Weights and measures. See also Ezek. 45:11.
11*a* Prov. 23:30 (29–32).
b TG Drunkenness; Word of Wisdom.
12*a* Amos 6:5 (5–6).
b Ps. 28:5. TG Rebellion.

the work of the Lord, neither consider the operation of his hands.
13 Therefore, my people are gone
into [a]captivity, because they have
no [b]knowledge; and their honorable
men are famished, and their multitude dried up with thirst.
14 Therefore, hell hath enlarged her-
self, and opened her mouth without
measure; and their glory, and their
multitude, and their pomp, and he
that rejoiceth, shall descend into it.
15 And the mean man shall be
[a]brought down, and the [b]mighty
man shall be humbled, and the
eyes of the [c]lofty shall be humbled.
16 But the Lord of Hosts shall be
exalted in [a]judgment, and God that
is holy shall be sanctified in righteousness.
17 Then shall the lambs feed after
their manner, and the waste places
of the [a]fat ones shall strangers eat.
18 Wo unto them that draw iniquity with cords of [a]vanity, and sin
as it were with a cart rope;
19 That say: Let him [a]make speed,
[b]hasten his work, that we may [c]see
it; and let the counsel of the Holy
One of Israel draw nigh and come,
that we may know it.
20 Wo unto them that [a]call [b]evil
good, and good evil, that put [c]dark-
ness for light, and light for darkness, that put bitter for sweet, and
sweet for bitter!
21 Wo unto the [a]wise in their own
eyes and [b]prudent in their own sight!
22 Wo unto the mighty to drink
[a]wine, and men of strength to mingle strong drink;
23 Who justify the wicked for [a]re-
ward, and take away the righteousness of the righteous from him!
24 Therefore, as the [a]fire devoureth
the [b]stubble, and the flame consumeth the [c]chaff, their [d]root shall
be rottenness, and their blossoms
shall go up as dust; because they
have cast away the law of the Lord
of Hosts, and [e]despised the word of
the Holy One of Israel.
25 Therefore, is the [a]anger of the
Lord kindled against his people,
and he hath stretched forth his
hand against them, and hath smitten them; and the hills did tremble, and their carcasses were torn
in the midst of the streets. For all
this his anger is not turned away,
but his hand is stretched out still.
26 And he will lift up an [a]ensign
to the [b]nations from far, and will
hiss unto them from the [c]end of the
earth; and behold, they shall [d]come
with speed swiftly; none shall be
weary nor stumble among them.
27 None shall slumber nor sleep;
neither shall the girdle of their
loins be loosed, nor the latchet of
their shoes be broken;
28 Whose arrows shall be sharp,
and all their bows bent, and their
horses' hoofs shall be counted like
flint, and their wheels like a whirlwind, their roaring like a lion.
29 They shall roar like young [a]li-
ons; yea, they shall roar, and lay
hold of the prey, and shall carry
away safe, and none shall deliver.
30 And in that [a]day they shall roar
against them like the roaring of the

13 *a* Lam. 1:3 (1–3).
b Isa. 1:3; Hosea 4:6. TG Knowledge.
15 *a* Isa. 2:17 (11, 17).
b 2 Ne. 12:11.
c TG Haughtiness.
16 *a* TG Jesus Christ, Judge.
17 *a* Isa. 10:16.
18 *a* TG Vanity.
19 *a* Jer. 17:15.
b TG Haste.
c TG Sign Seekers.
20 *a* D&C 64:16; 121:16.
b Moro. 7:14 (14, 18).
c 1 Jn. 1:6.
21 *a* Prov. 3:7 (5–7); 2 Ne. 28:15.
b TG Prudence.
22 *a* Prov. 31:4 (3–9).
23 *a* TG Bribe.
24 *a* Obad. 1:18; 2 Ne. 20:17; 3 Ne. 20:16.
b Joel 2:5; 1 Ne. 22:15 (15, 23); 2 Ne. 26:6 (4, 6); D&C 64:24 (23–24); 133:64.
c Luke 3:17; Mosiah 7:30 (29–31).
d Job 18:16 (16–21).
e 2 Sam. 12:9 (7–9).
25 *a* Deut. 32:21; D&C 63:32; Moses 6:27.
26 *a* TG Ensign.
b TG Nations.
c 2 Ne. 29:2.
d TG Israel, Gathering of.
29 *a* 3 Ne. 21:12 (12–13).
30 *a* TG Day of the Lord.

sea; and if they look unto the land, behold, darkness and sorrow, and the light is darkened in the heavens thereof.

CHAPTER 16

Isaiah sees the Lord—Isaiah's sins are forgiven—He is called to prophesy—He prophesies of the rejection by the Jews of Christ's teachings—A remnant will return—Compare Isaiah 6. About 559–545 B.C.

[a]IN the [b]year that king Uzziah died, I [c]saw also the Lord sitting upon a throne, high and lifted up, and his train filled the temple.

2 Above it stood the [a]seraphim; each one had six wings; with twain he covered his face, and with twain he covered his feet, and with twain he did fly.

3 And one cried unto another, and said: Holy, holy, holy, is the Lord of Hosts; the whole earth is full of his [a]glory.

4 And the posts of the door moved at the voice of him that cried, and the house was filled with smoke.

5 Then said I: Wo is unto me! for I am undone; because I am a man of unclean lips; and I dwell in the midst of a people of unclean lips; for mine eyes have [a]seen the King, the Lord of Hosts.

6 Then flew one of the seraphim unto me, having a live coal in his hand, which he had taken with the tongs from off the altar;

7 And he laid it upon my mouth, and said: Lo, this has touched thy lips; and thine [a]iniquity is taken away, and thy sin purged.

8 Also I heard the voice of the Lord, saying: [a]Whom shall I send, and who will go for us? Then I said: Here am I; send me.

9 And he said: Go and tell this people—Hear ye indeed, but they understood not; and see ye indeed, but they perceived not.

10 Make the heart of this people fat, and make their ears heavy, and shut their eyes—lest they see with their eyes, and [a]hear with their ears, and understand with their [b]heart, and be converted and be healed.

11 Then said I: Lord, how long? And he said: Until the cities be wasted without inhabitant, and the houses without man, and the land be utterly desolate;

12 And the Lord have [a]removed men far away, for there shall be a great forsaking in the midst of the land.

13 But yet there shall be a tenth, and they shall return, and shall be eaten, as a teil tree, and as an oak whose substance is in them when they cast their leaves; so the [a]holy seed shall be the substance thereof.

CHAPTER 17

Ephraim and Syria wage war against Judah—Christ will be born of a virgin—Compare Isaiah 7. About 559–545 B.C.

[a]AND it came to pass in the days of [b]Ahaz the son of [c]Jotham, the son of Uzziah, king of Judah, that [d]Rezin, king of Syria, and [e]Pekah the son of Remaliah, king of Israel, went up toward Jerusalem to war against it, but could not prevail against it.

2 And it was told the house of David, saying: Syria is confederate with Ephraim. And his heart was moved, and the heart of his people, as the trees of the wood are moved with the wind.

3 Then said the Lord unto Isaiah: Go forth now to meet Ahaz, thou

16 1*a* Isa. 6:1 (1–13).
b IE about 750 B.C.
c John 12:41; 2 Ne. 11:2.
2*a* TG Cherubim. BD Seraphim.
3*a* Ps. 72:19 (19–20). TG Jesus Christ, Glory of.
5*a* TG Jesus Christ, Appearances, Antemortal.
7*a* TG Cleanse; Remission of Sins.
8*a* TG Called of God.
10*a* Matt. 13:14 (14–15); John 12:40; Acts 28:26–27; Rom. 11:8.
b Prov. 2:2.
12*a* 2 Kgs. 17:18 (18, 20); 25:21.
13*a* Ezra 9:2.
17 1*a* Isa. 7:1 (1–25).
b 2 Kgs. 16:5; 2 Chr. 28:5 (5–6).
c 2 Kgs. 15:32.
d 2 Kgs. 15:37 (36–38).
e 2 Kgs. 15:25.

and Shearjashub thy son, at the end
of the [a]conduit of the upper pool
in the highway of the fuller's field;
4 And say unto him: Take heed,
and be quiet; fear not, neither be
faint-hearted for the two tails of
these smoking firebrands, for the
fierce anger of Rezin with Syria,
and of the son of Remaliah.
5 Because Syria, Ephraim, and the
son of Remaliah, have taken evil
counsel against thee, saying:
6 Let us go up against Judah and
vex it, and let us make a breach
therein for us, and set a king in the
midst of it, yea, the son of Tabeal.
7 Thus saith the Lord God: [a]It shall
not stand, neither shall it come to
pass.
8 For the head of Syria is Damascus, and the head of Damascus,
Rezin; and within threescore and
five years shall Ephraim be [a]broken
that it be not a people.
9 And the head of Ephraim is
Samaria, and the head of Samaria
is Remaliah's son. If ye will [a]not
believe surely ye shall not be established.
10 Moreover, the Lord spake again
unto Ahaz, saying:
11 Ask thee a [a]sign of the Lord thy
God; ask it either in the depths, or
in the heights above.
12 But Ahaz said: I will not ask,
neither will I [a]tempt the Lord.
13 And he said: Hear ye now, O
house of David; is it a small thing
for you to weary men, but will ye
weary my God also?
14 Therefore, the Lord himself shall
give you a sign—Behold, a [a]virgin
shall conceive, and shall bear a son,
and shall call his name [b]Immanuel.
15 Butter and [a]honey shall he eat,
that he may know to refuse the evil
and to choose the good.
16 For [a]before the child shall know
to refuse the evil and choose the
good, the land that thou abhorrest
shall be forsaken of [b]both her kings.
17 The Lord shall [a]bring upon thee,
and upon thy people, and upon thy
father's house, days that have not
come from the day that [b]Ephraim
departed from Judah, the king of
Assyria.
18 And it shall come to pass in
that day that the Lord shall hiss
for the fly that is in the uttermost
part of Egypt, and for the bee that
is in the land of Assyria.
19 And they shall come, and shall
rest all of them in the desolate val-
leys, and in the holes of the rocks,
and upon all thorns, and upon all
bushes.
20 In the same day shall the Lord
shave with a [a]razor that is hired,
by them beyond the river, by the
king of Assyria, the head, and the
hair of the feet; and it shall also
consume the beard.
21 And it shall come to pass in that
day, a man shall nourish a young
cow and two sheep;
22 And it shall come to pass, for
the abundance of milk they shall
give he shall eat butter; for butter
and honey shall every one eat that
is left in the land.
23 And it shall come to pass in
that day, every place shall be, where
there were a thousand vines at a
thousand silverlings, which shall
be for briers and thorns.
24 With arrows and with bows
shall men come thither, because
all the land shall become briers
and thorns.
25 And all hills that shall be digged
with the mattock, there shall not
come thither the fear of briers and
thorns; but it shall be for the sending forth of oxen, and the treading
of lesser cattle.

3*a* 2 Kgs. 18:17; Isa. 36:2.
7*a* Prov. 21:30; Isa. 8:10 (9–10).
8*a* TG Israel, Scattering of.
9*a* 2 Chr. 20:20. TG Unbelief.
11*a* Judg. 6:39 (36–40). TG Signs.
12*a* IE test, try, or prove.
14*a* Isa. 7:14.
b Isa. 8:8; 2 Ne. 18:8, 10.
15*a* 2 Sam. 17:29.
16*a* Isa. 8:4; 2 Ne. 18:4.
b 2 Kgs. 15:30; 16:9.
17*a* 2 Chr. 28:19 (19–21).
b 1 Kgs. 12:19 (16–19).
20*a* 2 Kgs. 16:7 (7–8); 2 Chr. 28:20 (20–21).

CHAPTER 18

Christ will be as a stone of stumbling and a rock of offense—Seek the Lord, not peeping wizards—Turn to the law and to the testimony for guidance—Compare Isaiah 8. About 559–545 B.C.

MOREOVER, the word of the Lord
said unto me: Take thee a great [a]roll,
and write in it with a man's pen,
concerning [b]Maher-shalal-hash-baz.
2 And I took unto me faithful
[a]witnesses to record, Uriah the
priest, and Zechariah the son of
Jeberechiah.
3 And I went unto the prophetess;
and she conceived and bare a son.
Then said the Lord to me: [a]Call his
name, Maher-shalal-hash-baz.
4 For behold, [a]the child shall [b]not
have knowledge to cry, My father,
and my mother, before the riches
of Damascus and the [c]spoil of [d]Samaria shall be taken away before
the king of [e]Assyria.
5 The Lord spake also unto me
again, saying:
6 Forasmuch as this people refuseth the waters of [a]Shiloah that go
softly, and rejoice in [b]Rezin and
Remaliah's son;
7 Now therefore, behold, the Lord
bringeth up upon them the waters
of the river, strong and many, even
the king of [a]Assyria and all his glory;
and he shall come up over all his
channels, and go over all his banks.
8 And he shall pass through Judah; he shall overflow and go over,
he shall [a]reach even to the neck;
and the stretching out of his wings
shall fill the breadth of thy land,
O Immanuel.
9 [a]Associate yourselves, O ye
people, and ye shall be broken in
pieces; and give ear all ye of far
countries; gird yourselves, and ye
shall be broken in pieces; gird yourselves, and ye shall be broken in
pieces.
10 Take counsel together, and it
shall come to naught; speak the
word, and it shall not stand; for
God is with us.
11 For the Lord spake thus to me
with a strong hand, and instructed
me that I should not walk in the
way of this people, saying:
12 Say ye not, A confederacy, to
all to whom this people shall say, A
[a]confederacy; neither fear ye their
fear, nor be afraid.
13 Sanctify the Lord of Hosts himself, and let him be your fear, and
let him be your dread.
14 And he shall be for a sanctuary;
but for a [a]stone of [b]stumbling, and
for a [c]rock of [d]offense to both the
houses of Israel, for a gin and a [e]snare
to the inhabitants of Jerusalem.
15 And many among them shall
[a]stumble and fall, and be broken,
and be snared, and be taken.
16 [a]Bind up the testimony, seal the
law among my disciples.
17 And I will wait upon the Lord,
that [a]hideth his face from the house
of Jacob, and I will look for him.
18 Behold, I and the children
whom the Lord hath given me are
for [a]signs and for wonders in Israel from the Lord of Hosts, which
dwelleth in Mount Zion.
19 And when they shall say unto
you: Seek unto them that have
[a]familiar spirits, and unto [b]wizards

---

18 1*a* Isa. 8:1 (1–22).
b HEB To speed to the spoil, he hasteneth the prey.
2*a* TG Witness.
3*a* 2 Ne. 18:18.
4*a* 2 Ne. 17:16.
b Isa. 8:4.
c 2 Kgs. 15:29 (29–30).
d 2 Kgs. 17:6.
e 2 Kgs. 16:7 (7–18); 2 Ne. 20:12. TG Israel, Scattering of.
6*a* Neh. 3:15; John 9:7.
b Isa. 7:1 (1–6).
7*a* Isa. 10:12.
8*a* Isa. 30:28.
9*a* Joel 3:9 (9–14).
12*a* Isa. 31:1 (1–3).
14*a* Rom. 9:33 (32–33). TG Cornerstone; Jesus Christ, Prophecies about.
b Isa. 8:14 (13–15); Luke 2:34; 1 Pet. 2:8 (4–8); Jacob 4:15.
c TG Rock.
d Luke 7:23.
e Mosiah 7:29.
15*a* Matt. 21:44.
16*a* Dan. 12:9.
17*a* Isa. 54:8.
18*a* 2 Ne. 18:3 (1–3).
19*a* Moro. 10:30. TG Sorcery.
b Lev. 20:6.

that peep and mutter—[c]should not a people seek unto their God for the living to hear from the dead?

20 To the [a]law and to the testimony; and if they speak not according to this word, it is because there is no light in them.

21 And they shall pass through it hardly bestead and hungry; and it shall come to pass that when they shall be hungry, they shall fret themselves, and curse their king and their God, and look upward.

22 And they shall look unto the earth and behold trouble, and [a]darkness, dimness of anguish, and shall be driven to darkness.

CHAPTER 19

Isaiah speaks messianically—The people in darkness will see a great light—Unto us a child is born—He will be the Prince of Peace and will reign on David's throne—Compare Isaiah 9. About 559–545 B.C.

[a]NEVERTHELESS, the dimness shall not be such as was in her vexation, when at first he lightly afflicted the [b]land of [c]Zebulun, and the land of [d]Naphtali, and afterwards did more grievously afflict by the way of the Red Sea beyond Jordan in Galilee of the nations.

2 The people that walked in darkness have seen a great light; they that dwell in the land of the shadow of death, upon them hath the light shined.

3 Thou hast multiplied the nation, and [a]increased the joy—they joy before thee according to the joy in harvest, and as men rejoice when they divide the spoil.

4 For thou hast broken the yoke of [a]his burden, and the staff of his shoulder, the rod of his [b]oppressor.

5 For every battle of the warrior is with confused noise, and garments rolled in blood; but [a]this shall be with burning and fuel of fire.

6 For unto us a [a]child is born, unto us a son is given; and the [b]government shall be upon his shoulder; and his name shall be called, Wonderful, Counselor, The [c]Mighty God, The [d]Everlasting Father, The Prince of [e]Peace.

7 Of the increase of [a]government and peace [b]there is no end, upon the throne of [c]David, and upon his kingdom to order it, and to establish it with judgment and with justice from henceforth, even forever. The zeal of the Lord of Hosts will perform this.

8 The Lord sent his word unto Jacob and it hath lighted upon Israel.

9 And all the people shall know, even Ephraim and the inhabitants of Samaria, that say in the pride and stoutness of heart:

10 The bricks are fallen down, but we will build with hewn [a]stones; the sycamores are cut down, but we will change them into [b]cedars.

11 Therefore the Lord shall set up the adversaries of [a]Rezin against him, and join his enemies together;

12 The Syrians before and the Philistines behind; and they shall [a]devour Israel with open mouth. For all this his [b]anger is not turned away, but his hand is stretched out still.

13 For the people turneth not unto [a]him that smiteth them, neither do they seek the Lord of Hosts.

14 Therefore will the Lord cut off

---

18 19*c* 1 Sam. 28:11 (8–20).
20*a* Luke 16:29 (29–31).
22*a* Isa. 5:30.
19 1*a* Isa. 9:1 (1–21).
b Matt. 4:15 (15–16).
c Josh. 19:10 (10–16).
d Josh. 19:33 (32–39).
3*a* Isa. 9:3.
4*a* IE Israel, the nation mentioned in v. 3.
b TG Oppression.
5*a* Mal. 4:1.
6*a* Isa. 7:14; Luke 2:11.
b Matt. 28:18.
c Titus 2:13; Mosiah 7:27. TG Jesus Christ, Jehovah; Jesus Christ, Power of.
d 2 Ne. 26:12; Mosiah 3:5; Alma 11:39 (38–39, 44); Moro. 7:22; 8:18.
e Micah 5:5; D&C 27:16; 111:8.
7*a* TG Kingdom of God, on Earth.
b Dan. 2:44.
c Ezek. 37:24.
10*a* 1 Kgs. 5:17.
b 1 Kgs. 5:6.
11*a* 2 Kgs. 16:9 (7–9).
12*a* 2 Kgs. 17:6 (1–18).
b Isa. 5:25; 10:4; Jer. 4:8.
13*a* Amos 4:10 (6–12).

from Israel head and tail, branch and rush [a]in one day.

15 The [a]ancient, he is the head; and the prophet that teacheth lies, he is the tail.

16 For the [a]leaders of this people cause them to err; and they that are [b]led of them are destroyed.

17 Therefore the Lord shall have no joy in their young men, neither shall have [a]mercy on their fatherless and [b]widows; for [c]every one of them is a hypocrite and an [d]evildoer, and every mouth speaketh [e]folly. For all this his anger is not turned away, but his [f]hand is stretched out still.

18 For [a]wickedness burneth as the fire; it shall devour the briers and thorns, and shall kindle in the thickets of the forests, and they shall mount up like the lifting up of smoke.

19 Through the wrath of the Lord of Hosts is the [a]land darkened, and the people shall be as the fuel of the fire; [b]no man shall spare his brother.

20 And he [a]shall snatch on the right hand and be hungry; and he shall [b]eat on the left hand and they shall not be satisfied; they shall eat every man the flesh of his own arm—

21 Manasseh, [a]Ephraim; and Ephraim, Manasseh; they together shall be against [b]Judah. For all this his anger is not turned away, but his hand is stretched out still.

CHAPTER 20

The destruction of Assyria is a type of the destruction of the wicked at the Second Coming—Few people will be left after the Lord comes again—The remnant of Jacob will return in that day—Compare Isaiah 10. About 559–545 B.C.

[a]Wo unto them that decree [b]unrighteous decrees, and that write grievousness which they have prescribed;

2 To turn away the needy from judgment, and to take away the right from the [a]poor of my people, that [b]widows may be their prey, and that they may rob the fatherless!

3 And what will ye do in the day of visitation, and in the desolation which shall come from far? to whom will ye flee for help? and where will ye leave your glory?

4 Without me they shall bow down under the prisoners, and they shall fall under the slain. For all this his anger is not turned away, but his hand is stretched out still.

5 O Assyrian, the rod of mine anger, and the staff in their hand is [a]their indignation.

6 I will send him [a]against a hypocritical nation, and against the people of my wrath will I give him a charge to take the spoil, and to take the prey, and to tread them down like the mire of the streets.

7 Howbeit he meaneth not so, neither doth his heart think so; but in his heart it is to destroy and cut off nations not a few.

8 For he saith: Are not my [a]princes altogether kings?

9 Is not [a]Calno as [b]Carchemish? Is not Hamath as Arpad? Is not Samaria as [c]Damascus?

10 As [a]my hand hath founded the

14*a* Isa. 10:17.
15*a* Isa. 9:15.
16*a* Isa. 1:23. TG Leadership.
b TG Trust Not in the Arm of Flesh.
17*a* TG Mercy.
b TG Widows.
c Micah 7:2 (2–3).
d Prov. 1:16; D&C 64:16.
e Eccl. 10:12 (1–3, 12); 2 Ne. 9:28 (28–29); D&C 35:7.
f 2 Ne. 28:32; Jacob 5:47; 6:4.
18*a* Mal. 4:1.
19*a* Isa. 8:22.
b Micah 7:2 (2–6).
20*a* Lev. 26:26 (26, 29).
b Deut. 28:53 (53–57).
21*a* TG Israel, Joseph, People of.
b TG Israel, Judah, People of.
20 1*a* Isa. 10:1 (1–34).
b TG Injustice.
2*a* Amos 4:1.
b TG Widows.
5*a* Isa. 10:5.
6*a* IE against Israel. TG Hypocrisy.
8*a* 2 Kgs. 18:33 (33–35); 19:10 (10–13).
9*a* Amos 6:2 (1–2).
b 2 Chr. 35:20.
c 2 Kgs. 16:9.
10*a* IE the king of Assyria's hand (vv. 10–11).

kingdoms of the idols, and whose
graven images did excel them of
Jerusalem and of Samaria;
11 Shall I not, as I have done unto
Samaria and her [a]idols, so do to Jerusalem and to her idols?
12 Wherefore it shall come to pass
that when the Lord hath performed
his whole work upon Mount Zion
and upon Jerusalem, I will punish
the fruit of the stout heart of the
king of [a]Assyria, and the glory of
his high looks.
13 For [a]he saith: By the strength
of [b]my hand and by my wisdom I
have done these things; for I am
prudent; and I have moved the borders of the people, and have robbed
their treasures, and I have put down
the inhabitants like a valiant man;
14 And my hand hath found as a
nest the riches of the people; and
as one gathereth eggs that are left
have I gathered all the earth; and
there was none that moved the wing,
or opened the mouth, or peeped.
15 Shall the [a]ax boast itself against
him that heweth therewith? Shall
the saw magnify itself against him
that shaketh it? As if the rod should
shake itself against them that lift it
up, or as if the staff should lift up
itself as if it were no wood!
16 Therefore shall the Lord, the
Lord of Hosts, send among his fat
ones, leanness; and under his glory
he shall kindle a burning like the
burning of a fire.
17 And the light of Israel shall be for
a [a]fire, and his Holy One for a flame,
and shall burn and shall devour his
thorns and his briers in one day;
18 And shall consume the glory
of his forest, and of his fruitful
field, both soul and body; and they
shall be as when a standard-bearer
fainteth.
19 And the [a]rest of the trees of
his forest shall be few, that a child
may write them.
20 And it shall come to pass in that
day, that the remnant of Israel, and
such as are escaped of the [a]house
of Jacob, shall no more again [b]stay
upon him that smote them, but
shall stay upon the Lord, the Holy
One of Israel, in truth.
21 The [a]remnant shall return, yea,
even the remnant of Jacob, unto the
mighty God.
22 For though thy people [a]Israel
be as the sand of the sea, yet a remnant of them shall [b]return; the [c]con-
sumption decreed shall overflow
with righteousness.
23 For the Lord God of Hosts shall
make a [a]consumption, even determined in all the land.
24 Therefore, thus saith the Lord
God of Hosts: O my people that
dwellest in Zion, [a]be not afraid of
the Assyrian; he shall smite thee
with a rod, and shall lift up his
staff against thee, after the [b]man-
ner of Egypt.
25 For yet a very little while, and
the [a]indignation shall cease, and
mine anger in their destruction.
26 And the Lord of Hosts shall [a]stir
up a scourge for him according to
the slaughter of [b]Midian at the rock
of Oreb; and as his rod was upon
the sea so shall he lift it up after
the manner of [c]Egypt.

11*a* Ezek. 36:18 (16–20).
12*a* 2 Kgs. 16:7 (7–18); Zeph. 2:13; 2 Ne. 18:4 (4–7).
13*a* IE the king of Assyria (vv. 13–14).
b Isa. 37:24 (24–38).
15*a* IE Can the king prosper against God?
17*a* Obad. 1:18; 2 Ne. 15:24; 3 Ne. 20:16.
19*a* IE the remnants of the army of Assyria.
20*a* Amos 9:8 (8–9); 2 Ne. 6:11 (10–11).
b IE depend upon. 2 Kgs. 16:8 (7–9); 2 Chr. 28:21 (20–21).
21*a* Isa. 11:11. TG Israel, Remnant of.
22*a* Gen. 22:17; Rom. 9:27.
b TG Israel, Gathering of.
c Isa. 28:22. TG World, End of.
23*a* Dan. 9:27.
24*a* Isa. 37:6 (6–7).
b TG Israel, Bondage of, in Egypt; Israel, Bondage of, in Other Lands.
25*a* Isa. 10:25; Dan. 11:36.
26*a* 2 Kgs. 19:35.
b Gen. 25:2 (1–6); Judg. 7:25; Isa. 9:4.
c Ex. 14:27 (26–27).

27 And it shall come to pass in that day that his [a]burden shall be taken away from off thy shoulder, and his yoke from off thy neck, and the yoke shall be destroyed because of the [b]anointing.

28 [a]He is come to Aiath, he is passed to Migron; at Michmash he hath laid up his carriages.

29 They are gone over the [a]passage; they have taken up their lodging at [b]Geba; Ramath is afraid; [c]Gibeah of Saul is fled.

30 Lift up the voice, O daughter of [a]Gallim; cause it to be heard unto Laish, O poor [b]Anathoth.

31 Madmenah is removed; the inhabitants of Gebim gather themselves to flee.

32 As yet shall he remain at [a]Nob that day; he shall shake his hand against the mount of the daughter of Zion, the hill of Jerusalem.

33 Behold, the Lord, the Lord of Hosts shall lop the bough with terror; and the [a]high ones of stature shall be [b]hewn down; and the [c]haughty shall be humbled.

34 And he shall cut down the thickets of the forests with iron, and Lebanon shall fall by a mighty one.

CHAPTER 21

The stem of Jesse (Christ) will judge in righteousness—The knowledge of God will cover the earth in the Millennium—The Lord will raise an ensign and gather Israel—Compare Isaiah 11. About 559–545 B.C.

[a]AND there shall [b]come forth a rod out of the [c]stem of Jesse, and a [d]branch shall grow out of his roots.

2 And the [a]Spirit of the Lord shall rest upon him, the spirit of [b]wisdom and [c]understanding, the spirit of counsel and might, the spirit of knowledge and of the fear of the Lord;

3 And shall make him of quick understanding in the fear of the Lord; and he shall not [a]judge after the sight of his eyes, neither reprove after the hearing of his ears.

4 But with [a]righteousness shall he [b]judge the poor, and reprove with equity for the [c]meek of the earth; and he shall [d]smite the earth with the [e]rod of his mouth, and with the breath of his lips shall he slay the wicked.

5 And [a]righteousness shall be the girdle of his loins, and faithfulness the girdle of his reins.

6 The [a]wolf also shall dwell with the lamb, and the leopard shall lie down with the kid, and the calf and the young lion and fatling together; and a little child shall lead them.

7 And the cow and the bear shall feed; their young ones shall lie down together; and the lion shall eat straw like the ox.

8 And the sucking child shall play on the hole of the asp, and the weaned child shall put his hand on the cockatrice's den.

9 They shall [a]not hurt nor [b]destroy in all my holy mountain, for the [c]earth shall be full of the [d]knowledge

---

27*a* Isa. 14:25.
b TG Jesus Christ, Messiah.
28*a* IE The Assyrian invasion forces introduced in v. 5 progress toward Jerusalem, vv. 28–32.
29*a* 1 Sam. 13:23.
b Neh. 11:31.
c 1 Sam. 11:4.
30*a* 1 Sam. 25:44.
b Josh. 21:18.
32*a* 1 Sam. 21:1; 22:19; Neh. 11:32.
33*a* Obad. 1:3 (3–4); Hel. 4:12 (12–13); D&C 101:42.
b Ezek. 17:24; Amos 2:9; D&C 112:8 (3–8).
c Ps. 18:27; 3 Ne. 25:1; D&C 29:9.
21 1*a* Isa. 11:1 (1–16).
b Isa. 53:2; Rev. 5:5.
c D&C 113:2 (1–2).
d TG Jesus Christ, Davidic Descent of.
2*a* Isa. 61:1 (1–3).
b 1 Kgs. 3:28.
c 1 Kgs. 3:11 (10–11).
3*a* 2 Ne. 12:4.
4*a* Ps. 50:6; Mosiah 29:12.
b Ps. 72:4 (2–4). TG Jesus Christ, Judge.
c TG Meek.
d Ps. 2:9.
e 2 Thes. 2:8; Rev. 19:15.
5*a* TG Jesus Christ, Millennial Reign.
6*a* Isa. 65:25.
9*a* Isa. 2:4.
b TG War.
c Hab. 2:14.
d Ps. 66:4; D&C 88:104. TG Knowledge; Millennium.

of the Lord, as the waters cover
the sea.
10 And in that day there shall be
a [a]root of Jesse, which shall stand
for an ensign of the people; to it
shall the [b]Gentiles seek; and his
[c]rest shall be glorious.
11 And it shall come to pass in
that day that the Lord shall set his
hand again the [a]second time to recover the remnant of his people
which shall be left, from [b]Assyria,
and from Egypt, and from Pathros,
and from Cush, and from Elam, and
from [c]Shinar, and from Hamath,
and from the islands of the sea.
12 And he shall set up an [a]ensign
for the nations, and shall assemble
the [b]outcasts of Israel, and [c]gather
together the dispersed of Judah
from the four corners of the earth.
13 The [a]envy of Ephraim also shall
depart, and the adversaries of Judah
shall be cut off; Ephraim shall not
[b]envy [c]Judah, and Judah shall not
vex Ephraim.
14 But they shall fly upon the
shoulders of the [a]Philistines towards
the west; they shall spoil them of
the east together; they shall lay
their hand upon [b]Edom and [c]Moab;
and the children of Ammon shall
obey them.
15 And the Lord shall utterly [a]de-
stroy the tongue of the Egyptian
sea; and with his mighty wind
he shall shake his hand over the
river, and shall smite it in the seven
streams, and make men go over [b]dry
shod.
16 And there shall be a [a]highway
for the remnant of his people which
shall be left, from Assyria, like as
it was to Israel in the day that he
came up out of the land of Egypt.

CHAPTER 22

In the millennial day all men will praise the Lord—He will dwell among them—Compare Isaiah 12. About 559–545 B.C.

[a]AND in that day thou shalt say:
O Lord, I will praise thee; though
thou wast angry with me thine anger is turned away, and thou com-
fortedst me.
2 Behold, God is my salvation; I
will [a]trust, and not be afraid; for
the Lord [b]JEHOVAH is my [c]strength
and my [d]song; he also has become
my salvation.
3 Therefore, with joy shall ye draw
[a]water out of the wells of salvation.
4 And in that day shall ye say:
[a]Praise the Lord, call upon his name,
declare his doings among the people, make mention that his name
is exalted.
5 [a]Sing unto the Lord; for he hath
done excellent things; this is known
in all the earth.
6 [a]Cry out and shout, thou inhabitant of Zion; for great is the Holy
One of Israel in the midst of thee.

CHAPTER 23

The destruction of Babylon is a type of the destruction at the Second Coming—It will be a day of wrath and vengeance

10*a* Rom. 15:12;
D&C 113:5 (5–6).
b D&C 45:9 (9–10).
c D&C 19:9.
TG Earth, Renewal of.
11*a* 2 Ne. 6:14; 25:17; 29:1.
b Zech. 10:10.
c Gen. 10:10.
12*a* TG Ensign.
b 3 Ne. 15:15; 16:1 (1–4).
c Neh. 1:9;
1 Ne. 22:12 (10–12);
D&C 45:25 (24–25).
TG Israel, Gathering of.
13*a* Jer. 3:18.
b Ezek. 37:22 (16–22).
TG Envy.
c TG Israel, Joseph, People of;
Israel, Judah, People of.
14*a* Obad. 1:19 (18–19).
b Lam. 4:21.
c Gen. 19:37 (30–38).
15*a* Zech. 10:11.
b Rev. 16:12.
16*a* Isa. 11:16; 19:23;
35:8 (8–10);
D&C 133:27.
TG Earth, Renewal of.
22 1*a* Isa. 12:1 (1–6).
2*a* Ps. 36:7 (7–8);
Mosiah 4:6;
Hel. 12:1.
b Ex. 15:2;
Ps. 83:18.
TG Jesus Christ, Jehovah.
c TG Strength.
d TG Singing.
3*a* TG Living Water.
4*a* TG Praise;
Thanksgiving.
5*a* Ps. 57:7 (7–11);
108:1 (1–5);
Alma 26:8;
D&C 136:28.
6*a* Isa. 54:1 (1–8);
Zeph. 3:14 (14–20);
Zech. 2:10 (10–13).

—Babylon (the world) will fall forever—
Compare Isaiah 13. About 559–545 B.C.

[a]THE burden of [b]Babylon, which
Isaiah the son of Amoz did see.
2 Lift ye up a banner upon the
high mountain, exalt the voice unto
them, [a]shake the hand, that they
may go into the gates of the nobles.
3 I have commanded my sanctified
ones, I have also called my [a]mighty
ones, for mine anger is not upon
them that rejoice in my highness.
4 The noise of the multitude in
the mountains like as of a great
people, a tumultuous noise of the
[a]kingdoms of nations [b]gathered together, the Lord of Hosts mustereth
the hosts of the battle.
5 They come from a far country,
from the end of heaven, yea, the
Lord, and the weapons of his indignation, to destroy the whole land.
6 Howl ye, for the [a]day of the Lord
is at hand; it shall come as a destruction from the Almighty.
7 Therefore shall all hands be
faint, every man's heart shall [a]melt;
8 And they shall be afraid; pangs
and sorrows shall take hold of them;
they shall be amazed one at another;
their faces shall be as flames.
9 Behold, the day of the Lord
cometh, cruel both with wrath and
fierce anger, to lay the land desolate; and he shall [a]destroy the sinners thereof out of it.
10 For the [a]stars of heaven and
the [b]constellations thereof shall not
give their [c]light; the [d]sun shall be
darkened in his going forth, and
the moon shall not cause her light
to shine.
11 And I will [a]punish the world
for evil, and the [b]wicked for their
iniquity; I will cause the arrogancy
of the [c]proud to cease, and will lay
down the haughtiness of the terrible.
12 I will make a [a]man more precious than fine gold; even a man
than the golden wedge of Ophir.
13 Therefore, I will [a]shake the
heavens, and the earth shall [b]re-
move out of her place, in the wrath
of the Lord of Hosts, and in the day
of his fierce anger.
14 And it shall be as the chased roe,
and as a sheep that no man taketh
up; and they shall every man turn
to his own people, and flee every
one into his own [a]land.
15 Every one that is proud shall
be thrust through; yea, and every
one that is [a]joined to the wicked
shall fall by the sword.
16 Their [a]children also shall be
[b]dashed to pieces before their eyes;
their houses shall be spoiled and
their wives ravished.
17 Behold, I will stir up the [a]Medes
against them, which shall not re-
gard silver and gold, nor shall they
delight in it.
18 Their bows shall also dash the
young men to pieces; and they shall
have no [a]pity on the fruit of the
womb; their eyes shall not spare
children.
19 And [a]Babylon, the glory of kingdoms, the beauty of the Chaldees'
excellency, shall be as when God
overthrew [b]Sodom and Gomorrah.

---

23 1*a* Isa. 13:1 (1–22).
b TG Babylon.
2*a* IE wave the hand, give a signal.
3*a* Joel 3:11.
4*a* Joel 3:14 (11, 14); Zeph. 3:8; Zech. 14:2 (2–3).
b Zech. 12:3 (2–9).
6*a* TG Day of the Lord.
7*a* Jer. 9:7; D&C 133:41.
9*a* TG Earth, Cleansing of.
10*a* Isa. 24:23; Ezek. 32:7 (7–8); Rev. 6:13 (12–13).
b TG Astronomy.
c Joel 3:15.
d TG World, End of.
11*a* Isa. 24:6; Mal. 4:1.
b Ex. 34:7; Prov. 21:12.
c Job 40:11; 2 Ne. 12:12; D&C 64:24.
12*a* Isa. 4:1 (1–4).
13*a* Hag. 2:6 (6–7); Heb. 12:26.
b TG Earth, Renewal of.
14*a* TG Lands of Inheritance.
15*a* Lam. 2:9; Alma 59:6 (5–6).
16*a* Job 27:14 (13–15).
b Ps. 137:9 (8–9).
17*a* Isa. 21:2.
18*a* Lam. 2:2 (2, 17, 21).
19*a* Isa. 14:15 (4–27).
b Gen. 19:24 (24–25); Deut. 29:23; Jer. 49:18; 2 Ne. 13:9.

20 It shall never be [a]inhabited,
neither shall it be dwelt in from
generation to generation: neither
shall the Arabian pitch tent there;
neither shall the shepherds make
their fold there.
21 But [a]wild beasts of the desert
shall lie there; and their houses
shall be full of doleful creatures;
and owls shall dwell there, and sa-
tyrs shall dance there.
22 And the wild beasts of the islands
shall cry in their desolate houses, and
dragons in their pleasant palaces;
and her time is near to come, and
her day shall not be prolonged. For I
will destroy her speedily; yea, for
I will be merciful unto my people,
but the wicked shall perish.

CHAPTER 24

Israel will be gathered and will enjoy millennial rest—Lucifer was cast out of heaven for rebellion—Israel will triumph over Babylon (the world)—Compare Isaiah 14. About 559–545 B.C.

[a]FOR the Lord will have mercy on
Jacob, and will yet [b]choose Israel,
and set them in their own land; and
the [c]strangers shall be joined with
them, and they shall cleave to the
house of Jacob.
2 And the people shall take them
and bring them to their place; yea,
from far unto the ends of the earth;
and they shall return to their [a]lands
of promise. And the house of Israel
shall [b]possess them, and the land
of the Lord shall be for [c]servants
and handmaids; and they shall take
them captives unto whom they were
captives; and they shall [d]rule over
their oppressors.
3 And it shall come to pass in that
day that the Lord shall give thee
[a]rest, from thy sorrow, and from thy
fear, and from the hard bondage
wherein thou wast made to serve.
4 And it shall come to pass in
that day, that thou shalt take up
this proverb [a]against the king of
[b]Babylon, and say: How hath the
oppressor ceased, the golden city
ceased!
5 The Lord hath broken the staff
of the [a]wicked, the scepters of the
rulers.
6 [a]He who smote the people in
wrath with a continual stroke, he
that ruled the nations in anger, is
persecuted, and none hindereth.
7 The whole earth is at [a]rest, and is
quiet; they break forth into [b]singing.
8 Yea, the fir trees rejoice at thee,
and also the cedars of Lebanon,
saying: Since thou art laid down no
feller is come up against us.
9 [a]Hell from beneath is moved for
thee to meet thee at thy coming; it
stirreth up the [b]dead for thee, even
all the chief ones of the earth; it
hath raised up from their thrones
all the kings of the nations.
10 All they shall speak and say unto
thee: Art thou also become weak
as we? Art thou become like unto us?
11 Thy pomp is brought down to
the grave; the noise of thy viols is
not heard; the worm is spread under thee, and the worms cover thee.
12 [a]How art thou fallen from
heaven, O [b]Lucifer, son of the
morning! Art thou cut down to
the ground, which did weaken the
nations!
13 For thou hast said in thy heart:
[a]I will ascend into heaven, I will

20*a* Jer. 50:39 (3, 39–40); 51:29 (29, 62).
21*a* Isa. 34:14 (11–15).
24 1*a* Isa. 14:1 (1–32).
b Zech. 1:17; 2:12.
c Isa. 60:3 (3–5, 10). TG Stranger.
2*a* TG Promised Lands.
b Amos 9:12.
c Isa. 60:14 (10–12, 14).
d TG Kingdom of God, on Earth.
3*a* Josh. 1:13; D&C 84:24.
4*a* Hab. 2:6 (6–8).
b TG Babylon.
5*a* TG Earth, Cleansing of; Wickedness.
6*a* IE Babylon.
7*a* TG Earth, Renewal of.
b Isa. 55:12 (12–13).
9*a* Ezek. 32:21. TG Hell.
b TG Spirits in Prison.
12*a* IE The fallen king of Babylon is typified by the fallen "son of the morning," Lucifer in vv. 12–15. D&C 76:26.
b TG Devil.
13*a* Moses 4:1 (1–4).

exalt my throne above the stars of
God; I will sit also upon the mount
of the congregation, in the sides of
the north;
14 [a]I will ascend above the heights
of the clouds; I will be like the
Most High.
15 Yet thou shalt be brought down
to hell, to the sides of the [a]pit.
16 They that see thee shall nar-
rowly look upon thee, and shall
consider thee, and shall say: Is this
the man that made the earth to
tremble, that did shake kingdoms?
17 And made the world as a wilderness, and destroyed the cities
thereof, and opened not the house
of his prisoners?
18 All the kings of the nations, yea,
all of them, lie in glory, every one
of them in his own house.
19 But thou art cast out of thy
grave like an abominable branch,
and the remnant of those that are
slain, thrust through with a sword,
that go down to the stones of the
pit; as a carcass trodden under feet.
20 Thou shalt not be joined with
them in burial, because thou hast
destroyed thy land and slain thy
people; the [a]seed of [b]evil-doers
shall never be renowned.
21 Prepare slaughter for his children for the [a]iniquities of their
fathers, that they do not rise, nor
possess the land, nor fill the face
of the world with cities.
22 For I will rise up against them,
saith the Lord of Hosts, and cut off
from Babylon the [a]name, and remnant, and son, and [b]nephew, saith
the Lord.
23 I will also make it a [a]possession
for the bittern, and pools of water;
and I will sweep it with the besom of
destruction, saith the Lord of Hosts.
24 The Lord of Hosts hath sworn,
saying: Surely as I have thought, so
shall it come to pass; and as I have
purposed, so shall it stand—
25 That I will bring the Assyrian in
my land, and upon my mountains
tread him under foot; then shall his
[a]yoke depart from off them, and
his burden depart from off their
shoulders.
26 This is the purpose that is purposed upon the whole earth; and
this is the hand that is stretched
out upon all nations.
27 For the Lord of Hosts hath purposed, and who shall disannul? And
his hand is stretched out, and who
shall turn it back?
28 In the year that king [a]Ahaz died
was this burden.
29 Rejoice not thou, whole Palestina, because the rod of him that
[a]smote thee is broken; for out of
the serpent's root shall come forth
a cockatrice, and his [b]fruit shall be
a [c]fiery flying serpent.
30 And the firstborn of the poor
shall feed, and the needy shall lie
down in safety; and I will kill thy
root with famine, and he shall slay
thy remnant.
31 Howl, O gate; cry, O city; thou,
whole Palestina, art dissolved; for
there shall come from the north a
smoke, and none shall be alone in
his appointed times.
32 What shall then answer the
messengers of the nations? That
the Lord hath founded [a]Zion, and
the [b]poor of his people shall trust
in it.

CHAPTER 25

Nephi glories in plainness—Isaiah's prophecies will be understood in the last days—The Jews will return from Babylon, crucify the Messiah, and be scattered and scourged—They will be restored when they believe in the

14*a* 2 Thes. 2:4.
15*a* Ps. 28:1; 88:4; 1 Ne. 14:3.
20*a* Ps. 21:10 (10–11); 37:28; 109:13.
b TG Wickedness.
21*a* Ex. 20:5.
22*a* Prov. 10:7; Jer. 51:62.
b Job 18:19.
23*a* Isa. 34:11 (11–15).
25*a* Isa. 10:27.
28*a* 2 Kgs. 16:20.
29*a* 2 Chr. 26:6.
b 2 Kgs. 18:8 (1, 8).
c TG Jesus Christ, Types of, in Anticipation.
32*a* TG Zion.
b Zeph. 3:12.

Messiah—He will first come six hundred years after Lehi left Jerusalem—The Nephites keep the law of Moses and believe in Christ, who is the Holy One of Israel. About 559–545 B.C.

NOW I, Nephi, do speak somewhat
concerning the words which I have
written, which have been spoken
by the mouth of Isaiah. For behold,
Isaiah spake many things which
were [a]hard for many of my people
to understand; for they know not
concerning the manner of prophesying among the Jews.
2 For I, Nephi, have not taught
them many things concerning the
manner of the Jews; for their [a]works
were works of darkness, and their
doings were doings of abominations.
3 Wherefore, I write unto my people, unto all those that shall receive
hereafter these things which I write,
[a]that they may know the judgments
of God, that they come upon all nations, according to the word which
he hath spoken.
4 Wherefore, hearken, O my people, which are of the house of Israel, and give ear unto my words;
for because the words of Isaiah are
not plain unto you, nevertheless
they are plain unto all those that
are filled with the [a]spirit of [b]proph-
ecy. But I give unto you a [c]prophecy,
according to the spirit which is in
me; wherefore I shall prophesy according to the [d]plainness which hath
been with me from the time that I
came out from Jerusalem with my
father; for behold, my soul delighteth in [e]plainness unto my people,
that they may learn.
5 Yea, and my soul delighteth in
the words of [a]Isaiah, for I came out
from Jerusalem, and mine eyes hath
beheld the things of the [b]Jews, and
I know that the Jews do [c]understand
the things of the prophets, and there
is none other people that understand the things which were spoken
unto the Jews like unto them, save
it be that they are taught after the
manner of the things of the Jews.
6 But behold, I, Nephi, have not
taught my children after the manner of the Jews; but behold, I, of
myself, have dwelt at Jerusalem,
wherefore I know concerning the
regions round about; and I have
made mention unto my children
concerning the judgments of God,
which [a]hath come to pass among the
Jews, unto my children, according
to all that which Isaiah hath spoken, and I do not write them.
7 But behold, I proceed with mine
own prophecy, according to my
[a]plainness; in the which I [b]know
that no man can err; nevertheless,
in the days that the prophecies of
Isaiah shall be fulfilled men shall
know of a surety, at the times when
they shall come to pass.
8 Wherefore, they are of [a]worth
unto the children of men, and he
that supposeth that they are not,
unto them will I speak particularly,
and confine the words unto mine
[b]own people; for I know that they
shall be of great worth unto them in
the [c]last days; for in that day shall
they understand them; wherefore,
for their good have I written them.
9 And as one generation hath
been [a]destroyed among the Jews because of iniquity, even so have they
been destroyed from generation to

25 1*a* Jacob 4:14.
TG Symbolism.
2*a* 2 Kgs. 17:13–20.
3*a* TG God, Knowledge about;
Prophets, Mission of;
Scriptures, Value of.
4*a* TG Holy Ghost, Source of Testimony.
b TG Prophecy.
c 2 Ne. 31:1.
d 2 Ne. 31:3; 33:5;
Jacob 2:11; 4:13.
e TG Communication;
Plainness.
5*a* 1 Ne. 19:23.
b TG Israel, Judah, People of.
c Matt. 13:11 (10–17).
6*a* 2 Ne. 6:8;
Hel. 8:20 (20–21).
7*a* 2 Ne. 32:7;
Alma 13:23;
Ether 12:39.
b Ezek. 12:23 (21–25).
8*a* TG Scriptures, Value of.
b 2 Ne. 27:6;
Enos 1:16 (13–16);
Morm. 5:12;
D&C 3:20 (16–20).
c TG Last Days.
9*a* Lam. 1–5;
Matt. 23:37.

generation according to their iniquities; and never hath any of
them been destroyed save it were
[b]foretold them by the prophets of
the Lord.
10 Wherefore, it hath been told
them concerning the destruction
which should come upon them, immediately after my father left [a]Jeru-
salem; nevertheless, they [b]hardened
their hearts; and according to my
prophecy they have been destroyed,
save it be those which are [c]carried
away [d]captive into Babylon.
11 And now this I speak because
of the [a]spirit which is in me. And
notwithstanding they have been
carried away they shall return
again, and possess the land of Jerusalem; wherefore, they shall be
[b]restored again to the [c]land of their
inheritance.
12 But, behold, they shall have
[a]wars, and rumors of wars; and when
the day cometh that the [b]Only Begotten of the Father, yea, even the
Father of heaven and of earth, shall
[c]manifest himself unto them in the
flesh, behold, they will reject him,
because of their iniquities, and the
hardness of their hearts, and the
stiffness of their necks.
13 Behold, they will [a]crucify him;
and after he is laid in a [b]sepulchre
for the space of [c]three days he shall
[d]rise from the dead, with healing in
his wings; and all those who shall
believe on his name shall be saved
in the kingdom of God. Wherefore,
my soul delighteth to prophesy concerning him, for I have [e]seen his
day, and my heart doth magnify
his holy name.
14 And behold it shall come to
pass that after the [a]Messiah hath
risen from the dead, and hath
manifested himself unto his people, unto as many as will believe on
his name, behold, Jerusalem shall
be [b]destroyed again; for [c]wo unto
them that fight against God and
the people of his [d]church.
15 Wherefore, the [a]Jews shall be
[b]scattered among all nations; yea,
and also [c]Babylon shall be destroyed; wherefore, the Jews shall be
scattered by other nations.
16 And after they have been
[a]scattered, and the Lord God hath
scourged them by other nations
for the space of many generations,
yea, even down from generation to
generation until they shall be per-
suaded to [b]believe in Christ, the Son
of God, and the atonement, which
is infinite for all mankind—and
when that day shall come that they
shall believe in Christ, and worship
the Father in his name, with pure
hearts and [c]clean hands, and look
not forward any more for [d]another
Messiah, then, at that time, the day
will come that it must needs be expedient that they should believe
these things.
17 And the Lord will set his hand

9*b* Ezek. 4:3; Amos 3:7; D&C 5:20.
10*a* 1 Ne. 7:13; 2 Ne. 6:8; Omni 1:15; Hel. 8:21 (20–21).
b TG Hardheartedness.
c 2 Kgs. 24:14 (14–15); Jer. 52:15 (3–15); 1 Ne. 1:13; 10:3.
d Lam. 1:3 (1–3).
11*a* TG Teaching with the Spirit.
b Jer. 24:6 (5–7).
c TG Lands of Inheritance.
12*a* TG War.
b TG Jesus Christ, Divine Sonship.
c TG Jesus Christ, Birth of.
13*a* TG Jesus Christ, Crucifixion of.
b Luke 23:53; John 19:41 (41–42); 1 Ne. 19:10.
c Mosiah 3:10.
d Mal. 4:2. TG Jesus Christ, Prophecies about; Jesus Christ, Resurrection; Resurrection.
e 1 Ne. 11:27 (13–34).
14*a* TG Jesus Christ, Messiah.
b Matt. 24:2 (1–2); Luke 21:24.
c Ps. 83:17 (2–17); D&C 71:7; Moses 7:15 (14–16).
d TG Jesus Christ, Head of the Church.
15*a* TG Israel, Judah, People of.
b Neh. 1:8 (7–9); 2 Ne. 10:6; 3 Ne. 16:8. TG Israel, Bondage of, in Other Lands; Israel, Scattering of.
c TG Babylon.
16*a* Ezek. 34:12; Morm. 5:14.
b 2 Ne. 10:7 (5–9); 30:7 (7–8).
c Job 17:9; D&C 88:86.
d TG False Christs.

again the second time to [a]restore his people from their lost and fallen state. Wherefore, he will proceed to do a [b]marvelous work and a wonder among the children of men.
18 Wherefore, he shall bring forth [a]his [b]words unto them, which words shall [c]judge them at the last day, for they shall be given them for the purpose of [d]convincing them of the true Messiah, who was rejected by them; and unto the convincing of them that they need not look forward any more for a Messiah to come, for there should not any come, save it should be a [e]false Messiah which should deceive the people; for there is save one [f]Messiah spoken of by the prophets, and that Messiah is he who should be rejected of the Jews.
19 For according to the words of the prophets, the [a]Messiah cometh in [b]six hundred years from the time that my father left Jerusalem; and according to the words of the prophets, and also the word of the [c]angel of God, his [d]name shall be Jesus Christ, the [e]Son of God.
20 And now, my brethren, I have spoken plainly that ye cannot err. And as the Lord God liveth that [a]brought Israel up out of the land of Egypt, and gave unto Moses power that he should [b]heal the nations after they had been bitten by the poisonous serpents, if they would cast their eyes unto the [c]serpent which he did raise up before them, and also gave him power that he should smite the [d]rock and the water should come forth; yea, behold I say unto you, that as these things are [e]true, and as the Lord God liveth, there is none other [f]name given under heaven save it be this Jesus Christ, of which I have spoken, whereby man can be saved.
21 Wherefore, for this cause hath the Lord God promised unto me that these things which I [a]write shall be kept and preserved, and handed down unto my seed, from generation to generation, that the promise may be fulfilled unto Joseph, that his seed should never [b]perish as long as the earth should stand.
22 Wherefore, these things shall go from generation to generation as long as the earth shall stand; and they shall go according to the will and pleasure of God; and the nations who shall possess them shall be [a]judged of them according to the words which are written.
23 For we labor diligently to write, to [a]persuade our children, and also our brethren, to believe in Christ, and to be reconciled to God; for we

17*a* Gen. 49:10; 2 Ne. 21:11; 29:1. TG Israel, Gathering of; Israel, Restoration of; Restoration of the Gospel.
b Isa. 29:14; 2 Ne. 27:26; 3 Ne. 28:32 (31–33).
18*a* 3 Ne. 16:4.
b 2 Ne. 29:11; 33:14 (11, 14–15); W of M 1:11; 3 Ne. 27:25 (23–27); Ether 5:4.
c TG Judgment, the Last.
d 2 Ne. 26:12; Morm. 3:21.
e TG False Christs.
f TG Jesus Christ, Messiah.
19*a* TG Jesus Christ, Betrayal of; Jesus Christ, Birth of.
b 1 Ne. 10:4; 19:8; 3 Ne. 1:1.
c 2 Ne. 10:3.
d TG Jesus Christ, Prophecies about.
e TG Jesus Christ, Divine Sonship.
20*a* Ex. 3:10 (2–10); 1 Ne. 17:24 (24, 31, 40); 19:10.
b John 3:14; 1 Ne. 17:41.
c 2 Kgs. 18:4; Alma 33:19; Hel. 8:14 (14–15).
d Ex. 17:6; Num. 20:11; Neh. 9:15; 1 Ne. 17:29; 20:21.
e 1 Ne. 14:30; Mosiah 1:6.
f Hosea 13:4; Acts 4:12; 1 Jn. 3:23 (19–24); 1 Ne. 10:6; 2 Ne. 2:6 (5–8); Mosiah 16:5 (4–5); Alma 12:22 (22–25). TG Jesus Christ, Savior.
21*a* 2 Ne. 27:6.
b Amos 5:15; Alma 46:24 (24–27).
22*a* 2 Ne. 29:11; 33:15 (10–15); 3 Ne. 27:25 (23–27); Ether 4:10 (8–10).
23*a* TG Family, Children, Responsibilities toward.

know that it is by [b]grace that we are
saved, after all we can [c]do.
24 And, notwithstanding we believe in Christ, we [a]keep the law
of Moses, and look forward with
steadfastness unto Christ, until the
law shall be fulfilled.
25 For, for this end was the [a]law
given; wherefore the law hath become [b]dead unto us, and we are
made alive in Christ because of our
faith; yet we keep the law because
of the commandments.
26 And we [a]talk of Christ, we rejoice in Christ, we preach of Christ,
we [b]prophesy of Christ, and we write
according to our prophecies, that
our [c]children may know to what
source they may look for a [d]remis-
sion of their sins.
27 Wherefore, we speak concerning the law that our children may
know the deadness of the law; and
they, by knowing the deadness of
the law, may look forward unto that
life which is in Christ, and know for
what end the law was given. And
after the law is fulfilled in Christ,
that they need not harden their
hearts against him when the law
ought to be done away.
28 And now behold, my people, ye
are a [a]stiffnecked people; wherefore,
I have spoken plainly unto you, that
ye cannot misunderstand. And the
words which I have spoken shall
stand as a [b]testimony against you;
for they are sufficient to [c]teach any
man the [d]right way; for the right
way is to believe in Christ and deny
him not; for by denying him ye also
deny the prophets and the law.
29 And now behold, I say unto you
that the right way is to believe in
Christ, and deny him not; and Christ
is the Holy One of Israel; wherefore
ye must bow down before him, and
[a]worship him with all your [b]might,
mind, and strength, and your whole
soul; and if ye do this ye shall in
nowise be cast out.
30 And, inasmuch as it shall be
expedient, ye must keep the [a]per-
formances and [b]ordinances of God
until the law shall be fulfilled which
was given unto Moses.

CHAPTER 26

Christ will minister to the Nephites—Nephi foresees the destruction of his people—They will speak from the dust—The Gentiles will build up false churches and secret combinations—The Lord forbids men to practice priestcrafts. About 559–545 B.C.

AND after Christ shall have [a]risen
from the dead he shall [b]show himself unto you, my children, and my
beloved brethren; and the words
which he shall speak unto you shall
be the [c]law which ye shall do.
2 For behold, I say unto you that I
have beheld that many generations
shall pass away, and there shall be
great wars and contentions among
my people.
3 And after the Messiah shall come
there shall be [a]signs given unto my
people of his [b]birth, and also of his
[c]death and resurrection; and great
and terrible shall that day be unto
the wicked, for they shall perish;
and they perish because they cast

23*b* Ps. 130:4 (3–4); Rom. 3:20 (20–24); 7:5; 2 Ne. 2:5 (4–10); Mosiah 13:32; Alma 42:14 (12–16); D&C 20:30; 138:4. TG Grace.
c James 2:24 (14–26). TG Good Works.
24*a* Jacob 4:5.
25*a* TG Law of Moses.
b Rom. 7:4 (4–6); D&C 74:5 (2–6).
26*a* Jacob 4:12; Jarom 1:11; Mosiah 3:13; 16:6.
b Luke 10:24 (23–24).
c TG Family, Children, Responsibilities toward.
d TG Remission of Sins.
28*a* Mosiah 3:14; Alma 9:31. TG Stiffnecked.
b TG Testimony.
c 1 Kgs. 8:36; 2 Ne. 33:10. TG Teaching.
d 1 Sam. 12:23; Isa. 45:19; 2 Pet. 2:15.
29*a* TG Worship.
b Deut. 6:5; Mark 12:30 (29–31).
30*a* 4 Ne. 1:12.
b TG Ordinance.
26 1*a* 3 Ne. 11:8 (1–12). TG Jesus Christ, Resurrection.
b 1 Ne. 11:7; 12:6.
c 3 Ne. 15:9 (2–10).
3*a* 1 Ne. 12:4 (4–6). TG Signs.
b TG Jesus Christ, Birth of.
c TG Jesus Christ, Death of.

out the [d]prophets, and the saints,
and stone them, and slay them;
wherefore the cry of the [e]blood of
the saints shall ascend up to God
from the ground against them.
4 Wherefore, all those who are
proud, and that do wickedly, the
day that cometh shall [a]burn them
up, saith the Lord of Hosts, for they
shall be as stubble.
5 And they that kill the [a]prophets,
and the saints, the depths of the
earth shall [b]swallow them up, saith
the Lord of Hosts; and [c]mountains
shall cover them, and whirlwinds
shall carry them away, and buildings shall fall upon them and crush
them to pieces and grind them to
powder.
6 And they shall be visited with
thunderings, and lightnings, and
earthquakes, and all manner of destructions, for the [a]fire of the anger
of the Lord shall be kindled against
them, and they shall be as stubble,
and the day that cometh shall consume them, saith the Lord of Hosts.
7 [a]O the pain, and the anguish
of my soul for the loss of the slain of
my people! For I, Nephi, have seen
it, and it well nigh consumeth me
before the presence of the Lord;
but I must cry unto my God: Thy
ways are [b]just.
8 But behold, the righteous that
hearken unto the words of the prophets, and destroy them not, but look
forward unto Christ with [a]steadfast-
ness for the signs which are given,
notwithstanding all [b]persecution—
behold, they are they which shall
[c]not perish.
9 But the Son of Righteousness
shall [a]appear unto them; and he
shall [b]heal them, and they shall have
[c]peace with him, until [d]three generations shall have passed away, and
many of the [e]fourth generation shall
have passed away in righteousness.
10 And when these things have
passed away a speedy [a]destruc-
tion cometh unto my people; for,
notwithstanding the pains of my
soul, I have seen it; wherefore, I
know that it shall come to pass; and
they sell themselves for naught; for,
for the reward of their pride and
their [b]foolishness they shall reap
destruction; for because they yield
unto the devil and [c]choose works of
[d]darkness rather than light, therefore they must go down to [e]hell.
11 For the Spirit of the Lord will
not always [a]strive with man. And
when the Spirit [b]ceaseth to strive
with man then cometh speedy destruction, and this grieveth my
soul.
12 And as I spake concerning the
[a]convincing of the [b]Jews, that Jesus
is the [c]very Christ, it must needs
be that the Gentiles be convinced
also that Jesus is the Christ, the
[d]Eternal [e]God;
13 And that he [a]manifesteth himself unto all those who believe in

---

3*d* TG Prophets, Rejection of.
e Gen. 4:10; 2 Ne. 28:10; Morm. 8:27.
4*a* 3 Ne. 8:14 (14–24); 9:3 (3–9).
5*a* Ps. 105:15.
b Num. 16:32; 1 Ne. 19:11; 3 Ne. 10:14.
c Hosea 10:8; Alma 12:14.
6*a* 3 Ne. 8:8; 9:3–11.
7*a* Morm. 6:17 (17–22).
b Rom. 3:5; Alma 42:1 (1, 13–25).
8*a* TG Steadfastness.
b TG Persecution.
c 3 Ne. 10:12 (12–13).
9*a* Alma 16:20.
b John 12:40; 3 Ne. 9:13 (13–14); 18:32; D&C 112:13.
c TG Peace.
d 1 Ne. 12:11 (11–12); 3 Ne. 27:32 (30–32).
e Alma 45:12 (10–12); Hel. 13:10 (5, 9–10).
10*a* Mosiah 12:8; Alma 45:11 (9–14); Hel. 13:6 (5–6).
b TG Foolishness.
c TG Agency.
d Job 38:15; John 3:19.
e Job 24:24 (17–24). TG Hell.
11*a* Gen. 6:3; Ether 2:15; Moses 8:17.
b TG Holy Ghost, Loss of.
12*a* 2 Ne. 25:18.
b 2 Ne. 30:7 (7–8); Morm. 5:14 (12–14); D&C 19:27. TG Israel, Judah, People of.
c Morm. 3:21.
d 2 Ne. 19:6; Mosiah 3:5; Alma 11:39 (38–39, 44); Moro. 7:22; 8:18.
e 1 Ne. 19:10 (7, 10); 2 Ne. 10:3; Mosiah 7:27; 27:31 (30–31); 3 Ne. 11:14.
13*a* TG God, Access to.

him, by the power of the [b]Holy
Ghost; yea, unto every nation, kindred, tongue, and people, working
mighty [c]miracles, signs, and wonders, among the children of men
according to their [d]faith.
14 But behold, I prophesy unto
you concerning the [a]last days; concerning the days when the Lord
God shall [b]bring these things forth
unto the children of men.
15 After my seed and the seed of
my brethren shall have [a]dwindled
in unbelief, and shall have been
smitten by the Gentiles; yea, after
the Lord God shall have [b]camped
against them round about, and shall
have laid siege against them with
a mount, and raised forts against
them; and after they shall have been
brought down low in the dust, even
that they are not, yet the words of
the righteous shall be written, and
the [c]prayers of the faithful shall
be heard, and all those who have
[d]dwindled in unbelief shall not be
forgotten.
16 For those who shall be destroyed
shall [a]speak unto them out of the
ground, and their speech shall be
low out of the dust, and their voice
shall be as one that hath a familiar spirit; for the Lord God will
give unto him power, that he may
whisper concerning them, even as
it were out of the ground; and their
speech shall whisper out of the dust.
17 For thus saith the Lord God:
They shall [a]write the things which
shall be done among them, and
they shall be written and [b]sealed
up in a book, and those who have
dwindled in [c]unbelief shall not
have them, for they [d]seek to destroy
the things of God.
18 Wherefore, as those who have
been destroyed have been destroyed
speedily; and the multitude of their
[a]terrible ones shall be as [b]chaff that
passeth away—yea, thus saith the
Lord God: It shall be at an instant,
suddenly—
19 And it shall come to pass, that
those who have dwindled in unbelief shall be [a]smitten by the hand
of the Gentiles.
20 And the Gentiles are lifted up
in the [a]pride of their eyes, and have
[b]stumbled, because of the greatness
of their [c]stumbling block, that they
have built up many [d]churches; nevertheless, they [e]put down the power
and miracles of God, and preach up
unto themselves their own wisdom
and their own [f]learning, that they
may get gain and [g]grind upon the
face of the poor.
21 And there are many churches
built up which cause [a]envyings,
and [b]strifes, and [c]malice.
22 And there are also secret [a]com-
binations, even as in times of old,
according to the combinations of
the [b]devil, for he is the founder of

13*b* TG Holy Ghost, Mission of.
c TG Miracle.
d TG Faith.
14*a* TG Last Days.
b TG Restoration of the Gospel.
15*a* 1 Ne. 12:22 (22–23); 15:13.
b Isa. 29:3.
c Ex. 3:9 (7, 9); Mosiah 21:15; D&C 109:49.
d D&C 3:18.
16*a* Isa. 29:4; 2 Ne. 3:20; 33:13; Morm. 8:23 (23, 26); 9:30; Moro. 10:27. TG Book of Mormon.
17*a* 1 Ne. 13:40 (39–42); 2 Ne. 27:6 (6–26); 29:12.
b TG Scriptures, Preservation of.
c TG Unbelief.
d Enos 1:14; Morm. 6:6.
18*a* Isa. 29:5.
b Hosea 13:3 (1–4); Morm. 5:16 (16–18).
19*a* 1 Ne. 13:14; 3 Ne. 16:8 (8–9); 20:27 (27–28); Morm. 5:9.
20*a* Prov. 11:2; D&C 38:39. TG Pride.
b 1 Ne. 13:34 (29, 34); 14:1 (1–3). TG Apostasy of the Early Christian Church.
c Ezek. 3:20; 14:4 (3–7).
d 1 Ne. 14:10 (9–10); 22:23; Morm. 8:28 (25–41).
e 2 Ne. 28:5 (4–6); Morm. 9:26 (7–26).
f 1 Tim. 6:20; 2 Ne. 9:28; 28:4 (4, 15); D&C 1:19. TG Learn.
g Isa. 3:15; 2 Ne. 13:15.
21*a* TG Envy.
b Rom. 16:17 (17–18). TG Strife.
c TG Malice.
22*a* TG Secret Combinations.
b 2 Ne. 28:21.

all these things; yea, the founder
of murder, and [c]works of darkness;
yea, and he leadeth them by the
neck with a flaxen cord, until he
bindeth them with his strong cords
forever.
23 For behold, my beloved brethren, I say unto you that the Lord
God worketh not in [a]darkness.
24 He doeth not [a]anything save it
be for the benefit of the world; for
he [b]loveth the world, even that he
layeth down his own life that he may
draw [c]all men unto him. Wherefore,
he commandeth none that they
shall not partake of his salvation.
25 Behold, doth he cry unto any,
saying: Depart from me? Behold,
I say unto you, Nay; but he saith:
[a]Come unto me all ye [b]ends of the
earth, [c]buy milk and honey, without
money and without price.
26 Behold, hath he commanded
any that they should [a]depart out of
the synagogues, or out of the houses
of worship? Behold, I say unto you,
Nay.
27 Hath he commanded any that
they should not partake of his [a]sal-
vation? Behold I say unto you, Nay;
but he hath [b]given it free for all
men; and he hath commanded his
people that they should persuade
all men to [c]repentance.
28 Behold, hath the Lord commanded any that they should not
partake of his goodness? Behold I
say unto you, Nay; but [a]all men are
privileged the one [b]like unto the
other, and none are forbidden.
29 He commandeth that there
shall be no [a]priestcrafts; for, behold,
priestcrafts are that men preach
and set [b]themselves up for a light
unto the world, that they may get
[c]gain and [d]praise of the world; but
they seek not the [e]welfare of Zion.
30 Behold, the Lord hath forbidden this thing; wherefore, the Lord
God hath given a commandment
that all men should have [a]charity,
which [b]charity is [c]love. And except
they should have charity they were
nothing. Wherefore, if they should
have charity they would not suffer
the laborer in Zion to perish.
31 But the [a]laborer in [b]Zion shall
labor for Zion; for if they labor for
[c]money they shall perish.
32 And again, the Lord God hath
[a]commanded that men should not
murder; that they should not lie;
that they should not [b]steal; that they
should not take the name of the Lord
their God in [c]vain; that they should
not [d]envy; that they should not have
[e]malice; that they should not contend one with another; that they
should not commit [f]whoredoms;
and that they should do none of
these things; for whoso doeth them
shall perish.
33 For none of these iniquities
come of the Lord; for he doeth that
which is good among the children of
men; and he doeth nothing save it
be plain unto the children of men;
and he [a]inviteth them [b]all to [c]come
unto him and partake of his goodness; and he [d]denieth none that come

22*c* Lev. 19:26.
23*a* Isa. 48:16 (16–18).
24*a* 2 Ne. 2:27; Jacob 5:41; Alma 26:37.
b John 3:16.
c John 12:32; 2 Ne. 9:5.
25*a* 1 Ne. 1:14; Alma 5:34 (33–36); 3 Ne. 9:14 (13–14).
b Mark 16:15–16.
c Isa. 55:1.
26*a* Mark 9:39 (38–40).
27*a* TG Salvation.
b Eph. 2:8.
c TG Repent.
28*a* Rom. 2:11; Alma 13:5.
b 1 Ne. 17:35 (33–35).
29*a* Acts 8:9; Alma 1:12; 3 Ne. 16:10. TG Priestcraft.
b TG Unrighteous Dominion.
c Ezek. 22:27.
d D&C 58:39; 121:35 (34–37).
e Ezek. 34:3.
30*a* TG Charity.
b Moro. 7:47 (47–48).
c TG God, Love of; Love.
31*a* TG Industry.
b TG Zion.
c Jacob 2:18 (17–19); D&C 11:7; 38:39.
32*a* TG Commandments of God; Law of Moses.
b TG Stealing.
c TG Profanity.
d TG Envy.
e TG Malice.
f TG Chastity; Whore.
33*a* Jude 1:3.
b Alma 19:36.
c TG God, Access to.
d Acts 10:28 (9–35, 44). TG Justice.

unto him, black and white, [e]bond
and free, male and female; and he
remembereth the [f]heathen; and all
are alike unto God, both Jew and
Gentile.

CHAPTER 27

Darkness and apostasy will cover the earth in the last days—The Book of Mormon will come forth—Three witnesses will testify of the book—The learned man will say he cannot read the sealed book—The Lord will do a marvelous work and a wonder—Compare Isaiah 29. About 559–545 B.C.

BUT, behold, in the [a]last days, or in
the days of the Gentiles—yea, behold all the nations of the Gentiles
and also the Jews, both those who
shall come upon this land and those
who shall be upon other lands, yea,
even upon all the lands of the earth,
behold, they will be [b]drunken with
iniquity and all manner of abominations—
2 And when that day shall come
they shall be [a]visited of the Lord of
Hosts, with thunder and with earth-
quake, and with a great noise, and
with storm, and with tempest, and
with the [b]flame of devouring fire.
3 And all the [a]nations that [b]fight
against Zion, and that distress her,
shall be as a dream of a night vision;
yea, it shall be unto them, even as unto
a hungry man which dreameth, and
behold he eateth but he awaketh
and his soul is empty; or like unto
a thirsty man which dreameth, and
behold he drinketh but he awaketh
and behold he is faint, and his soul
hath appetite; yea, even so shall the
multitude of all the nations be that
fight against Mount Zion.
4 For behold, all ye that doeth iniquity, stay yourselves and wonder,
for ye shall cry out, and cry; yea, ye
shall be [a]drunken but not with wine,
ye shall stagger but not with strong
drink.
5 For behold, the Lord hath poured
out upon you the spirit of deep
sleep. For behold, ye have closed
your [a]eyes, and ye have [b]rejected the
prophets; and your rulers, and the
seers hath he covered because of
your iniquity.
6 And it shall come to pass that
the Lord God shall bring forth unto
[a]you the words of a [b]book, and they
shall be the words of them which
have slumbered.
7 And behold the book shall be
[a]sealed; and in the book shall be a
[b]revelation from God, from the beginning of the world to the [c]ending
thereof.
8 Wherefore, because of the things
which are [a]sealed up, the things
which are sealed shall not be delivered in the day of the wickedness
and abominations of the people.
Wherefore the book shall be kept
from them.
9 But the book shall be delivered
unto a man, and he shall deliver
the words of the book, which are the
words of those who have slumbered
in the dust, and he shall deliver
these words unto [a]another;
10 But the words which are [a]sealed
he shall not deliver, neither shall he
deliver the book. For the book shall

33*e* Rom. 2:11; 1 Ne. 17:35 (35–40).
f Jonah 4:11 (10–11); 2 Ne. 29:12; Alma 26:37 (27, 37). TG Heathen.
27 1*a* TG Last Days.
b Isa. 29:9. TG Abomination; Iniquity; Wickedness.
2*a* Isa. 29:6 (6–10); Morm. 8:29.
b Isa. 24:6; 66:16; Jacob 6:3; 3 Ne. 25:1.
3*a* Isa. 29:7 (7–8).
b 1 Ne. 22:14. TG Protection, Divine.
4*a* Rev. 17:6 (1–6); 2 Ne. 8:21.
5*a* TG Spiritual Blindness.
b 2 Chr. 24:19; Jer. 26:5; 37:15; Zech. 1:4 (2–5).
6*a* Jarom 1:2; Morm. 5:12 (12–13).
b 2 Ne. 26:17 (16–17); 29:12. TG Book of Mormon.
7*a* Isa. 29:11 (11–12); Ether 3:27. TG Seal.
b Mosiah 8:19; Ether 3:25 (20–28); 4:4.
c Ether 1:2–4; 13:1–13.
8*a* 3 Ne. 26:9 (7–12, 18); Ether 4:5; 5:1; D&C 17:6.
9*a* JS—H 1:64.
10*a* Dan. 12:9; 1 Ne. 14:26; D&C 35:18; JS—H 1:65.

be sealed by the power of God, and
the revelation which was sealed
shall be kept in the book until the
own due time of the Lord, that they
may come forth; for behold, they [b]re-
veal all things from the foundation
of the world unto the end thereof.
11 And the day cometh that the
words of the book which were sealed
shall be read upon the house tops;
and they shall be read by the power
of Christ; and all things shall be
[a]revealed unto the children of men
which ever have been among the
children of men, and which ever will
be even unto the end of the earth.
12 Wherefore, at that day when
the book shall be delivered unto the
man of whom I have spoken, the
book shall be hid from the eyes of
the world, that the eyes of none shall
behold it save it be that [a]three [b]wit-
nesses shall behold it, by the power
of God, besides him to whom the
book shall be delivered; and they
shall testify to the truth of the book
and the things therein.
13 And there is [a]none other which
shall view it, save it be a few according to the will of God, to bear testimony of his word unto the children
of men; for the Lord God hath said
that the words of the faithful should
speak as if it were [b]from the dead.
14 Wherefore, the Lord God will
proceed to bring forth the words
of the book; and in the mouth of
as many witnesses as seemeth him
good will he establish his word; and
wo be unto him that [a]rejecteth the
word of God!
15 But behold, it shall come to
pass that the Lord God shall say
unto him to whom he shall deliver
the book: Take these words which
are not sealed and deliver them to
another, that he may show them
unto the learned, saying: [a]Read this,
I pray thee. And the learned shall
say: Bring hither the book, and I
will read them.
16 And now, because of the glory
of the world and to get [a]gain will
they say this, and not for the glory
of God.
17 And the man shall say: I cannot bring the book, for it is sealed.
18 Then shall the learned say: I
cannot read it.
19 Wherefore it shall come to pass,
that the Lord God will [a]deliver again
the book and the words thereof to
him that is not learned; and the
man that is not learned shall say:
I am not learned.
20 Then shall the Lord God say
unto him: The learned shall not read
them, for they have rejected them,
and I am [a]able to do mine own work;
wherefore thou shalt read the words
which I shall give unto thee.
21 [a]Touch not the things which are
sealed, for I will bring them forth in
mine own due time; for I will show
unto the children of men that I am
able to do mine own work.
22 Wherefore, when thou hast read
the words which I have commanded
thee, and obtained the [a]witnesses
which I have promised unto thee,
then shalt thou seal up the book
again, and hide it up unto me, that
I may preserve the words which
thou hast not read, until I shall see
fit in mine own [b]wisdom to [c]reveal
all things unto the children of men.
23 For behold, I am God; and I am
a God of [a]miracles; and I will show

10*b* Ether 4:15.
TG God, Omniscience of.
11*a* Luke 12:3;
Morm. 5:8;
D&C 121:26–31.
12*a* 2 Ne. 11:3;
Ether 5:3 (2–4);
D&C 5:11 (11, 15); 17:1.
b Deut. 19:15.
13*a* D&C 5:14 (3, 14).
b 2 Ne. 3:19 (19–20);
33:13 (13–15);
Morm. 9:30;
Moro. 10:27.
14*a* 2 Ne. 28:29 (29–30);
Ether 4:8.
15*a* Isa. 29:11.
16*a* TG Priestcraft.
19*a* Isa. 29:12.
20*a* Ex. 4:11 (11–12);
Jer. 1:7 (7–9).
21*a* Ether 5:1.
22*a* TG Witness.
b TG God, Wisdom of.
c Ether 4:7 (6–7).
TG Mysteries of
Godliness.
23*a* TG Marvelous;
Miracle.

unto the [b]world that I am the same
yesterday, today, and forever; and I
[c]work not among the children of men
save it be [d]according to their faith.
24 And again it shall come to pass
that the Lord shall say unto him
that shall read the words that shall
be delivered him:
25 [a]Forasmuch as this people draw
near unto me with their mouth,
and with their lips do [b]honor me,
but have removed their [c]hearts far
from me, and their fear towards me
is taught by the [d]precepts of men—
26 Therefore, I will proceed to do
a [a]marvelous work among this
people, yea, a [b]marvelous work and
a wonder, for the [c]wisdom of their
wise and [d]learned shall perish,
and the [e]understanding of their
[f]prudent shall be hid.
27 And [a]wo unto them that seek
deep to hide their [b]counsel from the
Lord! And their works are in the
[c]dark; and they say: Who seeth us,
and who knoweth us? And they also
say: Surely, your turning of things
upside down shall be esteemed as
the [d]potter's clay. But behold, I will
show unto them, saith the Lord of
Hosts, that I [e]know all their works.
For shall the work say of him that
made it, he made me not? Or shall
the thing framed say of him that
framed it, he had no understanding?
28 But behold, saith the Lord of
Hosts: I will show unto the children
of men that it is yet a very little
while and Lebanon shall be turned
into a fruitful field; and the [a]fruitful
field shall be esteemed as a forest.
29 [a]And in that day shall the [b]deaf
hear the words of the book, and
the eyes of the blind shall see out
of obscurity and out of darkness.
30 And the [a]meek also shall increase, and their [b]joy shall be in the
Lord, and the poor among men shall
rejoice in the Holy One of Israel.
31 For assuredly as the Lord liveth they shall see that the [a]terrible
one is brought to naught, and the
scorner is consumed, and all that
watch for iniquity are cut off;
32 And they that make a man an
[a]offender for a word, and lay a snare
for him that reproveth in the [b]gate,
and [c]turn aside the just for a thing
of naught.
33 Therefore, thus saith the Lord,
who redeemed Abraham, concerning the house of Jacob: Jacob shall
[a]not now be ashamed, neither shall
his face now wax pale.
34 But when he [a]seeth his children,
the work of my hands, in the midst
of him, they shall sanctify my name,
and sanctify the Holy One of Jacob,
and shall fear the God of Israel.
35 They also that [a]erred in spirit
shall come to understanding, and they
that murmured shall [b]learn doctrine.

CHAPTER 28

Many false churches will be built up in the last days—They will teach false, vain, and foolish doctrines—Apostasy will abound because of false teachers—The devil will rage in the hearts of men—He will teach all manner of false doctrines. About 559–545 B.C.

AND now, behold, my brethren, I
have spoken unto you, according

23*b* TG World.
c W of M 1:7.
d Heb. 11; Ether 12:12 (7–22).
25*a* Isa. 29:13 (13–24).
b Matt. 15:8 (7–9). TG Honor; Respect.
c TG Hardheartedness.
d 2 Ne. 28:31.
26*a* 1 Ne. 22:8; 2 Ne. 29:1 (1–2). TG Restoration of the Gospel.
b Isa. 29:14; 2 Ne. 25:17.
c TG Wisdom.
d TG Learn.
e TG Knowledge.
f TG Prudence.
27*a* Isa. 29:15 (15–16).
b TG Conspiracy; Counsel.
c TG Secret Combinations.
d Jer. 18:6.
e TG God, Omniscience of.
28*a* TG Earth, Renewal of.
29*a* Isa. 29:18.
b TG Deaf.
30*a* TG Meek.
b D&C 101:36.
31*a* Isa. 29:20.
32*a* Luke 11:54 (53–54); Acts 22:22. TG Offense.
b Amos 5:10 (7, 10).
c 2 Ne. 28:16.
33*a* TG Israel, Restoration of.
34*a* Isa. 29:23.
35*a* 2 Ne. 28:14; D&C 33:4.
b Dan. 12:4 (4–10).

as the Spirit hath constrained me;
wherefore, I know that they must
surely come to pass.
2 And the things which shall be
written out of the [a]book shall be of
great [b]worth unto the children of
men, and especially unto our seed,
which is a [c]remnant of the house
of Israel.
3 For it shall come to pass in that
day that the [a]churches which are built
up, and not unto the Lord, when the
one shall say unto the other: Behold,
I, I am the Lord's; and the others shall
say: I, I am the Lord's; and thus shall
every one say that hath built up
[b]churches, and not unto the Lord—
4 And they shall contend one with
another; and their priests shall contend one with another, and they
shall teach with their [a]learning,
and deny the [b]Holy Ghost, which
giveth utterance.
5 And they [a]deny the [b]power of
God, the Holy One of Israel; and
they say unto the people: Hearken
unto us, and hear ye our precept;
for behold there is [c]no God today,
for the Lord and the Redeemer hath
done his work, and he hath given
his power unto men;
6 Behold, hearken ye unto my
precept; if they shall say there is a
miracle wrought by the hand of the
Lord, believe it not; for this day he
is not a God of [a]miracles; he hath
done his work.
7 Yea, and there shall be many
which shall say: [a]Eat, drink, and be
merry, for tomorrow we die; and it
shall be well with us.
8 And there shall also be many
which shall say: [a]Eat, drink, and be
[b]merry; nevertheless, fear God—he
will [c]justify in committing a little
[d]sin; yea, [e]lie a little, take the advantage of one because of his words,
dig a [f]pit for thy neighbor; there is
[g]no harm in this; and do all these
things, for tomorrow we die; and if
it so be that we are guilty, God will
beat us with a few stripes, and at
last we shall be saved in the kingdom of God.
9 Yea, and there shall be many
which shall teach after this manner,
[a]false and vain and [b]foolish [c]doc-
trines, and shall be puffed up in
their hearts, and shall seek deep to
hide their counsels from the Lord;
and their works shall be in the dark.
10 And the [a]blood of the saints shall
cry from the ground against them.
11 Yea, they have all gone out of the
[a]way; they have become [b]corrupted.
12 Because of [a]pride, and because
of [b]false teachers, and [c]false doctrine, their churches have become
corrupted, and their churches are
lifted up; because of pride they are
puffed up.
13 They [a]rob the [b]poor because of
their fine sanctuaries; they rob the
poor because of their fine clothing;

---

28 2*a* TG Book of Mormon; Restoration of the Gospel.
b 1 Ne. 13:39 (34–42); 14:5 (1–5); 22:9; 2 Ne. 30:3; 3 Ne. 21:6.
c TG Israel, Remnant of.
3*a* 1 Cor. 1:13 (10–13); 1 Ne. 22:23; 4 Ne. 1:26 (25–29); Morm. 8:28 (28, 32–38).
b TG False Doctrine.
4*a* 2 Ne. 9:28; 26:20.
b 1 Cor. 2:4 (1–9).
5*a* 2 Ne. 26:20; Morm. 9:26 (7–26).
b 2 Tim. 3:5.
c Alma 30:28.
6*a* 3 Ne. 29:7; Morm. 8:26; 9:15 (15–26).
7*a* Prov. 16:25; 1 Cor. 15:32; Alma 30:17 (17–18).
8*a* Isa. 22:13.
b TG Worldliness.
c Morm. 8:31.
d Mal. 2:17.
e D&C 10:25; Moses 4:4. TG Lying.
f Job 6:27; Prov. 26:27; 1 Ne. 14:3; 22:14; D&C 109:25.
g Alma 30:17.
9*a* TG False Doctrine.
b Ezek. 13:3; Hel. 13:29.
c Matt. 15:9; Col. 2:22 (18–22).
10*a* Gen. 4:10; Rev. 6:10 (9–11); 18:24 (22–24); 19:2; 2 Ne. 26:3; Morm. 8:27; Ether 8:22 (22–24); D&C 87:7.
11*a* Hel. 6:31; D&C 132:25 (22–25).
b Morm. 8:28 (28–41); D&C 33:4.
12*a* Prov. 28:25. TG Pride.
b Jer. 23:21 (21–32); 50:6; 3 Ne. 14:15. TG False Prophets.
c TG False Doctrine.
13*a* Ezek. 34:8; Morm. 8:37 (37–41).
b Ezek. 18:12; 2 Ne. 13:14 (14–15); Hel. 4:12 (11–13).

and they persecute the meek and the poor in heart, because in their [c]pride they are puffed up.

14 They wear [a]stiff necks and high heads; yea, and because of pride, and wickedness, and abominations, and [b]whoredoms, they have all [c]gone astray save it be a [d]few, who are the humble followers of Christ; nevertheless, they are [e]led, that in many instances they do [f]err because they are taught by the precepts of men.

15 O the [a]wise, and the learned, and the rich, that are puffed up in the [b]pride of their [c]hearts, and all those who preach [d]false doctrines, and all those who commit [e]whoredoms, and pervert the right way of the Lord, [f]wo, wo, wo be unto them, saith the Lord God Almighty, for they shall be thrust down to hell!

16 Wo unto them that [a]turn aside the just for a thing of naught and [b]revile against that which is good, and say that it is of no worth! For the day shall come that the Lord God will speedily visit the inhabitants of the earth; and in that day that they are [c]fully ripe in iniquity they shall perish.

17 But behold, if the inhabitants of the earth shall repent of their wickedness and abominations they shall not be destroyed, saith the Lord of Hosts.

18 But behold, that great and [a]abominable church, the [b]whore of all the earth, must [c]tumble to the earth, and great must be the fall thereof.

19 For the kingdom of the devil must [a]shake, and they which belong to it must needs be stirred up unto repentance, or the [b]devil will grasp them with his everlasting [c]chains, and they be stirred up to anger, and perish;

20 For behold, at that day shall he [a]rage in the [b]hearts of the children of men, and stir them up to anger against that which is good.

21 And others will he [a]pacify, and lull them away into carnal [b]security, that they will say: All is well in Zion; yea, Zion prospereth, all is well—and thus the [c]devil [d]cheateth their souls, and leadeth them away carefully down to hell.

22 And behold, others he [a]flattereth away, and telleth them there is no [b]hell; and he saith unto them: I am no devil, for there is none—and thus he whispereth in their ears, until he grasps them with his awful [c]chains, from whence there is no deliverance.

23 Yea, they are grasped with death, and hell; and death, and hell, and the devil, and all that have been seized therewith must stand before the throne of God, and be [a]judged according to their works, from whence they must go into the place prepared for them, even a [b]lake of fire and brimstone, which is endless torment.

24 Therefore, wo be unto him that is at [a]ease in Zion!

13*c* Alma 5:53; Morm. 8:36 (36–39).
14*a* Prov. 21:4. TG Stiffnecked.
b TG Whore.
c 2 Ne. 12:5; Mosiah 14:6; Alma 5:37.
d Morm. 8:36.
e 2 Pet. 3:17.
f Matt. 22:29; 2 Ne. 27:35 (34–35); D&C 33:4.
15*a* Prov. 3:7 (5–7); 2 Ne. 15:21.
b TG Pride.
c TG Hardheartedness.
d Matt. 5:19.
e Mosiah 11:2.
f 3 Ne. 29:5 (4–7); Morm. 9:26.
16*a* 2 Ne. 27:32.
b Mal. 2:17. TG Reviling.
c Ether 2:10 (8–11).
18*a* TG Devil, Church of.
b Rev. 19:2.
c 1 Ne. 14:3 (3, 17).
19*a* 1 Ne. 22:23 (22–23).
b Alma 34:35.
c Mosiah 23:12; Alma 12:11. TG Chain.
20*a* Rev. 13:7; 2 Ne. 2:18; D&C 10:27; 76:29.
b Alma 8:9; D&C 10:20.
21*a* Jacob 3:11; Alma 5:7 (6–7); Morm. 8:31.
b TG Apathy.
c 2 Ne. 9:39; 32:8; Alma 30:42 (42, 53).
d Rev. 13:14 (11–18).
22*a* TG Flatter.
b Mal. 2:17.
c 2 Ne. 9:45; Alma 36:18. TG Bondage, Spiritual.
23*a* TG Jesus Christ, Judge.
b Rev. 19:20; 21:8; 2 Ne. 9:16 (8–19, 26); Jacob 6:10.
24*a* Amos 6:1.

25 Wo be unto him that crieth:
All is well!
26 Yea, wo be unto him that [a]heark-
eneth unto the precepts of men, and
denieth the power of God, and the
gift of the Holy Ghost!
27 Yea, wo be unto him that saith:
We have received, and we [a]need
no more!
28 And in fine, wo unto all those
who tremble, and are [a]angry because
of [b]the truth of God! For behold, he
that is built upon the [c]rock [d]receiv-
eth it with gladness; and he that
is built upon a sandy foundation
trembleth lest he shall fall.
29 Wo be unto him that shall say:
We have received the word of God,
and we [a]need [b]no more of the word
of God, for we have enough!
30 For behold, thus saith the Lord
God: I will give unto the children of
men line upon line, [a]precept upon
precept, here a little and there a
little; and blessed are those who
hearken unto my precepts, and lend
an ear unto my counsel, for they
shall learn [b]wisdom; for unto him
that [c]receiveth I will give [d]more; and
from them that shall say, We have
enough, from them shall be taken
away even that which they have.
31 Cursed is he that putteth his
[a]trust in man, or maketh flesh his
arm, or shall hearken unto the [b]pre-
cepts of men, save their precepts
shall be given by the power of the
Holy Ghost.
32 [a]Wo be unto the Gentiles, saith
the Lord God of Hosts! For notwithstanding I shall lengthen out mine
arm unto them from day to day,
they will deny me; nevertheless, I
will be merciful unto them, saith
the Lord God, if they will repent
and [b]come unto me; for mine [c]arm
is lengthened out all the day long,
saith the Lord God of Hosts.

CHAPTER 29

Many Gentiles will reject the Book of Mormon—They will say, We need no more Bible—The Lord speaks to many nations—He will judge the world out of the books which will be written. About 559–545 B.C.

BUT behold, there shall be many—
at that day when I shall proceed to
do a [a]marvelous work among them,
that I may remember my [b]covenants
which I have made unto the children of men, that I may set my hand
again the [c]second time to recover
my people, which are of the house
of Israel;
2 And also, that I may remember
the promises which I have made
unto thee, Nephi, and also unto
thy father, that I would remember
your seed; and that the [a]words
of your seed should proceed forth
out of my mouth unto your seed;
and my words shall [b]hiss forth
unto the [c]ends of the earth, for a
[d]standard unto my people, which
are of the house of Israel;
3 And because my words shall hiss
forth—many of the Gentiles shall
say: A [a]Bible! A Bible! We have

26*a* 2 Ne. 9:29.
27*a* Alma 12:10 (10–11); 3 Ne. 26:10 (9–10); Ether 4:8.
28*a* 2 Ne. 9:40; 33:5. TG Rebellion.
b Matt. 7:25.
c TG Rock.
d TG Teachable.
29*a* 2 Ne. 29:10 (3–10).
b 2 Ne. 27:14; Ether 4:8.
30*a* Prov. 2:9 (9–11); Isa. 28:13 (9–13); D&C 98:12.
b Prov. 14:8. TG Wisdom.
c Luke 8:18.
d Alma 12:10; D&C 50:24.
31*a* D&C 1:19 (19–20). TG Trust Not in the Arm of Flesh.
b 2 Ne. 27:25.
32*a* 1 Ne. 14:6; 3 Ne. 16:8.
b TG God, Access to.
c 2 Ne. 19:17 (17–21); Jacob 5:47; 6:4; D&C 133:67.
29 1*a* 2 Ne. 27:26. TG Restoration of the Gospel.
b TG Abrahamic Covenant.
c 2 Ne. 6:14; 21:11; 25:17. TG Israel, Gathering of; Israel, Restoration of.
2*a* 2 Ne. 3:21.
b Isa. 5:26; Moro. 10:28.
c 2 Ne. 15:26.
d Ps. 60:4. TG Ensign.
3*a* 1 Ne. 13:24 (23–24). TG Bible; Book of Mormon.

got a Bible, and there cannot be
any more Bible.
4 But thus saith the Lord God: O
fools, they shall have a [a]Bible; and
it shall proceed forth from the [b]Jews,
mine ancient covenant people. And
what [c]thank they the [d]Jews for the
Bible which they receive from them?
Yea, what do the Gentiles mean? Do
they remember the travails, and the
labors, and the pains of the Jews, and
their diligence unto me, in bringing
forth salvation unto the Gentiles?
5 O ye Gentiles, have ye remembered
the Jews, mine ancient covenant
people? Nay; but ye have [a]cursed
them, and have [b]hated them, and
have not sought to recover them. But
behold, I will return all these things
upon your own heads; for I the Lord
have not forgotten my people.
6 Thou fool, that shall say: A [a]Bible,
we have got a Bible, and we need
no more Bible. Have ye obtained
a Bible save it were by the Jews?
7 Know ye not that there are more
[a]nations than one? Know ye not
that I, the Lord your God, have created all men, and that I remember
those who are upon the [b]isles of the
sea; and that I rule in the heavens
above and in the [c]earth beneath;
and I bring forth my [d]word unto the
children of men, yea, even upon all
the nations of the earth?
8 Wherefore murmur ye, because
that ye shall receive more of my
word? Know ye not that the [a]testimony of [b]two nations is a [c]witness
unto you that I am God, that I remember one [d]nation like unto another? Wherefore, I speak the same
words unto one nation like unto
another. And when the two [e]nations
shall run together the testimony of
the two nations shall run together
also.
9 And I do this that I may prove
unto many that I am the [a]same yesterday, today, and forever; and that
I speak forth my [b]words according
to mine own pleasure. And because that I have spoken one [c]word
ye need not suppose that I cannot
speak another; for my [d]work is not
yet finished; neither shall it be until
the end of man, neither from that
time henceforth and forever.
10 Wherefore, because that ye have
a Bible ye need not suppose that
it contains all my [a]words; neither
[b]need ye suppose that I have not
caused more to be written.
11 For I command [a]all men, both
in the east and in the west, and in
the north, and in the south, and
in the islands of the sea, that they
shall [b]write the words which I speak
unto them; for out of the [c]books
which shall be written I will [d]judge
the world, every man according to
their works, according to that which
is written.
12 For behold, I shall speak unto
the [a]Jews and they shall [b]write
it; and I shall also speak unto the

4a Rom. 3:2 (1–3).
b Neh. 1:10; 1 Ne. 13:25 (23–25); D&C 3:16.
c TG Ingratitude; Thanksgiving.
d TG Israel, Judah, People of.
5a Micah 6:16. TG Curse.
b 3 Ne. 29:8. TG Hate.
6a 1 Ne. 13:23, 38.
7a TG Jesus Christ, Creator; Man, Physical Creation of; Nations.
b Isa. 51:5; 1 Ne. 22:4; 2 Ne. 10:8 (8, 20); D&C 133:8.
c Deut. 10:14; 1 Ne. 11:6; D&C 55:1; Moses 6:44.
d D&C 5:6.
8a TG Testimony.
b Ezek. 37:17 (15–20); 1 Ne. 13:39 (38–41); 2 Ne. 3:12; 33:10 (10–11).
c Matt. 18:16.
d 2 Sam. 7:23; Alma 9:20.
e Hosea 1:11.
9a Heb. 13:8.
b TG Word of God; Word of the Lord.
c TG Revelation.
d Moses 1:4.
10a TG Scriptures to Come Forth.
b 2 Ne. 28:29.
11a Alma 29:8.
b 2 Tim. 3:16; Moses 1:40. TG Scriptures, Preservation of; Scriptures, Writing of.
c TG Book of Life.
d 2 Ne. 25:22 (18, 22); 33:14 (11, 14–15). TG Jesus Christ, Judge.
12a 1 Ne. 13:23 (23–29); 2 Ne. 3:12.
b TG Scriptures, Lost.

Nephites and they shall [c]write it;
and I shall also speak unto the
other tribes of the house of Israel,
which I have led away, and they
shall write it; and I shall also speak
unto [d]all nations of the earth and
they shall write it.
13 And it shall come to pass that
the [a]Jews shall have the words of
the Nephites, and the Nephites shall
have the words of the Jews; and the
Nephites and the Jews shall have
the words of the [b]lost tribes of Israel; and the lost tribes of Israel
shall have the words of the Nephites and the Jews.
14 And it shall come to pass that my
people, which are of the [a]house of
Israel, shall be gathered home unto
the [b]lands of their possessions; and
my word also shall be gathered in
[c]one. And I will show unto them that
fight against my word and against
my [d]people, who are of the [e]house
of Israel, that I am God, and that I
[f]covenanted with [g]Abraham that
I would remember his [h]seed [i]forever.

CHAPTER 30

Converted Gentiles will be numbered with the covenant people—Many Lamanites and Jews will believe the word and become delightsome—Israel will be restored and the wicked destroyed. About 559–545 B.C.

AND now behold, my beloved brethren, I would speak unto you; for
I, Nephi, would not suffer that ye
should suppose that ye are more
righteous than the Gentiles shall
be. For behold, except ye shall keep
the commandments of God ye shall
all likewise [a]perish; and because of
the words which have been spoken
ye need not suppose that the Gentiles are utterly destroyed.
2 For behold, I say unto you that
as many of the Gentiles as will repent are the [a]covenant people of
the Lord; and as many of the [b]Jews
as will not repent shall be [c]cast off;
for the Lord [d]covenanteth with none
save it be with them that [e]repent
and believe in his Son, who is the
Holy One of Israel.
3 And now, I would prophesy somewhat more concerning the Jews and
the Gentiles. For after the book of
which I have spoken shall come
forth, and be written unto the Gentiles, and sealed up again unto the
Lord, there shall be many which
shall [a]believe the words which are
written; and [b]they shall carry them
forth unto the [c]remnant of our seed.
4 And then shall the remnant of
our seed know concerning us, how
that we came out from Jerusalem,
and that they are descendants of
the Jews.
5 And the gospel of Jesus Christ
shall be declared among [a]them;
wherefore, [b]they shall be restored
unto the [c]knowledge of their fathers,
and also to the knowledge of Jesus
Christ, which was had among their
fathers.

12*c* 1 Ne. 13:40 (39–42); 2 Ne. 26:17 (16–17); 27:6 (6–26).
d 2 Ne. 26:33; Alma 29:8.
13*a* Morm. 5:14 (13–14).
b TG Israel, Ten Lost Tribes of.
14*a* Jer. 3:18 (17–19).
b TG Israel, Gathering of; Lands of Inheritance.
c Ezek. 37:17 (16–17).
d 1 Kgs. 8:51; 2 Ne. 3:9; 8:16.
e 1 Ne. 22:9; 2 Ne. 30:7 (7–8).
f Gen. 12:2 (1–3); 1 Ne. 17:40; 3 Ne. 20:27; Abr. 2:9. TG Abrahamic Covenant.
g Micah 7:20 (18–20).
h Ps. 102:28; D&C 132:30; Moses 7:52 (50–53). TG Seed of Abraham.
i Gen. 17:7 (5–7).
30 1*a* Luke 13:3 (1–5).
2*a* Gal. 3:29 (26–29); Abr. 2:10 (9–11).
b Matt. 8:12. TG Israel, Judah, People of.
c Luke 3:9 (3–9); Rom. 9:6; Jacob 5:6.
d Rom. 3:29.
e TG Repent.
3*a* 2 Ne. 28:2; 3 Ne. 16:6 (6–13).
b 1 Ne. 22:9 (5–10); 3 Ne. 5:25 (20–26).
c 2 Ne. 4:7 (7–11); Jacob 1:5. TG Israel, Remnant of.
5*a* 3 Ne. 21:5 (3–7, 24–26); Morm. 5:15.
b D&C 3:20.
c 1 Ne. 15:14; 2 Ne. 3:12; Morm. 7:9 (1, 9–10).

6 And then shall they rejoice; for they shall [a]know that it is a blessing unto them from the hand of God; and their [b]scales of darkness shall begin to fall from their eyes; and many generations shall not pass away among them, save they shall be a pure and a [c]delightsome people.

7 And it shall come to pass that the [a]Jews which are scattered also shall [b]begin to believe in Christ; and they shall begin to gather in upon the face of the land; and as many as shall believe in Christ shall also become a delightsome people.

8 And it shall come to pass that the Lord God shall commence his work among all nations, kindreds, tongues, and people, to bring about the [a]restoration of his people upon the earth.

9 And with righteousness shall the [a]Lord God [b]judge the poor, and reprove with equity for the [c]meek of the earth. And he shall smite the earth with the rod of his mouth; and with the breath of his lips shall he slay the wicked.

10 For the [a]time speedily cometh that the Lord God shall cause a great [b]division among the people, and the wicked will he [c]destroy; and he will [d]spare his people, yea, even if it so be that he must [e]destroy the wicked by fire.

11 And [a]righteousness shall be the girdle of his loins, and faithfulness the girdle of his reins.

12 [a]And then shall the wolf dwell with the lamb; and the leopard shall lie down with the kid, and the calf, and the young lion, and the fatling, together; and a little child shall lead them.

13 And the cow and the bear shall feed; their young ones shall lie down together; and the lion shall eat straw like the ox.

14 And the sucking child shall play on the hole of the asp, and the weaned child shall put his hand on the cockatrice's den.

15 They shall not hurt nor destroy in all my holy [a]mountain; for the earth shall be full of the [b]knowledge of the Lord as the waters cover the sea.

16 Wherefore, the things of [a]all nations shall be made known; yea, all things shall be made [b]known unto the children of men.

17 There is nothing which is secret save it shall be [a]revealed; there is no work of darkness save it shall be made manifest in the light; and there is nothing which is sealed upon the earth save it shall be loosed.

18 Wherefore, all things which have been revealed unto the children of men shall at that [a]day be revealed; and Satan shall have power over the hearts of the children of men [b]no more, for a long time. And now, my beloved brethren, I make an end of my sayings.

CHAPTER 31

Nephi tells why Christ was baptized—Men must follow Christ, be baptized, receive the Holy Ghost, and endure to the end to be saved—Repentance and

---

6*a* Alma 3:14.
b TG Darkness, Spiritual; Spiritual Blindness.
c W of M 1:8; D&C 49:24; 109:65.
7*a* 2 Ne. 29:14 (13–14); 3 Ne. 5:25 (23–26). TG Israel, Judah, People of.
b 2 Ne. 25:16 (16–17).
8*a* TG Israel, Restoration of; Millennium, Preparing a People for.
9*a* Isa. 11:4 (4–9).
b Ps. 19:9; 2 Ne. 9:15.
c TG Meek.
10*a* Jacob 5:29; 6:2. TG Last Days.
b D&C 63:54.
c Ps. 73:17 (3–17); D&C 29:17; JS—M 1:55.
d 1 Ne. 22:17 (15–22); 3 Ne. 22:13 (13–17); Moses 7:61.
e 1 Ne. 22:23 (15–17, 23); Jacob 5:69. TG Earth, Cleansing of.
11*a* Isa. 11:5 (5–9). TG Righteousness.
12*a* Isa. 65:25. TG Earth, Renewal of.
15*a* Joel 2:1.
b TG God, Knowledge about.
16*a* D&C 101:32 (32–35); 121:28 (26–32).
b Ether 4:7 (6–7, 13–17).
17*a* Luke 12:2 (2–3); D&C 1:3 (1–3).
18*a* Acts 3:21.
b Rev. 20:2 (2–3); Ether 8:26.

baptism are the gate to the strait and narrow path—Eternal life comes to those who keep the commandments after baptism. About 559–545 B.C.

AND now I, Nephi, make an end of
my [a]prophesying unto you, my beloved brethren. And I cannot write
but a few things, which I know must
surely come to pass; neither can I
write but a few of the [b]words of my
brother Jacob.
2 Wherefore, the things which I
have written sufficeth me, save it
be a few words which I [a]must speak
concerning the doctrine of Christ;
wherefore, I shall speak unto you
plainly, according to the plainness
of my prophesying.
3 For my soul delighteth in [a]plain-
ness; for after this manner doth the
Lord God work among the children
of men. For the Lord God giveth
light unto the [b]understanding; for
he speaketh unto men according
to their [c]language, unto their understanding.
4 Wherefore, I would that ye
should remember that I have spoken
unto you concerning that [a]prophet
which the Lord showed unto me,
that should baptize the [b]Lamb of
God, which should take away the
sins of the world.
5 And now, if the Lamb of God, he
being [a]holy, should have need to
be [b]baptized by water, to fulfil all
righteousness, O then, how much
more need have we, being unholy,
to be [c]baptized, yea, even by water!
6 And now, I would ask of you, my
beloved brethren, wherein the Lamb
of God did fulfil all righteousness
in being baptized by water?
7 Know ye not that he was holy?
But notwithstanding he being holy,
he showeth unto the children of
men that, according to the flesh he
humbleth himself before the Father,
and witnesseth unto the Father that
he would be [a]obedient unto him in
keeping his commandments.
8 Wherefore, after he was baptized
with water the Holy Ghost descended
upon him in the [a]form of a [b]dove.
9 And again, it showeth unto the
children of men the straitness of the
path, and the narrowness of the [a]gate,
by which they should enter, he having set the [b]example before them.
10 And he said unto the children
of men: [a]Follow thou me. Wherefore, my beloved brethren, can we
[b]follow Jesus save we shall be willing to keep the commandments of
the Father?
11 And the Father said: Repent ye,
repent ye, and be baptized in the
name of my Beloved Son.
12 And also, the voice of the Son
came unto me, saying: He that is
baptized in my name, to him will
the Father [a]give the Holy Ghost,
like unto me; wherefore, [b]follow
me, and do the things which ye
have seen me do.
13 Wherefore, my beloved brethren, I know that if ye shall [a]follow
the Son, with full purpose of heart,
acting no [b]hypocrisy and no de-
ception before God, but with real
[c]intent, repenting of your sins, wit-
nessing unto the Father that ye are
[d]willing to take upon you the [e]name

---

31 1*a* 2 Ne. 25:4 (1–4).
b 2 Ne. 11:1.
2*a* 2 Ne. 11:4 (4–6).
3*a* 2 Ne. 25:7 (7–8); 32:7.
b TG Understanding.
c D&C 1:24.
TG Language.
4*a* 1 Ne. 10:7; 11:27.
b TG Jesus Christ, Lamb of God.
5*a* 1 Jn. 3:3.
b Matt. 3:11 (11–17).
TG Jesus Christ, Baptism of.
c TG Baptism, Essential.
7*a* John 5:30.
TG Obedience.
8*a* 1 Ne. 11:27.
b TG Holy Ghost, Dove, Sign of.
9*a* 2 Ne. 9:41;
3 Ne. 14:14 (13–14);
D&C 22:4; 43:7.
b TG Example.
10*a* Matt. 4:19; 8:22; 9:9.
b Matt. 8:19; Moro. 7:11;
D&C 56:2.
12*a* TG Holy Ghost, Gift of.
b Matt. 16:24 (24–26);
Luke 9:59 (57–62);
John 12:26; 1 Jn. 2:6.
TG God, the Standard of Righteousness.
13*a* TG Jesus Christ, Exemplar.
b TG Hypocrisy.
c TG Integrity;
Sincere.
d TG Agency;
Commitment.
e TG Jesus Christ, Taking the Name of.

of Christ, by [f]baptism—yea, by following your Lord and your Savior down into the water, according to his word, behold, then shall ye receive the Holy Ghost; yea, then cometh the [g]baptism of fire and of the Holy Ghost; and then can ye speak with the [h]tongue of angels, and shout praises unto the Holy One of Israel.
14 But, behold, my beloved brethren, thus came the voice of the Son unto me, saying: After ye have repented of your sins, and witnessed unto the Father that ye are willing to keep my commandments, by the baptism of water, and have received the baptism of fire and of the Holy Ghost, and can speak with a new tongue, yea, even with the tongue of angels, and after this should [a]deny me, it would have been [b]better for you that ye had not known me.
15 And I heard a voice from the Father, saying: Yea, the [a]words of my Beloved are true and faithful. He that [b]endureth to the [c]end, the same shall be saved.
16 And now, my beloved brethren, I know by this that unless a man shall [a]endure to the end, in following the [b]example of the Son of the living God, he cannot be saved.
17 Wherefore, do the things which I have told you I have seen that your Lord and your Redeemer should do; for, for this cause have they been shown unto me, that ye might know the gate by which ye should enter. For the gate by which ye should enter is repentance and [a]baptism by water; and then cometh a [b]remission of your sins by fire and by the Holy Ghost.
18 And then are ye in this [a]strait and narrow [b]path which leads to eternal life; yea, ye have entered in by the gate; ye have done according to the commandments of the Father and the Son; and ye have received the Holy Ghost, which [c]witnesses of the [d]Father and the Son, unto the fulfilling of the promise which he hath made, that if ye entered in by the way ye should receive.
19 And now, my beloved brethren, after ye have gotten into this strait and narrow [a]path, I would ask if all is [b]done? Behold, I say unto you, Nay; for ye have not come thus far save it were by the word of Christ with unshaken [c]faith in him, [d]relying wholly upon the merits of him who is mighty to [e]save.
20 Wherefore, ye must press forward with a [a]steadfastness in Christ, having a perfect brightness of [b]hope, and a [c]love of God and of all men. Wherefore, if ye shall press forward, feasting upon the word of Christ, and [d]endure to the end, behold, thus saith the Father: Ye shall have [e]eternal life.
21 And now, behold, my beloved brethren, this is the [a]way; and there

13*f* Gal. 3:27 (26–27).
g TG Holy Ghost, Baptism of.
h 2 Ne. 32:2 (2–3). TG Holy Ghost, Gifts of.
14*a* Matt. 10:33 (32–33); Rom. 1:16 (15–18); 2 Tim. 2:12 (10–15); Alma 24:30; D&C 101:5 (1–5). TG Holy Ghost, Unpardonable Sin against.
b Heb. 6:4 (4–6); 2 Pet. 2:21.
15*a* D&C 64:31; 66:11.
b Jacob 6:11 (7–11). TG Endure; Steadfastness.
c Alma 5:13.
16*a* Mark 13:13; Alma 38:2; D&C 20:29; 53:7.
b TG Example; Jesus Christ, Exemplar.
17*a* Mosiah 18:10. TG Baptism.
b TG Holy Ghost, Mission of; Remission of Sins.
18*a* 1 Ne. 8:20.
b Prov. 4:18. TG Gate; Path; Way.
c TG Holy Ghost, Mission of; Holy Ghost, Source of Testimony.
d 3 Ne. 28:11; Moses 6:66.
19*a* Hosea 14:9 (8–9).
b Mosiah 4:10.
c TG Faith.
d Moro. 6:4; D&C 3:20; Moses 7:53.
e TG Jesus Christ, Atonement through.
20*a* TG Commitment; Dedication; Perseverance; Steadfastness; Walking with God.
b TG Hope.
c TG God, Love of; Love.
d James 5:8 (7–11); Rev. 2:25 (25–26); 3 Ne. 15:9.
e 1 Jn. 2:25; 5:13 (10–21). TG Objectives.
21*a* Ex. 33:13 (12–13); Acts 4:12; 2 Ne. 9:41; Alma 37:46; D&C 132:22 (22, 25).

is [b]none other way nor [c]name given under heaven whereby man can be saved in the kingdom of God. And now, behold, this is the [d]doctrine of Christ, and the only and true doctrine of the [e]Father, and of the Son, and of the Holy Ghost, which is [f]one God, without end. Amen.

CHAPTER 32

Angels speak by the power of the Holy Ghost—Men must pray and gain knowledge for themselves from the Holy Ghost. About 559–545 B.C.

AND now, behold, my beloved brethren, I suppose that ye ponder somewhat in your hearts concerning that which ye should do after ye have entered in by the way. But, behold, why do ye ponder these things in your hearts?

2 Do ye not remember that I said unto you that after ye had [a]received the Holy Ghost ye could speak with the [b]tongue of angels? And now, how could ye speak with the tongue of angels save it were by the Holy Ghost?

3 [a]Angels speak by the power of the Holy Ghost; wherefore, they speak the words of Christ. Wherefore, I said unto you, [b]feast upon the [c]words of Christ; for behold, the words of Christ will [d]tell you all things what ye should do.

4 Wherefore, now after I have spoken these words, if ye cannot understand them it will be because ye [a]ask not, neither do ye knock; wherefore, ye are not brought into the light, but must perish in the dark.

5 For behold, again I say unto you that if ye will enter in by the way, and receive the Holy Ghost, it will [a]show unto you all things what ye should do.

6 Behold, this is the doctrine of Christ, and there will be no more doctrine given until after he shall [a]manifest himself unto you in the flesh. And when he shall manifest himself unto you in the flesh, the things which he shall say unto you shall ye observe to do.

7 And now I, Nephi, cannot say more; the Spirit stoppeth mine utterance, and I am left to mourn because of the [a]unbelief, and the wickedness, and the ignorance, and the [b]stiffneckedness of men; for they will [c]not search [d]knowledge, nor understand great knowledge, when it is given unto them in [e]plainness, even as plain as word can be.

8 And now, my beloved brethren, I perceive that ye ponder still in your hearts; and it grieveth me that I must speak concerning this thing. For if ye would hearken unto the [a]Spirit which teacheth a man to [b]pray, ye would know that ye must [c]pray; for the [d]evil spirit teacheth not a man to pray, but teacheth him that he must not pray.

9 But behold, I say unto you that ye must [a]pray always, and not faint; that ye must not perform any thing unto the Lord save in the first place ye shall [b]pray unto the Father in

---

21 *b* 2 Ne. 25:20; Mosiah 3:17.
c TG Jesus Christ, Taking the Name of.
d Matt. 7:28; John 7:16.
e TG Godhead.
f Deut. 6:4; Gal. 3:20; 1 Ne. 13:41; 3 Ne. 28:10; Morm. 7:7. TG Unity.
32 2 *a* Alma 36:24; 3 Ne. 9:20.
b 2 Ne. 31:13.
3 *a* TG Angels.
b Jer. 15:16. TG Bread of Life; Study.
c Col. 3:16.
d Ex. 4:15. TG Problem-Solving.
4 *a* TG Ask.
5 *a* 3 Ne. 16:6; Ether 4:11 (11–12); D&C 28:15; Moses 8:24. TG Holy Ghost, Gifts of; Revelation.
6 *a* 1 Ne. 12:6.
7 *a* TG Doubt; Unbelief.
b TG Stiffnecked.
c 2 Pet. 3:5.
d TG Knowledge.
e 2 Ne. 25:7 (7–8); 31:3; Jacob 4:13; Alma 13:23; Ether 12:39.
8 *a* TG Discernment, Spiritual.
b TG Prayer.
c Jacob 3:1.
d 2 Ne. 9:39; 28:21 (20–22); Mosiah 2:32; 4:14; Alma 30:42 (42, 53). TG Spirits, Evil or Unclean.
9 *a* Mosiah 26:39; 3 Ne. 20:1; D&C 75:11.
b 3 Ne. 18:19.

the [c]name of Christ, that he will [d]consecrate thy performance unto thee, that thy performance may be for the [e]welfare of thy soul.

CHAPTER 33

Nephi's words are true—They testify of Christ—Those who believe in Christ will believe Nephi's words, which will stand as a witness before the judgment bar. About 559–545 B.C.

AND now I, Nephi, cannot write all the things which were taught among my people; neither am I [a]mighty in writing, like unto speaking; for when a man [b]speaketh by the power of the Holy Ghost the power of the Holy Ghost carrieth it unto the hearts of the children of men.

2 But behold, there are many that [a]harden their [b]hearts against the [c]Holy Spirit, that it hath no place in them; wherefore, they cast many things away which are written and esteem them as things of naught.

3 But I, Nephi, have written what I have written, and I esteem it as of great [a]worth, and especially unto my people. For I [b]pray continually for them by day, and mine [c]eyes water my pillow by night, because of them; and I cry unto my God in faith, and I know that he will hear my cry.

4 And I know that the Lord God will consecrate my prayers for the gain of my people. And the words which I have written in weakness will be made strong unto them; for it [a]persuadeth them to do good; it maketh known unto them of their fathers; and it speaketh of Jesus, and persuadeth them to believe in him, and to endure to the end, which is life [b]eternal.

5 And it speaketh [a]harshly against sin, according to the [b]plainness of the truth; wherefore, no man will be angry at the words which I have written save he shall be of the spirit of the devil.

6 I [a]glory in [b]plainness; I glory in truth; I glory in my Jesus, for he hath [c]redeemed my soul from hell.

7 I have [a]charity for my people, and great faith in Christ that I shall meet many souls spotless at his judgment-seat.

8 I have charity for the [a]Jew—I say Jew, because I mean them from whence I came.

9 I also have charity for the Gentiles. But behold, for none of [a]these can I hope except they shall be [b]reconciled unto Christ, and enter into the [c]narrow [d]gate, and [e]walk in the [f]strait path which leads to life, and continue in the path until the end of the day of [g]probation.

10 And now, my beloved brethren, and also [a]Jew, and all ye ends of the earth, hearken unto these words and [b]believe in Christ; and if ye believe not in these words believe in Christ.

9*c* Col. 3:17; Moses 5:8.
d Micah 4:13; 2 Ne. 2:2.
e Alma 34:27.
33 1*a* Ether 12:23 (23–27).
b Rom. 10:17 (13–17); D&C 100:8 (7–8). TG Holy Ghost, Gifts of.
2*a* Num. 15:31 (30–31); 1 Ne. 19:7; Jacob 4:14; D&C 3:7 (4–13). TG Hardheartedness.
b TG Spiritual Blindness.
c TG Holy Ghost, Loss of.
3*a* TG Scriptures, Value of.
b Gen. 20:7; Num. 21:7; 1 Sam. 7:5; Jer. 42:4; Enos 1:9 (9–12); W of M 1:8; Moro. 9:22.
c Ps. 6:6; Jer. 13:17; Acts 20:19.
4*a* Ether 8:26; Moro. 7:13 (12–17). TG Motivations.
b TG Eternal Life.
5*a* 1 Ne. 16:2 (1–3); 2 Ne. 9:40; 28:28; Enos 1:23; W of M 1:17.
b 2 Ne. 25:4; Jacob 2:11; 4:13.
6*a* Ps. 44:8 (4–8); D&C 76:61.
b 2 Ne. 31:3.
c Enos 1:27.
7*a* TG Charity.
8*a* TG Israel, Judah, People of. BD Judah, Kingdom of.
9*a* Eph. 3:6 (1–7); 2 Ne. 10:18; 3 Ne. 21:14.
b TG Reconciliation.
c 2 Ne. 9:41; Hel. 3:29 (29–30).
d Matt. 7:14.
e TG Walking with God.
f D&C 132:22.
g TG Probation.
10*a* TG Israel, Judah, People of.
b TG Believe.

And if ye shall [c]believe in Christ ye
will believe in these [d]words, for they
are the [e]words of Christ, and he hath
given them unto me; and they [f]teach
all men that they should do good.
11 And if they are not the words
of Christ, judge ye—for Christ will
show unto you, with [a]power and
great [b]glory, that they are his words,
at the last day; and you and I shall
stand face to face before his bar; and
ye shall know that I have been commanded of him to write these things,
notwithstanding my weakness.
12 And I pray the Father in the
name of Christ that many of us, if
not all, may be saved in his [a]king-
dom at that great and last day.
13 And now, my beloved brethren,
all those who are of the house of
Israel, and all ye ends of the earth,
I speak unto you as the voice of one
[a]crying from the dust: Farewell until that great day shall come.
14 And you that will not partake
of the goodness of God, and respect
the words of the [a]Jews, and also my
[b]words, and the words which shall
proceed forth out of the mouth of
the Lamb of God, behold, I bid you
an everlasting farewell, for these
words shall [c]condemn you at the
last day.
15 For what I seal on earth, shall
be brought against you at the [a]judg-
ment bar; for thus hath the Lord
commanded me, and I must [b]obey.
Amen.

THE BOOK OF JACOB

THE BROTHER OF NEPHI

The words of his preaching unto his brethren. He confoundeth a man who seeketh to overthrow the doctrine of Christ. A few words concerning the history of the people of Nephi.

CHAPTER 1

Jacob and Joseph seek to persuade men to believe in Christ and keep His commandments—Nephi dies—Wickedness prevails among the Nephites. About 544–421 B.C.

FOR behold, it came to pass
that fifty and five years had
passed away from the time
that Lehi left Jerusalem; wherefore, Nephi gave me, Jacob, a [a]com-
mandment concerning the [b]small
plates, upon which these things are
engraven.
2 And he gave me, Jacob, a commandment that I should [a]write upon
[b]these plates a few of the things
which I considered to be most
precious; that I should not touch,
save it were lightly, concerning the
history of this people which are
called the people of Nephi.
3 For he said that the history of his

10*c* John 8:47.
d TG Book of Mormon.
e Isa. 51:16; Moro. 10:27 (27–29); D&C 1:24.
f 1 Kgs. 8:36; 2 Ne. 25:28.
11*a* Ether 5:4 (4–6); Moro. 7:35.
b TG Jesus Christ, Glory of.
12*a* TG Kingdom of God, in Heaven; Kingdom of God, on Earth.
13*a* Isa. 29:4; 2 Ne. 27:13; Morm. 8:26.
14*a* TG Bible.
b TG Book of Mormon.
c 2 Ne. 29:11; W of M 1:11.
15*a* 2 Ne. 25:22; 3 Ne. 27:25 (23–27); Ether 4:10 (8–10).
b TG Obedience.

[JACOB]

1 1*a* Jacob 7:27; Jarom 1:15 (1–2, 15); Omni 1:3.
b 2 Ne. 5:31 (28–33); Jacob 3:13 (13–14).
2*a* TG Scribe; Scriptures, Writing of.
b 1 Ne. 6:6.

people should be engraven upon his
[a]other plates, and that I should [b]pre-
serve these plates and hand them
down unto my seed, from generation
to generation.
4 And if there were preaching
which was [a]sacred, or revelation
which was great, or prophesying,
that I should engraven the [b]heads of
them upon these plates, and touch
upon them as much as it were possible, for Christ's sake, and for the
sake of our people.
5 For because of faith and great
anxiety, it truly had been made
manifest unto us concerning our
people, what things should [a]hap-
pen unto them.
6 And we also had many revelations,
and the spirit of much prophecy;
wherefore, we knew of [a]Christ and
his kingdom, which should come.
7 Wherefore we labored diligently
among our people, that we might
persuade them to [a]come unto Christ,
and partake of the goodness of God,
that they might enter into his [b]rest,
lest by any means he should swear
in his wrath they should not [c]enter
in, as in the [d]provocation in the days
of temptation while the children of
Israel were in the [e]wilderness.
8 Wherefore, we would to God that
we could persuade all men [a]not to
rebel against God, to [b]provoke him
to anger, but that all men would believe in Christ, and view his death,
and suffer his [c]cross and bear the
shame of the world; wherefore, I,
Jacob, take it upon me to fulfil the
commandment of my brother Nephi.
9 Now Nephi began to be old,
and he saw that he must soon [a]die;
wherefore, he [b]anointed a man to be
a king and a ruler over his people
now, according to the reigns of the
[c]kings.
10 The people having loved Nephi
exceedingly, he having been a great
protector for them, having wielded
the [a]sword of Laban in their defence,
and having labored in all his days
for their welfare—
11 Wherefore, the people were desirous to retain in remembrance his
name. And whoso should reign in
his stead were called by the people,
second Nephi, third Nephi, and so
forth, according to the reigns of the
kings; and thus they were called by
the people, let them be of whatever
name they would.
12 And it came to pass that Nephi
died.
13 Now the people which were not
[a]Lamanites were Nephites; nevertheless, they were called Nephites,
Jacobites, Josephites, [b]Zoramites,
Lamanites, Lemuelites, and Ishmaelites.
14 But I, Jacob, shall not hereafter
distinguish [a]them by these names,
but I shall [b]call them Lamanites
that seek to destroy the people of
Nephi, and those who are friendly
to Nephi I shall call [c]Nephites, or
the [d]people of Nephi, according to
the reigns of the kings.

3*a* 2 Ne. 5:33 (29–33); Jacob 3:13 (13–14).
b TG Scriptures, Preservation of.
4*a* TG Sacred.
b IE the dominant, important items.
5*a* See 1 Ne. 12–15. See also 1 Ne. 22:7 (7–8); 2 Ne. 1:9 (5–10); 4:7 (7–11); 30:3 (3–6).
6*a* 1 Ne. 10:4 (4–11); 19:8 (8–14).
7*a* 2 Ne. 9:41 (41, 45, 51); Omni 1:26 (25–26); Moro. 10:32.
b TG Rest.
c Num. 14:23; Deut. 1:35 (35–37); D&C 84:24 (23–25).
d Heb. 3:8.
e Num. 26:65; 1 Ne. 17:31 (23–31).
8*a* TG Loyalty; Rebellion.
b Num. 14:11 (11–12); 1 Kgs. 16:33; 1 Ne. 17:30 (23–31); Alma 12:37 (36–37); Hel. 7:18.
c Luke 14:27.
9*a* Gen. 47:29 (28–29); 2 Ne. 1:14.
b TG Anointing.
c 2 Ne. 6:2; Jarom 1:7 (7, 14).
10*a* 1 Ne. 4:9; 2 Ne. 5:14; W of M 1:13; Mosiah 1:16; D&C 17:1.
13*a* Enos 1:13; Alma 23:17; D&C 3:18.
b 1 Ne. 4:35; Alma 54:23; 4 Ne. 1:36 (36–37).
14*a* W of M 1:16.
b Mosiah 25:12; Alma 2:11.
c 2 Ne. 4:11.
d 2 Ne. 5:9.

15 And now it came to pass that the people of Nephi, under the reign of the second king, began to grow hard in their hearts, and indulge themselves somewhat in wicked practices, such as like unto David of old desiring many [a]wives and [b]concubines, and also Solomon, his son.
16 Yea, and they also began to search much [a]gold and silver, and began to be lifted up somewhat in pride.
17 Wherefore I, Jacob, gave unto them these words as I taught them in the [a]temple, having first obtained mine [b]errand from the Lord.
18 For I, Jacob, and my brother Joseph had been [a]consecrated priests and [b]teachers of this people, by the hand of Nephi.
19 And we did [a]magnify our office unto the Lord, taking upon us the [b]responsibility, answering the sins of the people upon our own heads if we did not [c]teach them the word of God with all diligence; wherefore, by laboring with our might their [d]blood might not come upon our garments; otherwise their blood would come upon our garments, and we would not be found spotless at the last day.

CHAPTER 2

Jacob denounces the love of riches, pride, and unchastity—Men may seek riches to help their fellowmen—The Lord commands that no man among the Nephites may have more than one wife—The Lord delights in the chastity of women. About 544–421 B.C.

THE [a]words which Jacob, the brother of Nephi, spake unto the people of Nephi, after the death of Nephi:
2 Now, my beloved brethren, I, Jacob, according to the [a]responsibility which I am under to God, to [b]magnify mine office with [c]soberness, and that I might [d]rid my garments of your sins, I come up into the temple this day that I might declare unto you the word of God.
3 And ye yourselves know that I have hitherto been diligent in the office of my calling; but I this day am weighed down with much more desire and anxiety for the [a]welfare of your souls than I have hitherto been.
4 For behold, as yet, ye have been obedient unto the word of the Lord, which I have given unto you.
5 But behold, hearken ye unto me, and know that by the help of the all-powerful Creator of heaven and earth I can tell you concerning your [a]thoughts, how that ye are beginning to labor in sin, which sin appeareth very abominable unto me, yea, and abominable unto God.
6 Yea, it grieveth my soul and causeth me to shrink with shame before the presence of my Maker, that I must testify unto you concerning the wickedness of your hearts.
7 And also it grieveth me that I must use so much [a]boldness of speech concerning you, before your wives and your children, many of whose feelings are exceedingly tender and [b]chaste and delicate

15*a* Deut. 17:17; 1 Sam. 25:43 (42–43); D&C 132:38 (38–39).
b 2 Sam. 20:3; 1 Chr. 3:9.
16*a* Mosiah 2:12.
17*a* 2 Ne. 5:16; Alma 16:13; Hel. 3:14 (9, 14); 3 Ne. 11:1. TG Temple.
b TG Called of God.
18*a* 2 Ne. 5:26. TG Delegation of Responsibility; Setting Apart.
b TG Teacher.
19*a* Jacob 2:2; D&C 24:3. TG Leadership; Priesthood, Magnifying Callings within.
b Ezek. 34:10. TG Accountability; Stewardship.
c 1 Sam. 8:9; Moro. 9:6.
d Lev. 20:27; Acts 20:26; 2 Ne. 9:44; Mosiah 2:27; D&C 88:85; 112:33.
2 1*a* 2 Ne. 6:1.
2*a* TG Stewardship.
b Rom. 11:13; Jacob 1:19; D&C 24:3.
c TG Sincere.
d Mosiah 2:28.
3*a* 2 Ne. 6:3; Mosiah 25:11.
5*a* Amos 4:13; Alma 12:3 (3–7); D&C 6:16. TG God, Omniscience of.
7*a* Lev. 19:17; D&C 121:43.
b TG Chastity.

before God, which thing is pleasing unto God;

8 And it supposeth me that they have come up hither to hear the pleasing [a]word of God, yea, the word which healeth the wounded soul.

9 Wherefore, it burdeneth my soul that I should be constrained, because of the strict commandment which I have received from God, to [a]admonish you according to your crimes, to enlarge the wounds of those who are already wounded, instead of consoling and healing their wounds; and those who have not been wounded, instead of feasting upon the pleasing word of God have daggers placed to pierce their souls and wound their delicate minds.

10 But, notwithstanding the greatness of the task, I must do according to the strict [a]commands of God, and tell you concerning your wickedness and abominations, in the presence of the pure in heart, and the broken heart, and under the glance of the [b]piercing eye of the Almighty God.

11 Wherefore, I must tell you the truth according to the [a]plainness of the [b]word of God. For behold, as I inquired of the Lord, thus came the word unto me, saying: Jacob, get thou up into the temple on the morrow, and declare the word which I shall give thee unto this people.

12 And now behold, my brethren, this is the word which I declare unto you, that many of you have begun to search for gold, and for silver, and for all manner of precious [a]ores, in the which this land, which is a [b]land of promise unto you and to your seed, doth abound most plentifully.

13 And the hand of providence hath smiled upon you most pleasingly, that you have obtained many riches; and because some of you have obtained more abundantly than that of your brethren ye are [a]lifted up in the pride of your hearts, and wear stiff necks and high heads because of the costliness of your apparel, and persecute your brethren because ye suppose that ye are better than they.

14 And now, my brethren, do ye suppose that God justifieth you in this thing? Behold, I say unto you, Nay. But he condemneth you, and if ye persist in these things his judgments must speedily come unto you.

15 O that he would show you that he can pierce you, and with one glance of his [a]eye he can smite you to the dust!

16 O that he would rid you from this iniquity and abomination. And, O that ye would listen unto the word of his commands, and let not this [a]pride of your hearts destroy your souls!

17 Think of your [a]brethren like unto yourselves, and be familiar with all and free with your [b]substance, that [c]they may be rich like unto you.

18 But [a]before ye seek for [b]riches, seek ye for the [c]kingdom of God.

19 And after ye have obtained a hope in Christ ye shall obtain riches, if ye seek them; and ye will seek them for the intent to [a]do good—

8*a* Micah 2:7; Alma 31:5; 36:26; Hel. 3:29 (29–30). TG Gospel.
9*a* TG Warn.
10*a* TG Commandments of God.
b 2 Ne. 9:44. TG God, Omniscience of.
11*a* 2 Ne. 25:4; 33:5; Jacob 4:13.
b Jacob 7:5.
12*a* 1 Ne. 18:25; 2 Ne. 5:15 (14–16); Hel. 6:9 (9–11); Ether 9:17; 10:23 (12, 23).
b 1 Ne. 4:14; 17:13 (13–14). TG Promised Lands.
13*a* 2 Kgs. 14:10; Alma 1:32; 31:25; Morm. 8:28 (28, 36–40).
15*a* TG God, Indignation of; God, Omniscience of.
16*a* TG Pride.
17*a* James 5:3 (1–6). TG Love.
b TG Almsgiving; Generosity; Welfare.
c Alma 4:12; 5:55; 4 Ne. 1:3 (3, 24–26).
18*a* Mark 10:24 (17–27).
b 1 Kgs. 3:11 (11–13); Prov. 27:24 (24–27); 2 Ne. 26:31; Alma 39:14; D&C 6:7. TG Worldliness.
c Luke 12:31 (22–31).
19*a* Mosiah 4:26; 3 Ne. 12:42; 4 Ne. 1:3. TG Good Works.

to clothe the naked, and to feed the
hungry, and to liberate the captive,
and administer relief to the sick
and the afflicted.
20 And now, my brethren, I have
spoken unto you concerning pride;
and those of you which have afflicted your neighbor, and persecuted him because ye were proud in
your hearts, of the things which God
hath given you, what say ye of it?
21 Do ye not suppose that such
things are abominable unto him
who created all flesh? And the one
being is as precious in his sight as
the other. And all flesh is of the
dust; and for the selfsame end hath
he created them, that they should
keep his [a]commandments and glorify him forever.
22 And now I make an end of
speaking unto you concerning this
pride. And were it not that I must
speak unto you concerning a grosser
crime, my heart would rejoice exceedingly because of you.
23 But the word of God burdens
me because of your grosser crimes.
For behold, thus saith the Lord: This
people begin to wax in iniquity; they
understand not the scriptures, for
they seek to excuse themselves in
committing [a]whoredoms, because of
the things which were written concerning David, and Solomon his son.
24 Behold, David and [a]Solomon
truly had many [b]wives and concubines, which thing was [c]abominable
before me, saith the Lord.
25 Wherefore, thus saith the Lord,
I have led this people forth out of
the land of Jerusalem, by the power
of mine arm, that I might raise up
unto me a [a]righteous branch from
the fruit of the loins of Joseph.
26 Wherefore, I the Lord God will
not suffer that this people shall do
like unto them of old.
27 Wherefore, my brethren, hear
me, and hearken to the word of
the Lord: For there shall not any
[a]man among you have save it be
[b]one [c]wife; and concubines he shall
have none;
28 For I, the Lord God, delight in
the [a]chastity of women. And [b]whore-
doms are an abomination before
me; thus saith the Lord of Hosts.
29 Wherefore, this people shall
keep my commandments, saith the
Lord of Hosts, or [a]cursed be the land
for their sakes.
30 For if I will, saith the Lord of
Hosts, raise up [a]seed unto me, I will
command my people; otherwise
they shall hearken unto these things.
31 For behold, I, the Lord, have
seen the sorrow, and heard the
mourning of the daughters of my
people in the land of Jerusalem,
yea, and in all the lands of my people, because of the wickedness and
[a]abominations of their [b]husbands.
32 And I will not suffer, saith the
Lord of Hosts, that the cries of the
fair daughters of this people, which
I have led out of the land of Jerusalem, shall come up unto me against
the men of my people, saith the
Lord of Hosts.
33 For they shall not lead away
captive the daughters of my people
because of their tenderness, save I
shall visit them with a sore curse,
even unto destruction; for they
shall not commit [a]whoredoms, like

21*a* D&C 11:20;
Abr. 3:25 (25–26).
23*a* TG Whore.
24*a* 1 Kgs. 11:1;
Neh. 13:26 (25–27).
b Deut. 17:17 (14–17);
2 Sam. 5:13;
D&C 132:39 (38–39).
c Deut. 7:3 (1–4);
1 Kgs. 11:3;
Ezra 9:2 (1–2).
25*a* Gen. 49:22 (22–26);
Ezek. 17:22 (22–24);
Amos 5:15;
2 Ne. 3:5; 14:2;
Alma 26:36.
TG Israel, Joseph,
People of.
27*a* TG Marriage, Husbands.
b Jacob 3:5 (5–7);
D&C 49:16.
TG Marriage, Plural.
c TG Marriage, Wives.
28*a* TG Chastity.
b TG Sexual Immorality;
Whore.
29*a* Ether 2:11 (8–12).
TG Curse.
30*a* Mal. 2:15;
D&C 132:63 (61–66).
31*a* TG Family, Children,
Responsibilities toward.
b TG Marriage, Husbands.
33*a* Ezek. 16:25 (20–34).
TG Sensuality.

unto them of old, saith the Lord
of Hosts.
34 And now behold, my brethren,
ye know that these commandments
were given to our [a]father, Lehi;
wherefore, ye have known them before; and ye have come unto great
condemnation; for ye have done
these things which ye ought not
to have done.
35 Behold, ye have done [a]greater
iniquities than the Lamanites, our
brethren. Ye have broken the hearts
of your tender wives, and lost the
confidence of your children, because of your bad examples before
them; and the sobbings of their
hearts ascend up to God against
you. And because of the [b]strictness
of the word of God, which cometh
down against you, many hearts died,
pierced with deep wounds.

CHAPTER 3

The pure in heart receive the pleasing word of God—Lamanite righteousness exceeds that of the Nephites—Jacob warns against fornication, lasciviousness, and every sin. About 544–421 B.C.

BUT behold, I, Jacob, would speak
unto you that are pure in heart.
Look unto God with firmness of
mind, and [a]pray unto him with exceeding faith, and he will [b]console
you in your [c]afflictions, and he will
plead your cause, and send down
[d]justice upon those who seek your
destruction.
2 O all ye that are pure in heart,
lift up your heads and receive the
pleasing word of God, and feast
upon his [a]love; for ye may, if your
[b]minds are [c]firm, forever.
3 But, wo, wo, unto you that are
not pure in heart, that are filthy
this day before God; for except ye
repent the land is [a]cursed for your
sakes; and the Lamanites, which
are not [b]filthy like unto you, nevertheless they are [c]cursed with a
sore cursing, shall scourge you even
unto destruction.
4 And the time speedily cometh,
that except ye repent they shall possess the land of your inheritance,
and the Lord God will [a]lead away
the righteous out from among you.
5 Behold, the Lamanites your
brethren, whom ye hate because
of their filthiness and the cursing
which hath come upon their skins,
are more righteous than you; for they
have not [a]forgotten the commandment of the Lord, which was given
unto our father—that they should
have save it were [b]one wife, and
[c]concubines they should have none,
and there should not be [d]whoredoms
committed among them.
6 And now, this commandment
they observe to keep; wherefore,
because of this observance, in keeping this commandment, the Lord
God will not destroy them, but will
be [a]merciful unto them; and one
day they shall [b]become a blessed
people.
7 Behold, their [a]husbands [b]love
their [c]wives, and their wives love their
husbands; and their husbands and
their wives love their children;
and their [d]unbelief and their hatred
towards you is because of the iniquity of their fathers; wherefore,

34*a* 1 Ne. 1:16 (16–17).
35*a* Jacob 3:5 (5–7).
b Gen. 2:24.
3 1*a* 2 Ne. 32:8.
b TG Comfort; Consolation; Purity.
c TG Affliction.
d TG Deliver; Protection, Divine.
2*a* TG God, Love of.
b TG Steadfastness.
c Alma 57:27.
3*a* TG Earth, Curse of.
b TG Filthiness.
c 1 Ne. 12:23.
4*a* Omni 1:12 (5–7, 12–13).
5*a* Jacob 2:35.
b Jacob 2:27.
c Mosiah 11:2 (2–14); Ether 10:5.
d TG Chastity.
6*a* 1 Ne. 13:31; 2 Ne. 4:7; 10:18 (18–19); Hel. 15:12 (10–17); Morm. 5:20 (20–21).
b 1 Ne. 15:14 (13–18); 22:8.
7*a* TG Marriage, Husbands.
b TG Family, Love within; Marriage, Continuing Courtship in.
c TG Marriage, Wives.
d D&C 3:18. TG Unbelief.

how much better are you than they,
in the sight of your great Creator?
8 O my brethren, I fear that unless
ye shall repent of your sins that their
skins will be [a]whiter than yours,
when ye shall be brought with them
before the throne of God.
9 Wherefore, a commandment I
give unto you, which is the word
of God, that ye [a]revile no more
against them because of the darkness of their skins; neither shall ye
revile against them because of their
filthiness; but ye shall remember
your own filthiness, and remember
that their filthiness came because
of their fathers.
10 Wherefore, ye shall remember
your [a]children, how that ye have
grieved their hearts because of the
[b]example that ye have set before
them; and also, remember that ye
may, because of your filthiness,
bring your children unto destruction, and their sins be heaped upon
your heads at the last day.
11 O my brethren, hearken unto
my words; [a]arouse the faculties of
your souls; shake yourselves that
ye may [b]awake from the slumber
of death; and loose yourselves from
the pains of [c]hell that ye may not
become [d]angels to the devil, to be
cast into that lake of fire and brimstone which is the second [e]death.
12 And now I, Jacob, spake many
more things unto the people of
Nephi, [a]warning them against [b]for-
nication and [c]lasciviousness, and
every kind of sin, telling them the
awful consequences of them.
13 And a hundredth part of the
proceedings of this people, which
now began to be numerous, cannot be written upon [a]these plates;
but many of their proceedings are
written upon the [b]larger plates, and
their wars, and their contentions,
and the reigns of their kings.
14 [a]These plates are called the
plates of Jacob, and they were [b]made
by the hand of Nephi. And I make
an end of speaking these words.

CHAPTER 4

All the prophets worshiped the Father in the name of Christ—Abraham's offering of Isaac was in similitude of God and His Only Begotten—Men should reconcile themselves to God through the Atonement—The Jews will reject the foundation stone. About 544–421 B.C.

NOW behold, it came to pass that
I, Jacob, having ministered much
unto my people in word, (and I
cannot write but a [a]little of my
words, because of the [b]difficulty of
engraving our words upon plates)
and we know that the things which
we write upon plates must remain;
2 But whatsoever things we write
upon anything save it be upon
[a]plates must perish and vanish away;
but we can write a few words upon
plates, which will give our children, and also our beloved brethren, a small degree of knowledge
concerning us, or concerning their
fathers—
3 Now in this thing we do rejoice;
and we labor diligently to engraven
these words upon plates, hoping
that our beloved brethren and our
children will receive them with
thankful hearts, and look upon
them that they may learn with joy
and not with sorrow, neither with
contempt, concerning their first
[a]parents.

8*a* 3 Ne. 2:15.
9*a* TG Reviling.
10*a* TG Family, Children, Responsibilities toward; Family, Love within.
b TG Example.
11*a* TG Apathy.
b 2 Ne. 28:21; Alma 5:7 (6–7).
c TG Hell.
d 2 Ne. 9:9 (8–9). TG Spirits, Evil or Unclean.
e TG Death, Spiritual, Second.
12*a* TG Warn.
b TG Fornication.
c TG Lust.
13*a* Jacob 1:1 (1–4); 4:1 (1–4).
b Jarom 1:14.
14*a* Jarom 1:2 (1–2).
b 1 Ne. 19:2 (2–3).
4 1*a* 1 Ne. 6:6; Jarom 1:14; Omni 1:30.
b Ether 12:24 (23–26).
2*a* TG Scriptures, Preservation of.
3*a* TG Scriptures, Value of.

4 For, for this intent have we written these things, that they may
know that we [a]knew of Christ, and
we had a hope of his [b]glory many
hundred years before his coming;
and not only we ourselves had a
hope of his glory, but also all the
holy [c]prophets which were before us.
5 Behold, they believed in Christ
and [a]worshiped the Father in his
name, and also we worship the
Father in his [b]name. And for this
intent we [c]keep the [d]law of Moses,
it [e]pointing our souls to him; and
for this cause it is sanctified unto
us for righteousness, even as it was
accounted unto Abraham in the
wilderness to be obedient unto the
commands of God in offering up his
son Isaac, which is a [f]similitude of
God and his [g]Only Begotten Son.
6 Wherefore, we search the prophets, and we have many revelations
and the spirit of [a]prophecy; and
having all these [b]witnesses we obtain a hope, and our faith becometh
unshaken, insomuch that we truly
can [c]command in the [d]name of
Jesus and the very trees obey us,
or the mountains, or the waves of
the sea.
7 Nevertheless, the Lord God
showeth us our [a]weakness that we
may know that it is by his [b]grace,
and his great condescensions unto
the children of men, that we have
power to do these things.
8 Behold, great and marvelous are
the [a]works of the Lord. How [b]un-
searchable are the depths of the
[c]mysteries of him; and it is impossible that man should find out all
his ways. And no man [d]knoweth
of his [e]ways save it be revealed unto
him; wherefore, brethren, despise
not the [f]revelations of God.
9 For behold, by the power of his
[a]word [b]man came upon the face of
the earth, which earth was [c]created
by the power of his word. Wherefore, if God being able to speak and
the world was, and to speak and man
was created, O then, why not able
to command the [d]earth, or the
workmanship of his hands upon
the face of it, according to his will
and pleasure?
10 Wherefore, brethren, seek not to
[a]counsel the Lord, but to take counsel from his hand. For behold, ye
yourselves know that he counseleth
in [b]wisdom, and in justice, and in
great mercy, over all his works.
11 Wherefore, beloved brethren,
be [a]reconciled unto him through
the [b]atonement of Christ, his [c]Only

4*a* TG Jesus Christ, Prophecies about; Testimony.
b TG Jesus Christ, Glory of.
c Luke 24:27; 1 Pet. 1:11; Jacob 7:11 (11–12); Mosiah 13:33 (33–35); D&C 20:26.
5*a* Moses 5:8.
b Gen. 4:26; Hel. 8:16 (16–20). TG Name of the Lord.
c 2 Ne. 25:24; Jacob 7:7; Mosiah 13:30.
d Jarom 1:11; Alma 25:15 (15–16). TG Law of Moses.
e Gal. 3:24; Ether 12:19 (18–19).
f TG Jesus Christ, Types of, in Anticipation.
g Gen. 22:2 (1–14); John 3:16 (16–21); Heb. 11:17. TG Jesus Christ, Divine Sonship.
6*a* TG Prophecy.
b TG Witness.
c 3 Ne. 28:20 (19–22). TG God, Power of.
d Acts 3:6 (6–16); 3 Ne. 8:1.
7*a* Ether 12:27; D&C 66:3.
b TG Grace.
8*a* Ps. 106:2.
b Rom. 11:34 (33–36); Mosiah 4:9.
c D&C 19:10; 76:114 (114–16). TG Mysteries of Godliness.
d Dan. 1:17; 1 Cor. 2:11 (9–16); Alma 26:21 (21–22). TG God, Knowledge about.
e Isa. 55:8 (8–9).
f D&C 3:7.
9*a* Morm. 9:17; Moses 1:32.
b TG Man, Physical Creation of.
c TG Creation; God, Creator; Jesus Christ, Creator.
d Hel. 12:16 (8–17).
10*a* Josh. 9:14; Prov. 15:22; Isa. 45:9; 2 Ne. 9:28–29; Alma 37:12, 37; D&C 3:4, 13; 22:4.
b TG God, Justice of; God, Wisdom of.
11*a* Lev. 6:30. TG Jesus Christ, Mission of; Reconciliation.
b TG Jesus Christ, Atonement through.
c TG Jesus Christ, Divine Sonship.

Begotten Son, and ye may obtain
a [d]resurrection, according to the
[e]power of the resurrection which
is in Christ, and be presented as
the [f]first-fruits of Christ unto God,
having faith, and obtained a good
hope of glory in him before he
manifesteth himself in the flesh.
12 And now, beloved, marvel not
that I tell you these things; for
why not [a]speak of the atonement
of Christ, and attain to a perfect
knowledge of him, as to attain to
the knowledge of a resurrection
and the world to come?
13 Behold, my brethren, he that
prophesieth, let him prophesy to the
understanding of men; for the [a]Spirit
speaketh the [b]truth and lieth not.
Wherefore, it speaketh of things as
they really [c]are, and of things as they
really will be; wherefore, these things
are manifested unto us [d]plainly,
for the salvation of our souls. But
behold, we are not witnesses alone
in these things; for God also [e]spake
them unto prophets of old.
14 But behold, the Jews were a
[a]stiffnecked people; and they [b]de-
spised the words of [c]plainness, and
[d]killed the prophets, and sought for
things that they could not understand. Wherefore, because of their
[e]blindness, which [f]blindness came
by looking beyond the [g]mark, they
must needs fall; for God hath taken
away his plainness from them, and
delivered unto them many things
which they [h]cannot understand, because they desired it. And because
they desired it God hath done it,
that they may [i]stumble.
15 And now I, Jacob, am led on by
the Spirit unto prophesying; for I
perceive by the workings of the Spirit
which is in me, that by the [a]stum-
bling of the [b]Jews they will [c]reject
the [d]stone upon which they might
build and have safe foundation.
16 But behold, according to the
scriptures, this [a]stone shall become
the great, and the last, and the only
sure [b]foundation, upon which the
Jews can build.
17 And now, my beloved, how is
it possible that these, after having
rejected the sure foundation, can
[a]ever build upon it, that it may become the head of their corner?
18 Behold, my beloved brethren,
I will unfold this mystery unto
you; if I do not, by any means, get
shaken from my firmness in the
Spirit, and stumble because of my
over anxiety for you.

CHAPTER 5

Jacob quotes Zenos relative to the allegory of the tame and wild olive trees—They are a likeness of Israel and the Gentiles—The scattering and gathering of Israel are prefigured—Allusions are made to the Nephites and Lamanites and all the house of Israel—The Gentiles will be grafted into Israel—Eventually the vineyard will be burned. About 544–421 B.C.

11*d* TG Resurrection.
e TG God, Power of.
f Mosiah 15:21 (21–23); 18:9; Alma 40:16 (16–21).
12*a* 2 Ne. 25:26.
13*a* TG Holy Ghost, Mission of.
b John 17:17. TG Honesty.
c D&C 93:24.
d Neh. 8:8; Jacob 2:11; Alma 13:23.
e TG Witness of the Father.
14*a* Deut. 9:13; Neh. 9:16; 2 Ne. 25:2. TG Stiffnecked.
b Num. 15:31 (30–31); Ezek. 20:13 (13–16); 1 Ne. 17:30 (30–31); 19:7; 2 Ne. 33:2; D&C 3:7 (4–13).
c 2 Cor. 11:3.
d Zech. 1:4 (2–5).
e Isa. 44:18.
f Rom. 11:25. TG Spiritual Blindness.
g John 7:47 (45–53).
h 2 Ne. 25:1.
i Isa. 57:14.
15*a* Isa. 8:14 (13–15); 1 Cor. 1:23; 2 Ne. 18:14 (13–15).
b TG Israel, Judah, People of.
c Rom. 11:1, 20 (1–36); 1 Ne. 10:11; Morm. 5:14 (14–20).
d TG Cornerstone; Jesus Christ, Prophecies about; Rock.
16*a* Ps. 118:22 (22–23).
b Isa. 28:16 (14–17); Hel. 5:12.
17*a* Matt. 19:30; Jacob 5:63 (62–64); D&C 29:30.

BEHOLD, my brethren, do ye not remember to have read the words of
the prophet [a]Zenos, which he spake
unto the house of Israel, saying:
2 Hearken, O ye house of Israel,
and hear the words of me, a prophet
of the Lord.
3 For behold, thus saith the Lord,
I will liken thee, O house of [a]Israel,
like unto a tame [b]olive tree, which
a man took and nourished in his
[c]vineyard; and it grew, and waxed
old, and began to [d]decay.
4 And it came to pass that the master of the vineyard went forth, and
he saw that his olive tree began to
decay; and he said: I will [a]prune
it, and dig about it, and nourish
it, that perhaps it may shoot forth
young and tender branches, and it
perish not.
5 And it came to pass that he
[a]pruned it, and digged about it, and
nourished it according to his word.
6 And it came to pass that after
many days it began to put forth
somewhat a little, young and tender
branches; but behold, the main [a]top
thereof began to perish.
7 And it came to pass that the master of the vineyard saw it, and he
said unto his [a]servant: It grieveth me
that I should lose this tree; wherefore, go and pluck the branches from
a [b]wild olive tree, and bring them
hither unto me; and we will pluck
off those main branches which are
beginning to wither away, and we
will cast them into the fire that
they may be burned.
8 And behold, saith the Lord of
the vineyard, I take [a]away many of
these young and tender branches,
and I will graft them [b]whitherso-
ever I will; and it mattereth not that
if it so be that the root of this tree
will perish, I may preserve the fruit
thereof unto myself; wherefore, I
will take these young and tender
branches, and I will graft them
whithersoever I will.
9 Take thou the branches of the
wild olive tree, and graft them in, in
the [a]stead thereof; and these which
I have plucked off I will cast into
the fire and burn them, that they
may not cumber the ground of my
vineyard.
10 And it came to pass that the
servant of the Lord of the vineyard did according to the word
of the Lord of the vineyard, and
grafted in the branches of the [a]wild
olive tree.
11 And the Lord of the vineyard
caused that it should be digged
about, and pruned, and nourished,
saying unto his servant: It grieveth
me that I should lose this tree; wherefore, that perhaps I might preserve
the roots thereof that they perish
not, that I might preserve them
unto myself, I have done this thing.
12 Wherefore, go thy way; watch
the tree, and nourish it, according
to my words.
13 And these will I [a]place in the
nethermost part of my vineyard,
whithersoever I will, it mattereth
not unto thee; and I do it that I may
preserve unto myself the natural
branches of the tree; and also, that I
may lay up fruit thereof against the
season, unto myself; for it grieveth
me that I should lose this tree and
the fruit thereof.
14 And it came to pass that the
Lord of the vineyard went his way,
and hid the natural [a]branches of the
tame olive tree in the nethermost

5 1*a* 1 Ne. 19:12 (12, 16); Jacob 6:1. TG Scriptures, Lost.
3*a* TG Israel, Twelve Tribes of.
b Ezek. 36:8 (8–15); Rom. 11:21 (1–36); 1 Ne. 10:12; Jacob 6:1 (1–7). TG Israel, Mission of; Vineyard of the Lord.
c Matt. 21:33 (33–41); D&C 101:44.
d TG Apostasy of Israel.
4*a* TG Prophets, Mission of.
5*a* 2 Kgs. 17:13 (13–18).
6*a* Luke 3:9 (8–9); 2 Ne. 30:2. TG Chief Priest.
7*a* TG Servant.
b Rom. 11:17 (17, 24).
8*a* TG Israel, Scattering of.
b Ezek. 17:22 (4–10, 22).
9*a* Acts 9:15; 14:27; Rom. 1:13; Gal. 3:14.
10*a* TG Gentiles.
13*a* Hosea 8:8; 1 Ne. 10:12.
14*a* TG Israel, Bondage of, in Other Lands.

parts of the vineyard, some in one
and some in another, according to
his will and pleasure.
15 And it came to pass that a long
time passed away, and the Lord
of the vineyard said unto his servant: Come, let us go down into
the vineyard, that we may [a]labor
in the vineyard.
16 And it came to pass that the
Lord of the vineyard, and also the
servant, went down into the vineyard to labor. And it came to pass
that the servant said unto his master:
Behold, look here; behold the tree.
17 And it came to pass that the
Lord of the vineyard looked and beheld the tree in the which the wild
olive branches had been grafted;
and it had sprung forth and begun
to bear [a]fruit. And he beheld that it
was good; and the fruit thereof was
like unto the natural fruit.
18 And he said unto the servant:
Behold, the branches of the wild
tree have taken hold of the mois-
ture of the root thereof, that the
root thereof hath brought forth
much strength; and because of the
much strength of the root thereof
the wild branches have brought
forth tame fruit. Now, if we had not
grafted in these branches, the tree
thereof would have perished. And
now, behold, I shall lay up much
fruit, which the tree thereof hath
brought forth; and the fruit thereof
I shall lay up against the season,
unto mine own self.
19 And it came to pass that the
Lord of the vineyard said unto
the servant: Come, let us go to the
nethermost part of the vineyard,
and behold if the natural branches
of the tree have not brought forth
much fruit also, that I may lay up
of the fruit thereof against the season, unto mine own self.
20 And it came to pass that they
went forth whither the master had
hid the natural branches of the
tree, and he said unto the servant:
Behold these; and he beheld the
[a]first that it had [b]brought forth
much fruit; and he beheld also that
it was good. And he said unto the
servant: Take of the fruit thereof,
and lay it up against the season,
that I may preserve it unto mine
own self; for behold, said he, this
long time have I nourished it, and
it hath brought forth much fruit.
21 And it came to pass that the
servant said unto his master: How
comest thou hither to plant this
tree, or this branch of the tree? For
behold, it was the poorest spot in
all the land of thy vineyard.
22 And the Lord of the vineyard
said unto him: Counsel me not; I
knew that it was a poor spot of
ground; wherefore, I said unto thee,
I have nourished it this long time,
and thou beholdest that it hath
brought forth much fruit.
23 And it came to pass that the
Lord of the vineyard said unto his
servant: Look hither; behold I have
planted another branch of the tree
also; and thou knowest that this spot
of ground was poorer than the first.
But, behold the tree. I have nourished it this long time, and it hath
brought forth much fruit; therefore,
gather it, and lay it up against the
season, that I may preserve it unto
mine own self.
24 And it came to pass that the
Lord of the vineyard said again unto
his servant: Look hither, and behold
another [a]branch also, which I have
planted; behold that I have nourished it also, and it hath brought
forth fruit.
25 And he said unto the servant:
Look hither and behold the last.
Behold, this have I planted in a
[a]good spot of ground; and I have

15*a* TG Millennium, Preparing a People for.
17*a* Matt. 12:33; John 15:16; Gal. 3:9 (7–9, 29); Col. 1:6 (3–8).
20*a* Jacob 5:39.
b TG Israel, Restoration of.
24*a* Ezek. 17:22 (22–24); Alma 16:17.
25*a* Ezek. 17:8; 1 Ne. 2:20; Jacob 5:43.

nourished it this long time, and
only a [b]part of the tree hath brought
forth tame fruit, and the [c]other part
of the tree hath brought forth wild
fruit; behold, I have nourished this
tree like unto the others.
26 And it came to pass that the
Lord of the vineyard said unto the
servant: Pluck off the branches that
have not brought forth good [a]fruit,
and cast them into the fire.
27 But behold, the servant said
unto him: Let us prune it, and dig
about it, and nourish it a little [a]lon-
ger, that perhaps it may bring forth
good fruit unto thee, that thou canst
lay it up against the season.
28 And it came to pass that the
Lord of the vineyard and the servant of the Lord of the vineyard did
nourish all the fruit of the vineyard.
29 And it came to pass that a [a]long
time had passed away, and the Lord
of the vineyard said unto his [b]ser-
vant: Come, let us go down into the
vineyard, that we may labor again
in the vineyard. For behold, the
time draweth near, and the [c]end
soon cometh; wherefore, I must lay
up fruit against the season, unto
mine own self.
30 And it came to pass that the
Lord of the vineyard and the servant went down into the vineyard;
and they came to the tree whose
natural branches had been broken
off, and the wild branches had been
grafted in; and behold all [a]sorts of
fruit did cumber the tree.
31 And it came to pass that the
Lord of the vineyard did [a]taste of
the fruit, every sort according to its
number. And the Lord of the vineyard said: Behold, this long time
have we nourished this tree, and
I have laid up unto myself against
the season much fruit.
32 But behold, this time it hath
brought forth much [a]fruit, and there
is [b]none of it which is good. And
behold, there are all kinds of bad
fruit; and it profiteth me nothing,
notwithstanding all our labor; and
now it grieveth me that I should
lose this tree.
33 And the Lord of the vineyard
said unto the servant: What shall
we do unto the tree, that I may preserve again good fruit thereof unto
mine own self?
34 And the servant said unto his
master: Behold, because thou didst
graft in the branches of the wild
olive tree they have nourished the
roots, that they are alive and they
have not perished; wherefore thou
beholdest that they are yet good.
35 And it came to pass that the
Lord of the vineyard said unto his
servant: The tree profiteth me nothing, and the roots thereof profit me
nothing so long as it shall bring
forth evil fruit.
36 Nevertheless, I know that the
roots are good, and for mine own
purpose I have preserved them; and
because of their much strength they
have hitherto brought forth, from
the wild branches, good fruit.
37 But behold, the wild branches
have grown and have [a]overrun the
roots thereof; and because that
the wild branches have overcome the
roots thereof it hath brought forth
much evil fruit; and because that
it hath brought forth so much evil
fruit thou beholdest that it beginneth to perish; and it will soon become ripened, that it may be cast
into the fire, except we should do
something for it to preserve it.
38 And it came to pass that the
Lord of the vineyard said unto his
servant: Let us go down into the
nethermost parts of the vineyard,
and behold if the natural branches
have also brought forth evil fruit.
39 And it came to pass that they

25*b* Hel. 15:3 (3–4).
c Alma 26:36.
26*a* Matt. 7:19 (15–20); Alma 5:36; D&C 97:7.
27*a* Jacob 5:50 (50–51); Alma 42:4.
29*a* TG Last Days.
b D&C 101:55; 103:21.
c 2 Ne. 30:10; Jacob 6:2.
30*a* TG Apostasy of Israel.
31*a* TG Jesus Christ, Judge; Judgment.
32*a* Hosea 10:1.
b JS—H 1:19.
37*a* D&C 45:30.

went down into the nethermost parts of the vineyard. And it came to pass that they beheld that the fruit of the natural branches had become corrupt also; yea, the [a]first and the second and also the last; and they had all become corrupt.

40 And the [a]wild fruit of the last had overcome that part of the tree which brought forth good fruit, even that the branch had withered away and died.

41 And it came to pass that the Lord of the vineyard wept, and said unto the servant: [a]What could I have done more for my vineyard?

42 Behold, I knew that all the fruit of the vineyard, save it were these, had become [a]corrupted. And now these which have once brought forth good fruit have also become corrupted; and now all the trees of my vineyard are good for nothing save it be to be [b]hewn down and cast into the fire.

43 And behold this last, whose branch hath withered away, I did plant in a [a]good spot of ground; yea, even that which was choice unto me above all other parts of the land of my vineyard.

44 And thou beheldest that I also cut down that which [a]cumbered this spot of ground, that I might plant this tree in the stead thereof.

45 And thou beheldest that a [a]part thereof brought forth good fruit, and a part thereof brought forth wild fruit; and because I plucked not the branches thereof and cast them into the fire, behold, they have overcome the good branch that it hath withered away.

46 And now, behold, notwithstanding all the care which we have taken of my vineyard, the trees thereof have become corrupted, that they bring forth no good [a]fruit; and these I had hoped to preserve, to have laid up fruit thereof against the season, unto mine own self. But, behold, they have become like unto the wild olive tree, and they are of no worth but to be [b]hewn down and cast into the fire; and it grieveth me that I should lose them.

47 But [a]what could I have done more in my vineyard? Have I slackened mine hand, that I have not nourished it? Nay, I have nourished it, and I have digged about it, and I have pruned it, and I have dunged it; and I have [b]stretched forth mine [c]hand almost all the day long, and the [d]end draweth nigh. And it grieveth me that I should hew down all the trees of my vineyard, and cast them into the fire that they should be burned. Who is it that has corrupted my vineyard?

48 And it came to pass that the servant said unto his master: Is it not the [a]loftiness of thy vineyard—have not the branches thereof overcome the roots which are good? And because the branches have overcome the roots thereof, behold they grew faster than the strength of the roots, [b]taking strength unto themselves. Behold, I say, is not this the cause that the trees of thy vineyard have become corrupted?

49 And it came to pass that the Lord of the vineyard said unto the servant: Let us go to and hew down the trees of the vineyard and cast them into the fire, that they shall not cumber the ground of my vineyard, for I have done all. What could I have done more for my vineyard?

50 But, behold, the servant said unto the Lord of the vineyard: Spare it a little [a]longer.

39*a* Jacob 5:20 (20, 23, 25).
40*a* Hel. 15:4 (3–4).
41*a* Isa. 5:4; 2 Ne. 2:27; 26:24; Jacob 5:47; Alma 26:37.
42*a* TG Apostasy of Israel.
b Matt. 3:10.
43*a* Ezek. 17:8; Jacob 5:25.
44*a* Moro. 9:23.
45*a* 1 Ne. 15:12 (12–17); 2 Ne. 3:5; 10:1; Alma 46:24 (24–25).
46*a* Luke 3:9.
b Alma 5:52; 3 Ne. 27:11.
47*a* Jacob 5:41 (41, 49).
b Isa. 9:12 (12, 17, 21).
c 2 Ne. 19:17 (17–21); 28:32; Jacob 6:4.
d TG World, End of.
48*a* TG Haughtiness; Pride.
b D&C 121:39. TG Unrighteous Dominion.
50*a* Jacob 5:27.

51 And the Lord said: Yea, I will spare it a little longer, for it grieveth me that I should lose the trees of my vineyard.

52 Wherefore, let us take of the [a]branches of these which I have planted in the nethermost parts of my vineyard, and let us graft them into the tree from whence they came; and let us pluck from the tree those branches whose fruit is most bitter, and graft in the natural branches of the tree in the stead thereof.

53 And this will I do that the tree may not perish, that, perhaps, I may preserve unto myself the roots thereof for mine [a]own purpose.

54 And, behold, the roots of the natural branches of the tree which I planted whithersoever I would are yet alive; wherefore, that I may preserve them also for mine own purpose, I will take of the [a]branches of this tree, and I will [b]graft them in unto them. Yea, I will graft in unto them the branches of their mother tree, that I may preserve the roots also unto mine own self, that when they shall be sufficiently strong perhaps they may bring forth good fruit unto me, and I may yet have glory in the fruit of my vineyard.

55 And it came to pass that they took from the natural tree which had become wild, and grafted in unto the natural trees, which also had become wild.

56 And they also took of the natural trees which had become wild, and [a]grafted into their mother tree.

57 And the Lord of the vineyard said unto the servant: Pluck not the wild branches from the trees, save it be those which are most bitter; and in them ye shall graft according to that which I have said.

58 And we will nourish again the trees of the vineyard, and we will trim up the [a]branches thereof; and we will pluck from the trees those branches which are ripened, that must perish, and cast them into the fire.

59 And this I do that, perhaps, the roots thereof may take strength because of their goodness; and because of the change of the branches, that the good may [a]overcome the evil.

60 And because that I have preserved the natural branches and the roots thereof, and that I have grafted in the natural branches again into their mother tree, and have preserved the roots of their mother tree, that, perhaps, the trees of my vineyard may bring forth again good [a]fruit; and that I may have joy again in the fruit of my vineyard, and, perhaps, that I may rejoice exceedingly that I have preserved the roots and the branches of the first fruit—

61 Wherefore, go to, and call [a]servants, that we may [b]labor diligently with our might in the vineyard, that we may [c]prepare the way, that I may bring forth again the natural fruit, which natural fruit is good and the most precious above all other fruit.

62 Wherefore, let us go to and labor with our might this last time, for behold the end draweth nigh, and this is for the last time that I shall [a]prune my vineyard.

63 Graft in the branches; begin at the [a]last that they may be first, and that the first may be [b]last, and dig about the trees, both old and young, the first and the last; and the last and the first, that all may be nourished once again for the last time.

64 Wherefore, dig about them,

52*a* TG Israel, Gathering of; Israel, Restoration of.
53*a* Ex. 19:6; Isa. 49:6.
54*a* 3 Ne. 21:6 (5–6); Morm. 5:15.
b 1 Ne. 15:16.
56*a* Jer. 24:6.
58*a* Isa. 27:11.
59*a* TG Triumph.
60*a* Isa. 27:6.
61*a* Jacob 6:2.
b D&C 24:19; 39:17; 95:4.
c TG Millennium, Preparing a People for.
62*a* D&C 75:2.
63*a* Matt. 20:16; Mark 10:31; Luke 13:30; 1 Ne. 13:42; Ether 13:12 (10–12).
b Matt. 19:30; Jacob 4:17; D&C 29:30.

and prune them, and dung them
once more, for the last time, for
the end draweth nigh. And if it be
so that these last grafts shall grow,
and bring forth the natural fruit,
then shall ye prepare the way for
them, that they may grow.
65 And as they begin to grow
ye shall [a]clear away the branches
which bring forth bitter fruit, according to the strength of the good
and the size thereof; and ye shall
not clear away the bad thereof all
at once, lest the roots thereof should
be too strong for the graft, and the
graft thereof shall perish, and I lose
the trees of my vineyard.
66 For it grieveth me that I should
lose the trees of my vineyard; wherefore ye shall clear away the bad according as the good shall grow, that
the root and the top may be equal
in strength, until the good shall
overcome the bad, and the bad be
hewn down and cast into the fire,
that they cumber not the ground of
my vineyard; and thus will I sweep
away the bad out of my vineyard.
67 And the branches of the natural tree will I graft in again into
the natural tree;
68 And the branches of the natural tree will I graft into the natural
branches of the tree; and thus will
I bring them together again, that
they shall bring forth the natural
[a]fruit, and they shall be one.
69 And the bad shall be [a]cast away,
yea, even out of all the land of my
vineyard; for behold, only this once
will I prune my vineyard.
70 And it came to pass that the
Lord of the vineyard sent his [a]ser-
vant; and the servant went and did
as the Lord had commanded him,
and brought other [b]servants; and
they were [c]few.
71 And the Lord of the vineyard
said unto them: Go to, and [a]labor
in the vineyard, with your might.
For behold, this is the [b]last time
that I shall [c]nourish my vineyard;
for the end is nigh at hand, and the
season speedily cometh; and if ye
labor with your might with me
ye shall have joy in the fruit which
I shall lay up unto myself against
the time which will soon come.
72 And it came to pass that the
servants did go and labor with their
mights; and the Lord of the vineyard
labored also with them; and they
did obey the commandments of the
Lord of the vineyard in all things.
73 And there began to be the natural fruit again in the vineyard; and
the natural branches began to grow
and thrive exceedingly; and the wild
branches began to be plucked off
and to be cast away; and they did
keep the root and the top thereof
equal, according to the strength
thereof.
74 And thus they labored, with
all diligence, according to the commandments of the Lord of the vineyard, even until the bad had been
cast away out of the vineyard, and
the Lord had preserved unto himself
that the trees had become again the
natural fruit; and they became like
unto [a]one body; and the fruits were
equal; and the Lord of the vineyard
had preserved unto himself the natural fruit, which was most precious
unto him from the beginning.
75 And it came to pass that when
the [a]Lord of the vineyard saw that
his fruit was good, and that his
vineyard was no more corrupt, he
called up his servants, and said unto
them: Behold, for this last time have
we nourished my vineyard; and
thou beholdest that I have done
according to my will; and I have
preserved the natural fruit, that it

65*a* D&C 86:6 (6–7).
68*a* TG Israel, Mission of.
69*a* 1 Ne. 22:23 (15–17, 23); 2 Ne. 30:10 (9–10).
70*a* D&C 101:55; 103:21.
b Matt. 9:37 (36–38).
c 1 Ne. 14:12.
71*a* Matt. 21:28; Jacob 6:2 (2–3); D&C 33:3 (3–4).
b D&C 39:17; 43:28 (28–30).
c TG Millennium, Preparing a People for.
74*a* D&C 38:27.
75*a* TG Jesus Christ, Millennial Reign.

is good, even like as it was in the
beginning. And [b]blessed art thou;
for because ye have been diligent in
laboring with me in my vineyard,
and have kept my commandments,
and have brought unto me again
the [c]natural fruit, that my vineyard
is no more corrupted, and the bad
is cast away, behold ye shall have
[d]joy with me because of the fruit
of my vineyard.
76 For behold, for a [a]long time will
I lay up of the fruit of my vineyard
unto mine own self against the season, which speedily cometh; and for
the last time have I nourished my
vineyard, and pruned it, and dug
about it, and dunged it; wherefore
I will lay up unto mine own self of
the fruit, for a long time, according
to that which I have spoken.
77 And when the time cometh that
evil fruit shall again come into my
vineyard, then will I cause the [a]good
and the bad to be gathered; and the
good will I preserve unto myself, and
the bad will I cast away into its own
place. And then cometh the [b]season
and the end; and my vineyard will
I cause to be [c]burned with [d]fire.

CHAPTER 6

The Lord will recover Israel in the last days—The world will be burned with fire—Men must follow Christ to avoid the lake of fire and brimstone. About 544–421 B.C.

AND now, behold, my brethren, as I
said unto you that I would prophesy, behold, this is my prophecy—
that the things which this prophet
[a]Zenos spake, concerning the house
of Israel, in the which he likened
them unto a tame [b]olive tree, must
surely come to pass.
2 And the day that he shall set
his hand again the second time to
[a]recover his people, is the day, yea,
even the last time, that the [b]ser-
vants of the Lord shall go forth in
his [c]power, to [d]nourish and prune
his [e]vineyard; and after that the
[f]end soon cometh.
3 And how [a]blessed are they who
have labored [b]diligently in his vineyard; and how [c]cursed are they who
shall be cast out into their own
place! And the [d]world shall be
[e]burned with fire.
4 And how merciful is our God
unto us, for he remembereth the
house of [a]Israel, both roots and
branches; and he stretches forth his
[b]hands unto them all the day long;
and they are a [c]stiffnecked and a
gainsaying people; but as many as
will not harden their hearts shall
be saved in the kingdom of God.
5 Wherefore, my beloved brethren, I beseech of you in words of
soberness that ye would repent, and
come with full purpose of heart,
and [a]cleave unto God as he cleaveth
unto you. And while his [b]arm of
mercy is extended towards you in

75*b* 1 Ne. 13:37; D&C 21:9.
c TG Israel, Restoration of.
d D&C 6:31; 18:15 (15–16).
76*a* 1 Ne. 22:26.
77*a* D&C 86:7.
b Rev. 20:3 (3–10); D&C 29:22; 43:31 (30–31); 88:111 (110–12).
c TG World, End of.
d Joel 1:19 (19–20); 2 Ne. 6:15 (14–15); Jacob 6:3.
6 1*a* Jacob 5:1; Alma 33:13 (13–15). TG Scriptures, Lost.
b Rom. 11:21 (1–36); 1 Ne. 10:12; Jacob 5:3 (3–77).
2*a* 1 Ne. 22:12 (10–12); D&C 110:11; 137:6. TG Israel, Gathering of; Israel, Restoration of.
b Jacob 5:61.
c 1 Ne. 14:1, 14.
d Jacob 5:71; D&C 101:56.
e Jer. 12:10; D&C 138:56. TG Vineyard of the Lord.
f 2 Ne. 30:10; Jacob 5:29; D&C 43:17 (17–20, 28).
3*a* Jacob 5:71.
b TG Diligence; Perseverance.
c D&C 41:1.
d TG World.
e Isa. 24:6; 2 Ne. 27:2; Jacob 5:77; 3 Ne. 25:1. TG World, End of.
4*a* 2 Sam. 7:24.
b Neh. 9:19 (18–26); 2 Ne. 19:17 (17–21); 28:32; Jacob 5:47.
c TG Stiffnecked.
5*a* Deut. 10:20; Josh. 23:8; 2 Kgs. 18:6; Hel. 4:25; D&C 11:19.
b Isa. 59:16; 2 Ne. 1:15; Alma 5:33; 3 Ne. 9:14.

the light of the day, harden not your hearts.

6 Yea, today, if ye will hear his voice, harden not your hearts; for why will ye [a]die?

7 For behold, after ye have been nourished by the good [a]word of God all the day long, will ye bring forth evil fruit, that ye must be [b]hewn down and cast into the fire?

8 Behold, will ye reject these words? Will ye reject the words of the [a]prophets; and will ye reject all the words which have been spoken concerning Christ, after so many have spoken concerning him; and [b]deny the good word of Christ, and the power of God, and the [c]gift of the Holy Ghost, and quench the Holy Spirit, and make a [d]mock of the great plan of redemption, which hath been laid for you?

9 Know ye not that if ye will do these things, that the power of the redemption and the resurrection, which is in Christ, will bring you to stand with [a]shame and [b]awful [c]guilt before the bar of God?

10 And according to the power of [a]justice, for justice cannot be denied, ye must go away into that [b]lake of fire and brimstone, whose flames are unquenchable, and whose smoke ascendeth up forever and ever, which lake of fire and brimstone is [c]endless [d]torment.

11 O then, my beloved brethren, repent ye, and enter in at the [a]strait gate, and [b]continue in the way which is narrow, until ye shall obtain eternal life.

12 O be [a]wise; what can I say more?

13 Finally, I bid you farewell, until I shall meet you before the [a]pleasing bar of God, which bar striketh the wicked with [b]awful dread and fear. Amen.

CHAPTER 7

Sherem denies Christ, contends with Jacob, demands a sign, and is smitten of God—All of the prophets have spoken of Christ and His Atonement—The Nephites lived out their days as wanderers, born in tribulation, and hated by the Lamanites. About 544–421 B.C.

AND now it came to pass after some years had passed away, there came a man among the people of Nephi, whose name was [a]Sherem.

2 And it came to pass that he began to preach among the people, and to declare unto them that there should be [a]no Christ. And he preached many things which were flattering unto the people; and this he did that he might [b]overthrow the doctrine of Christ.

3 And he labored diligently that he might lead away the hearts of the people, insomuch that he did lead away many hearts; and he knowing that I, Jacob, had faith in Christ who should come, he sought much opportunity that he might come unto me.

4 And he was [a]learned, that he had a perfect knowledge of the language of the people; wherefore, he could use much [b]flattery, and much power of speech, according to the [c]power of the devil.

5 And he had hope to shake me from the faith, notwithstanding the many [a]revelations and the many things which I had seen concerning

6*a* Ezek. 18:28 (26–28, 32).
7*a* Ps. 119:28.
b Alma 5:52; 3 Ne. 27:11 (11–12).
8*a* Jer. 26:5.
b TG Holy Ghost, Loss of.
c TG Holy Ghost, Gift of.
d TG Sacrilege.
9*a* TG Shame.
b Jacob 7:19; Mosiah 15:26.
c TG Guilt; Judgment, the Last.
10*a* TG God, Justice of; Justice.
b Rev. 19:20; 2 Ne. 28:23; Mosiah 3:27. TG Hell.
c Mosiah 2:33; D&C 19:11 (10–12).
d TG Damnation.
11*a* 2 Ne. 9:41.
b 2 Ne. 31:15. TG Commitment.
12*a* Matt. 10:16; Morm. 9:28.
13*a* Moro. 10:34.
b Alma 40:14.
7 1*a* TG False Prophets.
2*a* Alma 21:8; 30:12 (12, 22).
b TG False Doctrine.
4*a* TG Learn.
b TG Flatter.
c TG False Priesthoods.
5*a* 2 Ne. 10:3; 11:3; Jacob 2:11.

these things; for I truly had seen [b]angels, and they had ministered unto me. And also, I had [c]heard the voice of the Lord speaking unto me in very word, from time to time; wherefore, I could not be shaken.

6 And it came to pass that he came unto me, and on this wise did he speak unto me, saying: Brother Jacob, I have sought much opportunity that I might speak unto you; for I have heard and also know that thou goest about much, preaching that which ye call the [a]gospel, or the doctrine of Christ.

7 And ye have led away much of this people that they pervert the right way of God, and [a]keep not the law of Moses which is the right way; and convert the law of Moses into the worship of a being which ye say shall come many hundred years hence. And now behold, I, Sherem, declare unto you that this is [b]blasphemy; for no man knoweth of such things; for he cannot [c]tell of things to come. And after this manner did Sherem contend against me.

8 But behold, the Lord God poured in his [a]Spirit into my soul, insomuch that I did [b]confound him in all his words.

9 And I said unto him: Deniest thou the Christ who shall come? And he said: If there should be a Christ, I would not deny him; but I know that there is no Christ, neither has been, nor ever will be.

10 And I said unto him: Believest thou the scriptures? And he said, Yea.

11 And I said unto him: Then ye do not understand them; for they truly testify of Christ. Behold, I say unto you that none of the [a]prophets have written, nor [b]prophesied, save they have spoken concerning this Christ.

12 And this is not all—it has been made manifest unto me, for I have heard and seen; and it also has been made manifest unto me by the [a]power of the Holy Ghost; wherefore, I know if there should be no atonement made all mankind must be [b]lost.

13 And it came to pass that he said unto me: Show me a [a]sign by this power of the Holy Ghost, in the which ye know so much.

14 And I said unto him: What am I that I should [a]tempt God to show unto thee a sign in the thing which thou knowest to be [b]true? Yet thou wilt deny it, because thou art of the [c]devil. Nevertheless, not my will be done; but if God shall smite thee, let that be a [d]sign unto thee that he has power, both in heaven and in earth; and also, that Christ shall come. And thy will, O Lord, be done, and not mine.

15 And it came to pass that when I, Jacob, had spoken these words, the power of the Lord came upon him, insomuch that he fell to the earth. And it came to pass that he was nourished for the space of many days.

16 And it came to pass that he said unto the people: Gather together on the morrow, for I shall die; wherefore, I desire to speak unto the people before I shall die.

17 And it came to pass that on the morrow the multitude were gathered together; and he spake plainly unto them and denied the things which he had taught them, and confessed the Christ, and the power

---

5*b* 2 Ne. 2:4.
c Ex. 19:9 (9–13).
6*a* 2 Ne. 31:2.
7*a* Jacob 4:5.
b TG Blaspheme.
c Alma 30:13.
8*a* TG God, Spirit of; Holy Ghost, Mission of.
b Ps. 97:7. TG Confound.
11*a* 1 Ne. 10:5; 3 Ne. 20:24 (23–24). TG Jesus Christ, Prophecies about.
b 1 Pet. 1:11; Rev. 19:10; Jacob 4:4; Mosiah 13:33 (33–35); D&C 20:26.
12*a* TG Holy Ghost, Gifts of.
b 2 Ne. 2:21 (10–30).
13*a* John 6:30; Alma 30:43 (43–60); D&C 46:9 (8–9). TG Sign Seekers.
14*a* TG Test.
b Mosiah 12:30; Alma 30:42 (41–42).
c Alma 30:53.
d Num. 26:10; D&C 124:53 (50–53).

of the Holy Ghost, and the ministering of angels.
18 And he spake plainly unto them, that he had been [a]deceived by the power of the [b]devil. And he spake of hell, and of [c]eternity, and of eternal [d]punishment.
19 And he said: I [a]fear lest I have committed the [b]unpardonable sin, for I have lied unto God; for I denied the Christ, and said that I believed the scriptures; and they truly testify of him. And because I have thus lied unto God I greatly fear lest my case shall be [c]awful; but I confess unto God.
20 And it came to pass that when he had said these words he could say no more, and he [a]gave up the [b]ghost.
21 And when the multitude had witnessed that he spake these things as he was about to give up the ghost, they were astonished exceedingly; insomuch that the power of God came down upon them, and they were [a]overcome that they fell to the earth.
22 Now, this thing was pleasing unto me, Jacob, for I had requested it of my Father who was in heaven; for he had heard my cry and answered my prayer.
23 And it came to pass that peace and the [a]love of God was restored again among the people; and they [b]searched the scriptures, and hearkened no more to the words of this wicked man.
24 And it came to pass that many means were devised to [a]reclaim and restore the Lamanites to the knowledge of the truth; but it all was [b]vain, for they delighted in [c]wars and [d]bloodshed, and they had an eternal [e]hatred against us, their brethren. And they sought by the power of their arms to destroy us continually.
25 Wherefore, the people of Nephi did fortify against them with their arms, and with all their might, trusting in the God and [a]rock of their salvation; wherefore, they became as yet, conquerors of their enemies.
26 And it came to pass that I, Jacob, began to be old; and the record of this people being kept on the [a]other plates of Nephi, wherefore, I conclude this record, declaring that I have written according to the best of my knowledge, by saying that the time passed away with us, and also our [b]lives passed away like as it were unto us a [c]dream, we being a [d]lonesome and a solemn people, [e]wanderers, cast out from Jerusalem, born in tribulation, in a wilderness, and hated of our brethren, which caused wars and contentions; wherefore, we did mourn out our days.
27 And I, Jacob, saw that I must soon go down to my grave; wherefore, I said unto my son [a]Enos: Take these [b]plates. And I told him the things which my brother Nephi had [c]commanded me, and he promised obedience unto the commands. And I make an end of my writing upon these plates, which writing has been [d]small; and to the reader I bid farewell, hoping that many of my brethren may read my words. Brethren, adieu.

18*a* Gal. 3:1 (1–4); Alma 30:53 (53, 60).
b TG Deceit; Devil.
c TG Eternity.
d TG Punish.
19*a* TG Despair.
b TG Holy Ghost, Unpardonable Sin against; Sons of Perdition.
c Jacob 6:9; Mosiah 15:26.
20*a* Jer. 28:16 (15–17); Alma 30:59 (12–60).
b Gen. 49:33; Hel. 14:21.
21*a* Alma 19:6 (1–36).
23*a* TG God, Love of.
b Alma 17:2. TG Scriptures, Study of.
24*a* Enos 1:20.
b Enos 1:14.
c Mosiah 1:5; 10:12 (11–18); Alma 3:8; 9:16; D&C 93:39.
d Jarom 1:6; Alma 26:24 (23–25).
e 2 Ne. 5:1 (1–3); Mosiah 28:2. TG Malice.
25*a* TG Rock.
26*a* 1 Ne. 19:1 (1–6); Jarom 1:14 (1, 14–15).
b James 4:14.
c 1 Chr. 29:15; Ps. 144:4.
d Alma 13:23.
e Alma 26:36.
27*a* Enos 1:1.
b Omni 1:3.
c Jacob 1:1 (1–4).
d 1 Ne. 6:3 (1–6); Jarom 1:2 (2, 14).

THE BOOK OF ENOS

Enos prays mightily and gains a remission of his sins—The voice of the Lord comes into his mind, promising salvation for the Lamanites in a future day—The Nephites sought to reclaim the Lamanites—Enos rejoices in his Redeemer. About 420 B.C.

BEHOLD, it came to pass that
I, [a]Enos, knowing my father
that [b]he was a just man—for
he [c]taught me in his language, and
also in the [d]nurture and admoni-
tion of the Lord—and blessed be
the name of my God for it—
2 And I will tell you of the [a]wres-
tle which I had before God, before
I received a [b]remission of my sins.
3 Behold, I went to hunt beasts in
the forests; and the words which I
had often heard my father speak
concerning eternal life, and the [a]joy
of the saints, [b]sunk deep into my
heart.
4 And my soul [a]hungered; and I
[b]kneeled down before my Maker,
and I [c]cried unto him in mighty
[d]prayer and supplication for mine
own soul; and all the day long did
I cry unto him; yea, and when the
night came I did still raise my voice
high that it reached the heavens.
5 And there came a [a]voice unto me,
saying: Enos, thy sins are [b]forgiven
thee, and thou shalt be blessed.
6 And I, Enos, knew that God
[a]could not lie; wherefore, my guilt
was swept away.
7 And I said: Lord, how is it done?
8 And he said unto me: [a]Because
of thy [b]faith in Christ, whom thou
hast never before heard nor seen.
And many years pass away before
he shall manifest himself in the
flesh; wherefore, go to, thy faith
hath made thee [c]whole.
9 Now, it came to pass that when
I had heard these words I began to
feel a [a]desire for the [b]welfare of my
brethren, the Nephites; wherefore,
I did [c]pour out my whole soul unto
God for them.
10 And while I was thus strug-
gling in the spirit, behold, the voice
of the Lord came into my [a]mind
again, saying: I will visit thy brethren according to their diligence in
keeping my commandments. I have
[b]given unto them this land, and it
is a holy land; and I [c]curse it not
save it be for the cause of iniquity;
wherefore, I will visit thy brethren according as I have said; and
their [d]transgressions will I bring
down with sorrow upon their own
heads.
11 And after I, Enos, had heard
these words, my [a]faith began to
be [b]unshaken in the Lord; and I
[c]prayed unto him with many long

---

1 1*a* Jacob 7:27.
b 2 Ne. 2:3 (2–4).
c 1 Ne. 1:1; Mosiah 1:2.
d Eph. 6:4.
2*a* Gen. 32:24 (24–32); Alma 8:10. TG Repent.
b TG Remission of Sins.
3*a* TG Joy.
b 1 Ne. 10:17 (17–19); Alma 36:17. TG Teachable.
4*a* 2 Ne. 9:51; 3 Ne. 12:6. TG Meditation; Motivations.
b TG Reverence.
c Ps. 138:3. TG Perseverance.
d TG Prayer.
5*a* TG Revelation.
b TG Forgive.
6*a* TG God, the Standard of Righteousness.
8*a* Ether 3:13 (12–13).
b TG Faith.
c Matt. 9:22. TG Man, New, Spiritually Reborn; Steadfastness.
9*a* 1 Ne. 8:12; Alma 36:24.
b Alma 19:29. TG Benevolence.
c Num. 21:7; 1 Sam. 1:15; 7:5; Jer. 42:4; 2 Ne. 33:3; Alma 34:26 (26–27).
10*a* TG Inspiration; Mind.
b 1 Ne. 2:20.
c Gen. 8:21 (20–22); Ether 2:9 (7–12).
d TG Transgress.
11*a* TG Faith.
b TG Steadfastness.
c Gen. 20:7; 1 Sam. 7:5; 2 Ne. 33:3; W of M 1:8.

[d]strugglings for my brethren, the
Lamanites.
12 And it came to pass that after
I had [a]prayed and labored with all
diligence, the Lord said unto me: I
will grant unto thee according to
thy [b]desires, because of thy faith.
13 And now behold, this was the
desire which I desired of him—that
if it should so be, that my people,
the Nephites, should fall into transgression, and by any means be [a]de-
stroyed, and the Lamanites should
not be [b]destroyed, that the Lord
God would [c]preserve a record of
my people, the Nephites; even if it
so be by the power of his holy arm,
that it might be [d]brought forth at
some future day unto the Lamanites, that, perhaps, they might be
[e]brought unto salvation—
14 For at the present our strugglings were [a]vain in restoring them
to the true faith. And they swore in
their wrath that, if it were possible,
they would [b]destroy our records
and us, and also all the traditions
of our fathers.
15 Wherefore, I knowing that the
Lord God was able to [a]preserve our
records, I cried unto him continually, for he had said unto me: Whatsoever thing ye shall ask in faith,
believing that ye shall receive in the
name of Christ, ye shall receive it.
16 And I had faith, and I did cry
unto God that he would [a]preserve
the [b]records; and he covenanted
with me that he would [c]bring [d]them
forth unto the Lamanites in his own
due time.
17 And I, Enos, [a]knew it would be
according to the covenant which
he had made; wherefore my soul
did rest.
18 And the Lord said unto me:
Thy fathers have also required of
me this thing; and it shall be done
unto them according to their faith;
for their faith was like unto thine.
19 And now it came to pass that I,
Enos, went about among the people
of Nephi, prophesying of things to
come, and testifying of the things
which I had heard and seen.
20 And I bear record that the
people of Nephi did seek diligently
to [a]restore the Lamanites unto
the true faith in God. But our [b]la-
bors were vain; their [c]hatred was
fixed, and they were led by their
evil nature that they became wild,
and ferocious, and a [d]blood-thirsty
people, full of [e]idolatry and [f]filthi-
ness; feeding upon beasts of prey;
dwelling in [g]tents, and wandering
about in the wilderness with a short
skin girdle about their loins and
their heads shaven; and their skill
was in the [h]bow, and in the cimeter,
and the ax. And many of them did
eat nothing save it was raw meat;
and they were continually seeking
to destroy us.
21 And it came to pass that the
people of Nephi did till the land,
and [a]raise all manner of grain, and
of fruit, and [b]flocks of herds, and
flocks of all manner of cattle of every kind, and goats, and wild goats,
and also many horses.
22 And there were exceedingly

11*d* Eph. 6:18.
12*a* Morm. 5:21; 8:25 (24–26); 9:36 (36–37).
b Ps. 37:4; 1 Ne. 7:12; Hel. 10:5.
13*a* 1 Ne. 15:5; Morm. 6:1.
b Lev. 26:44.
c W of M 1:7 (6–11); Alma 37:2.
d 2 Ne. 3:15; Jacob 1:13; Alma 37:19; Morm. 7:9 (8–10); Ether 12:22; D&C 3:18.
e Alma 9:17; Hel. 15:16.
14*a* Jacob 7:24.
b 2 Ne. 26:17; Morm. 6:6.
15*a* TG Scriptures, Preservation of.
16*a* 3 Ne. 5:14 (13–15); D&C 3:19 (16–20); 10:47 (46–50).
b TG Book of Mormon.
c 2 Ne. 25:8; 27:6; Morm. 5:12.
d 1 Ne. 19:19. TG Israel, Restoration of.
17*a* TG Trust in God.
20*a* Jacob 7:24.
b Moro. 9:6.
c 2 Ne. 5:1. TG Hate.
d Jarom 1:6.
e Mosiah 9:12. TG Idolatry.
f TG Filthiness.
g Gen. 25:27.
h Mosiah 10:8; Alma 3:5 (4–5); 43:20 (18–21).
21*a* 1 Ne. 8:1; Mosiah 9:9.
b 1 Ne. 18:25; Ether 9:19 (18–19).

many [a]prophets among us. And the
people were a [b]stiffnecked people,
hard to understand.
23 And there was nothing save it
was exceeding [a]harshness, [b]preach-
ing and prophesying of wars, and
contentions, and destructions, and
continually [c]reminding them of
death, and the duration of eternity,
and the judgments and the power of
God, and all these things—stirring
them up [d]continually to keep them
in the fear of the Lord. I say there
was nothing short of these things,
and exceedingly great plainness of
speech, would keep them from going down speedily to destruction.
And after this manner do I write
concerning them.
24 And I saw [a]wars between the
Nephites and Lamanites in the
course of my days.
25 And it came to pass that I began to be old, and an hundred and
seventy and nine years had passed
away from the time that our father
Lehi [a]left Jerusalem.
26 And I saw that I [a]must soon
go down to my grave, having been
wrought upon by the power of God
that I must preach and prophesy
unto this people, and declare the
word according to the truth which
is in Christ. And I have declared it
in all my days, and have rejoiced
in it above that of the world.
27 And I soon go to the place of my
[a]rest, which is with my Redeemer;
for I know that in him I shall [b]rest.
And I rejoice in the day when my
[c]mortal shall put on [d]immortality,
and shall stand before him; then
shall I see his face with pleasure,
and he will say unto me: Come unto
me, ye blessed, there is a place prepared for you in the [e]mansions of
my Father. Amen.

THE BOOK OF JAROM

The Nephites keep the law of Moses, look forward to the coming of Christ, and prosper in the land—Many prophets labor to keep the people in the way of truth. About 399–361 B.C.

NOW behold, I, Jarom, write
a few words according to
the commandment of my
father, Enos, that our [a]genealogy
may be kept.
2 And as [a]these plates are [b]small,
and as these things are [c]written
for the intent of the benefit of our
brethren the [d]Lamanites, wherefore,
it must needs be that I write a little;
but I shall not write the things of
my prophesying, nor of my revelations. For what could I write more
than my fathers have written? For
have not they revealed the plan of
salvation? I say unto you, Yea; and
this sufficeth me.
3 Behold, it is expedient that much

22*a* W of M 1:16.
b Jarom 1:3.
23*a* 1 Ne. 16:2 (1–3); 2 Ne. 33:5; W of M 1:17.
b TG Preaching.
c Hel. 12:3.
d Jarom 1:12; Alma 4:19; 31:5.
24*a* 1 Ne. 12:2 (2–3); Morm. 8:7 (7–8). TG War.
25*a* 1 Ne. 2:2 (2–4).
26*a* 1 Cor. 9:16; Ether 12:2. TG Duty.
27*a* TG Rest.
b 2 Ne. 33:6.
c TG Mortality.
d TG Immortality.
e Ps. 65:4; John 14:2 (2–3); Ether 12:32 (32–34); D&C 72:4; 98:18.

[JAROM]
1 1*a* 1 Ne. 3:12; 5:14.
2*a* Jacob 3:14 (13–14); Omni 1:1.
b 1 Ne. 6:3 (1–6); Jacob 7:27.
c TG Scriptures, Writing of.
d 2 Ne. 27:6; Morm. 5:12 (12–13).

should be done among this people,
because of the hardness of their
hearts, and the deafness of their ears,
and the blindness of their minds,
and the [a]stiffness of their necks;
nevertheless, God is exceedingly
merciful unto them, and has not as
yet [b]swept them off from the face
of the land.
4 And there are many among us
who have many [a]revelations, for
they are not all [b]stiffnecked. And as
many as are not stiffnecked and
have faith, have [c]communion with
the Holy Spirit, which maketh manifest unto the children of men, according to their faith.
5 And now, behold, two hundred
years had passed away, and the
people of Nephi had waxed strong
in the land. They observed to [a]keep
the law of Moses and the [b]sabbath
day holy unto the Lord. And they
[c]profaned not; neither did they
[d]blaspheme. And the [e]laws of the
land were exceedingly strict.
6 And they were scattered upon
[a]much of the face of the land, and
the Lamanites also. And they were
exceedingly more [b]numerous than
were they of the Nephites; and they
loved [c]murder and would drink the
[d]blood of beasts.
7 And it came to pass that they
came many times against us, the
Nephites, to battle. But our [a]kings
and our [b]leaders were mighty men
in the faith of the Lord; and they
taught the people the ways of the
Lord; wherefore, we withstood the
Lamanites and swept them away out
of [c]our lands, and began to fortify
our cities, or whatsoever place of
our inheritance.
8 And we multiplied exceedingly,
and spread upon the face of the
land, and became exceedingly rich
in [a]gold, and in silver, and in precious things, and in fine [b]workman-
ship of wood, in buildings, and in
[c]machinery, and also in iron and
copper, and brass and steel, making
all manner of tools of every kind
to till the ground, and [d]weapons of
war—yea, the sharp pointed arrow,
and the quiver, and the dart, and
the javelin, and all preparations
for war.
9 And thus being prepared to meet
the Lamanites, they did not prosper
against us. But the word of the Lord
was verified, which he spake unto
our fathers, saying that: [a]Inasmuch
as ye will keep my commandments
ye shall [b]prosper in the land.
10 And it came to pass that the
prophets of the Lord did threaten
the people of Nephi, according to
the word of God, that if they did
not keep the commandments, but
should fall into transgression, they
should be [a]destroyed from off the
face of the land.
11 Wherefore, the prophets, and
the priests, and the [a]teachers, did
labor diligently, exhorting with all
long-suffering the people to [b]dili-
gence; teaching the [c]law of Moses,
and the intent for which it was
given; persuading them to [d]look
forward unto the Messiah, and believe in him to come [e]as though he

3*a* Enos 1:22 (22–23).
b Ether 2:8 (8–10).
4*a* Alma 26:22; Hel. 11:23; D&C 107:19 (18–19).
b TG Stiffnecked.
c TG Holy Ghost; Revelation.
5*a* 2 Ne. 25:24; Mosiah 2:3; Alma 30:3; 34:14 (13–14).
b Ex. 35:2. TG Sabbath.
c TG Profanity.
d TG Blaspheme.
e Alma 1:1.
6*a* Hel. 11:20 (19–20).
b Alma 2:27.
c Jacob 7:24; Enos 1:20; Alma 26:24 (23–25).
d TG Blood, Eating of.
7*a* 2 Ne. 5:18; 6:2; Jacob 1:9 (9, 11, 15); Mosiah 1:10.
b TG Leadership.
c W of M 1:14.
8*a* 2 Ne. 5:15.
b TG Art.
c TG Skill.
d 2 Ne. 5:14; Mosiah 10:8.
9*a* 2 Ne. 1:20; Omni 1:6.
b Josh. 1:7; Ps. 122:6.
10*a* 1 Ne. 12:19 (19–20); Omni 1:5.
11*a* TG Teacher.
b TG Diligence.
c Jacob 4:5; Alma 25:15 (15–16).
d 2 Ne. 11:4; Ether 12:19 (18–19).
e 2 Ne. 25:26 (24–27); Mosiah 3:13; 16:6.

already was. And after this manner did they teach them.

12 And it came to pass that by so doing they kept them from being [a]destroyed upon the face of the land; for they did [b]prick their hearts with the word, [c]continually stirring them up unto repentance.

13 And it came to pass that two hundred and thirty and eight years had passed away—after the manner of wars, and [a]contentions, and dissensions, for the space of [b]much of the time.

14 And I, Jarom, do not write more, for the plates are [a]small. But behold, my brethren, ye can go to the [b]other plates of Nephi; for behold, upon them the records of our wars are engraven, according to the writings of the [c]kings, or those which they caused to be written.

15 And I deliver these plates into the hands of my son Omni, that they may be kept according to the [a]commandments of my fathers.

THE BOOK OF OMNI

Omni, Amaron, Chemish, Abinadom, and Amaleki, each in turn, keep the records—Mosiah discovers the people of Zarahemla, who came from Jerusalem in the days of Zedekiah—Mosiah is made king over them—The descendants of Mulek at Zarahemla had discovered Coriantumr, the last of the Jaredites—King Benjamin succeeds Mosiah—Men should offer their souls as an offering to Christ. About 323–130 B.C.

BEHOLD, it came to pass that I, Omni, being commanded by my father, Jarom, that I should write somewhat upon [a]these plates, to preserve our genealogy—

2 Wherefore, in my days, I would that ye should know that I fought much with the sword to preserve my people, the Nephites, from falling into the hands of their enemies, the Lamanites. But behold, I of myself [a]am a wicked man, and I have not kept the statutes and the commandments of the Lord as I ought to have done.

3 And it came to pass that two hundred and seventy and six years had passed away, and we had many seasons of peace; and we had many [a]seasons of serious war and bloodshed. Yea, and in fine, two hundred and eighty and two years had passed away, and I had kept these plates according to the [b]commandments of my [c]fathers; and I [d]conferred them upon my son Amaron. And I make an end.

4 And now I, Amaron, write the things whatsoever I write, which are few, in the book of my father.

5 Behold, it came to pass that three hundred and twenty years had passed away, and the more wicked part of the Nephites were [a]destroyed.

6 For the Lord would not suffer, after he had led them out of the land of Jerusalem and kept and preserved them from falling into the hands of their enemies, yea, he would not suffer that the words should not be verified, which he

---

- 12*a* Ether 2:10 (8–10).
- *b* Alma 31:5.
- *c* Enos 1:23.
- 13*a* TG Contention.
- *b* Omni 1:3.
- 14*a* Jacob 4:1 (1–2); Omni 1:30.
- *b* Jacob 7:26 (26–27); W of M 1:3.
- *c* Omni 1:11; W of M 1:10.
- 15*a* Jacob 1:1 (1–4); Omni 1:3.

[OMNI]

- **1** 1*a* Jarom 1:2 (1–2); Omni 1:9.
- 2*a* TG Confession; Honesty; Humility.
- 3*a* Jarom 1:13.
- *b* Jacob 1:1 (1–4); 7:27; Jarom 1:15 (1–2, 15).
- *c* TG Patriarch.
- *d* TG Delegation of Responsibility.
- 5*a* Jarom 1:10.

spake unto our fathers, saying that: [a]Inasmuch as ye will not keep my commandments ye shall not [b]prosper in the land.

7 Wherefore, the Lord did visit them in great judgment; nevertheless, he did spare the righteous that they should not perish, but did deliver them out of the hands of their enemies.

8 And it came to pass that I did deliver the plates unto my brother Chemish.

9 Now I, Chemish, write what few things I write, in the same book with my brother; for behold, I saw the last which he wrote, that he wrote it with his own hand; and he wrote it in the day that he delivered them unto me. And after this manner we keep the [a]records, for it is according to the commandments of our fathers. And I make an end.

10 Behold, I, Abinadom, am the son of Chemish. Behold, it came to pass that I saw much war and contention between my people, the Nephites, and the Lamanites; and I, with my own sword, have taken the lives of many of the Lamanites in the defence of my brethren.

11 And behold, the [a]record of this people is engraven upon plates which is had by the [b]kings, according to the generations; and I know of no revelation save that which has been written, neither prophecy; wherefore, that which is sufficient is written. And I make an end.

12 Behold, I am Amaleki, the son of Abinadom. Behold, I will speak unto you somewhat concerning [a]Mosiah, who was made king over the [b]land of Zarahemla; for behold, he being [c]warned of the Lord that he should [d]flee out of the [e]land of [f]Nephi, and as many as would hearken unto the voice of the Lord should also [g]depart out of the land with him, into the wilderness—

13 And it came to pass that he did according as the Lord had commanded him. And they departed out of the land into the wilderness, as many as would hearken unto the voice of the Lord; and they were led by many preachings and prophesyings. And they were admonished continually by the word of God; and they were led by the power of his [a]arm, through the wilderness until they came down into the land which is called the [b]land of Zarahemla.

14 And they discovered a [a]people, who were called the people of Zarahemla. Now, there was great rejoicing among the people of Zarahemla; and also Zarahemla did rejoice exceedingly, because the Lord had sent the people of Mosiah with the [b]plates of brass which contained the record of the Jews.

15 Behold, it came to pass that Mosiah discovered that the people of [a]Zarahemla came out from Jerusalem at the time that [b]Zedekiah, king of Judah, was carried away captive into Babylon.

16 And they [a]journeyed in the wilderness, and were brought by the hand of the Lord across the great waters, into the land where Mosiah discovered them; and they had dwelt there from that time forth.

17 And at the time that Mosiah discovered them, they had become exceedingly numerous. Nevertheless, they had had many wars and serious contentions, and had fallen by the sword from time to time; and

---

6*a* Jarom 1:9; Mosiah 1:7.
b Deut. 28:29.
9*a* Omni 1:1. TG Record Keeping.
11*a* W of M 1:10.
b Jarom 1:14.
12*a* Omni 1:19.
b Alma 4:1.
c TG Warn.
d Mosiah 11:13.
e Omni 1:27; W of M 1:13.
f 2 Ne. 5:8; Mosiah 7:6 (6–7).
g Jacob 3:4.
13*a* Isa. 33:2; Mosiah 12:24.
b Mosiah 1:1; 2:4.
14*a* Mosiah 1:10.
b 1 Ne. 3:3 (3, 19–20); 5:10 (10–22).
15*a* Ezek. 17:22 (22–23); Mosiah 25:2 (2–4).
b Jer. 39:4 (1–10); 52:11 (9–11); Hel. 8:21.
16*a* 1 Ne. 16:9.

their [a]language had become corrupted; and they had brought no
[b]records with them; and they denied the being of their Creator; and
Mosiah, nor the people of Mosiah,
could understand them.
18 But it came to pass that Mosiah
caused that they should be taught
in his [a]language. And it came to
pass that after they were taught in
the language of Mosiah, Zarahemla
gave a genealogy of his fathers, according to his memory; and they
are written, but [b]not in these plates.
19 And it came to pass that the
people of Zarahemla, and of Mosiah,
did [a]unite together; and [b]Mosiah was
appointed to be their king.
20 And it came to pass in the days
of Mosiah, there was a large [a]stone
brought unto him with engravings
on it; and he did [b]interpret the
engravings by the gift and power
of God.
21 And they gave an account of
one [a]Coriantumr, and the slain of
his people. And Coriantumr was
discovered by the people of Zarahemla; and he dwelt with them for
the space of nine moons.
22 It also spake a few words concerning his fathers. And his first
parents came out from the [a]tower,
at the time the Lord [b]confounded
the language of the people; and the
severity of the Lord fell upon them
according to his judgments, which
are just; and their [c]bones lay scattered in the land northward.
23 Behold, I, Amaleki, was born in
the days of Mosiah; and I have lived
to see his death; and [a]Benjamin, [b]his
son, reigneth in his stead.
24 And behold, I have seen, in the
days of king Benjamin, a serious war
and much bloodshed between the
Nephites and the Lamanites. But
behold, the Nephites did obtain
much advantage over them; yea,
insomuch that king Benjamin did
drive them out of the land of Zarahemla.
25 And it came to pass that I began
to be old; and, having no seed, and
knowing king [a]Benjamin to be a just
man before the Lord, wherefore, I
shall [b]deliver up [c]these plates unto
him, exhorting all men to come
unto God, the Holy One of Israel,
and believe in prophesying, and in
revelations, and in the ministering
of angels, and in the gift of speaking with tongues, and in the gift of
interpreting languages, and in all
things which are [d]good; for there is
nothing which is good save it comes
from the Lord: and that which is
evil cometh from the devil.
26 And now, my beloved brethren,
I would that ye should [a]come unto
Christ, who is the Holy One of Israel,
and partake of his salvation, and
the power of his redemption. Yea,
come unto him, and [b]offer your
whole souls as an [c]offering unto him,
and continue in [d]fasting and praying, and endure to the end; and as
the Lord liveth ye will be saved.
27 And now I would speak somewhat concerning a certain [a]number
who went up into the wilderness to
[b]return to the [c]land of Nephi; for
there was a large number who were
desirous to possess the land of their
inheritance.
28 Wherefore, they went up into

17*a* 1 Ne. 3:19.
TG Language.
b Mosiah 1:3 (2–6).
18*a* Mosiah 24:4.
b 1 Ne. 9:4;
W of M 1:10.
19*a* Mosiah 25:13.
b Omni 1:12.
20*a* Mosiah 21:28 (27–28);
28:13.
b Mosiah 8:13 (13–19);
28:17.
TG Urim and Thummim.
21*a* Ether 12:1 (1–2);
13:20 (13–31); 15:32.
22*a* Ether 1:3 (1–6).
b Gen. 11:7 (6–9);
Mosiah 28:17;
Ether 1:33.
c Mosiah 8:8 (8–12).
23*a* W of M 1:3.
b Mosiah 2:11.
25*a* W of M 1:18 (17–18);
Mosiah 29:13.
b W of M 1:10.
c 1 Ne. 10:1.
d Alma 5:40;
Ether 4:12;
Moro. 7:16 (15–17).
26*a* Jacob 1:7;
Alma 29:2;
Moro. 10:32.
b TG Commitment;
Self-Sacrifice.
c 3 Ne. 9:20.
d TG Fast, Fasting.
27*a* Mosiah 9:3 (1–4).
b Mosiah 7:1.
c Omni 1:12.

the wilderness. And their leader being a strong and mighty man, and
a stiffnecked man, wherefore he
caused a contention among them;
and they were [a]all slain, save fifty,
in the wilderness, and they returned
again to the land of Zarahemla.
29 And it came to pass that they
also took others to a considerable
number, and took their journey
again into the wilderness.
30 And I, Amaleki, had a brother,
who also went with them; and I
have not since known concerning
them. And I am about to lie down
in my grave; and [a]these plates are
full. And I make an end of my
speaking.

THE WORDS OF MORMON

Mormon abridges the large plates of Nephi—He puts the small plates with the other plates—King Benjamin establishes peace in the land. About A.D. 385.

AND now I, Mormon, being about
to deliver up the [a]record which
I have been making into the
hands of my son Moroni, behold I
have witnessed almost all the destruction of my people, the Nephites.
2 And it is [a]many hundred years
after the coming of Christ that I deliver these records into the hands of
my son; and it supposeth me that he
will witness the entire [b]destruction
of my people. But may God grant
that he may survive them, that he
may write somewhat concerning
them, and somewhat concerning
Christ, that perhaps some day it
may [c]profit them.
3 And now, I speak somewhat concerning that which I have written;
for after I had made an [a]abridgment
from the [b]plates of Nephi, down to
the reign of this king Benjamin, of
whom Amaleki spake, I searched
among the [c]records which had been
delivered into my hands, and I found
these plates, which contained this
small account of the prophets, from
Jacob down to the reign of this king
[d]Benjamin, and also many of the
words of Nephi.
4 And the things which are upon
these plates [a]pleasing me, because
of the prophecies of the coming of
Christ; and my fathers knowing that
many of them have been fulfilled;
yea, and I also know that as many
things as have been [b]prophesied
concerning us down to this day
have been fulfilled, and as many
as go beyond this day must surely
come to pass—
5 Wherefore, I chose [a]these things,
to finish my [b]record upon them,
which remainder of my record I
shall take from the [c]plates of Nephi;
and I cannot write the [d]hundredth
part of the things of my people.
6 But behold, I shall take these

28*a* Mosiah 9:2 (1–4).
30*a* 1 Ne. 6:3 (3–6); Jacob 4:1 (1–2); Jarom 1:14.

[WORDS OF MORMON]

1 1*a* 3 Ne. 5:12 (9–12); Morm. 1:4 (1–4); 2:17 (17–18); 8:5 (1, 4–5, 14).
2*a* Morm. 6:5 (5–6).
b 1 Ne. 12:19.
c D&C 3:19 (16–20).
3*a* 1 Ne. 1:17 (16–17); D&C 10:44.
b Jarom 1:14; W of M 1:10; D&C 10:38 (38–40).
c Mosiah 1:6 (2–6); Hel. 3:13 (13–15); Morm. 4:23.
d Omni 1:23 (23–25).
4*a* 1 Ne. 6:5 (3–6).
b TG Jesus Christ, Prophecies about.
5*a* IE the things pleasing to him, mentioned in v. 4.
b 3 Ne. 5:17 (14–18); Morm. 1:1.
c 1 Ne. 9:2.
d Alma 13:31; 3 Ne. 5:8 (8–11); 26:6 (6–12).

plates, which contain these prophesyings and revelations, and put them with the remainder of my record, for they are choice unto me; and I know they will be choice unto my brethren.

7 And I do this for a [a]wise [b]purpose; for thus it whispereth me, according to the workings of the Spirit of the Lord which is in me. And now, I do not know all things; but the Lord [c]knoweth all things which are to come; wherefore, he [d]worketh in me to do according to his [e]will.

8 And my [a]prayer to God is concerning my brethren, that they may once again come to the knowledge of God, yea, the redemption of Christ; that they may once again be a [b]delightsome people.

9 And now I, Mormon, proceed to finish out my record, which I take from the plates of Nephi; and I make it according to the knowledge and the [a]understanding which God has given me.

10 Wherefore, it came to pass that after Amaleki had [a]delivered up these plates into the hands of king Benjamin, he took them and put them with the [b]other plates, which contained records which had been handed down by the [c]kings, from generation to generation until the days of king Benjamin.

11 And they were handed down from king Benjamin, from generation to generation until they have fallen into [a]my hands. And I, Mormon, pray to God that they may be preserved from this time henceforth. And I know that they will be preserved; for there are great things written upon them, out of which [b]my people and their brethren shall be [c]judged at the great and last day, according to the word of God which is written.

12 And now, concerning this king Benjamin—he had somewhat of contentions among his own people.

13 And it came to pass also that the armies of the Lamanites came down out of the [a]land of Nephi, to battle against his people. But behold, king Benjamin gathered together his armies, and he did stand against them; and he did fight with the strength of his own arm, with the [b]sword of Laban.

14 And in the [a]strength of the Lord they did contend against their enemies, until they had slain many thousands of the Lamanites. And it came to pass that they did contend against the Lamanites until they had driven them out of all the lands of their [b]inheritance.

15 And it came to pass that after there had been false [a]Christs, and their mouths had been shut, and they punished according to their crimes;

16 And after there had been [a]false prophets, and false preachers and teachers among the people, and all these having been punished according to their crimes; and after there having been much contention and many dissensions away [b]unto the Lamanites, behold, it came to pass that king Benjamin, with the assistance of the holy [c]prophets who were among his people—

17 For behold, king Benjamin was

7*a* 1 Ne. 9:5; 19:3;
Enos 1:13 (13–18);
Alma 37:2;
D&C 3:19 (9–20);
10:34 (1–19, 30–47).
b D&C 10:40 (20–46).
c TG God, Foreknowledge of;
God, Intelligence of;
God, Omniscience of.
d 2 Ne. 27:23.
e TG God, Will of.
8*a* 2 Ne. 33:3;
Enos 1:11 (11–12);
Moro. 9:22.
b 2 Ne. 30:6.
9*a* TG Understanding.
10*a* Omni 1:25 (25, 30).
b 1 Ne. 9:4;
Omni 1:11, 18;
W of M 1:3;
Mosiah 28:11.
c Jarom 1:14.
11*a* 3 Ne. 5:12 (8–12);
Morm. 1:4 (1–5).
b Hel. 15:3 (3–4).
c 2 Ne. 25:18; 29:11;
33:14 (11, 14–15);
3 Ne. 27:25 (23–27);
Ether 5:4.
13*a* Omni 1:12.
b 1 Ne. 4:9;
2 Ne. 5:14;
Jacob 1:10;
Mosiah 1:16;
D&C 17:1.
14*a* TG Strength.
b Jarom 1:7.
15*a* TG False Christs.
16*a* TG False Prophets.
b Jacob 1:14 (13–14).
c Enos 1:22.

a [a]holy man, and he did reign over
his people in righteousness; and
there were many holy men in the
land, and they did speak the word of
God with [b]power and with authority;
and they did use much [c]sharpness
because of the stiffneckedness of
the people—
18 Wherefore, with the help of
these, king [a]Benjamin, by laboring
with all the might of his body and
the [b]faculty of his whole soul, and
also the prophets, did once more
establish peace in the land.

THE BOOK OF MOSIAH

CHAPTER 1

King Benjamin teaches his sons the language and prophecies of their fathers—Their religion and civilization have been preserved because of the records kept on the various plates—Mosiah is chosen as king and is given custody of the records and other things. About 130–124 B.C.

AND now there was no more
contention in all the [a]land of
Zarahemla, among all the
people who belonged to king Benjamin, so that king Benjamin had
continual peace all the remainder of
his days.
2 And it came to pass that he had
three [a]sons; and he called their
names Mosiah, and Helorum, and
Helaman. And he caused that they
should be [b]taught in all the [c]lan-
guage of his fathers, that thereby
they might become men of understanding; and that they might know
concerning the prophecies which
had been spoken by the mouths of
their fathers, which were delivered
them by the hand of the Lord.
3 And he also taught them concerning the records which were
engraven on the [a]plates of brass, saying: My sons, I would that ye should
remember that were it not for these
[b]plates, which contain these records
and these commandments, we must
have suffered in [c]ignorance, even at
this present time, not knowing the
mysteries of God.
4 For it were not possible that our
father, Lehi, could have remembered
all these things, to have taught them
to his children, except it were for the
help of these plates; for he having
been taught in the [a]language of the
Egyptians therefore he could read
these engravings, and teach them to
his children, that thereby they could
teach them to their children, and
so fulfilling the commandments of
God, even down to this present time.
5 I say unto you, my sons, [a]were
it not for these things, which have
been kept and [b]preserved by the
hand of God, that we might [c]read and
understand of his [d]mysteries, and
have his [e]commandments always

17*a* Ex. 22:31; Alma 13:26; D&C 49:8; 107:29.
b Alma 17:3 (2–3). TG God, Power of.
c Enos 1:23; Moro. 9:4; D&C 121:43 (41–43).
18*a* Omni 1:25; Mosiah 29:13.
b 1 Ne. 15:25.

[MOSIAH]

1 1*a* Omni 1:13; Alma 2:15.
2*a* 1 Ne. 1:1; D&C 68:25 (25, 28).
b Enos 1:1; Mosiah 4:15 (14–15).
c Morm. 9:32.
3*a* 2 Ne. 5:12; Mosiah 1:16; 28:20.
b 1 Ne. 3:19 (19–20); Omni 1:17.
c Alma 37:8.
4*a* 1 Ne. 1:2; 3:19; Morm. 9:32 (32–33); JS—H 1:64.
5*a* Alma 37:9.
b TG Scriptures, Preservation of.
c Deut. 6:6 (6–8); 2 Chr. 34:21; 1 Ne. 15:24 (23–24). TG Scriptures, Value of.
d TG Mysteries of Godliness.
e 1 Ne. 4:15.

before our eyes, that even our
fathers would have dwindled in
unbelief, and we should have been
like unto our brethren, the Lamanites, who know nothing concerning
these things, or even do not believe
them when they are taught them,
because of the [f]traditions of their
fathers, which are not correct.
6 O my sons, I would that ye should
remember that these sayings are
true, and also that these records
are [a]true. And behold, also the plates
of Nephi, which contain the records
and the sayings of our fathers from
the time they left Jerusalem until
now, and they are true; and we can
know of their surety because we
have them before our eyes.
7 And now, my sons, I would that
ye should remember to [a]search
them diligently, that ye may profit
thereby; and I would that ye should
[b]keep the commandments of God,
that ye may [c]prosper in the land
according to the [d]promises which
the Lord made unto our fathers.
8 And many more things did king
Benjamin teach his sons, which are
not written in this book.
9 And it came to pass that after
king Benjamin had made an end
of teaching his sons, that he waxed
[a]old, and he saw that he must very
soon go the way of all the earth;
therefore, he thought it expedient
that he should confer the kingdom
upon one of his sons.
10 Therefore, he had Mosiah
brought before him; and these are
the words which he spake unto
him, saying: My son, I would that
ye should make a proclamation
throughout all this land among all
this [a]people, or the people of Zarahemla, and the people of Mosiah
who dwell in the land, that thereby
they may be gathered together; for
on the morrow I shall proclaim unto
this my people out of mine own
mouth that thou art a [b]king and a
ruler over this people, whom the
Lord our God hath given us.
11 And moreover, I shall give this
people a [a]name, that thereby they
may be distinguished above all the
people which the Lord God hath
brought out of the land of Jerusalem; and this I do because they have
been a [b]diligent people in keeping
the commandments of the Lord.
12 And I give unto them a name
that never shall be blotted out, except it be through [a]transgression.
13 Yea, and moreover I say unto
you, that if this highly favored
people of the Lord should fall into
[a]transgression, and become a wicked
and an adulterous people, that the
Lord will deliver them up, that
thereby they become [b]weak like
unto their brethren; and he will no
more [c]preserve them by his matchless and marvelous power, as he
has hitherto preserved our fathers.
14 For I say unto you, that if he
had not extended his arm in the
preservation of our fathers they
must have fallen into the hands of
the Lamanites, and become victims
to their hatred.
15 And it came to pass that after
king Benjamin had made an end
of these sayings to his son, that he
gave him [a]charge concerning all
the affairs of the kingdom.
16 And moreover, he also gave him
charge concerning the records which

5*f* Jacob 7:24; Mosiah 10:12 (11–17).
6*a* 1 Ne. 1:3; 14:30; 2 Ne. 25:20; Alma 3:12; Ether 5:3 (1–3).
7*a* TG Scriptures, Study of.
b Lev. 25:18 (18–19); Mosiah 2:22; Alma 50:20 (20–22).
c Josh. 1:7; Ps. 1:3 (2–3); 122:6; 1 Ne. 2:20.
d Omni 1:6; Alma 9:13 (13–14).
9*a* TG Old Age.
10*a* Omni 1:14; Mosiah 27:35.
b Gen. 41:43 (41–43); Jarom 1:7 (7, 14); Mosiah 2:30.
11*a* Mosiah 5:8 (8–12). TG Jesus Christ, Taking the Name of.
b TG Diligence.
12*a* TG Transgress.
13*a* Heb. 6:6 (4–6).
b Jer. 46:15 (15–17); Hel. 4:24 (24, 26).
c D&C 103:8.
15*a* 1 Kgs. 2:1; Ps. 72:1 (1–4).

were engraven on the [a]plates of
brass; and also the plates of Nephi;
and also, the [b]sword of Laban, and
the [c]ball or director, which led our
fathers through the wilderness,
which was prepared by the hand of
the Lord that thereby they might
be led, every one according to the
heed and diligence which they gave
unto him.
17 Therefore, as they were [a]unfaith-
ful they did not prosper nor progress
in their journey, but were [b]driven
back, and incurred the displeasure
of God upon them; and therefore
they were smitten with famine and
sore [c]afflictions, to stir them up in
[d]remembrance of their duty.
18 And now, it came to pass that
Mosiah went and did as his father
had commanded him, and proclaimed unto all the people who
were in the land of Zarahemla that
thereby they might gather themselves together, to go up to the
[a]temple to hear the words which
his father should speak unto them.

CHAPTER 2

King Benjamin addresses his people—He recounts the equity, fairness, and spirituality of his reign—He counsels them to serve their Heavenly King—Those who rebel against God will suffer anguish like unquenchable fire. About 124 B.C.

AND it came to pass that after Mosiah had done as his father had
commanded him, and had made
a proclamation throughout all the
land, that the people [a]gathered
themselves together throughout
all the land, that they might go up
to the [b]temple to [c]hear the [d]words
which king Benjamin should speak
unto them.
2 And there were a great number,
even so many that they did not
number them; for they had multiplied exceedingly and waxed great
in the land.
3 And they also took of the [a]first-
lings of their flocks, that they might
offer [b]sacrifice and [c]burnt [d]offerings
[e]according to the law of Moses;
4 And also that they might give
thanks to the Lord their God, who
had brought them out of the land
of Jerusalem, and who had delivered them out of the hands of their
enemies, and had [a]appointed just
men to be their [b]teachers, and also
a just man to be their king, who
had established peace in the [c]land
of Zarahemla, and who had taught
them to [d]keep the commandments
of God, that they might rejoice and
be filled with [e]love towards God
and all men.
5 And it came to pass that when
they came up to the temple, they
pitched their tents round about,
every man according to his [a]family,
consisting of his wife, and his
sons, and his daughters, and their
sons, and their daughters, from
the eldest down to the youngest,
every family being separate one
from another.
6 And they pitched their tents
round about the temple, every man
having his [a]tent with the door thereof towards the temple, that thereby
they might remain in their tents
and hear the words which king
Benjamin should speak unto them;

16*a* Mosiah 1:3.
b Jacob 1:10; W of M 1:13; D&C 17:1.
c 2 Ne. 5:12.
17*a* TG Disobedience.
b 1 Ne. 18:13 (12–13).
c Lam. 1:5. TG Affliction.
d Judg. 13:1; Hel. 12:3 (2–3).
18*a* 2 Ne. 5:16; Mosiah 2:1.
2 1*a* TG Assembly for Worship.
b Mosiah 1:18.
c 2 Chr. 34:30 (29–33).
d Mosiah 26:1.
3*a* Gen. 4:4 (2–7); Ex. 13:12 (12–13); Deut. 12:6; Moses 5:20 (5, 19–23).
b Ezra 6:10. TG Sacrifice.
c Lev. 1:3 (2–9); Deut. 33:10.
d Ezra 3:2 (2–5); 1 Ne. 5:9.
e 2 Ne. 25:24; Jarom 1:5; Alma 30:3; 34:14 (13–14).
4*a* TG Called of God.
b Mosiah 18:18 (18–22).
c Omni 1:13 (12–15).
d John 15:10; D&C 95:12.
e Deut. 11:1. TG Love.
5*a* TG Family, Patriarchal.
6*a* Ex. 33:8 (8–10).

7 For the multitude being so great
that king Benjamin could not teach
them all within the walls of the
temple, therefore he caused a [a]tower
to be erected, that thereby his people might hear the words which he
should speak unto them.
8 And it came to pass that he began to speak to his people from the
tower; and they could not all hear
his words because of the greatness
of the multitude; therefore he caused
that the words which he spake
should be written and sent forth
among those that were not under the
sound of his voice, that they might
also receive his words.
9 And these are the words which
he [a]spake and caused to be written,
saying: My brethren, all ye that have
assembled yourselves together, you
that can hear my words which I
shall speak unto you this day; for I
have not commanded you to come
up hither to [b]trifle with the words
which I shall speak, but that you
should [c]hearken unto me, and open
your ears that ye may hear, and your
[d]hearts that ye may understand, and
your [e]minds that the [f]mysteries of
God may be unfolded to your view.
10 I have not commanded you to
come up hither that ye should fear
[a]me, or that ye should think that I of
myself am more than a mortal man.
11 But I am like as yourselves,
subject to all manner of infirmities
in body and mind; yet I have been
chosen by this people, and [a]conse-
crated by [b]my father, and was suffered by the hand of the Lord that
I should be a ruler and a king over
this people; and have been kept and
preserved by his matchless power, to
serve you with all the might, mind
and strength which the Lord hath
granted unto me.
12 I say unto you that as I have
been suffered to [a]spend my days in
your service, even up to this time,
and have not sought [b]gold nor silver
nor any manner of riches of you;
13 Neither have I suffered that ye
should be confined in dungeons,
nor that ye should make slaves one
of another, nor that ye should murder, or plunder, or steal, or commit
adultery; nor even have I suffered
that ye should commit any manner
of wickedness, and have taught you
that ye should keep the commandments of the Lord, in all things
which he hath commanded you—
14 And even I, myself, have [a]la-
bored with mine own [b]hands that I
might serve you, and that ye should
not be [c]laden with taxes, and that
there should nothing come upon you
which was grievous to be borne—
and of all these things which I have
spoken, ye yourselves are witnesses
this day.
15 Yet, my brethren, I have not
done these things that I might
[a]boast, neither do I tell these things
that thereby I might accuse you;
but I tell you these things that ye
may know that I can answer a clear
[b]conscience before God this day.
16 Behold, I say unto you that
because I said unto you that I had
spent my days in your service, I do
not desire to boast, for I have only
been in the service of God.
17 And behold, I tell you these
things that ye may learn [a]wisdom;
that ye may learn that when ye are
in the [b]service of your [c]fellow beings

7*a* Gen. 35:21; Neh. 8:4 (4–5); Mosiah 11:12 (12–13).
9*a* Mosiah 8:3.
b D&C 6:12; 32:5. TG Mocking.
c TG Teachable.
d Prov. 8:5; Mosiah 12:27; 3 Ne. 19:33.
e TG Mind.
f TG Mysteries of Godliness.
10*a* TG Humility.
11*a* TG Setting Apart.
b Omni 1:23 (23–24). TG Serve; Service.
12*a* 1 Sam. 12:2 (1–25).
b 2 Kgs. 5:16; Acts 20:33 (33–34); Jacob 1:16.
14*a* Deut. 17:17; Neh. 5:14 (14–15); 1 Cor. 9:18 (4–18). TG Self-Sacrifice; Work, Value of.
b Acts 20:34 (33–35).
c Ezek. 46:18.
15*a* TG Boast.
b TG Conscience.
17*a* TG Wisdom.
b Matt. 25:40; D&C 42:31 (30–31). TG Service.
c TG Brotherhood and Sisterhood; Fellowshipping; Neighbor.

ye are only in the service of your
God.
18 Behold, ye have called me your
king; and if I, whom ye call your king,
do labor to [a]serve you, then ought
not ye to labor to serve one another?
19 And behold also, if I, whom
ye call your king, who has spent
his days in your service, and yet
has been in the service of God, do
merit any thanks from you, O how
you ought to [a]thank your heavenly
[b]King!
20 I say unto you, my brethren, that
if you should render all the [a]thanks
and [b]praise which your whole soul
has power to possess, to that God
who has created you, and has kept
and [c]preserved you, and has caused
that ye should [d]rejoice, and has
granted that ye should live in peace
one with another—
21 I say unto you that if ye should
[a]serve him who has created you
from the beginning, and is [b]pre-
serving you from day to day, by
lending you [c]breath, that ye may
live and move and do according to
your own [d]will, and even supporting
you from one moment to another—I
say, if ye should serve him with all
your [e]whole souls yet ye would be
[f]unprofitable servants.
22 And behold, all that he [a]re-
quires of you is to [b]keep his commandments; and he has [c]promised
you that if ye would keep his commandments ye should prosper in the
land; and he never doth [d]vary from
that which he hath said; therefore,
if ye do [e]keep his [f]commandments
he doth bless you and prosper you.
23 And now, in the first place, he
hath created you, and granted unto
you your lives, for which ye are indebted unto him.
24 And secondly, he doth [a]require
that ye should do as he hath commanded you; for which if ye do, he
doth immediately [b]bless you; and
therefore he hath paid you. And
ye are still indebted unto him, and
are, and will be, forever and ever;
therefore, of what have ye to boast?
25 And now I ask, can ye say aught
of yourselves? I answer you, Nay.
Ye cannot say that ye are even as
much as the dust of the earth; yet
ye were [a]created of the [b]dust of the
earth; but behold, it [c]belongeth to
him who created you.
26 And I, even I, whom ye call
your king, am [a]no better than ye
yourselves are; for I am also of the
dust. And ye behold that I am old,
and am about to yield up this mortal frame to its mother earth.
27 Therefore, as I said unto you that I
had [a]served you, [b]walking with a clear
conscience before God, even so I at
this time have caused that ye should
assemble yourselves together, that I
might be found blameless, and that
your [c]blood should not come upon
me, when I shall stand to be judged
of God of the things whereof he hath
commanded me concerning you.
28 I say unto you that I have
caused that ye should assemble
yourselves together that I might

18*a* Luke 22:26.
19*a* 1 Chr. 16:8.
TG Thanksgiving.
b TG Kingdom of God, in Heaven.
20*a* Job 1:21;
Ps. 34:1 (1–3);
D&C 59:21; 62:7; 78:19.
b 1 Sam. 12:24;
1 Ne. 18:16;
D&C 136:28.
c D&C 63:3.
d Neh. 12:43.
21*a* Job 22:3 (3–4).
b Neh. 9:6.
c 2 Ne. 9:26.
d TG Agency.
e TG Dedication.
f Luke 17:10 (7–10);
Rom. 3:12.
22*a* TG God, the Standard of Righteousness.
b Gen. 4:7;
Lev. 25:18 (18–19);
Mosiah 1:7;
Alma 50:20 (20–22).
c 1 Ne. 4:14;
Omni 1:6;
Ether 2:7 (7–12).
d TG God, Perfection of.
e Ps. 19:11 (9–11);
2 Ne. 1:20;
D&C 14:7; 58:2.
f TG Commandments of God.
24*a* TG Duty.
b Prov. 22:4 (4–5);
2 Ne. 1:20.
25*a* TG Man, Physical Creation of.
b Jacob 2:21;
Alma 42:2;
Hel. 12:7 (7–8);
Morm. 9:17.
c 1 Chr. 29:12;
Mosiah 4:22.
26*a* TG Equal.
27*a* TG Serve;
Service.
b TG Walking with God.
c Jacob 1:19.

[a]rid my garments of your blood, at this period of time when I am about to go down to my grave, that I might go down in peace, and my immortal [b]spirit may join the [c]choirs above in singing the praises of a just God.
29 And moreover, I say unto you that I have caused that ye should assemble yourselves together, that I might declare unto you that I can no longer be your teacher, nor your king;
30 For even at this time, my whole frame doth tremble exceedingly while attempting to speak unto you; but the Lord God doth support me, and hath suffered me that I should speak unto you, and hath commanded me that I should declare unto you this day, that my son Mosiah is a [a]king and a ruler over you.
31 And now, my brethren, I would that ye should do as ye have hitherto done. As ye have kept my commandments, and also the commandments of my father, and have prospered, and have been kept from falling into the hands of your enemies, even so if ye shall keep the commandments of my son, or the commandments of God which shall be delivered unto you by him, ye shall prosper in the land, and your enemies shall have no power over you.
32 But, O my people, beware lest there shall arise [a]contentions among you, and ye [b]list to [c]obey the evil spirit, which was spoken of by my father Mosiah.
33 For behold, there is a wo pronounced upon him who listeth to [a]obey that spirit; for if he listeth to obey him, and remaineth and dieth in his [b]sins, the same drinketh [c]damnation to his own soul; for he receiveth for his wages an [d]everlasting [e]punishment, having transgressed the law of God contrary to his own knowledge.
34 I say unto you, that there are not any among you, except it be your little children that have not been taught concerning these things, but what knoweth that ye are eternally [a]indebted to your heavenly Father, to render to him [b]all that you have and are; and also have been taught concerning the [c]records which contain the prophecies which have been spoken by the holy prophets, even down to the time our father, Lehi, left Jerusalem;
35 And also, all that has been spoken by our fathers until now. And behold, also, they spake that which was commanded them of the Lord; therefore, they are [a]just and true.
36 And now, I say unto you, my brethren, that after ye have known and have been taught all these things, if ye should transgress and go [a]contrary to that which has been spoken, that ye do [b]withdraw yourselves from the Spirit of the Lord, that it may have no place in you to guide you in wisdom's paths that ye may be blessed, prospered, and preserved—
37 I say unto you, that the man that doeth this, the same cometh out in open [a]rebellion against God; therefore he [b]listeth to obey the evil spirit, and becometh an enemy to

28*a* 2 Ne. 9:44; Jacob 2:2 (2, 16); D&C 61:34.
b TG Spirit Body.
c Morm. 7:7.
30*a* Mosiah 1:10; 6:3 (3–4). TG Kings, Earthly.
32*a* Eph. 4:27 (26–27); 3 Ne. 11:29. TG Contention.
b Alma 3:27 (26–27); 5:42 (41–42); 30:60; D&C 29:45.
c 2 Ne. 32:8; Mosiah 4:14; Alma 5:20.
33*a* TG Agency.
b TG Accountability.
c TG Damnation.
d Jacob 6:10; D&C 19:11 (10–12).
e TG Punish.
34*a* Philip. 3:8 (7–10). TG Debt.
b Rom. 12:1 (1–2).
c 1 Ne. 5:14; Alma 33:2.
35*a* Rom. 7:12; Rev. 15:3.
36*a* TG Disobedience.
b TG Holy Ghost, Loss of.
37*a* Mosiah 3:12; Hel. 8:25 (24–25). TG Holy Ghost, Unpardonable Sin against; Rebellion.
b Prov. 19:27; 1 Ne. 8:34 (33–34).

all righteousness; therefore, the Lord has no place in him, for he dwelleth not in [c]unholy temples.

38 Therefore if that man [a]repenteth not, and remaineth and dieth an enemy to God, the demands of divine [b]justice do awaken his immortal soul to a lively sense of his own [c]guilt, which doth cause him to shrink from the [d]presence of the Lord, and doth fill his breast with guilt, and [e]pain, and [f]anguish, which is like an unquenchable [g]fire, whose flame ascendeth up forever and ever.

39 And now I say unto you, that [a]mercy hath no claim on that man; therefore his final doom is to endure a never-ending [b]torment.

40 O, all ye [a]old men, and also ye young men, and you little children who can understand my words, for I have spoken plainly unto you that ye might understand, I pray that ye should awake to a [b]remembrance of the awful situation of those that have fallen into transgression.

41 And moreover, I would desire that ye should consider on the blessed and [a]happy state of those that keep the commandments of God. For behold, they are [b]blessed in all things, both temporal and spiritual; and if they hold out [c]faithful to the end they are received into [d]heaven, that thereby they may dwell with God in a state of never-ending happiness. O remember, remember that these things are true; for the Lord God hath spoken it.

CHAPTER 3

King Benjamin continues his address—The Lord Omnipotent will minister among men in a tabernacle of clay—Blood will come from every pore as He atones for the sins of the world—His is the only name whereby salvation comes—Men can put off the natural man and become Saints through the Atonement—The torment of the wicked will be as a lake of fire and brimstone. About 124 B.C.

AND again my brethren, I would call your attention, for I have somewhat more to speak unto you; for behold, I have things to tell you concerning that which is to come.

2 And the things which I shall tell you are made known unto me by an [a]angel from God. And he said unto me: [b]Awake; and I awoke, and behold he stood before me.

3 And he said unto me: Awake, and hear the words which I shall tell thee; for behold, I am come to declare unto you the [a]glad tidings of great [b]joy.

4 For the Lord hath heard thy prayers, and hath judged of thy [a]righteousness, and hath sent me to declare unto thee that thou mayest rejoice; and that thou mayest declare unto thy people, that they may also be filled with joy.

5 For behold, the time cometh, and is not far distant, that with power, the [a]Lord [b]Omnipotent who [c]reigneth, who was, and is from all [d]eternity to all eternity, shall come down from heaven among the

37*c* Alma 7:21; 34:36; Hel. 4:24.
38*a* TG Repent.
b TG God, Justice of.
c Mosiah 27:29 (25–29). TG Guilt.
d TG God, Presence of.
e TG Pain.
f TG Sorrow.
g TG Hell.
39*a* TG Mercy.
b TG Damnation; Punish.
40*a* TG Old Age.
b Alma 5:18 (7–18).
41*a* Matt. 11:29 (28–30); Alma 50:23; 4 Ne. 1:16 (15–18). TG Happiness; Joy.
b Gen. 39:3 (1–6); Ps. 37:25; Matt. 6:33; 1 Ne. 17:3 (1–5, 12–14).
c Ps. 31:23; Ether 4:19; D&C 6:13; 63:47.
d TG Heaven.
3 2*a* Mosiah 4:1; 5:5. TG Angels.
b Zech. 4:1 (1–2).
3*a* Isa. 52:7 (7–10); Luke 2:10 (10–11); Rom. 10:15; D&C 31:3.
b TG Joy.
4*a* TG Righteousness.
5*a* TG Jesus Christ, Jehovah.
b Rev. 1:8 (7–8). TG Jesus Christ, Power of.
c TG Jesus Christ, Authority of.
d 2 Ne. 26:12; Mosiah 16:15.

children of men, and shall dwell in
a [e]tabernacle of clay, and shall go
forth amongst men, working mighty
[f]miracles, such as healing the sick,
raising the dead, causing the lame
to walk, the [g]blind to receive their
sight, and the deaf to hear, and cur-
ing all manner of diseases.
6 And he shall cast out [a]devils, or
the [b]evil spirits which dwell in the
hearts of the children of men.
7 And lo, he shall [a]suffer [b]temp-
tations, and pain of body, [c]hunger,
thirst, and fatigue, even more than
man can [d]suffer, except it be unto
death; for behold, [e]blood cometh
from every pore, so great shall be
his [f]anguish for the wickedness and
the abominations of his people.
8 And he shall be called [a]Jesus
[b]Christ, the [c]Son of God, the [d]Father
of heaven and earth, the [e]Creator of
all things from the beginning; and
his [f]mother shall be called Mary.
9 And lo, he cometh unto his own,
that [a]salvation might come unto
the children of men even through
[b]faith on his name; and even after
all this they shall consider him a
man, and say that he hath a [c]devil,
and shall [d]scourge him, and shall
[e]crucify him.
10 And he shall [a]rise the [b]third
day from the dead; and behold, he
standeth to [c]judge the world; and
behold, all these things are done
that a righteous judgment might
come upon the children of men.
11 For behold, and also his [a]blood
[b]atoneth for the sins of those who
have [c]fallen by the transgression of
Adam, who have died not knowing
the [d]will of God concerning them,
or who have [e]ignorantly sinned.
12 But wo, wo unto him who
knoweth that he [a]rebelleth against
God! For salvation cometh to none
such except it be through repentance and faith on the [b]Lord Jesus
Christ.
13 And the Lord God hath sent his
holy [a]prophets among all the children of men, to declare these things
to every kindred, nation, and tongue,
that thereby whosoever should believe that Christ should come, the
same might receive [b]remission of
their sins, and rejoice with exceedingly great joy, even [c]as though
he had already come among them.

5*e* Mosiah 7:27; 15:2 (1–7); Alma 7:9 (9–13).
f Matt. 4:24 (23–24); 9:35; Acts 2:22; 1 Ne. 11:31. TG Death, Power over; Heal; Miracle.
g Matt. 9:28 (28–31); 20:30 (30–34); John 9:1 (1–4); 3 Ne. 17:9 (7–10); D&C 84:69.
6*a* Mark 1:34 (32–34); 1 Ne. 11:31.
b TG Spirits, Evil or Unclean.
7*a* Luke 12:50. TG Suffering.
b TG Jesus Christ, Temptation of; Temptation.
c Matt. 4:2 (1–2).
d D&C 19:16 (15–18).
e Matt. 26:39 (38–39); Luke 22:44.
f Isa. 53:4 (4–5).
8*a* TG Foreordination; Jesus Christ, Prophecies about.
b TG Jesus Christ, Messiah.
c Mosiah 15:3; Alma 7:10; 3 Ne. 1:14.
d Mosiah 15:4; Hel. 14:12; 3 Ne. 9:15; Ether 4:7.
e TG Jesus Christ, Creator.
f Matt. 1:16; 1 Ne. 11:18 (14–21).
9*a* TG Jesus Christ, Mission of.
b TG Faith.
c Luke 11:15 (14–22); John 8:48; 12:37; Hel. 13:26 (26–27).
d Luke 18:33; 1 Ne. 11:33; 2 Ne. 10:3.
e 1 Ne. 19:10 (10, 13); 2 Ne. 6:9; 3 Ne. 11:14 (14–15, 33). TG Jesus Christ, Crucifixion of.
10*a* TG Jesus Christ, Resurrection.
b 2 Ne. 25:13; Hel. 14:20 (20–27).
c TG Jesus Christ, Judge.
11*a* TG Blood, Symbolism of.
b TG Jesus Christ, Redeemer; Redemption.
c TG Fall of Man.
d TG God, Will of.
e Lev. 4:13 (13–35); Num. 15:27 (2–29); 2 Ne. 9:26 (25–26); Alma 9:16 (15–16); 42:21; 3 Ne. 6:18. TG Accountability; Ignorance.
12*a* Mosiah 2:37 (36–38); Hel. 8:25 (24–25). TG Rebellion.
b TG Jesus Christ, Lord.
13*a* TG Prophets, Mission of.
b TG Remission of Sins.
c 2 Ne. 25:26 (24–27); Jarom 1:11; Mosiah 16:6.

14 Yet the Lord God saw that his people were a [a]stiffnecked people, and he appointed unto them a [b]law, even the [c]law of Moses.

15 And many signs, and wonders, and [a]types, and shadows showed he unto them, concerning his coming; and also holy prophets spake unto them concerning his coming; and yet they [b]hardened their hearts, and understood not that the [c]law of Moses availeth nothing [d]except it were through the [e]atonement of his blood.

16 And even if it were possible that little [a]children could sin they could not be saved; but I say unto you they are [b]blessed; for behold, as in Adam, or by nature, they fall, even so the blood of Christ [c]atoneth for their sins.

17 And moreover, I say unto you, that there shall be [a]no other name given nor any other way nor means whereby [b]salvation can come unto the children of men, only in and through the name of Christ, the [c]Lord Omnipotent.

18 For behold he judgeth, and his judgment is just; and the infant perisheth not that dieth in his infancy; but men drink [a]damnation to their own souls except they humble themselves and [b]become as little children, and believe that [c]salvation was, and is, and is to come, in and through the [d]atoning blood of Christ, the Lord Omnipotent.

19 For the [a]natural [b]man is an [c]enemy to God, and has been from the [d]fall of Adam, and will be, forever and ever, unless he [e]yields to the enticings of the [f]Holy Spirit, and [g]putteth off the [h]natural man and becometh a [i]saint through the atonement of Christ the Lord, and becometh as a [j]child, [k]submissive, meek, humble, patient, full of love, willing to submit to all things which the Lord seeth fit to inflict upon him, even as a child doth submit to his father.

20 And moreover, I say unto you, that the time shall come when the [a]knowledge of a [b]Savior shall spread throughout [c]every nation, kindred, tongue, and people.

21 And behold, when that time cometh, none shall be found [a]blameless before God, except it be little children, only through repentance and faith on the name of the Lord God Omnipotent.

22 And even at this time, when thou shalt have taught thy people the things which the Lord thy God hath commanded thee, even then

14*a* 2 Ne. 25:28; Alma 9:31. TG Stiffnecked.
b Josh. 1:8; Mosiah 13:29 (29–32); Alma 25:15 (15–16); D&C 41:5 (4–5).
c TG Law of Moses.
15*a* TG Jesus Christ, Types of, in Anticipation; Passover; Symbolism.
b TG Hardheartedness.
c Heb. 10:1; Mosiah 12:31; 13:28 (27–32); Alma 25:16.
d 2 Ne. 11:6.
e Lev. 4:20; Matt. 26:54 (51–56).
16*a* TG Conceived in Sin.
b TG Salvation of Little Children.
c Moro. 8:8 (8–9); Moses 6:54 (54–56). TG Jesus Christ, Atonement through.
17*a* Acts 4:12 (10–12); 2 Ne. 31:21; Mosiah 4:8 (7–8); 3 Ne. 9:17.
b Matt. 7:14 (13–14). TG Jesus Christ, Savior; Salvation, Plan of.
c TG Jesus Christ, Lord.
18*a* 1 Cor. 11:29.
b Matt. 18:3.
c TG Salvation.
d Mosiah 4:2; Hel. 5:9.
19*a* Gen. 8:21; 1 Cor. 2:14 (11–14); 2 Pet. 2:12; Mosiah 16:3; Alma 41:11; Ether 3:2. TG Man, Natural, Not Spiritually Reborn; Worldliness.
b TG Mortality.
c James 4:4. TG Enemies.
d TG Fall of Man.
e 2 Chr. 30:8; Rom. 6:13 (12–14).
f Rom. 8:4 (1–9). TG Guidance, Divine.
g Alma 19:6.
h Col. 3:9; D&C 67:12.
i Luke 22:32 (31–38). TG Man, New, Spiritually Reborn; Saints; Spirituality.
j Matt. 18:3; 1 Pet. 2:2 (1–3); 3 Ne. 9:22.
k TG Self-Mastery; Submissiveness.
20*a* D&C 3:16.
b TG Jesus Christ, Savior.
c Mosiah 16:1. TG Missionary Work.
21*a* Col. 1:22; D&C 4:2. TG Accountability.

are they found no more blameless
in the sight of God, only according
to the words which I have spoken
unto thee.
23 And now I have spoken the
words which the Lord God hath
commanded me.
24 And thus saith the Lord: They
shall stand as a bright testimony
against this people, at the judgment
day; whereof they shall be judged,
every man according to his [a]works,
whether they be good, or whether
they be evil.
25 And if they be evil they are
consigned to an awful [a]view of their
own guilt and abominations, which
doth cause them to shrink from the
presence of the Lord into a state of
[b]misery and [c]endless torment, from
whence they can no more return;
therefore they have drunk damnation to their own souls.
26 Therefore, they have drunk out
of the [a]cup of the wrath of God,
which justice could no more deny
unto them than it could deny that
[b]Adam should fall because of his
partaking of the forbidden [c]fruit;
therefore, [d]mercy could have claim
on them no more forever.
27 And their [a]torment is as a [b]lake
of fire and brimstone, whose flames
are unquenchable, and whose smoke
ascendeth up [c]forever and ever.
Thus hath the Lord commanded
me. Amen.

CHAPTER 4

King Benjamin continues his address—Salvation comes because of the Atonement—Believe in God to be saved—Retain a remission of your sins through faithfulness—Impart of your substance to the poor—Do all things in wisdom and order. About 124 B.C.

AND now, it came to pass that when
king Benjamin had made an end
of speaking the words which had
been delivered unto him by the
[a]angel of the Lord, that he cast his
eyes round about on the multitude,
and behold they had [b]fallen to the
earth, for the [c]fear of the Lord had
come upon them.
2 And they had [a]viewed themselves
in their own [b]carnal state, even [c]less
than the dust of the earth. And they
all cried aloud with one voice, saying: O have mercy, and apply the
[d]atoning blood of Christ that we may
receive forgiveness of our sins, and
our hearts may be [e]purified; for we
believe in Jesus Christ, the Son of
God, who [f]created heaven and earth,
and all things; who shall come down
among the children of men.
3 And it came to pass that after they had spoken these words
the Spirit of the Lord came upon
them, and they were filled with
joy, having received a [a]remission
of their sins, and having peace of
[b]conscience, because of the exceeding [c]faith which they had in Jesus
Christ who should come, according
to the [d]words which king Benjamin
had spoken unto them.
4 And king Benjamin again opened
his mouth and began to speak
unto them, saying: My friends and
my brethren, my kindred and my
people, I would again call your
attention, that ye may hear and

24*a* TG Good Works.
25*a* 2 Ne. 9:14, 46; Alma 5:18; 11:43; 12:15 (14–15).
b Rom. 3:16; Morm. 8:38.
c TG Punish.
26*a* Ps. 75:8; Jer. 25:15; Lam. 4:21.
b Morm. 9:12; Moro. 8:8.
c Gen. 3:6; 2 Ne. 2:15 (15–19); Alma 12:22 (21–23).
d TG Mercy.
27*a* TG Hell.
b 2 Ne. 9:16; Jacob 6:10; Alma 12:17; D&C 76:36.
c Mosiah 5:5.
4 1*a* 1 Chr. 21:18; Mosiah 3:2.
b Neh. 8:9; Alma 19:17.
c Jer. 36:16; Heb. 12:28. TG Reverence.
2*a* TG Poor in Spirit.
b Neh. 9:1 (1–3). TG Carnal Mind.
c Gen. 18:27.
d Mosiah 3:18; Hel. 5:9.
e TG Purification.
f TG Jesus Christ, Creator.
3*a* TG Remission of Sins.
b TG Conscience.
c TG Faith.
d Neh. 8:12.

understand the remainder of my
words which I shall speak unto you.
5 For behold, if the knowledge of
the goodness of God at this time has
awakened you to a sense of your
[a]nothingness, and your worthless
and fallen state—
6 I say unto you, if ye have come
to a [a]knowledge of the goodness of
God, and his matchless power, and
his wisdom, and his patience, and his
long-suffering towards the children
of men; and also, the [b]atonement
which has been prepared from the
[c]foundation of the world, that thereby
salvation might come to him that
should put his [d]trust in the Lord,
and should be diligent in keeping his
commandments, and continue in the
faith even unto the end of his life, I
mean the life of the mortal body—
7 I say, that this is the man who
receiveth salvation, through the
atonement which was prepared
from the foundation of the world for
all mankind, which ever were since
the [a]fall of Adam, or who are, or who
ever shall be, even unto the end of
the world.
8 And this is the means whereby
salvation cometh. And there is [a]none
other salvation save this which hath
been spoken of; neither are there
any conditions whereby man can be
saved except the conditions which
I have told you.
9 Believe in [a]God; believe that he
is, and that he [b]created all things,
both in heaven and in earth; believe
that he has all [c]wisdom, and all
power, both in heaven and in earth;
believe that man doth not [d]compre-
hend all the things which the Lord
can comprehend.
10 And again, believe that ye must
[a]repent of your sins and forsake
them, and humble yourselves before God; and ask in [b]sincerity of
heart that he would [c]forgive you;
and now, if you [d]believe all these
things see that ye [e]do them.
11 And again I say unto you as I
have said before, that as ye have
come to the knowledge of the glory
of God, or if ye have known of his
goodness and have [a]tasted of his
love, and have received a [b]remis-
sion of your sins, which causeth
such exceedingly great joy in your
souls, even so I would that ye should
remember, and always retain in remembrance, the greatness of God,
and your own [c]nothingness, and
his [d]goodness and long-suffering
towards you, unworthy creatures,
and humble yourselves even in the
depths of [e]humility, [f]calling on the
name of the Lord daily, and standing [g]steadfastly in the faith of that
which is to come, which was spoken
by the mouth of the angel.
12 And behold, I say unto you that
if ye do this ye shall always rejoice,
and be filled with the [a]love of God,
and always [b]retain a remission of
your sins; and ye shall grow in the
[c]knowledge of the glory of him that
created you, or in the knowledge of
that which is just and true.
13 And ye will not have a [a]mind
to injure one another, but to live
[b]peaceably, and to render to every

5*a* Moses 1:10.
6*a* TG God, Knowledge about; God, Perfection of.
b TG Jesus Christ, Atonement through.
c Mosiah 15:19; 18:13.
d Ps. 36:7 (7–8); 2 Ne. 22:2; Hel. 12:1. TG Trust in God.
7*a* TG Fall of Man.
8*a* Acts 4:12; 2 Ne. 31:21; Mosiah 3:17.
9*a* Deut. 4:39.
b TG God, Creator; Jesus Christ, Creator.
c Rom. 11:34 (33–36); Jacob 4:8 (8–13). TG God, Perfection of.
d Isa. 55:9.
10*a* TG Repent.
b TG Sincere.
c Ps. 41:4; D&C 61:2.
d Matt. 7:24 (24–27); Acts 16:31 (30–31).
e 2 Ne. 31:19 (19–21).
11*a* Ps. 34:8; Alma 36:24 (24–26).
b TG Remission of Sins.
c Rom. 5:8 (6–8); Moses 1:10.
d Ex. 34:6 (5–7); Moro. 8:3.
e TG Humility.
f TG Prayer.
g TG Steadfastness.
12*a* TG God, Love of.
b Mosiah 4:26; Alma 4:14 (13–14); 5:26 (26–35); D&C 20:32 (31–34).
c TG God, Knowledge about.
13*a* TG Man, New, Spiritually Reborn.
b TG Peacemakers.

man according to that which is
his due.
14 And ye will not suffer your
[a]children that they go hungry, or
naked; neither will ye [b]suffer that
they transgress the laws of God, and
fight and [c]quarrel one with another,
and serve the devil, who is the master of sin, or who is the [d]evil spirit
which hath been spoken of by our
fathers, he being an enemy to all
righteousness.
15 But ye will [a]teach them to [b]walk
in the ways of truth and [c]soberness;
ye will teach them to [d]love one another, and to serve one another.
16 And also, ye yourselves will
[a]succor those that stand in need of
your succor; ye will administer
of your substance unto him that
standeth in need; and ye will not
suffer that the [b]beggar putteth up
his petition to you in vain, and turn
him out to perish.
17 Perhaps thou shalt [a]say: The
man has brought upon himself his
misery; therefore I will stay my
hand, and will not give unto him
of my food, nor impart unto him of
my substance that he may not suffer, for his punishments are just—
18 But I say unto you, O man,
whosoever doeth this the same hath
great cause to repent; and except
he repenteth of that which he hath
done he perisheth forever, and hath
no interest in the kingdom of God.
19 For behold, are we not all [a]beg-
gars? Do we not all depend upon
the same Being, even God, for all
the substance which we have, for
both food and raiment, and for gold,
and for silver, and for all the riches
which we have of every kind?
20 And behold, even at this time,
ye have been calling on his name,
and begging for a [a]remission of your
sins. And has he suffered that ye
have begged in vain? Nay; he has
poured out his [b]Spirit upon you, and
has caused that your hearts should
be filled with [c]joy, and has caused
that your mouths should be stopped
that ye could not find utterance,
so exceedingly great was your joy.
21 And now, if God, who has created you, on whom you are depen-
dent for your lives and for all that
ye have and are, doth grant unto
you whatsoever ye ask that is right,
in faith, believing that ye shall receive, O then, how ye ought to [a]im-
part of the substance that ye have
one to another.
22 And if ye [a]judge the man who
putteth up his petition to you for
your substance that he perish not,
and condemn him, how much more
just will be your [b]condemnation for
withholding your substance, which
doth not belong to you but to God,
to whom also your life [c]belongeth;
and yet ye put up no petition, nor
repent of the thing which thou
hast done.
23 I say unto you, wo be unto that
man, for his substance shall perish
with him; and now, I say these things
unto those who are [a]rich as pertaining to the things of this world.
24 And again, I say unto the poor,
ye who have not and yet have sufficient, that ye remain from day
to day; I mean all you who deny

14*a* 1 Tim. 5:8; D&C 83:4. TG Marriage, Fatherhood.
b Prov. 13:24.
c TG Contention.
d 2 Ne. 32:8; Mosiah 2:32.
15*a* Mosiah 1:2; Moses 6:58 (58–63). TG Family, Children, Responsibilities toward.
b TG Walking with God.
c TG Sincere.
d 1 Sam. 18:1; Mosiah 18:21. TG Family, Love within.
16*a* Prov. 19:17. TG Charity; Service; Welfare.
b Prov. 21:13; Isa. 10:2; Luke 3:11; D&C 38:16.
17*a* Prov. 17:5.
19*a* Prov. 22:2; 1 Cor. 4:7.
20*a* Rom. 2:4 (1–4).
b TG God, Spirit of.
c TG Joy.
21*a* Dan. 4:27. TG Generosity; Welfare.
22*a* Matt. 7:2 (1–2); John 7:24.
b 1 Jn. 3:17.
c Mosiah 2:25.
23*a* Luke 21:1 (1–4); D&C 56:16.

the beggar, because ye have not; I
would that ye say in your hearts
that: I [a]give not because I [b]have not,
but if I had I would [c]give.
25 And now, if ye say this in your
hearts ye remain guiltless, otherwise ye are [a]condemned; and your
condemnation is just for ye covet
that which ye have not received.
26 And now, for the sake of these
things which I have spoken unto
you—that is, for the sake of retaining a remission of your sins from
day to day, that ye may [a]walk guiltless before God—I would that ye
should [b]impart of your substance
to the [c]poor, every man according to that which he hath, such as
[d]feeding the hungry, clothing the
naked, visiting the sick and administering to their relief, both spiritually and temporally, according to
their wants.
27 And see that all these things are
done in wisdom and [a]order; for it
is not requisite that a man should
run [b]faster than he has strength.
And again, it is expedient that he
should be diligent, that thereby he
might win the prize; therefore, all
things must be done in order.
28 And I would that ye should
remember, that whosoever among
you [a]borroweth of his neighbor
should return the thing that he
borroweth, according as he doth
agree, or else thou shalt commit
sin; and perhaps thou shalt cause
thy neighbor to commit sin also.
29 And finally, I cannot tell you all
the things whereby ye may commit
sin; for there are divers ways and
means, even so many that I cannot
number them.
30 But this much I can tell you, that
if ye do not [a]watch yourselves, and
your [b]thoughts, and your [c]words,
and your deeds, and observe the commandments of God, and [d]continue
in the faith of what ye have heard
concerning the coming of our Lord,
even unto the end of your lives,
ye must perish. And now, O man,
remember, and perish not.

CHAPTER 5

The Saints become the sons and daughters of Christ through faith—They are then called by the name of Christ—King Benjamin exhorts them to be steadfast and immovable in good works. About 124 B.C.

AND now, it came to pass that when
king Benjamin had thus spoken to
his people, he sent among them,
desiring to know of his people if
they [a]believed the words which he
had spoken unto them.
2 And they all cried with one voice,
saying: Yea, we believe all the words
which thou hast spoken unto us;
and also, we know of their surety
and truth, because of the Spirit of
the Lord Omnipotent, which has
wrought a mighty [a]change in us,
or in our hearts, that we have no
more disposition to do [b]evil, but to
do good continually.
3 And we, ourselves, also, through
the infinite [a]goodness of God, and
the manifestations of his Spirit,
have great views of that which is
to come; and were it expedient, we
could prophesy of all things.
4 And it is the faith which we have
had on the things which our king
has spoken unto us that has brought

24*a* Deut. 16:17.
b Acts 3:6 (5–7).
c Mark 12:44.
25*a* D&C 56:17.
26*a* TG Walking with God.
b Jacob 2:19 (17–19); Mosiah 21:17; Alma 35:9.
c Job 29:12; Zech. 7:10; Luke 18:22; Alma 1:27. TG Almsgiving.
d Isa. 58:10 (9–11); Alma 4:12 (12–13); 3 Ne. 12:42.
27*a* TG Order.
b Eccl. 9:11; Alma 1:26; D&C 10:4.
28*a* TG Borrow; Debt; Honesty.
30*a* Deut. 4:9; Alma 12:14. TG Watch.
b Matt. 5:28 (27–28); Mark 7:23 (15–23).
c Matt. 15:18 (18–20). TG Gossip.
d TG Steadfastness.
5 1*a* 1 Ne. 11:4 (1–5).
2*a* Rom. 8:2 (1–4); Alma 5:14; 13:12. TG Man, New, Spiritually Reborn.
b Alma 19:33.
3*a* Ex. 34:6 (5–7).

us to this great knowledge, whereby
we do rejoice with such exceedingly
great joy.
5 And we are willing to enter into
a [a]covenant with our God to do his
will, and to be obedient to his commandments in all things that he
shall command us, all the remainder
of our days, that we may not bring
upon ourselves a [b]never-ending
torment, as has been spoken by the
[c]angel, that we may not drink out
of the cup of the wrath of God.
6 And now, these are the words
which king Benjamin desired of
them; and therefore he said unto
them: Ye have spoken the words
that I desired; and the covenant
which ye have made is a righteous
covenant.
7 And now, because of the covenant which ye have made ye shall
be called the [a]children of Christ,
his sons, and his daughters; for behold, this day he hath spiritually
begotten you; for ye say that your
hearts are [b]changed through faith
on his name; therefore, ye are [c]born
of him and have become his [d]sons
and his daughters.
8 And under this head ye are made
[a]free, and there is [b]no other head
whereby ye can be made free. There
is no other [c]name given whereby
salvation cometh; therefore, I would
that ye should [d]take upon you the
name of Christ, all you that have
entered into the covenant with God
that ye should be obedient unto the
end of your lives.
9 And it shall come to pass that
whosoever doeth this shall be found
at the right hand of God, for he
shall know the name by which he
is called; for he shall be called by
the name of Christ.
10 And now it shall come to pass,
that whosoever shall not take upon
him the name of Christ must be
called by some [a]other name; therefore, he findeth himself on the [b]left
hand of God.
11 And I would that ye should remember also, that this is the [a]name
that I said I should give unto you
that never should be blotted out,
except it be through transgression;
therefore, take heed that ye do not
transgress, that the name be not
blotted out of your hearts.
12 I say unto you, I would that
ye should remember to [a]retain the
name written always in your hearts,
that ye are not found on the left
hand of God, but that ye hear and
know the voice by which ye shall
be called, and also, the name by
which he shall call you.
13 For how [a]knoweth a man the
master whom he has not served,
and who is a stranger unto him,
and is far from the thoughts and
intents of his heart?
14 And again, doth a man take an
ass which belongeth to his neighbor, and keep him? I say unto you,
Nay; he will not even suffer that he
shall feed among his flocks, but will
drive him away, and cast him out.
I say unto you, that even so shall it
be among you if ye know not the
name by which ye are called.
15 Therefore, I would that ye should
be steadfast and immovable, always
abounding in [a]good works, that
Christ, the [b]Lord God Omnipotent,

5*a* 2 Chr. 15:12 (12–15); Neh. 10:29; Mosiah 6:3. TG Commitment.
b Mosiah 3:27 (25–27).
c Mosiah 3:2.
7*a* 1 Jn. 2:12; Mosiah 15:2; 27:25 (24–26); Moses 6:68 (64–68).
b TG Sanctification.
c John 1:13 (12–13); Mosiah 15:10. TG Man, New, Spiritually Reborn.
d Matt. 12:49 (49–50); D&C 11:30.
8*a* Rom. 6:18 (14–22); 1 Cor. 7:22; Gal. 5:1; D&C 88:86.
b Acts 4:12; Mosiah 4:8; Alma 21:9.
c Gal. 3:27; Mosiah 1:11; 26:18.
d Acts 11:26; Alma 46:15.
10*a* Alma 5:39 (38–42).
b Matt. 25:33.
11*a* Mosiah 1:11 (11–12). TG Jesus Christ, Taking the Name of.
12*a* Num. 6:27; Ps. 119:55; D&C 18:25.
13*a* Jer. 4:22; Mosiah 26:25 (24–27).
15*a* TG Good Works.
b TG Jesus Christ, Jehovah; Jesus Christ, Lord.

may [c]seal you his, that you may be
brought to heaven, that ye may have
everlasting salvation and eternal
life, through the wisdom, and power,
and justice, and mercy of him who
[d]created all things, in heaven and
in earth, who is God above all.
Amen.

CHAPTER 6

King Benjamin records the names of the people and appoints priests to teach them—Mosiah reigns as a righteous king. About 124–121 B.C.

AND now, king Benjamin thought
it was expedient, after having finished speaking to the people, that
he should [a]take the names of all
those who had entered into a covenant with God to keep his commandments.
2 And it came to pass that there
was not one soul, except it were little
children, but who had entered into
the covenant and had taken upon
them the name of Christ.
3 And again, it came to pass that
when king Benjamin had made an
end of all these things, and had
consecrated his son [a]Mosiah to be
a ruler and a king over his people,
and had given him all the charges
concerning the kingdom, and also
had [b]appointed [c]priests to [d]teach
the people, that thereby they might
hear and know the commandments
of God, and to stir them up in remembrance of the [e]oath which they
had made, he dismissed the multitude, and they returned, every one,
according to their [f]families, to their
own houses.
4 And Mosiah began to reign in
his father's stead. And he began to
reign in the thirtieth year of his
age, making in the whole, about
four hundred and seventy-six
years from the [a]time that Lehi left
Jerusalem.
5 And king Benjamin lived three
years and he died.
6 And it came to pass that king
Mosiah did [a]walk in the ways of the
Lord, and did observe his judgments
and his statutes, and did keep his
commandments in all things whatsoever he commanded him.
7 And king Mosiah did cause his
people that they should till the
earth. And he also, himself, did till
the earth, that thereby he might [a]not
become burdensome to his people,
that he might do according to that
which his father had done in all
things. And there was no contention among all his people for the
space of three years.

CHAPTER 7

Ammon finds the land of Lehi-Nephi, where Limhi is king—Limhi's people are in bondage to the Lamanites—Limhi recounts their history—A prophet (Abinadi) had testified that Christ is the God and Father of all things—Those who sow filthiness reap the whirlwind, and those who put their trust in the Lord will be delivered. About 121 B.C.

AND now, it came to pass that after king Mosiah had had continual
peace for the space of three years,
he was desirous to know concerning
the people who [a]went up to dwell
in the land of [b]Lehi-Nephi, or in
the city of Lehi-Nephi; for his people had heard nothing from them
from the time they left the land of
[c]Zarahemla; therefore, they wearied
him with their teasings.
2 And it came to pass that king
Mosiah granted that sixteen of their
strong men might go up to the land
of Lehi-Nephi, to inquire concerning their brethren.

15*c* TG Election.
d Col. 1:16; Mosiah 4:2; Alma 11:39.
6 1*a* D&C 128:8.
3*a* Mosiah 1:10; 2:30.
b TG Priesthood, Ordination.
c Mosiah 29:42.
d Alma 4:7.
e Mosiah 5:5 (5–7).
f Num. 1:2; Ether 1:41; D&C 48:6.
4*a* 1 Ne. 1:4; 2:4.
6*a* TG Walking with God.
7*a* 2 Cor. 11:9.
7 1*a* Omni 1:27 (27–30).
b 2 Ne. 5:8; Mosiah 9:6.
c Omni 1:13.

3 And it came to pass that on the morrow they started to go up, having with them one [a]Ammon, he being a strong and mighty man, and a [b]descendant of Zarahemla; and he was also their leader.

4 And now, they knew not the course they should travel in the wilderness to go up to the land of Lehi-Nephi; therefore they wandered many days in the wilderness, even [a]forty days did they wander.

5 And when they had wandered forty days they came to a [a]hill, which is north of the land of [b]Shilom, and there they pitched their tents.

6 And [a]Ammon took three of his brethren, and their names were Amaleki, Helem, and Hem, and they went down into the land of [b]Nephi.

7 And behold, they met the king of the people who were in the land of Nephi, and in the land of [a]Shilom; and they were surrounded by the king's guard, and were [b]taken, and were [c]bound, and were committed to [d]prison.

8 And it came to pass when they had been in prison two days they were again brought before the king, and their bands were loosed; and they stood before the king, and were permitted, or rather [a]commanded, that they should answer the questions which he should ask them.

9 And he said unto them: Behold, I am [a]Limhi, the son of Noah, who was the son of Zeniff, who came up out of the [b]land of Zarahemla to inherit this land, which was the land of their fathers, who was made a [c]king by the [d]voice of the people.

10 And now, [a]I desire to know the cause whereby ye were so bold as to come near the walls of the city, when I, myself, was with my guards without the [b]gate?

11 And now, for this cause have I suffered that ye should be preserved, that I might inquire of you, or else I should have caused that my guards should have put you to death. Ye are permitted to speak.

12 And now, when Ammon saw that he was permitted to speak, he went forth and [a]bowed himself before the king; and rising again he said: O king, I am very thankful before God this day that I am yet alive, and am permitted to speak; and I will endeavor to speak with boldness;

13 For I am assured that if ye had known me ye would not have suffered that I should have worn these bands. For I am Ammon, and am a [a]descendant of Zarahemla, and have come up out of the [b]land of Zarahemla to inquire concerning our brethren, whom [c]Zeniff brought up out of that land.

14 And now, it came to pass that after Limhi had heard the words of Ammon, he was exceedingly [a]glad, and said: Now, I know of a surety that my brethren who were in the land of Zarahemla are [b]yet alive. And now, I will rejoice; and on the morrow I will cause that my people shall rejoice also.

15 For behold, we are in bondage to the Lamanites, and are [a]taxed with a tax which is grievous to be borne. And now, behold, our brethren will deliver us out of our [b]bondage, or out of the hands of the

3*a* Mosiah 8:2.
b Omni 1:14.
4*a* Num. 13:25 (17–25).
5*a* Mosiah 11:13.
b Mosiah 9:14 (6, 8, 14); 11:12 (12–13); 22:11 (8, 11); Alma 23:12.
6*a* Mosiah 21:22, 26.
b 2 Ne. 5:8; Omni 1:12 (12, 27); Mosiah 9:1 (1, 3–4, 14); 28:1 (1, 5); Alma 50:8 (8, 11).
7*a* Mosiah 22:8.
b Mosiah 21:21.
c Alma 17:20.
d Mosiah 21:23 (22–24).
8*a* Alma 14:19.
9*a* Mosiah 11:1; 19:16.
b Omni 1:13.
c TG Kings, Earthly.
d Mosiah 19:26.
10*a* Mosiah 21:23 (23–24).
b Josh. 20:4.
12*a* Alma 47:22 (22–23).
13*a* Omni 1:14.
b Omni 1:13.
c Mosiah 8:2; 9:1.
14*a* Mosiah 21:24.
b Mosiah 21:25 (25–26).
15*a* Mosiah 19:15.
b TG Bondage, Physical.

Lamanites, and we will be their
[c]slaves; for it is better that we be
slaves to the Nephites than to pay
tribute to the king of the Lamanites.
16 And now, king Limhi commanded his guards that they should no
more bind Ammon nor his brethren,
but caused that they should go to
the hill which was north of Shilom,
and bring their brethren into the
city, that thereby they might eat,
and drink, and rest themselves from
the labors of their journey; for they
had suffered many things; they had
suffered hunger, thirst, and fatigue.
17 And now, it came to pass on
the morrow that king Limhi sent a
proclamation among all his people,
that thereby they might gather
themselves together to the [a]temple,
to hear the words which he should
speak unto them.
18 And it came to pass that when
they had gathered themselves together that he [a]spake unto them in
this wise, saying: O ye, my people,
lift up your heads and be comforted;
for behold, the time is at hand, or
is not far distant, when we shall no
longer be in subjection to our enemies, notwithstanding our many
strugglings, which have been in
vain; yet I trust there [b]remaineth
an effectual struggle to be made.
19 Therefore, lift up your heads,
and rejoice, and put your [a]trust in
[b]God, in that God who was the God
of Abraham, and Isaac, and Jacob;
and also, that God who [c]brought the
children of [d]Israel out of the land
of Egypt, and caused that they
should walk through the [e]Red Sea
on dry ground, and fed them with
[f]manna that they might not perish
in the wilderness; and many more
things did he do for them.
20 And again, that same God has
brought our fathers [a]out of the land
of Jerusalem, and has kept and preserved his people even until now;
and behold, it is [b]because of our iniquities and abominations that he
has brought us into bondage.
21 And ye all are witnesses this
day, that Zeniff, who was made king
over this people, he being [a]over-
zealous to inherit the land of his
fathers, therefore being deceived by
the cunning and craftiness of king
Laman, who having entered into a
treaty with king Zeniff, and having
yielded up into his hands the possessions of a part of the land, or even
the city of Lehi-Nephi, and the
city of Shilom; and the land round
about—
22 And all this he did, for the sole
purpose of [a]bringing this people into
subjection or into bondage. And behold, we at this time do pay [b]tribute
to the king of the Lamanites, to the
amount of one half of our corn, and
our barley, and even all our grain
of every kind, and one half of the
increase of our flocks and our herds;
and even one half of all we have or
possess the king of the Lamanites
doth exact of us, or our lives.
23 And now, is not this grievous
to be borne? And is not this, our
affliction, great? Now behold, how
great reason we have to [a]mourn.
24 Yea, I say unto you, great are the
reasons which we have to [a]mourn;
for behold how many of our brethren have been slain, and their blood
has been spilt in vain, and all because of iniquity.
25 For if this people had not fallen
into transgression the Lord would
not have suffered that this great evil
should come upon them. But behold,

15*c* TG Slavery.
17*a* 2 Ne. 5:16.
18*a* Mosiah 8:1.
b Mosiah 22:1 (1–16).
19*a* TG Trust in God.
b Ex. 3:6 (2–10); 1 Ne. 19:10; D&C 136:21.
c Ex. 12:51; 1 Ne. 17:40; Mosiah 12:34; Alma 36:28.
d TG Israel, Origins of.
e Josh. 2:10; 1 Ne. 4:2; 17:26.
f Ex. 16:15, 35; Num. 11:7 (7–8); Josh. 5:12; John 6:49; 1 Ne. 17:28.
20*a* 1 Ne. 2:2 (1–4).
b Deut. 28:15 (1–2, 15–68).
21*a* Mosiah 9:3 (1–3).
22*a* Mosiah 9:10; 10:18.
b TG Tribute.
23*a* Prov. 29:2.
24*a* Ezek. 24:23; Hel. 9:22.

they would not hearken unto his
words; but there arose contentions
among them, even so much that they
did shed blood among themselves.
26 And a [a]prophet of the Lord have
they [b]slain; yea, a chosen man of God,
who told them of their wickedness
and abominations, and prophesied
of many things which are to come,
yea, even the coming of Christ.
27 And because he said unto them
that Christ was the [a]God, the Father
of all things, and said that he should
take upon him the [b]image of man,
and it should be the [c]image after
which man was created in the beginning;
or in other words, he said
that man was created after the image
of [d]God, and that God should
come down among the children of
men, and take upon him flesh and
blood, and go forth upon the face
of the earth—
28 And now, because he said this,
they did [a]put him to death; and
many more things did they do
which brought down the wrath of
God upon them. Therefore, who
wondereth that they are in bondage,
and that they are smitten with
sore afflictions?
29 For behold, the Lord hath said:
I will not [a]succor my people in the
day of their transgression; but I
will hedge up their ways that they
prosper not; and their doings shall
be as a [b]stumbling block before
them.
30 And again, he saith: If my people
shall sow [a]filthiness they shall [b]reap
the [c]chaff thereof in the whirlwind;
and the effect thereof is poison.
31 And again he saith: If my
people shall sow filthiness they
shall reap the [a]east wind, which
bringeth immediate destruction.
32 And now, behold, the promise
of the Lord is fulfilled, and ye are
smitten and afflicted.
33 But if ye will [a]turn to the Lord
with full purpose of heart, and put
your trust in him, and serve him
with all [b]diligence of mind, if ye do
this, he will, according to his own
will and pleasure, deliver you out
of bondage.

CHAPTER 8

Ammon teaches the people of Limhi—He learns of the twenty-four Jaredite plates—Ancient records can be translated by seers—No gift is greater than seership. About 121 B.C.

AND it came to pass that after king
Limhi had made an end of [a]speaking
to his people, for he spake many
things unto them and only a few of
them have I written in this book, he
told his people all the things concerning
their brethren who were
in the land of Zarahemla.
2 And he caused that Ammon
should stand up before the multitude,
and rehearse unto them all
that had happened unto their brethren
from the time that [a]Zeniff went
up out of the land even until the
time that he [b]himself came up out
of the land.
3 And he also rehearsed unto them
the last words which king Benjamin
had [a]taught them, and explained
them to the people of king Limhi,
so that they might understand all
the words which he spake.

26*a* Mosiah 17:20 (12–20).
b TG Prophets, Rejection of.
27*a* Isa. 9:6; 2 Ne. 26:12; Mosiah 27:31 (30–31).
b TG God, Body of, Corporeal Nature.
c Gen. 1:26 (26–28); Ether 3:15 (14–17); D&C 20:18 (17–18).
d Mosiah 13:34; 15:2 (1–7); Alma 7:9 (9–13).
28*a* Mosiah 17:13.
29*a* Josh. 24:20; 1 Sam. 12:15; 2 Chr. 24:20.
b Jer. 6:21.
30*a* TG Filthiness.
b Hosea 8:7; Gal. 6:8 (7–8); D&C 6:33. TG Harvest.
c Luke 3:17; 2 Ne. 15:24.
31*a* Gen. 41:23; Jer. 18:17; Ezek. 27:26; Jonah 4:8; Mosiah 12:6.
33*a* Deut. 30:10; Lam. 5:21; Morm. 9:6; D&C 98:47.
b TG Diligence.
8 1*a* Mosiah 7:18 (18–33).
2*a* Mosiah 7:13.
b Mosiah 7:3.
3*a* Mosiah 2:9.

4 And it came to pass that after he
had done all this, that king Limhi
dismissed the multitude, and caused
that they should return every one
unto his own house.
5 And it came to pass that he caused
that the [a]plates which contained the
[b]record of his people from the time
that they left the [c]land of Zarahemla, should be brought before
Ammon, that he might read them.
6 Now, as soon as Ammon had
read the record, the king inquired
of him to know if he could [a]inter-
pret languages, and Ammon told
him that he could not.
7 And the king said unto him:
Being grieved for the afflictions of
my people, I caused that [a]forty and
three of my people should take a
journey into the wilderness, that
thereby they might find the land
of Zarahemla, that we might appeal
unto our brethren to deliver us out
of bondage.
8 And they were lost in the wilderness for the space of [a]many days,
yet they were diligent, and found
not the land of Zarahemla but returned to this land, having traveled
in a land among many waters, having discovered a land which was
covered with [b]bones of men, and of
beasts, and was also covered with
ruins of buildings of every kind,
having discovered a land which
had been peopled with a people
who were as numerous as the hosts
of Israel.
9 And for a testimony that the
things that they had said are true
they have brought [a]twenty-four
plates which are filled with engravings, and they are of pure gold.
10 And behold, also, they have
brought [a]breastplates, which are
large, and they are of [b]brass and
of copper, and are perfectly sound.
11 And again, they have brought
swords, the hilts thereof have perished, and the blades thereof were
cankered with rust; and there is no
one in the land that is able to interpret the language or the engravings
that are on the plates. Therefore I
said unto thee: Canst thou translate?
12 And I say unto thee again:
Knowest thou of any one that can
translate? For I am desirous that
these records should be translated
into our language; for, perhaps,
they will give us a knowledge of a
remnant of the people who have
been destroyed, from whence these
records came; or, perhaps, they will
give us a knowledge of this very
people who have been destroyed;
and I am desirous to know the cause
of their destruction.
13 Now Ammon said unto him: I
can assuredly tell thee, O king, of a
man that can [a]translate the records;
for he has wherewith that he can
look, and translate all records that
are of ancient date; and it is a gift
from God. And the things are called
[b]interpreters, and no man can look
in them except he be commanded,
lest he should look for that he ought
not and he should perish. And whosoever is commanded to look in
them, the same is called [c]seer.
14 And behold, the king of the people who are in the land of Zarahemla
is the man that is commanded to
do these things, and who has this
high gift from God.
15 And the king said that a [a]seer
is greater than a prophet.
16 And Ammon said that a seer is
a revelator and a prophet also; and
a gift which is greater can no man

5*a* See Mosiah 9–22.
b Mosiah 9:1; 22:14.
c Omni 1:13.
6*a* 1 Cor. 12:10; Mosiah 21:28.
7*a* Mosiah 21:25.
8*a* Alma 50:29; Hel. 3:4 (3–4); Morm. 6:4.
b Omni 1:22; Mosiah 21:26 (26–27).
9*a* Mosiah 21:27; 22:14.
10*a* Ex. 25:7; Ether 15:15.
b Ether 10:23.
13*a* Dan. 5:16; Omni 1:20 (20–22); Mosiah 28:17 (11–17).
b Ex. 28:30; Mosiah 21:28 (27–28). TG Urim and Thummim.
c TG Seer.
15*a* 1 Sam. 9:9; D&C 21:1.

have, except he should possess the
power of God, which no man can;
yet a man may have great power
given him from God.
17 But a seer can know of things
which are past, and also of things
which are to come, and by them shall
all things be revealed, or, rather,
shall secret things be made manifest, and hidden things shall come
to light, and things which are not
known shall be made known by
them, and also things shall be made
known by them which otherwise
could not be known.
18 Thus God has provided a means
that man, through faith, might
work mighty miracles; therefore
he becometh a great benefit to his
fellow beings.
19 And now, when Ammon had
made an end of speaking these words
the king rejoiced exceedingly, and
gave thanks to God, saying: Doubtless a [a]great mystery is contained
within these plates, and these interpreters were doubtless prepared for
the purpose of unfolding all such
mysteries to the children of men.
20 O how marvelous are the works
of the Lord, and how long doth he
suffer with his people; yea, and
how [a]blind and impenetrable are
the understandings of the children
of men; for they will not seek wisdom, neither do they desire that
[b]she should rule over them!
21 Yea, they are as a wild flock
which fleeth from the shepherd, and
scattereth, and are driven, and are
devoured by the beasts of the forest.

THE RECORD OF ZENIFF—An account of his people, from the time they left the land of Zarahemla until the time that they were delivered out of the hands of the Lamanites.

Comprising chapters 9 through 22.

CHAPTER 9

Zeniff leads a group from Zarahemla to possess the land of Lehi-Nephi—The Lamanite king permits them to inherit the land—There is war between the Lamanites and Zeniff's people. About 200–187 B.C.

[a]I, [b]ZENIFF, having been taught in
all the language of the Nephites,
and having had a knowledge of the
land of [c]Nephi, or of the land of our
fathers' first inheritance, and having been sent as a spy among the
Lamanites that I might spy out their
forces, that our army might come
upon them and destroy them—but
when I saw that which was good
among them I was desirous that
they should not be destroyed.
2 Therefore, I contended with my
brethren in the wilderness, for I would
that our ruler should make a treaty
with them; but he being an austere
and a blood-thirsty man commanded
that I should be slain; but I was res-
cued by the shedding of much blood;
for father fought against father, and
brother against brother, until the
greater number of our army was destroyed in the wilderness; and we returned, those of us that were spared,
to the land of Zarahemla, to relate that
tale to their wives and their children.
3 And yet, I being [a]over-zealous
to inherit the land of our fathers,
collected as many as were desirous
to go up to possess the land, and
started again on our [b]journey into
the wilderness to go up to the land;
but we were smitten with famine
and sore afflictions; for we were
slow to remember the Lord our God.
4 Nevertheless, after many days'
wandering in the wilderness we
pitched our tents in the place where
our brethren were slain, which was
near to the land of our fathers.
5 And it came to pass that I went
again with four of my men into the

19*a* Ether 3:26 (21–28); 4:4 (1–8).
20*a* TG Spiritual Blindness.
b IE Wisdom, a feminine noun in Hebrew and Greek. Prov. 9:1; Matt. 11:19.
9 1*a* Mosiah 8:5; 22:14.
b Mosiah 7:13.
c 2 Ne. 5:8; Omni 1:12 (12, 27); Mosiah 7:6 (6–7); 28:1 (1, 5).
3*a* Omni 1:27 (27–29); Mosiah 7:21.
b Mosiah 25:5.

city, in unto the king, that I might
know of the disposition of the king,
and that I might know if I might
go in with my people and possess
the land in peace.
6 And I went in unto the king, and
he covenanted with me that I might
possess the [a]land of Lehi-Nephi, and
the land of Shilom.
7 And he also commanded that
his people should depart out of the
land, and I and my people went into
the land that we might possess it.
8 And we began to build buildings, and to repair the walls of
the city, yea, even the walls of the
city of Lehi-Nephi, and the city of
Shilom.
9 And we began to till the ground,
yea, even with all manner of [a]seeds,
with seeds of corn, and of wheat,
and of barley, and with neas, and
with sheum, and with seeds of all
manner of fruits; and we did begin to multiply and prosper in the
land.
10 Now it was the cunning and
the craftiness of king [a]Laman, to
[b]bring my people into bondage,
that he yielded up the land that
we might possess it.
11 Therefore it came to pass, that
after we had dwelt in the land for
the space of twelve years that king
Laman began to grow uneasy, lest
by any means my people should
[a]wax strong in the land, and that
they could not overpower them and
bring them into bondage.
12 Now they were a [a]lazy and an
[b]idolatrous people; therefore they
were desirous to bring us into bondage, that they might glut themselves
with the labors of our hands; yea,
that they might feast themselves
upon the flocks of our fields.
13 Therefore it came to pass that
king Laman began to stir up his
people that they should contend
with my people; therefore there began to be wars and contentions in
the land.
14 For, in the thirteenth year of
my reign in the land of Nephi,
away on the south of the land of
[a]Shilom, when my people were wa-
tering and [b]feeding their flocks,
and tilling their lands, a numerous host of Lamanites came upon
them and began to slay them, and
to take off their flocks, and the corn
of their fields.
15 Yea, and it came to pass that
they fled, all that were not overtaken, even into the city of Nephi,
and did call upon me for protection.
16 And it came to pass that I did
arm them with bows, and with arrows, with swords, and with cimeters, and with clubs, and with slings,
and with all manner of weapons
which we could invent, and I and
my people did go forth against the
Lamanites to battle.
17 Yea, in the [a]strength of the Lord
did we go forth to battle against
the Lamanites; for I and my people did cry mightily to the Lord
that he would [b]deliver us out of the
hands of our enemies, for we were
awakened to a remembrance of the
deliverance of our fathers.
18 And God did [a]hear our cries
and did answer our prayers; and we
did go forth in his might; yea, we did
go forth against the Lamanites, and
in one day and a night we did slay
three thousand and forty-three; we
did slay them even until we had
driven them out of our land.
19 And I, myself, with mine own
hands, did help to bury their dead.
And behold, to our great sorrow
and lamentation, two hundred and
seventy-nine of our brethren were
slain.

6*a* 2 Ne. 5:8; Mosiah 7:1 (1–4, 21).
9*a* 1 Ne. 8:1; Enos 1:21; Mosiah 10:4.
10*a* Mosiah 24:3.
b Mosiah 7:22; 10:18.
11*a* Ex. 1:9 (9–10).
12*a* TG Laziness.
b Enos 1:20. TG Idolatry.
14*a* Mosiah 7:5; 11:12 (12–13).
b Mosiah 10:21.
17*a* TG Strength.
b Josh. 21:44; Alma 46:7.
18*a* Ex. 2:24 (23–24); Ps. 4:1 (1, 3); Dan. 10:12; D&C 35:3; Abr. 1:15 (15–16).

CHAPTER 10

King Laman dies—His people are wild and ferocious and believe in false traditions—Zeniff and his people prevail against them. About 187–160 B.C.

AND it came to pass that we again
began to establish the kingdom and
we again began to possess the land
in peace. And I caused that there
should be [a]weapons of war made
of every kind, that thereby I might
have weapons for my people against
the time the Lamanites should come
up again to war against my people.
2 And I set guards round about
the land, that the Lamanites might
not come upon us again unawares
and destroy us; and thus I did guard
my people and my flocks, and keep
them from falling into the hands
of our enemies.
3 And it came to pass that we did
inherit the land of our fathers for
many years, yea, for the space of
twenty and two years.
4 And I did cause that the men
should till the ground, and raise all
manner of [a]grain and all manner
of fruit of every kind.
5 And I did cause that the women
should spin, and toil, and work, and
work all manner of fine linen, yea,
and [a]cloth of every kind, that we
might clothe our nakedness; and
thus we did prosper in the land—
thus we did have continual peace
in the land for the space of twenty
and two years.
6 And it came to pass that king
[a]Laman died, and his son began to
reign in his stead. And he began
to stir his people up in rebellion
against my people; therefore they
began to prepare for war, and to
come up to battle against my people.
7 But I had sent my spies out round
about the land of [a]Shemlon, that I
might discover their preparations,
that I might guard against them,
that they might not come upon my
people and destroy them.
8 And it came to pass that they
came up upon the north of the
land of Shilom, with their numerous hosts, men [a]armed with [b]bows,
and with arrows, and with swords,
and with cimeters, and with
stones, and with slings; and they had
their heads shaved that they were
naked; and they were girded with a
leathern girdle about their loins.
9 And it came to pass that I caused
that the women and children of my
people should be hid in the wilderness; and I also caused that all my
old men that could bear arms, and
also all my young men that were
able to bear arms, should gather
themselves together to go to battle
against the Lamanites; and I did
place them in their ranks, every
man according to his age.
10 And it came to pass that we did
go up to battle against the Lamanites;
and I, even I, in my old age, did go
up to battle against the Lamanites.
And it came to pass that we did go up
in the [a]strength of the Lord to battle.
11 Now, the Lamanites knew nothing concerning the Lord, nor the
strength of the Lord, therefore they
depended upon their own strength.
Yet they were a strong people, as
to the [a]strength of men.
12 They were a [a]wild, and ferocious, and a blood-thirsty people,
believing in the [b]tradition of their
fathers, which is this—Believing
that they were driven out of the land
of Jerusalem because of the iniquities of their fathers, and that they
were [c]wronged in the wilderness by
their brethren, and they were also
wronged while crossing the sea;
13 And again, that they were

10 1*a* TG Weapon.
4*a* Mosiah 9:9.
5*a* Alma 1:29; Hel. 6:13. TG Clothing.
6*a* Mosiah 9:10 (10–11); 24:3.
7*a* Mosiah 11:12.
8*a* 2 Ne. 5:14; Jarom 1:8; Alma 2:12.
b Enos 1:20; Alma 3:5 (4–5).
10*a* TG Strength; Trust in God.
11*a* TG Trust Not in the Arm of Flesh.
12*a* Alma 17:14.
b 2 Ne. 5:1 (1–3); Mosiah 1:5; Alma 3:8.
c TG Injustice.

wronged while in the land of their [a]first inheritance, after they had crossed the sea, and all this because that Nephi was more faithful in keeping the commandments of the Lord—therefore [b]he was favored of the Lord, for the Lord heard his prayers and answered them, and he took the lead of their journey in the wilderness.

14 And his brethren were [a]wroth with him because they [b]understood not the dealings of the Lord; they were also wroth with him upon the waters because they hardened their hearts against the Lord.

15 And again, they were [a]wroth with him when they had arrived in the promised land, because they said that he had taken the [b]ruling of the people out of their hands; and they sought to kill him.

16 And again, they were wroth with him because he departed into the wilderness as the Lord had commanded him, and took the [a]records which were engraven on the plates of brass, for they said that he [b]robbed them.

17 And thus they have taught their children that they should hate them, and that they should murder them, and that they should rob and plunder them, and do all they could to destroy them; therefore they have an eternal hatred towards the children of Nephi.

18 For this very cause has king Laman, by his [a]cunning, and lying craftiness, and his fair promises, deceived me, that I have brought this my people up into this land, that they may destroy them; yea, and we have suffered these many years in the land.

19 And now I, Zeniff, after having told all these things unto my people concerning the Lamanites, I did stimulate them to go to battle with their might, putting their trust in the Lord; therefore, we did contend with them, face to face.

20 And it came to pass that we did drive them again out of our land; and we slew them with a great slaughter, even so many that we did not number them.

21 And it came to pass that we returned again to our own land, and my people again began to [a]tend their flocks, and to till their ground.

22 And now I, being old, did confer the kingdom upon one of my sons; therefore, I say no more. And may the Lord [a]bless my people. Amen.

CHAPTER 11

King Noah rules in wickedness—He revels in riotous living with his wives and concubines—Abinadi prophesies that the people will be taken into bondage—His life is sought by King Noah. About 160–150 B.C.

AND now it came to pass that Zeniff conferred the kingdom upon Noah, one of his sons; therefore Noah began to reign in his stead; and he did not walk in the ways of his father.

2 For behold, he did not keep the commandments of God, but he did walk after the desires of his own heart. And he had many wives and [a]concubines. And he did [b]cause his people to commit sin, and do that which was [c]abominable in the sight of the Lord. Yea, and they did commit [d]whoredoms and [e]all manner of wickedness.

3 And he laid a [a]tax of one fifth part of all they possessed, a fifth part of their gold and of their silver,

13 *a* 1 Ne. 18:23.
b 2 Ne. 5:5 (5–9).
14 *a* 1 Ne. 18:10 (10–11).
b 1 Ne. 15:8 (8–11); 2 Ne. 1:25 (24–27).
15 *a* 2 Ne. 5:1.
b 2 Ne. 5:3 (1–4).
16 *a* 2 Ne. 5:12; Mosiah 28:11.
b Alma 20:10 (10, 13).
18 *a* Mosiah 9:10; 19:28 (26, 28).
21 *a* Mosiah 9:14 (9, 14).
22 *a* Num. 6:24 (22–27).
11 2 *a* Jacob 3:5; Ether 10:5.
b 1 Kgs. 14:16; 15:26; 16:2; 21:22; 2 Kgs. 21:2 (1–9); Mosiah 23:12; 29:31.
c Mosiah 29:18.
d 2 Ne. 28:15.
e Mosiah 23:9.
3 *a* Gen. 47:24; Ether 10:5 (5–6).

and a fifth part of their [b]ziff, and of their copper, and of their brass and their iron; and a fifth part of their fatlings; and also a fifth part of all their grain.
4 And all this did he take to [a]support himself, and his wives and his [b]concubines; and also his priests, and their wives and their concubines; thus he had changed the affairs of the kingdom.
5 For he put down all the priests that had been consecrated by his father, and consecrated new [a]ones in their stead, such as were lifted up in the pride of their hearts.
6 Yea, and thus they were supported in their laziness, and in their idolatry, and in their whoredoms, by the taxes which king Noah had put upon his people; thus did the people labor exceedingly to support iniquity.
7 Yea, and they also became idolatrous, because they were deceived by the vain and flattering words of the king and priests; for they did speak flattering things unto them.
8 And it came to pass that king Noah built many elegant and spacious buildings; and he ornamented them with fine work of wood, and of all manner of [a]precious things, of gold, and of silver, and of iron, and of brass, and of ziff, and of copper;
9 And he also built him a spacious palace, and a throne in the midst thereof, all of which was of fine wood and was ornamented with gold and silver and with precious things.
10 And he also caused that his workmen should work all manner of fine work within the walls of the [a]temple, of fine wood, and of copper, and of brass.
11 And the seats which were set apart for the [a]high priests, which were above all the other seats, he did ornament with pure gold; and he caused a breastwork to be built before them, that they might rest their bodies and their arms upon while they should speak lying and vain words to his people.
12 And it came to pass that he built a [a]tower near the temple; yea, a very high tower, even so high that he could stand upon the top thereof and overlook the land of [b]Shilom, and also the land of [c]Shemlon, which was possessed by the Lamanites; and he could even look over all the land round about.
13 And it came to pass that he caused many buildings to be built in the land Shilom; and he caused a great tower to be built on the [a]hill north of the land Shilom, which had been a resort for the children of Nephi at the time they [b]fled out of the land; and thus he did do with the riches which he obtained by the taxation of his people.
14 And it came to pass that he placed his heart upon his riches, and he spent his time in [a]riotous living with his wives and his concubines; and so did also his priests spend their time with harlots.
15 And it came to pass that he planted vineyards round about in the land; and he built wine-presses, and made [a]wine in abundance; and therefore he became a wine-bibber, and also his people.
16 And it came to pass that the Lamanites began to come in upon his people, upon small numbers, and to slay them in their fields, and while they were tending their flocks.
17 And king Noah sent guards round about the land to keep them

3*b* HEB related words: adjective, "shining"; verb, "to overlay or plate with metal."
4*a* Prov. 29:3.
b TG Concubine.
5*a* 1 Kgs. 12:31; 2 Chr. 11:14 (13–14); Mosiah 11:11; 12:25 (17, 25).
8*a* Esth. 1:4.
10*a* 2 Ne. 5:16.
11*a* Mosiah 11:5 (5, 14); 12:17.
12*a* Gen. 35:21; Mosiah 2:7 (7–8); 19:5 (5–6).
b Mosiah 9:14 (6, 8, 14); 22:11 (8, 11).
c Mosiah 10:7.
13*a* Mosiah 7:5.
b Omni 1:12 (12–13).
14*a* TG Rioting and Reveling.
15*a* TG Drunkenness; Wine.

off; but he did not send a sufficient
number, and the Lamanites came
upon them and killed them, and
drove many of their flocks out of
the land; thus the Lamanites began
to destroy them, and to exercise
their hatred upon them.
18 And it came to pass that king
Noah sent his armies against them,
and they were driven back, or they
drove them back for a time; therefore, they returned rejoicing in
their spoil.
19 And now, because of this great
victory they were lifted up in the
pride of their hearts; they did [a]boast
in their own strength, saying that
their fifty could stand against thousands of the Lamanites; and thus
they did boast, and did delight
in blood, and the shedding of the
blood of their brethren, and this
because of the wickedness of their
king and priests.
20 And it came to pass that there
was a man among them whose name
was [a]Abinadi; and he went forth
among them, and began to prophesy, saying: Behold, thus saith the
Lord, and thus hath he commanded
me, saying, Go forth, and say unto
this people, thus saith the Lord—
Wo be unto this people, for I have
seen their abominations, and their
wickedness, and their whoredoms;
and except they repent I will [b]visit
them in mine anger.
21 And except they repent and
turn to the Lord their God, behold,
I will deliver them into the hands
of their enemies; yea, and they shall
be brought into [a]bondage; and they
shall be afflicted by the hand of
their enemies.
22 And it shall come to pass that
they shall [a]know that I am the Lord
their God, and am a [b]jealous God,
visiting the iniquities of my people.
23 And it shall come to pass that
except this people repent and turn
unto the Lord their God, they shall
be brought into bondage; and none
shall [a]deliver them, except it be the
Lord the Almighty God.
24 Yea, and it shall come to pass
that when they shall [a]cry unto me
I will be [b]slow to hear their cries;
yea, and I will suffer them that they
be smitten by their enemies.
25 And except they repent in [a]sack-
cloth and ashes, and cry mightily to
the Lord their God, I will not [b]hear
their prayers, neither will I deliver
them out of their afflictions; and
thus saith the Lord, and thus hath
he commanded me.
26 Now it came to pass that when
Abinadi had spoken these words
unto them they were wroth with
him, and sought to take away his
life; but the Lord [a]delivered him
out of their hands.
27 Now when king Noah had heard
of the words which Abinadi had
spoken unto the people, he was also
wroth; and he said: [a]Who is Abinadi, that I and my people should be
judged of him, or [b]who is the Lord,
that shall bring upon my people
such great affliction?
28 I command you to bring Abinadi
hither, that I may slay him, for he
has said these things that he might
[a]stir up my people to anger one
with another, and to raise contentions among my people; therefore
I will slay him.
29 Now the eyes of the people were
[a]blinded; therefore they [b]hardened
their hearts against the words of

19*a* Amos 6:13; D&C 3:4. TG Boast.
20*a* See accounts of Abinadi in Mosiah 11–17.
b TG Punish; Reproof.
21*a* Mosiah 12:2; D&C 101:79.
22*a* Ezek. 26:6; 1 Ne. 21:26 (25–26); D&C 43:25.
b Ex. 20:5; Deut. 6:15; 32:21; Mosiah 13:13.
23*a* Hosea 13:10 (4, 10).
24*a* Micah 3:4.
b Ps. 10:1; Jer. 2:27; Mosiah 21:15.
25*a* TG Sackcloth.
b Isa. 1:15 (15–17); 59:2.
26*a* TG Prophets, Rejection of; Protection, Divine.
27*a* Alma 9:6 (5–6).
b Ex. 5:2; Mosiah 12:13.
28*a* TG Provoking.
29*a* 1 Kgs. 15:26 (26–34). TG Spiritual Blindness.
b TG Hardheartedness.

Abinadi, and they sought from that
time forward to take him. And king
Noah hardened his heart against
the word of the Lord, and he did
not repent of his evil doings.

CHAPTER 12

Abinadi is imprisoned for prophesying the destruction of the people and the death of King Noah—The false priests quote the scriptures and pretend to keep the law of Moses—Abinadi begins to teach them the Ten Commandments. About 148 B.C.

AND it came to pass that after the
space of two years that Abinadi came
among them in disguise, that they
knew him not, and began to [a]proph-
esy among them, saying: Thus has
the Lord commanded me, saying—
Abinadi, go and prophesy unto this
my people, for they have hardened
their hearts against my words; they
have repented not of their evil doings; therefore, I will [b]visit them in
my anger, yea, in my fierce anger
will I visit them in their iniquities
and abominations.
2 Yea, wo be unto this generation!
And the Lord said unto me: Stretch
forth thy hand and prophesy, saying:
Thus saith the Lord, it shall come to
pass that this generation, because
of their iniquities, shall be brought
into [a]bondage, and shall be smitten on the [b]cheek; yea, and shall be
driven by men, and shall be slain;
and the vultures of the air, and the
dogs, yea, and the wild beasts, shall
devour their [c]flesh.
3 And it shall come to pass that the
[a]life of king Noah shall be valued
even as a garment in a hot [b]furnace;
for he shall know that I am the Lord.
4 And it shall come to pass that
I will smite this my people with
sore afflictions, yea, with famine
and with [a]pestilence; and I will
cause that they shall [b]howl all the
day long.
5 Yea, and I will cause that they
shall have [a]burdens lashed upon
their backs; and they shall be driven
before like a dumb ass.
6 And it shall come to pass that I
will send forth [a]hail among them,
and it shall smite them; and they
shall also be smitten with the [b]east
wind; and [c]insects shall pester their
land also, and devour their grain.
7 And they shall be smitten with a
great pestilence—and all this will I
do because of their [a]iniquities and
abominations.
8 And it shall come to pass that
except they repent I will utterly [a]de-
stroy them from off the face of the
earth; yet they shall leave a [b]record
behind them, and I will preserve
them for other nations which shall
possess the land; yea, even this will
I do that I may discover the abominations of this people to other nations. And many things did Abinadi
prophesy against this people.
9 And it came to pass that they
were angry with him; and they took
him and carried him bound before
the king, and said unto the king:
Behold, we have brought a man before thee who has prophesied evil
concerning thy people, and saith
that God will destroy them.
10 And he also prophesieth evil
concerning thy [a]life, and saith that
thy life shall be as a garment in a
furnace of fire.
11 And again, he saith that thou
shalt be as a stalk, even as a dry stalk

---

12 1*a* TG Missionary Work.
b Isa. 65:6 (6–7, 11); Jer. 9:9.
2*a* 1 Kgs. 8:46; Mosiah 11:21; 20:21.
b Lam. 3:30; Mosiah 21:3 (3–4, 13).
c Deut. 28:26.
3*a* Amos 7:11 (10–11); Mosiah 12:10 (10–12).
b Mosiah 19:20.
4*a* Luke 21:11 (10–13); 2 Ne. 6:15; D&C 97:26 (22–26).
b Mosiah 21:9 (1–15).
5*a* Mosiah 21:3.
6*a* Ex. 9:18 (13–35); Ezek. 13:13.
b Jer. 18:17; Ezek. 27:26; Mosiah 7:31.
c Ex. 10:4 (1–12).
7*a* D&C 3:18.
8*a* Gen. 6:13; Isa. 42:14 (14–15); 2 Ne. 26:10 (10–11); Alma 45:11 (9–14).
b Morm. 8:14 (14–16).
10*a* Amos 7:11 (10–11); Mosiah 12:3.

of the field, which is run over by
the beasts and trodden under foot.
12 And again, he saith thou shalt
be as the blossoms of a thistle,
which, when it is fully ripe, if the
wind bloweth, it is driven forth
upon the face of the land. And he
pretendeth the Lord hath spoken
it. And he saith all this shall come
upon thee except thou repent, and
this because of thine iniquities.
13 And now, O king, what great
evil hast thou done, or what great
sins have thy people committed,
that we should be [a]condemned of
God or judged of this man?
14 And now, O king, behold, we
are [a]guiltless, and thou, O king, hast
not sinned; therefore, this man has
[b]lied concerning you, and he has
prophesied in vain.
15 And behold, we are strong, we
shall not come into bondage, or be
taken captive by our enemies; yea,
and thou hast prospered in the
land, and thou shalt also prosper.
16 Behold, here is the man, we deliver him into thy hands; thou mayest
do with him as seemeth thee good.
17 And it came to pass that king
Noah caused that Abinadi should
be cast into prison; and he commanded that the [a]priests should
gather themselves together that
he might hold a council with them
what he should do with him.
18 And it came to pass that they
said unto the king: Bring him hither
that we may question him; and the
king commanded that he should be
brought before them.
19 And they began to question
him, that they might cross him, that
thereby they might have wherewith
to [a]accuse him; but he answered
them boldly, and withstood all their
questions, yea, to their astonishment; for he did [b]withstand them
in all their questions, and did
confound them in all their words.
20 And it came to pass that one of
them said unto him: [a]What meaneth
the words which are written, and
which have been taught by our
fathers, saying:
21 [a]How beautiful upon the mountains are the feet of him [b]that
bringeth good tidings; that publisheth peace; that bringeth good
tidings of good; that publisheth
salvation; that saith unto Zion, Thy
God reigneth;
22 [a]Thy watchmen shall lift up
the voice; with the voice together
shall they sing; for they shall see
eye to eye when the Lord shall bring
again Zion;
23 Break forth into joy; sing together ye waste places of Jerusalem;
for the Lord hath comforted his people, he hath redeemed Jerusalem;
24 The Lord hath made bare his
holy [a]arm in the eyes of all the nations, and all the ends of the earth
shall see the salvation of our God?
25 And now Abinadi said unto
them: Are you [a]priests, and pretend
to teach this people, and to understand the spirit of prophesying, and
yet desire to know of me what these
things mean?
26 I say unto you, wo be unto you
for perverting the ways of the Lord!
For if ye understand these things
ye have not taught them; therefore, ye have perverted the ways
of the Lord.
27 Ye have not applied your [a]hearts
to [b]understanding; therefore, ye
have not been wise. Therefore, what
teach ye this people?
28 And they said: We teach the
law of Moses.
29 And again he said unto them:

13*a* Mosiah 11:27.
14*a* Jer. 2:35; Alma 21:6.
b Hel. 13:26 (24–28).
17*a* Mosiah 11:11.
19*a* John 8:6.
b D&C 100:5 (5–6).
20*a* Mosiah 13:3.
21*a* Isa. 52:7 (7–10); Nahum 1:15.
b Mosiah 15:14; 27:37 (36–37).
22*a* Mosiah 15:29.
24*a* Isa. 33:2; Omni 1:13.
25*a* John 3:10 (7–10); Mosiah 11:5.
27*a* Prov. 8:5; Mosiah 2:9.
b TG Understanding.

If ye teach the [a]law of Moses why
do ye not keep it? Why do ye set
your hearts upon [b]riches? Why do
ye commit whoredoms and [c]spend
your strength with harlots, yea,
and cause this people to commit
sin, that the Lord has cause to send
me to prophesy against this people,
yea, even a great evil against this
people?
30 Know ye not that I speak the
[a]truth? Yea, ye know that I speak
the truth; and you ought to tremble
before God.
31 And it shall come to pass that
ye shall be smitten for your iniquities, for ye have said that ye teach
the law of Moses. And what know
ye concerning the law of Moses?
[a]Doth salvation come by the law
of Moses? What say ye?
32 And they answered and said
that salvation did come by the law
of Moses.
33 But now Abinadi said unto
them: I know if ye [a]keep the commandments of God ye shall be
saved; yea, if ye keep the commandments which the Lord delivered
unto Moses in the mount of [b]Sinai,
saying:
34 [a]I am the Lord thy God, who
hath [b]brought thee out of the land of
Egypt, out of the house of bondage.
35 Thou shalt have no [a]other God
before me.
36 [a]Thou shalt not make unto thee
any graven image, or any likeness of
any thing in heaven above, or things
which are in the earth beneath.
37 Now Abinadi said unto them,
Have ye done all this? I say unto
you, Nay, ye have not. And have ye
[a]taught this people that they should
do all these things? I say unto you,
Nay, ye have not.

CHAPTER 13

Abinadi is protected by divine power—He teaches the Ten Commandments—Salvation does not come by the law of Moses alone—God Himself will make an atonement and redeem His people. About 148 B.C.

AND now when the king had heard
these words, he said unto his priests:
Away with this fellow, and slay him;
for what have we to do with him, for
he is [a]mad.
2 And they stood forth and attempted to lay their hands on him;
but he withstood them, and said
unto them:
3 [a]Touch me not, for God shall
smite you if ye lay your hands
upon me, for I have not delivered
the message which the Lord sent
me to deliver; neither have I told
you that which ye [b]requested that I
should tell; therefore, God will not
suffer that I shall be destroyed at
this time.
4 But I must fulfil the commandments wherewith God has commanded me; and because I have told
you the truth ye are angry with me.
And again, because I have spoken
the word of God ye have judged me
that I am mad.
5 Now it came to pass after Abinadi had spoken these words that the
people of king Noah durst not lay
their hands on him, for the Spirit
of the Lord was upon him; and his
face [a]shone with exceeding luster,
even as Moses' did while in the
mount of Sinai, while speaking with
the Lord.
6 And he spake with [a]power and
authority from God; and he continued his words, saying:
7 Ye see that ye have not power to

29*a* TG Law of Moses.
b Jer. 48:7.
c TG Sexual Immorality.
30*a* Jacob 7:14; Alma 30:42 (41–42).
31*a* Mosiah 3:15; 13:28 (27–32); Alma 25:16.
33*a* Deut. 27:1; Neh. 9:13; 3 Ne. 25:4.
b Ex. 19:18 (9, 16–20); Mosiah 13:5.
34*a* Ex. 20:2 (2–4).
b Ex. 12:51; 1 Ne. 17:40; Mosiah 7:19.
35*a* Hosea 13:4. TG Idolatry.
36*a* Mosiah 13:12.
37*a* Mosiah 13:25 (25–26).
13 1*a* John 10:20 (19–20).
3*a* 1 Ne. 17:48.
b Mosiah 12:20 (20–24).
5*a* Ex. 34:29 (29–35).
6*a* TG Priesthood, Power of; Teaching with the Spirit.

slay me, therefore I finish my [a]message. Yea, and I perceive that it cuts you to your hearts because I tell you the truth concerning your iniquities.
8 Yea, and my words fill you with wonder and amazement, and with anger.
9 But I finish my message; and then it [a]matters not whither I go, if it so be that I am saved.
10 But this much I tell you, what you [a]do with me, after this, shall be as a [b]type and a shadow of things which are to come.
11 And now I read unto you the remainder of the [a]commandments of God, for I perceive that they are not written in your hearts; I perceive that ye have studied and taught [b]iniquity the most part of your lives.
12 And now, ye remember that I [a]said unto you: Thou shalt not make unto thee any graven image, or any likeness of things which are in heaven above, or which are in the earth beneath, or which are in the water under the earth.
13 And again: Thou shalt not [a]bow down thyself unto them, nor serve them; for I the Lord thy God am a jealous God, visiting the iniquities of the fathers upon the children, unto the third and fourth generations of them that hate me;
14 And showing mercy unto thousands of them that love me and keep my commandments.
15 Thou shalt not take the name of the Lord thy God in vain; for the Lord will not hold him [a]guiltless that taketh his name in vain.
16 Remember the [a]sabbath day, to keep it holy.
17 Six days shalt thou labor, and do all thy work;
18 But the seventh day, the sabbath of the Lord thy God, thou shalt not do any work, thou, nor thy son, nor thy daughter, thy man-servant, nor thy maid-servant, nor thy cattle, nor thy stranger that is within thy gates;
19 For in [a]six days the Lord made heaven and earth, and the sea, and all that in them is; wherefore the Lord blessed the sabbath day, and hallowed it.
20 [a]Honor thy [b]father and thy mother, that thy days may be long upon the land which the Lord thy God giveth thee.
21 Thou shalt not [a]kill.
22 Thou shalt not commit [a]adultery. Thou shalt not [b]steal.
23 Thou shalt not bear [a]false witness against thy neighbor.
24 Thou shalt not [a]covet thy neighbor's house, thou shalt not covet thy neighbor's wife, nor his man-servant, nor his maid-servant, nor his ox, nor his ass, nor anything that is thy neighbor's.
25 And it came to pass that after Abinadi had made an end of these sayings that he said unto them: Have ye [a]taught this people that they should observe to do all these things for to keep these commandments?
26 I say unto you, Nay; for if ye had, the Lord would not have caused me to come forth and to prophesy evil concerning this people.
27 And now ye have said that salvation cometh by the law of Moses. I say unto you that it is expedient that ye should [a]keep the law of Moses as yet; but I say unto you,

7*a* Prov. 15:10; 1 Ne. 16:2 (1–3); 2 Ne. 9:40.
9*a* Dan. 3:16 (16–18).
10*a* Alma 25:10.
b Jer. 26:14; Mosiah 17:18 (13–19).
11*a* Ex. 20:1 (1–17).
b Micah 2:1 (1–2).
12*a* Mosiah 12:36.
13*a* Ex. 20:5.
15*a* Ex. 20:7; Morm. 7:7; D&C 58:30.
16*a* Mosiah 18:23. TG Sabbath.
19*a* Gen. 1:31; Ex. 20:11.
20*a* TG Honoring Father and Mother.
b Prov. 20:20.
21*a* Ex. 20:13; Deut. 5:17; Matt. 5:21 (21–37); 3 Ne. 12:21 (21–37); D&C 42:18.
22*a* TG Adulterer.
b TG Stealing.
23*a* Prov. 24:28.
24*a* TG Covet.
25*a* Mosiah 12:37.
27*a* 2 Ne. 25:24.

that the time shall come when it
shall [b]no more be expedient to keep
the law of Moses.
28 And moreover, I say unto you,
that [a]salvation doth not come by
the [b]law alone; and were it not for
the [c]atonement, which God himself
shall make for the sins and iniquities of his people, that they must
unavoidably perish, notwithstanding the law of Moses.
29 And now I say unto you that
it was expedient that there should
be a law given to the children of
Israel, yea, even a very [a]strict law;
for they were a stiffnecked people,
[b]quick to do iniquity, and slow to
remember the Lord their God;
30 Therefore there was a [a]law given
them, yea, a law of performances
and of [b]ordinances, a law which they
were to [c]observe strictly from day to
day, to keep them in remembrance
of God and their duty towards him.
31 But behold, I say unto you,
that all these things were [a]types of
things to come.
32 And now, did they [a]understand
the law? I say unto you, Nay, they
did not all understand the law;
and this because of the hardness
of their hearts; for they understood
not that there could not any man
be saved [b]except it were through
the redemption of God.
33 For behold, did not Moses prophesy unto them concerning the
coming of the Messiah, and that
God should redeem his people? Yea,
and even [a]all the prophets who have
prophesied ever since the world
began—have they not spoken more
or less concerning these things?
34 Have they not said that [a]God
himself should come down among
the children of men, and take upon
him the form of man, and go forth
in mighty power upon the face of
the earth?
35 Yea, and have they not said also
that he should bring to pass the
[a]resurrection of the dead, and that
he, himself, should be oppressed
and afflicted?

CHAPTER 14

Isaiah speaks messianically—The Messiah's humiliation and sufferings are set forth—He makes His soul an offering for sin and makes intercession for transgressors—Compare Isaiah 53. About 148 B.C.

YEA, even doth not Isaiah say: Who
hath [a]believed our report, and to
whom is the arm of the Lord revealed?
2 For he shall grow up before him
as a tender plant, and as a root out
of dry ground; he hath no form
nor comeliness; and when we shall
see him there is no beauty that we
should desire him.
3 He is [a]despised and rejected of
men; a man of sorrows, and acquainted with grief; and we hid as
it were our faces from him; he was
despised, and we esteemed him not.
4 Surely he has [a]borne our [b]griefs,
and carried our sorrows; yet we did
esteem him stricken, smitten of God,
and afflicted.

27*b* 3 Ne. 9:19 (19–20); 15:4 (2–10).
28*a* Gal. 2:16; Mosiah 12:31; Alma 25:16. TG Redemption; Salvation, Plan of.
b Rom. 7:4 (4–25); Gal. 2:21; 3:2; Heb. 10:1; 2 Ne. 2:5; Mosiah 3:15 (14–15).
c TG Jesus Christ, Atonement through.
29*a* Josh. 1:8; Heb. 9:10 (8–10); Mosiah 3:14 (14–15); Alma 25:15 (15–16); D&C 41:5 (4–5).
b 1 Ne. 17:45; Alma 46:8.
30*a* Rom. 7:1 (1–3).
b TG Ordinance.
c 2 Ne. 25:24; Jacob 4:5.
31*a* Mosiah 16:14; Alma 25:15 (15–16). TG Jesus Christ, Types of, in Anticipation; Symbolism.
32*a* Ps. 111:10.
b 2 Ne. 25:23 (23–25).
33*a* 1 Pet. 1:11; 1 Ne. 10:5; Jacob 4:4; 7:11 (11–12); Alma 25:16 (10–16); 30:44. TG Jesus Christ, Prophecies about.
34*a* Mosiah 7:27; 15:1; 17:8; Alma 10:21. TG Jesus Christ, Jehovah.
35*a* Isa. 26:19; 2 Ne. 2:8.
14 1*a* Isa. 53:1 (1–12).
3*a* Ps. 22:6; 1 Ne. 19:14.
4*a* Alma 7:11.
b Matt. 8:17.

5 But he was [a]wounded for our
[b]transgressions, he was bruised for
our iniquities; the chastisement of
our peace was upon him; and with
his stripes we are [c]healed.
6 All we, like [a]sheep, have gone
astray; we have turned every one
to his own way; and the Lord hath
laid on him the iniquities of us all.
7 He was oppressed, and he was
afflicted, yet he [a]opened not his
mouth; he is brought as a [b]lamb to
the slaughter, and as a sheep before
her shearers is dumb so he opened
not his mouth.
8 He was taken from prison and
from judgment; and who shall declare his generation? For he was
cut off out of the land of the living;
for the transgressions of my people
was he stricken.
9 And he made his grave with the
wicked, and with the [a]rich in his
death; because he had done no [b]evil,
neither was any deceit in his mouth.
10 Yet it pleased the Lord to [a]bruise
him; he hath put him to grief; when
thou shalt make his soul an offering for sin he shall see his [b]seed,
he shall prolong his days, and the
pleasure of the Lord shall prosper
in his hand.
11 He shall see the travail of his
soul, and shall be satisfied; by
his knowledge shall my righteous
servant justify many; for he shall
[a]bear their iniquities.
12 Therefore will I divide him a
portion with the [a]great, and [b]he shall
divide the spoil with the strong; because he hath poured out his soul
unto death; and he was numbered
with the transgressors; and he bore
the sins of many, and made [c]inter-
cession for the transgressors.

CHAPTER 15

How Christ is both the Father and the Son—He will make intercession and bear the transgressions of His people—They and all the holy prophets are His seed—He brings to pass the Resurrection—Little children have eternal life. About 148 B.C.

AND now Abinadi said unto them:
I would that ye should understand
that [a]God himself shall [b]come down
among the children of men, and
shall [c]redeem his people.
2 And because he [a]dwelleth in
[b]flesh he shall be called the [c]Son of
God, and having subjected the flesh
to the [d]will of the [e]Father, being the
Father and the Son—
3 The Father, [a]because he was
[b]conceived by the power of God;
and the Son, because of the flesh;
thus becoming the Father and
Son—

5*a* TG Jesus Christ, Crucifixion of.
b Mosiah 15:9; Alma 11:40.
c 1 Pet. 2:24 (24–25).
6*a* Matt. 9:36; 2 Ne. 12:5; 28:14; Alma 5:37.
7*a* Isa. 53:7 (7–8); Mark 15:3 (2–14); John 19:9 (9–10); 1 Pet. 2:23 (22–23); Mosiah 15:6. TG Jesus Christ, Trials of.
b Jer. 11:19. TG Passover.
9*a* Matt. 27:57 (57–60); Mark 15:46 (27, 43–46). TG Jesus Christ, Death of.
b John 19:4.
10*a* Gen. 3:15; Rom. 16:20.
b Mosiah 15:10 (10–13).
11*a* Lev. 16:22 (21–22); 1 Pet. 3:18; D&C 19:16 (16–19).
12*a* Luke 24:26.
b Mosiah 15:12.
c 2 Ne. 2:9; Mosiah 15:8; Moro. 7:28 (27–28).
15 1*a* Isa. 54:5; 1 Tim. 3:16; Mosiah 13:34 (33–34).
b TG God, Manifestations of.
c TG Jesus Christ, Mission of.
2*a* Mosiah 3:5; 7:27; Alma 7:9 (9–13).
b TG Jesus Christ, Condescension of.
c John 19:7. TG Jesus Christ, Divine Sonship.
d TG God, Will of.
e Isa. 9:6; 64:8; John 10:30; 14:10 (8–10); Mosiah 5:7; Alma 11:39 (38–39); Ether 3:14.
3*a* D&C 93:4.
b Luke 1:32 (31–33); Mosiah 3:8 (8–9); Alma 7:10; 3 Ne. 1:14. TG Jesus Christ, Divine Sonship.

4 And they are [a]one God, yea, the very [b]Eternal [c]Father of heaven and of earth.

5 And thus the flesh becoming subject to the Spirit, or the Son to the Father, being one God, [a]suffereth temptation, and yieldeth not to the temptation, but suffereth himself to be mocked, and [b]scourged, and cast out, and disowned by his [c]people.

6 And after all this, after working many mighty miracles among the children of men, he shall be led, yea, even [a]as Isaiah said, as a sheep before the shearer is dumb, so he [b]opened not his mouth.

7 Yea, even so he shall be led, [a]crucified, and slain, the [b]flesh becoming subject even unto death, the [c]will of the Son being swallowed up in the will of the Father.

8 And thus God breaketh the [a]bands of death, having gained the [b]victory over death; giving the Son power to make [c]intercession for the children of men—

9 Having ascended into heaven, having the bowels of mercy; being filled with compassion towards the children of men; standing betwixt them and justice; having broken the bands of death, taken upon [a]himself their iniquity and their transgressions, having redeemed them, and [b]satisfied the demands of justice.

10 And now I say unto you, who shall declare his [a]generation? Behold, I say unto you, that when his soul has been made an offering for [b]sin he shall see his [c]seed. And now what say ye? And who shall be his seed?

11 Behold I say unto you, that whosoever has heard the words of the [a]prophets, yea, all the holy prophets who have prophesied concerning the coming of the Lord—I say unto you, that all those who have hearkened unto their words, and believed that the Lord would redeem his people, and have looked forward to that day for a remission of their sins, I say unto you, that these are his seed, or they are the heirs of the [b]kingdom of God.

12 For these are they whose sins [a]he has borne; these are they for whom he has died, to redeem them from their transgressions. And now, are they not his seed?

13 Yea, and are not the [a]prophets, every one that has opened his mouth to prophesy, that has not fallen into transgression, I mean all the holy prophets ever since the world began? I say unto you that they are his seed.

14 And these are [a]they who have published peace, who have brought good [b]tidings of good, who have [c]published salvation; and said unto Zion: Thy God reigneth!

4*a* Deut. 6:4. TG Godhead.
b Alma 11:39.
c Mosiah 3:8; Hel. 14:12; 3 Ne. 9:15; Ether 4:7.
5*a* Luke 4:2; Heb. 4:15. TG Jesus Christ, Temptation of.
b John 19:1.
c Matt. 21:42; Mark 8:31; Luke 17:25; 23:38.
6*a* Isa. 53:7.
b Luke 23:9; John 19:9 (9–10); Mosiah 14:7. TG Jesus Christ, Trials of.
7*a* TG Jesus Christ, Crucifixion of.
b Isa. 53:10.
c Luke 22:42; John 6:38; 3 Ne. 11:11.
8*a* Alma 5:7.
b Hosea 13:14; 1 Cor. 15:57 (55–57); Mosiah 16:7.
c 2 Ne. 2:9; Mosiah 14:12; Moro. 7:28 (27–28).
9*a* Mosiah 14:5 (5–12). TG Self-Sacrifice.
b TG Jesus Christ, Mission of.
10*a* Isa. 53:8.
b Lev. 6:25 (25–26).
c Isa. 53:10; Mosiah 5:7; 27:25; Moro. 7:19. TG God the Father, Jehovah.
11*a* Luke 10:16; D&C 84:36 (36–38).
b TG Kingdom of God, in Heaven; Kingdom of God, on Earth.
12*a* Mosiah 14:12; Alma 7:13; 11:40 (40–41).
13*a* Zech. 7:12; Matt. 11:13; 1 Ne. 3:20. TG Sons and Daughters of God.
14*a* Mosiah 12:21 (21–24); 27:37.
b Isa. 52:7.
c TG Missionary Work.

15 And O how beautiful upon the
mountains were their feet!
16 And again, how beautiful upon
the mountains are the feet of those
that are still publishing peace!
17 And again, how beautiful upon
the mountains are the feet of those
who shall hereafter publish peace,
yea, from this time henceforth and
forever!
18 And behold, I say unto you,
this is not all. For O how beautiful
upon the mountains are the [a]feet
of him that bringeth good tidings,
that is the founder of [b]peace, yea,
even the Lord, who has redeemed
his people; yea, him who has granted
salvation unto his people;
19 For were it not for the redemption which he hath made for his
people, which was prepared from
the [a]foundation of the world, I say
unto you, were it not for this, all
mankind must have [b]perished.
20 But behold, the bands of
death shall be broken, and the
Son reigneth, and hath power over
the dead; therefore, he bringeth to
pass the resurrection of the dead.
21 And there cometh a resurrection, even a [a]first resurrection; yea,
even a resurrection of those that
have been, and who are, and who
shall be, even until the resurrection
of Christ—for so shall he be called.
22 And now, the resurrection of
all the prophets, and all those that
have believed in their words, or all
those that have kept the commandments of God, shall come forth in
the first resurrection; therefore, they
are the first resurrection.
23 They are raised to [a]dwell with
God who has redeemed them; thus
they have eternal life through
Christ, who has [b]broken the bands
of death.
24 And these are those who have
part in the first resurrection; and
these are they that have died before
Christ came, in their ignorance, not
having [a]salvation declared unto
them. And thus the Lord bringeth
about the restoration of these; and
they have a part in the first resurrection, or have eternal life, being
redeemed by the Lord.
25 And little [a]children also have
eternal life.
26 But behold, and [a]fear, and
tremble before God, for ye ought
to tremble; for the Lord redeemeth
none such that [b]rebel against him
and [c]die in their sins; yea, even all
those that have perished in their
sins ever since the world began,
that have wilfully rebelled against
God, that have known the commandments of God, and would not keep
them; [d]these are they that have [e]no
part in the first [f]resurrection.
27 Therefore ought ye not to tremble? For salvation cometh to none
such; for the Lord hath redeemed
none such; yea, neither can the
Lord redeem such; for he cannot
deny himself; for he cannot deny
[a]justice when it has its claim.
28 And now I say unto you that
the time shall come that the [a]salva-
tion of the Lord shall be declared to
every nation, kindred, tongue, and
people.
29 Yea, Lord, [a]thy [b]watchmen
shall lift up their voice; with the
voice together shall they sing; for

18*a* Nahum 1:15;
3 Ne. 20:40;
D&C 128:19.
b Micah 5:5 (4–7);
John 16:33.
TG Peace of God.
19*a* Mosiah 4:6.
b 2 Ne. 9:7 (6–13).
21*a* Jacob 4:11;
Alma 40:16 (16–21).
TG Firstfruits.
23*a* Ps. 15:1 (1–5); 24:3 (3–4);
1 Ne. 15:33 (33–36);
D&C 76:62 (50–70).
b TG Death, Power over.
24*a* 2 Ne. 9:26 (25–26);
D&C 137:7.
25*a* D&C 29:46; 137:10.
TG Salvation of Little
Children.
26*a* Deut. 5:29;
Jacob 6:9; 7:19.
b Josh. 22:16;
Job 24:13;
Ps. 5:10;
1 Ne. 2:23 (21–24).
c Ezek. 18:26;
1 Ne. 15:33 (32–33);
Moro. 10:26.
d Alma 40:19.
e D&C 76:85.
f TG Telestial Glory.
27*a* Alma 12:32;
34:16 (15–16); 42:1.
28*a* Ps. 67:2 (1–2).
TG Missionary Work.
29*a* Isa. 52:8 (8–10);
Mosiah 12:22 (22–24).
b TG Watchman.

they shall see eye to eye, when the
Lord shall bring again Zion.
30 Break forth into joy, sing together, ye waste places of Jerusalem;
for the Lord hath comforted his people, he hath redeemed Jerusalem.
31 The Lord hath made bare his
holy arm in the eyes of all the nations; and all the ends of the earth
shall see the [a]salvation of our God.

CHAPTER 16

God redeems men from their lost and fallen state—Those who are carnal remain as though there were no redemption—Christ brings to pass a resurrection to endless life or to endless damnation. About 148 B.C.

AND now, it came to pass that after
Abinadi had spoken these words he
stretched forth his hand and said:
The time shall come when all shall
see the [a]salvation of the Lord; when
[b]every nation, kindred, tongue, and
people shall see eye to eye and shall
[c]confess before God that his [d]judg-
ments are just.
2 And then shall the [a]wicked be
[b]cast out, and they shall have cause
to howl, and [c]weep, and wail, and
gnash their teeth; and this because
they would not [d]hearken unto the
voice of the Lord; therefore the Lord
redeemeth them not.
3 For they are [a]carnal and devilish,
and the devil has power over them;
yea, even that old serpent that did
[b]beguile our first parents, which was
the [c]cause of their fall; which
was the cause of [d]all mankind becoming carnal, sensual, devilish,
[e]knowing evil from good, [f]subject-
ing themselves to the devil.
4 Thus all mankind were [a]lost;
and behold, they would have been
endlessly lost were it not that God
redeemed his people from their lost
and fallen state.
5 But remember that he that per-
sists in his own [a]carnal nature, and
goes on in the ways of sin and rebellion against God, remaineth in
his fallen state and the [b]devil hath
all power over him. Therefore he
is as though there was no [c]redemp-
tion made, being an enemy to God;
and also is the [d]devil an enemy
to God.
6 And now if Christ had not come
into the world, speaking of things to
come [a]as though they had already
come, there could have been no
redemption.
7 And if Christ had not risen from
the dead, or have broken the bands
of death that the grave should have
no victory, and that death should
have no [a]sting, there could have
been no resurrection.
8 But there is a [a]resurrection, therefore the grave hath no victory, and
the sting of [b]death is swallowed
up in Christ.
9 He is the [a]light and the life of the
world; yea, a light that is endless,

31*a* TG Salvation.
16 1*a* TG Salvation.
b Mosiah 3:20 (20–21).
c Mosiah 27:31; D&C 88:104.
d TG Justice.
2*a* Ps. 91:8; Jer. 12:1; D&C 1:9 (9–10).
b Ps. 52:5; D&C 63:54.
c Matt. 13:42 (41–42); Luke 13:28; Alma 40:13; Moses 1:22.
d Jer. 44:16; Ether 11:13.
3*a* Gal. 5:19 (16–26); Mosiah 3:19.
b Gen. 3:13; 2 Ne. 9:9; Ether 8:25; Moses 4:19 (5–19).
c Moses 5:13.
d Ps. 14:3. TG Man, Natural, Not Spiritually Reborn.
e Gen. 3:5; 2 Ne. 2:18 (18, 26); Alma 29:5; Moro. 7:16 (15–19).
f Alma 5:41 (41–42); D&C 29:40.
4*a* 2 Ne. 9:7; Alma 11:45; 12:36; 42:6 (6, 9, 14). TG Fall of Man.
5*a* TG Carnal Mind; Man, Natural, Not Spiritually Reborn.
b TG Bondage, Spiritual.
c 1 Ne. 10:6; 2 Ne. 2:6 (5–8); 25:20; Alma 12:22 (22–25).
d TG Devil.
6*a* 2 Ne. 25:26 (24–27); Jarom 1:11; Mosiah 3:13.
7*a* Hosea 13:14; Mosiah 15:8 (8, 20).
8*a* 2 Ne. 9:10; Alma 42:15 (6–15).
b Isa. 25:8; 1 Cor. 15:54–55; Morm. 7:5.
9*a* Ether 3:14; Moro. 7:18; D&C 88:13 (7–13). TG Jesus Christ, Light of the World.

that can never be darkened; yea, and also a life which is endless, that there can be no more death.
10 Even this mortal shall put on [a]immortality, and this [b]corruption shall put on incorruption, and shall be brought to [c]stand before the bar of God, to be judged of him according to their works whether they be good or whether they be evil—
11 If they be good, to the resurrection of [a]endless life and [b]happiness; and if they be evil, to the resurrection of [c]endless damnation, being delivered up to the devil, who hath subjected them, which is damnation—
12 Having gone according to their own carnal wills and desires; having never called upon the Lord while the arms of mercy were extended towards them; for the arms of mercy were extended towards them, and they would [a]not; they being warned of their iniquities and yet they would not depart from them; and they were commanded to repent and yet they would not repent.
13 And now, ought ye not to tremble and repent of your sins, and remember that only in and through Christ ye can be saved?
14 Therefore, if ye teach the [a]law of Moses, also teach that it is a [b]shadow of those things which are to come—
15 Teach them that redemption cometh through Christ the Lord, who is the very [a]Eternal Father. Amen.

CHAPTER 17

Alma believes and writes the words of Abinadi—Abinadi suffers death by fire—He prophesies disease and death by fire upon his murderers. About 148 B.C.

AND now it came to pass that when Abinadi had finished these sayings, that the king commanded that the [a]priests should take him and cause that he should be put to [b]death.
2 But there was one among them whose name was [a]Alma, he also being a descendant of Nephi. And he was a young man, and he [b]believed the words which Abinadi had spoken, for he knew concerning the iniquity which Abinadi had testified against them; therefore he began to plead with the king that he would not be angry with Abinadi, but suffer that he might depart in peace.
3 But the king was more wroth, and caused that Alma should be cast out from among them, and sent his servants after him that they might slay him.
4 But he fled from before them and [a]hid himself that they found him not. And he being concealed for many days did [b]write all the words which Abinadi had spoken.
5 And it came to pass that the king caused that his guards should surround Abinadi and take him; and they bound him and cast him into prison.
6 And after three days, having counseled with his [a]priests, he caused that he should again be brought before him.
7 And he said unto him: Abinadi, we have found an accusation against thee, and thou art worthy of death.
8 For thou hast said that [a]God himself should come down among

10*a* Alma 40:2.
TG Immortality.
b 1 Cor. 15:42.
c 3 Ne. 26:4.
TG Jesus Christ, Judge.
11*a* Dan. 12:2 (2–3);
John 5:29 (28–29).
b TG Happiness.
c Alma 9:11.
TG Damnation.
12*a* TG Prophets, Rejection of.
14*a* TG Law of Moses.
b Mosiah 13:31;
Alma 25:15 (15–16).
TG Jesus Christ, Types of, in Anticipation.
15*a* Mosiah 3:8.
17 1*a* TG False Priesthoods.
b Jer. 26:11.
2*a* Mosiah 23:9.
b Mosiah 26:15;
Alma 5:11.
4*a* 1 Kgs. 17:3 (1–16);
Ether 13:13 (13, 22).
b TG Scriptures, Writing of.
6*a* Mosiah 11:5.
8*a* Mosiah 7:27; 13:34.

the children of men; and now, for
this cause thou shalt be put to death
unless thou wilt recall all the words
which thou hast spoken evil concerning me and my people.
9 Now Abinadi said unto him: I
say unto you, I will [a]not recall the
words which I have spoken unto
you concerning this people, for they
are true; and that ye may know of
their surety I have suffered myself
that I have fallen into your hands.
10 Yea, and I will [a]suffer even until death, and I will not recall my
words, and they shall stand as a [b]tes-
timony against you. And if ye slay
me ye will shed [c]innocent blood,
and this shall also stand as a testimony against you at the last day.
11 And now king Noah was about
to release him, for he feared his
word; for he feared that the judgments of God would come upon him.
12 But the [a]priests lifted up their
voices against him, and began to
accuse him, saying: He has reviled
the king. Therefore the king was
stirred up in [b]anger against him,
and he delivered him up that he
might be slain.
13 And it came to pass that they
took him and bound him, and
[a]scourged his skin with faggots,
yea, even unto [b]death.
14 And now when the flames began to scorch him, he cried unto
them, saying:
15 Behold, even as ye have done
unto me, so shall it come to pass
that thy [a]seed shall cause that
many shall suffer the pains that I
do suffer, even the pains of [b]death
by fire; and this because they believe in the salvation of the Lord
their God.
16 And it will come to pass that ye
shall be afflicted with all manner of
[a]diseases because of your iniquities.
17 Yea, and ye shall be smitten
on every hand, and shall be driven
and scattered to and fro, even as a
wild flock is driven by wild and
ferocious beasts.
18 And in that day ye shall be
[a]hunted, and ye shall be taken by
the hand of your enemies, and then
ye shall suffer, as I suffer, the pains
of [b]death by fire.
19 Thus God executeth [a]vengeance
upon those that destroy his people.
O God, [b]receive my soul.
20 And now, when [a]Abinadi had
said these words, he fell, having
suffered death by fire; yea, having
been put to death because he would
not deny the commandments of
God, having sealed the truth of his
words by his [b]death.

CHAPTER 18

Alma preaches in private—He sets forth the covenant of baptism and baptizes at the waters of Mormon—He organizes the Church of Christ and ordains priests—They support themselves and teach the people—Alma and his people flee from King Noah into the wilderness. About 147–145 B.C.

AND now, it came to pass that Alma,
who had fled from the servants of
king Noah, [a]repented of his sins and
iniquities, and went about privately
among the people, and began to
teach the words of Abinadi—
2 Yea, concerning that which was
to come, and also concerning the
resurrection of the dead, and the [a]re-
demption of the people, which was
to be brought to pass through the

9*a* TG Courage; Integrity.
10*a* TG Persecution.
b TG Testimony.
c Jer. 26:15 (14–15); Lam. 4:13; Alma 14:11; 60:13.
12*a* Mosiah 11:5; 12:25 (17, 25).
b Prov. 20:2.
13*a* Dan. 3:6; James 5:10 (10–11); Alma 14:26 (20–27).
b Mosiah 7:28; 21:30; Alma 25:11.
15*a* Mosiah 13:10; Alma 25:12 (7–12).
b Alma 25:5.
16*a* Deut. 28:60 (25–60).
18*a* Alma 25:8.
b Mosiah 13:10; 19:20; Alma 25:11 (7–12).
19*a* Ps. 125:3.
b Luke 23:46; Acts 7:59.
20*a* Mosiah 7:26.
b Heb. 9:16 (16–17).
18 1*a* Mosiah 23:9.
2*a* TG Jesus Christ, Redeemer.

power, and sufferings, and [b]death
of Christ, and his resurrection and
ascension into heaven.
3 And as many as would hear his
word he did teach. And he taught
them privately, that it might not
come to the knowledge of the king.
And many did believe his words.
4 And it came to pass that as many
as did believe him did go forth to
a [a]place which was called Mormon,
having received its name from the
king, being in the [b]borders of the
land having been infested, by times
or at seasons, by wild beasts.
5 Now, there was in Mormon a
fountain of pure water, and Alma
resorted thither, there being near
the water a thicket of small trees,
where he did hide himself in the
daytime from the searches of the
king.
6 And it came to pass that as many
as believed him went thither to
hear his words.
7 And it came to pass after many
days there were a goodly number
gathered together at the place of
Mormon, to hear the words of Alma.
Yea, all were gathered together that
believed on his word, to hear him.
And he did [a]teach them, and did
preach unto them repentance, and
redemption, and faith on the Lord.
8 And it came to pass that he said
unto them: Behold, here are the waters of Mormon (for thus were they
called) and now, as ye are [a]desirous
to come into the [b]fold of God, and
to be called his people, and are willing to bear one another's burdens,
that they may be light;
9 Yea, and are [a]willing to mourn
with those that [b]mourn; yea, and
comfort those that stand in need of
comfort, and to stand as [c]witnesses
of God at all times and in all things,
and in all places that ye may be in,
even until death, that ye may be redeemed of God, and be numbered
with those of the [d]first resurrection,
that ye may have eternal life—
10 Now I say unto you, if this be
the desire of your hearts, what have
you against being [a]baptized in the
[b]name of the Lord, as a witness before him that ye have entered into
a [c]covenant with him, that ye will
serve him and keep his commandments, that he may pour out his
Spirit more abundantly upon you?
11 And now when the people had
heard these words, they clapped
their hands for joy, and exclaimed:
This is the desire of our hearts.
12 And now it came to pass that
Alma took Helam, he being one of
the first, and went and stood forth
in the water, and cried, saying: O
Lord, pour out thy Spirit upon thy
servant, that he may do this work
with holiness of heart.
13 And when he had said these
words, the [a]Spirit of the Lord was
upon him, and he said: Helam, I
baptize thee, having [b]authority
from the Almighty God, as a testimony that ye have entered into
a [c]covenant to serve him until you
are dead as to the mortal body; and
may the Spirit of the Lord be poured
out upon you; and may he grant
unto you eternal life, through the
redemption of Christ, whom he has
prepared from the [d]foundation of
the world.
14 And after Alma had said these
words, both Alma and Helam were

2*b* TG Jesus Christ, Ascension of; Jesus Christ, Death of.
4*a* Alma 5:3; 3 Ne. 5:12.
b Mosiah 18:31.
7*a* Alma 5:13.
8*a* D&C 20:36–37, 77.
b TG Brotherhood and Sisterhood; Conversion.
9*a* TG Baptism, Qualifications for.
b TG Comfort; Compassion.
c TG Missionary Work; Witness.
d Jacob 4:11.
10*a* 2 Ne. 31:17; Alma 4:4.
b TG Jesus Christ, Taking the Name of.
c Neh. 10:29. TG Commitment.
13*a* TG Holy Ghost, Mission of.
b Mosiah 21:33; Alma 5:3; 3 Ne. 11:25.
c Mosiah 21:31. TG Covenants.
d Mosiah 4:6; Alma 12:30 (25, 30).

[a]buried in the water; and they arose
and came forth out of the water rejoicing, being filled with the Spirit.
15 And again, Alma took another,
and went forth a second time into
the water, and baptized him according to the first, only he did not
bury [a]himself again in the water.
16 And after this manner he did
baptize every one that went forth
to the place of Mormon; and they
were in number about two hundred
and four souls; yea, and they were
[a]baptized in the waters of Mormon,
and were filled with the [b]grace
of God.
17 And they were called the church
of God, or the [a]church of Christ,
from that time forward. And it came
to pass that whosoever was baptized
by the power and authority of God
was added to his church.
18 And it came to pass that Alma,
having [a]authority from God, [b]or-
dained priests; even one priest to
every fifty of their number did he
ordain to preach unto them, and to
[c]teach them concerning the things
pertaining to the kingdom of God.
19 And he commanded them that
[a]they should [b]teach nothing save
it were the things which he had
taught, and which had been spoken
by the mouth of the holy prophets.
20 Yea, even he commanded them
that they should [a]preach nothing
save it were repentance and faith
on the Lord, who had redeemed
his people.
21 And he commanded them that
there should be no [a]contention one
with another, but that they should
look forward with [b]one eye, having
one faith and one baptism, having
their hearts [c]knit together in unity
and in love one towards another.
22 And thus he commanded them
to preach. And thus they became
the [a]children of God.
23 And he commanded them that
they should observe the [a]sabbath
day, and keep it holy, and also every day they should give thanks to
the Lord their God.
24 And he also commanded them
that the priests whom he had ordained [a]should [b]labor with their
own hands for their support.
25 And there was [a]one day in every
week that was set apart that they
should [b]gather themselves together
to teach the people, and to worship
the Lord their God, and also, as often as it was in their power, to [c]as-
semble themselves together.
26 And the priests were not to depend upon the people for their support; but for their labor they were
to receive the [a]grace of God, that
they might wax strong in the Spirit,
having the [b]knowledge of God, that
they might teach with power and
authority from God.
27 And again Alma commanded
that the people of the church should
impart of their substance, [a]every
one according to that which he
had; if he have more abundantly
he should impart more abundantly;
and of him that had but little, but

14*a* TG Baptism, Immersion.
15*a* JS—H 1:71 (70–71).
16*a* Mosiah 25:18.
b TG Grace.
17*a* Mosiah 21:34; 25:22 (18–23); 26:4; Alma 4:5 (4–5); 3 Ne. 26:21. TG Jesus Christ, Head of the Church.
18*a* Mosiah 23:16. TG Priesthood, Authority.
b TG Priesthood, History of.
c Mosiah 2:4; 23:14; 24:4 (4–8).
19*a* Mosiah 23:14.
b D&C 5:10.
20*a* TG Preaching; Repent.
21*a* TG Contention.
b Matt. 6:22; Morm. 8:15; D&C 4:5; 88:68.
c 1 Sam. 18:1; Rom. 15:5 (1–7); Mosiah 4:15; 23:15.
22*a* Moses 6:68.
23*a* Ex. 35:2; Mosiah 13:16 (16–19).
24*a* Acts 20:34 (33–35); Mosiah 27:5 (3–5); Alma 1:3, 26.
b 1 Cor. 9:18 (16–19); Alma 30:32.
25*a* Alma 32:11.
b TG Meetings.
c TG Assembly for Worship.
26*a* TG Blessing; Reward; Wages.
b Neh. 10:28 (28–31). TG God, Knowledge about.
27*a* Alma 16:16; 4 Ne. 1:3.

little should be required; and to him that had not should be given.
28 And thus they should impart of their [a]substance of their own free will and good desires towards God, and to those priests that stood in need, yea, and to every needy, naked soul.
29 And this he said unto them, having been commanded of God; and they did [a]walk uprightly before God, imparting to one another both temporally and spiritually according to their needs and their wants.
30 And now it came to pass that all this was done in Mormon, yea, by the [a]waters of Mormon, in the forest that was near the waters of Mormon; yea, the place of Mormon, the waters of Mormon, the forest of Mormon, how beautiful are they to the eyes of them who there came to the knowledge of their Redeemer; yea, and how blessed are they, for they shall [b]sing to his praise forever.
31 And these things were done in the [a]borders of the land, that they might not come to the knowledge of the king.
32 But behold, it came to pass that the king, having discovered a movement among the people, sent his servants to watch them. Therefore on the day that they were assembling themselves together to hear the word of the Lord they were discovered unto the king.
33 And now the king said that Alma was stirring up the people to rebellion against him; therefore he sent his [a]army to destroy them.
34 And it came to pass that Alma and the people of the Lord were [a]apprised of the coming of the king's army; therefore they took their tents and their families and [b]departed into the wilderness.
35 And they were in number about [a]four hundred and fifty souls.

CHAPTER 19

Gideon seeks to slay King Noah—The Lamanites invade the land—King Noah suffers death by fire—Limhi rules as a tributary monarch. About 145–121 B.C.

AND it came to pass that the [a]army of the king returned, having searched in vain for the people of the Lord.
2 And now behold, the forces of the king were small, having been reduced, and there began to be a division among the remainder of the people.
3 And the lesser part began to [a]breathe out threatenings against the king, and there began to be a great contention among them.
4 And now there was a man among them whose name was Gideon, and he being a strong man and an enemy to the king, therefore he drew his sword, and swore in his wrath that he would slay the king.
5 And it came to pass that he fought with the king; and when the king saw that he was about to overpower him, he fled and ran and got upon the [a]tower which was near the temple.
6 And Gideon pursued after him and was about to get upon the tower to slay the king, and the king cast his eyes round about towards the land of [a]Shemlon, and behold, the army of the Lamanites were within the borders of the land.
7 And now the king cried out in the anguish of his soul, saying: Gideon, [a]spare me, for the Lamanites are upon us, and they will destroy us; yea, they will destroy my people.
8 And now the king was not so much concerned about his people as

28*a* TG Generosity; Initiative.
29*a* TG Walking with God; Welfare.
30*a* Mosiah 26:15.
b TG Praise; Singing.
31*a* Mosiah 18:4.
33*a* Mosiah 19:1.
34*a* Mosiah 23:1.
b Mosiah 21:30; 23:13, 36.
35*a* Mosiah 23:10.
19 1*a* Mosiah 18:33.
3*a* Acts 9:1.
5*a* Judg. 9:51 (50–55); Mosiah 11:12.
6*a* Mosiah 10:7; 11:12; 20:1.
7*a* Deut. 13:8 (6–9).

he was about his [a]own life; nevertheless, Gideon did spare his life.
9 And the king commanded the
people that they should flee before the Lamanites, and he himself
did go before them, and they did
flee into the wilderness, with their
women and their children.
10 And it came to pass that the
Lamanites did pursue them, and
did overtake them, and began to
slay them.
11 Now it came to pass that the
king commanded them that all the
men should [a]leave their wives and
their children, and flee before the
Lamanites.
12 Now there were many that
would not leave them, but had
rather stay and perish with them.
And the rest left their wives and
their children and fled.
13 And it came to pass that those
who tarried with their wives and
their children caused that their fair
daughters should stand forth and
plead with the Lamanites that they
would not slay them.
14 And it came to pass that the Lamanites had compassion on them,
for they were charmed with the
beauty of their women.
15 Therefore the Lamanites did
spare their lives, and took them
captives and carried them back
to the land of Nephi, and granted
unto them that they might possess
the land, under the conditions that
they would deliver up king Noah
into the hands of the Lamanites, and
deliver up their property, even [a]one
half of all they possessed, one half
of their gold, and their silver, and
all their precious things, and thus
they should pay tribute to the king
of the Lamanites from year to year.
16 And now there was one of the
sons of the king among those that
were taken captive, whose name
was [a]Limhi.
17 And now Limhi was desirous
that his father should not be destroyed; nevertheless, Limhi was
not ignorant of the iniquities of his
father, he himself being a just man.
18 And it came to pass that Gideon
sent men into the wilderness secretly, to search for the king and
those that were with him. And it
came to pass that they met the people in the wilderness, all save the
king and his priests.
19 Now they had sworn in their
hearts that they would return to the
land of Nephi, and if their [a]wives
and their children were slain, and
also those that had tarried with
them, that they would seek revenge,
and also perish with them.
20 And the king commanded them
that they should not return; and
they were angry with the king, and
caused that he should suffer, even
unto [a]death by fire.
21 And they were about to take
the priests also and [a]put them to
death, and they fled before them.
22 And it came to pass that they
were about to return to the land
of Nephi, and they met the men
of Gideon. And the men of Gideon
told them of all that had happened
to their wives and their children;
and that the Lamanites had granted
unto them that they might possess
the land by paying a tribute to the
Lamanites of one half of all they
possessed.
23 And the people told the men
of [a]Gideon that they had slain the
king, and his [b]priests had fled from
them farther into the wilderness.
24 And it came to pass that after
they had ended the ceremony, that
they returned to the land of Nephi,
rejoicing, because their wives and
their children were not slain; and
they told Gideon what they had
done to the king.
25 And it came to pass that the

8*a* TG Selfishness.
11*a* Mosiah 19:19 (19–23).
15*a* Mosiah 7:15.
16*a* Mosiah 7:9; 11:1.
19*a* Mosiah 19:11.
20*a* Mosiah 12:3; 13:10; 17:18 (13–19); Alma 25:11 (7–12).
21*a* Mosiah 20:3.
23*a* Mosiah 20:17.
b Mosiah 17:12 (1, 6, 12–18); 20:23 (3, 18, 23).

king of the Lamanites made an [a]oath unto them, that his people should not slay them.

26 And also Limhi, being the son of the king, having the kingdom conferred upon him [a]by the people, made [b]oath unto the king of the Lamanites that his people should pay [c]tribute unto him, even one half of all they possessed.

27 And it came to pass that Limhi began to establish the kingdom and to establish [a]peace among his people.

28 And the king of the Lamanites set [a]guards round about the land, that he might [b]keep the people of Limhi in the land, that they might not depart into the wilderness; and he did support his guards out of the tribute which he did receive from the Nephites.

29 And now king Limhi did have continual peace in his kingdom for the space of two years, that the Lamanites did not molest them nor seek to destroy them.

CHAPTER 20

Some Lamanite daughters are abducted by the priests of Noah—The Lamanites wage war upon Limhi and his people—The Lamanite hosts are repulsed and pacified. About 145–123 B.C.

Now there was a place in [a]Shemlon where the daughters of the Lamanites did gather themselves together to sing, and to [b]dance, and to make themselves merry.

2 And it came to pass that there was one day a small number of them gathered together to sing and to dance.

3 And now the priests of king Noah, being ashamed to return to the city of Nephi, yea, and also fearing that the people would [a]slay them, therefore they durst not return to their wives and their [b]children.

4 And having tarried in the wilderness, and having discovered the daughters of the Lamanites, they laid and watched them;

5 And when there were but few of them gathered together to dance, they came forth out of their secret places and took them and carried them into the wilderness; yea, twenty and four of the [a]daughters of the Lamanites they carried into the wilderness.

6 And it came to pass that when the Lamanites found that their daughters had been missing, they were angry with the people of Limhi, for they thought it was the people of Limhi.

7 Therefore they sent their armies forth; yea, even the king himself went before his people; and they went up to the land of Nephi to destroy the people of Limhi.

8 And now Limhi had discovered them from the [a]tower, even all their preparations for war did he discover; therefore he gathered his people together, and laid wait for them in the fields and in the forests.

9 And it came to pass that when the Lamanites had come up, that the people of Limhi began to fall upon them from their waiting places, and began to slay them.

10 And it came to pass that the battle became exceedingly sore, for they fought like lions for their prey.

11 And it came to pass that the people of Limhi began to drive the Lamanites before them; yet they were not half so numerous as the Lamanites. But they [a]fought for their lives, and for their [b]wives, and for their children; therefore they exerted themselves and like dragons did they fight.

12 And it came to pass that they found the king of the Lamanites

25*a* Mosiah 21:3.
26*a* Mosiah 7:9.
b Mosiah 20:14, 22.
c Mosiah 22:7.
27*a* TG Peacemakers.
28*a* Mosiah 21:5; 22:6 (6–10).
b Mosiah 7:22; 9:10.
20 1*a* Mosiah 19:6.
b Judg. 21:21.
3*a* Mosiah 19:21.
b Mosiah 25:12.
5*a* Mosiah 21:20; 23:33 (30–35).
8*a* Mosiah 11:12.
11*a* Alma 43:45.
b Alma 46:12.

among the number of their dead;
yet he was not dead, having been
wounded and left upon the ground,
so speedy was the flight of his people.
13 And they took him and bound
up his wounds, and brought him before Limhi, and said: Behold, here
is the king of the Lamanites; he
having received a wound has fallen
among their dead, and they have left
him; and behold, we have brought
him before you; and now let us
slay him.
14 But Limhi said unto them: Ye
shall not slay him, but bring him
hither that I may see him. And they
brought him. And Limhi said unto
him: What cause have ye to come
up to war against my people? Behold, my people have not broken the
[a]oath that I made unto you; therefore, why should ye break the oath
which ye made unto my people?
15 And now the king said: I have
broken the oath because thy people did carry away the daughters of
my people; therefore, in my anger
I did cause my people to come up
to war against thy people.
16 And now Limhi had heard nothing concerning this matter; therefore he said: I will search among
my people and whosoever has done
this thing shall perish. Therefore he
caused a search to be made among
his people.
17 Now when [a]Gideon had heard
these things, he being the king's
captain, he went forth and said
unto the king: I pray thee forbear,
and do not search this people, and
lay not this thing to their charge.
18 For do ye not remember the
priests of thy father, whom this
people sought to destroy? And are
they not in the wilderness? And are
not they the ones who have stolen
the daughters of the Lamanites?
19 And now, behold, and tell the
king of these things, that he may
tell his people that they may be
pacified towards us; for behold
they are already preparing to come
against us; and behold also there
are but few of us.
20 And behold, they come with
their numerous hosts; and except
the king doth pacify them towards
us we must perish.
21 For are not the words of Abinadi [a]fulfilled, which he prophesied
against us—and all this because we
would not hearken unto the words
of the Lord, and turn from our iniquities?
22 And now let us pacify the king,
and we fulfil the [a]oath which we
have made unto him; for it is better that we should be in bondage
than that we should lose our [b]lives;
therefore, let us put a stop to the
shedding of so much blood.
23 And now Limhi told the king
all the things concerning his father,
and the [a]priests that had fled into
the wilderness, and attributed the
carrying away of their daughters
to them.
24 And it came to pass that the
king was pacified towards his people; and he said unto them: Let us
go forth to meet my people, without
arms; and I swear unto you with an
[a]oath that my people shall not slay
thy people.
25 And it came to pass that they
followed the king, and went forth
without arms to meet the Lamanites. And it came to pass that they
did meet the Lamanites; and the
king of the Lamanites did bow
himself down before them, and did
plead in behalf of the people of
Limhi.
26 And when the Lamanites saw
the people of Limhi, that they were
without arms, they had [a]compassion
on them and were pacified towards
them, and returned with their king
in peace to their own land.

14*a* Mosiah 19:26 (25–26).
17*a* Mosiah 19:23 (4–8, 23); 22:3; Alma 1:8 (8–9).
21*a* Mosiah 12:2 (1–8); 21:4.
22*a* Mosiah 19:26.
b TG Life, Sanctity of.
23*a* Mosiah 19:23 (21, 23); 23:9 (9, 12, 31).
24*a* Mosiah 21:3.
26*a* TG Compassion.

CHAPTER 21

*Limhi's people are smitten and defeated
by the Lamanites—Limhi's people meet
Ammon and are converted—They tell
Ammon of the twenty-four Jaredite
plates. About 122–121* B.C.

AND it came to pass that Limhi and
his people returned to the city of
Nephi, and began to dwell in the
land again in peace.
2 And it came to pass that after
many days the Lamanites began
again to be stirred up in anger
against the Nephites, and they began to come into the borders of the
land round about.
3 Now they durst not slay them,
because of the [a]oath which their
king had made unto Limhi; but they
would smite them on their [b]cheeks,
and exercise authority over them;
and began to put heavy [c]burdens
upon their backs, and drive them
as they would a dumb ass—
4 Yea, all this was done that the
[a]word of the Lord might be [b]ful-
filled.
5 And now the afflictions of the
Nephites were great, and there was
no way that they could deliver themselves out of their hands, for the
Lamanites had [a]surrounded them
on every side.
6 And it came to pass that the
people began to murmur with the
king because of their afflictions;
and they began to be desirous to
go against them to battle. And they
did afflict the king sorely with their
complaints; therefore he granted
unto them that they should do according to their desires.
7 And they gathered themselves
together again, and put on their
armor, and went forth against the
Lamanites to drive them out of their
land.
8 And it came to pass that the Lamanites did beat them, and drove
them back, and [a]slew many of them.
9 And now there was a great
[a]mourning and lamentation among
the people of Limhi, the widow
mourning for her husband, the
son and the daughter mourning
for their father, and the brothers
for their brethren.
10 Now there were a great many
[a]widows in the land, and they did
cry mightily from day to day, for
a great fear of the Lamanites had
come upon them.
11 And it came to pass that their
continual cries did stir up the remainder of the people of Limhi to
anger against the Lamanites; and
they went again to battle, but they
were driven back again, suffering
much loss.
12 Yea, they went again even the
third time, and suffered in the like
manner; and those that were not
slain returned again to the city of
Nephi.
13 And they did humble themselves even to the dust, subjecting
themselves to the [a]yoke of bondage,
[b]submitting themselves to be smitten, and to be driven to and fro, and
burdened, according to the desires
of their enemies.
14 And they did [a]humble themselves even in the depths of humility; and they did cry mightily
to God; yea, even all the day long
did they cry unto their God that
he would [b]deliver them out of their
afflictions.
15 And now the Lord was [a]slow
to hear their cry because of their
iniquities; nevertheless the Lord

---

21 3*a* Mosiah 19:25; 20:24.
b Lam. 3:30; Mosiah 12:2.
c Ex. 1:11 (10–11); Mosiah 12:5; 24:9.
4*a* D&C 3:19.
b Mosiah 20:21.
5*a* Mosiah 19:28; 22:6 (6–10).
8*a* Mosiah 21:29.
9*a* Mosiah 12:4. TG Mourning.
10*a* TG Widows.
13*a* Mosiah 19:28 (26, 28); 21:36.
b TG Submissiveness.
14*a* Mosiah 29:20.
b TG Deliver; Protection, Divine.
15*a* 1 Sam. 8:18; Prov. 15:29; Mosiah 11:24 (23–25); D&C 101:7 (7–9).

did hear their [b]cries, and began to
soften the hearts of the Lamanites
that they began to ease their burdens; yet the Lord did not see fit to
deliver them out of bondage.
16 And it came to pass that they
began to prosper by degrees in the
land, and began to raise grain more
abundantly, and flocks, and herds,
that they did not suffer with hunger.
17 Now there was a great number
of women, more than there was of
men; therefore king Limhi commanded that every man should [a]im-
part to the support of the [b]widows
and their children, that they might
not perish with hunger; and this
they did because of the greatness of
their number that had been slain.
18 Now the people of Limhi kept
together in a body as much as it was
possible, and secured their grain
and their flocks;
19 And the king himself did not
trust his person without the walls
of the city, unless he took his guards
with him, fearing that he might by
some means fall into the hands of
the Lamanites.
20 And he caused that his people
should watch the land round about,
that by some means they might take
those priests that fled into the wilderness, who had stolen the [a]daugh-
ters of the Lamanites, and that had
caused such a great destruction to
come upon them.
21 For they were desirous to take
them that they might [a]punish them;
for they had come into the land
of Nephi by night, and carried off
their grain and many of their precious things; therefore they laid
wait for them.
22 And it came to pass that there
was no more disturbance between
the Lamanites and the people of
Limhi, even until the time that
[a]Ammon and his brethren came
into the land.
23 And the king having been
without the gates of the city with
his guard, [a]discovered Ammon and
his brethren; and supposing them
to be priests of Noah therefore he
caused that they should be taken,
and bound, and cast into [b]prison.
And had they been the priests of
Noah he would have caused that
they should be put to death.
24 But when he found that they
were not, but that they were his
brethren, and had come from the
[a]land of Zarahemla, he was filled
with exceedingly great joy.
25 Now king Limhi had sent, previous to the coming of Ammon, a
[a]small number of men to [b]search
for the land of Zarahemla; but they
could not find it, and they were lost
in the wilderness.
26 Nevertheless, they did find a
land which had been peopled; yea,
a land which was covered with dry
[a]bones; yea, a land which had been
peopled and which had been destroyed; and they, having supposed
it to be the land of Zarahemla, returned to the land of Nephi, having
arrived in the borders of the land
not many days before the [b]coming
of Ammon.
27 And they brought a [a]record with
them, even a record of the people
whose bones they had found; and
it was engraven on plates of ore.
28 And now Limhi was again filled
with joy on learning from the mouth
of Ammon that king Mosiah had a
[a]gift from God, whereby he could
[b]interpret such engravings; yea, and
Ammon also did rejoice.
29 Yet Ammon and his brethren
were filled with sorrow because so

15*b* Ex. 3:9 (7, 9); 2 Ne. 26:15; D&C 109:49.
17*a* Mosiah 4:26 (16, 26).
b TG Widows.
20*a* Mosiah 20:5.
21*a* Mosiah 7:7 (7–11).
22*a* Mosiah 7:6 (6–13).
23*a* Mosiah 7:10.
b Mosiah 7:7 (6–8); Hel. 5:21.
24*a* Omni 1:13.
25*a* Mosiah 8:7.
b Mosiah 7:14.
26*a* Mosiah 8:8; Hel. 3:6 (3–12).
b Mosiah 7:6 (6–11).
27*a* Mosiah 8:9; 28:11.
28*a* Omni 1:20 (20–22); Mosiah 28:13 (11–19). TG God, Gifts of.
b 1 Cor. 12:10; Mosiah 8:6 (6, 12–13).

many of their brethren had been
[a]slain;
30 And also that king Noah and
his priests had caused the people
to commit so many sins and iniquities against God; and they also did
mourn for the [a]death of Abinadi;
and also for the [b]departure of Alma
and the people that went with him,
who had formed a church of God
through the strength and power of
God, and faith on the words which
had been spoken by Abinadi.
31 Yea, they did mourn for their departure, for they knew not whither
they had fled. Now they would have
gladly joined with them, for they
themselves had entered into a [a]covenant with God to serve him and
keep his commandments.
32 And now since the coming of
Ammon, king Limhi had also entered into a covenant with God, and
also many of his people, to serve
him and keep his commandments.
33 And it came to pass that king
Limhi and many of his people were
desirous to be baptized; but there
was none in the land that had [a]authority from God. And Ammon declined doing this thing, considering
himself an unworthy servant.
34 Therefore they did not at that
time form themselves into a [a]church,
waiting upon the Spirit of the Lord.
Now they were desirous to become
even as Alma and his brethren, who
had fled into the wilderness.
35 They were desirous to be baptized as a witness and a testimony
that they were willing to serve God
with all their hearts; nevertheless
they did prolong the time; and an
account of their baptism shall be
[a]given hereafter.
36 And now all the study of Ammon and [a]his people, and king
Limhi and his people, was to deliver themselves out of the hands of
the Lamanites and from [b]bondage.

CHAPTER 22

Plans are made for the people to escape from Lamanite bondage—The Lamanites are made drunk—The people escape, return to Zarahemla, and become subject to King Mosiah. About 121–120 B.C.

AND now it came to pass that Ammon and king Limhi began to consult with the people how they should [a]deliver themselves out of bondage; and even they did cause that all the people should gather themselves together; and this they did that they might have the voice of the people concerning the matter.
2 And it came to pass that they
could find no way to deliver themselves out of bondage, except it were
to take their women and children,
and their flocks, and their herds,
and their tents, and depart into the
wilderness; for the Lamanites being
so numerous, it was impossible for
the people of Limhi to contend with
them, thinking to deliver themselves
out of bondage by the sword.
3 Now it came to pass that [a]Gideon
went forth and stood before the
king, and said unto him: Now O
king, thou hast hitherto hearkened
unto my words many times when
we have been contending with our
brethren, the Lamanites.
4 And now O king, if thou hast
not found me to be an unprofitable
servant, or if thou hast hitherto listened to my words in any degree,
and they have been of service to
thee, even so I desire that thou
wouldst listen to my words at this
time, and I will be thy servant and
deliver this people out of bondage.
5 And the king granted unto him
that he might speak. And Gideon
said unto him:
6 Behold the back pass, through
the back wall, on the back side
of the city. The Lamanites, or the

29*a* Mosiah 21:8 (7–14); 25:9.
30*a* Mosiah 17:13 (12–20).
b Mosiah 18:34 (34–35).
31*a* Mosiah 18:13.
33*a* TG Baptism, Essential; Priesthood, Authority.
34*a* Mosiah 18:17.
35*a* Mosiah 25:18 (17–18).
36*a* Mosiah 7:3 (2–3).
b Mosiah 21:13.
22 1*a* Mosiah 7:18.
3*a* Mosiah 20:17; Alma 1:8 (8–9).

[a]guards of the Lamanites, by night
are [b]drunken; therefore let us send a
proclamation among all this people
that they gather together their flocks
and herds, that they may drive them
into the wilderness by night.
7 And I will go according to thy
command and pay the last [a]tribute
of wine to the Lamanites, and they
will be [b]drunken; and we will pass
through the secret pass on the left of
their camp when they are drunken
and asleep.
8 Thus we will depart with our
women and our children, our flocks,
and our herds into the wilderness;
and we will travel around the land
of [a]Shilom.
9 And it came to pass that the king
hearkened unto the words of Gideon.
10 And king Limhi caused that his
people should gather their flocks
together; and he sent the tribute of
wine to the Lamanites; and he also
sent more wine, as a present unto
them; and they did drink freely
of the wine which king Limhi did
send unto them.
11 And it came to pass that the
people of king Limhi did [a]depart
by night into the wilderness with
their flocks and their herds, and
they went round about the land
of [b]Shilom in the wilderness, and
bent their course towards the land
of Zarahemla, being led by Ammon
and his brethren.
12 And they had taken all their
gold, and silver, and their precious
things, which they could carry, and
also their provisions with them, into
the wilderness; and they pursued
their journey.
13 And after being many days in the
wilderness they [a]arrived in the land
of Zarahemla, and joined Mosiah's
people, and became his subjects.
14 And it came to pass that Mosiah
[a]received them with joy; and he also
received their [b]records, and also the
[c]records which had been found by
the people of Limhi.
15 And now it came to pass when
the Lamanites had found that the
people of Limhi had departed out
of the land by night, that they sent
an [a]army into the wilderness to
pursue them;
16 And after they had pursued
them two days, they could no longer
follow their tracks; therefore
they were lost in the wilderness.

An account of Alma and the people of the Lord, who were driven into the wilderness by the people of King Noah.

Comprising chapters 23 and 24.

CHAPTER 23

Alma refuses to be king—He serves as high priest—The Lord chastens His people, and the Lamanites conquer the land of Helam—Amulon, leader of King Noah's wicked priests, rules subject to the Lamanite monarch. About 145–121 B.C.

NOW Alma, having been [a]warned
of the Lord that the armies of king
Noah would come upon them, and
having made it known to his people,
therefore they gathered together
their flocks, and took of their grain,
and [b]departed into the wilderness
before the armies of king Noah.
2 And the Lord did strengthen
them, that the people of king Noah
could not overtake them to destroy
them.
3 And they fled [a]eight days' journey
into the wilderness.
4 And they came to a land, yea,
even a very beautiful and pleasant
land, a land of pure water.
5 And they pitched their tents,
and began to till the ground, and

6*a* Mosiah 19:28; 21:5.
b Alma 55:14 (8–17).
7*a* Mosiah 19:26.
b TG Drunkenness.
8*a* Mosiah 7:7 (5–16).
11*a* Mosiah 25:8.
b Mosiah 11:12 (12–13); Alma 23:12.
13*a* Mosiah 25:5.
14*a* Mosiah 24:25.
b Mosiah 8:5; 9:1.
c Mosiah 8:9.
15*a* Mosiah 23:30 (30–39).
23 1*a* Mosiah 18:34; Alma 5:4. TG Warn.
b Mosiah 27:16.
3*a* Mosiah 24:25.

began to build buildings; yea, they
were [a]industrious, and did labor
exceedingly.
6 And the people were desirous
that Alma should be their [a]king,
for he was beloved by his people.
7 But he said unto them: Behold,
it is not expedient that we should
have a king; for thus saith the Lord:
Ye shall [a]not esteem one flesh above
another, or one man shall not think
himself above another; therefore
I say unto you it is not expedient
that ye should have a king.
8 Nevertheless, if it [a]were possible
that ye could always have just men
to be your [b]kings it would be well
for you to have a king.
9 But remember the [a]iniquity of
king Noah and his [b]priests; and I
myself was [c]caught in a snare, and
did many things which were abominable in the sight of the Lord, which
caused me sore [d]repentance;
10 Nevertheless, [a]after much
[b]tribulation, the Lord did hear my
cries, and did answer my prayers,
and has made me an [c]instrument
in his hands in bringing [d]so many
of you to a knowledge of his truth.
11 Nevertheless, in this I do not
glory, for I am unworthy to glory
of myself.
12 And now I say unto you, ye have
been [a]oppressed by king Noah, and
have been in bondage to him and his
priests, and have been [b]brought into
iniquity by them; therefore ye were
bound with the [c]bands of iniquity.
13 And now as ye have been delivered by the power of God out of these
bonds; yea, even out of the [a]hands of
king Noah and his people, and also
from the [b]bonds of iniquity, even so
I desire that ye should [c]stand fast
in this [d]liberty wherewith ye have
been made free, and that ye trust
[e]no man to be a king over you.
14 And also trust no one to be your
[a]teacher nor your minister, except
he be a man of God, walking in his
ways and keeping his commandments.
15 Thus did Alma teach his people, that every man should [a]love
his [b]neighbor [c]as himself, that there
should be no [d]contention among
them.
16 And now, Alma was their [a]high
priest, he being the founder of their
church.
17 And it came to pass that none
received [a]authority to preach or to
teach except it were by him from
God. Therefore he [b]consecrated all
their priests and all their teachers;
and none were consecrated except
they were just men.
18 Therefore they did watch over
their people, and did [a]nourish them
with things pertaining to righteousness.
19 And it came to pass that they
began to prosper exceedingly in
the land; and they called the land
[a]Helam.
20 And it came to pass that they
did multiply and prosper exceedingly in the land of Helam; and they
built a city, which they called the
city of Helam.
21 Nevertheless the Lord seeth fit

5*a* TG Industry; Work, Value of.
6*a* 1 Sam. 8:5; 3 Ne. 6:30.
7*a* Mosiah 27:3 (3–5).
8*a* Mosiah 29:13.
b TG Governments.
9*a* Prov. 16:12; Mosiah 11:2 (1–15); 29:17 (17–19).
b Mosiah 17:12 (1, 6, 12–18).
c Mosiah 17:2 (1–4).
d Mosiah 18:1.
10*a* D&C 58:4.
b TG Tribulation.
c Alma 17:9 (9–11); 26:3.
d Mosiah 18:35.
12*a* TG Oppression; Unrighteous Dominion.
b Mosiah 11:2 (1–15).
c Isa. 58:6; 2 Ne. 28:19 (19–22); Alma 12:11.
13*a* Mosiah 18:34 (34–35).
b TG Bondage, Spiritual.
c Gal. 5:1.
d TG Liberty.
e Mosiah 29:13 (5–36).
14*a* Mosiah 2:4; 18:18 (18–22).
15*a* TG Love.
b TG Neighbor.
c Mosiah 18:21.
d 3 Ne. 11:29 (28–29).
16*a* Mosiah 18:18; 26:7.
17*a* TG Priesthood, Authority.
b Lev. 16:32; 2 Ne. 5:26.
18*a* Eph. 6:4; 1 Tim. 4:6.
19*a* Mosiah 27:16; Alma 24:1.

to [a]chasten his people; yea, he tri-
eth their [b]patience and their faith.
22 Nevertheless—whosoever putteth his [a]trust in him the same shall
be [b]lifted up at the last day. Yea,
and thus it was with this people.
23 For behold, I will show unto
you that they were brought into
[a]bondage, and none could deliver
them but the Lord their God, yea,
even the God of Abraham and Isaac
and of Jacob.
24 And it came to pass that he did
deliver them, and he did show forth
his mighty power unto them, and
great were their rejoicings.
25 For behold, it came to pass that
while they were in the land of Helam, yea, in the city of Helam, while
tilling the land round about, behold
an army of the Lamanites was in
the borders of the land.
26 Now it came to pass that the
brethren of Alma fled from their
fields, and gathered themselves
together in the city of Helam; and
they were much frightened because
of the appearance of the Lamanites.
27 But Alma went forth and stood
among them, and exhorted them
that they should not be frightened,
but that they should remember the
Lord their God and he would deliver them.
28 Therefore they hushed their
fears, and began to cry unto the
Lord that he would soften the hearts
of the Lamanites, that they would
spare them, and their wives, and
their children.
29 And it came to pass that the
Lord did soften the hearts of the
Lamanites. And Alma and his brethren went forth and delivered themselves up into their hands; and the
Lamanites took possession of the
land of Helam.
30 Now the [a]armies of the Lamanites, which had followed after the
people of king Limhi, had been lost
in the wilderness for many days.
31 And behold, they had found
those priests of king Noah, in a
place which they called [a]Amulon;
and they had begun to possess the
land of Amulon and had begun to
till the ground.
32 Now the name of the leader of
those priests was [a]Amulon.
33 And it came to pass that Amulon
did plead with the Lamanites; and
he also sent forth their wives, who
were the [a]daughters of the Lamanites, to plead with their brethren,
that they should not destroy their
husbands.
34 And the Lamanites had [a]com-
passion on Amulon and his brethren,
and did not destroy them, because
of their wives.
35 And [a]Amulon and his brethren
did join the Lamanites, and they
were traveling in the wilderness in
search of the land of Nephi when
they discovered the land of Helam,
which was possessed by Alma and
his brethren.
36 And it came to pass that the Lamanites promised unto Alma and
his brethren, that if they would show
them the [a]way which led to the land
of Nephi that they would grant unto
them their lives and their liberty.
37 But after Alma had shown
them the way that led to the land
of Nephi the Lamanites would not
keep their promise; but they set
[a]guards round about the land of
Helam, over Alma and his brethren.
38 And the remainder of them
went to the land of Nephi; and a
part of them returned to the land
of Helam, and also brought with
them the wives and the children
of the guards who had been left in
the land.

21*a* Deut. 11:2 (1–8);
Hel. 12:3;
D&C 98:21.
TG Chastening.
b TG Patience.
22*a* TG Trust in God.
b 1 Ne. 13:37;
Alma 26:7.
23*a* Alma 36:2.
30*a* Mosiah 22:15.
31*a* Mosiah 24:1;
Alma 23:14.
32*a* Mosiah 24:8.
33*a* Mosiah 20:5; 25:12.
34*a* TG Compassion.
35*a* Alma 25:4.
36*a* Mosiah 18:34.
37*a* Mosiah 24:9 (8–15);
Alma 5:5.

39 And the king of the Lamanites
had granted unto Amulon that he
should be a king and a ruler over
his people, who were in the land
of Helam; nevertheless he should
have no power to do anything contrary to the will of the king of the
Lamanites.

CHAPTER 24

Amulon persecutes Alma and his people—They are to be put to death if they pray—The Lord makes their burdens seem light—He delivers them from bondage, and they return to Zarahemla. About 145–120 B.C.

AND it came to pass that Amulon
did gain favor in the eyes of the
king of the Lamanites; therefore,
the king of the Lamanites granted
unto him and his brethren that they
should be appointed teachers over
his people, yea, even over the people
who were in the land of Shemlon,
and in the land of Shilom, and in
the [a]land of Amulon.
2 For the Lamanites had taken possession of all these lands; therefore,
the king of the Lamanites had appointed kings over all these lands.
3 And now the name of the king
of the Lamanites was [a]Laman, being called after the name of his
father; and therefore he was called
king Laman. And he was king over
a numerous people.
4 And he appointed [a]teachers of
the [b]brethren of Amulon in every
land which was possessed by his
people; and thus the [c]language of
Nephi began to be taught among all
the people of the Lamanites.
5 And they were a people friendly
one with another; nevertheless
they knew not God; neither did the
brethren of Amulon teach them
anything concerning the Lord their
God, neither the law of Moses; nor
did they teach them the words of
Abinadi;
6 But they taught them that they
should keep their record, and that
they might write one to another.
7 And thus the Lamanites began
to increase in riches, and began to
[a]trade one with another and wax
great, and began to be a cunning
and a wise people, as to the wisdom
of the world, yea, a very cunning
people, delighting in all manner of
wickedness and plunder, except it
were among their own brethren.
8 And now it came to pass that
[a]Amulon began to exercise [b]author-
ity over Alma and his brethren, and
began to persecute him, and cause
that his children should persecute
their children.
9 For Amulon knew Alma, that he
had been [a]one of the king's priests,
and that it was he that believed the
words of Abinadi and was driven
out before the king, and therefore
he was wroth with him; for he was
subject to king Laman, yet he exercised authority over them, and put
[b]tasks upon them, and put [c]task-
masters over them.
10 And it came to pass that so great
were their afflictions that they began to cry mightily to God.
11 And Amulon commanded them
that they should stop their cries; and
he [a]put guards over them to watch
them, that whosoever should be
found calling upon God should
be put to death.
12 And Alma and his people did
not raise their voices to the Lord
their God, but did pour out their
[a]hearts to him; and he did know the
[b]thoughts of their hearts.
13 And it [a]came to pass that the
voice of the Lord came to them in
their afflictions, saying: Lift up

24 1*a* Mosiah 23:31; Alma 21:3 (2–4).
3*a* Mosiah 9:10 (10–11); 10:6.
4*a* Mosiah 2:4; 18:18 (18–22); 23:14.
b Mosiah 23:9 (9, 12, 31).
c Omni 1:18.
7*a* Gen. 34:10 (10–21); 4 Ne. 1:46.
8*a* Mosiah 23:32.
b D&C 121:39.
9*a* Mosiah 17:2 (1–4); 23:9.
b Mosiah 21:3 (3–6).
c Mosiah 23:37 (37–39).
11*a* Dan. 6:7 (7–27).
12*a* TG Prayer.
b Ps. 139:2; Matt. 12:25.
13*a* Jer. 33:3 (1–3); Matt. 6:6.

your heads and be of good comfort, for I know of the covenant which ye have made unto me; and I will covenant with my people and deliver them out of bondage.
14 And I will also ease the [a]burdens which are put upon your shoulders, that even you cannot feel them upon your backs, even while you are in bondage; and this will I do that ye may stand as [b]witnesses for me hereafter, and that ye may know of a surety that I, the Lord God, do visit my people in their [c]afflictions.
15 And now it came to pass that the burdens which were laid upon Alma and his brethren were made light; yea, the Lord did [a]strengthen them that they could bear up their [b]burdens with ease, and they did submit cheerfully and with [c]patience to all the will of the Lord.
16 And it came to pass that so great was their faith and their patience that the voice of the Lord came unto them again, saying: Be of good comfort, for on the morrow I will deliver you out of bondage.
17 And he said unto Alma: Thou shalt go before this people, and I will go [a]with thee and deliver this people out of [b]bondage.
18 Now it came to pass that Alma and his people in the night-time gathered their flocks together, and also of their grain; yea, even all the night-time were they gathering their flocks together.
19 And in the morning the Lord caused a [a]deep sleep to come upon the Lamanites, yea, and all their task-masters were in a profound sleep.
20 And Alma and his people departed into the wilderness; and when they had traveled all day they pitched their tents in a valley, and they called the valley Alma, because he led their way in the wilderness.
21 Yea, and in the valley of Alma they poured out their [a]thanks to God because he had been merciful unto them, and eased their [b]burdens, and had delivered them out of bondage; for they were in bondage, and none could deliver them except it were the Lord their God.
22 And they gave [a]thanks to God, yea, all their men and all their women and all their children that could speak lifted their voices in the praises of their God.
23 And now the Lord said unto Alma: Haste thee and get thou and this people out of this land, for the Lamanites have awakened and do pursue thee; therefore get thee out of this land, and I will stop the Lamanites in this valley that they come no further in pursuit of this people.
24 And it came to pass that they departed out of the valley, and took their journey into the wilderness.
25 And after they had been in the wilderness [a]twelve days they arrived in the land of Zarahemla; and king Mosiah did also [b]receive them with joy.

CHAPTER 25

The descendants of Mulek at Zarahemla become Nephites—They learn of the people of Alma and of Zeniff—Alma baptizes Limhi and all his people—Mosiah authorizes Alma to organize the Church of God. About 120 B.C.

AND now king Mosiah caused that all the people should be gathered together.
2 Now there were not so many of the children of Nephi, or so many of those who were descendants of

14*a* Isa. 46:4 (3–4).
b TG Witness.
c TG Adversity; Affliction.
15*a* Matt. 11:28 (28–30).
b Alma 31:38; 33:23.
c 2 Cor. 4:16; D&C 54:10. TG Patience.
17*a* Ex. 3:12; 1 Ne. 17:55; Alma 38:4.
b Mosiah 25:10. TG Bondage, Physical.
19*a* 1 Sam. 26:12; Alma 55:15 (15–16).
21*a* TG Thanksgiving.
b Ps. 81:6 (5–6).
22*a* TG Thanksgiving.
25*a* Mosiah 23:3.
b Mosiah 22:14.

Nephi, as there were of the [a]people
of Zarahemla, who was a descendant of [b]Mulek, and those who came
with him into the wilderness.
3 And there were not so many of
the people of Nephi and of the people of Zarahemla as there were of
the Lamanites; yea, they were not
half so numerous.
4 And now all the people of Nephi
were assembled together, and also
all the people of Zarahemla, and
they were gathered together in
two bodies.
5 And it came to pass that Mosiah
did read, and caused to be read, the
records of Zeniff to his people; yea,
he read the records of the people
of Zeniff, from the time they [a]left
the land of Zarahemla until they
[b]returned again.
6 And he also read the account
of Alma and his brethren, and all
their afflictions, from the time they
left the land of Zarahemla until the
time they returned again.
7 And now, when Mosiah had made
an end of reading the records, his
people who tarried in the land were
struck with wonder and amazement.
8 For they knew not what to think;
for when they beheld those that
had been delivered [a]out of bondage
they were filled with exceedingly
great joy.
9 And again, when they thought of
their brethren who had been [a]slain
by the Lamanites they were filled
with sorrow, and even shed many
tears of sorrow.
10 And again, when they thought
of the immediate goodness of
God, and his power in delivering
Alma and his brethren out of the
hands of the Lamanites and of
[a]bondage, they did raise their voices
and give thanks to God.
11 And again, when they thought
upon the Lamanites, who were their
brethren, of their sinful and [a]pol-
luted state, they were filled with
[b]pain and anguish for the [c]welfare
of their souls.
12 And it came to pass that those
who [a]were the children of Amulon
and his brethren, who had taken to
wife the [b]daughters of the Lamanites, were displeased with the
conduct of their fathers, and they
would no longer be called by the
names of their fathers, therefore
they took upon themselves the
name of Nephi, that they might be
called the children of Nephi and
be numbered among those who
were [c]called Nephites.
13 And now all the people of
Zarahemla were [a]numbered with
the Nephites, and this because the
kingdom had been conferred upon
none but those who were descendants of Nephi.
14 And now it came to pass that
when Mosiah had made an end of
speaking and reading to the people, he desired that Alma should
also speak to the people.
15 And Alma did speak unto them,
when they were assembled together
in large bodies, and he went from
one body to another, preaching unto
the people repentance and faith on
the Lord.
16 And he did exhort the people of
Limhi and his brethren, all those that
had been delivered out of bondage,
that they should remember that it
was the Lord that did deliver them.
17 And it came to pass that after
Alma had taught the people many
things, and had made an end of
speaking to them, that king Limhi
was desirous that he might be
baptized; and all his people were

25 2*a* Hel. 6:10.
b Ezek. 17:22 (22–23); Omni 1:15 (14–19).
5*a* Mosiah 9:3 (3–4).
b Mosiah 22:13.
8*a* Mosiah 22:11 (11–13).
9*a* Mosiah 21:29 (8, 29).
10*a* Mosiah 24:17; 27:16.
11*a* TG Pollution.
b Mosiah 28:3 (3–4); Alma 13:27.
c 2 Ne. 6:3; Jacob 2:3. TG Worth of Souls.
12*a* Mosiah 20:3 (3–5).
b Mosiah 23:33.
c Jacob 1:14 (13–14); Alma 2:11.
13*a* Omni 1:19.

desirous that they might be baptized also.
18 Therefore, Alma did go forth into the water and did [a]baptize them; yea, he did baptize them after the manner he did his brethren in the [b]waters of Mormon; yea, and as many as he did baptize did belong to the church of God; and this because of their belief on the words of Alma.
19 And it came to pass that king Mosiah granted unto Alma that he might establish [a]churches throughout all the land of Zarahemla; and gave him power to [b]ordain [c]priests and [d]teachers over every church.
20 Now this was done because there were so many people that they could not all be governed by one teacher; neither could they all hear the word of God in one assembly;
21 Therefore they did [a]assemble themselves together in different bodies, being called churches; every church having their priests and their teachers, and every priest preaching the word according as it was delivered to him by the mouth of Alma.
22 And thus, notwithstanding there being many churches they were all one [a]church, yea, even the church of God; for there was nothing preached in all the churches except it were repentance and faith in God.
23 And now there were seven churches in the land of Zarahemla. And it came to pass that whosoever were desirous to take upon them the [a]name of Christ, or of God, they did join the churches of God;
24 And they were called the [a]people of God. And the Lord did pour out his [b]Spirit upon them, and they were blessed, and prospered in the land.

CHAPTER 26

Many members of the Church are led into sin by unbelievers—Alma is promised eternal life—Those who repent and are baptized gain forgiveness—Church members in sin who repent and confess to Alma and to the Lord will be forgiven; otherwise, they will not be numbered among the people of the Church. About 120–100 B.C.

NOW it came to pass that there were many of the rising generation that could not understand the [a]words of king Benjamin, being little children at the time he spake unto his people; and they did [b]not believe the tradition of their fathers.
2 They did not believe what had been said concerning the resurrection of the dead, neither did they believe concerning the coming of Christ.
3 And now because of their [a]unbelief they could not [b]understand the word of God; and their hearts were hardened.
4 And they would not be baptized; neither would they join the [a]church. And they were a separate people as to their faith, and remained so ever after, even in their [b]carnal and sinful state; for they would not call upon the Lord their God.
5 And now in the reign of Mosiah they were not half so numerous as the people of God; but because of the [a]dissensions among the brethren they became more numerous.
6 For it came to pass that they did [a]deceive many with their [b]flattering words, who were in the church, and did cause them to commit many sins; therefore it became expedient

18*a* Mosiah 21:35.
b Mosiah 18:16 (8–17).
19*a* Mosiah 26:17.
b TG Priesthood.
c TG Priest, Melchizedek Priesthood.
d TG Teacher.
21*a* TG Church.
22*a* Mosiah 18:17; 26:4.
23*a* TG Jesus Christ, Taking the Name of.
24*a* TG Sons and Daughters of God.
b TG God, Spirit of; Prosper.
26 1*a* Mosiah 2:1.
b TG Family, Children, Duties of.
3*a* TG Unbelief.
b TG Understanding.
4*a* Mosiah 25:22 (18–23); Alma 4:5 (4–5).
b TG Man, Natural, Not Spiritually Reborn.
5*a* TG Apostasy of Individuals.
6*a* Col. 2:18 (16–23). TG Deceit.
b TG Flatter.

that those who committed sin, that
were in the church, should be [c]ad-
monished by the church.
7 And it came to pass that they
were brought before the priests, and
delivered up unto the [a]priests by
the teachers; and the priests brought
them before Alma, who was the
[b]high priest.
8 Now king Mosiah had given Alma
the [a]authority over the [b]church.
9 And it came to pass that Alma
did not know concerning them;
but there were many [a]witnesses
against them; yea, the people stood
and testified of their iniquity in
abundance.
10 Now there had not any such
thing happened before in the
church; therefore Alma was troubled in his spirit, and he caused that
they should be brought before the
king.
11 And he said unto the king:
Behold, here are many whom we
have brought before thee, who are
accused of their brethren; yea, and
they have been taken in divers iniquities. And they do not repent of
their iniquities; therefore we have
brought them before thee, that thou
mayest judge them according to
their crimes.
12 But king Mosiah said unto Alma:
Behold, I judge them not; therefore
I [a]deliver them into thy hands to
be judged.
13 And now the spirit of Alma was
again troubled; and he went and inquired of the Lord what he should
do concerning this matter, for he
feared that he should do wrong in
the sight of God.
14 And it came to pass that after
he had poured out his whole soul
to God, the [a]voice of the Lord came
to him, saying:
15 Blessed art thou, Alma, and
blessed are they who were baptized
in the [a]waters of Mormon. Thou art
blessed because of thy exceeding
[b]faith in the words alone of my
servant Abinadi.
16 And blessed are they because of
their exceeding faith in the words
alone which thou hast spoken unto
them.
17 And blessed art thou because
thou hast established a [a]church
among this people; and they shall
be established, and they shall be
my people.
18 Yea, blessed is this people who
are willing to bear my [a]name; for
in my [b]name shall they be called;
and they are mine.
19 And because thou hast inquired
of me concerning the transgressor,
thou art blessed.
20 Thou art my servant; and I covenant with thee that thou shalt have
[a]eternal life; and thou shalt serve
me and go forth in my name, and
shalt gather together my sheep.
21 And he that will hear my voice
shall be my [a]sheep; and him shall
ye receive into the church, and him
will I also receive.
22 For behold, [a]this is my [b]church;
whosoever is [c]baptized shall be baptized unto repentance. And whomsoever ye receive shall [d]believe in
my name; and him will I freely
[e]forgive.
23 For it is I that taketh upon me
the [a]sins of the world; for it is I that
hath [b]created them; and it is I that
granteth unto him that believeth

6*c* Alma 5:57 (57–58); 6:3. TG Warn.
7*a* TG Priest, Melchizedek Priesthood.
b Mosiah 23:16; 29:42.
8*a* TG Delegation of Responsibility.
b TG Church Organization.
9*a* TG Witness.
12*a* D&C 42:87 (78–93).
14*a* TG Guidance, Divine.
15*a* Mosiah 18:30.
b Mosiah 17:2; D&C 46:14. TG Faith.
17*a* Mosiah 25:19 (19–24).
18*a* Mosiah 1:11; 5:8. TG Jesus Christ, Taking the Name of.
b Deut. 28:10.
20*a* TG Election.
21*a* TG Jesus Christ, Good Shepherd.
22*a* Mosiah 27:13.
b TG Jesus Christ, Head of the Church.
c 2 Ne. 9:23.
d TG Baptism, Qualifications for.
e TG Remission of Sins.
23*a* TG Jesus Christ, Redeemer.
b TG Jesus Christ, Creator.

unto the end a place at my right
hand.
24 For behold, in my name are they
called; and if they [a]know me they
shall come forth, and shall have a
place eternally at my right hand.
25 And it shall come to pass that
when the [a]second trump shall sound
then shall they that never [b]knew
me come forth and shall stand before me.
26 And then shall they know that
I am the Lord their God, that I am
their Redeemer; but they would not
be redeemed.
27 And then I will confess unto
them that I never [a]knew them; and
they shall [b]depart into [c]everlasting
fire prepared for the devil and his
angels.
28 Therefore I say unto you, that
he that will not [a]hear my voice, the
same shall ye not receive into my
church, for him I will not receive
at the last day.
29 Therefore I say unto you, Go;
and whosoever transgresseth against
me, him shall ye [a]judge [b]according
to the sins which he has committed; and if he [c]confess his sins before thee and me, and [d]repenteth
in the sincerity of his heart, him
shall ye [e]forgive, and I will forgive
him also.
30 Yea, and [a]as often as my people
[b]repent will I forgive them their
trespasses against me.
31 And ye shall also [a]forgive one
another your trespasses; for verily
I say unto you, he that forgiveth
not his [b]neighbor's trespasses when
he says that he repents, the same
hath brought himself under condemnation.
32 Now I say unto you, Go; and
whosoever will [a]not repent of his
sins the same shall not be numbered
among my people; and this shall be
observed from this time forward.
33 And it came to pass when Alma
had heard these words he [a]wrote
them down that he might have
them, and that he might judge the
people of that church according to
the commandments of God.
34 And it came to pass that Alma
went and judged those that had
been taken in iniquity, according
to the [a]word of the Lord.
35 And whosoever repented of
their sins and did [a]confess them,
them he did number among the
people of the church;
36 And those that would not confess their sins and repent of their iniquity, the same were not numbered
among the people of the church,
and their names were [a]blotted out.
37 And it came to pass that Alma
did regulate all the affairs of the
church; and they began again to
have peace and to prosper exceedingly in the affairs of the church,
walking circumspectly before God,
receiving many, and baptizing many.
38 And now all these things did
Alma and his [a]fellow laborers do
who were over the church, [b]walking
in all diligence, teaching the word
of God in all things, suffering all
manner of afflictions, being persecuted by all those who did not
belong to the church of God.
39 And they did admonish their

24*a* John 17:3.
25*a* Dan. 12:2 (1–2).
b 3 Ne. 14:23 (21–23); D&C 76:85 (81–86); 112:26.
27*a* Matt. 7:23 (21–23).
b Luke 13:27.
c 1 Ne. 15:35 (32–36).
28*a* 2 Ne. 9:31; D&C 1:14 (2, 11, 14); Moses 6:27.
29*a* TG Judgment.
b TG Accountability.
c Num. 5:7 (6–10); Alma 17:4; 3 Ne. 1:25. TG Confession.
d TG Repent.
e TG Forgive.
30*a* Moro. 6:8.
b Ezek. 33:11 (11, 15–16); Amos 5:4 (4–8); Acts 3:19 (19–20); 2 Ne. 1:20; Mosiah 29:20.
31*a* Col. 3:13 (12–14); 3 Ne. 13:14 (14–15); D&C 64:10 (9–10).
b TG Neighbor.
32*a* Alma 1:24. TG Excommunication.
33*a* TG Scriptures, Writing of.
34*a* 2 Ne. 33:14 (13–15).
35*a* TG Confession.
36*a* Ex. 32:33; Ps. 9:5; 109:13; Alma 1:24. TG Book of Life.
38*a* TG Church Organization.
b TG Walking with God.

brethren; and they were also [a]admonished, every one by the word of God, according to his sins, or to the sins which he had committed, being commanded of God to [b]pray without ceasing, and to give [c]thanks in all things.

CHAPTER 27

Mosiah forbids persecution and enjoins equality—Alma the younger and the four sons of Mosiah seek to destroy the Church—An angel appears and commands them to cease their evil course—Alma is struck dumb—All mankind must be born again to gain salvation—Alma and the sons of Mosiah declare glad tidings. About 100–92 B.C.

AND now it came to pass that the persecutions which were inflicted on the church by the unbelievers became so great that the church began to murmur, and complain to their leaders concerning the matter; and they did complain to Alma. And Alma laid the case before their king, Mosiah. And Mosiah [a]consulted with his priests.

2 And it came to pass that king Mosiah sent a proclamation throughout the land round about that there should not any unbeliever [a]persecute any of those who belonged to the church of God.

3 And there was a strict command throughout all the churches that there should be no [a]persecutions among them, that there should be an [b]equality among all men;

4 That they should let no pride nor haughtiness disturb their [a]peace; that every man should [b]esteem his [c]neighbor as himself, [d]laboring with their own hands for their support.

5 Yea, and all their priests and teachers [a]should [b]labor with their own hands for their support, in all cases save it were in sickness, or in much want; and doing these things, they did abound in the [c]grace of God.

6 And there began to be much peace again in the land; and the people began to be very numerous, and began to scatter abroad upon the face of the earth, yea, on the north and on the south, on the east and on the west, building large cities and villages in all quarters of the land.

7 And the Lord did [a]visit them and [b]prosper them, and they became a large and wealthy people.

8 Now the sons of Mosiah were numbered among the [a]unbelievers; and also one of the sons of Alma was numbered among them, he being called Alma, after his father; nevertheless, he became a very wicked and an [b]idolatrous man. And he was a man of many words, and did speak much [c]flattery to the people; therefore he [d]led many of the people to do after the manner of his [e]iniquities.

9 And he became a great hinderment to the prosperity of the church of God; [a]stealing away the hearts of the people; causing much dissension among the people; giving a chance for the enemy of God to exercise his [b]power over them.

10 And now it came to pass that while he was going about to [a]destroy the church of God, for he did go about secretly with the sons of Mosiah seeking to destroy the church,

39*a* TG Warn.
b 2 Ne. 32:9 (8–9).
c TG Thanksgiving.
27 1*a* TG Counsel.
2*a* TG Persecution.
3*a* TG Malice.
b Mosiah 23:7; 29:32; Alma 30:11.
4*a* TG Peace.
b TG Love.
c TG Neighbor.
d TG Industry; Labor.
5*a* Mosiah 18:24 (24, 26); Alma 1:3, 26.
b TG Work, Value of.
c TG Grace.
7*a* Ex. 3:16.
b TG Prosper.
8*a* 1 Sam. 3:13; 1 Ne. 2:12 (12–13); Moses 5:16. TG Unbelief.
b TG Idolatry.
c TG Flatter.
d TG Peer Influence.
e Mal. 2:8.
9*a* 2 Sam. 12:14 (1–14); 15:6 (1–6). TG Apostasy of Individuals.
b D&C 50:7; 93:39 (37, 39).
10*a* Acts 8:3; Mosiah 28:4 (3–4).

and to lead astray the people of the
Lord, contrary to the commandments of God, or even the king—
11 And as I said unto you, as they
were going about [a]rebelling against
God, behold, the [b]angel of the Lord
[c]appeared unto them; and he descended as it were in a [d]cloud; and
he spake as it were with a voice of
thunder, which caused the earth to
shake upon which they stood;
12 And so great was their astonishment, that they fell to the earth,
and understood not the words which
he spake unto them.
13 Nevertheless he cried again, saying: Alma, arise and stand forth, for
why persecutest thou the church of
God? For the Lord hath said: [a]This
is my church, and I will establish
it; and nothing shall [b]overthrow
it, save it is the transgression of
my people.
14 And again, the angel said:
Behold, the Lord hath [a]heard the
prayers of his people, and also
the [b]prayers of his servant, Alma,
who is thy father; for he has [c]prayed
with much faith concerning thee
that thou mightest be brought to
the [d]knowledge of the truth; therefore, for this purpose have I come
to [e]convince thee of the power and
authority of God, that the [f]prayers
of his servants might be answered
according to their faith.
15 And now behold, can ye dispute the power of God? For behold, doth not my voice shake the
earth? And can ye not also [a]be-
hold me before you? And I am sent
from God.
16 Now I say unto thee: Go, and
remember the captivity of thy
fathers in the land of [a]Helam, and
in the land of Nephi; and remember
how great things he has done for
them; for they were in [b]bondage,
and he has [c]delivered them. And
now I say unto thee, Alma, go thy
way, and seek to destroy the church
no more, that their prayers may be
answered, and this even if thou wilt
of [d]thyself be [e]cast off.
17 And now it came to pass that
these were the last words which
the angel spake unto Alma, and
he departed.
18 And now Alma and those that
were with him fell again to the
earth, for great was their astonishment; for with their own eyes
they had beheld an [a]angel of the
Lord; and his voice was as thunder,
which [b]shook the earth; and they
knew that there was nothing save
the power of God that could shake
the earth and cause it to tremble
as though it would part asunder.
19 And now the astonishment of
Alma was so great that he became
[a]dumb, that he could not open his
mouth; yea, and he became weak,
even that he could not move his
hands; therefore he was taken by
those that were with him, and carried helpless, even until he was laid
before his father.
20 And they rehearsed unto his
father all that had happened unto
them; and his father rejoiced, for
he knew that it was the power
of God.
21 And he caused that a multitude
should be gathered together that
they might witness what the Lord

11*a* TG Disobedience; Rebellion.
b Alma 21:5.
c Acts 9:3 (1–9); Mosiah 27:15; Alma 8:15; 17:2.
d Ex. 19:9 (9, 16).
13*a* Mosiah 26:22. TG Jesus Christ, Head of the Church.
b Hosea 13:9. TG Apostasy of Individuals.
14*a* Dan. 10:12; Abr. 1:16 (15–16).
b 2 Cor. 1:11; Alma 10:22.
c TG Family, Love within.
d Hosea 4:6.
e Alma 29:10.
f Alma 19:17; Morm. 9:36 (36–37).
15*a* Mosiah 27:11.
16*a* Mosiah 23:19; Alma 24:1.
b Mosiah 25:10; Alma 5:5 (5–6).
c Mosiah 23:1 (1–4).
d Alma 30:47.
e Micah 3:6 (1–7); Matt. 8:12 (11–12).
18*a* TG Angels.
b Isa. 6:4; Alma 36:7.
19*a* Dan. 10:15; Luke 1:20 (20–22).

had done for his son, and also for
those that were with him.
22 And he caused that the priests
should assemble themselves together;
and they began to fast,
and to pray to the Lord their God
that he would open the mouth of
Alma, that he might speak, and also
that his limbs might receive their
strength—that the eyes of the people
might be opened to see and know
of the goodness and glory of God.
23 And it came to pass after they
had fasted and prayed for the
space of [a]two days and two nights,
the limbs of Alma received their
strength, and he stood up and began
to speak unto them, bidding
them to be of good comfort:
24 For, said he, I have repented of
my sins, and have been [a]redeemed
of the Lord; behold I am born of
the Spirit.
25 And the Lord said unto me: Marvel
not that all mankind, yea, men
and women, all nations, kindreds,
tongues and people, must be [a]born
again; yea, [b]born of God, [c]changed
from their carnal and [d]fallen state,
to a state of righteousness, being redeemed
of God, becoming his [e]sons
and daughters;
26 And thus they become new
creatures; and unless they do this,
they can in [a]nowise inherit the
kingdom of God.
27 I say unto you, unless this be
the case, they must be cast off; and
this I know, because I was like to
be cast off.
28 Nevertheless, after [a]wading
through much [b]tribulation, repenting
nigh unto death, the Lord in
mercy hath seen fit to snatch me
out of an [c]everlasting burning, and
I am born of God.
29 My soul hath been [a]redeemed
from the gall of bitterness and
[b]bonds of iniquity. I was in the
darkest abyss; but now I behold
the marvelous light of God. My soul
was [c]racked with eternal torment;
but I am snatched, and my soul is
[d]pained no more.
30 I rejected my Redeemer, and
denied that which had been spoken
of by our fathers; but now that they
may foresee that he will come, and
that he remembereth every creature
of his creating, he will make
himself manifest unto [a]all.
31 Yea, [a]every knee shall bow, and
every tongue confess before him.
Yea, even at the last day, when all
men shall stand to be [b]judged of
him, then shall they confess that
he is [c]God; then shall they confess,
who live [d]without God in the world,
that the judgment of an everlasting
punishment is just upon them;
and they shall quake, and tremble,
and shrink beneath the glance of
his [e]all-searching eye.
32 And now it came to pass that
Alma began from this time forward
to teach the people, and those who
were with Alma at the time the
angel appeared unto them, traveling
round about through all the
land, publishing to all the people
the things which they had heard
and seen, and preaching the word
of God in much tribulation, being
greatly persecuted by those who
were unbelievers, being smitten by
many of them.

---

23 *a* Alma 36:10.
24 *a* Ps. 49:15; Alma 27:25; A of F 1:3.
25 *a* Rom. 6:3 (3–11). TG Conversion; Man, New, Spiritually Reborn.
b Mosiah 5:7; Alma 5:14 (14, 49).
c Moses 6:65.
d TG Man, Natural, Not Spiritually Reborn.
e Mosiah 15:10; Moro. 7:19.
26 *a* John 3:5.
28 *a* Alma 7:5.
b TG Tribulation.
c 2 Ne. 9:16.
29 *a* Isa. 38:17.
b Isa. 58:6.
c Mosiah 2:38.
d TG Pain.
30 *a* D&C 84:46 (45–46).
31 *a* Philip. 2:10 (9–11); Mosiah 16:1 (1–2); D&C 88:104; 138:23.
b TG Jesus Christ, Judge.
c Mosiah 7:27; Alma 11:39 (38–39).
d Eph. 2:12; Alma 41:11.
e TG God, Omniscience of.

33 But notwithstanding all this, they did impart much consolation to the church, confirming their faith, and exhorting them with long-suffering and much travail to keep the commandments of God.

34 And four of them were the [a]sons of Mosiah; and their names were Ammon, and Aaron, and Omner, and Himni; these were the names of the sons of Mosiah.

35 And they traveled throughout all the land of Zarahemla, and among all the [a]people who were under the reign of king Mosiah, [b]zealously striving to repair all the injuries which they had done to the church, [c]confessing all their sins, and publishing all the things which they had seen, and explaining the prophecies and the scriptures to all who desired to hear them.

36 And thus they were instruments in the hands of God in bringing many to the knowledge of the truth, yea, to the knowledge of their Redeemer.

37 And how blessed are they! For they did [a]publish [b]peace; they did publish good tidings of good; and they did declare unto the people that the Lord reigneth.

CHAPTER 28

The sons of Mosiah go to preach to the Lamanites—Using the two seer stones, Mosiah translates the Jaredite plates. About 92 B.C.

Now it came to pass that after the [a]sons of Mosiah had done all these things, they took a small number with them and returned to their father, the king, and desired of him that he would grant unto them that they might, with these whom they had [b]selected, go up to the land of [c]Nephi that they might preach the things which they had heard, and that they might impart the word of God to their brethren, the Lamanites—

2 [a]That perhaps they might bring them to the knowledge of the Lord their God, and convince them of the iniquity of their fathers; and that perhaps they might cure them of their [b]hatred towards the Nephites, that they might also be brought to rejoice in the Lord their God, that they might become friendly to one another, and that there should be no more contentions in all the land which the Lord their God had given them.

3 Now they were desirous that salvation should be declared to every creature, for they could not [a]bear that any human [b]soul should [c]perish; yea, even the very thoughts that any soul should endure [d]endless torment did cause them to quake and [e]tremble.

4 And thus did the Spirit of the Lord work upon them, for they were the very [a]vilest of sinners. And the Lord saw fit in his infinite [b]mercy to spare them; nevertheless they suffered much anguish of soul because of their iniquities, suffering much and fearing that they should be cast off forever.

5 And it came to pass that they did plead with their father many days that they might go up to the land of Nephi.

6 And king Mosiah went and [a]inquired of the Lord if he should let his sons go up among the Lamanites to preach the word.

34*a* Mosiah 28:1; 29:3; Alma 17:1.
35*a* Mosiah 1:10; 28:18.
b TG Zeal.
c Alma 39:13.
37*a* Mosiah 12:21; 15:14 (14–17).
b TG Peace of God.
28 1*a* Mosiah 27:34.
b Alma 17:8.
c Mosiah 9:1 (1, 3–4, 14); Alma 50:8 (8, 11).
2*a* Alma 17:16.
b Jacob 7:24; Mosiah 1:5; Alma 26:9.
3*a* 1 Ne. 7:8; Mosiah 25:11; Alma 13:27 (27–30); 31:2; 3 Ne. 17:14; Moses 7:41.
b TG Worth of Souls.
c Matt. 18:14.
d Jacob 6:10; Moro. 8:21; D&C 19:12 (10–12).
e 1 Cor. 2:3.
4*a* Mosiah 27:10; Alma 26:18 (17–18).
b TG God, Mercy of.
6*a* Ex. 18:15; Alma 43:23.

7 And the Lord said unto Mosiah:
Let them go up, for many shall
believe on their words, and they
shall have eternal life; and I will
[a]deliver thy sons out of the hands
of the Lamanites.
8 And it came to pass that Mosiah
granted that they might go and do
according to their request.
9 And they [a]took their journey into
the wilderness to go up to preach
the word among the Lamanites;
and I shall give an [b]account of their
proceedings hereafter.
10 Now king Mosiah had no one to
confer the kingdom upon, for there
was not any of his sons who [a]would
accept of the kingdom.
11 Therefore he took the records
which were engraven on the plates
of [a]brass, and also the plates of
[b]Nephi, and all the things which he
had kept and preserved according
to the commandments of God, after
having translated and caused to be
written the records which were on
the [c]plates of gold which had been
found by the people of Limhi, which
were delivered to him by the hand
of Limhi;
12 And this he did because of the
great anxiety of his people; for they
were desirous beyond measure to
know concerning those people [a]who
had been destroyed.
13 And now he translated them
by the means of those two [a]stones
which were fastened into the two
rims of a bow.
14 Now these things were prepared
from the beginning, and were
handed down from generation to
generation, for the purpose of interpreting languages;
15 And they have been kept and
preserved by the hand of the Lord,
that he should discover to every
creature who should possess the
land the iniquities and abominations of his people;
16 And whosoever has these things
is called [a]seer, after the manner of
old times.
17 Now after Mosiah had finished
[a]translating these [b]records, behold,
it gave an account of the people
who were [c]destroyed, from the time
that they were destroyed back to
the building of the [d]great tower, at
the time the Lord [e]confounded the
language of the people and they
were scattered abroad upon the
face of all the earth, yea, and even
from that time back until the creation of Adam.
18 Now this account did cause the
people of Mosiah to mourn exceedingly, yea, they were filled with
sorrow; nevertheless it gave them
much knowledge, in the which they
did rejoice.
19 And this account shall be [a]writ-
ten hereafter; for behold, it is expedient that all people should know
the things which are written in
this account.
20 And now, as I said unto you,
that after king Mosiah had done
these things, he took the plates of
[a]brass, and all the things which
he had kept, and [b]conferred them
upon Alma, who was the son of Alma;
yea, all the records, and also the
[c]interpreters, and conferred them
upon him, and commanded him
that he should keep and [d]preserve
them, and also keep a record of the
people, handing them down from

7a Alma 17:35; 19:23 (22–23).
9a Alma 17:6 (6–9); 26:1.
b IE in Alma 17–26.
10a Mosiah 29:3 (1–3).
11a Mosiah 10:16.
b W of M 1:10.
c Mosiah 21:27; Alma 37:21 (21–31).
12a Mosiah 8:8.
13a Ex. 28:30; Mosiah 21:28 (27–28); Abr. 3:1; JS—H 1:35.
16a Mosiah 8:13 (13–18). TG Seer.
17a Omni 1:20; Alma 9:21.
b TG Scriptures, Writing of.
c Mosiah 8:8 (7–12); Alma 22:30.
d Ether 1:3 (1–5).
e Gen. 11:7 (6–9); Omni 1:22.
19a Ether 1:1.
20a Mosiah 1:3 (3–4); Alma 37:3 (3–12).
b Alma 37:1.
c TG Urim and Thummim.
d TG Scriptures, Preservation of.

one generation to another, even as they had been handed down from the time that Lehi left Jerusalem.

CHAPTER 29

Mosiah proposes that judges be chosen in place of a king—Unrighteous kings lead their people into sin—Alma the younger is chosen chief judge by the voice of the people—He is also the high priest over the Church—Alma the elder and Mosiah die. About 92–91 B.C.

Now when Mosiah had done this he sent out throughout all the land, among all the people, desiring to know their will concerning who should be their king.

2 And it came to pass that the voice of the people came, saying: We are desirous that Aaron thy son should be our king and our ruler.

3 Now Aaron had gone up to the land of Nephi, therefore the king could not confer the kingdom upon him; [a]neither would Aaron take upon him the kingdom; neither were any of the [b]sons of Mosiah [c]willing to take upon them the kingdom.

4 Therefore king Mosiah sent again among the people; yea, even a written word sent he among the people. And these were the words that were written, saying:

5 Behold, O ye my people, or my brethren, for I esteem you as such, I desire that ye should consider the cause which ye are called to [a]consider—for ye are desirous to have a king.

6 Now I declare unto you that he to whom the kingdom doth rightly belong has declined, and will not take upon him the kingdom.

7 And now if there should be another appointed in his stead, behold I fear there would rise [a]contentions among you. And who knoweth but what my son, to whom the kingdom doth belong, should turn to be angry and [b]draw away a part of this people after him, which would cause wars and contentions among you, which would be the cause of shedding much blood and perverting the way of the Lord, yea, and destroy the souls of many people.

8 Now I say unto you let us be wise and consider these things, for we have no right to destroy my son, neither should we have any right to destroy another if he should be appointed in his stead.

9 And if my son should turn again to his pride and vain things he would recall the things which he had said, and claim his right to the kingdom, which would cause him and also this people to commit much sin.

10 And now let us be wise and look forward to these things, and do that which will make for the peace of this people.

11 Therefore I will be your king the remainder of my days; nevertheless, let [a]us appoint [b]judges, to judge this people according to our law; and we will newly arrange the affairs of this people, for we will appoint wise men to be judges, that will judge this people according to the commandments of God.

12 Now it is better that a man should be [a]judged of God than of man, for the judgments of God are always just, but the judgments of man are not always just.

13 Therefore, [a]if it were possible that you could have [b]just men to be your kings, who would establish the [c]laws of God, and judge this people according to his commandments,

---

29 3*a* Alma 17:6.
b Mosiah 27:34.
c Mosiah 28:10.
5*a* 1 Sam. 8:9 (9–19).
7*a* TG Contention.
b Judg. 8:23; 9:2 (1–55).
11*a* Mosiah 29:25 (25–27, 41).
b Ex. 18:13; Deut. 16:18; Ezra 7:25; Alma 46:4; D&C 107:74 (74, 78).
12*a* 2 Sam. 23:3; 2 Chr. 1:10; Ps. 50:6; 75:7; 2 Ne. 21:4; D&C 98:9; Moses 6:57. TG God, Justice of.
13*a* Mosiah 23:8, 13.
b 1 Kgs. 15:14 (11–14).
c Ex. 18:21; Neh. 7:2.

yea, if ye could have men for your
kings who would do even as my
father [d]Benjamin did for this
people—I say unto you, if this could
always be the case then it would
be expedient that ye should always
have kings to rule over you.
14 And even I myself have labored
with all the power and faculties
which I have possessed, to teach
you the commandments of God,
and to establish peace throughout
the land, that there should be no
wars nor contentions, no stealing,
nor plundering, nor murdering, nor
any manner of iniquity;
15 And whosoever has committed iniquity, him have I [a]punished
according to the crime which he
has committed, according to the
law which has been given to us by
our fathers.
16 Now I say unto you, that because
all men are not just it is not expedient that ye should have a [a]king
or kings to rule over you.
17 For behold, how much [a]iniquity
doth one [b]wicked king cause to be
committed, yea, and what great
destruction!
18 Yea, remember king Noah, his
[a]wickedness and his abominations,
and also the wickedness and abominations of his people. Behold what
great destruction did come upon
them; and also because of their
iniquities they were brought into
[b]bondage.
19 And were it not for the inter-
position of their all-wise Creator,
and this because of their sincere
repentance, they must unavoidably
remain in bondage until now.
20 But behold, he did deliver them
because they did [a]humble themselves before him; and because they
[b]cried mightily unto him he did
deliver them out of bondage; and
thus doth the Lord work with his
power in all cases among the children of men, extending the arm of
[c]mercy towards them that put their
[d]trust in him.
21 And behold, now I say unto
you, ye cannot dethrone an iniqui-
tous [a]king save it be through much
contention, and the shedding of
much blood.
22 For behold, he has his [a]friends
in iniquity, and he keepeth his
guards about him; and he teareth up
the laws of those who have reigned
in righteousness before him; and he
trampleth under his feet the commandments of God;
23 And he enacteth laws, and sendeth them forth among his people,
yea, laws after the manner of his
own wickedness; and whosoever
doth not obey his laws he [a]causeth
to be destroyed; and whosoever doth
rebel against him he will send his
armies against them to war, and if
he can he will destroy them; and
thus an unrighteous [b]king doth pervert the ways of all righteousness.
24 And now behold I say unto you,
it is not expedient that such abominations should come upon you.
25 Therefore, choose you by the
[a]voice of this people, judges, that
ye may be [b]judged according to the
[c]laws which have been given you
by our fathers, which are correct,
and which were given them by the
hand of the Lord.
26 Now it is not common that
the [a]voice of the people desireth

13*d* Omni 1:25;
W of M 1:18 (17–18).
15*a* Alma 1:32.
16*a* 1 Sam. 8:5 (4–22).
TG Kings, Earthly.
17*a* 1 Kgs. 16:26 (25–26);
Alma 46:9.
b Prov. 16:12;
Mosiah 23:9 (8–10).
18*a* Mosiah 11:2 (1–15).
b 1 Sam. 8:11 (10–18);
Mosiah 12:2 (2–8);
Ether 6:23.
20*a* Mosiah 21:14.
b Ex. 2:23 (23–25);
Alma 43:49 (49–50).
c Ezek. 33:11 (11, 15–16);
Mosiah 26:30.
d TG Trust in God.
21*a* 1 Sam. 8:9;
Prov. 25:5 (4–5).
22*a* 1 Kgs. 12:8 (8–15).
23*a* TG Tyranny;
Unrighteous Dominion.
b TG Kings, Earthly.
25*a* Mosiah 29:11;
Alma 2:3 (3–7).
TG Citizenship.
b Ex. 18:22 (19–27).
c Deut. 4:8;
Alma 34:11.
26*a* 1 Sam. 8:7;
Alma 29:4;
D&C 26:2.
TG Common Consent.

anything [b]contrary to that which
is right; but it is common for the
lesser part of the [c]people to desire
that which is not right; therefore
this shall ye observe and make it
your law—to do your business by
the voice of the people.
27 And [a]if the time comes that
the voice of the people doth choose
iniquity, then is the time that the
judgments of God will come upon
you; yea, then is the time he will
visit you with great destruction even
as he has hitherto visited this land.
28 And now if ye have judges, and
they do not [a]judge you according to
the law which has been given, ye
can cause that they may be judged
of a higher judge.
29 If your higher judges do not
judge righteous judgments, ye shall
cause that a small number of your
lower judges should be gathered
together, and they shall judge your
higher judges, according to the voice
of the people.
30 And I command you to do these
things in the fear of the Lord; and
I command you to do these things,
and that ye have no king; that if
these people commit sins and iniquities they shall be answered upon
their own heads.
31 For behold I say unto you, the
sins of many people have been
[a]caused by the iniquities of their
kings; therefore their iniquities
are answered upon the heads of
their kings.
32 And now I desire that this [a]in-
equality should be no more in this
land, especially among this my people; but I desire that this land be a
land of [b]liberty, and [c]every man may
enjoy his rights and privileges alike,
so long as the Lord sees fit that we
may live and inherit the land, yea,
even as long as any of our posterity
remains upon the face of the land.
33 And many more things did king
Mosiah write unto them, unfolding
unto them all the trials and [a]trou-
bles of a righteous king, yea, all the
travails of soul for their people, and
also all the murmurings of the people to their king; and he explained
it all unto them.
34 And he told them that these
things ought not to be; but that
the burden should come upon all
the people, that every man might
[a]bear his part.
35 And he also unfolded unto them
all the disadvantages they labored
under, by having an unrighteous
[a]king to rule over them;
36 Yea, all [a]his iniquities and
abominations, and all the wars, and
contentions, and bloodshed, and the
stealing, and the plundering, and
the committing of whoredoms, and
all manner of iniquities which cannot be enumerated—telling them
that these things ought not to be,
that they were expressly repugnant
to the commandments of God.
37 And now it came to pass, after
king Mosiah had sent these things
forth among the people they were
[a]convinced of the truth of his words.
38 Therefore they relinquished
their desires for a king, and became
exceedingly anxious that every
man should have an equal [a]chance
throughout all the land; yea, and
every man expressed a willingness
to answer for his own sins.
39 Therefore, it came to pass that
they assembled themselves together
in bodies throughout the land, to
cast in their [a]voices concerning who
should be their [b]judges, to judge
them according to the [c]law which
had been given them; and they were

26*b* TG Disobedience.
c TG Governments.
27*a* Alma 2:4 (3–7); 10:19; Hel. 4:21 (20–24); 5:2.
28*a* Deut. 17:8 (8–9).
31*a* 1 Kgs. 14:16; 15:26; 16:2; 21:22; Mosiah 29:36.
32*a* Mosiah 27:3; Alma 30:11. TG Injustice.
b 2 Ne. 1:7; 10:11; Alma 46:17 (10–28, 34). TG Liberty.
c Alma 27:9.
33*a* TG Stewardship.
34*a* TG Accountability.
35*a* TG Kings, Earthly.
36*a* Mosiah 29:31.
37*a* 1 Sam. 8:19.
38*a* TG Agency.
39*a* TG Common Consent.
b Alma 62:47.
c Alma 1:14.

exceedingly rejoiced because of the
[d]liberty which had been granted
unto them.
40 And they did wax strong in love
towards Mosiah; yea, they did esteem
him more than any other man; for
they did not look upon him as a
[a]tyrant who was seeking for gain, yea,
for that [b]lucre which doth [c]corrupt
the soul; for he had not exacted riches
of them, neither had he delighted in
the shedding of blood; but he had
established [d]peace in the land, and
he had granted unto his people that
they should be delivered from all
manner of bondage; therefore they
did esteem him, yea, exceedingly,
beyond measure.
41 And it came to pass that they did
[a]appoint [b]judges to rule over them,
or to judge them according to the
law; and this they did throughout
all the land.
42 And it came to pass that Alma
was appointed to be the first [a]chief
judge, he being also the [b]high priest,
his father having conferred the office upon him, and having given
him the charge concerning all the
affairs of the church.
43 And now it came to pass that
Alma did [a]walk in the ways of the
Lord, and he did keep his commandments, and he did judge righteous
judgments; and there was continual
peace through the land.
44 And thus commenced the [a]reign
of the judges throughout all the land
of Zarahemla, among all the people who were called the Nephites;
and Alma was the first and chief
judge.
45 And now it came to pass that
his father died, being eighty and
two years old, having lived to fulfil
the commandments of God.
46 And it came to pass that Mosiah [a]died also, in the thirty and
third year of his reign, being [b]sixty
and three years old; making in the
whole, five hundred and nine years
from the time Lehi left Jerusalem.
47 And thus ended the reign of the
kings over the people of Nephi; and
thus ended the days of Alma, who
was the founder of their church.

THE BOOK OF ALMA

THE SON OF ALMA

The account of Alma, who was the son of Alma, the first and chief judge over the people of Nephi, and also the high priest over the Church. An account of the reign of the judges, and the wars and contentions among the people. And also an account of a war between the Nephites and the Lamanites, according to the record of Alma, the first and chief judge.

CHAPTER 1

Nehor teaches false doctrines, establishes a church, introduces priestcraft, and slays Gideon—Nehor is executed for his crimes—Priestcrafts and persecutions spread among the people—The priests support themselves, the people care for the poor, and the Church prospers. About 91–88 B.C.

39*d* TG Liberty.
40*a* TG Tyranny.
b Titus 1:11.
c TG Bribe.
d TG Peacemakers.
41*a* Alma 11:4.
b Judg. 2:16; Mosiah 29:11.
42*a* Alma 2:16; 7:1.
b Mosiah 26:7; Alma 4:4.
43*a* TG Walking with God.
44*a* Alma 17:6.
46*a* Alma 1:1.
b Mosiah 6:4.

NOW it came to pass that in the first year of the reign of the judges over the people of Nephi, from this time forward, king Mosiah having [a]gone the way of all the earth, having warred a good warfare, walking uprightly before God, leaving none to reign in his stead; nevertheless he had established [b]laws, and they were acknowledged by the people; therefore they were obliged to abide by the [c]laws which he had made.

2 And it came to pass that in the first year of the reign of Alma in the judgment-seat, there was a [a]man brought before him to be judged, a man who was large, and was noted for his much strength.

3 And he had gone about among the people, preaching to them that which he [a]termed to be the word of God, bearing down [b]against the church; declaring unto the people that every priest and teacher ought to become [c]popular; and they ought [d]not to labor with their hands, but that they ought to be supported by the people.

4 And he also testified unto the people that [a]all mankind should be saved at the last day, and that they [b]need not fear nor tremble, but that they might lift up their heads and rejoice; for the Lord had [c]created all men, and had also [d]redeemed [e]all men; and, in the end, all men should have eternal life.

5 And it came to pass that he did teach these things so much that many did believe on his words, even so many that they began to support him and give him [a]money.

6 And he began to be lifted up in the pride of his heart, and to wear very costly [a]apparel, yea, and even began to [b]establish a [c]church after the manner of his preaching.

7 And it came to pass as he was going, to preach to those who believed on his word, he met a man who belonged to the church of God, yea, even one of their [a]teachers; and he began to contend with him sharply, that he might lead away the people of the church; but the man withstood him, admonishing him with the [b]words of God.

8 Now the name of the man was [a]Gideon; and it was he who was an instrument in the hands of God in delivering the people of Limhi out of bondage.

9 Now, because Gideon withstood him with the words of God he was wroth with Gideon, and drew his sword and began to smite him. Now Gideon being [a]stricken with many years, therefore he was not able to withstand his blows, therefore he was [b]slain by the sword.

10 And the man who slew him was taken by the people of the church, and was brought before Alma, to be [a]judged according to the crimes which he had committed.

11 And it came to pass that he stood before Alma and pled for himself with much boldness.

12 But Alma said unto him: Behold, this is the first time that [a]priestcraft has been introduced among this people. And behold, thou art not only guilty of priestcraft, but hast endeavored to enforce it by the sword; and were

---

1 1*a* Mosiah 29:46.
b Jarom 1:5; Alma 4:16; 8:17; Hel. 4:22.
c TG Citizenship.
2*a* Alma 1:15.
3*a* Ezek. 13:3 (1–4).
b TG Antichrist.
c Luke 6:26; 1 Ne. 22:23.
d Mosiah 18:24 (24, 26); 27:5 (3–5).
4*a* Alma 15:15; 21:6; 30:17; Morm. 8:31.
b TG Humility; Meek.
c TG Jesus Christ, Creator; Man, Physical Creation of.
d TG Jesus Christ, Redeemer; Redemption.
e Moses 4:1 (1–4).
5*a* Acts 8:18 (17–23).
6*a* TG Apparel.
b TG Unrighteous Dominion.
c TG Devil, Church of.
7*a* TG Teacher.
b TG Word of God; Word of the Lord.
8*a* Mosiah 20:17; 22:3; Alma 2:1.
9*a* Gen. 24:1; 1 Ne. 18:17.
b Alma 6:7.
10*a* Mosiah 29:42.
12*a* 2 Ne. 26:29; Alma 2:20; 14:16. TG Priestcraft.

[b]priestcraft to be enforced among
this people it would prove their
entire destruction.
13 And thou hast shed the [a]blood
of a righteous man, yea, a man who
has done much good among this
people; and were we to spare thee
his blood would come upon us for
[b]vengeance.
14 Therefore thou art condemned
to [a]die, according to the [b]law which
has been given us by Mosiah, our
last king; and it has been [c]acknowl-
edged by this people; therefore this
people must [d]abide by the law.
15 And it came to pass that they
took him; and his name was [a]Nehor;
and they carried him upon the top
of the hill Manti, and there he was
caused, or rather did acknowledge,
between the heavens and the earth,
that what he had taught to the people was contrary to the word of God;
and there he suffered an ignomini-
ous [b]death.
16 Nevertheless, this did not put an
end to the spreading of priestcraft
through the land; for there were
many who loved the vain things
of the world, and they went forth
preaching [a]false doctrines; and
this they did for the sake of [b]riches
and honor.
17 Nevertheless, they durst not
[a]lie, if it were known, for fear of
the law, for liars were punished;
therefore they pretended to preach
according to their belief; and now
the law could have no power on
any man for [b]his belief.
18 And they durst not [a]steal, for
fear of the law, for such were punished; neither durst they rob, nor
murder, for he that [b]murdered was
punished unto [c]death.
19 But it came to pass that whosoever did not belong to the church
of God began to persecute those
that did belong to the church of
God, and had taken upon them the
name of Christ.
20 Yea, they did persecute them,
and afflict them with all manner
of words, and this because of their
humility; because they were not
proud in their own eyes, and because they did impart the word
of God, one with another, without
[a]money and without price.
21 Now there was a strict law
among the people of the church, that
there should [a]not any man, belong-
ing to the church, arise and persecute those that did not belong to the
church, and that there should be
no persecution among themselves.
22 Nevertheless, there were many
among them who began to be proud,
and began to contend warmly with
their adversaries, even unto blows;
yea, they would smite one another
with their [a]fists.
23 Now this was in the second year
of the reign of Alma, and it was a
cause of much affliction to the
church; yea, it was the cause of much
trial with the church.
24 For the hearts of many were
hardened, and their names were
[a]blotted out, that they were remembered no more among the people
of God. And also many [b]withdrew
themselves from among them.
25 Now this was a great trial to
those that did stand fast in the faith;
nevertheless, they were [a]steadfast

12*b* Alma 21:4.
13*a* Prov. 28:17.
TG Blood, Shedding of.
b Luke 18:7;
D&C 121:5.
TG Vengeance.
14*a* TG Capital Punishment.
b Mosiah 29:39.
c Hel. 1:8.
d TG Citizenship.
15*a* Alma 1:2; 2:1 (1, 20).
b Deut. 13:5 (1–9).
16*a* TG False Doctrine.
b TG Riches;
Vanity.
17*a* TG Honesty;
Lying.
b Alma 30:7 (7–12);
A of F 1:11.
18*a* Alma 30:10.
TG Stealing.
b TG Murder.
c TG Capital Punishment.
20*a* Isa. 55:1 (1–2).
21*a* Alma 4:8.
TG Persecution.
22*a* Ex. 21:18 (18–19);
Isa. 58:4.
24*a* Ex. 32:33;
Mosiah 26:32, 36;
Alma 6:3.
TG Excommunication.
b Alma 46:7.
TG Apostasy of
Individuals.
25*a* TG Commitment;
Steadfastness.

and immovable in keeping the
commandments of God, and they
bore with [b]patience the persecution
which was heaped upon them.
26 And when the priests left their
[a]labor to impart the word of God
unto the people, the people also left
their labors to hear the word of God.
And when the priest had imparted
unto them the word of God they
all returned again diligently unto
their labors; and the priest, not es-
teeming himself above his hearers,
for the preacher was no better than
the hearer, neither was the teacher
any better than the learner; and
thus they were all equal, and they
did all labor, every man [b]according
to his strength.
27 And they did [a]impart of their
substance, every man according
to that which he had, to the [b]poor,
and the needy, and the sick, and
the afflicted; and they did not wear
costly [c]apparel, yet they were neat
and comely.
28 And thus they did establish
the affairs of the church; and thus
they began to have continual peace
again, notwithstanding all their
persecutions.
29 And now, because of the steadiness of the church they began to
be exceedingly [a]rich, having abundance of all things whatsoever
they stood in need—an abundance
of flocks and herds, and fatlings of
every kind, and also abundance of
grain, and of gold, and of silver, and
of precious things, and abundance
of [b]silk and fine-twined linen, and
all manner of good homely [c]cloth.
30 And thus, in their [a]prosperous
circumstances, they did not send
away any who were [b]naked, or that
were hungry, or that were athirst,
or that were sick, or that had not
been nourished; and they did not
set their hearts upon [c]riches; therefore they were [d]liberal to all, both
old and young, both bond and free,
both male and female, whether
out of the church or in the church,
having no [e]respect to persons as to
those who stood in need.
31 And thus they did [a]prosper and
become far more wealthy than those
who did not belong to their church.
32 For those who did not belong
to their church did indulge themselves in [a]sorceries, and in [b]idolatry
or [c]idleness, and in [d]babblings, and
in [e]envyings and [f]strife; wearing
costly apparel; being [g]lifted up in
the pride of their own eyes; per-
secuting, lying, thieving, robbing,
committing whoredoms, and murdering, and all manner of wickedness; nevertheless, the law was put in
force upon all those who did transgress it, inasmuch as it was possible.
33 And it came to pass that by
thus exercising the law upon them,
every man suffering according to
that which he had done, they became
more still, and durst not commit
any wickedness if it were known;
therefore, there was much peace
among the people of Nephi until the
fifth year of the reign of the judges.

CHAPTER 2

Amlici seeks to be king and is rejected by the voice of the people—His followers make him king—The Amlicites

25*b* TG Patience.
26*a* Mosiah 18:24 (24, 26); 27:5 (3–5).
b Mosiah 4:27; D&C 10:4.
27*a* TG Almsgiving; Consecration.
b Luke 18:22; Acts 20:35 (33–35); Mosiah 4:26; D&C 42:30 (29–31).
c TG Vanity.
29*a* TG Riches; Treasure.
b Alma 4:6.
c Mosiah 10:5; Hel. 6:13. TG Clothing.
30*a* 2 Cor. 8:14; Jacob 2:19 (17–19).
b TG Poor.
c Job 31:25. TG Wealth.
d TG Generosity.
e Deut. 10:17; Alma 16:14; D&C 1:35.
31*a* TG Prosper.
32*a* TG Sorcery.
b TG Idolatry.
c TG Laziness.
d TG Gossip.
e TG Envy.
f TG Strife.
g 2 Kgs. 14:10; Jacob 2:13; Alma 31:25; Morm. 8:28. TG Pride.

make war on the Nephites and are defeated—The Lamanites and Amlicites join forces and are defeated—Alma slays Amlici. About 87 B.C.

AND it came to pass in the commencement of the fifth year of their
reign there began to be a contention
among the people; for a certain
[a]man, being called Amlici, he being
a very cunning man, yea, a wise
man as to the wisdom of the world,
he being after the order of the man
that slew [b]Gideon by the sword, who
was executed according to the law—
2 Now this Amlici had, by his cunning, [a]drawn away much people
after him; even so much that they
began to be very powerful; and they
began to endeavor to establish Amlici to be a king over the people.
3 Now this was alarming to the
people of the church, and also to all
those who had not been drawn away
after the persuasions of Amlici;
for they knew that according to their
law that such things must be established by the [a]voice of the people.
4 Therefore, if it were possible
that Amlici should gain the voice
of the people, he, being a wicked
man, would [a]deprive them of their
rights and privileges of the church;
for it was his intent to destroy the
church of God.
5 And it came to pass that the people assembled themselves together
throughout all the land, every man
according to his mind, whether it
were for or against Amlici, in separate bodies, having much dispute
and wonderful [a]contentions one
with another.
6 And thus they did assemble
themselves together to cast in their
[a]voices concerning the matter; and
they were laid before the judges.
7 And it came to pass that the
[a]voice of the people came against
Amlici, that he was not made king
over the people.
8 Now this did cause much joy
in the hearts of those who were
against him; but Amlici did stir up
those who were in his favor to anger
against those who were not in his
favor.
9 And it came to pass that they
gathered themselves together, and
did [a]consecrate Amlici to be their
king.
10 Now when Amlici was made
king over them he commanded
them that they should take up arms
against their brethren; and this
he did that he might subject them
to him.
11 Now the people of Amlici were
distinguished by the name of Amlici, being called [a]Amlicites; and the
remainder were [b]called Nephites,
or the people of God.
12 Therefore the people of the
Nephites were aware of the intent
of the Amlicites, and therefore they
did prepare to meet them; yea,
they did arm themselves with swords,
and with cimeters, and with bows, and
with arrows, and with stones, and
with slings, and with all manner
of [a]weapons of war, of every kind.
13 And thus they were prepared
to meet the Amlicites at the time
of their coming. And there were
appointed [a]captains, and higher
captains, and chief captains, according to their numbers.
14 And it came to pass that Amlici
did arm his men with all manner of
weapons of war of every kind; and
he also appointed rulers and leaders over his people, to lead them to
war against their brethren.
15 And it came to pass that the

2 1*a* Alma 1:15; 16:11; 24:28 (28–30).
b Alma 1:8.
2*a* 2 Sam. 15:6 (1–10).
3*a* Mosiah 29:25 (25–27); Alma 4:16 (16–17).
4*a* Mosiah 29:27; Alma 10:19; Hel. 5:2.
5*a* 3 Ne. 11:29.
6*a* TG Common Consent.
7*a* Mosiah 29:25 (25–27).
9*a* TG Unrighteous Dominion.
11*a* Alma 3:4.
b Jacob 1:14 (13–14); Mosiah 25:12; Alma 3:11 (11, 17).
12*a* Mosiah 10:8; Hel. 1:14.
13*a* Alma 16:5.

Amlicites came upon the hill Am-
nihu, which was east of the [a]river
Sidon, which ran by the [b]land of
Zarahemla, and there they began
to make war with the Nephites.
16 Now Alma, being the [a]chief
judge and the [b]governor of the people of Nephi, therefore he went up
with his people, yea, with his captains, and chief captains, yea, at
the head of his armies, against the
Amlicites to battle.
17 And they began to slay the Amlicites upon the hill east of Sidon.
And the Amlicites did contend with
the Nephites with great strength,
insomuch that many of the Nephites did fall before the Amlicites.
18 Nevertheless the Lord did
strengthen the hand of the Nephites,
that they slew the Amlicites with
great slaughter, that they began to
flee before them.
19 And it came to pass that the
Nephites did pursue the Amlicites
all that day, and did slay them with
much slaughter, insomuch that there
were [a]slain of the Amlicites twelve
thousand five hundred thirty and
two souls; and there were slain of
the Nephites six thousand five hundred sixty and two souls.
20 And it came to pass that when
Alma could pursue the Amlicites
no longer he caused that his people should pitch their tents in the
[a]valley of Gideon, the valley being
called after that Gideon who was
slain by the hand of [b]Nehor with
the sword; and in this valley the
Nephites did pitch their tents for
the night.
21 And Alma sent spies to follow
the remnant of the Amlicites, that
he might know of their plans and
their plots, whereby he might guard
himself against them, that he might
preserve his people from being
destroyed.
22 Now those whom he had sent
out to watch the camp of the Amlicites were called Zeram, and Amnor,
and Manti, and Limher; these were
they who went out with their men
to watch the camp of the Amlicites.
23 And it came to pass that on the
morrow they returned into the camp
of the Nephites in great haste, being greatly astonished, and struck
with much fear, saying:
24 Behold, we followed the [a]camp
of the [b]Amlicites, and to our great
astonishment, in the land of Mi-
non, above the land of Zarahemla,
in the course of the land of [c]Nephi,
we saw a numerous host of the Lamanites; and behold, the Amlicites
have joined them;
25 And they are upon our brethren
in that land; and they are fleeing
before them with their flocks, and
their wives, and their children, towards our city; and except we make
haste they obtain possession of our
city, and our fathers, and our wives,
and our children be slain.
26 And it came to pass that the
people of Nephi took their tents,
and departed out of the valley of
Gideon towards their [a]city, which
was the city of [b]Zarahemla.
27 And behold, as they were crossing the river Sidon, the Lamanites
and the Amlicites, being as [a]nu-
merous almost, as it were, as the
sands of the sea, came upon them
to destroy them.
28 Nevertheless, the Nephites being [a]strengthened by the hand of
the Lord, having prayed mightily
to him that he would deliver them
out of the hands of their enemies,
therefore the Lord did hear their
cries, and did strengthen them, and
the Lamanites and the Amlicites
did fall before them.
29 And it came to pass that Alma
fought with Amlici with the sword,

15*a* Alma 3:3.
b Omni 1:13; Mosiah 1:1.
16*a* Mosiah 29:42.
b Mosiah 1:10.
19*a* Alma 3:1 (1–2, 26); 4:2.
20*a* Alma 6:7; 8:1.
b Alma 1:12 (7–15); 14:16.
24*a* Alma 3:20.
b Alma 3:4 (4, 13–18).
c 2 Ne. 5:8; Alma 20:1.
26*a* Alma 6:4.
b Omni 1:14 (14, 18).
27*a* Jarom 1:6.
28*a* Deut. 31:6.

face to face; and they did contend mightily, one with another.

30 And it came to pass that Alma, being a man of God, being exercised with much [a]faith, cried, saying: O Lord, have mercy and [b]spare my life, that I may be an instrument in thy hands to save and preserve this people.

31 Now when Alma had said these words he contended again with Amlici; and he was strengthened, insomuch that he slew Amlici with the sword.

32 And he also contended with the king of the Lamanites; but the king of the Lamanites fled back from before Alma and sent his guards to contend with Alma.

33 But Alma, with his guards, contended with the guards of the king of the Lamanites until he slew and drove them back.

34 And thus he cleared the ground, or rather the bank, which was on the west of the river Sidon, throwing the bodies of the Lamanites who had been slain into the waters of Sidon, that thereby his people might have room to cross and contend with the Lamanites and the Amlicites on the west side of the river Sidon.

35 And it came to pass that when they had all crossed the river Sidon that the Lamanites and the Amlicites began to flee before them, notwithstanding they were so numerous that they could not be numbered.

36 And they fled before the Nephites towards the wilderness which was west and north, away beyond the borders of the land; and the Nephites did pursue them with their might, and did slay them.

37 Yea, they were met on every hand, and slain and driven, until they were scattered on the west, and on the north, until they had reached the wilderness, which was called Hermounts; and it was that part of the wilderness which was infested by wild and ravenous beasts.

38 And it came to pass that many died in the wilderness of their wounds, and were devoured by those beasts and also the vultures of the air; and their bones have been found, and have been heaped up on the earth.

CHAPTER 3

The Amlicites had marked themselves according to the prophetic word—The Lamanites had been cursed for their rebellion—Men bring their own curses upon themselves—The Nephites defeat another Lamanite army. About 87–86 B.C.

AND it came to pass that the Nephites who were not [a]slain by the weapons of war, after having buried those who had been slain—now the number of the slain were not numbered, because of the greatness of their number—after they had finished burying their dead they all returned to their lands, and to their houses, and their wives, and their children.

2 Now many women and children had been slain with the sword, and also many of their flocks and their herds; and also many of their fields of grain were destroyed, for they were trodden down by the hosts of men.

3 And now as many of the Lamanites and the Amlicites who had been slain upon the bank of the river Sidon were cast into the [a]waters of Sidon; and behold their bones are in the depths of the [b]sea, and they are many.

4 And the [a]Amlicites were distinguished from the Nephites, for they had [b]marked themselves with red in their foreheads after the manner of the Lamanites; nevertheless they had not shorn their heads like unto the Lamanites.

5 Now the heads of the Lamanites were shorn; and they were [a]naked,

---

30*a* TG Faith.
b Alma 3:22.
3 1*a* Alma 2:19; 4:2.
3*a* Alma 2:15; 4:4.
b Alma 44:22.
4*a* Alma 2:11, 24.
b Alma 3:13 (13–19).
5*a* Enos 1:20; Mosiah 10:8; Alma 43:20 (18–21).

save it were skin which was girded
about their loins, and also their
armor, which was girded about
them, and their bows, and their
arrows, and their stones, and their
slings, and so forth.
6 And the skins of the Lamanites
were dark, according to the mark
which was set upon their fathers,
which was a [a]curse upon them because of their transgression and
their rebellion against their brethren, who consisted of Nephi, Jacob,
and Joseph, and Sam, who were just
and holy men.
7 And their brethren sought to
destroy them, therefore they were
cursed; and the Lord God set a
[a]mark upon them, yea, upon Laman
and Lemuel, and also the sons of
Ishmael, and Ishmaelitish women.
8 And this was done that their seed
might be distinguished from the
seed of their brethren, that thereby
the Lord God might preserve his
people, that they might not [a]mix
and believe in incorrect [b]traditions
which would prove their destruction.
9 And it came to pass that whosoever did mingle his seed with that
of the Lamanites did bring the same
curse upon his seed.
10 Therefore, whosoever suffered
himself to be led away by the Lamanites was called under that
head, and there was a mark set
upon him.
11 And it came to pass that whosoever would not believe in the [a]tradi-
tion of the Lamanites, but believed
those records which were brought
out of the land of Jerusalem, and
also in the tradition of their fathers,
which were correct, who believed
in the commandments of God and
kept them, were [b]called the Nephites, or the people of Nephi, from
that time forth—
12 And it is they who have kept
the records which are [a]true of their
people, and also of the people of
the Lamanites.
13 Now we will return again to
the Amlicites, for they also had a
[a]mark set upon them; yea, they set
the mark upon themselves, yea,
even a mark of red upon their
foreheads.
14 Thus the word of God is fulfilled, for these are the words which
he said to Nephi: Behold, the Lamanites have I cursed, and I will
set a mark on them that they and
their seed may be [a]separated from
thee and thy seed, from this time
henceforth and forever, except they
repent of their wickedness and
[b]turn to me that I may have mercy
upon them.
15 And again: I will set a mark
upon him that mingleth his seed
with thy brethren, that they may
be cursed also.
16 And again: I will set a mark
upon him that fighteth against thee
and thy seed.
17 And again, I say he that de-
parteth from thee shall no more
be called thy seed; and I will bless
thee, and whomsoever shall be
called thy seed, henceforth and
forever; and these were the promises of the Lord unto Nephi and to
his seed.
18 Now the Amlicites knew not
that they were fulfilling the words
of God when they began to mark
themselves in their foreheads; nevertheless they had come out in open
[a]rebellion against God; therefore it
was expedient that the curse should
fall upon them.
19 Now I would that ye should
see that they brought upon themselves the [a]curse; and even so doth
every man that is cursed bring

6a 2 Ne. 5:21; 26:33. TG Curse.
7a 1 Ne. 12:23.
8a TG Marriage, Interfaith; Separation.
b Mosiah 10:12 (11–18); Alma 9:16.
11a Alma 17:9 (9–11).
b Alma 2:11.
12a Mosiah 1:6; Ether 4:11 (6–11).
13a Alma 3:4.
14a TG Separation.
b 2 Ne. 30:6 (4–7).
18a Josh. 22:18; 4 Ne. 1:38. TG Rebellion.
19a 2 Ne. 5:21 (21–25); Alma 17:15.

upon himself his own condemnation.
20 Now it came to pass that not
many days after the battle which
was fought in the land of Zarahemla, by the Lamanites and the
Amlicites, that there was another
army of the Lamanites came in
upon the people of Nephi, in the
[a]same place where the first army
met the Amlicites.
21 And it came to pass that there
was an army sent to drive them out
of their land.
22 Now Alma himself being afflicted with a [a]wound did not go
up to battle at this time against the
Lamanites;
23 But he sent up a numerous army
against them; and they went up and
slew many of the Lamanites, and
drove the remainder of them out of
the borders of their land.
24 And then they returned again
and began to establish peace in the
land, being troubled no more for a
time with their enemies.
25 Now all these things were done,
yea, all these wars and contentions
were commenced and ended in
the fifth year of the reign of the
judges.
26 And in one year were thousands and tens of thousands of souls
sent to the eternal world, that they
might reap their [a]rewards according
to their works, whether they were
good or whether they were bad, to
reap eternal happiness or eternal
misery, according to the spirit which
they listed to obey, whether it be a
good spirit or a bad one.
27 For every man receiveth [a]wages
of him whom he listeth to [b]obey, and
this according to the words of the
spirit of prophecy; therefore let it
be according to the truth. And thus
endeth the fifth year of the reign
of the judges.

CHAPTER 4

Alma baptizes thousands of converts—Iniquity enters the Church, and the Church's progress is hindered—Nephihah is appointed chief judge—Alma, as high priest, devotes himself to the ministry. About 86–83 B.C.

Now it came to pass in the sixth
year of the reign of the judges over
the people of Nephi, there were no
contentions nor wars in the [a]land
of Zarahemla;
2 But the people were afflicted,
yea, greatly afflicted for the loss of
their brethren, and also for the [a]loss
of their flocks and herds, and also
for the loss of their fields of grain,
which were trodden under foot and
destroyed by the Lamanites.
3 And so great were their afflictions that every soul had cause to
mourn; and they believed that it
was the judgments of God sent upon
them because of their wickedness
and their abominations; therefore
they were [a]awakened to a remembrance of their duty.
4 And they began to establish the
[a]church more fully; yea, and many
were [b]baptized in the [c]waters of Sidon and were joined to the church
of God; yea, they were baptized by
the hand of Alma, who had been
consecrated the [d]high priest over
the people of the church, by the
hand of his father Alma.
5 And it came to pass in the seventh
year of the reign of the judges there
were about three thousand five hundred souls that united themselves to
the [a]church of God and were baptized.
And thus ended the seventh year of
the reign of the judges over the people

20*a* Alma 2:24.
22*a* Alma 2:30 (29–33).
26*a* Ps. 7:16.
TG Agency;
Reward.
27*a* Mosiah 2:32 (32–33);
Alma 5:42 (41–42).
TG Wages.
b Rom. 6:16 (14–18);
Hel. 14:31 (29–31).
4 1*a* Omni 1:12 (12–19).
2*a* Alma 2:19;
3:1 (1–2, 26).
3*a* 1 Cor. 15:34 (33–34).
4*a* TG Church Organization.
b Mosiah 18:10 (10–17).
c Alma 3:3; 6:7.
d Mosiah 29:42.
TG High Priest,
Melchizedek Priesthood.
5*a* Mosiah 25:22 (18–23);
3 Ne. 26:21.

of Nephi; and there was continual
peace in all that time.
6 And it came to pass in the eighth
year of the reign of the judges,
that the people of the church began to wax proud, because of their
exceeding [a]riches, and their [b]fine
silks, and their fine-twined linen,
and because of their many flocks
and herds, and their gold and their
silver, and all manner of precious
things, which they had obtained
by their [c]industry; and in all these
things were they lifted up in the
pride of their eyes, for they began
to wear very costly [d]apparel.
7 Now this was the cause of much
affliction to Alma, yea, and to many
of the people whom Alma had consecrated to be [a]teachers, and [b]priests,
and [c]elders over the church; yea,
many of them were sorely grieved
for the wickedness which they saw
had begun to be among their people.
8 For they saw and beheld with
great sorrow that the people of the
church began to be lifted up in the
pride of their eyes, and to set their
[a]hearts upon riches and upon the
vain things of the world, that they
began to be scornful, one towards
another, and they began to persecute
those that did [b]not believe according to their own will and pleasure.
9 And thus, in this eighth year of
the reign of the judges, there began
to be great [a]contentions among the
people of the church; yea, there were
[b]envyings, and [c]strife, and malice,
and persecutions, and pride, even
to exceed the pride of those who
did not belong to the church of God.
10 And thus ended the eighth
year of the reign of the judges; and
the wickedness of the church was
a great [a]stumbling-block to those
who did not belong to the church;
and thus the church began to fail
in its progress.
11 And it came to pass in the commencement of the ninth year, Alma
saw the wickedness of the church,
and he saw also that the [a]example
of the church began to lead those
who were unbelievers on from one
piece of iniquity to another, thus
bringing on the destruction of the
people.
12 Yea, he saw great inequality
among the people, some lifting
themselves up with their pride, de-
spising others, turning their backs
upon the [a]needy and the naked and
those who were [b]hungry, and those
who were athirst, and those who
were sick and afflicted.
13 Now this was a great cause for
lamentations among the people,
while others were abasing themselves, succoring those who stood in
need of their succor, such as imparting their substance to the [a]poor and
the needy, feeding the hungry, and
suffering all manner of [b]afflictions,
for Christ's [c]sake, who should come
according to the spirit of prophecy;
14 Looking forward to that day,
thus [a]retaining a [b]remission of
their sins; being filled with great
[c]joy because of the resurrection of
the dead, according to the will and
power and [d]deliverance of Jesus
Christ from the bands of death.
15 And now it came to pass that
Alma, having seen the afflictions of
the humble followers of God, and

6*a* TG Riches.
b Alma 1:29.
c TG Industry.
d TG Apparel.
7*a* Mosiah 6:3.
TG Teacher.
b TG Church Organization.
c Alma 4:16.
TG Elder.
8*a* TG Pride;
Vanity;
Worldliness.
b Alma 1:21.
9*a* TG Contention.
b TG Envy.
c Alma 16:18.
TG Strife.
10*a* TG Stumblingblock.
11*a* 2 Sam. 12:14;
Alma 39:11.
TG Example.
12*a* Isa. 3:14;
Ezek. 22:12 (6–13);
Amos 3:10;
Jacob 2:17.
b Mosiah 4:26.
13*a* TG Almsgiving.
b TG Affliction.
c 2 Cor. 12:10.
14*a* Mosiah 4:12;
Alma 5:26 (26–35);
D&C 20:32 (31–34).
b TG Justification.
c TG Joy.
d TG Deliver.

the persecutions which were heaped upon them by the remainder of his people, and seeing all their [a]inequality, began to be very sorrowful; nevertheless the Spirit of the Lord did not fail him.
16 And he selected a wise man who was among the [a]elders of the church, and gave him power according to the [b]voice of the people, that he might have power to enact [c]laws according to the laws which had been given, and to put them in force according to the wickedness and the crimes of the people.
17 Now this man's name was [a]Nephihah, and he was appointed [b]chief judge; and he sat in the judgment-seat to judge and to govern the people.
18 Now Alma did not grant unto him the office of being [a]high priest over the church, but he retained the office of high priest unto himself; but he delivered the judgment-seat unto [b]Nephihah.
19 And this he did that he [a]himself might go forth among his people, or among the people of Nephi, that he might [b]preach the [c]word of God unto them, to [d]stir them up in [e]remembrance of their duty, and that he might pull down, by the word of God, all the pride and craftiness and all the contentions which were among his people, seeing no way that he might reclaim them save it were in bearing down in pure [f]testimony against them.
20 And thus in the commencement of the ninth year of the reign of the judges over the people of Nephi, Alma delivered up the judgment-seat to [a]Nephihah, and confined himself wholly to the [b]high priesthood of the holy order of God, to the [c]testimony of the word, according to the spirit of revelation and prophecy.

The words which Alma, the High Priest according to the holy order of God, delivered to the people in their cities and villages throughout the land.

Beginning with chapter 5.

CHAPTER 5

To gain salvation, men must repent and keep the commandments, be born again, cleanse their garments through the blood of Christ, be humble and strip themselves of pride and envy, and do the works of righteousness—The Good Shepherd calls His people—Those who do evil works are children of the devil—Alma testifies of the truth of his doctrine and commands men to repent—The names of the righteous will be written in the book of life. About 83 B.C.

Now it came to pass that Alma began to [a]deliver the word of [b]God unto the people, first in the land of Zarahemla, and from thence throughout all the land.
2 And these are the words which he spake to the people in the church which was established in the city of Zarahemla, according to his own record, saying:
3 I, Alma, having been [a]consecrated by my father, Alma, to be a [b]high priest over the church of God, he having power and [c]authority from God to do these things, behold, I say unto you that he began to

---

15*a* 2 Cor. 8:14; D&C 49:20.
16*a* Alma 4:7.
b Alma 2:3 (3–7); 50:39.
c Alma 1:1 (1, 14, 18).
17*a* Alma 27:20.
b Alma 30:29; 50:37.
18*a* TG High Priest, Melchizedek Priesthood.
b Alma 7:2.
19*a* Alma 7:1.
b Alma 5:1.
c Alma 31:5; D&C 11:2.
d Enos 1:23.
e 2 Chr. 35:6; Alma 16:16; D&C 108:7.
f TG Testimony.
20*a* Alma 8:12.
b Mosiah 29:42; Alma 5:3 (3, 44, 49).
c TG Preaching.
5 1*a* Alma 4:19.
b Alma 5:61.
3*a* TG Priesthood, Authority.
b Alma 4:20 (4, 18, 20); 8:23 (11, 23).
c Mosiah 18:13; 3 Ne. 11:25.

establish a church in the [d]land which was in the borders of Nephi; yea, the land which was called the land of Mormon; yea, and he did baptize his brethren in the waters of Mormon.

4 And behold, I say unto you, they were [a]delivered out of the hands of the people of king Noah, by the mercy and power of God.

5 And behold, after that, they were brought into [a]bondage by the hands of the Lamanites in the wilderness; yea, I say unto you, they were in captivity, and again the Lord did deliver them out of [b]bondage by the power of his word; and we were brought into this land, and here we began to establish the church of God throughout this land also.

6 And now behold, I say unto you, my brethren, you that belong to this church, have you sufficiently retained in [a]remembrance the captivity of your fathers? Yea, and have you sufficiently retained in remembrance his mercy and long-suffering towards them? And moreover, have ye sufficiently retained in remembrance that he has [b]delivered their souls from hell?

7 Behold, he changed their hearts; yea, he awakened them out of a deep sleep, and they awoke unto God. Behold, they were in the midst of darkness; nevertheless, their souls were illuminated by the light of the everlasting word; yea, they were encircled about by the [a]bands of death, and the [b]chains of hell, and an everlasting destruction did await them.

8 And now I ask of you, my brethren, were they destroyed? Behold, I say unto you, Nay, they were not.

9 And again I ask, were the bands of death broken, and the [a]chains of hell which encircled them about, were they loosed? I say unto you, Yea, they were loosed, and their souls did expand, and they did [b]sing redeeming love. And I say unto you that they are saved.

10 And now I ask of you on what conditions are they [a]saved? Yea, what grounds had they to hope for salvation? What is the cause of their being loosed from the bands of death, yea, and also the chains of hell?

11 Behold, I can tell you—did not my father Alma believe in the words which were delivered by the [a]mouth of Abinadi? And was he not a holy prophet? Did he not speak the words of God, and my father Alma believe them?

12 And according to his faith there was a mighty [a]change wrought in his heart. Behold I say unto you that this is all true.

13 And behold, he [a]preached the word unto your fathers, and a mighty change was also wrought in their hearts, and they humbled themselves and put their [b]trust in the true and [c]living God. And behold, they were faithful until the [d]end; therefore they were saved.

14 And now behold, I ask of you, my brethren of the church, have ye [a]spiritually been [b]born of God? Have ye received his image in your countenances? Have ye experienced this mighty [c]change in your hearts?

15 Do ye exercise faith in the

3*d* Mosiah 18:4; 3 Ne. 5:12.
4*a* Mosiah 23:1 (1–3).
5*a* Mosiah 23:37 (37–39); 24:9 (8–15).
b Mosiah 24:17; 25:10; 27:16.
6*a* 2 Pet. 3:1 (1–2).
b TG Deliver.
7*a* Mosiah 15:8. TG Bondage, Spiritual; Man, Natural, Not Spiritually Reborn.
b Alma 12:11 (9–11); D&C 138:23. TG Hell.
9*a* Alma 12:6.
b Ps. 147:1 (1–7).
10*a* TG Save.
11*a* Mosiah 17:2 (2–4).
12*a* TG Conversion.
13*a* Mosiah 18:7 (1–31).
b TG Trust in God.
c 1 Sam. 17:26; Ps. 42:2; Morm. 9:28; D&C 20:19.
d 2 Ne. 31:15.
14*a* TG Spirituality.
b Mosiah 27:25 (24–27); Alma 22:15.
c Rom. 7:22; 8:11 (11–17); Col. 3:10 (9–10); Mosiah 5:2; Moses 6:65. TG Sanctification.

redemption of him who [a]created
you? Do you look forward with an
eye of faith, and view this mortal
body raised in immortality, and
this corruption [b]raised in incorruption, to stand before God to
be [c]judged according to the deeds
which have been done in the mortal
body?
16 I say unto you, can you imagine
to yourselves that ye hear the voice
of the Lord, saying unto you, in that
day: Come unto me ye [a]blessed, for
behold, your works have been the
works of righteousness upon the
face of the earth?
17 Or do ye [a]imagine to yourselves
that ye can lie unto the Lord in
that day, and [b]say—Lord, our works
have been righteous works upon
the face of the earth—and that he
will save you?
18 Or otherwise, can ye imagine
yourselves brought before the tri-
bunal of God with your souls filled
with guilt and remorse, having a
remembrance of all your guilt, yea,
a perfect [a]remembrance of all your
wickedness, yea, a remembrance
that ye have set at defiance the
commandments of God?
19 I say unto you, can ye look up
to God at that day with a pure heart
and clean hands? I say unto you,
can you look up, having the [a]image
of God engraven upon your countenances?
20 I say unto you, can ye think of
being saved when you have yielded
yourselves to become [a]subjects to
the devil?
21 I say unto you, ye will know at
that day that ye cannot be [a]saved;
for there can no man be saved
except his [b]garments are washed
white; yea, his garments must be
[c]purified until they are cleansed
from all stain, through the blood
of him of whom it has been spoken by our fathers, who should
come to redeem his people from
their sins.
22 And now I ask of you, my brethren, how will any of you feel, if ye
shall stand before the bar of God,
having your garments stained with
[a]blood and all manner of [b]filthiness?
Behold, what will these things testify against you?
23 Behold will they not [a]testify
that ye are murderers, yea, and also
that ye are [b]guilty of all manner of
wickedness?
24 Behold, my brethren, do ye
suppose that such an one can have
a place to sit down in the kingdom of God, with [a]Abraham, with
Isaac, and with Jacob, and also all
the holy prophets, whose garments
are cleansed and are spotless, pure
and white?
25 I say unto you, Nay; except ye
make our Creator a liar from the
beginning, or suppose that he is a
liar from the beginning, ye cannot
suppose that such can have place
in the kingdom of heaven; but
they shall be cast out for they are
the [a]children of the kingdom of
the devil.
26 And now behold, I say unto you,
my brethren, if ye have experienced
a [a]change of heart, and if ye have
felt to sing the [b]song of redeeming love, I would ask, [c]can ye feel
so now?

15*a* TG Jesus Christ, Creator.
b TG Immortality; Redemption; Resurrection.
c TG Jesus Christ, Judge; Judgment, the Last.
16*a* Matt. 25:34 (31–46).
17*a* Alma 7:3.
b 3 Ne. 14:22 (21–23).
18*a* Ezek. 20:43; 2 Ne. 9:14; Mosiah 2:40; 3:25; Alma 11:43.
19*a* 1 Jn. 3:2 (1–3).
20*a* Mosiah 2:32.
21*a* TG Salvation, Plan of.
b 1 Ne. 12:10; Alma 13:11 (11–13); 3 Ne. 27:19 (19–20).
c D&C 138:59. TG Purification.
22*a* Isa. 59:3.
b TG Filthiness.
23*a* Isa. 59:12.
b TG Guilt.
24*a* Luke 13:28.
25*a* Deut. 32:5; 2 Ne. 9:9.
26*a* TG Change; Conversion; Man, New, Spiritually Reborn.
b Alma 26:13.
c Mosiah 4:12; Alma 4:14 (13–14); D&C 20:32 (31–34).

27 Have ye walked, keeping yourselves [a]blameless before God? Could ye say, if ye were called to die at this time, within yourselves, that ye have been sufficiently [b]humble? That your garments have been [c]cleansed and made white through the blood of Christ, who will come to [d]redeem his people from their sins?

28 Behold, are ye stripped of [a]pride? I say unto you, if ye are not ye are not prepared to meet God. Behold ye must prepare quickly; for the kingdom of heaven is soon at hand, and such an one hath not eternal life.

29 Behold, I say, is there one among you who is not stripped of [a]envy? I say unto you that such an one is not prepared; and I would that he should prepare [b]quickly, for the hour is close at hand, and he knoweth not when the time shall come; for such an one is not found guiltless.

30 And again I say unto you, is there one among you that doth make a [a]mock of his brother, or that heapeth upon him persecutions?

31 Wo unto such an one, for he is not prepared, and the [a]time is at hand that he must repent or he cannot be saved!

32 Yea, even wo unto all ye [a]workers of iniquity; repent, repent, for the Lord God hath spoken it!

33 Behold, he sendeth an invitation unto [a]all men, for the [b]arms of mercy are extended towards them, and he saith: Repent, and I will receive you.

34 Yea, he saith: [a]Come unto me and ye shall partake of the [b]fruit of the tree of life; yea, ye shall eat and drink of the [c]bread and the waters of life [d]freely;

35 Yea, come unto me and bring forth works of righteousness, and ye shall not be hewn down and cast into the fire—

36 For behold, the time is at hand that whosoever [a]bringeth forth not good fruit, or whosoever doeth not the works of righteousness, the same have cause to wail and mourn.

37 O ye workers of iniquity; ye that are [a]puffed up in the vain things of the world, ye that have professed to have known the ways of righteousness nevertheless have gone [b]astray, as [c]sheep having no [d]shepherd, notwithstanding a shepherd hath [e]called after you and is still calling after you, but ye will not [f]hearken unto his voice!

38 Behold, I say unto you, that the good [a]shepherd doth call you; yea, and in his own name he doth call you, which is the name of Christ; and if ye will not [b]hearken unto the voice of the [c]good shepherd, to the [d]name by which ye are called, behold, ye are not the sheep of the good shepherd.

39 And now if ye are not the [a]sheep of the good shepherd, of what fold are ye? Behold, I say unto you, that the [b]devil is your shepherd, and ye are of his fold; and now,

---

27*a* 1 Jn. 3:21 (19 24). TG Justification.
b TG Humility.
c Rev. 19:8.
d 1 Cor. 15:3. TG Jesus Christ, Mission of.
28*a* TG Pride.
29*a* TG Envy.
b TG Procrastination.
30*a* TG Backbiting; Mocking.
31*a* TG Procrastination.
32*a* Ps. 5:5 (4–6).
33*a* Alma 19:36; 3 Ne. 18:25.
b Isa. 59:16; 2 Ne. 1:15; Jacob 6:5; 3 Ne. 9:14.
34*a* 1 Ne. 1:14; 2 Ne. 26:25 (24–28); 3 Ne. 9:14 (13–14).
b 1 Ne. 8:11; 15:36.
c TG Bread of Life.
d 2 Ne. 9:50 (50–51); Alma 42:27.
36*a* Matt. 3:10; 7:19 (15–20); Jacob 5:26 (26–60); 3 Ne. 14:19; D&C 97:7.
37*a* TG Worldliness.
b 2 Ne. 12:5; 28:14; Mosiah 14:6.
c Matt. 9:36.
d TG Shepherd.
e Prov. 1:24 (24–27); Isa. 65:12; 1 Ne. 17:13; 2 Ne. 7:2.
f 2 Chr. 33:10; Jer. 26:4; Alma 10:6 (5–6).
38*a* TG Jesus Christ, Good Shepherd.
b Lev. 26:14 (14–20); D&C 101:7.
c 3 Ne. 15:24; 18:31.
d Mosiah 5:8; Alma 34:38.
39*a* Matt. 6:24; Luke 16:13.
b Mosiah 5:10. TG Devil, Church of.

who can deny this? Behold, I say
unto you, whosoever denieth this
is a [c]liar and a [d]child of the devil.
40 For I say unto you that whatsoever is [a]good cometh from God,
and whatsoever is [b]evil cometh
from the devil.
41 Therefore, if a man bringeth
forth [a]good works he hearkeneth
unto the voice of the good shepherd,
and he doth follow him; but whosoever bringeth forth evil works,
the same becometh a [b]child of the
devil, for he hearkeneth unto his
voice, and doth follow him.
42 And whosoever doeth this must
receive his [a]wages of him; therefore, for his [b]wages he receiveth
[c]death, as to things pertaining unto
righteousness, being dead unto all
good works.
43 And now, my brethren, I would
that ye should hear me, for I speak
in the [a]energy of my soul; for behold,
I have spoken unto you plainly that
ye cannot err, or have spoken according to the commandments of God.
44 For I am called to speak after
this manner, according to the [a]holy
order of God, which is in Christ
Jesus; yea, I am commanded to
stand and testify unto this people
the things which have been spoken by our fathers concerning the
things which are to come.
45 And this is not all. Do ye not
suppose that I [a]know of these things
myself? Behold, I testify unto you
that I do know that these things
whereof I have spoken are true. And
how do ye suppose that I know of
their surety?
46 Behold, I say unto you they
are made [a]known unto me by the
Holy Spirit of God. Behold, I have
[b]fasted and prayed many days that
I might know these things of myself. And now I do know of myself
that they are true; for the Lord God
hath made them manifest unto me
by his Holy Spirit; and this is the
spirit of [c]revelation which is in me.
47 And moreover, I say unto you
that it has thus been revealed unto
me, that the words which have been
spoken by our fathers are true, even
so according to the spirit of prophecy which is in me, which is also
by the manifestation of the Spirit
of God.
48 I say unto you, that I know of
myself that whatsoever I shall say
unto you, concerning that which
is to come, is true; and I say unto
you, that I know that Jesus Christ
shall come, yea, the Son, the Only
Begotten of the Father, full of grace,
and mercy, and truth. And behold,
it is he that cometh to take away
the sins of the world, yea, the sins
of every man who steadfastly believeth on his name.
49 And now I say unto you that
this is the [a]order after which I am
called, yea, to preach unto my beloved brethren, yea, and every one
that dwelleth in the land; yea, to
preach unto all, both old and young,
both bond and free; yea, I say unto
you the aged, and also the middle
aged, and the rising generation; yea,
to cry unto them that they must
repent and be [b]born again.
50 Yea, thus saith the Spirit: Repent,
all ye ends of the earth, for the
kingdom of heaven is soon at hand;
yea, the Son of God cometh in his
[a]glory, in his might, majesty, power,

39*c* 1 Jn. 2:22.
d 2 Ne. 9:9.
40*a* Ezra 3:11; Ps. 85:12; Omni 1:25; Ether 4:12; Moro. 7:16 (15–17).
b Isa. 45:7; Amos 3:6; Moro. 7:12.
41*a* 3 Ne. 14:17 (16–20). TG Good Works.
b Mosiah 16:3 (3–5); Alma 11:23.
42*a* Alma 3:27 (26–27); D&C 29:45.
b Rom. 6:23.
c Hel. 14:18 (16–18).
43*a* Alma 7:5.
44*a* Mosiah 29:42.
45*a* Alma 36:4.
46*a* 1 Cor. 2:10 (9–16).
b Alma 10:7.
c Rev. 19:10.
49*a* TG Called of God; Priesthood.
b TG Man, New, Spiritually Reborn.
50*a* Ps. 24:8; 72:19. TG Jesus Christ, Glory of.

and dominion. Yea, my beloved
brethren, I say unto you, that the
Spirit saith: Behold the glory of
the [b]King of all the earth; and
also the King of heaven shall very
soon shine forth among all the children of men.
51 And also the Spirit saith unto
me, yea, crieth unto me with a
mighty voice, saying: Go forth and
say unto this people—Repent, for
except ye repent ye can in nowise
inherit the [a]kingdom of [b]heaven.
52 And again I say unto you,
the Spirit saith: Behold, the [a]ax is
laid at the root of the tree; therefore every tree that bringeth not
forth good fruit shall be [b]hewn
down and cast into the fire, yea,
a fire which cannot be consumed,
even an unquenchable fire. Behold,
and remember, the Holy One hath
spoken it.
53 And now my beloved brethren,
I say unto you, can ye withstand
these sayings; yea, can ye lay aside
these things, and [a]trample the Holy
One under your feet; yea, can ye be
[b]puffed up in the pride of your hearts;
yea, will ye still persist in the wearing of [c]costly apparel and setting
your hearts upon the vain things
of the world, upon your [d]riches?
54 Yea, will ye persist in supposing
that ye are better one than another;
yea, will ye persist in the persecution of your brethren, who humble
themselves and do walk after the
holy order of God, wherewith they
have been brought into this church,
having been [a]sanctified by the Holy
Spirit, and they do bring forth works
which are meet for repentance—
55 Yea, and will you persist in
turning your backs upon the [a]poor,
and the needy, and in withholding
your substance from them?
56 And finally, all ye that will persist in your wickedness, I say unto
you that these are they who shall
be hewn down and cast into the
fire except they speedily repent.
57 And now I say unto you, all
you that are desirous to follow the
voice of the [a]good shepherd, come
ye out from the wicked, and be
ye [b]separate, and touch not their
unclean things; and behold, their
names shall be [c]blotted out, that
the names of the wicked shall not
be numbered among the names
of the righteous, that the word of
God may be fulfilled, which saith:
The names of the wicked shall
not be mingled with the names of
my people;
58 For the names of the righteous
shall be written in the [a]book of life,
and unto them will I grant an inheritance at my right hand. And now,
my brethren, what have ye to say
against this? I say unto you, if ye
speak against it, it matters not, for
the word of God must be fulfilled.
59 For what shepherd is there
among you having many sheep
doth not watch over them, that the
wolves enter not and devour his
flock? And behold, if a wolf enter
his [a]flock doth he not drive him
out? Yea, and at the last, if he can,
he will destroy him.
60 And now I say unto you that
the good shepherd doth call after
you; and if you will hearken unto
his voice he will bring you into his

50*b* Ps. 74:12; 149:2; Matt. 2:2; Luke 23:2; 2 Ne. 10:14; D&C 38:21 (21–22); 128:22 (22–23); Moses 7:53. TG Jesus Christ, King; Kingdom of God, on Earth.
51*a* TG Kingdom of God, in Heaven.
b TG Heaven.
52*a* Luke 3:9; D&C 97:7.
b Jacob 5:46; 6:7; 3 Ne. 27:11 (11–12).
53*a* TG Sacrilege.
b 1 Cor. 5:2.
c 2 Ne. 28:13 (11–14); Morm. 8:36 (36–39).
d Ps. 62:10; D&C 56:16 (16–18).
54*a* TG Sanctification.
55*a* Ps. 109:16 (15–16); Jacob 2:17; Hel. 6:39 (39–40); D&C 56:16.
57*a* TG Jesus Christ, Good Shepherd.
b Ezra 6:21; 9:1; Neh. 9:2; 2 Thes. 3:6; D&C 133:5 (5, 14).
c Deut. 29:20; Ps. 109:13.
58*a* TG Book of Life.
59*a* Prov. 27:23.

fold, and ye are his sheep; and he commandeth you that ye suffer no ravenous wolf to enter among you, that ye may not be destroyed.

61 And now I, Alma, do command you in the language of [a]him who hath commanded me, that ye observe to do the words which I have spoken unto you.

62 I speak by way of command unto you that belong to the church; and unto those who do not belong to the church I speak by way of invitation, saying: Come and be baptized unto repentance, that ye also may be partakers of the fruit of the [a]tree of life.

CHAPTER 6

The Church in Zarahemla is cleansed and set in order—Alma goes to Gideon to preach. About 83 B.C.

AND now it came to pass that after Alma had made an end of speaking unto the people of the church, which was established in the city of Zarahemla, he [a]ordained [b]priests and elders, by laying on his [c]hands according to the order of God, to preside and [d]watch over the church.

2 And it came to pass that whosoever did not belong to the church who [a]repented of their sins were baptized unto repentance, and were received into the church.

3 And it also came to pass that whosoever did belong to the church that did not [a]repent of their wickedness and humble themselves before God—I mean those who were lifted up in the [b]pride of their hearts—the same were rejected, and their names were [c]blotted out, that their names were not numbered among those of the righteous.

4 And thus they began to establish the order of the church in the [a]city of Zarahemla.

5 Now I would that ye should understand that the word of God was liberal unto all, that none were deprived of the privilege of assembling themselves together to hear the word of God.

6 Nevertheless the children of God were commanded that they should gather themselves together oft, and join in [a]fasting and mighty prayer in behalf of the welfare of the souls of those who knew not God.

7 And now it came to pass that when Alma had made these regulations he departed from them, yea, from the church which was in the city of Zarahemla, and went over upon the east of the [a]river Sidon, into the [b]valley of Gideon, there having been a city built, which was called the city of Gideon, which was in the valley that was called Gideon, being called after the man who was [c]slain by the hand of Nehor with the sword.

8 And Alma went and began to declare the word of God unto the church which was established in the valley of Gideon, according to the revelation of the truth of the word which had been spoken by his fathers, and according to the spirit of prophecy which was in him, according to the [a]testimony of Jesus Christ, the Son of God, who should come to redeem his people from their sins, and the holy order by which he was called. And thus it is written. Amen.

The words of Alma which he delivered to the people in Gideon, according to his own record.

Comprising chapter 7.

61*a* Alma 5:1 (1, 44).
62*a* 1 Ne. 8:10; 11:21 (21–23).
6 1*a* TG Ordain; Priesthood.
b TG Elder; Priest, Melchizedek Priesthood.
c TG Hands, Laying on of.
d D&C 52:39.
2*a* TG Baptism, Qualifications for.
3*a* Mosiah 26:6.
b 1 Cor. 5:2.
c Ex. 32:33; Mosiah 26:36; Alma 1:24; 5:57 (57–58). TG Excommunication.
4*a* Alma 2:26.
6*a* TG Fast, Fasting.
7*a* Alma 4:4; 8:3.
b Alma 2:20.
c Alma 1:9.
8*a* Rev. 19:10.

CHAPTER 7

Christ will be born of Mary—He will loose the bands of death and bear the sins of His people—Those who repent, are baptized, and keep the commandments will have eternal life—Filthiness cannot inherit the kingdom of God—Humility, faith, hope, and charity are required. About 83 B.C.

BEHOLD my beloved brethren, seeing that I have been permitted to
come unto you, therefore I attempt
to address you in my language; yea,
by my [a]own mouth, seeing that it
is the first time that I have spoken unto you by the words of my
mouth, I having been wholly confined to the [b]judgment-seat, having
had much business that I could not
come unto you.
2 And even I could not have come
now at this time were it not that
the judgment-seat hath been [a]given
to another, to reign in my stead;
and the Lord in much mercy hath
granted that I should come unto you.
3 And behold, I have come having
great hopes and much desire that
I should find that ye had humbled
yourselves before God, and that ye
had continued in the supplicating
of his grace, that I should find that
ye were blameless before him, that I
should find that ye were not in the
awful [a]dilemma that our brethren
were in at Zarahemla.
4 But blessed be the name of God,
that he hath given me to know, yea,
hath given unto me the exceedingly
great joy of knowing that they are
established again in the way of his
righteousness.
5 And I trust, according to the
Spirit of God which is in me, that I
shall also have joy over you; nevertheless I do not desire that my joy
over you should come by the cause
of so much afflictions and sorrow
which I have had for the brethren
at Zarahemla, for behold, my joy
cometh over them after wading
through much affliction and sorrow.
6 But behold, I trust that ye are
not in a state of so much unbelief
as were your brethren; I trust that
ye are not lifted up in the pride
of your hearts; yea, I trust that ye
have not set your hearts upon riches
and the vain things of the world;
yea, I trust that you do not worship
[a]idols, but that ye do worship the
true and the [b]living God, and that
ye look forward for the remission
of your sins, with an everlasting
faith, which is to come.
7 For behold, I say unto you there
be many things to come; and behold, there is one thing which is
of more importance than they all—
for behold, the [a]time is not far distant that the Redeemer liveth and
cometh among his people.
8 Behold, I do not say that he will
come among us at the [a]time of his
dwelling in his mortal tabernacle;
for behold, the Spirit hath not said
unto me that this should be the
case. Now as to this thing I do not
know; but this much I do know,
that the Lord God hath power to do
all things which are according to
his word.
9 But behold, the Spirit hath said
this much unto me, saying: Cry unto
this people, saying—[a]Repent ye,
and prepare the way of the Lord,
and walk in his paths, which are
straight; for behold, the kingdom
of heaven is at hand, and the Son
of God [b]cometh upon the face of
the earth.
10 And behold, he shall be [a]born
of Mary, at [b]Jerusalem which is the
[c]land of our forefathers, she being
a [d]virgin, a precious and chosen

7 1*a* Alma 4:19.
b Mosiah 29:42.
2*a* Alma 4:18 (16–18).
3*a* Alma 5:17 (16–17).
6*a* 2 Ne. 9:37; Hel. 6:31.
b Dan. 6:26.
7*a* Alma 9:26.
8*a* 1 Ne. 12:6 (4–8); Alma 16:20.
9*a* Matt. 3:2 (2–3); Alma 9:25 (25–26).
b Mosiah 3:5; 7:27; 15:2 (1–7).
10*a* Isa. 7:14; Luke 1:27; Mosiah 3:8.
b Luke 2:4.
c 1 Chr. 9:3; 2 Chr. 15:9; 1 Ne. 1:4; 3 Ne. 20:29.
d 1 Ne. 11:13 (13–21).

vessel, who shall be overshadowed
and [e]conceive by the power of the
Holy Ghost, and bring forth a son,
yea, even the Son of God.
11 And he shall go forth, suffering
pains and [a]afflictions and [b]tempta-
tions of every kind; and this that the
word might be fulfilled which saith
he will [c]take upon him the pains
and the sicknesses of his people.
12 And he will take upon him
[a]death, that he may [b]loose the bands
of death which bind his people;
and he will take upon him their
infirmities, that his bowels may be
filled with mercy, according to the
flesh, that he may know according
to the flesh how to [c]succor his people according to their infirmities.
13 Now the Spirit [a]knoweth all
things; nevertheless the Son of God
suffereth according to the [b]flesh that
he might [c]take upon him the sins of
his people, that he might blot out
their transgressions according to
the power of his deliverance; and
now behold, this is the testimony
which is in me.
14 Now I say unto you that ye
must [a]repent, and be born again;
for the Spirit saith if ye are not
born again ye cannot inherit the
kingdom of heaven; therefore come
and be baptized unto repentance,
that ye may be washed from your
sins, that ye may have faith on the
Lamb of God, who taketh away the
sins of the world, who is mighty
to save and to cleanse from all un-
righteousness.
15 Yea, I say unto you come and
fear not, and lay aside every sin,
which easily doth [a]beset you, which
doth bind you down to destruction,
yea, come and go forth, and show
unto your God that ye are willing
to repent of your sins and enter
into a covenant with him to keep
his commandments, and witness
it unto him this day by going into
the waters of baptism.
16 And whosoever doeth this,
and keepeth the commandments
of God from thenceforth, the same
will [a]remember that I say unto him,
yea, he will remember that I have
said unto him, he shall have eternal life, according to the testimony
of the Holy Spirit, which testifieth
in me.
17 And now my beloved brethren,
do you believe these things? Behold, I say unto you, yea, I know
that ye believe them; and the way
that I know that ye believe them is
by the manifestation of the Spirit
which is in me. And now because
your faith is strong concerning that,
yea, concerning the things which I
have spoken, great is my joy.
18 For as I said unto you from the
beginning, that I had much desire
that ye were not in the state of [a]di-
lemma like your brethren, even so
I have found that my desires have
been gratified.
19 For I perceive that ye are in
the paths of righteousness; I perceive that ye are in the path which
leads to the kingdom of God; yea,
I perceive that ye are making his
[a]paths straight.
20 I perceive that it has been made
known unto you, by the testimony
of his word, that he cannot [a]walk
in crooked paths; neither doth he
vary from that which he hath said;
neither hath he a shadow of turning
from the right to the left, or from
that which is right to that which is
wrong; therefore, his course is one
eternal round.

10*e* Matt. 1:20;
Mosiah 15:3.
11*a* Isa. 53:5 (3–5).
b TG Jesus Christ, Temptation of.
c Mosiah 14:4 (3–5).
12*a* TG Jesus Christ, Death of.
b Ps. 116:16 (15–16);
2 Ne. 2:8;
Alma 12:25 (24–25);
42:23.
c Heb. 2:18; 4:15;
D&C 62:1.
13*a* TG God, Omniscience of.
b TG Jesus Christ, Condescension of.
c Mosiah 15:12.
14*a* TG Purification.
15*a* 2 Ne. 4:18.
16*a* Ether 12:4;
Moro. 7:3.
18*a* James 1:8.
19*a* Matt. 3:3.
20*a* 1 Ne. 10:19;
Alma 37:12;
D&C 3:2.

21 And he doth not dwell in [a]unholy temples; neither can filthiness or anything which is unclean be received into the kingdom of God; therefore I say unto you the time shall come, yea, and it shall be at the last day, that he who is [b]filthy shall remain in his filthiness.

22 And now my beloved brethren, I have said these things unto you that I might awaken you to a sense of your duty to God, that ye may walk blameless before him, that ye may walk after the holy order of God, after which ye have been received.

23 And now I would that ye should be [a]humble, and be [b]submissive and gentle; easy to be entreated; full of patience and long-suffering; being temperate in all things; being diligent in keeping the commandments of God at all times; asking for whatsoever things ye stand in need, both spiritual and temporal; always returning thanks unto God for whatsoever things ye do receive.

24 And see that ye have [a]faith, hope, and charity, and then ye will always abound in good works.

25 And may the Lord bless you, and keep your garments spotless, that ye may at last be brought to sit down with [a]Abraham, Isaac, and Jacob, and the holy prophets who have been ever since the world began, having your garments [b]spotless even as their garments are spotless, in the kingdom of heaven to go no more out.

26 And now my beloved brethren, I have spoken these words unto you according to the Spirit which testifieth in me; and my soul doth exceedingly rejoice, because of the exceeding diligence and heed which ye have given unto my word.

27 And now, may the [a]peace of God rest upon you, and upon your houses and lands, and upon your flocks and herds, and all that you possess, your women and your children, according to your faith and good works, from this time forth and forever. And thus I have spoken. Amen.

CHAPTER 8

Alma preaches and baptizes in Melek—He is rejected in Ammonihah and leaves—An angel commands him to return and cry repentance unto the people—He is received by Amulek, and the two of them preach in Ammonihah. About 82 B.C.

AND now it came to pass that Alma returned from the [a]land of Gideon, after having taught the people of Gideon many things which cannot be written, having established the [b]order of the church, according as he had before done in the land of Zarahemla, yea, he returned to his own house at Zarahemla to rest himself from the labors which he had performed.

2 And thus ended the ninth year of the reign of the judges over the people of Nephi.

3 And it came to pass in the commencement of the tenth year of the reign of the judges over the people of Nephi, that Alma departed from thence and took his journey over into the land of [a]Melek, on the west of the [b]river Sidon, on the west by the borders of the wilderness.

4 And he began to teach the people in the land of Melek according to the [a]holy order of God, by which he had been called; and he began to teach the people throughout all the land of Melek.

5 And it came to pass that the people came to him throughout all

21*a* 1 Cor. 3:17 (16–17); 6:19; Mosiah 2:37; Alma 34:36.
b 1 Ne. 15:33 (33–35); 2 Ne. 9:16; Morm. 9:14; D&C 88:35.
23*a* Prov. 18:12.
b TG Submissiveness.
24*a* 1 Cor. 13:13 (1–13); Ether 12:31 (30–35); Moro. 7:44 (33–48).
25*a* D&C 27:10.
b 2 Pet. 3:14.
27*a* TG Peace of God.
8 1*a* Alma 2:20; 6:7.
b TG Church Organization.
3*a* Alma 31:6.
b Alma 6:7; 16:6 (6–7).
4*a* D&C 107:3 (2–4). TG Priesthood.

the borders of the land which was by
the wilderness side. And they were
baptized throughout all the land;
6 So that when he had finished his
work at Melek he departed thence,
and traveled three days' journey on
the north of the land of Melek; and
he came to a city which was called
[a]Ammonihah.
7 Now it was the custom of the
people of Nephi to call their lands,
and their cities, and their villages,
yea, even all their small villages, after the [a]name of him who first possessed them; and thus it was with
the land of Ammonihah.
8 And it came to pass that when
Alma had come to the city of Ammonihah he began to preach the
word of God unto them.
9 Now Satan had gotten great [a]hold
upon the hearts of the people of the
city of Ammonihah; therefore they
would not hearken unto the words
of Alma.
10 Nevertheless Alma [a]labored
much in the spirit, [b]wrestling with
God in [c]mighty prayer, that he
would pour out his Spirit upon the
people who were in the city; that
he would also grant that he might
baptize them unto repentance.
11 Nevertheless, they hardened
their hearts, saying unto him: Behold,
we know that thou art Alma; and we
know that thou art high priest over
the church which thou hast established in many parts of the land,
according to your tradition; and we
are not of thy church, and we do not
believe in such foolish traditions.
12 And now we know that because
we are not of thy church we know
that thou hast no power over us; and
thou hast delivered up the judgment-
seat unto [a]Nephihah; therefore thou
art not the chief judge over us.
13 Now when the people had said
this, and withstood all his words,
and [a]reviled him, and spit upon
him, and caused that he should be
[b]cast out of their city, he departed
thence and took his journey towards
the city which was called Aaron.
14 And it came to pass that while
he was journeying thither, being
weighed down with sorrow, wading
through much [a]tribulation and anguish of soul, because of the wickedness of the people who were in the
city of Ammonihah, it came to pass
while Alma was thus weighed down
with sorrow, behold an [b]angel of the
Lord appeared unto him, saying:
15 Blessed art thou, Alma; therefore, lift up thy head and rejoice, for
thou hast great cause to rejoice;
for thou hast been faithful in keeping the commandments of God from
the time which thou receivedst thy
first message from him. Behold, I
am he that [a]delivered it unto you.
16 And behold, I am sent to [a]com-
mand thee that thou return to the
city of Ammonihah, and preach
again unto the people of the city;
yea, preach unto them. Yea, say unto
them, except they repent the Lord
God will [b]destroy them.
17 For behold, they do study at
this time that they may destroy
the liberty of thy people, (for thus
saith the Lord) which is contrary to
the [a]statutes, and judgments, and
commandments which he has given
unto his people.
18 Now it came to pass that after
Alma had received his message from
the angel of the Lord he returned
speedily to the land of Ammonihah.
And he entered the city by another
way, yea, by the way which is on
the south of the city of Ammonihah.
19 And as [a]he entered the city he

6*a* Alma 9:1.
7*a* Ether 2:13.
9*a* 2 Ne. 28:20 (19–22); D&C 10:20.
10*a* Alma 17:5.
b Enos 1:2 (1–12).
c 3 Ne. 27:1; D&C 5:24; 29:2.
12*a* Alma 4:20.
13*a* 1 Cor. 4:12.
b Alma 8:24.
14*a* TG Tribulation.
b Mosiah 3:2 (2–3); Alma 10:20 (7–10, 20).
15*a* Mosiah 27:11 (11–16).
16*a* Gal. 2:2; Hel. 13:3.
b Alma 9:12 (4, 12, 18, 24).
17*a* Alma 1:1 (1, 14). TG Commandments of God.
19*a* Alma 10:8.

was an hungered, and he said to
a man: Will ye give to an humble
servant of God something to eat?
20 And the man said unto him: I
am a Nephite, and I know that thou
art a holy prophet of God, for thou
art the man whom an [a]angel said in
a vision: Thou shalt receive. Therefore, go with me into my house
and I will impart unto thee of my
[b]food; and I know that thou wilt be
a blessing unto me and my house.
21 And it came to pass that the
man received him into his house;
and the man was called Amulek;
and he brought forth bread and
meat and set before Alma.
22 And it came to pass that Alma
ate bread and was filled; and he
[a]blessed Amulek and his house, and
he gave thanks unto God.
23 And after he had eaten and
was filled he said unto Amulek: I
am Alma, and am the [a]high priest
over the church of God throughout
the land.
24 And behold, I have been called
to preach the word of God among all
this people, according to the spirit
of revelation and prophecy; and I
was in this land and they would
not receive me, but they [a]cast me
out and I was about to set my back
towards this land forever.
25 But behold, I have been commanded that I should turn again and
prophesy unto this people, yea, and
to testify against them concerning
their iniquities.
26 And now, Amulek, because thou
hast fed me and taken me in, thou
art blessed; for I was an hungered,
for I had fasted many days.
27 And Alma [a]tarried many days
with Amulek before he began to
preach unto the people.
28 And it came to pass that the
people did wax more gross in their
iniquities.
29 And the word came to Alma,
saying: Go; and also say unto my servant [a]Amulek, go forth and prophesy
unto this people, saying—Repent
ye, for thus saith the Lord, except
ye repent I will visit this people in
mine anger; yea, and I will not turn
my [b]fierce anger away.
30 And Alma went forth, and also
Amulek, among the people, to declare the words of God unto them;
and they were filled with the Holy
Ghost.
31 And they had [a]power given unto
them, insomuch that they could
not be confined in dungeons; neither was it possible that any man
could slay them; nevertheless they
did not exercise their [b]power until they were bound in bands and
cast into prison. Now, this was done
that the Lord might show forth his
power in them.
32 And it came to pass that they
went forth and began to preach
and to prophesy unto the people,
according to the spirit and power
which the Lord had given them.

The words of Alma, and also the words of Amulek, which were declared unto the people who were in the land of Ammonihah. And also they are cast into prison, and delivered by the miraculous power of God which was in them, according to the record of Alma.

Comprising chapters 9 through 14.

CHAPTER 9

Alma commands the people of Ammonihah to repent—The Lord will be merciful to the Lamanites in the last days—If the Nephites forsake the light, they will be destroyed by the Lamanites—The Son of God will come soon—He will redeem those who repent, are baptized, and have faith in His name. About 82 B.C.

20*a* Alma 10:7 (7–9).
b 1 Kgs. 17:11 (8–13).
22*a* Alma 10:11.
23*a* Alma 5:3 (3, 44, 49); 13:1 (1–20).
24*a* Alma 8:13.
27*a* Alma 10:10.
29*a* Alma 10:1.
b Alma 9:12, 18.
31*a* Alma 14:10.
b Alma 14:25 (17–29).

AND again, I, Alma, having been
commanded of God that I should
take Amulek and go forth and
preach again unto this people, or
the people who were in the city of
[a]Ammonihah, it came to pass as I
began to preach unto them, they
began to contend with me, saying:
2 Who art thou? Suppose ye that we
shall believe the testimony of [a]one
man, although he should preach
unto us that the earth should pass
away?
3 Now they understood not the
words which they spake; for they
knew not that the earth should
pass away.
4 And they said also: We will not
believe thy words if thou shouldst
prophesy that this great city should
be destroyed in [a]one day.
5 Now they knew not that God
could do such marvelous [a]works,
for they were a hard-hearted and
a stiffnecked people.
6 And they said: [a]Who is God, that
sendeth [b]no more authority than one
man among this people, to declare
unto them the truth of such great
and marvelous things?
7 And they stood forth to lay their
hands on me; but behold, they did
not. And I stood with boldness to
declare unto them, yea, I did boldly
testify unto them, saying:
8 Behold, O ye wicked and perverse
[a]generation, how have ye forgotten
the [b]tradition of your fathers; yea,
how soon ye have forgotten the
commandments of God.
9 Do ye not remember that our
father, Lehi, was brought out of Jerusalem by the [a]hand of God? Do
ye not remember that they were all
led by him through the wilderness?
10 And have ye forgotten so soon
how many times he [a]delivered our
fathers out of the hands of their
enemies, and preserved them from
being destroyed, even by the hands
of their own brethren?
11 Yea, and if it had not been for
his matchless power, and his mercy,
and his [a]long-suffering towards us,
we should unavoidably have been
cut off from the face of the earth
long before this period of time, and
perhaps been consigned to a state
of [b]endless misery and woe.
12 Behold, now I say unto you that
he commandeth you to repent; and
except ye repent, ye can in nowise
inherit the kingdom of God. But
behold, this is not all—he has commanded you to repent, or he will
utterly [a]destroy you from off the
face of the earth; yea, he will visit
you in his [b]anger, and in his [c]fierce
anger he will not turn away.
13 Behold, do ye not remember the
words which he spake unto Lehi, saying that: [a]Inasmuch as ye shall keep
my commandments, ye shall prosper in the land? And again it is said
that: Inasmuch as ye will not keep
my commandments ye shall be cut
off from the presence of the Lord.
14 Now I would that ye should
remember, that inasmuch as the
Lamanites have not kept the commandments of God, they have been
[a]cut off from the presence of the
Lord. Now we see that the word of
the Lord has been verified in this
thing, and the Lamanites have been
cut off from his presence, from the
beginning of their transgressions
in the land.
15 Nevertheless I say unto you,
that it shall be more [a]tolerable for
them in the day of judgment than
for you, if ye remain in your sins,

9 1*a* Alma 8:6.
2*a* Deut. 17:6.
4*a* Alma 16:10 (9–10).
5*a* TG God, Works of.
6*a* Ex. 5:2; Mosiah 11:27; Moses 5:16.
b Alma 10:12.
8*a* Matt. 3:7; Alma 10:17 (17–25).
b TG Birthright.
9*a* 1 Ne. 2:2 (1–7).
10*a* TG Deliver.
11*a* TG Long-Suffering.
b Mosiah 16:11.
12*a* Alma 8:16; 10:27 (19, 23, 27).
b Jer. 18:10 (6–10).
c Alma 8:29.
13*a* 2 Ne. 1:20; Mosiah 1:7; Alma 37:13.
14*a* 2 Ne. 5:20 (20–24); Alma 38:1.
15*a* Matt. 11:22 (22, 24).

yea, and even more tolerable for
them in this life than for you, except ye repent.
16 For there are many promises
which are [a]extended to the Lamanites; for it is because of the [b]tradi-
tions of their fathers that caused
them to remain in their state of
[c]ignorance; therefore the Lord will
be merciful unto them and [d]prolong
their existence in the land.
17 And at some period of time
they will be [a]brought to believe in
his word, and to know of the incor-
rectness of the traditions of their
fathers; and many of them will be
saved, for the Lord will be merciful unto all who [b]call on his name.
18 But behold, I say unto you that
if ye persist in your wickedness that
your days shall not be [a]prolonged
in the land, for the [b]Lamanites shall
be sent upon you; and if ye repent
not they shall come in a time when
you know not, and ye shall be visited with [c]utter destruction; and
it shall be according to the fierce
[d]anger of the Lord.
19 For he will not suffer you that
ye shall live in your iniquities,
to [a]destroy his people. I say unto
you, Nay; he would rather suffer
that the Lamanites might destroy
all his people who are called the
people of Nephi, if it were possible
that they could [b]fall into sins and
transgressions, after having had
so much light and so much knowledge given unto them of the Lord
their God;
20 Yea, after having been such a
highly favored people of the Lord;
yea, after having been favored
above every other [a]nation, kindred,
tongue, or people; after having had
all things [b]made known unto them,
according to their desires, and their
faith, and prayers, of that which has
been, and which is, and which is
to come;
21 Having been [a]visited by the
Spirit of God; having conversed
with angels, and having been spoken unto by the voice of the Lord;
and having the spirit of prophecy,
and the spirit of revelation, and also
many gifts, the gift of speaking with
tongues, and the gift of preaching,
and the gift of the Holy Ghost, and
the gift of [b]translation;
22 Yea, and after having been
[a]delivered of God out of the land
of Jerusalem, by the hand of the
Lord; having been [b]saved from
famine, and from sickness, and all
manner of diseases of every kind;
and they having waxed strong in
battle, that they might not be destroyed; having been brought out of
[c]bondage time after time, and having been kept and preserved until
now; and they have been prospered
until they are rich in all manner of
things—
23 And now behold I say unto you,
that if this people, who have received so many blessings from the
hand of the Lord, should transgress
[a]contrary to the light and knowledge which they do have, I say unto
you that if this be the case, that if
they should fall into transgression,
it would be far more [b]tolerable for
the Lamanites than for them.
24 For behold, the [a]promises of the
Lord are extended to the Lamanites,
but they are not unto you if ye transgress; for has not the Lord expressly

16*a* Alma 17:15.
b Alma 3:8; 17:15.
c 2 Ne. 9:26 (25–26); Mosiah 3:11; Alma 42:21.
d Deut. 11:9 (8–9); 32:47; Hel. 15:11 (10–11); D&C 5:33.
17*a* Enos 1:13.
b Ps. 81:7; Alma 38:5; D&C 3:8.
18*a* Deut. 6:2.
b Alma 16:3.
c Alma 16:9.
d Alma 8:29.
19*a* 1 Ne. 12:19 (15, 19–20); Alma 45:11 (10–14).
b Alma 24:30.
20*a* 2 Sam. 7:23; Abr. 2:9.
b TG Prophets, Mission of.
21*a* Ex. 3:16; 2 Ne. 4:26; Morm. 1:15.
b Omni 1:20; Mosiah 8:13 (13–19); 28:17 (11–17).
22*a* 2 Ne. 1:4.
b TG Protection, Divine.
c Mosiah 27:16.
23*a* TG Disobedience.
b Matt. 11:22 (22–24).
24*a* 2 Ne. 30:6 (4–7); D&C 3:20.

promised and firmly decreed, that
if ye will rebel against him that ye
shall [b]utterly be destroyed from off
the face of the earth?
25 And now for this cause, that ye
may not be destroyed, the Lord has
sent his angel to visit many of his
people, declaring unto them that
they must go forth and cry mightily
unto this people, saying: [a]Repent
ye, for the kingdom of heaven is
nigh at hand;
26 And [a]not many days hence the
Son of God shall come in his [b]glory;
and his glory shall be the glory of
the Only Begotten of the Father,
full of [c]grace, equity, and truth,
full of patience, [d]mercy, and long-
suffering, quick to [e]hear the cries
of his people and to answer their
prayers.
27 And behold, he cometh to [a]re-
deem those who will be [b]baptized
unto repentance, through faith on
his name.
28 Therefore, prepare ye the way
of the Lord, for the time is at hand
that all men shall reap a [a]reward
of their [b]works, according to that
which they have been—if they have
been righteous they shall [c]reap the
salvation of their souls, according to
the power and deliverance of Jesus
Christ; and if they have been evil
they shall reap the [d]damnation of
their souls, according to the power
and captivation of the devil.
29 Now behold, this is the voice of
the angel, crying unto the people.
30 And now, my [a]beloved brethren, for ye are my brethren, and ye
ought to be beloved, and ye ought
to bring forth works which are meet
for repentance, seeing that your
hearts have been grossly hardened
against the word of God, and seeing that ye are a [b]lost and a fallen
people.
31 Now it came to pass that when
I, Alma, had spoken these words,
behold, the people were wroth
with me because I said unto them
that they were a hard-hearted and
a [a]stiffnecked people.
32 And also because I said unto
them that they were a lost and a
fallen people they were angry with
me, and sought to lay their hands
upon me, that they might cast me
into prison.
33 But it came to pass that the
Lord did not suffer them that they
should take me [a]at that time and
cast me into prison.
34 And it came to pass that Amulek went and stood forth, and began to preach unto them also. And
now the [a]words of Amulek are not
all written, nevertheless a part of
his words are written in this book.

CHAPTER 10

Lehi descended from Manasseh—Amulek recounts the angelic command that he care for Alma—The prayers of the righteous cause the people to be spared—Unrighteous lawyers and judges lay the foundation of the destruction of the people. About 82 B.C.

NOW these are the [a]words which
[b]Amulek preached unto the people
who were in the land of Ammonihah, saying:
2 I am Amulek; I am the son of Giddonah, who was the son of Ishmael,
who was a descendant of Aminadi;
and it was that same Aminadi who
interpreted the [a]writing which
was upon the wall of the temple,
which was written by the finger
of God.

24*b* Alma 16:9 (2–9); Morm. 6:15 (15–22).
25*a* Matt. 3:2 (2–3); Alma 7:9; Hel. 5:32.
26*a* Alma 7:7.
b TG Jesus Christ, Glory of.
c TG Grace.
d TG God, Mercy of.
e Deut. 26:7; Isa. 65:24.
27*a* TG Redemption.
b TG Baptism, Essential.
28*a* TG Reward.
b Job 34:11; D&C 1:10; 6:33.
c Ps. 7:16.
d TG Damnation.
30*a* 1 Jn. 4:11.
b Alma 12:22.
31*a* 2 Ne. 25:28; Mosiah 3:14.
33*a* Alma 14:17 (17–18).
34*a* Alma 10:1 (1–11).
10 1*a* Alma 9:34.
b Alma 8:29 (21–29).
2*a* Dan. 5:16.

3 And Aminadi was a descendant of Nephi, who was the son of Lehi, who came out of the land of Jerusalem, who was a descendant of [a]Manasseh, who was the son of [b]Joseph who was [c]sold into Egypt by the hands of his brethren.

4 And behold, I am also a man of no small [a]reputation among all those who know me; yea, and behold, I have many kindreds and [b]friends, and I have also acquired much riches by the hand of my [c]industry.

5 Nevertheless, after all this, I never have known much of the ways of the Lord, and his [a]mysteries and marvelous power. I said I never had known much of these things; but behold, I mistake, for I have seen much of his mysteries and his marvelous power; yea, even in the preservation of the lives of this people.

6 Nevertheless, I did harden my heart, for I was [a]called many times and I would not [b]hear; therefore I knew concerning these things, yet I would not know; therefore I went on rebelling [c]against God, in the wickedness of my heart, even until the fourth day of this seventh month, which is in the tenth year of the reign of the judges.

7 As I was journeying to see a very near kindred, behold an [a]angel of the Lord appeared unto me and said: Amulek, return to thine own house, for thou shalt feed a prophet of the Lord; yea, a holy man, who is a chosen man of God; for he has [b]fasted many days because of the sins of this people, and he is an hungered, and thou shalt [c]receive him into thy house and feed him, and he shall bless thee and thy house; and the blessing of the Lord shall rest upon thee and thy house.

8 And it came to pass that I obeyed the voice of the angel, and returned towards my house. And as I was going thither I found the [a]man whom the angel said unto me: Thou shalt receive into thy house—and behold it was this same man who has been speaking unto you concerning the things of God.

9 And the angel said unto me he is a [a]holy man; wherefore I know he is a holy man because it was said by an angel of God.

10 And again, I know that the things whereof he hath testified are true; for behold I say unto you, that as the Lord liveth, even so has he sent his [a]angel to make these things manifest unto me; and this he has done while this Alma hath [b]dwelt at my house.

11 For behold, he hath [a]blessed mine house, he hath blessed me, and my women, and my children, and my father and my kinsfolk; yea, even all my kindred hath he blessed, and the blessing of the Lord hath rested upon us according to the words which he spake.

12 And now, when Amulek had spoken these words the people began to be astonished, seeing there was [a]more than one witness who testified of the things whereof they were accused, and also of the things which were to come, according to the spirit of prophecy which was in them.

13 Nevertheless, there were some among them who thought to question them, that by their cunning [a]devices they might catch them in their words, that they might [b]find

3*a* Gen. 41:51; Josh. 17:1; 1 Chr. 7:14; 9:3; 1 Ne. 5:14.
b TG Israel, Joseph, People of.
c Gen. 37:36 (29–36).
4*a* Acts 5:34 (34–39).
b Alma 15:16.
c TG Industry; Work, Value of.
5*a* TG Mysteries of Godliness.
6*a* 2 Chr. 33:10; Isa. 50:2; Alma 5:37.
b D&C 39:9.
c Acts 9:5.
7*a* Alma 8:20.
b Alma 5:46; 6:6.
c Acts 10:30 (30–35). TG Hospitality.
8*a* Alma 8:19 (19–21).
9*a* TG Holiness.
10*a* Mosiah 3:2 (2–3); Alma 11:31.
b Alma 8:27.
11*a* 1 Sam. 2:20; Alma 8:22.
12*a* Alma 9:6.
13*a* Jer. 11:19; Lam. 3:62 (60–62); Alma 11:21.
b Mark 14:55 (55–60).

witness against them, that they
might deliver them to their judges
that they might be judged according to the law, and that they might
be slain or cast into prison, according to the crime which they could
make appear or witness against
them.
14 Now it was those men who
sought to destroy them, who were
[a]lawyers, who were hired or appointed by the people to administer the law at their times of trials,
or at the trials of the crimes of the
people before the judges.
15 Now these lawyers were learned
in all the arts and [a]cunning of the
people; and this was to enable them
that they might be skilful in their
profession.
16 And it came to pass that they
began to question Amulek, that
thereby they might make him [a]cross
his words, or contradict the words
which he should speak.
17 Now they knew not that Amulek could [a]know of their designs.
But it came to pass as they began
to question him, he [b]perceived their
thoughts, and he said unto them: O
ye wicked and perverse [c]generation,
ye lawyers and hypocrites, for ye
are laying the foundations of the
devil; for ye are laying [d]traps and
snares to catch the holy ones of God.
18 Ye are laying plans to [a]pervert
the ways of the righteous, and to
bring down the wrath of God upon
your heads, even to the utter destruction of this people.
19 Yea, well did Mosiah say, who
was our last king, when he was about
to deliver up the kingdom, having
no one to confer it upon, causing
that this people should be governed
by their own voices—yea, well did
he say that if the time should come
that the voice of this people should
[a]choose iniquity, that is, if the time
should come that this people should
fall into transgression, they would
be ripe for destruction.
20 And now I say unto you that
well doth the Lord [a]judge of your
iniquities; well doth he cry unto this
people, by the voice of his [b]angels:
Repent ye, repent, for the kingdom
of heaven is at hand.
21 Yea, well doth he cry, by the
voice of his angels that: [a]I will come
down among my people, with equity
and justice in my hands.
22 Yea, and I say unto you that if
it were not for the [a]prayers of the
righteous, who are now in the land,
that ye would even now be visited
with utter destruction; yet it would
not be by [b]flood, as were the people
in the days of [c]Noah, but it would
be by famine, and by pestilence,
and the [d]sword.
23 But it is by the [a]prayers of the
righteous that ye are spared; now
therefore, if ye will [b]cast out the
righteous from among you then will
not the Lord stay his hand; but in
his fierce anger he will come out
against you; then ye shall be smitten by famine, and by pestilence,
and by the sword; and the [c]time is
soon at hand except ye repent.
24 And now it came to pass that
the people were more angry with
Amulek, and they cried out, saying:
This man doth revile against our
laws which are just, and our wise
[a]lawyers whom we have selected.
25 But Amulek stretched forth
his hand, and cried the mightier
unto them, saying: O ye wicked and

14*a* Alma 10:24; 11:21 (20–37); 14:18 (18, 23); 3 Ne. 6:11.
15*a* Luke 20:23.
16*a* Mark 12:13.
17*a* Luke 5:22.
b Alma 12:3; D&C 6:16.
c Matt. 3:7; Alma 9:8.
d D&C 10:25 (21–27).
18*a* Acts 13:10.
19*a* Mosiah 29:27; Alma 2:4 (3–7); Hel. 5:2.
20*a* TG Jesus Christ, Judge.
b Alma 8:14 (14–16, 20); 13:22.
21*a* Mosiah 13:34 (28–35).
22*a* 1 Sam. 7:9 (7–10); Mosiah 27:14 (14–16).
b Gen. 8:21; 3 Ne. 22:9 (8–10). TG Flood.
c TG Earth, Cleansing of.
d Deut. 32:25; JS—H 1:45.
23*a* TG Prayer.
b 2 Chr. 13:9; Moro. 9:14.
c TG Procrastination.
24*a* Alma 10:14.

perverse generation, why hath Satan got such great hold upon your hearts? Why will ye yield yourselves unto him that he may have power over you, to [a]blind your eyes, that ye will not understand the words which are spoken, according to their truth?

26 For behold, have I testified against your law? Ye do not understand; ye say that I have spoken against your law; but I have not, but I have spoken in favor of your law, to your condemnation.

27 And now behold, I say unto you, that the foundation of the [a]destruction of this people is beginning to be laid by the [b]unrighteousness of your [c]lawyers and your judges.

28 And now it came to pass that when Amulek had spoken these words the people cried out against him, saying: Now we know that this man is a [a]child of the devil, for he hath [b]lied unto us; for he hath spoken against our law. And now he says that he has not spoken against it.

29 And again, he has reviled against our lawyers, and our judges.

30 And it came to pass that the lawyers put it into their hearts that they should remember these things against him.

31 And there was one among them whose name was Zeezrom. Now he was the foremost to [a]accuse Amulek and Alma, he being one of the most expert among them, having much business to do among the people.

32 Now the object of these lawyers was to get gain; and they got gain [a]according to their employ.

CHAPTER 11

The Nephite monetary system is set forth—Amulek contends with Zeezrom—Christ will not save people in their sins—Only those who inherit the kingdom of heaven are saved—All men will rise in immortality—There is no death after the Resurrection. About 82 B.C.

Now it was in the law of Mosiah that every man who was a judge of the law, or those who were appointed to be judges, should receive [a]wages [b]according to the time which they labored to judge those who were brought before them to be judged.

2 Now if a man owed another, and he would not [a]pay that which he did owe, he was complained of to the judge; and the judge executed authority, and sent forth officers that the man should be brought before him; and he judged the man according to the law and the evidences which were brought against him, and thus the man was compelled to pay that which he owed, or be stripped, or be cast out from among the people as a thief and a robber.

3 And the judge received for his wages [a]according to his time—a [b]senine of gold for a day, or a senum of silver, which is equal to a senine of gold; and this is according to the law which was given.

4 Now these are the names of the different pieces of their gold, and of their silver, according to their value. And the names are given by the Nephites, for they did not reckon after the [a]manner of the Jews who were at Jerusalem; neither did they measure after the manner of the Jews; but they altered their reckoning and their measure, according to the minds and the circumstances of the people, in every generation, until the reign of the judges, they having been [b]established by king Mosiah.

25*a* 2 Cor. 4:4 (3–4); Alma 14:6; Moses 6:27.
27*a* Alma 8:16; 9:12 (4, 12, 18, 24).
b TG Injustice.
c Luke 11:46 (45–52); 2 Ne. 28:16.
28*a* John 7:20.
b Alma 14:2.
31*a* Alma 11:21 (20–36).
32*a* Alma 11:1 (1–3).
11 1*a* TG Wages.
b Alma 10:32.
2*a* TG Justice.
3*a* Alma 10:32.
b Alma 30:33; 3 Ne. 12:26.
4*a* BD Money.
b Mosiah 29:41 (40–44).

5 Now the reckoning is thus—a senine of gold, a seon of gold, a shum
of gold, and a limnah of gold.
6 A senum of silver, an amnor of
silver, an ezrom of silver, and an
onti of silver.
7 A senum of silver was equal
to a senine of gold, and either for
a measure of barley, and also for a
measure of every kind of grain.
8 Now the amount of a seon of
gold was twice the value of a senine.
9 And a shum of gold was twice
the value of a seon.
10 And a limnah of gold was the
value of them all.
11 And an amnor of silver was as
great as two senums.
12 And an ezrom of silver was as
great as four senums.
13 And an onti was as great as
them all.
14 Now this is the value of the
lesser numbers of their reckoning—
15 A shiblon is half of a senum;
therefore, a shiblon for half a measure of barley.
16 And a shiblum is a half of a
shiblon.
17 And a leah is the half of a
shiblum.
18 Now this is their number, according to their reckoning.
19 Now an antion of gold is equal
to three shiblons.
20 Now, it was for the sole purpose
to get [a]gain, because they received
their wages according to their [b]em-
ploy, therefore, they did [c]stir up the
people to [d]riotings, and all manner
of disturbances and wickedness,
that they might have more employ, that they might [e]get [f]money
according to the suits which were
brought before them; therefore they
did stir up the people against Alma
and Amulek.
21 And this Zeezrom began to
question Amulek, saying: Will ye
answer me a few questions which I
shall ask you? Now Zeezrom was a
man who was [a]expert in the [b]devices
of the devil, that he might destroy
that which was good; therefore, he
said unto Amulek: Will ye answer
the questions which I shall put
unto you?
22 And Amulek said unto him:
Yea, if it be according to the [a]Spirit
of the Lord, which is in me; for I
shall say nothing which is contrary to the Spirit of the Lord. And
Zeezrom said unto him: Behold,
here are six onties of silver, and all
these will I [b]give thee if thou wilt
deny the existence of a Supreme
Being.
23 Now Amulek said: O thou [a]child
of hell, why [b]tempt ye me? Knowest
thou that the righteous yieldeth to
no such temptations?
24 Believest thou that there is
no God? I say unto you, Nay, thou
knowest that there is a God, but thou
lovest that [a]lucre more than him.
25 And now thou hast lied before God unto me. Thou saidst
unto me—Behold these six onties,
which are of great worth, I will
give unto thee—when thou hadst
it in thy heart to retain them from
me; and it was only thy desire that
I should deny the true and living
God, that thou mightest have cause
to destroy me. And now behold, for
this great evil thou shalt have thy
reward.
26 And Zeezrom said unto him:
Thou sayest there is a true and living God?
27 And Amulek said: Yea, there is
a true and living God.
28 Now Zeezrom said: Is there more
than one God?

20*a* TG Selfishness.
b Prov. 28:8.
c TG Provoking.
d TG Rioting and Reveling.
e Alma 10:32.
f Luke 11:52 (45–54).
21*a* Alma 10:31; 14:7 (6–7, 18, 23).
b Lam. 3:62 (60–62); Alma 10:13.
22*a* TG God, Spirit of; Holy Ghost, Mission of.
b TG Bribe.
23*a* Acts 13:10 (8–12); Alma 5:41.
b TG Temptation; Test.
24*a* Luke 16:14; John 12:43 (42–43); Acts 19:27 (27, 36–38); Titus 1:11.

29 And he answered, No.
30 Now Zeezrom said unto him
again: How knowest thou these
things?
31 And he said: An [a]angel hath
made them known unto me.
32 And Zeezrom said again: Who
is he that shall come? Is it the Son
of God?
33 And he said unto him, Yea.
34 And Zeezrom said again: Shall
he save his people [a]in their sins?
And Amulek answered and said
unto him: I say unto you he shall
not, for it is impossible for him to
deny his word.
35 Now Zeezrom said unto the
people: See that ye remember these
things; for he said there is but one
God; yet he saith that the Son of
God shall come, but he shall [a]not
save his people—as though he had
authority to command God.
36 Now Amulek saith again unto
him: Behold thou hast [a]lied, for
thou sayest that I spake as though
I had authority to command God
because I said he shall not save his
people in their sins.
37 And I say unto you again that
he cannot save them in their [a]sins;
for I cannot deny his word, and he
hath said that [b]no unclean thing
can inherit the [c]kingdom of heaven;
therefore, how can ye be saved,
except ye inherit the kingdom of
heaven? Therefore, ye cannot be
saved in your sins.
38 Now Zeezrom saith again unto
him: Is the Son of God the very
Eternal Father?
39 And Amulek said unto him:
Yea, he is the very [a]Eternal Father
of heaven and of earth, and [b]all
things which in them are; he is the
beginning and the end, the first
and the last;
40 And he shall come into the
[a]world to [b]redeem his people; and
he shall [c]take upon him the transgressions
of those who believe on
his name; and these are they that
shall have eternal life, and salvation
cometh to none else.
41 Therefore the wicked remain as
though there had been [a]no redemption
made, except it be the loosing
of the bands of death; for behold,
the day cometh that [b]all shall rise
from the dead and stand before
God, and be [c]judged according to
their works.
42 Now, there is a death which
is called a temporal death; and
the death of Christ shall loose the
[a]bands of this temporal death, that
all shall be raised from this temporal
death.
43 The spirit and the body shall
be [a]reunited again in its [b]perfect
form; both limb and joint shall be
restored to its proper frame, even
as we now are at this time; and we
shall be brought to stand before
God, [c]knowing even as we know
now, and have a bright [d]recollection
of all our [e]guilt.
44 Now, this restoration shall
come to all, both old and young,
both bond and free, both male and
female, both the wicked and the
righteous; and even there shall not
so much as a hair of their heads be
lost; but every thing shall be [a]restored
to its perfect frame, as it is
now, or in the body, and shall be

31*a* Alma 10:10.
34*a* Hel. 5:10 (10–11).
35*a* Alma 14:5.
36*a* Alma 12:1.
37*a* 1 Cor. 6:9 (9–10).
b 1 Ne. 15:33; Alma 40:26; 3 Ne. 27:19. TG Uncleanness.
c TG Kingdom of God, in Heaven.
39*a* Isa. 9:6; 64:8; Mosiah 15:4 (2–4); Moro. 7:22; 8:18.
b Col. 1:16; Mosiah 4:2.
40*a* TG World.
b Luke 2:34; Rom. 11:26 (26–27).
c Ex. 34:7; 1 Jn. 2:2; Mosiah 14:5 (5, 8); 15:12; D&C 19:17 (16–18); 29:17.
41*a* Alma 12:18; D&C 88:33.
b Rev. 20:13 (12–13); Alma 28:12; 42:23.
c TG Judgment, the Last.
42*a* Alma 12:16 (16, 24, 36).
43*a* 2 Ne. 9:13; Alma 40:23.
b TG Perfection.
c D&C 130:18.
d 2 Ne. 9:14; Mosiah 3:25; Alma 5:18.
e Matt. 12:36 (36–37). TG Guilt.
44*a* Rev. 20:12 (12–15).

brought and be arraigned before the
bar of Christ the Son, and God the
[b]Father, and the Holy Spirit, which
is [c]one Eternal God, to be [d]judged
according to their works, whether
they be good or whether they be
evil.
45 Now, behold, I have spoken
unto you concerning the [a]death of
the mortal body, and also concerning the [b]resurrection of the mortal
body. I say unto you that this mortal body is [c]raised to an [d]immortal
body, that is from death, even from
the first death unto life, that they
can [e]die no more; their spirits uniting with their bodies, never to be
divided; thus the whole becoming
[f]spiritual and immortal, that they
can no more see corruption.
46 Now, when Amulek had finished
these words the people began again
to be astonished, and also Zeezrom
began to tremble. And thus ended
the words of Amulek, or this is all
that I have written.

CHAPTER 12

Alma speaks to Zeezrom—The mysteries of God can be given only to the faithful—Men are judged by their thoughts, beliefs, words, and works—The wicked will suffer a spiritual death—This mortal life is a probationary state—The plan of redemption brings to pass the Resurrection and, through faith, a remission of sins—The repentant have a claim on mercy through the Only Begotten Son. About 82 B.C.

NOW Alma, seeing that the words of
Amulek had silenced Zeezrom, for
he beheld that Amulek had caught
him in his [a]lying and deceiving to destroy him, and seeing that he began
to tremble under a [b]consciousness
of his guilt, he opened his mouth
and began to speak unto him, and
to establish the words of Amulek,
and to explain things beyond, or to
unfold the scriptures beyond that
which Amulek had done.
2 Now the words that Alma spake
unto Zeezrom were heard by the
people round about; for the multitude was great, and he spake on
this wise:
3 Now Zeezrom, seeing that thou
hast been taken in thy lying and
craftiness, for thou hast not lied
unto men only but thou hast lied
unto God; for behold, he knows all
thy [a]thoughts, and thou seest that
thy [b]thoughts are made known unto
us by his Spirit;
4 And thou seest that we know
that thy plan was a very [a]subtle
plan, as to the subtlety of the devil,
for to lie and to deceive this people that thou mightest set them
against us, to [b]revile us and to cast
us out—
5 Now this was a plan of thine [a]ad-
versary, and he hath exercised his
power in thee. Now I would that ye
should remember that what I say
unto thee I say unto all.
6 And behold I say unto you all
that this was a [a]snare of the adversary, which he has laid to catch
this people, that he might bring
you into subjection unto him, that
he might encircle you about with
his [b]chains, that he might chain
you down to everlasting destruction, according to the power of his
captivity.
7 Now when Alma had spoken
these words, Zeezrom began to
tremble more exceedingly, for he
was convinced more and more of
the power of God; and he was also

44*b* TG Godhead.
c 3 Ne. 11:27 (27–28, 36). TG God, Eternal Nature of.
d 2 Pet. 2:9. TG Jesus Christ, Judge.
45*a* Alma 12:12.
b Alma 40:23; D&C 88:16.
c TG Death, Power over.
d TG Immortality.
e Rev. 21:4; Alma 12:18 (18, 20); D&C 63:49; 88:116.
f 1 Cor. 15:44.
12 1*a* Alma 11:36 (20–38).
b Alma 62:45; D&C 6:11; 18:44. TG Conscience.
3*a* Jacob 2:5; D&C 6:16.
b Alma 10:17.
4*a* D&C 123:12.
b TG Slander.
5*a* TG Devil.
6*a* Prov. 29:6 (3–8).
b Alma 5:9 (7–10).

convinced that Alma and Amulek had a knowledge of him, for he was convinced that they [a]knew the thoughts and intents of his heart; for power was given unto them that they might know of these things according to the spirit of prophecy.

8 And Zeezrom began to inquire of them diligently, that he might know more concerning the kingdom of God. And he said unto Alma: What does this mean which Amulek hath spoken concerning the resurrection of the dead, that all shall rise from the dead, both the [a]just and the unjust, and are brought to stand before God to be [b]judged according to their works?

9 And now Alma began to expound these things unto him, saying: It is given unto many to [a]know the [b]mysteries of God; nevertheless they are laid under a strict command that they shall not impart [c]only according to the portion of his word which he doth grant unto the children of men, according to the heed and diligence which they give unto him.

10 And therefore, he that will [a]harden his heart, the same receiveth the [b]lesser portion of the word; and he that will [c]not harden his heart, to him is [d]given the greater portion of the word, until it is given unto him to know the mysteries of God until he know them in full.

11 And they that will harden their hearts, to them is given the lesser [a]portion of the word until they [b]know nothing concerning his mysteries; and then they are taken captive by the devil, and led by his will down to destruction. Now this is what is meant by the [c]chains of [d]hell.

12 And Amulek hath spoken plainly concerning [a]death, and being raised from this mortality to a state of immortality, and being brought before the bar of God, to be [b]judged according to our works.

13 Then if our hearts have been hardened, yea, if we have hardened our hearts against the word, insomuch that it has not been found in us, then will our state be awful, for then we shall be condemned.

14 For our [a]words will condemn us, yea, all our works will condemn us; we shall not be found spotless; and our thoughts will also condemn us; and in this awful state we shall not dare to look up to our God; and we would fain be glad if we could command the rocks and the [b]mountains to fall upon us to [c]hide us from his presence.

15 But this cannot be; we must come forth and stand before him in his glory, and in his power, and in his might, majesty, and dominion, and acknowledge to our everlasting [a]shame that all his [b]judgments are just; that he is just in all his works, and that he is merciful unto the children of men, and that he has all power to save every man that believeth on his name and bringeth forth fruit meet for repentance.

16 And now behold, I say unto you then cometh a death, even a second [a]death, which is a spiritual death;

7*a* Alma 14:2.
8*a* Dan. 12:2.
b TG Judgment, the Last.
9*a* Dan. 1:17.
b Alma 26:22.
TG Mysteries of Godliness.
c John 16:12;
Alma 29:8;
3 Ne. 26:10 (6–11);
Ether 4:7 (1–7).
10*a* 2 Ne. 28:27;
3 Ne. 26:10 (9–10);
Ether 4:8.
b D&C 93:39.
c TG Teachable.
d Dan. 2:21; 2 Ne. 28:30;
D&C 50:24; 71:5.
11*a* Matt. 25:29 (29–30).
b TG Apostasy of Individuals.
c Prov. 5:22;
John 8:34 (31–36);
2 Ne. 28:19 (19–22);
Mosiah 23:12;
Alma 26:14.
TG Bondage, Spiritual.
d Prov. 9:18; 1 Ne. 14:7;
2 Ne. 2:29 (26–29).
TG Hell.
12*a* Alma 11:45 (41–45).
b TG Judgment, the Last.
14*a* Prov. 18:21; Matt. 12:36;
James 3:6 (1–13);
Mosiah 4:30 (29–30).
b Hosea 10:8;
2 Ne. 26:5.
c Job 34:22; Amos 9:3;
2 Ne. 12:10.
15*a* Mosiah 3:25.
TG Shame.
b 2 Pet. 2:9.
TG Justice.
16*a* TG Death, Spiritual, Second.

then is a time that whosoever dieth
in his sins, as to a temporal [b]death,
shall also [c]die a spiritual death; yea,
he shall die as to things pertaining
unto righteousness.
17 Then is the time when their
torments shall be as a [a]lake of fire
and brimstone, whose flame ascendeth up forever and ever; and
then is the time that they shall be
chained down to an everlasting destruction, according to the power
and captivity of Satan, he having
subjected them according to his will.
18 Then, I say unto you, they shall
be as though there had been [a]no redemption made; for they cannot be
redeemed according to God's justice;
and they cannot [b]die, seeing there
is no more corruption.
19 Now it came to pass that when
Alma had made an end of speaking
these words, the people began to be
more astonished;
20 But there was one Antionah,
who was a chief ruler among them,
came forth and said unto him: What
is this that thou hast said, that man
should rise from the dead and be
changed from this mortal to an
[a]immortal state, that the soul can
never die?
21 What does the scripture mean,
which saith that God placed [a]cheru-
bim and a flaming sword on the
east of the garden of [b]Eden, lest our
first parents should enter and partake of the fruit of the tree of life,
and live forever? And thus we see
that there was no possible chance
that they should live forever.
22 Now Alma said unto him: This
is the thing which I was about to
explain. Now we see that Adam
did [a]fall by the partaking of the
forbidden [b]fruit, according to the
word of God; and thus we see, that
by his fall, all mankind became a
[c]lost and fallen people.
23 And now behold, I say unto
you that if it had been possible for
Adam to have [a]partaken of the fruit
of the tree of life at that time, there
would have been no death, and the
word would have been void, making God a liar, for he said: [b]If thou
eat thou shalt surely die.
24 And we see that [a]death comes
upon mankind, yea, the death which
has been spoken of by Amulek,
which is the temporal death; nevertheless there was a space granted
unto [b]man in which he might repent;
therefore this life became a [c]pro-
bationary state; a time to [d]prepare
to meet God; a time to prepare for
that endless state which has been
spoken of by us, which is after the
resurrection of the dead.
25 Now, if it had not been for the
plan of redemption, which was laid
from the foundation of the world,
there could have been no [a]resur-
rection of the dead; but there was
a plan of [b]redemption laid, which
shall bring to pass the resurrection of the dead, of which has been
spoken.
26 And now behold, if it were possible that our first parents could
have gone forth and partaken of the
[a]tree of life they would have been
forever miserable, having no preparatory state; and thus the [b]plan

16*b* Alma 11:42 (40–45).
c 1 Ne. 15:33; Alma 40:26.
17*a* Rev. 19:20; 21:8; Mosiah 3:27; Alma 14:14.
18*a* Alma 11:41.
b Rev. 21:4; Alma 11:45; D&C 63:49; 88:116.
20*a* TG Immortality.
21*a* Gen. 3:24; Alma 42:2; Moses 4:31.
b TG Cherubim.
b TG Eden.
22*a* TG Fall of Man.
b Gen. 3:6; 2 Ne. 2:15 (15–19); Mosiah 3:26.
c Mosiah 16:5 (4–5); Alma 9:30 (30–32).
23*a* Alma 42:5 (2–9).
b Gen. 2:17.
24*a* TG Death.
b 2 Ne. 2:21; Moses 5:8–12.
c 1 Pet. 2:20 (20–21). TG Earth, Purpose of; Probation.
d Alma 34:32 (32–35).
25*a* 2 Ne. 2:8; Alma 7:12; 42:23.
b TG Redemption.
26*a* Gen. 2:9; 1 Ne. 15:36 (22, 28, 36); 2 Ne. 2:15; Alma 32:40.
b Alma 34:9 (8–16); 42:8 (6–28); Moses 6:62.

of redemption would have been frustrated, and the word of God would have been void, taking none effect.
27 But behold, it was not so; but it was [a]appointed unto men that they must die; and after death, they must come to [b]judgment, even that same judgment of which we have spoken, which is the end.
28 And after God had appointed that these things should come unto man, behold, then he saw that it was expedient that man should know concerning the things whereof he had appointed unto them;
29 Therefore he sent [a]angels to converse with them, who caused men to behold of his glory.
30 And they began from that time forth to call on his name; therefore God [a]conversed with men, and made known unto them the [b]plan of redemption, which had been prepared from the [c]foundation of the world; and this he made known unto them according to their faith and repentance and their [d]holy works.
31 Wherefore, he gave [a]commandments unto men, they having first transgressed the [b]first commandments as to things which were temporal, and becoming as gods, [c]knowing good from evil, placing themselves in a state to [d]act, or being placed in a state to act according to their wills and pleasures, whether to do evil or to do good—
32 Therefore God gave unto them commandments, after having made [a]known unto them the plan of redemption, that they should not do evil, the penalty thereof being a second [b]death, which was an everlasting [c]death as to things pertaining unto righteousness; for on such the plan of redemption could have no power, for the works of [d]justice could not be destroyed, according to the supreme [e]goodness of God.
33 But God did call on men, in the name of his Son, (this being the [a]plan of redemption which was laid) saying: If ye will [b]repent, and harden not your hearts, then will I have mercy upon you, through mine Only Begotten Son;
34 Therefore, whosoever repenteth, and hardeneth not his heart, he shall have claim on [a]mercy through mine Only Begotten Son, unto a [b]remission of his sins; and these shall enter into my [c]rest.
35 And whosoever will harden his heart and will do [a]iniquity, behold, I swear in my wrath that he shall not enter into my rest.
36 And now, my brethren, behold I say unto you, that if ye will harden your hearts ye shall not enter into the rest of the Lord; therefore your iniquity [a]provoketh him that he sendeth down his [b]wrath upon you as in the [c]first provocation, yea, according to his word in the last provocation as well as the first, to the everlasting [d]destruction of your souls; therefore, according to his word, unto the last death, as well as the first.
37 And now, my brethren, seeing we know these things, and they are true, let us repent, and harden not

27*a* Job 7:1; Heb. 9:27; D&C 42:48; 121:25.
b TG Judgment, the Last.
29*a* Moro. 7:25 (25, 31); D&C 29:42.
30*a* Moses 1:1; 5:4 (4–5); 6:51 (4, 51–68).
b TG Salvation, Plan of.
c Gen. 2:16 (16–17); Mosiah 18:13; Alma 13:3 (3, 5, 7–8); Abr. 3:26 (24–26).
d Luke 8:15 (14–15).
31*a* TG Commandments of God.
b Gen. 2:17 (16–17); 2 Ne. 2:19 (18–19).
c Gen. 3:22; Moses 4:11.
d 2 Ne. 2:16. TG Agency.
32*a* Moses 5:9 (4–9).
b TG Death, Spiritual, Second.
c TG Damnation.
d Mosiah 15:27; Alma 34:16 (15–16); 42:15.
e TG Goodness.
33*a* TG Salvation, Plan of.
b Moses 5:8.
34*a* 2 Cor. 4:1.
b TG Remission of Sins.
c D&C 84:24. TG Rest.
35*a* Moses 5:15.
36*a* 1 Kgs. 16:33. TG Provoking.
b TG God, Indignation of.
c Heb. 3:8; 2 Ne. 9:7; Jacob 1:7 (7–8); Mosiah 16:4 (4–7); Alma 11:45; 42:6 (6, 9, 14).
d TG Damnation.

our hearts, that we [a]provoke not
the Lord our God to pull down his
wrath upon us in these his second
commandments which he has given
unto us; but let us enter into the
[b]rest of God, which is prepared according to his word.

CHAPTER 13

Men are called as high priests because of their exceeding faith and good works—They are to teach the commandments—Through righteousness they are sanctified and enter into the rest of the Lord—Melchizedek was one of these—Angels are declaring glad tidings throughout the land—They will declare the actual coming of Christ. About 82 B.C.

AND again, my brethren, I would
cite your minds forward to the time
when the Lord God gave these commandments unto his children; and
I would that ye should remember
that the Lord God [a]ordained priests,
after his holy order, which was after
the order of his Son, to teach these
things unto the people.
2 And those priests were ordained
after the [a]order of his Son, in a
[b]manner that thereby the people
might know in what manner to look
forward to his Son for redemption.
3 And this is the manner after
which they were ordained—being
[a]called and [b]prepared from the
[c]foundation of the world according
to the [d]foreknowledge of God, on account of their exceeding faith and
good works; in the first place being
left to [e]choose good or evil; therefore they having chosen good, and
exercising exceedingly great [f]faith,
are [g]called with a holy calling, yea,
with that holy calling which was
prepared with, and according to, a
preparatory redemption for such.
4 And thus they have been [a]called
to this holy calling on account of
their faith, while others would reject the Spirit of God on account
of the hardness of their hearts and
[b]blindness of their minds, while, if
it had not been for this they might
have had as great [c]privilege as their
brethren.
5 Or in fine, in the first place they
were on the [a]same standing with
their brethren; thus this holy calling
being prepared from the foundation
of the world for such as would not
harden their hearts, being in and
through the atonement of the Only
Begotten Son, who was prepared—
6 And thus being called by this
holy calling, and ordained unto the
high priesthood of the holy order of
God, to teach his commandments
unto the children of men, that they
also might enter into his [a]rest—
7 This high priesthood being after
the order of his Son, which order was
from the foundation of the world;
or in other words, being [a]without
beginning of days or end of years,
being prepared from [b]eternity to
all eternity, according to his [c]fore-
knowledge of all things—
8 Now they were [a]ordained after
this manner—being called with
a holy calling, and ordained with a
holy ordinance, and taking upon
them the high priesthood of the holy
order, which calling, and ordinance,

37*a* Num. 14:11 (11–12); 1 Ne. 17:30 (23–31); Jacob 1:8; Hel. 7:18.
b Alma 13:6 (6–29); 16:17; D&C 84:24.
13 1*a* Alma 8:23 (11, 23); D&C 84:17 (17–19); Moses 6:7; Abr. 2:9 (9, 11).
2*a* D&C 107:3 (2–4).
b Alma 13:16.
3*a* D&C 127:2. TG Election; Foreordination.
b D&C 138:56.
c Alma 12:30 (25, 30); 22:13. TG Man, Antemortal Existence of.
d TG God, Foreknowledge of.
e TG Agency.
f TG Priesthood, Qualifying for.
g TG Called of God.
4*a* Ether 12:10.
b TG Spiritual Blindness.
c 1 Ne. 17:35 (32–35).
5*a* Rom. 2:11; 2 Ne. 26:28.
6*a* Alma 12:37; 16:17. TG Rest.
7*a* Heb. 7:3; Abr. 1:3 (2–4).
b TG Eternity.
c TG God, Foreknowledge of; God, Omniscience of.
8*a* TG Priesthood, Melchizedek; Priesthood, Oath and Covenant.

and high priesthood, is without
beginning or end—
9 Thus they become [a]high priests
forever, after the order of the Son,
the Only Begotten of the Father, who
is without beginning of days or end
of years, who is full of [b]grace, equity,
and truth. And thus it is. Amen.
10 Now, as I said concerning the
holy order, or this [a]high priesthood, there were many who were
ordained and became high priests of
God; and it was on account of their
exceeding [b]faith and [c]repentance,
and their righteousness before God,
they choosing to repent and work
righteousness rather than to perish;
11 Therefore they were called after this holy order, and were [a]sanc-
tified, and their [b]garments were
washed white through the blood
of the Lamb.
12 Now they, after being [a]sanc-
tified by the [b]Holy Ghost, having
their garments made white, being
[c]pure and spotless before God, could
not look upon [d]sin save it were with
[e]abhorrence; and there were many,
exceedingly great many, who were
made pure and entered into the rest
of the Lord their God.
13 And now, my brethren, I would
that ye should humble yourselves
before God, and bring forth [a]fruit
meet for repentance, that ye may
also enter into that rest.
14 Yea, humble yourselves even as
the people in the days of [a]Melchi-
zedek, who was also a high priest
after this same order which I have
spoken, who also took upon him
the high priesthood forever.
15 And it was this same Melchizedek
to whom Abraham paid [a]tithes; yea,
even our father Abraham paid tithes
of one-tenth part of all he possessed.
16 Now these [a]ordinances were
given after this [b]manner, that thereby the people might look forward
on the Son of God, it being a [c]type
of his order, or it being his order,
and this that they might look forward to him for a remission of their
sins, that they might enter into the
rest of the Lord.
17 Now this Melchizedek was a
king over the land of Salem; and
his people had waxed strong in iniquity and abomination; yea, they
had all gone astray; they were full
of all manner of wickedness;
18 But Melchizedek having exercised mighty faith, and received the
office of the high priesthood according to the [a]holy order of God, did
preach repentance unto his people.
And behold, they did repent; and
Melchizedek did establish peace in
the land in his days; therefore he
was called the prince of peace, for
he was the king of Salem; and he
did reign under his father.
19 Now, there were [a]many before
him, and also there were many afterwards, but [b]none were greater;
therefore, of him they have more
particularly made mention.
20 Now I need not rehearse the
matter; what I have said may suffice. Behold, the [a]scriptures are

9*a* TG High Priest, Melchizedek Priesthood.
b John 1:17 (14, 17); 2 Ne. 2:6; Moses 1:6. TG Grace.
10*a* D&C 84:18 (6–22); 107:53 (40–55).
b TG Priesthood, Magnifying Callings within.
c TG Spirituality.
11*a* Lev. 8:30; Moses 6:60 (59–60).
b 1 Ne. 12:10; Alma 5:21 (21–27); 3 Ne. 27:19 (19–20).
12*a* Rom. 8:1 (1–9); D&C 11:12 (12–13). TG Sanctification.
b TG Holy Ghost, Baptism of.
c TG Purity.
d Rom. 12:9; 2 Ne. 4:31; Mosiah 5:2; Alma 19:33.
e Prov. 8:13; Alma 37:29.
13*a* Luke 3:8.
14*a* JST Gen. 14:25–40 (Bible Appendix); D&C 84:14. TG Priesthood, History of.
15*a* Gen. 14:20 (18–20); Mal. 3:10 (8–10). TG Tithing.
16*a* A of F 1:5. TG Ordinance.
b Alma 13:2.
c TG Jesus Christ, Types of, in Anticipation.
18*a* TG Priesthood.
19*a* Hel. 8:18; D&C 84:14 (6–16); 107:53 (40–55).
b D&C 107:2 (1–4).
20*a* Alma 14:1 (1, 8, 14). TG Scriptures, Value of.

before you; if ye will [b]wrest them
it shall be to your own destruction.
21 And now it came to pass that
when Alma had said these words
unto them, he stretched forth his
hand unto them and cried with a
mighty voice, saying: [a]Now is the
time to repent, for the day of salvation draweth nigh;
22 Yea, and the voice of the Lord,
by the [a]mouth of angels, doth declare it unto all nations; yea, doth
declare it, that they may have glad
tidings of great joy; yea, and he doth
sound these glad tidings among all
his people, yea, even to them that
are scattered abroad upon the face
of the earth; wherefore they have
come unto us.
23 And they are made known unto
us in [a]plain terms, that we may understand, that we cannot err; and
this because of our being [b]wander-
ers in a strange land; therefore, we
are thus highly favored, for we have
these glad tidings declared unto us
in all parts of our vineyard.
24 For behold, [a]angels are declaring it unto many at this time in our
land; and this is for the purpose of
preparing the hearts of the children
of men to receive his word at the
time of his coming in his glory.
25 And now we only wait to hear
the joyful news declared unto us
by the mouth of angels, of his coming; for the time cometh, we [a]know
not how soon. Would to God that
it might be in my day; but let it be
sooner or later, in it I will rejoice.
26 And it shall be made known unto
[a]just and holy men, by the mouth
of angels, at the time of his coming,
that the words of our fathers may
be fulfilled, according to that which
they have spoken concerning him,
which was according to the spirit
of prophecy which was in them.
27 And now, my brethren, I [a]wish
from the inmost part of my heart,
yea, with great [b]anxiety even unto
pain, that ye would hearken unto
my words, and cast off your sins,
and not [c]procrastinate the day of
your repentance;
28 But that ye would humble
yourselves before the Lord, and
call on his holy name, and [a]watch
and pray continually, that ye may
not be [b]tempted above that which
ye can bear, and thus be [c]led by
the Holy Spirit, becoming humble,
[d]meek, submissive, patient, full of
love and all long-suffering;
29 [a]Having faith on the Lord; having a hope that ye shall receive
eternal life; having the [b]love of God
always in your hearts, that ye may
be lifted up at the last day and enter into his [c]rest.
30 And may the Lord grant unto
you repentance, that ye may not
bring down his wrath upon you,
that ye may not be [a]bound down
by the chains of [b]hell, that ye may
not suffer the second [c]death.
31 And Alma spake many more
words unto the people, which are
not written in [a]this book.

CHAPTER 14

Alma and Amulek are imprisoned and smitten—The believers and their holy scriptures are burned by fire—These martyrs are received by the Lord

20*b* 2 Pet. 3:16; Alma 41:1.
21*a* TG Procrastination.
22*a* Alma 10:20 (7–10, 20).
23*a* 2 Ne. 25:7 (7–8); 31:3; 32:7; Jacob 4:13; Ether 12:39.
b Jacob 7:26.
24*a* Alma 10:10; 39:19.
25*a* 1 Ne. 10:4; 3 Ne. 1:1.
26*a* Ex. 22:31; Amos 3:7; W of M 1:17; D&C 49:8; 107:29.
27*a* Mosiah 28:3 (3–4).
b Mosiah 25:11.
c TG Apathy; Procrastination.
28*a* TG Prayer; Watch.
b Rom. 7:23 (23–24); 1 Cor. 10:13; D&C 64:20.
c Alma 22:1; Morm. 5:17.
d TG Forbear; Love; Meek.
29*a* Alma 7:24.
b Ps. 18:1; D&C 20:31; 76:116. TG God, Love of.
c D&C 84:24.
30*a* TG Bondage, Spiritual.
b TG Damnation; Hell.
c TG Death, Spiritual, Second.
31*a* W of M 1:5; 3 Ne. 5:9 (8–12).

in glory—The prison walls are rent and fall—Alma and Amulek are delivered, and their persecutors are slain. About 82–81 B.C.

AND it came to pass after he had made an end of speaking unto the people many of them did believe on his words, and began to repent, and to search the [a]scriptures.

2 But the more part of them were desirous that they might destroy Alma and Amulek; for they were angry with Alma, because of the [a]plainness of his words unto Zeezrom; and they also said that Amulek had [b]lied unto them, and had reviled against their law and also against their lawyers and judges.

3 And they were also angry with Alma and Amulek; and because they had [a]testified so plainly against their wickedness, they sought to [b]put them away privily.

4 But it came to pass that they did not; but they took them and bound them with strong cords, and took them before the chief judge of the land.

5 And the people went forth and witnessed against them—testifying that they had reviled against the law, and their lawyers and judges of the land, and also of all the people that were in the land; and also testified that there was but one God, and that he should send his Son among the people, but he should [a]not save them; and many such things did the people testify against Alma and Amulek. Now this was done before the chief judge of the land.

6 And it came to pass that Zeezrom was astonished at the words which had been spoken; and he also knew concerning the [a]blindness of the minds, which he had caused among the people by his [b]lying words; and his soul began to be [c]harrowed up under a [d]consciousness of his own guilt; yea, he began to be encircled about by the pains of hell.

7 And it came to pass that he began to cry unto the people, saying: Behold, I am [a]guilty, and these men are spotless before God. And he began to plead for them from that time forth; but they reviled him, saying: Art thou also possessed with the devil? And they spit upon him, and [b]cast him out from among them, and also all those who believed in the words which had been spoken by Alma and Amulek; and they cast them out, and sent men to cast stones at them.

8 And they brought their wives and children together, and whosoever believed or had been taught to believe in the word of God they caused that they should be [a]cast into the fire; and they also brought forth their records which contained the holy scriptures, and cast them into the fire also, that they might be [b]burned and destroyed by fire.

9 And it came to pass that they took Alma and Amulek, and carried them forth to the place of [a]martyrdom, that they might witness the destruction of those who were consumed by fire.

10 And when Amulek saw the pains of the women and children who were consuming in the fire, he also was pained; and he said unto Alma: How can we witness this awful scene? Therefore let us stretch forth our hands, and exercise the [a]power of God which is in us, and save them from the flames.

11 But Alma said unto him: The Spirit constraineth me that I must not stretch forth mine hand; for behold the Lord receiveth them up

14 1*a* 2 Kgs. 22:11 (8–13); Acts 17:2 (2–3, 11); Alma 13:20.
2*a* Alma 12:7 (3–7).
b Alma 10:28 (24–32).
3*a* Prov. 26:26; Alma 37:21.
b Acts 23:12 (12–15).
5*a* Alma 11:35 (33–37).
6*a* TG Spiritual Blindness.
b Alma 10:31 (25–31).
c Alma 15:5.
d TG Conscience.
7*a* Alma 10:31; 11:21 (21–36); 15:3.
b Alma 15:1.
8*a* Alma 15:2.
b Jer. 36:23 (21–28).
9*a* TG Martyrdom.
10*a* Alma 8:31 (30–31).

unto himself, in [a]glory; and he doth
suffer that they may do this thing,
or that the people may do this thing
unto them, according to the hardness of their hearts, that the [b]judg-
ments which he shall exercise upon
them in his wrath may be just; and
the [c]blood of the [d]innocent shall
stand as a witness against them,
yea, and cry mightily against them
at the last day.
12 Now Amulek said unto Alma:
Behold, perhaps they will burn us
also.
13 And Alma said: Be it according
to the will of the Lord. But, behold,
our work is not finished; therefore
they burn us not.
14 Now it came to pass that when
the bodies of those who had been
cast into the fire were consumed,
and also the records which were cast
in with them, the chief judge of the
land came and stood before Alma
and Amulek, as they were bound;
and he smote them with his hand
upon their [a]cheeks, and said unto
them: After what ye have seen, will
ye preach again unto this people,
that they shall be cast into a [b]lake
of fire and brimstone?
15 Behold, ye see that ye had not
power to save those who had been
cast into the fire; neither has God
saved them because they were of
thy faith. And the judge smote them
again upon their cheeks, and asked:
What say ye for yourselves?
16 Now this judge was after the
order and faith of [a]Nehor, who slew
Gideon.
17 And it came to pass that Alma
and Amulek answered him [a]noth-
ing; and he smote them again, and
delivered them to the officers to be
[b]cast into prison.
18 And when they had been cast
into prison three days, there came
many [a]lawyers, and judges, and
priests, and teachers, who were of
the profession of Nehor; and they
came in unto the prison to see them,
and they questioned them about
many words; but they answered
them nothing.
19 And it came to pass that the
judge stood before them, and said:
Why do ye not answer the words
of this people? Know ye not that I
have [a]power to deliver you up unto
the flames? And he [b]commanded
them to speak; but they answered
nothing.
20 And it came to pass that they
departed and went their ways, but
came again on the morrow; and
the judge also smote them again
on their cheeks. And many came
forth also, and smote them, saying:
Will ye stand again and judge this
people, and condemn our law? If
ye have such great power why do
ye not [a]deliver yourselves?
21 And many such things did they
say unto them, gnashing their teeth
upon them, and spitting upon them,
and saying: How shall we look when
we are damned?
22 And many such things, yea, all
manner of such things did they say
unto them; and thus they did [a]mock
them for many days. And they
did withhold food from them that
they might hunger, and water
that they might thirst; and they also
did take from them their clothes
that they were naked; and thus they
were [b]bound with strong cords, and
confined in [c]prison.
23 And it came to pass after they
had thus suffered for many days,
(and it was on the twelfth day, in
the tenth month, in the tenth year
of the reign of the judges over the

11*a* TG Exaltation.
b Ex. 23:7; Ps. 37:9 (8–13); Alma 60:13; D&C 103:3. TG Justice.
c TG Cruelty; Martyrdom.
d Lam. 4:13; Mosiah 17:10.
14*a* 1 Kgs. 22:24 (14–27).
b Alma 12:17. TG Damnation.
16*a* Alma 1:12 (7–15); 2:20; 21:4.
17*a* Matt. 27:12 (12–14).
b Alma 9:33.
18*a* Alma 10:14; 11:21 (20–37).
19*a* John 19:10 (9–10).
b Mosiah 7:8.
20*a* Matt. 27:40 (39–43).
22*a* TG Mocking.
b Acts 16:23 (23–40); D&C 122:6.
c Gen. 39:20; Mosiah 7:7.

people of Nephi) that the chief
judge over the land of [a]Ammoni-
hah and many of their teachers
and their lawyers went in unto the
prison where Alma and Amulek
were bound with cords.
24 And the chief judge stood before them, and smote them again,
and said unto them: If ye have the
[a]power of God deliver yourselves
from these bands, and then we will
believe that the Lord will destroy
this people according to your words.
25 And it came to pass that they all
went forth and smote them, saying
the same words, even until the last;
and when the last had spoken unto
them the [a]power of God was upon
Alma and Amulek, and they rose
and stood upon their feet.
26 And Alma cried, saying: How
long shall we suffer these great
[a]afflictions, O Lord? O Lord, [b]give
us strength according to our faith
which is in Christ, even unto [c]de-
liverance. And they broke the cords
with which they were bound; and
when the people saw this, they began to flee, for the fear of destruction had come upon them.
27 And it came to pass that so great
was their fear that they fell to the
earth, and did not obtain the outer
door of the [a]prison; and the earth
shook mightily, and the walls of
the prison were rent in twain, so
that they fell to the earth; and the
chief judge, and the lawyers, and
priests, and teachers, who smote
upon Alma and Amulek, were slain
by the fall thereof.
28 And Alma and Amulek came
forth out of the prison, and they
were not hurt; for the Lord had
granted unto them [a]power, according to their faith which was in Christ.
And they straightway came forth
out of the prison; and they were
[b]loosed from their [c]bands; and the
prison had fallen to the earth, and
every soul within the walls thereof,
save it were Alma and Amulek, was
slain; and they straightway came
forth into the city.
29 Now the people having heard a
great noise came running together by
multitudes to know the cause of it;
and when they saw Alma and Amulek coming forth out of the prison,
and the walls thereof had fallen to
the earth, they were struck with
great fear, and fled from the presence of Alma and Amulek even as a
goat fleeth with her young from two
lions; and thus they did flee from
the presence of Alma and Amulek.

CHAPTER 15

Alma and Amulek go to Sidom and establish a church—Alma heals Zeezrom, who joins the Church—Many are baptized, and the Church prospers—Alma and Amulek go to Zarahemla. About 81 B.C.

AND it came to pass that Alma and
Amulek were commanded to depart
out of that city; and they departed,
and came out even into the land of
Sidom; and behold, there they found
all the people who had departed out
of the land of [a]Ammonihah, who had
been [b]cast out and stoned, because
they believed in the words of Alma.
2 And they related unto them all
that had happened unto their [a]wives
and children, and also concerning
themselves, and of their [b]power of
deliverance.
3 And also Zeezrom lay sick at Sidom, with a burning fever, which
was caused by the great tribulations

23*a* Alma 8:6; 15:1 (1, 15–16).
24*a* TG Sign Seekers.
25*a* Alma 8:31.
26*a* James 5:10 (10–11); Mosiah 17:13 (10–20); JS—H 1:22.
b Ps. 69:14 (1–2, 14); D&C 121:3.
c TG Deliver.
27*a* Acts 12:4 (4–6); 16:26; Hel. 5:21 (21–50); 3 Ne. 28:19 (19–20); 4 Ne. 1:30; Ether 12:13.
28*a* Alma 15:2.
b 1 Ne. 7:17 (17–18); Jacob 4:6; 3 Ne. 28:20 (19–22).
c Alma 36:27.
15 1*a* Alma 14:23; 16:2 (2–3, 9, 11).
b Alma 14:7.
2*a* Alma 14:8 (8–14).
b Alma 14:28 (26–29).

of his mind on account of his [a]wick-
edness, for he supposed that Alma
and Amulek were no more; and he
supposed that they had been slain
because of his iniquity. And this
great sin, and his many other sins,
did harrow up his mind until it did
become exceedingly sore, having no
deliverance; therefore he began to
be scorched with a burning heat.
4 Now, when he heard that Alma
and Amulek were in the land of Sidom, his heart began to take courage;
and he sent a message immediately
unto them, desiring them to come
unto him.
5 And it came to pass that they
went immediately, obeying the message which he had sent unto them;
and they went in unto the house
unto Zeezrom; and they found him
upon his bed, sick, being very low
with a burning fever; and his mind
also was [a]exceedingly sore because
of his iniquities; and when he saw
them he stretched forth his hand,
and besought them that they would
heal him.
6 And it came to pass that Alma
said unto him, taking him by the
hand: [a]Believest thou in the power
of Christ unto salvation?
7 And he answered and said: Yea,
I believe all the words that thou
hast taught.
8 And Alma said: If thou believest
in the redemption of Christ thou
canst be [a]healed.
9 And he said: Yea, I believe according to thy words.
10 And then Alma cried unto the
Lord, saying: O Lord our God, have
[a]mercy on this man, and [b]heal him
according to his faith which is in
Christ.
11 And when Alma had said these
words, [a]Zeezrom leaped upon his
feet, and began to walk; and this was
done to the great astonishment of
all the people; and the knowledge
of this went forth throughout all the
land of Sidom.
12 And Alma baptized Zeezrom
unto the Lord; and he began from
that time forth to preach unto the
people.
13 And Alma established a church
in the land of Sidom, and consecrated [a]priests and [b]teachers in the
land, to baptize unto the Lord whosoever were desirous to be baptized.
14 And it came to pass that they
were many; for they did flock in
from all the region round about
Sidom, and were baptized.
15 But as to the people that were
in the land of Ammonihah, they yet
remained a hard-hearted and a stiffnecked people; and they repented
not of their sins, [a]ascribing all the
power of Alma and Amulek to the
devil; for they were of the profession of [b]Nehor, and did not believe
in the repentance of their sins.
16 And it came to pass that Alma
and Amulek, Amulek having [a]for-
saken all his gold, and silver, and
his precious things, which were in
the land of Ammonihah, for the
word of God, he being [b]rejected by
those who were once his friends and
also by his father and his kindred;
17 Therefore, after Alma having
established the church at Sidom,
seeing a great [a]check, yea, seeing
that the people were checked as to
the pride of their hearts, and began
to [b]humble themselves before God,
and began to assemble themselves
together at their [c]sanctuaries to [d]wor-
ship God before the [e]altar, [f]watching
and praying continually, that they
might be delivered from Satan, and
from [g]death, and from destruction—

3a Alma 14:7 (6–7).
5a Alma 14:6.
6a Mark 9:23.
8a TG Administrations to the Sick; Heal.
10a TG Mercy.
b Mark 2:11 (1–12).
11a Acts 3:8 (1–11).
13a Alma 4:20 (7, 16, 18, 20); 16:18.
b TG Teacher.
15a Matt. 12:24 (24–27).
b Alma 1:15 (2–15).
16a Luke 14:33; Alma 10:4.
b TG Prophets, Rejection of.
17a Alma 16:21.
b Ezra 10:1 (1–5).
c Ps. 150:1; Alma 16:13.
d TG Worship.
e Ex. 27:1 (1–8).
f TG Watch.
g TG Death, Spiritual, First.

18 Now as I said, Alma having
seen all these things, therefore he
took Amulek and came over to the
land of Zarahemla, and took him
to his [a]own house, and did administer unto him in his tribulations,
and [b]strengthened him in the Lord.
19 And thus ended the tenth year
of the reign of the judges over the
people of Nephi.

CHAPTER 16

The Lamanites destroy the people of Ammonihah—Zoram leads the Nephites to victory over the Lamanites—Alma and Amulek and many others preach the word—They teach that after His Resurrection Christ will appear to the Nephites. About 81–77 B.C.

AND it came to pass in the eleventh
year of the reign of the judges over
the people of Nephi, on the fifth day
of the second month, there having
been much peace in the land of
Zarahemla, there having been no
wars nor contentions for a certain
number of years, even until the
fifth day of the second month in
the eleventh year, there was a cry
of war heard throughout the land.
2 For behold, the armies of the
Lamanites had come in upon the
wilderness side, into the borders
of the land, even into the city of
[a]Ammonihah, and began to slay the
people and destroy the city.
3 And now it came to pass, before
the Nephites could raise a sufficient
army to drive them out of the land,
they had [a]destroyed the people who
were in the city of Ammonihah,
and also some around the borders
of Noah, and taken others captive
into the wilderness.
4 Now it came to pass that the
Nephites were desirous to obtain
those who had been carried away
captive into the wilderness.
5 Therefore, he that had been
appointed chief captain over the
armies of the Nephites, (and his
name was Zoram, and he had two
sons, Lehi and Aha)—now Zoram
and his two sons, knowing that Alma
was high priest over the church,
and having heard that he had the
spirit of prophecy, therefore they
went unto him and desired of him
to know whither the Lord would
that they should go into the wilderness in search of their brethren,
who had been taken captive by the
Lamanites.
6 And it came to pass that Alma
[a]inquired of the Lord concerning
the matter. And Alma returned
and said unto them: Behold, the
Lamanites will cross the river Sidon
in the south wilderness, away up
beyond the borders of the land of
[b]Manti. And behold there shall ye
meet them, on the east of the river
Sidon, and there the Lord will deliver unto thee thy brethren who
have been taken captive by the
Lamanites.
7 And it came to pass that Zoram
and his sons crossed over the river Sidon, with their armies, and marched
away beyond the borders of Manti
into the south wilderness, which was
on the east side of the river Sidon.
8 And they came upon the armies
of the Lamanites, and the Lamanites were scattered and driven into
the wilderness; and they took their
brethren who had been taken captive by the Lamanites, and there was
not one soul of them had been lost
that were taken captive. And they
were brought by their brethren to
possess their own lands.
9 And thus ended the eleventh
year of the judges, the Lamanites
having been driven out of the land,
and the people of Ammonihah were
[a]destroyed; yea, [b]every living soul

18*a* Alma 27:20.
b Zech. 10:12 (11–12).
16 2*a* Alma 15:1 (1, 15–16); 49:3 (1–15).
3*a* Alma 9:18.
6*a* 2 Kgs. 6:8–12; Alma 43:23 (23–24); 48:16; 3 Ne. 3:20 (18–21).
b Alma 17:1; 22:27; 56:14.
9*a* Alma 8:16; 9:24 (18–24); Morm. 6:15 (15–22).
b Alma 14:11.

of the Ammonihahites was [c]destroyed, and also their [d]great city, which they said God could not destroy, because of its greatness.

10 But behold, in [a]one day it was left desolate; and the [b]carcasses were mangled by dogs and wild beasts of the wilderness.

11 Nevertheless, after many days their [a]dead bodies were heaped up upon the face of the earth, and they were covered with a shallow covering. And now so great was the scent thereof that the people did not go in to possess the land of Ammonihah for many years. And it was called Desolation of [b]Nehors; for they were of the profession of Nehor, who were slain; and their lands remained desolate.

12 And the Lamanites did not come again to war against the Nephites until the fourteenth year of the reign of the judges over the people of Nephi. And thus for three years did the people of Nephi have continual peace in all the land.

13 And Alma and Amulek went forth preaching repentance to the people in their [a]temples, and in their [b]sanctuaries, and also in their [c]synagogues, which were built after the manner of the Jews.

14 And as many as would hear their words, unto them they did impart the word of God, without any [a]respect of persons, continually.

15 And thus did Alma and Amulek go forth, and also many more who had been chosen for the work, to preach the word throughout all the land. And the establishment of the church became general throughout the land, in all the region round about, among all the people of the Nephites.

16 And there was [a]no inequality among them; the Lord did pour out his Spirit on all the face of the land to prepare the minds of the children of men, or to prepare their [b]hearts to receive the word which should be taught among them at the time of his coming—

17 That they might not be hardened against the word, that they might not be unbelieving, and go on to destruction, but that they might receive the word with joy, and as a [a]branch be grafted into the true vine, that they might enter into the [b]rest of the Lord their God.

18 Now those [a]priests who did go forth among the people did preach against all [b]lyings, and [c]deceivings, and [d]envyings, and [e]strifes, and malice, and revilings, and stealing, robbing, plundering, murdering, committing adultery, and all manner of lasciviousness, crying that these things ought not so to be—

19 Holding forth things which must shortly come; yea, holding forth the [a]coming of the Son of God, his sufferings and death, and also the resurrection of the dead.

20 And many of the people did inquire concerning the place where the Son of God should come; and they were taught that he would [a]appear unto them [b]after his resurrection; and this the people did hear with great joy and gladness.

21 And now after the church had been established throughout all the land—having got the [a]victory over

9 *c* Alma 25:2.
d Alma 49:3.
10 *a* Alma 9:4.
b Jer. 19:7.
11 *a* Alma 28:11.
b Alma 1:15; 2:1 (1, 20); 24:28 (28–30).
13 *a* 2 Ne. 5:16; Hel. 3:14 (9, 14).
b Alma 15:17; 21:6.
c Alma 21:20 (4–6, 20).
14 *a* Deut. 10:17; Alma 1:30.
16 *a* Mosiah 18:27 (19–29); 4 Ne. 1:3.
b Acts 16:14. TG Teachable.
17 *a* Jacob 5:24. TG Vineyard of the Lord.
b Alma 12:37; 13:6 (6–29).
18 *a* Alma 15:13; 30:20 (20–23, 31).
b 3 Ne. 30:2.
c TG Deceit.
d TG Envy.
e Alma 4:9 (8–9). TG Strife.
19 *a* TG Jesus Christ, Prophecies about.
20 *a* 2 Ne. 26:9; 3 Ne. 11:8 (7–14).
b 1 Ne. 12:6 (4–8); Alma 7:8.
21 *a* Alma 15:17.

the devil, and the word of God being preached in its purity in all the
land, and the Lord pouring out his
blessings upon the people—thus
ended the fourteenth year of the
reign of the judges over the people of
Nephi.

An account of the sons of Mosiah, who rejected their rights to the kingdom for the word of God, and went up to the land of Nephi to preach to the Lamanites; their sufferings and deliverance—according to the record of Alma.

Comprising chapters 17 through 27.

CHAPTER 17

The sons of Mosiah have the spirit of prophecy and of revelation—They go their several ways to declare the word to the Lamanites—Ammon goes to the land of Ishmael and becomes the servant of King Lamoni—Ammon saves the king's flocks and slays his enemies at the water of Sebus. Verses 1–3, about 77 B.C.; verse 4, about 91–77 B.C.; and verses 5–39, about 91 B.C.

AND now it came to pass that as
Alma was journeying from the land
of Gideon southward, away to the
land of [a]Manti, behold, to his astonishment, he [b]met with the [c]sons
of Mosiah journeying towards the
land of Zarahemla.
2 Now these sons of Mosiah were
with Alma at the time the angel
[a]first appeared unto him; therefore
Alma did rejoice exceedingly to
see his brethren; and what added
more to his joy, they were still his
brethren in the Lord; yea, and they
had waxed strong in the knowledge
of the truth; for they were men of
a sound understanding and they
had [b]searched the scriptures diligently, that they might know the
word of God.
3 But this is not all; they had
given themselves to much prayer,
and [a]fasting; therefore they had the
spirit of prophecy, and the spirit of
revelation, and when they taught,
they taught with [b]power and authority of God.
4 And they had been teaching the
word of God for the space of fourteen
years among the Lamanites, having
had much [a]success in bringing many
to the [b]knowledge of the truth; yea,
by the power of their words many
were brought before the altar of God,
to call on his name and [c]confess
their sins before him.
5 Now these are the circumstances
which attended them in their journeyings, for they had many afflictions; they did suffer much, both in
body and in mind, such as hunger,
thirst and fatigue, and also much
[a]labor in the spirit.
6 Now these were their journeyings: Having [a]taken leave of their
father, Mosiah, in the [b]first year of
the judges; having [c]refused the kingdom which their father was desirous to confer upon them, and also
this was the minds of the people;
7 Nevertheless they departed out
of the land of Zarahemla, and took
their swords, and their spears,
and their bows, and their arrows,
and their slings; and this they did
that they might [a]provide food for
themselves while in the wilderness.
8 And thus they departed into
the wilderness with their numbers
which they had [a]selected, to go up
to the land of Nephi, to preach the
word of God unto the Lamanites.
9 And it came to pass that they

---

17 1*a* Alma 16:6.
b Alma 27:16.
c Mosiah 27:34.
2*a* Mosiah 27:11 (11–17).
b Jacob 7:23; D&C 84:85. TG Scriptures, Study of.
3*a* TG Fast, Fasting.
b W of M 1:17. TG Authority; Teaching with the Spirit.
4*a* Alma 29:14.
b TG Missionary Work.
c Num. 5:7 (6–10); Mosiah 26:29 (29, 35); 3 Ne. 1:25.
5*a* Alma 8:10.
6*a* Mosiah 28:9 (1, 5–9); Alma 26:1.
b Mosiah 29:44 (41–44).
c Mosiah 29:3.
7*a* 1 Ne. 16:15 (15–32).
8*a* Mosiah 28:1.

journeyed many days in the wilderness, and they fasted much and [a]prayed much that the Lord would grant unto them a portion of his Spirit to go with them, and abide with them, that they might be an [b]instrument in the hands of God to bring, if it were possible, their brethren, the Lamanites, to the knowledge of the truth, to the knowledge of the baseness of the [c]traditions of their fathers, which were not correct.

10 And it came to pass that the Lord did [a]visit them with his [b]Spirit, and said unto them: Be [c]comforted. And they were comforted.

11 And the Lord said unto them also: Go forth among the Lamanites, thy brethren, and establish my word; yet ye shall be [a]patient in long-suffering and afflictions, that ye may show forth good [b]examples unto them in me, and I will make an instrument of thee in my hands unto the salvation of many souls.

12 And it came to pass that the hearts of the sons of Mosiah, and also those who were with them, took courage to go forth unto the Lamanites to declare unto them the word of God.

13 And it came to pass when they had arrived in the borders of the land of the Lamanites, that they [a]separated themselves and departed one from another, trusting in the Lord that they should meet again at the close of their [b]harvest; for they supposed that great was the work which they had undertaken.

14 And assuredly it was great, for they had undertaken to preach the word of God to a [a]wild and a hardened and a ferocious people; a people who delighted in murdering the Nephites, and robbing and plundering them; and their hearts were set upon riches, or upon gold and silver, and precious stones; yet they sought to obtain these things by murdering and plundering, that they might not labor for them with their own hands.

15 Thus they were a very indolent people, many of whom did worship idols, and the [a]curse of God had fallen upon them because of the [b]traditions of their fathers; notwithstanding the promises of the Lord were extended unto them on the conditions of repentance.

16 Therefore, this was the [a]cause for which the sons of Mosiah had undertaken the work, that perhaps they might bring them unto repentance; that perhaps they might bring them to know of the plan of redemption.

17 Therefore they separated themselves one from another, and went forth among them, every man alone, according to the word and power of God which was given unto him.

18 Now Ammon being the chief among them, or rather he did administer unto them, and he departed from them, after having [a]blessed them according to their several stations, having imparted the word of God unto them, or administered unto them before his departure; and thus they took their several journeys throughout the land.

19 And Ammon went to the land of [a]Ishmael, the land being called after the sons of [b]Ishmael, who also became Lamanites.

20 And as Ammon entered the land of Ishmael, the Lamanites took him and [a]bound him, as was their custom to bind all the Nephites who fell into their hands, and carry them before the king; and thus it was left to the pleasure of the king to slay them, or to retain them in captivity,

9*a* Alma 25:17. TG Guidance, Divine.
b Mosiah 23:10; Alma 26:3.
c Alma 3:11.
10*a* 1 Ne. 2:16; D&C 5:16.
b TG God, Spirit of.
c Alma 26:27.
11*a* Alma 20:29; 26:27. TG Forbear; Patience.
b TG Example.
13*a* Alma 21:1.
b Matt. 9:37.
14*a* Mosiah 10:12.
15*a* Alma 3:19 (6–19); 3 Ne. 2:15 (15–16).
b Alma 9:16 (16–24); 18:5.
16*a* Mosiah 28:2 (1–3).
18*a* TG Blessing.
19*a* Alma 21:18 (18, 20); 22:1 (1, 4); 25:13.
b 1 Ne. 7:6 (4–6).
20*a* Mosiah 7:7 (7–10).

or to cast them into prison, or to
cast them out of his land, according
to his will and pleasure.
21 And thus Ammon was carried
before the king who was over the
land of Ishmael; and his name was
Lamoni; and he was a descendant
of Ishmael.
22 And the king inquired of Ammon if it were his desire to dwell
in the land among the Lamanites,
or among his people.
23 And Ammon said unto him:
Yea, I desire to [a]dwell among this
people for a time; yea, and perhaps
until the day I die.
24 And it came to pass that king
Lamoni was much pleased with
Ammon, and caused that his bands
should be loosed; and he would
that Ammon should take one of his
daughters to wife.
25 But Ammon said unto him: Nay,
but I will be thy servant. Therefore
Ammon became a [a]servant to king
Lamoni. And it came to pass that
he was set among other servants to
watch the flocks of Lamoni, according to the custom of the Lamanites.
26 And after he had been in the
service of the king three days, as he
was with the Lamanitish servants
going forth with their flocks to the
place of [a]water, which was called
the water of Sebus, and all the Lamanites drive their flocks hither,
that they may have water—
27 Therefore, as Ammon and the
servants of the king were driving
forth their flocks to this place of
water, behold, a certain number of
the Lamanites, who had been with
their flocks to water, stood and
[a]scattered the flocks of Ammon and
the servants of the king, and they
scattered them insomuch that they
fled many ways.
28 Now the servants of the king
began to murmur, saying: Now
the king will slay us, as he has our
brethren because their flocks were
scattered by the wickedness of these
men. And they began to weep exceedingly, saying: Behold, our flocks
are scattered already.
29 Now they wept because of the
fear of being slain. Now when Ammon saw this his heart was swollen
within him with joy; for, said he,
I will show forth my power unto
these my fellow-servants, or the
power which is in me, in restoring
these flocks unto the king, that I
may win the hearts of these my
fellow-servants, that I may lead
them to [a]believe in my words.
30 And now, these were the
thoughts of Ammon, when he saw
the afflictions of those whom he
termed to be his brethren.
31 And it came to pass that he flattered them by his words, saying: My
brethren, be of good cheer and let
us go in search of the flocks, and
we will gather them together and
bring them back unto the place of
water; and thus we will preserve
the flocks unto the king and he
will not slay us.
32 And it came to pass that they
went in search of the flocks, and
they did follow Ammon, and they
rushed forth with much swiftness
and did head the flocks of the
king, and did gather them together
again to the place of water.
33 And those men again stood to
scatter their flocks; but Ammon
said unto his brethren: Encircle
the flocks round about that they
flee not; and I go and contend with
these men who do scatter our flocks.
34 Therefore, they did as Ammon
commanded them, and he went forth
and stood to contend with those
who stood by the waters of Sebus;
and they were in number not a few.
35 Therefore they did not fear
Ammon, for they supposed that
one of their men could slay him
according to their pleasure, for
they knew not that the Lord had

23*a* Alma 19:19.
25*a* Alma 21:19.
26*a* Ex. 2:17 (15–20).
27*a* Alma 18:3 (3–7); 19:21 (20–21).
29*a* 2 Kgs. 5:8.
35*a* Mosiah 28:7; Alma 19:23 (22–23).

promised Mosiah that he would [a]deliver his sons out of their hands; neither did they know anything concerning the Lord; therefore they delighted in the destruction of their brethren; and for this cause they stood to scatter the flocks of the king.

36 But [a]Ammon stood forth and began to cast stones at them with his sling; yea, with mighty power he did sling stones amongst them; and thus he slew a [b]certain number of them insomuch that they began to be astonished at his power; nevertheless they were angry because of the slain of their brethren, and they were determined that he should fall; therefore, seeing that they [c]could not hit him with their stones, they came forth with clubs to slay him.

37 But behold, every man that lifted his club to smite Ammon, he smote off their arms with his sword; for he did withstand their blows by smiting their arms with the edge of his sword, insomuch that they began to be astonished, and began to flee before him; yea, and they were not few in number; and he caused them to flee by the strength of his arm.

38 Now six of them had fallen by the sling, but he [a]slew none save it were their leader with his sword; and he smote off as many of their arms as were lifted against him, and they were not a few.

39 And when he had driven them afar off, he returned and they watered their flocks and returned them to the pasture of the king, and then went in unto the king, bearing the arms which had been smitten off by the sword of Ammon, of those who sought to slay him; and they were carried in unto the king for a testimony of the things which they had done.

CHAPTER 18

King Lamoni supposes that Ammon is the Great Spirit—Ammon teaches the king about the Creation, God's dealings with men, and the redemption that comes through Christ—Lamoni believes and falls to the earth as if dead. About 90 B.C.

AND it came to pass that king Lamoni caused that his [a]servants should stand forth and testify to all the things which they had seen concerning the matter.

2 And when they had all testified to the things which they had seen, and he had learned of the faithfulness of Ammon in preserving his flocks, and also of his [a]great power in contending against those who sought to slay him, he was astonished exceedingly, and said: Surely, this is more than a man. Behold, is not this the Great Spirit who doth send such great punishments upon this people, because of their murders?

3 And they answered the king, and said: Whether he be the Great Spirit or a man, we know not; but this much we do know, that he [a]cannot be slain by the enemies of the king; neither can they [b]scatter the king's flocks when he is with us, because of his expertness and [c]great strength; therefore, we know that he is a friend to the king. And now, O king, we do not believe that a man has such great power, for we know he cannot be slain.

4 And now, when the king heard these words, he said unto them: Now I know that it is the Great Spirit; and he has come down at this time to preserve your lives, that I might not [a]slay you as I did your brethren. Now this is the Great Spirit of whom our fathers have spoken.

5 Now this was the [a]tradition of Lamoni, which he had received

36*a* Ether 12:15.
b Alma 18:16 (16, 20).
c Alma 18:3.
38*a* Alma 19:22.

18 1*a* Alma 19:15.
2*a* Alma 22:9 (9–11).
3*a* Alma 17:36 (34–38).
b Alma 17:27; 19:21 (20–21).
c Alma 22:20.
4*a* Alma 17:28 (28–31).
5*a* Alma 17:15; 60:32.

from his father, that there was a
[b]Great Spirit. Notwithstanding they
believed in a Great Spirit, they supposed that [c]whatsoever they did was
right; nevertheless, Lamoni began
to fear exceedingly, with fear lest
he had done wrong in slaying his
servants;
6 For he had slain many of them
because their brethren had scattered
their flocks at the place of water;
and thus, because they had had their
flocks scattered they were slain.
7 Now it was the practice of these
Lamanites to stand by the [a]waters
of Sebus to scatter the flocks of the
people, that thereby they might
drive away many that were scattered unto their own land, it being
a practice of plunder among them.
8 And it came to pass that king
Lamoni inquired of his servants,
saying: Where is this man that has
such great power?
9 And they said unto him: Behold,
he is feeding thy [a]horses. Now the
king had commanded his servants,
previous to the time of the water-
ing of their flocks, that they should
prepare his horses and chariots,
and conduct him forth to the land
of Nephi; for there had been a
[b]great [c]feast appointed at the land
of Nephi, by the father of Lamoni,
who was king over all the land.
10 Now when king Lamoni heard
that Ammon was preparing his
horses and his [a]chariots he was more
astonished, because of the faithfulness of Ammon, saying: Surely there
has not been any servant among all
my servants that has been so faithful as this man; for even he doth
remember all my commandments
to execute them.
11 Now I surely know that this is
the Great Spirit, and I would desire
him that he come in unto me, but
I durst not.
12 And it came to pass that when
Ammon had made ready the horses
and the chariots for the king and
his servants, he went in unto the
king, and he saw that the [a]coun-
tenance of the king was changed;
therefore he was about to return
out of his presence.
13 And one of the king's servants
said unto him, [a]Rabbanah, which
is, being interpreted, powerful or
great king, considering their kings
to be powerful; and thus he said
unto him: Rabbanah, the king desireth thee to stay.
14 Therefore Ammon turned himself unto the king, and said unto
him: What wilt thou that I should
do for thee, O king? And the king
answered him not for the space of
an [a]hour, according to their time,
for he knew not what he should
say unto him.
15 And it came to pass that Ammon said unto him again: What
desirest thou of me? But the king
answered him not.
16 And it came to pass that Ammon, being filled with the [a]Spirit
of God, therefore he perceived the
[b]thoughts of the king. And he said
unto him: Is it because thou hast
heard that I defended thy servants
and thy flocks, and slew [c]seven of
their brethren with the sling and
with the sword, and smote off the
arms of others, in order to defend thy
flocks and thy servants; behold, is
it this that causeth thy marvelings?
17 I say unto you, what is it, that
thy marvelings are so great? Behold,
I am a [a]man, and am thy servant;
therefore, whatsoever thou desirest
which is right, that will I do.
18 Now when the king had heard

5*b* Alma 19:25 (25–27). TG God, Knowledge about.
c Alma 30:17.
7*a* Alma 17:26; 19:20 (20–21).
9*a* Enos 1:21; Alma 20:6.
b Alma 20:9 (9, 12).
c Esth. 1:3.
10*a* Alma 20:6; 3 Ne. 3:22.
12*a* Dan. 5:6.
13*a* John 20:16.
14*a* 3 Ne. 8:19.
16*a* Gen. 41:38; 1 Ne. 1:12; Mosiah 27:24.
b Alma 12:3.
c Alma 17:36.
17*a* Dan. 2:30.

these words, he marveled again,
for he beheld that Ammon could
[a]discern his thoughts; but notwithstanding this, king Lamoni did open
his mouth, and said unto him: Who
art thou? Art thou that Great Spirit,
who [b]knows all things?
19 Ammon answered and said unto
him: I am not.
20 And the king said: How knowest thou the thoughts of my heart?
Thou mayest speak boldly, and tell
me concerning these things; and also
tell me by what power ye slew and
smote off the arms of my brethren
that scattered my flocks—
21 And now, [a]if thou wilt tell me
concerning these things, whatsoever thou desirest I will give unto
thee; and if it were needed, I would
guard thee with my armies; but I
know that thou art more powerful
than all they; nevertheless, whatsoever thou desirest of me I will
grant it unto thee.
22 Now Ammon being [a]wise, yet
harmless, he said unto Lamoni: Wilt
thou hearken unto my words, if I
tell thee by what power I do these
things? And this is the thing that I
desire of thee.
23 And the king answered him,
and said: Yea, I [a]will believe all
thy words. And thus he was caught
with [b]guile.
24 And Ammon began to speak
unto him with [a]boldness, and
said unto him: Believest thou that
there is a God?
25 And he answered, and said
unto him: I do not know what that
meaneth.
26 And then Ammon said: Believest
thou that there is a [a]Great Spirit?
27 And he said, Yea.
28 And Ammon said: This is God.
And Ammon said unto him again:
Believest thou that this Great Spirit,
who is God, created all things which
are in heaven and in the earth?
29 And he said: Yea, I believe that
he created all things which are in
the earth; but I do not know the
heavens.
30 And Ammon said unto him:
The heavens is a place where God
dwells and all his holy angels.
31 And king Lamoni said: Is it
above the earth?
32 And Ammon said: Yea, and he
looketh down upon all the children of men; and he [a]knows all the
thoughts and [b]intents of the heart;
for by his hand were they all created from the beginning.
33 And king Lamoni said: I believe
all these things which thou hast
spoken. Art thou [a]sent from God?
34 Ammon said unto him: I am a
[a]man; and man in the beginning was
created after the image of God, and I
am called by his [b]Holy Spirit to teach
these things unto this people, that
they may be brought to a knowledge
of that which is just and true;
35 And a portion of that [a]Spirit
dwelleth in me, which giveth me
[b]knowledge, and also power according to my faith and desires which
are in God.
36 Now when Ammon had said
these words, he began at the creation of the world, and also the
creation of Adam, and told him all
the things concerning the fall of
man, and [a]rehearsed and laid before him the [b]records and the holy
scriptures of the people, which had
been spoken by the [c]prophets, even
down to the time that their father,
Lehi, left Jerusalem.
37 And he also rehearsed unto

18*a* TG Discernment, Spiritual.
b TG God, Omniscience of.
21*a* Dan. 5:16.
22*a* Gen. 41:39; Alma 48:11 (11–17).
23*a* Alma 18:40.
b Josh. 9:22.
24*a* Alma 38:12.
26*a* Alma 22:9 (9–10).
32*a* TG God, Omniscience of.
b Amos 4:13; 3 Ne. 28:6.
33*a* 2 Chr. 24:19.
34*a* Mosiah 7:27; Ether 3:15 (13–16).
b TG Teaching with the Spirit.
35*a* TG Inspiration.
b TG Knowledge.
36*a* Mosiah 1:4; Alma 22:12; 36:1; 37:9; Hel. 5:13 (1–13); Moses 6:58.
b Alma 63:12. TG Scriptures, Value of.
c Acts 3:18 (18–21); 28:23.

them (for it was unto the king and to
his servants) all the journeyings of
their fathers in the wilderness, and
all their sufferings with hunger and
thirst, and their travail, and so forth.
38 And he also rehearsed unto them
concerning the [a]rebellions of Laman
and Lemuel, and the sons of Ishmael,
yea, all their rebellions did he relate
unto them; and he expounded unto
them all the [b]records and scriptures
from the time that Lehi left Jerusalem down to the present time.
39 But this is not all; for he [a]ex-
pounded unto them the [b]plan of
redemption, which was prepared
from the foundation of the world;
and he also made known unto them
concerning the coming of Christ,
and all the works of the Lord did
he make known unto them.
40 And it came to pass that after
he had said all these things, and
expounded them to the king, that
the king [a]believed all his words.
41 And he began to cry unto the
Lord, saying: O Lord, have mercy;
according to thy abundant [a]mercy
which thou hast had upon the people of Nephi, have upon me, and
my people.
42 And now, when he had said
this, he [a]fell unto the earth, [b]as if
he were dead.
43 And it came to pass that his
[a]servants took him and carried him
in unto his wife, and laid him upon
a bed; and he lay as if he were dead
for the space of two days and two
nights; and his wife, and his sons,
and his daughters mourned over
him, after the manner of the Lamanites, greatly lamenting his loss.

CHAPTER 19

Lamoni receives the light of everlasting life and sees the Redeemer—His household falls into a trance, and many see angels—Ammon is preserved miraculously—He baptizes many and establishes a church among them. About 90 B.C.

AND it came to pass that after two
days and two nights they were about
to take his [a]body and lay it in a sepulchre, which they had made for
the purpose of burying their dead.
2 Now the queen having heard of
the fame of Ammon, therefore she
sent and desired that he should
come in unto her.
3 And it came to pass that Ammon
did as he was commanded, and
went in unto the queen, and desired
to know what she would that he
should do.
4 And she said unto him: The [a]ser-
vants of my husband have made it
known unto me that thou art a
[b]prophet of a holy God, and that
thou hast [c]power to do many mighty
works in his name;
5 Therefore, if this is the case, I
would that ye should go in and
see my husband, for he has been
laid upon his bed for the space
of two days and two nights; and
some say that he is not dead, but
others say that he is dead and that
he [a]stinketh, and that he ought to
be placed in the sepulchre; but as
for myself, to me he doth not stink.
6 Now, this was what Ammon desired, for he knew that king Lamoni was under the power of God; he
knew that the dark [a]veil of [b]unbe-
lief was being cast away from his
mind, and the [c]light which did light
up his mind, which was the light of
the glory of God, which was a marvelous light of his goodness—yea,
this light had infused such joy into
his soul, the cloud of darkness having been dispelled, and that the
light of everlasting life was lit up in

38*a* 2 Ne. 1:2.
b 1 Ne. 9:2.
39*a* Alma 19:31.
TG Missionary Work.
b TG Salvation, Plan of.
40*a* Alma 18:23.
41*a* TG God, Mercy of.
42*a* Alma 19:1 (1, 5–12).
b Alma 22:18.
43*a* Alma 19:4 (4–5).
19 1*a* Alma 18:42 (42–43).
4*a* Alma 18:43.
b TG Prophets, Mission of.
c D&C 3:4.
5*a* John 11:39.
6*a* 2 Cor. 4:4 (3–4).
TG Veil.
b TG Unbelief.
c TG Light [noun].

his soul, yea, he knew that this had
[d]overcome his natural frame, and
he was carried away in God—
7 Therefore, what the queen desired of him was his only desire.
Therefore, he went in to see the
king according as the queen had
desired him; and he saw the king,
and he knew that he was not dead.
8 And he said unto the queen:
He is not dead, but he sleepeth in
God, and on the morrow he shall
rise again; therefore bury him not.
9 And Ammon said unto her:
[a]Believest thou this? And she said
unto him: I have had no witness
save thy word, and the word of our
servants; nevertheless I [b]believe
that it shall be according as thou
hast said.
10 And Ammon said unto her:
Blessed art thou because of thy
exceeding faith; I say unto thee,
woman, there has not been such
great faith among all the people of
the [a]Nephites.
11 And it came to pass that she
watched over the bed of her husband, from that time even until that
time on the morrow which Ammon
had appointed that he should rise.
12 And it came to pass that he
arose, according to the words of Ammon; and as he arose, he stretched
forth his hand unto the woman,
and said: Blessed be the name of
God, and blessed art thou.
13 For as sure as thou livest, behold, I have [a]seen my Redeemer;
and he shall come forth, and be
[b]born of a [c]woman, and he shall redeem all mankind who believe on
his name. Now, when he had said
these words, his heart was swollen
within him, and he sunk again with
joy; and the queen also sunk down,
being overpowered by the Spirit.
14 Now Ammon seeing the Spirit
of the Lord poured out according to
his [a]prayers upon the Lamanites, his
brethren, who had been the cause
of so much mourning among the
Nephites, or among all the people
of God because of their iniquities
and their [b]traditions, he fell upon
his knees, and began to pour out his
soul in prayer and thanksgiving to
God for what he had done for his
brethren; and he was also overpowered with [c]joy; and thus they all
three had [d]sunk to the earth.
15 Now, when the servants of the
king had seen that they had fallen,
they also began to cry unto God,
for the fear of the Lord had come
upon them also, for it was [a]they
who had stood before the king and
testified unto him concerning the
great power of Ammon.
16 And it came to pass that they
did call on the name of the Lord, in
their might, even until they had all
fallen to the earth, save it were one
of the Lamanitish [a]women, whose
name was Abish, she having been
converted unto the Lord for many
years, on account of a remarkable
vision of her father—
17 Thus, having been converted to
the Lord, and never having made
it [a]known, therefore, when she saw
that all the servants of Lamoni had
[b]fallen to the earth, and also her
mistress, the queen, and the king,
and Ammon lay [c]prostrate upon
the earth, she knew that it was the
power of God; and supposing that
this opportunity, by making known
unto the people what had happened
among them, that by beholding this
scene it would [d]cause them to believe in the power of God, therefore
she ran forth from house to house,
making it known unto the people.
18 And they began to assemble
themselves together unto the house

6*d* Jacob 7:21; Mosiah 3:19.
9*a* John 11:26 (22–45).
b Mosiah 26:15 (15–16).
10*a* Luke 7:9.
13*a* TG God, Privilege of Seeing; Jesus Christ, Appearances, Antemortal.
b TG Jesus Christ, Birth of.
c 1 Ne. 11:18 (13–21).
14*a* D&C 42:14.
b Mosiah 1:5.
c TG Joy.
d Alma 27:17.
15*a* Alma 18:1 (1–2).
16*a* Alma 19:28.
17*a* JS—H 1:74.
b Mosiah 4:1.
c Moses 1:9 (9–10).
d Mosiah 27:14.

of the king. And there came a multitude, and to their astonishment, they beheld the king, and the queen, and their servants prostrate upon the earth, and they all lay there as though they were dead; and they also saw Ammon, and behold, he was a Nephite.

19 And now the people began to murmur among themselves; some saying that it was a great evil that had come upon them, or upon the king and his house, because he had suffered that the Nephite should [a]remain in the land.

20 But others rebuked them, saying: The king hath brought this evil upon his house, because he slew his servants who had had their flocks scattered at the [a]waters of Sebus.

21 And they were also rebuked by those men who had stood at the waters of Sebus and [a]scattered the flocks which belonged to the king, for they were angry with Ammon because of the number which he had slain of their brethren at the waters of Sebus, while defending the flocks of the king.

22 Now, one of them, whose brother had been [a]slain with the sword of Ammon, being exceedingly angry with Ammon, drew his sword and went forth that he might let it fall upon Ammon, to slay him; and as he lifted the sword to smite him, behold, he fell dead.

23 Now we see that Ammon could not be slain, for the [a]Lord had said unto Mosiah, his father: I will spare him, and it shall be unto him according to thy faith—therefore, Mosiah [b]trusted him unto the Lord.

24 And it came to pass that when the multitude beheld that the man had fallen dead, who lifted the sword to slay Ammon, [a]fear came upon them all, and they durst not put forth their hands to touch him or any of those who had fallen; and they began to marvel again among themselves what could be the cause of this great power, or what all these things could mean.

25 And it came to pass that there were many among them who said that Ammon was the [a]Great Spirit, and others said he was sent by the Great Spirit;

26 But others rebuked them all, saying that he was a [a]monster, who had been sent from the Nephites to torment them.

27 And there were some who said that Ammon was sent by the Great Spirit to afflict them because of their iniquities; and that it was the Great Spirit that had always attended the Nephites, who had ever delivered them out of their hands; and they said that it was this Great Spirit who had destroyed so many of their brethren, the Lamanites.

28 And thus the contention began to be exceedingly sharp among them. And while they were thus contending, the [a]woman servant who had caused the multitude to be gathered together came, and when she saw the contention which was among the multitude she was exceedingly sorrowful, even unto tears.

29 And it came to pass that she went and took the queen by the [a]hand, that perhaps she might raise her from the ground; and as soon as she touched her hand she arose and stood upon her feet, and cried with a loud voice, saying: O blessed Jesus, who has saved me from an [b]awful hell! O blessed God, have [c]mercy on this people!

30 And when she had said this, she clasped her hands, being filled with joy, speaking many words which were not understood; and when she had done this, she took the king,

19*a* Alma 17:23 (22–23).
20*a* Alma 17:26; 18:7.
21*a* Alma 17:27; 18:3.
22*a* Alma 17:38.
23*a* Mosiah 28:7; Alma 17:35.
b TG Family, Love within; Trust in God.
24*a* Luke 7:16; Moses 6:39 (37–40).
25*a* Alma 18:5 (2–5).
26*a* Moses 6:38 (37–39).
28*a* Alma 19:16.
29*a* Alma 22:22.
b 1 Ne. 14:3.
c Enos 1:9; Alma 36:24.

Lamoni, by the hand, and behold
he arose and stood upon his feet.
31 And he, immediately, seeing
the contention among his people,
went forth and began to rebuke
them, and to teach them the [a]words
which he had heard from the mouth
of Ammon; and as many as heard
his words believed, and were converted unto the Lord.
32 But there were [a]many among
them who would not hear his words;
therefore they went their way.
33 And it came to pass that when
Ammon arose he also administered
unto them, and also did all the servants of Lamoni; and they did all
declare unto the people the selfsame
thing—that their hearts had been
[a]changed; that they had no more
desire to do [b]evil.
34 And behold, many did declare
unto the people that they had seen
[a]angels and had conversed with them;
and thus they had told them things
of God, and of his righteousness.
35 And it came to pass that there
were many that did [a]believe in their
words; and as many as did believe
were baptized; and they became a
righteous people, and they did establish a church among them.
36 And thus the work of the Lord
did commence among the Lamanites; thus the Lord did begin to pour
out his [a]Spirit upon them; and we
see that his arm is extended to [b]all
people who will repent and believe
on his name.

CHAPTER 20

The Lord sends Ammon to Middoni to deliver his imprisoned brethren—Ammon and Lamoni meet Lamoni's father, who is king over all the land—Ammon compels the old king to approve the release of his brethren. About 90 B.C.

AND it came to pass that when they
had established a church in that
[a]land, that king Lamoni desired that
Ammon should go with him to the
land of Nephi, that he might show
him unto his father.
2 And the voice of the Lord came
to Ammon, saying: Thou shalt not go
up to the land of Nephi, for behold,
the king will seek thy life; but thou
shalt go to the land of [a]Middoni; for
behold, thy brother Aaron, and also
Muloki and Ammah are in prison.
3 Now it came to pass that when
Ammon had heard this, he said unto
Lamoni: Behold, my brother and
brethren are in prison at Middoni,
and I go that I may deliver them.
4 Now Lamoni said unto Ammon:
I know, in the [a]strength of the Lord
thou canst do all things. But behold,
I will go with thee to the land of
Middoni; for the king of the land
of Middoni, whose name is Anti-
omno, is a friend unto me; therefore
I go to the land of Middoni, that I
may flatter the king of the land,
and he will cast thy brethren out
of [b]prison. Now Lamoni said unto
him: Who told thee that thy brethren were in prison?
5 And Ammon said unto him: No
one hath told me, save it be God;
and he said unto me—Go and deliver thy brethren, for they are in
prison in the land of Middoni.
6 Now when Lamoni had heard
this he caused that his servants
should make ready his [a]horses and
his chariots.
7 And he said unto Ammon: Come,
I will go with thee down to the land
of Middoni, and there I will plead
with the king that he will cast thy
brethren out of prison.
8 And it came to pass that as Ammon and Lamoni were journeying

31*a* Alma 18:39 (36–39).
32*a* John 12:37 (35–37).
33*a* TG Man, New, Spiritually Reborn.
b Jonah 3:8; Mosiah 5:2; Alma 13:12; 3 Ne. 20:26.
34*a* TG Angels; Vision.
35*a* TG Baptism, Qualifications for.
36*a* TG God, Spirit of.
b 2 Ne. 26:33; Alma 5:33; 3 Ne. 18:25.
20 1*a* 2 Ne. 5:8; Alma 2:24.
2*a* Alma 21:12 (12–13, 18); 23:10.
4*a* TG Strength.
b Alma 20:22; 22:2.
6*a* Alma 18:9.

thither, they met the father of
Lamoni, who was king [a]over all
the land.
9 And behold, the father of Lamoni said unto him: Why did ye
[a]not come to the [b]feast on that great
day when I made a feast unto my
sons, and unto my people?
10 And he also said: Whither art
thou going with this Nephite, who
is one of the children of a [a]liar?
11 And it came to pass that Lamoni rehearsed unto him whither
he was going, for he feared to offend
him.
12 And he also told him all the
cause of his tarrying in his own
kingdom, that he did not go unto
his father to the feast which he had
prepared.
13 And now when Lamoni had rehearsed unto him all these things,
behold, to his astonishment, his
father was angry with him, and said:
Lamoni, thou art going to deliver
these Nephites, who are sons of a
liar. Behold, he robbed our fathers;
and now his children are also come
amongst us that they may, by their
cunning and their lyings, deceive
us, that they again may rob us of
our property.
14 Now the father of Lamoni commanded him that he should slay
Ammon with the sword. And he
also commanded him that he should
not go to the land of Middoni, but
that he should return with him to
the land of [a]Ishmael.
15 But Lamoni said unto him: I
will not slay Ammon, neither will
I return to the land of Ishmael, but
I go to the land of Middoni that I
may release the brethren of Ammon,
for I know that they are just men
and holy prophets of the true God.
16 Now when his father had heard
these words, he was angry with
him, and he drew his sword that
he might smite him to the earth.
17 But Ammon stood forth and
said unto him: Behold, thou shalt
not slay thy son; nevertheless, it
were [a]better that he should fall than
thee, for behold, he has [b]repented
of his sins; but if thou shouldst fall
at this time, in thine anger, thy soul
could not be saved.
18 And again, it is expedient that
thou shouldst forbear; for if thou
shouldst [a]slay thy son, he being an
innocent man, his blood would cry
from the ground to the Lord his
God, for vengeance to come upon
thee; and perhaps thou wouldst
lose thy [b]soul.
19 Now when Ammon had said
these words unto him, he answered
him, saying: I know that if I should
slay my son, that I should shed innocent blood; for it is thou that hast
sought to destroy him.
20 And he stretched forth his hand
to slay Ammon. But Ammon withstood his blows, and also smote his
arm that he could not use it.
21 Now when the king saw that
Ammon could slay him, he began
to plead with Ammon that he would
spare his life.
22 But Ammon raised his sword,
and said unto him: Behold, I will
smite thee except thou wilt grant
unto me that my brethren may be
[a]cast out of prison.
23 Now the king, fearing he should
lose his life, said: If thou wilt spare
me I will grant unto thee whatsoever thou wilt ask, even to half of
the kingdom.
24 Now when Ammon saw that he
had wrought upon the old king according to his desire, he said unto
him: If thou wilt grant that my
brethren may be cast out of prison,
and also that Lamoni may retain his
kingdom, and that ye be not displeased with him, but grant that he
may do according to his own desires
in [a]whatsoever thing he thinketh,

8*a* Alma 22:1.
9*a* 1 Sam. 20:27.
b Alma 18:9.
10*a* Mosiah 10:16 (12–17).
14*a* Alma 17:19.
17*a* Alma 48:23.
b Alma 22:6.
18*a* TG Murder.
b D&C 42:18.
22*a* Alma 20:4.
24*a* Alma 21:21 (21–22); 22:1.

then will I spare thee; otherwise I
will smite thee to the earth.
25 Now when Ammon had said
these words, the king began to rejoice because of his life.
26 And when he saw that Ammon
had no desire to destroy him, and
when he also saw the great [a]love
he had for his son Lamoni, he was
astonished exceedingly, and said:
Because this is all that thou hast
desired, that I would [b]release thy
brethren, and suffer that my son
Lamoni should retain his kingdom,
behold, I will grant unto you that
my son may retain his kingdom
from this time and forever; and I
will govern him no more—
27 And I will also grant unto thee
that thy brethren may be cast out
of prison, and thou and thy brethren may come unto me, in my kingdom; for I shall greatly desire to
see thee. For the king was greatly
astonished at the words which he
had spoken, and also at the words
which had been spoken by his son
Lamoni, therefore he was [a]desirous to
learn them.
28 And it came to pass that Ammon and Lamoni proceeded on
their journey towards the land of
Middoni. And Lamoni found favor
in the eyes of the king of the land;
therefore the brethren of Ammon
were brought forth out of prison.
29 And when Ammon did meet
them he was exceedingly sorrowful,
for behold they were naked, and
their skins were worn exceedingly
because of being bound with strong
cords. And they also had [a]suffered
hunger, thirst, and all kinds of afflictions; nevertheless they were
[b]patient in all their sufferings.
30 And, as it happened, it was their
lot to have fallen into the hands of
a more hardened and a more [a]stiff-
necked people; therefore they would
not hearken unto their words, and
they had cast them out, and had
smitten them, and had driven them
from house to house, and from
place to place, even until they had
arrived in the land of Middoni; and
there they were taken and cast into
prison, and bound with [b]strong
cords, and kept in prison for many
days, and were delivered by Lamoni
and Ammon.

An account of the preaching of Aaron, and Muloki, and their brethren, to the Lamanites.

Comprising chapters 21 through 25.

CHAPTER 21

Aaron teaches the Amalekites about Christ and His Atonement—Aaron and his brethren are imprisoned in Middoni—After their deliverance, they teach in the synagogues and make many converts—Lamoni grants religious freedom to the people in the land of Ishmael. About 90–77 B.C.

NOW when Ammon and his brethren [a]separated themselves in the
borders of the land of the Lamanites, behold Aaron took his journey
towards the land which was called
by the Lamanites, [b]Jerusalem, calling it after the land of their fathers'
nativity; and it was away joining
the borders of Mormon.
2 Now the Lamanites and the
Amalekites and the people of [a]Amu-
lon had built a great city, which
was called Jerusalem.
3 Now the Lamanites of themselves
were sufficiently hardened, but
the Amalekites and the Amulonites
were still harder; therefore they
did cause the Lamanites that they
should harden their hearts, that
they should wax strong in wickedness and their abominations.
4 And it came to pass that Aaron
came to the city of Jerusalem, and

26*a* 2 Sam. 1:26.
TG Loyalty.
b Alma 22:2.
27*a* TG Teachable.
29*a* Alma 21:14.
b Alma 17:11.
30*a* TG Stiffnecked.
b Alma 26:29.
21 1*a* Alma 17:13 (13, 17).
b Alma 24:1;
3 Ne. 9:7.
2*a* Mosiah 23:31; 24:1;
Alma 24:1 (1, 28–30);
25:7 (4–9).

first began to preach to the Amalekites. And he began to preach to
them in their [a]synagogues, for they
had built synagogues after the [b]or-
der of the Nehors; for many of the
Amalekites and the Amulonites
were after the order of the Nehors.
5 Therefore, as Aaron entered into
one of their [a]synagogues to preach
unto the people, and as he was
speaking unto them, behold there
arose an Amalekite and began to
contend with him, saying: What is
that thou hast testified? Hast thou
seen an [b]angel? Why do not angels
appear unto us? Behold [c]are not
this people as good as thy people?
6 Thou also sayest, except we repent we shall perish. How knowest
thou the thought and intent of our
hearts? How knowest thou that we
have cause to repent? How knowest
thou that we are not a [a]righteous people? Behold, we have built [b]sanctu-
aries, and we do assemble ourselves
together to worship [c]God. We do
believe that God will save all men.
7 Now Aaron said unto him: Believest thou that the Son of God
shall come to redeem mankind
from their sins?
8 And the man said unto him: We
do not [a]believe that thou knowest
any such thing. We do not believe
in these foolish traditions. We do
not believe that thou knowest of
things to come, neither do we believe that thy fathers and also that
our fathers did know concerning
the things which they spake, of that
which is to come.
9 Now Aaron began to open the
[a]scriptures unto them concerning the coming of Christ, and also
concerning the resurrection of the
dead, and that there could be [b]no
redemption for mankind [c]save it
were through the [d]death and sufferings of Christ, and the atonement of
his blood.
10 And it came to pass as he began
to expound these things unto them
they were angry with him, and began to [a]mock him; and they would
not hear the words which he spake.
11 Therefore, when he saw that
they would not hear his words, he
departed out of their synagogue,
and came over to a village which
was called Ani-Anti, and there he
found Muloki preaching the word
unto them; and also Ammah and
his brethren. And they contended
with many about the word.
12 And it came to pass that they
saw that the people would harden
their hearts, therefore they departed
and came over into the land of
[a]Middoni. And they did preach the
word unto many, and [b]few believed
on the words which they taught.
13 Nevertheless, Aaron and a certain number of his brethren were
taken and cast into [a]prison, and the
remainder of them fled out of the
land of Middoni unto the regions
round about.
14 And those who were cast into
prison [a]suffered many things, and
they were delivered by the hand
of Lamoni and Ammon, and they
were fed and clothed.
15 And they went forth again to
declare the word, and thus they were
delivered for the first time out of
prison; and thus they had suffered.
16 And they went forth whithersoever they were led by the [a]Spirit
of the Lord, preaching the word
of God in every synagogue of the
Amalekites, or in every assembly
of the Lamanites where they could
be admitted.
17 And it came to pass that the

4*a* D&C 66:7.
b Alma 1:12 (2–15); 14:16; 24:28.
5*a* Alma 16:13.
b Mosiah 27:11 (11–15).
c Moses 8:21.
6*a* Jer. 2:35; Mosiah 12:14 (9–15).
b Alma 15:17; 16:13; 23:2; Hel. 3:14 (9, 14).
c Alma 1:4.
8*a* Jacob 7:2 (1–7).
9*a* Alma 25:6.
b Alma 22:14 (13–14).
c Mosiah 5:8; Alma 38:9.
d TG Jesus Christ, Death of.
10*a* TG Mocking.
12*a* Alma 23:10.
b Matt. 7:14.
13*a* Alma 20:2.
14*a* Alma 20:29.
16*a* Acts 16:6; Alma 22:1 (1–4).

Lord began to bless them, insomuch that they brought many to the knowledge of the truth; yea, they did [a]convince many of their sins, and of the traditions of their fathers, which were not correct.

18 And it came to pass that Ammon and Lamoni returned from the land of Middoni to the land of [a]Ishmael, which was the land of their inheritance.

19 And king Lamoni would not suffer that Ammon should serve him, or be his [a]servant.

20 But he caused that there should be [a]synagogues built in the land of Ishmael; and he caused that his people, or the people who were under his reign, should assemble themselves together.

21 And he did rejoice over them, and he did teach them many things. And he did also declare unto them that they were a people who were under him, and that they were a [a]free people, that they were free from the oppressions of the king, his father; for that his father had granted unto him that he might reign over the people who were in the land of Ishmael, and in all the land round about.

22 And he also declared unto them that they might have the [a]liberty of worshiping the Lord their God according to their desires, in whatsoever place they were in, if it were in the land which was under the reign of king Lamoni.

23 And Ammon did preach unto the people of king Lamoni; and it came to pass that he did teach them all things concerning things pertaining to righteousness. And he did exhort them daily, with all diligence; and they gave heed unto his word, and they were [a]zealous for keeping the commandments of God.

CHAPTER 22

Aaron teaches Lamoni's father about the Creation, the Fall of Adam, and the plan of redemption through Christ—The king and all his household are converted—The division of the land between the Nephites and the Lamanites is explained. About 90–77 B.C.

NOW, as Ammon was thus teaching the people of Lamoni continually, we will return to the account of Aaron and his brethren; for after he departed from the land of Middoni he was [a]led by the Spirit to the land of Nephi, even to the house of the king which was [b]over all the land [c]save it were the land of Ishmael; and he was the father of Lamoni.

2 And it came to pass that he went in unto him into the king's palace, with his brethren, and bowed himself before the king, and said unto him: Behold, O king, we are the brethren of Ammon, whom thou hast [a]delivered out of [b]prison.

3 And now, O king, if thou wilt spare our lives, we will be thy servants. And the king said unto them: Arise, for I will grant unto you your lives, and I will not suffer that ye shall be my servants; but I will insist that ye shall administer unto me; for I have been somewhat [a]troubled in mind because of the [b]generosity and the greatness of the words of thy brother Ammon; and I desire to know the cause why he has not come up out of Middoni with thee.

4 And Aaron said unto the king: Behold, the Spirit of the Lord has called him another way; he has gone [a]to the land of Ishmael, to teach the people of Lamoni.

5 Now the king said unto them: What is this that ye have said concerning the Spirit of the Lord?

17*a* Alma 62:45; D&C 18:44.
18*a* Alma 17:19; 22:1 (1, 4); 25:13.
19*a* Alma 17:25.
20*a* Alma 16:13.
21*a* Alma 20:24; 22:1.
22*a* Luke 4:8; D&C 93:19; 134:4 (1–4); A of F 1:11. TG Liberty.
23*a* TG Zeal.
22 1*a* Gen. 24:27; Acts 16:6; Alma 21:16 (16–17).
b Alma 20:8.
c Alma 20:24; 21:21 (21–22).
2*a* Alma 20:26.
b Alma 20:4.
3*a* Acts 2:37 (37–38).
b Alma 20:26.
4*a* Alma 21:18.

Behold, this is the thing which doth
trouble me.
6 And also, what is this that Ammon said—[a]If ye will repent ye shall
be saved, and if ye will not repent,
ye shall be cast off at the last day?
7 And Aaron answered him and
said unto him: Believest thou that
there is a God? And the king said: I
know that the Amalekites say that
there is a God, and I have granted
unto them that they should build
sanctuaries, that they may assemble themselves together to worship
him. And if now thou sayest there
is a God, behold I will [a]believe.
8 And now when Aaron heard this,
his heart began to rejoice, and he
said: Behold, assuredly as thou livest, O king, there is a God.
9 And the king said: Is God that
[a]Great Spirit that brought our
fathers out of the land of Jerusalem?
10 And Aaron said unto him: Yea,
he is that Great Spirit, and he [a]cre-
ated all things both in heaven and
in earth. Believest thou this?
11 And he said: Yea, I believe that
the Great Spirit created all things,
and I desire that ye should tell me
concerning all these things, and I
will [a]believe thy words.
12 And it came to pass that when
Aaron saw that the king would
believe his words, he began from
the creation of Adam, [a]reading the
scriptures unto the king—how God
[b]created man after his own image,
and that God gave him commandments, and that because of transgression, man had fallen.
13 And Aaron did expound unto
him the scriptures from the [a]cre-
ation of Adam, laying the fall of man
before him, and their carnal state
and also the [b]plan of [c]redemption,
which was prepared [d]from the foundation of the world, through Christ,
for all whosoever would believe on
his name.
14 And since man had [a]fallen he
could not [b]merit anything of himself; but the sufferings and [c]death
of Christ [d]atone for their sins,
through faith and repentance, and
so forth; and that he breaketh the
bands of death, that the [e]grave shall
have no victory, and that the sting
of death should be swallowed up
in the hopes of glory; and Aaron
did expound all these things unto
the king.
15 And it came to pass that after
Aaron had expounded these things
unto him, the king said: [a]What shall
I do that I may have this eternal life
of which thou hast spoken? Yea,
what shall I do that I may be [b]born
of God, having this wicked spirit
[c]rooted out of my breast, and receive
his Spirit, that I may be filled with
joy, that I may not be cast off at the
last day? Behold, said he, I will give
up [d]all that I possess, yea, I will forsake my kingdom, that I may receive
this great joy.
16 But Aaron said unto him: If
thou desirest this thing, if thou wilt
[a]bow down before God, yea, if thou
wilt repent of all thy sins, and will
bow down before God, and call on
his name in faith, believing that ye
shall receive, then shalt thou receive
the [b]hope which thou desirest.
17 And it came to pass that when
Aaron had said these words, the
king did [a]bow down before the Lord,
upon his knees; yea, even he did

6*a* Alma 20:17 (17–18).
7*a* D&C 46:14 (13–14).
9*a* Alma 18:2, 26 (18–28).
10*a* TG Creation.
11*a* TG Believe.
12*a* 1 Ne. 5:18 (10–18); Alma 18:36; 37:9.
b TG Man, Physical Creation of.
13*a* Gen. 1:26 (26–28); 2:7.
b TG Salvation, Plan of.
c TG Redemption.
d 2 Ne. 9:18; Alma 13:3 (3, 5, 7–9).
14*a* TG Fall of Man.
b Eph. 2:8 (8–9); Alma 42:14 (10–25).
c TG Jesus Christ, Death of.
d 2 Ne. 2:10; Alma 33:22; 34:9 (8–16).
e Isa. 25:8; 1 Cor. 15:55 (34–57).
15*a* Acts 2:37.
b Alma 5:14 (14, 49); 36:23 (23, 26).
c Rom. 7:18.
d Matt. 13:46 (44–46); 19:21 (16–22).
16*a* TG Conversion.
b Ether 12:4.
17*a* D&C 5:24.

prostrate himself upon the earth,
and cried [b]mightily, saying:
18 O God, Aaron hath told me that
there is a God; and if there is a God,
and if thou art God, wilt thou make
thyself known unto me, and I will
give away all my sins to know thee,
and that I may be raised from the
dead, and be saved at the last day.
And now when the king had said
these words, he was struck [a]as if he
were dead.
19 And it came to pass that his
servants ran and told the queen all
that had happened unto the king.
And she came in unto the king; and
when she saw him lay as if he were
dead, and also Aaron and his brethren standing as though they had
been the cause of his fall, she was
angry with them, and commanded
that her servants, or the servants
of the king, should take them and
slay them.
20 Now the servants had seen the
cause of the king's fall, therefore
they durst not lay their hands on
Aaron and his brethren; and they
pled with the queen saying: Why
commandest thou that we should
slay these men, when behold one
of them is [a]mightier than us all?
Therefore we shall fall before them.
21 Now when the queen saw the
fear of the servants she also began to fear exceedingly, lest there
should some evil come upon her.
And she commanded her servants
that they should go and call the
people, that they might slay Aaron
and his brethren.
22 Now when Aaron saw the determination of the queen, he, also
knowing the hardness of the hearts
of the people, feared lest that a
multitude should assemble themselves together, and there should
be a great contention and a disturbance among them; therefore he
put forth his [a]hand and raised the
king from the earth, and said unto
him: Stand. And he stood upon his
feet, receiving his strength.
23 Now this was done in the presence of the queen and many of the
servants. And when they saw it
they greatly marveled, and began
to fear. And the king stood forth,
and began to [a]minister unto them.
And he did minister unto them, insomuch that his [b]whole household
were [c]converted unto the Lord.
24 Now there was a multitude
gathered together because of the
commandment of the queen, and
there began to be great murmurings among them because of Aaron
and his brethren.
25 But the king stood forth among
them and administered unto them.
And they were [a]pacified towards
Aaron and those who were with him.
26 And it came to pass that when
the king saw that the people were
pacified, he caused that Aaron and
his brethren should stand forth in the
midst of the multitude, and that they
should preach the word unto them.
27 And it came to pass that the
king sent a [a]proclamation throughout all the land, amongst all his
people who were in all his land,
who were in all the regions round
about, which was bordering even
to the sea, on the east and on the
[b]west, and which was divided from
the land of [c]Zarahemla by a narrow
strip of wilderness, which ran from
the sea east even to the sea west,
and round about on the borders of
the seashore, and the borders of the
wilderness which was on the north
by the land of Zarahemla, through
the borders of [d]Manti, by the head
of the [e]river Sidon, running from
the east towards the west—and
thus were the Lamanites and the
Nephites divided.

17*b* TG Prayer.
18*a* Alma 18:42 (42–43).
20*a* Alma 18:3 (1–3).
22*a* Alma 19:29.
23*a* TG Minister; Ministration; Ministry.
b Alma 23:3.
c TG Conversion.
25*a* TG Peace; Peacemakers.
27*a* Alma 23:1 (1–4).
b Hel. 3:8; 11:20.
c Omni 1:13.
d Alma 17:1; 56:14.
e Alma 16:6 (6–7); 43:22 (22–53).

28 Now, the more [a]idle part of the Lamanites lived in the wilderness, and dwelt in tents; and they were spread through the wilderness on the west, in the land of Nephi; yea, and also on the west of the land of Zarahemla, in the borders by the seashore, and on the west in the land of Nephi, in the place of their fathers' first inheritance, and thus bordering along by the seashore.

29 And also there were many Lamanites on the east by the seashore, whither the Nephites had driven them. And thus the Nephites were nearly surrounded by the Lamanites; nevertheless the Nephites had taken possession of all the northern parts of the land bordering on the wilderness, at the head of the river Sidon, from the east to the west, round about on the wilderness side; on the north, even until they came to the land which they called [a]Bountiful.

30 And it bordered upon the land which they called [a]Desolation, it being so far northward that it came into the land which had been peopled and been destroyed, of whose [b]bones we have spoken, which was discovered by the [c]people of Zarahemla, it being the place of their [d]first landing.

31 And they came from there [a]up into the south wilderness. Thus the [b]land on the northward was called [c]Desolation, and the land on the southward was called Bountiful, it being the wilderness which is filled with all manner of wild animals of every kind, a part of which had come from the land northward for food.

32 And now, it was only the [a]distance of a day and a half's journey for a Nephite, on the line Bountiful and the land Desolation, from the east to the west sea; and thus the land of Nephi and the land of Zarahemla were nearly surrounded by water, there being a small [b]neck of land between the land northward and the land southward.

33 And it came to pass that the Nephites had inhabited the land Bountiful, even from the east unto the west sea, and thus the Nephites in their wisdom, with their guards and their armies, had hemmed in the Lamanites on the south, that thereby they should have no more possession on the north, that they might not overrun the land northward.

34 Therefore the Lamanites could have no more possessions only in the land of Nephi, and the wilderness round about. Now this was wisdom in the Nephites—as the Lamanites were an enemy to them, they would not suffer their afflictions on every hand, and also that they might have a country whither they might flee, according to their desires.

35 And now I, after having said this, return again to the account of Ammon and Aaron, Omner and Himni, and their brethren.

CHAPTER 23

Religious freedom is proclaimed—The Lamanites in seven lands and cities are converted—They call themselves Anti-Nephi-Lehies and are freed from the curse—The Amalekites and the Amulonites reject the truth. About 90–77 B.C.

BEHOLD, now it came to pass that the king of the Lamanites sent a [a]proclamation among all his people, that they should not lay their hands on Ammon, or Aaron, or Omner, or Himni, nor either of their brethren who should go forth preaching the word of God, in whatsoever place

28*a* 2 Ne. 5:24 (22–25).
29*a* Alma 52:9, 17, 27; 63:5.
30*a* Alma 46:17; 50:34; Morm. 3:5 (5, 7); 4:3 (1–3).
b Mosiah 8:8 (7–12); 28:17 (11–19).
c Omni 1:21 (20–22).
d Ether 6:12; 7:6.
31*a* Hel. 6:10.
b Alma 46:17; 63:4.
c Hel. 3:6 (5–6).
32*a* Hel. 4:7.
b Alma 50:34; 52:9.
23 1*a* Alma 22:27.

they should be, in any part of their land.

2 Yea, he sent a decree among them, that they should not lay their hands on them to bind them, or to cast them into prison; neither should they spit upon them, nor smite them, nor cast them out of their [a]synagogues, nor scourge them; neither should they cast stones at them, but that they should have free access to their houses, and also their temples, and their [b]sanctuaries.

3 And thus they might go forth and preach the word according to their desires, for the king had been converted unto the Lord, and [a]all his [b]household; therefore he sent his proclamation throughout the land unto his people, that the word of God might have no obstruction, but that it might go forth throughout all the land, that his people might be convinced concerning the wicked [c]traditions of their fathers, and that they might be convinced that they were all brethren, and that they ought not to murder, nor to plunder, nor to steal, nor to commit adultery, nor to commit any manner of wickedness.

4 And now it came to pass that when the king had sent forth this proclamation, that Aaron and his brethren went forth from [a]city to city, and from one house of worship to another, establishing churches, and consecrating [b]priests and teachers throughout the land among the Lamanites, to preach and to teach the word of God among them; and thus they began to have great success.

5 And [a]thousands were brought to the knowledge of the Lord, yea, thousands were brought to believe in the [b]traditions of the Nephites; and they were taught the [c]records and prophecies which were handed down even to the present time.

6 And as sure as the Lord liveth, so sure as many as believed, or as many as were brought to the knowledge of the truth, through the preaching of Ammon and his brethren, according to the spirit of revelation and of prophecy, and the power of God working [a]miracles in them—yea, I say unto you, as the Lord liveth, as many of the Lamanites as believed in their preaching, and were [b]converted unto the Lord, [c]never did fall away.

7 For they became a righteous people; they did lay down the weapons of their rebellion, that they did not fight against God any more, neither against any of their brethren.

8 Now, these are [a]they who were converted unto the Lord:

9 The people of the Lamanites who were in the land of Ishmael;

10 And also of the people of the Lamanites who were in the land of [a]Middoni;

11 And also of the people of the Lamanites who were in the city of Nephi;

12 And also of the people of the Lamanites who were in the land of [a]Shilom, and who were in the land of Shemlon, and in the city of Lemuel, and in the city of Shimnilom.

13 And these are the names of the cities of the Lamanites which were [a]converted unto the Lord; and these are they that laid down the weapons of their rebellion, yea, all their weapons of war; and they were all Lamanites.

14 And the Amalekites were not

2*a* Alma 21:20 (4–6, 20); 26:29.
b Hel. 3:14 (9, 14).
3*a* Alma 22:23.
b Gen. 18:19.
c Alma 26:24.
4*a* Luke 8:1; D&C 66:5; 75:18.
b Alma 30:31.
5*a* Alma 26:4.
b Alma 37:19.
c Alma 63:12. TG Scriptures, Value of.
6*a* Ex. 8:19; 1 Ne. 19:22; D&C 84:3; 121:12.
b TG Commitment; Conversion.
c Alma 27:27.
8*a* Alma 26:3, 31.
10*a* Alma 20:2; 21:12 (12–13, 18).
12*a* Mosiah 22:11 (8, 11).
13*a* Alma 53:10.

[a]converted, save only one; neither were any of the [b]Amulonites; but they did harden their hearts, and also the hearts of the Lamanites in that part of the land wheresoever they dwelt, yea, and all their villages and all their cities.

15 Therefore, we have named all the cities of the Lamanites in which they did repent and come to the knowledge of the truth, and were converted.

16 And now it came to pass that the king and those who were converted were desirous that they might have a name, that thereby they might be distinguished from their brethren; therefore the king consulted with Aaron and many of their priests, concerning the name that they should take upon them, that they might be distinguished.

17 And it came to pass that they called their names [a]Anti-Nephi-Lehies; and they were called by this name and were no more called [b]Lamanites.

18 And they began to be a very [a]industrious people; yea, and they were friendly with the Nephites; therefore, they did [b]open a correspondence with them, and the [c]curse of God did no more follow them.

CHAPTER 24

The Lamanites come against the people of God—The Anti-Nephi-Lehies rejoice in Christ and are visited by angels—They choose to suffer death rather than to defend themselves—More Lamanites are converted. About 90–77 B.C.

AND it came to pass that the Amalekites and the Amulonites and the Lamanites who were in the land of [a]Amulon, and also in the land of [b]Helam, and who were in the land of [c]Jerusalem, and in fine, in all the land round about, who had not been converted and had not taken upon them the name of [d]Anti-Nephi-Lehi, were stirred up by the Amalekites and by the Amulonites to anger against their brethren.

2 And their hatred became exceedingly sore against them, even insomuch that they began to rebel against their king, insomuch that they would not that he should be their king; therefore, they took up arms against the people of Anti-Nephi-Lehi.

3 Now the king conferred the kingdom upon his son, and he called his name Anti-Nephi-Lehi.

4 And the king died in that selfsame year that the Lamanites began to make preparations for war against the people of God.

5 Now when Ammon and his brethren and all those who had come up with him saw the preparations of the Lamanites to destroy their brethren, they came forth to the land of Midian, and there Ammon met all his brethren; and from thence they came to the land of Ishmael that they might hold a [a]council with Lamoni and also with his brother Anti-Nephi-Lehi, what they should do to defend themselves against the Lamanites.

6 Now there was not one soul among all the people who had been converted unto the Lord that would take up arms against their brethren; nay, they would not even make any preparations for war; yea, and also their king commanded them that they should not.

7 Now, these are the words which he said unto the people concerning the matter: I thank my God, my beloved people, that our great God has in goodness sent these our brethren, the Nephites, unto us to

14*a* Alma 24:29.
b Mosiah 23:31 (31–39).
17*a* Alma 24:1 (1–3, 5, 20).
b Jacob 1:13.
18*a* TG Industry.
b Alma 24:8.
c 1 Ne. 2:23; 2 Ne. 30:6 (5–6); 3 Ne. 2:15 (14–16).
24 1*a* Alma 21:3 (2–4); 25:7 (4–9).
b Mosiah 23:19; 27:16.
c Alma 21:1.
d Alma 23:17; 25:13 (1, 13).
5*a* Alma 27:4.

preach unto us, and to convince us of
the [a]traditions of our wicked fathers.
8 And behold, I thank my great
God that he has given us a portion
of his Spirit to soften our hearts, that
we have [a]opened a correspondence
with these brethren, the Nephites.
9 And behold, I also thank my God,
that by opening this correspondence we have been convinced of
our [a]sins, and of the many murders
which we have committed.
10 And I also thank my God, yea,
my great God, that he hath granted
unto us that we might repent of
these things, and also that he hath
[a]forgiven us of those our many sins
and murders which we have committed, and taken away the [b]guilt
from our hearts, through the merits of his Son.
11 And now behold, my brethren,
since it has been all that we could
do (as we were the most lost of all
mankind) to repent of all our sins
and the many murders which we
have committed, and to get God to
[a]take them away from our hearts,
for it was all we could do to repent
sufficiently before God that he
would take away our stain—
12 Now, my best beloved brethren, since God hath taken away
our stains, and our swords have become bright, then let us stain our
swords no more with the blood of
our brethren.
13 Behold, I say unto you, Nay, let
us retain our swords that they be
not stained with the blood of our
brethren; for perhaps, if we should
stain our swords [a]again they can no
more be [b]washed bright through
the blood of the Son of our great
God, which shall be shed for the
atonement of our sins.
14 And the great God has had
mercy on us, and made these things
known unto us that we might not
perish; yea, and he has made these
things known unto us beforehand,
because he loveth our [a]souls as well
as he loveth our children; therefore,
in his mercy he doth visit us by his
angels, that the [b]plan of salvation
might be made known unto us as
well as unto future generations.
15 Oh, how merciful is our God!
And now behold, since it has been
as much as we could do to get our
stains taken away from us, and our
swords are made bright, let us [a]hide
them away that they may be kept
bright, as a testimony to our God at
the last day, or at the day that we
shall be brought to stand before
him to be judged, that we have not
stained our swords in the blood of
our brethren since he imparted
his word unto us and has made us
[b]clean thereby.
16 And now, my brethren, if our
brethren seek to destroy us, behold,
we will hide away our swords, yea,
even we will bury them deep in the
earth, that they may be kept bright,
as a testimony that we have never
used them, at the last day; and if
our brethren destroy us, behold,
we shall [a]go to our God and shall
be saved.
17 And now it came to pass that
when the king had made an end of
these sayings, and all the people
were assembled together, they took
their swords, and all the weapons
which were used for the shedding
of man's blood, and they did [a]bury
them up deep in the earth.
18 And this they did, it being in
their view a testimony to God, and
also to men, that they [a]never would
use weapons again for the shedding
of man's blood; and this they did,
vouching and [b]covenanting with
God, that rather than shed the

7*a* Mosiah 1:5.
8*a* Alma 23:18.
9*a* Micah 3:8; Hel. 13:26; D&C 18:44.
10*a* Dan. 9:9.
b TG Guilt.
11*a* Isa. 53:6 (4–6).
13*a* D&C 42:26.
b Rev. 1:5.
14*a* TG Worth of Souls.
b TG Jesus Christ, Prophecies about; Salvation, Plan of.
15*a* Alma 25:14; 26:32.
b TG Purification.
16*a* Alma 40:11 (11–15).
17*a* Hel. 15:9.
18*a* Alma 53:11.
b TG Covenants.

blood of their brethren they would
[c]give up their own lives; and rather
than take away from a brother they
would give unto him; and rather
than spend their days in idleness
they would labor abundantly with
their hands.
19 And thus we see that, when
these Lamanites were brought to
[a]believe and to know the truth, they
were [b]firm, and would suffer even
unto death rather than commit sin;
and thus we see that they buried
their weapons of peace, or they buried the weapons of war, for peace.
20 And it came to pass that their
brethren, the Lamanites, made preparations for war, and came up to
the land of Nephi for the purpose
of destroying the king, and to place
[a]another in his stead, and also of
destroying the people of Anti-
Nephi-Lehi out of the land.
21 Now when the people saw that
they were coming against them they
went out to meet them, and [a]pros-
trated themselves before them to the
earth, and began to call on the name
of the Lord; and thus they were
in this attitude when the Lamanites began to fall upon them, and
began to slay them with the sword.
22 And thus without meeting any
resistance, they did slay a [a]thousand
and five of them; and we know that
they are blessed, for they have gone
to dwell with their God.
23 Now when the Lamanites saw
that their brethren would not flee
from the sword, neither would they
turn aside to the right hand or to the
left, but that they would lie down
and [a]perish, and [b]praised God even
in the very act of perishing under
the sword—
24 Now when the Lamanites saw
this they did [a]forbear from slaying
them; and there were many whose
hearts had [b]swollen in them for those
of their brethren who had fallen
under the sword, for they repented
of the things which they had done.
25 And it came to pass that they
threw down their weapons of war,
and they would not take them
again, for they were stung for the
murders which they had committed;
and they came down even as their
brethren, relying upon the mercies
of those whose arms were lifted to
slay them.
26 And it came to pass that the
people of God were joined that day
by more than the number who had
been slain; and those who had been
slain were righteous people, therefore we have no reason to doubt but
what they were [a]saved.
27 And there was not a wicked man
slain among them; but there were
more than a thousand brought to
the knowledge of the truth; thus we
see that the Lord worketh in many
[a]ways to the salvation of his people.
28 Now the greatest number of
those of the Lamanites who slew so
many of their brethren were Amalekites and Amulonites, the greatest
number of whom were after the
[a]order of the [b]Nehors.
29 Now, among those who joined
the people of the Lord, there were
[a]none who were Amalekites or Amulonites, or who were of the order of
Nehor, but they were actual descendants of Laman and Lemuel.
30 And thus we can plainly dis-
cern, that after a people have been
once [a]enlightened by the [b]Spirit of
God, and have had great [c]knowledge
of things pertaining to righteousness, and then have [d]fallen away into

18*c* TG Self-Sacrifice.
19*a* TG Faith.
b TG Integrity.
20*a* Isa. 7:6.
21*a* Alma 27:3.
22*a* Alma 26:34.
23*a* Alma 26:32.
b Mosiah 16:7.
24*a* Alma 25:1.
b TG Compassion; Repent.
26*a* Isa. 57:1; Rev. 14:13.
27*a* 2 Kgs. 5:15; Isa. 55:8 (8–9); Alma 37:7 (6–7).
28*a* Alma 21:4.
b Alma 1:15; 2:1 (1, 20); 16:11.
29*a* Alma 23:14.
30*a* Matt. 12:45.
b TG God, Spirit of.
c Heb. 10:26 (26–27); Alma 47:36.
d 2 Ne. 31:14; Alma 9:19; 31:8; D&C 93:19. TG Apostasy of Individuals; Holy Ghost, Loss of.

sin and transgression, they become more [e]hardened, and thus their state becomes [f]worse than though they had never known these things.

CHAPTER 25

Lamanite aggressions spread—The seed of the priests of Noah perish as Abinadi prophesied—Many Lamanites are converted and join the people of Anti-Nephi-Lehi—They believe in Christ and keep the law of Moses. About 90–77 B.C.

AND behold, now it came to pass that those Lamanites were more angry because they had slain their brethren; therefore they swore vengeance upon the Nephites; and they did [a]no more attempt to slay the people of [b]Anti-Nephi-Lehi at that time.
2 But they took their armies and went over into the borders of the land of Zarahemla, and fell upon the people who were in the land of Ammonihah and [a]destroyed them.
3 And after that, they had [a]many battles with the Nephites, in the which they were driven and slain.
4 And among the Lamanites who were slain were almost all the [a]seed of Amulon and his brethren, who were the priests of Noah, and they were slain by the hands of the Nephites;
5 And the remainder, having fled into the east wilderness, and having usurped the power and [a]authority over the Lamanites, caused that many of the Lamanites should [b]perish by fire because of their belief—
6 For many of [a]them, after having suffered much loss and so many afflictions, began to be stirred up in remembrance of the [b]words which Aaron and his brethren had preached to them in their land; therefore they began to disbelieve the [c]traditions of their fathers, and to believe in the Lord, and that he gave great power unto the Nephites; and thus there were many of them converted in the wilderness.
7 And it came to pass that those rulers who were the remnant of the children of [a]Amulon caused that they should be put to [b]death, yea, all those that believed in these things.
8 Now this martyrdom caused that many of their brethren should be stirred up to anger; and there began to be contention in the wilderness; and the Lamanites began to [a]hunt the seed of Amulon and his brethren and began to slay them; and they fled into the east wilderness.
9 And behold they are hunted at this day by the Lamanites. Thus the words of Abinadi were brought to pass, which he said concerning the seed of the priests who caused that he should suffer death by fire.
10 For he said unto them: What ye shall [a]do unto me shall be a type of things to come.
11 And now Abinadi was the first that suffered [a]death by fire because of his belief in God; now this is what he meant, that many should suffer death by fire, according as he had suffered.
12 And he said unto the priests of Noah that their seed should cause many to be put to death, in the like manner as he was, and that they should be scattered abroad and slain, even as a sheep having no shepherd is driven and slain by wild beasts; and now behold, these words were verified, for they were driven by the Lamanites, and they were hunted, and they were smitten.
13 And it came to pass that when

30*e* TG Hardheartedness.
f 2 Chr. 33:9; Ezek. 5:6; 2 Pet. 2:20 (20–21).
25 1*a* Alma 24:24 (20–25).
b Alma 27:2.
2*a* Alma 8:16; 16:9.
3*a* Alma 27:1.
4*a* Mosiah 23:35.
5*a* TG Authority.
b Mosiah 17:15.
6*a* IE the Lamanites.
b Alma 21:9 (5–12).
c Alma 26:24.
7*a* Alma 21:3 (2–4); 24:1 (1, 28–30).
b TG Martyrdom.
8*a* Mosiah 17:18.
10*a* Mosiah 13:10.
11*a* Mosiah 17:13 (13–20).

the Lamanites saw that they could not overpower the Nephites they returned again to their own land; and many of them came over to dwell in the land of [a]Ishmael and the land of Nephi, and did join themselves to the people of God, who were the people of [b]Anti-Nephi-Lehi.

14 And they did also [a]bury their weapons of war, according as their brethren had, and they began to be a righteous people; and they did walk in the ways of the Lord, and did observe to keep his commandments and his statutes.

15 Yea, and they did keep the law of Moses; for it was expedient that they should keep the law of Moses as yet, for it was not all fulfilled. But notwithstanding the [a]law of Moses, they did look forward to the coming of Christ, considering that the law of Moses was a [b]type of his coming, and believing that they must keep those [c]outward [d]performances until the time that he should be revealed unto them.

16 Now they did not suppose that [a]salvation came by the [b]law of Moses; but the law of Moses did serve to strengthen their faith in Christ; and thus they did retain a [c]hope through faith, unto eternal salvation, relying upon the spirit of prophecy, which spake of those things to come.

17 And now behold, Ammon, and Aaron, and Omner, and Himni, and their brethren did rejoice exceedingly, for the success which they had had among the Lamanites, seeing that the Lord had granted unto them according to their [a]prayers, and that he had also verified his word unto them in every particular.

CHAPTER 26

Ammon glories in the Lord—The faithful are strengthened by the Lord and are given knowledge—By faith men may bring thousands of souls unto repentance—God has all power and comprehends all things. About 90–77 B.C.

AND now, these are the words of Ammon to his brethren, which say thus: My brothers and my brethren, behold I say unto you, how great reason have we to rejoice; for could we have supposed when we [a]started from the land of Zarahemla that God would have granted unto us such great blessings?

2 And now, I ask, what great blessings has he bestowed upon us? Can ye tell?

3 Behold, I answer for you; for our brethren, the Lamanites, were in darkness, yea, even in the darkest abyss, but behold, how [a]many of them are brought to behold the marvelous light of God! And this is the blessing which hath been bestowed upon us, that we have been made [b]instruments in the hands of God to bring about this great work.

4 Behold, [a]thousands of them do rejoice, and have been brought into the fold of God.

5 Behold, the [a]field was ripe, and blessed are ye, for ye did thrust in the [b]sickle, and did reap with your might, yea, all the day long did ye labor; and behold the number of your [c]sheaves! And they shall be

13*a* Alma 22:1 (1, 4).
b Alma 24:1 (1–3, 5, 20); 27:21 (2, 21, 25).
14*a* Alma 24:15; 26:32.
15*a* Jacob 4:5; Jarom 1:11.
b Mosiah 16:14. TG Jesus Christ, Types of, in Anticipation.
c Josh. 1:8; Mosiah 3:14 (14–15); 13:29 (29–32); D&C 41:5 (4–5).
d TG Ordinance.
16*a* Mosiah 3:15; 12:31; 13:28 (27–33).
b 2 Ne. 11:4; Jacob 4:5; Jarom 1:11; Ether 12:19 (18–19).
c Alma 33:22 (19–23); 37:46 (45–46).
17*a* Alma 17:9 (7–11).
26 1*a* Mosiah 28:9; Alma 17:6 (6–11).
3*a* Alma 23:8 (8–13).
b 2 Cor. 4:5; Mosiah 23:10.
4*a* Alma 23:5; 26:31.
5*a* John 4:35; D&C 4:4.
b Joel 3:13.
c D&C 33:9; 75:5. TG Reward.

gathered into the garners, that they
are not wasted.
6 Yea, they shall not be beaten
down by the storm at the last day;
yea, neither shall they be harrowed
up by the whirlwinds; but when the
[a]storm cometh they shall be gathered together in their place, that
the storm cannot penetrate to them;
yea, neither shall they be driven
with fierce winds whithersoever
the enemy listeth to carry them.
7 But behold, they are in the hands
of the Lord of the [a]harvest, and they
are his; and he will [b]raise them up
at the last day.
8 [a]Blessed be the name of our God;
let us [b]sing to his praise, yea, let us
give [c]thanks to his holy name, for
he doth work righteousness forever.
9 For if we had not come up out
of the land of Zarahemla, these
our dearly beloved brethren, who
have so dearly beloved us, would
still have been racked with [a]hatred
against us, yea, and they would also
have been [b]strangers to God.
10 And it came to pass that when
Ammon had said these words, his
brother Aaron rebuked him, saying:
Ammon, I fear that thy joy doth
carry thee away unto boasting.
11 But Ammon said unto him: I
do not [a]boast in my own strength,
nor in my own wisdom; but behold,
my [b]joy is full, yea, my heart is
brim with [c]joy, and I will rejoice in
my God.
12 Yea, I know that I am [a]noth-
ing; as to my strength I am weak;
therefore I will [b]not boast of myself,
but I will [c]boast of my God, for in
his [d]strength I can do all [e]things;
yea, behold, many mighty miracles we have wrought in this land,
for which we will praise his name
forever.
13 Behold, how many thousands of
our brethren has he loosed from the
pains of [a]hell; and they are brought
to [b]sing redeeming love, and this
because of the power of his word
which is in us, therefore have we
not great reason to rejoice?
14 Yea, we have reason to praise
him forever, for he is the Most High
God, and has loosed our brethren
from the [a]chains of hell.
15 Yea, they were encircled about
with everlasting [a]darkness and
destruction; but behold, he has
brought them into his everlasting
[b]light, yea, into everlasting salvation;
and they are encircled about with
the matchless bounty of his love;
yea, and we have been instruments
in his hands of doing this great
and marvelous work.
16 Therefore, let us [a]glory, yea,
we will [b]glory in the Lord; yea, we
will rejoice, for our joy is full; yea,
we will praise our God forever. Behold, who can glory too much in the
Lord? Yea, who can say too much of
his great power, and of his [c]mercy,
and of his long-suffering towards
the children of men? Behold, I say
unto you, I cannot say the smallest
part which I feel.
17 Who could have supposed that
our God would have been so merciful as to have snatched us from our
awful, sinful, and [a]polluted state?
18 Behold, we went forth even in

6*a* Hel. 5:12;
3 Ne. 14:25 (25, 27).
7*a* TG Harvest.
b Mosiah 23:22;
Alma 36:28.
8*a* Ps. 41:13.
b Ps. 57:7 (7–11);
108:1 (1–5);
2 Ne. 22:5 (5–6).
c TG Thanksgiving.
9*a* Mosiah 28:2.
b TG Stranger.
11*a* 2 Cor. 7:14 (13–16).
b 1 Thes. 3:9;
D&C 18:16 (14–16).
c TG Joy.
12*a* TG Poor in Spirit.
b Alma 29:9.
c Jer. 9:24;
Rom. 15:17.
d Isa. 45:24;
Philip. 4:13 (12–13);
1 Ne. 17:3.
e Ps. 18:32 (32–40);
1 Ne. 7:12.
13*a* TG Hell.
b Alma 5:26.
14*a* Alma 12:11.
15*a* Prov. 20:20.
b TG Light [noun].
16*a* Rom. 15:17;
1 Cor. 1:31.
b Ps. 44:8 (4–8);
2 Cor. 10:17 (15–18);
D&C 76:61.
c Ps. 36:5 (5–6);
Morm. 6:22;
D&C 97:6.
17*a* TG Pollution.

wrath, with mighty threatenings to
[a]destroy his church.
19 Oh then, why did he not con-
sign us to an awful destruction, yea,
why did he not let the sword of his
justice fall upon us, and doom us
to eternal [a]despair?
20 Oh, my soul, almost as it were,
fleeth at the thought. Behold, he did
not exercise his justice upon us, but
in his great mercy hath brought us
over that everlasting [a]gulf of death
and misery, even to the salvation
of our souls.
21 And now behold, my brethren,
what [a]natural man is there that
knoweth these things? I say unto
you, there is [b]none that [c]knoweth
these things, save it be the penitent.
22 Yea, he that [a]repenteth and exerciseth faith, and bringeth forth
good [b]works, and prayeth continually without ceasing—unto such
it is given to know the [c]mysteries
of God; yea, unto such it shall be
[d]given to [e]reveal things which never
have been revealed; yea, and it
shall be given unto such to bring
thousands of souls to repentance,
even as it has been given unto
us to bring these our brethren to
repentance.
23 Now do ye remember, my brethren, that we said unto our brethren
in the land of Zarahemla, we go up
to the land of Nephi, to preach unto
our brethren, the Lamanites, and
they [a]laughed us to scorn?
24 For they said unto us: Do ye suppose that ye can bring the Lamanites to the knowledge of the truth?
Do ye suppose that ye can convince
the Lamanites of the [a]incorrectness
of the [b]traditions of their fathers,
as [c]stiffnecked a people as they are;
whose hearts delight in the [d]shed-
ding of blood; whose days have
been spent in the grossest iniquity;
whose ways have been the ways of
a transgressor from the beginning?
Now my brethren, ye remember that
this was their language.
25 And moreover they did say: Let
us take up arms against them, that
we destroy them and their iniquity
out of the land, lest they overrun
us and destroy us.
26 But behold, my beloved brethren, we came into the wilderness
not with the intent to destroy our
brethren, but with the intent that
perhaps we might save some few
of their souls.
27 Now when our hearts were depressed, and we were about to [a]turn
back, behold, the Lord [b]comforted
us, and said: Go amongst thy brethren, the Lamanites, and bear with
[c]patience thine [d]afflictions, and I
will give unto you success.
28 And now behold, we have come,
and been forth amongst them; and
we have been patient in our sufferings, and we have suffered every pri-
vation; yea, we have traveled from
house to house, relying upon the
mercies of the world—not upon
the mercies of the world alone but
upon the mercies of God.
29 And we have entered into their
houses and taught them, and we
have taught them in their streets;
yea, and we have taught them upon
their hills; and we have also entered
into their temples and their [a]syna-
gogues and taught them; and we
have been cast out, and mocked,
and spit upon, and smote upon our

18a Mosiah 27:10; 28:4 (3–4); Alma 36:6 (6–11).
19a TG Despair.
20a 2 Ne. 1:13; Hel. 3:29.
21a TG Man, Natural, Not Spiritually Reborn.
b Alma 36:5.
c 1 Cor. 2:11 (9–16); Jacob 4:8 (8–10, 13).
22a TG Repent.
b TG Good Works.
c Luke 8:10; Alma 12:9. TG Mysteries of Godliness.
d Dan. 2:22 (19–22, 28).
e Jarom 1:4; Hel. 11:23; D&C 107:19 (18–19).
23a 2 Chr. 30:10; Neh. 2:19; Luke 8:53. TG Laughter.
24a Mosiah 1:5; 28:2.
b Alma 23:3; 25:6.
c TG Stiffnecked.
d Jacob 7:24; Jarom 1:6.
27a Hel. 13:2 (2–3).
b Alma 17:10.
c Alma 17:11. TG Patience.
d Alma 7:5. TG Affliction.
29a Alma 23:2 (2, 4).

cheeks; and we have been [b]stoned,
and taken and bound with [c]strong
cords, and cast into prison; and
through the power and wisdom of
God we have been delivered again.
30 And we have suffered all manner
of afflictions, and all this, that perhaps we might be the means of saving some soul; and we supposed that
our [a]joy would be full if perhaps we
could be the means of saving some.
31 Now behold, we can look forth
and see the [a]fruits of our labors; and
are they few? I say unto you, Nay,
they are [b]many; yea, and we can
witness of their sincerity, because
of their love towards their brethren
and also towards us.
32 For behold, they had rather
[a]sacrifice their lives than even to
take the life of their enemy; and
they have [b]buried their weapons of
war deep in the earth, because of
their love towards their brethren.
33 And now behold I say unto you,
has there been so great love in all
the land? Behold, I say unto you,
Nay, there has not, even among the
Nephites.
34 For behold, they would take
up arms against their brethren;
they would not suffer themselves
to be slain. But behold how [a]many
of these have laid down their lives;
and we know that they have gone
to their God, because of their love
and of their hatred to sin.
35 Now have we not reason to
rejoice? Yea, I say unto you, there
never were men that had so great
reason to rejoice as we, since the
world began; yea, and my joy is
carried away, even unto boasting
in my God; for he has all [a]power,
[b]all wisdom, and all understanding;
he comprehendeth all things, and
he is a [c]merciful Being, even unto
salvation, to those who will repent
and believe on his name.
36 Now if this is [a]boasting, even so
will I boast; for this is my life and
my light, my joy and my salvation,
and my redemption from everlasting wo. Yea, blessed is the name
of my God, who has been mindful of
this people, who are a [b]branch of the
tree of Israel, and has been [c]lost
from its body in a strange land; yea,
I say, blessed be the name of my
God, who has been mindful of us,
[d]wanderers in a strange land.
37 Now my brethren, we see that
God is [a]mindful of every [b]people,
whatsoever land they may be in;
yea, he numbereth his people, and
his bowels of mercy are over all the
earth. Now this is my joy, and my
great thanksgiving; yea, and I will
give thanks unto my God forever.
Amen.

CHAPTER 27

The Lord commands Ammon to lead the people of Anti-Nephi-Lehi to safety—Upon meeting Alma, Ammon's joy exhausts his strength—The Nephites give the Anti-Nephi-Lehies the land of Jershon—They are called the people of Ammon. About 90–77 B.C.

Now it came to pass that when
those Lamanites who had gone
to war against the Nephites had
found, after their [a]many struggles
to destroy them, that it was in vain
to seek their destruction, they returned again to the land of Nephi.
2 And it came to pass that the
Amalekites, because of their loss,
were exceedingly angry. And when
they saw that they could not seek
revenge from the Nephites, they began to [a]stir up the people in anger

29*b* 2 Cor. 11:23 (23–29).
c Alma 20:30 (29–30).
30*a* D&C 18:15 (15–16).
31*a* Acts 21:19 (19–20).
b Alma 23:8 (8–13); 26:4.
32*a* Alma 24:23 (20–24).
b Alma 24:15; 25:14.
34*a* Alma 24:22.
35*a* TG God, Intelligence of; God, Perfection of; God, Wisdom of.
b D&C 88:41.
c TG God, Mercy of.
36*a* Rom. 3:27.
b Gen. 49:22 (22–26); Ezek. 17:22; Jacob 2:25.
c Jacob 5:25 (25, 40–45).
d Jacob 7:26.
37*a* 2 Ne. 2:27; 26:24; Jacob 5:41.
b Jonah 4:11 (10–11); Acts 10:35 (9–35, 44); 2 Ne. 26:33.
27 1*a* Alma 25:3.
2*a* Acts 13:50.

against their [b]brethren, the people of [c]Anti-Nephi-Lehi; therefore they began again to destroy them.

3 Now this people [a]again refused to take their arms, and they suffered themselves to be slain according to the desires of their enemies.

4 Now when Ammon and his brethren saw this work of destruction among those whom they so dearly beloved, and among those who had so dearly beloved them—for they were treated as though they were angels sent from God to save them from everlasting destruction—therefore, when Ammon and his brethren saw this great work of destruction, they were moved with compassion, and they [a]said unto the king:

5 Let us gather together this people of the Lord, and let us go down to the land of Zarahemla to our brethren the Nephites, and flee out of the hands of our enemies, that we be not destroyed.

6 But the king said unto them: Behold, the Nephites will destroy us, because of the many murders and sins we have committed against them.

7 And Ammon said: I will go and inquire of the Lord, and if he say unto us, go down unto our brethren, will ye go?

8 And the king said unto him: Yea, if the Lord saith unto us go, we will go down unto our brethren, and we will be their slaves until we repair unto them the many murders and sins which we have committed against them.

9 But Ammon said unto him: It is against the law of our brethren, which was established by my father, that there should be any [a]slaves among them; therefore let us go down and rely upon the mercies of our brethren.

10 But the king said unto him: Inquire of the Lord, and if he saith unto us go, we will go; otherwise we will perish in the land.

11 And it came to pass that Ammon went and inquired of the Lord, and the Lord said unto him:

12 Get this people [a]out of this land, that they perish not; for Satan has great hold on the hearts of the Amalekites, who do stir up the Lamanites to anger against their brethren to slay them; therefore get thee out of this land; and blessed are this people in this generation, for I will [b]preserve them.

13 And now it came to pass that Ammon went and told the king all the words which the Lord had said unto him.

14 And they gathered together all their people, yea, all the people of the Lord, and did gather together all their flocks and herds, and departed out of the land, and came into the wilderness which divided the land of Nephi from the land of Zarahemla, and came over near the borders of the land.

15 And it came to pass that Ammon said unto them: Behold, I and my brethren will go forth into the land of Zarahemla, and ye shall remain here until we return; and we will [a]try the hearts of our brethren, whether they will that ye shall come into their land.

16 And it came to pass that as Ammon was going forth into the land, that he and his brethren met Alma, over in the [a]place of which has been spoken; and behold, this was a joyful meeting.

17 Now the [a]joy of Ammon was so great even that he was full; yea, he was swallowed up in the joy of his God, even to the [b]exhausting of his strength; and he fell [c]again to the earth.

2*b* Alma 43:11.
c Alma 25:1.
3*a* Alma 24:21 (21–26).
4*a* Alma 24:5 (3–5).
9*a* Mosiah 29:32 (32, 38, 40).
12*a* TG Separation.
b TG Protection, Divine.
15*a* Judg. 7:4.
16*a* Alma 17:1 (1–4).
17*a* TG Joy.
b Dan. 10:8 (8–12); 1 Ne. 1:7.
c Alma 19:14 (14, 17).

18 Now was not this [a]exceeding joy? Behold, this is joy which none receiveth save it be the truly penitent and humble seeker of [b]happiness.
19 Now the joy of Alma in meeting his [a]brethren was truly great, and also the joy of Aaron, of Omner, and Himni; but behold their joy was not that to exceed their strength.
20 And now it came to pass that Alma conducted his brethren back to the land of Zarahemla; even to his [a]own house. And they went and told the [b]chief judge all the things that had happened unto them in the land of Nephi, among their brethren, the Lamanites.
21 And it came to pass that the chief judge sent a proclamation throughout all the land, desiring the voice of the people concerning the admitting their brethren, who were the people of [a]Anti-Nephi-Lehi.
22 And it came to pass that the voice of the people came, saying: Behold, we will give up the [a]land of [b]Jershon, which is on the east by the sea, which joins the land Bountiful, which is on the south of the land Bountiful; and this land Jershon is the land which we will give unto our brethren for an inheritance.
23 And behold, we will set our armies between the land Jershon and the land Nephi, that we may [a]protect our brethren in the land Jershon; and this we do for our brethren, on account of their fear to take up arms against their brethren lest they should commit sin; and this their great fear came because of their sore repentance which they had, on account of their many murders and their awful wickedness.
24 And now behold, this will we do unto our brethren, that they may inherit the land Jershon; and we will guard them from their enemies with our armies, on condition that they will give us a [a]portion of their substance to assist us that we may maintain our armies.
25 Now, it came to pass that when Ammon had heard this, he returned to the people of Anti-Nephi-Lehi, and also Alma with him, into the wilderness, where they had pitched their tents, and made known unto them all these things. And Alma also related unto them his [a]conversion, with Ammon and Aaron, and his brethren.
26 And it came to pass that it did cause great joy among them. And they went down into the land of Jershon, and took possession of the land of Jershon; and they were called by the Nephites the [a]people of Ammon; therefore they were distinguished by that name ever after.
27 And they were among the people of Nephi, and also numbered among the people who were of the church of God. And they were also distinguished for their [a]zeal towards God, and also towards men; for they were perfectly [b]honest and upright in all things; and they were [c]firm in the faith of Christ, even unto the end.
28 And they did look upon shedding the blood of their brethren with the greatest abhorrence; and they never could be prevailed upon to take up arms against their brethren; and they never did look upon death with any degree of terror, for their hope and views of Christ and the resurrection; therefore, death was swallowed up to them by the victory of Christ over it.
29 Therefore, they would suffer

18*a* Alma 28:8.
b TG Happiness; Objectives.
19*a* TG Friendship.
20*a* Alma 15:18.
b Alma 4:17 (16–18).
21*a* Alma 25:13 (1, 13); 43:11.
22*a* Alma 43:12.
b Alma 28:1 (1, 8).
23*a* Alma 43:12.
24*a* Alma 43:13.
25*a* Mosiah 27:24 (10–25).
26*a* Alma 30:1.
27*a* TG Zeal.
b Prov. 19:1; D&C 124:20 (15, 20). TG Honesty.
c Alma 23:6; Hel. 15:8 (6–10).

[a]death in the most aggravating and
distressing manner which could be
inflicted by their brethren, before
they would take the sword or cimeter to smite them.
30 And thus they were a zealous
and beloved people, a highly favored people of the Lord.

CHAPTER 28

The Lamanites are defeated in a tremendous battle—Tens of thousands are slain—The wicked are consigned to a state of endless woe; the righteous attain a never-ending happiness. About 77–76 B.C.

AND now it came to pass that after
the people of Ammon were established in the land of [a]Jershon, and
a church also established in the
land of Jershon, and the armies of
the Nephites were set round about
the land of Jershon, yea, in all the
borders round about the land of
Zarahemla; behold the armies of
the Lamanites had followed their
brethren into the wilderness.
2 And thus there was a tremendous battle; yea, even such an one
as never had been known among
all the people in the land from the
time Lehi left Jerusalem; yea, and
tens of thousands of the Lamanites
were slain and scattered abroad.
3 Yea, and also there was a tremendous slaughter among the people of
Nephi; nevertheless, the Lamanites
were [a]driven and scattered, and the
people of Nephi returned again to
their land.
4 And now this was a time that
there was a great [a]mourning and
lamentation heard throughout all
the land, among all the people of
Nephi—
5 Yea, the cry of [a]widows mourning for their husbands, and also of
fathers mourning for their sons,
and the daughter for the brother,
yea, the brother for the father;
and thus the cry of mourning was
heard among all of them, mourning for their kindred who had
been slain.
6 And now surely this was a sorrowful day; yea, a time of solem-
nity, and a time of much [a]fasting
and prayer.
7 And thus endeth the fifteenth
year of the reign of the judges over
the people of Nephi;
8 And [a]this is the account of Ammon and his brethren, their journeyings in the land of Nephi, their
sufferings in the land, their sorrows,
and their afflictions, and their [b]in-
comprehensible joy, and the reception and safety of the brethren in
the land of Jershon. And now may
the Lord, the Redeemer of all men,
bless their souls forever.
9 And this is the account of the
wars and contentions among the
Nephites, and also the wars between
the Nephites and the Lamanites;
and the fifteenth year of the reign
of the judges is ended.
10 And from the [a]first year to the
fifteenth has brought to pass the
destruction of many thousand lives;
yea, it has brought to pass an awful
scene of bloodshed.
11 And the bodies of many thousands are laid low in the earth,
while the bodies of many thousands
are [a]moldering in heaps upon the
face of the earth; yea, and many
thousands are [b]mourning for the
loss of their kindred, because they
have reason to fear, according to the
promises of the Lord, that they are
consigned to a state of endless wo.
12 While many thousands of others
truly [a]mourn for the loss of their
kindred, yet they rejoice and exult
in the hope, and even know, according to the [b]promises of the Lord, that

---

29a Alma 24:23 (20–23).
28 1a Alma 27:22; 30:19 (1, 19).
3a Alma 30:1.
4a TG Mourning.
5a TG Widows.
6a Matt. 5:4; Alma 30:2; 3 Ne. 12:4.
8a IE the account covered in Alma 17–28.
b Alma 27:18 (16–19).
10a IE the years recounted in Alma 1–28.
11a Alma 16:11.
b Alma 48:23; D&C 42:45.
12a Gen. 50:10.
b Alma 11:41.

they are raised to dwell at the right
hand of God, in a state of never-
ending [c]happiness.
13 And thus we see how great
the [a]inequality of man is because
of sin and [b]transgression, and the
power of the devil, which comes
by the cunning [c]plans which he
hath devised to ensnare the hearts
of men.
14 And thus we see the great call
of [a]diligence of men to labor in the
vineyards of the Lord; and thus we
see the great reason of sorrow, and
also of rejoicing—sorrow because
of death and destruction among
men, and joy because of the [b]light
of Christ unto life.

CHAPTER 29

Alma desires to cry repentance with angelic zeal—The Lord grants teachers for all nations—Alma glories in the Lord's work and in the success of Ammon and his brethren. About 76 B.C.

O THAT I were an angel, and could
have the wish of mine heart, that I
might go forth and speak with the
[a]trump of God, with a voice to shake
the earth, and cry repentance unto
every people!
2 Yea, I would declare unto every
soul, as with the voice of thunder,
repentance and the plan of redemption, that they should repent and
[a]come unto our God, that there
might not be more sorrow upon all
the face of the earth.
3 But behold, I am a man, and do
sin in my wish; for I ought to be
content with the things which the
Lord hath allotted unto me.
4 I ought not to harrow up in my
desires the firm decree of a just God,
for I know that he granteth unto men
according to their [a]desire, whether
it be unto death or unto life; yea,
I know that he allotteth unto men,
yea, decreeth unto them decrees
which are unalterable, according to
their [b]wills, whether they be unto
salvation or unto destruction.
5 Yea, and I know that good and
evil have come before all men; he
that knoweth not good from evil is
[a]blameless; but he that [b]knoweth
good and evil, to him it is given according to his desires, whether he
desireth good or evil, life or death,
joy or remorse of [c]conscience.
6 Now, seeing that I know these
things, why should I desire more
than to [a]perform the work to which
I have been called?
7 Why should I desire that I were
an angel, that I could speak unto
all the ends of the earth?
8 For behold, the Lord doth [a]grant
unto [b]all nations, of their own nation and [c]tongue, to teach his word,
yea, in wisdom, all that he [d]seeth
fit that they should have; therefore
we see that the Lord doth counsel
in wisdom, according to that which
is just and true.
9 I know that which the Lord hath
commanded me, and I glory in it.
I do [a]not [b]glory of myself, but I
glory in that which the Lord hath
commanded me; yea, and this is
my glory, that perhaps I may be an
instrument in the hands of God to
bring some soul to repentance; and
this is my joy.
10 And behold, when I see many
of my brethren truly penitent, and
coming to the Lord their God, then
is my soul filled with joy; then do I
remember [a]what the Lord has done

12*c* Alma 56:11.
13*a* 1 Ne. 17:35.
b TG Transgress.
c 2 Ne. 9:28.
14*a* TG Diligence; Vineyard of the Lord.
b TG Light of Christ.
29 1*a* Isa. 58:1; D&C 29:4.
2*a* Omni 1:26 (25–26); 3 Ne. 21:20.
4*a* Ps. 21:2; 37:4.
b TG Agency.
5*a* TG Accountability.
b Gen. 3:5; 2 Ne. 2:18 (18, 26); Mosiah 16:3; Moro. 7:16 (15–19). TG Discernment, Spiritual.
c Job 27:6. TG Conscience.
6*a* TG Stewardship.
8*a* 3 Ne. 26:8 (7–10); D&C 11:22.
b 2 Ne. 2:27; 29:12.
c D&C 90:11.
d Alma 12:9 (9–11).
9*a* Alma 26:12.
b TG Glory.
10*a* Mosiah 27:14 (11–31).

for me, yea, even that he hath heard my prayer; yea, then do I remember his merciful arm which he extended towards me.

11 Yea, and I also remember the captivity of my fathers; for I surely do know that the [a]Lord did deliver them out of bondage, and by this did establish his church; yea, the Lord God, the God of Abraham, the God of Isaac, and the God of Jacob, did deliver them out of bondage.

12 Yea, I have always remembered the captivity of my fathers; and that same God who [a]delivered them out of the hands of the Egyptians did deliver them out of [b]bondage.

13 Yea, and that same God did establish his church among them; yea, and that same God hath called me by a [a]holy calling, to [b]preach the word unto this people, and hath given me much success, in the which my joy is full.

14 But I do not joy in my own [a]success alone, but my joy is more full because of the success of my brethren, who have been up to the land of Nephi.

15 Behold, they have labored exceedingly, and have brought forth much fruit; and how great shall be their reward!

16 Now, when I think of the success of these my brethren my soul is carried away, even to the separation of it from the body, as it were, so great is my [a]joy.

17 And now may God grant unto these, my brethren, that they may sit down in the kingdom of God; yea, and also all those who are the fruit of their labors that they may go no more out, but that they may praise him forever. And may God grant that it may be done according to my words, even as I have spoken. Amen.

CHAPTER 30

Korihor, the anti-Christ, ridicules Christ, the Atonement, and the spirit of prophecy—He teaches that there is no God, no fall of man, no penalty for sin, and no Christ—Alma testifies that Christ will come and that all things denote there is a God—Korihor demands a sign and is struck dumb—The devil had appeared to Korihor as an angel and taught him what to say—Korihor is trodden down and dies. About 76–74 B.C.

BEHOLD, now it came to pass that after the [a]people of Ammon were established in the land of Jershon, yea, and also after the Lamanites were [b]driven out of the land, and their dead were buried by the people of the land—

2 Now their dead were not numbered because of the greatness of their numbers; neither were the dead of the Nephites numbered—but it came to pass after they had buried their dead, and also after the days of [a]fasting, and [b]mourning, and prayer, (and it was in the sixteenth year of the reign of the judges over the people of Nephi) there began to be continual peace throughout all the land.

3 Yea, and the people did observe to keep the commandments of the Lord; and they were strict in observing the [a]ordinances of God, according to the law of Moses; for they were taught to [b]keep the law of Moses until it should be fulfilled.

4 And thus the people did have no disturbance in all the sixteenth year of the reign of the judges over the people of Nephi.

5 And it came to pass that in the commencement of the seventeenth year of the reign of the judges, there was continual peace.

6 But it came to pass in the latter end of the seventeenth year, there came a man into the land of

---

11*a* Ex. 3:6; Alma 36:2.
12*a* Micah 6:4.
b Alma 5:5 (5–6); 36:29 (2, 29).
13*a* Alma 5:3.
b TG Preaching.
14*a* Alma 17:4 (1–4).
16*a* TG Joy.
30 1*a* Alma 27:26.
b Alma 28:3 (2–3).
2*a* Alma 28:6.
b TG Mourning.
3*a* TG Ordinance.
b 2 Ne. 25:24; Jarom 1:5; Mosiah 2:3; Alma 34:14 (13–14).

Zarahemla, and he was [a]Anti-Christ,
for he began to preach unto the people [b]against the prophecies which
had been spoken by the prophets,
concerning the coming of Christ.
7 Now there was no law against a
[a]man's [b]belief; for it was strictly contrary to the commands of God that
there should be a law which should
bring men on to unequal grounds.
8 For thus saith the scripture:
[a]Choose ye this day, whom ye will
serve.
9 Now if a man desired to serve
God, it was his privilege; or rather,
if he believed in God it was his privilege to serve him; but if he did not
believe in him there was no law to
punish him.
10 But if he [a]murdered he was
punished unto [b]death; and if he
[c]robbed he was also punished; and
if he stole he was also punished;
and if he committed [d]adultery he
was also punished; yea, for all this
wickedness they were punished.
11 For there was a law that men
should be judged according to their
crimes. Nevertheless, there was no
law against a man's belief; therefore,
a man was punished only for the
crimes which he had done; therefore
all men were on [a]equal grounds.
12 And this [a]Anti-Christ, whose
name was Korihor, (and the law
could have no hold upon him) began to preach unto the people that
there should be [b]no Christ. And after
this manner did he preach, saying:
13 O ye that are bound down under a [a]foolish and a vain hope, why
do ye yoke yourselves with such
foolish things? Why do ye look for
a Christ? For no man can [b]know of
anything which is to come.
14 Behold, these things which ye
call prophecies, which ye say are
handed down by holy prophets,
behold, they are foolish traditions
of your fathers.
15 How do ye know of their surety?
Behold, ye cannot know of things
which ye do not [a]see; therefore ye
cannot know that there shall be a
Christ.
16 Ye look forward and say that
ye see a remission of your sins. But
behold, it is the effect of a [a]frenzied
mind; and this derangement of your
minds comes because of the traditions of your fathers, which lead
you away into a belief of things
which are not so.
17 And many more such things
did he say unto them, telling them
that there could be no atonement
made for the sins of men, but every
man [a]fared in this life according to
the management of the creature;
therefore every man prospered
according to his genius, and that
every man conquered according
to his strength; and [b]whatsoever a
man did was [c]no crime.
18 And thus he did preach unto
them, leading away the hearts of
many, causing them to lift up their
heads in their wickedness, yea, leading away many women, and also
men, to commit whoredoms—telling
them that when a man was dead,
that was the end thereof.
19 Now this man went over to the
land of [a]Jershon also, to preach
these things among the people of
Ammon, who were once the people
of the Lamanites.
20 But behold they were more wise
than many of the Nephites; for they
took him, and bound him, and carried him before Ammon, who was
a [a]high priest over that people.

6a TG Antichrist; False Prophets.
b TG False Doctrine; Prophets, Rejection of.
7a Alma 1:17.
b Acts 18:13.
8a Josh. 24:15. TG Agency.
10a TG Murder.
b TG Capital Punishment.
c Alma 1:18.
d TG Adulterer.
11a Mosiah 27:3; 29:32.
12a TG Antichrist.
b Jacob 7:2 (2, 9); Alma 31:16 (16, 29); 34:5.
13a 1 Cor. 1:25 (18–25).
b Jacob 7:7.
15a Hel. 16:20; Ether 12:5 (5–6, 19). TG Spiritual Blindness.
16a Acts 26:24 (24–25).
17a Prov. 16:25; 2 Ne. 28:7 (5–9).
b Alma 18:5.
c Alma 1:4; Morm. 8:31.
19a Alma 28:1 (1, 8); 31:3.
20a Alma 46:38.

21 And it came to pass that he caused that he should be carried out of the land. And he came over into the land of Gideon, and began to preach unto them also; and here he did not have much success, for he was taken and bound and carried before the high priest, and also the chief judge over the land.

22 And it came to pass that the high priest said unto him: Why do ye go about perverting the ways of the Lord? Why do ye teach this people that there shall be no Christ, to interrupt their rejoicings? Why do ye speak against all the prophecies of the holy prophets?

23 Now the high priest's name was Giddonah. And Korihor said unto him: Because I do not teach the foolish traditions of your fathers, and because I do not teach this people to bind themselves down under the foolish ordinances and performances which are laid down by ancient priests, to usurp power and authority over them, to keep them in ignorance, that they may not lift up their heads, but be brought down according to thy words.

24 Ye say that this people is a free people. Behold, I say they are in bondage. Ye say that those ancient prophecies are true. Behold, I say that ye do not know that they are true.

25 Ye say that this people is a guilty and a fallen people, because of the transgression of a parent. Behold, I say that a child is not guilty because of its parents.

26 And ye also say that Christ shall come. But behold, I say that ye do not know that there shall be a Christ. And ye say also that he shall be slain for the [a]sins of the world—

27 And thus ye lead away this people after the foolish traditions of your fathers, and according to your own desires; and ye keep them down, even as it were in bondage, that ye may glut yourselves with the labors of their hands, that they durst not look up with boldness, and that they durst not enjoy their rights and privileges.

28 Yea, they durst not make use of that which is their own lest they should offend their priests, who do yoke them according to their desires, and have brought them to believe, by their traditions and their dreams and their whims and their visions and their pretended mysteries, that they should, if they did not do according to their words, offend some unknown being, who they say is God—a being who [a]never has been seen or known, who [b]never was nor ever will be.

29 Now when the high priest and the [a]chief judge saw the hardness of his heart, yea, when they saw that he would [b]revile even against God, they would not make any reply to his words; but they caused that he should be bound; and they delivered him up into the hands of the officers, and sent him to the land of Zarahemla, that he might be brought before Alma, and the chief judge who was governor over all the land.

30 And it came to pass that when he was brought before Alma and the chief judge, he did go on in the same manner as he did in the land of Gideon; yea, he went on to [a]blaspheme.

31 And he did rise up in great [a]swelling words before Alma, and did revile against the [b]priests and teachers, accusing them of leading away the people after the silly traditions of their fathers, for the sake of glutting on the labors of the people.

32 Now Alma said unto him: Thou knowest that we do not glut ourselves upon the labors of this people; for behold I have [a]labored even from

26*a* Isa. 53:6 (4–12).
28*a* 2 Ne. 28:5.
b Alma 30:53.
29*a* Alma 4:17.
b TG Reviling.
30*a* TG Blaspheme.
31*a* Hel. 13:22.
TG Boast.
b Alma 23:4.
32*a* TG Labor; Self-Sacrifice.

the commencement of the reign of
the judges until now, with mine
[b]own hands for my support, notwithstanding my many travels round
about the land to declare the word
of God unto my people.
33 And notwithstanding the many
labors which I have performed in
the church, I have never received
so much as even one [a]senine for my
labor; neither has any of my brethren, save it were in the judgment-
seat; and then we have received
only according to law for our time.
34 And now, if we do not receive
anything for our labors in the
church, what doth it profit us to
labor in the church save it were to
declare the truth, that we may have
rejoicings in the [a]joy of our brethren?
35 Then why sayest thou that we
preach unto this people to get gain,
when thou, of thyself, knowest that
we receive no gain? And now, believest thou that we deceive this
people, that [a]causes such joy in
their hearts?
36 And Korihor answered him, Yea.
37 And then Alma said unto him:
Believest thou that there is a God?
38 And he answered, Nay.
39 Now Alma said unto him: Will ye
deny again that there is a God, and
also deny the Christ? For behold, I
say unto you, I know there is a God,
and also that Christ shall come.
40 And now what evidence have ye
that there is no [a]God, or that Christ
cometh not? I say unto you that ye
have none, save it be your word only.
41 But, behold, I have all things as
a [a]testimony that these things are
true; and ye also have all things
as a testimony unto you that they
are true; and will ye deny them?
Believest thou that these things
are true?
42 Behold, I know that thou [a]be-
lievest, but thou art possessed with
a [b]lying spirit, and ye have put
[c]off the Spirit of God that it may
have no place in you; but the devil
has power over you, and he doth
carry you about, working devices
that he may destroy the children
of God.
43 And now Korihor said unto
Alma: If thou wilt show me a [a]sign,
that I may be convinced that there
is a God, yea, show unto me that he
hath power, and then will I be convinced of the truth of thy words.
44 But Alma said unto him: Thou
hast had signs enough; will ye tempt
your God? Will ye say, Show unto
me a sign, when ye have the testimony of [a]all these thy brethren,
and also all the holy prophets? The
scriptures are laid before thee, yea,
and all things denote there is a
God; yea, even the [b]earth, and [c]all
things that are upon the face of it,
yea, and its [d]motion, yea, and also
all the [e]planets which move in their
regular form do witness that there
is a Supreme Creator.
45 And yet do ye go about, leading away the hearts of this people,
testifying unto them there is no
God? And yet will ye deny against
all these [a]witnesses? And he said:
Yea, I will deny, except ye shall show
me a sign.
46 And now it came to pass that
Alma said unto him: Behold, I am
grieved because of the hardness of
your heart, yea, that ye will still resist the spirit of the truth, that thy
soul may be destroyed.
47 But behold, it is [a]better that thy

32*b* Acts 20:34 (33–35);
1 Thes. 2:9;
Mosiah 18:24.
33*a* Alma 11:3.
34*a* TG Joy.
35*a* Matt. 7:16.
40*a* Ps. 14:1.
41*a* TG Testimony.
42*a* Acts 26:27;
Jacob 7:14;
Mosiah 12:30;
Alma 30:52.
b Jer. 27:10;
Rom. 3:3–4;
Mosiah 2:32.
c 1 Sam. 16:14.
43*a* John 6:30;
Jacob 7:13 (13–21);
D&C 46:9 (8–9).
TG Sign Seekers.
44*a* Mosiah 13:33 (33–34).
b Job 12:8 (7–10).
TG Nature, Earth.
c D&C 88:47.
d Hel. 12:15 (11–15).
e Moses 6:63.
TG Astronomy.
45*a* TG Witness.
47*a* 1 Ne. 4:13.

soul should be [b]lost than that thou
shouldst be the means of bringing
many souls down to destruction,
by thy lying and by thy flattering
words; therefore if thou shalt deny
again, behold God shall smite thee,
that thou shalt become dumb, that
thou shalt never open thy mouth
any more, that thou shalt not deceive this people any more.
48 Now Korihor said unto him: I do
not deny the existence of a God, but
I do not believe that there is a God;
and I say also, that ye do not know
that there is a God; and except ye
show me a sign, I will not believe.
49 Now Alma said unto him: This
will I give unto thee for a sign, that
thou shalt be [a]struck dumb, according to my words; and I say, that in
the name of God, ye shall be struck
dumb, that ye shall no more have
utterance.
50 Now when Alma had said these
words, Korihor was struck dumb,
that he could not have utterance,
according to the words of Alma.
51 And now when the chief judge
saw this, he put forth his hand and
wrote unto Korihor, saying: Art thou
convinced of the power of God?
In whom did ye desire that Alma
should show forth his sign? Would
ye that he should afflict others, to
show unto thee a sign? Behold, he
has showed unto you a sign; and
now will ye dispute more?
52 And Korihor put forth his hand
and wrote, saying: I know that I
am dumb, for I cannot speak; and
I know that nothing save it were
the [a]power of God could bring this
upon me; yea, and I always [b]knew
that there was a God.
53 But behold, the devil hath
[a]deceived me; for he [b]appeared
unto me in the [c]form of an angel,
and said unto me: Go and reclaim
this people, for they have all gone
astray after an unknown God. And
he said unto me: There is [d]no God;
yea, and he taught me that which
I should say. And I have taught his
words; and I taught them because
they were pleasing unto the [e]car-
nal mind; and I taught them, even
until I had much success, insomuch
that I verily believed that they were
true; and for this cause I withstood
the truth, even until I have brought
this great [f]curse upon me.
54 Now when he had said this, he
besought that Alma should pray
unto God, that the [a]curse might be
taken from him.
55 But Alma said unto him: If this
curse should be taken from thee thou
wouldst again lead away the hearts
of this people; therefore, it shall
be unto thee even as the Lord will.
56 And it came to pass that the
curse was not taken off of Korihor; but he was [a]cast out, and went
about from house to house begging
for his food.
57 Now the knowledge of what
had happened unto Korihor was
immediately published throughout
all the land; yea, the proclamation
was sent forth by the chief judge to
all the people in the land, declaring unto those who had believed
in the words of Korihor that they
must speedily repent, [a]lest the same
judgments would come unto them.
58 And it came to pass that they
were all convinced of the wickedness of Korihor; therefore they were
all converted again unto the Lord;
and this put an end to the iniquity
after the manner of Korihor. And
Korihor did go about from house to
house, begging food for his support.
59 And it came to pass that as he
went forth among the people, yea,
among a people who had separated
themselves from the Nephites and
called themselves [a]Zoramites, being

47*b* Mosiah 27:16.
49*a* Luke 1:20;
Acts 13:11 (8–12).
52*a* 2 Chr. 13:20.
b Alma 30:42 (41–42).
53*a* Jacob 7:14 (14, 18).
b 2 Ne. 9:9.
c 2 Cor. 11:14.
d Ps. 10:4 (2–11);
Alma 30:28.
e TG Carnal Mind.
f TG Curse.
54*a* Num. 12:13 (9–15).
56*a* Dan. 5:21.
57*a* John 5:14.
59*a* Alma 31:7 (7–8).

led by a man whose name was
Zoram—and as he went forth
amongst them, behold, he was run
upon and trodden down, even until
he was [b]dead.
60 And thus we see the end of
him who [a]perverteth the ways of
the Lord; and thus we see that the
devil will not [b]support his children
at the last day, but doth speedily
drag them down to [c]hell.

CHAPTER 31

Alma heads a mission to reclaim the apostate Zoramites—The Zoramites deny Christ, believe in a false concept of election, and worship with set prayers—The missionaries are filled with the Holy Spirit—Their afflictions are swallowed up in the joy of Christ. About 74 B.C.

Now it came to pass that after the end
of Korihor, Alma having received
tidings that the Zoramites were perverting the ways of the Lord, and
that Zoram, who was their leader,
was leading the hearts of the people to [a]bow down to dumb [b]idols,
his heart again began to [c]sicken because of the iniquity of the people.
2 For it was the cause of great [a]sor-
row to Alma to know of iniquity
among his people; therefore his
heart was exceedingly [b]sorrowful
because of the separation of the
Zoramites from the Nephites.
3 Now the Zoramites had gathered themselves together in a land
which they called [a]Antionum, which
was east of the land of Zarahemla,
which lay nearly bordering upon the
seashore, which was south of the land
of [b]Jershon, which also bordered
upon the wilderness south, which
wilderness was full of the Lamanites.
4 Now the Nephites greatly feared
that the Zoramites would enter into
a [a]correspondence with the Lamanites, and that it would be the
means of great loss on the part of
the Nephites.
5 And now, as the [a]preaching of
the [b]word had a great tendency to
[c]lead the people to do that which
was just—yea, it had had more powerful effect upon the minds of the
people than the sword, or anything
else, which had happened unto
them—therefore Alma thought it
was expedient that they should try
the virtue of the word of God.
6 Therefore he took Ammon, and
Aaron, and Omner; and Himni he
did leave in the church in Zarahemla; but the former three he
took with him, and also [a]Amulek
and Zeezrom, who were at [b]Melek;
and he also took two of his sons.
7 Now the eldest of his sons he
took not with him, and his name
was Helaman; but the names of
those whom he took with him were
[a]Shiblon and [b]Corianton; and these
are the names of those who went
with him among the [c]Zoramites, to
preach unto them the word.
8 Now the Zoramites were [a]dis-
senters from the Nephites; therefore they had had the word of God
preached unto them.
9 But they had [a]fallen into great
errors, for they would not observe
to keep the commandments of God,

59*b* Jer. 28:16 (15–17); Jacob 7:20 (1–20).
60*a* TG Lying.
b Alma 3:27 (26–27); 5:42 (41–42); D&C 29:45.
c TG Hell.
31 1*a* Ex. 20:5; Mosiah 13:13.
b 2 Ne. 9:37. TG Idolatry.
c Alma 35:15.
2*a* 1 Ne. 7:8; Mosiah 28:3; 3 Ne. 17:14; Moses 7:41.
b Isa. 22:4.
3*a* Alma 43:5 (5, 15, 22).
b Alma 27:22.
4*a* TG Conspiracy.
5*a* Ex. 24:7; Jonah 3:5; Rom. 10:17; Enos 1:23; Alma 4:19. TG Preaching.
b 2 Kgs. 22:11; Heb. 4:12; Jacob 2:8; Alma 36:26.
c Jarom 1:12; Alma 45:21; Hel. 5:51 (50–52); D&C 11:2. TG Gospel.
6*a* Hel. 5:41.
b Alma 8:3; 35:13; 45:18.
7*a* Alma 31:32; 35:14.
b Alma 39:1.
c Alma 30:59; 38:3.
8*a* Alma 24:30; 53:8; Hel. 1:15; D&C 93:19.
9*a* TG Apostasy of Individuals.

and his statutes, according to the law of Moses.

10 Neither would they observe the [a]performances of the church, to continue in prayer and supplication to God daily, that they might not enter into temptation.

11 Yea, in fine, they did pervert the ways of the Lord in very many instances; therefore, for this cause, Alma and his brethren went into the land to preach the word unto them.

12 Now, when they had come into the land, behold, to their astonishment they found that the Zoramites had built synagogues, and that they did gather themselves together on one day of the week, which day they did call the day of the Lord; and they did [a]worship after a manner which Alma and his brethren had never beheld;

13 For they had a place built up in the center of their synagogue, a place for standing, which was high above the head; and the top thereof would only admit one person.

14 Therefore, whosoever desired to [a]worship must go forth and stand upon the top thereof, and stretch forth his hands towards heaven, and cry with a loud voice, saying:

15 Holy, holy God; we believe that thou art God, and we believe that thou art holy, and that thou wast a [a]spirit, and that thou art a spirit, and that thou wilt be a spirit forever.

16 Holy God, we believe that thou hast separated us from our brethren; and we do not believe in the tradition of our brethren, which was handed down to them by the childishness of their fathers; but we believe that thou hast [a]elected us to be thy [b]holy children; and also thou hast made it known unto us that [c]there shall be [d]no Christ.

17 But thou art the same yesterday, today, and forever; and thou hast [a]elected us that we shall be saved, whilst all around us are elected to be cast by thy wrath down to hell; for the which holiness, O God, we thank thee; and we also thank thee that thou hast elected us, that we may not be led away after the foolish traditions of our brethren, which doth [b]bind them down to a belief of Christ, which doth lead their hearts to wander far from thee, our God.

18 And again we thank thee, O God, that we are a chosen and a holy people. Amen.

19 Now it came to pass that after Alma and his brethren and his sons had heard these prayers, they were astonished beyond all measure.

20 For behold, every man did go forth and offer up these same [a]prayers.

21 Now the place was called by them Rameumptom, which, being interpreted, is the holy stand.

22 Now, from this stand they did offer up, every man, the selfsame prayer unto God, thanking their God that they were chosen of him, and that he did not lead them away after the tradition of their brethren, and that their hearts were not stolen away to believe in things to come, which they knew nothing about.

23 Now, after the people had all offered up thanks after this manner, they returned to their homes, [a]never speaking of their God again until they had assembled themselves together again to the holy stand, to offer up thanks after their manner.

24 Now when Alma saw this his heart was [a]grieved; for he saw that they were a wicked and a perverse people; yea, he saw that their hearts were set upon gold, and upon silver, and upon all manner of fine goods.

10*a* TG Ordinance.
12*a* TG Worship.
14*a* Matt. 6:5 (1–7).
15*a* Alma 18:4 (4–5).
16*a* Luke 18:11; Alma 38:14 (13–14).
b Isa. 65:5 (1–5).
c Alma 34:5.
d Jacob 7:2 (2, 9); Alma 30:12 (12, 22).
17*a* TG Conceit; Pride.
b TG False Doctrine.
20*a* Matt. 6:7.
23*a* James 1:22 (21–25).
24*a* Gen. 6:6; 1 Ne. 2:18.

25 Yea, and he also saw that their
hearts were [a]lifted up unto great
boasting, in their pride.
26 And he lifted up his voice to
heaven, and [a]cried, saying: O, how
long, O Lord, wilt thou suffer that
thy servants shall dwell here below
in the flesh, to behold such gross
wickedness among the children of
men?
27 Behold, O God, they [a]cry unto
thee, and yet their hearts are swallowed up in their pride. Behold, O
God, they cry unto thee with their
mouths, while they are [b]puffed up,
even to greatness, with the vain
things of the [c]world.
28 Behold, O my God, their costly
apparel, and their ringlets, and their
[a]bracelets, and their ornaments of
gold, and all their precious things
which they are ornamented with;
and behold, their hearts are set upon
them, and yet they cry unto thee
and say—We thank thee, O God, for
we are a chosen people unto thee,
while others shall perish.
29 Yea, and they say that thou hast
made it known unto them that there
shall be no Christ.
30 O Lord God, how long wilt thou
suffer that such wickedness and in-
fidelity shall be among this people?
O Lord, wilt thou give me strength,
that I may [a]bear with mine infirmities. For I am infirm, and such
wickedness among this people doth
pain my soul.
31 O Lord, my heart is exceedingly
sorrowful; wilt thou comfort my soul
[a]in Christ. O Lord, wilt thou grant
unto me that I may have strength,
that I may suffer with patience
these [b]afflictions which shall come
upon me, because of the iniquity
of this people.
32 O Lord, wilt thou comfort my
soul, and give unto me success, and
also my fellow laborers who are with
me—yea, Ammon, and Aaron, and
Omner, and also [a]Amulek and Zeezrom, and also my [b]two sons—yea,
even all these wilt thou comfort, O
Lord. Yea, wilt thou comfort their
souls in Christ.
33 Wilt thou grant unto them that
they may have strength, that they
may [a]bear their afflictions which
shall come upon them because of
the iniquities of this people.
34 O Lord, wilt thou grant [a]unto us
that we may have success in bringing them again unto thee in Christ.
35 Behold, O Lord, their [a]souls are
precious, and many of them are
our brethren; therefore, give unto
us, O Lord, power and wisdom that
we may bring these, our brethren,
again unto thee.
36 Now it came to pass that when
Alma had said these words, that
he [a]clapped his [b]hands upon all
them who were with him. And behold, as he clapped his hands upon
them, they were filled with the
Holy Spirit.
37 And after that they did separate themselves one from another,
[a]taking no thought for themselves
what they should eat, or what they
should drink, or what they should
put on.
38 And the Lord provided for
them that they should hunger not,
neither should they thirst; yea,
and he also gave them strength,
that they should suffer no manner
of [a]afflictions, save it were swallowed up in the joy of Christ. Now
this was according to the prayer of
Alma; and this because he prayed
in [b]faith.

25*a* 2 Kgs. 14:10; Jacob 2:13; Alma 1:32.
26*a* Moses 7:44 (41–58).
27*a* Isa. 29:13. TG Hypocrisy.
b TG Pride; Selfishness.
c TG Worldliness.
28*a* Isa. 3:19 (16–24).
30*a* Num. 11:14.
31*a* John 16:33. TG Comfort; Peace of God.
b TG Affliction.
32*a* Alma 8:21; 34:1.
b Alma 31:7.
33*a* Rom. 15:1.
34*a* 2 Ne. 26:33.
35*a* TG Worth of Souls.
36*a* 3 Ne. 18:37.
b TG Hands, Laying on of.
37*a* Matt. 6:25 (25–34); 3 Ne. 13:25 (25–34).
38*a* Matt. 5:10 (10–12); Mosiah 24:15 (13–15); Alma 33:23.
b TG Faith.

CHAPTER 32

Alma teaches the poor whose afflictions had humbled them—Faith is a hope in that which is not seen which is true—Alma testifies that angels minister to men, women, and children—Alma compares the word unto a seed—It must be planted and nourished—Then it grows into a tree from which the fruit of eternal life is picked. About 74 B.C.

AND it came to pass that they did
go forth, and began to preach the
word of God unto the people, enter-
ing into their synagogues, and into
their houses; yea, and even they did
preach the word in their streets.
2 And it came to pass that after
much labor among them, they began to have success among the [a]poor
class of people; for behold, they
were cast out of the synagogues
because of the coarseness of their
apparel—
3 Therefore they were not permitted to enter into their synagogues
to worship God, being esteemed
as filthiness; therefore they were
poor; yea, they were esteemed by
their brethren as [a]dross; therefore
they were [b]poor as to things of the
world; and also they were poor
in heart.
4 Now, as Alma was teaching and
speaking unto the people upon the
hill [a]Onidah, there came a great
[b]multitude unto him, who were
those of whom we have been speaking, of whom were [c]poor in heart,
because of their poverty as to the
things of the world.
5 And they came unto Alma; and
the one who was the foremost among
them said unto him: Behold, [a]what
shall these my brethren do, for they
are [b]despised of all men because of
their poverty, yea, and more especially by our priests; for they have
[c]cast us out of our synagogues which
we have labored abundantly to build
with our own hands; and they have
cast us out because of our exceeding poverty; and we have [d]no place
to worship our God; and behold,
[e]what shall we do?
6 And now when Alma heard
this, he turned him about, his face
immediately towards him, and he
beheld with great joy; for he beheld that their [a]afflictions had
truly [b]humbled them, and that
they were in a [c]preparation to hear
the word.
7 Therefore he did say no more to
the other multitude; but he stretched
forth his hand, and cried unto those
whom he beheld, who were truly
penitent, and said unto them:
8 I behold that ye are [a]lowly in
heart; and if so, blessed are ye.
9 Behold thy brother hath said,
What shall we do?—for we are cast
out of our synagogues, that we cannot worship our God.
10 Behold I say unto you, do ye
suppose that ye [a]cannot worship
God save it be in your synagogues
only?
11 And moreover, I would ask, do
ye suppose that ye must not worship
God only [a]once in a week?
12 I say unto you, it is well that ye
are cast out of your synagogues, that
ye may be humble, and that ye may
learn [a]wisdom; for it is necessary
that ye should learn wisdom; for
it is because that ye are cast out,
that ye are despised of your brethren
because of your exceeding [b]poverty,
that ye are brought to a lowliness of
heart; for ye are necessarily brought
to be humble.

---

32 2*a* Luke 6:20; 7:22. TG Poor.
3*a* Luke 18:9.
b Alma 34:40.
4*a* Alma 47:5.
b TG Assembly for Worship.
c TG Poor in Spirit.
5*a* Prov. 18:23.
b TG Oppression.
c Alma 33:10.
d Alma 33:2.
e Acts 2:37 (37–38); Alma 34:3.
6*a* TG Adversity.
b TG Humility; Teachable.
c Prov. 16:1; Alma 16:16 (16–17); D&C 101:8.
8*a* Matt. 5:5 (3–5).
10*a* TG Worship.
11*a* Mosiah 18:25.
12*a* Eccl. 4:13.
b Prov. 16:8; 28:11.

13 And now, because ye are compelled to be humble blessed are ye; for a man sometimes, if he is compelled to be humble, seeketh [a]repentance; and now surely, whosoever repenteth shall find mercy; and he that findeth mercy and [b]endureth to the end the same shall be saved.

14 And now, as I said unto you, that because ye were compelled to be [a]humble ye were blessed, do ye not suppose that they are more blessed who truly humble themselves because of the word?

15 Yea, he that truly humbleth himself, and repenteth of his sins, and endureth to the end, the same shall be blessed—yea, much more blessed than they who are compelled to be humble because of their exceeding poverty.

16 Therefore, blessed are they who [a]humble themselves without being [b]compelled to be humble; or rather, in other words, blessed is he that believeth in the word of God, and is baptized without [c]stubbornness of heart, yea, without being brought to know the word, or even compelled to know, before they will believe.

17 Yea, there are many who do say: If thou wilt show unto us a [a]sign from heaven, then we shall know of a surety; then we shall believe.

18 Now I ask, is this faith? Behold, I say unto you, Nay; for if a man knoweth a thing he hath no cause to [a]believe, for he knoweth it.

19 And now, how much [a]more [b]cursed is he that [c]knoweth the [d]will of God and doeth it not, than he that only believeth, or only hath cause to believe, and falleth into [e]transgression?

20 Now of this thing ye must judge. Behold, I say unto you, that it is on the one hand even as it is on the other; and it shall be unto every man according to his work.

21 And now as I said concerning faith—[a]faith is not to have a perfect knowledge of things; therefore if ye have faith ye [b]hope for things which are [c]not seen, which are true.

22 And now, behold, I say unto you, and I would that ye should remember, that God is [a]merciful unto all who believe on his name; therefore he desireth, in the first place, that ye should believe, yea, even on his word.

23 And now, he imparteth his word by angels unto men, yea, [a]not only men but women also. Now this is not all; little [b]children do have words given unto them many times, which [c]confound the wise and the learned.

24 And now, my beloved brethren, as ye have desired to know of me what ye shall do because ye are afflicted and cast out—now I do not desire that ye should suppose that I mean to judge you only according to that which is true—

25 For I do not mean that ye all of you have been compelled to humble yourselves; for I verily believe that there are some among you who [a]would humble themselves, let them be in whatsoever circumstances they might.

26 Now, as I said concerning faith—that it was not a perfect knowledge—even so it is with my words. Ye cannot know of their surety at first, unto perfection, any more than faith is a perfect knowledge.

27 But behold, if ye will awake and arouse your faculties, even to an experiment upon my words, and

---

13*a* TG Objectives.
b Alma 38:2; 3 Ne. 15:9; 27:6 (6–17). TG Perseverance; Steadfastness.
14*a* 2 Kgs. 22:19.
16*a* TG Humility.
b TG Initiative.
c TG Stubbornness.
17*a* TG Signs; Sign Seekers.
18*a* Luke 16:30 (27–31); Ether 12:12 (12, 18).
19*a* D&C 41:1.
b TG Curse.
c John 15:24 (22–24).
d TG God, Will of.
e TG Transgress.
21*a* John 20:29; Heb. 11:1 (1–40).
b TG Hope.
c Ether 12:6.
22*a* TG God, Mercy of.
23*a* Joel 2:29 (28–29).
b Matt. 11:25; Luke 10:21; 3 Ne. 26:14 (14–16); D&C 128:18.
c D&C 133:58.
25*a* TG Initiative; Sincere.

exercise a particle of faith, yea, even
if ye can no more than [a]desire to
believe, let this desire work in you,
even until ye believe in a manner
that ye can give place for a portion
of my words.
28 Now, we will compare the word
unto a [a]seed. Now, if ye give place,
that a [b]seed may be planted in your
[c]heart, behold, if it be a true seed, or
a good seed, if ye do not cast it out
by your [d]unbelief, that ye will resist
the Spirit of the Lord, behold, it will
begin to swell within your breasts;
and when you feel these swell-
ing motions, ye will begin to say
within yourselves—It must needs be
that this is a good seed, or that the
word is good, for it beginneth to enlarge my soul; yea, it beginneth to
[e]enlighten my [f]understanding, yea,
it beginneth to be delicious to me.
29 Now behold, would not this increase your faith? I say unto you,
Yea; nevertheless it hath not grown
up to a perfect knowledge.
30 But behold, as the seed swelleth, and sprouteth, and beginneth
to grow, then you must needs say
that the seed is good; for behold it
swelleth, and sprouteth, and beginneth to grow. And now, behold, will
not this strengthen your faith? Yea,
it will strengthen your faith: for ye
will say I know that this is a good
seed; for behold it sprouteth and
beginneth to grow.
31 And now, behold, are ye sure
that this is a good seed? I say unto
you, Yea; for every seed bringeth
forth unto its own [a]likeness.
32 Therefore, if a seed groweth it
is good, but if it groweth not, behold it is not good, therefore it is
cast away.
33 And now, behold, because ye
have tried the experiment, and
planted the seed, and it swelleth
and sprouteth, and beginneth to
grow, ye must needs know that the
seed is good.
34 And now, behold, is your [a]knowl-
edge [b]perfect? Yea, your knowledge
is perfect in that thing, and your
[c]faith is dormant; and this because
you know, for ye know that the
word hath swelled your souls, and
ye also know that it hath sprouted
up, that your understanding doth
begin to be enlightened, and your
[d]mind doth begin to expand.
35 O then, is not this real? I say
unto you, Yea, because it is [a]light;
and whatsoever is light, is [b]good,
because it is discernible, therefore
ye must know that it is good; and
now behold, after ye have tasted
this light is your knowledge perfect?
36 Behold I say unto you, Nay; neither must ye lay aside your faith, for
ye have only exercised your faith
to plant the seed that ye might try
the experiment to know if the seed
was good.
37 And behold, as the tree beginneth to grow, ye will say: Let us
nourish it with great care, that it
may get root, that it may grow up,
and bring forth fruit unto us. And
now behold, if ye nourish it with
much care it will get root, and grow
up, and bring forth fruit.
38 But if ye [a]neglect the tree, and
take no thought for its nourishment,
behold it will not get any root; and
when the heat of the sun cometh
and scorcheth it, because it hath no
root it withers away, and ye pluck
it up and cast it out.
39 Now, this is not because the
seed was not good, neither is it because the fruit thereof would not
be desirable; but it is because your
[a]ground is [b]barren, and ye will not
nourish the tree, therefore ye cannot have the fruit thereof.

27*a* TG Motivations; Teachable.
28*a* Alma 33:1.
b Luke 8:11 (11–15).
c TG Heart.
d TG Doubt; Unbelief.
e TG Discernment, Spiritual; Edification.
f TG Intelligence; Testimony; Understanding.
31*a* Gen. 1:12 (11–12).
34*a* TG Knowledge.
b Ps. 19:7.
c Ether 3:19.
d TG Mind.
35*a* TG Light [noun].
b Gen. 1:4.
38*a* TG Apostasy of Individuals.
39*a* Matt. 13:5 (3–8).
b TG Barren.

40 And thus, if ye will not nourish
the word, looking forward with an
eye of faith to the fruit thereof, ye
can never pluck of the fruit of the
[a]tree of life.
41 But if ye will nourish the word,
yea, nourish the tree as it beginneth
to grow, by your faith with great
diligence, and with [a]patience, looking
forward to the fruit thereof, it
shall take root; and behold it shall
be a tree [b]springing up unto everlasting
life.
42 And because of your [a]diligence
and your faith and your patience
with the word in nourishing it, that
it may take root in you, behold, by
and by ye shall pluck the [b]fruit
thereof, which is most precious,
which is sweet above all that is
sweet, and which is white above all
that is white, yea, and pure above
all that is pure; and ye shall feast
upon this fruit even until ye are
filled, that ye hunger not, neither
shall ye thirst.
43 Then, my brethren, ye shall
[a]reap the [b]rewards of your faith,
and your diligence, and patience,
and long-suffering, waiting for the
tree to bring forth [c]fruit unto you.

CHAPTER 33

Zenos taught that men should pray and worship in all places, and that judgments are turned away because of the Son—Zenock taught that mercy is bestowed because of the Son—Moses had lifted up in the wilderness a type of the Son of God. About 74 B.C.

Now after Alma had spoken these
words, they sent forth unto him desiring
to know whether they should
believe in [a]one God, that they might
obtain this fruit of which he had
spoken, or [b]how they should plant
the [c]seed, or the word of which he
had spoken, which he said must be
planted in their hearts; or in what
manner they should begin to exercise
their faith.
2 And Alma said unto them: Behold,
ye have said that ye [a]could
not [b]worship your God because ye
are cast out of your synagogues. But
behold, I say unto you, if ye suppose
that ye cannot worship God, ye do
greatly err, and ye ought to search
the [c]scriptures; if ye suppose that
they have taught you this, ye do not
understand them.
3 Do ye remember to have read
what [a]Zenos, the prophet of old, has
said concerning prayer or [b]worship?
4 For he said: Thou art merciful, O
God, for thou hast heard my prayer,
even when I was [a]in the wilderness;
yea, thou wast merciful when I
prayed concerning those who were
mine [b]enemies, and thou didst turn
them to me.
5 Yea, O God, and thou wast merciful
unto me when I did cry unto
thee in my [a]field; when I did cry
unto thee in my prayer, and thou
didst hear me.
6 And again, O God, when I did
turn to my house thou didst hear
me in my prayer.
7 And when I did turn unto my
[a]closet, O Lord, and prayed unto
thee, thou didst hear me.
8 Yea, thou art merciful unto thy
children when they cry unto thee,
to be heard of thee and not of men,
and thou [a]wilt hear them.
9 Yea, O God, thou hast been merciful
unto me, and heard my cries
in the midst of thy congregations.

40*a* Gen. 2:9; 1 Ne. 15:36 (22, 28, 36).
41*a* TG Patience.
b Alma 33:23; D&C 63:23.
42*a* TG Diligence.
b Matt. 13:23; Col. 1:6; 1 Ne. 8:10 (10–18); 3 Ne. 14:16; D&C 52:34 (18, 34).
43*a* TG Harvest.
b TG Reward.
c Alma 33:23.
33 1*a* 2 Ne. 31:21; Mosiah 15:4; Alma 11:28 (28–35).
b Alma 33:23.
c Alma 32:28 (28–43).
2*a* Alma 32:5.
b TG Worship.
c Mosiah 2:34; Alma 37:8 (3–10). TG Prayer.
3*a* Alma 34:7. TG Scriptures, Lost.
b TG Worship.
4*a* 1 Kgs. 8:47 (44–52).
b Matt. 5:44.
5*a* Alma 34:20 (20–25).
7*a* Matt. 6:6 (5–6); Alma 34:26 (17–27).
8*a* TG God, Access to.

10 Yea, and thou hast also heard
me when I have been [a]cast out and
have been despised by mine enemies; yea, thou didst hear my cries,
and wast angry with mine enemies,
and thou didst [b]visit them in thine
anger with speedy destruction.
11 And thou didst hear me because of mine afflictions and my
[a]sincerity; and it is because of thy
Son that thou hast been thus merciful unto me, therefore I will cry
unto thee in all mine [b]afflictions,
for in thee is my joy; for thou hast
turned thy judgments away from
me, [c]because of thy Son.
12 And now Alma said unto them:
Do ye [a]believe those scriptures which
have been written by them of old?
13 Behold, if ye do, ye must believe what [a]Zenos said; for, behold
he said: Thou hast turned away thy
judgments because of thy Son.
14 Now behold, my brethren, I
would ask if ye have read the scriptures? If ye have, how can ye [a]dis-
believe on the Son of God?
15 For it is [a]not written that Zenos alone spake of these things, but
[b]Zenock also spake of these things—
16 For behold, he said: Thou art
angry, O Lord, with this people, because they [a]will not understand thy
mercies which thou hast bestowed
upon them because of thy Son.
17 And now, my brethren, ye see
that a second prophet of old has
testified of the Son of God, and because the people would not understand his words they [a]stoned him
to death.
18 But behold, this is not all; these
are not the only ones who have
spoken concerning the Son of God.
19 Behold, he was spoken of by
[a]Moses; yea, and behold a [b]type was
[c]raised up in the wilderness, that
whosoever would look upon it might
live. And many did look and live.
20 But few understood the meaning of those things, and this because
of the hardness of their hearts.
But there were many who were so
hardened that they would not look,
therefore they perished. Now the
reason they would not look is because they did not believe that it
would [a]heal them.
21 O my brethren, if ye could be
healed by merely casting about
your eyes that ye might be healed,
would ye not behold quickly, or
would ye rather harden your hearts
in [a]unbelief, and be [b]slothful, that
ye would not cast about your eyes,
that ye might perish?
22 If so, wo shall come upon you;
but if not so, then cast about your
eyes and [a]begin to believe in the
Son of God, that he will come to redeem his people, and that he shall
suffer and die to [b]atone for their
sins; and that he shall [c]rise again
from the dead, which shall bring
to pass the [d]resurrection, that all
men shall stand before him, to be
[e]judged at the last and judgment
day, according to their [f]works.
23 And now, my brethren, I desire
that ye shall [a]plant this word in your
hearts, and as it beginneth to swell
even so nourish it by your faith. And
behold, it will become a tree, [b]spring-
ing up in you unto [c]everlasting

10*a* Alma 32:5.
b Ps. 3:7; 18:17.
11*a* TG Sincere.
b TG Affliction.
c TG Jesus Christ, Atonement through.
12*a* TG Scriptures, Value of.
13*a* Jacob 6:1; Alma 34:7.
14*a* John 5:39.
15*a* Jacob 4:4; Mosiah 15:11 (11–13).
b 1 Ne. 19:10; Alma 34:7.
16*a* 2 Pet. 3:5 (4–5).
17*a* TG Martyrdom.
19*a* Deut. 18:15 (15, 18); Alma 34:7.
b Num. 21:9; 1 Ne. 17:41; 2 Ne. 25:20. TG Jesus Christ, Types of, in Anticipation; Symbolism.
c John 3:14; Hel. 8:14.
20*a* Hosea 11:3; 1 Ne. 17:41 (40–41).
21*a* TG Doubt; Unbelief.
b TG Apathy; Laziness.
22*a* Alma 25:16; 37:46 (45–46).
b 2 Ne. 2:10; Alma 22:14; 34:9 (8–16).
c TG Jesus Christ, Resurrection.
d Alma 11:44. TG Resurrection.
e TG Jesus Christ, Judge.
f TG Good Works.
23*a* Alma 33:1; 34:4.
b Alma 32:41; D&C 63:23.
c Alma 32:43.

life. And then may God grant unto
you that your [d]burdens may be
light, through the joy of his Son. And
even all this can ye do if ye [e]will.
Amen.

CHAPTER 34

Amulek testifies that the word is in Christ unto salvation—Unless an atonement is made, all mankind must perish—The whole law of Moses points toward the sacrifice of the Son of God—The eternal plan of redemption is based on faith and repentance—Pray for temporal and spiritual blessings—This life is the time for men to prepare to meet God—Work out your salvation with fear before God. About 74 B.C.

AND now it came to pass that after
Alma had spoken these words unto
them he sat down upon the ground,
and [a]Amulek arose and began to
teach them, saying:
2 My brethren, I think that it is
impossible that ye should be ignorant of the things which have been
spoken concerning the coming of
Christ, who is taught by us to be
the Son of God; yea, I know that
[a]these things were taught unto you
bountifully before your dissension
from among us.
3 And as ye have desired of my beloved brother that he should make
known unto you [a]what ye should
do, because of your afflictions; and
he hath spoken somewhat unto you
to prepare your minds; yea, and he
hath exhorted you unto faith and
to patience—
4 Yea, even that ye would have so
much faith as even to [a]plant the
word in your hearts, that ye may
try the experiment of its goodness.
5 And we have beheld that the
great question which is in your
minds is whether the word be in the
Son of God, or whether there shall
be [a]no Christ.
6 And ye also beheld that my
brother has proved unto you, in
many instances, that the [a]word is
in Christ unto salvation.
7 My brother has called upon the
words of [a]Zenos, that redemption
cometh through the Son of God, and
also upon the words of [b]Zenock; and
also he has appealed unto [c]Moses,
to prove that these things are true.
8 And now, behold, I will [a]testify
unto you of myself that these things
are true. Behold, I say unto you, that
I do know that Christ shall come
among the children of men, to take
upon him the [b]transgressions of his
people, and that he shall [c]atone for
the sins of the world; for the Lord
God hath spoken it.
9 For it is expedient that an [a]atone-
ment should be made; for according
to the great [b]plan of the Eternal God
there must be an atonement made,
or else all mankind must unavoidably perish; yea, all are hardened;
yea, all are [c]fallen and are lost, and
must perish except it be through
the atonement which it is expedient
should be made.
10 For it is expedient that there
should be a great and last [a]sacrifice;
yea, not a [b]sacrifice of man, neither
of beast, neither of any manner of
fowl; for it shall not be a human
sacrifice; but it must be an [c]infinite
and [d]eternal [e]sacrifice.

23*d* Mosiah 24:15 (13–15); Alma 31:38.
e TG Agency.
34 1*a* Alma 8:21; 31:32.
2*a* Alma 16:15 (13–21).
3*a* Alma 32:5.
4*a* Alma 33:23.
5*a* Jacob 7:2 (2, 9); Alma 30:12 (12, 22); 31:16 (16, 29).
6*a* John 1:14 (1, 14).
7*a* Alma 33:13; Hel. 8:19.
b Alma 33:15; Hel. 8:20 (19–20).
c Alma 33:19.
8*a* TG Testimony; Witness.
b TG Jesus Christ, Redeemer.
c TG Jesus Christ, Atonement through.
9*a* 2 Ne. 2:10; 9:7 (7–9); Alma 22:14; 33:22.
b Alma 12:26 (22–33); 42:8 (6–28); Moses 6:62.
c TG Fall of Man.
10*a* 1 Chr. 6:49; Moses 5:7 (6–7).
b TG Blood, Symbolism of.
c 2 Ne. 9:7.
d Isa. 45:17; Heb. 5:9.
e TG Sacrifice.

11 Now there is not any man that
can sacrifice his own blood which
will atone for the sins of another.
Now, if a man murdereth, behold
will our law, which is [a]just, take
the life of his brother? I say unto
you, Nay.
12 But the law requireth the [a]life
of him who hath [b]murdered; therefore there can be nothing which is
short of an infinite atonement which
will suffice for the sins of the world.
13 Therefore, it is expedient that
there should be a great and last
sacrifice, and then shall there be,
or it is expedient there should be,
a [a]stop to the shedding of [b]blood;
then shall the [c]law of Moses be fulfilled; yea, it shall be all fulfilled,
every jot and tittle, and none shall
have passed away.
14 And behold, this is the whole
[a]meaning of the [b]law, every whit
[c]pointing to that great and last [d]sacri-
fice; and that great and last [e]sacrifice
will be the Son of God, yea, [f]infinite
and eternal.
15 And thus he shall bring [a]sal-
vation to all those who shall believe on his name; this being the
intent of this last sacrifice, to bring
about the bowels of mercy, which
overpowereth justice, and bringeth
about means unto men that they
may have faith unto repentance.
16 And thus [a]mercy can satisfy
the demands of [b]justice, and encircles them in the arms of safety,
while he that exercises no faith
unto repentance is exposed to the
whole law of the demands of [c]jus-
tice; therefore only unto him that
has faith unto repentance is brought
about the great and eternal [d]plan of
[e]redemption.
17 Therefore may God grant unto
you, my brethren, that ye may begin
to exercise your [a]faith unto repentance, that ye begin to [b]call upon
his holy name, that he would have
mercy upon you;
18 Yea, cry unto him for mercy;
for he is [a]mighty to save.
19 Yea, humble yourselves, and
continue in [a]prayer unto him.
20 Cry unto him when ye are in
your [a]fields, yea, over all your flocks.
21 [a]Cry unto him in your houses,
yea, over all your household, both
morning, mid-day, and evening.
22 Yea, cry unto him against the
power of your [a]enemies.
23 Yea, [a]cry unto him against the
[b]devil, who is an enemy to all [c]righ-
teousness.
24 Cry unto him over the crops
of your fields, that ye may prosper
in them.
25 Cry over the flocks of your
fields, that they may increase.
26 But this is not all; ye must
[a]pour out your souls in your [b]clos-
ets, and your secret places, and in
your wilderness.
27 Yea, and when you do not cry
unto the Lord, let your [a]hearts be
[b]full, drawn out in prayer unto him
continually for your [c]welfare, and
also for the welfare of [d]those who
are around you.

11*a* Deut. 24:16; Mosiah 29:25.
12*a* TG Blood, Shedding of; Life, Sanctity of.
b TG Capital Punishment; Murder.
13*a* 3 Ne. 9:19.
b TG Blood, Symbolism of.
c 3 Ne. 1:24; 15:5.
14*a* 2 Ne. 25:24; Jarom 1:5; Mosiah 2:3; Alma 30:3.
b TG Law of Moses.
c TG Jesus Christ, Types of, in Anticipation.
d Ex. 12:21 (1–30).
e D&C 138:35.
f D&C 20:17 (17, 28).
15*a* TG Salvation.
16*a* TG Mercy.
b TG God, Justice of.
c Mosiah 15:27; Alma 12:32.
d TG Salvation, Plan of.
e TG Redemption.
17*a* TG Faith.
b TG God, Access to; Prayer.
18*a* Heb. 7:25 (24–25).
19*a* TG Prayer.
20*a* Alma 33:5 (4–5).
21*a* Ps. 5:3 (1–3); Dan. 6:10; 3 Ne. 18:21.
22*a* TG Enemies.
23*a* 3 Ne. 18:15 (15, 18).
b TG Devil.
c TG Righteousness.
26*a* 1 Sam. 1:15; Enos 1:9.
b Matt. 6:6 (5–6); Alma 33:7 (4–11).
27*a* TG Heart.
b TG Meditation.
c 2 Ne. 32:9. TG Welfare.
d D&C 108:7.

28 And now behold, my beloved brethren, I say unto you, do not suppose that this is all; for after ye have done all these things, if ye [a]turn away the [b]needy, and the [c]naked, and visit not the sick and afflicted, and [d]impart of your substance, if ye have, to those who stand in need—I say unto you, if ye do not any of these things, behold, your [e]prayer is [f]vain, and availeth you nothing, and ye are as [g]hypocrites who do deny the faith.

29 Therefore, if ye do not remember to be [a]charitable, ye are as dross, which the refiners do cast out, (it being of no worth) and is trodden under foot of men.

30 And now, my brethren, I would that, after ye have [a]received so many witnesses, seeing that the holy scriptures testify of these things, ye come forth and bring [b]fruit unto repentance.

31 Yea, I would that ye would come forth and [a]harden not your hearts any longer; for behold, now is the time and the [b]day of your [c]salvation; and therefore, if ye will repent and [d]harden not your hearts, immediately shall the great plan of redemption be brought about unto you.

32 For behold, this [a]life is the time for men to [b]prepare to meet God; yea, behold the day of [c]this life is the day for men to perform their [d]labors.

33 And now, as I said unto you before, as ye have had so many [a]witnesses, therefore, I beseech of you that ye do not [b]procrastinate the day of your [c]repentance until the end; for after this day of life, which is given us to prepare for eternity, behold, if we do not improve our time while in this life, then cometh the [d]night of [e]darkness wherein there can be no labor performed.

34 Ye cannot say, when ye are brought to that awful [a]crisis, that I will repent, that I will return to my God. Nay, ye cannot say this; for that same spirit which doth [b]possess your bodies at the time that ye go out of this life, that same spirit will have power to possess your body in that eternal world.

35 For behold, if ye have procrastinated the day of your repentance even until death, behold, ye have become [a]subjected to the spirit of the devil, and he doth [b]seal you his; therefore, the Spirit of the Lord hath withdrawn from you, and hath no place in you, and the devil hath all power over you; and this is the final state of the wicked.

36 And this I know, because the Lord hath said he dwelleth not in [a]unholy temples, but in the [b]hearts of the [c]righteous doth he dwell; yea, and he has also said that the righteous shall sit down in his kingdom, to go no more out; but their garments should be made white through the [d]blood of the Lamb.

37 And now, my beloved brethren, I desire that ye should remember

28*a* TG Apathy.
b TG Poor.
c Ezek. 18:7 (5–9).
d TG Almsgiving; Good Works.
e Ezek. 33:31; Matt. 15:8 (7–8).
f Isa. 58:3; Moro. 7:6 (6–8).
g TG Hypocrisy.
29*a* TG Charity; Generosity.
30*a* TG Witness.
b Matt. 3:8; Alma 13:13.
31*a* TG Self-Mastery.
b Rom. 13:12 (11–12).
c Matt. 11:20; 3 Ne. 9:3; D&C 84:114.
d TG Hardheartedness.
32*a* TG Mortality.
b 2 Cor. 6:2; 2 Ne. 2:21; Alma 12:24; 42:4 (4–6). TG Self-Mastery.
c D&C 138:57.
d TG Good Works; Industry.
33*a* TG Witness.
b Job 27:8; Hel. 13:38; D&C 45:2. TG Apathy; Idleness; Procrastination.
c TG Repent.
d Eccl. 9:10; John 9:4.
e TG Darkness, Spiritual.
34*a* Alma 40:14 (13–14); Ether 9:34.
b Rom. 6:16 (14–18).
35*a* 2 Ne. 28:19 (19–23).
b 2 Ne. 9:9; 3 Ne. 2:10. TG Devil; Sealing.
36*a* Mosiah 2:37; Alma 7:21; Hel. 4:24. TG Cleanliness.
b D&C 130:3.
c TG Righteousness.
d Rev. 12:11.

these things, and that ye should [a]work out your salvation with fear before God, and that ye should no more deny the coming of Christ;

38 That ye [a]contend no more against the Holy Ghost, but that ye receive it, and take upon you the [b]name of Christ; that ye humble yourselves even to the dust, and [c]worship God, in whatsoever place ye may be in, in spirit and in truth; and that ye live in [d]thanksgiving daily, for the many [e]mercies and blessings which he doth bestow upon you.

39 Yea, and I also [a]exhort you, my brethren, that ye be [b]watchful unto prayer continually, that ye may not be led away by the [c]temptations of the devil, that he may not overpower you, that ye may not become his subjects at the last day; for behold, he rewardeth you [d]no good thing.

40 And now my beloved brethren, I would exhort you to have [a]patience, and that ye bear with all manner of [b]afflictions; that ye do not [c]revile against those who do cast you out because of your [d]exceeding poverty, lest ye become sinners like unto them;

41 But that ye have [a]patience, and bear with those [b]afflictions, with a firm hope that ye shall one day rest from all your afflictions.

CHAPTER 35

The preaching of the word destroys the craft of the Zoramites—They expel the converts, who then join the people of Ammon in Jershon—Alma sorrows because of the wickedness of the people. About 74 B.C.

Now it came to pass that after Amulek had made an end of these words, they withdrew themselves from the multitude and came over into the land of [a]Jershon.

2 Yea, and the rest of the brethren, after they had preached the word unto the [a]Zoramites, also came over into the land of Jershon.

3 And it came to pass that after the more popular part of the Zoramites had consulted together concerning the words which had been preached unto them, they were angry because of the word, for it did destroy their [a]craft; therefore they would not hearken unto the words.

4 And they sent and gathered together throughout all the land all the people, and consulted with them concerning the words which had been spoken.

5 Now their rulers and their priests and their teachers did not let the people know concerning their desires; therefore they found out privily the minds of all the people.

6 And it came to pass that after they had found out the minds of all the people, those who were in favor of the words which had been spoken by Alma and his brethren were cast out of the land; and they were [a]many; and they came over also into the land of Jershon.

7 And it came to pass that Alma and his brethren did minister unto them.

8 Now the people of the Zoramites were angry with the [a]people of Ammon who were in Jershon, and the [b]chief ruler of the Zoramites, being a very wicked man, sent over unto the people of Ammon desiring them that they should cast out of their land all those who came over from them into their land.

9 And he breathed out many

37*a* Philip. 2:12 (12–16).
38*a* TG Holy Ghost, Loss of.
b Mosiah 5:8; Alma 5:38. TG Jesus Christ, Taking the Name of.
c TG Worship.
d Ps. 69:30 (30–31); D&C 46:7. TG Thanksgiving.
e Gen. 32:10; 1 Ne. 1:20; D&C 46:15.
39*a* Heb. 3:13.
b TG Watch.
c TG Temptation.
d Alma 30:60.
40*a* TG Patience; Steadfastness.
b TG Affliction.
c TG Reviling.
d Alma 32:3.
41*a* TG Patience.
b Job 23:2 (2–5).
35 1*a* Alma 28:1.
2*a* Alma 30:59.
3*a* TG Priestcraft.
6*a* Alma 35:14.
8*a* Alma 27:26.
b Alma 30:59.

threatenings against them. And
now the people of Ammon did not
fear their words; therefore they did
not cast them out, but they did receive all the poor of the Zoramites
that came over unto them; and they
did [a]nourish them, and did clothe
them, and did give unto them lands
for their inheritance; and they did
administer unto them according to
their wants.
10 Now this did [a]stir up the Zoramites to [b]anger against the people of
Ammon, and they began to mix with
the Lamanites and to stir them up
also to anger against them.
11 And thus the Zoramites and the
Lamanites began to make preparations for war against the people of Ammon, and also against the Nephites.
12 And thus ended the seventeenth
year of the reign of the judges over
the people of Nephi.
13 And the people of Ammon departed out of the land of Jershon,
and came over into the land of Melek, and gave place in the land of
Jershon for the armies of the Nephites, that they might contend with
the armies of the Lamanites and the
armies of the Zoramites; and thus
commenced a war betwixt the Lamanites and the Nephites, in the
eighteenth year of the reign of
the judges; and an [a]account shall
be given of their wars hereafter.
14 And Alma, and Ammon, and
their brethren, and also the [a]two
sons of Alma returned to the land
of Zarahemla, after having been
instruments in the hands of God
of bringing [b]many of the [c]Zoram-
ites to repentance; and as many as
were brought to repentance were
driven out of their land; but they
have lands for their inheritance in
the land of Jershon, and they have
taken up arms to defend themselves,
and their wives, and children, and
their lands.
15 Now Alma, being [a]grieved for
the iniquity of his people, yea for the
wars, and the bloodsheds, and the
contentions which were among
them; and having been to declare
the word, or sent to declare the word,
among all the people in every city;
and seeing that the hearts of the
people began to wax hard, and that
they began to be [b]offended because
of the strictness of the word, his
heart was exceedingly sorrowful.
16 Therefore, he caused that his
sons should be gathered together,
that he might give unto them every
one his [a]charge, separately, concerning the things pertaining unto
righteousness. And we have an account of his commandments, which
he gave unto them according to
his own record.

The commandments of Alma to his son Helaman.

Comprising chapters 36 and 37.

CHAPTER 36

Alma testifies to Helaman of his conversion after seeing an angel—He suffered the pains of a damned soul; he called upon the name of Jesus, and was then born of God—Sweet joy filled his soul—He saw concourses of angels praising God—Many converts have tasted and seen as he has tasted and seen. About 74 B.C.

MY [a]son, give ear to my words; for
I swear unto you, that inasmuch as
ye shall keep the commandments
of God ye shall prosper in the land.
2 I would that ye should do as
I have done, in remembering the
captivity of our fathers; for they
were in [a]bondage, and none could

9*a* Mosiah 4:26; D&C 42:43. TG Nourish; Welfare.
10*a* Alma 47:1; Hel. 1:17.
b TG Anger; War.
13*a* Alma 43:3.
14*a* Alma 31:7.
b Alma 35:6.
c Alma 30:59.
15*a* Alma 31:1.
b TG Prophets, Rejection of.
16*a* TG Stewardship.
36 1*a* Hel. 5:13 (1–13); Moses 6:58.
2*a* Mosiah 23:23; 24:17 (17–21). TG Israel, Bondage of, in Egypt.

[b]deliver them except it was the
[c]God of Abraham, and the God of
Isaac, and the God of Jacob; and
he surely did deliver them in their
afflictions.
3 And now, O my son Helaman,
behold, thou art in thy youth, and
therefore, I beseech of thee that
thou wilt hear my words and learn
of me; for I do know that whosoever
shall put their [a]trust in God shall be
supported in their [b]trials, and their
troubles, and their afflictions, and
shall be [c]lifted up at the last day.
4 And I would not that ye think
that I [a]know of myself—not of the
temporal but of the spiritual, not of
the [b]carnal mind but of God.
5 Now, behold, I say unto you, if I
had not been [a]born of God I should
[b]not have known these things; but
God has, by the mouth of his holy
[c]angel, made these things known
unto me, not of any [d]worthiness
of myself;
6 For I went about with the sons
of Mosiah, seeking to [a]destroy the
church of God; but behold, God sent
his holy angel to stop us by the way.
7 And behold, he spake unto us,
as it were the voice of thunder,
and the whole earth did [a]tremble
beneath our feet; and we all fell to
the earth, for the [b]fear of the Lord
came upon us.
8 But behold, the voice said unto
me: Arise. And I arose and stood
up, and beheld the angel.
9 And he said unto me: If thou
wilt of thyself be destroyed, seek no
more to destroy the church of God.
10 And it came to pass that I fell to
the earth; and it was for the space
of [a]three days and three nights
that I could not open my mouth,
neither had I the use of my limbs.
11 And the angel spake more
things unto me, which were heard
by my brethren, but I did [a]not hear
them; for when I heard the words—
If thou wilt be destroyed of thyself,
seek no more to destroy the church
of God—I was struck with such great
fear and amazement lest perhaps I
should be destroyed, that I fell to
the earth and I did hear no more.
12 But I was racked with [a]eternal
[b]torment, for my soul was [c]harrowed
up to the greatest degree and racked
with all my sins.
13 Yea, I did remember all my sins
and iniquities, for which I was [a]tor-
mented with the [b]pains of hell; yea,
I saw that I had [c]rebelled against
my God, and that I had not kept his
holy commandments.
14 Yea, and I had [a]murdered many
of his children, or rather led them
away unto destruction; yea, and in
fine so great had been my iniquities, that the very thought of coming into the presence of my God
did rack my soul with inexpressible
horror.
15 Oh, thought I, that I [a]could be
banished and become extinct both
soul and body, that I might not be
brought to stand in the presence of
my God, to be judged of my [b]deeds.
16 And now, for three days and
for three nights was I racked, even
with the [a]pains of a [b]damned soul.
17 And it came to pass that as I was
thus [a]racked with torment, while I

2*b* Deut. 26:8.
c Ex. 3:6;
Alma 29:11.
3*a* TG Trust in God.
b Rom. 8:28.
c Mosiah 23:22 (21–22).
4*a* 1 Cor. 2:11;
Alma 5:45 (45–46).
TG Knowledge.
b TG Carnal Mind.
5*a* TG Man, New, Spiritually
Reborn.
b Alma 26:21 (21–22).
c Mosiah 27:11 (11–18).
d TG Worthiness.
6*a* Mosiah 27:10; 28:4 (3–4).
7*a* Isa. 6:4;
Mosiah 27:18.
b Prov. 2:5.
TG Fear of God.
10*a* Mosiah 27:23 (19–23);
Alma 38:8.
11*a* Dan. 10:7;
Acts 9:7 (3–7).
12*a* D&C 19:11 (11–15).
b TG Despair.
c TG Poor in Spirit;
Repent;
Sorrow.
13*a* TG Guilt.
b Moses 1:20.
c TG Disobedience.
14*a* Matt. 10:28.
15*a* Rev. 6:16 (15–17);
Alma 12:14.
b Isa. 59:18;
Alma 41:3 (2–5); 42:27;
D&C 1:10 (9–10).
16*a* TG Pain.
b TG Damnation.
17*a* Ps. 119:67.

was [b]harrowed up by the [c]memory
of my many sins, behold, I [d]remem-
bered also to have heard my father
prophesy unto the people concerning the coming of one Jesus Christ,
a Son of God, to atone for the sins
of the world.
18 Now, as my mind caught hold
upon this thought, I cried within
my heart: O Jesus, thou Son of God,
[a]have mercy on me, who am [b]in the
[c]gall of bitterness, and am encircled
about by the everlasting [d]chains of
[e]death.
19 And now, behold, when I thought
this, I could remember my [a]pains
[b]no more; yea, I was harrowed up
by the memory of my sins no more.
20 And oh, what [a]joy, and what
marvelous light I did behold; yea,
my soul was filled with joy as exceeding as was my pain!
21 Yea, I say unto you, my son, that
there could be nothing so exquisite
and so bitter as were my pains. Yea,
and again I say unto you, my son,
that on the other hand, there can
be nothing so exquisite and sweet
as was my joy.
22 Yea, methought I saw, even as
our father [a]Lehi saw, God sitting
upon his throne, surrounded with
numberless concourses of angels, in
the attitude of singing and [b]prais-
ing their God; yea, and my soul did
long to be there.
23 But behold, my limbs did receive
their [a]strength again, and I stood
upon my feet, and did manifest
unto the people that I had been
[b]born of God.
24 Yea, and from that time even
until now, I have labored without
ceasing, that I might bring souls
unto [a]repentance; that I might bring
them to [b]taste of the exceeding joy
of which I did taste; that they might
also be [c]born of God, and be [d]filled
with the Holy Ghost.
25 Yea, and now behold, O my
son, the Lord doth [a]give me exceedingly great joy in the fruit of my
[b]labors;
26 For because of the [a]word which
he has imparted unto me, behold,
many have been born of God, and
have [b]tasted as I have tasted, and have
seen eye to eye as I have seen; therefore they do know of these things of
which I have spoken, as I do know;
and the knowledge which I have
is of God.
27 And I have been supported under trials and troubles of every kind,
yea, and in all manner of afflictions;
yea, God has [a]delivered me from
prison, and from bonds, and from
death; yea, and I do put my trust in
him, and he will still [b]deliver me.
28 And I know that he will [a]raise
me up at the last day, to dwell with
him in [b]glory; yea, and I will [c]praise
him forever, for he has [d]brought
our fathers out of Egypt, and he
has swallowed up the [e]Egyptians in
the Red Sea; and he led them by his
power into the promised land; yea,
and he has delivered them out of

17*b* 2 Cor. 7:10 (8–11).
c Alma 11:43; D&C 18:44.
d 1 Ne. 10:17 (17–19); Enos 1:3.
18*a* Matt. 15:22.
b IE in extreme remorse.
c Jonah 2:2; Acts 8:23.
d Prov. 5:22; 2 Ne. 9:45; 28:22; Alma 12:11 (10–11); Moses 7:26.
e TG Death, Spiritual, First.
19*a* TG Peace of God.
b Jer. 31:34; D&C 19:16.
20*a* Moses 5:11. TG Forgive; Joy.
22*a* 1 Ne. 1:8. TG God, Manifestations of.
b Isa. 6:3 (1–4).
23*a* Moses 1:10.
b Alma 22:15; 38:6. TG Conversion.
24*a* Alma 19:29.
b Ps. 34:8; 1 Ne. 8:12; Mosiah 4:11.
c TG Holy Ghost, Baptism of.
d 2 Ne. 32:2 (2, 5); 3 Ne. 9:20. TG Holy Ghost, Mission of.
25*a* TG Reward.
b TG Work, Value of.
26*a* Prov. 10:11; Jacob 2:8; Alma 31:5; D&C 108:7.
b 1 Pet. 2:3 (1–3).
27*a* Alma 14:28 (26–29).
b Ps. 34:17.
28*a* Alma 26:7; 3 Ne. 15:1.
b TG Exaltation.
c Ezra 3:11 (11–13); 2 Ne. 9:49.
d Mosiah 12:34; D&C 103:16.
e Ex. 14:27 (26–27).

bondage and captivity from time
to time.
29 Yea, and he has also brought
our fathers out of the land of Jerusalem; and he has also, by his everlasting power, delivered them out of
[a]bondage and captivity, from time
to time even down to the present
day; and I have always retained in
remembrance their captivity; yea,
and ye also ought to retain in remembrance, as I have done, their
captivity.
30 But behold, my son, this is not
all; for ye ought to know as I do
know, that [a]inasmuch as ye shall
keep the commandments of God ye
shall [b]prosper in the land; and ye
ought to know also, that inasmuch
as ye will not keep the commandments of God ye shall be cut off from
his presence. Now this is according
to his word.

CHAPTER 37

The plates of brass and other scriptures are preserved to bring souls to salvation—The Jaredites were destroyed because of their wickedness—Their secret oaths and covenants must be kept from the people—Counsel with the Lord in all your doings—As the Liahona guided the Nephites, so the word of Christ leads men to eternal life. About 74 B.C.

AND now, my son Helaman, I command you that ye take the [a]records
which have been [b]entrusted with me;
2 And I also command you that ye
keep a [a]record of this people, according as I have done, upon the plates
of Nephi, and keep all these things
sacred which I have kept, even as I
have kept them; for it is for a [b]wise
purpose that they are kept.
3 And these [a]plates of brass, which
contain these engravings, which
have the records of the holy scriptures upon them, which have the
[b]genealogy of our forefathers, even
from the beginning—
4 Behold, it has been prophesied
by our fathers, that they should be
kept and [a]handed down from one
generation to another, and be kept
and preserved by the hand of the
Lord until they should go forth unto
every nation, kindred, tongue, and
people, that they shall know of the
[b]mysteries contained thereon.
5 And now behold, if they are
kept they must retain their brightness; yea, and they will retain their
brightness; yea, and also shall all
the plates which do contain that
which is holy writ.
6 Now ye may suppose that this is
[a]foolishness in me; but behold I say
unto you, that by [b]small and sim-
ple things are great things brought
to pass; and small means in many
instances doth confound the wise.
7 And the Lord God doth work
by [a]means to bring about his great
and eternal purposes; and by very
[b]small means the Lord doth [c]con-
found the wise and bringeth about
the salvation of many souls.
8 And now, it has hitherto been
wisdom in God that these things
should be preserved; for behold,
[a]they have [b]enlarged the memory
of this people, yea, and convinced
many of the error of their ways, and
brought them to the [c]knowledge of

29*a* Mosiah 24:17; 25:10; 27:16; Alma 5:5 (5–6); 29:12 (11–12).
30*a* 2 Ne. 1:20.
b Mosiah 1:7; Alma 37:13; 50:20.
37 1*a* Alma 45:2 (2–8); 50:38; 63:1.
b Mosiah 28:20.
2*a* TG Record Keeping.
b Enos 1:13 (13–18); W of M 1:7 (6–11); Alma 37:12. TG Restoration of the Gospel.
3*a* Mosiah 28:20; Alma 63:12 (1, 11–14).
b 1 Ne. 5:14.
4*a* 1 Ne. 5:19 (16–19); Alma 63:13; Hel. 3:16.
b TG Mysteries of Godliness.
6*a* 1 Cor. 2:14.
b 1 Ne. 16:29; D&C 64:33; 123:16.
7*a* Isa. 55:8 (8–9); Alma 24:27.
b 2 Kgs. 5:13; Alma 37:41.
c 1 Cor. 1:27; D&C 133:58 (58–59).
8*a* Mosiah 2:34; Alma 33:2.
b Mosiah 1:3 (3–5).
c TG Education; Scriptures, Value of.

their God unto the salvation of
their souls.
9 Yea, I say unto you, [a]were it not
for these things that these records do
contain, which are on these plates,
Ammon and his brethren could not
have [b]convinced so many thousands
of the Lamanites of the incorrect
tradition of their fathers; yea, these
records and their [c]words brought
them unto repentance; that is, they
brought them to the knowledge of
the Lord their God, and to rejoice
in Jesus Christ their Redeemer.
10 And who knoweth but what
they will be the [a]means of bringing
many thousands of them, yea, and
also many thousands of our [b]stiff-
necked brethren, the Nephites, who
are now hardening their hearts in
sin and iniquities, to the knowledge
of their Redeemer?
11 Now these mysteries are not yet
fully made known unto me; therefore I shall forbear.
12 And it may suffice if I only
say they are preserved for a [a]wise
purpose, which purpose is known
unto God; for he doth [b]counsel in
wisdom over all his works, and his
paths are straight, and his course
is [c]one eternal round.
13 O remember, remember, my son
Helaman, how [a]strict are the commandments of God. And he said: [b]If
ye will keep my commandments ye
shall [c]prosper in the land—but if
ye keep not his commandments ye
shall be cut off from his presence.
14 And now remember, my son,
that God has [a]entrusted you with
these things, which are [b]sacred,
which he has kept sacred, and also
which he will keep and [c]preserve
for a [d]wise purpose in him, that he
may show forth his power unto future generations.
15 And now behold, I tell you by
the spirit of prophecy, that if ye
transgress the commandments of
God, behold, these things which
are sacred shall be taken away from
you by the power of God, and ye
shall be delivered up unto Satan,
that he may sift you as chaff before
the wind.
16 But if ye keep the commandments of God, and do with these
things which are sacred according
to that which the Lord doth command you, (for you must appeal
unto the Lord for all things whatsoever ye must do with them) behold,
no power of earth or hell can [a]take
them from you, for God is powerful
to the fulfilling of all his words.
17 For he will fulfil all his [a]prom-
ises which he shall make unto you,
for he has fulfilled his promises
which he has made unto our fathers.
18 For he promised unto them that
he would [a]preserve these things
for a wise purpose in him, that he
might show forth his power unto
future generations.
19 And now behold, one purpose
hath he fulfilled, even to the restoration of [a]many thousands of the
Lamanites to the knowledge of
the truth; and he hath shown forth
his power in them, and he will also
still show forth his power in them
unto [b]future generations; therefore
they shall be preserved.
20 Therefore I command you, my
son Helaman, that ye be diligent in
fulfilling all my words, and that ye
be diligent in keeping the commandments of God as they are written.
21 And now, I will speak unto

9*a* Mosiah 1:5.
b Alma 18:36; 22:12.
c TG Gospel.
10*a* 2 Ne. 3:15.
b TG Stiffnecked.
12*a* Alma 37:2.
b Prov. 15:22; 2 Ne. 9:28; Jacob 4:10.
c 1 Ne. 10:19; Alma 7:20.
13*a* Luke 13:24 (22–30).
b Alma 9:13 (13–14); 3 Ne. 5:22.
c Ps. 122:6; Mosiah 1:7; Alma 36:30; 50:20.
14*a* D&C 3:5.
b TG Sacred.
c TG Scriptures, Preservation of.
d 1 Ne. 9:5 (3–6).
16*a* JS—H 1:59.
17*a* 2 Kgs. 10:10. TG Promise.
18*a* D&C 5:9.
19*a* Alma 23:5 (5–13).
b 2 Ne. 3:15; Enos 1:13 (12–18); Morm. 7:9 (8–10).

you concerning those [a]twenty-four
plates, that ye keep them, that the
[b]mysteries and the works of darkness, and their secret works, or the
secret works of those people who
have been destroyed, may be made
[c]manifest unto this people; yea, all
their murders, and robbings, and
their plunderings, and all their
wickedness and abominations, may
be made manifest unto this people;
yea, and that ye preserve these [d]in-
terpreters.
22 For behold, the Lord saw that
his people began to work in darkness, yea, work secret murders and
abominations; therefore the Lord
said, if they did not repent they
should be destroyed from off the
face of the earth.
23 And the Lord said: I will prepare
unto my servant Gazelem, a [a]stone,
which shall shine forth in darkness
unto light, that I may [b]discover unto
my people who serve me, that I
may discover unto them the works
of their brethren, yea, their secret
works, their works of darkness, and
their wickedness and abominations.
24 And now, my son, these [a]inter-
preters were prepared that the word
of God might be fulfilled, which he
spake, saying:
25 I will [a]bring forth out of darkness unto light all their secret works
and their abominations; and except
they repent I will [b]destroy them from
off the face of the earth; and I will
bring to light all their secrets and
abominations, unto every nation
that shall hereafter possess the land.
26 And now, my son, we see that
they did not repent; therefore they
have been destroyed, and thus far
the word of God has been fulfilled;
yea, their [a]secret abominations have
been brought out of darkness and
made known unto us.
27 And now, my son, I command
you that ye retain all their oaths,
and their covenants, and their agree-
ments in their secret abominations;
yea, and all their [a]signs and their
wonders ye shall [b]keep from this
people, that they know them not,
lest peradventure they should fall
into darkness also and be destroyed.
28 For behold, there is a [a]curse
upon all this land, that destruction
shall come upon all those workers
of darkness, according to the power
of God, when they are fully ripe;
therefore I desire that this people
might not be destroyed.
29 Therefore ye shall keep these
secret plans of their [a]oaths and
their covenants from this people,
and only their wickedness and
their murders and their abominations shall ye make known unto
them; and ye shall teach them to
[b]abhor such wickedness and abominations and murders; and ye shall
also teach them that these people
were destroyed on account of their
wickedness and abominations and
their murders.
30 For behold, they [a]murdered all
the prophets of the Lord who came
among them to declare unto them
concerning their iniquities; and
the blood of those whom they murdered did cry unto the Lord their
God for vengeance upon those who
were their murderers; and thus the
judgments of God did come upon
these workers of darkness and secret [b]combinations.
31 Yea, and [a]cursed be the land forever and ever unto those workers of

21*a* Mosiah 8:9; 21:27; 28:11; Ether 1:2 (1–5); 15:33.
b TG Secret Combinations.
c Prov. 26:26; Alma 14:3 (2–3).
d TG Urim and Thummim.
23*a* Mosiah 8:13.
b IE reveal, make known.
24*a* TG Urim and Thummim.
25*a* Ps. 64:5 (4–6); D&C 88:108 (108–9).
b Mosiah 21:26.
26*a* 2 Ne. 10:15.
27*a* Hel. 6:22. TG Signs.
b Alma 63:12.
28*a* Ether 2:8 (7–12).
29*a* Hel. 6:25.
b Deut. 32:19; Alma 13:12. TG Hate.
30*a* TG Prophets, Rejection of.
b TG Secret Combinations.
31*a* Alma 45:16. TG Earth, Curse of.

darkness and secret combinations,
even unto destruction, except they
repent before they are fully [b]ripe.
32 And now, my son, remember
the words which I have spoken unto
you; trust not those secret plans
unto this people, but teach them
an everlasting [a]hatred against sin
and iniquity.
33 [a]Preach unto them repentance,
and faith on the Lord Jesus Christ;
teach them to humble themselves
and to be [b]meek and lowly in heart;
teach them to [c]withstand every
[d]temptation of the devil, with their
faith on the Lord Jesus Christ.
34 Teach them to never be weary
of good works, but to be meek and
lowly in heart; for such shall find
[a]rest to their souls.
35 O, remember, my son, and [a]learn
[b]wisdom in thy [c]youth; yea, learn
in thy youth to keep the commandments of God.
36 Yea, and [a]cry unto God for all
thy support; yea, let all thy [b]do-
ings be unto the Lord, and whithersoever thou goest let it be in the
Lord; yea, let all thy [c]thoughts be
directed unto the Lord; yea, let the
affections of thy heart be placed
upon the Lord forever.
37 [a]Counsel with the Lord in all
thy doings, and he will direct thee
for [b]good; yea, when thou liest down
at night lie down unto the Lord,
that he may watch over you in your
sleep; and when thou risest in the
[c]morning let thy heart be full of
thanks unto God; and if ye do these
things, ye shall be lifted up at the
last day.
38 And now, my son, I have
somewhat to say concerning the
thing which our fathers call a ball,
or director—or our fathers called
it [a]Liahona, which is, being interpreted, a compass; and the Lord
prepared it.
39 And behold, there cannot any
man work after the manner of so
curious a workmanship. And behold, it was prepared to show unto
our fathers the course which they
should travel in the wilderness.
40 And it did work for them
according to their [a]faith in God;
therefore, if they had faith to believe that God could cause that
those spindles should point the
way they should go, behold, it was
done; therefore they had this miracle, and also many other miracles
wrought by the power of God, day
by day.
41 Nevertheless, because those
miracles were worked by [a]small
means it did show unto them marvelous works. They were [b]slothful,
and forgot to exercise their faith
and diligence and then those marvelous works ceased, and they did
not progress in their journey;
42 Therefore, they tarried in the
wilderness, or did [a]not travel a direct course, and were afflicted with
hunger and thirst, because of their
transgressions.
43 And now, my son, I would that
ye should understand that these
things are not without a [a]shadow;
for as our fathers were slothful to
give heed to this compass (now
these things were temporal) they

31*b* Gen. 15:16; Hel. 13:14; D&C 61:31; 101:11.
32*a* 2 Ne. 4:31; Alma 43:7.
33*a* TG Mission of Early Saints; Preaching.
b TG Meek.
c TG Perseverance; Self-Mastery.
d TG Temptation.
34*a* Matt. 11:29 (28–30).
35*a* TG Education; Learn.
b TG Wisdom.
c Eccl. 12:1; Lam. 3:27.
36*a* TG Prayer.
b Ps. 37:5 (4–7).
c D&C 6:36. TG Motivations.
37*a* Josh. 9:14; Ps. 34:4 (4, 6, 10); Prov. 3:5 (5–6); Lam. 3:25; Heb. 11:6; Jacob 4:10; D&C 3:4.
b TG Abundant Life.
c 1 Chr. 16:8 (7–36); Ps. 5:3; Ether 6:9; D&C 46:32.
38*a* 1 Ne. 16:10 (10, 16, 26); 18:12 (12, 21); 2 Ne. 5:12; D&C 17:1.
40*a* 1 Ne. 16:28.
41*a* 1 Ne. 16:29; Alma 37:7 (6–8).
b TG Apathy; Laziness.
42*a* 1 Ne. 16:28.
43*a* Col. 2:17; Heb. 8:5; Mosiah 3:15.

did not prosper; even so it is with things which are spiritual.

44 For behold, it is as easy to give heed to the [a]word of Christ, which will point to you a straight course to eternal bliss, as it was for our fathers to give heed to this compass, which would point unto them a straight course to the promised land.

45 And now I say, is there not a [a]type in this thing? For just as surely as this director did bring our fathers, by following its course, to the promised land, shall the words of Christ, if we follow their course, carry us beyond this vale of sorrow into a far better land of promise.

46 O my son, do not let us be [a]slothful because of the [b]easiness of the [c]way; for so was it with our fathers; for so was it prepared for them, that if they would [d]look they might [e]live; even so it is with us. The way is prepared, and if we will look we may live forever.

47 And now, my son, see that ye take [a]care of these sacred things, yea, see that ye [b]look to God and live. Go unto this people and declare the word, and be sober. My son, farewell.

The commandments of Alma to his son Shiblon.

Comprising chapter 38.

CHAPTER 38

Shiblon was persecuted for righteousness' sake—Salvation is in Christ, who is the life and the light of the world—Bridle all your passions. About 74 B.C.

My [a]son, give ear to my words, for I say unto you, even as I said unto Helaman, that [b]inasmuch as ye shall keep the commandments of God ye shall prosper in the land; and inasmuch as ye will not keep the commandments of God ye shall be [c]cut off from his [d]presence.

2 And now, my son, I trust that I shall have great joy in you, because of your [a]steadiness and your faithfulness unto God; for as you have commenced in your youth to look to the Lord your God, even so I hope that you will continue in keeping his commandments; for blessed is he that [b]endureth to the end.

3 I say unto you, my son, that I have had great joy in thee already, because of thy faithfulness and thy diligence, and thy patience and thy long-suffering among the people of the [a]Zoramites.

4 For I know that thou wast in bonds; yea, and I also know that thou wast stoned for the word's sake; and thou didst bear all these things with [a]patience because the Lord was [b]with thee; and now thou knowest that the Lord did deliver thee.

5 And now my son, Shiblon, I would that ye should remember, that as much as ye shall put your [a]trust in God even so much ye shall be [b]delivered out of your trials, and your [c]troubles, and your afflictions, and ye shall be lifted up at the last day.

6 Now, my son, I would not that ye should think that I know these

---

44*a* Ps. 119:105.
45*a* TG Jesus Christ, Types of, in Anticipation.
46*a* Luke 6:46 (46–49); 1 Ne. 17:41 (40–41).
b Matt. 11:30.
c Ex. 33:13 (12–13); 2 Ne. 9:41; 31:21 (17–21); D&C 132:22 (22, 25).
d Alma 25:16; 33:22 (19–23).
e John 11:25; Hel. 8:15; 3 Ne. 15:9.
47*a* TG Scriptures, Preservation of.
b Amos 5:6; Ether 12:41.
38 1*a* Alma 31:7; 63:1.
b Alma 36:30.
c 1 Ne. 2:21; 2 Ne. 5:20 (20–24); Alma 9:14 (13–15).
d TG God, Presence of.
2*a* TG Commitment.
b Matt. 10:22; Mark 13:13; 2 Ne. 31:16 (15–20); Alma 32:13 (13–15); 3 Ne. 15:9; 27:6 (6–17); D&C 20:29; 53:7.
3*a* Alma 31:7; 39:2.
4*a* TG Patience.
b Ex. 3:12; 1 Ne. 17:55; Mosiah 24:17.
5*a* Ps. 50:15; D&C 100:17.
b Matt. 11:28 (28–30).
c Ps. 81:7; Alma 9:17; D&C 3:8.

things of myself, but it is the Spirit
of God which is in me which maketh these things known unto me;
for if I had not been [a]born of God I
should not have known these things.
7 But behold, the Lord in his great
mercy sent his [a]angel to declare
unto me that I must stop the work
of [b]destruction among his people;
yea, and I have seen an angel face
to face, and he spake with me, and
his voice was as thunder, and it
shook the whole earth.
8 And it came to pass that I was
[a]three days and three nights in
the most bitter [b]pain and [c]anguish
of soul; and never, until I did cry
out unto the Lord Jesus Christ for
mercy, did I receive a [d]remission of
my sins. But behold, I did cry unto
him and I did find peace to my soul.
9 And now, my son, I have told
you this that ye may learn wisdom, that ye may learn of me that
there is [a]no other way or means
whereby man can be saved, only in
and through Christ. Behold, he is
the life and the [b]light of the world.
Behold, he is the word of truth and
[c]righteousness.
10 And now, as ye have begun to
teach the word even so I would that
ye should continue to teach; and I
would that ye would be diligent
and [a]temperate in all things.
11 See that ye are not lifted up
unto pride; yea, see that ye do not
[a]boast in your own wisdom, nor of
your much strength.
12 Use [a]boldness, but not overbear-
ance; and also see that ye [b]bridle
all your passions, that ye may be
filled with love; see that ye refrain
from idleness.
13 Do not [a]pray as the Zoramites
do, for ye have seen that they pray to
be heard of men, and to be praised
for their wisdom.
14 Do not say: O God, I thank thee
that we are [a]better than our brethren; but rather say: O Lord, forgive
my [b]unworthiness, and remember
my brethren in mercy—yea, acknowledge your unworthiness before God at all times.
15 And may the Lord bless your
soul, and receive you at the last day
into his kingdom, to sit down in
peace. Now go, my son, and teach
the word unto this people. Be [a]so-
ber. My son, farewell.

The commandments of Alma to his son Corianton.

Comprising chapters 39 through 42.

CHAPTER 39

Sexual sin is an abomination—Corianton's sins kept the Zoramites from receiving the word—Christ's redemption is retroactive in saving the faithful who preceded it. About 74 B.C.

AND now, my [a]son, I have somewhat
more to say unto thee than what I
said unto thy brother; for behold,
have ye not observed the steadiness
of thy brother, his faithfulness, and
his diligence in keeping the commandments of God? Behold, has he
not set a good [b]example for thee?
2 For thou didst not give so much
heed unto my words as did thy
brother, among the people of the
[a]Zoramites. Now this is what I have
against thee; thou didst go on unto

6*a* Alma 36:23 (23, 26); D&C 5:16. TG Holy Ghost, Baptism of; Man, Natural, Not Spiritually Reborn; Man, New, Spiritually Reborn.
7*a* Mosiah 27:11 (11–17).
b Mosiah 28:4 (3–4); Alma 26:18 (17–18); 36:6 (6–11).
8*a* Alma 36:10 (10, 16).
b TG Pain.
c TG Sorrow.
d TG Remission of Sins.
9*a* Alma 21:9.
b TG Jesus Christ, Light of the World.
c Ether 4:12.
10*a* TG Temperance.
11*a* TG Boast; Pride.
12*a* Alma 18:24.
b TG Priesthood, Magnifying Callings within; Self-Mastery.
13*a* TG Hypocrisy.
14*a* Alma 31:16.
b Luke 18:13 (10–14). TG Ingratitude; Poor in Spirit.
15*a* 1 Pet. 5:8.
39 1*a* Alma 31:7.
b TG Example.
2*a* Alma 38:3.

boasting in thy strength and thy
wisdom.
3 And this is not all, my son. Thou
didst do that which was grievous
unto me; for thou didst forsake the
ministry, and did go over into the
land of Siron among the borders
of the Lamanites, after the [a]harlot
Isabel.
4 Yea, she did [a]steal away the
hearts of many; but this was no excuse for thee, my son. Thou shouldst
have tended to the ministry wherewith thou wast entrusted.
5 Know ye not, my son, that these
things are an abomination in the
sight of the Lord; yea, most [a]abomi-
nable above all sins save it be the
shedding of innocent [b]blood or denying the Holy Ghost?
6 For behold, if ye [a]deny the Holy
Ghost when it once has had place
in you, and ye know that ye deny
it, behold, this is a sin which is
[b]unpardonable; yea, and whosoever
murdereth against the light and
knowledge of God, it is not easy for
him to obtain [c]forgiveness; yea, I
say unto you, my son, that it is not
easy for him to obtain a forgiveness.
7 And now, my son, I would to God
that ye had not been [a]guilty of so
great a crime. I would not dwell
upon your crimes, to harrow up
your soul, if it were not for your
good.
8 But behold, ye cannot [a]hide your
crimes from God; and except ye repent they will stand as a testimony
against you at the last day.
9 Now my son, I would that ye
should repent and forsake your sins,
and go no more after the [a]lusts of
your eyes, but [b]cross yourself in all
these things; for except ye do this ye
can in nowise inherit the kingdom
of God. Oh, remember, and take it
upon you, and [c]cross yourself in
these things.
10 And I command you to take it
upon you to counsel with your elder
brothers in your undertakings; for
behold, thou art in thy youth, and
ye stand in need to be nourished
by your brothers. And give heed to
their counsel.
11 Suffer not yourself to be led
away by any vain or foolish thing;
suffer not the devil to lead away
your heart again after those wicked
harlots. Behold, O my son, how
great [a]iniquity ye brought upon the
[b]Zoramites; for when they saw your
[c]conduct they would not believe in
my words.
12 And now the Spirit of the Lord
doth say unto me: [a]Command thy
children to do good, lest they [b]lead
away the hearts of many people to
destruction; therefore I command
you, my son, in the fear of God, that
ye [c]refrain from your iniquities;
13 That ye turn to the Lord with
all your mind, might, and strength;
that ye lead away the hearts of no
more to do wickedly; but rather return unto them, and [a]acknowledge
your faults and that wrong which
ye have done.
14 [a]Seek not after riches nor the
vain things of this world; for behold,
you cannot carry them with you.

3*a* 1 Sam. 2:22 (22–25); Prov. 5:3. TG Sensuality.
4*a* Prov. 7:18 (6–27).
5*a* TG Adulterer; Fornication; Sexual Immorality.
b TG Life, Sanctity of.
6*a* Moro. 8:28; D&C 76:35. TG Holy Ghost, Loss of.
b TG Holy Ghost, Unpardonable Sin against.
c Rom. 9:18; D&C 64:10. TG Forgive.
7*a* TG Guilt.
8*a* TG God, Omniscience of.
9*a* Prov. 5:8. TG Carnal Mind; Chastity; Covet; Lust.
b TG Self-Mastery.
c 3 Ne. 12:30.
11*a* 1 Sam. 2:24 (22–25).
b Alma 35:14 (2–14); 43:4 (4–6, 13).
c 2 Sam. 12:14; Ezek. 5:5; Rom. 2:21 (21–23); 14:13; 1 Cor. 9:14 (13–14); 1 Ne. 21:6; Alma 4:11; D&C 103:9 (8–9). TG Example.
12*a* TG Commandments of God; Teaching.
b TG Peer Influence.
c TG Abstain.
13*a* Mosiah 27:35.
14*a* Matt. 6:33 (25–34); Jacob 2:18 (18–19); D&C 6:7 (6–7); 68:31 (31–32). TG Treasure.

15 And now, my son, I would say somewhat unto you concerning the [a]coming of Christ. Behold, I say unto you, that it is he that surely shall come to take away the sins of the world; yea, he cometh to declare glad tidings of salvation unto his people.

16 And now, my son, this was the ministry unto which ye were called, to declare these glad tidings unto this people, to prepare their minds; or rather that salvation might come unto them, that they may prepare the minds of their [a]children to hear the word at the time of his coming.

17 And now I will ease your mind somewhat on this subject. Behold, you marvel why these things should be known so long beforehand. Behold, I say unto you, is not a soul at this time as precious unto God as a soul will be at the time of his coming?

18 Is it not as necessary that the plan of redemption should be [a]made known unto this people as well as unto their children?

19 Is it not as easy at this time for the Lord to [a]send his angel to declare these glad tidings unto us as unto our children, or as after the time of his coming?

CHAPTER 40

Christ brings to pass the resurrection of all men—The righteous dead go to paradise and the wicked to outer darkness to await the day of their resurrection—All things will be restored to their proper and perfect frame in the Resurrection. About 74 B.C.

Now my son, here is somewhat more I would say unto thee; for I perceive that thy mind is worried concerning the resurrection of the dead.

2 Behold, I say unto you, that there is no resurrection—or, I would say, in other words, that this mortal does not put on [a]immortality, this corruption does not [b]put on incorruption—[c]until after the coming of Christ.

3 Behold, he bringeth to pass the [a]resurrection of the dead. But behold, my son, the resurrection is not yet. Now, I unfold unto you a mystery; nevertheless, there are many [b]mysteries which are [c]kept, that no one knoweth them save God himself. But I show unto you one thing which I have inquired diligently of God that I might know—that is concerning the resurrection.

4 Behold, there is a time appointed that all shall [a]come forth from the dead. Now when this time cometh no one knows; but God knoweth the time which is appointed.

5 Now, whether there shall be one time, or a [a]second time, or a third time, that men shall come forth from the dead, it mattereth not; for God [b]knoweth all these things; and it sufficeth me to know that this is the case—that there is a time appointed that all shall rise from the dead.

6 Now there must needs be a space betwixt the time of death and the time of the resurrection.

7 And now I would inquire what becometh of the [a]souls of men [b]from this time of death to the time appointed for the resurrection?

8 Now whether there is more than one [a]time appointed for men to rise it mattereth not; for all do not die at once, and this mattereth not; all is

---

15*a* TG Jesus Christ, Mission of.
16*a* TG Family, Children, Responsibilities toward.
18*a* Jacob 4:4 (4–6).
19*a* Mosiah 3:2 (2–3).
40 2*a* Mosiah 16:10 (10–13). TG Immortality.
b 1 Cor. 15:53 (42–54).
c 1 Cor. 15:20 (20–23).
3*a* TG Resurrection.
b TG Mysteries of Godliness.
c D&C 25:4; 121:26; 124:41.
4*a* John 5:29 (28–29).
5*a* 1 Thes. 4:16; Mosiah 26:25 (24–25); D&C 43:18; 76:85.
b TG God, Omniscience of.
7*a* Alma 40:21; D&C 138. TG Soul.
b TG Spirits, Disembodied.
8*a* 2 Pet. 3:8. TG Time.

as one day with God, and time only is measured unto men.

9 Therefore, there is a time appointed unto men that they shall rise from the dead; and there is a space between the time of death and the resurrection. And now, concerning this space of time, what becometh of the souls of men is the thing which I have inquired diligently of the Lord to know; and this is the thing of which I do know.

10 And when the time cometh when all shall rise, then shall they know that God [a]knoweth all the [b]times which are appointed unto man.

11 Now, concerning the [a]state of the soul between [b]death and the resurrection—Behold, it has been made known unto me by an angel, that the spirits of all men, as soon as they are departed from this mortal body, yea, the spirits of all men, whether they be good or evil, are [c]taken [d]home to that God who gave them life.

12 And then shall it come to pass, that the spirits of those who are righteous are received into a state of [a]happiness, which is called [b]paradise, a state of rest, a state of [c]peace, where they shall rest from all their troubles and from all care, and sorrow.

13 And then shall it come to pass, that the [a]spirits of the wicked, yea, who are evil—for behold, they have no part nor portion of the Spirit of the Lord; for behold, they chose evil works rather than good; therefore the spirit of the [b]devil did enter into them, and take possession of their house—and these shall be cast out into [c]outer darkness; there shall be [d]weeping, and wailing, and gnashing of teeth, and this because of their own iniquity, being led captive by the will of the devil.

14 Now this is the state of the [a]souls of the [b]wicked, yea, in darkness, and a state of awful, [c]fearful looking for the fiery [d]indignation of the wrath of God upon them; thus they remain in this [e]state, as well as the righteous in paradise, until the time of their resurrection.

15 Now, there are some that have understood that this state of happiness and this state of misery of the soul, before the resurrection, was a first resurrection. Yea, I admit it may be termed a resurrection, the [a]raising of the spirit or the soul and their consignation to happiness or misery, according to the words which have been spoken.

16 And behold, again it hath been spoken, that there is a [a]first [b]resurrection, a resurrection of all those who have been, or who are, or who shall be, down to the resurrection of Christ from the dead.

17 Now, we do not suppose that this first resurrection, which is spoken of in this manner, can be the resurrection of the souls and their [a]consignation to happiness or misery. Ye cannot suppose that this is what it meaneth.

18 Behold, I say unto you, Nay; but it meaneth the [a]reuniting of the

10*a* TG God, Foreknowledge of.
b Acts 17:26.
11*a* John 20:17.
b Job 14:10; Luke 16:22 (22–26); 1 Ne. 15:31 (31–36); Alma 11:45; D&C 76:73 (71–74).
c Alma 40:15.
d Eccl. 12:7; 2 Ne. 9:38; Alma 24:16; Hel. 8:23.
12*a* Isa. 51:11; Luke 16:22; D&C 138:15. TG Happiness.
b TG Paradise.
c 2 Kgs. 22:20; Alma 7:27; D&C 45:46. TG Peace of God.
13*a* TG Spirits in Prison.
b TG Bondage, Spiritual.
c TG Damnation; Darkness, Spiritual; Hell.
d Matt. 8:12; Mosiah 16:2.
14*a* TG Spirits in Prison.
b D&C 138:20.
c Jacob 6:13; Moses 7:1.
d TG God, Indignation of.
e Alma 34:34.
15*a* Alma 40:11.
16*a* Jacob 4:11; Mosiah 15:21 (21–23); 18:9.
b TG Jesus Christ, Resurrection.
17*a* D&C 76:17 (17, 32, 50). TG Judgment, the Last.
18*a* Matt. 27:52.

soul with the body, of those from the days of Adam down to the resurrection of Christ.

19 Now, whether the souls and the bodies of those of whom has been spoken shall all be reunited at once, the wicked as well as the righteous, I do not say; let it suffice, that I say that they all come forth; or in other words, their resurrection cometh to pass [a]before the resurrection of those who die after the resurrection of Christ.

20 Now, my son, I do not say that their resurrection cometh at the resurrection of Christ; but behold, I give it as my opinion, that the souls and the bodies are reunited, of the righteous, at the resurrection of Christ, and his [a]ascension into heaven.

21 But whether it be at his resurrection or after, I do not say; but this much I say, that there is a [a]space between death and the resurrection of the body, and a state of the soul in [b]happiness or in [c]misery until the time which is appointed of God that the dead shall come forth, and be reunited, both soul and body, and be [d]brought to stand before God, and be judged according to their works.

22 Yea, this bringeth about the restoration of those things of which has been spoken by the mouths of the prophets.

23 The [a]soul shall be [b]restored to the [c]body, and the body to the soul; yea, and every limb and joint shall be restored to its body; yea, even a [d]hair of the head shall not be lost; but all things shall be restored to their proper and [e]perfect frame.

24 And now, my son, this is the restoration of which has been [a]spoken by the mouths of the prophets—

25 And then shall the [a]righteous shine forth in the kingdom of God.

26 But behold, an awful [a]death cometh upon the wicked; for they die as to things pertaining to things of righteousness; for they are unclean, and [b]no unclean thing can inherit the kingdom of God; but they are cast out, and consigned to partake of the fruits of their labors or their works, which have been evil; and they drink the dregs of a bitter [c]cup.

CHAPTER 41

In the Resurrection men come forth to a state of endless happiness or endless misery—Wickedness never was happiness—Carnal men are without God in the world—Every person receives again in the Restoration the characteristics and attributes acquired in mortality. About 74 B.C.

AND now, my son, I have somewhat to say concerning the restoration of which has been spoken; for behold, some have [a]wrested the scriptures, and have gone far [b]astray because of this thing. And I perceive that thy mind has been [c]worried also concerning this thing. But behold, I will explain it unto thee.

2 I say unto thee, my son, that the plan of restoration is requisite with the justice of God; for it is requisite that all things should be restored to their proper order. Behold, it is requisite and just, according to the power and resurrection of Christ,

---

19*a* Mosiah 15:26.
20*a* TG Jesus Christ, Ascension of.
21*a* Luke 23:43 (39–43).
b TG Paradise.
c TG Spirits in Prison.
d Alma 42:23.
23*a* Ezek. 37:14 (6–14); D&C 88:15 (15–17). TG Soul.
b 2 Ne. 9:13; Alma 11:45 (40–45).
c TG Body, Sanctity of.
d Luke 21:18; Alma 41:2; D&C 29:25.
e Philip. 3:21. TG Perfection.
24*a* Isa. 26:19. TG Resurrection.
25*a* Dan. 12:3; Matt. 13:43.
26*a* Ps. 94:3 (1–11); 1 Cor. 6:9 (9–10); 1 Ne. 15:33; Alma 12:16; D&C 29:41. TG Hell.
b Eph. 5:5; Alma 11:37. TG Uncleanness.
c Ps. 75:8.
41 1*a* 2 Pet. 1:20; 3:16; Alma 13:20.
b TG Apostasy of Individuals.
c TG Problem-Solving.

that the soul of man should be restored to its body, and that every
[a]part of the body should be restored
to itself.
3 And it is requisite with the [a]jus-
tice of God that men should be
[b]judged according to their [c]works;
and if their works were good in this
life, and the desires of their hearts
were good, that they should also, at
the last day, be [d]restored unto that
which is good.
4 And if their works are evil they
shall be [a]restored unto them for evil.
Therefore, all things shall be [b]re-
stored to their proper order, every
thing to its natural frame—[c]mortality
raised to [d]immortality, [e]corruption
to incorruption—raised to [f]endless
happiness to [g]inherit the kingdom
of God, or to endless misery to inherit the kingdom of the devil, the
one on one hand, the other on the
other—
5 The one raised to [a]happiness according to his desires of happiness,
or good according to his desires of
good; and the other to evil according
to his desires of evil; for as he has
desired to do evil all the day long
even so shall he have his reward of
evil when the night cometh.
6 And so it is on the other hand.
If he hath repented of his sins, and
desired righteousness until the end
of his days, even so he shall be rewarded unto righteousness.
7 [a]These are they that are redeemed
of the Lord; yea, these are they that
are taken out, that are delivered from
that endless night of darkness; and
thus they stand or fall; for behold,
they are their own [b]judges, whether
to do good or do evil.
8 Now, the decrees of God are
[a]unalterable; therefore, the way is
prepared that [b]whosoever will may
[c]walk therein and be saved.
9 And now behold, my son, do not
risk [a]one more offense against your
God upon those points of doctrine,
which ye have hitherto risked to
commit sin.
10 Do not suppose, because it has
been spoken concerning restoration,
that ye shall be restored from sin to
happiness. Behold, I say unto you,
[a]wickedness never was [b]happiness.
11 And now, my son, all men that
are in a state of [a]nature, or I would
say, in a [b]carnal state, are in the [c]gall
of bitterness and in the [d]bonds of
iniquity; they are [e]without God in
the world, and they have gone [f]con-
trary to the nature of God; therefore, they are in a state contrary to
the nature of happiness.
12 And now behold, is the meaning
of the word restoration to take a
thing of a natural state and place it
in an unnatural state, or to place
it in a state opposite to its nature?
13 O, my son, this is not the case;
but the meaning of the word restoration is to bring back again [a]evil
for evil, or carnal for carnal, or devilish for devilish—good for that which
is good; righteous for that which is
righteous; just for that which is just;
merciful for that which is merciful.

2*a* Alma 40:23.
3*a* TG God, Justice of; Justice.
b TG Accountability; Judgment, the Last.
c Isa. 59:18; Alma 36:15; 42:27; D&C 1:10 (9–10).
d Hel. 14:31.
4*a* Alma 42:28.
b 2 Ne. 9:13 (10–13); D&C 138:17. TG Resurrection.
c TG Mortality.
d TG Immortality.
e 1 Cor. 15:50 (50–53).
f TG Eternal Life.
g TG Exaltation.
5*a* TG Happiness.
7*a* D&C 76:65.
b 2 Ne. 2:26; Alma 42:27; Hel. 14:30. TG Agency.
8*a* Morm. 9:19.
b Alma 42:27.
c TG Walking with God.
9*a* Prov. 26:11; Matt. 12:45 (43–45); D&C 42:26 (23–28).
10*a* Ps. 32:10; Isa. 57:21; Hel. 13:38. TG Evil; Wickedness.
b Alma 50:21; Morm. 2:13. TG Happiness; Peace of God.
11*a* Mosiah 3:19. TG Man, Natural, Not Spiritually Reborn.
b TG Carnal Mind; Fall of Man.
c Acts 8:23; Morm. 8:31.
d TG Bondage, Spiritual.
e Eph. 2:12; Mosiah 27:31.
f Hel. 13:38.
13*a* Dan. 12:10; Rev. 22:12 (6–16).

14 Therefore, my son, see that you are merciful unto your brethren; deal [a]justly, [b]judge righteously, and do [c]good continually; and if ye do all these things then shall ye receive your [d]reward; yea, ye shall have [e]mercy restored unto you again; ye shall have justice restored unto you again; ye shall have a righteous judgment restored unto you again; and ye shall have good rewarded unto you again.

15 For that which ye do [a]send out shall return unto you again, and be restored; therefore, the word restoration more fully condemneth the sinner, and justifieth him not at all.

CHAPTER 42

Mortality is a probationary time to enable man to repent and serve God—The Fall brought temporal and spiritual death upon all mankind—Redemption comes through repentance—God Himself atones for the sins of the world—Mercy is for those who repent—All others are subject to God's justice—Mercy comes because of the Atonement—Only the truly penitent are saved. About 74 B.C.

AND now, my son, I perceive there is somewhat more which doth worry your mind, which ye cannot understand—which is concerning the [a]justice of God in the [b]punishment of the sinner; for ye do try to suppose that it is [c]injustice that the sinner should be consigned to a state of misery.

2 Now behold, my son, I will explain this thing unto thee. For behold, after the Lord God sent our first parents forth from the garden of [a]Eden, to till the [b]ground, from whence they were taken—yea, he drew out the man, and he placed at the east end of the garden of Eden, [c]cherubim, and a flaming sword which turned every way, to keep the tree of life—

3 Now, we see that the man had become as God, knowing good and evil; and lest he should put forth his hand, and take also of the tree of life, and eat and live forever, the Lord God placed [a]cherubim and the flaming sword, that he should not partake of the fruit—

4 And thus we see, that there was a [a]time granted unto man to repent, yea, a [b]probationary time, a time to repent and serve God.

5 For behold, if Adam had put forth his hand immediately, and [a]partaken of the [b]tree of life, he would have lived forever, according to the word of God, having no space for repentance; yea, and also the word of God would have been void, and the great plan of salvation would have been frustrated.

6 But behold, it was appointed unto man to [a]die—therefore, as they were cut off from the tree of life they should be cut off from the face of the earth—and man became [b]lost forever, yea, they became [c]fallen man.

7 And now, ye see by this that our first parents were [a]cut off both temporally and spiritually from the [b]presence of the Lord; and thus we see they became subjects to follow after their own [c]will.

8 Now behold, it was not expedient

14*a* TG Honesty.
b Matt. 7:1 (1–5); D&C 11:12.
c TG Benevolence.
d TG Reward.
e TG Mercy.
15*a* Prov. 19:17; Eccl. 11:1; Alma 42:27 (27–28).
42 1*a* Mosiah 15:27. TG God, Justice of.
b TG Punish.
c Rom. 3:5; 2 Ne. 26:7. TG Injustice.
2*a* TG Eden.
b Jacob 2:21; Mosiah 2:25; Morm. 9:17.
c Gen. 3:24; Alma 12:21; Moses 4:31.
3*a* TG Cherubim.
4*a* Jacob 5:27.
b Alma 34:32. TG Earth, Purpose of; Probation.
5*a* Alma 12:23; Moses 4:28.
b Gen. 2:9; 3:24 (22–24); 1 Ne. 8:10 (10–12); Moses 3:9.
6*a* TG Death.
b 2 Ne. 9:7; Mosiah 16:4 (4–7); Alma 11:45; 12:36.
c TG Fall of Man.
7*a* 2 Ne. 2:5; 9:6 (6–15); Hel. 14:16 (15–18).
b TG God, Presence of.
c TG Agency.

that man should be reclaimed from this [a]temporal death, for that would destroy the great [b]plan of happiness.

9 Therefore, as the soul could never die, and the [a]fall had brought upon all mankind a spiritual [b]death as well as a temporal, that is, they were cut off from the presence of the Lord, it was expedient that mankind should be reclaimed from this spiritual death.

10 Therefore, as they had become [a]carnal, sensual, and devilish, by [b]nature, this [c]probationary state became a state for them to prepare; it became a preparatory state.

11 And now remember, my son, if it were not for the plan of redemption, (laying it aside) as soon as they were dead their souls were [a]miserable, being cut off from the presence of the Lord.

12 And now, there was no means to reclaim men from this fallen state, which [a]man had brought upon himself because of his own [b]disobedience;

13 Therefore, according to justice, the [a]plan of [b]redemption could not be brought about, only on conditions of repentance of men in this probationary state, yea, this preparatory state; for except it were for these conditions, mercy could not take effect except it should destroy the work of justice. Now the work of justice could not be destroyed; if so, God would [c]cease to be God.

14 And thus we see that all mankind were [a]fallen, and they were in the grasp of [b]justice; yea, the justice of God, which consigned them forever to be cut off from his presence.

15 And now, the plan of mercy could not be brought about except an atonement should be made; therefore God himself [a]atoneth for the sins of the world, to bring about the plan of [b]mercy, to appease the demands of [c]justice, that God might be a [d]perfect, just God, and a [e]merciful God also.

16 Now, repentance could not come unto men except there were a [a]punishment, which also was [b]eternal as the life of the soul should be, affixed [c]opposite to the plan of happiness, which was as [d]eternal also as the life of the soul.

17 Now, how could a man repent except he should [a]sin? How could he sin if there was no [b]law? How could there be a law save there was a punishment?

18 Now, there was a punishment affixed, and a just law given, which brought remorse of [a]conscience unto man.

19 Now, if there was no law given—if a man [a]murdered he should [b]die—would he be afraid he would die if he should murder?

20 And also, if there was no law given against sin men would not be afraid to sin.

21 And if there was [a]no law given, if men sinned what could justice do, or mercy either, for they would have no claim upon the creature?

22 But there is a law given, and a

8*a* Gen. 3:22 (22–24).
b Alma 12:26 (22–33); 34:9 (8–16); Moses 6:62.
9*a* TG Fall of Man.
b Moses 5:4. TG Death, Spiritual, First.
10*a* TG Carnal Mind.
b TG Man, Natural, Not Spiritually Reborn.
c TG Mortality; Probation.
11*a* 2 Ne. 9:9 (7–9).
12*a* 1 Cor. 15:22.
b TG Disobedience.
13*a* TG Salvation, Plan of.
b TG Redemption; Repent.
c 2 Ne. 2:13 (13–14).
14*a* Eph. 2:8 (8–9); Alma 22:14 (13–14).
b Rom. 7:5; 2 Ne. 2:5 (4–10); 25:23.
15*a* 2 Ne. 9:10; Mosiah 16:8 (7–8). TG Jesus Christ, Atonement through; Jesus Christ, Redeemer.
b TG Jesus Christ, Mission of.
c Alma 12:32. TG Justice.
d TG God, Perfection of.
e TG God, Mercy of.
16*a* TG Punish.
b D&C 19:11 (10–12).
c TG Opposition.
d TG Eternity.
17*a* Rom. 7:8 (1–25). TG Sin.
b Rom. 4:15; 5:13; 2 Ne. 9:25.
18*a* TG Conscience.
19*a* TG Murder.
b TG Blood, Shedding of.
21*a* 2 Ne. 9:26 (25–26); Mosiah 3:11; Alma 9:16 (15–16).

[a]punishment affixed, and a [b]repentance granted; which repentance, mercy claimeth; otherwise, justice claimeth the creature and executeth the [c]law, and the law inflicteth the punishment; if not so, the works of justice would be destroyed, and God would cease to be God.

23 But God ceaseth not to be God, and [a]mercy claimeth the penitent, and mercy cometh because of the [b]atonement; and the atonement bringeth to pass the [c]resurrection of the dead; and the [d]resurrection of the dead bringeth [e]back men into the presence of God; and thus they are restored into his presence, to be [f]judged according to their works, according to the law and justice.

24 For behold, justice exerciseth all his demands, and also [a]mercy claimeth all which is her own; and thus, none but the truly penitent are saved.

25 What, do ye suppose that [a]mercy can rob [b]justice? I say unto you, Nay; not one whit. If so, God would cease to be God.

26 And thus God bringeth about his great and eternal [a]purposes, which were prepared [b]from the foundation of the world. And thus cometh about the salvation and the redemption of men, and also their destruction and misery.

27 Therefore, O my son, [a]whosoever will come may come and partake of the waters of life freely; and whosoever will not come the same is not compelled to come; but in the last day it shall be [b]restored unto him according to his [c]deeds.

28 If he has desired to do [a]evil, and has not repented in his days, behold, evil shall be done unto him, according to the restoration of God.

29 And now, my son, I desire that ye should let these things [a]trouble you no more, and only let your sins trouble you, with that trouble which shall bring you down unto repentance.

30 O my son, I desire that ye should deny the [a]justice of God no more. Do not endeavor to excuse yourself in the least point because of your sins, by denying the justice of God; but do you let the justice of God, and his [b]mercy, and his long-suffering have full sway in your heart; and let it bring you down to the dust in [c]humility.

31 And now, O my son, ye are called of God to [a]preach the word unto this people. And now, my son, go thy way, declare the word with truth and soberness, that thou mayest [b]bring souls unto repentance, that the great plan of mercy may have claim upon them. And may God grant unto you even according to my words. Amen.

CHAPTER 43

Alma and his sons preach the word—The Zoramites and other Nephite dissenters become Lamanites—The Lamanites come against the Nephites in war—Moroni arms the Nephites with defensive armor—The Lord

22*a* TG Punish.
b TG Repent.
c Gal. 3:13; D&C 76:48.
23*a* TG God, Mercy of.
b TG Jesus Christ, Atonement through.
c 2 Ne. 2:8; Alma 7:12; 12:25 (24–25).
d 2 Ne. 9:4; Alma 11:41 (41–45); Hel. 14:15 (15–18); Morm. 9:13.
e Alma 40:21 (21–24).
f TG Jesus Christ, Judge.
24*a* TG God, Mercy of.
25*a* TG Mercy.
b TG Justice.
26*a* Matt. 5:48; Rom. 8:17 (14–21); 2 Ne. 2:15 (14–30); D&C 29:43 (42–44); Moses 1:39. TG Earth, Purpose of.
b Alma 13:3 (3, 5, 7–8); 3 Ne. 1:14.
27*a* Alma 5:34; 41:7 (7–8); Hel. 14:30. TG Agency.
b Alma 41:15.
c Isa. 59:18; Alma 36:15; D&C 1:10 (9–10).
28*a* Alma 41:4 (2–5).
29*a* 2 Cor. 7:10 (8–11); Morm. 2:13.
30*a* TG Justice.
b TG God, Mercy of.
c TG Humility.
31*a* D&C 11:15.
b TG Mission of Early Saints.

reveals to Alma the strategy of the Lamanites—The Nephites defend their homes, liberties, families, and religion—The armies of Moroni and Lehi surround the Lamanites. About 74 B.C.

AND now it came to pass that the sons of Alma did go forth among the people, to declare the word unto them. And Alma, also, himself, could not [a]rest, and he also went forth.
2 Now [a]we shall say no more concerning their preaching, except that they preached the word, and the truth, according to the spirit of prophecy and revelation; and they preached after the [b]holy order of God by which they were called.
3 And now [a]I return to an [b]account of the wars between the Nephites and the Lamanites, in the eighteenth year of the reign of the judges.
4 For behold, it came to pass that the [a]Zoramites became Lamanites; therefore, in the commencement of the eighteenth year the people of the Nephites saw that the Lamanites were coming upon them; therefore they made preparations for war; yea, they gathered together their armies in the land of Jershon.
5 And it came to pass that the Lamanites came with their thousands; and they came into the land of [a]Antionum, which is the land of the Zoramites; and a man by the name of [b]Zerahemnah was their leader.
6 And now, as the [a]Amalekites were of a more wicked and murderous disposition than the Lamanites were, in and of themselves, therefore, Zerahemnah appointed chief [b]captains over the Lamanites, and they were all Amalekites and [c]Zoramites.
7 Now this he did that he might preserve their [a]hatred towards the Nephites, that he might bring them into subjection to the accomplishment of his designs.
8 For behold, his [a]designs were to [b]stir up the Lamanites to anger against the Nephites; this he did that he might usurp great power over them, and also that he might gain power over the Nephites by bringing them into [c]bondage.
9 And now the design of the Nephites was to support their lands, and their houses, and their [a]wives, and their children, that they might preserve them from the hands of their enemies; and also that they might preserve their [b]rights and their privileges, yea, and also their [c]liberty, that they might worship God according to their desires.
10 For they knew that if they should fall into the hands of the Lamanites, that whosoever should [a]worship God in [b]spirit and in truth, the true and the living God, the Lamanites would [c]destroy.
11 Yea, and they also knew the extreme hatred of the Lamanites towards their [a]brethren, who were the [b]people of Anti-Nephi-Lehi, who were called the people of Ammon—and they would not take up arms, yea, they had entered into a covenant and they would not break it—therefore, if they should fall into the hands of the Lamanites they would be destroyed.
12 And the Nephites would not suffer that they should be destroyed; therefore they gave them lands for their inheritance.

43 1*a* Ether 12:2 (2–3).
2*a* W of M 1:9 (1–9).
b Alma 30:20 (20–23, 31); 46:38.
TG Priesthood.
3*a* Morm. 5:9.
b Alma 35:13.
4*a* Alma 30:59; 35:14 (2–14); 52:33 (20, 33).
5*a* Alma 31:3.
b Alma 44:1.
6*a* Alma 21:4 (2–16).
b Alma 48:5.
c Alma 43:44.
7*a* Alma 37:32.
8*a* Alma 43:29.
b Alma 27:12; 47:1.
c Alma 44:2.
9*a* Alma 44:5; 46:12; 48:10 (10, 24).
b TG Citizenship.
c TG Liberty.
10*a* TG Worship.
b John 4:23 (23–24).
c Dan. 6:7 (4–17).
11*a* Alma 23:17; 24:1 (1–3, 5, 20); 25:13 (1, 13); 27:2 (2, 21–26).
b Alma 47:29.

13 And the people of Ammon did
give unto the Nephites a large portion of their substance to [a]support
their armies; and thus the Nephites
were compelled, alone, to withstand
against the Lamanites, who were a
compound of Laman and Lemuel,
and the sons of Ishmael, and all
those who had dissented from the
Nephites, who were Amalekites and
Zoramites, and the [b]descendants of
the priests of Noah.
14 Now those descendants were
as numerous, nearly, as were the
Nephites; and thus the Nephites
were obliged to contend with their
brethren, even unto bloodshed.
15 And it came to pass as the
armies of the Lamanites had gathered together in the land of Antionum, behold, the armies of the
Nephites were prepared to meet
them in the [a]land of Jershon.
16 Now, the leader of the Nephites, or the man who had been [a]ap-
pointed to be the [b]chief captain
over the Nephites—now the chief
captain took the command of all
the armies of the Nephites—and
his name was Moroni;
17 And Moroni took all the command, and the government of their
wars. And he was only twenty
and five years old when he was
appointed chief captain over the
armies of the Nephites.
18 And it came to pass that he met
the Lamanites in the borders of Jershon, and his people were armed
with swords, and with cimeters,
and all manner of [a]weapons of war.
19 And when the armies of the
Lamanites saw that the people of
Nephi, or that Moroni, had [a]pre-
pared his people with [b]breastplates
and with arm-shields, yea, and also
shields to defend their heads, and
also they were dressed with thick
clothing—
20 Now the army of Zerahemnah
was not prepared with any such
thing; they had only their [a]swords
and their cimeters, their bows and
their arrows, their [b]stones and their
slings; and they were [c]naked, save
it were a skin which was girded
about their loins; yea, all were naked, save it were the Zoramites and
the Amalekites;
21 But they were not armed with
breastplates, nor shields—therefore,
they were exceedingly afraid of the
armies of the Nephites because of
their armor, notwithstanding their
number being so much greater than
the Nephites.
22 Behold, now it came to pass
that they durst not come against
the Nephites in the borders of Jershon; therefore they departed out
of the land of Antionum into the
wilderness, and took their journey
round about in the wilderness, away
by the head of the river Sidon, that
they might come into the land of
[a]Manti and take possession of the
land; for they did not suppose that
the armies of Moroni would know
whither they had gone.
23 But it came to pass, as soon as
they had departed into the wilderness Moroni sent spies into the wilderness to watch their camp; and
Moroni, also, knowing of the prophecies of Alma, sent certain men unto
him, desiring him that he should
[a]inquire of the Lord [b]whither the
armies of the Nephites should go
to defend themselves against the
Lamanites.
24 And it came to pass that the
[a]word of the Lord came unto Alma,
and Alma informed the messengers
of Moroni, that the armies of the

13*a* Alma 56:27.
b Alma 25:4.
15*a* Alma 27:26.
16*a* Alma 46:34.
b Alma 46:11.
18*a* TG Weapon.
19*a* TG Skill.
b Alma 49:24.
20*a* Mosiah 10:8; Alma 3:5 (4–5); 44:8.
b 1 Ne. 16:15; Alma 49:2.
c Enos 1:20.
22*a* Alma 22:27; 56:14.
23*a* Ex. 18:15; 2 Kgs. 6:12 (8–18); Mosiah 28:6.
b Alma 16:6 (5–8); 48:16; 3 Ne. 3:20 (18–21).
24*a* Isa. 31:5; Alma 43:47; D&C 134:11. TG Guidance, Divine.

Lamanites were marching round about in the wilderness, that they might come over into the land of Manti, that they might commence an attack upon the weaker part of the people. And those messengers went and delivered the message unto Moroni.
25 Now Moroni, leaving a part of his army in the land of Jershon, lest by any means a part of the Lamanites should come into that land and take possession of the city, took the remaining part of his army and marched over into the land of Manti.
26 And he caused that all the people in that quarter of the land should gather themselves together to battle against the Lamanites, to defend their lands and their country, their rights and their liberties; therefore they were prepared against the time of the coming of the Lamanites.
27 And it came to pass that Moroni caused that his army should be secreted in the valley which was near the bank of the river Sidon, which was on the west of the river Sidon in the wilderness.
28 And Moroni placed spies round about, that he might know when the camp of the Lamanites should come.
29 And now, as Moroni knew the [a]intention of the Lamanites, that it was their intention to destroy their brethren, or to [b]subject them and bring them into bondage that they might establish a kingdom unto themselves over all the land;
30 And he also knowing that it was the [a]only desire of the Nephites to preserve their lands, and their [b]liberty, and their church, therefore he thought it no sin that he should defend them by [c]stratagem; therefore, he found by his spies which course the Lamanites were to take.
31 Therefore, he divided his army and brought a part over into the valley, and [a]concealed them on the east, and on the south of the hill Riplah;
32 And the remainder he concealed in the west [a]valley, on the west of the river Sidon, and so down into the borders of the land Manti.
33 And thus having placed his army according to his desire, he was prepared to meet them.
34 And it came to pass that the Lamanites came up on the north of the hill, where a part of the army of Moroni was concealed.
35 And as the Lamanites had passed the hill Riplah, and came into the valley, and began to cross the river Sidon, the army which was concealed on the south of the hill, which was led by a man whose name was [a]Lehi, and he led his army forth and encircled the Lamanites about on the east in their rear.
36 And it came to pass that the Lamanites, when they saw the Nephites coming upon them in their rear, turned them about and began to contend with the army of Lehi.
37 And the work of death commenced on both sides, but it was more dreadful on the part of the Lamanites, for their [a]nakedness was exposed to the heavy blows of the Nephites with their swords and their cimeters, which brought death almost at every stroke.
38 While on the other hand, there was now and then a man fell among the Nephites, by their swords and the loss of blood, they being shielded from the more vital parts of the body, or the more vital parts of the body being shielded from the strokes of the Lamanites, by their [a]breastplates, and their armshields, and their head-plates; and thus the Nephites did carry on the work of death among the Lamanites.

29 *a* Alma 43:8.
b Alma 49:7.
30 *a* Alma 44:5; 46:12 (12–20); 48:10 (10–16).
b Alma 46:35.
c Judg. 7:16 (15–25).
31 *a* Josh. 8:13; Alma 52:21 (21–31); 58:16 (15–21).
32 *a* Alma 43:41.
35 *a* Alma 49:16.
37 *a* Alma 3:5.
38 *a* Alma 44:9.

39 And it came to pass that the
Lamanites became frightened, because of the great destruction among
them, even until they began to flee
towards the river Sidon.
40 And they were pursued by Lehi
and his men; and they were driven
by Lehi into the waters of Sidon,
and they crossed the waters of Sidon. And Lehi retained his armies
upon the bank of the river Sidon
that they should not cross.
41 And it came to pass that Moroni
and his army met the Lamanites in
the [a]valley, on the other side of the
river Sidon, and began to fall upon
them and to slay them.
42 And the Lamanites did flee
again before them, towards the land
of Manti; and they were met again
by the armies of Moroni.
43 Now in this case the Lamanites
did fight exceedingly; yea, never
had the Lamanites been known to
fight with such exceedingly great
strength and courage, no, not even
from the beginning.
44 And they were inspired by the
[a]Zoramites and the Amalekites, who
were their chief captains and leaders, and by Zerahemnah, who was
their chief captain, or their chief
leader and commander; yea, they did
fight like dragons, and many of the
Nephites were slain by their hands,
yea, for they did smite in two many
of their head-plates, and they did
pierce many of their breastplates,
and they did smite off many of their
arms; and thus the Lamanites did
smite in their fierce anger.
45 Nevertheless, the Nephites were
inspired by a [a]better cause, for they
were not [b]fighting for monarchy
nor power but they were fighting
for their homes and their [c]liberties,
their wives and their children, and
their all, yea, for their rites of worship and their church.
46 And they were doing that which
they felt was the [a]duty which they
owed to their God; for the Lord had
said unto them, and also unto their
fathers, that: [b]Inasmuch as ye are
not guilty of the [c]first offense, neither the second, ye shall not suffer
yourselves to be slain by the hands
of your enemies.
47 And again, the Lord has said
that: Ye shall [a]defend your families
even unto [b]bloodshed. Therefore
for this cause were the Nephites
contending with the Lamanites, to
defend themselves, and their families, and their lands, their country,
and their rights, and their religion.
48 And it came to pass that when
the men of Moroni saw the fierceness and the anger of the Lamanites,
they were about to shrink and flee
from them. And Moroni, perceiving
their intent, sent forth and inspired
their hearts with these thoughts—
yea, the thoughts of their lands,
their liberty, yea, their freedom
from bondage.
49 And it came to pass that they
turned upon the Lamanites, and
they [a]cried with one voice [b]unto
the Lord their God, for their [c]liberty
and their freedom from bondage.
50 And they [a]began to stand
against the Lamanites with power;
and in that selfsame hour that they
cried unto the Lord for their freedom, the Lamanites began to flee
before them; and they fled even to
the waters of Sidon.
51 Now, the Lamanites were more
[a]numerous, yea, by more than
double the number of the Nephites; nevertheless, they were driven

---

41*a* Alma 43:32.
44*a* Alma 43:6.
45*a* Alma 44:1.
b Mosiah 20:11; Alma 44:5.
c TG Liberty.
46*a* TG Duty.
b Alma 48:14 (14–16); D&C 98:33 (23–36).
c Luke 6:29; 3 Ne. 3:21 (20–21); Morm. 3:10 (10–11); D&C 98:23 (22–48).
47*a* Isa. 31:5; Alma 43:24; 61:14; Morm. 7:4; D&C 134:11. TG Family, Children, Responsibilities toward; War.
b Josh. 1:18.
49*a* Ex. 2:23 (23–25); Mosiah 29:20.
b Ps. 59:1 (1–5).
c TG Liberty.
50*a* Ex. 17:11 (8–13).
51*a* Alma 46:30.

insomuch that they were gathered together in one body in the valley, upon the bank by the river Sidon.

52 Therefore the armies of Moroni encircled them about, yea, even on both sides of the river, for behold, on the east were the men of Lehi.

53 Therefore when Zerahemnah saw the men of Lehi on the east of the river Sidon, and the armies of Moroni on the west of the river Sidon, that they were encircled about by the Nephites, they were struck with terror.

54 Now Moroni, when he saw their [a]terror, commanded his men that they should stop shedding their blood.

CHAPTER 44

Moroni commands the Lamanites to make a covenant of peace or be destroyed—Zerahemnah rejects the offer, and the battle resumes—Moroni's armies defeat the Lamanites. About 74–73 B.C.

AND it came to pass that they did stop and withdrew a pace from them. And Moroni said unto [a]Zerahemnah: Behold, Zerahemnah, that we do [b]not desire to be men of blood. Ye know that ye are in our hands, yet we do not desire to slay you.

2 Behold, we have not come out to battle against you that we might shed your blood for power; neither do we desire to bring any one to the [a]yoke of bondage. But this is the [b]very cause for which ye have come against us; yea, and ye are angry with us because of our religion.

3 But now, ye behold that the Lord is with us; and ye behold that he has delivered you into our hands. And now I would that ye should understand that this is done unto us [a]because of our religion and our faith in Christ. And now ye see that ye cannot destroy this our faith.

4 Now ye see that this is the true faith of God; yea, ye see that God will support, and keep, and preserve us, so long as we are [a]faithful unto him, and unto our faith, and our religion; and never will the Lord suffer that we shall be destroyed except we should fall into transgression and deny our faith.

5 And now, Zerahemnah, I command you, in the name of that all-powerful God, who has strengthened our arms that we have gained power over you, [a]by our faith, by our religion, and by our [b]rites of worship, and by our church, and by the sacred support which we owe to our [c]wives and our children, by that [d]liberty which binds us to our lands and our country; yea, and also by the maintenance of the sacred word of God, to which we owe all our happiness; and by all that is most dear unto us—

6 Yea, and this is not all; I command you by all the desires which ye have for life, that ye [a]deliver up your weapons of war unto us, and we will seek not your blood, but we will [b]spare your lives, if ye will go your way and come not again to war against us.

7 And now, if ye do not this, behold, ye are in our hands, and I will command my men that they shall fall upon you, and [a]inflict the wounds of death in your bodies, that ye may become extinct; and then we will see who shall have power over this people; yea, we will see who shall be brought into bondage.

8 And now it came to pass that when Zerahemnah had heard these sayings he came forth and delivered up his [a]sword and his cimeter, and his bow into the hands of Moroni, and said unto him: Behold, here are

---

54*a* Alma 47:2.
44 1*a* Alma 43:5.
b Alma 43:45.
2*a* TG Bondage, Physical.
b Alma 43:8.
3*a* Alma 38:1.
TG Protection, Divine.
4*a* Mark 4:40 (35–41).
5*a* Alma 43:45 (9, 45); 46:12 (12–20).
b TG Ordinance.
c Gen. 2:24 (23–24).
d TG Liberty.
6*a* Alma 52:25 (25, 32).
b TG Benevolence.
7*a* Alma 62:11.
8*a* Alma 43:20.

our weapons of war; we will deliver
them up unto you, but we will not
suffer ourselves to take an [b]oath
unto you, which we know that we
shall break, and also our children;
but take our weapons of war, and
suffer that we may depart into the
wilderness; otherwise we will retain our swords, and we will perish
or conquer.
9 Behold, we are [a]not of your faith;
we do not believe that it is God that
has delivered us into your hands; but
we believe that it is your cunning
that has preserved you from our
swords. Behold, it is your [b]breast-
plates and your shields that have
preserved you.
10 And now when Zerahemnah
had made an end of speaking these
words, Moroni returned the sword
and the weapons of war, which he
had received, unto Zerahemnah,
saying: Behold, we will end the
conflict.
11 Now I cannot recall the words
which I have spoken, therefore
as the Lord liveth, ye shall not
depart except ye depart with an
oath that ye will not return again
against us to war. Now as ye are in
our hands we will spill your blood
upon the ground, or ye shall submit to the conditions which I have
proposed.
12 And now when Moroni had said
these words, Zerahemnah retained
his sword, and he was angry with
Moroni, and he rushed forward
that he might slay Moroni; but as
he raised his sword, behold, one of
Moroni's soldiers smote it even to
the earth, and it broke by the hilt;
and he also smote Zerahemnah that
he took off his scalp and it fell to
the earth. And Zerahemnah withdrew from before them into the
midst of his soldiers.
13 And it came to pass that the
soldier who stood by, who smote
off the scalp of Zerahemnah, took
up the scalp from off the ground by
the hair, and laid it upon the point
of his sword, and stretched it forth
unto them, saying unto them with
a loud voice:
14 Even as this scalp has fallen
to the earth, which is the scalp of
your chief, so shall ye fall to the
earth except ye will deliver up your
weapons of war and depart with a
covenant of peace.
15 Now there were many, when
they heard these words and saw
the scalp which was upon the
sword, that were struck with fear;
and many came forth and threw
down their weapons of war at
the feet of Moroni, and entered
into a [a]covenant of peace. And as
many as entered into a covenant
they suffered to [b]depart into the
wilderness.
16 Now it came to pass that Zerahemnah was exceedingly wroth,
and he did stir up the remainder
of his soldiers to anger, to contend more powerfully against the
Nephites.
17 And now Moroni was angry,
because of the stubbornness of
the Lamanites; therefore he commanded his people that they should
fall upon them and slay them. And
it came to pass that they began to
slay them; yea, and the Lamanites
did contend with their swords and
their might.
18 But behold, their naked skins
and their bare heads were exposed
to the sharp swords of the Nephites;
yea, behold they were pierced and
smitten, yea, and did fall exceedingly fast before the swords of the
Nephites; and they began to be
swept down, even as the soldier of
Moroni had prophesied.
19 Now Zerahemnah, when he
saw that they were all about to
be destroyed, cried mightily unto
Moroni, promising that he would
covenant and also his people with
them, if they would spare the remainder of their lives, that they

8*b* TG Oath.
9*a* TG Unbelief.
b Alma 43:38; 46:13.
15*a* 1 Ne. 4:37;
Alma 50:36.
b Hel. 1:33.

[a]never would come to war again
against them.
20 And it came to pass that Moroni
caused that the work of death should
[a]cease again among the people. And
he took the weapons of war from
the Lamanites; and after they had
entered into a [b]covenant with him
of peace they were suffered to depart into the wilderness.
21 Now the number of their dead
was not numbered because of the
greatness of the number; yea, the
number of their dead was exceedingly great, both on the Nephites
and on the Lamanites.
22 And it came to pass that they
did cast their dead into the waters
of Sidon, and they have gone forth
and are buried in the depths of
the [a]sea.
23 And the armies of the Nephites,
or of Moroni, returned and came to
their houses and their lands.
24 And thus ended the eighteenth
year of the reign of the judges over
the people of Nephi. And thus ended
the record of Alma, which was written upon the plates of Nephi.

The account of the people of Nephi, and their wars and dissensions, in the days of Helaman, according to the record of Helaman, which he kept in his days.

Comprising chapters 45 through 62.

CHAPTER 45

Helaman believes the words of Alma—Alma prophesies the destruction of the Nephites—He blesses and curses the land—Alma may have been taken up by the Spirit, even as Moses—Dissension grows in the Church. About 73 B.C.

BEHOLD, now it came to pass that the
people of Nephi were exceedingly
rejoiced, because the Lord had again
[a]delivered them out of the hands of
their enemies; therefore they gave
thanks unto the Lord their God; yea,
and they did [b]fast much and pray
much, and they did worship God
with exceedingly great joy.
2 And it came to pass in the nineteenth year of the reign of the judges
over the people of Nephi, that Alma
came unto his son Helaman and
said unto him: Believest thou the
words which I spake unto thee concerning those [a]records which have
been kept?
3 And Helaman said unto him:
Yea, I [a]believe.
4 And Alma said again: Believest
thou in Jesus Christ, who shall come?
5 And he said: Yea, I believe all
the words which thou hast spoken.
6 And Alma said unto him again:
Will ye [a]keep my commandments?
7 And he said: Yea, I will keep thy
commandments with all my heart.
8 Then Alma said unto him: Blessed
art thou; and the Lord shall [a]pros-
per thee in this land.
9 But behold, I have somewhat
to [a]prophesy unto thee; but what
I prophesy unto thee ye shall not
make known; yea, what I prophesy
unto thee shall not be made known,
even until the prophecy is fulfilled;
therefore write the words which I
shall say.
10 And these are the words: Behold, I perceive that this very people, the Nephites, according to the
spirit of revelation which is in me,
in [a]four hundred years from the
time that Jesus Christ shall manifest
himself unto them, shall dwindle in
[b]unbelief.
11 Yea, and then shall they see
wars and pestilences, yea, famines and bloodshed, even until the

---

19*a* Alma 47:6.
20*a* Alma 46:7.
b Alma 55:28; 62:16 (16–17).
22*a* Alma 3:3.
45 1*a* TG Deliver.
b TG Fast, Fasting.
2*a* Alma 37:1 (1–32); 50:38.
3*a* 1 Ne. 11:5.
6*a* TG Commandments of God; Obedience.
8*a* 1 Ne. 4:14; Alma 48:15, 25.
9*a* TG Prophecy.
10*a* 1 Ne. 12:12 (10–15); Hel. 13:9; Morm. 8:6.
b TG Apostasy of Individuals.

people of Nephi shall become [a]extinct—
12 Yea, and this because they shall dwindle in unbelief and fall into the works of darkness, and [a]lasciviousness, and all manner of iniquities; yea, I say unto you, that because they shall sin against so great light and knowledge, yea, I say unto you, that from that day, even the [b]fourth generation shall not all pass away before this great iniquity shall come.
13 And when that great day cometh, behold, the time very soon cometh that those who are now, or the seed of those who are now numbered among the people of Nephi, shall [a]no more be numbered among the people of Nephi.
14 But whosoever remaineth, and is not destroyed in that great and dreadful day, shall be [a]numbered among the [b]Lamanites, and shall become like unto them, all, save it be a few who shall be called the disciples of the Lord; and them shall the Lamanites pursue even [c]until they shall become extinct. And now, because of iniquity, this prophecy shall be fulfilled.
15 And now it came to pass that after Alma had said these things to Helaman, he [a]blessed him, and also his other sons; and he also blessed the earth for the [b]righteous' sake.
16 And he said: Thus saith the Lord God—[a]Cursed shall be the land, yea, this land, unto every nation, kindred, tongue, and people, unto destruction, which do [b]wickedly, when they are fully ripe; and as I have said so shall it be; for this is the cursing and the [c]blessing of God upon the land, for the Lord cannot look upon sin with the [d]least degree of allowance.
17 And now, when Alma had said these words he blessed the [a]church, yea, all those who should stand fast in the faith from that time henceforth.
18 And when Alma had done this he [a]departed out of the land of Zarahemla, as if to go into the land of [b]Melek. And it came to pass that he was never heard of more; as to his death or burial we know not of.
19 Behold, this we know, that he was a righteous man; and the saying went abroad in the church that he was taken up by the [a]Spirit, or [b]buried by the hand of the Lord, even as Moses. But behold, the scriptures saith the Lord took Moses unto himself; and we suppose that he has also received Alma in the spirit, unto himself; therefore, for this cause we know nothing concerning his death and burial.
20 And now it came to pass in the commencement of the nineteenth year of the reign of the judges over the people of Nephi, that Helaman went forth among the people to declare the [a]word unto them.
21 For behold, because of their wars with the Lamanites and the many little dissensions and disturbances which had been among the people, it became expedient that the [a]word of God should be declared among them, yea, and that a [b]regulation should be made throughout the church.
22 Therefore, [a]Helaman and his brethren went forth to establish the church again in all the land, yea, in every city throughout all the land which was possessed by the people

11*a* Jarom 1:10; Hel. 13:6 (5–19).
12*a* TG Lust.
b 2 Ne. 26:9; 3 Ne. 27:32.
13*a* Hel. 3:16.
14*a* Moro. 9:24.
b 1 Ne. 13:30; D&C 3:17.
c Moro. 1:2 (1–3).
15*a* Gen. 49:1 (1–27); Alma 8:22.
b Alma 46:10; 62:40.
16*a* 2 Ne. 1:7; Alma 37:31; Morm. 1:17; Ether 2:11 (8–12). TG Earth, Curse of.
b Jer. 44:5 (5–6).
c D&C 130:21.
d D&C 1:31.
17*a* TG Church.
18*a* 3 Ne. 1:3 (2–3).
b Alma 35:13.
19*a* 2 Kgs. 2:16.
b Deut. 34:6 (5–6). TG Translated Beings.
20*a* Alma 46:1.
21*a* Alma 31:5.
b Alma 6:7; 62:44 (44–47).
22*a* Alma 48:19.

of Nephi. And it came to pass that they did appoint [b]priests and [c]teachers throughout all the land, over all the churches.

23 And now it came to pass that after Helaman and his brethren had appointed priests and teachers over the churches that there arose a [a]dissension among them, and they would not give heed to the words of Helaman and his brethren;

24 But they grew proud, being lifted up in their hearts, because of their exceedingly great [a]riches; therefore they grew rich in their own eyes, and would not give heed to their words, to [b]walk uprightly before God.

CHAPTER 46

Amalickiah conspires to be king—Moroni raises the title of liberty—He rallies the people to defend their religion—True believers are called Christians—A remnant of Joseph will be preserved—Amalickiah and the dissenters flee to the land of Nephi—Those who will not support the cause of freedom are put to death. About 73–72 B.C.

AND it came to pass that as many as would not hearken to the [a]words of Helaman and his brethren were gathered together against their brethren.

2 And now behold, they were exceedingly wroth, insomuch that they were determined to slay them.

3 Now the leader of those who were wroth against their brethren was a large and a strong man; and his name was [a]Amalickiah.

4 And Amalickiah was desirous to be a [a]king; and those people who were wroth were also desirous that he should be their king; and they were the greater part of them the lower [b]judges of the land, and they were seeking for power.

5 And they had been led by the [a]flatteries of Amalickiah, that if they would support him and establish him to be their king that he would make them rulers over the people.

6 Thus they were led away by Amalickiah to dissensions, notwithstanding the preaching of Helaman and his brethren, yea, notwithstanding their exceedingly great care over the church, for they were [a]high priests over the church.

7 And there were many in the church who believed in the [a]flattering words of Amalickiah, therefore they [b]dissented even from the church; and thus were the affairs of the people of Nephi exceedingly precarious and dangerous, notwithstanding their great [c]victory which they had had over the Lamanites, and their great rejoicings which they had had because of their [d]deliverance by the hand of the Lord.

8 Thus we see how [a]quick the children of men do [b]forget the Lord their God, yea, how quick to do [c]iniquity, and to be led away by the evil one.

9 Yea, and we also see the great [a]wickedness one very wicked man can cause to take place among the children of men.

10 Yea, we see that Amalickiah, because he was a man of cunning device and a man of many flattering words, that he led away the hearts of many people to do wickedly; yea, and to seek to [a]destroy the church of God, and to destroy the foundation of [b]liberty which God had granted

---

22*b* TG Church Organization.
c TG Teacher.
23*a* 3 Ne. 11:29 (28–29).
24*a* TG Treasure.
b TG Pride; Walking in Darkness.
46 1*a* Alma 45:20.
3*a* Alma 49:25.
4*a* Alma 2:2.
b Mosiah 29:11 (11–44).
5*a* Prov. 29:5.
6*a* Alma 46:38.
7*a* TG Flatter.
b Alma 1:24.
c Alma 44:20.
d Josh. 21:44; 1 Kgs. 5:3; Mosiah 9:17. TG Deliver.
8*a* Ex. 32:8; Judg. 2:17; Hel. 4:26; 6:32; 12:2 (2, 4–5).
b Deut. 6:12.
c Mosiah 13:29.
9*a* 2 Kgs. 10:29; Mosiah 29:17 (17–18).
10*a* TG Tyranny.
b 2 Ne. 1:7; Mosiah 29:32. TG Liberty.

unto them, or which blessing God
had sent upon the face of the land
for the [c]righteous' sake.
11 And now it came to pass that
when Moroni, who was the [a]chief
commander of the armies of the
Nephites, had heard of these dissensions, he was angry with Amalickiah.
12 And it came to pass that he rent
his coat; and he took a piece thereof,
and wrote upon it—[a]In memory of
our God, our religion, and freedom,
and our peace, our wives, and our
children—and he fastened it upon
the end of a pole.
13 And he fastened on his head-
plate, and his [a]breastplate, and his
shields, and girded on his armor
about his loins; and he took the pole,
which had on the end thereof his
rent coat, (and he called it the [b]title
of liberty) and he [c]bowed himself
to the earth, and he prayed mightily unto his God for the blessings
of liberty to rest upon his brethren, so long as there should a band
of [d]Christians remain to possess
the land—
14 For thus were all the true believers of Christ, who belonged
to the church of God, called by
those who did not belong to the
church.
15 And those who did belong to
the church were [a]faithful; yea, all
those who were true believers in
Christ [b]took upon them, gladly, the
name of Christ, or [c]Christians as
they were called, because of their
belief in Christ who should come.
16 And therefore, at this time,
Moroni prayed that the cause of the
Christians, and the [a]freedom of the
land might be favored.
17 And it came to pass that when
he had poured out his soul to God,
he named all the land which was
[a]south of the land [b]Desolation, yea,
and in fine, all the land, both on the
[c]north and on the south—A chosen
land, and the land of [d]liberty.
18 And he said: Surely God shall
not [a]suffer that we, who are despised
because we take upon us the name
of Christ, shall be trodden down and
destroyed, until we bring it upon us
by our own [b]transgressions.
19 And when Moroni had said
these words, he went forth among
the people, waving the [a]rent part of
his garment in the air, that all might
see the writing which he had written upon the rent part, and crying
with a loud voice, saying:
20 Behold, whosoever will maintain this title upon the land, let
them come forth in the strength
of the Lord, and [a]enter into a covenant that they will [b]maintain their
rights, and their religion, that the
Lord God may bless them.
21 And it came to pass that when
Moroni had proclaimed these words,
behold, the people came running
[a]together with their armor girded
about their loins, [b]rending their garments in token, or as a [c]covenant,
that they would not forsake the
Lord their God; or, in other words,
if they should transgress the commandments of God, or fall into
transgression, and be [d]ashamed to
take upon them the name of Christ,
the Lord should rend them even as
they had rent their garments.

10*c* Alma 45:15 (15–16); 62:40.
11*a* Alma 43:16.
12*a* 2 Sam. 10:12; Neh. 4:14 (10–14); Alma 44:5; 48:10 (10, 24).
13*a* Alma 44:9; 49:6 (6, 24).
b Alma 51:20. TG Citizenship.
c TG Reverence.
d Alma 48:10.
15*a* TG Faithful; Loyalty.
b TG Jesus Christ, Taking the Name of.
c Acts 11:26.
16*a* Alma 51:13.
17*a* 3 Ne. 3:24; Morm. 3:5.
b Alma 22:30; 50:34.
c Alma 22:31; 63:4.
d 2 Ne. 1:7; Mosiah 29:32.
18*a* TG Protection, Divine.
b TG Transgress.
19*a* TG Ensign.
20*a* Alma 48:13.
b TG Citizenship.
21*a* 2 Sam. 20:14 (11–14).
b TG Rend.
c TG Commitment.
d Jer. 17:13; Rom. 1:16; 2 Tim. 1:8; 1 Ne. 8:25; Morm. 8:38.

22 Now this was the covenant which they made, and they [a]cast their garments at the feet of Moroni, saying: We [b]covenant with our God, that we shall be destroyed, even as our brethren in the land northward, if we shall fall into transgression; yea, he may cast us at the feet of our enemies, even as we have cast our garments at thy feet to be trodden under foot, if we shall fall into transgression.

23 Moroni said unto them: Behold, we are a [a]remnant of the seed of Jacob; yea, we are a remnant of the seed of [b]Joseph, whose [c]coat was rent by his brethren into many pieces; yea, and now behold, let us remember to keep the commandments of God, or our garments shall be rent by our brethren, and we be cast into prison, or be sold, or be slain.

24 Yea, let us preserve our liberty as a [a]remnant of Joseph; yea, let us remember the words of Jacob, before his death, for behold, he saw that a [b]part of the [c]remnant of the coat of Joseph was [d]preserved and had not decayed. And he said—Even as this remnant of garment of my son hath been preserved, so shall a [e]remnant of the seed of my son be preserved by the hand of God, and be taken unto himself, while the remainder of the seed of Joseph shall perish, even as the remnant of his garment.

25 Now behold, this giveth my soul sorrow; nevertheless, my soul hath joy in my son, because of that part of his seed which shall be taken unto God.

26 Now behold, this was the language of Jacob.

27 And now who knoweth but what the remnant of the seed of Joseph, which shall perish as his garment, are those who have dissented from us? Yea, and even it shall be ourselves if we do not stand fast in the faith of Christ.

28 And now it came to pass that when Moroni had said these words he went forth, and also sent forth in all the parts of the land where there were dissensions, and gathered together all the people who were desirous to maintain their liberty, to stand against Amalickiah and those who had dissented, who were called Amalickiahites.

29 And it came to pass that when Amalickiah saw that the people of Moroni were more numerous than the Amalickiahites—and he also saw that his people were [a]doubtful concerning the justice of the cause in which they had undertaken—therefore, fearing that he should not gain the point, he took those of his people who would and departed into the [b]land of Nephi.

30 Now Moroni thought it was not expedient that the Lamanites should have any more [a]strength; therefore he thought to cut off the people of Amalickiah, or to take them and bring them back, and put Amalickiah to death; yea, for he knew that he would stir up the Lamanites to anger against them, and cause them to come to battle against them; and this he knew that Amalickiah would do that he might obtain his purposes.

31 Therefore Moroni thought it was expedient that he should take his armies, who had gathered themselves together, and armed themselves, and entered into a covenant to keep the peace—and it came to pass that he took his army and marched out with his tents into the wilderness, to cut off the course of Amalickiah in the wilderness.

32 And it came to pass that he did

22*a* Acts 7:58; 22:20.
b TG Commitment.
23*a* TG Israel, Remnant of.
b TG Israel, Joseph, People of.
c Gen. 37:3 (3, 31–36).
24*a* 2 Ne. 10:1; Jacob 5:45 (43–45).
b Gen. 44:28.
c 3 Ne. 5:23 (23–24); 10:17.
d 2 Ne. 3:5 (5–24); 25:21; Ether 13:7.
e Ether 13:6.
29*a* TG Doubt.
b Alma 47:20.
30*a* Alma 43:51.

according to his desires, and marched forth into the wilderness, and headed the armies of Amalickiah.

33 And it came to pass that Amalickiah [a]fled with a small number of his men, and the remainder were delivered up into the hands of Moroni and were taken back into the land of Zarahemla.

34 Now, Moroni being a man who was [a]appointed by the chief judges and the voice of the people, therefore he had power according to his will with the armies of the Nephites, to establish and to exercise authority over them.

35 And it came to pass that whomsoever of the Amalickiahites that would not enter into a covenant to support the [a]cause of freedom, that they might maintain a free [b]government, he caused to be put to death; and there were but few who denied the covenant of freedom.

36 And it came to pass also, that he caused the [a]title of liberty to be hoisted upon every tower which was in all the land, which was possessed by the Nephites; and thus Moroni planted the standard of liberty among the Nephites.

37 And they began to have peace again in the land; and thus they did maintain peace in the land until nearly the end of the nineteenth year of the reign of the judges.

38 And Helaman and the [a]high priests did also maintain order in the church; yea, even for the space of four years did they have much peace and rejoicing in the church.

39 And it came to pass that there were many who died, firmly [a]believing that their souls were redeemed by the Lord Jesus Christ; thus they went out of the world rejoicing.

40 And there were some who died with fevers, which at some seasons of the year were very frequent in the land—but not so much so with fevers, because of the excellent qualities of the many [a]plants and roots which God had prepared to remove the cause of [b]diseases, to which men were subject by the nature of the climate—

41 But there were many who died with [a]old age; and those who died in the faith of Christ are [b]happy in him, as we must needs suppose.

CHAPTER 47

Amalickiah uses treachery, murder, and intrigue to become king of the Lamanites—The Nephite dissenters are more wicked and ferocious than the Lamanites. About 72 B.C.

Now we will return in our record to Amalickiah and those who had [a]fled with him into the wilderness; for, behold, he had taken those who went with him, and went up in the [b]land of Nephi among the Lamanites, and did [c]stir up the Lamanites to anger against the people of Nephi, insomuch that the king of the Lamanites sent a proclamation throughout all his land, among all his people, that they should gather themselves together again to go to battle against the Nephites.

2 And it came to pass that when the proclamation had gone forth among them they were exceedingly afraid; yea, they [a]feared to displease the king, and they also feared to go to battle against the Nephites lest they should lose their lives. And it came to pass that they would not, or the more part of them would not, obey the commandments of the king.

3 And now it came to pass that

33 *a* Alma 47:1.
34 *a* Alma 43:16.
35 *a* Alma 43:30.
b TG Governments.
36 *a* Alma 62:4.
38 *a* Alma 43:2; 46:6; 49:30.
39 *a* Moro. 7:41 (3, 41).
40 *a* D&C 59:17 (17–20); 89:10.
b Ezek. 47:12.
TG Health; Sickness.
41 *a* TG Old Age.
b Rev. 14:13.
47 1 *a* Alma 46:33.
b 2 Ne. 5:8; Omni 1:12; Alma 49:10.
c Alma 27:12; 35:10; 43:8; Hel. 1:17.
TG Provoking.
2 *a* Alma 43:54 (49–54).

the king was wroth because of
their disobedience; therefore he
gave Amalickiah the command of
that part of his army which was
obedient unto his commands, and
commanded him that he should go
forth and [a]compel them to arms.
4 Now behold, this was the desire
of Amalickiah; for he being a very
[a]subtle man to do evil therefore he
laid the plan in his heart to [b]de-
throne the king of the Lamanites.
5 And now he had got the command of those parts of the Lamanites who were in favor of the king;
and he sought to gain favor of those
who were not obedient; therefore
he went forward to the place which
was called [a]Onidah, for thither had
all the Lamanites fled; for they
discovered the army coming, and,
supposing that they were coming to
destroy them, therefore they fled to
Onidah, to the place of arms.
6 And they had appointed a man
to be a king and a leader over them,
being fixed in their minds with
a determined resolution that they
would [a]not be subjected to go
against the Nephites.
7 And it came to pass that they
had gathered themselves together
upon the top of the mount which
was called Antipas, in preparation
to battle.
8 Now it was not Amalickiah's intention to give them battle according to the commandments of the
king; but behold, it was his intention to gain favor with the armies of
the Lamanites, that he might place
himself at their head and dethrone
the king and take possession of the
kingdom.
9 And behold, it came to pass that
he caused his army to pitch their
tents in the valley which was near
the mount Antipas.
10 And it came to pass that when it
was night he sent a secret embassy
into the mount Antipas, desiring
that the leader of those who were
upon the mount, whose name was
Lehonti, that he should come down
to the foot of the mount, for he desired to speak with him.
11 And it came to pass that when
Lehonti received the message he
durst not go down to the foot of
the mount. And it came to pass that
Amalickiah sent again the second
time, desiring him to come down.
And it came to pass that Lehonti
would not; and he sent again the
third time.
12 And it came to pass that when
Amalickiah found that he could
not get Lehonti to come down off
from the mount, he went up into
the mount, nearly to Lehonti's camp;
and he sent again the fourth time
his message unto Lehonti, desiring
that he would come down, and that
he would bring his guards with him.
13 And it came to pass that when
Lehonti had come down with his
guards to Amalickiah, that Amalickiah desired him to come down
with his army in the night-time, and
surround those men in their camps
over whom the king had given him
command, and that he would deliver
them up into Lehonti's hands, if he
would make him (Amalickiah) a
second [a]leader over the whole army.
14 And it came to pass that Lehonti
came down with his men and surrounded the men of Amalickiah, so
that before they awoke at the dawn
of day they were surrounded by the
armies of Lehonti.
15 And it came to pass that when
they saw that they were surrounded,
they pled with Amalickiah that he
would suffer them to fall in with
their brethren, that they might not
be destroyed. Now this was the very
thing which Amalickiah desired.
16 And it came to pass that he
delivered his men, [a]contrary to
the commands of the king. Now
this was the thing that Amalickiah

3*a* Alma 47:16 (16, 21).
4*a* 2 Sam. 13:3 (3–14).
b Alma 47:35 (8, 35).
5*a* Alma 32:4.
6*a* Alma 44:19 (8, 19).
13*a* Alma 49:10.
16*a* Alma 47:3.

desired, that he might accomplish
his designs in dethroning the king.
17 Now it was the custom among
the Lamanites, if their chief leader
was killed, to appoint the second
leader to be their chief leader.
18 And it came to pass that Amalickiah caused that one of his servants should administer [a]poison by
degrees to Lehonti, that he died.
19 Now, when Lehonti was dead,
the Lamanites appointed Amalickiah to be their leader and their chief
commander.
20 And it came to pass that Amalickiah marched with his armies (for
he had gained his desires) to the
[a]land of Nephi, to the city of Nephi,
which was the chief city.
21 And the king came out to meet
him with his guards, for he supposed
that Amalickiah had [a]fulfilled his
commands, and that Amalickiah
had gathered together so great an
army to go against the Nephites
to battle.
22 But behold, as the king came
out to meet him Amalickiah caused
that his servants should go forth to
meet the king. And they went and
[a]bowed themselves before the king,
as if to reverence him because of
his greatness.
23 And it came to pass that the
king put forth his hand to raise
them, as was the custom with the Lamanites, as a token of peace, which
custom they had taken from the
Nephites.
24 And it came to pass that when
he had raised the first from the
ground, behold he stabbed the king
to the heart; and he fell to the earth.
25 Now the servants of the king
fled; and the servants of Amalickiah raised a cry, saying:
26 Behold, the servants of the king
have stabbed him to the heart, and
he has fallen and they have fled;
behold, come and see.
27 And it came to pass that
Amalickiah commanded that his
armies should march forth and see
what had happened to the king; and
when they had come to the spot, and
found the king lying in his gore,
Amalickiah pretended to be wroth,
and said: Whosoever loved the king,
let him go forth, and pursue his servants that they may be slain.
28 And it came to pass that all
they who loved the king, when
they heard these words, came forth
and pursued after the servants of
the king.
29 Now when the [a]servants of the
king saw an army pursuing after
them, they were frightened again,
and fled into the wilderness, and
came over into the land of Zarahemla and joined the [b]people of
Ammon.
30 And the army which pursued
after them returned, having pursued after them in vain; and thus
Amalickiah, by his [a]fraud, gained
the hearts of the people.
31 And it came to pass on the morrow he entered the city Nephi with
his armies, and took possession of
the city.
32 And now it came to pass that the
queen, when she had heard that
the king was slain—for Amalickiah
had sent an embassy to the queen
informing her that the king had
been slain by his servants, that he
had pursued them with his army,
but it was in vain, and they had
made their escape—
33 Therefore, when the queen had
received this message she sent unto
Amalickiah, desiring him that he
would spare the people of the city;
and she also desired him that he
should come in unto her; and she
also desired him that he should
bring [a]witnesses with him to testify
concerning the death of the king.
34 And it came to pass that Amalickiah took the same servant that
slew the king, and all them who

18*a* Alma 54:7.
20*a* Alma 46:29.
21*a* Alma 47:3.
22*a* Mosiah 7:12.
29*a* Alma 55:5.
b Alma 43:11; 62:17.
30*a* Alma 55:1.
TG Fraud.
33*a* TG Witness.

were with him, and went in unto the queen, unto the place where she sat; and they all [a]testified unto her that the king was slain by his own servants; and they said also: They have fled; does not this testify against them? And thus they satisfied the queen concerning the death of the king.

35 And it came to pass that Amalickiah sought the [a]favor of the queen, and took her unto him to wife; and thus by his [b]fraud, and by the assistance of his cunning servants, he [c]obtained the kingdom; yea, he was acknowledged king throughout all the land, among all the people of the Lamanites, who were [d]composed of the Lamanites and the Lemuelites and the Ishmaelites, and all the dissenters of the Nephites, from the reign of Nephi down to the present time.

36 Now these [a]dissenters, having the same instruction and the same information of the Nephites, yea, having been instructed in the same [b]knowledge of the Lord, nevertheless, it is strange to relate, not long after their dissensions they became more hardened and [c]impenitent, and more wild, wicked and ferocious than the Lamanites—drinking in with the [d]traditions of the Lamanites; giving way to [e]indolence, and all manner of lasciviousness; yea, entirely forgetting the Lord their God.

CHAPTER 48

Amalickiah incites the Lamanites against the Nephites—Moroni prepares his people to defend the cause of the Christians—He rejoices in liberty and freedom and is a mighty man of God. About 72 B.C.

AND now it came to pass that, as soon as [a]Amalickiah had obtained the kingdom he began to [b]inspire the hearts of the Lamanites against the people of Nephi; yea, he did appoint men to speak unto the Lamanites from their [c]towers, against the Nephites.

2 And thus he did inspire their hearts against the Nephites, insomuch that in the latter end of the [a]nineteenth year of the reign of the judges, he having accomplished his designs thus far, yea, having been made king over the Lamanites, he [b]sought also to [c]reign over all the land, yea, and all the people who were in the land, the Nephites as well as the Lamanites.

3 Therefore he had accomplished his design, for he had hardened the hearts of the Lamanites and blinded their minds, and stirred them up to anger, insomuch that he had gathered together a numerous host to go to battle against the Nephites.

4 For he was determined, because of the greatness of the number of his people, to [a]overpower the Nephites and to bring them into bondage.

5 And thus he did appoint [a]chief captains of the [b]Zoramites, they being the most acquainted with the strength of the Nephites, and their places of resort, and the weakest parts of their cities; therefore he appointed them to be chief captains over his armies.

6 And it came to pass that they took their camp, and moved forth toward the land of Zarahemla in the wilderness.

7 Now it came to pass that while Amalickiah had thus been obtaining power by fraud and deceit, Moroni, on the other hand, had been [a]preparing

---

34*a* TG False; Lying.
35*a* Prov. 19:6 (6–7).
b TG Conspiracy; Tyranny.
c Alma 47:4.
d Jacob 1:13 (13–14).
36*a* TG Apostasy of Individuals.
b Heb. 10:26 (26–27); Alma 24:30.
c Jer. 8:12.
d TG Peer Influence.
e 3 Ne. 4:5.
48 1*a* Alma 52:3 (1–3); 54:5.
b Alma 62:35.
c Mosiah 2:8.
2*a* Alma 48:21.
b D&C 121:39.
c Alma 54:24.
4*a* TG Tyranny.
5*a* Alma 43:6; 49:5 (5, 23).
b Alma 52:20 (20, 33).
7*a* Alma 49:8.

the minds of the people to be faithful unto the Lord their God.

8 Yea, he had been strengthening the armies of the Nephites, and erecting small [a]forts, or places of resort; throwing up banks of earth round about to enclose his armies, and also building [b]walls of stone to encircle them about, round about their cities and the borders of their lands; yea, all round about the land.

9 And in their weakest fortifications he did place the greater number of men; and thus he did fortify and strengthen the land which was possessed by the Nephites.

10 And thus he was preparing to [a]support their liberty, their lands, their wives, and their children, and their peace, and that they might live unto the Lord their God, and that they might maintain that which was called by their enemies the cause of [b]Christians.

11 And Moroni was a [a]strong and a mighty man; he was a man of a perfect [b]understanding; yea, a man that did not delight in bloodshed; a man whose soul did joy in the liberty and the freedom of his country, and his brethren from bondage and slavery;

12 Yea, a man whose heart did swell with thanksgiving to his God, for the many privileges and blessings which he bestowed upon his people; a man who did labor exceedingly for the [a]welfare and safety of his people.

13 Yea, and he was a man who was firm in the faith of Christ, and he had [a]sworn with an oath to defend his people, his rights, and his country, and his religion, even to the loss of his blood.

14 Now the Nephites were taught to defend themselves against their enemies, even to the shedding of blood if it were necessary; yea, and they were also taught [a]never to give an offense, yea, and never to raise the sword except it were against an enemy, except it were to preserve their lives.

15 And this was their [a]faith, that by so doing God would [b]prosper them in the land, or in other words, if they were faithful in keeping the commandments of God that he would prosper them in the land; yea, warn them to flee, or to prepare for war, according to their danger;

16 And also, that God would make it known unto them [a]whither they should go to defend themselves against their enemies, and by so doing, the Lord would deliver them; and this was the faith of Moroni, and his heart did glory in it; [b]not in the shedding of blood but in doing good, in preserving his people, yea, in keeping the commandments of God, yea, and resisting iniquity.

17 Yea, verily, verily I say unto you, if all men had been, and were, and ever would be, like unto [a]Moroni, behold, the very powers of hell would have been shaken forever; yea, the [b]devil would never have power over the hearts of the children of men.

18 Behold, he was a man like unto [a]Ammon, the son of Mosiah, yea, and even the other sons of Mosiah, yea, and also Alma and his sons, for they were all men of God.

19 Now behold, Helaman and his brethren were no less [a]serviceable unto the people than was Moroni; for they did preach the word of God, and they did baptize unto

8a Alma 49:13 (2–13, 18–24).
b Deut. 3:5.
10a Alma 44:5; 46:12.
b Alma 46:13.
11a TG Strength.
b Alma 18:22. TG Understanding.
12a TG Welfare.
13a Alma 46:20 (20–22). TG Dependability.
14a Alma 43:46 (46–47); 3 Ne. 3:21 (20–21); Morm. 3:10 (10–11); D&C 98:16.
15a TG Steadfastness.
b Alma 45:8.
16a Alma 16:6 (5–8); 43:23 (23–24); 3 Ne. 3:20 (18–21). TG Guidance, Divine.
b Alma 55:19.
17a Alma 53:2.
b 1 Ne. 22:26; 3 Ne. 6:15; D&C 35:24.
18a Alma 28:8.
19a Alma 45:22.

repentance all men whosoever would hearken unto their words.

20 And thus they went forth, and the people did [a]humble themselves because of their [b]words, insomuch that they were highly [c]favored of the Lord, and thus they were free from wars and contentions among themselves, yea, even for the space of four years.

21 But, as I have said, in the [a]latter end of the nineteenth year, yea, notwithstanding their peace amongst themselves, they were compelled reluctantly to contend with their brethren, the Lamanites.

22 Yea, and in fine, their wars never did cease for the space of many years with the Lamanites, notwithstanding their much reluctance.

23 Now, they were [a]sorry to take up arms against the Lamanites, because they did not delight in the shedding of blood; yea, and this was not all—they were [b]sorry to be the means of sending so many of their brethren out of this world into an eternal world, [c]unprepared to meet their God.

24 Nevertheless, they could not suffer to lay down their lives, that their [a]wives and their children should be [b]massacred by the barbarous [c]cruelty of those who were once their brethren, yea, and had [d]dissented from their church, and had left them and had gone to destroy them by joining the Lamanites.

25 Yea, they could not bear that their brethren should rejoice over the blood of the Nephites, so long as there were any who should keep the commandments of God, for the promise of the Lord was, if they should keep his commandments they should [a]prosper in the land.

CHAPTER 49

The invading Lamanites are unable to take the fortified cities of Ammonihah and Noah—Amalickiah curses God and swears to drink the blood of Moroni—Helaman and his brethren continue to strengthen the Church. About 72 B.C.

AND now it came to pass in the eleventh month of the nineteenth year, on the tenth day of the month, the armies of the Lamanites were seen approaching towards the land of [a]Ammonihah.

2 And behold, the city had been rebuilt, and Moroni had stationed an army by the borders of the city, and they had [a]cast up dirt round about to shield them from the arrows and the [b]stones of the Lamanites; for behold, they fought with stones and with arrows.

3 Behold, I said that the city of [a]Ammonihah had been rebuilt. I say unto you, yea, that it was in part rebuilt; and because the Lamanites had destroyed it once because of the iniquity of the people, they supposed that it would again become an easy prey for them.

4 But behold, how great was their disappointment; for behold, the Nephites had dug up a [a]ridge of earth round about them, which was so high that the Lamanites could not cast their stones and their arrows at them that they might take effect, neither could they come upon them save it was by their place of [b]entrance.

5 Now at this time the chief [a]captains of the Lamanites were astonished exceedingly, because of the wisdom of the Nephites in preparing their places of security.

6 Now the leaders of the Lamanites

20*a* TG Humility.
b 1 Ne. 15:20; Hel. 6:5.
c 1 Ne. 17:35.
21*a* Alma 48:2.
23*a* Alma 28:11 (11–12); D&C 42:45.
b 3 Ne. 12:44.
c Amos 4:12; Alma 20:17.
24*a* Alma 46:12.
b TG Martyrdom.
c TG Cruelty.
d TG Apostasy of Individuals.
25*a* Alma 45:8.

49 1*a* Alma 8:6.
2*a* Alma 48:8.
b 1 Ne. 16:15; Alma 43:20.
3*a* Alma 16:2 (2–3, 9, 11).
4*a* Alma 48:8; 50:1.
b Alma 49:20.
5*a* Alma 52:19.

had supposed, because of the greatness of their numbers, yea, they supposed that they should be privileged to come upon them as they had hitherto done; yea, and they had also prepared themselves with shields, and with [a]breastplates; and they had also prepared themselves with garments of skins, yea, very thick garments to cover their nakedness.

7 And being thus prepared they supposed that they should easily overpower and [a]subject their brethren to the yoke of bondage, or slay and massacre them according to their pleasure.

8 But behold, to their uttermost astonishment, they were [a]prepared for them, in a manner which never had been known among the children of Lehi. Now they were prepared for the Lamanites, to battle after the manner of the instructions of Moroni.

9 And it came to pass that the Lamanites, or the Amalickiahites, were exceedingly astonished at their manner of preparation for war.

10 Now, if king Amalickiah had come down out of the [a]land of Nephi, at the head of his army, perhaps he would have caused the Lamanites to have attacked the Nephites at the city of Ammonihah; for behold, he did care not for the blood of his people.

11 But behold, Amalickiah did not come down himself to battle. And behold, his chief captains durst not attack the Nephites at the city of Ammonihah, for Moroni had altered the management of affairs among the Nephites, insomuch that the Lamanites were disappointed in their places of retreat and they could not come upon them.

12 Therefore they retreated into the wilderness, and took their camp and marched towards the land of [a]Noah, supposing that to be the next best place for them to come against the Nephites.

13 For they knew not that Moroni had fortified, or had built [a]forts of security, for every city in all the land round about; therefore, they marched forward to the land of Noah with a firm determination; yea, their chief captains came forward and took an [b]oath that they would destroy the people of that city.

14 But behold, to their astonishment, the city of Noah, which had hitherto been a weak place, had now, by the means of Moroni, become strong, yea, even to exceed the strength of the city Ammonihah.

15 And now, behold, this was wisdom in Moroni; for he had supposed that they would be frightened at the city Ammonihah; and as the city of Noah had hitherto been the weakest part of the land, therefore they would march thither to battle; and thus it was according to his desires.

16 And behold, Moroni had appointed Lehi to be chief captain over the men of that city; and it was that [a]same Lehi who fought with the Lamanites in the valley on the east of the river Sidon.

17 And now behold it came to pass, that when the Lamanites had found that Lehi commanded the city they were again disappointed, for they feared Lehi exceedingly; nevertheless their chief captains had [a]sworn with an oath to attack the city; therefore, they brought up their armies.

18 Now behold, the Lamanites could not get into their forts of security by any other way save by the entrance, because of the highness of the bank which had been thrown up, and the depth of the

6*a* Alma 46:13; Hel. 1:14.
7*a* Alma 43:29.
8*a* Alma 48:7 (7–10).
10*a* 2 Ne. 5:8; Omni 1:12; Alma 47:1 (1, 13–24).
12*a* Alma 16:3.
13*a* Alma 48:8; 50:10 (1–6, 10).
b Alma 49:17.
16*a* Alma 43:35.
17*a* Alma 49:13.

ditch which had been dug round
about, save it were by the entrance.
19 And thus were the Nephites prepared to destroy all such as should
attempt to climb up to enter the fort
by any other way, by casting over
stones and arrows at them.
20 Thus they were prepared, yea,
a body of their strongest men, with
their swords and their slings, to
smite down all who should attempt
to come into their place of security by the place of [a]entrance; and
thus were they prepared to defend
themselves against the Lamanites.
21 And it came to pass that the
captains of the Lamanites brought
up their armies before the place
of entrance, and began to contend
with the Nephites, to get into their
place of security; but behold, they
were driven back from time to time,
insomuch that they were slain with
an immense slaughter.
22 Now when they found that
they could not obtain power over
the Nephites by the pass, they began to dig down their banks of
earth that they might obtain a pass
to their armies, that they might
have an equal chance to fight; but
behold, in these attempts they were
swept off by the stones and arrows
which were thrown at them; and
instead of filling up their ditches
by pulling down the banks of earth,
they were filled up in a measure
with their dead and wounded
bodies.
23 Thus the Nephites had all power
over their enemies; and thus the Lamanites did attempt to destroy the
Nephites until their [a]chief captains
were all slain; yea, and more than
a thousand of the Lamanites were
slain; while, on the other hand,
there was not a single soul of the
Nephites which was slain.
24 There were about fifty who
were wounded, who had been exposed to the arrows of the Lamanites
through the pass, but they were
shielded by their [a]shields, and their
breastplates, and their head-plates,
insomuch that their wounds were
upon their legs, many of which were
very severe.
25 And it came to pass, that when
the Lamanites saw that their chief
captains were all slain they fled
into the wilderness. And it came to
pass that they returned to the land
of Nephi, to inform their king,
Amalickiah, who was a [a]Nephite by
birth, concerning their great [b]loss.
26 And it came to pass that he was
exceedingly angry with his people,
because he had not obtained his
desire over the Nephites; he had
not subjected them to the yoke of
bondage.
27 Yea, he was exceedingly wroth,
and he did [a]curse God, and also Moroni, swearing with an [b]oath that
he would drink his blood; and this
because Moroni had kept the commandments of God in preparing
for the safety of his people.
28 And it came to pass, that on the
other hand, the people of Nephi did
[a]thank the Lord their God, because
of his matchless power in delivering them from the hands of their
enemies.
29 And thus ended the nineteenth
year of the reign of the judges over
the people of Nephi.
30 Yea, and there was continual
peace among them, and exceedingly
great prosperity in the church because of their heed and diligence
which they gave unto the word of
God, which was declared unto them
by Helaman, and Shiblon, and Corianton, and Ammon and his brethren, yea, and by all those who had
been ordained by the [a]holy order
of God, being baptized unto repentance, and sent forth to preach
among the people.

20*a* Alma 49:4 (4, 18, 21, 24).
23*a* Alma 48:5.
24*a* Alma 43:19.
25*a* Alma 46:3.
b Alma 51:11.
27*a* TG Blaspheme.
b Acts 23:12; Alma 51:9.
28*a* TG Thanksgiving.
30*a* Alma 30:20 (20–23, 31); 43:2; 46:38.

CHAPTER 50

Moroni fortifies the lands of the Nephites—They build many new cities—Wars and destructions befell the Nephites in the days of their wickedness and abominations—Morianton and his dissenters are defeated by Teancum—Nephihah dies, and his son Pahoran fills the judgment seat. About 72–67 B.C.

AND now it came to pass that Moroni did not stop making preparations for war, or to defend his people against the Lamanites; for he caused that his armies should commence in the commencement of the twentieth year of the reign of the judges, that they should commence in digging up [a]heaps of earth round about all the cities, throughout all the land which was possessed by the Nephites.

2 And upon the top of these ridges of earth he caused that there should be [a]timbers, yea, works of timbers built up to the height of a man, round about the cities.

3 And he caused that upon those works of timbers there should be a frame of pickets built upon the timbers round about; and they were strong and high.

4 And he caused towers to be erected that overlooked those works of pickets, and he caused places of security to be built upon those [a]towers, that the stones and the arrows of the Lamanites could not hurt them.

5 And they were prepared that they could cast stones from the top thereof, according to their pleasure and their strength, and slay him who should attempt to approach near the walls of the city.

6 Thus Moroni did prepare strongholds against the coming of their enemies, round about every city in all the land.

7 And it came to pass that Moroni caused that his armies should go forth into the east wilderness; yea, and they went forth and drove all the Lamanites who were in the east wilderness into their own lands, which were [a]south of the land of Zarahemla.

8 And the land of [a]Nephi did run in a straight course from the east sea to the west.

9 And it came to pass that when Moroni had driven all the Lamanites out of the east wilderness, which was north of the lands of their own possessions, he caused that the inhabitants who were in the land of Zarahemla and in the land round about should go forth into the east wilderness, even to the borders by the seashore, and possess the land.

10 And he also placed armies on the south, in the borders of their possessions, and caused them to erect [a]fortifications that they might secure their armies and their people from the hands of their enemies.

11 And thus he cut off all the strongholds of the Lamanites in the east wilderness, yea, and also on the west, fortifying the line between the Nephites and the Lamanites, between the land of Zarahemla and the land of Nephi, from the west sea, running by the head of the [a]river Sidon—the Nephites possessing all the land [b]northward, yea, even all the land which was northward of the land Bountiful, according to their pleasure.

12 Thus Moroni, with his armies, which did increase daily because of the assurance of protection which his works did bring forth unto them, did seek to cut off the strength and the power of the Lamanites from off the lands of their possessions, that they should have no power upon the lands of their possession.

13 And it came to pass that the Nephites began the foundation of a

50 1*a* Alma 48:8; 49:4; 52:6.
2*a* Alma 53:4.
4*a* 2 Chr. 14:7 (7–8).
7*a* Alma 22:32.
8*a* 2 Ne. 5:8; Omni 1:12 (12, 27); Mosiah 7:6 (6–7); 9:1 (1, 3–4, 14).
10*a* Alma 49:13 (13, 18–24); 53:3 (3–7).
11*a* Alma 2:15; 22:29.
b Morm. 2:3.

city, and they called the name of the city [a]Moroni; and it was by the east sea; and it was on the south by the line of the possessions of the Lamanites.
14 And they also began a foundation for a city between the city of Moroni and the city of Aaron, joining the borders of Aaron and Moroni; and they called the name of the city, or the land, [a]Nephihah.
15 And they also began in that same year to build many cities on the north, one in a particular manner which they called [a]Lehi, which was in the north by the borders of the seashore.
16 And thus ended the twentieth year.
17 And in these prosperous circumstances were the people of Nephi in the commencement of the twenty and first year of the reign of the judges over the people of Nephi.
18 And they did prosper [a]exceedingly, and they became exceedingly rich; yea, and they did multiply and wax strong in the land.
19 And thus we see how merciful and just are all the dealings of the Lord, to the fulfilling of all his words unto the children of men; yea, we can behold that his words are verified, even at this time, which he spake unto Lehi, saying:
20 Blessed art thou and thy children; and they shall be blessed, inasmuch as they shall keep my [a]commandments they shall prosper in the land. But remember, inasmuch as they will not keep my commandments they shall be [b]cut off from the presence of the Lord.
21 And we see that these promises have been verified to the people of Nephi; for it has been their quarrelings and their contentions, yea, their murderings, and their plunderings, their idolatry, their whoredoms, and their abominations, which were among themselves, which [a]brought upon them their wars and their destructions.
22 And those who were faithful in keeping the commandments of the Lord were delivered at all times, whilst thousands of their wicked brethren have been consigned to bondage, or to perish by the sword, or to dwindle in unbelief, and mingle with the Lamanites.
23 But behold there never was a [a]happier time among the people of Nephi, since the days of Nephi, than in the days of Moroni, yea, even at this time, in the twenty and first year of the reign of the judges.
24 And it came to pass that the twenty and second year of the reign of the judges also ended in peace; yea, and also the twenty and third year.
25 And it came to pass that in the commencement of the twenty and fourth year of the reign of the judges, there would also have been peace among the people of Nephi had it not been for a [a]contention which took place among them concerning the land of [b]Lehi, and the land of [c]Morianton, which joined upon the borders of Lehi; both of which were on the borders by the seashore.
26 For behold, the people who possessed the land of Morianton did claim a part of the land of Lehi; therefore there began to be a warm [a]contention between them, insomuch that the people of Morianton took up arms against their brethren, and they were determined by the sword to slay them.
27 But behold, the people who possessed the land of Lehi fled to the camp of Moroni, and appealed unto

13*a* Alma 51:22 (22–24); 62:32 (32, 34); 3 Ne. 8:9.
14*a* Alma 51:24 (24–26); 59:5; 62:18 (14, 18, 26).
15*a* Alma 51:26 (24–26); 62:30.
18*a* Alma 1:29.
20*a* Lev. 25:18 (18–19); Ps. 1:3 (2–3); Alma 37:13; 62:48.
b Ps. 37:2; D&C 1:14.
21*a* Alma 41:10.
23*a* 2 Ne. 5:27; Mosiah 2:41; 4 Ne. 1:16 (15–18).
25*a* TG Contention.
b Hel. 6:10.
c Alma 51:26.
26*a* 3 Ne. 11:29.

him for assistance; for behold they were not in the wrong.

28 And it came to pass that when the people of Morianton, who were led by a man whose name was Morianton, found that the people of Lehi had fled to the camp of Moroni, they were exceedingly fearful lest the army of Moroni should come upon them and destroy them.

29 Therefore, Morianton put it into their hearts that they should flee to the land which was northward, which was covered with [a]large bodies of water, and take possession of the land which was [b]northward.

30 And behold, they would have carried this plan into effect, (which would have been a cause to have been lamented) but behold, Morianton being a man of much passion, therefore he was angry with one of his maid servants, and he fell upon her and beat her much.

31 And it came to pass that she fled, and came over to the camp of Moroni, and told Moroni all things concerning the matter, and also concerning their intentions to flee into the land northward.

32 Now behold, the people who were in the land Bountiful, or rather Moroni, feared that they would hearken to the words of Morianton and unite with his people, and thus he would obtain possession of those parts of the land, which would lay a foundation for serious consequences among the people of Nephi, yea, which [a]consequences would lead to the overthrow of their [b]liberty.

33 Therefore Moroni sent an army, with their camp, to head the people of Morianton, to stop their flight into the land northward.

34 And it came to pass that they did not [a]head them until they had come to the borders of the land [b]Desolation; and there they did head them, by the narrow pass which led by the sea into the land northward, yea, by the sea, on the west and on the east.

35 And it came to pass that the army which was sent by Moroni, which was led by a man whose name was Teancum, did meet the people of Morianton; and so stubborn were the people of Morianton, (being inspired by his wickedness and his [a]flattering words) that a battle commenced between them, in the which Teancum did [b]slay Morianton and defeat his army, and took them prisoners, and returned to the camp of Moroni. And thus ended the twenty and fourth year of the reign of the judges over the people of Nephi.

36 And thus were the people of Morianton brought back. And upon their [a]covenanting to keep the peace they were restored to the land of Morianton, and a union took place between them and the people of Lehi; and they were also restored to their lands.

37 And it came to pass that in the same year that the people of Nephi had peace restored unto them, that Nephihah, the [a]second chief judge, died, having filled the judgment-seat with [b]perfect uprightness before God.

38 Nevertheless, he had refused Alma to take possession of those [a]records and those things which were esteemed by Alma and his fathers to be most sacred; therefore Alma had conferred [b]them upon his son, Helaman.

39 Behold, it came to pass that the son of Nephihah was appointed to fill the judgment-seat, in the stead of his father; yea, he was appointed

29*a* Mosiah 8:8; Hel. 3:4 (3–4).
b Alma 22:31 (29–31); 51:30.
32*a* TG Contention; Division.
b TG Liberty.
34*a* Hel. 1:28 (28–30).
b Alma 46:17; Morm. 3:5 (5, 7).
35*a* Mosiah 27:8; Hel. 1:7; 2:5.
b Alma 51:29.
36*a* 1 Ne. 4:37; Alma 44:15.
37*a* Alma 4:17 (16–18).
b TG Perfection.
38*a* Alma 37:1 (1–5); 45:2 (2–8).
b 3 Ne. 1:2.

chief judge and [a]governor over the
people, with an [b]oath and sacred ordinance to judge righteously, and to
keep the peace and the [c]freedom of
the people, and to grant unto them
their sacred privileges to worship
the Lord their God, yea, to support
and maintain the cause of God all
his days, and to bring the wicked
to justice according to their crime.
40 Now behold, his name was [a]Pa-
horan. And Pahoran did fill the seat
of his father, and did commence
his reign in the end of the twenty
and fourth year, over the people
of Nephi.

CHAPTER 51

The king-men seek to change the law and set up a king—Pahoran and the freemen are supported by the voice of the people—Moroni compels the king-men to defend their country or be put to death—Amalickiah and the Lamanites capture many fortified cities—Teancum repels the Lamanite invasion and slays Amalickiah in his tent. About 67–66 B.C.

AND now it came to pass in the
commencement of the twenty and
fifth year of the reign of the judges
over the people of Nephi, they having established peace between the
people of Lehi and the people of
Morianton concerning their lands,
and having commenced the twenty
and fifth year in [a]peace;
2 Nevertheless, they did not long
maintain an entire peace in the land,
for there began to be a contention
among the people concerning the
chief judge Pahoran; for behold,
there were a part of the people who
desired that a few particular points
of the [a]law should be altered.
3 But behold, Pahoran would not
alter nor suffer the law to be altered;
therefore, he did not hearken to
those who had sent in their voices
with their petitions concerning the
altering of the law.
4 Therefore, those who were desirous that the law should be altered were angry with him, and
desired that he should no longer be
chief judge over the land; therefore
there arose a warm [a]dispute concerning the matter, but not unto
bloodshed.
5 And it came to pass that those
who were desirous that Pahoran
should be dethroned from the
judgment-seat were called [a]king-
men, for they were desirous that the
law should be altered in a manner to
overthrow the free government and
to establish a [b]king over the land.
6 And those who were desirous
that Pahoran should remain chief
judge over the land took upon them
the name of [a]freemen; and thus was
the [b]division among them, for the
freemen had sworn or [c]covenanted
to maintain their rights and the
privileges of their religion by a free
government.
7 And it came to pass that this
matter of their contention was settled by the [a]voice of the people.
And it came to pass that the voice
of the people came in favor of the
freemen, and Pahoran retained
the judgment-seat, which caused
much rejoicing among the brethren of Pahoran and also many of
the people of liberty, who also put
the king-men to silence, that they
durst not oppose but were obliged
to maintain the cause of freedom.
8 Now those who were in favor
of kings were those of [a]high birth,
and they sought to be [b]kings; and
they were supported by those who
sought power and authority over
the people.

39*a* Alma 60:1.
b TG Oath; Ordinance.
c Alma 4:16 (16–17); Hel. 1:5 (3–5, 13).
40*a* Alma 59:3; 61:1; Hel. 1:2.
51 1*a* TG Peacemakers.
2*a* Alma 1:1.
4*a* TG Disputations.
5*a* Alma 60:16; 62:9. TG Kings, Earthly; Unrighteous Dominion.
b 3 Ne. 6:30.
6*a* Alma 61:3 (3–4); 62:6.
b 1 Kgs. 16:21 (21–22).
c Alma 48:13; 60:25 (25–27).
7*a* Alma 4:16; Hel. 1:5.
8*a* TG Haughtiness; Pride.
b TG Tyranny.

9 But behold, this was a critical time for such contentions to be among the people of Nephi; for behold, Amalickiah had again [a]stirred up the hearts of the people of the Lamanites against the people of the Nephites, and he was gathering together soldiers from all parts of his land, and arming them, and preparing for war with all diligence; for he had [b]sworn to drink the blood of Moroni.

10 But behold, we shall see that his promise which he made was [a]rash; nevertheless, he did prepare himself and his armies to come to battle against the Nephites.

11 Now his armies were not so great as they had hitherto been, because of the many thousands who had been [a]slain by the hand of the Nephites; but notwithstanding their great loss, Amalickiah had gathered together a wonderfully great army, insomuch that he feared not to come down to the land of Zarahemla.

12 Yea, even Amalickiah did himself come down, at the head of the Lamanites. And it was in the twenty and fifth year of the reign of the judges; and it was at the same time that they had begun to settle the affairs of their contentions concerning the chief judge, Pahoran.

13 And it came to pass that when the men who were called king-men had heard that the Lamanites were coming down to battle against them, they were glad in their hearts; and they refused to take up arms, for they were so wroth with the chief judge, and also with the [a]people of [b]liberty, that they would not take up arms to defend their country.

14 And it came to pass that when Moroni saw this, and also saw that the Lamanites were coming into the borders of the land, he was exceedingly wroth because of the [a]stubbornness of those people whom he had labored with so much diligence to preserve; yea, he was exceedingly wroth; his soul was filled with anger against them.

15 And it came to pass that he sent a petition, with the voice of the people, unto the governor of the land, desiring that he should read it, and give him (Moroni) power to compel those dissenters to defend their country or to put them to death.

16 For it was his first care to put an end to such contentions and dissensions among the people; for behold, this had been hitherto a cause of all their destruction. And it came to pass that it was granted according to the voice of the people.

17 And it came to pass that Moroni commanded that his army should go against those king-men, to pull down their pride and their nobility and level them with the earth, or they should take up arms and support the cause of liberty.

18 And it came to pass that the armies did march forth against them; and they did pull down their pride and their nobility, insomuch that as they did lift their weapons of war to fight against the men of Moroni they were hewn down and leveled to the earth.

19 And it came to pass that there were four thousand of those [a]dissenters who were hewn down by the sword; and those of their leaders who were not slain in battle were taken and [b]cast into prison, for there was no time for their trials at this period.

20 And the remainder of those dissenters, rather than be smitten down to the earth by the sword, yielded to the standard of liberty, and were compelled to hoist the [a]title of liberty upon their towers, and in their cities, and to take up arms in defence of their country.

9*a* Alma 63:14.
b Acts 23:12; Alma 49:27 (26–27).
10*a* TG Rashness.
11*a* Alma 49:25 (22–25).
13*a* Alma 46:16 (10–16).
b TG Liberty.
14*a* TG Stubbornness.
19*a* Alma 60:16.
b Alma 62:9.
20*a* Alma 46:13 (12–13).

21 And thus Moroni put an end to
those king-men, that there were not
any known by the appellation of
king-men; and thus he put an end
to the stubbornness and the pride
of those people who professed the
blood of nobility; but they were
brought down to humble themselves like unto their brethren, and
to fight [a]valiantly for their freedom
from bondage.
22 Behold, it came to pass that
while Moroni was thus breaking
down the wars and contentions
among his own people, and subjecting them to peace and civilization,
and making regulations to prepare
for war against the Lamanites, behold, the Lamanites had come into
the [a]land of Moroni, which was in
the borders by the seashore.
23 And it came to pass that the
Nephites were not sufficiently
strong in the city of Moroni; therefore Amalickiah did drive them,
slaying many. And it came to pass
that Amalickiah took possession of
the city, yea, possession of all their
fortifications.
24 And those who fled out of the
[a]city of Moroni came to the city of
Nephihah; and also the people of
the city of Lehi gathered themselves
together, and made preparations
and were ready to receive the Lamanites to battle.
25 But it came to pass that Amalickiah would not suffer the Lamanites
to go against the city of Nephihah
to battle, but kept them down by
the seashore, leaving men in every
city to maintain and defend it.
26 And thus he went on, taking
possession of [a]many cities, the city
of [b]Nephihah, and the city of [c]Lehi,
and the city of [d]Morianton, and
the city of Omner, and the city of
[e]Gid, and the city of [f]Mulek, all of
which were on the east borders by
the seashore.
27 And thus had the Lamanites
obtained, by the cunning of Amalickiah, so many cities, by their
numberless hosts, all of which were
strongly fortified after the manner
of the [a]fortifications of Moroni; all
of which afforded strongholds for
the Lamanites.
28 And it came to pass that they
marched to the [a]borders of the land
Bountiful, driving the Nephites before them and slaying many.
29 But it came to pass that they
were met by Teancum, who had
[a]slain Morianton and had [b]headed
his people in his flight.
30 And it came to pass that he
headed Amalickiah also, as he was
marching forth with his numerous
army that he might take possession
of the land Bountiful, and also the
land [a]northward.
31 But behold he met with a disappointment by being repulsed
by Teancum and his men, for they
were great warriors; for every man
of Teancum did exceed the Lamanites in their strength and in
their skill of war, insomuch that
they did gain advantage over the
Lamanites.
32 And it came to pass that they
did harass them, insomuch that
they did slay them even until it was
dark. And it came to pass that Teancum and his men did pitch their
tents in the borders of the land
Bountiful; and Amalickiah did
pitch his tents in the borders on
the beach by the seashore, and after
this manner were they driven.
33 And it came to pass that when
the night had come, Teancum and
his servant stole forth and went out
by night, and went into the camp
of Amalickiah; and behold, sleep

21 *a* TG Courage.
22 *a* Alma 50:13; 62:32 (32, 34); 3 Ne. 8:9.
24 *a* Alma 50:14.
26 *a* Alma 58:31.
b Alma 50:14; 62:18 (14, 18, 26).
c Alma 50:15; 62:30.
d Alma 50:25; 55:33.
e Alma 55:7.
f Alma 52:2 (2, 16, 22); 53:6 (2, 6).
27 *a* Alma 48:8 (8–9).
28 *a* Alma 52:12.
29 *a* Alma 50:35.
b Hel. 1:28 (28–30).
30 *a* Alma 50:29; 52:9.

had overpowered them because of their much fatigue, which was caused by the labors and heat of the day.

34 And it came to pass that Teancum stole privily into the tent of the king, and [a]put a javelin to his heart; and he did cause the [b]death of the king immediately that he did not awake his servants.

35 And he returned again privily to his own camp, and behold, his men were asleep, and he awoke them and told them all the things that he had done.

36 And he caused that his armies should stand in [a]readiness, lest the Lamanites had awakened and should come upon them.

37 And thus endeth the twenty and fifth year of the reign of the judges over the people of Nephi; and thus endeth the days of Amalickiah.

CHAPTER 52

Ammoron succeeds Amalickiah as king of the Lamanites—Moroni, Teancum, and Lehi lead the Nephites in a victorious war against the Lamanites—The city of Mulek is retaken, and Jacob the Zoramite is slain. About 66–64 B.C.

AND now, it came to pass in the twenty and sixth year of the reign of the judges over the people of Nephi, behold, when the Lamanites awoke on the first morning of the first month, behold, they found Amalickiah was dead in his own tent; and they also saw that Teancum was [a]ready to give them battle on that day.

2 And now, when the Lamanites saw this they were affrighted; and they abandoned their design in marching into the land northward, and retreated with all their army into the city of [a]Mulek, and sought protection in their fortifications.

3 And it came to pass that the [a]brother of Amalickiah was appointed king over the people; and his name was [b]Ammoron; thus king Ammoron, the brother of king Amalickiah, was appointed to reign in his stead.

4 And it came to pass that he did command that his people should maintain those cities, which they had taken by the shedding of blood; for they had not taken any cities save they had lost much blood.

5 And now, Teancum saw that the Lamanites were determined to maintain those cities which they had taken, and those parts of the land which they had obtained possession of; and also seeing the enormity of their number, Teancum thought it was not expedient that he should attempt to attack them in their forts.

6 But he kept his men round about, as if making preparations for war; yea, and truly he was preparing to defend himself against them, by [a]casting up walls round about and preparing places of resort.

7 And it came to pass that he kept thus preparing for war until Moroni had sent a large number of men to strengthen his army.

8 And Moroni also sent orders unto him that he should retain all the prisoners who fell into his hands; for as the Lamanites had taken many prisoners, that he should retain all the prisoners of the Lamanites as a [a]ransom for those whom the Lamanites had taken.

9 And he also sent orders unto him that he should fortify the land [a]Bountiful, and secure the [b]narrow pass which led into the land [c]northward, lest the Lamanites should obtain that point and should have power to harass them on every side.

34*a* Alma 62:36.
b Alma 54:16.
36*a* Alma 52:1.
52 1*a* Alma 51:36.
2*a* Alma 51:26.
3*a* Alma 48:1 (1–6); 54:5.
b Alma 54:1; Hel. 1:16.
6*a* Alma 50:1; 53:3.
8*a* Alma 54:2 (1–2).
9*a* Alma 22:29; 53:3 (3–4); 63:5; Hel. 1:23.
b Alma 22:32; Morm. 2:29.
c Alma 51:30.

10 And Moroni also sent unto him, desiring him that he would be [a]faithful in maintaining that quarter of the land, and that he would seek every opportunity to scourge the Lamanites in that quarter, as much as was in his power, that perhaps he might take again by stratagem or some other way those cities which had been taken out of their hands; and that he also would fortify and strengthen the cities round about, which had not fallen into the hands of the Lamanites.
11 And he also said unto him, I would come unto you, but behold, the Lamanites are upon us in the borders of the land by the west sea; and behold, I go against them, therefore I cannot come unto you.
12 Now, the king (Ammoron) had [a]departed out of the land of Zarahemla, and had made known unto the queen concerning the death of his brother, and had gathered together a large number of men, and had marched forth against the Nephites on the borders by the west sea.
13 And thus he was endeavoring to harass the Nephites, and to draw away a part of their forces to that part of the land, while he had commanded those whom he had left to possess the cities which he had taken, that they should also harass the Nephites on the borders by the east sea, and should take possession of their lands as much as it was in their power, according to the power of their armies.
14 And thus were the Nephites in those dangerous circumstances in the ending of the twenty and sixth year of the reign of the judges over the people of Nephi.
15 But behold, it came to pass in the twenty and seventh year of the reign of the judges, that Teancum, by the command of Moroni—who had established armies to protect the south and the west borders of the land, and had begun his march towards the land Bountiful, that he might assist Teancum with his men in retaking the cities which they had lost—
16 And it came to pass that Teancum had received orders to make an attack upon the city of Mulek, and retake it if it were possible.
17 And it came to pass that Teancum made preparations to make an attack upon the city of Mulek, and march forth with his army against the Lamanites; but he saw that it was impossible that he could overpower them while they were in their fortifications; therefore he abandoned his designs and returned again to the city Bountiful, to wait for the coming of Moroni, that he might receive strength to his army.
18 And it came to pass that Moroni did arrive with his army at the land of Bountiful, in the latter end of the twenty and seventh year of the reign of the judges over the people of Nephi.
19 And in the commencement of the twenty and eighth year, Moroni and Teancum and many of the chief [a]captains held a council of war—what they should do to cause the Lamanites to come out against them to battle; or that they might by some means flatter them out of their strongholds, that they might gain advantage over them and take again the city of Mulek.
20 And it came to pass they sent embassies to the army of the Lamanites, which protected the city of Mulek, to their leader, whose name was Jacob, desiring him that he would come out with his armies to meet them upon the plains between the two cities. But behold, Jacob, who was a [a]Zoramite, would not come out with his army to meet them upon the plains.
21 And it came to pass that Moroni, having no hopes of meeting them upon fair grounds, therefore, he resolved upon a plan that he might

10*a* TG Trustworthiness.
12*a* Alma 51:28.
19*a* Alma 49:5; 55:23.
20*a* Alma 48:5.

[a]decoy the Lamanites out of their strongholds.

22 Therefore he caused that Teancum should take a small number of men and march down near the seashore; and Moroni and his army, by night, marched in the wilderness, on the west of the city [a]Mulek; and thus, on the morrow, when the guards of the Lamanites had discovered Teancum, they ran and told it unto Jacob, their leader.

23 And it came to pass that the armies of the Lamanites did march forth against Teancum, supposing by their numbers to overpower Teancum because of the smallness of his numbers. And as Teancum saw the armies of the Lamanites coming out against him he began to retreat down by the seashore, northward.

24 And it came to pass that when the Lamanites saw that he began to flee, they took courage and pursued them with vigor. And while Teancum was thus leading away the Lamanites who were pursuing them in vain, behold, Moroni commanded that a part of his army who were with him should march forth into the city, and take possession of it.

25 And thus they did, and slew all those who had been left to protect the city, yea, all those who would not [a]yield up their weapons of war.

26 And thus Moroni had obtained possession of the city Mulek with a part of his army, while he marched with the remainder to meet the Lamanites when they should return from the pursuit of Teancum.

27 And it came to pass that the Lamanites did pursue Teancum until they came near the city Bountiful, and then they were met by Lehi and a small army, which had been left to protect the city Bountiful.

28 And now behold, when the chief captains of the Lamanites had beheld Lehi with his army coming against them, they fled in much confusion, lest perhaps they should not obtain the city Mulek before Lehi should overtake them; for they were wearied because of their march, and the men of Lehi were fresh.

29 Now the Lamanites did not know that Moroni had been in their rear with his army; and all they feared was Lehi and his men.

30 Now Lehi was not desirous to overtake them till they should meet Moroni and his army.

31 And it came to pass that before the Lamanites had retreated far they were surrounded by the Nephites, by the men of Moroni on one hand, and the men of Lehi on the other, all of whom were fresh and full of strength; but the Lamanites were wearied because of their long march.

32 And Moroni commanded his men that they should fall upon them until they had given up their weapons of war.

33 And it came to pass that Jacob, being their leader, being also a [a]Zoramite, and having an unconquerable spirit, he led the Lamanites forth to battle with exceeding fury against Moroni.

34 Moroni being in their course of march, therefore Jacob was determined to slay them and cut his way through to the city of Mulek. But behold, Moroni and his men were more powerful; therefore they did not give way before the Lamanites.

35 And it came to pass that they fought on both hands with exceeding fury; and there were many slain on both sides; yea, and Moroni was wounded and Jacob was killed.

36 And Lehi pressed upon their rear with such fury with his strong men, that the Lamanites in the rear delivered up their weapons of war; and the remainder of them, being much confused, knew not whither to go or to strike.

37 Now Moroni seeing their confusion, he said unto them: If ye will

21*a* Josh. 8:13; Alma 43:31 (30–43); 56:30.
22*a* Alma 51:26; 53:6 (2, 6).
25*a* Alma 44:6.
33*a* Alma 30:59.

bring forth your weapons of war and deliver them up, behold we will forbear shedding your blood.

38 And it came to pass that when the Lamanites had heard these words, their chief captains, all those who were not slain, came forth and threw down their weapons of war [a]at the feet of Moroni, and also commanded their men that they should do the same.

39 But behold, there were many that would not; and those who would not deliver up their swords were taken and bound, and their weapons of war were taken from them, and they were compelled to march with their brethren forth into the land Bountiful.

40 And now the number of prisoners who were taken exceeded more than the number of those who had been slain, yea, more than those who had been slain on both sides.

CHAPTER 53

The Lamanite prisoners are used to fortify the city Bountiful—Dissensions among the Nephites give rise to Lamanite victories—Helaman takes command of the two thousand stripling sons of the people of Ammon. About 64–63 B.C.

AND it came to pass that they did set guards over the prisoners of the Lamanites, and did compel them to go forth and bury their dead, yea, and also the dead of the Nephites who were slain; and Moroni placed men over them to guard them while they should perform their labors.

2 And Moroni went to the city of Mulek with Lehi, and took command of the city and gave it unto Lehi. Now behold, this Lehi was a man who had been with Moroni in the more part of all his battles; and he was a man [a]like unto Moroni, and they rejoiced in each other's safety; yea, they were beloved by each other, and also beloved by all the people of Nephi.

3 And it came to pass that after the Lamanites had finished burying their dead and also the dead of the Nephites, they were marched back into the land Bountiful; and Teancum, by the orders of Moroni, caused that they should commence laboring in [a]digging a ditch round about the land, or the city, [b]Bountiful.

4 And he caused that they should build a [a]breastwork of timbers upon the inner bank of the ditch; and they cast up dirt out of the ditch against the breastwork of timbers; and thus they did cause the Lamanites to labor until they had encircled the city of Bountiful round about with a strong wall of timbers and earth, to an exceeding height.

5 And this city became an exceeding stronghold ever after; and in this city they did guard the prisoners of the Lamanites; yea, even within a wall which they had caused them to [a]build with their own hands. Now Moroni was compelled to cause the Lamanites to labor, because it was easy to guard them while at their labor; and he desired all his forces when he should make an attack upon the Lamanites.

6 And it came to pass that Moroni had thus gained a victory over one of the greatest of the armies of the Lamanites, and had obtained possession of the city of [a]Mulek, which was one of the strongest holds of the Lamanites in the land of Nephi; and thus he had also built a stronghold to retain his prisoners.

7 And it came to pass that he did no more attempt a battle with the Lamanites in that year, but he did employ his men in preparing for war, yea, and in making fortifications to guard against the Lamanites, yea, and also delivering their women and their children from famine and

38*a* Alma 55:23.
53 2*a* Alma 48:17.
3*a* Alma 52:6.
b Alma 52:9 (9, 17, 27); 63:5.
4*a* Alma 50:2 (2–3).
5*a* Alma 55:25 (25–26).
6*a* Alma 51:26; 52:22.

affliction, and providing food for
their armies.
8 And now it came to pass that
the armies of the Lamanites, on the
west sea, south, while in the absence
of Moroni on account of some intrigue amongst the Nephites, which
caused [a]dissensions amongst them,
had gained some ground over the
Nephites, yea, insomuch that they
had obtained possession of a number of their cities in that part of
the land.
9 And thus because of [a]iniquity
amongst themselves, yea, because
of dissensions and intrigue among
themselves they were placed in the
most dangerous circumstances.
10 And now behold, I have somewhat to say concerning the [a]people
of Ammon, who, in the beginning,
were Lamanites; but by Ammon
and his brethren, or rather by the
power and word of God, they had
been [b]converted unto the Lord; and
they had been brought down into
the land of Zarahemla, and had
ever since been protected by the
Nephites.
11 And because of their oath they
had been kept from taking up arms
against their brethren; for they had
taken an oath that they [a]never would
shed blood more; and according
to their oath they would have perished; yea, they would have suffered
themselves to have fallen into the
hands of their brethren, had it not
been for the pity and the exceeding
love which Ammon and his brethren had had for them.
12 And for this cause they were
brought down into the land of
Zarahemla; and they ever had been
[a]protected by the Nephites.
13 But it came to pass that when
they saw the danger, and the many
[a]afflictions and tribulations which
the Nephites bore for them, they
were moved with compassion and
were [b]desirous to take up arms in
the defence of their country.
14 But behold, as they were about
to take their weapons of war, they
were overpowered by the persuasions of Helaman and his brethren,
for they were about to [a]break the
[b]oath which they had made.
15 And Helaman feared lest by
so doing they should lose their
souls; therefore all those who had
entered into this covenant were
compelled to behold their brethren
wade through their afflictions, in
their dangerous circumstances at
this time.
16 But behold, it came to pass
they had many [a]sons, who had not
entered into a covenant that they
would not take their weapons of
war to defend themselves against
their enemies; therefore they did
assemble themselves together at this
time, as many as were able to take
up arms, and they called themselves
Nephites.
17 And they entered into a covenant to fight for the liberty of the
Nephites, yea, to protect the land
unto the [a]laying down of their lives;
yea, even they covenanted that they
never would give up their [b]liberty,
but they would fight in all cases to
protect the Nephites and themselves
from bondage.
18 Now behold, there were two
thousand of those young men, who
entered into this covenant and took
their weapons of war to defend
their country.
19 And now behold, as they never
had hitherto been a disadvantage
to the Nephites, they became now
at this period of time also a great
support; for they took their weapons of war, and they would that
Helaman should be their leader.
20 And they were all young men,

8*a* Alma 31:8;
Hel. 1:15.
9*a* Josh. 7:4.
10*a* Alma 27:26.
b Alma 23:13 (8–13).
11*a* Alma 24:18 (17–19).
12*a* Alma 27:23.
13*a* TG Affliction;
Tribulation.
b Alma 24:18 (17–19); 56:7.
14*a* Num. 30:2.
b TG Oath.
16*a* Alma 57:6.
17*a* TG Self-Sacrifice.
b Alma 56:47.
TG Liberty.

and they were exceedingly valiant for [a]courage, and also for strength and activity; but behold, this was not all—they were men who were true at all times in whatsoever thing they were entrusted.

21 Yea, they were men of truth and [a]soberness, for they had been taught to keep the commandments of God and to [b]walk uprightly before him.

22 And now it came to pass that Helaman did march at the head of his [a]two thousand stripling soldiers, to the support of the people in the borders of the land on the south by the west sea.

23 And thus ended the twenty and eighth year of the reign of the judges over the people of Nephi.

CHAPTER 54

Ammoron and Moroni negotiate for the exchange of prisoners—Moroni demands that the Lamanites withdraw and cease their murderous attacks—Ammoron demands that the Nephites lay down their arms and become subject to the Lamanites. About 63 B.C.

AND now it came to pass in the commencement of the twenty and ninth year of the judges, that [a]Ammoron sent unto Moroni desiring that he would exchange prisoners.

2 And it came to pass that Moroni felt to [a]rejoice exceedingly at this request, for he desired the provisions which were imparted for the support of the Lamanite prisoners for the support of his own people; and he also desired his own people for the strengthening of his army.

3 Now the Lamanites had taken many women and children, and there was not a woman nor a child among all the prisoners of Moroni, or the prisoners whom Moroni had taken; therefore Moroni resolved upon a stratagem to obtain as many prisoners of the Nephites from the Lamanites as it were possible.

4 Therefore he wrote an epistle, and sent it by the servant of Ammoron, the same who had brought an epistle to Moroni. Now these are the words which he wrote unto Ammoron, saying:

5 Behold, Ammoron, I have written unto you somewhat concerning this war which ye have waged against my people, or rather which thy [a]brother hath waged against them, and which ye are still determined to carry on after his death.

6 Behold, I would tell you somewhat concerning the [a]justice of God, and the sword of his almighty wrath, which doth hang over you except ye repent and withdraw your armies into your own lands, or the land of your possessions, which is the land of Nephi.

7 Yea, I would tell you these things if ye were capable of hearkening unto them; yea, I would tell you concerning that awful [a]hell that awaits to receive such [b]murderers as thou and thy brother have been, except ye repent and withdraw your murderous purposes, and return with your armies to your own lands.

8 But as ye have once rejected these things, and have fought against the people of the Lord, even so I may expect you will do it again.

9 And now behold, we are prepared to receive you; yea, and except you withdraw your purposes, behold, ye will pull down the [a]wrath of that God whom you have rejected upon you, even to your utter destruction.

10 But, as the Lord liveth, our armies shall come upon you except ye withdraw, and ye shall soon be visited with [a]death, for we will retain our cities and our lands; yea,

20*a* TG Courage; Dependability; Integrity.
21*a* TG Sobriety.
b TG Walking with God.
22*a* Alma 56:3 (1–9).

54 1*a* Alma 52:3.
2*a* Alma 52:8.
5*a* Alma 48:1 (1–6); 52:3 (1–3).
6*a* TG God, Indignation of; God, Justice of.

7*a* TG Hell.
b Alma 47:18 (18, 22–34). TG Murder.
9*a* TG Punish.
10*a* Alma 43:47.

and we will maintain our religion and the cause of our God.

11 But behold, it supposeth me that I talk to you concerning these things in vain; or it supposeth me that thou art a [a]child of hell; therefore I will close my epistle by telling you that I will not exchange prisoners, save it be on conditions that ye will deliver up a man and his wife and his children, for one prisoner; if this be the case that ye will do it, I will exchange.

12 And behold, if ye do not this, I will come against you with my armies; yea, even I will arm my women and my children, and I will come against you, and I will follow you even into your own land, which is the land of [a]our first inheritance; yea, and it shall be blood for blood, yea, life for life; and I will give you battle even until you are destroyed from off the face of the earth.

13 Behold, I am in my anger, and also my people; ye have sought to [a]murder us, and we have only sought to defend ourselves. But behold, if ye seek to destroy us more we will seek to destroy you; yea, and we will seek our land, the land of our first inheritance.

14 Now I close my epistle. I am Moroni; I am a leader of the people of the Nephites.

15 Now it came to pass that Ammoron, when he had received this epistle, was angry; and he wrote another epistle unto Moroni, and these are the words which he wrote, saying:

16 I am Ammoron, the king of the Lamanites; I am the brother of Amalickiah whom ye have [a]murdered. Behold, I will avenge his blood upon you, yea, and I will come upon you with my armies for I fear not your threatenings.

17 For behold, your fathers did wrong their brethren, insomuch that they did rob them of their [a]right to the [b]government when it rightly belonged unto them.

18 And now behold, if ye will lay down your arms, and subject yourselves to be governed by those to whom the government doth rightly belong, then will I cause that my people shall lay down their weapons and shall be at war no more.

19 Behold, ye have breathed out many threatenings against me and my people; but behold, we fear not your threatenings.

20 Nevertheless, I will grant to exchange prisoners according to your request, gladly, that I may preserve my food for my men of war; and we will wage a war which shall be eternal, either to the subjecting the Nephites to our authority or to their eternal extinction.

21 And as concerning that God whom ye say we have rejected, behold, we [a]know not such a being; neither do ye; but if it so be that there is such a being, we know not but that he hath made us as well as you.

22 And if it so be that there is a devil and a hell, behold will he not send you there to dwell with my brother whom ye have murdered, whom ye have hinted that he hath gone to such a place? But behold these things matter not.

23 I am Ammoron, and a descendant of [a]Zoram, whom your fathers pressed and brought out of Jerusalem.

24 And behold now, I am a bold Lamanite; behold, this war hath been waged to avenge their wrongs, and [a]to maintain and to obtain their rights to the government; and I close my epistle to Moroni.

CHAPTER 55

Moroni refuses to exchange prisoners—The Lamanite guards are enticed

11*a* John 8:44 (43–44).
12*a* 2 Ne. 5:8 (5–8).
13*a* Alma 55:2.
16*a* Alma 51:34.
17*a* 2 Ne. 5:3 (1–4); Mosiah 10:15 (12–17).
b TG Governments.
21*a* TG Unbelief.
23*a* 1 Ne. 4:35; Jacob 1:13; 4 Ne. 1:36 (36–37).
24*a* Alma 48:2 (1–4).

to become drunk, and the Nephite prisoners are freed—The city of Gid is taken without bloodshed. About 63–62 B.C.

NOW it came to pass that when Moroni had received this epistle he was more angry, because he knew that Ammoron had a perfect knowledge of his [a]fraud; yea, he knew that Ammoron knew that it was not a just cause that had caused him to wage a war against the people of Nephi.
2 And he said: Behold, I will not exchange prisoners with Ammoron save he will withdraw his [a]purpose, as I have stated in my epistle; for I will not grant unto him that he shall have any more power than what he hath got.
3 Behold, I know the place where the Lamanites do guard my people whom they have taken prisoners; and as Ammoron would not grant unto me mine epistle, behold, I will give unto him according to my words; yea, I will seek death among them until they shall sue for peace.
4 And now it came to pass that when Moroni had said these words, he caused that a search should be made among his men, that perhaps he might find a man who was a descendant of Laman among them.
5 And it came to pass that they found one, whose name was Laman; and he was [a]one of the servants of the king who was murdered by Amalickiah.
6 Now Moroni caused that Laman and a small number of his men should go forth unto the guards who were over the Nephites.
7 Now the Nephites were guarded in the city of [a]Gid; therefore Moroni appointed Laman and caused that a small number of men should go with him.
8 And when it was evening Laman went to the guards who were over the Nephites, and behold, they saw him coming and they hailed him; but he saith unto them: Fear not; behold, I am a Lamanite. Behold, we have escaped from the Nephites, and they sleep; and behold we have taken of their wine and brought with us.
9 Now when the Lamanites heard these words they received him with joy; and they said unto him: Give us of your wine, that we may drink; we are glad that ye have thus taken wine with you for we are weary.
10 But Laman said unto them: Let us keep of our wine till we go against the Nephites to battle. But this saying only made them more desirous to drink of the wine;
11 For, said they: We are weary, therefore let us take of the wine, and by and by we shall receive wine for our rations, which will strengthen us to go against the Nephites.
12 And Laman said unto them: You may do according to your desires.
13 And it came to pass that they did take of the wine freely; and it was pleasant to their taste, therefore they took of it more freely; and it was strong, having been prepared in its [a]strength.
14 And it came to pass they did drink and were merry, and by and by they were all [a]drunken.
15 And now when Laman and his men saw that they were all drunken, and were in a [a]deep sleep, they returned to Moroni and told him all the things that had happened.
16 And now this was according to the design of Moroni. And Moroni had prepared his men with weapons of war; and he went to the city Gid, while the Lamanites were in a deep sleep and drunken, and cast in [a]weapons of war unto the prisoners, insomuch that they were all armed;
17 Yea, even to their women, and all those of their children, as many as were able to use a weapon of war,

55 1*a* Neh. 6:8; Alma 47:30 (12–35).
2*a* Alma 54:13.
5*a* Alma 47:29.
7*a* Alma 51:26.
13*a* Prov. 20:1. TG Wine.
14*a* Mosiah 22:6 (6–11).
15*a* 1 Sam. 26:12; Mosiah 24:19.
16*a* Alma 62:22 (21–23).

when Moroni had armed all those
prisoners; and all those things were
done in a profound silence.
18 But had they awakened the Lamanites, behold they were drunken
and the Nephites could have slain
them.
19 But behold, this was not the
desire of Moroni; he did not [a]delight
in murder or bloodshed, but he delighted in the saving of his people
from destruction; and for this cause
he might not bring upon him injustice, he would not fall upon the
Lamanites and destroy them in their
drunkenness.
20 But he had obtained his desires;
for he had armed those prisoners of
the Nephites who were within the
wall of the city, and had given them
power to gain possession of those
parts which were within the walls.
21 And then he caused the men
who were with him to withdraw a
pace from them, and surround the
armies of the Lamanites.
22 Now behold this was done in
the night-time, so that when the
Lamanites awoke in the morning
they beheld that they were surrounded by the Nephites without,
and that their prisoners were armed
within.
23 And thus they saw that the
Nephites had power over them; and
in these circumstances they found
that it was not expedient that they
should fight with the Nephites;
therefore their chief [a]captains de-
manded their weapons of war, and
they brought them forth and [b]cast
them at the feet of the Nephites,
pleading for mercy.
24 Now behold, this was the desire
of Moroni. He took them prisoners
of war, and took possession of the
city, and caused that all the prisoners should be liberated, who were
Nephites; and they did join the
army of Moroni, and were a great
strength to his army.
25 And it came to pass that he did
cause the Lamanites, whom he had
taken prisoners, that they should
commence a [a]labor in strengthening the fortifications round about
the city Gid.
26 And it came to pass that when
he had fortified the city Gid, according to his desires, he caused
that his prisoners should be taken
to the city Bountiful; and he also
guarded that city with an exceedingly strong force.
27 And it came to pass that they
did, notwithstanding all the in-
trigues of the Lamanites, keep and
protect all the prisoners whom they
had taken, and also maintain all the
ground and the advantage which
they had retaken.
28 And it came to pass that the
Nephites began [a]again to be victorious, and to reclaim their rights
and their privileges.
29 Many times did the Lamanites
attempt to encircle them about by
night, but in these attempts they
did lose many prisoners.
30 And many times did they attempt to administer of their wine
to the Nephites, that they might
destroy them with poison or with
drunkenness.
31 But behold, the Nephites were
not slow to [a]remember the Lord
their God in this their time of affliction. They could not be taken
in their snares; yea, they would not
partake of their wine, save they had
first given to some of the Lamanite
prisoners.
32 And they were thus cautious
that no poison should be administered among them; for if their
wine would poison a Lamanite it
would also poison a Nephite; and
thus they did try all their liquors.
33 And now it came to pass that it
was expedient for Moroni to make
preparations to attack the city [a]Mori-
anton; for behold, the Lamanites

19*a* Alma 48:16; 55:30 (30–32).
23*a* Alma 52:19; 56:12.
b Alma 52:38.
25*a* Alma 53:5 (3–5).
28*a* Alma 44:20 (12–23).
31*a* Hosea 5:15; Alma 62:49 (49–51).
33*a* Alma 50:25; 51:26.

had, by their labors, fortified the
city Morianton until it had become
an exceeding stronghold.
34 And they were continually
bringing new forces into that city,
and also new supplies of provisions.
35 And thus ended the twenty and
ninth year of the reign of the judges
over the people of Nephi.

CHAPTER 56

Helaman sends an epistle to Moroni, recounting the state of the war with the Lamanites—Antipus and Helaman gain a great victory over the Lamanites—Helaman's two thousand stripling sons fight with miraculous power, and none of them are slain. Verse 1, about 62 B.C.*; verses 2–19, about 66* B.C.*; and verses 20–57, about 65–64* B.C.

AND now it came to pass in the
commencement of the thirtieth
year of the reign of the judges, on
the second day in the first month,
[a]Moroni received an [b]epistle from
Helaman, stating the affairs of the
people in [c]that quarter of the land.
2 And these are the words which
he wrote, saying: My dearly beloved
brother, Moroni, as well in the Lord
as in the tribulations of our warfare;
behold, my beloved brother,
I have somewhat to tell you concerning
our warfare in this part of
the land.
3 Behold, [a]two thousand of the sons
of those men whom Ammon brought
down out of the land of Nephi—now
ye have known that these were descendants
of Laman, who was the
eldest son of our father Lehi;
4 Now I need not rehearse unto
you concerning their traditions or
their unbelief, for thou knowest
concerning all these things—
5 Therefore it sufficeth me that
I tell you that two thousand of
these young men have taken their
weapons of war, and would that I
should be their leader; and we have
come forth to defend our country.
6 And now ye also know concerning
the [a]covenant which their
fathers made, that they would not
take up their weapons of war against
their brethren to shed blood.
7 But in the twenty and sixth year,
when they saw our afflictions and
our tribulations for them, they were
about to [a]break the covenant which
they had made and take up their
weapons of war in our defence.
8 But I would not suffer them that
they should break this [a]covenant
which they had made, supposing
that God would strengthen us, insomuch
that we should not suffer
more because of the fulfilling the
[b]oath which they had taken.
9 But behold, here is one thing in
which we may have great joy. For
behold, in the twenty and sixth
year, I, Helaman, did march at the
head of these [a]two thousand young
men to the city of [b]Judea, to assist
Antipus, whom ye had appointed a
leader over the people of that part
of the land.
10 And I did join my two thousand
[a]sons, (for they are worthy to
be called sons) to the army of Antipus,
in which strength Antipus
did rejoice exceedingly; for behold,
his army had been reduced by the
Lamanites because their forces had
slain a vast number of our men,
for which cause we have to mourn.
11 Nevertheless, we may console
ourselves in this point, that they
have died in the cause of their
country and of their God, yea, and
they are [a]happy.
12 And the Lamanites had also retained
many prisoners, all of whom
are chief [a]captains, for none other
have they spared alive. And we
suppose that they are now at this

56 1*a* Alma 58:35.
b Alma 59:1.
c Alma 53:22 (8, 22).
3*a* Alma 53:22.
6*a* TG Covenants.
7*a* Alma 24:18 (17–19); 53:13 (13–15).
8*a* TG Honesty.
b TG Vow.
9*a* Alma 53:22.
b Alma 57:11.
10*a* Alma 56:17.
11*a* Alma 28:12.
12*a* Alma 52:19.

time in the land of Nephi; it is so
if they are not slain.
13 And now these are the cities of
which the Lamanites have obtained
possession by the shedding of the
blood of so many of our valiant men:
14 The land of [a]Manti, or the city
of Manti, and the city of Zeezrom,
and the city of [b]Cumeni, and the
city of Antiparah.
15 And these are the cities which
they possessed when I arrived at
the city of Judea; and I found Antipus and his men toiling with their
might to fortify the city.
16 Yea, and they were depressed
in body as well as in spirit, for they
had fought valiantly by day and
toiled by night to maintain their
cities; and thus they had suffered
great afflictions of every kind.
17 And now they were determined
to conquer in this place or die; therefore you may well suppose that this
little force which I brought with
me, yea, those [a]sons of mine, gave
them great hopes and much joy.
18 And now it came to pass that
when the Lamanites saw that Antipus had received a greater strength
to his army, they were compelled
by the orders of Ammoron to not
come against the city of Judea, or
against us, to battle.
19 And thus were we favored of
the Lord; for had they come upon
us in this our weakness they might
have perhaps destroyed our little
army; but thus were we preserved.
20 They were commanded by
Ammoron to maintain those cities
which they had taken. And thus
ended the twenty and sixth year.
And in the commencement of the
twenty and seventh year we had
prepared our city and ourselves for
defence.
21 Now we were desirous that
the Lamanites should come upon
us; for we were not desirous to
make an attack upon them in their
strongholds.
22 And it came to pass that we kept
spies out round about, to watch the
movements of the Lamanites, that
they might not pass us by night
nor by day to make an attack upon
our other cities which were on the
northward.
23 For we knew in those cities
they were not sufficiently strong
to meet them; therefore we were
desirous, if they should pass by us,
to fall upon them in their rear, and
thus bring them up in the rear at
the same time they were met in the
front. We supposed that we could
overpower them; but behold, we
were disappointed in this our desire.
24 They durst not pass by us with
their whole army, neither durst
they with a part, lest they should
not be sufficiently strong and they
should fall.
25 Neither durst they march down
against the city of Zarahemla; neither durst they cross the head of
Sidon, over to the city of Nephihah.
26 And thus, with their forces,
they were determined to maintain
those cities which they had taken.
27 And now it came to pass in the
second month of this year, there was
brought unto us many provisions
from the fathers of those my two
thousand sons.
28 And also there were sent two
thousand men unto us from the
land of Zarahemla. And thus we
were prepared with ten thousand
men, and provisions for them,
and also for their wives and their
children.
29 And the Lamanites, thus seeing
our forces increase daily, and provisions arrive for our support, they
began to be fearful, and began to
sally forth, if it were possible to put
an end to our receiving provisions
and strength.
30 Now when we saw that the
Lamanites began to grow uneasy
on this wise, we were desirous to
bring a stratagem into effect upon
them; therefore Antipus ordered
that I should march forth with my

14*a* Alma 43:22.
b Alma 57:7 (7–34).
17*a* Alma 56:10.

little sons to a neighboring city, [a]as
if we were carrying provisions to a
neighboring city.
31 And we were to march near the
city of Antiparah, as if we were going to the city beyond, in the borders by the seashore.
32 And it came to pass that we did
march forth, as if with our provisions, to go to that city.
33 And it came to pass that Antipus did march forth with a part of
his army, leaving the remainder to
maintain the city. But he did not
march forth until I had gone forth
with my little army, and came near
the city Antiparah.
34 And now, in the city Antiparah
were stationed the strongest army
of the Lamanites; yea, the most
numerous.
35 And it came to pass that when
they had been informed by their
spies, they came forth with their
army and marched against us.
36 And it came to pass that we did
flee before them, northward. And
thus we did lead away the most
powerful army of the Lamanites;
37 Yea, even to a considerable distance, insomuch that when they
saw the army of Antipus pursuing
them, with their might, they did
not turn to the right nor to the
left, but pursued their march in a
straight course after us; and, as we
suppose, it was their intent to slay
us before Antipus should overtake
them, and this that they might not
be surrounded by our people.
38 And now Antipus, beholding
our danger, did speed the march of
his army. But behold, it was night;
therefore they did not overtake
us, neither did Antipus overtake
them; therefore we did camp for
the night.
39 And it came to pass that before
the dawn of the morning, behold,
the Lamanites were pursuing us.
Now we were not sufficiently strong
to contend with them; yea, I would
not suffer that my little sons should
fall into their hands; therefore we
did continue our march, and we
took our march into the wilderness.
40 Now they durst not turn to the
right nor to the left lest they should
be surrounded; neither would I turn
to the right nor to the left lest they
should overtake me, and we could
not stand against them, but be slain,
and they would make their escape;
and thus we did flee all that day
into the wilderness, even until it
was dark.
41 And it came to pass that again,
when the light of the morning came
we saw the Lamanites upon us, and
we did flee before them.
42 But it came to pass that they
did not pursue us far before they
halted; and it was in the morning of
the third day of the seventh month.
43 And now, whether they were
overtaken by Antipus we knew not,
but I said unto my men: Behold, we
know not but they have halted for
the purpose that we should come
against them, that they might catch
us in their snare;
44 Therefore what say ye, my sons,
will ye go against them to battle?
45 And now I say unto you, my
beloved brother Moroni, that never
had I seen [a]so great [b]courage, nay,
not amongst all the Nephites.
46 For as I had ever called them
my sons (for they were all of them
very young) even so they said unto
me: Father, behold our God is with
us, and he will [a]not suffer that we
should fall; then let us go forth;
we would not slay our brethren if
they would let us alone; therefore
let us go, lest they should overpower
the army of Antipus.
47 Now they never had fought,
yet they did not fear death; and
they did think more upon the
[a]liberty of their [b]fathers than they
did upon their lives; yea, they had

30*a* Alma 52:21; 58:1.
45*a* Alma 19:10.
b TG Courage.
46*a* Alma 61:10 (10–11).
47*a* TG Birthright; Liberty.
b Alma 53:17 (15–18). TG Honoring Father and Mother.

been taught by their [c]mothers, that if they did not doubt, God would deliver them.

48 And they rehearsed unto me the words of their [a]mothers, saying: We [b]do not doubt our mothers knew it.

49 And it came to pass that I did return with my two thousand against these Lamanites who had pursued us. And now behold, the armies of Antipus had overtaken them, and a terrible battle had commenced.

50 The army of Antipus being weary, because of their long march in so short a space of time, were about to fall into the hands of the Lamanites; and had I not returned with my two thousand they would have obtained their purpose.

51 For Antipus had fallen by the sword, and many of his leaders, because of their weariness, which was occasioned by the speed of their march—therefore the men of Antipus, being confused because of the fall of their leaders, began to give way before the Lamanites.

52 And it came to pass that the Lamanites took courage, and began to pursue them; and thus were the Lamanites pursuing them with great vigor when [a]Helaman came upon their rear with his two thousand, and began to slay them exceedingly, insomuch that the whole army of the Lamanites halted and turned upon Helaman.

53 Now when the people of Antipus saw that the Lamanites had turned them about, they gathered together their men and came again upon the rear of the Lamanites.

54 And now it came to pass that we, the people of Nephi, the people of Antipus, and I with my two thousand, did surround the Lamanites, and did slay them; yea, insomuch that they were compelled to deliver up their weapons of war and also themselves as prisoners of war.

55 And now it came to pass that when they had surrendered themselves up unto us, behold, I numbered those young men who had fought with me, fearing lest there were many of them slain.

56 But behold, to my great joy, there had [a]not one soul of them fallen to the earth; yea, and they had fought as if with the [b]strength of God; yea, never were men known to have fought with such miraculous strength; and with such mighty power did they fall upon the Lamanites, that they did frighten them; and for this cause did the Lamanites deliver themselves up as prisoners of war.

57 And as we had no place for our prisoners, that we could guard them to keep them from the armies of the Lamanites, therefore we sent them to the land of Zarahemla, and a part of those men who were not slain of Antipus, with them; and the remainder I took and joined them to my stripling [a]Ammonites, and took our march back to the city of Judea.

CHAPTER 57

Helaman recounts the taking of Antiparah and the surrender and later the defense of Cumeni—His Ammonite striplings fight valiantly; all are wounded, but none are slain—Gid reports the slaying and the escape of the Lamanite prisoners. About 63 B.C.

AND now it came to pass that I received an epistle from Ammoron, the king, stating that if I would deliver up those prisoners of war whom we had taken that he would deliver up the city of Antiparah unto us.

2 But I sent an epistle unto the king, that we were sure our forces were sufficient to take the city of

47*c* Alma 57:21. TG Marriage, Motherhood.
48*a* TG Family, Love within.
b D&C 46:14.
52*a* Morm. 6:6. IE Mormon here abridges some of the material in the letter of Helaman.
56*a* Alma 57:25; 58:39.
b TG Strength.
57*a* Alma 27:26.

Antiparah by our force; and by delivering up the prisoners for that
city we should suppose ourselves
unwise, and that we would only deliver up our prisoners on exchange.
3 And Ammoron refused mine
epistle, for he would not exchange
prisoners; therefore we began to
make preparations to go against
the city of Antiparah.
4 But the people of Antiparah did
leave the city, and fled to their other
cities, which they had possession of,
to fortify them; and thus the city
of Antiparah fell into our hands.
5 And thus ended the twenty
and eighth year of the reign of
the judges.
6 And it came to pass that in the
commencement of the twenty and
ninth year, we received a supply
of provisions, and also an addition
to our army, from the land of Zarahemla, and from the land round
about, to the number of six thousand men, besides sixty of the [a]sons
of the Ammonites who had come to
join their brethren, my little band
of two thousand. And now behold,
we were strong, yea, and we had
also plenty of provisions brought
unto us.
7 And it came to pass that it was
our desire to wage a battle with the
army which was placed to protect
the city [a]Cumeni.
8 And now behold, I will show unto
you that we soon accomplished our
desire; yea, with our strong force, or
with a part of our strong force, we
did surround, by night, the city
Cumeni, a little before they were
to receive a supply of provisions.
9 And it came to pass that we did
camp round about the city for many
nights; but we did sleep upon our
swords, and keep guards, that the
Lamanites could not come upon us
by night and slay us, which they attempted many times; but as many
times as they attempted this their
blood was spilt.
10 At length their provisions did
arrive, and they were about to enter
the city by night. And we, instead
of being Lamanites, were Nephites;
therefore, we did take them and
their provisions.
11 And notwithstanding the Lamanites being cut off from their
support after this manner, they were
still determined to maintain the
city; therefore it became expedient
that we should take those provisions
and send them to [a]Judea, and our
prisoners to the land of Zarahemla.
12 And it came to pass that not
many days had passed away before
the Lamanites began to lose all hopes
of succor; therefore they yielded up
the city unto our hands; and thus
we had accomplished our designs
in obtaining the city Cumeni.
13 But it came to pass that our
prisoners were so numerous that,
notwithstanding the enormity of
our numbers, we were obliged to
employ all our force to keep them,
or to put them to death.
14 For behold, they would break
out in great numbers, and would
fight with stones, and with clubs,
or whatsoever thing they could get
into their hands, insomuch that we
did slay upwards of two thousand
of them after they had surrendered
themselves prisoners of war.
15 Therefore it became expedient
for us, that we should put an end
to their lives, or guard them, sword
in hand, down to the land of Zarahemla; and also our provisions were
not any more than sufficient for
our own people, notwithstanding
that which we had taken from the
Lamanites.
16 And now, in those critical circumstances, it became a very serious matter to determine concerning
these prisoners of war; nevertheless,
we did resolve to send them down
to the land of Zarahemla; therefore we selected a part of our men,
and gave them charge over our
prisoners to go down to the land of
Zarahemla.

57 6*a* Alma 53:16. | 7*a* Alma 56:14. | 11*a* Alma 56:9.

17 But it came to pass that on the
morrow they did return. And now
behold, we did not [a]inquire of them
concerning the prisoners; for behold, the Lamanites were upon us,
and they returned in season to save
us from falling into their hands.
For behold, Ammoron had sent to
their support a new supply of provisions and also a numerous army
of men.
18 And it came to pass that those
men whom we sent with the prisoners did arrive in season to check
them, as they were about to overpower us.
19 But behold, my little band of
two thousand and sixty fought most
desperately; yea, they were firm
before the Lamanites, and did [a]ad-
minister death unto all those who
opposed them.
20 And as the remainder of our
army were about to give way before the Lamanites, behold, those
two thousand and sixty were firm
and undaunted.
21 Yea, and they did [a]obey and
observe to perform every word
of command with exactness; yea,
and even according to their faith it
was done unto them; and I did remember the words which they said
unto me that their [b]mothers had
taught them.
22 And now behold, it was these
my sons, and those men who had
been selected to convey the prisoners, to whom we owe this great victory; for it was they who did beat
the Lamanites; therefore they were
driven back to the city of Manti.
23 And we retained our city Cumeni, and were not all destroyed
by the sword; nevertheless, we had
suffered great loss.
24 And it came to pass that after
the Lamanites had fled, I immediately gave orders that my men
who had been wounded should be
taken from among the dead, and
caused that their wounds should
be dressed.
25 And it came to pass that there
were two hundred, out of my two
thousand and sixty, who had fainted
because of the loss of blood; nevertheless, according to the goodness of
God, and to our great astonishment,
and also the joy of our whole army,
there was [a]not one soul of them who
did perish; yea, and neither was
there one soul among them who
had not received many wounds.
26 And now, their [a]preservation
was astonishing to our whole army,
yea, that they should be spared
while there was a thousand of our
brethren who were slain. And we
do justly ascribe it to the miraculous [b]power of God, because of their
exceeding [c]faith in that which they
had been taught to believe—that
there was a just God, and whosoever did not doubt, that they should
be preserved by his marvelous
power.
27 Now this was the [a]faith of these
of whom I have spoken; they are
young, and their minds are [b]firm,
and they do put their trust in God
continually.
28 And now it came to pass that
after we had thus taken care of our
wounded men, and had buried our
dead and also the dead of the Lamanites, who were many, behold,
we did inquire of Gid concerning the [a]prisoners whom they had
started to go down to the land of
Zarahemla with.
29 Now Gid was the chief captain
over the band who was appointed
to guard them down to the land.
30 And now, these are the words
which Gid said unto me: Behold,
we did start to go down to the land
of Zarahemla with our prisoners.
And it came to pass that we did
meet the spies of our armies, who

17*a* Alma 57:28.
19*a* Alma 62:11.
21*a* TG Trustworthiness.
b Alma 56:47 (47–48).
25*a* Alma 56:56.
26*a* 1 Chr. 5:20 (18–22).
b TG God, Power of.
c TG Faith.
27*a* Alma 58:40.
b Jacob 3:2.
28*a* Alma 57:17 (16–17).

had been sent out to watch the camp
of the Lamanites.
31 And they cried unto us, saying—Behold, the armies of the Lamanites are marching towards the
city of Cumeni; and behold, they
will fall upon them, yea, and will
destroy our people.
32 And it came to pass that our
prisoners did hear their cries, which
caused them to take courage; and
they did rise up in rebellion against
us.
33 And it came to pass because of
their rebellion we did cause that
our swords should come upon them.
And it came to pass that they did
in a body run upon our swords, in
the which, the greater number of
them were slain; and the remainder
of them broke through and fled
from us.
34 And behold, when they had fled
and we could not overtake them, we
took our march with speed towards
the city Cumeni; and behold, we did
arrive in time that we might assist
our brethren in preserving the city.
35 And behold, we are again delivered out of the hands of our enemies. And blessed is the name of
our God; for behold, it is he that
has delivered us; yea, that has done
this great thing for us.
36 Now it came to pass that when
I, Helaman, had heard these words
of Gid, I was filled with exceeding
joy because of the goodness of God
in preserving us, that we might
not all perish; yea, and I trust that
the souls of them who have been
slain have [a]entered into the rest of
their God.

CHAPTER 58

Helaman, Gid, and Teomner take the city of Manti by a stratagem—The Lamanites withdraw—The sons of the people of Ammon are preserved as they stand fast in defense of their liberty and faith. About 63–62 B.C.

AND behold, now it came to pass
that our next object was to obtain
the city of Manti; but behold, there
was no way that we could lead them
out of the city by our small bands.
For behold, they remembered that
which we had hitherto done; therefore we could not [a]decoy them away
from their strongholds.
2 And they were so much more
numerous than was our army that
we durst not go forth and attack
them in their strongholds.
3 Yea, and it became expedient
that we should employ our men to
the maintaining those parts of the
land which we had regained of our
possessions; therefore it became expedient that we should wait, that we
might receive more strength from
the land of Zarahemla and also a
new supply of provisions.
4 And it came to pass that I thus
did send an embassy to the governor
of our land, to acquaint him concerning the affairs of our people.
And it came to pass that we did wait
to receive provisions and strength
from the land of Zarahemla.
5 But behold, this did profit us but
little; for the Lamanites were also
receiving great strength from day
to day, and also many provisions;
and thus were our circumstances
at this period of time.
6 And the Lamanites were sallying
forth against us from time to time,
resolving by stratagem to destroy us;
nevertheless we could not come to
battle with them, because of their
[a]retreats and their strongholds.
7 And it came to pass that we did
wait in these difficult circumstances
for the space of many months, even
until we were about to [a]perish for
the want of food.
8 But it came to pass that we did
receive food, which was guarded to
us by an army of two thousand men
to our assistance; and this is all the
assistance which we did receive, to
defend ourselves and our country

36*a* Alma 12:34.
58 1*a* Alma 52:21; 56:30.
6*a* 1 Sam. 24:22; 3 Ne. 4:1.
7*a* Alma 60:9.

from falling into the hands of our enemies, yea, to contend with an enemy which was innumerable.

9 And now the cause of these our embarrassments, or the cause why they did not send more strength unto us, we knew not; therefore we were grieved and also filled with fear, lest by any means the judgments of God should come upon our land, to our overthrow and utter destruction.

10 Therefore we did pour out our souls in prayer to God, that he would strengthen us and deliver us out of the hands of our enemies, yea, and also give us strength that we might retain our cities, and our lands, and our possessions, for the support of our people.

11 Yea, and it came to pass that the Lord our God did visit us with assurances that he would deliver us; yea, insomuch that he did speak peace to our souls, and did grant unto us great faith, and did cause us that we should hope for our [a]deliverance in him.

12 And we did take courage with our small force which we had received, and were fixed with a determination to conquer our enemies, and to [a]maintain our lands, and our possessions, and our wives, and our children, and the cause of our [b]liberty.

13 And thus we did go forth with all our might against the Lamanites, who were in the city of Manti; and we did pitch our tents by the wilderness side, which was near to the city.

14 And it came to pass that on the morrow, that when the Lamanites saw that we were in the borders by the wilderness which was near the city, that they sent out their spies round about us that they might discover the number and the strength of our army.

15 And it came to pass that when they saw that we were not strong, according to our numbers, and fearing that we should cut them off from their support except they should come out to battle against us and kill us, and also supposing that they could easily destroy us with their numerous hosts, therefore they began to make preparations to come out against us to battle.

16 And when we saw that they were making preparations to come out against us, behold, I caused that Gid, with a small number of men, should [a]secrete himself in the wilderness, and also that Teomner and a small number of men should secrete themselves also in the wilderness.

17 Now Gid and his men were on the right and the others on the left; and when they had thus secreted themselves, behold, I remained, with the remainder of my army, in that same place where we had first pitched our tents against the time that the Lamanites should come out to battle.

18 And it came to pass that the Lamanites did come out with their numerous army against us. And when they had come and were about to fall upon us with the sword, I caused that my men, those who were with me, should retreat into the wilderness.

19 And it came to pass that the Lamanites did follow after us with great speed, for they were exceedingly desirous to overtake us that they might slay us; therefore they did follow us into the wilderness; and we did pass by in the midst of Gid and Teomner, insomuch that they were not discovered by the Lamanites.

20 And it came to pass that when the Lamanites had passed by, or when the army had passed by, Gid and Teomner did rise up from their secret places, and did cut off the spies of the Lamanites that they should not return to the city.

11*a* TG Deliver.
12*a* Alma 46:12; 3 Ne. 2:12; Morm. 2:23.
b TG Liberty.
16*a* Josh. 8:13; Alma 43:31 (30–43); 52:21 (21–31).

21 And it came to pass that when
they had cut them off, they ran to
the city and fell upon the guards
who were left to guard the city, insomuch that they did destroy them
and did take possession of the city.
22 Now this was done because the
Lamanites did suffer their whole
army, save a few guards only, to be
led away into the wilderness.
23 And it came to pass that Gid
and Teomner by this means had
obtained possession of their strongholds. And it came to pass that we
took our course, after having traveled much in the wilderness towards
the land of Zarahemla.
24 And when the Lamanites saw
that they were marching towards
the land of Zarahemla, they were
exceedingly afraid, lest there was
a plan laid to lead them on to destruction; therefore they began to
retreat into the wilderness again,
yea, even back by the same way
which they had come.
25 And behold, it was night and
they did pitch their tents, for the
chief [a]captains of the Lamanites
had supposed that the Nephites
were weary because of their march;
and supposing that they had driven
their whole army therefore they
took no thought concerning the
city of Manti.
26 Now it came to pass that when
it was night, I caused that my men
should not sleep, but that they
should march forward by another
way towards the land of Manti.
27 And because of this our march
in the night-time, behold, on the
morrow we were beyond the Lamanites, insomuch that we did arrive
before them at the city of Manti.
28 And thus it came to pass, that
by this stratagem we did take possession of the city of Manti without
the shedding of blood.
29 And it came to pass that when
the armies of the Lamanites did
arrive near the city, and saw that
we were prepared to meet them,
they were astonished exceedingly
and struck with great fear, insomuch that they did [a]flee into the
wilderness.
30 Yea, and it came to pass that
the armies of the Lamanites did flee
out of all this quarter of the land.
But behold, they have carried with
them many women and children
out of the land.
31 And [a]those cities which had
been taken by the Lamanites, all of
them are at this period of time in
our possession; and our fathers and
our women and our children are returning to their homes, all save it be
those who have been taken prisoners
and carried off by the Lamanites.
32 But behold, our armies are small
to maintain so great a number of
cities and so great possessions.
33 But behold, we [a]trust in our God
who has given us victory over those
lands, insomuch that we have obtained those cities and those lands,
which were our own.
34 Now we do not know the [a]cause
that the government does not grant
us more strength; neither do those
men who came up unto us know
why we have not received greater
strength.
35 Behold, we do not know but
what [a]ye are unsuccessful, and ye
have drawn away the forces into
that quarter of the land; if so, we
do not desire to murmur.
36 And if it is not so, behold, we
fear that there is some [a]faction in
the government, that they do not
send more men to our assistance;
for we know that they are more
numerous than that which they
have sent.
37 But, behold, it mattereth not—
we trust God will [a]deliver us, notwithstanding the weakness of our
armies, yea, and deliver us out of
the hands of our enemies.

25*a* Alma 59:12.
29*a* Alma 59:6.
31*a* Alma 56:14; 59:1.
33*a* TG Trust in God.
34*a* Alma 59:13.
35*a* Alma 56:1.
36*a* Alma 61:3.
37*a* 2 Kgs. 17:39.

38 Behold, this is the twenty and ninth year, in the latter end, and we are in the possession of our lands; and the Lamanites have fled to the land of Nephi.

39 And those sons of the people of Ammon, of whom I have so highly spoken, are with me in the city of Manti; and the Lord has supported them, yea, and kept them from falling by the sword, insomuch that even [a]one soul has not been slain.

40 But behold, they have received many wounds; nevertheless they [a]stand fast in that [b]liberty wherewith God has made them free; and they are strict to remember the Lord their God from day to day; yea, they do observe to keep his statutes, and his judgments, and his commandments continually; and their faith is strong in the prophecies concerning that which is to come.

41 And now, my beloved brother, Moroni, may the Lord our God, who has redeemed us and made us free, keep you continually in his presence; yea, and may he favor this people, even that ye may have success in obtaining the possession of all that which the Lamanites have taken from us, which was for our support. And now, behold, I close mine epistle. I am Helaman, the son of Alma.

CHAPTER 59

Moroni asks Pahoran to strengthen the forces of Helaman—The Lamanites take the city of Nephihah—Moroni is angry with the government. About 62 B.C.

Now it came to pass in the thirtieth year of the reign of the judges over the people of Nephi, after Moroni had received and had read Helaman's [a]epistle, he was exceedingly rejoiced because of the welfare, yea, the exceeding success which Helaman had had, in obtaining [b]those lands which were lost.

2 Yea, and he did make it known unto all his people, in all the land round about in that part where he was, that they might rejoice also.

3 And it came to pass that he immediately sent [a]an epistle to [b]Pahoran, desiring that he should cause men to be gathered together to strengthen Helaman, or the armies of Helaman, insomuch that he might with ease maintain that part of the land which he had been so miraculously prospered in regaining.

4 And it came to pass when Moroni had sent this epistle to the land of Zarahemla, he began again to lay a plan that he might obtain the remainder of those possessions and cities which the Lamanites had taken from them.

5 And it came to pass that while Moroni was thus making preparations to go against the Lamanites to battle, behold, the people of [a]Nephihah, who were gathered together from the city of Moroni and the city of Lehi and the city of Morianton, were attacked by the Lamanites.

6 Yea, even those who had been [a]compelled to flee from the land of Manti, and from the land round about, had come over and joined the Lamanites in this part of the land.

7 And thus being exceedingly numerous, yea, and receiving strength from day to day, by the command of Ammoron they came forth against the people of Nephihah, and they did begin to slay them with an exceedingly great slaughter.

8 And their armies were so numerous that the remainder of the people of [a]Nephihah were [b]obliged to flee before them; and they came even and joined the army of Moroni.

39*a* Alma 56:56.
40*a* Alma 61:21.
TG Trustworthiness.
b TG Liberty.

59 1*a* Alma 56:1.
b Alma 58:31 (31, 41).
3*a* Alma 60:1 (1–3).
b Alma 50:40.

5*a* Alma 50:14.
6*a* Alma 58:29 (29–30).
8*a* Alma 62:26.
b Alma 60:17.

9 And now as Moroni had supposed
that there [a]should be men sent to
the city of Nephihah, to the assistance of the people to maintain that
city, and knowing that it was easier
to keep the city from falling into
the hands of the Lamanites than to
retake it from them, he supposed
that they would easily maintain
that city.
10 Therefore he retained all his
force to maintain those places which
he had recovered.
11 And now, when Moroni saw
that the city of Nephihah was [a]lost
he was exceedingly sorrowful, and
began to doubt, because of the wickedness of the people, whether they
should not fall into the hands of
their brethren.
12 Now this was the case with all
his chief captains. They doubted
and marveled also because of the
wickedness of the people, and this
because of the success of the Lamanites over them.
13 And it came to pass that Moroni was angry with the government, because of their [a]indifference
concerning the freedom of their
country.

CHAPTER 60

Moroni complains to Pahoran of the government's neglect of the armies—The Lord suffers the righteous to be slain—The Nephites must use all of their power and means to deliver themselves from their enemies—Moroni threatens to fight against the government unless help is supplied to his armies. About 62 B.C.

AND it came to pass that he wrote
[a]again to the governor of the land,
who was Pahoran, and these are
the words which he wrote, saying:
Behold, I direct mine epistle to
Pahoran, in the city of Zarahemla,
who is the chief judge and the [b]governor over the land, and also to all
those who have been chosen by this
people to govern and manage the
affairs of this war.
2 For behold, I have somewhat to
say unto them by the way of [a]condemnation; for behold, ye yourselves
know that ye have been appointed
to gather together men, and arm
them with swords, and with cimeters, and all manner of weapons of
war of every kind, and send forth
against the Lamanites, in whatsoever parts they should come into
our land.
3 And now behold, I say unto you
that myself, and also my men, and
also Helaman and his men, have
suffered exceedingly great [a]sufferings; yea, even hunger, thirst, and
fatigue, and all manner of afflictions of every kind.
4 But behold, were this all we had
suffered we would not murmur nor
complain.
5 But behold, great has been the
slaughter among our people; yea,
thousands have fallen by the sword,
while it might have otherwise been
if ye had rendered unto our armies
sufficient strength and succor for
them. Yea, great has been your neglect towards us.
6 And now behold, we desire to
know the cause of this exceedingly
great neglect; yea, we desire to
know the cause of your thoughtless state.
7 Can you think to sit upon your
thrones in a state of thoughtless
[a]stupor, while your enemies are
spreading the work of death around
you? Yea, while they are murdering
thousands of your brethren—
8 Yea, even they who have looked
up to you for protection, yea, have
placed you in a situation that ye
might have succored them, yea,
ye might have sent armies unto
them, to have strengthened them,
and have saved thousands of them
from falling by the sword.

9*a* Alma 60:15.
11*a* Alma 62:14.
13*a* Alma 58:34; 61:3.
60 1*a* Alma 59:3.
b Alma 50:39.
2*a* TG Reproof.
3*a* Alma 61:2.
7*a* TG Apathy.

9 But behold, this is not all—ye
have withheld your provisions from
them, insomuch that many have
fought and bled out their lives because of their great desires which
they had for the welfare of this people; yea, and this they have done
when they were about to [a]perish with
hunger, because of your exceedingly
great neglect towards them.
10 And now, my beloved brethren—for ye ought to be beloved; yea,
and ye ought to have stirred yourselves more diligently for the welfare and the freedom of this people;
but behold, ye have neglected them
insomuch that the blood of thousands shall come upon your heads
for vengeance; yea, for [a]known
unto God were all their cries, and
all their sufferings—
11 Behold, could ye suppose that
ye could sit upon your thrones, and
because of the exceeding goodness
of God ye could do nothing and he
would deliver you? Behold, if ye
have supposed this ye have supposed in vain.
12 Do ye [a]suppose that, because so
many of your brethren have been
killed it is because of their wickedness? I say unto you, if ye have supposed this ye have supposed in vain;
for I say unto you, there are many
who have fallen by the sword; and
behold it is to your condemnation;
13 For the Lord suffereth the
[a]righteous to be slain that his justice and [b]judgment may come upon
the wicked; therefore ye need not
suppose that the righteous are lost
because they are slain; but behold,
they do enter into the rest of the
Lord their God.
14 And now behold, I say unto
you, I fear exceedingly that the
judgments of God will come upon
this people, because of their exceeding [a]slothfulness, yea, even the
slothfulness of our government, and
their exceedingly great neglect towards their brethren, yea, towards
those who have been slain.
15 For were it not for the wickedness which first commenced at
our head, we [a]could have withstood
our enemies that they could have
gained no power over us.
16 Yea, had it not been for the war
which broke out [a]among ourselves;
yea, were it not for these [b]king-men,
who caused so much bloodshed
among ourselves; yea, at the time we
were contending among ourselves,
if we had united our strength as we
hitherto have done; yea, had it not
been for the desire of power and authority which those king-men had
over us; had they been true to the
cause of our freedom, and united
with us, and gone forth against our
enemies, instead of taking up their
swords against us, which was the
cause of so much bloodshed among
ourselves; yea, if we had gone forth
against them in the strength of the
Lord, we should have dispersed our
enemies, for it would have been
done, according to the [c]fulfilling
of his word.
17 But behold, now the Lamanites are coming upon us, taking
[a]possession of our lands, and they
are murdering our people with the
sword, yea, our women and our
children, and also carrying them
away captive, causing them that
they should suffer all manner of
afflictions, and this because of the
great wickedness of those who are
seeking for power and authority,
yea, even those king-men.
18 But why should I say much concerning this matter? For we know
not but what ye yourselves are seeking for authority. We know not but
what ye are also [a]traitors to your
country.

9*a* Alma 58:7 (7–9).
10*a* Ex. 3:9;
Ps. 9:12.
12*a* Luke 13:2 (1–2).
13*a* Lam. 4:13;
D&C 42:46.
b Alma 14:11 (10–11);
D&C 103:3.
14*a* TG Laziness.
15*a* Alma 59:9.
16*a* Alma 51:19 (5–7, 13–27).
b Alma 62:9.
c Alma 38:1.
17*a* Alma 59:8 (5–8).
18*a* Alma 62:1.

19 Or is it that ye have neglected
us because ye are in the heart of our
country and ye are [a]surrounded by
security, that ye do not cause food
to be sent unto us, and also men to
strengthen our armies?
20 Have ye forgotten the commandments of the Lord your God?
Yea, have ye forgotten the captivity
of our fathers? Have ye forgotten the
many times we have been delivered
out of the hands of our enemies?
21 Or do ye suppose that the Lord
[a]will still deliver us, while we sit
upon our thrones and do not make
use of the means which the Lord
has provided for us?
22 Yea, will ye sit in idleness while
ye are surrounded with thousands
of those, yea, and tens of thousands,
who do also sit in idleness, while
there are thousands round about
in the borders of the land who are
falling by the sword, yea, wounded
and bleeding?
23 Do ye suppose that God will
look upon you as guiltless while ye
sit still and behold these things?
Behold I say unto you, Nay. Now
I would that ye should remember
that God has said that the [a]inward
vessel shall be [b]cleansed first,
and then shall the outer vessel be
cleansed also.
24 And now, except ye do repent
of that which ye have done, and
begin to be up and doing, and send
forth food and men unto us, and also
unto Helaman, that he may support
those parts of our country which
he has regained, and that we may
also recover the remainder of our
possessions in these parts, behold it
will be expedient that we contend
no more with the Lamanites until
we have first cleansed our inward
vessel, yea, even the great head of
our government.
25 And except ye grant mine epistle, and come out and show unto
me a true [a]spirit of freedom, and
strive to strengthen and fortify our
armies, and grant unto them food
for their support, behold I will leave
a part of my freemen to maintain
this part of our land, and I will
leave the strength and the blessings
of God upon them, that none other
power can operate against them—
26 And this because of their exceeding faith, and their patience
in their [a]tribulations—
27 And I will come unto you, and
if there be any among you that
has a desire for freedom, yea, if
there be even a spark of freedom
remaining, behold I will stir up in-
surrections among you, even until
those who have desires to usurp
power and authority shall become
extinct.
28 Yea, behold I do not fear your
power nor your authority, but it
is my [a]God whom I fear; and it is
according to his commandments
that I do take my sword to defend
the cause of my country, and it is
because of your iniquity that we
have suffered so much loss.
29 Behold it is time, yea, the time
is now at hand, that except ye do
bestir yourselves in the defence of
your country and your little ones,
the [a]sword of justice doth hang over
you; yea, and it shall fall upon you
and visit you even to your utter
destruction.
30 Behold, I wait for assistance
from you; and, except ye do administer unto our relief, behold, I
come unto you, even in the land of
Zarahemla, and smite you with the
sword, insomuch that ye can have no
more power to impede the progress
of this people in the cause of our
freedom.
31 For behold, the Lord will not
suffer that ye shall live and wax
strong in your iniquities to destroy
his righteous people.
32 Behold, can you suppose that
the Lord will spare you and come

19*a* TG Apathy.
21*a* 1 Ne. 17:23 (23–35).
23*a* Matt. 23:26 (25–26).
b TG Purification.
25*a* Alma 51:6 (6–7); 61:15.
26*a* TG Tribulation.
28*a* Acts 5:29 (26–29).
29*a* Isa. 1:20 (19–20);
Hel. 13:5;
3 Ne. 2:19.

out in judgment against the Lamanites, when it is the [a]tradition of their
fathers that has caused their hatred,
yea, and it has been redoubled by
those who have dissented from us,
while your iniquity is for the cause
of your love of glory and the vain
things of the world?
33 Ye know that ye do transgress
the laws of God, and ye do know that
ye do trample them under your feet.
Behold, the Lord saith unto me: If
those whom ye have appointed your
governors do not repent of their sins
and [a]iniquities, ye shall [b]go up to
battle against them.
34 And now behold, I, Moroni, am
constrained, according to the covenant which I have made to keep the
commandments of my God; therefore I would that ye should adhere
to the word of God, and send speedily unto me of your provisions and
of your men, and also to Helaman.
35 And behold, if ye will not do this
I come unto you speedily; for behold,
God will not suffer that we should
perish with hunger; therefore he
will give unto us of your food,
even if it must be by the sword. Now
see that ye fulfil the word of God.
36 Behold, I am Moroni, your chief
captain. I [a]seek not for power, but to
pull it down. I [b]seek not for honor
of the world, but for the glory of
my God, and the freedom and welfare of my country. And thus I close
mine epistle.

CHAPTER 61

Pahoran tells Moroni of the insurrection and rebellion against the government—The king-men take Zarahemla and are in league with the Lamanites—Pahoran asks for military aid against the rebels. About 62 B.C.

BEHOLD, now it came to pass that
soon after Moroni had sent his
epistle unto the chief governor, he
received an epistle from [a]Pahoran,
the chief governor. And these are
the words which he received:
2 I, Pahoran, who am the chief
governor of this land, do send these
words unto Moroni, the chief captain over the army. Behold, I say
unto you, Moroni, that I do not joy
in your great [a]afflictions, yea, it
grieves my soul.
3 But behold, there are those who
do joy in your afflictions, yea, insomuch that they have risen up in
[a]rebellion against me, and also those
of my people who are [b]freemen,
yea, and those who have risen up
are exceedingly numerous.
4 And it is those who have sought
to take away the judgment-seat
from me that have been the cause
of this great iniquity; for they have
used great [a]flattery, and they have
[b]led away the hearts of many people, which will be the cause of
sore affliction among us; they have
withheld our provisions, and have
daunted our [c]freemen that they
have not come unto you.
5 And behold, they have driven
me out before them, and I have
fled to the land of Gideon, with as
many men as it were possible that
I could get.
6 And behold, I have sent a proclamation throughout this part of the
land; and behold, they are [a]flock-
ing to us [b]daily, to their arms, in
the defence of their country and
their [c]freedom, and to avenge our
[d]wrongs.
7 And they have come unto us, insomuch that those who have risen
up in rebellion against us are set at
defiance, yea, insomuch that they
do fear us and durst not come out
against us to battle.

32a Alma 17:15.
33a Alma 61:18.
b Alma 61:20.
36a Alma 61:9; D&C 121:39.
b TG Motivations.
61 1a Alma 50:40.
2a Alma 60:3 (3–9).
3a Alma 58:36; 59:13.
b Alma 51:6 (6–7).
4a TG Flatter.
b TG Peer Influence.
c Alma 51:6 (6–7); 62:6.
6a Alma 62:5.
b Acts 2:47.
c TG Liberty.
d TG Injustice.

8 They have [a]got possession of the
land, or the city, of Zarahemla; they
have appointed a [b]king over them,
and he hath written unto the king
of the Lamanites, in the which he
hath joined an alliance with him; in
the which alliance he hath agreed
to maintain the city of Zarahemla,
which maintenance he supposeth
will enable the Lamanites to conquer the remainder of the land,
and he shall be placed king over
this people when they shall be conquered [c]under the Lamanites.
9 And now, in your epistle you
have [a]censured me, but it mattereth
not; I am not angry, but do rejoice
in the greatness of your heart. I,
Pahoran, do not [b]seek for power,
save only to retain my judgment-
seat that I may preserve the rights
and the liberty of my people. My
soul standeth fast in that liberty in
the which God hath made us [c]free.
10 And now, behold, we will resist
wickedness even unto bloodshed.
We would [a]not shed the blood of
the Lamanites if they would stay
in their own land.
11 We would not shed the blood
of our brethren if they would not
rise up in rebellion and take the
sword against us.
12 We would subject ourselves
to the [a]yoke of bondage if it were
requisite with the justice of God, or
if he should command us so to do.
13 But behold he doth not command us that we shall subject ourselves to our enemies, but that we
should put our [a]trust in him, and
he will deliver us.
14 Therefore, my beloved brother,
Moroni, let us resist evil, and whatsoever evil we cannot resist with
our [a]words, yea, such as rebellions
and dissensions, let us [b]resist them
with our swords, that we may retain
our freedom, that we may rejoice in
the great privilege of our church,
and in the cause of our Redeemer
and our God.
15 Therefore, come unto me speedily with a few of your men, and
leave the remainder in the charge
of Lehi and Teancum; give unto
them power to conduct the [a]war in
that part of the land, according to
the [b]Spirit of God, which is also the
[c]spirit of freedom which is in them.
16 Behold I have sent a few provisions unto them, that they may not
perish until ye can come unto me.
17 Gather together whatsoever
force ye can upon your march hither,
and we will go speedily against
those dissenters, in the strength
of our God according to the faith
which is in us.
18 And we will [a]take possession of
the city of Zarahemla, that we may
obtain more food to send forth unto
Lehi and Teancum; yea, we will go
forth against them in the strength
of the Lord, and we will put an end
to this great iniquity.
19 And now, Moroni, I do joy in
receiving your epistle, for I was
somewhat worried concerning what
we should do, whether it should be
just in us to go against our brethren.
20 But ye have said, except they
repent the Lord [a]hath commanded
you that ye should go against them.
21 See that ye [a]strengthen Lehi and
Teancum in the Lord; tell them to
fear not, for God will deliver them,
yea, and also all those who [b]stand
fast in that liberty wherewith God
hath made them free. And now I
close mine epistle to my beloved
brother, Moroni.

8*a* Alma 61:18.
b Alma 62:6. TG Tyranny.
c Mosiah 7:21.
9*a* D&C 101:5. TG Reproof.
b Alma 60:36; D&C 121:39.
c John 8:36; Gal. 5:1; D&C 88:86.
10*a* Alma 56:46.
12*a* TG Bondage, Physical; Submissiveness.
13*a* TG Trust in God.
14*a* TG Reproof.
b Alma 43:47.
15*a* TG War.
b 2 Cor. 3:17. TG God, Spirit of.
c Alma 60:25.
18*a* Alma 61:8.
20*a* Alma 60:33.
21*a* Zech. 10:12.
b Alma 58:40.

CHAPTER 62

Moroni marches to the aid of Pahoran in the land of Gideon—The king-men who refuse to defend their country are put to death—Pahoran and Moroni retake Nephihah—Many Lamanites join the people of Ammon—Teancum slays Ammoron and is in turn slain—The Lamanites are driven from the land, and peace is established—Helaman returns to the ministry and builds up the Church. About 62–57 B.C.

AND now it came to pass that when
Moroni had received this epistle
his heart did take courage, and was
filled with exceedingly great joy because of the faithfulness of Pahoran,
that he was not also a [a]traitor to the
freedom and cause of his country.
2 But he did also mourn exceedingly because of the iniquity of those
who had driven Pahoran from the
judgment-seat, yea, in fine because
of those who had rebelled against
their country and also their God.
3 And it came to pass that Moroni
took a small number of men, according to the desire of Pahoran,
and gave Lehi and Teancum command over the remainder of his
army, and took his march towards
the land of Gideon.
4 And he did raise the [a]standard
of [b]liberty in whatsoever place he
did enter, and gained whatsoever
force he could in all his march towards the land of Gideon.
5 And it came to pass that thousands did [a]flock unto his standard,
and did take up their swords in the
defence of their freedom, that they
might not come into bondage.
6 And thus, when Moroni had
gathered together whatsoever men
he could in all his march, he came
to the land of Gideon; and uniting
his forces with those of Pahoran
they became exceedingly strong,
even stronger than the men of
Pachus, who was the [a]king of those
dissenters who had driven the
[b]freemen out of the land of Zarahemla and had taken possession
of the land.
7 And it came to pass that Moroni and Pahoran went down with
their armies into the land of Zarahemla, and went forth against the
city, and did meet the men of Pachus, insomuch that they did come
to battle.
8 And behold, Pachus was slain
and his men were taken prisoners,
and Pahoran was restored to his
judgment-seat.
9 And the men of Pachus received
their trial, according to the law, and
also those king-men who had been
taken and [a]cast into prison; and
they were [b]executed according to
the law; yea, those men of Pachus
and those [c]king-men, whosoever
would not take up arms in the defence of their country, but would
fight against it, were put to death.
10 And thus it became expedient
that this law should be strictly observed for the safety of their country; yea, and whosoever was found
denying their freedom was speedily [a]executed according to the law.
11 And thus ended the thirtieth
year of the reign of the judges over
the people of Nephi; Moroni and
Pahoran having restored peace to
the land of Zarahemla, among their
own people, having [a]inflicted death
upon all those who were not true
to the cause of freedom.
12 And it came to pass in the
commencement of the thirty and
first year of the reign of the judges
over the people of Nephi, Moroni
immediately caused that provisions
should be sent, and also an army
of six thousand men should be sent
unto Helaman, to assist him in preserving that part of the land.
13 And he also caused that an

62 1*a* Alma 60:18.
4*a* Alma 46:36 (12–13, 36).
b TG Liberty.
5*a* Alma 61:6.
6*a* Alma 61:8 (4–8).
b Alma 51:6 (6–7).
9*a* Alma 51:19.
b TG Capital Punishment.
c Alma 51:5 (5, 17, 21); 60:16.
10*a* 1 Kgs. 2:46.
11*a* Alma 44:7; 57:19.

army of six thousand men, with a sufficient quantity of food, should be sent to the armies of Lehi and Teancum. And it came to pass that this was done to fortify the land against the Lamanites.

14 And it came to pass that Moroni and Pahoran, leaving a large body of men in the land of Zarahemla, took their march with a large body of men towards the land of Nephihah, being determined to [a]overthrow the Lamanites in that city.

15 And it came to pass that as they were marching towards the land, they took a large body of men of the Lamanites, and slew many of them, and took their provisions and their weapons of war.

16 And it came to pass after they had taken them, they caused them to enter into a [a]covenant that they would no more take up their weapons of war against the Nephites.

17 And when they had entered into this covenant they sent them to [a]dwell with the people of Ammon, and they were in number about four thousand who had not been slain.

18 And it came to pass that when they had sent them away they pursued their march towards the land of [a]Nephihah. And it came to pass that when they had come to the city of Nephihah, they did pitch their tents in the plains of Nephihah, which is near the city of Nephihah.

19 Now Moroni was desirous that the Lamanites should come out to battle against them, upon the plains; but the Lamanites, knowing of their exceedingly great courage, and beholding the greatness of their numbers, therefore they durst not come out against them; therefore they did not come to battle in that day.

20 And when the night came, Moroni went forth in the darkness of the night, and came upon the top of the wall to spy out in what part of the city the Lamanites did camp with their army.

21 And it came to pass that they were on the east, by the entrance; and they were all asleep. And now Moroni returned to his army, and caused that they should prepare in haste strong cords and ladders, to be let down from the top of the [a]wall into the inner part of the wall.

22 And it came to pass that Moroni caused that his men should march forth and come upon the top of the wall, and let [a]themselves down into that part of the city, yea, even on the west, where the Lamanites did not camp with their armies.

23 And it came to pass that they were all let down into the city by night, by the means of their strong cords and their ladders; thus when the morning came they were all within the walls of the city.

24 And now, when the Lamanites awoke and saw that the armies of Moroni were within the walls, they were affrighted exceedingly, insomuch that they did flee out by the pass.

25 And now when Moroni saw that they were fleeing before him, he did cause that his men should march forth against them, and slew many, and surrounded many others, and took them prisoners; and the remainder of them fled into the land of Moroni, which was in the borders by the seashore.

26 Thus had Moroni and Pahoran obtained the [a]possession of the city of Nephihah without the loss of one soul; and there were many of the Lamanites who were slain.

27 Now it came to pass that many of the Lamanites that were prisoners were desirous to [a]join the people of Ammon and become a free people.

28 And it came to pass that as many as were desirous, unto them it was granted according to their desires.

29 Therefore, all the prisoners of

14*a* Alma 59:11 (5–11).
16*a* Alma 44:15, 20; 3 Ne. 5:4.
17*a* Alma 47:29.
18*a* Alma 50:14; 51:26 (24–26).
21*a* Alma 49:13 (13, 18–24).
22*a* Alma 55:16.
26*a* Alma 59:8.
27*a* Alma 24:26 (25–27).

the Lamanites did join the people of Ammon, and did begin to labor exceedingly, tilling the ground, raising all manner of grain, and flocks and herds of every kind; and thus were the Nephites relieved from a great burden; yea, insomuch that they were relieved from all the prisoners of the Lamanites.

30 Now it came to pass that Moroni, after he had obtained possession of the city of Nephihah, having taken many prisoners, which did reduce the armies of the Lamanites exceedingly, and having regained many of the Nephites who had been taken prisoners, which did strengthen the army of Moroni exceedingly; therefore Moroni went forth from the land of Nephihah to the land of [a]Lehi.

31 And it came to pass that when the Lamanites saw that Moroni was coming against them, they were again frightened and fled before the army of Moroni.

32 And it came to pass that [a]Moroni and his army did pursue them from city to city, until they were met by Lehi and Teancum; and the Lamanites fled from Lehi and Teancum, even down upon the borders by the seashore, until they came to the land of Moroni.

33 And the armies of the Lamanites were all gathered together, insomuch that they were all in one body in the land of Moroni. Now Ammoron, the king of the Lamanites, was also with them.

34 And it came to pass that Moroni and Lehi and Teancum did encamp with their armies round about in the borders of the land of Moroni, insomuch that the Lamanites were encircled about in the borders by the wilderness on the south, and in the borders by the wilderness on the east.

35 And thus they did encamp for the night. For behold, the Nephites and the Lamanites also were weary because of the greatness of the march; therefore they did not resolve upon any stratagem in the night-time, save it were Teancum; for he was exceedingly angry with Ammoron, insomuch that he considered that Ammoron, and Amalickiah his brother, had been the [a]cause of this great and lasting war between them and the Lamanites, which had been the cause of so much war and bloodshed, yea, and so much famine.

36 And it came to pass that Teancum in his anger did go forth into the camp of the Lamanites, and did let himself down over the walls of the city. And he went forth with a cord, from place to place, insomuch that he did find the king; and he did [a]cast a javelin at him, which did pierce him near the heart. But behold, the king did awaken his servants before he died, insomuch that they did pursue Teancum, and slew him.

37 Now it came to pass that when Lehi and Moroni knew that Teancum was dead they were exceedingly sorrowful; for behold, he had been a man who had [a]fought valiantly for his country, yea, a true friend to liberty; and he had suffered very many exceedingly sore afflictions. But behold, he was dead, and had gone the way of all the earth.

38 Now it came to pass that Moroni marched forth on the morrow, and came upon the Lamanites, insomuch that they did slay them with a great slaughter; and they did drive them out of the land; and they did flee, even that they did not return at that time against the Nephites.

39 And thus ended the thirty and first year of the reign of the judges over the people of Nephi; and thus they had had wars, and bloodsheds, and famine, and affliction, for the space of many years.

40 And there had been murders,

30*a* Alma 50:15; 51:26 (24–26).
32*a* Alma 50:13; 51:22 (22–23); 3 Ne. 8:9.
35*a* Alma 48:1.
36*a* Alma 51:34.
37*a* IE throughout the Amalickiah-Ammoron wars. Alma 50:35; 51:29–34; 52; 61; 62:3–37.

and contentions, and dissensions,
and all manner of iniquity among
the people of Nephi; nevertheless
for the [a]righteous' sake, yea, because
of the prayers of the righteous, they
were spared.
41 But behold, because of the exceedingly great length of the war
between the Nephites and the Lamanites many had become hardened, because of the exceedingly
great length of the war; and many
were softened because of their [a]af-
flictions, insomuch that they did
humble themselves before God, even
in the depth of humility.
42 And it came to pass that after
Moroni had fortified those parts of
the land which were most exposed
to the Lamanites, until they were
sufficiently strong, he returned to
the city of Zarahemla; and also Helaman returned to the place of his
inheritance; and there was once
more peace established among the
people of Nephi.
43 And Moroni yielded up the
[a]command of his armies into the
hands of his son, whose name was
[b]Moronihah; and he retired to his
own house that he might spend the
remainder of his days in peace.
44 And Pahoran did return to his
judgment-seat; and Helaman did
take upon him again to preach unto
the people the word of God; for
because of so many wars and contentions it had become expedient
that a [a]regulation should be made
again in the church.
45 Therefore, Helaman and his
brethren went forth, and did declare the word of God with much
power unto the [a]convincing of many
people of their wickedness, which
did cause them to repent of their
sins and to be baptized unto the
Lord their God.
46 And it came to pass that they
did establish again the church of
God, throughout all the land.
47 Yea, and regulations were made
concerning the law. And their
[a]judges, and their chief judges were
chosen.
48 And the people of Nephi began to [a]prosper again in the land,
and began to multiply and to wax
exceedingly strong again in the
land. And they began to grow exceedingly rich.
49 But notwithstanding their
riches, or their strength, or their
prosperity, they were not lifted up
in the pride of their eyes; neither
were they [a]slow to remember the
Lord their God; but they did humble
themselves exceedingly before him.
50 Yea, they did remember how
great things the Lord had done for
them, that he had [a]delivered them
from death, and from bonds, and
from prisons, and from all manner
of [b]afflictions, and he had [c]deliv-
ered them out of the hands of their
enemies.
51 And they did pray unto the
Lord their God continually, insomuch that the Lord did bless them,
according to his word, so that they
did wax strong and [a]prosper in the
land.
52 And it came to pass that all
these things were done. And [a]He-
laman died, in the thirty and fifth
year of the reign of the judges over
the people of Nephi.

CHAPTER 63

Shiblon and later Helaman take possession of the sacred records—Many Nephites travel to the land northward—Hagoth builds ships, which sail forth in the west sea—Moronihah defeats the Lamanites in battle. About 56–52 B.C.

40*a* Alma 45:15 (15–16); 46:10.
41*a* TG Adversity; Affliction.
43*a* Hel. 4:16 (10, 16).
b Alma 63:15.
44*a* Alma 45:21.
45*a* Alma 21:17; D&C 18:44.
47*a* Mosiah 29:39.
48*a* Alma 50:20.
49*a* Alma 55:31.
50*a* 2 Cor. 11:26 (24–33).
b TG Adversity.
c TG Deliver.
51*a* Gen. 26:22. TG Prosper.
52*a* His great career spans Alma 31–62.

AND it came to pass in the commencement of the thirty and sixth year of the reign of the judges over the people of Nephi, that [a]Shiblon took possession of those [b]sacred things which had been delivered unto Helaman by Alma.

2 And he was a just man, and he did walk uprightly before God; and he did observe to do good continually, to keep the commandments of the Lord his God; and also did his brother.

3 And it came to pass that [a]Moroni died also. And thus ended the thirty and sixth year of the reign of the judges.

4 And it came to pass that in the thirty and seventh year of the reign of the judges, there was a large company of men, even to the amount of five thousand and four hundred men, with their wives and their children, departed out of the land of Zarahemla into the land which was [a]northward.

5 And it came to pass that Hagoth, he being an [a]exceedingly curious man, therefore he went forth and built him an exceedingly large ship, on the borders of the land [b]Bountiful, by the land Desolation, and launched it forth into the west sea, by the [c]narrow neck which led into the land northward.

6 And behold, there were many of the Nephites who did enter therein and did sail forth with much provisions, and also many women and children; and they took their course northward. And thus ended the thirty and seventh year.

7 And in the thirty and eighth year, this man built [a]other ships. And the first ship did also return, and many more people did enter into it; and they also took much provisions, and set out again to the land northward.

8 And it came to pass that they were never heard of more. And we suppose that they were drowned in the depths of the sea. And it came to pass that one other ship also did sail forth; and whither she did go we know not.

9 And it came to pass that in this year there were many people who went forth into the land [a]northward. And thus ended the thirty and eighth year.

10 And it came to pass in the thirty and ninth year of the reign of the judges, [a]Shiblon died also, and Corianton had gone forth to the land northward in a ship, to carry forth provisions unto the people who had gone forth into that land.

11 Therefore it became expedient for [a]Shiblon to confer those sacred things, before his death, upon the son of [b]Helaman, who was called [c]Helaman, being called after the name of his father.

12 Now behold, all those [a]engravings which were in the possession of Helaman were written and sent forth among the children of men throughout all the land, save it were those parts which had been commanded by Alma should [b]not go forth.

13 Nevertheless, these things were to be kept sacred, and [a]handed down from one generation to another; therefore, in this year, they had been conferred upon Helaman, before the death of Shiblon.

14 And it came to pass also in this year that there were some dissenters

63 1*a* Alma 38:1 (1–2); 49:30.
b Mosiah 1:3; Alma 37:1 (1–12). TG Sacred.
3*a* See Alma 43–63 for his great contributions.
4*a* Alma 22:31; 46:17; Hel. 3:3.
5*a* Hel. 3:10 (10, 14).
b Alma 53:3 (3–4); Hel. 1:23.
c Alma 22:32; Morm. 2:29; Ether 10:20.
7*a* Hel. 3:10.
9*a* Hel. 3:12 (11–12); 6:6.
10*a* Alma 31:7.
11*a* Alma 63:1.
b See heading to the book of Helaman.
c Hel. 3:37.
12*a* Alma 18:36; 3 Ne. 1:2.
b Alma 37:27 (27–32).
13*a* Alma 37:4.

who had gone forth unto the Lamanites; and they were [a]stirred up
again to anger against the Nephites.
15 And also in this same year
they came down with a numerous
army to war against the people
of [a]Moronihah, or against the army of
Moronihah, in the which they were
beaten and driven back again to
their own lands, suffering great loss.
16 And thus ended the thirty and
ninth year of the reign of the judges
over the people of Nephi.
17 And thus ended the account of
[a]Alma, and Helaman his son, and
also Shiblon, who was his son.

THE BOOK OF HELAMAN

An account of the Nephites. Their wars and contentions, and their dissensions. And also the prophecies of many holy prophets, before the coming of Christ, according to the records of Helaman, who was the son of Helaman, and also according to the records of his sons, even down to the coming of Christ. And also many of the Lamanites are converted. An account of their conversion. An account of the righteousness of the Lamanites, and the wickedness and abominations of the Nephites, according to the record of Helaman and his sons, even down to the coming of Christ, which is called the book of Helaman, and so forth.

CHAPTER 1

Pahoran the second becomes chief judge and is murdered by Kishkumen—Pacumeni fills the judgment seat—Coriantumr leads the Lamanite armies, takes Zarahemla, and slays Pacumeni—Moronihah defeats the Lamanites and retakes Zarahemla, and Coriantumr is slain. About 52–50 B.C.

AND now behold, it came to pass
in the commencement of the
fortieth year of the reign of
the judges over the people of Nephi,
there began to be a serious difficulty
among the people of the Nephites.
2 For behold, [a]Pahoran had died,
and gone the way of all the earth;
therefore there began to be a serious
contention concerning who should
have the judgment-seat among the
brethren, who were the sons of
Pahoran.
3 Now these are their names who
did contend for the judgment-seat,
who did also cause the people to
contend: Pahoran, Paanchi, and
Pacumeni.
4 Now these are not all the sons
of Pahoran (for he had many), but
these are they who did contend for
the judgment-seat; therefore, they
did cause three [a]divisions among
the people.
5 Nevertheless, it came to pass
that Pahoran was appointed by
the [a]voice of the people to be chief
judge and a governor over the people
of Nephi.
6 And it came to pass that Pacumeni, when he saw that he could
not obtain the judgment-seat, he
did [a]unite with the voice of the
people.
7 But behold, Paanchi, and that
part of the people that were desirous that he should be their governor,
was exceedingly wroth; therefore,

14*a* Alma 51:9; Hel. 4:4.
15*a* Alma 62:43.
17*a* Alma 1:2 (1–2).

[HELAMAN]

1 2*a* Alma 50:40.
4*a* Matt. 12:25.
5*a* Mosiah 29:11; Alma 51:7; Hel. 5:2.
6*a* TG Unity.

he was about to [a]flatter away those
people to rise up in rebellion against
their brethren.
8 And it came to pass as he was
about to do this, behold, he was
taken, and was tried according to
the [a]voice of the people, and condemned unto death; for he had
raised up in rebellion and sought to
destroy the [b]liberty of the people.
9 Now when those people who
were desirous that he should be
their governor saw that he was
condemned unto death, therefore
they were angry, and behold, they
sent forth one [a]Kishkumen, even to
the judgment-seat of Pahoran, and
murdered Pahoran as he sat upon
the judgment-seat.
10 And he was pursued by the
servants of Pahoran; but behold, so
speedy was the flight of Kishkumen
that no man could overtake him.
11 And he went unto those that
sent him, and they all entered into
a covenant, yea, [a]swearing by their
everlasting Maker, that they would
tell no man that Kishkumen had
murdered Pahoran.
12 Therefore, Kishkumen was not
known among the people of Nephi,
for he was in disguise at the time
that he murdered Pahoran. And
Kishkumen and his band, who had
covenanted with him, did mingle
themselves among the people, in a
manner that they all could not be
found; but as many as were found
were condemned unto [a]death.
13 And now behold, Pacumeni was
appointed, according to the [a]voice
of the people, to be a chief judge
and a governor over the people, to
reign in the stead of his brother
Pahoran; and it was according to
his right. And all this was done in
the fortieth year of the reign of the
judges; and it had an end.
14 And it came to pass in the forty
and first year of the reign of the
judges, that the Lamanites had
gathered together an innumerable
army of men, and [a]armed them with
swords, and with cimeters and
with bows, and with arrows, and with
head-plates, and with breastplates,
and with all manner of shields of
every kind.
15 And they came down again that
they might pitch battle against the
Nephites. And they were led by a
man whose name was [a]Coriantumr;
and he was a descendant of Zarahemla; and he was a [b]dissenter from
among the Nephites; and he was a
large and a mighty man.
16 Therefore, the king of the Lamanites, whose name was Tubal-
oth, who was the son of [a]Ammoron,
supposing that Coriantumr, being
a mighty man, could stand against
the Nephites, with his strength and
also with his great [b]wisdom, insomuch that by sending him forth
he should gain power over the
Nephites—
17 Therefore he did [a]stir them up
to anger, and he did gather together
his armies, and he did appoint Coriantumr to be their leader, and
did cause that they should march
down to the land of Zarahemla to
battle against the Nephites.
18 And it came to pass that because
of so much contention and so much
difficulty in the government, that
they had not kept sufficient guards
in the land of Zarahemla; for they
had supposed that the Lamanites
durst not come into the heart of
their lands to attack that great city
Zarahemla.
19 But it came to pass that Coriantumr did march forth at the head
of his numerous host, and came
upon the inhabitants of the city,
and their march was with such
exceedingly great speed that there

7a Mosiah 27:8; Alma 50:35; Hel. 2:5; Ether 8:2.
8a Alma 1:14 (10–15).
b TG Liberty.
9a Hel. 2:3.
11a Gen. 24:3; Ether 8:14 (13–14).
12a TG Capital Punishment.
13a Hel. 1:5; 2:2.
14a Alma 2:12; 49:6 (6, 24).
15a Hel. 1:30.
b Alma 31:8; 53:8; Hel. 4:8.
16a Alma 52:3.
b Ezek. 28:5 (4–5).
17a Alma 35:10; 47:1.

was no time for the Nephites to
gather together their armies.
20 Therefore Coriantumr did cut
down the watch by the entrance
of the city, and did march forth
with his whole army into the city,
and they did slay every one who
did oppose them, insomuch that
they did take possession of the
whole city.
21 And it came to pass that Pacumeni, who was the chief judge, did
flee before Coriantumr, even to
the walls of the city. And it came
to pass that Coriantumr did smite
him against the wall, insomuch that
he died. And thus ended the days
of Pacumeni.
22 And now when Coriantumr
saw that he was in possession of
the city of Zarahemla, and saw that
the Nephites had fled before them,
and were slain, and were taken, and
were cast into prison, and that he
had obtained the possession of the
strongest hold in all the land, his
heart [a]took courage insomuch that
he was about to go forth against all
the land.
23 And now he did not tarry in
the land of Zarahemla, but he did
march forth with a large army, even
towards the city of [a]Bountiful; for
it was his determination to go forth
and cut his way through with the
sword, that he might obtain the
north parts of the land.
24 And, supposing that their greatest strength was in the center of the
land, therefore he did march forth,
giving them no time to assemble
themselves together save it were in
small bodies; and in this manner
they did fall upon them and cut
them down to the earth.
25 But behold, this march of Coriantumr through the center of the
land gave Moronihah great advantage over them, notwithstanding
the greatness of the number of the
Nephites who were slain.
26 For behold, Moronihah had
supposed that the Lamanites durst
not come into the center of the
land, but that they would attack the
cities round about in the borders
as they had hitherto done; therefore Moronihah had caused that
their strong armies should maintain those parts round about by the
borders.
27 But behold, the Lamanites were
not frightened according to his desire, but they had come into the
center of the land, and had taken
the capital city which was the city
of Zarahemla, and were marching
through the most capital parts of
the land, slaying the people with a
great slaughter, both men, women,
and children, taking possession of
many cities and of many strongholds.
28 But when Moronihah had discovered this, he immediately sent
forth Lehi with an army round about
to [a]head them before they should
come to the land Bountiful.
29 And thus he did; and he did
head them before they came to the
land Bountiful, and gave unto them
battle, insomuch that they began
to retreat back towards the land
of Zarahemla.
30 And it came to pass that Moronihah did head them in their retreat,
and did give unto them battle, insomuch that it became an exceedingly bloody battle; yea, many were
slain, and among the number who
were slain [a]Coriantumr was also
found.
31 And now, behold, the Lamanites
could not retreat either way, neither
on the north, nor on the south, nor on
the east, nor on the west, for they
were surrounded on every hand by
the Nephites.
32 And thus had Coriantumr
plunged the Lamanites into the
midst of the Nephites, insomuch
that they were in the power of the
Nephites, and he himself was slain,
and the Lamanites did [a]yield themselves into the hands of the Nephites.

22*a* TG Pride.
23*a* Alma 22:29.
28*a* Alma 50:34; 51:29 (29–30).
30*a* Hel. 1:15.
32*a* Hel. 4:3.

33 And it came to pass that Moronihah took possession of the city of
Zarahemla again, and caused that
the Lamanites who had been taken
prisoners should depart out of the
land in [a]peace.
34 And thus ended the forty and
first year of the reign of the judges.

CHAPTER 2

Helaman, the son of Helaman, becomes chief judge—Gadianton leads the band of Kishkumen—Helaman's servant slays Kishkumen, and the Gadianton band flees into the wilderness. About 50–49 B.C.

AND it came to pass in the forty
and second year of the reign of
the judges, after Moronihah had
established again peace between
the Nephites and the Lamanites,
behold there was no one to fill the
judgment-seat; therefore there began to be a contention again among
the people concerning who should
fill the judgment-seat.
2 And it came to pass that [a]Hela-
man, who was the son of Helaman,
was appointed to fill the judgment-
seat, by the [b]voice of the people.
3 But behold, [a]Kishkumen, who
had murdered Pahoran, did lay
wait to destroy Helaman also; and
he was upheld by his band, who
had entered into a covenant that no
one should know his wickedness.
4 For there was one [a]Gadianton,
who was exceedingly expert in many
words, and also in his craft, to carry
on the secret work of murder and
of robbery; therefore he became the
leader of the band of Kishkumen.
5 Therefore he did [a]flatter them,
and also Kishkumen, that if they
would place him in the judgment-
seat he would grant unto those
who belonged to his band that they
should be placed in power and authority among the people; therefore Kishkumen sought to destroy
Helaman.
6 And it came to pass as he went
forth towards the judgment-seat
to destroy Helaman, behold one of
the servants of Helaman, having
been out by night, and having obtained, through disguise, a knowledge of those plans which had
been laid by this band to destroy
Helaman—
7 And it came to pass that he met
Kishkumen, and he gave unto him
a sign; therefore Kishkumen made
known unto him the object of his
desire, desiring that he would conduct him to the judgment-seat that
he might murder Helaman.
8 And when the servant of Helaman had known all the heart of
Kishkumen, and how that it was his
[a]object to murder, and also that it
was the object of all those who belonged to his band to murder, and
to rob, and to gain power, (and this
was their [b]secret plan, and their
combination) the servant of Helaman said unto Kishkumen: Let us
go forth unto the judgment-seat.
9 Now this did please Kishkumen
exceedingly, for he did suppose that
he should accomplish his design;
but behold, the servant of Helaman,
as they were going forth unto the
judgment-seat, did stab Kishkumen
even to the heart, that he fell dead
without a groan. And he ran and
told Helaman all the things which
he had seen, and heard, and done.
10 And it came to pass that Helaman did send forth to take this
band of robbers and [a]secret murderers, that they might be executed
according to the law.
11 But behold, when Gadianton
had found that Kishkumen did not
return he feared lest that he should
be destroyed; therefore he caused
that his band should follow him.
And they took their flight out of

33*a* Alma 44:15.
2 2*a* Hel. 3:20.
b Hel. 1:13.
3*a* Hel. 1:9.
4*a* Hel. 3:23; 6:18 (18, 29).
5*a* Mosiah 27:8; Alma 50:35; Hel. 1:7; Ether 8:2. TG Flatter.
8*a* TG Conspiracy.
b 2 Ne. 10:15; Moses 5:31 (18–31). TG Secret Combinations.
10*a* Hel. 3:23.

the land, by a secret way, into the
wilderness; and thus when Helaman
sent forth to take them they could
nowhere be found.
12 And more of this Gadianton
shall be spoken hereafter. And thus
ended the forty and second year
of the reign of the judges over the
people of Nephi.
13 And behold, in the end of this
book ye shall see that this [a]Gadian-
ton did prove the overthrow, yea,
almost the entire destruction of the
people of Nephi.
14 Behold I do not mean the end
of the [a]book of Helaman, but I
mean the end of the book of Nephi,
from which I have taken all the
account which I have written.

CHAPTER 3

Many Nephites migrate to the land northward—They build houses of cement and keep many records—Tens of thousands are converted and baptized—The word of God leads men to salvation—Nephi the son of Helaman fills the judgment seat. About 49–39 B.C.

AND now it came to pass in the forty
and third year of the reign of the
judges, there was no contention
among the people of Nephi save
it were a little pride which was in
the church, which did cause some
little dissensions among the people,
which affairs were settled in the
ending of the forty and third year.
2 And there was no contention
among the people in the forty
and fourth year; neither was there
much contention in the forty and
fifth year.
3 And it came to pass in the forty
and sixth, yea, there was much contention and many dissensions; in the
which there were an exceedingly
great many who departed out of
the land of Zarahemla, and went
forth unto the land [a]northward to
inherit the land.
4 And they did travel to an exceedingly great distance, insomuch
that they came to [a]large bodies of
water and many rivers.
5 Yea, and even they did spread
forth into all parts of the land,
into whatever parts it had not been
rendered desolate and without timber, because of the many inhabitants who had before inherited the
land.
6 And now no part of the land was
desolate, save it were for timber;
but because of the greatness of the
[a]destruction of the people who had
before inhabited the land it was
called [b]desolate.
7 And there being but little timber
upon the face of the land, nevertheless the people who went forth
became exceedingly [a]expert in the
working of cement; therefore they
did build houses of cement, in the
which they did dwell.
8 And it came to pass that they
did multiply and spread, and did
go forth from the land southward
to the land northward, and did
spread insomuch that they began
to cover the face of the whole earth,
from the sea south to the sea north,
from the [a]sea west to the sea east.
9 And the people who were in the
land northward did dwell in [a]tents,
and in houses of cement, and they
did suffer whatsoever tree should
spring up upon the face of the
land that it should grow up, that
in time they might have timber to
build their houses, yea, their cities,
and their temples, and their [b]syna-
gogues, and their sanctuaries, and
all manner of their buildings.
10 And it came to pass as timber
was exceedingly scarce in the land
northward, they did send forth
much by the way of [a]shipping.

13*a* Hel. 6:18; 3 Ne. 4:1.
14*a* W of M 1:9; 3 Ne. 5:10.
3 3*a* Alma 63:4.
4*a* Mosiah 8:8; Alma 50:29; Morm. 6:4.
6*a* Mosiah 8:8; 21:26 (26–27).
b Alma 22:31.
7*a* TG Skill.
8*a* Alma 22:27 (27, 32–33); Hel. 11:20.
9*a* Gen. 25:27; Ether 2:13.
b Alma 16:13.
10*a* Alma 63:7 (5–8).

11 And thus they did enable the people in the land northward that they might build many cities, both of wood and of cement.

12 And it came to pass that there were many of the [a]people of Ammon, who were Lamanites by birth, did also go forth into this land.

13 And now there are many [a]records kept of the proceedings of this people, by many of this people, which are particular and very large, concerning them.

14 But behold, a [a]hundredth part of the proceedings of this people, yea, the account of the Lamanites and of the Nephites, and their wars, and contentions, and dissensions, and their preaching, and their prophecies, and their shipping and their building of ships, and their building of [b]temples, and of synagogues and their [c]sanctuaries, and their righteousness, and their wickedness, and their murders, and their robbings, and their plundering, and all manner of abominations and whoredoms, cannot be contained in this work.

15 But behold, there are many books and many [a]records of every kind, and they have been kept chiefly by the Nephites.

16 And they have been [a]handed down from one generation to another by the Nephites, even until they have fallen into transgression and have been murdered, plundered, and hunted, and driven forth, and slain, and [b]scattered upon the face of the earth, and mixed with the Lamanites until they are [c]no more called the Nephites, becoming wicked, and wild, and ferocious, yea, even becoming Lamanites.

17 And now I return again to mine account; therefore, what I have spoken had passed after there had been great contentions, and disturbances, and wars, and dissensions, among the people of Nephi.

18 The forty and sixth year of the reign of the judges ended;

19 And it came to pass that there was still great contention in the land, yea, even in the forty and seventh year, and also in the forty and eighth year.

20 Nevertheless [a]Helaman did fill the judgment-seat with justice and equity; yea, he did observe to keep the statutes, and the judgments, and the commandments of God; and he did do that which was right in the sight of God continually; and he did walk after the ways of his father, insomuch that he did prosper in the land.

21 And it came to pass that he had two sons. He gave unto the eldest the name of [a]Nephi, and unto the youngest, the name of Lehi. And they began to grow up unto the Lord.

22 And it came to pass that the wars and contentions began to cease, in a small degree, among the people of the Nephites, in the latter end of the forty and eighth year of the reign of the judges over the people of Nephi.

23 And it came to pass in the forty and ninth year of the reign of the judges, there was continual peace established in the land, all save it were the [a]secret combinations which [b]Gadianton the robber had established in the more settled parts of the land, which at that time were not known unto those who were at the head of government; therefore they were not destroyed out of the land.

24 And it came to pass that in this same year there was exceedingly great prosperity in the church, insomuch that there were thousands who did [a]join themselves unto the

12*a* Alma 27:26; 63:9 (4–9); Hel. 6:6.
13*a* W of M 1:3 (1–11).
14*a* 3 Ne. 5:8; 26:6 (6–11).
b 2 Ne. 5:16; Jacob 1:17; 3 Ne. 11:1.
c Alma 23:2.
15*a* 3 Ne. 5:9; 4 Ne. 1:48.
16*a* 1 Ne. 5:18 (16–19); Alma 37:4.
b Ezek. 36:19 (16–20).
c Alma 45:13 (12–14).
20*a* Hel. 2:2.
21*a* Hel. 3:37; 4:14; 5:4–5; 3 Ne. 1:2.
23*a* 2 Ne. 10:15; Hel. 2:10 (8–10); 7:25 (4–5, 21, 25).
b Hel. 2:4; 6:18.
24*a* Mosiah 25:23.

church and were baptized unto repentance.

25 And so great was the prosperity of the church, and so many the blessings which were poured out upon the people, that even the high priests and the teachers were themselves astonished beyond measure.

26 And it came to pass that the work of the Lord did prosper unto the baptizing and uniting to the church of God, many souls, yea, even tens of thousands.

27 Thus we may see that the Lord is merciful unto all who will, in the sincerity of their hearts, call upon his holy name.

28 Yea, thus we see that the [a]gate of heaven is open unto [b]all, even to those who will believe on the name of Jesus Christ, who is the Son of God.

29 Yea, we see that whosoever will may lay hold upon the [a]word of God, which is [b]quick and powerful, which shall [c]divide asunder all the cunning and the snares and the wiles of the devil, and lead the man of Christ in a strait and [d]narrow course across that everlasting [e]gulf of misery which is prepared to engulf the wicked—

30 And land their souls, yea, their immortal souls, at the [a]right hand of God in the kingdom of heaven, to sit down with Abraham, and Isaac, and with Jacob, and with all our holy fathers, to go no more out.

31 And in this year there was continual rejoicing in the land of Zarahemla, and in all the regions round about, even in all the land which was possessed by the Nephites.

32 And it came to pass that there was peace and exceedingly great joy in the remainder of the forty and ninth year; yea, and also there was continual peace and great joy in the fiftieth year of the reign of the judges.

33 And in the fifty and first year of the reign of the judges there was peace also, save it were the pride which began to enter into the church—not into the church of God, but into the hearts of the people who [a]professed to belong to the church of God—

34 And they were lifted up in [a]pride, even to the persecution of many of their brethren. Now this was a great evil, which did cause the more humble part of the people to suffer great persecutions, and to wade through much affliction.

35 Nevertheless they did [a]fast and [b]pray oft, and did wax stronger and stronger in their [c]humility, and firmer and firmer in the faith of Christ, unto the filling their souls with joy and consolation, yea, even to the [d]purifying and the [e]sanctification of their hearts, which sanctification cometh because of their [f]yielding their hearts unto God.

36 And it came to pass that the fifty and second year ended in peace also, save it were the exceedingly great pride which had gotten into the hearts of the people; and it was because of their exceedingly great [a]riches and their prosperity in the land; and it did grow upon them from day to day.

37 And it came to pass in the fifty and third year of the reign of the judges, [a]Helaman died, and his eldest son [b]Nephi began to reign in his stead. And it came to pass that he did fill the judgment-seat with justice and equity; yea, he did keep

28*a* Isa. 26:2.
b Acts 10:28 (9–35, 44); Rom. 2:11 (10–11).
29*a* Micah 2:7; Jacob 2:8; D&C 11:2; 33:1. TG Gospel.
b Heb. 4:12; D&C 27:1.
c D&C 6:2.
d 2 Ne. 9:41; 33:9.
e 1 Ne. 12:18; 15:28 (28–30).
30*a* Matt. 25:34 (31–46).
33*a* D&C 112:26.
34*a* TG Pride.
35*a* TG Fast, Fasting.
b TG Prayer.
c TG Humility.
d TG Cleanliness; Purification; Purity.
e TG Sanctification.
f 2 Chr. 30:8; Rom. 6:13 (12–14). TG Submissiveness; Teachable.
36*a* TG Treasure.
37*a* Alma 63:11; Hel. 16:25.
b Hel. 3:21; 5:1.

the commandments of God, and
did walk in the ways of his father.

CHAPTER 4

Nephite dissenters and the Lamanites join forces and take the land of Zarahemla—The Nephites' defeats come because of their wickedness—The Church dwindles, and the people become weak like the Lamanites. About 38–30 B.C.

AND it came to pass in the fifty and
fourth year there were many dissensions in the church, and there
was also a [a]contention among the
people, insomuch that there was
much bloodshed.
2 And the rebellious part were
slain and driven out of the land,
and they did go unto the king of
the Lamanites.
3 And it came to pass that they did
endeavor to stir up the Lamanites
to [a]war against the Nephites; but
behold, the Lamanites were [b]exceed-
ingly afraid, insomuch that they
would not hearken to the words of
those dissenters.
4 But it came to pass in the fifty
and sixth year of the reign of the
judges, there were [a]dissenters who
went up from the Nephites unto the
Lamanites; and they succeeded with
those others in [b]stirring them up to
anger against the Nephites; and they
were all that year preparing for war.
5 And in the fifty and seventh
year they did come down against
the Nephites to battle, and they
did commence the work of death;
yea, insomuch that in the fifty and
eighth year of the reign of the judges
they succeeded in obtaining [a]pos-
session of the land of Zarahemla;
yea, and also all the lands, even unto
the land which was near the land
Bountiful.
6 And the Nephites and the armies
of Moronihah were driven even into
the land of Bountiful;
7 And there they did fortify against
the Lamanites, from the west sea,
even unto the east; it being a [a]day's
journey for a Nephite, on the line
which they had fortified and stationed their armies to defend their
north country.
8 And thus those [a]dissenters of
the Nephites, with the help of a
numerous army of the Lamanites,
had obtained all the possession of
the Nephites which was in the land
southward. And all this was done
in the fifty and eighth and ninth
years of the reign of the judges.
9 And it came to pass in the sixti-
eth year of the reign of the judges,
Moronihah did succeed with his
armies in obtaining many parts of
the land; yea, they regained many
cities which had fallen into the
hands of the Lamanites.
10 And it came to pass in the sixty
and first year of the reign of the
judges they succeeded in regaining
even the half of all their possessions.
11 Now this great loss of the Nephites, and the great slaughter which
was among them, [a]would not have
happened had it not been for their
[b]wickedness and their abomination
which was among them; yea, and it
was among those also who professed
to belong to the church of God.
12 And it was because of the [a]pride
of their hearts, because of their exceeding [b]riches, yea, it was because
of their oppression to the [c]poor,
withholding their food from the
hungry, withholding their clothing
from the naked, and smiting their
humble brethren upon the cheek,
making a [d]mock of that which
was sacred, denying the spirit of
prophecy and of revelation, murdering, plundering, lying, stealing,

4 1*a* 3 Ne. 11:29.
3*a* Hel. 11:24.
b Hel. 1:32 (30–33).
4*a* Hel. 5:17.
b Alma 63:14.
5*a* Hel. 5:16, 52.
7*a* Alma 22:32.
8*a* Hel. 1:15.
11*a* D&C 82:10.
b Mosiah 27:13.
12*a* Obad. 1:3 (3–4); 2 Ne. 20:33; D&C 101:42.
b 1 Tim. 6:17; 2 Ne. 9:42; 3 Ne. 6:12 (10–16).
c Ezek. 18:12; Zech. 7:10; D&C 42:30 (30–39, 71).
d TG Mocking; Sacrilege.

committing adultery, rising up in great contentions, and deserting away into the land of Nephi, among the Lamanites—

13 And because of this their great wickedness, and their [a]boastings in their own strength, they were left in their own strength; therefore they did not prosper, but were afflicted and smitten, and driven before the Lamanites, until they had lost possession of almost all their lands.

14 But behold, Moronihah did [a]preach many things unto the people because of their iniquity, and also [b]Nephi and Lehi, who were the sons of Helaman, did preach many things unto the people, yea, and did prophesy many things unto them concerning their iniquities, and what should come unto them if they did not repent of their sins.

15 And it came to pass that they did repent, and inasmuch as they did repent they did begin to prosper.

16 For when Moronihah saw that they did repent he did venture to [a]lead them forth from place to place, and from city to city, even until they had regained the one-half of their property and the one-half of all their lands.

17 And thus ended the sixty and first year of the reign of the judges.

18 And it came to pass in the sixty and second year of the reign of the judges, that Moronihah could obtain no more possessions over the Lamanites.

19 Therefore they did abandon their design to obtain the remainder of their lands, for so numerous were the Lamanites that it became impossible for the Nephites to obtain more power over them; therefore Moronihah did employ all his armies in maintaining those parts which he had taken.

20 And it came to pass, because of the greatness of the number of the Lamanites the Nephites were in great fear, lest they should be overpowered, and trodden down, and slain, and destroyed.

21 Yea, they began to remember the [a]prophecies of Alma, and also the [b]words of Mosiah; and they saw that they had been a [c]stiffnecked people, and that they had set at [d]naught the commandments of God;

22 And that they had altered and trampled under their feet the [a]laws of Mosiah, or that which the Lord commanded him to give unto the people; and they saw that their laws had become corrupted, and that they had become a wicked people, insomuch that they were wicked even like unto the Lamanites.

23 And because of their iniquity the church had begun to [a]dwindle; and they began to disbelieve in the spirit of prophecy and in the spirit of revelation; and the judgments of God did stare them in the face.

24 And they saw that they had become [a]weak, like unto their brethren, the Lamanites, and that the Spirit of the Lord did no more preserve them; yea, it had withdrawn from them because the Spirit of the Lord doth not [b]dwell in [c]unholy [d]temples—

25 Therefore the Lord did cease to preserve them by his miraculous and matchless power, for they had fallen into a state of [a]unbelief and awful wickedness; and they saw that the Lamanites were exceedingly more numerous than they, and except they should [b]cleave unto the Lord their God they must unavoidably perish.

26 For behold, they saw that the strength of the Lamanites was as

13*a* Ezek. 35:13.
TG Boast;
Trust Not in the Arm of Flesh.
14*a* Hel. 5:17 (14–20).
b Hel. 3:21.
16*a* Alma 62:43.
21*a* Alma 5:53 (1–62).
b Mosiah 29:27.
c TG Stiffnecked.
d Prov. 1:25.
22*a* Alma 1:1.
23*a* TG Apostasy of Individuals.
24*a* Jer. 46:15 (15–17);
Mosiah 1:13.
b TG Holy Ghost, Loss of.
c Mosiah 2:37;
Alma 7:21; 34:36.
d TG Temple.
25*a* TG Unbelief.
b Josh. 23:8;
Jacob 6:5;
D&C 11:19.

great as their strength, even man for
man. And thus had they fallen into
this great transgression; yea, thus
had they become [a]weak, because
of their transgression, in the space of
[b]not many years.

CHAPTER 5

Nephi and Lehi devote themselves to preaching—Their names invite them to pattern their lives after their forebears—Christ redeems those who repent—Nephi and Lehi make many converts and are imprisoned, and fire encircles them—A cloud of darkness overshadows three hundred people—The earth shakes, and a voice commands men to repent—Nephi and Lehi converse with angels, and the multitude is encircled by fire. About 30 B.C.

AND it came to pass that in this same
year, behold, [a]Nephi [b]delivered up
the judgment-seat to a man whose
name was [c]Cezoram.
2 For as their laws and their governments were established by the
[a]voice of the people, and they who
[b]chose evil were [c]more numerous
than they who chose good, therefore
they were [d]ripening for destruction,
for the laws had become corrupted.
3 Yea, and this was not all; they
were a [a]stiffnecked people, insomuch that they could not be governed by the law nor justice, save
it were to their destruction.
4 And it came to pass that Nephi
had become weary because of their
iniquity; and he yielded up the
judgment-seat, and took it upon
him to preach the word of God all
the remainder of his days, and his
brother Lehi also, all the remainder of his days;
5 For they remembered the words
which their [a]father Helaman spake
unto them. And these are the words
which he spake:
6 Behold, my sons, I desire that
ye should remember to keep the
commandments of God; and I
would that ye should declare unto
the people these words. Behold, I
have given unto you the names of
our first [a]parents who came out
of the land of Jerusalem; and this
I have done that when you remember your names ye may remember
them; and when ye remember them
ye may remember their works; and
when ye remember their works ye
may know how that it is said, and
also written, that they were [b]good.
7 Therefore, my sons, I would that
ye should do that which is good,
that it may be said of you, and also
written, even as it has been said and
written of them.
8 And now my sons, behold I have
somewhat more to desire of you,
which desire is, that ye may not
do these things that ye may boast,
but that ye may do these things to
lay up for yourselves a [a]treasure in
heaven, yea, which is eternal, and
which fadeth not away; yea, that
ye may have that [b]precious gift of
eternal life, which we have reason
to suppose hath been given to our
fathers.
9 O remember, remember, my sons,
the [a]words which king Benjamin
spake unto his people; yea, remember that there is no other way nor
means whereby man can be saved,
only through the [b]atoning blood
of Jesus Christ, who shall come;
yea, remember that he cometh to
[c]redeem the [d]world.

26*a* Ezek. 19:8 (6–9).
TG Weak.
b Alma 46:8;
Hel. 6:32; 7:6; 11:26; 12:2.
5 1*a* Hel. 3:37.
b Alma 4:20 (15–20).
c Hel. 6:15.
2*a* Mosiah 29:25 (25–27);
Hel. 1:5 (3–5, 13).
b Alma 10:19.
c 4 Ne. 1:40.
d Hel. 6:40; 10:11;
D&C 18:6; 61:31.
3*a* TG Stiffnecked.
5*a* Hel. 3:21 (21, 37).
6*a* 1 Ne. 1:4 (1, 4).
b 2 Ne. 4:12; 33:3 (1–15);
Jacob 1:10 (9–12).
8*a* Hel. 8:25;
3 Ne. 13:20 (19–21).
TG Treasure.
b 1 Ne. 15:36.
9*a* Mosiah 2:9.
b Mosiah 3:18; 4:2.
TG Jesus Christ,
Atonement through.
c TG Jesus Christ,
Redeemer.
d TG World.

10 And remember also the words
which Amulek spake unto Zeezrom, [a]in the city of Ammonihah;
for he said unto him that the Lord
surely should come to redeem his
people, but that he should not come
to redeem them in their sins, but to
redeem them from their sins.
11 And he hath power given unto
him from the Father to redeem
them from their sins because of repentance; therefore he hath [a]sent
his angels to declare the tidings
of the conditions of repentance,
which bringeth unto the power of
the Redeemer, unto the salvation of
their souls.
12 And now, my sons, remember,
remember that it is upon the [a]rock
of our Redeemer, who is Christ, the
Son of God, that ye must build your
[b]foundation; that when the devil
shall send forth his mighty winds,
yea, his shafts in the whirlwind, yea,
when all his hail and his mighty
[c]storm shall beat upon you, it shall
have no power over you to drag you
down to the gulf of misery and endless wo, because of the rock upon
which ye are built, which is a sure
foundation, a foundation whereon
if men build they cannot fall.
13 And it came to pass that these
were the words which Helaman
[a]taught to his sons; yea, he did
teach them many things which are
not written, and also many things
which are written.
14 And they did remember his
words; and therefore they went
forth, keeping the commandments
of God, to teach the word of God
among all the people of Nephi, beginning at the city Bountiful;
15 And from thenceforth to the
city of Gid; and from the city of
Gid to the city of Mulek;
16 And even from one city to another, until they had gone forth
[a]among all the people of Nephi
who were in the land southward;
and from thence into the land of
Zarahemla, among the Lamanites.
17 And it came to pass that they
did [a]preach with great [b]power, insomuch that they did confound many
of those [c]dissenters who had gone
over from the Nephites, insomuch
that they came forth and did confess their sins and were baptized
unto repentance, and immediately
returned to the Nephites to endeavor
to repair unto them the wrongs
which they had done.
18 And it came to pass that Nephi
and Lehi did preach unto the Lamanites with such great power and authority, for they had power and authority
given unto them that they might
[a]speak, and they also had what they
should speak given unto them—
19 Therefore they did speak unto
the great astonishment of the Lamanites, to the convincing them,
insomuch that there were eight thousand of the Lamanites who were in
the land of Zarahemla and round
about [a]baptized unto repentance,
and were convinced of the [b]wick-
edness of the [c]traditions of their
fathers.
20 And it came to pass that Nephi
and Lehi did proceed from thence
to go to the [a]land of Nephi.
21 And it came to pass that they
were taken by an army of the Lamanites and cast into [a]prison; yea,
even in that same prison in which
Ammon and his brethren were cast
by the servants of Limhi.

10*a* Alma 11:34.
11*a* Alma 13:24 (24–25); 39:19.
12*a* Ps. 71:3; Matt. 7:24 (24–27); D&C 6:34; Moses 7:53. TG Cornerstone; Rock.
b Isa. 28:16 (14–17); Jacob 4:16.
c Alma 26:6; 3 Ne. 14:25 (25, 27).
13*a* Mosiah 1:4; Alma 18:36; 36:1; Moses 6:58.
16*a* Hel. 4:5.
17*a* Hel. 4:14.
b TG Teaching with the Spirit.
c Hel. 4:4 (2, 4).
18*a* D&C 24:6; 100:5 (5–8). TG Prophets, Mission of.
19*a* TG Missionary Work.
b Mal. 2:6.
c Hel. 15:4.
20*a* Alma 22:1.
21*a* Mosiah 7:7 (6–8); 21:23 (22–24).

22 And after they had been cast
into prison many days without
food, behold, they went forth into
the prison to take them that they
might slay them.
23 And it came to pass that Nephi
and Lehi were encircled about [a]as
if by [b]fire, even insomuch that they
durst not lay their hands upon them
for fear lest they should be burned.
Nevertheless, Nephi and Lehi were
not burned; and they were as standing in the midst of fire and were
not burned.
24 And when they saw that they
were encircled about with a [a]pillar
of fire, and that it burned them not,
their hearts did take courage.
25 For they saw that the Lamanites durst not lay their hands upon
them; neither durst they come near
unto them, but stood as if they were
struck dumb with amazement.
26 And it came to pass that Nephi
and Lehi did stand forth and began
to speak unto them, saying: [a]Fear
not, for behold, it is God that has
shown unto you this marvelous
thing, in the which is shown unto
you that ye cannot lay your hands
on us to slay us.
27 And behold, when they had
said these words, the earth shook
exceedingly, and the walls of the
prison did shake as if they were
about to tumble to the earth; but
behold, they did not fall. And behold, they that were in the prison
were Lamanites and Nephites who
were dissenters.
28 And it came to pass that they
were overshadowed with a cloud
of [a]darkness, and an awful solemn
fear came upon them.
29 And it came to pass that there
came a [a]voice as if it were above the
cloud of darkness, saying: Repent ye,
repent ye, and seek no more to destroy my [b]servants whom I have sent
unto you to declare good tidings.
30 And it came to pass when they
heard this [a]voice, and beheld that
it was not a voice of thunder, neither was it a voice of a great tumultuous noise, but behold, it was
a [b]still voice of perfect mildness,
as if it had been a whisper, and it
did pierce even to the very soul—
31 And notwithstanding the mildness of the voice, behold the earth
shook exceedingly, and the walls of
the prison trembled again, as if it
were about to tumble to the earth;
and behold the cloud of darkness,
which had overshadowed them, did
not disperse—
32 And behold the voice came
again, saying: [a]Repent ye, repent
ye, for the kingdom of heaven is at
hand; and seek no more to destroy
my servants. And it came to pass
that the earth shook again, and the
walls trembled.
33 And also again the third time the
voice came, and did speak unto them
marvelous words which [a]cannot be
uttered by man; and the walls did
tremble again, and the earth shook
as if it were about to divide asunder.
34 And it came to pass that the
Lamanites could not flee because
of the cloud of darkness which did
overshadow them; yea, and also they
were immovable because of the fear
which did come upon them.
35 Now there was one among them
who was a Nephite by birth, who
had once belonged to the church of
God but had dissented from them.
36 And it came to pass that he
turned him about, and behold, he
saw through the cloud of darkness
the faces of Nephi and Lehi; and behold, they did [a]shine exceedingly,

23*a* Ex. 24:17; D&C 137:2.
b Ex. 3:2; Dan. 3:25 (25, 27).
24*a* Ex. 14:24; 1 Ne. 1:6; D&C 29:12; JS—H 1:16. TG Protection, Divine.
26*a* Dan. 10:12.
28*a* Ex. 14:20.
29*a* Deut. 4:33; 3 Ne. 11:3 (3–14).
b TG Servant.
30*a* Moses 1:25.
b 1 Kgs. 19:12; D&C 85:6 (6–7).
32*a* Matt. 3:2 (2–3); Alma 7:9; 9:25 (25–26).
33*a* Rom. 8:26.
36*a* Ex. 34:29 (29–35); Acts 6:15.

even as the faces of angels. And he beheld that they did lift their eyes to heaven; and they were in the attitude as if talking or lifting their voices to some being whom they beheld.

37 And it came to pass that this man did cry unto the multitude, that they might turn and look. And behold, there was power given unto them that they did turn and look; and they did behold the faces of Nephi and Lehi.

38 And they said unto the man: Behold, what do all these things mean, and who is it with whom these men do converse?

39 Now the man's name was Aminadab. And Aminadab said unto them: They do converse with the angels of God.

40 And it came to pass that the Lamanites said unto him: [a]What shall we do, that this cloud of darkness may be removed from overshadowing us?

41 And Aminadab said unto them: You must [a]repent, and cry unto the voice, even until ye shall have [b]faith in Christ, who was taught unto you by Alma, and [c]Amulek, and Zeezrom; and when ye shall do this, the cloud of darkness shall be removed from overshadowing you.

42 And it came to pass that they all did begin to cry unto the voice of him who had shaken the earth; yea, they did cry even until the cloud of darkness was dispersed.

43 And it came to pass that when they cast their eyes about, and saw that the cloud of darkness was dispersed from overshadowing them, behold, they saw that they were [a]encircled about, yea every soul, by a pillar of fire.

44 And [a]Nephi and [b]Lehi were in the midst of them; yea, they were encircled about; yea, they were as if in the midst of a flaming fire, yet it did harm them not, neither did it take hold upon the walls of the prison; and they were filled with that [c]joy which is unspeakable and full of glory.

45 And behold, the [a]Holy Spirit of God did come down from heaven, and did enter into their hearts, and they were filled as if with fire, and they could [b]speak forth marvelous words.

46 And it came to pass that there came a voice unto them, yea, a pleasant voice, as if it were a whisper, saying:

47 [a]Peace, peace be unto you, because of your faith in my Well Beloved, who was from the foundation of the world.

48 And now, when they heard this they cast up their eyes as if to behold from whence the voice came; and behold, they saw the [a]heavens open; and angels came down out of heaven and ministered unto them.

49 And there were about three hundred souls who saw and heard these things; and they were bidden to go forth and marvel not, neither should they doubt.

50 And it came to pass that they did go forth, and did minister unto the people, declaring throughout all the regions round about all the things which they had heard and seen, insomuch that the more part of the Lamanites were [a]convinced of them, because of the greatness of the evidences which they had received.

51 And as many as were [a]convinced did lay down their weapons of war, and also their hatred and the tradition of their fathers.

52 And it came to pass that they did [a]yield up unto the Nephites the lands of their possession.

40*a* Acts 2:37 (37–39).
41*a* TG Repent.
b TG Faith.
c Alma 31:6 (5–38).
43*a* 3 Ne. 17:24; 19:14.
44*a* Hel. 6:6.
b Hel. 11:19.
c TG Joy.
45*a* 3 Ne. 9:20; 19:14 (13–14); Ether 12:14.
b TG Holy Ghost, Gifts of.
47*a* TG Peace of God.
48*a* Acts 7:56 (55–56); 1 Ne. 1:8.
50*a* Ether 12:14.
51*a* Alma 31:5.
52*a* Hel. 4:5 (5, 18–19).

CHAPTER 6

The righteous Lamanites preach to the wicked Nephites—Both peoples prosper during an era of peace and plenty—Lucifer, the author of sin, stirs up the hearts of the wicked and the Gadianton robbers in murder and wickedness—The robbers take over the Nephite government. About 29–23 B.C.

AND it came to pass that when the
sixty and second year of the reign
of the judges had ended, all these
things had happened and the Lamanites had become, the more part
of them, a righteous people, insomuch that their [a]righteousness did
exceed that of the Nephites, because
of their firmness and their steadiness in the faith.
2 For behold, there were many of
the Nephites who had become [a]hard-
ened and impenitent and grossly
wicked, insomuch that they did
reject the word of God and all the
preaching and prophesying which
did come among them.
3 Nevertheless, the people of the
church did have great joy because
of the conversion of the Lamanites, yea, because of the church of
God, which had been established
among them. And they did [a]fellow-
ship one with another, and did rejoice one with another, and did have
great joy.
4 And it came to pass that many
of the Lamanites did come down
into the land of Zarahemla, and
did declare unto the people of the
Nephites the manner of their [a]con-
version, and did exhort them to
faith and repentance.
5 Yea, and many did [a]preach with
exceedingly great power and authority, unto the bringing down many
of them into the depths of humility, to be the humble followers of
God and the Lamb.
6 And it came to pass that many of
the Lamanites did go into the land
northward; and also [a]Nephi and
[b]Lehi went into the [c]land northward,
to preach unto the people. And thus
ended the sixty and third year.
7 And behold, there was peace in
all the land, insomuch that the Nephites did go into whatsoever part of
the land they would, whether among
the Nephites or the Lamanites.
8 And it came to pass that the Lamanites did also go whithersoever
they would, whether it were among
the Lamanites or among the Nephites; and thus they did have free
intercourse one with another, to
[a]buy and to sell, and to get gain,
according to their desire.
9 And it came to pass that they
became exceedingly rich, both the
Lamanites and the Nephites; and
they did have an exceeding plenty
of [a]gold, and of silver, and of all
manner of precious metals, both in
the land south and in the land north.
10 Now the land south was called
[a]Lehi, and the land north was called
[b]Mulek, which was after the [c]son of
Zedekiah; for the Lord did bring
Mulek into the land north, and Lehi
into the land south.
11 And behold, there was all manner of gold in both these lands, and
of silver, and of precious ore of every kind; and there were also curious workmen, who did [a]work all
kinds of ore and did refine it; and
thus they did become rich.
12 They did raise grain in abundance, both in the north and in the
south; and they did flourish exceedingly, both in the north and in the

---

6 1*a* Hel. 13:1.
2*a* Rom. 1:28 (28–32); Hel. 6:21. TG Hardheartedness.
3*a* TG Fellowshipping.
4*a* TG Conversion.
5*a* 1 Ne. 15:20; Alma 48:20.
6*a* Hel. 7:1.
b Hel. 5:44 (36–44); 11:19.
c Alma 63:9 (4–9); Hel. 3:12 (11–12).
8*a* 3 Ne. 6:11.
9*a* 1 Ne. 18:25; 2 Ne. 5:15 (14–16); Jacob 2:12 (12–13); Ether 9:17; 10:23 (12, 23).
10*a* Alma 50:25.
b Omni 1:14; Mosiah 25:2 (2–4); Hel. 8:21.
c Jer. 39:6; 52:10; Ezek. 17:22 (22–23); Alma 22:31.
11*a* TG Industry.

south. And they did multiply and
wax exceedingly strong in the land.
And they did raise many flocks and
herds, yea, many fatlings.
13 Behold their women did toil
and spin, and did [a]make all manner
of [b]cloth, of fine-twined linen and
cloth of every kind, to clothe their
nakedness. And thus the sixty and
fourth year did pass away in peace.
14 And in the sixty and fifth year
they did also have great joy and peace,
yea, much preaching and many
prophecies concerning that which
was to come. And thus passed away
the sixty and fifth year.
15 And it came to pass that in the
sixty and sixth year of the reign of
the judges, behold, [a]Cezoram was
murdered by an unknown hand as
he sat upon the judgment-seat. And
it came to pass that in the same
year, that his son, who had been appointed by the people in his stead,
was also murdered. And thus ended
the sixty and sixth year.
16 And in the commencement
of the sixty and seventh year the
people began to grow exceedingly
wicked again.
17 For behold, the Lord had blessed
them so long with the [a]riches of
the world that they had not been
stirred up to anger, to wars, nor to
bloodshed; therefore they began to
set their hearts upon their riches;
yea, they began to seek to get gain
that they might be lifted up one
above another; therefore they began
to commit [b]secret murders, and to
rob and to plunder, that they might
get gain.
18 And now behold, those murderers and plunderers were a band who
had been formed by Kishkumen and
[a]Gadianton. And now it had come
to pass that there were many, even
among the Nephites, of Gadianton's
band. But behold, they were more
numerous among the more wicked
part of the Lamanites. And they
were called Gadianton's robbers and
murderers.
19 And it was they who did murder the chief judge [a]Cezoram, and
his son, while in the judgment-seat;
and behold, they were not found.
20 And now it came to pass that
when the Lamanites found that
there were robbers among them they
were exceedingly sorrowful; and
they did use every means in their
power to destroy them off the face
of the earth.
21 But behold, Satan did stir up
the [a]hearts of the more part of the
Nephites, insomuch that they did
unite with those bands of robbers,
and did enter into their covenants
and their oaths, that they would
protect and preserve one another in
whatsoever difficult circumstances
they should be placed, that they
should not suffer for their murders,
and their plunderings, and their
[b]stealings.
22 And it came to pass that they
did have their signs, yea, their [a]se-
cret signs, and their [b]secret words;
and this that they might distinguish
a brother who had entered into the
covenant, that whatsoever wickedness his brother should do he should
not be injured by his brother, nor by
those who did belong to his band,
who had taken this covenant.
23 And thus they might murder,
and plunder, and steal, and commit
[a]whoredoms and all manner of
wickedness, contrary to the laws
of their country and also the laws of
their God.
24 And whosoever of those who belonged to their band should reveal
unto the world of their [a]wickedness
and their abominations, should be

13*a* TG Art.
b Mosiah 10:5; Alma 1:29.
15*a* Hel. 5:1; 6:19.
17*a* TG Treasure.
b 3 Ne. 6:23; 9:9.
18*a* Hel. 2:4 (4, 12–13); 3:23.
19*a* Hel. 6:15.
21*a* Hel. 6:2.
b TG Stealing.
22*a* Alma 37:27. TG Secret Combinations.
b Hel. 11:2; 3 Ne. 3:7.
23*a* TG Whore.
24*a* TG Wickedness.

tried, not according to the laws of
their country, but according to the
laws of their wickedness, which
had been given by Gadianton and
Kishkumen.
25 Now behold, it is these secret
[a]oaths and covenants which Alma
commanded his son should not
go forth unto the world, lest they
should be a means of bringing down
the people unto destruction.
26 Now behold, those [a]secret oaths
and covenants did not come forth
unto Gadianton from the [b]records
which were delivered unto Helaman;
but behold, they were put into the
heart of [c]Gadianton by that [d]same being who did entice our first parents
to partake of the forbidden fruit—
27 Yea, that same being who did
plot with [a]Cain, that if he would
murder his brother Abel it should
not be known unto the world. And
he did plot with Cain and his followers from that time forth.
28 And also it is that same being
who put it into the hearts of the
people to [a]build a tower sufficiently
high that they might get to heaven.
And it was that same being who led
on the people who came from that
tower into this land; who spread
the works of darkness and abominations over all the face of the land,
until he dragged the people down
to an [b]entire destruction, and to an
everlasting hell.
29 Yea, it is that same being who
put it into the heart of [a]Gadianton
to still carry on the work of darkness, and of secret murder; and he
has brought it forth from the beginning of man even down to this time.
30 And behold, it is he who is the
[a]author of all sin. And behold, he
doth carry on his works of darkness
and secret murder, and doth hand
down their plots, and their oaths,
and their covenants, and their plans
of awful wickedness, from generation to generation according as he
can get hold upon the hearts of the
children of men.
31 And now behold, he had got
great hold upon the hearts of the
Nephites; yea, insomuch that they
had become exceedingly wicked; yea,
the more part of them had turned
out of the [a]way of righteousness,
and did [b]trample under their feet
the commandments of God, and did
turn unto their own ways, and
did build up unto themselves [c]idols
of their gold and their silver.
32 And it came to pass that all
these iniquities did come unto them
in the space of [a]not many years,
insomuch that a more part of it had
come unto them in the sixty and
seventh year of the reign of the
judges over the people of Nephi.
33 And they did grow in their iniquities in the sixty and eighth year
also, to the great sorrow and lamentation of the righteous.
34 And thus we see that the [a]Neph-
ites did begin to dwindle in unbelief, and grow in wickedness and
abominations, while the Lamanites
began to grow exceedingly in the
knowledge of their God; yea, they
did begin to keep his statutes and
commandments, and to walk in
truth and uprightness before him.
35 And thus we see that the Spirit
of the Lord began to [a]withdraw
from the Nephites, because of the
wickedness and the hardness of
their hearts.
36 And thus we see that the Lord
began to pour out his [a]Spirit upon
the Lamanites, because of their

25*a* Alma 37:29 (27–32).
26*a* 3 Ne. 3:9; Ether 8:9 (9–19); Moses 5:29 (29, 49–52).
b 3 Ne. 6:28.
c Hel. 8:28.
d Moses 4:6 (6–12).
27*a* Moses 5:25 (18–33).
28*a* Gen. 11:4 (1–4); Ether 1:3.
b Ether 8:21 (9, 15–25).
29*a* Hel. 2:4 (4–13).
30*a* Alma 5:40 (39–42); Moro. 7:12 (12, 17); Moses 4:4.
31*a* Gen. 6:12; 2 Ne. 28:11.
b 1 Ne. 19:7.
c Judg. 2:17; 2 Ne. 9:37; Alma 7:6.
32*a* Alma 46:8; Hel. 4:26; 7:6; 11:26.
34*a* Moro. 9:20.
35*a* Matt. 13:15; Mosiah 2:36; D&C 121:37.
36*a* TG God, Spirit of.

easiness and [b]willingness to believe
in his words.
37 And it came to pass that the
Lamanites did hunt the band of
robbers of Gadianton; and they
did preach the word of God among
the more wicked part of them, insomuch that this band of robbers
was utterly destroyed from among
the Lamanites.
38 And it came to pass on the
other hand, that the Nephites did
build them up and support them,
beginning at the more wicked part
of them, until they had overspread
all the land of the Nephites, and
had seduced the more part of the
righteous until they had come down
to believe in their works and partake of their spoils, and to join with
them in their secret murders and
combinations.
39 And thus they did obtain the
sole management of the government, insomuch that they did trample under their feet and smite and
rend and turn their backs upon the
[a]poor and the meek, and the humble followers of God.
40 And thus we see that they were
in an awful state, and [a]ripening for
an everlasting destruction.
41 And it came to pass that thus
ended the sixty and eighth year
of the reign of the judges over the
people of Nephi.

THE PROPHECY OF NEPHI, THE SON OF HELAMAN—God threatens the people of Nephi that he will visit them in his anger, to their utter destruction except they repent of their wickedness. God smiteth the people of Nephi with pestilence; they repent and turn unto him. Samuel, a Lamanite, prophesies unto the Nephites.

Comprising chapters 7 through 16.

CHAPTER 7

Nephi is rejected in the north and returns to Zarahemla—He prays upon his garden tower and then calls upon the people to repent or perish. About 23–21 B.C.

BEHOLD, now it came to pass in the
sixty and ninth year of the reign of
the judges over the people of the
Nephites, that Nephi, the son of
Helaman, [a]returned to the land of
Zarahemla from the land northward.
2 For he had been forth among the
people who were in the land northward, and did preach the word of
God unto them, and did prophesy
many things unto them;
3 And they did [a]reject all his words,
insomuch that he could not stay
among them, but returned again
unto the land of his nativity.
4 And seeing the people in a state
of such awful wickedness, and
those Gadianton robbers filling the
judgment-seats—having [a]usurped
the power and authority of the land;
laying aside the commandments
of God, and not in the least aright
before him; doing no justice unto
the children of men;
5 Condemning the righteous because of their righteousness; letting
the guilty and the wicked go [a]un-
punished because of their [b]money;
and moreover to be held in office
at the head of government, to rule
and do according to their wills,
that they might get gain and glory
of the [c]world, and, moreover, that
they might the more easily commit
adultery, and steal, and kill, and
do according to their own wills—
6 Now this great iniquity had come
upon the Nephites, in the space of
[a]not many years; and when Nephi
saw it, his heart was swollen with
sorrow within his breast; and he did
exclaim in the agony of his soul:

36*b* Ex. 25:2 (1–7).
39*a* Ps. 109:16 (15–16); Ezek. 22:7 (7–13); Amos 5:12; Alma 5:55 (54–56); D&C 56:16.
40*a* Hel. 5:2; 11:37; D&C 18:6; 61:31.
7 1*a* Hel. 6:6.
3*a* TG Prophets, Rejection of.
4*a* TG Tyranny; Unrighteous Dominion.
5*a* Job 12:6; 21:7; Ps. 73:12.
b TG Bribe.
c Matt. 13:22; D&C 39:9.
6*a* IE six years; see Hel. 4:26; 6:6, 32; 11:26.

7 Oh, that I could have had my
days in the days when my father
Nephi first came out of the land of
Jerusalem, that I could have [a]joyed
with him in the promised land; then
were his people easy to be entreated,
[b]firm to keep the commandments
of God, and slow to be led to do iniquity; and they were quick to hearken
unto the words of the Lord—
8 Yea, if my days could have been
in those days, then would my soul
have had joy in the righteousness
of my brethren.
9 But behold, I am consigned that
these are my days, and that my soul
shall be filled with [a]sorrow because of
this the wickedness of my brethren.
10 And behold, now it came to pass
that it was upon a tower, which was
in the [a]garden of Nephi, which
was by the highway which led to
the chief market, which was in the
city of Zarahemla; therefore, Nephi
had bowed himself upon the tower
which was in his garden, which
tower was also near unto the garden
gate by which led the highway.
11 And it came to pass that there
were certain men passing by and
saw Nephi as he was pouring out his
soul unto God upon the [a]tower; and
they ran and told the people what
they had seen, and the people came
together in multitudes that they
might know the cause of so great
mourning for the wickedness of
the people.
12 And now, when Nephi arose he
beheld the multitudes of people
who had gathered together.
13 And it came to pass that he
opened his mouth and said unto
them: Behold, [a]why have ye gathered yourselves together? That I
may tell you of your iniquities?
14 Yea, because I have got upon
my tower that I might pour out
my soul unto my God, because of
the exceeding sorrow of my heart,
which is because of your iniquities!
15 And because of my [a]mourning
and lamentation ye have gathered
yourselves together, and do marvel; yea, and ye have great need
to marvel; yea, ye ought to marvel
because ye are given away that the
devil has got so great hold upon
your hearts.
16 Yea, how could you have given
way to the enticing of him who
is seeking to hurl away your souls
down to [a]everlasting misery and
endless wo?
17 O repent ye, repent ye! [a]Why
will ye die? Turn ye, turn ye unto
the Lord your God. Why has he
forsaken you?
18 It is because you have hardened your hearts; yea, ye will not
[a]hearken unto the voice of the [b]good
shepherd; yea, ye have [c]provoked
him to anger against you.
19 And behold, instead of [a]gath-
ering you, except ye will repent,
behold, he shall scatter you forth
that ye shall become meat for dogs
and wild beasts.
20 O, how could you have [a]forgot-
ten your God in the very day that
he has delivered you?
21 But behold, it is to get [a]gain, to
be [b]praised of men, yea, and that
ye might get gold and silver. And
ye have set your hearts upon the
[c]riches and the vain things of this
world, for the which ye do murder,
and plunder, and steal, and bear
[d]false witness against your neighbor, and do all manner of iniquity.
22 And for this cause [a]wo shall come
unto you except ye shall repent.

7*a* 2 Ne. 5:27 (26–28).
b D&C 5:22.
9*a* Jer. 9:1 (1–3).
10*a* Hel. 9:8.
11*a* Alma 50:4.
13*a* Matt. 3:7 (5–8).
15*a* TG Mourning.
16*a* Alma 26:20.
17*a* Isa. 1:5 (5–6); Ezek. 18:23 (23, 32).
18*a* TG Disobedience.
b Ezek. 34:12; John 10:14; Alma 5:60 (38–60). TG Jesus Christ, Good Shepherd.
c Num. 14:11 (11–12); 1 Ne. 17:30 (23–31); Jacob 1:8; Alma 12:37 (36–37).
19*a* 3 Ne. 10:4 (4–7).
20*a* Isa. 17:10 (4–11).
21*a* TG Selfishness.
b TG Peer Influence.
c TG Treasure.
d Matt. 15:19 (19–20). TG Slander.
22*a* Rev. 8:13; D&C 5:5.

For if ye will not repent, behold, this [b]great city, and also all those great cities which are round about, which are in the land of our possession, shall be taken away that ye shall have no place in them; for behold, the Lord will not grant unto you [c]strength, as he has hitherto done, to withstand against your enemies.

23 For behold, thus saith the Lord: I will not show unto the wicked of my strength, to one more than the other, save it be unto those who repent of their sins, and hearken unto my words. Now therefore, I would that ye should behold, my brethren, that it shall be [a]better for the Lamanites than for you except ye shall repent.

24 For behold, they are more righteous than you, for they have not sinned against that great knowledge which ye have received; therefore the Lord will be merciful unto them; yea, he will [a]lengthen out their days and increase their seed, even when thou shalt be utterly [b]destroyed except thou shalt repent.

25 Yea, wo be unto you because of that great abomination which has come among you; and ye have united yourselves unto it, yea, to that [a]secret band which was established by Gadianton!

26 Yea, [a]wo shall come unto you because of that pride which ye have suffered to enter your hearts, which has lifted you up beyond that which is good because of your exceedingly great riches!

27 Yea, wo be unto you because of your wickedness and abominations!

28 And except ye repent ye shall perish; yea, even your lands shall be taken from you, and ye shall be destroyed from off the face of the earth.

29 Behold now, I do not say that these things shall be, of myself, because it is not of myself that I [a]know these things; but behold, I [b]know that these things are true because the Lord God has made them known unto me, therefore I testify that they shall be.

CHAPTER 8

Corrupt judges seek to incite the people against Nephi—Abraham, Moses, Zenos, Zenock, Ezias, Isaiah, Jeremiah, Lehi, and Nephi all testified of Christ—By inspiration Nephi announces the murder of the chief judge. About 23–21 B.C.

AND now it came to pass that when Nephi had said these words, behold, there were men who were judges, who also belonged to the secret band of Gadianton, and they were angry, and they cried out against him, saying unto the people: Why do ye not seize upon this man and bring him forth, that he may be condemned according to the crime which he has done?

2 Why seest thou this man, and hearest him revile against this people and against our law?

3 For behold, Nephi had spoken unto them concerning the corruptness of their law; yea, many things did Nephi speak which cannot be written; and nothing did he speak which was contrary to the commandments of God.

4 And those judges were angry with him because he [a]spake plainly unto them concerning their secret works of darkness; nevertheless, they durst not lay their own hands upon him, for they feared the people lest they should cry out against them.

5 Therefore they did cry unto the people, saying: Why do you suffer this man to revile against us? For

22*b* Hel. 8:5.
c Mosiah 7:29.
23*a* Hel. 15:14 (11–15).
24*a* Ex. 20:12; 1 Ne. 17:55; Alma 9:16; D&C 5:33.
b Alma 9:19; Hel. 10:14.
25*a* 2 Ne. 10:15; Hel. 3:23.
26*a* Isa. 5:8 (8–25).
29*a* Hel. 8:8.
b Hel. 8:12.
8 4*a* 1 Ne. 16:2 (2–3).

behold he doth condemn all this
people, even unto destruction; yea,
and also that these our [a]great cities shall be taken from us, that we
shall have no place in them.
6 And now we know that this is
impossible, for behold, we are [a]pow-
erful, and our cities great, therefore
our enemies can have no power
over us.
7 And it came to pass that thus
they did [a]stir up the people to anger
against Nephi, and raised contentions among them; for there were
some who did cry out: [b]Let this man
alone, for he is a good man, and
those things which he saith will
surely come to pass except we repent;
8 Yea, behold, all the judgments
will come upon us which he has
testified unto us; for we know that
he has testified aright unto us concerning our iniquities. And behold
they are many, and he [a]knoweth as
well all things which shall befall
us as he knoweth of our iniquities;
9 Yea, and behold, if he had not
been a prophet he could not have
[a]testified concerning those things.
10 And it came to pass that those
people who sought to destroy Nephi
were compelled because of their fear,
that they did not lay their hands
on him; therefore he began again
to speak unto them, seeing that
he had gained favor in the eyes of
some, insomuch that the remainder
of them did fear.
11 Therefore he was constrained
to speak more unto them saying:
Behold, my brethren, have ye not
read that God gave power unto one
man, even Moses, to smite upon the
waters of the [a]Red Sea, and they
parted hither and thither, insomuch
that the Israelites, who were our
fathers, came through upon dry
ground, and the waters closed upon
the armies of the Egyptians and
swallowed them up?
12 And now behold, if God gave
unto this man such power, then
why should ye dispute among yourselves, and say that he hath given
unto me no power whereby I may
[a]know concerning the judgments
that shall come upon you except
ye repent?
13 But, behold, ye not only deny
my words, but ye also deny all the
words which have been spoken
by our fathers, and also the words
which were spoken by this man,
Moses, who had such great power
given unto him, yea, the words
which he hath spoken concerning
the coming of the Messiah.
14 Yea, did he not bear record that
the Son of God should come? And
as he [a]lifted up the brazen serpent
in the wilderness, even so shall he
be lifted up who should come.
15 And as many as should look
upon that serpent should [a]live, even
so as many as should look upon the
Son of God with faith, having a contrite spirit, might [b]live, even unto
that life which is eternal.
16 And now behold, Moses did
not only testify of these things, but
also [a]all the holy prophets, from his
days even to the days of Abraham.
17 Yea, and behold, [a]Abraham saw
of his coming, and was filled with
gladness and did rejoice.
18 Yea, and behold I say unto you,
that Abraham not only knew of
these things, but there were [a]many
before the days of Abraham who
were called by the [b]order of God;

5*a* Hel. 7:22.
6*a* Moses 8:21 (20–22).
7*a* TG Provoking.
b Acts 5:38 (37–40).
8*a* Hel. 7:29.
TG God, Foreknowledge of.
9*a* TG Testimony.
11*a* Ex. 14:16;
Josh. 2:10;
Neh. 9:11;
1 Ne. 17:26;
Mosiah 7:19;
D&C 8:3;
Moses 1:25.
12*a* Hel. 7:29 (28–29).
14*a* Num. 21:9 (6–9);
2 Ne. 25:20;
Alma 33:19 (19–22).
TG Jesus Christ, Types of, in Anticipation.
15*a* 1 Ne. 17:41;
Alma 37:46 (46–47);
3 Ne. 15:9.
b John 11:25.
16*a* Luke 24:27;
Rev. 19:10;
Jacob 4:4 (4–5); 7:11.
17*a* Gen. 22:8 (8–14);
John 8:56 (53, 56).
18*a* Alma 13:19;
D&C 84:14 (6–16); 136:37.
b TG Priesthood.

yea, even after the order of his Son;
and this that it should be shown
unto the people, a great many
thousand years before his coming,
that even redemption should come
unto them.
19 And now I would that ye should
know, that even since the days of
Abraham there have been many
prophets that have testified these
things; yea, behold, the prophet
[a]Zenos did testify boldly; for the
which he was slain.
20 And behold, also [a]Zenock, and
also [b]Ezias, and also [c]Isaiah, and
[d]Jeremiah, (Jeremiah being that
same prophet who testified of the
destruction of [e]Jerusalem) and
now we know that Jerusalem was
destroyed according to the words
of Jeremiah. O then why not the
Son of God come, according to his
prophecy?
21 And now will you dispute that
[a]Jerusalem was destroyed? Will ye
say that the [b]sons of Zedekiah were
not slain, all except it were [c]Mulek?
Yea, and do ye not behold that the
seed of Zedekiah are with us, and
they were driven out of the land
of Jerusalem? But behold, this is
not all—
22 Our father Lehi was driven
out of Jerusalem because he [a]tes-
tified of these things. Nephi also
testified of these things, and also
almost all of our fathers, even down
to this time; yea, they have testified
of the [b]coming of Christ, and have
looked forward, and have rejoiced
in his day which is to come.
23 And behold, he is God, and he
is [a]with them, and he did manifest
himself unto them, that they were
redeemed by him; and they gave
unto him glory, because of that
which is to come.
24 And now, seeing ye know these
things and cannot deny them except ye shall lie, therefore in this
ye have sinned, for ye have rejected
all these things, notwithstanding
so many [a]evidences which ye have
received; yea, even ye have received
[b]all things, both things in heaven,
and all things which are in the
earth, as a witness that they are
true.
25 But behold, ye have rejected the
truth, and [a]rebelled against your
holy God; and even at this time,
instead of laying up for yourselves
[b]treasures in heaven, where nothing
doth corrupt, and where nothing can
come which is unclean, ye are heap-
ing up for yourselves wrath against
the day of [c]judgment.
26 Yea, even at this time ye are
ripening, because of your murders
and your [a]fornication and wickedness, for everlasting destruction;
yea, and except ye repent it will
come unto you soon.
27 Yea, behold it is now even at
your doors; yea, go ye in unto the
judgment-seat, and search; and behold, your judge is murdered, and
he [a]lieth in his blood; and he hath
been murdered [b]by his brother, who
seeketh to sit in the judgment-seat.
28 And behold, they both belong
to your secret band, whose [a]author
is Gadianton and the evil one who
seeketh to destroy the souls of men.

19 *a* Alma 34:7; Hel. 15:11.
20 *a* 1 Ne. 19:10; Alma 33:15; 34:7; 3 Ne. 10:16 (15–16).
b TG Scriptures, Lost.
c Isa. 53:2 (1–12).
d 1 Ne. 5:13; 7:14.
e Jer. 26:18 (17–19); 1 Ne. 1:4 (4–18); 2 Ne. 6:8; 25:6.
21 *a* Omni 1:15.
b 2 Kgs. 25:7; Jer. 39:6; 52:10.
c Ezek. 17:22 (22–23); Hel. 6:10; Morm. 7:2.
22 *a* D&C 138:49.
b TG Jesus Christ, Prophecies about.
23 *a* Alma 40:11 (11–12).
24 *a* 2 Kgs. 17:13; 1 Ne. 10:5.
b Alma 30:44; Moses 6:63.
25 *a* Ps. 5:10; Mosiah 2:37 (36–38); 3:12.
b Hel. 5:8; 3 Ne. 13:20 (19–21). TG Treasure.
c Ps. 109:7 (3–7); D&C 10:23 (20–23); 121:24 (23–25).
26 *a* TG Fornication.
27 *a* Hel. 9:3, 15.
b Hel. 9:6 (6, 26–38).
28 *a* Hel. 6:26 (26–30).

CHAPTER 9

Messengers find the chief judge dead at the judgment seat—They are imprisoned and later released—By inspiration Nephi identifies Seantum as the murderer—Nephi is accepted by some as a prophet. About 23–21 B.C.

BEHOLD, now it came to pass that when Nephi had spoken these words, certain men who were among them ran to the judgment-seat; yea, even there were [a]five who went, and they said among themselves, as they went:

2 Behold, now we will know of a surety whether this man be a prophet and God hath commanded him to prophesy such marvelous things unto us. Behold, we do not [a]believe that he hath; yea, we do not believe that he is a prophet; nevertheless, if this thing which he has said concerning the chief judge be true, that he be dead, then will we believe that the other words which he has spoken are true.

3 And it came to pass that they ran in their might, and came in unto the judgment-seat; and behold, the chief judge had fallen to the earth, and did [a]lie in his blood.

4 And now behold, when they saw this they were astonished exceedingly, insomuch that they fell to the earth; for they had not believed the words which Nephi had spoken concerning the chief judge.

5 But now, when they saw they believed, and fear came upon them lest all the judgments which Nephi had spoken [a]should come upon the people; therefore they did quake, and had fallen to the earth.

6 Now, immediately when the judge had been murdered—he being stabbed by his brother by a garb of secrecy, and he fled, and the servants ran and told the people, raising the cry of murder among them;

7 And behold the people did gather themselves together unto the place of the judgment-seat—and behold, to their astonishment they saw those [a]five men who had fallen to the earth.

8 And now behold, the people knew nothing concerning the multitude who had gathered together at the [a]garden of Nephi; therefore they said among themselves: These men are they who have murdered the judge, and God has smitten them that they could not flee from us.

9 And it came to pass that they laid hold on them, and bound them and cast them into prison. And there was a proclamation sent abroad that the judge was slain, and that the murderers had been taken and were cast into prison.

10 And it came to pass that on the morrow the people did assemble themselves together to [a]mourn and to [b]fast, at the burial of the great chief judge who had been slain.

11 And thus also those judges who were at the garden of Nephi, and heard his words, were also gathered together at the burial.

12 And it came to pass that they inquired among the people, saying: Where are the five who were sent to inquire concerning the chief judge whether he was dead? And they answered and said: Concerning this five whom ye say ye have sent, we know not; but there are five who are the murderers, whom we have cast into prison.

13 And it came to pass that the judges desired that they should be brought; and they were brought, and behold they were the five who were sent; and behold the judges inquired of them to know concerning the matter, and they told them all that they had done, saying:

14 We ran and came to the place of the judgment-seat, and when we saw all things even as Nephi had testified, we were astonished

9 1*a* Hel. 9:7 (7, 12).
2*a* Dan. 2:9.
3*a* Hel. 8:27.
5*a* 2 Kgs. 22:13 (8–20).
7*a* Hel. 9:1.
8*a* Hel. 7:10 (10–11, 14).
10*a* TG Mourning.
b TG Fast, Fasting.

insomuch that we fell to the earth; and when we were recovered from our astonishment, behold they cast us into [a]prison.

15 Now, as for the murder of this man, we know not who has done it; and only this much we know, we ran and came [a]according as ye desired, and behold he was dead, according to the words of Nephi.

16 And now it came to pass that the judges did expound the matter unto the people, and did cry out against Nephi, saying: Behold, we know that this Nephi must have agreed with some one to slay the judge, and then he might declare it unto us, that he might convert us unto his faith, that he might raise himself to be a great man, chosen of God, and a prophet.

17 And now behold, we will detect this man, and he shall confess his fault and make known unto us the true murderer of this judge.

18 And it came to pass that the five were liberated on the day of the burial. Nevertheless, they did rebuke the judges in the words which they had spoken against Nephi, and did contend with them one by one, insomuch that they did confound them.

19 Nevertheless, they caused that Nephi should be taken and bound and brought before the multitude, and they began to question him in divers ways that they might cross him, that they might accuse him to death—

20 Saying unto him: Thou art confederate; who is this man that hath done this murder? Now tell us, and acknowledge thy fault; saying, Behold here is [a]money; and also we will grant unto thee thy life if thou wilt tell us, and acknowledge the agreement which thou hast made with him.

21 But Nephi said unto them: O ye [a]fools, ye uncircumcised of heart, ye blind, and ye [b]stiffnecked people, do ye know how long the Lord your God will suffer you that ye shall go on in this your way of sin?

22 O ye ought to begin to howl and [a]mourn, because of the great destruction which at this time doth await you, except ye shall repent.

23 Behold ye say that I have agreed with a man that he should murder Seezoram, our chief judge. But behold, I say unto you, that this is because I have testified unto you that ye might know concerning this thing; yea, even for a witness unto you, that I did know of the wickedness and abominations which are among you.

24 And because I have done this, ye say that I have agreed with a man that he should do this thing; yea, because I showed unto you this sign ye are angry with me, and seek to destroy my life.

25 And now behold, I will show unto you another sign, and see if ye will in this thing seek to destroy me.

26 Behold I say unto you: Go to the house of Seantum, who is the [a]brother of Seezoram, and say unto him—

27 Has Nephi, the pretended prophet, who doth prophesy so much evil concerning this people, agreed with thee, in the which ye have murdered Seezoram, who is your brother?

28 And behold, he shall say unto you, Nay.

29 And ye shall say unto him: Have ye murdered your brother?

30 And he shall stand with fear, and wist not what to say. And behold, he shall deny unto you; and he shall make as if he were astonished; nevertheless, he shall declare unto you that he is innocent.

31 But behold, ye shall examine

14*a* Gen. 39:20.
15*a* Hel. 8:27.
20*a* 1 Sam. 8:3 (1–4); Ether 9:11. TG Bribe.
21*a* Ps. 75:4; Luke 24:25; Acts 7:51.
b TG Stiffnecked.
22*a* Ezek. 24:23; Mosiah 7:24.
26*a* Hel. 8:27.

him, and ye shall find blood upon
the skirts of his cloak.
32 And when ye have seen this,
ye shall say: From whence cometh
this blood? Do we not know that it
is the blood of your brother?
33 And then shall he tremble, and
shall look pale, even as if death had
come upon him.
34 And then shall ye say: Because
of this fear and this paleness which
has come upon your face, behold,
we know that thou art guilty.
35 And then shall greater fear
come upon him; and then shall he
confess unto you, and deny no more
that he has done this murder.
36 And then shall he say unto
you, that I, Nephi, know nothing
concerning the matter save it were
given unto me by the power of God.
And then shall ye know that I am
an honest man, and that I am sent
unto you from God.
37 And it came to pass that they
went and did, even according as
Nephi had said unto them. And behold, the words which he had said
were true; for according to the words
he did deny; and also according to
the words he did confess.
38 And he was brought to prove
that he himself was the very murderer, insomuch that the five were
set at liberty, and also was Nephi.
39 And there were some of the
Nephites who believed on the words
of Nephi; and there were some
also, who believed because of the
testimony of the five, for they had
been converted while they were
in prison.
40 And now there were some
among the people, who said that
Nephi was a prophet.
41 And there were others who said:
Behold, he is a god, for except he
was a god he could not [a]know of
all things. For behold, he has told
us the thoughts of our hearts, and
also has told us things; and even
he has brought unto our knowledge the true murderer of our chief
judge.

CHAPTER 10

The Lord gives Nephi the sealing power—He is empowered to bind and loose on earth and in heaven—He commands the people to repent or perish—The Spirit carries him from multitude to multitude. About 21–20 B.C.

AND it came to pass that there arose
a division among the people, insomuch that they divided hither and
thither and went their ways, leaving
Nephi alone, as he was standing in
the midst of them.
2 And it came to pass that Nephi
went his way towards his own house,
[a]pondering upon the things which
the Lord had shown unto him.
3 And it came to pass as he was
thus pondering—being much cast
down because of the wickedness of
the people of the Nephites, their
secret works of darkness, and their
murderings, and their plunderings,
and all manner of iniquities—and
it came to pass as he was thus pondering in his heart, behold, a [a]voice
came unto him saying:
4 [a]Blessed art thou, Nephi, for those
things which thou hast done; for
I have beheld how thou hast with
[b]unwearyingness declared the word,
which I have given unto thee, unto
this people. And thou hast not feared
them, and hast not sought thine
[c]own life, but hast sought my [d]will,
and to keep my commandments.
5 And now, because thou hast done
this with such unwearyingness, behold, I will bless thee forever; and I
will make thee mighty in word and
in deed, in faith and in works; yea,
even that [a]all things shall be [b]done

41*a* TG God, Omniscience of.
10 2*a* TG Meditation.
3*a* TG Guidance, Divine.
4*a* Acts 23:11.
b Acts 20:31.
TG Dedication; Dependability; Priesthood, Magnifying Callings within; Steadfastness.
c TG Self-Sacrifice.
d Mosiah 24:15; 3 Ne. 11:11.
5*a* 3 Ne. 18:20; D&C 88:64 (63–65).
b Ex. 33:17.

unto thee according to thy [c]word,
for thou shalt [d]not ask that which
is contrary to my will.
6 Behold, thou art Nephi, and I
am God. Behold, I declare it unto
thee in the presence of mine angels,
that ye shall have power over this
people, and shall smite the earth
with [a]famine, and with pestilence,
and destruction, according to the
wickedness of this people.
7 Behold, I give unto you [a]power,
that whatsoever ye shall [b]seal on
earth shall be sealed in heaven;
and whatsoever ye shall loose on
earth shall be loosed in heaven; and
thus shall ye have power among
this people.
8 And thus, if ye shall say unto this
temple it shall be rent in twain, it
shall be done.
9 And if ye shall say unto this
[a]mountain, Be thou cast down and
become smooth, it shall be done.
10 And behold, if ye shall say that
God shall smite this people, it shall
come to pass.
11 And now behold, I command
you, that ye shall go and declare
unto this people, that thus saith the
Lord God, who is the Almighty: Except ye repent ye shall be smitten,
even unto [a]destruction.
12 And behold, now it came to
pass that when the Lord had spoken
these words unto Nephi, he did stop
and did not go unto his own house,
but did return unto the multitudes
who were scattered about upon
the face of the land, and began to
declare unto them the word of the
Lord which had been spoken unto
him, concerning their destruction
if they did not repent.
13 Now behold, [a]notwithstanding
that great miracle which Nephi
had done in telling them concerning the death of the chief judge,
they did harden their hearts and
did not hearken unto the words of
the Lord.
14 Therefore Nephi did declare
unto them the word of the Lord,
saying: Except ye repent, thus saith
the Lord, ye shall be [a]smitten even
unto destruction.
15 And it came to pass that when
Nephi had declared unto them the
word, behold, they did still harden
their hearts and would not hearken
unto his words; therefore they did
[a]revile against him, and did seek to
lay their hands upon him that they
might cast him into prison.
16 But behold, the power of God
was with him, and they could not
take him to cast him into prison,
for he was taken by the Spirit and
[a]conveyed away out of the midst
of them.
17 And it came to pass that thus
he did go forth in the Spirit, from
multitude to multitude, declaring
the word of God, even until he had
declared it unto them all, or sent it
forth among all the people.
18 And it came to pass that they
would not hearken unto his words;
and there began to be contentions,
insomuch that they were divided
against themselves and began to
slay one another with the sword.
19 And thus ended the seventy and
first year of the reign of the judges
over the people of Nephi.

CHAPTER 11

Nephi persuades the Lord to replace their war with a famine—Many people perish—They repent, and Nephi importunes the Lord for rain—Nephi and Lehi receive many revelations—The Gadianton robbers entrench themselves in the land. About 20–6 B.C.

5*c* 1 Kgs. 17:1; Enos 1:12.
d James 4:3 (1–3); 2 Ne. 4:35; D&C 46:30.
6*a* Hel. 11:4 (4–18). TG Drought.
7*a* Hel. 11:18.
b Matt. 16:19. TG Priesthood, Authority.
9*a* Matt. 17:20; Jacob 4:6; Morm. 8:24; Ether 12:30.
11*a* Hel. 5:2; 11:8.
13*a* Mark 6:6 (4–6).
14*a* Hel. 7:24.
15*a* TG Reviling.
16*a* Acts 8:39 (39–40).

AND now it came to pass in the seventy and second year of the reign
of the judges that the contentions
did increase, insomuch that there
were wars throughout all the land
among all the people of Nephi.
2 And it was this [a]secret band of
robbers who did carry on this work
of destruction and wickedness. And
this war did last all that year; and
in the seventy and third year it did
also last.
3 And it came to pass that in this
year Nephi did cry unto the Lord,
saying:
4 O Lord, do not suffer that this
people shall be destroyed by the
sword; but O Lord, rather [a]let there
be a [b]famine in the land, to stir
them up in remembrance of the
Lord their God, and perhaps they
will repent and turn unto thee.
5 And so it was done, according
to the words of Nephi. And there
was a great famine upon the land,
among all the people of Nephi. And
thus in the seventy and fourth year
the famine did continue, and the
work of destruction did cease by the
sword but became sore by famine.
6 And this work of destruction did
also continue in the seventy and
fifth year. For the earth was smitten
that it was [a]dry, and did not yield
forth grain in the season of grain;
and the whole earth was smitten,
even among the Lamanites as well
as among the Nephites, so that they
were smitten that they did perish
by thousands in the more wicked
parts of the land.
7 And it came to pass that the
people saw that they were about to
perish by famine, and they began
to [a]remember the Lord their God;
and they began to remember the
words of Nephi.
8 And the people [a]began to plead
with their chief judges and their
leaders, that they would say unto
Nephi: Behold, we know that thou
art a man of God, and therefore
cry unto the Lord our God that he
turn away from us this famine, lest
all the words which thou hast spoken concerning our [b]destruction
be fulfilled.
9 And it came to pass that the
judges did say unto Nephi, according to the words which had been
desired. And it came to pass that
when Nephi saw that the people
had [a]repented and did humble
themselves in sackcloth, he cried
again unto the Lord, saying:
10 O Lord, behold this people repenteth; and they have swept away
the band of Gadianton from amongst
them insomuch that they have become extinct, and they have concealed their secret plans in the earth.
11 Now, O Lord, because of this
their humility wilt thou turn away
thine anger, and let thine anger
be appeased in the destruction of
those wicked men whom thou hast
already destroyed.
12 O Lord, wilt thou turn away
thine anger, yea, thy fierce anger, and
cause that this famine may cease in
this land.
13 O Lord, wilt thou hearken unto
me, and cause that it may be done according to my words, and send forth
[a]rain upon the face of the earth,
that she may bring forth her fruit,
and her grain in the season of grain.
14 O Lord, thou didst hearken unto
[a]my words when I said, Let there
be a famine, that the pestilence of
the sword might cease; and I know
that thou wilt, even at this time,
hearken unto my words, for thou
saidst that: If this people repent I
will spare them.
15 Yea, O Lord, and thou seest
that they have repented, because of
the famine and the pestilence and

11 2*a* Hel. 6:22 (18–24); 11:26 (25–26).
4*a* Hel. 11:14.
b 1 Kgs. 8:35; 1 Chr. 21:12; Hel. 10:6. TG Famine.
6*a* TG Drought.
7*a* Amos 4:7 (6–10); Hel. 12:3.
8*a* Ex. 10:7.
b Hel. 10:11 (11–14).
9*a* Morm. 2:12.
13*a* 1 Kgs. 18:41 (1, 41–46).
14*a* Hel. 11:4.

destruction which has come unto them.
16 And now, O Lord, wilt thou turn away thine anger, and try again if they will serve thee? And if so, O Lord, thou canst bless them according to thy words which thou hast said.
17 And it came to pass that in the seventy and sixth year the Lord did turn away his anger from the people, and caused that [a]rain should fall upon the earth, insomuch that it did bring forth her fruit in the season of her fruit. And it came to pass that it did bring forth her grain in the season of her grain.
18 And behold, the people did rejoice and glorify God, and the whole face of the land was filled with rejoicing; and they did no more seek to destroy Nephi, but they did esteem him as a [a]great prophet, and a man of God, having great power and authority given unto him from God.
19 And behold, Lehi, his brother, was not a [a]whit behind him as to things pertaining to righteousness.
20 And thus it did come to pass that the people of Nephi began to prosper again in the land, and began to build up their waste places, and began to multiply and spread, even until they did [a]cover the whole face of the land, both on the northward and on the southward, from the sea west to the sea east.
21 And it came to pass that the seventy and sixth year did end in peace. And the seventy and seventh year began in peace; and the [a]church did spread throughout the face of all the land; and the more part of the people, both the Nephites and the Lamanites, did belong to the church; and they did have exceedingly great peace in the land; and thus ended the seventy and seventh year.
22 And also they had peace in the seventy and eighth year, save it were a few contentions concerning the points of doctrine which had been laid down by the prophets.
23 And in the seventy and ninth year there began to be much strife. But it came to pass that Nephi and Lehi, and many of their brethren who knew concerning the true points of doctrine, having many [a]revelations daily, therefore they did preach unto the people, insomuch that they did put an end to their strife in that same year.
24 And it came to pass that in the eightieth year of the reign of the judges over the people of Nephi, there were a certain number of the dissenters from the people of Nephi, who had some years before gone over unto the Lamanites, and taken upon themselves the name of Lamanites, and also a certain number who were real descendants of the Lamanites, being stirred up to anger by them, or by those dissenters, therefore they commenced a [a]war with their brethren.
25 And they did commit murder and plunder; and then they would retreat back into the mountains, and into the wilderness and secret places, hiding themselves that they could not be discovered, receiving daily an addition to their numbers, inasmuch as there were dissenters that went forth unto them.
26 And thus in time, yea, even in the space of [a]not many years, they became an exceedingly great band of robbers; and they did search out all the [b]secret plans of Gadianton; and thus they became robbers of Gadianton.
27 Now behold, these robbers did make great havoc, yea, even great destruction among the people of Nephi, and also among the people of the Lamanites.

17*a* Deut. 11:14 (13–17); Ether 2:24; D&C 117:1.
18*a* Hel. 10:7 (5–11).
19*a* Hel. 5:44 (36–44); 6:6.
20*a* Jarom 1:6; Alma 22:27 (27, 32–33); Hel. 3:8; 3 Ne. 1:17.
21*a* TG Church; Peace.
23*a* Jarom 1:4; Alma 26:22; D&C 107:19.
24*a* Hel. 4:3.
26*a* Hel. 4:26; 6:32; 7:6.
b Hel. 11:2.

28 And it came to pass that it was expedient that there should be a stop put to this work of destruction; therefore they sent an army of strong men into the wilderness and upon the mountains to search out this band of robbers, and to destroy them.
29 But behold, it came to pass that in that same year they were driven back even into their own lands. And thus ended the eightieth year of the reign of the judges over the people of Nephi.
30 And it came to pass in the commencement of the eighty and first year they did go forth again against this band of robbers, and did destroy many; and they were also visited with much destruction.
31 And they were again obliged to return out of the wilderness and out of the [a]mountains unto their own lands, because of the exceeding greatness of the numbers of those robbers who infested the mountains and the wilderness.
32 And it came to pass that thus ended this year. And the robbers did still increase and wax strong, insomuch that they did defy the whole armies of the Nephites, and also of the Lamanites; and they did cause great fear to come unto the people upon all the face of the land.
33 Yea, for they did visit many parts of the land, and did do great destruction unto them; yea, did kill many, and did carry away others captive into the wilderness, yea, and more especially their women and their children.
34 Now this great evil, which came unto the people because of their iniquity, did stir them up again in [a]remembrance of the Lord their God.
35 And thus ended the eighty and first year of the reign of the judges.
36 And in the eighty and second year they began again to [a]forget the Lord their God. And in the eighty and third year they began to wax strong in iniquity. And in the eighty and fourth year they did not mend their ways.
37 And it came to pass in the eighty and fifth year they did wax stronger and stronger in their pride, and in their wickedness; and thus they were [a]ripening again for destruction.
38 And thus ended the eighty and fifth year.

CHAPTER 12

Men are unstable and foolish and quick to do evil—The Lord chastens His people—The nothingness of men is compared with the power of God—In the day of judgment, men will gain everlasting life or everlasting damnation. About 6 B.C.

AND thus we can behold how false, and also the unsteadiness of the hearts of the children of men; yea, we can see that the Lord in his great infinite goodness doth bless and [a]prosper those who put their [b]trust in him.
2 Yea, and we may see at the very [a]time when he doth [b]prosper his people, yea, in the increase of their fields, their flocks and their herds, and in gold, and in silver, and in all manner of [c]precious things of every kind and art; sparing their lives, and delivering them out of the hands of their enemies; softening the hearts of their enemies that they should not declare wars against them; yea, and in fine, doing all things for the welfare and happiness of his people; yea, then is the time that they do [d]harden their hearts, and do [e]forget the Lord their God, and do [f]trample under their feet the

31 *a* 3 Ne. 1:27.
34 *a* Hosea 5:15.
36 *a* Mosiah 13:29.
37 *a* Hel. 6:40.
12 1 *a* 2 Chr. 26:5; Ps. 1:3 (2–3).
b Ps. 36:7 (7–8); 2 Ne. 22:2; Mosiah 4:6. TG Trust in God.
2 *a* Alma 46:8; Hel. 4:26; 6:32.
b Ps. 62:10.
c TG Treasure.
d TG Apostasy of Individuals.
e Deut. 8:11 (10–20).
f Alma 5:53; 3 Ne. 28:35. TG Sacrilege.

Holy One—yea, and this because of
their ease, and their exceedingly
great prosperity.
3 And thus we see that except the
Lord doth [a]chasten his people with
many afflictions, yea, except he doth
visit them with [b]death and with terror, and with famine and with all
manner of pestilence, they will not
[c]remember him.
4 O how [a]foolish, and how vain,
and how evil, and devilish, and how
[b]quick to do iniquity, and how slow
to do good, are the children of men;
yea, how quick to hearken unto the
words of the evil one, and to set
their [c]hearts upon the vain things of
the world!
5 Yea, how quick to be lifted up
in [a]pride; yea, how quick to [b]boast,
and do all manner of that which is
iniquity; and how slow are they to
remember the Lord their God, and
to give ear unto his counsels, yea,
how slow to [c]walk in wisdom's paths!
6 Behold, they do not desire that
the Lord their God, who hath [a]cre-
ated them, should [b]rule and reign
over them; notwithstanding his
great goodness and his mercy towards them, they do set at [c]naught
his counsels, and they will not that
he should be their guide.
7 O how great is the [a]nothingness of
the children of men; yea, even they
are [b]less than the dust of the earth.
8 For behold, the dust of the earth
moveth hither and thither, to the
dividing asunder, at the command
of our great and everlasting God.
9 Yea, behold at his [a]voice do the
hills and the mountains tremble
and [b]quake.
10 And by the [a]power of his voice
they are broken up, and become
smooth, yea, even like unto a valley.
11 Yea, by the power of his voice
doth the [a]whole earth shake;
12 Yea, by the power of his voice,
do the foundations rock, even to
the very center.
13 Yea, and if he say unto the
earth—Move—it is moved.
14 Yea, if he say unto the [a]earth—
Thou shalt [b]go back, that it [c]lengthen
out the day for many hours—it is
done;
15 And thus, according to his
word the [a]earth goeth back, and it
appeareth unto man that the [b]sun
standeth still; yea, and behold, this
is so; for surely it is the earth that
moveth and not the sun.
16 And behold, also, if he say unto
the [a]waters of the great deep—[b]Be
thou dried up—it is done.
17 Behold, if he say unto this
mountain—Be thou raised up, and
[a]come over and fall upon that city,
that it be buried up—behold it is
done.
18 And behold, if a man [a]hide up a
treasure in the earth, and the Lord
shall say—Let it be [b]accursed, because of the iniquity of him who
hath hid it up—behold, it shall be
accursed.
19 And if the Lord shall say—Be
thou accursed, that no man shall
find thee from this time henceforth
and forever—behold, no man getteth
it henceforth and forever.

3*a* Deut. 11:2 (1–8); Ezek. 20:26; Mosiah 23:21; D&C 98:21; 101:8.
b Ps. 78:34.
c Amos 4:6 (6–11); Jonah 2:7; Mosiah 1:17.
4*a* TG Foolishness.
b Ex. 32:8; Judg. 2:17; Isa. 59:7; Jer. 4:22.
c Gen. 6:5; Matt. 15:19; Heb. 3:12.
5*a* Prov. 29:23.
b TG Boast.
c TG Walking in Darkness; Walking with God.
6*a* Isa. 45:9 (9–10); D&C 58:30.
b Judg. 8:23 (22–23); D&C 60:4.
c Jer. 8:7.
7*a* Isa. 40:17 (15, 17); Dan. 4:35; Moses 1:10.
b Gen. 18:27.
9*a* Ezek. 1:24.
b Judg. 5:5; 3 Ne. 22:10.
10*a* 1 Ne. 17:46.
11*a* Morm. 5:23; Ether 4:9.
14*a* Josh. 10:12 (12–14).
b Isa. 38:8 (7–8).
c 2 Kgs. 20:9 (8–11).
15*a* Alma 30:44.
b Hab. 3:11.
16*a* Matt. 8:27 (23–27); Jacob 4:9.
b Isa. 44:27; 51:10.
17*a* 3 Ne. 8:10 (10, 25); 9:8 (5–6, 8).
18*a* Hel. 13:18 (18–23); Morm. 1:18 (17–19); Ether 14:1.
b Hel. 13:17.

20 And behold, if the Lord shall
say unto a man—Because of thine
iniquities, thou shalt be accursed
[a]forever—it shall be done.
21 And if the Lord shall say—Because of thine iniquities thou shalt
be [a]cut off from my presence—he
will cause that it shall be so.
22 And wo unto him to whom he
shall say this, for it shall be unto
him that will do iniquity, and he
cannot be [a]saved; therefore, for this
cause, that men might be saved, hath
repentance been declared.
23 Therefore, blessed are they who
will repent and hearken unto the
voice of the Lord their God; for these
are they that shall be saved.
24 And may God grant, in his great
fulness, that men might be brought
unto repentance and good works, that
they might be restored unto grace
for [a]grace, according to their works.
25 And I would that all men might
be saved. But we read that in the
[a]great and last day there are some
who shall be cast out, yea, who shall
be cast off from the [b]presence of
the Lord;
26 Yea, who shall be consigned to
a state of endless misery, fulfilling
the words which say: They that have
done good shall have [a]everlasting
life; and they that have done evil
shall have everlasting [b]damnation.
And thus it is. Amen.

The prophecy of Samuel, the Lamanite, to the Nephites.

Comprising chapters 13 through 15.

CHAPTER 13

Samuel the Lamanite prophesies the destruction of the Nephites unless they repent—They and their riches are cursed—They reject and stone the prophets, are encircled about by demons, and seek for happiness in doing iniquity. About 6 B.C.

AND now it came to pass in the
eighty and sixth year, the Nephites
did still remain in wickedness, yea,
in great wickedness, while the [a]La-
manites did observe strictly to keep
the commandments of God, according to the law of Moses.
2 And it came to pass that in this
year there was one [a]Samuel, a [b]La-
manite, came into the land of Zarahemla, and began to preach unto the
people. And it came to pass that he
did preach, many days, repentance
unto the people, and they did [c]cast
him out, and he was about to [d]return
to his own land.
3 But behold, the [a]voice of the Lord
came unto him, that he should return again, and prophesy unto the
people whatsoever things should
come into his [b]heart.
4 And it came to pass that they
would not suffer that he should enter into the city; therefore he went
and got upon the [a]wall thereof, and
stretched forth his hand and cried
with a loud voice, and [b]prophesied
unto the people whatsoever things
the Lord put into his heart.
5 And he said unto them: Behold,
I, Samuel, a Lamanite, do speak the
words of the Lord which he doth put
into my heart; and behold he hath
put it into my heart to say unto this
people that the [a]sword of justice
hangeth over this people; and four
hundred years pass not away save
the sword of justice falleth upon
this people.
6 Yea, heavy [a]destruction awaiteth

20*a* Mosiah 27:31.
21*a* Jer. 23:39 (39–40); D&C 63:4.
22*a* TG Salvation.
24*a* TG Grace.
25*a* Mal. 4:5; 3 Ne. 26:4.
b TG God, Presence of.
26*a* Dan. 12:2 (2–3); D&C 19:7.
b TG Damnation.
13 1*a* Hel. 6:1; 15:5.
2*a* Hel. 14:1; 3 Ne. 23:9 (9–10).
b Hel. 16:7.
c Hel. 14:10.
d Alma 26:27.
3*a* Gal. 2:2; Alma 8:16; 20:2; 3 Ne. 1:12.
b D&C 100:5.
4*a* Hel. 14:11; 16:1.
b TG Teaching with the Spirit.
5*a* Alma 60:29; 3 Ne. 2:19.
6*a* Alma 45:11 (10–14); Hel. 15:17.

this people, and it surely cometh unto this people, and nothing can save this people save it be repentance and faith on the Lord Jesus Christ, who surely shall come into the world, and shall suffer many things and shall be slain for his people.

7 And behold, an [a]angel of the Lord hath declared it unto me, and he did bring [b]glad tidings to my soul. And behold, I was sent unto you to declare it unto you also, that ye might have glad tidings; but behold ye would [c]not receive me.

8 Therefore, thus saith the Lord: Because of the hardness of the hearts of the people of the Nephites, except they repent I will take away my word from them, and I will [a]withdraw my Spirit from them, and I will suffer them no longer, and I will turn the hearts of their brethren against them.

9 And [a]four hundred years shall not pass away before I will cause that they shall be smitten; yea, I will visit them with the sword and with famine and with pestilence.

10 Yea, I will visit them in my fierce anger, and there shall be those of the [a]fourth generation who shall live, of your enemies, to behold your utter destruction; and this shall surely come except ye repent, saith the Lord; and those of the fourth generation shall visit your destruction.

11 But if ye will repent and [a]return unto the Lord your God I will turn away mine anger, saith the Lord; yea, thus saith the Lord, blessed are they who will repent and turn unto me, but wo unto him that repenteth not.

12 Yea, [a]wo unto this great city of Zarahemla; for behold, it is because of those who are righteous that it is saved; yea, wo unto this great city, for I perceive, saith the Lord, that there are many, yea, even the more part of this great city, that will harden their hearts against me, saith the Lord.

13 But blessed are they who will repent, for them will I spare. But behold, if it were not for the righteous who are in this great city, behold, I would cause that [a]fire should come down out of heaven and [b]destroy it.

14 But behold, it is for the righteous' sake that it is spared. But behold, the time cometh, saith the Lord, that when ye shall cast out the righteous from among you, then shall ye be [a]ripe for destruction; yea, wo be unto this great city, because of the wickedness and abominations which are in her.

15 Yea, and wo be unto the city of Gideon, for the wickedness and abominations which are in her.

16 Yea, and wo be unto all the cities which are in the land round about, which are possessed by the Nephites, because of the wickedness and abominations which are in them.

17 And behold, a [a]curse shall come upon the land, saith the Lord of Hosts, because of the people's sake who are upon the land, yea, because of their wickedness and their abominations.

18 And it shall come to pass, saith the Lord of Hosts, yea, our great and true God, that whoso shall [a]hide up treasures in the earth shall find them again no more, because of the great curse of the land, save he be a righteous man and shall hide it up unto the Lord.

19 For I will, saith the Lord, that they shall hide up their [a]treasures

7*a* Alma 13:26; Hel. 14:26 (9, 26, 28).
b Isa. 52:7.
c TG Prophets, Rejection of.
8*a* Ex. 23:21 (20–21).
9*a* Alma 45:10.
10*a* 1 Ne. 12:12; 2 Ne. 26:9; Alma 45:12; 3 Ne. 27:32.
11*a* 1 Sam. 7:3; 3 Ne. 10:6 (5–7).
12*a* 3 Ne. 8:24 (8, 24); 9:3.
13*a* 2 Kgs. 1:10 (9–16); 3 Ne. 9:11.
b Gen. 18:23; 1 Ne. 22:16; D&C 64:24.
14*a* Gen. 15:16; Alma 37:31; D&C 61:31; 101:11.
17*a* Hel. 12:18.
18*a* Morm. 1:18 (17–19); Ether 14:1.
19*a* Prov. 13:11.

unto me; and cursed be they who
hide not up their treasures unto me;
for none hideth up their treasures
unto me save it be the righteous; and
he that hideth not up his treasures
unto me, cursed is he, and also the
treasure, and none shall redeem it
because of the curse of the land.
20 And the day shall come that
they shall hide up their treasures,
because they have set their hearts
upon riches; and because they have
set their hearts upon their riches,
and will hide up their treasures
when they shall flee before their
enemies; because they will not
hide them up unto me, cursed be
they and also their treasures; and
in that day shall they be smitten,
saith the Lord.
21 Behold ye, the people of this
great city, and hearken unto my
words; yea, hearken unto the words
which the Lord saith; for behold, he
saith that ye are [a]cursed because
of your riches, and also are your
riches cursed because ye have set
your hearts upon them, and have
not [b]hearkened unto the words of
him who gave them unto you.
22 Ye do not remember the Lord
your God in the things with which
he hath blessed you, but ye do always remember your [a]riches, not to
thank the Lord your God for them;
yea, your hearts are not drawn out
unto the Lord, but they do swell
with great pride, unto [b]boasting,
and unto great [c]swelling, [d]envy-
ings, strifes, malice, persecutions,
and murders, and all manner of
iniquities.
23 For this cause hath the Lord
God caused that a curse should come
upon the land, and also upon your
riches, and this because of your
iniquities.
24 Yea, wo unto this people, because of this time which has arrived,
that ye do [a]cast out the prophets,
and do mock them, and cast stones
at them, and do slay them, and do
all manner of iniquity unto them,
even as they did of old time.
25 And now when ye talk, ye say:
If our days had been in the days of
our [a]fathers of old, we would not
have [b]slain the prophets; we would
not have stoned them, and cast
them out.
26 Behold ye are worse than they;
for as the Lord liveth, if a [a]prophet
come among you and declareth unto
you the word of the Lord, which testifieth of your [b]sins and iniquities,
ye are [c]angry with him, and cast him
out and seek all manner of ways to
destroy him; yea, you will say that
he is a [d]false [e]prophet, and that he
is a sinner, and of the devil, because he [f]testifieth that your deeds
are evil.
27 But behold, if a man shall come
among you and shall say: Do this,
and there is no iniquity; do that and
ye shall not suffer; yea, he will say:
[a]Walk after the pride of your own
hearts; yea, walk after the pride of
your eyes, and do whatsoever your
heart desireth—and if a man shall
come among you and say this, ye
will receive him, and say that he
is a [b]prophet.
28 Yea, ye will lift him up, and ye
will give unto him of your substance;
ye will give unto him of your gold,
and of your silver, and ye will clothe
him with costly apparel; and because he speaketh [a]flattering words
unto you, and he saith that all is

21*a* TG Curse.
b TG Disobedience.
22*a* Luke 12:34.
b TG Boast.
c Alma 30:31.
d TG Envy.
24*a* 2 Chr. 36:16 (15–16);
Neh. 9:26;
Jer. 20:2;
1 Ne. 1:20;
Hel. 16:6.
25*a* Matt. 23:32;
Acts 7:51 (51–52).
b TG Prophets, Rejection of.
26*a* 2 Chr. 18:7;
Luke 16:31 (19–31).
b Micah 3:8.
c Isa. 30:9 (9–10).
d Mosiah 12:14.
e Luke 11:15 (14–22);
Mosiah 3:9 (9–12).
f Gal. 4:16.
27*a* TG Walking in Darkness.
b Lam. 2:14; 4:13;
Micah 2:11.
TG False Prophets.
28*a* 2 Tim. 4:3 (3–4).

well, then ye will not find fault with him.

29 O ye wicked and ye perverse generation; ye hardened and ye [a]stiffnecked people, how long will ye suppose that the Lord will suffer you? Yea, how long will ye suffer yourselves to be led by [b]foolish and [c]blind guides? Yea, how long will ye [d]choose darkness rather than [e]light?

30 Yea, behold, the anger of the Lord is already kindled against you; behold, he hath cursed the land because of your iniquity.

31 And behold, the time cometh that he curseth your riches, that they become [a]slippery, that ye cannot hold them; and in the days of your poverty ye cannot retain them.

32 And in the days of your poverty ye shall cry unto the Lord; and in vain shall ye cry, for your desolation is already come upon you, and your destruction is made sure; and then shall ye weep and howl in that day, saith the Lord of Hosts. And then shall ye lament, and say:

33 O [a]that I had repented, and had not killed the prophets, and [b]stoned them, and cast them out. Yea, in that day ye shall say: O that we had remembered the Lord our God in the day that he gave us our riches, and then they would not have become slippery that we should lose them; for behold, our riches are gone from us.

34 Behold, we lay a tool here and on the morrow it is gone; and behold, our swords are taken from us in the day we have sought them for battle.

35 Yea, we have hid up our [a]treasures and they have slipped away from us, because of the curse of the land.

36 O that we had repented in the day that the word of the Lord came unto us; for behold the land is cursed, and all things are become slippery, and we cannot hold them.

37 Behold, we are surrounded by [a]demons, yea, we are encircled about by the angels of him who hath sought to destroy our souls. Behold, our iniquities are great. O Lord, canst thou not turn away thine anger from us? And this shall be your language in those days.

38 But behold, your [a]days of probation are past; ye have [b]procrastinated the day of your salvation until it is everlastingly too late, and your destruction is made sure; yea, for ye have sought all the days of your lives for that which ye could not obtain; and ye have sought for [c]happiness in doing iniquity, which thing is [d]contrary to the nature of that righteousness which is in our great and Eternal Head.

39 O ye people of the land, that ye would hear my words! And I pray that the anger of the Lord be turned away from you, and that ye would repent and be saved.

CHAPTER 14

Samuel predicts light during the night and a new star at Christ's birth—Christ redeems men from temporal and spiritual death—The signs of His death include three days of darkness, the rending of the rocks, and great upheavals of nature. About 6 B.C.

AND now it came to pass that [a]Samuel, the Lamanite, did prophesy a great many more things which cannot be written.

2 And behold, he said unto them: Behold, I give unto you a sign; for [a]five years more cometh, and behold, then cometh the Son of God

29*a* TG Stiffnecked.
b Ezek. 13:3; 2 Ne. 28:9.
c Matt. 15:14; 23:16.
d John 3:19.
e Job 24:13 (2–16).
31*a* Jer. 48:36 (35–36); Morm. 1:18 (17–19).
33*a* Morm. 2:10 (10–15).
b Matt. 23:37.
35*a* TG Treasure.
37*a* Mosiah 2:32.
38*a* Morm. 2:15 (10–15). TG Probation.
b Alma 34:33 (33–34). TG Apathy; Procrastination.
c Alma 41:10. TG Abundant Life; Happiness.
d Alma 41:11 (10–12).
14 1*a* Hel. 13:2; 3 Ne. 23:9 (9–10).
2*a* Hel. 16:4; 3 Ne. 1:5 (5–21).

to redeem all those who shall believe on his name.
3 And behold, this will I give unto
you for a [a]sign at the time of his
coming; for behold, there shall be
great lights in heaven, insomuch
that in the night before he cometh
there shall be no darkness, insomuch
that it shall appear unto man as if
it was day.
4 Therefore, there shall be one
[a]day and a night and a day, as if
it were one day and there were no
night; and this shall be unto you
for a sign; for ye shall know of the
rising of the sun and also of its setting; therefore they shall know of a
surety that there shall be two days
and a night; nevertheless the night
shall not be darkened; and it shall
be the night before he is [b]born.
5 And behold, there shall a new
[a]star arise, such an one as ye never
have beheld; and this also shall be
a sign unto you.
6 And behold this is not all, there
shall be many [a]signs and wonders
in heaven.
7 And it shall come to pass that ye
shall all be amazed, and wonder, insomuch that ye shall [a]fall to the earth.
8 And it shall come to pass that
whosoever shall [a]believe on the Son
of God, the same shall have everlasting life.
9 And behold, thus hath the Lord
commanded me, by his angel, that
I should come and tell this thing
unto you; yea, he hath commanded
that I should prophesy these things
unto you; yea, he hath said unto
me: Cry unto this people, repent
and prepare the way of the Lord.
10 And now, because I am a Lamanite, and have spoken unto you
the words which the Lord hath
commanded me, and because it was
hard against you, ye are angry with
me and do seek to destroy me, and
have [a]cast me out from among you.
11 And ye shall [a]hear my words,
for, for this intent have I come up
upon the walls of this city, that ye
might hear and know of the judgments of God which do await you
because of your iniquities, and also
that ye might know the conditions
of repentance;
12 And also that ye might know of
the coming of Jesus Christ, the Son
of God, the [a]Father of heaven and of
earth, the Creator of all things from
the beginning; and that ye might
know of the signs of his coming,
to the intent that ye might believe
on his name.
13 And if ye [a]believe on his name
ye will repent of all your sins, that
thereby ye may have a remission of
them through his [b]merits.
14 And behold, again, another
sign I give unto you, yea, a sign of
his [a]death.
15 For behold, he surely must
die that [a]salvation may come; yea,
it behooveth him and becometh
expedient that he [b]dieth, to bring to
pass the [c]resurrection of the dead,
that thereby men may be brought
into the [d]presence of the Lord.
16 Yea, behold, this death bringeth
to pass the [a]resurrection, and [b]re-
deemeth all mankind from the first
death—that spiritual death; for all
mankind, by the [c]fall of Adam being [d]cut off from the presence of

3*a* Hel. 16:13;
3 Ne. 1:15 (8–20).
4*a* 3 Ne. 1:8.
b TG Jesus Christ, Birth of.
5*a* Matt. 2:2 (1–2);
3 Ne. 1:21.
TG Astronomy.
6*a* 3 Ne. 2:1.
7*a* 3 Ne. 1:16 (16–17).
8*a* John 3:16.
10*a* Hel. 13:2 (2–7).
11*a* Ezek. 2:7 (6–7).
12*a* Mosiah 3:8; 15:4;
3 Ne. 9:15;
Ether 4:7.
TG Jesus Christ, Creator.
13*a* Acts 16:31 (30–31).
b D&C 19:16 (16–20).
14*a* TG Jesus Christ,
Death of.
15*a* TG Jesus Christ, Savior.
b 1 Cor. 15:36.
c 2 Ne. 9:4;
Alma 42:23;
Morm. 9:13.
TG Resurrection.
d TG God, Presence of.
16*a* John 20:9;
D&C 18:12 (11–12).
b TG Salvation, Plan of.
c TG Fall of Man.
d 2 Ne. 2:5; 9:6 (6–15);
Alma 11:42 (40–45);
12:16 (16, 24, 36);
42:7 (6–11).

the Lord, are considered as [e]dead,
both as to things temporal and to
things spiritual.
17 But behold, the resurrection of
Christ [a]redeemeth mankind, yea,
even all mankind, and bringeth
them back into the presence of the
Lord.
18 Yea, and it bringeth to pass
the condition of repentance, that
whosoever repenteth the same is
not [a]hewn down and cast into the
fire; but whosoever repenteth not is
hewn down and cast into the fire;
and there cometh upon them again
a [b]spiritual death, yea, a second
death, for they are cut off again as to
things pertaining to righteousness.
19 Therefore repent ye, repent ye,
lest by knowing these things and
not doing them ye shall suffer yourselves to come under condemnation,
and ye are brought down unto this
second death.
20 But behold, as I said unto you
concerning another [a]sign, a sign of
his death, behold, in that day that
he shall suffer death the sun shall
be darkened and refuse to give his
[b]light unto you; and also the moon
and the stars; and there shall be no
light upon the face of this land, even
from the time that he shall suffer
death, for the space of [c]three days,
to the time that he shall rise again
from the dead.
21 Yea, at the time that he shall
yield up the [a]ghost there shall be
[b]thunderings and lightnings for the
space of many hours, and the earth
shall shake and tremble; and the
[c]rocks which are upon the face of
this earth, which are both above the
earth and beneath, which ye know
at this time are solid, or the more
part of it is one solid mass, shall be
[d]broken up;
22 Yea, they shall be rent in twain,
and shall ever after be [a]found in
seams and in cracks, and in broken fragments upon the face of the
whole earth, yea, both above the
earth and beneath.
23 And behold, there shall be
great [a]tempests, and there shall be
many mountains laid low, like unto
a valley, and there shall be many
places which are now called [b]val-
leys which shall become mountains,
whose height is great.
24 And [a]many highways shall be
broken up, and many cities shall
become desolate.
25 And many [a]graves shall be
opened, and shall yield up many of
their dead; and many saints shall
appear unto many.
26 And behold, thus hath the [a]an-
gel spoken unto me; for he said unto
me that there should be thunderings and lightnings for the space
of many hours.
27 And he said unto me that while
the thunder and the lightning
lasted, and the tempest, that these
things should be, and that [a]darkness
should cover the face of the whole
earth for the space of three days.
28 And the angel said unto me
that many shall see greater things
than these, to the intent that they
might believe that [a]these signs and
these wonders should come to pass
upon all the face of this land, to
the intent that there should be no
cause for unbelief among the children of men—
29 And this to the intent that whosoever will believe might be saved,
and that whosoever will not believe,

16*e* TG Death, Spiritual, First.
17*a* TG Redemption.
18*a* Luke 13:7.
b TG Death, Spiritual, Second.
20*a* 3 Ne. 8:5 (5–25); 11:2.
b Luke 23:44.
c Mosiah 3:10.
21*a* Matt. 27:50 (50–54).
b 1 Ne. 19:11; 3 Ne. 8:6 (5–23).
c 3 Ne. 10:9.
d Gen. 7:11; 1 Ne. 12:4.
22*a* 3 Ne. 8:18.
23*a* 3 Ne. 10:14.
b Isa. 40:4; Luke 3:5; D&C 49:23; 109:74.
24*a* 3 Ne. 8:14 (8–10, 14); 9:12 (3–12); 10:7.
25*a* Matt. 27:52 (52–53); 3 Ne. 23:11 (7–13).
26*a* Alma 13:26; Hel. 13:7.
27*a* 1 Ne. 19:10; 3 Ne. 8:3; 10:9.
28*a* 1 Ne. 12:4 (4–5); 19:12 (10–12); 3 Ne. 10:11.

a [a]righteous judgment might come
upon them; and also if they are condemned they bring upon themselves
their own condemnation.
30 And now remember, remember,
my brethren, that whosoever perisheth, perisheth unto [a]himself; and
whosoever doeth iniquity, doeth it
unto himself; for behold, ye are [b]free;
ye are permitted to act for yourselves; for behold, God hath given
unto you a [c]knowledge and he hath
made you free.
31 He hath given unto you that ye
might [a]know good from evil, and he
hath given unto you that ye might
[b]choose life or death; and ye can
do good and be [c]restored unto that
which is good, or have that which is
good restored unto you; or ye can
do evil, and have that which is evil
restored unto you.

CHAPTER 15

The Lord chastened the Nephites because He loved them—Converted Lamanites are firm and steadfast in the faith—The Lord will be merciful unto the Lamanites in the latter days. About 6 B.C.

AND now, my beloved brethren, behold, I declare unto you that except
ye shall repent your houses shall
be left unto you [a]desolate.
2 Yea, except ye repent, your women
shall have great cause to mourn in
the day that they shall give suck; for
ye shall attempt to flee and there
shall be no place for [a]refuge; yea,
and wo unto them which are [b]with
child, for they shall be heavy and
cannot flee; therefore, they shall
be trodden down and shall be left
to perish.
3 Yea, wo unto this [a]people who
are called the [b]people of Nephi except they shall repent, when they
shall see all these signs and wonders
which shall be showed unto them;
for behold, they have been a chosen
people of the Lord; yea, the people
of Nephi hath he loved, and also
hath he [c]chastened them; yea, in
the days of their iniquities hath he
chastened them because he loveth
them.
4 But behold my brethren, the
[a]Lamanites hath he hated because
their deeds have been evil continually, and this because of the iniquity
of the [b]tradition of their fathers.
But behold, salvation hath come
unto them through the preaching
of the Nephites; and for this intent hath the Lord [c]prolonged their
days.
5 And I would that ye should behold that the [a]more part of them
are in the path of their duty, and
they do walk circumspectly before
God, and they do observe to keep
his commandments and his statutes
and his judgments according to the
law of Moses.
6 Yea, I say unto you, that the more
part of them are doing this, and
they are striving with [a]unwearied
diligence that they may bring the
remainder of their brethren to the
knowledge of the truth; therefore
there are many who do add to their
numbers daily.
7 And behold, ye do know of yourselves, for ye have witnessed it, that
as many of them as are brought to
the knowledge of the truth, and to
know of the wicked and abominable
traditions of their fathers, and are
led to believe the holy scriptures,
yea, the prophecies of the holy
prophets, which are written, which

29*a* TG Judgment.
30*a* 3 Ne. 3:11.
b Gal. 5:1; 2 Ne. 2:27 (26–27); Alma 41:7; Moses 6:56. TG Agency.
c TG Knowledge.
31*a* Moro. 7:16.
b Rom. 6:16 (14–18); Alma 3:27 (26–27).
c Alma 41:3 (1–15).
15 1*a* Isa. 5:9; Matt. 23:38.
2*a* TG Refuge.
b Matt. 24:19.
3*a* W of M 1:11.
b Jacob 5:25.
c Prov. 3:12; Heb. 12:6 (5–11); D&C 95:1.
4*a* Jacob 5:40.
b Ezek. 20:18; Hel. 5:19. TG Traditions of Men.
c Alma 9:16.
5*a* Hel. 13:1; 16:6.
6*a* TG Dedication.

leadeth them to faith on the Lord,
and unto repentance, which faith
and repentance bringeth a [a]change
of heart unto them—
8 Therefore, as many as have come
to this, ye know of yourselves are
[a]firm and steadfast in the faith, and
in the thing wherewith they have
been made free.
9 And ye know also that they have
[a]buried their weapons of war, and
they fear to take them up lest by
any means they should sin; yea, ye
can see that they fear to sin—for
behold they will suffer themselves
that they be trodden down and slain
by their enemies, and will not lift
their swords against them, and this
because of their [b]faith in Christ.
10 And now, because of their
[a]steadfastness when they do believe
in that thing which they do believe,
for because of their firmness when
they are once enlightened, behold,
the Lord shall bless them and prolong their days, notwithstanding
their iniquity—
11 Yea, even if they should dwindle
in unbelief the Lord shall [a]prolong
their days, until the time shall come
which hath been spoken of by our
fathers, and also by the prophet
[b]Zenos, and many other prophets,
concerning the [c]restoration of our
brethren, the Lamanites, again to
the knowledge of the truth—
12 Yea, I say unto you, that in the
latter times the [a]promises of the
Lord have been extended to our
brethren, the Lamanites; and notwithstanding the many afflictions
which they shall have, and notwithstanding they shall be [b]driven to
and fro upon the face of the earth,
and be hunted, and shall be smitten and scattered abroad, having no
place for [c]refuge, the Lord shall be
[d]merciful unto them.
13 And this is according to the
prophecy, that they shall again be
[a]brought to the true knowledge,
which is the knowledge of their
Redeemer, and their great and true
[b]shepherd, and be numbered among
his [c]sheep.
14 Therefore I say unto you, it
shall be [a]better for them than for
you except ye repent.
15 For behold, [a]had the mighty
works been shown unto them which
have been shown unto you, yea,
unto them who have dwindled in
unbelief because of the traditions
of their fathers, ye can see of yourselves that they never would again
have dwindled in unbelief.
16 Therefore, saith the Lord: I will
not utterly destroy them, but I
will cause that in the day of my
wisdom they shall [a]return again
unto me, saith the Lord.
17 And now behold, saith the
Lord, concerning the people of the
Nephites: If they will not repent,
and observe to do my will, I will utterly [a]destroy them, saith the Lord,
because of their unbelief notwithstanding the many mighty works
which I have done among them;
and as surely as the Lord liveth
shall these things be, saith the Lord.

CHAPTER 16

The Nephites who believe Samuel are baptized by Nephi—Samuel cannot be slain with the arrows and stones of the unrepentant Nephites—Some harden their hearts, and others see angels—The unbelievers say it is not reasonable to believe in Christ and His coming in Jerusalem. About 6–1 B.C.

7*a* TG Conversion.
8*a* Alma 23:6; 27:27; 3 Ne. 6:14.
9*a* Alma 24:17 (17–26).
b Mark 5:34 (34–36).
10*a* TG Steadfastness.
11*a* Deut. 11:9 (8–9); Alma 9:16.
b Hel. 8:19; 3 Ne. 10:16.
c Morm. 5:12 (9, 12); 7:1.
12*a* Enos 1:13 (12–13).
b Morm. 5:15.
c TG Refuge.
d 1 Ne. 13:31; 2 Ne. 4:7; 10:18 (18–19); Jacob 3:6 (5–9); Morm. 5:20 (20–21).
13*a* 3 Ne. 16:12.
b TG Jesus Christ, Good Shepherd.
c TG Sheep.
14*a* Hel. 7:23.
15*a* Matt. 11:21 (20–24).
16*a* Enos 1:13.
17*a* Hel. 13:6 (5–10); Morm. 3:2.

AND now, it came to pass that there
were many who heard the words
of Samuel, the Lamanite, which he
spake upon the [a]walls of the city.
And as many as believed on his word
went forth and sought for Nephi;
and when they had come forth and
found him they confessed unto him
their sins and denied not, desiring
that they might be [b]baptized unto
the Lord.
2 But as many as there were who
did not believe in the words of Samuel were [a]angry with him; and they
cast stones at him upon the wall,
and also many shot arrows at him
as he stood upon the wall; but the
Spirit of the Lord was with him,
insomuch that they could not hit
him with their stones neither with
their arrows.
3 Now when they saw that they
could not hit him, there were many
more who did believe on his words,
insomuch that they went away unto
Nephi to be baptized.
4 For behold, Nephi was baptizing,
and prophesying, and preaching,
crying repentance unto the people,
showing signs and wonders, working
[a]miracles among the people, that
they might know that the Christ
must [b]shortly come—
5 Telling them of things which
must shortly come, that they might
know and remember at the time of
their coming that they had been
made known unto them beforehand,
to the intent that they might believe;
therefore as many as believed on the
words of Samuel went forth unto
him to be baptized, for they came
repenting and confessing their sins.
6 But the [a]more part of them did
not believe in the words of Samuel;
therefore when they saw that they
could not hit him with their stones
and their arrows, they cried unto
their captains, saying: [b]Take this
fellow and bind him, for behold
he [c]hath a devil; and because of the
power of the devil which is in him
we cannot hit him with our stones
and our arrows; therefore take him
and bind him, and away with him.
7 And as they went forth to lay
their hands on him, behold, he did
cast himself down from the wall,
and did flee out of their lands, yea,
even unto his own country, and
began to preach and to prophesy
[a]among his own people.
8 And behold, he was never heard
of more among the Nephites; and
thus were the affairs of the people.
9 And thus ended the eighty and
sixth year of the reign of the judges
over the people of Nephi.
10 And thus ended also the eighty
and seventh year of the reign of the
judges, the more part of the people
remaining in their pride and wickedness, and the lesser part walking
more circumspectly before God.
11 And these were the conditions
also, in the eighty and eighth year
of the reign of the judges.
12 And there was but little altera-
tion in the affairs of the people,
save it were the people began to be
more hardened in iniquity, and do
more and more of that which was
[a]contrary to the commandments of
God, in the eighty and ninth year
of the reign of the judges.
13 But it came to pass in the ninetieth year of the reign of the judges,
there were [a]great signs given unto
the people, and wonders; and the
words of the prophets [b]began to
be fulfilled.
14 And [a]angels did appear unto
men, wise men, and did declare
unto them glad tidings of great joy;
thus in this year the scriptures began to be fulfilled.
15 Nevertheless, the people began
to harden their hearts, all save it
were the most believing part of them,
both of the Nephites and also of the

16 1*a* Hel. 13:4.
b Alma 9:27.
2*a* Prov. 29:10.
4*a* TG Miracle.
b Hel. 14:2.
6*a* Hel. 15:5; 3 Ne. 1:22.
b Hel. 13:24.
c John 7:20.
7*a* Hel. 13:2.
12*a* TG Disobedience.
13*a* 3 Ne. 1:4.
b Hel. 14:3 (3–7).
14*a* Alma 13:26.

Lamanites, and began to depend
upon their [a]own strength and upon
their own wisdom, saying:
16 Some things they may have
guessed right, among so many; but
behold, we know that all these great
and marvelous works cannot come
to pass, of which has been spoken.
17 And they began to reason and to
contend among themselves, saying:
18 That it is [a]not reasonable that
such a being as a Christ shall come;
if so, and he be the Son of God, the
Father of heaven and of earth, as it
has been spoken, why will he not
show himself unto us as well as unto
them who shall be at Jerusalem?
19 Yea, why will he not show himself in this land as well as in the
land of Jerusalem?
20 But behold, we know that this is
a wicked [a]tradition, which has been
handed down unto us by our fathers,
to cause us that we should believe
in some great and marvelous thing
which should come to pass, but not
among us, but in a land which is
far distant, a land which we know
not; therefore they can keep us in
ignorance, for we cannot [b]witness
with our own eyes that they are true.
21 And they will, by the cunning
and the mysterious arts of the evil
one, work some great mystery which
we cannot understand, which will
keep us down to be servants to
their words, and also servants unto
them, for we depend upon them to
teach us the word; and thus will
they keep us in ignorance if we will
yield ourselves unto them, all the
days of our lives.
22 And many more things did the
people [a]imagine up in their hearts,
which were foolish and [b]vain; and
they were much disturbed, for Satan did stir them up to do iniquity
continually; yea, he did go about
spreading [c]rumors and contentions
upon all the face of the land, that
he might harden the hearts of the
people against that which was good
and against that which should come.
23 And notwithstanding the
signs and the wonders which were
wrought among the people of the
Lord, and the many miracles which
they did, Satan did get great hold
upon the hearts of the people upon
all the face of the land.
24 And thus ended the ninetieth
year of the reign of the judges over
the people of Nephi.
25 [a]And thus ended the book of
Helaman, according to the record
of Helaman and his sons.

THIRD NEPHI
THE BOOK OF NEPHI

THE SON OF NEPHI, WHO WAS THE SON OF HELAMAN

And Helaman was the son of Helaman, who was the son of Alma, who was the son of Alma, being a descendant of Nephi who was the son of Lehi, who came out of Jerusalem in the first year of the reign of Zedekiah, the king of Judah.

CHAPTER 1

Nephi, the son of Helaman, departs out of the land, and his son Nephi keeps the records—Though signs and wonders abound, the wicked plan to slay the righteous—The night of Christ's birth arrives—The sign is given, and a

15*a* Isa. 5:21.
18*a* Alma 30:53.
20*a* TG Traditions of Men.
b Alma 30:15; Ether 12:5 (5–6, 19).
22*a* Gen. 6:5.
b 4 Ne. 1:43.
c Prov. 6:18 (16–19).
25*a* Hel. 3:37.

*new star arises—Lyings and deceivings
increase, and the Gadianton robbers
slaughter many. About* A.D. *1–4.*

NOW it came to pass that the
ninety and first year had
passed away and it was [a]six
hundred years from the time that
Lehi left Jerusalem; and it was in
the year that [b]Lachoneus was the
chief judge and the governor over
the land.
2 And [a]Nephi, the son of Helaman, had departed out of the land
of Zarahemla, giving charge unto
his son [b]Nephi, who was his eldest
son, concerning the [c]plates of brass,
and [d]all the records which had been
kept, and all those things which
had been kept sacred from the departure of Lehi out of Jerusalem.
3 Then he [a]departed out of the
land, and [b]whither he went, no man
knoweth; and his son Nephi did
keep the records in his stead, yea,
the record of this people.
4 And it came to pass that in the
commencement of the ninety and
second year, behold, the prophecies
of the prophets began to be fulfilled
more fully; for there began to be
[a]greater signs and greater miracles
wrought among the people.
5 But there were some who began
to say that the time was past for the
words to be fulfilled, which were
[a]spoken by Samuel, the Lamanite.
6 And they began to [a]rejoice over
their brethren, saying: Behold the
time is past, and the words of Samuel are not fulfilled; therefore, your
joy and your faith concerning this
thing hath been vain.
7 And it came to pass that they did
make a great uproar throughout the
land; and the people who believed
began to be very sorrowful, lest
by any means those things which
had been spoken might not come
to pass.
8 But behold, they did watch steadfastly for [a]that day and that night
and that day which should be as
one day as if there were no night,
that they might know that their
faith had not been vain.
9 Now it came to pass that there
was a day set apart by the [a]unbe-
lievers, that all those who believed
in those traditions should be [b]put to
death except the [c]sign should come
to pass, which had been given by
Samuel the prophet.
10 Now it came to pass that when
Nephi, the son of Nephi, saw this
wickedness of his people, his heart
was exceedingly sorrowful.
11 And it came to pass that he
went out and bowed himself down
upon the earth, and cried mightily
to his God in behalf of his people,
yea, those who were about to be
destroyed because of their faith in
the tradition of their fathers.
12 And it came to pass that he
cried mightily unto the Lord [a]all
that day; and behold, the [b]voice of
the Lord came unto him, saying:
13 Lift up your head and be of
good cheer; for behold, the time is
at hand, and on this night shall the
[a]sign be given, and on the [b]morrow
come I into the world, to show unto
the world that I will fulfil all that
which I have caused to be [c]spoken
by the mouth of my holy prophets.
14 Behold, I [a]come unto my own,
to [b]fulfil all things which I have
made known unto the children of
men from the [c]foundation of the

1 1*a* 2 Ne. 25:19; Alma 13:25.
b 3 Ne. 3:1; 6:19.
2*a* Hel. 3:21 (20–21).
b 3 Ne. 7:15 (15, 20, 23).
c Alma 37:3 (3–12); 63:12 (1, 11–14).
d Alma 50:38.
3*a* Alma 45:18 (18–19).
b 3 Ne. 2:9.
4*a* Hel. 16:13 (13, 23).
5*a* Hel. 14:2.
6*a* TG Mocking.
8*a* Hel. 14:4 (3–4).
9*a* TG Unbelief.
b 3 Ne. 1:16. TG Martyrdom.
c Hel. 14:3 (2–7).
12*a* Enos 1:4; Alma 5:46.
b Alma 20:2; Hel. 13:3.
13*a* Matt. 2:2.
b Luke 2:11 (10–11).
c TG Jesus Christ, Prophecies about.
14*a* John 1:11.
b Matt. 5:17 (17–18); Luke 24:44.
c Alma 42:26; 3 Ne. 26:5.

world, and to do the [d]will, [e]both [f]of
the Father and of the Son—of the
Father because of me, and of the
Son because of my flesh. And behold, the time is at hand, and this
night shall the sign be given.
15 And it came to pass that the
words which came unto Nephi
were fulfilled, according as they
had been spoken; for behold, at the
going down of the [a]sun there was
[b]no darkness; and the people began
to be astonished because there was
no darkness when the night came.
16 And there were many, who
had not believed the words of the
prophets, who [a]fell to the earth and
became as if they were dead, for
they knew that the great [b]plan of
destruction which they had laid for
those who believed in the words of
the prophets had been frustrated;
for the sign which had been given
was already at hand.
17 And they began to know that
the Son of God must shortly appear;
yea, in fine, all the people upon the
face of the whole earth from the
[a]west to the east, both in the land
north and in the land south, were
so exceedingly astonished that they
fell to the earth.
18 For they knew that the prophets had testified of these things for
many years, and that the sign which
had been given was already at hand;
and they began to fear because of
their iniquity and their unbelief.
19 And it came to pass that there
was no darkness in all that night,
but it was as light as though it was
mid-day. And it came to pass that the
sun did rise in the morning again,
according to its proper order; and
they knew that it was the day that
the Lord should be [a]born, because
of the [b]sign which had been given.
20 And it had come to pass, yea,
all things, every whit, according to
the words of the prophets.
21 And it came to pass also that
a new [a]star did appear, according
to the word.
22 And it came to pass that from
this time forth there began to be
[a]lyings sent forth among the people,
by Satan, to harden their hearts, to
the intent that they might not believe in those [b]signs and wonders
which they had seen; but notwithstanding these lyings and deceivings
the [c]more part of the people did
believe, and were converted unto
the Lord.
23 And it came to pass that Nephi
went forth among the people, and
also many others, baptizing unto
repentance, in the which there was
a great [a]remission of sins. And thus
the people began again to have
peace in the land.
24 And there were no contentions,
save it were a few that began to
preach, endeavoring to prove by
the [a]scriptures that it was no more
expedient to observe the law of
Moses. Now in this thing they did
err, having not understood the
scriptures.
25 But it came to pass that they
soon became converted, and were
convinced of the error which they
were in, for it was made known
unto them that the law was not yet
[a]fulfilled, and that it must be fulfilled in every whit; yea, the word
came unto them that it must be
fulfilled; yea, that one jot or tittle
should not pass away till it should
all be fulfilled; therefore in this
same year were they brought to a
knowledge of their error and did
[b]confess their faults.
26 And thus the ninety and second

14*d* TG God, Will of.
e D&C 93:4 (4, 14).
f Mosiah 15:3.
15*a* Josh. 10:13.
b Hel. 14:3.
16*a* Hel. 14:7.
b 3 Ne. 1:9 (9, 11).
17*a* Hel. 11:20.
19*a* TG Jesus Christ, Birth of.
b Hel. 14:3.
21*a* Matt. 2:2 (1–2); Hel. 14:5.
22*a* Moses 5:13.
b TG Signs.
c Hel. 16:6.
23*a* TG Remission of Sins.
24*a* Alma 34:13.
25*a* Matt. 5:18; 2 Ne. 25:24.
b Num. 5:7 (6–10); Mosiah 26:29 (29, 35); Alma 17:4.

year did pass away, bringing [a]glad
tidings unto the people because of
the signs which did come to pass,
according to the words of the prophecy of all the holy prophets.
27 And it came to pass that the
ninety and third year did also pass
away in peace, save it were for the
Gadianton robbers, who dwelt upon
the [a]mountains, who did infest the
land; for so strong were their holds
and their secret places that the
people could not overpower them;
therefore they did commit many
murders, and did do much slaughter among the people.
28 And it came to pass that in the
ninety and fourth year they began
to increase in a great degree, because there were many dissenters
of the Nephites who did flee unto
them, which did cause much sorrow unto those Nephites who did
remain in the land.
29 And there was also a cause of
much sorrow among the Lamanites;
for behold, they had many children
who did grow up and began to wax
strong in years, that they became for
themselves, and were [a]led away by
some who were [b]Zoramites, by their
lyings and their flattering words,
to join those Gadianton robbers.
30 And thus were the Lamanites
afflicted also, and began to decrease
as to their faith and righteousness,
because of the wickedness of the
[a]rising generation.

CHAPTER 2

Wickedness and abominations increase among the people—The Nephites and Lamanites unite to defend themselves against the Gadianton robbers—Converted Lamanites become white and are called Nephites. About A.D. *5–16.*

AND it came to pass that thus
passed away the ninety and fifth
year also, and the people began to
forget those [a]signs and wonders
which they had heard, and began
to be less and less astonished at a
sign or a wonder from heaven, insomuch that they began to be hard
in their hearts, and blind in their
minds, and began to disbelieve all
which they had heard and seen—
2 [a]Imagining up some vain thing
in their hearts, that it was wrought
by men and by the power of the
devil, to lead away and [b]deceive
the hearts of the people; and thus
did Satan get possession of the
hearts of the people again, insomuch that he did blind their eyes
and lead them away to believe that
the doctrine of Christ was a [c]foolish
and a vain thing.
3 And it came to pass that the
people began to wax strong in wickedness and abominations; and they
did not believe that there should be
any more signs or wonders given;
and Satan did [a]go about, leading
away the hearts of the people,
tempting them and causing them
that they should do great wickedness
in the land.
4 And thus did pass away the
ninety and sixth year; and also
the ninety and seventh year; and
also the ninety and eighth year;
and also the ninety and ninth year;
5 And also an hundred years
had passed away since the days of
[a]Mosiah, who was king over the
people of the Nephites.
6 And six hundred and nine years
had passed away since Lehi left
Jerusalem.
7 And nine years had passed away
from the time when the sign was
given, which was spoken of by the
prophets, that Christ should come
into the world.
8 Now the Nephites began to
[a]reckon their time from this period

26*a* Luke 2:10.
27*a* Hel. 11:31 (25–31); 3 Ne. 2:11.
29*a* TG Peer Influence.
b Alma 30:59; 43:4.
30*a* Judg. 2:10.
2 1*a* Hel. 14:6.
2*a* Heb. 3:12.
b TG Deceit.
c 1 Cor. 1:23 (23–25); Alma 30:13 (12–18).
3*a* Job 1:7; D&C 10:27.
5*a* Mosiah 29:46 (46–47).
8*a* 3 Ne. 5:7; 8:2.

when the sign was given, or from
the coming of Christ; therefore, nine
years had passed away.
9 And Nephi, who was the father
of Nephi, who had the charge of the
records, [a]did not return to the land
of Zarahemla, and could nowhere
be found in all the land.
10 And it came to pass that the people did still [a]remain in wickedness,
notwithstanding the much preaching and prophesying which was
sent among them; and thus passed
away the tenth year also; and the
eleventh year also passed away in
iniquity.
11 And it came to pass in the
thirteenth year there began to be
wars and contentions throughout
all the land; for the [a]Gadianton robbers had become so [b]numerous, and
did slay so many of the people,
and did lay waste so many cities, and
did spread so much death and
carnage throughout the land, that
it became expedient that all the
people, both the Nephites and the
Lamanites, should take up arms
against them.
12 Therefore, all the Lamanites
who had become converted unto the
Lord did unite with their brethren,
the Nephites, and were compelled,
for the [a]safety of their lives and their
women and their children, to take
up arms against those Gadianton
robbers, yea, and also to maintain
their rights, and the privileges of
their church and of their worship,
and their freedom and their [b]liberty.
13 And it came to pass that before
this thirteenth year had passed away
the Nephites were threatened with
utter destruction because of this
war, which had become exceedingly
sore.
14 And it came to pass that those
Lamanites who had united with the
Nephites were numbered among
the Nephites;
15 And their [a]curse was taken from
them, and their skin became [b]white
like unto the Nephites;
16 And their young men and their
daughters became exceedingly fair,
and they were numbered among
the Nephites, and were called Nephites. And thus ended the thirteenth
year.
17 And it came to pass in the commencement of the fourteenth year,
the war between the robbers and
the people of Nephi did continue
and did become exceedingly sore;
nevertheless, the people of Nephi
did gain some advantage of the
robbers, insomuch that they did
drive them back out of their lands
into the mountains and into their
secret places.
18 And thus ended the fourteenth
year. And in the fifteenth year they
did come forth against the people
of Nephi; and because of the wickedness of the people of Nephi, and
their many contentions and dissensions, the Gadianton robbers did
gain many advantages over them.
19 And thus ended the fifteenth
year, and thus were the people in
a state of many afflictions; and the
[a]sword of destruction did hang over
them, insomuch that they were
about to be smitten down by it,
and this because of their iniquity.

CHAPTER 3

Giddianhi, the Gadianton leader, demands that Lachoneus and the Nephites surrender themselves and their lands—Lachoneus appoints Gidgiddoni as chief captain of the armies—The Nephites assemble in Zarahemla and Bountiful to defend themselves. About A.D. *16–18.*

AND now it came to pass that in the
sixteenth year from the coming of
Christ, [a]Lachoneus, the governor of
the land, received an epistle from

9*a* 3 Ne. 1:3 (2–3).
10*a* Alma 34:35.
11*a* 3 Ne. 1:27.
b Morm. 2:8.
12*a* Alma 58:12; 3 Ne. 3:2.
b TG Liberty.
15*a* Alma 17:15; 23:18.
b 2 Ne. 5:21; 30:6; Jacob 3:8.
19*a* Alma 60:29; Hel. 13:5; 3 Ne. 3:3.
3 1*a* 3 Ne. 1:1; 6:6.

the leader and the governor of this
band of robbers; and these were the
words which were written, saying:
2 Lachoneus, most noble and chief
governor of the land, behold, I write
this epistle unto you, and do give
unto you exceedingly great praise
because of your firmness, and also
the firmness of your people, in
[a]maintaining that which ye suppose
to be your right and [b]liberty; yea,
ye do stand well, as if ye were supported by the hand of a god, in the
defence of your liberty, and your
property, and your country, or that
which ye do call so.
3 And it seemeth a pity unto me,
most noble Lachoneus, that ye
should be so foolish and vain as to
suppose that ye can stand against
so many brave men who are at my
command, who do now at this time
stand in their arms, and do await
with great anxiety for the word—
Go down upon the Nephites and
[a]destroy them.
4 And I, knowing of their unconquerable spirit, having proved them
in the field of battle, and knowing of
their everlasting hatred towards you
because of the many wrongs which
ye have done unto them, therefore
if they should come down against
you they would visit you with utter
destruction.
5 Therefore I have written this
epistle, sealing it with mine own
hand, feeling for your welfare, because of your firmness in that which
ye believe to be right, and your noble
spirit in the field of battle.
6 Therefore I write unto you, desiring that ye would yield up unto this
my people, your cities, your lands,
and your possessions, rather than
that they should visit you with the
sword and that destruction should
come upon you.
7 Or in other words, yield yourselves up unto us, and unite with
us and become acquainted with
our [a]secret works, and become our
brethren that ye may be like unto
us—not our slaves, but our brethren
and partners of all our substance.
8 And behold, I [a]swear unto you,
if ye will do this, with an oath, ye
shall not be destroyed; but if ye will
not do this, I swear unto you with
an oath, that on the morrow month I
will command that my armies shall
come down against you, and they
shall not stay their hand and shall
spare not, but shall slay you, and
shall let fall the sword upon you
even until ye shall become extinct.
9 And behold, I am [a]Giddianhi;
and I am the governor of this the
[b]secret society of Gadianton; which
society and the works thereof I
know to be [c]good; and they are of
[d]ancient date and they have been
handed down unto us.
10 And I write this epistle unto
you, Lachoneus, and I hope that ye
will deliver up your lands and your
possessions, without the shedding
of blood, that this my people may
recover their rights and [a]govern-
ment, who have dissented away
from you because of your wickedness in retaining from them their
rights of government, and except ye
do this, I will avenge their wrongs.
I am Giddianhi.
11 And now it came to pass when
Lachoneus received this epistle he
was exceedingly astonished, because of the boldness of Giddianhi
demanding the possession of the
land of the Nephites, and also of
threatening the people and aveng-
ing the wrongs of those that had
received no wrong, save it were
they had [a]wronged themselves by
dissenting away unto those wicked
and abominable robbers.
12 Now behold, this Lachoneus,

2*a* 3 Ne. 2:12.
b TG Liberty.
3*a* 3 Ne. 2:19.
7*a* Hel. 6:22 (22–26).
8*a* Hel. 1:11;
Ether 8:14 (13–14).
9*a* 3 Ne. 4:14.
b TG Secret Combinations.
c Alma 30:53.
d Hel. 6:26 (26–30);
Ether 8:9 (9–19);
Moses 5:29 (29, 49–52).
10*a* TG Governments.
11*a* Hel. 14:30.

the governor, was a just man, and
could not be frightened by the
demands and the threatenings of
a [a]robber; therefore he did not
hearken to the epistle of Giddianhi,
the governor of the robbers, but he
did cause that his people should cry
unto the Lord for [b]strength against
the time that the robbers should
come down against them.
13 Yea, he sent a proclamation
among all the people, that they
should [a]gather together their women,
and their children, their flocks and
their herds, and all their substance,
save it were their land, unto one place.
14 And he caused that [a]fortifica-
tions should be built round about
them, and the strength thereof
should be exceedingly great. And
he caused that armies, both of the
Nephites and of the Lamanites, or of
all them who were numbered among
the Nephites, should be placed as
guards round about to watch them,
and to guard them from the robbers
day and night.
15 Yea, he said unto them: As the
Lord liveth, except ye repent of all
your iniquities, and cry unto the
Lord, ye will in nowise be [a]delivered
out of the hands of those Gadianton
robbers.
16 And so great and marvelous
were the words and prophecies of
Lachoneus that they did cause fear
to come upon all the people; and
they did exert themselves in their
might to do according to the words
of Lachoneus.
17 And it came to pass that Lachoneus did appoint chief captains
over all the armies of the Nephites,
to command them at the time that
the robbers should come down out
of the wilderness against them.
18 Now the chiefest among all the
chief captains and the great commander of all the armies of the
Nephites was appointed, and his
name was [a]Gidgiddoni.
19 Now it was the custom among
all the Nephites to appoint for their
chief captains, (save it were in their
times of wickedness) some one that
had the [a]spirit of revelation and
also prophecy; therefore, this Gidgiddoni was a great prophet among
them, as also was the chief judge.
20 Now the people said unto Gidgiddoni: [a]Pray unto the Lord, and let
us go up upon the mountains and
into the wilderness, that we may
fall upon the robbers and destroy
them in their own lands.
21 But Gidgiddoni saith unto them:
The Lord [a]forbid; for if we should
go up against them the Lord would
[b]deliver us into their hands; therefore we will prepare ourselves in
the center of our lands, and we will
gather all our armies together, and
we will not go against them, but we
will wait till they shall come against
us; therefore as the Lord liveth, if
we do this he will deliver them into
our hands.
22 And it came to pass in the seventeenth year, in the latter end of
the year, the proclamation of Lachoneus had gone forth throughout
all the face of the land, and they
had taken their [a]horses, and their
chariots, and their cattle, and all
their flocks, and their herds, and
their grain, and all their substance,
and did march forth by thousands
and by tens of thousands, until they
had all gone forth to the [b]place
which [c]had been appointed that
they should gather themselves together, to defend themselves against
their enemies.
23 And the [a]land which was

12*a* 1 Kgs. 20:3 (2–3); Alma 54:7 (5–11).
b TG Strength.
13*a* 3 Ne. 3:22; 4:1.
14*a* Morm. 2:4.
15*a* TG Deliver; Protection, Divine.
18*a* 3 Ne. 4:13 (13, 24, 26); 6:6.
19*a* TG Guidance, Divine.
20*a* Alma 16:6 (5–8); 43:23 (23–24); 48:16.
21*a* Alma 43:46 (46–47); 48:14; Morm. 3:10 (10–11).
b 1 Sam. 14:12; 2 Kgs. 3:18; 1 Ne. 3:29.
22*a* 3 Ne. 4:4.
b Morm. 2:7.
c 3 Ne. 3:13.
23*a* 3 Ne. 4:16.

appointed was the land of Zarahemla, and the land which was
between the land Zarahemla and
the land [b]Bountiful, yea, to the
line which was between the [c]land
Bountiful and the land Desolation.
24 And there were a great many
thousand people who were called
Nephites, who did gather themselves together in this land. Now
Lachoneus did cause that they
should gather themselves together
in the land [a]southward, because of
the great curse which was upon the
[b]land northward.
25 And they did fortify themselves
against their enemies; and they did
dwell in one land, and in one body,
and they did fear the words which
had been spoken by Lachoneus,
insomuch that they did repent of
all their sins; and they did put up
their [a]prayers unto the Lord their
God, that he would deliver them in
the time that their enemies should
come down against them to battle.
26 And they were exceedingly sorrowful because of their enemies.
And Gidgiddoni did cause that they
should make [a]weapons of war of every kind, and they should be strong
with armor, and with shields, and
with bucklers, after the manner of
his instruction.

CHAPTER 4

The Nephite armies defeat the Gadianton robbers—Giddianhi is slain, and his successor, Zemnarihah, is hanged—The Nephites praise the Lord for their victories. About A.D. 19–22.

AND it came to pass that in the latter end of the eighteenth year those
armies of [a]robbers had prepared
for battle, and began to come down
and to sally forth from the hills,
and out of the mountains, and the
wilderness, and their strongholds,
and their [b]secret places, and began to take possession of the lands,
both which were in the land south
and which were in the land north,
and began to take possession of all
the lands which had been [c]deserted
by the Nephites, and the cities which
had been left desolate.
2 But behold, there were no wild
beasts nor [a]game in those lands
which had been deserted by the
Nephites, and there was no game
for the robbers save it were in the
wilderness.
3 And the robbers could not exist
save it were in the wilderness, for
the want of food; for the Nephites
had left their lands desolate, and
had gathered their flocks and their
herds and all their substance, and
they were in one body.
4 Therefore, there was no chance
for the robbers to plunder and to
obtain food, save it were to come
up in open battle against the Nephites; and the Nephites being in one
body, and having so great a number, and having reserved for themselves provisions, and [a]horses and
cattle, and flocks of every kind, that
they might subsist for the space
of [b]seven years, in the which time
they did hope to destroy the robbers from off the face of the land;
and thus the eighteenth year did
pass away.
5 And it came to pass that in the
nineteenth year Giddianhi found
that it was expedient that he should
go up to battle against the Nephites, for there was [a]no way that they
could subsist save it were to plunder and rob and murder.
6 And they durst not spread themselves upon the face of the land insomuch that they could raise grain,
lest the Nephites should come upon

23*b* Alma 22:29; 3 Ne. 11:1.
c Morm. 3:7; 4:2.
24*a* Alma 46:17; Morm. 3:5.
b Alma 22:31 (30–31).
25*a* TG Trust in God.
26*a* 2 Ne. 5:14; Jarom 1:8; Mosiah 10:8; Alma 2:12; Hel. 1:14.
4 1*a* Hel. 2:13 (11–13).
b Alma 58:6.
c 3 Ne. 3:13 (13–14, 22).
2*a* 1 Ne. 18:25; 2 Ne. 5:24; 3 Ne. 4:20.
4*a* 3 Ne. 3:22; 6:1 (1–2).
b Gen. 41:36 (29–36); 3 Ne. 4:18.
5*a* Alma 47:36.

them and slay them; therefore Giddianhi gave commandment unto his armies that in this year they should go up to battle against the Nephites.
7 And it came to pass that they did come up to battle; and it was in the sixth month; and behold, great and terrible was the day that they did come up to battle; and they were girded about after the manner of robbers; and they had a lamb-skin about their loins, and they were dyed in blood, and their heads were shorn, and they had head-plates upon them; and great and terrible was the appearance of the armies of Giddianhi, because of their armor, and because of their being dyed in blood.
8 And it came to pass that the armies of the Nephites, when they saw the appearance of the army of Giddianhi, had all fallen to the earth, and did lift their cries to the Lord their God, that he would spare them and deliver them out of the hands of their enemies.
9 And it came to pass that when the armies of Giddianhi saw this they began to shout with a loud voice, because of their joy, for they had supposed that the Nephites had fallen with fear because of the terror of their armies.
10 But in this thing they were disappointed, for the Nephites did not [a]fear them; but they did fear their God and did supplicate him for [b]protection; therefore, when the armies of Giddianhi did rush upon them they were prepared to meet them; yea, in the strength of the Lord they did receive them.
11 And the battle commenced in this the sixth month; and great and terrible was the battle thereof, yea, great and terrible was the [a]slaughter thereof, insomuch that there never was known so great a slaughter among all the people of Lehi since he left Jerusalem.
12 And notwithstanding the [a]threatenings and the oaths which Giddianhi had made, behold, the Nephites did beat them, insomuch that they did fall back from before them.
13 And it came to pass that [a]Gidgiddoni commanded that his armies should pursue them as far as the borders of the wilderness, and that they should not spare any that should fall into their hands by the way; and thus they did pursue them and did slay them, to the borders of the wilderness, even until they had fulfilled the commandment of Gidgiddoni.
14 And it came to pass that Giddianhi, who had stood and fought with boldness, was pursued as he fled; and being weary because of his much fighting he was overtaken and slain. And thus was the end of Giddianhi the robber.
15 And it came to pass that the armies of the Nephites did return again to their place of security. And it came to pass that this nineteenth year did pass away, and the robbers did not come again to battle; neither did they come again in the twentieth year.
16 And in the twenty and first year they did not come up to battle, but they came up on all sides to lay siege round about the people of Nephi; for they did suppose that if they should cut off the people of Nephi from their [a]lands, and should hem them in on every side, and if they should cut them off from all their outward privileges, that they could cause them to yield themselves up according to their wishes.
17 Now they had appointed unto themselves another leader, whose name was Zemnarihah; therefore it was Zemnarihah that did cause that this siege should take place.
18 But behold, this was an advantage to the Nephites; for it was impossible for the robbers to lay

10*a* TG Reverence.
b Jer. 17:17 (17–18).
11*a* Alma 28:11 (8–12).
12*a* 3 Ne. 3:8 (4–10).
13*a* 3 Ne. 3:18.
16*a* 3 Ne. 3:23.

siege sufficiently long to have any
effect upon the Nephites, because
of their [a]much [b]provision which
they had laid up in store,
19 And because of the scantiness
of provisions among the robbers;
for behold, they had nothing save
it were meat for their subsistence,
which meat they did obtain in the
wilderness;
20 And it came to pass that the
[a]wild game became scarce in the wilderness insomuch that the robbers
were about to perish with hunger.
21 And the Nephites were continually marching out by day and by
night, and falling upon their armies,
and cutting them off by thousands
and by tens of thousands.
22 And thus it became the desire of
the people of Zemnarihah to withdraw from their design, because of
the great destruction which came
upon them by night and by day.
23 And it came to pass that Zemnarihah did give command unto his
people that they should withdraw
themselves from the siege, and
march into the furthermost parts
of the land northward.
24 And now, Gidgiddoni being
aware of their design, and knowing
of their weakness because of the
want of food, and the great slaughter which had been made among
them, therefore he did send out his
armies in the night-time, and did
cut off the way of their retreat, and
did place his armies in the way of
their retreat.
25 And this did they do in the
night-time, and got on their march
beyond the robbers, so that on the
morrow, when the robbers began
their march, they were met by the
armies of the Nephites both in their
front and in their rear.
26 And the robbers who were on
the south were also cut off in their
places of retreat. And all these
things were done by command of
Gidgiddoni.
27 And there were many thousands who did yield themselves up
prisoners unto the Nephites, and
the remainder of them were slain.
28 And their leader, Zemnarihah,
was taken and hanged upon a tree,
yea, even upon the top thereof until he was dead. And when they
had hanged him until he was dead
they did fell the tree to the earth,
and did cry with a loud voice,
saying:
29 May the Lord preserve his people in righteousness and in holiness
of heart, that they may cause to be
felled to the earth all who shall seek
to slay them because of power and
secret combinations, even as this
man hath been felled to the earth.
30 And they did rejoice and cry
again with one voice, saying: May
the [a]God of Abraham, and the God
of Isaac, and the God of Jacob, protect this people in righteousness, so
long as they shall [b]call on the name
of their God for [c]protection.
31 And it came to pass that they
did break forth, all as one, in singing, and [a]praising their God for
the great thing which he had done
for them, in preserving them from
falling into the hands of their
enemies.
32 Yea, they did cry: Hosanna to
the Most High God. And they did
cry: Blessed be the name of the Lord
God [a]Almighty, the Most High God.
33 And their hearts were swollen
with joy, unto the gushing out of
many tears, because of the great
goodness of God in delivering them
out of the hands of their enemies;
and they knew it was because of
their repentance and their humility
that they had been delivered from
an everlasting destruction.

18*a* 3 Ne. 4:4.
b Gen. 41:36 (33–57); D&C 4:4.
20*a* 1 Ne. 18:25; 2 Ne. 5:24; 3 Ne. 4:2.
30*a* Alma 29:11.
b Gen. 4:26; Ether 4:15; Moro. 2:2.
c TG Protection, Divine.
31*a* Alma 26:8. TG Thanksgiving.
32*a* 1 Ne. 1:14.

CHAPTER 5

The Nephites repent and forsake their sins—Mormon writes the history of his people and declares the everlasting word to them—Israel will be gathered in from her long dispersion. About A.D. *22–26.*

AND now behold, there was not a
living soul among all the people
of the Nephites who did [a]doubt in
the least the words of all the holy
prophets who had spoken; for they
knew that it must needs be that
they must be fulfilled.
2 And they knew that it must be
expedient that Christ had come, because of the many signs which had
been given, according to the words
of the prophets; and because of the
things which had come to pass already they knew that it must needs
be that all things should come to
pass according to that which had
been spoken.
3 Therefore they did forsake all
their sins, and their abominations,
and their whoredoms, and did serve
God with all diligence day and night.
4 And now it came to pass that
when they had taken all the robbers prisoners, insomuch that none
did escape who were not slain, they
did cast their prisoners into prison,
and did cause the word of God to be
preached unto them; and as many
as would repent of their sins and
[a]enter into a [b]covenant that they
would murder no more were set at
[c]liberty.
5 But as many as there were who
did not enter into a covenant, and
who did still continue to have those
[a]secret murders in their hearts, yea,
as many as were found breathing
out threatenings against their brethren were condemned and punished
according to the law.
6 And thus they did put an end
to all those wicked, and secret,
and abominable combinations,
in the which there was so much
wickedness, and so many murders
committed.
7 And thus had the [a]twenty and
second year passed away, and the
twenty and third year also, and the
twenty and fourth, and the twenty
and fifth; and thus had twenty and
five years passed away.
8 And there had many things transpired which, in the eyes of some,
would be great and marvelous; nevertheless, they cannot all be written
in this book; yea, this book cannot
contain even a [a]hundredth part
of what was done among so many
people in the space of twenty and
five years;
9 But behold there are [a]records
which do contain [b]all the proceedings of this people; and a [c]shorter
but true account was given by
Nephi.
10 Therefore I have made my
[a]record of these things according
to the record of Nephi, which was
engraven on the plates which were
called the [b]plates of Nephi.
11 And behold, I do make the
record on plates which I have made
with mine own hands.
12 And behold, I am called [a]Mor-
mon, being called after the [b]land of
Mormon, the land in which Alma
did establish the church among the
people, yea, the first church which
was established among them after
their transgression.
13 Behold, I am a disciple of Jesus
Christ, the Son of God. I have been
[a]called of him to declare his word
among his people, that they might
have everlasting life.
14 And it hath become expedient
that I, according to the will of God,
that the prayers of those who have

---

5 1*a* TG Doubt.
4*a* 3 Ne. 6:3.
b Alma 44:15; 62:16 (16–17).
c TG Liberty.
5*a* 2 Ne. 10:15.
7*a* 3 Ne. 2:8.
8*a* W of M 1:5;
3 Ne. 26:6 (6–12).
9*a* Hel. 3:15 (13–15).
b W of M 1:5;
Alma 13:31.
c Morm. 2:18.
10*a* Hel. 2:14.
b W of M 1:1;
Morm. 1:4 (1–4);
2:17 (17–18);
8:5 (1, 4–5, 14).
12*a* W of M 1:11.
b Mosiah 18:4;
Alma 5:3.
13*a* 3 Ne. 30:1; Moro. 7:2.

gone hence, who were the holy ones,
should be fulfilled according to their
faith, should make a [a]record of these
things which have been done—
15 Yea, a [a]small record of that which
hath taken place from the time that
Lehi left Jerusalem, even down until the present time.
16 Therefore I do make my record
from the accounts which have been
given by those who were before me,
until the commencement of my day;
17 And then I do make a [a]record of
the things which I have seen with
mine own eyes.
18 And I know the record which I
make to be a just and a true record;
nevertheless there are many things
which, according to our [a]language,
we are not able to [b]write.
19 And now I make an end of my
saying, which is of myself, and
proceed to give my account of the
things which have been before me.
20 I am Mormon, and a pure [a]de-
scendant of Lehi. I have reason to
bless my God and my Savior Jesus
Christ, that he brought our fathers
out of the land of Jerusalem, (and
[b]no one knew it save it were himself and those whom he brought
out of that land) and that he hath
given me and my people so much
knowledge unto the salvation of
our souls.
21 Surely he hath [a]blessed the
house of [b]Jacob, and hath been
[c]merciful unto the seed of Joseph.
22 And [a]insomuch as the children
of Lehi have kept his commandments he hath blessed them and
prospered them according to his
word.
23 Yea, and surely shall he again
bring a [a]remnant of the seed of Joseph to the [b]knowledge of the Lord
their God.
24 And as surely as the Lord liveth, will he [a]gather in from the four
quarters of the earth all the remnant of the [b]seed of Jacob, who are
scattered abroad upon all the face
of the earth.
25 And as he hath [a]covenanted with
all the house of Jacob, even so shall
the covenant wherewith he hath
covenanted with the house of Jacob
be fulfilled in his own due time,
unto the [b]restoring all the house
of Jacob unto the knowledge of the
covenant that he hath covenanted
with them.
26 And then shall they [a]know their
Redeemer, who is Jesus Christ, the
Son of God; and then shall they be
gathered in from the four quarters
of the earth unto their own lands,
from whence they have been dispersed; yea, as the Lord liveth so
shall it be. Amen.

CHAPTER 6

The Nephites prosper—Pride, wealth, and class distinctions arise—The Church is rent with dissensions—Satan leads the people in open rebellion—Many prophets cry repentance and are slain—Their murderers conspire to take over the government. About A.D. *26–30.*

AND now it came to pass that the
people of the Nephites did all return
to their own lands in the twenty
and sixth year, every man, with
his family, his flocks and his herds,
his [a]horses and his cattle, and all

14*a* Enos 1:16 (13–18); D&C 3:19; 10:47 (46–50).
15*a* Morm. 7:9; 8:12.
17*a* W of M 1:5; Morm. 1:1.
18*a* TG Language.
b 3 Ne. 19:32 (32–34); Morm. 9:33 (32–33); Ether 12:25 (24–25); D&C 76:116.
20*a* Morm. 1:5; 8:13.
b 1 Ne. 4:36; 3 Ne. 15:14.
21*a* TG Israel, Blessings of.
b Gen. 32:28 (24–32); Ps. 135:4; D&C 49:24 (23–25).
c Ps. 98:3.
22*a* 2 Ne. 1:20; Jarom 1:9; Omni 1:6; Mosiah 1:7; Alma 9:13 (13–14); 37:13.
23*a* Alma 46:24; 3 Ne. 10:17.
b 2 Ne. 3:12; Morm. 7:5 (5, 10).
24*a* TG Israel, Gathering of.
b Gen. 46:8.
25*a* 3 Ne. 15:8; 16:5.
b 2 Ne. 30:3 (1–6); 3 Ne. 16:13 (6–13).
26*a* 2 Ne. 30:7 (7–8); 3 Ne. 20:31 (29–34).
6 1*a* 3 Ne. 3:22 (21–23).

things whatsoever did belong unto
them.
2 And it came to pass that they had
[a]not eaten up all their provisions;
therefore they did take with them
all that they had not devoured, of
all their grain of every kind, and
their gold, and their silver, and all
their precious things, and they did
return to their own lands and their
possessions, both on the north and
on the south, both on the land northward and on the land southward.
3 And they granted unto those
robbers who had [a]entered into a
covenant to keep the peace of the
land, who were desirous to remain
Lamanites, lands, according to their
numbers, that they might have, with
their labors, wherewith to subsist
upon; and thus they did establish
peace in all the land.
4 And they began again to prosper
and to wax great; and the twenty
and sixth and seventh years passed
away, and there was great [a]order
in the land; and they had formed
their laws according to equity and
justice.
5 And now there was nothing in
all the land to hinder the people
from prospering continually, except
they should fall into transgression.
6 And now it was [a]Gidgiddoni, and
the judge, [b]Lachoneus, and those
who had been appointed leaders,
who had established this great peace
in the land.
7 And it came to pass that there
were many cities built anew, and
there were many old cities repaired.
8 And there were many [a]highways
cast up, and many roads made,
which led from city to city, and
from land to land, and from place
to place.
9 And thus passed away the twenty
and eighth year, and the people had
continual peace.
10 But it came to pass in the twenty
and ninth year there began to be
some disputings among the people;
and some were lifted up unto pride
and [a]boastings because of their exceedingly great riches, yea, even
unto great persecutions;
11 For there were many [a]mer-
chants in the land, and also many
[b]lawyers, and many officers.
12 And the people began to be
distinguished by ranks, according
to their [a]riches and their chances
for learning; yea, some were [b]igno-
rant because of their poverty, and
others did receive great [c]learning
because of their riches.
13 Some were lifted up in pride, and
others were exceedingly humble;
some did return railing for railing,
while others would receive railing
and [a]persecution and all manner
of [b]afflictions, and would not turn
and [c]revile again, but were humble
and penitent before God.
14 And thus there became a great
inequality in all the land, insomuch
that the church began to be broken
up; yea, insomuch that in the thirtieth year the church was broken up
in all the land save it were among
a few of the Lamanites who were
converted unto the true faith; and
[a]they would not depart from it, for
they were firm, and steadfast, and
immovable, willing with all [b]dili-
gence to keep the commandments
of the Lord.
15 Now the cause of this iniquity
of the people was this—[a]Satan had
great [b]power, unto the stirring up
of the people to do all manner of
iniquity, and to the puffing them up

2*a* 3 Ne. 4:4.
3*a* 3 Ne. 5:4.
4*a* TG Order.
6*a* 3 Ne. 3:18.
b 3 Ne. 3:1.
8*a* 3 Ne. 8:13.
10*a* TG Boast.
11*a* Hel. 6:8.
b Alma 10:14 (14–17, 27);
14:5 (5, 18–27).
12*a* 1 Tim. 6:17;
Hel. 4:12 (11–13).
b TG Ignorance.
c TG Learn.
13*a* TG Persecution.
b TG Affliction.
c 3 Ne. 12:39;
4 Ne. 1:34;
D&C 98:23 (23–27).
TG Reviling.
14*a* Alma 23:6; 27:27;
Hel. 15:8 (5–16).
b TG Dedication;
Diligence.
15*a* Moses 6:15.
b 1 Ne. 22:26;
Alma 48:17.

with pride, tempting them to seek
for power, and authority, and [c]riches,
and the vain things of the world.
16 And thus Satan did lead away
the hearts of the people to do all
manner of iniquity; therefore they
had enjoyed peace but a few years.
17 And thus, in the commencement
of the thirtieth year—the people
having been [a]delivered up for the
space of a long time to be carried
about by the [b]temptations of the
devil whithersoever he desired to
carry them, and to do whatsoever
iniquity he desired they should—
and thus in the commencement of
this, the thirtieth year, they were in
a state of awful wickedness.
18 Now they did not sin [a]igno-
rantly, for they knew the [b]will of God
concerning them, for it had been
taught unto them; therefore they
did wilfully [c]rebel against God.
19 And now it was in the days of
Lachoneus, the son of [a]Lachoneus,
for Lachoneus did fill the seat of his
father and did govern the people
that year.
20 And there began to be men [a]in-
spired from heaven and sent forth,
standing among the people in all
the land, preaching and testifying
boldly of the sins and iniquities of
the people, and testifying unto them
concerning the redemption which
the Lord would make for his people, or in other words, the resurrection of Christ; and they did testify
boldly of his [b]death and sufferings.
21 Now there were many of the
people who were exceedingly angry because of those who testified
of these things; and those who were
angry were chiefly the chief judges,
and they who [a]had been high priests
and lawyers; yea, all those who were
lawyers were angry with those who
testified of these things.
22 Now there was no lawyer nor
judge nor high priest that could
have power to condemn any one to
death save their condemnation was
signed by the governor of the land.
23 Now there were many of those
[a]who testified of the things pertaining to Christ who testified boldly,
who were taken and put to death
[b]secretly by the judges, that the
knowledge of their death came not
unto the governor of the land until
after their death.
24 Now behold, this was contrary
to the laws of the land, that any
man should be put to death except
they had power from the governor
of the land—
25 Therefore a complaint came up
unto the land of Zarahemla, to the
governor of the land, against these
judges who had condemned the
prophets of the Lord unto [a]death,
not according to the law.
26 Now it came to pass that they
were taken and brought up before
the judge, to be judged of the crime
which they had done, according to
the [a]law which had been given by
the people.
27 Now it came to pass that those
judges had many friends and kindreds; and the remainder, yea, even
almost all the lawyers and the high
priests, did gather themselves together, and unite with the kindreds
of those judges who were to be tried
according to the law.
28 And they did enter into a [a]cov-
enant one with another, yea, even
into that covenant which was given
by them of old, which covenant was
given and administered by the [b]devil,
to combine against all righteousness.

15*c* TG Selfishness.
17*a* Moses 5:23.
b TG Temptation.
18*a* Num. 15:27 (2–29);
Mosiah 3:11.
TG Ignorance.
b TG God, Will of.
c TG Rebellion.
19*a* 3 Ne. 1:1.
20*a* TG Inspiration;
Prophets, Mission of.
b TG Jesus Christ,
Death of.
21*a* D&C 121:37.
TG Apostasy of
Individuals.
23*a* 3 Ne. 7:14.
b Hel. 6:17 (17–38).
25*a* 3 Ne. 9:9.
26*a* Mosiah 29:25;
Alma 1:14.
28*a* TG Secret
Combinations.
b Hel. 6:26;
Ether 8:9 (9, 15–16).

29 Therefore they did combine against the people of the Lord, and enter into a covenant to destroy them, and to deliver those who were guilty of murder from the grasp of justice, which was about to be administered according to the law.
30 And they did set at defiance the law and the rights of their country; and they did covenant one with another to destroy the governor, and to establish a [a]king over the land, that the land should no more be at [b]liberty but should be subject unto kings.

CHAPTER 7

The chief judge is murdered, the government is destroyed, and the people divide into tribes—Jacob, an anti-Christ, becomes king of a secret combination—Nephi preaches repentance and faith in Christ—Angels minister to him daily, and he raises his brother from the dead—Many repent and are baptized. About A.D. *30–33.*

NOW behold, I will show unto you that they did not establish a king over the land; but in this same year, yea, the thirtieth year, they did destroy upon the judgment-seat, yea, did murder the chief judge of the land.
2 And the people were divided one against another; and they did [a]separate one from another into tribes, every man according to his family and his kindred and friends; and thus they did destroy the government of the land.
3 And every tribe did appoint a chief or a leader over them; and thus they became tribes and leaders of tribes.
4 Now behold, there was no man among them save he had much family and many kindreds and friends; therefore their tribes became exceedingly great.
5 Now all this was done, and there were no wars as yet among them; and all this iniquity had come upon the people [a]because they did [b]yield themselves unto the power of Satan.
6 And the regulations of the government were destroyed, because of the [a]secret combination of the friends and kindreds of those who murdered the prophets.
7 And they did cause a great contention in the land, insomuch that the more righteous part of the people had nearly all become wicked; yea, there were but few righteous men among them.
8 And thus six years had not passed away since the more part of the people had turned from their righteousness, like the dog to his [a]vomit, or like the sow to her wallowing in the mire.
9 Now this secret combination, which had brought so great iniquity upon the people, did gather themselves together, and did place at their head a man whom they did call Jacob;
10 And they did call him their king; therefore he became a king over this wicked band; and he was one of the chiefest who had given his voice against the prophets who testified of Jesus.
11 And it came to pass that they were not so strong in number as the tribes of the people, who were united together save it were their leaders did establish their laws, every one according to his tribe; nevertheless they were enemies; notwithstanding they were not a righteous people, yet they were united in the hatred of those who had entered into a covenant to [a]destroy the government.
12 Therefore, Jacob seeing that their enemies were more numerous than they, he being the king of the band, therefore he commanded his

30*a* 1 Sam. 8:5; Alma 51:5; 3 Ne. 7:12. TG Tyranny.
b TG Liberty.
7 2*a* TG Unity.
5*a* Moses 4:6.
b Rom. 6:16 (13–20); Alma 10:25.
6*a* 2 Ne. 9:9.
8*a* Prov. 26:11; 2 Pet. 2:22.
11*a* 3 Ne. 9:9.

people that they should take their flight into the northernmost part of the land, and there build up unto themselves a [a]kingdom, until they were joined by dissenters, (for he flattered them that there would be many dissenters) and they become sufficiently strong to contend with the tribes of the people; and they did so.

13 And so speedy was their march that it could not be impeded until they had gone forth out of the reach of the people. And thus ended the thirtieth year; and thus were the affairs of the people of Nephi.

14 And it came to pass in the thirty and first year that they were divided into tribes, every man according to his family, kindred and friends; nevertheless they had come to an agreement that they would not go to war one with another; but they were not united as to their laws, and their manner of government, for they were established according to the minds of those who were their chiefs and their leaders. But they did establish very strict laws that one tribe should not trespass against another, insomuch that in some degree they had peace in the land; nevertheless, their hearts were turned from the Lord their God, and they did stone the [a]prophets and did cast them out from among them.

15 And it came to pass that [a]Nephi—having been visited by angels and also the voice of the Lord, therefore having seen angels, and being eye-witness, and having had power given unto him that he might know concerning the ministry of Christ, and also being eye-witness to their quick return from righteousness unto their wickedness and abominations;

16 Therefore, being [a]grieved for the hardness of their hearts and the blindness of their minds—went forth among them in that same year, and began to testify, boldly, repentance and remission of sins through faith on the Lord Jesus Christ.

17 And he did minister many things unto them; and all of them cannot be written, and a part of them would not suffice, therefore they are not written in this book. And Nephi did minister with [a]power and with great authority.

18 And it came to pass that they were angry with him, even because he had greater power than they, for it were [a]not possible that they could disbelieve his words, for so great was his faith on the Lord Jesus Christ that angels did minister unto him daily.

19 And in the name of Jesus did he cast out devils and [a]unclean spirits; and even his [b]brother did he [c]raise from the dead, after he had been stoned and suffered death by the people.

20 And the people saw it, and did witness of it, and were angry with him because of his power; and he did also do [a]many more miracles, in the sight of the people, in the name of Jesus.

21 And it came to pass that the thirty and first year did pass away, and there were but few who were converted unto the Lord; but as many as were converted did truly signify unto the people that they had been [a]visited by the power and [b]Spirit of God, which was in Jesus Christ, in whom they believed.

22 And as many as had devils cast out from them, and were [a]healed of their sicknesses and their infirmities, did truly manifest unto the

12*a* 3 Ne. 6:30.
14*a* 3 Ne. 6:23 (23–25).
15*a* 3 Ne. 1:2 (2–3, 10); 11:18.
16*a* Gen. 6:6; 1 Ne. 2:18; Alma 31:24; Moses 8:25.
17*a* TG Priesthood, Power of.
18*a* Alma 4:19.
19*a* TG Spirits, Evil or Unclean.
b 3 Ne. 19:4.
c TG Death, Power over.
20*a* 3 Ne. 8:1.
21*a* TG God, Manifestations of.
b TG God, Spirit of.
22*a* Mark 2:11 (11–12); Acts 8:7.

people that they had been wrought
upon by the Spirit of God, and had
been healed; and they did show
forth signs also and did do some
miracles among the people.
23 Thus passed away the thirty
and second year also. And Nephi
did cry unto the people in the commencement of the thirty and third
year; and he did preach unto them
repentance and remission of sins.
24 Now I would have you to remember also, that there were none
who were brought unto [a]repentance
who were not baptized with water.
25 Therefore, there were ordained
of Nephi, men unto this ministry,
that all such as should come unto
them should be [a]baptized with water, and this as a witness and a testimony before God, and unto the
people, that they had repented and
received a [b]remission of their sins.
26 And there were many in the
commencement of this year that
were baptized unto repentance;
and thus the more part of the year
did pass away.

CHAPTER 8

Tempests, earthquakes, fires, whirlwinds, and physical upheavals attest the crucifixion of Christ—Many people are destroyed—Darkness covers the land for three days—Those who remain bemoan their fate. About A.D. *33–34.*

AND now it came to pass that according to our record, and we know
our record to be [a]true, for behold,
it was a [b]just man who did keep
the record—for he truly did [c]many
[d]miracles in the [e]name of Jesus; and
there was not any man who could
do a miracle in the name of Jesus
save he were cleansed every whit
from his iniquity—
2 And now it came to pass, if
there was no mistake made by
this man in the reckoning of our
time, the [a]thirty and third year had
passed away;
3 And the people began to look
with great earnestness for the sign
which had been given by the prophet
Samuel, the Lamanite, yea, for the
time that there should be [a]darkness
for the space of three days over the
face of the land.
4 And there began to be great
[a]doubtings and [b]disputations among
the people, notwithstanding so
many signs had been given.
5 And it came to pass in the [a]thirty
and fourth year, in the first month,
on the fourth day of the month,
there arose a great [b]storm, such an
one as never had been known in all
the land.
6 And there was also a great and
terrible tempest; and there was terrible [a]thunder, insomuch that it did
[b]shake the whole earth as if it was
about to divide asunder.
7 And there were exceedingly
sharp lightnings, such as never had
been known in all the land.
8 And the [a]city of Zarahemla did
take fire.
9 And the city of [a]Moroni did [b]sink
into the depths of the sea, and the
inhabitants thereof were drowned.
10 And the earth was carried up
upon the city of [a]Moronihah, that in
the place of the city there became
a great [b]mountain.

24*a* TG Baptism, Qualifications for.
25*a* TG Baptism.
b D&C 20:37. TG Remission of Sins.
8 1*a* John 21:24.
b 3 Ne. 23:7.
c 3 Ne. 7:20 (19–20).
d John 6:14; Morm. 9:18 (18–19).
e Acts 3:6 (6–16); Jacob 4:6.
2*a* 3 Ne. 2:8.
3*a* 1 Ne. 19:10; Hel. 14:27 (20, 27); 3 Ne. 10:9. TG Darkness, Physical.
4*a* TG Doubt.
b TG Disputations.
5*a* Hel. 14:20 (20–27); 3 Ne. 11:2.
b TG Jesus Christ, Crucifixion of; Jesus Christ, Death of.
6*a* 1 Ne. 19:11; Hel. 14:21 (20–27).
b Matt. 27:51 (45, 50–51).
8*a* 4 Ne. 1:7–8.
9*a* Alma 50:13.
b 3 Ne. 9:4 (4–5).
10*a* 3 Ne. 8:25.
b Hel. 12:17; 3 Ne. 9:8 (6–8).

11 And there was a great and terrible destruction in the land southward.

12 But behold, there was a more great and terrible destruction in the land northward; for behold, the [a]whole face of the land was changed, because of the tempest and the whirlwinds, and the thunderings and the lightnings, and the exceedingly great quaking of the whole earth;

13 And the [a]highways were broken up, and the level roads were spoiled, and many smooth places became rough.

14 And many [a]great and notable cities were [b]sunk, and many were [c]burned, and many were shaken till the buildings thereof had fallen to the earth, and the inhabitants thereof were slain, and the places were left desolate.

15 And there were some cities which remained; but the damage thereof was exceedingly great, and there were many in them who were slain.

16 And there were some who were carried away in the [a]whirlwind; and whither they went no man knoweth, save they know that they were carried away.

17 And thus the face of the whole earth became deformed, because of the tempests, and the thunderings, and the lightnings, and the quaking of the earth.

18 And behold, the rocks were rent in twain; they were broken up upon the face of the whole earth, insomuch that they were [a]found in broken fragments, and in seams and in cracks, upon all the face of the land.

19 And it came to pass that when the thunderings, and the lightnings, and the storm, and the tempest, and the quakings of the earth did cease—for behold, they did last for about the space of [a]three [b]hours; and it was said by some that the time was greater; nevertheless, all these great and terrible things were done in about the space of three hours—and then behold, there was [c]darkness upon the face of the land.

20 And it came to pass that there was thick darkness upon all the face of the land, insomuch that the inhabitants thereof who had not fallen could [a]feel the [b]vapor of darkness;

21 And there could be no light, because of the darkness, neither candles, neither torches; neither could there be fire kindled with their fine and exceedingly dry wood, so that there could not be any light at all;

22 And there was not any light seen, neither fire, nor glimmer, neither the sun, nor the moon, nor the stars, for so great were the mists of darkness which were upon the face of the land.

23 And it came to pass that it did last for the space of three days that there was no light seen; and there was great mourning and [a]howling and weeping among all the people continually; yea, great were the groanings of the people, because of the darkness and the great destruction which had come upon them.

24 And in one place they were heard to cry, saying: O that we had repented [a]before this great and terrible day, and then would our brethren have been spared, and they would not have been [b]burned in that great city Zarahemla.

25 And in another place they were heard to cry and mourn, saying: O that we had repented before this great and terrible day, and had not killed and stoned the prophets, and cast them out; then would our

12*a* 3 Ne. 11:1.
13*a* Hel. 14:24; 3 Ne. 6:8.
14*a* 3 Ne. 9:12; 10:4.
b 1 Ne. 12:4.
c 2 Ne. 26:4; 3 Ne. 9:3 (3–9).
16*a* Dan. 11:40; 3 Ne. 10:13 (13–14).
18*a* Hel. 14:22 (21–22).
19*a* Luke 23:44 (44–45).
b Alma 18:14.
c 1 Ne. 19:10; 3 Ne. 10:9.
20*a* Ex. 10:21.
b 1 Ne. 12:5; 19:11.
23*a* 3 Ne. 10:8 (2, 8).
24*a* TG Procrastination.
b Hel. 13:12; 3 Ne. 9:3.

mothers and our fair daughters, and
our children have been spared, and
not have been buried up in that
great city [a]Moronihah. And thus
were the howlings of the people
great and terrible.

CHAPTER 9

In the darkness, the voice of Christ proclaims the destruction of many people and cities for their wickedness—He also proclaims His divinity, announces that the law of Moses is fulfilled, and invites men to come unto Him and be saved. About A.D. *34.*

AND it came to pass that there was a
[a]voice heard among all the inhabitants of the earth, upon all the face
of this land, crying:
2 Wo, wo, wo unto this people; wo
unto the inhabitants of the whole
earth except they shall [a]repent; for
the devil [b]laugheth, and his angels
rejoice, because of the slain of the
fair sons and daughters of my people; and it is because of their iniquity and abominations that they
are fallen!
3 Behold, that great city Zarahemla
have I [a]burned with fire, and the
inhabitants thereof.
4 And behold, that great city Moroni have I caused to be [a]sunk in the
depths of the sea, and the inhabitants thereof to be drowned.
5 And behold, that great city [a]Mo-
ronihah have I covered with earth,
and the inhabitants thereof, to hide
their iniquities and their abominations from before my face, that the
blood of the prophets and the saints
shall not come any more unto me
against them.
6 And behold, the city of Gilgal
have I caused to be sunk, and the
inhabitants thereof to be buried up
in the depths of the earth;
7 Yea, and the city of Onihah and
the inhabitants thereof, and the
city of Mocum and the inhabitants
thereof, and the city of [a]Jerusalem
and the inhabitants thereof; and
[b]waters have I caused to come up
in the stead thereof, to hide their
wickedness and abominations from
before my face, that the [c]blood of
the prophets and the saints shall
[d]not come up any more unto me
against them.
8 And behold, the city of Gadiandi,
and the city of Gadiomnah, and
the city of Jacob, and the city of
Gimgimno, all these have I caused
to be sunk, and made [a]hills and val-
leys in the places thereof; and the
inhabitants thereof have I [b]buried
up in the depths of the earth, to
hide their wickedness and abominations from before my face, that
the blood of the prophets and the
saints should not come up any more
unto me against them.
9 And behold, that great city
Jacobugath, which was inhabited
by the people of king Jacob, have I
caused to be burned with fire because of their sins and their [a]wick-
edness, which was above all the
wickedness of the whole earth, because of their [b]secret murders and
combinations; for it was they that did
[c]destroy the peace of my people and
the government of the land; therefore I did cause them to be burned,
to [d]destroy them from before my
face, that the blood of the prophets
and the saints should not come up
unto me any more against them.

25*a* 3 Ne. 8:10; 9:5.
9 1*a* 1 Ne. 19:11.
2*a* TG Repent.
b Moses 7:26.
3*a* Matt. 11:20; Hel. 13:12; 3 Ne. 8:14 (14–24).
4*a* 3 Ne. 8:9; 4 Ne. 1:9.
5*a* 3 Ne. 8:25 (10, 25).
7*a* Alma 21:1; 24:1.
b Ezek. 26:19.
c Rev. 16:6 (5–7).
d Jonah 1:2.
8*a* 1 Ne. 19:11; 3 Ne. 10:13 (13–14); Moses 7:14.
b Num. 16:32; Hel. 12:17; 3 Ne. 8:10 (10, 25).
9*a* Gen. 6:5 (5–6); Morm. 4:12 (10–12); D&C 112:23; Moses 7:36 (36–37); 8:22 (22, 28–30).
b Hel. 6:17 (17–38); 3 Ne. 6:23.
c 3 Ne. 7:11 (9–13).
d Gen. 6:13; 1 Ne. 17:31; 2 Ne. 1:17; Mosiah 12:8.

10 And behold, the city of Laman,
and the city of Josh, and the city
of Gad, and the city of Kishkumen,
have I caused to be burned with
fire, and the inhabitants thereof,
because of their wickedness in casting out the prophets, and stoning
those whom I did send to declare
unto them concerning their wickedness and their abominations.
11 And because they did cast
them all out, that there were none
righteous among them, I did send
down [a]fire and destroy them, that
their wickedness and abominations
might be hid from before my [b]face,
that the blood of the prophets and
the saints whom I sent among them
might not cry unto me [c]from the
ground against them.
12 And [a]many great destructions
have I caused to come upon this land,
and upon this people, because of
their wickedness and their abominations.
13 O all ye that are [a]spared because
ye were more [b]righteous than they,
will ye not now return unto me, and
repent of your sins, and be converted, that I may [c]heal you?
14 Yea, verily I say unto you, if ye
will [a]come unto me ye shall have
[b]eternal life. Behold, mine [c]arm of
mercy is extended towards you, and
whosoever will come, him will I
receive; and blessed are those who
come unto me.
15 Behold, I am Jesus Christ the
Son of God. I [a]created the heavens
and the earth, and all things that in
them are. I was with the Father from
the beginning. [b]I am in the Father,
and the Father in me; and in me
hath the Father glorified his name.
16 I came unto my own, and my
own [a]received me not. And the
scriptures [b]concerning my coming
are fulfilled.
17 And as many as have received
me, to them have I [a]given to become
the sons of God; and even so will I
to as many as shall believe on my
name, for behold, by me [b]redemp-
tion cometh, and [c]in me is the [d]law
of Moses fulfilled.
18 I am the [a]light and the life of
the world. I am [b]Alpha and Omega,
the beginning and the end.
19 And ye shall offer up unto me
[a]no more the shedding of blood;
yea, your sacrifices and your burnt
offerings shall be done away, for I
will accept none of your sacrifices
and your burnt offerings.
20 And ye shall offer for a [a]sacri-
fice unto me a broken heart and a
contrite spirit. And whoso cometh
unto me with a broken heart and a
contrite spirit, him will I [b]baptize
with fire and with the Holy Ghost,
even as the Lamanites, because of
their faith in me at the time of their
conversion, were baptized with fire
and with the Holy Ghost, and they
knew it not.
21 Behold, I have come unto the
world to bring [a]redemption unto
the world, to save the world from sin.

11*a* 2 Kgs. 1:10 (9–16); Hel. 13:13.
b Deut. 31:18.
c Gen. 4:10.
12*a* Hel. 14:24; 3 Ne. 8:14 (8–10, 14); 10:7 (4–7).
13*a* 3 Ne. 10:6 (6, 12); 27:31.
b Gen. 18:26.
c Jer. 3:22; 17:14; Matt. 13:15; 3 Ne. 18:32.
14*a* 1 Ne. 1:14; 2 Ne. 26:25 (24–28); Alma 5:34 (33–36).
b John 3:16.
c Isa. 59:16; Alma 19:36.
15*a* John 1:3 (1–3); Col. 1:16; Heb. 1:2 (1–3); Mosiah 15:4; Hel. 14:12; Ether 4:7; D&C 14:9.
b 3 Ne. 11:27 (7, 11, 27); 19:23 (23, 29).
16*a* John 1:11; D&C 6:21.
b 3 Ne. 15:5.
17*a* John 1:12. TG Man, Potential to Become like Heavenly Father; Sons and Daughters of God.
b Ps. 107:2. TG Jesus Christ, Redeemer.
c 3 Ne. 15:8 (2–8).
d Heb. 8:13; 3 Ne. 12:19 (19, 46–47).
18*a* TG Jesus Christ, Light of the World.
b Rev. 1:8. TG Jesus Christ, Firstborn.
19*a* Mosiah 13:27; Alma 34:13; 3 Ne. 15:4 (2–10).
20*a* Ps. 51:17; Omni 1:26; 3 Ne. 12:19; D&C 64:34.
b TG Holy Ghost, Baptism of.
21*a* TG Jesus Christ, Atonement through.

22 Therefore, whoso [a]repenteth and cometh unto me [b]as a [c]little child, him will I receive, for of such is the kingdom of God. Behold, for such I have [d]laid down my life, and have taken it up again; therefore repent, and come unto me ye ends of the earth, and be saved.

CHAPTER 10

There is silence in the land for many hours—The voice of Christ promises to gather His people as a hen gathers her chickens—The more righteous part of the people have been preserved. About A.D. *34–35.*

AND now behold, it came to pass that all the people of the land did [a]hear these sayings, and did witness of it. And after these sayings there was silence in the land for the space of many hours;

2 For so great was the astonishment of the people that they did cease lamenting and howling for the loss of their kindred which had been slain; therefore there was silence in all the land for the space of many hours.

3 And it came to pass that there came a voice again unto the people, and all the people did hear, and did witness of it, saying:

4 O ye people of these [a]great cities which have fallen, who are descendants of Jacob, yea, who are of the house of Israel, how oft have I [b]gathered you as a hen gathereth her chickens under her wings, and have [c]nourished you.

5 And again, [a]how oft would I have gathered you as a hen gathereth her chickens under her wings, yea, O ye people of the house of Israel, who have fallen; yea, O ye people of the house of Israel, ye that dwell at Jerusalem, as ye that have fallen; yea, how oft would I have gathered you as a hen gathereth her chickens, and ye would not.

6 O ye house of Israel whom I have [a]spared, how oft will I gather you as a hen gathereth her chickens under her wings, if ye will repent and [b]return unto me with full purpose of [c]heart.

7 But if not, O house of Israel, the places of your dwellings shall become [a]desolate until the time of the fulfilling of the [b]covenant to your fathers.

8 And now it came to pass that after the people had heard these words, behold, they began to weep and howl [a]again because of the loss of their kindred and friends.

9 And it came to pass that thus did the three days pass away. And it was in the morning, and the [a]darkness dispersed from off the face of the land, and the earth did cease to tremble, and the [b]rocks did cease to rend, and the dreadful groanings did cease, and all the tumultuous noises did pass away.

10 And the earth did cleave together again, that it stood; and the [a]mourning, and the weeping, and the wailing of the people who were spared alive did cease; and their mourning was turned into joy, and their lamentations into the [b]praise and thanksgiving unto the Lord Jesus Christ, their Redeemer.

11 And thus far were the [a]scriptures [b]fulfilled which had been spoken by the prophets.

12 And it was the [a]more righteous part of the people who were saved, and it was they who received the

---

22 *a* TG Repent.
b Mark 10:15.
c Mosiah 3:19; 3 Ne. 11:37 (37–38).
d John 10:15 (15–18). TG Jesus Christ, Death of; Self-Sacrifice.

10 1 *a* 1 Ne. 19:11.
4 *a* 3 Ne. 8:14 (8–16); 9:12 (3–12).
b Hel. 7:19.
c Luke 16:29 (29–31); 1 Ne. 17:3; Jacob 5:25.
5 *a* Matt. 23:37; D&C 43:24 (24–25).
6 *a* 3 Ne. 9:13.
b 1 Sam. 7:3; Hel. 13:11; 3 Ne. 24:7.
c Ezek. 36:26.
7 *a* Ezek. 26:19.
b Enos 1:16 (12–18).
8 *a* 3 Ne. 8:23 (23–25).
9 *a* 3 Ne. 8:19 (3, 19–23).
b Hel. 14:21.
10 *a* TG Mourning.
b Acts 16:25.
11 *a* 1 Ne. 19:12 (10–12).
b Acts 3:18 (18–21).
12 *a* 2 Ne. 26:8; 3 Ne. 9:13 (11–13); 27:31.

prophets and stoned them not; and it
was they who had not shed the blood
of the saints, who were spared—
13 And they were spared and were
not sunk and buried up in the earth;
and they were not drowned in the
depths of the sea; and they were not
burned by fire, neither were they
fallen upon and crushed to death;
and they were not carried away in
the whirlwind; neither were they
overpowered by the vapor of smoke
and of darkness.
14 And now, whoso readeth, let him
understand; he that hath the scriptures, let him [a]search them, and see
and behold if all these deaths and
destructions by fire, and by smoke,
and by [b]tempests, and by whirlwinds, and by the [c]opening of the
earth to receive them, and all these
things are not unto the fulfilling
of the prophecies of many of the
holy prophets.
15 Behold, I say unto you, Yea,
many have testified of these things
at the coming of Christ, and were
[a]slain because they testified of these
things.
16 Yea, the prophet [a]Zenos did
testify of these things, and also
Zenock spake [b]concerning these
things, because they testified particularly concerning us, who are the
remnant of their seed.
17 Behold, our father Jacob also
testified concerning a [a]remnant of
the seed of Joseph. And behold, are
not we a remnant of the seed of
Joseph? And these things which testify of us, are they not written upon
the plates of brass which our father
Lehi brought out of Jerusalem?
18 And it came to pass that in the
ending of the thirty and fourth year,
behold, I will show unto you that the
people of Nephi who were spared,
and also those who had been called
[a]Lamanites, who had been spared,
did have great favors shown unto
them, and great [b]blessings poured
out upon their heads, insomuch that
soon after the [c]ascension of Christ
into heaven he did truly manifest
himself unto them—
19 [a]Showing his body unto them,
and ministering unto them; and
an account of his ministry shall be
given hereafter. Therefore for this
time I make an end of my sayings.

Jesus Christ did show himself unto the people of Nephi, as the multitude were gathered together in the land Bountiful, and did minister unto them; and on this wise did he show himself unto them.

Comprising chapters 11 through 26.

CHAPTER 11

The Father testifies of His Beloved Son—Christ appears and proclaims His Atonement—The people feel the wound marks in His hands and feet and side—They cry Hosanna—He sets forth the mode and manner of baptism—The spirit of contention is of the devil—Christ's doctrine is that men should believe and be baptized and receive the Holy Ghost. About A.D. *34.*

AND now it came to pass that there
were a great multitude [a]gathered
together, of the people of Nephi,
round about the temple which was
in the land [b]Bountiful; and they
were marveling and wondering one
with another, and were showing one
to another the [c]great and marvelous change which had taken place.
2 And they were also conversing
about this Jesus Christ, of whom
the [a]sign had been given concerning his death.

14*a* TG Scriptures, Study of.
b Hel. 14:23.
c Num. 16:32; 1 Ne. 19:11; 2 Ne. 26:5.
15*a* TG Martyrdom.
16*a* Hel. 8:20 (19–20).
b 1 Ne. 19:21.
17*a* Alma 46:24; 3 Ne. 5:23 (23–24).
18*a* 4 Ne. 1:20.
b TG Blessing.
c Acts 1:9 (9–11).
19*a* 3 Ne. 11:12 (12–15).

11 1*a* Hel. 3:14 (9, 14).
b Alma 22:29; 3 Ne. 3:23.
c 3 Ne. 8:12 (11–14).
2*a* Hel. 14:20 (20–27); 3 Ne. 8:5 (5–25).

3 And it came to pass that while
they were thus conversing one with
another, they heard a [a]voice as if it
came out of heaven; and they cast
their eyes round about, for they
understood not the voice which
they heard; and it was not a harsh
voice, neither was it a loud voice;
nevertheless, and notwithstanding
it being a [b]small voice it did [c]pierce
them that did hear to the center,
insomuch that there was no part
of their frame that it did not cause
to quake; yea, it did pierce them to
the very soul, and did cause their
hearts to burn.
4 And it came to pass that again
they heard the voice, and they [a]un-
derstood it not.
5 And again the third time they did
hear the voice, and did [a]open their
ears to hear it; and their eyes were
towards the sound thereof; and they
did look steadfastly towards heaven,
from whence the sound came.
6 And behold, the third time they
did understand the voice which
they heard; and it said unto them:
7 Behold my [a]Beloved Son, [b]in
whom I am well pleased, in whom
I have glorified my name—hear
ye him.
8 And it came to pass, as they understood they cast their eyes up
again towards heaven; and behold,
they [a]saw a Man [b]descending out
of heaven; and he was clothed in a
white robe; and he came down and
stood in the midst of them; and the
eyes of the whole multitude were
turned upon him, and they durst
not open their mouths, even one to
another, and wist not what it meant,
for they thought it was an angel that
had appeared unto them.
9 And it came to pass that he
stretched forth his hand and spake
unto the people, saying:
10 Behold, I am Jesus Christ, whom
the prophets testified shall come
into the world.
11 And behold, I am the [a]light
and the life of the world; and I
have drunk out of that bitter [b]cup
which the Father hath given me, and
have glorified the Father in [c]taking
upon me the sins of the world, in
the which I have suffered the [d]will
of the Father in all things from the
beginning.
12 And it came to pass that when
Jesus had spoken these words the
whole multitude [a]fell to the earth;
for they remembered that it had
been [b]prophesied among them
that Christ should [c]show himself
unto them after his ascension into
heaven.
13 And it came to pass that the
[a]Lord spake unto them saying:
14 Arise and come forth unto me,
that ye may [a]thrust your hands
into my side, and also that ye may
[b]feel the prints of the nails in my
hands and in my feet, that ye may
know that I am the [c]God of Israel,
and the God of the whole [d]earth,
and have been slain for the sins of
the world.
15 And it came to pass that the
multitude went forth, and thrust
their hands into his side, and [a]did
feel the prints of the nails in his
hands and in his feet; and this they

3*a* Deut. 4:33; Ezek. 1:24; Hel. 5:29 (28–36).
b 1 Kgs. 19:12 (11–13); D&C 85:6.
c 1 Sam. 3:11; Jer. 20:9.
4*a* Ezek. 1:24 (24–28); 1 Cor. 14:2.
5*a* Job 36:15; D&C 101:92.
7*a* Matt. 3:17; 17:5; JS—H 1:17. TG Witness of the Father.
b 3 Ne. 9:15.
8*a* 1 Ne. 12:6; 2 Ne. 26:1 (1, 9); Alma 16:20; Ether 3:17 (17–18).
b Acts 1:9 (9–11).
11*a* TG Jesus Christ, Light of the World.
b John 18:11.
c John 1:29.
d Mark 14:36 (32–42); Luke 22:42; John 6:38; Hel. 10:4; D&C 19:2.
12*a* TG Reverence.
b Alma 16:20.
c 3 Ne. 10:19.
13*a* TG Jesus Christ, Lord.
14*a* John 20:27.
b Luke 24:39 (36–39); D&C 129:2.
c Isa. 45:3; 3 Ne. 15:5; D&C 36:1; 127:3.
d Ex. 9:29; 1 Ne. 11:6.
15*a* 3 Ne. 18:25. TG Jesus Christ, Appearances, Postmortal.

did do, going forth one by one until they had all gone forth, and did
see with their eyes and did feel
with their hands, and did know of
a surety and did bear record, that
it was he, of whom it was written
by the prophets, that should come.
16 And when they had all gone
forth and had witnessed for themselves, they did cry out with one
accord, saying:
17 Hosanna! Blessed be the name
of the Most High God! And they did
fall down at the feet of Jesus, and
did [a]worship him.
18 And it came to pass that he
spake unto [a]Nephi (for Nephi was
among the multitude) and he commanded him that he should come
forth.
19 And Nephi arose and went forth,
and [a]bowed himself before the Lord
and did [b]kiss his feet.
20 And the Lord commanded him
that he should [a]arise. And he arose
and stood before him.
21 And the Lord said unto him: I
give unto you [a]power that ye shall
[b]baptize this people when I am again
ascended into heaven.
22 And again the Lord called [a]oth-
ers, and said unto them likewise;
and he gave unto them power to
baptize. And he said unto them: On
this wise shall ye baptize; and there
shall be [b]no disputations among you.
23 Verily I say unto you, that whoso
repenteth of his sins through your
[a]words, and [b]desireth to be baptized
in my name, on this wise shall ye
baptize them—Behold, ye shall go
down and [c]stand in the water, and
in my name shall ye baptize them.
24 And now behold, these are the
words which ye shall say, calling
them by name, saying:
25 Having [a]authority given me of
Jesus Christ, I baptize you in the
name of the [b]Father, and of the Son,
and of the Holy Ghost. Amen.
26 And then shall ye [a]immerse
them in the water, and come forth
again out of the water.
27 And after this manner shall ye
[a]baptize in my name; for behold, verily I say unto you, that the Father,
and the Son, and the Holy Ghost are
[b]one; and I am in the Father, and
the Father in me, and the Father
and I are one.
28 And according as I have commanded you thus shall ye baptize.
And there shall be no [a]disputations
among you, as there have hitherto
been; neither shall there be disputations among you concerning the
points of my doctrine, as there have
hitherto been.
29 For verily, verily I say unto you,
he that hath the spirit of [a]conten-
tion is not of me, but is of the [b]devil,
who is the father of contention, and
he stirreth up the hearts of men
to contend with anger, one with
another.
30 Behold, this is not my doctrine,
to stir up the hearts of men with
anger, one against another; but this

17*a* TG Worship.
18*a* 3 Ne. 1:2 (2–3, 10); 7:15 (15, 20, 23).
19*a* Ex. 34:8; Ether 6:12.
b 3 Ne. 17:10.
20*a* Josh. 7:10; Ezek. 2:1 (1–2).
21*a* TG Church Organization; Priesthood, Authority.
b TG Baptism, Essential.
22*a* 1 Ne. 12:7; 3 Ne. 12:1.
b 1 Cor. 11:16 (16–19); 3 Ne. 18:34. TG Disputations.
23*a* Mosiah 26:15 (15–16); 3 Ne. 12:2.
b TG Baptism, Qualifications for.
c 3 Ne. 19:11 (10–13).
25*a* Mosiah 18:13; Alma 5:3; D&C 20:73. TG Delegation of Responsibility; Priesthood, Authority.
b TG Godhead.
26*a* Moses 6:52. TG Baptism, Immersion; Jesus Christ, Types of, in Memory.
27*a* TG Baptism.
b Alma 11:44; 3 Ne. 28:10; Morm. 7:7; D&C 20:28.
28*a* Acts 4:32; 1 Cor. 1:10 (10–13); Eph. 4:13 (11–14); D&C 38:27. TG Disputations.
29*a* 2 Tim. 2:24 (23–24); Mosiah 23:15. TG Contention.
b Eph. 4:27 (26–27); Mosiah 2:32 (32–33); Alma 2:5; 45:23; Hel. 4:1.

is my doctrine, that such things
[a]should be done away.
31 Behold, verily, verily, I say
unto you, I will declare unto you
my [a]doctrine.
32 And this is my [a]doctrine, and
it is the doctrine which the Father
hath given unto me; and I bear
[b]record of the Father, and the Father
beareth record of me, and the [c]Holy
Ghost beareth record of the Father
and me; and I bear record that the
Father commandeth all men, everywhere, to repent and believe in me.
33 And whoso believeth in me,
and is [a]baptized, the same shall be
[b]saved; and they are they who shall
[c]inherit the kingdom of God.
34 And whoso believeth not in
me, and is not [a]baptized, shall be
damned.
35 Verily, verily, I say unto you,
that this is my doctrine, and I bear
record of it from the Father; and
whoso [a]believeth in me believeth
in the Father also; and unto him
will the Father bear record of me,
for he will visit him [b]with fire and
with the [c]Holy Ghost.
36 And thus will the Father bear
record of me, and the [a]Holy Ghost
will bear record unto him of the
Father and me; for the Father, and
I, and the Holy Ghost are [b]one.
37 And again I say unto you, ye
must repent, and [a]become as a [b]little
child, and be baptized in my name,
or ye can in nowise receive these
things.
38 And again I say unto you, ye
must repent, and be baptized in my
name, and become as a little [a]child,
or ye can in nowise inherit the
kingdom of God.
39 Verily, verily, I say unto you,
that this is my [a]doctrine, and whoso
[b]buildeth upon this buildeth upon
my rock, and the [c]gates of hell shall
not prevail against them.
40 And whoso shall [a]declare more
or less than this, and establish it
for my doctrine, the same cometh
of evil, and is not built upon my
rock; but he buildeth upon a [b]sandy
foundation, and the gates of hell
stand open to receive such when
the floods come and the winds beat
upon them.
41 Therefore, go forth unto this
people, and declare the words which
I have spoken, unto the ends of
the earth.

CHAPTER 12

Jesus calls and commissions the twelve disciples—He delivers to the Nephites a discourse similar to the Sermon on the Mount—He speaks the Beatitudes—His teachings transcend and take precedence over the law of Moses—Men are commanded to be perfect even as He and His Father are perfect—Compare Matthew 5. About A.D. *34.*

[a]AND it came to pass that when
Jesus had spoken these words unto
Nephi, and to those who had been
called, (now the number of them
who had been called, and received
power and authority to [b]baptize, was
[c]twelve) and behold, he stretched
forth his hand unto the multitude,

30*a* Mark 9:50; John 16:33.
31*a* John 18:37; 2 Ne. 31:21 (2–21).
32*a* TG Jesus Christ, Teaching Mode of.
b 1 Jn. 5:7 (6–9). TG Jesus Christ, Relationships with the Father.
c 3 Ne. 28:11; Ether 5:4; Moses 1:24.
33*a* Mark 16:16. TG Baptism, Essential.
b TG Salvation, Plan of.
c TG Exaltation.
34*a* TG Baptism.
35*a* Ether 4:12.
b 3 Ne. 9:20; 12:2.
c TG Holy Ghost, Baptism of.
36*a* TG Holy Ghost, Source of Testimony.
b TG Godhead; Unity.
37*a* Mark 10:15; Luke 18:17.
b 3 Ne. 9:22.
38*a* TG Baptism, Qualifications for.
39*a* Mark 4:2.
b Matt. 7:24 (24–29); 1 Pet. 2:6 (4–8); 1 Ne. 13:36. TG Rock.
c Matt. 16:18; 3 Ne. 18:13 (12–13); D&C 17:8.
40*a* Rom. 16:17 (17–19); 1 Tim. 1:3.
b 3 Ne. 14:26 (24–27).
12 1*a* Matt. 5:1 (1–48).
b Mark 16:16 (15–16); John 4:2 (1–2).
c 3 Ne. 11:22; 13:25.

and cried unto them, saying: [d]Blessed
are ye if ye shall give heed unto the
words of these twelve whom I have
[e]chosen from among you to minister unto you, and to be your servants; and unto them I have given
power that they may baptize you
with water; and after that ye are
baptized with water, behold, I will
baptize you with fire and with the
Holy Ghost; therefore blessed are
ye if ye shall believe in me and be
baptized, after that ye have seen me
and know that I am.
2 And again, more blessed are they
who shall [a]believe in your words
because that ye shall testify that
ye have seen me, and that ye know
that I am. Yea, blessed are they who
shall [b]believe in your [c]words, and
[d]come down into the depths of humility and be baptized, for they
shall be visited [e]with fire and with
the Holy Ghost, and shall receive a
remission of their sins.
3 Yea, blessed are the [a]poor in spirit
who [b]come unto me, for theirs is
the kingdom of heaven.
4 And again, blessed are all they that
[a]mourn, for they shall be [b]comforted.
5 And blessed are the [a]meek, for
they shall inherit the [b]earth.
6 And blessed are all they who
do [a]hunger and [b]thirst after [c]righ-
teousness, for they shall be [d]filled
with the Holy Ghost.
7 And blessed are the [a]merciful,
for they shall obtain mercy.
8 And blessed are all the [a]pure in
heart, for they shall [b]see God.
9 And blessed are all the [a]peace-
makers, for they shall be called the
[b]children of God.
10 And blessed are all they who
are [a]persecuted for my name's sake,
for theirs is the kingdom of heaven.
11 And blessed are ye when men
shall [a]revile you and persecute, and
shall say all manner of evil against
you falsely, for my sake;
12 For [a]ye shall have great joy and
be exceedingly glad, for great shall
be your [b]reward in heaven; for so
[c]persecuted they the prophets who
were before you.
13 Verily, verily, I say unto you, I
give unto you to be the [a]salt of the
earth; but if the salt shall lose its
savor wherewith shall the earth be
salted? The salt shall be thenceforth
good for nothing, but to be cast out
and to be trodden under foot of men.
14 Verily, verily, I say unto you, I
give unto you to be the light of this
people. A city that is set on a hill
cannot be hid.
15 Behold, do men light a [a]candle
and put it under a bushel? Nay, but
on a candlestick, and it giveth light
to all that are in the house;
16 Therefore let your [a]light so
shine before this people, that they
may see your good works and [b]glo-
rify your Father who is in heaven.
17 Think not that I am come to
destroy the law or the prophets.

1*d* TG Blessing.
e TG Called of God.
2*a* TG Teachable.
b Mosiah 26:15 (15–16); D&C 46:14.
c 3 Ne. 11:23.
d Ether 4:13.
e 3 Ne. 11:35; 19:13 (13–14).
3*a* Ps. 86:1; Eccl. 4:13 (13–14); Matt. 5:3; D&C 56:18 (17–18). TG Poor in Spirit.
b Matt. 11:28 (28–30).
4*a* Morm. 2:11 (11–14). TG Mourning.
b Matt. 5:4; Alma 28:6. TG Comfort.
5*a* Zeph. 2:3 (1–3); Rom. 12:16. TG Meek.
b TG Earth, Destiny of.
6*a* Matt. 5:6; 2 Ne. 9:51; Enos 1:4.
b Jer. 29:13.
c Prov. 21:21.
d TG Spirituality.
7*a* TG Mercy.
8*a* TG Purity.
b TG God, Privilege of Seeing.
9*a* TG Peacemakers.
b TG Sons and Daughters of God.
10*a* Matt. 5:10; D&C 122:5 (5–9).
11*a* TG Reviling.
12*a* Matt. 5:12.
b TG Reward.
c 2 Cor. 7:4. TG Prophets, Rejection of.
13*a* 2 Chr. 13:5; Matt. 5:13; D&C 101:39 (39–40). TG Mission of Early Saints; Salt.
15*a* Luke 8:16.
16*a* 3 Ne. 18:24. TG Example.
b John 11:4 (1–4); Ether 12:4.

I am not come to destroy but to
fulfil;
18 For verily I say unto you, [a]one
jot nor one tittle hath not passed
away from the [b]law, but in me it
hath all been fulfilled.
19 And behold, I have given you
the law and the commandments
of my Father, that ye shall believe
in me, and that ye shall repent of
your sins, and come unto me with a
[a]broken heart and a contrite spirit.
Behold, ye have the commandments before you, and the [b]law is
fulfilled.
20 Therefore [a]come unto me and
be ye saved; for verily I say unto
you, that except ye shall keep my
[b]commandments, which I have commanded you at this time, ye shall
in no case enter into the kingdom
of heaven.
21 Ye have heard that it hath been
said by them of old time, and it is
also written before you, that thou
shalt not [a]kill, and whosoever shall
kill shall be in danger of the judgment of God;
22 But I say unto you, that whosoever is [a]angry with his brother shall
be in danger of his judgment. And
whosoever shall say to his brother,
Raca, shall be in danger of the
council; and whosoever shall say,
Thou fool, shall be in danger of
hell fire.
23 Therefore, [a]if ye shall come
unto me, or shall desire to come
unto me, and rememberest that thy
brother hath aught against thee—
24 Go thy way unto thy brother, and
first be [a]reconciled to thy brother,
and then come unto me with full
[b]purpose of heart, and I will receive you.
25 [a]Agree with thine adversary
quickly while thou art in the way
with him, lest at any time he shall
get thee, and thou shalt be cast into
prison.
26 Verily, verily, I say unto thee,
thou shalt by no means come out
thence until thou hast paid the uttermost senine. And while ye are in
prison can ye pay even one [a]senine?
Verily, verily, I say unto you, Nay.
27 Behold, it is written by them of
old time, that thou shalt not commit [a]adultery;
28 But I say unto you, that whosoever looketh on a woman, to [a]lust
after her, hath committed adultery
already in his heart.
29 Behold, I give unto you a commandment, that ye suffer [a]none
of these things to enter into your
[b]heart;
30 For it is better that ye should
deny yourselves of these things,
wherein ye will take up your [a]cross,
than that ye should be cast into
hell.
31 It hath been written, that whosoever shall put away his wife, let him
give her a writing of [a]divorcement.
32 Verily, verily, I say unto you,
that whosoever shall [a]put away his
wife, saving for the cause of [b]for-
nication, causeth her to commit
[c]adultery; and whoso shall marry
her who is divorced committeth
adultery.
33 And again it is written, thou
shalt not [a]forswear thyself, but

18*a* Matt. 5:18.
b TG Law of Moses.
19*a* 3 Ne. 9:20.
TG Contrite Heart.
b 3 Ne. 9:17.
20*a* Isa. 55:3.
b 3 Ne. 15:10.
21*a* Ex. 20:13 (13–17);
Deut. 5:17 (17–21);
Matt. 5:21;
Mosiah 13:21 (21–24);
D&C 42:18.
TG Life, Sanctity of.
22*a* Matt. 5:22.
23*a* Matt. 5:23.
24*a* TG Forgive;
Reconciliation.
b 3 Ne. 18:29 (28–33);
D&C 46:4.
25*a* Matt. 5:25 (25–26).
26*a* Alma 11:3; 30:33.
27*a* Matt. 5:27;
2 Ne. 9:36;
D&C 59:6.
28*a* TG Lust.
29*a* D&C 42:23.
b Acts 8:22.
30*a* Matt. 10:38; 16:24;
Luke 9:23; 14:27;
D&C 23:6.
31*a* TG Divorce.
32*a* Matt. 5:32;
Mark 10:11 (11–12);
Luke 16:18.
b TG Fornication.
c TG Adulterer.
33*a* TG Swearing.

shalt [b]perform unto the Lord thine
[c]oaths;
34 But verily, verily, I say unto
you, [a]swear not at all; neither by
heaven, for it is God's throne;
35 Nor by the earth, for it is his
footstool;
36 Neither shalt thou swear by thy
head, because thou canst not make
one hair black or white;
37 But let your [a]communication be
[b]Yea, yea; Nay, nay; for whatsoever
cometh of more than these is evil.
38 And behold, it is written, an [a]eye
for an eye, and a tooth for a tooth;
39 But I say unto you, that ye shall
not [a]resist evil, but whosoever shall
smite thee on thy right [b]cheek, [c]turn
to him the other also;
40 And if any man will sue thee at
the law and take away thy coat, [a]let
him have thy cloak also;
41 And whosoever shall compel
thee to [a]go a mile, go with him twain.
42 [a]Give to him that asketh thee,
and from him that would [b]borrow
of thee turn thou not away.
43 And behold it is written also,
that thou shalt love thy neighbor and
hate thine enemy;
44 But behold I say unto you, love
your [a]enemies, bless them that curse
you, do [b]good to them that hate you,
and [c]pray for them who despitefully
use you and persecute you;
45 That ye may be the children of
your Father who is in heaven; for
he maketh his sun to rise [a]on the
evil and on the good.
46 Therefore those things which
were of old time, which were under the law, in me are all [a]fulfilled.
47 [a]Old things are done away, and
all things have become [b]new.
48 Therefore I would that ye should
be [a]perfect even as I, or your Father
who is in heaven is perfect.

CHAPTER 13

Jesus teaches the Nephites the Lord's Prayer—They are to lay up treasures in heaven—The twelve disciples in their ministry are commanded to take no thought for temporal things—Compare Matthew 6. About A.D. 34.

[a]VERILY, verily, I say that I would
that ye should do alms unto the
poor; but take heed that ye do not
your alms before men to be seen of
them; otherwise ye have no reward
of your Father who is in heaven.
2 Therefore, when ye shall do your
alms do not sound a trumpet before
you, as will hypocrites do in the
synagogues and in the streets, that
they may have [a]glory of men. Verily I say unto you, they have their
reward.
3 But when thou doest alms let
not thy left hand know what thy
right hand doeth;
4 That thine alms may be in secret; and thy Father who seeth in
secret, himself shall reward thee
openly.
5 And when thou [a]prayest thou
shalt not do as the [b]hypocrites, for

33*b* TG Dependability.
c TG Oath.
34*a* Lev. 5:4; Morm. 3:14. TG Profanity.
37*a* TG Communication.
b TG Honesty.
38*a* Lev. 24:20; Matt. 5:38 (38–42). TG Punish.
39*a* 3 Ne. 6:13; 4 Ne. 1:34; D&C 98:23 (23–27). TG Submissiveness.
b Lam. 3:30.
c TG Forbear; Patience.
40*a* TG Charity; Initiative.
41*a* TG Generosity.
42*a* Jacob 2:19 (17–19); Mosiah 4:26.
b TG Borrow.
44*a* Prov. 24:17; 25:21 (21–22); Alma 48:23. TG Enemies.
b TG Benevolence.
c Acts 7:60 (59–60); 2 Tim. 4:16.
45*a* Matt. 5:45.
46*a* Heb. 8:13.
47*a* 3 Ne. 9:17; 15:2 (2, 7); D&C 22:1.
b Jer. 31:31 (31–33); Ether 13:9.
48*a* Matt. 5:48; 3 Ne. 19:29 (28–29); 27:27. TG God, Perfection of; God, the Standard of Righteousness; Jesus Christ, Exemplar; Man, New, Spiritually Reborn; Man, Potential to Become like Heavenly Father.
13 1*a* Matt. 6:1 (1–34). TG Almsgiving.
2*a* D&C 121:35 (34–35).
5*a* TG Prayer.
b TG Hypocrisy.

they love to pray, standing in the
synagogues and in the corners of
the streets, that they may be seen
of men. Verily I say unto you, they
have their reward.
6 But thou, when thou prayest,
enter into thy closet, and when
thou hast [a]shut thy door, pray to
thy Father who is in secret; and thy
Father, who [b]seeth in secret, shall
reward thee openly.
7 But when ye pray, use not [a]vain
repetitions, as the [b]heathen, for they
think that they shall be heard for
their much speaking.
8 Be not ye therefore like unto
them, for your Father [a]knoweth
what things ye have need of before
ye [b]ask him.
9 After this [a]manner therefore
[b]pray ye: Our [c]Father who art in
heaven, hallowed be thy name.
10 Thy will be done on earth as it
is in heaven.
11 And forgive us our debts, as we
forgive our debtors.
12 And [a]lead us not into temptation, but deliver us from evil.
13 For thine is the kingdom, and the
power, and the glory, forever. Amen.
14 For, if ye [a]forgive men their
trespasses your heavenly Father
will also forgive you;
15 But if ye forgive not men their
trespasses neither will your Father
forgive your trespasses.
16 Moreover, when ye [a]fast be not
as the [b]hypocrites, of a sad countenance, for they disfigure their faces
that they may appear unto men to
fast. Verily I say unto you, they have
their reward.
17 But thou, when thou fastest,
anoint thy head, and [a]wash thy face;
18 That thou appear not unto
men to fast, but unto thy Father, who
is in [a]secret; and thy Father, who
seeth in secret, shall reward thee
openly.
19 Lay not up for yourselves treasures upon earth, where [a]moth and
rust doth corrupt, and thieves break
through and steal;
20 But lay up for yourselves [a]treasures in heaven, where neither moth
nor rust doth corrupt, and where
thieves do not break through nor
steal.
21 For where your treasure is, there
will your heart be also.
22 The [a]light of the body is the [b]eye;
if, therefore, thine eye be [c]single,
thy whole body shall be full of
light.
23 But if thine eye be evil, thy
whole body shall be full of darkness. If, therefore, the light that is in
thee be darkness, how great is that
darkness!
24 No man can [a]serve [b]two masters;
for either he will hate the one and
love the other, or else he will hold
to the one and despise the other.
Ye cannot serve God and Mammon.
25 And now it came to pass that
when Jesus had spoken these words
he looked upon the [a]twelve whom
he had chosen, and said unto them:
Remember the words which I have
spoken. For behold, ye are they
whom I have chosen to [b]minister
unto this people. Therefore I say
unto you, [c]take no thought for your
life, what ye shall eat, or what ye

6*a* 2 Kgs. 4:33.
b TG God, Omniscience of.
7*a* TG Sincere.
b TG Heathen.
8*a* D&C 84:83.
b Ezek. 36:37.
9*a* Matt. 6:9 (9–13).
b TG Prayer.
c TG God the Father, Elohim.
12*a* JST Matt. 6:14 (Matt. 6:13 note *a*).
14*a* Mosiah 26:31. TG Forgive.
16*a* Isa. 58:5 (5–7); Zech. 7:5 (5–6). TG Fast, Fasting.
b TG Hypocrisy.
17*a* TG Wash.
18*a* Isa. 45:15; D&C 38:7.
19*a* 3 Ne. 27:32.
20*a* Hel. 5:8; 8:25. TG Treasure.
22*a* Ezra 9:8.
b Matt. 6:22 (20–25).
c D&C 88:67. TG Dedication.
24*a* 1 Sam. 7:3; Alma 5:41 (39–42); Moses 1:15.
b Hosea 10:2.
25*a* Matt. 6:25; 3 Ne. 12:1; 15:11.
b TG Church Organization; Delegation of Responsibility.
c Alma 31:37; D&C 84:81 (79–85).

shall drink; nor yet for your body, what ye shall put on. Is not the life more than meat, and the body than [d]raiment?

26 Behold the [a]fowls of the air, for they sow not, neither do they reap nor gather into barns; yet your heavenly Father feedeth them. Are ye not much better than they?

27 Which of you by taking thought can add one cubit unto his stature?

28 And why take ye thought for raiment? Consider the [a]lilies of the field how they grow; they toil not, neither do they spin;

29 And yet I say unto you, that even Solomon, in all his glory, was not arrayed like one of these.

30 Wherefore, if God so clothe the grass of the field, which today is, and tomorrow is cast into the oven, even so will he clothe you, if ye are not of little faith.

31 Therefore take no thought, saying, What shall we eat? or, What shall we drink? or, Wherewithal shall we be clothed?

32 For your heavenly Father knoweth that ye have need of all these things.

33 But [a]seek ye first the [b]kingdom of God and his righteousness, and all these things shall be added unto you.

34 Take therefore no thought for the morrow, for the morrow shall take thought for the things of itself. [a]Sufficient is the day unto the evil thereof.

CHAPTER 14

Jesus commands: Judge not; ask of God; beware of false prophets—He promises salvation to those who do the will of the Father—Compare Matthew 7. About A.D. *34.*

[a]AND now it came to pass that when Jesus had spoken these words he turned again to the multitude, and did open his mouth unto them again, saying: Verily, verily, I say unto you, Judge not, that ye be not judged.

2 [a]For with what judgment ye judge, ye shall be judged; and with what measure ye mete, it shall be measured to you again.

3 And why beholdest thou the mote that is in thy brother's eye, but considerest not the beam that is in thine own eye?

4 Or how wilt thou say to thy brother: Let me pull the mote out of thine eye—and behold, a beam is in thine own eye?

5 Thou [a]hypocrite, first cast the [b]beam out of thine own eye; and then shalt thou see clearly to cast the mote out of thy brother's eye.

6 Give not that which is [a]holy unto the dogs, neither cast ye your pearls before swine, lest they trample them under their feet, and turn again and rend you.

7 [a]Ask, and it shall be given unto you; [b]seek, and ye shall find; knock, and it shall be opened unto you.

8 For every one that asketh, receiveth; and he that seeketh, findeth; and to him that knocketh, it shall be opened.

9 Or what man is there of you, who, if his son ask bread, will give him a stone?

10 Or if he ask a fish, will he give him a serpent?

11 If ye then, being evil, know how to give good gifts unto your children, how much more shall your Father who is in heaven give good things to them that ask him?

12 Therefore, all things whatsoever ye would that men should do to you, [a]do ye even so to them, for this is the law and the prophets.

25*d* Job 27:16 (16–17).
26*a* D&C 117:6.
28*a* TG Nature, Earth.
33*a* TG Commitment.
b Luke 12:31 (22–34). TG Objectives.
34*a* Matt. 6:34.

14 1*a* Matt. 7:1 (1–27); JST Matt. 7:1–2 (Matt. 7:1 note *a*).
2*a* Morm. 8:19.
5*a* TG Hypocrisy.
b John 8:7 (3–11).
6*a* TG Holiness.
7*a* 3 Ne. 27:29. TG Prayer.
b TG Initiative; Objectives.
12*a* TG Benevolence; Compassion; Courtesy.

13 Enter ye in at the [a]strait gate;
for wide is the gate, and [b]broad is
the way, which leadeth to destruction, and many there be who go in
thereat;
14 Because strait is the [a]gate, and
[b]narrow is the way, which leadeth
unto life, and [c]few there be that
find it.
15 Beware of [a]false prophets, who
come to you in sheep's clothing, but
inwardly they are ravening wolves.
16 Ye shall know them by their
[a]fruits. Do men gather grapes of
thorns, or figs of thistles?
17 Even so every [a]good tree bringeth forth good fruit; but a corrupt
tree bringeth forth evil fruit.
18 A good tree cannot bring forth
evil fruit, neither a corrupt tree
bring forth good fruit.
19 Every tree that [a]bringeth not
forth good fruit is hewn down, and
cast into the fire.
20 Wherefore, by their [a]fruits ye
shall know them.
21 Not every one that saith unto
me, Lord, Lord, shall [a]enter into
the kingdom of heaven; but he that
doeth the will of my Father who is
in heaven.
22 Many will [a]say to me in that day:
Lord, Lord, have we not prophesied
in thy name, and in thy name have
cast out devils, and in thy name
done many wonderful works?
23 And then will [a]I profess unto
them: I never [b]knew you; [c]depart
from me, ye that work iniquity.
24 Therefore, whoso heareth these
sayings of mine and doeth them,
I will liken him unto a wise man,
who built his house upon a [a]rock—
25 And the [a]rain descended, and
the floods came, and the winds blew,
and beat upon that house; and it
[b]fell not, for it was founded upon
a rock.
26 And every one that heareth
these sayings of mine and doeth
them not shall be likened unto a
[a]foolish man, who built his house
upon the [b]sand—
27 And the rain descended, and
the floods came, and the winds
blew, and beat upon that house; and
it fell, and great was the fall of it.

CHAPTER 15

Jesus announces that the law of Moses is fulfilled in Him—The Nephites are the other sheep of whom He spoke in Jerusalem—Because of iniquity, the Lord's people in Jerusalem do not know of the scattered sheep of Israel. About A.D. 34.

AND now it came to pass that when
Jesus had ended these sayings he
cast his eyes round about on the
multitude, and said unto them:
Behold, ye have heard the things
which I [a]taught before I ascended
to my Father; therefore, whoso remembereth these sayings of mine
and [b]doeth them, him will I [c]raise
up at the last day.
2 And it came to pass that when
Jesus had said these words he perceived that there were some among
them who marveled, and wondered
what he would concerning the law

13*a* Luke 13:24;
3 Ne. 27:33.
b D&C 132:25.
14*a* 2 Ne. 9:41; 31:9 (9, 17–18);
D&C 22:4.
b 1 Ne. 8:20.
c Matt. 7:14;
1 Ne. 14:12.
15*a* Jer. 23:21 (21–32);
2 Ne. 28:12 (9, 12, 15).
TG False Prophets.
16*a* Col. 1:6;
Alma 32:42 (28–42);
D&C 52:34 (18, 34).
17*a* Alma 5:41.
19*a* Matt. 3:10;
Alma 5:36 (36–41);
D&C 97:7.
20*a* Matt. 7:17 (16–20); 12:33;
Luke 6:43 (43–45);
Moro. 7:5.
21*a* 1 Jn. 2:17.
22*a* Alma 5:17.
23*a* Matt. 7:23.
b Mosiah 5:13;
26:25 (24–27);
D&C 112:26.
c Ps. 119:115;
Luke 13:27.
24*a* TG Rock.
25*a* Alma 26:6;
Hel. 5:12.
b Prov. 12:7.
26*a* TG Foolishness.
b 3 Ne. 11:40.
15 1*a* IE in Galilee and Judea.
b James 1:22 (22–24).
c John 6:39;
1 Ne. 13:37;
Mosiah 23:22;
Alma 26:7;
D&C 5:35.

of Moses; for they understood not
the saying that [a]old things had
passed away, and that all things
had become new.
3 And he said unto them: Marvel
not that I said unto you that old
things had passed away, and that
all things had become [a]new.
4 Behold, I say unto you that the
[a]law is fulfilled that was given unto
Moses.
5 Behold, [a]I am he that gave the
law, and I am he who covenanted
with my people Israel; therefore,
the law in me is fulfilled, for I have
come to [b]fulfil the law; therefore it
hath an end.
6 Behold, I do [a]not destroy the
prophets, for as many as have not
been fulfilled in me, verily I say unto
you, shall all be fulfilled.
7 And because I said unto you that
old things have passed away, I do not
destroy that which hath been spoken
concerning things which are to come.
8 For behold, the [a]covenant which
I have made with my people is not
all fulfilled; but the law which was
given unto Moses hath an end in me.
9 Behold, I am the [a]law, and the
[b]light. Look unto me, and endure to
the end, and ye shall [c]live; for unto
him that [d]endureth to the end will
I give eternal life.
10 Behold, I have given unto you
the [a]commandments; therefore keep
my commandments. And this is the
law and the prophets, for they truly
[b]testified of me.
11 And now it came to pass that
when Jesus had spoken these words,
he [a]said unto those twelve whom
he had chosen:
12 Ye are my [a]disciples; and ye are
a [b]light unto this people, who are a
remnant of the house of [c]Joseph.
13 And behold, this is the [a]land of
your inheritance; and the Father
hath given it unto you.
14 And not at any time hath the
Father given me commandment that
I should [a]tell it unto your brethren
at Jerusalem.
15 Neither at any time hath the
Father given me commandment that
I should tell unto them concerning
the [a]other tribes of the house of
Israel, whom the Father hath led
away out of the land.
16 This much did the Father [a]com-
mand me, that I should tell unto
them:
17 That other sheep I have which
are not of this fold; them also I
must bring, and they shall hear my
voice; and there shall be one fold,
and one [a]shepherd.
18 And now, because of [a]stiff-
neckedness and [b]unbelief they [c]un-
derstood not my word; therefore I
was commanded to say no more of
the [d]Father concerning this thing
unto them.
19 But, verily, I say unto you that
the Father hath commanded me,
and I tell it unto you, that ye were
[a]separated from among them because of their iniquity; therefore it

2*a* 3 Ne. 12:47 (46–47).
3*a* Heb. 8:13; Ether 13:9.
4*a* Mosiah 13:27 (27–31); 3 Ne. 9:17 (17–20).
5*a* 1 Cor. 10:4 (1–4); 3 Ne. 11:14. TG Jesus Christ, Jehovah.
b Alma 34:13. TG Jesus Christ, Mission of.
6*a* 3 Ne. 20:11 (11–12); 23:3 (1–3).
8*a* 3 Ne. 5:25 (24–26); 16:5. TG Covenants; Restoration of the Gospel.
9*a* 2 Ne. 26:1.
b TG Jesus Christ, Light of the World.
c Lev. 18:5; John 11:25; D&C 84:44.
d Matt. 10:22 (22–33); Mark 13:13; 2 Ne. 31:20; Alma 32:13 (13–15); 3 Ne. 27:6 (6–17).
10*a* 3 Ne. 12:20.
b Mosiah 13:33.
11*a* 3 Ne. 13:25; Moro. 2:1.
12*a* TG Church Organization.
b TG Example; Leadership.
c TG Israel, Joseph, People of.
13*a* 1 Ne. 18:23; 3 Ne. 16:16.
14*a* 3 Ne. 5:20.
15*a* 2 Ne. 21:12; 3 Ne. 16:1 (1–4). TG Israel, Ten Lost Tribes of.
16*a* John 15:15; 16:12.
17*a* TG Shepherd.
18*a* TG Stiffnecked.
b TG Doubt; Unbelief.
c D&C 10:59.
d John 12:50.
19*a* 1 Kgs. 8:53; John 17:6 (6–22).

is because of their iniquity that
they know not of you.
20 And verily, I say unto you again
that the other tribes hath the Father
separated from them; and it is because of their iniquity that they
know not of them.
21 And verily I say unto you, that
ye are they of whom I said: [a]Other
sheep I have which are not of this
fold; them also I must bring, and
they shall hear my voice; and there
shall be one fold, and one [b]shepherd.
22 And they understood me not,
for they supposed it had been the
[a]Gentiles; for they understood not
that the Gentiles should be [b]con-
verted through their preaching.
23 And they understood me not
that I said they shall hear my voice;
and they understood me not that
the [a]Gentiles should not at any time
hear my voice—that I should not
manifest myself unto them save it
were by the [b]Holy Ghost.
24 But behold, ye have both heard
[a]my voice, and seen me; and ye are
my sheep, and ye are numbered
among those whom the Father hath
[b]given me.

CHAPTER 16

Jesus will visit others of the lost sheep of Israel—In the latter days the gospel will go to the Gentiles and then to the house of Israel—The Lord's people will see eye to eye when He brings again Zion. About A.D. *34.*

AND verily, verily, I say unto you
that I have [a]other sheep, which are
not of this land, neither of the land
of Jerusalem, neither in any parts
of that land round about whither
I have been to minister.
2 For they of whom I speak are
they who have not as yet heard my
voice; neither have I at any time
manifested myself unto them.
3 But I have received a [a]command-
ment of the Father that I shall go
unto them, and that they shall [b]hear
my voice, and shall be numbered
among my sheep, that there may be
one fold and one shepherd; therefore I go to show myself unto them.
4 And I command you that ye shall
[a]write these sayings after I am gone,
that if it so be that my people at
Jerusalem, they who have seen me
and been with me in my ministry,
do not ask the Father in my name,
that they may receive a knowledge
of you by the Holy Ghost, and also
of the other tribes whom they know
not of, that these sayings which ye
shall write shall be kept and shall
be manifested unto the [b]Gentiles,
that through the fulness of the Gentiles, the remnant of their seed, who
shall be scattered forth upon the
face of the earth because of their
[c]unbelief, may be brought in, or
may be brought to a [d]knowledge
of me, their Redeemer.
5 And then will I [a]gather them in
from the four quarters of the earth;
and then will I fulfil the [b]covenant
which the Father hath made unto
all the people of the [c]house of Israel.
6 And blessed are the [a]Gentiles,
because of their belief in me, in and
of the Holy Ghost, which [b]witnesses
unto them of me and of the Father.

21 *a* John 10:16 (14–16).
b TG Jesus Christ, Good Shepherd.
22 *a* TG Gentiles.
b Acts 10:45 (34–48).
23 *a* Matt. 15:24.
b 1 Ne. 10:11. TG Holy Ghost, Mission of.
24 *a* Alma 5:38; 3 Ne. 16:3 (1–5); 18:31.
b John 6:37; D&C 27:14.
16 1 *a* 1 Ne. 19:10; 2 Ne. 21:12; 3 Ne. 15:15. TG Israel, Ten Lost Tribes of.
3 *a* 3 Ne. 18:27.
b 3 Ne. 17:4.
4 *a* 2 Ne. 25:18. TG Scriptures to Come Forth.
b 1 Ne. 10:14; 3 Ne. 21:6 (1–11).
c TG Unbelief.
d Ezek. 20:42 (42–44); Micah 7:9 (8–9); 3 Ne. 20:13. TG Israel, Restoration of.
5 *a* TG Israel, Gathering of.
b 3 Ne. 5:25 (24–26); 15:8.
c 1 Ne. 22:9; 3 Ne. 21:27 (26–29).
6 *a* 1 Ne. 13:39 (23, 30–42); 2 Ne. 30:3; 3 Ne. 20:27.
b 2 Ne. 32:5; 3 Ne. 11:32 (32, 35–36). TG Holy Ghost, Source of Testimony.

7 Behold, because of their belief
in me, saith the Father, and because
of the unbelief of you, O house of
Israel, in the [a]latter day shall the
truth come unto the [b]Gentiles, that
the fulness of these things shall be
made known unto them.
8 But wo, saith the Father, unto the
[a]unbelieving of the Gentiles—for
notwithstanding they have come
forth upon the face of this land,
and have [b]scattered my people who
are of the house of Israel; and my
people who are of the house of Israel have been [c]cast out from among
them, and have been trodden under
feet by them;
9 And because of the mercies of the
Father unto the Gentiles, and also
the judgments of the Father upon
my people who are of the house of
Israel, verily, verily, I say unto you,
that after all this, and I have caused
my people who are of the house of
Israel to be smitten, and to be afflicted, and to be [a]slain, and to be
cast out from among them, and to
become [b]hated by them, and to become a hiss and a byword among
them—
10 And thus commandeth the
Father that I should say unto you:
At that day when the Gentiles shall
[a]sin against my gospel, and shall reject the fulness of my gospel, and
shall be [b]lifted up in the pride of
their hearts above all nations, and
above all the people of the whole
earth, and shall be filled with all
manner of lyings, and of deceits,
and of mischiefs, and all manner
of hypocrisy, and [c]murders, and
[d]priestcrafts, and whoredoms, and
of secret abominations; and if they
shall do all those things, and shall
[e]reject the fulness of my gospel,
behold, saith the Father, I will
bring the fulness of my gospel from
among them.
11 And then will I [a]remember my
covenant which I have made unto
my people, O house of Israel, and
I will bring my gospel unto them.
12 And I will show unto thee, O
house of Israel, that the Gentiles
shall not have power over you; but
I will remember my covenant unto
you, O house of Israel, and ye shall
come unto the [a]knowledge of the
fulness of my gospel.
13 But if the Gentiles will repent
and return unto me, saith the
Father, behold they shall be [a]num-
bered among my people, O house
of Israel.
14 And I will not suffer my people,
who are of the house of Israel, to
go through among them, and tread
them down, saith the Father.
15 But if they will not turn unto
me, and hearken unto my voice, I
will suffer them, yea, I will suffer
my people, O house of Israel, that
they shall go through among them,
and shall [a]tread them down, and
they shall be as salt that hath lost
its savor, which is thenceforth good
for nothing but to be cast out, and
to be trodden under foot of my
people, O house of Israel.
16 Verily, verily, I say unto you,
thus hath the Father commanded

7*a* TG Restoration of the Gospel.
b D&C 19:27; 107:33. TG Mission of Latter-day Saints.
8*a* 2 Ne. 6:15; 28:15 (15–32); Ether 2:9 (8–11).
b 1 Ne. 13:14; 2 Ne. 26:19; Morm. 5:9 (9, 15).
c 3 Ne. 20:28.
9*a* Amos 9:1 (1–4).
b Jer. 23:40; Lam. 2:16 (15–16); Joel 2:17; 1 Ne. 19:14.
10*a* 3 Ne. 20:15.
b Morm. 8:36 (35–41).
c 3 Ne. 30:2; Morm. 8:31.
d 2 Ne. 26:29. TG Priestcraft.
e 3 Ne. 20:28 (27–28); D&C 6:31.
11*a* Isa. 44:21; 3 Ne. 20:29 (28–31); 21:4 (1–11); Morm. 5:20.
12*a* Hel. 15:13. TG Israel, Restoration of; Knowledge.
13*a* Gal. 3:7 (7, 29); 1 Ne. 15:13 (13–17); 22:9 (5–10); 2 Ne. 10:18 (18–19); 3 Ne. 30:2; Abr. 2:10 (9–11).
15*a* Micah 5:8 (8–15); 3 Ne. 20:16; 21:12 (12–21); D&C 87:5.

me—that I should give unto [a]this people this land for their inheritance.

17 And then the [a]words of the prophet Isaiah shall be fulfilled, which say:

18 [a]Thy [b]watchmen shall lift up the voice; with the voice together shall they sing, for they shall see eye to eye when the Lord shall bring again Zion.

19 Break forth into joy, sing together, ye waste places of Jerusalem; for the Lord hath comforted his people, he hath redeemed Jerusalem.

20 The Lord hath made bare his holy arm in the eyes of all the nations; and all the ends of the earth shall see the salvation of God.

CHAPTER 17

Jesus directs the people to ponder His words and pray for understanding—He heals their sick—He prays for the people, using language that cannot be written—Angels minister to and fire encircles their little ones. About A.D. *34.*

BEHOLD, now it came to pass that when Jesus had spoken these words he looked round about again on the multitude, and he said unto them: Behold, my [a]time is at hand.

2 I [a]perceive that ye are weak, that ye cannot [b]understand all my words which I am commanded of the Father to speak unto you at this time.

3 Therefore, go ye unto your homes, and [a]ponder upon the things which I have said, and ask of the Father, in my name, that ye may understand, and [b]prepare your minds for the [c]morrow, and I come unto you again.

4 But now I [a]go unto the Father, and also to [b]show myself unto the lost tribes of Israel, for they are not [c]lost unto the Father, for he knoweth whither he hath taken them.

5 And it came to pass that when Jesus had thus spoken, he cast his eyes round about again on the multitude, and beheld they were [a]in tears, and did look steadfastly upon him as if they would ask him to tarry a little longer with them.

6 And he said unto them: Behold, my bowels are filled with [a]compassion towards you.

7 Have ye any that are [a]sick among you? Bring them hither. Have ye any that are lame, or blind, or halt, or maimed, or [b]leprous, or that are withered, or that are deaf, or that are afflicted in any manner? Bring them hither and I will [c]heal them, for I have compassion upon you; my bowels are filled with mercy.

8 For I perceive that ye desire that I should show unto you what I have done unto your brethren at Jerusalem, for I see that your [a]faith is [b]sufficient that I should heal you.

9 And it came to pass that when he had thus spoken, all the multitude, with one accord, did go forth with their sick and their afflicted, and their lame, and with their [a]blind, and with their dumb, and with all them that were afflicted in any manner; and he did heal them every one as they were brought forth unto him.

16*a* 3 Ne. 15:13.
17*a* 3 Ne. 20:11.
18*a* Isa. 52:8 (8–10); 3 Ne. 20:32.
b Ezek. 33:2 (2, 7); D&C 101:45 (45, 53–54). TG Watchman.
17 1*a* IE to return to the Father. See v. 4.
2*a* TG Jesus Christ, Teaching Mode of.
b John 16:12; D&C 50:40; 78:18 (17–18).
3*a* TG Meditation.
b Ezra 7:10; D&C 29:8; 132:3.
c 3 Ne. 19:2.
4*a* 3 Ne. 18:39.
b 3 Ne. 16:3. TG Jesus Christ, Appearances, Postmortal.
c TG Israel, Ten Lost Tribes of.
5*a* TG God, Love of.
6*a* TG Compassion.
7*a* TG Sickness.
b TG Leprosy.
c TG Administrations to the Sick; Heal.
8*a* Matt. 8:10 (1–17); Luke 18:42.
b 2 Ne. 27:23; Ether 12:12.
9*a* Matt. 9:28 (28–31); Mosiah 3:5; 3 Ne. 26:15; D&C 84:69.

10 And they did all, both they who
had been healed and they who were
whole, bow down at his feet, and
did worship him; and as many as
could come for the multitude did
[a]kiss his feet, insomuch that they
did bathe his feet with their tears.
11 And it came to pass that he
commanded that their [a]little children should be brought.
12 So they brought their little
children and set them down upon
the ground round about him, and
Jesus stood in the midst; and the
multitude gave way till they had
all been brought unto him.
13 And it came to pass that when
they had all been brought, and Jesus
stood in the midst, he commanded
the multitude that they should
[a]kneel down upon the ground.
14 And it came to pass that when
they had knelt upon the ground,
Jesus groaned within himself, and
said: Father, I am [a]troubled because
of the wickedness of the people of
the house of Israel.
15 And when he had said these
words, he himself also [a]knelt upon
the earth; and behold he [b]prayed
unto the Father, and the things
which he prayed cannot be written,
and the multitude did bear record
who heard him.
16 And after this manner do they
bear record: The [a]eye hath never
seen, neither hath the ear heard,
before, so great and marvelous
things as we saw and heard Jesus
speak unto the Father;
17 And no [a]tongue can speak, neither can there be written by any
man, neither can the hearts of men
conceive so great and marvelous
things as we both saw and heard
Jesus speak; and no one can conceive
of the joy which filled our souls at
the time we heard him pray for us
unto the Father.
18 And it came to pass that when
Jesus had made an end of praying
unto the Father, he arose; but so
great was the [a]joy of the multitude
that they were overcome.
19 And it came to pass that Jesus
spake unto them, and bade them
arise.
20 And they arose from the earth,
and he said unto them: Blessed are
ye because of your faith. And [a]now
behold, my joy is full.
21 And when he had said these
words, he [a]wept, and the multitude
bare record of it, and he took their
little children, one by one, and
[b]blessed them, and prayed unto the
Father for them.
22 And when he had done this he
wept again;
23 And he spake unto the multitude, and said unto them: Behold
your little ones.
24 And as they looked to behold
they cast their eyes towards heaven,
and they saw the heavens open, and
they saw angels descending out of
heaven as it were in the midst of fire;
and they came down and [a]encircled
those little ones about, and they
were encircled about with fire; and
the angels did minister unto them.
25 And the multitude did see and
[a]hear and bear record; and they
know that their record is true for
they all of them did see and hear,
every man for himself; and they
were in number about two thousand and five hundred souls; and
they did consist of men, women,
and children.

10*a* Luke 7:38 (38, 45); 3 Ne. 11:19.
11*a* Matt. 19:13 (13–14); Mark 10:13; 3 Ne. 26:14 (14, 16). TG Children.
13*a* Acts 9:40; 20:36; 3 Ne. 19:6 (6, 16–17).
14*a* Mosiah 28:3; Alma 31:2; 3 Ne. 17:20; 27:32; Moses 7:41.
15*a* 3 Ne. 19:19 (19, 27).
b TG Jesus Christ, Relationships with the Father.
16*a* Isa. 64:4; 1 Cor. 2:9; 3 Ne. 19:32 (30–36); D&C 76:10, 116 (114–19).
17*a* 2 Cor. 12:4; 3 Ne. 19:34 (32–34).
18*a* TG Joy.
20*a* 3 Ne. 17:14.
21*a* John 11:35. TG Sincere.
b Mark 10:16 (14–16).
24*a* Hel. 5:43 (23–24, 43–45); 3 Ne. 19:14. TG Transfiguration.
25*a* Ex. 19:9 (9–13).

CHAPTER 18

Jesus institutes the sacrament among the Nephites—They are commanded to pray always in His name—Those who eat His flesh and drink His blood unworthily are damned—The disciples are given power to confer the Holy Ghost. About A.D. 34.

AND it came to pass that Jesus commanded his disciples that they
should bring forth some [a]bread and
wine unto him.
2 And while they were gone for
bread and wine, he commanded
the multitude that they should sit
themselves down upon the earth.
3 And when the disciples had come
with [a]bread and wine, he took of
the bread and brake and blessed it;
and he gave unto the disciples and
commanded that they should eat.
4 And when they had eaten and
were filled, he commanded that
they should give unto the multitude.
5 And when the multitude had
eaten and were filled, he said unto
the disciples: Behold there shall one
be [a]ordained among you, and to
him will I give power that he shall
[b]break [c]bread and bless it and give
it unto the people of my [d]church,
unto all those who shall believe and
be baptized in my name.
6 And this shall ye always observe
to [a]do, even as I have done, even as
I have broken bread and blessed it
and given it unto you.
7 And this shall ye do in [a]remem-
brance of my [b]body, which I have
shown unto you. And it shall be
a testimony unto the Father that
ye do always remember me. And if ye
do always remember me ye shall
have my Spirit to be with you.
8 And it came to pass that when
he said these words, he commanded
his disciples that they should take
of the [a]wine of the cup and drink
of it, and that they should also give
unto the multitude that they might
drink of it.
9 And it came to pass that they
did so, and did drink of it and were
filled; and they gave unto the multitude, and they did drink, and they
were filled.
10 And when the disciples had
done this, Jesus said unto them:
Blessed are ye for this thing which
ye have done, for this is fulfilling
my commandments, and this doth
witness unto the Father that ye are
[a]willing to do that which I have
commanded you.
11 And this shall ye always do to
those who repent and are baptized
in my name; and ye shall do it in
[a]remembrance of my [b]blood, which
I have shed for you, that ye may
witness unto the Father that ye do
always remember me. And if ye
do always remember me ye shall
have my Spirit to be with you.
12 And I give unto you a commandment that ye shall do these
things. And if ye shall always do
these things blessed are ye, for ye
are built upon my [a]rock.
13 But whoso among you shall
do [a]more or less than these are not
built upon my rock, but are built
upon a sandy foundation; and when
the rain descends, and the floods
come, and the winds blow, and beat
upon them, they shall [b]fall, and the
[c]gates of hell are ready open to receive them.
14 Therefore blessed are ye if ye
shall keep my commandments,
which the Father hath commanded
me that I should give unto you.

---

18 1*a* Matt. 26:26; 3 Ne. 20:3 (3–9); 26:13.
3*a* TG Jesus Christ, Types of, in Memory.
5*a* TG Church Organization.
b Moro. 4:1.
c Matt. 14:19 (19–21); 3 Ne. 20:6 (6–7).
d TG Church.
6*a* TG Jesus Christ, Exemplar.
7*a* 3 Ne. 20:8; Moro. 4:3. TG Sacrament.
b TG Bread of Life.
8*a* Matt. 26:27 (27–29). TG Jesus Christ, Types of, in Memory.
10*a* TG Commitment.
11*a* Moro. 5:1.
b TG Blood, Symbolism of.
12*a* TG Rock.
13*a* Josh. 1:7; D&C 3:2.
b TG Apostasy of Individuals.
c Matt. 16:18; 3 Ne. 11:39.

15 Verily, verily, I say unto you, ye
must watch and [a]pray always, lest
ye be tempted by the devil, and ye
be led away captive by him.
16 And as I have prayed among
you even so shall ye pray in my
[a]church, among my people who
do repent and are baptized in my
name. Behold I am the [b]light; I have
set an [c]example for you.
17 And it came to pass that when
Jesus had spoken these words unto
his disciples, he turned again unto
the multitude and said unto them:
18 Behold, verily, verily, I say unto
you, ye must watch and pray always
lest ye enter into temptation; for
[a]Satan desireth to have you, that
he may sift you as wheat.
19 Therefore ye must always pray
unto the Father in my name;
20 And [a]whatsoever ye shall ask
the Father in my name, which is
right, believing that ye shall receive,
behold it shall be given unto you.
21 [a]Pray in your families unto the
Father, always in my name, that
your wives and your children may
be blessed.
22 And behold, ye shall [a]meet together oft; and ye shall not forbid
any man from coming unto you
when ye shall meet together, but
suffer them that they may come
unto you and forbid them not;
23 But ye shall [a]pray for them, and
shall not cast them out; and if it so
be that they come unto you oft ye
shall pray for them unto the Father,
in my name.
24 Therefore, hold up your [a]light
that it may shine unto the world.
Behold I am the [b]light which ye
shall hold up—that which ye have
seen me do. Behold ye see that I
have prayed unto the Father, and
ye all have witnessed.
25 And ye see that I have commanded that [a]none of you should go
away, but rather have commanded
that ye should come unto me, that
ye might [b]feel and see; even so shall
ye do unto the world; and whosoever breaketh this commandment
suffereth himself to be led into
temptation.
26 And now it came to pass that
when Jesus had spoken these words,
he turned his eyes again upon the
[a]disciples whom he had chosen, and
said unto them:
27 Behold verily, verily, I say unto
you, I give unto you another commandment, and then I must go
unto my [a]Father that I may fulfil
[b]other commandments which he
hath given me.
28 And now behold, this is the
commandment which I give unto
you, that ye shall not suffer any
one knowingly to [a]partake of my
flesh and blood [b]unworthily, when
ye shall minister it;
29 For whoso eateth and drinketh
my flesh and [a]blood [b]unworthily
eateth and drinketh damnation to
his soul; therefore if ye know that
a man is unworthy to eat and drink
of my flesh and blood ye shall forbid him.
30 Nevertheless, ye shall not [a]cast
him out from among you, but ye

15*a* Alma 34:23; D&C 93:49.
16*a* TG Jesus Christ, Head of the Church.
b TG Jesus Christ, Light of the World.
c TG God, the Standard of Righteousness; Jesus Christ, Exemplar.
18*a* Luke 22:31; 2 Ne. 2:18 (17–18); D&C 10:22 (22–27).
20*a* Isa. 58:9 (8–9); Matt. 21:22 (21–22); Mark 11:24; Hel. 10:5; Morm. 9:21; Moro. 7:26; D&C 88:64 (63–65).
21*a* Alma 34:21. TG Family, Children, Responsibilities toward.
22*a* TG Meetings.
23*a* 3 Ne. 18:30. TG Missionary Work.
24*a* TG Jesus Christ, Light of the World.
b Matt. 5:16; Mark 4:21; 3 Ne. 12:16.
25*a* Alma 5:33; 19:36.
b 3 Ne. 11:15 (14–16).
26*a* 3 Ne. 13:25.
27*a* TG God the Father, Elohim.
b 3 Ne. 16:3.
28*a* Ex. 12:43; 1 Cor. 11:27 (27–30); 4 Ne. 1:27.
b Lev. 7:18; Morm. 9:29.
29*a* TG Blood, Symbolism of.
b 3 Ne. 12:24 (23–26); D&C 46:4.
30*a* D&C 46:3.

shall [b]minister unto him and shall
pray for him unto the Father, in
my name; and if it so be that he repenteth and is baptized in my name,
then shall ye receive him, and shall
minister unto him of my flesh and
blood.
31 But if he repent not he shall
not be numbered among my people,
that he may not destroy my people,
for behold I [a]know [b]my sheep, and
they are numbered.
32 Nevertheless, ye shall not cast
him out of your [a]synagogues, or
your places of worship, for unto
such shall ye continue to minister;
for ye know not but what they will
return and repent, and come unto
me with full purpose of heart, and
I shall [b]heal them; and ye shall be
the means of bringing salvation
unto them.
33 Therefore, keep these sayings
which I have commanded you that
ye come not under [a]condemnation;
for wo unto him whom the Father
condemneth.
34 And I give you these commandments because of the disputations
which have been among you. And
blessed are ye if ye have [a]no disputations among you.
35 And now I go unto the Father,
because it is expedient that I should
go unto the Father [a]for your sakes.
36 And it came to pass that when
Jesus had made an end of these sayings, he touched with his [a]hand the
[b]disciples whom he had chosen, one
by one, even until he had touched
them all, and spake unto them as
he touched them.
37 And the multitude heard not
the words which he spake, therefore
they did not bear record; but the
disciples bare record that he gave
them [a]power to give the [b]Holy Ghost.
And I will show unto you [c]hereafter
that this record is true.
38 And it came to pass that when
Jesus had touched them all, there
came a [a]cloud and overshadowed
the multitude that they could not
see Jesus.
39 And while they were overshadowed he [a]departed from them, and
ascended into heaven. And the disciples saw and did bear record that
he ascended again into heaven.

CHAPTER 19

The twelve disciples minister unto the people and pray for the Holy Ghost—The disciples are baptized and receive the Holy Ghost and the ministering of angels—Jesus prays using words that cannot be written—He attests to the exceedingly great faith of these Nephites. About A.D. 34.

AND now it came to pass that when
Jesus had ascended into heaven,
the multitude did disperse, and
every man did take his wife and his
children and did return to his own
home.
2 And it was noised abroad among
the people immediately, before it
was yet dark, that the multitude had
seen Jesus, and that he had ministered unto them, and that he would
also show himself on the [a]morrow
unto the multitude.
3 Yea, and even all the night it was
noised abroad concerning Jesus; and
insomuch did they send forth unto
the people that there were many,
yea, an exceedingly great number,
did labor exceedingly all that night,
that they might be on the morrow in
the place where Jesus should show
himself unto the multitude.

30*b* 3 Ne. 18:23.
31*a* D&C 27:14.
b John 10:14; Alma 5:38; 3 Ne. 15:24.
32*a* Alma 16:13; Moro. 7:1.
b Jer. 3:22; 3 Ne. 9:13 (13–14); D&C 112:13.
33*a* TG Condemnation.
34*a* 3 Ne. 11:28 (28–30). TG Disputations.
35*a* 1 Jn. 2:1; 2 Ne. 2:9; Moro. 7:28 (27–28); D&C 29:5.
36*a* TG Hands, Laying on of.
b 1 Ne. 12:7; 3 Ne. 15:11; 19:4 (4–12).
37*a* TG Holy Ghost, Gift of; Priesthood, Authority.
b Alma 31:36.
c 3 Ne. 26:17; 28:18; Moro. 2:2 (2–3).
38*a* Ex. 19:9 (9, 16); 2 Chr. 5:14 (11–14).
39*a* 3 Ne. 17:4.
19 2*a* 3 Ne. 17:3.

4 And it came to pass that on the
morrow, when the multitude was
gathered together, behold, Nephi
and his [a]brother whom he had raised
from the [b]dead, whose name was
Timothy, and also his son, whose
name was Jonas, and also Mathoni,
and Mathonihah, his brother, and
Kumen, and Kumenonhi, and Jeremiah, and Shemnon, and Jonas,
and Zedekiah, and Isaiah—now
these were the [c]names of the [d]dis-
ciples whom Jesus had chosen—
and it came to pass that they went
forth and stood in the midst of the
multitude.
5 And behold, the multitude was
[a]so great that they did cause that
they should be separated into twelve
bodies.
6 And the twelve did teach the
multitude; and behold, they did
cause that the multitude should
[a]kneel down upon the face of the
earth, and should pray unto the
Father in the name of Jesus.
7 And the disciples did pray unto
the Father also in the name of Jesus.
And it came to pass that they arose
and ministered unto the people.
8 And when they had ministered
those same words which Jesus had
spoken—nothing varying from the
words which Jesus had spoken—behold, they knelt again and prayed
to the Father in the name of Jesus.
9 And they did pray for that which
they most desired; and they desired
that the [a]Holy Ghost should be given
unto them.
10 And when they had thus prayed
they went down unto the water's
edge, and the multitude followed
them.
11 And it came to pass that Nephi
went down [a]into the water and was
[b]baptized.
12 And he came up out of the
water and began to baptize. And
he baptized all those whom Jesus
had chosen.
13 And it came to pass when they
were all baptized and had come [a]up
out of the water, the [b]Holy Ghost
did fall upon them, and they were
filled with the Holy Ghost and
with fire.
14 And behold, they were [a]en-
circled about as if it were by fire;
and it came down from heaven, and
the multitude did witness it, and did
bear record; and angels did come
down out of heaven and did minister unto them.
15 And it came to pass that while
the angels were ministering unto
the disciples, behold, Jesus came
and stood in the midst and ministered unto them.
16 And it came to pass that he
spake unto the multitude, and
commanded them that they should
kneel down again upon the earth,
and also that his disciples should
kneel down upon the earth.
17 And it came to pass that when
they had all knelt down upon the
earth, he commanded his disciples
that they should pray.
18 And behold, they began to
pray; and they did pray unto Jesus,
calling him their Lord and their
God.
19 And it came to pass that Jesus
departed out of the midst of them,
and went a little way off from
them and [a]bowed himself to the
earth, and he said:
20 Father, I thank thee that thou
hast given the Holy Ghost unto these
whom I have [a]chosen; and it is because of their belief in me that I
have chosen them out of the world.
21 Father, I pray thee that thou wilt
give the Holy Ghost unto all them
that shall believe in their words.

4*a* 3 Ne. 7:19.
b TG Death, Power over.
c 3 Ne. 28:25.
d 3 Ne. 18:36 (36–37); 26:17.
5*a* Mosiah 2:7.
6*a* 3 Ne. 17:13.
9*a* 3 Ne. 9:20.
11*a* 3 Ne. 11:23.
b Matt. 3:14 (13–15); JS—H 1:71 (70–71).
13*a* TG Baptism, Immersion.
b 3 Ne. 12:2; Morm. 7:10. TG Holy Ghost, Baptism of.
14*a* Hel. 5:43 (23–24, 43–45); 3 Ne. 17:24.
19*a* 3 Ne. 17:15.
20*a* TG Church Organization.

22 Father, thou hast given them the Holy Ghost because they believe in [a]me; and thou seest that they believe in me because thou hearest them, and they pray unto me; and they pray unto me because I am with them.

23 And now Father, I [a]pray unto thee for them, and also for all those who shall believe on their words, that they may believe in me, that I may be in them [b]as thou, Father, art in me, that we may be [c]one.

24 And it came to pass that when Jesus had thus prayed unto the Father, he came unto his disciples, and behold, they did still continue, without ceasing, to pray unto him; and they did not [a]multiply many words, for it was given unto them what they should [b]pray, and they were filled with desire.

25 And it came to pass that Jesus blessed them as they did pray unto him; and his [a]countenance did smile upon them, and the light of his [b]countenance did [c]shine upon them, and behold they were as [d]white as the countenance and also the garments of Jesus; and behold the whiteness thereof did exceed all the whiteness, yea, even there could be nothing upon earth so white as the whiteness thereof.

26 And Jesus said unto them: Pray on; nevertheless they did not cease to pray.

27 And he turned from them again, and went a little way off and bowed himself to the earth; and he prayed again unto the Father, saying:

28 Father, I thank thee that thou hast [a]purified those whom I have chosen, because of their faith, and I pray for them, and also for them who shall believe on their words, that they may be purified in me, through faith on their words, even as they are purified in me.

29 Father, I pray not for the world, but for those whom thou hast given me [a]out of the world, because of their faith, that they may be purified in me, that I may be in them as thou, Father, art in me, that we may be one, that I may be glorified in them.

30 And when Jesus had spoken these words he came again unto his disciples; and behold they did pray steadfastly, without ceasing, unto him; and he did smile upon them again; and behold they were [a]white, even as Jesus.

31 And it came to pass that he went again a little way off and prayed unto the Father;

32 And tongue cannot speak the words which he prayed, neither can be [a]written by man the words which he prayed.

33 And the multitude did hear and do bear record; and their [a]hearts were open and they did understand in their hearts the words which he prayed.

34 Nevertheless, so great and marvelous were the words which he prayed that they cannot be written, neither can they be [a]uttered by man.

35 And it came to pass that when Jesus had made an end of praying he came again to the disciples, and said unto them: [a]So great [b]faith have I never seen among all the Jews; wherefore I could not show unto them so great [c]miracles, because of their [d]unbelief.

22*a* Acts 7:59.
23*a* TG Jesus Christ, Relationships with the Father.
b 3 Ne. 9:15; 11:27.
c John 17:22 (1–22); 1 Cor. 6:17.
24*a* Matt. 6:7.
b Hel. 10:5; D&C 46:30.
25*a* Num. 6:25 (23–27).
b Ps. 4:6.
c Dan. 9:17.
d TG Transfiguration.
28*a* Neh. 12:30; Moro. 7:48; D&C 50:29 (28–29); 88:74 (74–75). TG Purity.
29*a* John 17:6.
30*a* Matt. 17:2.
32*a* 3 Ne. 5:18; D&C 76:116.
33*a* Prov. 2:2; 8:5; Isa. 44:18; Mosiah 2:9; 12:27.
34*a* 2 Cor. 12:4; 3 Ne. 17:17.
35*a* Matt. 8:10.
b TG Faith.
c John 11:47 (47–48).
d Matt. 13:58. TG Doubt; Unbelief.

36 Verily I say unto you, there are none of them that have seen so great things as ye have seen; neither have they heard so great things as ye have heard.

CHAPTER 20

Jesus provides bread and wine miraculously and again administers the sacrament unto the people—The remnant of Jacob will come to the knowledge of the Lord their God and will inherit the Americas—Jesus is the prophet like unto Moses, and the Nephites are children of the prophets—Others of the Lord's people will be gathered to Jerusalem. About A.D. 34.

AND it came to pass that he commanded the multitude that they should [a]cease to [b]pray, and also his disciples. And he commanded them that they should not cease to pray in their hearts.

2 And he commanded them that they should arise and stand up upon their feet. And they arose up and stood upon their feet.

3 And it came to pass that he [a]brake [b]bread again and blessed it, and gave to the disciples to eat.

4 And when they had eaten he commanded them that they should break bread, and give unto the multitude.

5 And when they had given unto the multitude he also gave them wine to drink, and commanded them that they should give unto the multitude.

6 Now, there had been no [a]bread, neither wine, brought by the disciples, neither by the multitude;

7 But he truly [a]gave unto them bread to eat, and also wine to drink.

8 And he said unto them: He that eateth this bread eateth of [a]my body to his soul; and he that drinketh of this wine drinketh of my blood to his soul; and his soul shall never hunger nor thirst, but shall be filled.

9 Now, when the multitude had all eaten and drunk, behold, they were filled with the Spirit; and they did cry out with one voice, and gave glory to Jesus, whom they both saw and heard.

10 And it came to pass that when they had all given glory unto Jesus, he said unto them: Behold now I finish the commandment which the Father hath commanded me concerning this people, who are a remnant of the house of Israel.

11 Ye remember that I spake unto you, and said that when the [a]words of [b]Isaiah should be fulfilled—behold they are written, ye have them before you, therefore search them—

12 And verily, verily, I say unto you, that when they shall be fulfilled then is the fulfilling of the [a]covenant which the Father hath made unto his people, O house of Israel.

13 And then shall the [a]remnants, which shall be [b]scattered abroad upon the face of the earth, be [c]gathered in from the east and from the west, and from the south and from the north; and they shall be brought to the [d]knowledge of the Lord their God, who hath redeemed them.

14 And the Father hath [a]commanded me that I should give unto you this [b]land, for your inheritance.

15 And I say unto you, that if the Gentiles do not [a]repent after

---

20 1*a* 1 Sam. 7:8; 2 Ne. 32:9.
b Mosiah 24:12.
3*a* Mark 6:41 (36–44).
b 3 Ne. 18:1; 26:13.
6*a* Matt. 14:19 (19–21).
7*a* John 6:14.
8*a* John 6:51 (50–58); 1 Cor. 11:24 (20–26); 3 Ne. 18:7; Moro. 4:3.
11*a* 3 Ne. 16:17 (17–20); 23:3 (1–3).
b 2 Ne. 25:5 (1–5); Morm. 8:23.
12*a* Gen. 17:11 (9–12); 3 Ne. 15:7.
13*a* 3 Ne. 16:13 (6–13); 21:3 (2–7).
b TG Israel, Scattering of.
c Jer. 46:27 (2–28); 3 Ne. 22:7 (6–17). TG Israel, Gathering of.
d Ezek. 20:42 (42–44); 3 Ne. 16:4 (4–5).
14*a* TG Jesus Christ, Authority of.
b TG Promised Lands.
15*a* 3 Ne. 16:10 (10–14).

the [b]blessing which they shall receive, after they have scattered my
people—
16 Then shall ye, who are a [a]rem-
nant of the house of Jacob, go forth
among them; and ye shall be in the
midst of them who shall be many;
and ye shall be among them as a lion
among the beasts of the forest, and
as a young [b]lion among the flocks
of sheep, who, if he goeth through
both [c]treadeth down and teareth in
pieces, and none can deliver.
17 Thy hand shall be lifted up
upon thine adversaries, and all thine
enemies shall be cut off.
18 And I will [a]gather my people
together as a man gathereth his
sheaves into the floor.
19 For I will make my [a]people with
whom the Father hath covenanted,
yea, I will make thy [b]horn iron, and
I will make thy hoofs brass. And
thou shalt [c]beat in pieces many
people; and I will consecrate their
gain unto the Lord, and their substance unto the Lord of the whole
earth. And behold, I am he who
doeth it.
20 And it shall come to pass, saith
the Father, that the [a]sword of my
justice shall hang over them at that
day; and except they repent it shall
fall upon them, saith the Father,
yea, even upon all the nations of
the Gentiles.
21 And it shall come to pass that I
will establish my [a]people, O house
of Israel.
22 And behold, this [a]people will
I establish in this land, unto the
fulfilling of the [b]covenant which I
made with your father Jacob; and
it shall be a [c]New Jerusalem. And
the [d]powers of heaven shall be in
the midst of this people; yea, even
[e]I will be in the midst of you.
23 Behold, I am he of whom Moses spake, saying: [a]A prophet shall
the Lord your God raise up unto
you of your brethren, like unto
me; him shall ye hear in all things
whatsoever he shall say unto you.
And it shall come to pass that every
soul who will not hear that prophet
shall be cut off from among the
people.
24 Verily I say unto you, yea, and
[a]all the prophets from Samuel and
those that follow after, as many as
have spoken, have testified of me.
25 And behold, ye are the [a]children
of the prophets; and ye are of the
house of Israel; and ye are of the
[b]covenant which the Father made
with your fathers, saying unto Abraham: And [c]in thy seed shall all the
kindreds of the earth be blessed.
26 The Father having raised me
up unto you first, and sent me to
[a]bless you in [b]turning away every
one of you from his iniquities; and
this because ye are the children of
the covenant—
27 And after that ye were blessed
then fulfilleth the Father the covenant which he made with Abra-
ham, saying: [a]In thy seed shall all the
kindreds of the earth be blessed—
unto the pouring out of the Holy

15*b* 3 Ne. 20:27.
16*a* TG Israel, Remnant of.
b Gen. 49:9; Morm. 5:24; D&C 87:5 (4–5); 109:65 (65–67). TG Israel, Deliverance of.
c Micah 5:8 (8–9); 3 Ne. 16:15 (14–15); 21:12 (11–21).
18*a* Micah 4:12.
19*a* Lev. 26:12; D&C 63:1 (1–6).
b TG Last Days.
c Micah 4:13.
20*a* 1 Ne. 14:17; 22:16 (15–16); 3 Ne. 29:4.
21*a* 1 Kgs. 8:51; 3 Ne. 16:8 (8–15); 21:23 (12–24).
22*a* TG Israel, Joseph, People of.
b Gen. 49:26 (22–26).
c Isa. 2:3 (2–5); 3 Ne. 21:23 (23–24); Ether 13:3 (1–12); D&C 84:2 (2–4). TG Jerusalem, New.
d 3 Ne. 21:25.
e Isa. 59:20 (20–21); 3 Ne. 24:1.
23*a* Deut. 18:15 (15–19); Acts 3:22 (22–23); 1 Ne. 22:20 (20–21); D&C 133:63.
24*a* Acts 3:24 (24–26); 1 Ne. 10:5; Jacob 7:11.
25*a* Rom. 4:24 (23–24).
b TG Abrahamic Covenant.
c Gen. 12:3 (1–3); 22:18 (9, 18). TG Seed of Abraham.
26*a* TG Israel, Blessings of.
b Prov. 16:6; Alma 19:33.
27*a* Gen. 12:2 (1–3); Gal. 3:8 (7–29); 2 Ne. 29:14; Abr. 2:9.

Ghost through me upon the Gentiles,
which [b]blessing upon the [c]Gentiles
shall make them mighty above all,
unto the [d]scattering of my people,
O house of Israel.
28 And they shall be a [a]scourge
unto the people of this land. Nevertheless, when they shall have
received the fulness of my gospel,
then if they shall harden their hearts
against me I will return their [b]iniqui-
ties upon their own heads, saith the
Father.
29 And I will [a]remember the covenant which I have made with my
people; and I have covenanted with
them that I would [b]gather them
together in mine own due time,
that I would give unto them again
the [c]land of their fathers for their
inheritance, which is the land of
Jerusalem, which is the promised
land unto them forever, saith the
Father.
30 And it shall come to pass that
the time cometh, when the fulness
of my gospel shall be preached
unto them;
31 And they shall [a]believe in me,
that I am Jesus Christ, the Son of
God, and shall pray unto the Father
in my name.
32 Then shall their [a]watchmen lift
up their voice, and with the voice
together shall they sing; for they
shall see eye to eye.
33 Then will the Father gather
them together again, and give unto
them [a]Jerusalem for the [b]land of
their inheritance.
34 Then shall they break forth
into joy—[a]Sing together, ye waste
places of Jerusalem; for the Father
hath comforted his people, he hath
redeemed Jerusalem.
35 The Father hath made bare his
holy arm in the eyes of all the nations; and all the ends of the earth
shall see the salvation of the Father;
and the Father and I are one.
36 And then shall be brought to
pass that which is written: [a]Awake,
awake again, and put on thy strength,
O Zion; put on thy beautiful garments, O Jerusalem, the holy city,
for henceforth there shall no more
come into thee the uncircumcised
and the unclean.
37 Shake thyself from the dust;
arise, sit down, O Jerusalem; loose
thyself from the bands of thy neck,
O captive daughter of Zion.
38 For thus saith the Lord: Ye
have sold yourselves for naught,
and ye shall be redeemed without
money.
39 Verily, verily, I say unto you,
that my people shall know my
name; yea, in that day they shall
know that I am he that doth speak.
40 And then shall they say: [a]How
beautiful upon the mountains are
the feet of him that bringeth good
tidings unto them, that [b]publisheth
peace; that bringeth good tidings
unto them of good, that publisheth
salvation; that saith unto Zion: Thy
God reigneth!
41 And then shall a cry go forth:
[a]Depart ye, depart ye, go ye out from
thence, touch not that which is [b]un-
clean; go ye out of the midst of her;
be ye [c]clean that bear the vessels
of the Lord.

27*b* 3 Ne. 20:15.
c 3 Ne. 16:6 (6–7); Morm. 5:19.
d 3 Ne. 16:8 (8–9); Morm. 5:9.
28*a* Josh. 23:13; 1 Ne. 2:24; 3 Ne. 16:8 (8–10).
b Isa. 51:23.
29*a* Isa. 44:21; 3 Ne. 16:11 (11–12).
b TG Israel, Gathering of.
c Amos 9:15; Alma 7:10; D&C 133:24. TG Israel, Land of.
31*a* 3 Ne. 5:26 (21–26); 21:26 (26–29).
32*a* Isa. 52:8 (8–9); 3 Ne. 16:18 (18–20). TG Watchman.
33*a* Isa. 18:7; D&C 84:2. TG Jerusalem.
b Deut. 11:11. TG Israel, Land of; Lands of Inheritance.
34*a* Isa. 54:1.
36*a* Isa. 52:1 (1–3); D&C 113:7 (7–10). TG Priesthood, Power of.
40*a* Isa. 52:7; Nahum 1:15; Mosiah 15:18 (13–18); D&C 128:19.
b Mark 13:10; 1 Ne. 13:37.
41*a* Isa. 52:11 (11–15).
b TG Uncleanness.
c D&C 133:5. TG Cleanliness.

42 For ye shall [a]not go out with
[b]haste nor go by flight; for the Lord
will go before you, and the God of
Israel shall be your rearward.
43 Behold, my servant shall deal
prudently; he shall be exalted and
extolled and be very high.
44 As many were astonished at
thee—his visage was so marred,
more than any man, and his form
more than the sons of men—
45 So shall he [a]sprinkle many
nations; the kings shall shut their
mouths at him, for that which had
not been told them shall they see;
and that which they had not heard
shall they [b]consider.
46 Verily, verily, I say unto you, all
these things shall surely come, even
as the Father hath commanded me.
Then shall this covenant which the
Father hath covenanted with his
people be fulfilled; and then shall
[a]Jerusalem be inhabited again with
my people, and it shall be the land
of their inheritance.

CHAPTER 21

Israel will be gathered when the Book of Mormon comes forth—The Gentiles will be established as a free people in America—They will be saved if they believe and obey; otherwise, they will be cut off and destroyed—Israel will build the New Jerusalem, and the lost tribes will return. About A.D. *34.*

AND verily I say unto you, I give
unto you a [a]sign, that ye may know
the [b]time when these things shall
be about to take place—that I shall
gather in, from their long dispersion, my people, O house of Israel,
and shall establish again among
them my Zion;
2 And behold, this is the thing
which I will give unto you for a
sign—for verily I say unto you that
[a]when these things which I declare unto you, and which I shall
declare unto you hereafter of myself, and by the power of the Holy
Ghost which shall be given unto you
of the Father, shall be made known
unto the Gentiles that they may
know concerning this people who
are a remnant of the house of Jacob,
and concerning this my people who
shall be scattered by them;
3 Verily, verily, I say unto you, when
these things shall be made [a]known
unto them of the Father, and shall
come forth of the Father, [b]from
them unto you;
4 For it is wisdom in the Father
that they should be established in
this land, and be set up as a [a]free
people by the power of the Father,
that these things might come forth
from them unto a remnant of your
seed, that the [b]covenant of the
Father may be fulfilled which he
hath covenanted with his people,
O house of Israel;
5 Therefore, when these works and
the works which shall be wrought
among you hereafter shall come
forth [a]from the Gentiles, unto your
[b]seed which shall dwindle in unbelief because of iniquity;
6 For thus it behooveth the Father
that it should come forth from the
[a]Gentiles, that he may show forth
his power unto the Gentiles, for this
cause that the Gentiles, if they will
not harden their hearts, that they

42*a* 3 Ne. 21:29.
b TG Haste; Rashness.
45*a* Lev. 1:5; Isa. 52:15; Ezek. 36:25.
b 3 Ne. 21:8; D&C 101:94.
46*a* Joel 2:18; Ether 13:5 (5, 11).
21 1*a* Isa. 66:19.
b TG Last Days.
2*a* 1 Ne. 10:14; Ether 4:17; D&C 20:9 (8–11); JS—H 1:34.
3*a* TG Witness of the Father.
b 3 Ne. 20:13; Morm. 5:15 (10–21).
4*a* John 8:32 (32–36); 1 Ne. 13:19 (17–19); D&C 101:77 (77–80).
b Ps. 89:35; 3 Ne. 16:11 (8–12); Morm. 5:20. TG Abrahamic Covenant.
5*a* 3 Ne. 26:8.
b 2 Ne. 30:5; Morm. 5:15; D&C 3:18.
6*a* 1 Ne. 10:14; Jacob 5:54; 3 Ne. 16:4 (4–7); 21:24 (24–26); Morm. 5:15.

may repent and come unto me and
be baptized in my name and know
of the true points of my doctrine,
that they may be [b]numbered among
my people, O house of Israel;
7 And when these things come
to pass that thy [a]seed shall begin to
know these things—it shall be a
sign unto them, that they may know
that the work of the Father hath already commenced unto the fulfilling of the covenant which he hath
made unto the people who are of
the house of Israel.
8 And when that day shall come, it
shall come to pass that kings shall
shut their mouths; for that which
had not been told them shall they
see; and that which they had not
heard shall they [a]consider.
9 For in that day, for my sake shall
the Father [a]work a work, which
shall be a great and a [b]marvelous
[c]work among them; and there shall
be among them those who will not
believe it, although a man shall declare it unto them.
10 But behold, the life of my servant shall be in my hand; therefore
they shall not hurt him, although he
shall be [a]marred because of them.
Yet I will heal him, for I will show unto
them that [b]my wisdom is greater
than the cunning of the devil.
11 Therefore it shall come to pass
that whosoever will not believe in
my words, who am Jesus Christ,
which the Father shall cause [a]him
to bring forth unto the [b]Gentiles,
and shall give unto him power that
he shall bring them forth unto the
Gentiles, (it shall be done even as
Moses said) they shall be [c]cut off
from among my people who are of
the covenant.
12 And my people who are a remnant of Jacob shall be among the
Gentiles, yea, in the midst of them as
a [a]lion among the beasts of the forest, as a young lion among the flocks
of sheep, who, if he go through both
treadeth down and teareth in pieces,
and none can deliver.
13 Their hand shall be lifted up
upon their [a]adversaries, and all their
enemies shall be cut off.
14 Yea, wo be unto the Gentiles
except they [a]repent; for it shall
come to pass in that day, saith the
Father, that I will cut off thy horses
out of the midst of thee, and I will
destroy thy [b]chariots;
15 And I will cut off the cities of
thy land, and throw down all thy
[a]strongholds;
16 And I will cut off [a]witchcrafts
out of thy land, and thou shalt have
no more soothsayers;
17 Thy [a]graven images I will also
cut off, and thy standing images
out of the midst of thee, and thou
shalt no more worship the works
of thy hands;
18 And I will pluck up thy [a]groves
out of the midst of thee; so will I
destroy thy cities.
19 And it shall come to pass that
all [a]lyings, and deceivings, and en-
vyings, and strifes, and priestcrafts,
and whoredoms, shall be done away.
20 For it shall come to pass, saith
the Father, that at that [a]day whosoever will not repent and come
unto my Beloved Son, them will I

6*b* Gal. 3:7 (7, 29); 2 Ne. 30:3; 3 Ne. 16:13; Abr. 2:10 (9–11).
7*a* 3 Ne. 5:23 (21–26); 21:26.
8*a* 3 Ne. 20:45.
9*a* TG God, Works of.
b 1 Ne. 22:8. TG Restoration of the Gospel.
c Acts 13:41 (40–41).
10*a* D&C 135:1 (1–3).
b D&C 10:43.
11*a* 2 Ne. 3:11 (6–15); Morm. 8:16 (16, 25); Ether 3:28 (21–28).
b 1 Ne. 21:6.
c D&C 1:14; 133:63.
12*a* Isa. 5:29; Micah 5:8 (8–15); Mal. 4:3; 2 Ne. 15:29; 3 Ne. 16:15 (7–15); 20:16; 25:3; D&C 87:5.
13*a* 1 Ne. 21:17 (17–19).
14*a* Eph. 3:6 (1–7); 2 Ne. 10:18; 33:9.
b Lev. 26:22 (21–22); Hel. 14:24.
15*a* 2 Ne. 12:15.
16*a* TG Sorcery; Superstitions.
17*a* Ex. 20:4 (3–4, 23); Isa. 41:29 (24, 29); Mosiah 13:12; D&C 1:16. TG Idolatry.
18*a* 1 Kgs. 16:33 (32–33).
19*a* 3 Ne. 30:2; D&C 109:30.
20*a* Amos 5:18; Alma 29:2; Morm. 9:27.

[b]cut off from among my people, O
house of Israel;
21 And I will execute [a]vengeance
and [b]fury upon them, even as upon
the heathen, such as they have not
heard.
22 But if they will repent and heark-
en unto my words, and [a]harden not
their hearts, I will [b]establish my
church among them, and they shall
come in unto the covenant and be
[c]numbered among this the remnant
of Jacob, unto whom I have given
this land for their [d]inheritance;
23 And they shall assist my [a]peo-
ple, the remnant of Jacob, and also
as many of the house of Israel as
shall come, that they may build a
city, which shall be called the [b]New
Jerusalem.
24 And then shall [a]they assist my
people that they may be gathered
in, who are scattered upon all the
face of the land, in unto the New
Jerusalem.
25 And then shall the [a]power of
heaven come down among them;
and [b]I also will be in the midst.
26 And then shall the work of
the Father commence at that day,
even [a]when this gospel shall be
preached among the remnant of
[b]this people. Verily I say unto you,
at that day shall the work of the
Father commence among all the
dispersed of my people, yea, even the
tribes which have been [c]lost, which
the Father hath led away out of
Jerusalem.
27 Yea, the work shall commence
among all the [a]dispersed of my
people, with the Father to prepare
the way whereby they may [b]come
unto me, that they may call on the
Father in my name.
28 Yea, and then shall the work
commence, with the Father among
all nations in preparing the way
whereby his people may be [a]gath-
ered home to the land of their inheritance.
29 And they shall go out from all
nations; and they shall [a]not go out
in [b]haste, nor go by flight, for I will
go before them, saith the Father,
and I will be their rearward.

CHAPTER 22

In the last days, Zion and her stakes will be established, and Israel will be gathered in mercy and tenderness—They will triumph—Compare Isaiah 54. About A.D. *34.*

AND then shall that which is written come to pass: Sing, O [a]barren,
thou that didst not bear; break forth
into [b]singing, and cry aloud, thou
that didst not travail with child;
for more are the children of the
[c]desolate than the children of the
married wife, saith the Lord.
2 Enlarge the place of thy tent,
and let them stretch forth the cur-
tains of thy habitations; spare not,
lengthen thy cords and strengthen
thy [a]stakes;
3 For thou shalt break forth on
the right hand and on the left, and
thy seed shall [a]inherit the [b]Gentiles
and make the desolate cities to be
inhabited.

20*b* Jer. 44:8 (6–8).
21*a* Isa. 34:8; 61:2; Jer. 23:19 (19–20); Mal. 4:1 (1, 3); D&C 97:26 (25–28).
b Ezek. 21:17 (14–17).
22*a* TG Hardheartedness.
b 1 Ne. 14:12 (12, 14). TG Dispensations; Millennium, Preparing a People for.
c 2 Ne. 10:18 (18–19); 3 Ne. 16:13; 30:2.
d TG Lands of Inheritance.
23*a* 3 Ne. 16:8 (8–15).
b 3 Ne. 20:22 (21–22, 39); Ether 13:3 (1–12). TG Jerusalem, New.
24*a* 3 Ne. 21:6.
25*a* 1 Ne. 13:37; 3 Ne. 20:22.
b Isa. 2:2 (2–4); 59:20 (20–21); 3 Ne. 24:1.
26*a* 3 Ne. 20:31 (29–34); Morm. 5:14.
b 1 Ne. 14:17; 3 Ne. 21:6 (6–7).
c TG Israel, Ten Lost Tribes of.
27*a* 3 Ne. 16:5 (4–5).
b TG Israel, Restoration of.
28*a* TG Israel, Gathering of.
29*a* 3 Ne. 20:42.
b Isa. 52:12 (11–12).
22 1*a* Isa. 54:1 (1–17).
b TG Singing.
c Isa. 49:21.
2*a* TG Stake.
3*a* Obad. 1:19 (19–21).
b TG Gentiles.

4 Fear not, for thou shalt not be ashamed; neither be thou confounded, for thou shalt not be put to [a]shame; for thou shalt forget the [b]shame of thy youth, and shalt not remember the [c]reproach of thy youth, and shalt not remember the reproach of thy widowhood any more.

5 For thy maker, thy [a]husband, the Lord of Hosts is his name; and thy Redeemer, the Holy One of Israel—the God of the whole earth shall he be called.

6 For the Lord hath called thee [a]as a woman forsaken and grieved in spirit, and a wife of youth, when thou wast refused, saith thy God.

7 For a small moment have I [a]forsaken thee, but with great mercies will I gather thee.

8 In a little wrath I hid my face from thee for a moment, but with everlasting [a]kindness will I have [b]mercy on thee, saith the Lord thy Redeemer.

9 For [a]this, the [b]waters of Noah unto me, for as I have sworn that the waters of Noah should no more go over the earth, so have I sworn that I would not be wroth with thee.

10 For the [a]mountains shall depart and the hills be removed, but my [b]kindness shall not [c]depart from thee, neither shall the covenant of my peace be removed, saith the Lord that hath mercy on thee.

11 O thou afflicted, tossed with tempest, and not comforted! Behold, I will lay thy [a]stones with fair colors, and lay thy foundations with sapphires.

12 And I will make thy windows of agates, and thy gates of carbuncles, and all thy borders of pleasant stones.

13 And [a]all thy children shall be taught of the Lord; and great shall be the [b]peace of thy children.

14 In [a]righteousness shalt thou be established; thou shalt be far from oppression for thou shalt not fear, and from terror for it shall not come near thee.

15 Behold, they shall surely gather together [a]against thee, not by me; whosoever shall gather together against thee shall fall for thy sake.

16 Behold, I have created the smith that bloweth the coals in the fire, and that bringeth forth an instrument for his work; and I have created the waster to destroy.

17 No weapon that is formed against thee shall prosper; and every tongue that shall revile against thee in judgment thou shalt condemn. This is the heritage of the [a]servants of the Lord, and their righteousness is of me, saith the Lord.

CHAPTER 23

Jesus approves the words of Isaiah—He commands the people to search the prophets—The words of Samuel the Lamanite concerning the Resurrection are added to their records. About A.D. 34.

AND now, behold, I say unto you, that ye ought to [a]search these things. Yea, a commandment I give unto you that ye search these things diligently; for great are the words of [b]Isaiah.

2 For surely he spake as touching all things concerning my people which are of the house of Israel;

4a Joel 2:26 (26–27); 2 Ne. 6:13 (7, 13).
b TG Shame.
c TG Reproach.
5a Hosea 3:5 (4–5).
6a Isa. 62:4.
7a Jer. 46:27 (2–28); 3 Ne. 20:13 (11–13).
8a TG Kindness.
b TG God, Mercy of.
9a Isa. 54:9.
b Gen. 8:21; Matt. 24:37 (36–38); Alma 10:22. TG Earth, Cleansing of.
10a Isa. 40:4 (4–5). TG Earth, Renewal of.
b TG Israel, Blessings of.
c Ps. 94:14; D&C 35:25.
11a Rev. 21:19 (18–21). TG Rock.
13a Isa. 60:21; Jer. 31:34 (33–34).
b 1 Ne. 22:17 (15–22); 2 Ne. 30:10; Moses 7:61.
14a TG Righteousness.
15a 1 Ne. 22:14.
17a TG Servant.
23 1a TG Scriptures, Study of.
b 2 Ne. 25:5 (1–5); 3 Ne. 20:11; Morm. 8:23.

[a]therefore it must needs be that he must speak also to the Gentiles.

3 And all things that he spake have been and [a]shall be, even according to the words which he spake.

4 Therefore give heed to my words; write the things which I have told you; and according to the time and the will of the Father [a]they shall go forth unto the Gentiles.

5 And whosoever will hearken unto my words and repenteth and is baptized, the same shall be saved. Search the [a]prophets, for many there be that testify of these things.

6 And now it came to pass that when Jesus had said these words he said unto them again, after he had expounded all the scriptures unto them which they had received, he said unto them: Behold, other scriptures I would that ye should write, that ye have not.

7 And it came to pass that he said unto [a]Nephi: Bring forth the record which ye have kept.

8 And when Nephi had brought forth the records, and laid them before him, he cast his eyes upon them and said:

9 Verily I say unto you, I commanded my servant [a]Samuel, the Lamanite, that he should testify unto this people, that at the day that the Father should glorify his name in me that there were [b]many [c]saints who should [d]arise from the dead, and should appear unto many, and should minister unto them. And he said unto them: Was it not so?

10 And his disciples answered him and said: Yea, Lord, Samuel did prophesy according to thy words, and they were all fulfilled.

11 And Jesus said unto them: How be it that ye have not [a]written this thing, that many [b]saints did arise and appear unto many and did minister unto them?

12 And it came to pass that Nephi remembered that this thing had not been written.

13 And it came to pass that Jesus commanded that it should be [a]written; therefore it was written according as he commanded.

14 And now it came to pass that when Jesus had [a]expounded all the scriptures in one, which they had written, he commanded them that they should [b]teach the things which he had expounded unto them.

CHAPTER 24

The Lord's messenger will prepare the way for the Second Coming—Christ will sit in judgment—Israel is commanded to pay tithes and offerings—A book of remembrance is kept—Compare Malachi 3. About A.D. 34.

AND it came to pass that he commanded them that they should write the words which the Father had given unto Malachi, which he should tell unto them. And it came to pass that after they were written he expounded them. And these are the words which he did tell unto them, saying: Thus said the Father unto Malachi—Behold, I will [a]send my [b]messenger, and he shall prepare the way before me, and the Lord whom ye seek shall suddenly [c]come to his temple, even the [d]messenger of the covenant, whom ye delight in; behold, he shall come, saith the Lord of Hosts.

2 But who may [a]abide the day of his coming, and who shall stand when he appeareth? For he is like

---

2*a* Isa. 49:6.
3*a* 3 Ne. 15:6; 20:11 (11–12).
4*a* Morm. 8:26.
5*a* Luke 24:27 (25–27).
7*a* 3 Ne. 8:1; 4 Ne. 1:19.
9*a* Hel. 13:2.
b Hel. 14:25 (1, 21–26).
c TG Saints.
d TG Resurrection.
11*a* TG Jesus Christ, Teaching Mode of.
b Matt. 27:52 (52–53).
13*a* TG Record Keeping.
14*a* Luke 24:44 (27, 44).
b TG Scriptures, Study of; Teaching.
24 1*a* Mal. 3:1 (1–18).
b D&C 45:9.
c Isa. 59:20 (20–21); 3 Ne. 20:22; 21:25.
d TG Jesus Christ, Messenger of the Covenant.
2*a* 3 Ne. 25:1.

a [b]refiner's fire, and like fuller's soap.
3 And he shall sit as a refiner and purifier of silver; and he shall [a]purify the [b]sons of Levi, and purge them as gold and silver, that they may [c]offer unto the Lord an offering in righteousness.
4 Then shall the offering of Judah and Jerusalem be pleasant unto the Lord, as in the days of old, and as in former years.
5 And I will come [a]near to you to judgment; and I will be a swift witness against the [b]sorcerers, and against the adulterers, and against false [c]swearers, and against those that [d]oppress the hireling in his wages, the widow and the [e]fatherless, and that turn aside the [f]stranger, and fear not me, saith the Lord of Hosts.
6 For [a]I am the Lord, I change not; therefore ye sons of Jacob are not consumed.
7 Even from the days of your fathers ye are gone away from mine [a]ordinances, and have not kept them. [b]Return unto me and I will return unto you, saith the Lord of Hosts. But ye say: Wherein shall we return?
8 Will a man rob God? Yet ye have robbed me. But ye say: Wherein have we robbed thee? In [a]tithes and [b]offerings.
9 Ye are cursed with a curse, for ye have robbed me, even this whole nation.
10 Bring ye all the [a]tithes into the storehouse, that there may be [b]meat in my house; and prove me now herewith, saith the Lord of Hosts, if I will not open you the [c]windows of heaven, and pour you out a [d]blessing that there shall not be room enough to receive it.
11 And I will rebuke the [a]devourer for your sakes, and he shall not destroy the fruits of your ground; neither shall your vine cast her fruit before the time in the fields, saith the Lord of Hosts.
12 And all nations shall call you blessed, for ye shall be a delightsome land, saith the Lord of Hosts.
13 Your words have been stout against me, saith the Lord. Yet ye say: What have we spoken against thee?
14 Ye have [a]said: It is [b]vain to serve God, and what doth it profit that we have kept his [c]ordinances and that we have walked mournfully before the Lord of Hosts?
15 And now we call the proud happy; yea, they that work wickedness are set up; yea, they that tempt God are even delivered.
16 Then they that feared the Lord [a]spake often one to another, and the Lord hearkened and heard; and a book of [b]remembrance was written before him for them that feared the Lord, and that thought upon his name.
17 And they shall be [a]mine, saith the Lord of Hosts, in that day when I [b]make up my jewels; and I will

2*b* Deut. 4:24; Zech. 13:9; D&C 128:24. TG Earth, Cleansing of; Jesus Christ, Second Coming.
3*a* TG Purification.
b Deut. 10:8; D&C 84:31 (31–34); 128:24.
c D&C 13.
5*a* Ezek. 43:7 (1–7).
b TG Sorcery.
c Hosea 10:4; D&C 104:5 (4–5). TG Swearing.
d Ps. 94:6. TG Oppression.
e Ps. 10:14; 68:5; James 1:27; D&C 136:8.
f TG Stranger.
6*a* 2 Ne. 6:7; Moses 1:6.
7*a* TG Ordinance.
b 1 Sam. 7:3; Hel. 13:11; 3 Ne. 10:6 (5–7); Moro. 9:22.
8*a* TG Tithing.
b Neh. 10:32. TG Sacrifice.
10*a* D&C 64:23; 119:4 (1–7).
b TG Food.
c Gen. 7:11.
d TG Blessing.
11*a* D&C 86:3.
14*a* Job 16:11 (11–17); Jer. 20:7 (7–8); Hab. 1:2 (1–4).
b Mal. 3:14 (14–15).
c TG Ordinance.
16*a* 4 Ne. 1:12; Moro. 6:5 (5–6).
b D&C 85:9 (7–9); Moses 6:5. TG Book of Remembrance.
17*a* Lev. 20:26.
b D&C 101:3.

spare them as a man spareth his
own son that serveth him.
18 Then shall ye return and [a]dis-
cern between the righteous and the
wicked, between him that serveth
God and him that serveth him not.

CHAPTER 25

At the Second Coming, the proud and wicked will be burned as stubble—Elijah will return before that great and dreadful day—Compare Malachi 4. About A.D. 34.

[a]FOR behold, the day cometh that
shall [b]burn as an oven; and all the
[c]proud, yea, and all that do wickedly, shall be stubble; and the day
that cometh shall burn them up,
saith the Lord of Hosts, that it shall
leave them neither root nor branch.
2 But unto you that fear my name,
shall the [a]Son of Righteousness
arise with healing in his wings; and
ye shall go forth and [b]grow up as
[c]calves in the stall.
3 And ye shall [a]tread down the
wicked; for they shall be ashes under the soles of your feet in the day
that I shall do this, saith the Lord
of Hosts.
4 Remember ye the law of Moses,
my servant, which I commanded
unto him in [a]Horeb for all Israel,
with the statutes and judgments.
5 Behold, I will send you [a]Elijah
the prophet before the coming
of the great and dreadful [b]day of
the Lord;
6 And he shall [a]turn the heart of
the [b]fathers to the children, and
the heart of the children to their
fathers, lest I come and [c]smite the
earth with a curse.

CHAPTER 26

Jesus expounds all things from the beginning to the end—Babes and children utter marvelous things that cannot be written—Those in the Church of Christ have all things in common among them. About A.D. 34.

AND now it came to pass that when
Jesus had told these things he expounded them unto the multitude;
and he did expound all things unto
them, both great and small.
2 And he saith: [a]These scriptures,
which ye had not with you, the
Father commanded that I should
give unto you; for it was wisdom
in him that they should be given
unto future generations.
3 And he did expound all things,
even from the beginning until the
[a]time that he should come in his
[b]glory—yea, even all things which
should come upon the face of the
earth, even until the [c]elements
should melt with fervent heat, and
the earth should be [d]wrapt together
as a scroll, and the heavens and the
earth should pass away;
4 And even unto the [a]great and last
day, when all people, and all kindreds, and all nations and tongues
shall [b]stand before God, to be judged

18*a* TG Discernment, Spiritual.
25 1*a* Mal. 4:1 (1–6).
b Ps. 21:9 (8–10); Isa. 24:6; 66:16; 1 Ne. 22:15; 3 Ne. 24:2; D&C 29:9; 64:23 (23–24); 133:64; JS—H 1:37. TG Earth, Cleansing of.
c Ps. 18:27; 2 Ne. 20:33. TG Pride.
2*a* Ps. 84:11; Mal. 4:2; Ether 9:22.
b D&C 45:58.
c Amos 6:4; 1 Ne. 22:24.
3*a* 3 Ne. 21:12.
4*a* Ex. 3:1; 19:18 (9, 16–20); 1 Kgs. 19:8; Neh. 9:13; Mosiah 12:33; 13:5.
5*a* 2 Kgs. 2:2; D&C 2:1; 35:4; 110:13 (13–16); 128:17 (17–18). TG Genealogy and Temple Work.
b TG Day of the Lord.
6*a* D&C 98:16 (16–17).
b TG Family, Eternal; Salvation for the Dead.
c Mal. 4:6; D&C 110:15 (13–16).
26 2*a* IE Mal. 3–4, quoted in 3 Ne. 24–25.
3*a* TG Day of the Lord.
b Ps. 72:19. TG Jesus Christ, Glory of.
c Amos 9:13; 2 Pet. 3:10 (10, 12); Morm. 9:2. TG Earth, Cleansing of; Earth, Destiny of; World, End of.
d Morm. 5:23.
4*a* Mal. 4:5; Hel. 12:25; 3 Ne. 28:31.
b Mosiah 16:10 (1–2, 10–11). TG Judgment, the Last.

of their works, whether they be good
or whether they be evil—
5 If they be good, to the [a]resur-
rection of everlasting life; and if
they be evil, to the resurrection of
damnation; being on a parallel, the
one on the one hand and the other
on the other hand, according to the
mercy, and the [b]justice, and the holiness which is in Christ, who was
[c]before the world began.
6 And now there cannot be written in this book even a [a]hundredth
part of the things which Jesus did
truly teach unto the people;
7 But behold the [a]plates of Nephi
do contain the more part of the
things which he taught the people.
8 And these things have I written, which are a [a]lesser part of the
things which he taught the people;
and I have written them to the intent that they may be brought again
unto this people, [b]from the Gentiles,
according to the words which Jesus
hath spoken.
9 And when they shall have received this, which is expedient that
they should have first, to try their
faith, and if it shall so be that they
shall believe these things then shall
the [a]greater things be made manifest unto them.
10 And if it so be that they will not
believe these things, then shall the
[a]greater things be [b]withheld from
them, unto their condemnation.
11 Behold, I was about to write
them, all which were engraven
upon the plates of Nephi, but the
Lord [a]forbade it, saying: I will [b]try
the faith of my people.
12 Therefore I, [a]Mormon, do
write the things which have been
commanded me of the Lord. And
now I, [b]Mormon, make an end of
my sayings, and proceed to write
the things which have been commanded me.
13 Therefore, I would that ye
should behold that the Lord truly
did teach the people, for the space
of three days; and after that he did
[a]show himself unto them oft, and
did break [b]bread oft, and bless it,
and give it unto them.
14 And it came to pass that he did
teach and minister unto the [a]chil-
dren of the multitude of whom
hath been spoken, and he did [b]loose
their [c]tongues, and they did speak
unto their fathers great and marvelous things, even greater than he
had revealed unto the people; and
he loosed their tongues that they
could utter.
15 And it came to pass that after
he had ascended into heaven—the
second time that he showed himself unto them, and had gone unto
the Father, after having [a]healed
all their sick, and their lame, and
opened the eyes of their blind
and unstopped the ears of the deaf,
and even had done all manner of
cures among them, and raised a
man from the [b]dead, and had shown
forth his power unto them, and had
ascended unto the Father—
16 Behold, it came to pass on the
morrow that the multitude gathered
themselves together, and they both
saw and heard these children; yea,
even [a]babes did open their mouths

5*a* Dan. 12:2.
b TG God, Justice of; Justice.
c 3 Ne. 1:14; Ether 3:14. TG Man, Antemortal Existence of.
6*a* John 21:25; W of M 1:5; 3 Ne. 5:8 (8–11); Ether 15:33.
7*a* Jarom 1:14; 4 Ne. 1:19.
8*a* 3 Ne. 28:33; D&C 11:22.
b 3 Ne. 21:5 (5–6).
9*a* John 16:12; 2 Ne. 27:8 (7–11, 21); Morm. 8:12; Ether 4:8 (4–10).
10*a* Ether 4:7 (1–8).
b 2 Ne. 28:27; Alma 12:10 (9–11); D&C 6:26 (26–27).
11*a* 3 Ne. 26:18.
b Ether 12:6.
12*a* 3 Ne. 28:24.
b W of M 1:1 (1–2).
13*a* John 21:14; 3 Ne. 27:2.
b 3 Ne. 18:1; 20:3 (3–9). TG Bread; Sacrament.
14*a* Luke 10:21; Alma 32:23; 3 Ne. 17:11; D&C 128:18.
b D&C 23:3.
c 3 Ne. 19:32; 28:14 (14, 16).
15*a* 3 Ne. 17:9. TG Administrations to the Sick; Heal.
b TG Death, Power over.
16*a* Matt. 11:25.

and utter marvelous things; and the things which they did utter were [b]forbidden that there should not any man write them.

17 And it came to pass that the [a]disciples whom Jesus had chosen began [b]from that time forth to [c]baptize and to teach as many as did come unto them; and as many as were baptized in the name of Jesus were filled with the Holy Ghost.

18 And many of them saw and heard unspeakable things, which are [a]not lawful to be written.

19 And they taught, and did [a]minister one to another; and they had [b]all things [c]common among them, every man dealing justly, one with another.

20 And it came to pass that they did do all things even as Jesus had commanded them.

21 And they who were baptized in the name of Jesus were called the [a]church of Christ.

CHAPTER 27

Jesus commands them to call the Church in His name—His mission and atoning sacrifice constitute His gospel—Men are commanded to repent and be baptized that they may be sanctified by the Holy Ghost—They are to be even as Jesus is. About A.D. 34–35.

AND it came to pass that as the disciples of Jesus were journeying and were preaching the things which they had both heard and seen, and were baptizing in the name of Jesus, it came to pass that the disciples were gathered together and were [a]united in [b]mighty prayer and [c]fasting.

2 And Jesus again [a]showed himself unto them, for they were praying unto the Father in his name; and Jesus came and stood in the midst of them, and said unto them: What will ye that I shall give unto you?

3 And they said unto him: Lord, we will that thou wouldst tell us the [a]name whereby we shall call this church; for there are disputations among the people concerning this matter.

4 And the Lord said unto them: Verily, verily, I say unto you, why is it that the people should murmur and dispute because of this thing?

5 Have they not read the scriptures, which say ye must take upon you the [a]name of Christ, which is my name? For by this name shall ye be called at the last day;

6 And whoso taketh upon him my name, and [a]endureth to the end, the same shall be saved at the last day.

7 Therefore, whatsoever ye shall do, ye shall do it in my name; therefore ye shall call the church in my name; and ye shall call upon the Father in my name that he will bless the church for my sake.

8 And how be it [a]my [b]church save it be called in my name? For if a church be called in Moses' name then it be Moses' church; or if it be called in the name of a man then it be the church of a man; but if it be called in my name then it is my church, if it so be that they are built upon my gospel.

9 Verily I say unto you, that ye are built upon my gospel; therefore ye shall call whatsoever things ye do call, in my name; therefore if ye call upon the Father, for the church, if it be in my name the Father will hear you;

10 And if it so be that the church

16*b* 3 Ne. 27:23.
17*a* 3 Ne. 19:4 (4–12); 4 Ne. 1:14.
b Ether 12:31.
c 4 Ne. 1:1.
18*a* 3 Ne. 26:11.
19*a* TG Benevolence.
b 4 Ne. 1:3 (3, 25–26).
c TG Consecration.
21*a* Mosiah 18:17; Alma 4:5 (4–5). TG Church.
27 1*a* D&C 29:6; 84:1.
b Alma 8:10; D&C 5:24; 29:2.
c Mosiah 27:22; Alma 5:46; 6:6. TG Fast, Fasting.
2*a* 3 Ne. 26:13. TG Jesus Christ, Appearances, Postmortal.
3*a* D&C 1:1; 20:1.
5*a* TG Jesus Christ, Taking the Name of.
6*a* Alma 32:13 (13–15); 38:2; 3 Ne. 15:9.
8*a* 1 Cor. 1:12 (11–13); D&C 115:4.
b TG Jesus Christ, Head of the Church.

is built upon my gospel then will
the Father show forth his own works
in it.
11 But if it be not built upon my
gospel, and is built upon the works
of men, or upon the works of the
devil, verily I say unto you they have
joy in their works for a season,
and by and by the end cometh, and
they are [a]hewn down and cast into
the [b]fire, from whence there is no
return.
12 For their works do [a]follow them,
for it is because of their works that
they are hewn down; therefore remember the things that I have told
you.
13 Behold I have given unto you
my [a]gospel, and this is the gospel
which I have given unto you—that I
came into the world to do the [b]will
of my Father, because my Father
sent me.
14 And my Father sent me that I
might be [a]lifted up upon the [b]cross;
and after that I had been lifted up
upon the [c]cross, that I might [d]draw
all men unto me, that as I have been
lifted up by men even so should
men be lifted up by the Father, to
stand before me, to be [e]judged of
their works, whether they be good
or whether they be evil—
15 And for this cause have I been
[a]lifted up; therefore, according to
the power of the Father I will draw
all men unto me, that they may be
judged according to their [b]works.
16 And it shall come to pass, that
whoso [a]repenteth and is baptized
in my [b]name shall be filled; and if
he [c]endureth to the end, behold,
him will I hold guiltless before
my Father at that day when I shall
stand to judge the world.
17 And he that endureth not unto
the end, the same is he that is also
hewn down and cast into the fire,
from whence they can no more
return, because of the [a]justice of
the Father.
18 And this is the word which he
hath given unto the children of men.
And for this cause he fulfilleth the
words which he hath given, and he
lieth not, but fulfilleth all his words.
19 And [a]no unclean thing can
enter into his kingdom; therefore
nothing entereth into his [b]rest save
it be those who have [c]washed their
garments in my blood, because of
their faith, and the repentance of
all their sins, and their faithfulness
unto the end.
20 Now this is the commandment:
[a]Repent, all ye ends of the earth,
and come unto me and be [b]baptized
in my name, that ye may be [c]sanc-
tified by the reception of the Holy
Ghost, that ye may stand [d]spotless
before me at the last day.
21 Verily, verily, I say unto you,
this is my [a]gospel; and ye know
the things that ye must [b]do in my
church; for the works which ye
have seen me do that shall ye also
do; for that which ye have seen me
do even that shall ye do;

11*a* Jacob 5:46; 6:7; Alma 5:52; D&C 132:13.
b TG Hell.
12*a* Rev. 14:13; D&C 59:2.
13*a* Acts 10:36 (36–40); D&C 76:40 (40–42). TG Gospel.
b John 6:39. TG Jesus Christ, Mission of.
14*a* 3 Ne. 15:1; Morm. 2:19.
b Moses 7:55.
c Luke 9:44 (44–45); 1 Ne. 11:33.
d John 6:44; 2 Ne. 9:5; D&C 17:8; 27:18.
e TG Jesus Christ, Judge.
15*a* TG Jesus Christ, Atonement through.
b 1 Sam. 2:3.
16*a* TG Repent.
b TG Baptism, Qualifications for.
c 1 Ne. 13:37. TG Endure; Steadfastness.
17*a* TG God, Justice of.
19*a* Alma 11:37. TG Uncleanness.
b D&C 84:24. TG Rest.
c Rev. 1:5 (1–6); 7:14; 1 Ne. 12:10; Alma 5:21 (21–27); 13:11 (11–13).
20*a* Ether 4:18; Moro. 7:34.
b TG Baptism, Essential.
c TG Sanctification.
d 1 Cor. 1:8; D&C 4:2.
21*a* 1 Ne. 13:36. TG Gospel; Salvation, Plan of.
b TG Jesus Christ, Exemplar.

22 Therefore, if ye do these things blessed are ye, for ye shall be lifted up at the last day.

23 [a]Write the things which ye have seen and heard, save it be those which are [b]forbidden.

24 Write the works of this people, which shall be, even as hath been written, of that which hath been.

25 For behold, out of the books which have been written, and which shall be written, shall this people be [a]judged, for by them shall their [b]works be known unto men.

26 And behold, all things are [a]written by the Father; therefore out of the books which shall be written shall the world be judged.

27 And know ye that [a]ye shall be [b]judges of this people, according to the judgment which I shall give unto you, which shall be just. Therefore, what [c]manner of men ought ye to be? Verily I say unto you, even [d]as I am.

28 And now I [a]go unto the Father. And verily I say unto you, whatsoever things ye shall ask the Father in my name shall be given unto you.

29 Therefore, [a]ask, and ye shall receive; knock, and it shall be opened unto you; for he that asketh, receiveth; and unto him that knocketh, it shall be opened.

30 And now, behold, my joy is great, even unto fulness, because of you, and also this generation; yea, and even the Father rejoiceth, and also all the holy angels, because of you and this generation; for [a]none of them are lost.

31 Behold, I would that ye should understand; for I mean them who are [a]now alive of [b]this generation; and none of them are lost; and in them I have fulness of [c]joy.

32 But behold, it [a]sorroweth me because of the [b]fourth generation from this generation, for they are led away captive by him even as was the [c]son of perdition; for they will sell me for silver and for gold, and for that which [d]moth doth corrupt and which thieves can break through and steal. And in that day will I visit them, even in turning their works upon their own heads.

33 And it came to pass that when Jesus had ended these sayings he said unto his disciples: Enter ye in at the [a]strait gate; for strait is the gate, and narrow is the way that leads to life, and few there be that find it; but wide is the gate, and broad the way which leads to death, and many there be that travel therein, until the night cometh, wherein no man can work.

CHAPTER 28

Nine of the twelve disciples desire and are promised an inheritance in Christ's kingdom when they die—The Three Nephites desire and are given power over death so as to remain on the earth until Jesus comes again—They are translated and see things not lawful to utter, and they are now ministering among men. About A.D. *34–35.*

1 AND it came to pass when Jesus had said these words, he spake unto his disciples, one by one, saying unto them: What is it that ye [a]desire of

23*a* TG Record Keeping.
b 3 Ne. 26:16 (16, 18).
25*a* 2 Ne. 33:15 (10–15); W of M 1:11.
b Ps. 33:15 (13–15); 1 Ne. 15:33 (26–36).
26*a* 3 Ne. 24:16. TG Book of Life.
27*a* 1 Ne. 12:10 (9–10); Morm. 3:19.
b Rev. 20:4 (4–6).
c 2 Pet. 3:11. TG Godliness; Jesus Christ, Exemplar; Man, Potential to Become like Heavenly Father.
d Matt. 5:48; 3 Ne. 12:48.
28*a* John 16:10; 20:17.
29*a* Matt. 7:7; 3 Ne. 14:7.
30*a* John 17:12.
31*a* 3 Ne. 9:13 (11–13); 10:12.
b 3 Ne. 28:23.
c TG Joy.
32*a* Gen. 6:6; 3 Ne. 17:14.
b 1 Ne. 12:11 (11–12); 2 Ne. 26:9 (9–10); Alma 45:12 (10, 12); Hel. 13:6 (5–19).
c John 17:12; 3 Ne. 29:7.
d Matt. 6:19; 3 Ne. 13:19 (19–21).
33*a* Matt. 7:13 (13–14); Luke 13:24; 3 Ne. 14:13; D&C 22:4 (1–4).
28 1*a* 2 Chr. 1:7 (7–12); D&C 7:1 (1–8).

me, after that I am gone to the
Father?
2 And they all spake, save it were
three, saying: We desire that after
we have lived unto the age of man,
that our ministry, wherein thou
hast called us, may have an end,
that we may speedily come unto
thee in thy kingdom.
3 And he said unto them: Blessed
are ye because ye desired this thing
of me; therefore, after that ye are
[a]seventy and two years old ye shall
come unto me in my [b]kingdom; and
with me ye shall find [c]rest.
4 And when he had spoken unto
them, he turned himself unto the
three, and said unto them: What
will ye that I should do unto you,
when I am gone unto the Father?
5 And they sorrowed in their
hearts, for they durst not speak unto
him the thing which they desired.
6 And he said unto them: Behold,
I [a]know your thoughts, and ye have
desired the thing which [b]John, my
beloved, who was with me in my
ministry, before that I was lifted up
by the Jews, desired of me.
7 Therefore, more blessed are ye,
for ye shall [a]never taste of [b]death;
but ye shall live to behold all the doings of the Father unto the children
of men, even until all things shall
be fulfilled according to the will of
the Father, when I shall come in my
glory with the [c]powers of heaven.
8 And ye shall never endure the
pains of death; but when I shall
come in my glory ye shall be
changed in the twinkling of an eye
from [a]mortality to [b]immortality;
and then shall ye be blessed in the
kingdom of my Father.
9 And again, ye shall not have pain
while ye shall dwell in the flesh,
neither sorrow save it be for the
[a]sins of the world; and all this will
I do because of the thing which ye
have desired of me, for ye have desired that ye might [b]bring the souls
of men unto me, while the world
shall stand.
10 And for this cause ye shall have
[a]fulness of joy; and ye shall sit down
in the kingdom of my Father; yea,
your joy shall be full, even as the
Father hath given me fulness of
joy; and ye shall be even as I am,
and I am even as the Father; and
the Father and I are [b]one;
11 And the [a]Holy Ghost beareth
record of the Father and me; and
the Father giveth the Holy Ghost
unto the children of men, because
of me.
12 And it came to pass that when
Jesus had spoken these words, he
touched every one of them with his
finger save it were the [a]three who
were to tarry, and then he departed.
13 And behold, the heavens were
opened, and they were [a]caught up
into heaven, and saw and heard
unspeakable things.
14 And it was [a]forbidden them
that they should utter; neither was
it given unto them [b]power that they
could utter the things which they
saw and heard;
15 And whether they were in the
body or out of the body, they could
not tell; for it did seem unto them
like a [a]transfiguration of them, that

3*a* 4 Ne. 1:14.
b TG Election.
c TG Rest.
6*a* Amos 4:13;
Alma 18:32.
b John 21:22 (21–23);
D&C 7:3 (1–8).
7*a* 4 Ne. 1:37 (14, 37);
Morm. 8:10 (10–12);
Ether 12:17.
b Luke 9:27.
TG Translated Beings.
c 3 Ne. 20:22.
8*a* 3 Ne. 28:36 (36–40).
TG Mortality.
b TG Immortality.
9*a* 4 Ne. 1:44;
Morm. 8:10.
b Philip. 1:24 (23–24);
3 Ne. 28:27;
D&C 7:5 (1–8).
10*a* John 16:15;
D&C 76:59;
84:38 (37–38).
b Deut. 6:4;
Gal. 3:20;
2 Ne. 31:21;
3 Ne. 11:27 (27–28, 36);
Morm. 7:7;
D&C 20:28.
11*a* 2 Ne. 31:18 (17–21);
3 Ne. 11:32;
Ether 5:4;
Moses 6:66.
12*a* 4 Ne. 1:14 (14, 37);
Morm. 1:13.
13*a* 2 Cor. 12:4 (2–4).
14*a* D&C 76:115.
b 3 Ne. 19:32; 26:14.
15*a* Moses 1:11.
TG Transfiguration.

they were changed from this body
of flesh into an immortal state,
that they could behold the things
of God.
16 But it came to pass that they
did again minister upon the face
of the earth; nevertheless they did
not minister of the things which
they had heard and seen, because
of the commandment which was
given them in heaven.
17 And now, whether they were
mortal or immortal, from the day
of their transfiguration, I know not;
18 But this much I know, according to the record which hath been
given—they did go forth upon the
face of the land, and did minister
unto all the people, uniting as many
to the church as would believe in
their preaching; baptizing them,
and as many as were baptized did
receive the Holy Ghost.
19 And they were cast into prison
by them who did not belong to the
church. And the [a]prisons could not
hold them, for they were rent in
twain.
20 And they were cast down into
the earth; but they did smite the
earth with the word of God, insomuch that by his [a]power they were
delivered out of the depths of the
earth; and therefore they could not
dig pits sufficient to hold them.
21 And thrice they were cast into
a [a]furnace and received no harm.
22 And twice were they cast into
a [a]den of wild beasts; and behold
they did play with the beasts as a
child with a suckling lamb, and received no harm.
23 And it came to pass that thus
they did go forth among all the
people of Nephi, and did preach
the [a]gospel of Christ unto all people upon the face of the land; and
they were converted unto the Lord,
and were united unto the church of
Christ, and thus the people of [b]that
generation were blessed, according
to the word of Jesus.
24 And now I, [a]Mormon, make an
end of speaking concerning these
things for a time.
25 Behold, I was about to write the
[a]names of those who were never to
taste of death, but the Lord forbade;
therefore I write them not, for they
are hid from the world.
26 But behold, [a]I have seen them,
and they have ministered unto me.
27 And behold they will be [a]among
the Gentiles, and the Gentiles shall
know them not.
28 They will also be among the
Jews, and the Jews shall know
them not.
29 And it shall come to pass, when
the Lord seeth fit in his wisdom
that they shall minister unto all the
[a]scattered tribes of Israel, and unto
all nations, kindreds, tongues and
people, and shall bring out of them
unto Jesus many souls, that their
desire may be fulfilled, and also
because of the convincing power
of God which is in them.
30 And they are as the [a]angels of
God, and if they shall pray unto the
Father in the name of Jesus they can
show themselves unto whatsoever
man it seemeth them good.
31 Therefore, great and marvelous
works shall be wrought by them,
before the [a]great and coming day
when all people must surely stand
before the judgment-seat of Christ;
32 Yea even among the Gentiles
shall there be a [a]great and marvelous work wrought by them, before
that judgment day.
33 And if ye had [a]all the scriptures
which give an account of all the

19*a* Acts 16:26; Alma 14:27 (26–28); 4 Ne. 1:30; Morm. 8:24.
20*a* 1 Ne. 7:17 (17–18); Jacob 4:6.
21*a* Dan. 3:25; 4 Ne. 1:32; Morm. 8:24.
22*a* Dan. 6:16 (16–27); 4 Ne. 1:33.
23*a* TG Gospel.
b 3 Ne. 27:31 (30–31).
24*a* 3 Ne. 26:12.
25*a* 3 Ne. 19:4.
26*a* Morm. 8:11.
27*a* 3 Ne. 28:9.
29*a* TG Israel, Scattering of; Israel, Ten Lost Tribes of.
30*a* TG Angels.
31*a* Mal. 4:5; Hel. 12:25; 3 Ne. 26:4; Morm. 9:2.
32*a* 2 Ne. 25:17.
33*a* 3 Ne. 26:8 (6–12).

marvelous works of Christ, ye
would, according to the words of
Christ, know that these things must
surely come.
34 And wo be unto him that will
[a]not hearken unto the words of Jesus,
and also to them whom he hath
chosen and [b]sent among them; for
whoso [c]receiveth not the words of
Jesus and the words of those whom
he hath sent receiveth not him; and
therefore he will not receive them
at the last day;
35 And it would be better for them
if they had not been born. For do ye
suppose that ye can get rid of the
justice of an [a]offended God, who hath
been [b]trampled under feet of men,
that thereby salvation might come?
36 And now behold, as I spake
concerning those whom the Lord
hath chosen, yea, even three who
were caught up into the heavens,
that I knew not whether they were
[a]cleansed from [b]mortality to immortality—
37 But behold, since I wrote, I have
inquired of the Lord, and he hath
made it manifest unto me that there
must needs be a change wrought
upon their bodies, or else it needs
be that they must taste of death;
38 Therefore, that they might not
taste of death there was a [a]change
wrought upon their bodies, that
they might not [b]suffer pain nor
sorrow save it were for the sins of
the world.
39 Now this change was not equal
to that which shall take place at the
last day; but there was a change
wrought upon them, insomuch
that Satan could have no power
over them, that he could not [a]tempt
them; and they were [b]sanctified in
the flesh, that they were [c]holy, and
that the powers of the earth could
not hold them.
40 And in this state they were to
remain until the judgment day of
Christ; and at that day they were
to receive a greater change, and to
be received into the kingdom of
the Father to go no more out, but
to dwell with God eternally in the
heavens.

CHAPTER 29

The coming forth of the Book of Mormon is a sign that the Lord has commenced to gather Israel and fulfill His covenants—Those who reject His latter-day revelations and gifts will be cursed. About A.D. *34–35.*

AND now behold, I say unto you
that when the Lord shall see fit, in
his wisdom, that these sayings shall
[a]come unto the Gentiles according
to his word, then ye may know that
the [b]covenant which the Father
hath made with the children of Israel, concerning their restoration
to the [c]lands of their inheritance,
is already beginning to be fulfilled.
2 And ye may know that the words
of the Lord, which have been spoken by the holy prophets, shall all
be fulfilled; and ye need not say
that the Lord [a]delays his coming
unto the children of Israel.
3 And ye need not imagine in
your hearts that the words which
have been spoken are vain, for behold, the Lord will remember his
covenant which he hath made unto
his people of the house of Israel.
4 And when ye shall see these sayings coming forth among you, then
ye need not any longer spurn at the
doings of the Lord, for the [a]sword
of his [b]justice is in his right hand;

34*a* Ether 4:8 (8–12).
b Matt. 10:5 (5–42).
c TG Prophets, Rejection of.
35*a* TG Blaspheme.
b Hel. 12:2.
36*a* TG Purification.
b 3 Ne. 28:8 (8–9). TG Immortality; Mortality.
38*a* TG Translated Beings.
b TG Suffering.
39*a* TG Temptation; Test.
b TG Sanctification.
c TG Holiness.
29 1*a* 2 Ne. 30:3 (3–8); Morm. 3:17.
b Ezek. 20:37; Morm. 5:14 (14, 20).
c TG Lands of Inheritance.
2*a* Matt. 24:48; Luke 12:45.
4*a* 3 Ne. 20:20.
b TG Justice.

and behold, at that day, if ye shall
spurn at his doings he will cause
that it shall soon overtake you.
5 [a]Wo unto him that [b]spurneth at
the doings of the Lord; yea, wo unto
him that shall [c]deny the Christ and
his works!
6 Yea, [a]wo unto him that shall deny
the revelations of the Lord, and that
shall say the Lord no longer worketh
by revelation, or by prophecy, or by
[b]gifts, or by tongues, or by healings,
or by the power of the Holy Ghost!
7 Yea, and wo unto him that shall
say at that day, to get [a]gain, that there
can be [b]no miracle wrought by Jesus
Christ; for he that doeth this shall
become [c]like unto the son of perdition, for whom there was no mercy,
according to the word of Christ!
8 Yea, and ye need not any longer
[a]hiss, nor [b]spurn, nor make game of
the [c]Jews, nor any of the remnant
of the house of Israel; for behold,
the Lord remembereth his covenant
unto them, and he will do unto
them according to that which he
hath sworn.
9 Therefore ye need not suppose
that ye can turn the right hand of
the Lord unto the left, that he may
not execute judgment unto the fulfilling of the covenant which he
hath made unto the house of Israel.

CHAPTER 30

The latter-day Gentiles are commanded to repent, come unto Christ, and be numbered with the house of Israel. About A.D. 34–35.

HEARKEN, O ye Gentiles, and hear
the words of Jesus Christ, the Son
of the living God, which he hath
[a]commanded me that I should speak
concerning you, for, behold he commandeth me that I should write,
saying:
2 Turn, all ye [a]Gentiles, from your
wicked ways; and [b]repent of your
evil doings, of your [c]lyings and deceivings, and of your whoredoms,
and of your secret abominations,
and your idolatries, and of your
[d]murders, and your [e]priestcrafts,
and your [f]envyings, and your strifes,
and from all your wickedness and
abominations, and come unto me,
and be baptized in my name, that ye
may receive a remission of your sins,
and be filled with the Holy Ghost,
that ye may be [g]numbered with
my people who are of the house of
Israel.

---

5 *a* 2 Ne. 28:15; Morm. 9:26.
b Morm. 8:17; Ether 4:8 (8–10).
c Matt. 10:33 (32–33); Moro. 1:3.
6 *a* Morm. 9:7 (7–11, 15).
b TG Holy Ghost, Gifts of.
7 *a* TG Priestcraft.
b 2 Ne. 28:6 (4–6); Morm. 8:26; 9:15 (15–26).
c 2 Ne. 9:9; 3 Ne. 27:32. TG Sons of Perdition.
8 *a* 1 Ne. 19:14.
b 2 Ne. 29:5 (4–5). TG Backbiting.
c TG Israel, Judah, People of.
30 1 *a* 3 Ne. 5:13 (12–13).
2 *a* Rom. 15:10 (8–21).
b TG Repent.
c Alma 16:18; 3 Ne. 21:19 (19–21).
d 3 Ne. 16:10; Morm. 8:31.
e TG Priestcraft.
f TG Envy.
g Gal. 3:29 (27–29); 2 Ne. 10:18 (18–19); 3 Ne. 21:22 (22–25); Abr. 2:10.

FOURTH NEPHI
THE BOOK OF NEPHI

WHO IS THE SON OF NEPHI—ONE OF THE DISCIPLES OF JESUS CHRIST

An account of the people of Nephi, according to his record.

The Nephites and the Lamanites are all converted unto the Lord—They have all things in common, work miracles, and prosper in the land—After two centuries, divisions, evils, false churches, and persecutions arise—After three hundred years, both the Nephites and the Lamanites are wicked—Ammaron hides up the sacred records. About A.D. 35–321.

AND it came to pass that the thirty and fourth year passed away, and also the thirty and fifth, and behold the disciples of Jesus had formed a church of Christ in all the lands round about. And as many as did come unto them, and did truly repent of their sins, were [a]baptized in the name of Jesus; and they did also receive the Holy Ghost.

2 And it came to pass in the thirty and sixth year, the people were all converted unto the Lord, upon all the face of the land, both Nephites and Lamanites, and there were no contentions and disputations among them, and every man did deal justly one with another.

3 And they had [a]all things common among them; therefore there were not rich and poor, bond and free, but they were all made free, and partakers of the heavenly [b]gift.

4 And it came to pass that the thirty and seventh year passed away also, and there still continued to be [a]peace in the land.

5 And there were great and marvelous works wrought by the disciples of Jesus, insomuch that they did [a]heal the sick, and [b]raise the dead, and cause the lame to walk, and the blind to receive their sight, and the deaf to hear; and all manner of [c]miracles did they work among the children of men; and in nothing did they work miracles save it were in the name of Jesus.

6 And thus did the thirty and eighth year pass away, and also the thirty and ninth, and forty and first, and the forty and second, yea, even until forty and nine years had passed away, and also the fifty and first, and the fifty and second; yea, and even until fifty and nine years had passed away.

7 And the Lord did prosper them exceedingly in the land; yea, insomuch that they did build cities again where there had been cities burned.

8 Yea, even that great [a]city Zarahemla did they cause to be built again.

9 But there were many cities which had been [a]sunk, and waters came up in the stead thereof; therefore these cities could not be renewed.

10 And now, behold, it came to pass that the people of Nephi did wax strong, and did multiply exceedingly fast, and became an exceedingly [a]fair and delightsome people.

---

1 1*a* 3 Ne. 26:17.
3*a* Jacob 2:19 (17–19); Mosiah 4:26; 18:27 (19–29); Alma 16:16; 3 Ne. 12:42; 26:19. TG Consecration.
b TG God, Gifts of.
4*a* TG Peace.
5*a* TG Heal.
b TG Death, Power over.
c John 14:12 (12–14). TG Miracle.
8*a* 3 Ne. 8:8 (8, 24).
9*a* 3 Ne. 9:4 (4, 7).
10*a* 1 Ne. 13:15; 2 Ne. 5:21; Morm. 9:6.

11 And they were married, and given in marriage, and were blessed according to the multitude of the [a]promises which the Lord had made unto them.

12 And they did not walk any more after the [a]performances and [b]ordinances of the [c]law of Moses; but they did walk after the commandments which they had received from their Lord and their God, continuing in [d]fasting and prayer, and in meeting together oft both to pray and to hear the word of the Lord.

13 And it came to pass that there was no contention among all the people, in all the land; but there were mighty miracles wrought among the disciples of Jesus.

14 And it came to pass that the seventy and first year passed away, and also the seventy and second year, yea, and in fine, till the seventy and ninth year had passed away; yea, even an hundred years had passed away, and the [a]disciples of Jesus, whom he had chosen, had all gone to the [b]paradise of God, save it were the [c]three who should tarry; and there were other [d]disciples [e]ordained in their stead; and also many of that [f]generation had passed away.

15 And it came to pass that there was no [a]contention in the land, because of the [b]love of God which did dwell in the hearts of the people.

16 And there were no [a]envyings, nor [b]strifes, nor [c]tumults, nor whoredoms, nor lyings, nor murders, nor any manner of [d]lasciviousness; and surely there could not be a [e]happier people among all the people who had been created by the hand of God.

17 There were no robbers, nor murderers, neither were there Lamanites, nor any manner of -ites; but they were in [a]one, the children of Christ, and heirs to the kingdom of God.

18 And how blessed were they! For the Lord did bless them in all their doings; yea, even they were blessed and prospered until an hundred and ten years had passed away; and the first generation from Christ had passed away, and there was no contention in all the land.

19 And it came to pass that [a]Nephi, he that kept this last record, (and he kept it upon the [b]plates of Nephi) died, and his son Amos kept it in his stead; and he kept it upon the plates of Nephi also.

20 And he kept it eighty and four years, and there was still peace in the land, save it were a small part of the people who had revolted from the church and taken upon them the name of Lamanites; therefore there began to be [a]Lamanites again in the land.

21 And it came to pass that [a]Amos died also, (and it was an hundred and ninety and four years from the coming of Christ) and his son Amos kept the record in his stead; and he also kept it upon the plates of Nephi; and it was also written in the book of Nephi, which is this book.

22 And it came to pass that two hundred years had passed away; and the second generation had all passed away save it were a few.

23 And now I, Mormon, would that ye should know that the people had multiplied, insomuch that they were spread upon all the face of the land,

---

11*a* TG Promise.
12*a* 2 Ne. 25:30.
b TG Ordinance.
c 3 Ne. 9:19; 15:4 (2–8). TG Law of Moses.
d Moro. 6:5; D&C 88:76.
14*a* 3 Ne. 28:3; Morm. 3:19.
b TG Paradise.
c 3 Ne. 28:12. TG Translated Beings.
d TG Apostles.
e TG Priesthood, History of.
f 1 Ne. 12:12.
15*a* TG Contention.
b TG God, Love of.
16*a* TG Envy.
b TG Strife.
c TG Rioting and Reveling.
d TG Lust.
e Prov. 14:34; Mosiah 2:41; Alma 50:23. TG Happiness.
17*a* John 17:21 (21–23). TG Zion.
19*a* 4 Ne. heading.
b 3 Ne. 26:7.
20*a* 3 Ne. 10:18; Morm. 1:9.
21*a* 4 Ne. 1:47.

and that they had become exceedingly [a]rich, because of their prosperity in Christ.
24 And now, in this two hundred
and first year there began to be
among them those who were lifted
up in [a]pride, such as the wearing of
costly apparel, and all manner of
fine pearls, and of the fine things
of the world.
25 And from that time forth they
did have their goods and their substance no more [a]common among
them.
26 And they began to be divided
into classes; and they began to build
up [a]churches unto themselves to get
[b]gain, and began to deny the true
church of Christ.
27 And it came to pass that when
two hundred and ten years had
passed away there were many
churches in the land; yea, there were
many churches which professed to
know the Christ, and yet they did
[a]deny the more parts of his gospel,
insomuch that they did receive all
manner of wickedness, and did administer that which was sacred unto
him to whom it had been [b]forbidden
because of unworthiness.
28 And this church did multiply
exceedingly because of iniquity,
and because of the power of [a]Satan
who did get hold upon their [b]hearts.
29 And again, there was another
church which denied the Christ;
and they did [a]persecute the true
[b]church of Christ, because of their
humility and their belief in Christ;
and they did despise them because
of the many miracles which were
wrought among them.
30 Therefore they did exercise
power and authority over the disciples of Jesus who did tarry with
them, and they did cast them into
[a]prison; but by the power of the
word of God, which was in them,
the prisons were rent in twain, and
they went forth doing mighty miracles among them.
31 Nevertheless, and notwithstanding all these miracles, the people
did harden their hearts, and did
seek to kill them, even as the Jews
at Jerusalem sought to kill Jesus,
according to his word.
32 And they did cast them into
[a]furnaces of [b]fire, and they came
forth receiving no harm.
33 And they also cast them into
[a]dens of wild beasts, and they did
play with the wild beasts even as a
child with a lamb; and they did come
forth from among them, receiving
no harm.
34 Nevertheless, the people did
harden their hearts, for they were
led by many priests and [a]false
prophets to build up many churches,
and to do all manner of iniquity.
And they did [b]smite upon the people of Jesus; but the people of Jesus
did not smite again. And thus they
did dwindle in unbelief and wickedness, from year to year, even until
two hundred and thirty years had
passed away.
35 And now it came to pass in this
year, yea, in the two hundred and
thirty and first year, there was a
great division among the people.
36 And it came to pass that in this
year there arose a people who were
called the [a]Nephites, and they were
true believers in Christ; and among
them there were those who were
called by the Lamanites—Jacobites,
and Josephites, and [b]Zoramites;
37 Therefore the true believers in
Christ, and the true worshipers of

23*a* TG Treasure.
24*a* TG Pride; Selfishness.
25*a* TG Consecration.
26*a* 1 Ne. 22:23; 2 Ne. 28:3 (3–32); Morm. 8:28 (28, 32–38).
b Ezek. 22:27; D&C 10:56. TG Priestcraft.
27*a* TG Apostasy of Individuals.
b 3 Ne. 18:28 (28–29).
28*a* TG Devil, Church of.
b TG Hardheartedness.
29*a* TG Persecution.
b TG Jesus Christ, Head of the Church.
30*a* 3 Ne. 28:19 (19–20).
32*a* 3 Ne. 28:21.
b Dan. 3:27.
33*a* 3 Ne. 28:22.
34*a* TG False Prophets.
b 3 Ne. 6:13; 12:39; D&C 98:23 (23–27).
36*a* Morm. 1:8.
b Jacob 1:13.

Christ, (among whom were the [a]three
disciples of Jesus who should tarry)
were called Nephites, and Jacobites,
and Josephites, and Zoramites.
38 And it came to pass that they
who rejected the gospel were called
Lamanites, and Lemuelites, and Ishmaelites; and they did not dwindle
in [a]unbelief, but they did [b]wilfully
rebel against the gospel of Christ;
and they did teach their children
that they should not believe, even
as their fathers, from the beginning,
did dwindle.
39 And it was because of the
wickedness and abomination of
their fathers, even as it was in the
beginning. And they were [a]taught
to hate the children of God, even
as the Lamanites were taught to
[b]hate the children of Nephi from
the beginning.
40 And it came to pass that two
hundred and forty and four years
had passed away, and thus were the
affairs of the people. And the [a]more
wicked part of the people did wax
strong, and became exceedingly
more numerous than were the people of God.
41 And they did still continue to
build up churches unto themselves,
and adorn them with all manner
of precious things. And thus did
two hundred and fifty years pass
away, and also two hundred and
sixty years.
42 And it came to pass that the
wicked part of the people began
again to build up the secret oaths
and [a]combinations of Gadianton.
43 And also the people who were
called the people of Nephi began to
be proud in their hearts, because of
their exceeding riches, and become
[a]vain like unto their brethren, the
Lamanites.
44 And from this time the disciples began to sorrow for the [a]sins
of the world.
45 And it came to pass that when
three hundred years had passed
away, both the people of Nephi
and the Lamanites had become
exceedingly wicked one like unto
another.
46 And it came to pass that the robbers of [a]Gadianton did spread over
all the face of the land; and there
were none that were righteous save
it were the disciples of Jesus. And
gold and silver did they lay up in
store in abundance, and did [b]traffic
in all manner of traffic.
47 And it came to pass that after
three hundred and five years had
passed away, (and the people did
still remain in wickedness) [a]Amos
died; and his brother, Ammaron,
did keep the record in his stead.
48 And it came to pass that when
three hundred and twenty years
had passed away, [a]Ammaron, being
constrained by the Holy Ghost, did
[b]hide up the [c]records which were
[d]sacred—yea, even all the sacred
records which had been handed
down from generation to generation,
which were sacred—even until the
three hundred and twentieth year
from the coming of Christ.
49 And he did hide them up unto
the Lord, that they might [a]come
again unto the remnant of the house
of Jacob, according to the prophecies and the promises of the Lord.
And thus is the end of the record
of Ammaron.

37*a* 3 Ne. 28:7; Morm. 8:10 (10–12).
38*a* TG Unbelief.
b Josh. 22:18; Morm. 1:16.
39*a* Mosiah 10:17.
b TG Hate; Malice.
40*a* Hel. 5:2.
42*a* TG Secret Combinations.
43*a* Hel. 16:22.
44*a* Eccl. 3:16 (16–17); 3 Ne. 28:9; Morm. 8:10 (9–10).
46*a* Morm. 2:8; Ether 8:20.
b Mosiah 24:7; Ether 10:22.
47*a* 4 Ne. 1:21.
48*a* Morm. 1:2.
b Morm. 2:17.
c TG Scriptures, Preservation of.
d Hel. 3:15 (13, 15–16).
49*a* Enos 1:13; Morm. 5:9.

THE BOOK OF MORMON

CHAPTER 1

Ammaron instructs Mormon concerning the sacred records—War commences between the Nephites and the Lamanites—The Three Nephites are taken away—Wickedness, unbelief, sorceries, and witchcraft prevail. About A.D. *321–26.*

AND now I, Mormon, make a
[a]record of the things which I
have both seen and heard, and
call it the [b]Book of Mormon.
2 And about the time that [a]Am-
maron hid up the records unto the
Lord, he came unto me, (I being
about ten years of age, and I began
to be [b]learned somewhat after the
manner of the learning of my people) and Ammaron said unto me: I
perceive that thou art a [c]sober child,
and art quick to observe;
3 Therefore, when ye are about
twenty and four years old I would
that ye should remember the things
that ye have observed concerning
this people; and when ye are of that
age go to the [a]land Antum, unto a
hill which shall be called [b]Shim;
and there have I deposited unto
the Lord all the sacred engravings
concerning this people.
4 And behold, ye shall take the
[a]plates of Nephi unto yourself, and
the remainder shall ye leave in the
place where they are; and ye shall
engrave on the plates of Nephi all
the things that ye have observed
concerning this people.
5 And I, Mormon, being a descendant of [a]Nephi, (and my father's
name was Mormon) I remembered
the things which Ammaron commanded me.
6 And it came to pass that I, being
eleven years old, was carried by my
father into the land southward, even
to the land of Zarahemla.
7 The whole face of the land had
become covered with buildings, and
the people were as numerous almost,
as it were the sand of the sea.
8 And it came to pass in this year
there began to be a war between
the [a]Nephites, who consisted of the
Nephites and the Jacobites and the
Josephites and the Zoramites; and
this war was between the Nephites,
and the Lamanites and the Lemuelites and the Ishmaelites.
9 Now the [a]Lamanites and the
Lemuelites and the Ishmaelites were
called Lamanites, and the two par-
ties were Nephites and Lamanites.
10 And it came to pass that the
war began to be among them in
the borders of Zarahemla, by the
waters of Sidon.
11 And it came to pass that the
Nephites had gathered together a
great number of men, even to exceed the number of thirty thousand.
And it came to pass that they did
have in this same year a number
of [a]battles, in which the Nephites
did beat the Lamanites and did slay
many of them.
12 And it came to pass that the
Lamanites withdrew their design,
and there was peace settled in the
land; and peace did remain for the
space of about four years, that there
was no bloodshed.
13 But wickedness did prevail
upon the face of the whole land,
insomuch that the Lord did take
away his [a]beloved disciples, and
the work of miracles and of healing
did cease because of the iniquity of
the people.
14 And there were no [a]gifts from

1 1*a* 3 Ne. 5:11 (11–18); Morm. 8:5.
b W of M 1:5; Morm. 5:9.
2*a* 4 Ne. 1:48 (47–49).
b Enos 1:1; Mosiah 1:3 (3–5).
c TG Sobriety; Trustworthiness.
3*a* Morm. 2:17.
b Morm. 4:23; Ether 9:3.
4*a* W of M 1:1 (1, 11); 3 Ne. 5:10 (9–12); Morm. 2:17 (17–18); 8:5 (1, 4–5, 14).
5*a* 3 Ne. 5:20 (12, 20).
8*a* 4 Ne. 1:36.
9*a* 4 Ne. 1:20.
11*a* 2 Ne. 1:12; Morm. 4:1 (1–23).
13*a* 3 Ne. 28:12 (2, 12).
14*a* 1 Sam. 3:1.

the Lord, and the [b]Holy Ghost did not come upon any, because of their wickedness and [c]unbelief.
15 And I, being [a]fifteen years of age and being somewhat of a [b]sober mind, therefore I was [c]visited of the Lord, and [d]tasted and knew of the goodness of Jesus.
16 And I did endeavor to preach unto this people, but my mouth was shut, and I was forbidden that I should preach unto them; for behold they had [a]wilfully rebelled against their God; and the beloved disciples were [b]taken away out of the land, because of their iniquity.
17 But I did remain among them, but I was forbidden to [a]preach unto them, because of the hardness of their hearts; and because of the hardness of their hearts the land was [b]cursed for their sake.
18 And these Gadianton robbers, who were among the Lamanites, did infest the land, insomuch that the inhabitants thereof began to [a]hide up their [b]treasures in the earth; and they became slippery, because the Lord had cursed the land, that they could not hold them, nor retain them again.
19 And it came to pass that there were [a]sorceries, and witchcrafts, and magics; and the power of the evil one was wrought upon all the face of the land, even unto the fulfilling of all the words of Abinadi, and also [b]Samuel the Lamanite.

CHAPTER 2

Mormon leads the Nephite armies—Blood and carnage sweep the land—The Nephites lament and mourn with the sorrowing of the damned—Their day of grace is passed—Mormon obtains the plates of Nephi—Wars continue. About A.D. 327–50.

AND it came to pass in that same year there began to be a war again between the Nephites and the Lamanites. And notwithstanding I being [a]young, was large in stature; therefore the people of Nephi appointed me that I should be their leader, or the leader of their armies.
2 Therefore it came to pass that in my sixteenth year I did go forth at the head of an army of the Nephites, against the Lamanites; therefore three hundred and twenty and six years had passed away.
3 And it came to pass that in the three hundred and twenty and seventh year the Lamanites did come upon us with [a]exceedingly great power, insomuch that they did frighten my armies; therefore they would not fight, and they began to retreat towards the [b]north countries.
4 And it came to pass that we did come to the city of Angola, and we did take possession of the city, and make preparations to defend ourselves against the Lamanites. And it came to pass that we did [a]fortify the city with our might; but notwithstanding all our fortifications the Lamanites did come upon us and did drive us out of the city.
5 And they did also drive us forth out of the land of David.
6 And we marched forth and came to the land of Joshua, which was in the borders west by the seashore.
7 And it came to pass that we did gather in our people as fast as it were

14*b* TG Holy Ghost, Loss of.
c TG Unbelief.
15*a* Morm. 2:1 (1–2).
b TG Sobriety.
c Ex. 3:16; 2 Ne. 4:26; Alma 9:21.
d Ps. 34:8.
16*a* 4 Ne. 1:38. TG Rebellion.
b Morm. 8:10.
17*a* Micah 3:6 (5–7).
b 2 Ne. 1:7; Alma 45:16 (10–14, 16); Ether 2:11 (8–12).
18*a* Hel. 12:18; Morm. 2:10 (10–14); Ether 14:1 (1–2).
b Hel. 13:18–23, 30–37. TG Treasure.
19*a* TG Sorcery.
b Morm. 2:10 (10–15).
2 1*a* Morm. 1:15 (12, 15–16).
3*a* Morm. 4:13 (13–17); 5:6.
b Alma 50:11; Morm. 2:29.
4*a* 3 Ne. 3:14 (14, 25); Morm. 2:21.

possible, that we might get them together in [a]one body.

8 But behold, the land was [a]filled with [b]robbers and with Lamanites; and notwithstanding the great destruction which hung over my people, they did not repent of their evil doings; therefore there was blood and carnage spread throughout all the face of the land, both on the part of the Nephites and also on the part of the Lamanites; and it was one complete revolution throughout all the face of the land.

9 And now, the Lamanites had a king, and his name was [a]Aaron; and he came against us with an army of forty and four thousand. And behold, I withstood him with forty and two thousand. And it came to pass that I beat him with my army that he fled before me. And behold, all this was done, and three hundred and thirty years had passed away.

10 And it came to pass that the Nephites began to repent of their iniquity, and began to cry even as had been prophesied by Samuel the prophet; for behold no man could [a]keep that which was his own, for the thieves, and the robbers, and the murderers, and the magic art, and the witchcraft which was in the land.

11 Thus there began to be a [a]mourning and a lamentation in all the land because of these things, and more especially among the people of Nephi.

12 And it came to pass that when I, Mormon, saw their lamentation and their [a]mourning and their sorrow before the Lord, my heart did begin to rejoice within me, knowing the mercies and the long-suffering of the Lord, therefore supposing that he would be merciful unto them that they would [b]again become a righteous people.

13 But behold this my joy was vain, for their [a]sorrowing was not unto repentance, because of the goodness of God; but it was rather the [b]sorrowing of the [c]damned, because the Lord would not always suffer them to take [d]happiness in sin.

14 And they did not come unto Jesus with broken [a]hearts and contrite spirits, but they did [b]curse God, and wish to die. Nevertheless they would struggle with the sword for their lives.

15 And it came to pass that my sorrow did return unto me again, and I saw that the [a]day of [b]grace [c]was passed with them, both temporally and spiritually; for I saw thousands of them hewn down in open [d]rebellion against their God, and heaped up as [e]dung upon the face of the land. And thus three hundred and forty and four years had passed away.

16 And it came to pass that in the three hundred and forty and fifth year the Nephites did begin to flee before the Lamanites; and they were pursued until they came even to the land of Jashon, before it was possible to stop them in their retreat.

17 And now, the city of Jashon was near the [a]land where Ammaron had [b]deposited the records unto the Lord, that they might not be destroyed. And behold I had gone according to the word of Ammaron, and taken the [c]plates of Nephi, and did make a record according to the words of Ammaron.

18 And upon the plates of Nephi I

7*a* 3 Ne. 3:22 (22–25).
8*a* 3 Ne. 2:11.
b 4 Ne. 1:46; Morm. 8:9; Ether 8:20.
9*a* Moro. 9:17.
10*a* Hel. 12:18; 13:18 (17–23); Morm. 1:18 (17–19); Ether 14:1 (1–2).
11*a* 3 Ne. 12:4.
12*a* TG Mourning.
b Hel. 11:9 (8–17).
13*a* 2 Cor. 7:10; Alma 42:29.
b Hosea 7:14; Ether 8:7.
c TG Damnation.
d Alma 41:10.
14*a* TG Contrite Heart.
b TG Blaspheme.
15*a* Hel. 13:38.
b TG Grace.
c Jer. 8:20.
d TG Rebellion.
e Jer. 8:2 (1–3).
17*a* Morm. 1:3 (1–4).
b 4 Ne. 1:48 (48–49).
c Morm. 8:5 (1, 4–5, 14).

did make a full account of all the wickedness and abominations; but upon [a]these plates I did forbear to make a full account of their wickedness and abominations, for behold, a continual scene of wickedness and abominations has been before mine eyes ever since I have been sufficient to behold the ways of man.

19 And wo is me because of their wickedness; for my heart has been filled with sorrow because of their wickedness, all my days; nevertheless, I know that I shall be [a]lifted up at the last day.

20 And it came to pass that in this year the people of Nephi again were hunted and driven. And it came to pass that we were driven forth until we had come northward to the land which was called Shem.

21 And it came to pass that we did [a]fortify the city of Shem, and we did gather in our people as much as it were possible, that perhaps we might save them from destruction.

22 And it came to pass in the three hundred and forty and sixth year they began to come upon us again.

23 And it came to pass that I did speak unto my people, and did urge them with great energy, that they would stand boldly before the Lamanites and [a]fight for their [b]wives, and their children, and their houses, and their homes.

24 And my words did arouse them somewhat to vigor, insomuch that they did not flee from before the Lamanites, but did stand with boldness against them.

25 And it came to pass that we did contend with an army of thirty thousand against an army of fifty thousand. And it came to pass that we did stand before them with such firmness that they did flee from before us.

26 And it came to pass that when they had fled we did pursue them with our armies, and did meet them again, and did [a]beat them; nevertheless the [b]strength of the Lord was not with us; yea, we were left to ourselves, that the Spirit of the Lord did not abide in us; therefore we had become weak like unto our brethren.

27 And my heart did sorrow because of this the great calamity of my people, because of their wickedness and their abominations. But behold, we did go forth against the Lamanites and the robbers of Gadianton, until we had again taken possession of the lands of our inheritance.

28 And the three hundred and forty and ninth year had passed away. And in the three hundred and fiftieth year we made a treaty with the Lamanites and the robbers of Gadianton, in which we did get the lands of our inheritance divided.

29 And the Lamanites did give unto us the land [a]northward, yea, even to the [b]narrow passage which led into the land southward. And we did give unto the Lamanites all the land southward.

CHAPTER 3

Mormon cries repentance unto the Nephites—They gain a great victory and glory in their own strength—Mormon refuses to lead them, and his prayers for them are without faith—The Book of Mormon invites the twelve tribes of Israel to believe the gospel. About A.D. *360–62.*

AND it came to pass that the Lamanites did not come to battle again until ten years more had passed away. And behold, I had employed my people, the Nephites, in preparing their lands and their arms against the time of battle.

2 And it came to pass that the Lord did say unto me: Cry unto

---

18*a* 3 Ne. 5:15 (8–20).
19*a* Mosiah 23:22; Ether 4:19.
21*a* Morm. 2:4.
23*a* Alma 58:12.
b Ether 14:2.
26*a* Morm. 3:8 (7–8, 13).
b TG God, Spirit of; Strength.
29*a* Morm. 2:3.
b Alma 22:32; 52:9; 63:5.

this people—Repent ye, and come
unto me, and be ye baptized, and
build up again my church, and ye
shall be [a]spared.
3 And I did cry unto this people,
but it was [a]in vain; and they did
[b]not realize that it was the Lord
that had spared them, and granted
unto them a chance for repentance.
And behold they did harden their
hearts against the Lord their God.
4 And it came to pass that after
this tenth year had passed away,
making, in the whole, three hundred
and sixty years from the coming of
Christ, the king of the Lamanites
sent an epistle unto me, which gave
unto me to know that they were
preparing to come again to battle
against us.
5 And it came to pass that I did
cause my people that they should
gather themselves together at the
land [a]Desolation, to a city which was
in the borders, by the narrow pass
which led into the land [b]southward.
6 And there we did place our
armies, that we might stop the
armies of the Lamanites, that they
might not get possession of any of
our lands; therefore we did fortify
against them with all our force.
7 And it came to pass that in the
three hundred and sixty and first
year the Lamanites did come down
to the [a]city of Desolation to battle
against us; and it came to pass that
in that year we did beat them, insomuch that they did return to their
own lands again.
8 And in the three hundred and
sixty and second year they did
come down [a]again to battle. And
we did beat them again, and did
slay a great number of them, and
their dead were cast into the sea.
9 And now, because of this great
thing which my people, the Nephites, had done, they began to [a]boast
in their own strength, and began
to swear before the heavens that
they would avenge themselves of
the blood of their brethren who
had been slain by their enemies.
10 And they did [a]swear by the
heavens, and also by the throne
of God, that they [b]would go up to
battle against their enemies, and
would cut them off from the face of
the land.
11 And it came to pass that I, Mormon, did utterly [a]refuse from this
time forth to be a commander and
a leader of this people, because of
their wickedness and abomination.
12 Behold, I had led them, notwithstanding their wickedness I had led
them many times to battle, and had
loved them, according to the [a]love of
God which was in me, with all my
heart; and my soul had been poured
out in prayer unto my God all the
day long for them; nevertheless, it
was [b]without faith, because of the
[c]hardness of their hearts.
13 And [a]thrice have I delivered
them out of the hands of their enemies, and they have repented not
of their sins.
14 And when they had sworn by
all that had been [a]forbidden them
by our Lord and Savior Jesus Christ,
that they would go up unto their
enemies to battle, and avenge themselves of the blood of their brethren, behold the voice of the Lord
came unto me, saying:
15 [a]Vengeance is mine, and I will

---

3 2*a* Hel. 15:17 (16–17); Morm. 6:11 (11–15).
3*a* Morm. 4:18.
b TG Hardheartedness; Ingratitude.
5*a* Alma 50:34; Morm. 4:3 (1–3).
b Ether 9:31 (31–32); 10:21.
7*a* 3 Ne. 3:23; Morm. 4:2 (2, 19).
8*a* Morm. 2:26; 3:13.
9*a* Prov. 14:16; 2 Ne. 4:34; Morm. 4:8.
10*a* TG Swearing.
b Alma 43:46 (46–47); 48:14; 3 Ne. 3:21 (20–21); Morm. 4:4.
11*a* Morm. 5:1.
12*a* TG God, Love of.
b James 1:6; Morm. 5:2.
c Neh. 9:16 (16–17).
13*a* Morm. 2:26; 3:8 (7–8).
14*a* 3 Ne. 12:34.
15*a* Isa. 35:4; Rom. 12:19. TG Vengeance.

[b]repay; and because this people
repented not after I had delivered
them, behold, they shall be cut off
from the face of the earth.
16 And it came to pass that I utterly refused to go up against mine
enemies; and I did even as the Lord
had commanded me; and I did stand
as an idle witness to manifest unto
the world the things which I saw
and heard, according to the manifestations of the Spirit which had
testified of things to come.
17 Therefore I write [a]unto you,
Gentiles, and also unto you, house
of Israel, when the work shall commence, that ye shall be about to prepare to return to the land of your
inheritance;
18 Yea, behold, I write unto all the
ends of the earth; yea, unto you,
twelve tribes of Israel, who shall be
[a]judged according to your works by
the twelve whom Jesus chose to be
his disciples in the land of Jerusalem.
19 And I write also unto the remnant of this people, who shall also
be judged by the [a]twelve whom
Jesus chose in this land; and they
shall be judged by the other twelve
whom Jesus chose in the land of
Jerusalem.
20 And these things doth the Spirit
manifest unto me; therefore I write
unto you all. And for this cause I
write unto you, that ye may know
that ye must all stand before the
[a]judgment-seat of Christ, yea, every
soul who belongs to the whole human [b]family of Adam; and ye must
stand to be judged of your works,
whether they be good or evil;
21 And also that ye may [a]believe
the gospel of Jesus Christ, which
ye shall [b]have among you; and also
that the [c]Jews, the covenant people
of the Lord, shall have other [d]wit-
ness besides him whom they saw
and heard, that Jesus, whom they
slew, was the [e]very Christ and the
very God.
22 And I would that I could persuade [a]all ye ends of the earth to
repent and prepare to stand before
the judgment-seat of Christ.

CHAPTER 4

War and carnage continue—The wicked punish the wicked—Greater wickedness prevails than ever before in all Israel—Women and children are sacrificed to idols—The Lamanites begin to sweep the Nephites before them. About A.D. 363–75.

AND now it came to pass that in the
three hundred and sixty and third
year the Nephites did go up with their
armies to [a]battle against the Lamanites, out of the land Desolation.
2 And it came to pass that the
armies of the Nephites were driven
back again to the land of Desolation.
And while they were yet weary, a
fresh army of the Lamanites did
come upon them; and they had a
sore battle, insomuch that the Lamanites did take possession of the
[a]city Desolation, and did slay many
of the Nephites, and did take many
prisoners.
3 And the remainder did flee and
join the inhabitants of the city Teancum. Now the city Teancum lay
in the borders by the seashore; and
it was also near the city [a]Desolation.
4 And it was [a]because the armies
of the Nephites went up unto the
Lamanites that they began to be
smitten; for were it not for that, the

15*b* 2 Sam. 16:12 (9–12); D&C 82:23. TG God, Justice of.
17*a* 2 Ne. 30:3 (3–8); 3 Ne. 29:1.
18*a* Matt. 19:28; Luke 22:30 (29–30); D&C 29:12.
19*a* 1 Ne. 12:10 (9–10); 3 Ne. 27:27.
20*a* TG Jesus Christ, Judge; Judgment, the Last.
b D&C 27:11.
21*a* D&C 3:20.
b 1 Ne. 13:23 (20–29, 41).
c TG Israel, Judah, People of.
d 2 Ne. 25:18.
e 2 Ne. 26:12; Mosiah 7:27.
22*a* Alma 29:1.
4 1*a* 2 Ne. 1:12; Morm. 1:11 (11–19).
2*a* 3 Ne. 3:23; Morm. 3:7.
3*a* Morm. 3:5.
4*a* Morm. 3:10 (10–11).

Lamanites could have had no power
over them.
5 But, behold, the judgments of
God will overtake the [a]wicked; and
it is by the wicked that the wicked
are [b]punished; for it is the wicked
that stir up the hearts of the children of men unto bloodshed.
6 And it came to pass that the
Lamanites did make preparations
to come against the city Teancum.
7 And it came to pass in the
three hundred and sixty and fourth
year the Lamanites did come
against the city Teancum, that they
might take possession of the city
Teancum also.
8 And it came to pass that they
were repulsed and driven back by
the Nephites. And when the Nephites saw that they had driven the
Lamanites they did again [a]boast
of their own strength; and they
went forth in their own might, and
took possession again of the city
Desolation.
9 And now all these things had
been done, and there had been
thousands slain on both sides, both
the Nephites and the Lamanites.
10 And it came to pass that the
three hundred and sixty and sixth
year had passed away, and the Lamanites came again upon the Nephites to battle; and yet the Nephites
repented not of the evil they had
done, but persisted in their wickedness continually.
11 And it is impossible for the
tongue to describe, or for man to
write a perfect description of the
horrible scene of the blood and
carnage which was among the
people, both of the Nephites and
of the Lamanites; and every heart
was hardened, so that they [a]de-
lighted in the shedding of blood
continually.
12 And there never had been so
great [a]wickedness among all the
children of Lehi, nor even among
all the house of Israel, according
to the words of the Lord, as was
among this people.
13 And it came to pass that the
Lamanites did take possession of
the city Desolation, and this because their [a]number did exceed the
number of the Nephites.
14 And they did also march forward against the city Teancum, and
did drive the inhabitants forth out
of her, and did take many prisoners
both women and children, and did
offer them up as [a]sacrifices unto
their idol gods.
15 And it came to pass that in
the three hundred and sixty and
seventh year, the Nephites being
angry because the Lamanites had
sacrificed their women and their
children, that they did go against
the Lamanites with exceedingly
great anger, insomuch that they
did beat again the Lamanites, and
drive them out of their lands.
16 And the Lamanites did not
come again against the Nephites
until the three hundred and seventy and fifth year.
17 And in this year they did come
down against the Nephites with all
their powers; and they were not
numbered because of the greatness
of their number.
18 And [a]from this time forth did
the Nephites gain no power over the
Lamanites, but began to be swept
off by them even as a dew before
the sun.
19 And it came to pass that the
Lamanites did come down against
the [a]city Desolation; and there was
an exceedingly sore battle fought in
the land Desolation, in the which
they did beat the Nephites.

5*a* Nahum 1:3.
b 2 Pet. 2:12; D&C 63:33.
8*a* Morm. 3:9.
11*a* Moro. 9:5 (5, 23). TG Blood, Shedding of.
12*a* Gen. 6:5 (5–6); 3 Ne. 9:9; D&C 112:23; Moses 7:36 (36–37); 8:22 (22, 28–30).
13*a* Morm. 2:3; 5:6.
14*a* Jer. 19:5; Alma 17:15; Abr. 1:8 (6–14). TG Idolatry; Sacrifice.
18*a* Morm. 3:3.
19*a* Morm. 3:7.

20 And they fled again from before them, and they came to the city Boaz; and there they did stand against the Lamanites with exceeding boldness, insomuch that the Lamanites did not beat them until they had come again the second time.
21 And when they had come the second time, the Nephites were driven and slaughtered with an exceedingly great slaughter; their women and their [a]children were again sacrificed unto idols.
22 And it came to pass that the Nephites did again flee from before them, taking all the inhabitants with them, both in towns and villages.
23 And now I, Mormon, seeing that the Lamanites were about to overthrow the land, therefore I did go to the hill [a]Shim, and did take up all the [b]records which Ammaron had hid up unto the Lord.

CHAPTER 5

Mormon again leads the Nephite armies in battles of blood and carnage—The Book of Mormon will come forth to convince all Israel that Jesus is the Christ—Because of their unbelief, the Lamanites will be scattered, and the Spirit will cease to strive with them—They will receive the gospel from the Gentiles in the latter days. About A.D. *375–84.*

AND it came to pass that I did go forth among the Nephites, and did repent of the [a]oath which I had made that I would no more assist them; and they gave me command again of their armies, for they looked upon me as though I could deliver them from their afflictions.
2 But behold, I was [a]without hope, for I knew the judgments of the Lord which should come upon them; for they repented not of their iniquities, but did struggle for their lives without calling upon that Being who created them.
3 And it came to pass that the Lamanites did come against us as we had fled to the city of Jordan; but behold, they were driven back that they did not take the city at that time.
4 And it came to pass that they came against us again, and we did maintain the city. And there were also other cities which were maintained by the Nephites, which strongholds did cut them off that they could not get into the country which lay before us, to destroy the inhabitants of our land.
5 But it came to pass that whatsoever lands we had passed by, and the inhabitants thereof were not gathered in, were destroyed by the Lamanites, and their towns, and villages, and cities were burned with fire; and thus three hundred and seventy and nine years passed away.
6 And it came to pass that in the three hundred and eightieth year the Lamanites did come again against us to battle, and we did stand against them boldly; but it was all in vain, for so [a]great were their numbers that they did tread the people of the Nephites under their feet.
7 And it came to pass that we did again take to flight, and those whose flight was swifter than the Lamanites' did escape, and those whose flight did not exceed the Lamanites' were swept down and destroyed.
8 And now behold, I, Mormon, do not desire to harrow up the souls of men in casting before them such an awful scene of blood and carnage as was laid before mine eyes; but I, knowing that these things must surely be made known, and that all things which are hid must be [a]revealed upon the house-tops—
9 And also that a knowledge of these things must [a]come unto the remnant of these people, and also unto the Gentiles, who the Lord

21*a* 2 Kgs. 17:31. TG Idolatry.
23*a* Morm. 1:3; Ether 9:3.
b W of M 1:3.
5 1*a* Morm. 3:11 (11, 16). TG Vow.
2*a* Morm. 3:12.
6*a* Morm. 2:3; 4:13 (13–17).
8*a* Matt. 10:26 (26–33); Luke 12:3; 2 Ne. 27:11; D&C 1:3; 88:108.
9*a* 4 Ne. 1:49.

hath said should [b]scatter this people,
and this people should be counted
as naught among them—therefore
[c]I write a [d]small abridgment, dar-
ing not to give a full account of the
things which I have seen, because
of the commandment which I have
received, and also that ye might
not have too great sorrow because
of the wickedness of this people.
10 And now behold, this I speak
unto their seed, and also to the Gentiles who have care for the house of
Israel, that realize and know from
whence their blessings come.
11 For I know that such will sorrow for the calamity of the house
of Israel; yea, they will sorrow for
the destruction of this people; they
will sorrow that this people had
not repented that they might have
been clasped in the arms of Jesus.
12 Now [a]these things are [b]written
unto the [c]remnant of the house of
Jacob; and they are written after this
manner, because it is known of God
that wickedness will not bring them
forth unto them; and they are to be
[d]hid up unto the Lord that they may
come forth in his own due time.
13 And this is the commandment
which I have received; and behold,
they [a]shall come forth according to the commandment of the
Lord, when he shall see fit, in his
wisdom.
14 And behold, they shall go unto
the [a]unbelieving of the [b]Jews; and
for this intent shall they go—that
they may be [c]persuaded that Jesus
is the Christ, the Son of the living
God; that the Father may bring
about, through his most Beloved,
his great and eternal purpose, in
restoring the Jews, or all the house
of Israel, to the [d]land of their inheritance, which the Lord their God
hath given them, unto the fulfilling
of his [e]covenant;
15 And also that the seed of [a]this
people may more fully believe his
gospel, which shall [b]go forth unto
them from the Gentiles; for this
people shall be [c]scattered, and shall
[d]become a dark, a filthy, and a loathsome people, beyond the description of that which ever hath been
amongst us, yea, even that which
hath been among the Lamanites, and
this because of their unbelief and
idolatry.
16 For behold, the Spirit of the
Lord hath already ceased to [a]strive
with their fathers; and they are
without Christ and God in the world;
and they are driven about as [b]chaff
before the wind.
17 They were once a delightsome
people, and they had Christ for their
[a]shepherd; yea, they were led even
by God the Father.
18 But now, behold, they are [a]led
about by Satan, even as chaff is
driven before the wind, or as a vessel is tossed about upon the waves,
without sail or anchor, or without
anything wherewith to steer her;
and even as she is, so are they.
19 And behold, the Lord hath reserved their blessings, which they

9*b* 3 Ne. 16:8 (8–9).
c Alma 43:3.
d Morm. 1:1.
12*a* 1 Ne. 19:19; Enos 1:16; Hel. 15:11 (11–13); Morm. 7:1 (1, 9–10).
b TG Book of Mormon; Scriptures to Come Forth.
c 2 Ne. 25:8; 27:6; Jarom 1:2; D&C 3:20 (16–20).
d Morm. 8:4 (4, 13–14); Moro. 10:2 (1–2). TG Scriptures, Preservation of.
13*a* 2 Ne. 3:18.
14*a* Rom. 11:20 (1–36); 1 Ne. 10:11; Jacob 4:15 (15–18). TG Unbelief.
b 2 Ne. 26:12; 29:13; 30:7 (7–8). TG Israel, Judah, People of.
c John 20:31; 2 Ne. 25:16 (16–17). TG Israel, Restoration of.
d TG Lands of Inheritance.
e Ezek. 20:37; 3 Ne. 29:1 (1–3).
15*a* 2 Ne. 30:5; 3 Ne. 21:5 (3–7, 24–26).
b 1 Ne. 13:38 (20–29, 38); Morm. 7:8 (8–9).
c 1 Ne. 10:12 (12–14); 3 Ne. 16:8.
d 2 Ne. 26:33.
16*a* Gen. 6:3; Ether 2:15; Moro. 8:28.
b Ps. 1:4 (1–4); Hosea 13:3 (1–4).
17*a* TG Jesus Christ, Good Shepherd.
18*a* 2 Ne. 28:21.

might have received in the land, for the [a]Gentiles who shall possess the land.
20 But behold, it shall come to pass that they shall be driven and scattered by the Gentiles; and after they have been driven and scattered by the Gentiles, behold, then will the Lord [a]remember the [b]covenant which he made unto Abraham and unto all the house of Israel.
21 And also the Lord will remember the [a]prayers of the righteous, which have been put up unto him for them.
22 And then, O ye Gentiles, how can ye stand before the power of God, except ye shall repent and turn from your evil ways?
23 Know ye not that ye are in the [a]hands of God? Know ye not that he hath all power, and at his great command the [b]earth shall be [c]rolled together as a scroll?
24 Therefore, repent ye, and humble yourselves before him, lest he shall come out in justice against you—lest a [a]remnant of the seed of Jacob shall go forth among you as a [b]lion, and tear you in pieces, and there is none to deliver.

CHAPTER 6

The Nephites gather to the land of Cumorah for the final battles—Mormon hides the sacred records in the hill Cumorah—The Lamanites are victorious, and the Nephite nation is destroyed—Hundreds of thousands are slain with the sword. About A.D. *385.*

AND now I finish my record concerning the [a]destruction of my people, the Nephites. And it came to pass that we did march forth before the Lamanites.
2 And I, Mormon, wrote an epistle unto the king of the Lamanites, and desired of him that he would grant unto us that we might gather together our people unto the [a]land of [b]Cumorah, by a hill which was called Cumorah, and there we could give them battle.
3 And it came to pass that the king of the Lamanites did grant unto me the thing which I desired.
4 And it came to pass that we did march forth to the land of Cumorah, and we did pitch our tents around about the hill Cumorah; and it was in a land of [a]many waters, rivers, and fountains; and here we had hope to gain advantage over the Lamanites.
5 And when [a]three hundred and eighty and four years had passed away, we had gathered in all the remainder of our people unto the land of Cumorah.
6 And it came to pass that when we had gathered in all our people in one to the land of Cumorah, behold I, Mormon, began to be old; and knowing it to be the last struggle of my people, and having been commanded of the Lord that I should not suffer the records which had been handed down by our fathers, which were [a]sacred, to fall into the hands of the Lamanites, (for the Lamanites would [b]destroy them) therefore I made [c]this record out of the plates of Nephi, and [d]hid up in the hill Cumorah all the records which had been entrusted to me by the hand of the Lord, save it were [e]these few plates which I gave unto my son [f]Moroni.

19*a* 3 Ne. 20:27.
20*a* 1 Ne. 13:31; 3 Ne. 16:11 (8–12).
b TG Abrahamic Covenant.
21*a* Enos 1:12 (12–18); Morm. 8:25 (24–26); 9:36 (36–37).
23*a* Ether 1:1; D&C 87:6 (6–7).
b Hel. 12:11 (8–18); Morm. 9:2.
c 3 Ne. 26:3.
24*a* TG Israel, Remnant of.
b 3 Ne. 20:16 (15–16).
6 1*a* 1 Ne. 12:19 (19–20); Jarom 1:10; Alma 45:11 (9–14); Hel. 13:5 (5–11).
2*a* Ether 9:3.
b Morm. 8:2; D&C 128:20.
4*a* Mosiah 8:8; Alma 50:29; Hel. 3:4 (3–4).
5*a* W of M 1:2.
6*a* TG Sacred.
b 2 Ne. 26:17; Enos 1:14.
c Morm. 2:18.
d Ether 15:11.
e Moro. 9:24; 10:2; D&C 17:1; JS—H 1:52.
f Morm. 8:1.

7 And it came to pass that my people, with their wives and their children, did now behold the [a]armies
of the Lamanites marching towards
them; and with that awful [b]fear of
death which fills the breasts of all
the wicked, did they await to receive them.
8 And it came to pass that they
came to battle against us, and every
soul was filled with terror because
of the greatness of their numbers.
9 And it came to pass that they
did fall upon my people with the
sword, and with the bow, and with
the arrow, and with the ax, and with
all manner of weapons of war.
10 And it came to pass that my men
were hewn down, yea, even my [a]ten
thousand who were with me, and I
fell wounded in the midst; and they
passed by me that they did not put
an end to my life.
11 And when they had gone through
and hewn down [a]all my people save
it were twenty and four of us, (among
whom was my son Moroni) and
we having survived the dead of our
people, did behold on the morrow,
when the Lamanites had returned
unto their camps, from the top of
the hill Cumorah, the ten thousand
of my people who were hewn down,
being led in the front by me.
12 And we also beheld the ten
thousand of my people who were
led by my son Moroni.
13 And behold, the ten thousand
of Gidgiddonah had fallen, and he
also in the midst.
14 And Lamah had fallen with his
ten thousand; and Gilgal had fallen
with his ten thousand; and Lim-
hah had fallen with his ten thousand; and Jeneum had fallen with
his ten thousand; and Cumenihah,
and Moronihah, and Antionum,
and Shiblom, and Shem, and Josh,
had fallen with their ten thousand
each.
15 And it came to pass that there
were ten more who did fall by the
sword, with their ten thousand each;
yea, even [a]all my people, save it were
those twenty and four who were
with me, and also a [b]few who had
escaped into the south countries,
and a few who had deserted over
unto the Lamanites, had fallen; and
their flesh, and bones, and blood
lay upon the face of the earth, being
left by the hands of those who slew
them to molder upon the land, and
to crumble and to return to their
mother earth.
16 And my soul was rent with [a]an-
guish, because of the slain of my
people, and I cried:
17 [a]O ye fair ones, how could ye
have departed from the ways of the
Lord! O ye fair ones, how could ye
have rejected that Jesus, who stood
with open arms to receive you!
18 Behold, if ye had not done this,
ye would not have fallen. But behold,
ye are fallen, and I [a]mourn your loss.
19 O ye [a]fair sons and daughters,
ye fathers and mothers, ye husbands
and wives, ye fair ones, how is it
that ye could have [b]fallen!
20 But behold, ye are gone, and my
sorrows cannot bring your return.
21 And the day soon cometh that
your mortal must put on immortality, and these bodies which are
now moldering in corruption must
soon become [a]incorruptible bodies;
and then ye must stand before
the judgment-seat of Christ, to be
judged according to your works;
and if it so be that ye are righteous,
then are ye blessed with your fathers
who have gone before you.
22 O that ye had repented before
this great [a]destruction had come
upon you. But behold, ye are gone,

7*a* 1 Ne. 12:15.
b TG Fearful.
10*a* Judg. 1:4.
11*a* 1 Ne. 12:19 (19–20); Hel. 15:17 (16–17); Morm. 3:2.
15*a* Alma 9:24.
b Morm. 8:2.
16*a* TG Despair; Mourning; Sorrow.
17*a* 2 Ne. 26:7.
18*a* Lam. 2:11.
19*a* Ether 13:17.
b 1 Ne. 13:15.
21*a* 1 Cor. 15:53 (53–54).
22*a* 2 Sam. 1:27 (17–27).

and the Father, yea, the Eternal
Father of heaven, [b]knoweth your
state; and he doeth with you according to his [c]justice and [d]mercy.

CHAPTER 7

Mormon invites the Lamanites of the latter days to believe in Christ, accept His gospel, and be saved—All who believe the Bible will also believe the Book of Mormon. About A.D. *385.*

AND now, behold, I would speak
somewhat unto the [a]remnant of this
people who are spared, if it so be
that God may give unto them my
words, that they may know of the
things of their fathers; yea, I speak
unto you, ye remnant of the house
of Israel; and these are the words
which I speak:
2 Know ye that ye are of the [a]house
of Israel.
3 Know ye that ye must come unto
repentance, or ye cannot be saved.
4 Know ye that ye must lay down
your weapons of war, and delight no
more in the shedding of blood, and
take them not again, save it be that
God shall [a]command you.
5 Know ye that ye must come to
the [a]knowledge of your fathers, and
repent of all your sins and iniquities,
and [b]believe in Jesus Christ, that he
is the Son of God, and that he was
slain by the Jews, and by the power
of the Father he hath risen again,
whereby he hath gained the [c]vic-
tory over the grave; and also in him
is the sting of death swallowed up.
6 And he bringeth to pass the [a]res-
urrection of the dead, whereby man
must be raised to stand before his
[b]judgment-seat.
7 And he hath brought to pass the
[a]redemption of the [b]world, whereby
he that is found [c]guiltless before him
at the judgment day hath it given
unto him to [d]dwell in the presence
of God in his kingdom, to sing cease-
less praises with the [e]choirs above,
unto the Father, and unto the Son,
and unto the Holy Ghost, which are
[f]one God, in a state of [g]happiness
which hath no end.
8 Therefore repent, and be baptized
in the name of Jesus, and lay hold
upon the [a]gospel of Christ, which
shall be set before you, not only in
this record but also in the record
which shall come unto the Gentiles
[b]from the Jews, which record shall
come from the Gentiles [c]unto you.
9 For behold, [a]this is [b]written for
the intent that ye may [c]believe
that; and if [d]ye believe that ye will
believe this also; and if ye believe
this ye will know concerning your
fathers, and also the marvelous
works which were wrought by the
power of God among them.
10 And ye will also know that ye
are a [a]remnant of the seed of Jacob;
therefore ye are numbered among
the people of the first covenant; and
if it so be that ye believe in Christ,
and are baptized, first [b]with water,
then with fire and with the Holy
Ghost, following the [c]example of
our Savior, according to that which

22*b* 2 Sam. 7:20; D&C 6:16.
c TG God, Justice of.
d Ps. 36:5 (5–6); Alma 26:16; D&C 97:6.
7 1*a* Hel. 15:11 (11–13); Morm. 5:12 (9, 12).
2*a* 1 Ne. 5:14; Alma 10:3; Hel. 6:10; 8:21.
4*a* Alma 43:47.
5*a* 2 Ne. 3:12; 3 Ne. 5:23.
b TG Faith.
c Isa. 25:8; Mosiah 16:8 (7–8); Alma 24:23.
6*a* TG Resurrection.
b TG Jesus Christ, Judge.
7*a* TG Redemption.
b TG World.
c Mosiah 13:15; D&C 58:30. TG Justification.
d Ps. 27:4; 1 Ne. 10:21; D&C 76:62 (50–62); Moses 6:57.
e Mosiah 2:28.
f Deut. 6:4; Gal. 3:20; D&C 20:28.
g TG Happiness.
8*a* TG Gospel.
b 2 Ne. 29:4 (4–13).
c 1 Ne. 13:38 (20–29, 38); Morm. 5:15.
9*a* 1 Ne. 19:19; Enos 1:16 (12–18); 3 Ne. 5:15 (12–17); Morm. 5:12. TG Israel, Restoration of.
b TG Book of Mormon.
c 1 Ne. 13:40 (38–42).
d 2 Ne. 3:15 (12–15); Alma 37:19 (1–20).
10*a* TG Israel, Remnant of.
b 3 Ne. 19:13 (13–14); Ether 12:14.
c TG God, the Standard of Righteousness.

he hath commanded us, it shall be well with you in the day of judgment. Amen.

CHAPTER 8

The Lamanites seek out and destroy the Nephites—The Book of Mormon will come forth by the power of God—Woes pronounced upon those who breathe out wrath and strife against the work of the Lord—The Nephite record will come forth in a day of wickedness, degeneracy, and apostasy. About A.D. 400–421.

BEHOLD I, [a]Moroni, do finish the [b]record of my father, Mormon. Behold, I have but few things to write, which things I have been commanded by my father.
2 And now it came to pass that after the [a]great and tremendous battle at Cumorah, behold, the Nephites who had escaped into the country southward were hunted by the [b]Lamanites, until they were all destroyed.
3 And my father also was killed by them, and I even [a]remain [b]alone to write the sad tale of the destruction of my people. But behold, they are gone, and I fulfil the commandment of my father. And whether they will slay me, I know not.
4 Therefore I will write and [a]hide up the records in the earth; and whither I go it mattereth not.
5 Behold, my father hath made [a]this record, and he hath written the intent thereof. And behold, I would write it also if I had room upon the [b]plates, but I have not; and ore I have none, for I am alone. My father hath been slain in battle, and all my kinsfolk, and I have not friends nor whither to go; and [c]how long the Lord will suffer that I may live I know not.
6 Behold, [a]four hundred years have passed away since the coming of our Lord and Savior.
7 And behold, the Lamanites have hunted my people, the Nephites, down from city to city and from place to place, even until they are no more; and great has been their [a]fall; yea, great and marvelous is the destruction of my people, the Nephites.
8 And behold, it is the hand of the Lord which hath done it. And behold also, the Lamanites are at [a]war one with another; and the whole face of this land is one continual round of murder and bloodshed; and no one knoweth the end of the war.
9 And now, behold, I say no more concerning them, for there are none save it be the Lamanites and [a]robbers that do exist upon the face of the land.
10 And there are none that do know the true God save it be the [a]disciples of Jesus, who did tarry in the land until the wickedness of the people was so great that the Lord would not suffer them to [b]remain with the people; and whether they be upon the face of the land no man knoweth.
11 But behold, my [a]father and I have seen [b]them, and they have ministered unto us.
12 And whoso receiveth [a]this record, and shall not condemn it because of the imperfections which are in it, the same shall know of [b]greater things than these. Behold, I am Moroni; and were it possible, I would make all things known unto you.

---

8 1a Morm. 6:6; Moro. 9:24.
b TG Record Keeping.
2a Morm. 6:15 (2–15).
b D&C 3:18.
3a Moro. 9:22.
b Ether 4:3.
4a Morm. 5:12; Moro. 10:2 (1–2).
5a Morm. 2:17 (17–18).
b Morm. 6:6.
c Moro. 1:1; 10:1 (1–2).
6a Alma 45:10.
7a 1 Ne. 12:2 (2–3); Enos 1:24.
8a 1 Ne. 12:21 (20–23).
9a 4 Ne. 1:46; Morm. 2:8 (8, 28); Ether 8:20.
10a 3 Ne. 28:7; 4 Ne. 1:37 (14, 37); Ether 12:17.
b Morm. 1:16.
11a 3 Ne. 28:26.
b TG Translated Beings.
12a 3 Ne. 5:15 (8–18).
b John 16:12; 3 Ne. 26:9 (6–11); D&C 42:15.

13 Behold, I make an end of speaking concerning this people. I am the
son of Mormon, and my father was
a [a]descendant of Nephi.
14 And I am the same who [a]hid-
eth up this record unto the Lord;
the plates thereof are of no worth,
because of the commandment of
the Lord. For he truly saith that no
one shall have them [b]to get gain;
but the record thereof is of [c]great
worth; and whoso shall bring it to
light, him will the Lord bless.
15 For none can have power to
bring it to light save it be given him
of God; for God wills that it shall
be done with an [a]eye single to his
glory, or the welfare of the ancient
and long dispersed covenant people
of the Lord.
16 And blessed be [a]he that shall
bring this thing to light; for it shall
be [b]brought out of darkness unto
light, according to the word of God;
yea, it shall be brought out of the
earth, and it shall shine forth out of
darkness, and come unto the knowledge of the people; and it shall be
done by the power of God.
17 And if there be [a]faults they
be the faults of a man. But behold,
we know no fault; nevertheless
God knoweth all things; therefore,
he that [b]condemneth, let him be
aware lest he shall be in danger of
hell fire.
18 And he that saith: Show unto
me, or ye shall be [a]smitten—let him
beware lest he commandeth that
which is forbidden of the Lord.
19 For behold, the same that [a]judg-
eth [b]rashly shall be judged rashly
again; for according to his works
shall his wages be; therefore, he
that smiteth shall be smitten again,
of the Lord.
20 Behold what the scripture
says—man shall not [a]smite, neither
shall he [b]judge; for judgment is
mine, saith the Lord, and vengeance
is mine also, and I will repay.
21 And he that shall breathe out
[a]wrath and [b]strifes against the work
of the Lord, and against the [c]cov-
enant people of the Lord who are
the house of Israel, and shall say: We
will destroy the work of the Lord,
and the Lord will not remember
his covenant which he hath made
unto the house of Israel—the same
is in danger to be hewn down and
cast into the fire;
22 For the eternal [a]purposes of
the Lord shall roll on, until all his
promises shall be fulfilled.
23 Search the prophecies of [a]Isaiah.
Behold, I cannot write them. Yea, behold I say unto you, that those saints
who have gone before me, who have
possessed this land, shall [b]cry, yea,
even from the dust will they cry unto
the Lord; and as the Lord liveth he
will remember the covenant which
he hath made with them.
24 And he knoweth their [a]prayers,
that they were in behalf of their
brethren. And he knoweth their
faith, for in his name could they remove [b]mountains; and in his name
could they cause the earth to shake;
and by the power of his word did
they cause [c]prisons to tumble to the
earth; yea, even the fiery furnace
could not harm them, neither wild

13*a* Alma 10:3; 3 Ne. 5:20.
14*a* Ether 4:3; Moro. 10:2 (1–2).
b JS—H 1:53. TG Scriptures, Preservation of.
c 2 Ne. 3:7 (6–9).
15*a* Matt. 6:22; D&C 4:5.
16*a* 3 Ne. 21:11 (8–11); Ether 3:28 (21–28).
b TG Scriptures to Come Forth.
17*a* 1 Ne. 19:6; Morm. 9:31 (31, 33); Ether 12:23 (22–28, 35).
b 3 Ne. 29:5 (1–9); Ether 4:8 (8–10).
18*a* JS—H 1:60 (60–61).
19*a* 3 Ne. 14:2; Moro. 7:14. TG Gossip.
b TG Rashness.
20*a* TG Violence.
b James 4:12 (11–12).
21*a* Prov. 19:19.
b TG Strife.
c 1 Ne. 14:17.
22*a* D&C 3:3.
23*a* Isa. 29:4; 3 Ne. 20:11; 23:1 (1–3).
b 2 Ne. 3:20; 26:16.
24*a* Enos 1:13 (12–18); Morm. 9:36 (34–37); D&C 10:46 (46–49).
b Jacob 4:6; Hel. 10:9.
c 3 Ne. 28:19 (19–21).

beasts nor poisonous serpents, because of the power of his word.
25 And behold, their [a]prayers
were also in behalf of him that the
Lord should suffer to bring these
things forth.
26 And no one need say they shall
not come, for they surely shall, for
the Lord hath spoken it; for [a]out of
the earth shall they come, by the
hand of the Lord, and none can stay
it; and it shall come in a day when it
shall be said that [b]miracles are done
away; and it shall come even as if
one should speak [c]from the dead.
27 And it shall come in a day when
the [a]blood of saints shall cry unto
the Lord, because of secret [b]combi-
nations and the works of darkness.
28 Yea, it shall come in a day when
the power of God shall be [a]denied,
and [b]churches become defiled and
be [c]lifted up in the pride of their
hearts; yea, even in a day when leaders of churches and teachers shall
rise in the pride of their hearts,
even to the envying of them who
belong to their churches.
29 Yea, it shall come in a day when
[a]there shall be heard of fires, and
tempests, and [b]vapors of smoke in
foreign lands;
30 And there shall also be heard
of [a]wars, rumors of wars, and earthquakes in divers places.
31 Yea, it shall come in a day when
there shall be great [a]pollutions upon
the face of the earth; there shall be
[b]murders, and robbing, and lying,
and deceivings, and whoredoms, and
all manner of abominations; when
there shall be many who will say,
Do this, or do that, and it [c]mattereth
not, for the Lord will [d]uphold such
at the last day. But wo unto such,
for they are in the [e]gall of bitterness and in the [f]bonds of iniquity.
32 Yea, it shall come in a day when
there shall be [a]churches built up
that shall say: Come unto me, and
for your money you shall be forgiven of your sins.
33 O ye wicked and perverse and
[a]stiffnecked people, why have ye
built up churches unto yourselves
to get [b]gain? Why have ye [c]trans-
figured the holy word of God, that
ye might bring [d]damnation upon
your souls? Behold, look ye unto
the [e]revelations of God; for behold,
the time cometh at that day when
all these things must be fulfilled.
34 Behold, the Lord hath shown
unto me great and marvelous things
concerning that which must shortly
come, at that day when these things
shall come forth among you.
35 Behold, I speak unto you as if
ye were present, and yet ye are not.
But behold, Jesus Christ hath shown
you unto me, and I know your
doing.
36 And I know that ye do [a]walk in
the pride of your hearts; and there
are none save a few only who do
not [b]lift themselves up in the pride
of their hearts, unto the wearing of
[c]very fine apparel, unto envying,

25*a* Morm. 5:21.
26*a* 3 Ne. 23:4.
b 3 Ne. 29:7; Morm. 9:15 (15–26); Moro. 7:37 (27–37).
c 2 Ne. 26:16 (15–16); 33:13; Morm. 9:30; Moro. 10:27.
27*a* Gen. 4:10; Rev. 6:10 (1, 10); 2 Ne. 28:10; Ether 8:22 (22–24); D&C 87:7.
b TG Secret Combinations.
28*a* TG Unbelief.
b 2 Tim. 3:1 (1–7); 1 Ne. 14:10 (9–10); 2 Ne. 28:3 (3–32); D&C 33:4.
c 2 Kgs. 14:10; Jacob 2:13.
29*a* Joel 2:30 (28–32); 2 Ne. 27:2 (1–3).
b 1 Ne. 19:11; D&C 45:41 (40–41).
30*a* Matt. 24:6; 1 Ne. 14:16 (15–17).
31*a* TG Pollution.
b 3 Ne. 16:10; 30:2.
c 2 Ne. 28:21; Alma 1:4; 30:17.
d 2 Ne. 28:8.
e Acts 8:23; Alma 41:11.
f TG Bondage, Spiritual.
32*a* TG Devil, Church of.
33*a* D&C 5:8.
b TG Priestcraft.
c 1 Ne. 13:26 (20–41). TG Apostasy of the Early Christian Church.
d TG Damnation.
e 1 Ne. 14:23 (18–27); Ether 4:16.
36*a* TG Walking in Darkness.
b Jacob 2:13; 3 Ne. 16:10.
c 2 Ne. 28:13 (11–14); Alma 5:53.

and strifes, and malice, and persecutions, and all manner of iniquities; and your churches, yea, even every one, have become polluted because of the pride of your hearts.

37 For behold, ye do love [a]money, and your substance, and your fine apparel, and the adorning of your churches, more than ye love the poor and the needy, the sick and the afflicted.

38 O ye pollutions, ye hypocrites, ye teachers, who sell yourselves for that which will canker, why have ye polluted the holy church of God? Why are ye [a]ashamed to take upon you the name of Christ? Why do ye not think that greater is the value of an endless happiness than that [b]misery which never dies—because of the [c]praise of the world?

39 Why do ye adorn yourselves with that which hath no life, and yet suffer the hungry, and the needy, and the naked, and the sick and the afflicted to pass by you, and notice them not?

40 Yea, why do ye build up your [a]secret abominations to get gain, and cause that widows should mourn before the Lord, and also orphans to mourn before the Lord, and also the blood of their fathers and their husbands to cry unto the Lord from the ground, for vengeance upon your heads?

41 Behold, the sword of vengeance hangeth over you; and the time soon cometh that he avengeth the [a]blood of the saints upon you, for he will not suffer their cries any longer.

CHAPTER 9

Moroni calls upon those who do not believe in Christ to repent—He proclaims a God of miracles, who gives revelations and pours out gifts and signs upon the faithful—Miracles cease because of unbelief—Signs follow those who believe—Men are exhorted to be wise and keep the commandments. About A.D. *401–21.*

AND now, I speak also concerning those who do not believe in Christ.

2 Behold, will ye believe in the day of your visitation—behold, when the Lord shall come, yea, even that [a]great day when the [b]earth shall be rolled together as a scroll, and the elements shall [c]melt with fervent heat, yea, in that great day when ye shall be brought to stand before the Lamb of God—then will ye say that there is no God?

3 Then will ye longer deny the Christ, or can ye behold the Lamb of God? Do ye suppose that ye shall dwell with him under a [a]consciousness of your guilt? Do ye suppose that ye could be happy to dwell with that holy Being, when your souls are racked with a consciousness of guilt that ye have ever abused his laws?

4 Behold, I say unto you that ye would be more miserable to dwell with a holy and just God, under a consciousness of your [a]filthiness before him, than ye would to dwell with the [b]damned souls in [c]hell.

5 For behold, when ye shall be brought to see your [a]nakedness before God, and also the glory of God, and the [b]holiness of Jesus Christ, it will kindle a flame of unquenchable fire upon you.

6 O then ye [a]unbelieving, [b]turn ye unto the Lord; cry mightily unto the Father in the name of Jesus, that perhaps ye may be found spotless,

37*a* Ezek. 34:8; 1 Ne. 13:7; 2 Ne. 28:13 (9–16).
38*a* Rom. 1:16; 2 Tim. 1:8; 1 Ne. 8:25; Alma 46:21.
b Rom. 3:16; Mosiah 3:25.
c 1 Ne. 13:9.
40*a* TG Secret Combinations.
41*a* 1 Ne. 22:14; D&C 136:36.
9 2*a* Mal. 4:5; 3 Ne. 28:31.
b Morm. 5:23; D&C 63:21 (20–21). TG World, End of.
c Amos 9:13; 3 Ne. 26:3.
3*a* TG Conscience; Guilt.
4*a* TG Filthiness.
b TG Damnation.
c TG Hell.
5*a* Ex. 32:25; 2 Ne. 9:14.
b TG Holiness.
6*a* TG Unbelief.
b Ezek. 18:23, 32; D&C 98:47.

[c]pure, fair, and white, having been
cleansed by the blood of the [d]Lamb,
at that great and last day.
7 And again I speak unto you who
[a]deny the revelations of God, and say
that they are done away, that there
are no revelations, nor prophecies,
nor gifts, nor healing, nor speaking
with tongues, and the [b]interpreta-
tion of tongues;
8 Behold I say unto you, he that
denieth these things knoweth not
the [a]gospel of Christ; yea, he has not
read the scriptures; if so, he does
not [b]understand them.
9 For do we not read that God is the
[a]same [b]yesterday, today, and forever,
and in him there is no [c]variableness
neither shadow of changing?
10 And now, if ye have imagined
up unto yourselves a god who doth
vary, and in whom there is shadow
of changing, then have ye imagined
up unto yourselves a god who is not
a God of miracles.
11 But behold, I will show unto you
a God of [a]miracles, even the God
of Abraham, and the God of Isaac,
and the God of Jacob; and it is that
same [b]God who created the heavens
and the earth, and all things that
in them are.
12 Behold, he created Adam, and
by [a]Adam came the [b]fall of man.
And because of the fall of man came
Jesus Christ, even the Father and
the Son; and because of Jesus Christ
came the [c]redemption of man.
13 And because of the redemption of man, which came by Jesus
Christ, they are brought back into
the [a]presence of the Lord; yea, this
is wherein all men are redeemed,
because the death of Christ bringeth
to pass the [b]resurrection, which
bringeth to pass a redemption from
an endless [c]sleep, from which sleep
all men shall be awakened by the
power of God when the trump shall
sound; and they shall come forth,
both small and great, and all shall
stand before his bar, being redeemed and loosed from this eternal [d]band of death, which death is a
temporal death.
14 And then cometh the [a]judgment
of the Holy One upon them; and
then cometh the time that he that
is [b]filthy shall be filthy still; and
he that is righteous shall be righteous still; he that is happy shall be
happy still; and he that is unhappy
shall be unhappy still.
15 And now, O all ye that have
imagined up unto yourselves a god
who can do [a]no miracles, I would
ask of you, have all these things
passed, of which I have spoken? Has
the end come yet? Behold I say unto
you, Nay; and God has not ceased
to be a God of miracles.
16 Behold, are not the things that
God hath wrought marvelous in our
eyes? Yea, and who can comprehend
the marvelous [a]works of God?
17 Who shall say that it was not
a miracle that by his [a]word the
heaven and the earth should be; and
by the power of his word man was
[b]created of the [c]dust of the earth;
and by the power of his word have
miracles been wrought?

6*c* TG Cleanliness; Purification.
d TG Jesus Christ, Lamb of God.
7*a* 3 Ne. 29:6.
b 1 Cor. 12:10; A of F 1:7.
8*a* TG Gospel.
b Matt. 22:29.
9*a* Heb. 13:8; 1 Ne. 10:18 (18–19); Alma 7:20; Moro. 8:18; D&C 20:12.
b TG God, Eternal Nature of.
c TG God, Perfection of.
11*a* TG God, Power of.
b Gen. 1:1; Mosiah 4:2; D&C 76:24 (20–24).
12*a* Mosiah 3:26; Moro. 8:8.
b TG Fall of Man.
c TG Jesus Christ, Redeemer.
13*a* TG God, Presence of.
b Hel. 14:15 (15–18).
c Dan. 12:2; D&C 43:18.
d Alma 36:18; D&C 138:16.
14*a* TG Judgment, the Last.
b Alma 7:21; D&C 88:35.
15*a* Morm. 8:26; Moro. 7:35; D&C 35:8. TG Miracle.
16*a* Ps. 40:5; 92:5; D&C 76:114; Moses 1:4 (3–5).
17*a* Jacob 4:9.
b TG Man, Physical Creation of.
c Gen. 2:7; Mosiah 2:25; D&C 77:12; 93:35 (33–35).

18 And who shall say that Jesus
Christ did not do many mighty
[a]miracles? And there were many
[b]mighty miracles wrought by the
hands of the apostles.
19 And if there were [a]miracles
wrought then, why has God ceased
to be a God of miracles and yet be
an unchangeable Being? And behold, I say unto you he [b]changeth
not; if so he would cease to be God;
and he ceaseth not to be God, and
is a God of miracles.
20 And the reason why he ceaseth
to do [a]miracles among the children
of men is because that they dwindle
in unbelief, and depart from the
right way, and know not the God
in whom they should [b]trust.
21 Behold, I say unto you that
whoso believeth in Christ, doubting
nothing, [a]whatsoever he shall ask
the Father in the name of Christ
it shall be granted him; and this
[b]promise is unto all, even unto the
ends of the earth.
22 For behold, thus said Jesus
Christ, the Son of God, unto his
disciples who should tarry, yea,
and also to [a]all his disciples, in the
hearing of the multitude: Go ye
into all the world, and preach the
gospel to every creature;
23 And he that [a]believeth and is
baptized shall be saved, but he that
believeth not shall be [b]damned;
24 And [a]these signs shall follow
them that believe—in my name
shall they cast out [b]devils; they shall
speak with new tongues; they shall
take up serpents; and if they drink
any deadly thing it shall not hurt
them; they shall lay [c]hands on the
sick and they shall recover;
25 And whosoever shall believe in
my name, doubting nothing, unto
him will I [a]confirm all my words,
even unto the ends of the earth.
26 And now, behold, who can stand
[a]against the works of the Lord?
[b]Who can deny his sayings? Who
will rise up against the almighty
power of the Lord? Who will despise the works of the Lord? Who
will despise the children of Christ?
Behold, all ye who are [c]despisers of
the works of the Lord, for ye shall
wonder and perish.
27 O then despise not, and wonder
not, but hearken unto the words of
the Lord, and ask the Father in the
name of Jesus for what things soever ye shall stand in need. [a]Doubt
not, but be believing, and begin as
in times of old, and [b]come unto the
Lord with all your [c]heart, and [d]work
out your own salvation with fear
and trembling before him.
28 Be [a]wise in the days of your
[b]probation; strip yourselves of all
uncleanness; ask not, that ye may
consume it on your [c]lusts, but ask
with a firmness unshaken, that ye
will yield to no temptation, but
that ye will serve the true and
[d]living God.
29 See that ye are not baptized
[a]unworthily; see that ye partake
not of the sacrament of Christ
[b]unworthily; but see that ye do all

18a John 6:14;
3 Ne. 8:1.
b Mark 6:5.
19a Rom. 15:19 (18–19);
D&C 63:10 (7–10).
b TG God, Perfection of.
20a Judg. 6:13 (11–13);
Ether 12:12 (12–18);
Moro. 7:37.
b TG Trust in God.
21a Matt. 21:22 (18–22);
3 Ne. 18:20.
b TG Promise.
22a Mark 16:15.
TG Missionary Work;
World.
23a Mark 16:16.
b TG Damnation.
24a Mark 16:17 (17–18).
TG Signs.
b Mark 5:15 (15–20);
1 Ne. 11:31.
c TG Administrations to
the Sick;
Hands, Laying on of.
25a TG Testimony.
26a 2 Ne. 26:20; 28:5 (4–6, 15).
b 3 Ne. 29:5 (4–7).
c Prov. 13:13.
27a TG Doubt.
b 3 Ne. 21:20;
Ether 5:5;
Moro. 10:30 (30–32).
c Josh. 22:5;
D&C 64:34 (22, 34).
TG Commitment.
d Philip. 2:12 (12–16).
28a Matt. 10:16;
Jacob 6:12.
b TG Probation.
c TG Covet;
Lust.
d Alma 5:13.
29a TG Baptism,
Qualifications for.
b Lev. 22:3;
1 Cor. 11:27 (27–30);
3 Ne. 18:29 (28–32).

things in [c]worthiness, and do it in the name of Jesus Christ, the Son of the living God; and if ye do this, and endure to the end, ye will in nowise be cast out.
30 Behold, I speak unto you as though I [a]spake from the dead; for I know that ye shall have my words.
31 Condemn me not because of mine [a]imperfection, neither my father, because of his imperfection, neither them who have written before him; but rather give thanks unto God that he hath made manifest unto you our imperfections, that ye may learn to be more wise than we have been.
32 And now, behold, we have written this record according to our knowledge, in the characters which are called among us the [a]reformed Egyptian, being handed down and altered by us, according to our manner of speech.
33 And if our plates had been [a]sufficiently large we should have written in Hebrew; but the Hebrew hath been altered by us also; and if we could have written in Hebrew, behold, ye would have had no [b]imperfection in our record.
34 But the Lord knoweth the things which we have written, and also that none other people knoweth our language; and because that none other people knoweth our language, therefore he hath prepared [a]means for the interpretation thereof.
35 And these things are written that we may rid our garments of the blood of our [a]brethren, who have dwindled in unbelief.
36 And behold, these things which we have [a]desired concerning our brethren, yea, even their restoration to the knowledge of Christ, are according to the prayers of all the saints who have dwelt in the land.
37 And may the Lord Jesus Christ grant that their prayers may be answered according to their faith; and may God the Father remember the covenant which he hath made with the house of Israel; and may he bless them forever, through faith on the name of Jesus Christ. Amen.

THE BOOK OF ETHER

The record of the Jaredites, taken from the twenty-four plates found by the people of Limhi in the days of King Mosiah.

CHAPTER 1

Moroni abridges the writings of Ether—Ether's genealogy is set forth—The language of the Jaredites is not confounded at the Tower of Babel—The Lord promises to lead them to a choice land and make them a great nation.

AND now I, Moroni, proceed to give an [a]account of those ancient inhabitants who were destroyed by the [b]hand of the Lord upon the face of this north country.
2 And I take mine account from the [a]twenty and four plates which

29*c* TG Worthiness.
30*a* Morm. 8:26; Moro. 10:27.
31*a* Morm. 8:17; Ether 12:23 (22–28, 35).
32*a* 1 Ne. 1:2; Mosiah 1:2 (2–4).
33*a* Jarom 1:14 (2, 14).
b 3 Ne. 5:18.
34*a* Mosiah 8:13 (13–18); Ether 3:23 (23, 28); D&C 17:1.
35*a* 2 Ne. 26:15.
36*a* Morm. 5:21; 8:24 (24–26); D&C 10:46 (46–49).

[ETHER]
1 1*a* Mosiah 28:19.
b 1 Sam. 5:9; Morm. 5:23; D&C 87:6 (6–7).
2*a* Alma 37:21 (21–31); Ether 15:33.

were found by the people of Limhi, which is called the Book of Ether.
3 And as I suppose that the [a]first part of this record, which speaks concerning the creation of the world, and also of Adam, and an account from that time even to the great [b]tower, and whatsoever things transpired among the children of men until that time, is had among the Jews—
4 Therefore I do not write those things which transpired from the [a]days of Adam until that time; but they are had upon the plates; and whoso findeth them, the same will have power that he may get the full account.
5 But behold, I give not the full account, but a [a]part of the account I give, from the tower down until they were destroyed.
6 And on this wise do I give the account. He that wrote this record was [a]Ether, and he was a descendant of Coriantor.
7 Coriantor was the son of Moron.
8 And Moron was the son of Ethem.
9 And Ethem was the son of Ahah.
10 And Ahah was the son of Seth.
11 And Seth was the son of Shiblon.
12 And Shiblon was the son of Com.
13 And Com was the son of Coriantum.
14 And Coriantum was the son of Amnigaddah.
15 And Amnigaddah was the son of Aaron.
16 And Aaron was a descendant of Heth, who was the son of Hearthom.
17 And Hearthom was the son of Lib.
18 And Lib was the son of Kish.
19 And Kish was the son of Corom.
20 And Corom was the son of Levi.
21 And Levi was the son of Kim.
22 And Kim was the son of Morianton.
23 And Morianton was a descendant of Riplakish.
24 And Riplakish was the son of Shez.
25 And Shez was the son of Heth.
26 And Heth was the son of Com.
27 And Com was the son of Coriantum.
28 And Coriantum was the son of Emer.
29 And Emer was the son of Omer.
30 And Omer was the son of Shule.
31 And Shule was the son of Kib.
32 And [a]Kib was the son of [b]Orihah, who was the son of Jared;
33 Which [a]Jared came forth with his brother and their families, with some others and their families, from the great tower, at the time the Lord [b]confounded the language of the people, and swore in his wrath that they should be scattered upon all the [c]face of the earth; and according to the word of the Lord the people were scattered.
34 And the [a]brother of Jared being a large and mighty man, and a man highly favored of the Lord, Jared, his brother, said unto him: Cry unto the Lord, that he will not confound us that we may not [b]understand our words.
35 And it came to pass that the brother of Jared did cry unto the Lord, and the Lord had compassion upon Jared; therefore he did not confound the [a]language of Jared; and Jared and his brother were not confounded.
36 Then Jared said unto his brother: Cry again unto the Lord, and it may be that he will turn away his anger from them who are our [a]friends, that he confound not their language.
37 And it came to pass that the brother of Jared did cry unto the Lord, and the Lord had compassion

3a Ether 8:9.
b Gen. 11:4 (1–9); Omni 1:22; Mosiah 28:17; Hel. 6:28.
4a IE covering same period as Genesis 1–10.
5a Ether 3:17; 15:33.
6a Ether 11:23; 12:2; 15:34.
32a Ether 7:3.
b Ether 6:27.
33a Gen. 11:9 (6–9).
b Omni 1:22.
c Mosiah 28:17.
34a Ether 2:13; 6:1.
b TG Communication.
35a Zeph. 3:9; Ether 3:24; Moses 6:6 (5–6).
36a Ether 2:1.

upon their friends and their families
also, that they were not confounded.
38 And it came to pass that Jared
spake again unto his brother, saying: Go and [a]inquire of the Lord
whether he will drive us out of the
land, and if he will drive us out of
the land, cry unto him whither we
shall go. And who knoweth but the
Lord will carry us forth into a land
which is [b]choice above all the earth?
And if it so be, let us be faithful
unto the Lord, that we may receive
it for our inheritance.
39 And it came to pass that the
brother of Jared did cry unto the
Lord according to that which had
been spoken by the mouth of Jared.
40 And it came to pass that the
Lord did hear the brother of Jared,
and [a]had compassion upon him,
and said unto him:
41 Go to and gather together thy
[a]flocks, both male and female, of
every kind; and also of the [b]seed of
the earth of every kind; and [c]thy
[d]families; and also Jared thy brother
and his family; and also thy [e]friends
and their families, and the friends
of Jared and their families.
42 And when thou hast done this
thou shalt [a]go at the head of them
down into the valley which is northward. And there will I meet thee,
and I will go [b]before thee into a
land which is [c]choice above all the
lands of the earth.
43 And there will I bless thee and
thy seed, and raise up unto me of thy
seed, and of the seed of thy brother,
and they who shall go with thee,
a great nation. And [a]there shall be
none [b]greater than the nation which
I will raise up unto me of thy seed,
upon all the face of the earth. And
thus I will do unto thee because this
long time ye have cried unto me.

CHAPTER 2

The Jaredites prepare for their journey to a promised land—It is a choice land whereon men must serve Christ or be swept off—The Lord talks to the brother of Jared for three hours—The Jaredites build barges—The Lord asks the brother of Jared to propose how the barges will be lighted.

AND it came to pass that Jared and
his brother, and their families,
and also the [a]friends of Jared and
his brother and their families, went
down into the valley which was
northward, (and the name of the
valley was [b]Nimrod, being called
after the mighty hunter) with their
[c]flocks which they had gathered together, male and female, of every
kind.
2 And they did also lay snares and
catch [a]fowls of the air; and they
did also prepare a vessel, in which
they did carry with them the fish
of the waters.
3 And they did also carry with
them deseret, which, by interpretation, is a honey bee; and thus they
did carry with them [a]swarms of bees,
and all manner of that which was
upon the face of the land, [b]seeds
of every kind.
4 And it came to pass that when
they had come down into the valley
of Nimrod the Lord came down and
talked with the brother of Jared; and
he was in a [a]cloud, and the brother
of Jared saw him not.
5 And it came to pass that the Lord
commanded them that they should
[a]go forth into the wilderness, yea,

38*a* 2 Chr. 18:4 (4–7).
b 1 Ne. 2:20. TG Lands of Inheritance.
40*a* Ether 3:3.
41*a* Ether 2:1 (1–3).
b 1 Ne. 8:1; 16:11; Ether 9:17.
c Ether 6:20.
d Num. 1:2; Mosiah 6:3; D&C 48:6.
e Ether 6:16.
42*a* Gen. 12:1; Num. 9:17; 1 Ne. 2:2; Ether 2:5; Abr. 2:3.
b Judg. 4:14; D&C 84:88 (87–88).
c 1 Ne. 13:30.
43*a* Gen. 26:3; Deut. 28:8.
b Ether 15:2.
2 1*a* Ether 1:36.
b Gen. 10:8; 1 Chr. 1:10.
c Ether 1:41; 6:4; 9:18 (18–19).
2*a* Gen. 7:3 (1–3).
3*a* 1 Ne. 17:5; 18:6.
b 1 Ne. 16:11.
4*a* Num. 11:25; D&C 34:7 (7–9); JS—H 1:68 (68–71).
5*a* Num. 9:17; Ether 1:42.

into that quarter where there never had man been. And it came to pass that the Lord did go before them, and did talk with them as he stood in a [b]cloud, and gave [c]directions whither they should travel.

6 And it came to pass that they did travel in the wilderness, and did [a]build [b]barges, in which they did cross many waters, being directed continually by the hand of the Lord.

7 And the Lord would not suffer that they should stop beyond the sea in the wilderness, but he would that they should come forth even unto the [a]land of promise, which was choice above all other lands, which the Lord God had [b]preserved for a righteous people.

8 And he had sworn in his wrath unto the brother of Jared, that whoso should possess this land of promise, from that time henceforth and forever, should [a]serve him, the true and only God, or they should be [b]swept off when the fulness of his wrath should come upon them.

9 And now, we can behold the decrees of God concerning this land, that it is a land of promise; and whatsoever nation shall possess it shall serve God, or they shall be [a]swept off when the fulness of his [b]wrath shall come upon them. And the fulness of his wrath cometh upon them when they are [c]ripened in iniquity.

10 For behold, this is a land which is choice above all other lands; wherefore he that doth possess it shall serve God or shall be [a]swept off; for it is the everlasting decree of God. And it is not until the [b]fulness of iniquity among the children of the land, that they are [c]swept off.

11 And this cometh unto you, O ye [a]Gentiles, that ye may know the decrees of God—that ye may repent, and not continue in your iniquities until the fulness come, that ye may not bring down the fulness of the [b]wrath of God upon you as the inhabitants of the land have hitherto done.

12 Behold, this is a choice land, and whatsoever nation shall possess it shall be [a]free from bondage, and from captivity, and from all other nations under heaven, if they will but [b]serve the God of the land, who is Jesus Christ, who hath been manifested by the things which we have written.

13 And now I proceed with my record; for behold, it came to pass that the Lord did bring Jared and his brethren forth even to that great sea which divideth the lands. And as they came to the sea they pitched their tents; and they called the name of the place [a]Moriancumer; and they dwelt in [b]tents, and dwelt in tents upon the seashore for the space of four years.

14 And it came to pass at the end of four years that the Lord came again unto the brother of Jared, and stood in a cloud and [a]talked with him. And for the space of three hours did the Lord talk with the brother of Jared, and [b]chastened him because he remembered not to [c]call upon the name of the Lord.

15 And the brother of Jared repented of the evil which he had done, and did call upon the name of the Lord for his brethren who were with him. And the Lord said unto him: I will forgive thee and thy brethren of their sins; but thou shalt not sin

5*b* Ex. 13:21.
c TG Guidance, Divine.
6*a* TG Skill.
b Gen. 6:14 (14–15); Ether 2:16.
7*a* TG Promised Lands.
b 1 Ne. 4:14.
8*a* Ether 13:2.
b Jarom 1:3 (3, 10); Alma 37:28; Ether 9:20.
9*a* 2 Ne. 6:15.
b TG God, Indignation of.
c Gen. 15:16; 1 Ne. 14:6.
10*a* Jarom 1:12.
b 2 Ne. 28:16.
c 1 Ne. 17:37.
11*a* 1 Ne. 14:6; 2 Ne. 28:32.
b Alma 45:16 (10–14, 16); Morm. 1:17.
12*a* 1 Ne. 13:19. TG Liberty.
b Isa. 60:12.
13*a* Alma 8:7; Ether 1:34.
b Gen. 25:27; Hel. 3:9.
14*a* Ex. 25:22.
b 1 Ne. 16:25. TG Chastening; Reproof.
c TG Prayer.

any more, for ye shall remember that
my [a]Spirit will not always [b]strive
with man; wherefore, if ye will sin
until ye are fully ripe ye shall be cut
off from the presence of the Lord.
And these are my [c]thoughts upon
the land which I shall give you for
your inheritance; for it shall be a
land [d]choice above all other lands.
16 And the Lord said: Go to work
and build, after the manner of
[a]barges which ye have hitherto
built. And it came to pass that the
brother of Jared did go to work, and
also his brethren, and built barges
after the manner which they had
built, according to the [b]instructions
of the Lord. And they were small,
and they were light upon the water, even like unto the lightness of
a fowl upon the water.
17 And they were built after a
manner that they were exceedingly
[a]tight, even that they would hold water like unto a dish; and the bottom
thereof was tight like unto a dish;
and the sides thereof were tight like
unto a dish; and the ends thereof
were peaked; and the top thereof
was tight like unto a dish; and the
length thereof was the length of a
tree; and the door thereof, when
it was shut, was tight like unto
a dish.
18 And it came to pass that the
brother of Jared cried unto the Lord,
saying: O Lord, I have performed the
work which thou hast commanded
me, and I have made the barges according as thou hast directed me.
19 And behold, O Lord, in them
there is no light; whither shall we
steer? And also we shall perish, for
in them we cannot breathe, save it
is the air which is in them; therefore we shall perish.
20 And the Lord said unto the
brother of Jared: Behold, thou shalt
make a hole in the top, and also in
the bottom; and when thou shalt
suffer for air thou shalt unstop the
hole and receive air. And if it be so
that the water come in upon thee,
behold, ye shall stop the hole, that ye
may not perish in the flood.
21 And it came to pass that the
brother of Jared did so, according
as the Lord had commanded.
22 And he cried again unto the
Lord saying: O Lord, behold I have
done even as thou hast commanded
me; and I have prepared the vessels
for my people, and behold there is
no light in them. Behold, O Lord,
wilt thou suffer that we shall cross
this great water in darkness?
23 And the Lord said unto the
brother of Jared: What will ye that
I should do that ye may have light
in your vessels? For behold, ye cannot have [a]windows, for they will be
dashed in pieces; neither shall ye
take fire with you, for ye shall not
go by the light of fire.
24 For behold, ye shall be as a
[a]whale in the midst of the sea; for
the mountain waves shall dash upon
you. Nevertheless, I will bring you
up again out of the depths of the
sea; for the [b]winds have gone forth
[c]out of my mouth, and also the [d]rains
and the floods have I sent forth.
25 And behold, I prepare you
against these things; for ye cannot
cross this great deep save I prepare
you against the waves of the sea, and
the winds which have gone forth,
and the floods which shall come.
Therefore what will ye that I should
prepare for you that ye may have
light when ye are swallowed up in
the depths of the sea?

15*a* TG God, Spirit of.
b Gen. 6:3;
2 Ne. 26:11;
Morm. 5:16;
Moses 8:17.
c TG Earth, Purpose of.
d Ether 9:20.
16*a* Ether 2:6.
b Ex. 25:40;
Prov. 16:9;
1 Ne. 17:51 (50–51).
17*a* Ether 6:7.
23*a* Gen. 6:16.
24*a* Gen. 1:21;
Ether 6:10.
b Ether 6:5.
c Job 37:2 (2–13).
d Ps. 148:8;
D&C 117:1.

CHAPTER 3

The brother of Jared sees the finger of the Lord as He touches sixteen stones—Christ shows His spirit body to the brother of Jared—Those who have a perfect knowledge cannot be kept from within the veil—Interpreters are provided to bring the Jaredite record to light.

AND it came to pass that the brother of Jared, (now the number of the vessels which had been prepared was eight) went forth unto the [a]mount, which they called the mount [b]Shelem, because of its exceeding height, and did [c]molten out of a rock sixteen small stones; and they were white and clear, even as transparent [d]glass; and he did carry them in his hands upon the top of the mount, and cried again unto the Lord, saying:

2 O Lord, thou hast said that we must be encompassed about by the floods. Now behold, O Lord, and do not be [a]angry with thy servant because of his weakness before thee; for we know that thou art holy and dwellest in the heavens, and that we are [b]unworthy before thee; because of the [c]fall our [d]natures have become evil continually; nevertheless, O Lord, thou hast given us a commandment that we must call upon thee, that from thee we may receive according to our desires.

3 Behold, O Lord, thou hast smitten us because of our iniquity, and hast driven us forth, and for these many years we have been in the wilderness; nevertheless, thou hast been [a]merciful unto us. O Lord, look upon me in pity, and turn away thine anger from this thy people, and suffer not that they shall go forth across this raging deep in darkness; but behold these [b]things which I have molten out of the rock.

4 And I know, O Lord, that thou hast all [a]power, and can do whatsoever thou wilt for the benefit of man; therefore touch these stones, O Lord, with thy [b]finger, and prepare them that they may shine forth in darkness; and they shall shine forth unto us in the vessels which we have prepared, that we may have [c]light while we shall cross the sea.

5 Behold, O Lord, thou canst do this. We know that thou art able to show forth great power, which [a]looks small unto the understanding of men.

6 And it came to pass that when the brother of Jared had said these words, behold, the [a]Lord stretched forth his hand and touched the stones one by one with his [b]finger. And the [c]veil was taken from off the eyes of the brother of Jared, and he saw the finger of the Lord; and it was as the finger of a man, like unto flesh and blood; and the brother of Jared [d]fell down before the Lord, for he was struck with [e]fear.

7 And the Lord saw that the brother of Jared had fallen to the earth; and the Lord said unto him: Arise, why hast thou fallen?

8 And he saith unto the Lord: I saw the finger of the Lord, and I feared lest he should [a]smite me; for I knew not that the Lord had flesh and blood.

9 And the Lord said unto him: Because of thy faith thou hast seen that I shall take upon me [a]flesh and blood; and never has man come before me with [b]such exceeding faith as thou hast; for were it not so ye

---

3 1*a* Ex. 24:13 (12–13); Deut. 10:1; 1 Ne. 11:1.
b Ether 4:1.
c TG Skill.
d Rev. 21:21.
2*a* Gen. 18:32 (25–33).
b Moses 1:10.
c TG Fall of Man.
d Mosiah 3:19.
3*a* Ether 1:40 (34–43).
b Ether 6:2 (2–3, 10).
4*a* TG God, Power of.
b Ether 12:20 (19–21).
c TG Light [noun].
5*a* Isa. 55:8 (8–9).
6*a* TG Jesus Christ, Lord.
b Dan. 5:5; Abr. 3:12 (11–12).
c Ether 12:19 (19, 21).
d Ezek. 1:28; Acts 9:4 (3–5).
e Ex. 3:6; JS—H 1:32.
8*a* Moses 1:11.
9*a* TG Flesh and Blood; Jesus Christ, Condescension of.
b Matt. 8:10; Alma 19:10.

could not have seen my finger. Saw-
est thou more than this?
10 And he answered: Nay; Lord,
[a]show thyself unto me.
11 And the Lord said unto him:
[a]Believest thou the words which I
shall speak?
12 And he answered: Yea, Lord, I
know that thou speakest the truth,
for thou art a God of truth, and
[a]canst not lie.
13 And when he had said these
words, behold, the Lord [a]showed
himself unto him, and said: [b]Be-
cause thou knowest these things ye
are redeemed from the fall; therefore ye are brought back into my
[c]presence; therefore I [d]show myself
unto you.
14 Behold, I am he who was [a]pre-
pared from the foundation of the
world to [b]redeem my people. Behold,
I am Jesus Christ. I am the [c]Father
and the Son. In me shall all mankind have [d]life, and that eternally,
even they who shall believe on my
name; and they shall become my
[e]sons and my daughters.
15 And never have I [a]showed myself unto man whom I have created,
for never has man [b]believed in me
as thou hast. Seest thou that ye are
created after mine own [c]image? Yea,
even all men were created in the
beginning after mine own image.
16 Behold, this [a]body, which ye
now [b]behold, is the [c]body of my
[d]spirit; and man have I created after the body of my spirit; and even
as I appear unto thee to be in the
spirit will I appear unto my people
in the flesh.
17 And now, as I, Moroni, said I
could [a]not make a full account of
these things which are written,
therefore it sufficeth me to say
that Jesus showed himself unto
this man in the spirit, even after
the manner and in the likeness of
the same body even as he [b]showed
himself unto the Nephites.
18 And he ministered unto him
even as he ministered unto the
Nephites; and all this, that this man
might know that he was God, because
of the many great works which the
Lord had showed unto him.
19 And because of the [a]knowledge
of this man he could not be kept
from beholding within the [b]veil; and
he saw the finger of Jesus, which,
when he saw, he fell with fear; for
he knew that it was the finger of
the Lord; and he had [c]faith no longer, for he knew, nothing [d]doubting.
20 Wherefore, having this perfect
knowledge of God, he could [a]not be
kept from within the veil; therefore
he [b]saw Jesus; and he did minister
unto him.
21 And it came to pass that the
Lord said unto the brother of Jared:
Behold, thou shalt not suffer these
things which ye have seen and heard
to go forth unto the world, until the
[a]time cometh that I shall glorify my
name in the flesh; wherefore, ye
shall [b]treasure up the things which
ye have seen and heard, and show
it to no man.

10*a* Ex. 33:18 (17–18).
11*a* 1 Ne. 11:4 (4–5).
12*a* Num. 23:19; Heb. 6:18.
13*a* 1 Sam. 3:21; D&C 67:11 (11–12).
b Enos 1:8 (6–8).
c TG God, Presence of; God, Privilege of Seeing.
d TG Jesus Christ, Appearances, Antemortal.
14*a* TG Jesus Christ, Foreordained.
b TG Jesus Christ, Redeemer.
c Mosiah 15:2.
d Mosiah 16:9; D&C 88:13 (7–13).
e TG Sons and Daughters of God.
15*a* Ex. 3:6; 33:20 (11–23); John 1:18; D&C 107:54; Moses 1:2. TG God, Privilege of Seeing.
b TG Faith.
c Gen. 1:26 (26–28); Mosiah 7:27; D&C 20:18 (17–18). TG God, Body of, Corporeal Nature.
16*a* TG God, Manifestations of.
b D&C 17:1.
c TG Spirit Body.
d TG Man, Antemortal Existence of.
17*a* Ether 1:5; 15:33.
b 3 Ne. 11:8 (8–16).
19*a* TG Knowledge.
b TG Veil.
c Alma 32:34.
d TG Doubt.
20*a* Ether 12:21 (19–21).
b TG Jesus Christ, Appearances, Antemortal.
21*a* Ether 4:1.
b Luke 2:19 (17–20).

22 And behold, when ye shall come
unto me, ye shall write them and
shall seal them up, that no one can
interpret them; for ye shall write
them in a [a]language that they cannot be read.
23 And behold, these [a]two stones
will I give unto thee, and ye shall
seal them up also with the things
which ye shall write.
24 For behold, the [a]language which
ye shall write I have confounded;
wherefore I will cause in my own
due time that these stones shall
magnify to the eyes of men these
things which ye shall write.
25 And when the Lord had said
these words, he [a]showed unto the
brother of Jared [b]all the inhabitants of the earth which had been,
and also all that would be; and he
[c]withheld them not from his sight,
even unto the ends of the earth.
26 For he had said unto him in
times before, that [a]if he would [b]be-
lieve in him that he could show unto
him [c]all things—it should be shown
unto him; therefore the Lord could
not withhold anything from him,
for he knew that the Lord could
show him all things.
27 And the Lord said unto him:
Write these things and [a]seal them
up; and I will show them in mine
own due time unto the children of
men.
28 And it came to pass that the
Lord commanded him that he
should seal up the two [a]stones which
he had received, and show them not,
until the Lord should show them
unto the children of [b]men.

CHAPTER 4

Moroni is commanded to seal up the writings of the brother of Jared—They will not be revealed until men have faith even as the brother of Jared—Christ commands men to believe His words and those of His disciples—Men are commanded to repent, believe the gospel, and be saved.

AND the Lord commanded the
brother of Jared to go down out of
the [a]mount from the presence of the
Lord, and [b]write the things which
he had seen; and they were forbidden to come unto the children of
men [c]until after that he should be
lifted up upon the cross; and for this
cause did king Mosiah keep them,
that they should not come unto the
world until after Christ should show
himself unto his people.
2 And after Christ truly had showed
himself unto his people he commanded that they should be made
manifest.
3 And now, after that, they have
all dwindled in unbelief; and there
is [a]none save it be the Lamanites,
and they have rejected the gospel of
Christ; therefore I am commanded
that I should [b]hide them up again
in the earth.
4 Behold, I have written upon these
plates the [a]very things which the
brother of Jared saw; and there never
were [b]greater things made manifest than those which were made
manifest unto the brother of Jared.
5 Wherefore the Lord hath commanded me to write them; and I have
written them. And he commanded

22*a* Mosiah 8:11 (11–12). TG Language.
23*a* Mosiah 8:13 (13–18); Morm. 9:34; D&C 17:1. TG Urim and Thummim.
24*a* Ether 1:35.
25*a* 2 Ne. 27:7. TG God, Omniscience of; Revelation.
b Moses 1:8.
c Luke 24:16 (10–24); D&C 25:4.
26*a* Ether 3:11–13.
b TG Believe.
c 2 Ne. 27:7 (7–8, 10–11); Mosiah 8:19; Ether 4:4 (1–8).
27*a* 2 Ne. 27:7 (6–23).
28*a* D&C 17:1.
b 2 Ne. 3:6; 3 Ne. 21:11 (8–11); Morm. 8:16 (16, 25).
4 1*a* Ether 3:1.
b Ether 12:24. TG Record Keeping; Scriptures, Writing of.
c Ether 3:21.
3*a* Morm. 8:3 (2–3).
b Morm. 8:14. TG Scriptures, Preservation of.
4*a* Ether 5:1.
b 2 Ne. 27:7 (7–8, 10–11); Mosiah 8:19; Ether 3:26 (21–28).

me that I should [a]seal them up;
and he also hath commanded that
I should seal up the interpretation
thereof; wherefore I have sealed up
the [b]interpreters, according to the
commandment of the Lord.
6 For the Lord said unto me: They
shall not go forth unto the Gentiles
until the day that they shall repent
of their iniquity, and become clean
before the Lord.
7 And in that day that they shall
exercise [a]faith in me, saith the Lord,
even as the brother of Jared did, that
they may become [b]sanctified in me,
then will I [c]manifest unto them the
things which the brother of Jared
saw, even to the unfolding unto
them all my [d]revelations, saith Jesus
Christ, the Son of God, the [e]Father
of the heavens and of the earth, and
all things that in them are.
8 And he that will [a]contend against
the word of the Lord, let him be
accursed; and he that shall [b]deny
these things, let him be accursed;
for unto them will I show [c]no greater
things, saith Jesus Christ; for I am
he who speaketh.
9 And at my command the heavens are opened and are [a]shut; and
at my word the [b]earth shall shake;
and at my command the inhabitants
thereof shall pass away, even so as
by fire.
10 And he that believeth not my
words believeth not my disciples;
and if it so be that I do not speak,
judge ye; for ye shall know that it
is I that speaketh, at the [a]last day.
11 But he that [a]believeth these
things which I have spoken, him
will I visit with the manifestations
of my Spirit, and he shall [b]know
and bear record. For because of
my Spirit he shall [c]know that these
things are [d]true; for it persuadeth
men to do good.
12 And whatsoever thing persuadeth men to do good is of me; for
[a]good cometh of none save it be of
me. I am the same that leadeth men
to all good; he that will [b]not believe
my words will not believe me—that
I am; and he that will not believe me
will not believe the Father who sent
me. For behold, I am the Father, I
am the [c]light, and the [d]life, and the
[e]truth of the world.
13 [a]Come unto me, O ye Gentiles,
and I will show unto you the greater
things, the knowledge which is hid
up because of unbelief.
14 Come unto me, O ye house of
Israel, and it shall be made [a]mani-
fest unto you how great things the
Father hath laid up for you, from
the foundation of the world; and it
hath not come unto you, because of
unbelief.
15 Behold, when ye shall rend that
veil of unbelief which doth cause
you to remain in your awful state of
wickedness, and hardness of heart,
and blindness of mind, then shall
the great and marvelous things
which have been [a]hid up from the
foundation of the world from you—
yea, when ye shall [b]call upon the
Father in my name, with a broken
heart and a contrite spirit, then
shall ye know that the Father hath

5a Dan. 12:9; 3 Ne. 26:9 (7–12, 18); Ether 5:1; D&C 17:6; 35:18; JS—H 1:65.
b Morm. 6:6; D&C 17:1; JS—H 1:52. TG Urim and Thummim.
7a D&C 5:28.
b TG Sanctification.
c 2 Ne. 30:16; Alma 12:9; 3 Ne. 26:10 (6–11).
d 2 Ne. 27:22.
e Mosiah 3:8.
8a Job 9:3 (1–4); 3 Ne. 29:5 (1–9); Morm. 8:17.
b 2 Ne. 27:14; 28:29 (29–31); 3 Ne. 28:34.
c Alma 12:10 (10–11); 3 Ne. 26:10 (9–10).
9a 1 Kgs. 8:35; D&C 77:8.
b Hel. 12:11 (8–18); Morm. 5:23.
10a 2 Ne. 25:22; 33:15 (10–15); 3 Ne. 27:25 (23–27).
11a D&C 5:16.
b 2 Ne. 32:5; 3 Ne. 16:6.
c TG Testimony.
d Alma 3:12; Ether 5:3 (1–4); Moro. 10:4 (1–5).
12a Omni 1:25; Alma 5:40; Moro. 7:16 (12–17).
b 3 Ne. 11:35; 28:34.
c TG Jesus Christ, Light of the World.
d Col. 3:4.
e Alma 38:9.
13a 3 Ne. 12:2 (2–3).
14a D&C 121:26 (26–29).
15a 2 Ne. 27:10.
b Gen. 4:26; Moro. 2:2.

remembered the covenant which
he made unto your fathers, O house
of Israel.
16 And then shall my [a]revelations
which I have caused to be written
by my servant John be unfolded in
the eyes of all the people. Remember, when ye see these things, ye
shall know that the time is at hand
that they shall be made manifest in
very deed.
17 Therefore, [a]when ye shall receive this record ye may know that
the work of the Father has commenced upon all the face of the land.
18 Therefore, [a]repent all ye ends
of the earth, and come unto me,
and believe in my gospel, and be
[b]baptized in my name; for he that
believeth and is baptized shall be
saved; but he that believeth not shall
be damned; and [c]signs shall follow
them that believe in my name.
19 And blessed is he that is found
[a]faithful unto my name at the last
day, for he shall be [b]lifted up to
dwell in the kingdom prepared for
him [c]from the foundation of the
world. And behold it is I that hath
spoken it. Amen.

CHAPTER 5

Three witnesses and the work itself will stand as a testimony of the truthfulness of the Book of Mormon.

AND now I, Moroni, have written
the words which were commanded
me, according to my memory; and
I have told you the things which I
have [a]sealed up; therefore touch
them not in order that ye may
translate; for that thing is forbidden
you, except by and by it shall be
wisdom in God.
2 And behold, ye may be privileged that ye may show the plates
unto [a]those who shall assist to bring
forth this work;
3 And unto [a]three shall they be
shown by the power of God; wherefore they shall [b]know of a surety
that these things are [c]true.
4 And in the mouth of three [a]wit-
nesses shall these things be established; and the [b]testimony of three,
and this work, in the which shall be
shown forth the power of God and
also his word, of which the Father,
and the Son, and the Holy Ghost
bear record—and all this shall stand
as a testimony against the world at
the last day.
5 And if it so be that they repent
and [a]come unto the Father in the
name of Jesus, they shall be received
into the kingdom of God.
6 And now, if I have no authority
for these things, judge ye; for ye shall
know that I have authority when
ye shall see me, and we shall stand
before God at the last day. Amen.

CHAPTER 6

The Jaredite barges are driven by the winds to the promised land—The people praise the Lord for His goodness—Orihah is appointed king over them—Jared and his brother die.

AND now I, Moroni, proceed to give
the record of [a]Jared and his brother.
2 For it came to pass after the Lord
had prepared the [a]stones which
the brother of Jared had carried up
into the mount, the brother of Jared

16*a* Rev. 1:1;
1 Ne. 14:23 (18–27).
17*a* 3 Ne. 21:2 (1–11, 28).
18*a* 3 Ne. 27:20;
Moro. 7:34.
b John 3:5 (3–5).
TG Baptism, Essential.
c TG Holy Ghost, Gifts of.
19*a* Ps. 31:23;
Mosiah 2:41;
D&C 6:13; 63:47.
TG Jesus Christ, Taking the Name of.
b Morm. 2:19.
c 2 Ne. 9:18;
Alma 42:26;
Ether 3:14.
5 1*a* 2 Ne. 27:8 (7–11, 21);
Ether 4:5 (4–7);
D&C 17:6.
2*a* 2 Ne. 27:14 (13–14);
D&C 5:15 (1–16).
3*a* 2 Ne. 11:3; 27:12 (12–14);
D&C 17:3 (3–5).
b D&C 5:25.
c Ether 4:11 (6–11);
Moro. 10:4 (1–4).
4*a* 2 Ne. 27:12 (12–14);
D&C 14:8; 17:1.
b 2 Ne. 25:18; 29:11.
5*a* Morm. 9:27;
Moro. 10:30 (30–32).
6 1*a* Ether 1:34.
2*a* Ether 3:3.

came down out of the mount, and
he did put forth the stones into the
vessels which were prepared, one
in each end thereof; and behold,
they did give light unto the vessels.
3 And thus the Lord caused stones
to shine in darkness, to give light
unto men, women, and children, that
they might not cross the great waters
in darkness.
4 And it came to pass that when
they had prepared all manner of
[a]food, that thereby they might subsist upon the water, and also food for
their flocks and herds, and [b]what-
soever beast or animal or fowl that
they should carry with them—and
it came to pass that when they had
done all these things they got aboard
of their vessels or barges, and set
forth into the sea, commending
themselves unto the Lord their God.
5 And it came to pass that the Lord
God caused that there should be a
[a]furious wind blow upon the face
of the waters, [b]towards the promised land; and thus they were tossed
upon the waves of the sea before
the wind.
6 And it came to pass that they
were many times buried in the
depths of the sea, because of the
mountain waves which broke upon
them, and also the great and terrible tempests which were caused by
the fierceness of the wind.
7 And it came to pass that when
they were buried in the deep there
was no water that could hurt them,
their vessels being [a]tight like unto
a dish, and also they were tight
like unto the [b]ark of Noah; therefore when they were encompassed
about by many waters they did cry
unto the Lord, and he did bring
them forth again upon the top of
the waters.
8 And it came to pass that the wind
did never cease to blow towards
the promised land while they were
upon the waters; and thus they were
[a]driven forth before the wind.
9 And they did [a]sing praises unto
the Lord; yea, the brother of Jared
did sing praises unto the Lord, and
he did [b]thank and praise the Lord
all the day long; and when the night
came, they did not cease to praise
the Lord.
10 And thus they were driven forth;
and no monster of the sea could
break them, neither [a]whale that
could mar them; and they did have
light continually, whether it was
above the water or under the water.
11 And thus they were driven
forth, [a]three hundred and forty and
four days upon the water.
12 And they did [a]land upon the
shore of the [b]promised land. And
when they had set their feet upon
the shores of the promised land they
bowed themselves down upon the
face of the land, and did humble
themselves before the Lord, and did
shed tears of joy before the Lord,
because of the multitude of his
[c]tender mercies over them.
13 And it came to pass that they
went forth upon the face of the
land, and began to till the earth.
14 And Jared had four [a]sons; and
they were called Jacom, and Gilgah,
and Mahah, and Orihah.
15 And the brother of Jared also
begat sons and daughters.
16 And the [a]friends of Jared and
his brother were in number about
twenty and two souls; and they
also begat sons and daughters before they came to the promised
land; and therefore they began to
be many.
17 And they were taught to [a]walk

4*a* TG Food.
b Ether 2:1; 9:18 (18–19).
5*a* Ether 2:24 (24–25).
b 1 Ne. 18:8.
7*a* Ether 2:17.
b Gen. 6:14; Moses 7:43.
8*a* 1 Ne. 18:13 (8–13).
9*a* TG Singing.
b 1 Chr. 16:8 (7–36); Ps. 34:1 (1–3); Alma 37:37; D&C 46:32.
10*a* Gen. 1:21; Ether 2:24.
11*a* Gen. 7:11; 8:13.
12*a* Ether 7:16.
b Alma 22:30 (29–34); Ether 7:6.
c Ether 7:27; 10:2.
14*a* Ether 6:27.
16*a* Ether 1:41.
17*a* TG Walking with God.

humbly before the Lord; and they were also [b]taught from on high.

18 And it came to pass that they began to spread upon the face of the land, and to multiply and to till the earth; and they did wax strong in the land.

19 And the brother of Jared began to be old, and saw that he must soon go down to the grave; wherefore he said unto Jared: Let us gather together our people that we may number them, that we may know of them what they will desire of us before we go down to our graves.

20 And accordingly the people were gathered together. Now the number of the sons and the daughters of the brother of Jared were twenty and two souls; and the number of sons and daughters of Jared were twelve, he having four sons.

21 And it came to pass that they did number their people; and after that they had numbered them, they did desire of them the things which they would that they should do before they went down to their graves.

22 And it came to pass that the people desired of them that they should [a]anoint one of their sons to be a king over them.

23 And now behold, this was grievous unto them. And the brother of Jared said unto them: Surely this thing [a]leadeth into captivity.

24 But Jared said unto his brother: Suffer them that they may have a king. And therefore he said unto them: Choose ye out from among our sons a king, even whom ye will.

25 And it came to pass that they chose even the firstborn of the brother of Jared; and his name was Pagag. And it came to pass that he refused and would not be their [a]king. And the people would that his father should constrain him, but his father would not; and he commanded them that they should constrain no man to be their king.

26 And it came to pass that they chose all the brothers of Pagag, and they would not.

27 And it came to pass that neither would the [a]sons of Jared, even all save it were one; and [b]Orihah was anointed to be king over the people.

28 And he began to reign, and the people began to [a]prosper; and they became exceedingly rich.

29 And it came to pass that Jared died, and his brother also.

30 And it came to pass that Orihah did walk humbly before the Lord, and did remember how great things the Lord had done for his father, and also taught his people how great things the Lord had done for their fathers.

CHAPTER 7

Orihah reigns in righteousness—Amid usurpation and strife, the rival kingdoms of Shule and Cohor are set up—Prophets condemn the wickedness and idolatry of the people, who then repent.

AND it came to pass that Orihah did execute judgment upon the land in righteousness all his days, whose days were exceedingly many.

2 And he begat sons and daughters; yea, he begat thirty and one, among whom were twenty and three sons.

3 And it came to pass that he also begat [a]Kib in his [b]old age. And it came to pass that Kib reigned in his stead; and Kib begat Corihor.

4 And when Corihor was thirty and two years old he rebelled against his father, and went over and dwelt in the land of Nehor; and he begat sons and daughters, and they became exceedingly fair; wherefore Corihor drew away many people after him.

5 And when he had gathered together an army he came up unto the

---

17*b* TG Guidance, Divine; Revelation.
22*a* TG Anointing.
23*a* 1 Sam. 8:11 (10–18); Mosiah 29:18 (16–23); Ether 7:5.
25*a* TG Kings, Earthly.
27*a* Ether 6:14.
b Ether 1:32.
28*a* TG Prosper.

7 3*a* Ether 1:32 (31–32).
b Gen. 18:12 (11–12); Ether 7:26; 9:23.

land of [a]Moron where the king
dwelt, and took him captive, which
[b]brought to pass the saying of the
brother of Jared that they would
be brought into captivity.
6 Now the [a]land of Moron, where
the king dwelt, was near the land
which is called Desolation by the
Nephites.
7 And it came to pass that Kib
dwelt in [a]captivity, and his people
under Corihor his son, until he became exceedingly old; nevertheless
Kib begat Shule in his old age, while
he was yet in captivity.
8 And it came to pass that Shule
was angry with his brother; and
Shule waxed strong, and became
mighty as to the strength of a man;
and he was also mighty in judgment.
9 Wherefore, he came to the hill
Ephraim, and he did molten out of
the hill, and made swords out of
[a]steel for those whom he had drawn
away with him; and after he had
armed them with swords he returned
to the city Nehor, and gave battle
unto his brother Corihor, by which
means he obtained the kingdom
and restored it unto his father Kib.
10 And now because of the thing
which Shule had done, his father
bestowed upon him the kingdom;
therefore he began to reign in the
stead of his father.
11 And it came to pass that he did
execute judgment in righteousness;
and he did spread his kingdom upon
all the face of the land, for the people
had become exceedingly numerous.
12 And it came to pass that Shule
also begat many sons and daughters.
13 And Corihor repented of the
many evils which he had done;
wherefore Shule gave him power
in his kingdom.
14 And it came to pass that Corihor
had many sons and daughters. And
among the sons of Corihor there was
one whose name was Noah.
15 And it came to pass that Noah
rebelled against Shule, the king, and
also his father Corihor, and drew
away Cohor his brother, and also all
his brethren and many of the people.
16 And he gave battle unto Shule,
the king, in which he did obtain the
land of their [a]first inheritance; and
he became a king over that part of
the land.
17 And it came to pass that he gave
battle again unto Shule, the king;
and he took Shule, the king, and carried him away captive into Moron.
18 And it came to pass as he was
about to put him to death, the sons
of Shule crept into the house of
Noah by night and slew him, and
broke down the door of the prison
and brought out their father, and
placed him upon his throne in his
own kingdom.
19 Wherefore, the son of Noah did
build up his kingdom in his stead;
nevertheless they did not gain power
any more over Shule the king, and
the people who were under the
reign of Shule the king did prosper
exceedingly and wax great.
20 And the country was [a]divided;
and there were two kingdoms, the
kingdom of Shule, and the kingdom
of Cohor, the son of Noah.
21 And Cohor, the son of Noah,
caused that his people should give
battle unto Shule, in which Shule
did beat them and did slay Cohor.
22 And now Cohor had a son who
was called Nimrod; and Nimrod
gave up the kingdom of Cohor unto
Shule, and he did gain favor in the
eyes of Shule; wherefore Shule did
bestow great favors upon him, and
he did do in the kingdom of Shule
according to his desires.
23 And also in the reign of Shule
there came [a]prophets among the people, who were sent from the Lord,
prophesying that the wickedness and
[b]idolatry of the people was bringing a
curse upon the land, and they should
be destroyed if they did not repent.

5*a* Ether 14:6 (6, 11).
b Ether 6:23.
6*a* Ether 6:12.
7*a* Ether 8:4 (3–4); 10:14.
9*a* 1 Ne. 16:18.
16*a* Ether 6:12.
20*a* 2 Ne. 5:7 (1–14).
23*a* Ether 9:28; 11:1 (1, 12, 20).
b TG Idolatry.

24 And it came to pass that the people did [a]revile against the prophets,
and did mock them. And it came
to pass that king Shule did execute
judgment against all those who did
revile against the prophets.
25 And he did execute a law
throughout all the land, which
gave power unto the prophets that
they should go whithersoever they
would; and by this cause the people were brought unto repentance.
26 And because the people did repent of their iniquities and idolatries the Lord did spare them, and
they began to prosper again in the
land. And it came to pass that Shule
[a]begat sons and daughters in his
old age.
27 And there were no more wars
in the days of Shule; and he remembered the great things that the Lord
had done for his fathers in bringing
them [a]across the great deep into the
promised land; wherefore he did
execute judgment in righteousness
all his days.

CHAPTER 8

There is strife and contention over the kingdom—Akish forms an oath-bound secret combination to slay the king—Secret combinations are of the devil and result in the destruction of nations—Modern Gentiles are warned against the secret combination that will seek to overthrow the freedom of all lands, nations, and countries.

AND it came to pass that he begat
Omer, and Omer reigned in his stead.
And Omer begat Jared; and Jared
begat sons and daughters.
2 And Jared rebelled against his
father, and came and dwelt in the
land of Heth. And it came to pass
that he did [a]flatter many people, because of his cunning words, until he
had gained the half of the kingdom.
3 And when he had gained the half
of the kingdom he gave battle unto
his father, and he did carry away
his father into captivity, and did
make him serve in captivity;
4 And now, in the days of the
reign of Omer he was in [a]captivity
the half of his days. And it came to
pass that he begat sons and daughters, among whom were Esrom and
Coriantumr;
5 And they were exceedingly angry because of the doings of Jared
their brother, insomuch that they
did raise an army and gave battle
unto Jared. And it came to pass
that they did give battle unto him
by night.
6 And it came to pass that when
they had slain the army of Jared
they were about to slay him also;
and he pled with them that they
would not slay him, and he would
give up the kingdom unto his father.
And it came to pass that they did
grant unto him his life.
7 And now Jared became exceedingly [a]sorrowful because of the loss
of the kingdom, for he had set his
heart upon the kingdom and upon
the glory of the world.
8 Now the daughter of Jared being
exceedingly expert, and seeing the
sorrows of her father, thought to
devise a plan whereby she could redeem the kingdom unto her father.
9 Now the daughter of Jared was
exceedingly fair. And it came to pass
that she did talk with her father,
and said unto him: Whereby hath
my father so much sorrow? Hath
he not read the [a]record which our
fathers brought across the great
deep? Behold, is there not an [b]ac-
count concerning them of [c]old, that
they by their [d]secret plans did
obtain kingdoms and great glory?
10 And now, therefore, let my
father send for Akish, the son of

24*a* Mosiah 27:2 (1–3).
TG Prophets, Rejection of; Reviling.
26*a* Ether 7:3 (3, 7); 9:23.
27*a* Ether 6:12 (1–12).

8 2*a* Hel. 1:7; 2:5.
4*a* Ether 7:7 (5–7); 10:14.
7*a* Morm. 2:13.
9*a* Ether 1:3.
b 3 Ne. 6:28.
c Hel. 6:26 (26–30); 3 Ne. 3:9.
d Hel. 6:27; Ether 13:18; Moses 5:30 (18–52).

Kimnor; and behold, I am fair, and
I will dance before him, and I will
please him, that he will desire me
to wife; wherefore if he shall desire
of thee that ye shall give unto him
me to wife, then shall ye say: I will
give her if ye will bring unto me
the [a]head of my father, the king.
11 And now Omer was a friend
to Akish; wherefore, when Jared
had sent for Akish, the daughter
of Jared danced before him that
she pleased him, insomuch that he
desired her to wife. And it came to
pass that he said unto Jared: Give
her unto me to wife.
12 And Jared said unto him: I will
give her unto you, if ye will bring
unto me the head of my father, the
king.
13 And it came to pass that Akish
gathered in unto the house of Jared
all his kinsfolk, and said unto them:
Will ye swear unto me that ye will
be faithful unto me in the thing
which I shall desire of you?
14 And it came to pass that they
all [a]sware unto him, by the God of
heaven, and also by the heavens,
and also by the earth, and by their
heads, that whoso should vary from
the assistance which Akish desired
should lose his head; and whoso
should divulge whatsoever thing
Akish made known unto them, the
same should lose his life.
15 And it came to pass that thus
they did agree with [a]Akish. And
Akish did administer unto them the
oaths which were given by them of
old who also sought power, which
had been handed down even from
[b]Cain, who was a murderer from
the beginning.
16 And they were kept up by the
[a]power of the devil to administer
these oaths unto the people, to keep
them in darkness, to help such as
sought power to gain power, and to
murder, and to plunder, and to lie,
and to commit all manner of wickedness and whoredoms.
17 And it was the daughter of
Jared who put it into his heart to
search up these things of old; and
Jared put it into the heart of Akish;
wherefore, Akish administered it
unto his kindred and friends, leading them away by fair promises to
do whatsoever thing he desired.
18 And it came to pass that they
formed a [a]secret combination, even
as they of old; which combination is
most abominable and wicked above
all, in the sight of God;
19 For the Lord worketh not in secret combinations, neither doth he
will that man should shed blood,
but in all things hath forbidden it,
from the beginning of man.
20 And now I, Moroni, do not write
the manner of their oaths and combinations, for it hath been made
known unto me that they are had
[a]among all people, and they are
had among the Lamanites.
21 And they have caused the [a]de-
struction of this people of whom I
am now speaking, and also the destruction of the people of Nephi.
22 And whatsoever [a]nation shall
uphold such secret combinations,
to get power and gain, until they
shall spread over the nation, behold,
they shall be destroyed; for the Lord
will not suffer that the [b]blood of his
saints, which shall be shed by them,
shall always cry unto him from the
ground for [c]vengeance upon them
and yet he avenge them not.
23 Wherefore, O ye Gentiles, it is
wisdom in God that these things
should be shown unto you, that
thereby ye may repent of your sins,
and suffer not that these murderous
combinations shall get above you,

10*a* Mark 6:24 (22–28).
14*a* Hel. 1:11;
3 Ne. 3:8.
TG Swearing.
15*a* Ether 9:1.
b Gen. 4:7 (7–8);
Moses 5:25.
16*a* Moses 4:6; 5:13.
18*a* TG Secret Combinations.
20*a* 4 Ne. 1:46;
Morm. 2:8; 8:9.
21*a* Hel. 6:28;
D&C 38:13 (13–16).
22*a* TG Governments.
b Rev. 6:10 (1–11); 19:2;
2 Ne. 28:10;
Morm. 8:27 (27, 40–41);
D&C 87:7.
c TG God, Justice of;
Vengeance.

which are built up to get [a]power and
gain—and the work, yea, even the
work of [b]destruction come upon you,
yea, even the sword of the justice of
the Eternal God shall fall upon you,
to your overthrow and destruction
if ye shall suffer these things to be.
24 Wherefore, the Lord commandeth you, when ye shall see these
things come among you that ye
shall awake to a sense of your awful situation, because of this [a]secret
combination which shall be among
you; or wo be unto it, because of
the blood of them who have been
slain; for they cry from the dust for
vengeance upon it, and also upon
those who built it up.
25 For it cometh to pass that whoso
buildeth it up seeketh to overthrow
the [a]freedom of all lands, nations,
and countries; and it bringeth to
pass the destruction of all people,
for it is built up by the devil, who is
the father of all lies; even that same
liar who [b]beguiled our first parents,
yea, even that same liar who hath
caused man to commit murder from
the beginning; who hath [c]hardened
the hearts of men that they have
[d]murdered the prophets, and stoned
them, and cast them out from the
beginning.
26 Wherefore, I, Moroni, am commanded to write these things that
evil may be done away, and that
the time may come that Satan may
have [a]no power upon the hearts of
the children of men, but that they
may be [b]persuaded to do good continually, that they may come unto
the fountain of all [c]righteousness
and be saved.

CHAPTER 9

The kingdom passes from one to another by descent, intrigue, and murder—Emer saw the Son of Righteousness—Many prophets cry repentance—A famine and poisonous serpents plague the people.

AND now I, Moroni, proceed with my record. Therefore, behold, it came to pass that because of the [a]secret combinations of Akish and his friends, behold, they did overthrow the kingdom of Omer.
2 Nevertheless, the Lord was mer-
ciful unto Omer, and also to his sons
and to his daughters who did not
seek his destruction.
3 And the Lord [a]warned Omer
in a dream that he should depart
out of the land; wherefore Omer
[b]departed out of the land with his
family, and traveled many days, and
came over and passed by the hill of
[c]Shim, and came over by the place
[d]where the Nephites were destroyed,
and from thence eastward, and
came to a place which was called
Ablom, by the seashore, and there
he pitched his tent, and also his
sons and his daughters, and all his
household, save it were Jared and
his family.
4 And it came to pass that Jared
was anointed king over the people,
by the hand of wickedness; and he
gave unto Akish his daughter to wife.
5 And it came to pass that Akish
[a]sought the life of his father-in-law;
and he applied unto those whom
he had sworn by the [b]oath of the
ancients, and they obtained the
head of his father-in-law, as he sat
upon his throne, giving audience
to his people.
6 For so great had been the spreading of this wicked and secret society
that it had corrupted the hearts of
all the people; therefore Jared was
murdered upon his throne, and
Akish reigned in his stead.

23*a* Moses 6:15.
b Luke 13:3 (1–5).
24*a* D&C 42:64.
25*a* TG Liberty.
b Gen. 3:13 (1–13); 2 Ne. 9:9; Mosiah 16:3; Moses 4:19 (5–19).
c TG Hardheartedness.
d TG Prophets, Rejection of.
26*a* 2 Ne. 30:18.
b 2 Ne. 33:4; Moro. 7:13 (12–17).
c TG Righteousness.
9 1*a* Ether 8:15 (13–17).
3*a* TG Dream; Warn.
b Ether 9:13.
c Morm. 1:3; 4:23.
d Morm. 6:2 (1–15).
5*a* Esth. 2:21.
b TG Oath.

7 And it came to pass that Akish
began to be [a]jealous of his son,
therefore he shut him up in prison,
and kept him upon little or no food
until he had suffered death.
8 And now the brother of him that
suffered death, (and his name was
Nimrah) was angry with his father
because of that which his father
had done unto his brother.
9 And it came to pass that Nimrah
gathered together a small number of
men, and fled out of the land, and
came over and dwelt with Omer.
10 And it came to pass that Akish
begat other sons, and they won the
hearts of the people, notwithstanding they had sworn unto him to do
all manner of iniquity according to
that which he desired.
11 Now the people of Akish were
desirous for gain, even as Akish was
desirous for [a]power; wherefore, the
sons of Akish did offer them [b]money,
by which means they drew away the
more part of the people after them.
12 And there began to be a war
between the sons of Akish and
Akish, which lasted for the space
of many years, yea, unto the destruction of nearly all the people
of the kingdom, yea, even all, save
it were thirty souls, and they who
fled with the house of Omer.
13 Wherefore, Omer was restored
again to the [a]land of his inheritance.
14 And it came to pass that Omer
began to be old; nevertheless, in
his old age he begat Emer; and he
anointed Emer to be king to reign
in his stead.
15 And after that he had anointed
Emer to be king he saw peace in
the land for the space of two years,
and he died, having seen exceedingly many days, which were full
of sorrow. And it came to pass that
Emer did reign in his stead, and did
fill the steps of his father.
16 And the Lord began again to
take the curse from off the land, and
the house of Emer did prosper exceedingly under the reign of Emer;
and in the space of sixty and two
years they had become exceedingly
strong, insomuch that they became
exceedingly rich—
17 Having [a]all manner of fruit,
and of grain, and of [b]silks, and of
fine linen, and of [c]gold, and of silver, and of precious things;
18 And also [a]all manner of cattle,
of oxen, and cows, and of sheep,
and of swine, and of goats, and also
many other kinds of animals which
were useful for the food of man.
19 And they also had [a]horses, and
asses, and there were elephants
and cureloms and cumoms; all of
which were useful unto man, and
more especially the elephants and
cureloms and cumoms.
20 And thus the Lord did pour out
his blessings upon this land, which
was [a]choice above all other lands;
and he commanded that whoso
should possess the land should
possess it unto the Lord, or they
should be [b]destroyed when they
were ripened in iniquity; for upon
such, saith the Lord: I will pour out
the fulness of my wrath.
21 And Emer did execute judgment in righteousness all his days,
and he begat many sons and daughters; and he begat Coriantum, and
he anointed Coriantum to reign in
his stead.
22 And after he had anointed
Coriantum to reign in his stead he
lived four years, and he saw peace
in the land; yea, and he even saw
the [a]Son of Righteousness, and did
rejoice and glory in his day; and he
died in peace.
23 And it came to pass that Coriantum did walk in the steps of his
father, and did build many mighty

7*a* TG Jealous.
11*a* TG Tyranny.
b 1 Sam. 8:3 (1–4); Hel. 9:20. TG Bribe.
13*a* Ether 9:3.
17*a* Ether 1:41.
b Ether 10:24.
c Hel. 6:9 (9–11); Ether 10:12 (12, 23).
18*a* Ether 6:4.
19*a* 1 Ne. 18:25; Enos 1:21; 3 Ne. 6:1.
20*a* Ether 2:15.
b Deut. 31:4 (4–5); Ether 2:8 (8–11).
22*a* 3 Ne. 25:2.

cities, and did administer that which was good unto his people in all his days. And it came to pass that he had no children even until he was exceedingly [a]old.

24 And it came to pass that his wife died, being an hundred and two years old. And it came to pass that Coriantum took to wife, in his old age, a young maid, and begat sons and daughters; wherefore he lived until he was an hundred and forty and two years old.

25 And it came to pass that he begat Com, and Com reigned in his stead; and he reigned forty and nine years, and he begat Heth; and he also begat other sons and daughters.

26 And the people had spread again over all the face of the land, and there began again to be an exceedingly great wickedness upon the face of the land, and [a]Heth began to embrace the secret plans again of old, to destroy his father.

27 And it came to pass that he did dethrone his father, for he slew him with his own sword; and he did reign in his stead.

28 And there came prophets in the land [a]again, crying repentance unto them—that they must prepare the way of the Lord or there should come a curse upon the face of the land; yea, even there should be a great famine, in which they should be destroyed if they did not repent.

29 But the people believed not the words of the prophets, but they cast them out; and some of them they cast into [a]pits and left them to perish. And it came to pass that they did all these things according to the commandment of the king, Heth.

30 And it came to pass that there began to be a great [a]dearth upon the land, and the inhabitants began to be destroyed exceedingly fast because of the dearth, for there was no rain upon the face of the earth.

31 And there came forth [a]poisonous serpents also upon the face of the land, and did poison many people. And it came to pass that their flocks began to flee before the poisonous serpents, towards the land [b]southward, which was called by the Nephites [c]Zarahemla.

32 And it came to pass that there were many of them which did perish by the way; nevertheless, there were some which fled into the land southward.

33 And it came to pass that the Lord did cause the [a]serpents that they should pursue them no more, but that they should hedge up the way that the people could not pass, that whoso should attempt to pass might fall by the poisonous serpents.

34 And it came to pass that the people did follow the course of the beasts, and did devour the [a]carcasses of them which fell by the way, until they had devoured them all. Now when the people saw that they must [b]perish they began to [c]repent of their iniquities and cry unto the Lord.

35 And it came to pass that when they had [a]humbled themselves sufficiently before the Lord he did send rain upon the face of the earth; and the people began to revive again, and there began to be fruit in the north countries, and in all the countries round about. And the Lord did show forth his power unto them in preserving them from famine.

CHAPTER 10

One king succeeds another—Some of the kings are righteous; others are wicked—When righteousness prevails, the people are blessed and prospered by the Lord.

AND it came to pass that Shez, who was a descendant of Heth—for

23*a* Ether 7:3 (3, 7).
26*a* Ether 10:1.
28*a* Ether 7:23; 11:1 (1, 12, 20).
29*a* Jer. 38:6 (4–13).
30*a* TG Drought; Famine.
31*a* Ether 10:19.
b Morm. 3:5; Ether 10:21.
c Omni 1:13.
33*a* Deut. 8:15; 1 Ne. 17:41. TG Plague.
34*a* Jer. 7:33 (32–33).
b Alma 34:34.
c D&C 101:8.
35*a* D&C 5:24.

[a]Heth had perished by the famine,
and all his household save it were
Shez—wherefore, Shez began to
build up again a broken people.
2 And it came to pass that Shez
did remember the destruction of
his fathers, and he did build up a
righteous kingdom; for he remembered what the Lord had done in
bringing Jared and his brother
[a]across the deep; and he did walk
in the ways of the Lord; and he begat sons and daughters.
3 And his eldest son, whose name
was Shez, did [a]rebel against him;
nevertheless, Shez was smitten by
the hand of a robber, because of his
exceeding riches, which brought
peace again unto his father.
4 And it came to pass that his
father did build up many cities
upon the face of the land, and the
people began again to spread over
all the face of the land. And Shez
did live to an exceedingly old age;
and he begat Riplakish. And he died,
and Riplakish reigned in his stead.
5 And it came to pass that Riplakish did not do that which was
right in the sight of the Lord, for he
did have many wives and [a]concu-
bines, and did lay that upon men's
shoulders which was grievous to be
borne; yea, he did [b]tax them with
heavy taxes; and with the taxes he
did build many spacious buildings.
6 And he did erect him an exceedingly beautiful throne; and he did
build many prisons, and whoso
would not be subject unto taxes he
did [a]cast into prison; and whoso was
not able to pay taxes he did cast
into prison; and he did cause that
they should labor continually for
their support; and whoso refused
to labor he did cause to be put
to death.
7 Wherefore he did obtain all his
fine work, yea, even his fine [a]gold
he did cause to be refined in prison;
and all manner of fine [b]workman-
ship he did cause to be wrought
in prison. And it came to pass that
he did afflict the people with his
whoredoms and abominations.
8 And when he had reigned for the
space of forty and two years the people did rise up in rebellion against
him; and there began to be war
again in the land, insomuch that
Riplakish was killed, and his descendants were driven out of the land.
9 And it came to pass after the
space of many years, Morianton, (he
being a descendant of Riplakish)
gathered together an army of out-
casts, and went forth and gave battle unto the people; and he gained
power over many cities; and the war
became exceedingly sore, and did
last for the space of many years;
and he did gain power over all the
land, and did establish himself king
over all the land.
10 And after that he had established himself king he did ease the
burden of the people, by which he
did gain favor in the eyes of the
people, and they did anoint him
to be their king.
11 And he did do justice unto
the people, but not unto himself
because of his many [a]whoredoms;
wherefore he was cut off from the
presence of the Lord.
12 And it came to pass that Morianton built up many cities, and the
people became exceedingly rich
under his reign, both in buildings,
and in [a]gold and silver, and in raising grain, and in flocks, and herds,
and such things which had been
restored unto them.
13 And Morianton did live to an
exceedingly great age, and then he
begat Kim; and Kim did reign in
the stead of his father; and he did
reign eight years, and his father
died. And it came to pass that Kim
did [a]not reign in righteousness,

10 1*a* Ether 9:26 (25–29).
2*a* Ether 6:12 (1–12).
3*a* Mosiah 10:6.
5*a* Esth. 2:14; Jacob 3:5; Mosiah 11:2 (2–14).
b Gen. 47:24.
6*a* TG Oppression; Tyranny.
7*a* Esth. 1:4.
b TG Art.
11*a* TG Whore.
12*a* Ether 9:17 (17–18).
13*a* 1 Ne. 17:35 (34–35).

wherefore he was not favored of
the Lord.
14 And his brother did rise up in
rebellion against him, by which he
did bring him into [a]captivity; and
he did remain in captivity all his
days; and he begat sons and daughters in captivity, and in his old age
he begat Levi; and he died.
15 And it came to pass that Levi
did serve in captivity after the
death of his father, for the space
of forty and two years. And he did
make war against the king of the
land, by which he did obtain unto
himself the kingdom.
16 And after he had obtained
unto himself the kingdom he did
that which was right in the sight
of the Lord; and the people did
prosper in the land; and he did live
to a good [a]old age, and begat sons
and daughters; and he also begat
Corom, whom he anointed king in
his stead.
17 And it came to pass that Corom
did that which was good in the sight
of the Lord all his days; and he begat many sons and daughters; and
after he had seen many days he did
pass away, even like unto the rest
of the earth; and Kish reigned in
his stead.
18 And it came to pass that Kish
passed away also, and Lib reigned
in his stead.
19 And it came to pass that Lib
also did that which was good in the
sight of the Lord. And in the days
of Lib the [a]poisonous serpents were
destroyed. Wherefore they did go
into the land southward, to hunt
food for the people of the land, for
the land was covered with animals
of the forest. And Lib also himself
became a great [b]hunter.
20 And they built a great city by
the [a]narrow neck of land, by the
place where the sea divides the land.
21 And they did preserve the land
[a]southward for a wilderness, to get
game. And the whole face of the
land northward was covered with
inhabitants.
22 And they were exceedingly
[a]industrious, and they did buy and
sell and [b]traffic one with another,
that they might get gain.
23 And they did [a]work in all manner of [b]ore, and they did make gold,
and silver, and [c]iron, and [d]brass,
and all manner of metals; and they
did dig it out of the earth; wherefore, they did cast up mighty heaps
of earth to get ore, of gold, and of
silver, and of iron, and of copper.
And they did [e]work all manner of
fine work.
24 And they did have [a]silks, and
fine-twined [b]linen; and they did
work all manner of [c]cloth, that they
might clothe themselves from their
nakedness.
25 And they did make all manner of tools to till the earth, both
to plow and to sow, to reap and to
hoe, and also to thrash.
26 And they did make all manner
of tools with which they did work
their beasts.
27 And they did make all manner
of [a]weapons of war. And they did
work all manner of work of exceedingly curious workmanship.
28 And never could be a people
more blessed than were they, and
more prospered by the hand of the
Lord. And they were in a land that
was choice above all lands, for the
Lord had spoken it.
29 And it came to pass that Lib
did live many years, and begat sons
and daughters; and he also begat
Hearthom.

14*a* Ether 7:7; 8:4 (3–4); 10:30 (30–31).
16*a* TG Old Age.
19*a* Ether 9:31.
b Gen. 25:27; Ether 2:1.
20*a* Alma 63:5.
21*a* Morm. 3:5; Ether 9:31 (31–32).
22*a* TG Industry.
b Gen. 34:10 (10–21); Mosiah 24:7; 4 Ne. 1:46.
23*a* TG Skill.
b Hel. 6:9 (9–11); Ether 9:17.
c 2 Ne. 5:15; Moses 5:46.
d Gen. 4:22; Mosiah 8:10.
e TG Art.
24*a* Ether 9:17.
b Ex. 25:4 (4–5); 1 Ne. 13:7 (7–8).
c TG Clothing.
27*a* Ether 15:15.

30 And it came to pass that
Hearthom reigned in the stead of
his father. And when Hearthom had
reigned twenty and four years, behold, the kingdom was taken away
from him. And he served many
years in [a]captivity, yea, even all the
remainder of his days.
31 And he begat Heth, and Heth
lived in captivity all his days. And
Heth begat Aaron, and Aaron dwelt
in captivity all his days; and he begat Amnigaddah, and Amnigaddah
also dwelt in captivity all his days;
and he begat Coriantum, and Coriantum dwelt in captivity all his
days; and he begat Com.
32 And it came to pass that Com
drew away the half of the kingdom.
And he reigned over the half of
the kingdom forty and two years;
and he went to battle against the
king, Amgid, and they fought for
the space of many years, during
which time Com gained power over
Amgid, and obtained power over the
remainder of the kingdom.
33 And in the days of Com there
began to be robbers in the land; and
they adopted the old plans, and administered [a]oaths after the manner
of the ancients, and sought again
to destroy the kingdom.
34 Now Com did fight against
them much; nevertheless, he did
not prevail against them.

CHAPTER 11

Wars, dissensions, and wickedness dominate Jaredite life—Prophets predict the utter destruction of the Jaredites unless they repent—The people reject the words of the prophets.

AND there came also in the days of
Com many [a]prophets, and prophesied of the destruction of that great
people except they should repent,
and turn unto the Lord, and forsake
their murders and wickedness.
2 And it came to pass that the
prophets were [a]rejected by the
people, and they fled unto Com for
protection, for the people sought to
destroy them.
3 And they prophesied unto Com
many things; and he was blessed in
all the remainder of his days.
4 And he lived to a good old age,
and begat Shiblom; and Shiblom
reigned in his stead. And the brother
of Shiblom rebelled against him,
and there began to be an exceedingly great war in all the land.
5 And it came to pass that the
brother of Shiblom caused that all
the prophets who prophesied of the
destruction of the people should be
put to [a]death;
6 And there was great calamity in
all the land, for they had testified
that a great curse should come upon
the land, and also upon the people,
and that there should be a great destruction among them, such an one
as never had been upon the face of
the earth, and their bones should
become as [a]heaps of earth upon the
face of the land except they should
repent of their wickedness.
7 And they hearkened not unto the
voice of the Lord, because of their
wicked combinations; wherefore,
there began to be wars and [a]conten-
tions in all the land, and also many
famines and pestilences, insomuch
that there was a great destruction,
such an one as never had been
known upon the face of the earth;
and all this came to pass in the days
of Shiblom.
8 And the people began to repent
of their iniquity; and inasmuch as
they did the Lord did have [a]mercy
on them.
9 And it came to pass that Shiblom
was slain, and Seth was brought
into [a]captivity, and did dwell in
captivity all his days.
10 And it came to pass that Ahah,

30*a* Ether 10:14; 11:9.
33*a* TG Secret Combinations.
11 1*a* Ether 7:23; 9:28.
2*a* TG Prophets, Rejection of.
5*a* TG Persecution.
6*a* Omni 1:22; Ether 14:21.
7*a* TG Contention.
8*a* TG Mercy.
9*a* Ether 10:30; 11:18 (18–19).

his son, did obtain the kingdom; and
he did reign over the people all his
days. And he did do all manner of
iniquity in his days, by which he
did cause the shedding of much
blood; and few were his days.
11 And Ethem, being a descendant
of Ahah, did obtain the kingdom;
and he also did do that which was
wicked in his days.
12 And it came to pass that in the
days of Ethem there came many
prophets, and prophesied again
unto the people; yea, they did prophesy that the Lord would utterly
[a]destroy them from off the face of
the earth except they repented of
their iniquities.
13 And it came to pass that the
people hardened their hearts, and
would not [a]hearken unto their words;
and the prophets [b]mourned and
withdrew from among the people.
14 And it came to pass that Ethem
did execute judgment in wickedness all his days; and he begat Moron. And it came to pass that Moron
did reign in his stead; and Moron did
that which was wicked before the
Lord.
15 And it came to pass that there
arose a [a]rebellion among the people,
because of that secret [b]combination
which was built up to get power and
gain; and there arose a mighty man
among them in iniquity, and gave
battle unto Moron, in which he did
overthrow the half of the kingdom;
and he did maintain the half of the
kingdom for many years.
16 And it came to pass that Moron
did overthrow him, and did obtain
the kingdom again.
17 And it came to pass that there
arose another mighty man; and he
was a descendant of the brother
of Jared.
18 And it came to pass that he did
overthrow Moron and obtain the
kingdom; wherefore, Moron dwelt
in [a]captivity all the remainder of
his days; and he begat Coriantor.
19 And it came to pass that
Coriantor dwelt in captivity all
his days.
20 And in the days of Coriantor
there also came many prophets,
and prophesied of great and marvelous things, and cried repentance
unto the people, and except they
should repent the Lord God would
execute [a]judgment against them to
their utter destruction;
21 And that the Lord God would
send or bring forth [a]another people to possess the [b]land, by his
power, after the manner by which
he brought their fathers.
22 And they did [a]reject all the
words of the prophets, because of
their [b]secret society and wicked
abominations.
23 And it came to pass that Coriantor begat [a]Ether, and he died, having dwelt in captivity all his days.

CHAPTER 12

The prophet Ether exhorts the people to believe in God—Moroni recounts the wonders and marvels done by faith—Faith enabled the brother of Jared to see Christ—The Lord gives men weakness that they may be humble—The brother of Jared moved Mount Zerin by faith—Faith, hope, and charity are essential to salvation—Moroni saw Jesus face to face.

AND it came to pass that the days
of Ether were in the days of [a]Cori-
antumr; and Coriantumr was king
over all the land.
2 And [a]Ether was a prophet of the
Lord; wherefore Ether came forth

12*a* Ether 12:3.
13*a* Jer. 44:16; Mosiah 16:2.
b TG Mourning.
15*a* TG Rebellion.
b TG Secret Combinations.
18*a* Ether 11:9.
20*a* TG Judgment.
21*a* Omni 1:21; Ether 13:21 (20–21).
b Deut. 29:28.
22*a* TG Prophets, Rejection of.
b TG Secret Combinations.
23*a* Ether 1:6; 12:2; 15:34 (33–34).
12 1*a* Omni 1:21; Ether 13:20 (13–31).
2*a* Ether 1:6; 11:23; 15:34 (33–34).

in the days of Coriantumr, and began to prophesy unto the people,
for he could not be [b]restrained
because of the Spirit of the Lord
which was in him.
3 For he did [a]cry from the [b]morn-
ing, even until the going down of
the sun, exhorting the people to
believe in God unto repentance lest
they should be [c]destroyed, saying
unto them that [d]by [e]faith all things
are fulfilled—
4 Wherefore, whoso believeth in
God might with [a]surety [b]hope for
a better world, yea, even a place at
the right hand of God, which [c]hope
cometh of [d]faith, maketh an [e]anchor
to the souls of men, which would
make them sure and steadfast, always abounding in [f]good works,
being led to [g]glorify God.
5 And it came to pass that Ether
did prophesy great and marvelous
things unto the people, which they
did not believe, because they [a]saw
them not.
6 And now, I, Moroni, would speak
somewhat concerning these things;
I would show unto the world that
[a]faith is things which are [b]hoped
for and [c]not seen; wherefore, dispute not because ye see not, for ye
receive no [d]witness until after the
[e]trial of your faith.
7 For it was by faith that Christ
showed himself unto our fathers,
after he had risen from the dead;
and he showed not himself unto
them until after they had faith
in him; wherefore, it must needs
be that some had faith in him,
for he showed himself [a]not unto
the world.
8 But because of the faith of men
he has shown himself unto the
world, and glorified the name of
the Father, and prepared a way that
thereby others might be partakers
of the heavenly gift, that they might
hope for those things which they
have not seen.
9 Wherefore, ye may also have
hope, and be partakers of the gift,
if ye will but have faith.
10 Behold it was by faith that they
of old were [a]called after the holy
order of God.
11 Wherefore, by faith was the law
of Moses given. But in the [a]gift of
his Son hath God prepared a more
[b]excellent way; and it is by faith
that it hath been fulfilled.
12 For if there be no [a]faith among
the children of men God can do no
[b]miracle among them; wherefore,
he showed not himself until after
their faith.
13 Behold, it was the faith of Alma
and Amulek that caused the [a]prison
to tumble to the earth.
14 Behold, it was the faith of
Nephi and Lehi that wrought the
[a]change upon the Lamanites, that
they were baptized with fire and
with the [b]Holy Ghost.
15 Behold, it was the faith of
[a]Ammon and his brethren which
[b]wrought so great a miracle among
the Lamanites.
16 Yea, and even all they who

2*b* Jer. 20:9; Enos 1:26; Alma 43:1.
3*a* D&C 112:5.
b Jer. 26:5.
c Ether 11:12 (12, 20–22).
d Heb. 11:7 (1–40).
e 1 Cor. 13:13 (1–13); Moro. 7:1; 8:14; 10:20 (20–23).
4*a* Heb. 7:22.
b Alma 7:16; 22:16; Moro. 7:3; D&C 25:10; 138:14.
c Heb. 11:1; Moro. 7:40.
d Luke 7:50.
e Heb. 6:19.
f 1 Cor. 15:58; 1 Tim. 2:10.
g John 11:4 (1–4); 3 Ne. 12:16.
5*a* Heb. 11:3; Alma 30:15; Hel. 16:20.
6*a* Heb. 11:1.
b Rom. 8:25 (24–25).
c Alma 32:21.
d Lev. 9:6 (6, 23); 2 Ne. 1:15. TG Sign Seekers.
e 3 Ne. 26:11. TG Test.
7*a* Acts 10:41.
10*a* Alma 13:4 (3–4). TG Authority.
11*a* TG God, Gifts of.
b 1 Cor. 12:31.
12*a* Luke 16:30 (27–31); Alma 32:18 (17–18); Moro. 7:37.
b Ps. 78:41; Matt. 13:58; Morm. 9:20.
13*a* Alma 14:27 (26–29).
14*a* Hel. 5:50 (50–52).
b Hel. 5:45; 3 Ne. 9:20.
15*a* Alma 17:29 (29–39).
b IE as told in Alma 17–26.

wrought [a]miracles wrought them by
[b]faith, even those who were before
Christ and also those who were after.
17 And it was by faith that the
three disciples obtained a promise
that they should [a]not taste of death;
and they obtained not the promise
until after their faith.
18 And neither at any time hath
any wrought miracles until after
their faith; wherefore they first
believed in the Son of God.
19 And there were many whose
faith was so exceedingly strong,
even [a]before Christ came, who could
not be kept from within the [b]veil,
but truly saw with their eyes the
things which they had beheld with
an eye of faith, and they were glad.
20 And behold, we have seen in
this record that one of these was the
brother of Jared; for so great was
his faith in God, that when God put
forth his [a]finger he could not hide
it from the sight of the brother of
Jared, because of his word which he
had spoken unto him, which word
he had obtained by faith.
21 And after the brother of Jared
had beheld the finger of the Lord,
because of the [a]promise which the
brother of Jared had obtained by
faith, the Lord could not withhold
anything from his sight; wherefore
he showed him all things, for he could
no longer be kept without the [b]veil.
22 And it is by faith that my fathers
have obtained the [a]promise that
these things should come unto
their brethren through the Gentiles;
therefore the Lord hath commanded
me, yea, even Jesus Christ.
23 And I said unto him: Lord, the
Gentiles will [a]mock at these things,
because of our [b]weakness in writing;
for Lord thou hast made us [c]mighty
in word by faith, but thou hast not
made us mighty in writing; for thou
hast made all this people that they
could speak much, because of the
Holy Ghost which thou hast given
them;
24 And thou hast made us that we
could write but little, because of
the [a]awkwardness of our hands. Behold, thou hast not made us mighty
in [b]writing like unto the brother
of Jared, for thou madest him that
the things which he [c]wrote were
mighty even as thou art, unto the
overpowering of man to read them.
25 Thou hast also made our words
powerful and great, even that we
[a]cannot write them; wherefore, when
we write we behold our [b]weakness,
and stumble because of the placing of our words; and I fear lest the
Gentiles shall [c]mock at our words.
26 And when I had said this, the
Lord spake unto me, saying: [a]Fools
[b]mock, but they shall mourn; and
my grace is sufficient for the meek,
that they shall take no advantage
of your weakness;
27 And if men come unto me I
will show unto them their [a]weak-
ness. I [b]give unto men weakness
that they may be humble; and my
[c]grace is sufficient for all men that
[d]humble themselves before me; for
if they humble themselves before
me, and have faith in me, then will
I make [e]weak things become strong
unto them.

16*a* TG Miracle.
b Heb. 11:7 (7–40).
17*a* 3 Ne. 28:7;
4 Ne. 1:37 (14, 37);
Morm. 8:10 (10–12).
19*a* 2 Ne. 11:4; Jacob 4:5;
Jarom 1:11;
Alma 25:16 (15–16).
b Ether 3:6.
TG Veil.
20*a* Ether 3:4.
21*a* Ether 3:26 (25–26).
b Ether 3:20;
D&C 67:10 (10–13).
22*a* Enos 1:13.
23*a* Ether 12:36.
b 1 Cor. 2:3 (1–5);
1 Ne. 19:6;
Morm. 8:17 (13–17);
9:31 (31, 33).
c 2 Ne. 33:1.
24*a* Jacob 4:1.
b TG Language.
c Ether 4:1.
25*a* 3 Ne. 5:18.
b Ether 12:37.
c 1 Cor. 2:14.
26*a* Prov. 14:9; 20:3.
b Gal. 6:7; D&C 124:71.
TG Mocking; Offense.
27*a* Jacob 4:7.
b Ex. 4:11;
1 Cor. 1:27 (26–31).
c TG Grace.
d D&C 1:28.
TG Humility; Teachable.
e Deut. 11:8; Joel 3:10;
Luke 9:48 (46–48);
18:14 (10–14);
2 Cor. 12:9 (7–10);
Heb. 11:34;
1 Ne. 14:1.

28 Behold, I will show unto the
Gentiles their weakness, and I will
show unto them that [a]faith, hope
and charity bringeth unto me—the
fountain of all [b]righteousness.
29 And I, Moroni, having heard
these words, was [a]comforted, and
said: O Lord, thy righteous will be
done, for I know that thou workest
unto the children of men according
to their faith;
30 For the brother of Jared said
unto the mountain Zerin, [a]Remove—and it was removed. And if
he had not had faith it would not
have moved; wherefore thou workest after men have faith.
31 For thus didst thou manifest
thyself unto thy disciples; for [a]after
they had [b]faith, and did speak in
thy name, thou didst show thyself
unto them in great power.
32 And I also remember that thou
hast said that thou hast prepared a
house for man, yea, even among the
[a]mansions of thy Father, in which
man might have a more excellent
[b]hope; wherefore man must hope,
or he cannot receive an inheritance in the place which thou hast
prepared.
33 And again, I remember that
thou hast said that thou hast [a]loved
the world, even unto the laying
down of thy life for the world, that
thou mightest take it again to prepare a place for the children of men.
34 And now I know that this [a]love
which thou hast had for the children of men is charity; wherefore,
except men shall have charity they
cannot inherit that place which thou
hast prepared in the mansions of
thy Father.
35 Wherefore, I know by this thing
which thou hast said, that if the
Gentiles have not [a]charity, because
of our weakness, that thou wilt
prove them, and [b]take away their
[c]talent, yea, even that which they
have received, and give unto them
who shall have more abundantly.
36 And it came to pass that I prayed
unto the Lord that he would give unto
the Gentiles [a]grace, that they might
have charity.
37 And it came to pass that the
Lord said unto me: If they have not
charity it mattereth not unto thee,
thou hast been faithful; wherefore,
thy garments shall be made [a]clean.
And because thou hast seen thy
[b]weakness thou shalt be made strong,
even unto the sitting down in the
place which I have prepared in
the mansions of my Father.
38 And now I, Moroni, bid farewell
unto the Gentiles, yea, and also unto
my brethren whom I love, until we
shall meet before the [a]judgment-seat of Christ, where all men shall
know that my [b]garments are not
spotted with your blood.
39 And then shall ye know that I
have [a]seen Jesus, and that he hath
talked with me [b]face to face, and
that he told me in [c]plain humility,
even as a man telleth another in
mine own language, concerning
these things;
40 And only a few have I written,
because of my weakness in writing.
41 And now, I would commend
you to [a]seek this Jesus of whom the

28*a* Alma 7:24.
b TG God, the Standard of Righteousness.
29*a* TG Comfort.
30*a* Matt. 17:20; Jacob 4:6; Hel. 10:9. TG God, Power of.
31*a* 3 Ne. 26:17 (17–21).
b 1 Cor. 13:13 (1–13); Moro. 7:44 (33–48).
32*a* John 14:2; Enos 1:27; D&C 72:4; 98:18.
b TG Hope.
33*a* John 3:16 (16–18).
34*a* Moro. 7:47. TG Love.
35*a* 1 Cor. 13:2 (1–2).
b Matt. 25:28 (14–30).
c TG Talents.
36*a* Ether 12:23. TG Grace.
37*a* Job 15:14; 25:4; D&C 38:42; 88:74 (74–75); 135:5 (4–5). TG Cleanliness; Purification.
b Ether 12:25 (25–27).
38*a* TG Jesus Christ, Judge.
b Acts 20:26; Jacob 1:19.
39*a* TG Jesus Christ, Appearances, Postmortal.
b Gen. 32:30; Ex. 33:11; Num. 12:8.
c 2 Ne. 32:7; Alma 13:23.
41*a* Ezra 8:22 (22–23); Ps. 27:8; Amos 5:6; Alma 37:47; D&C 88:63; 101:38.

prophets and apostles have written, that the grace of God the Father, and also the Lord Jesus Christ, and the Holy Ghost, which beareth [b]record of them, may be and abide in you forever. Amen.

CHAPTER 13

Ether speaks of a New Jerusalem to be built in America by the seed of Joseph—He prophesies, is cast out, writes the Jaredite history, and foretells the destruction of the Jaredites—War rages over all the land.

AND now I, Moroni, proceed to finish my record concerning the destruction of the people of whom I have been writing.

2 For behold, they rejected all the words of Ether; for he truly told them of all things, from the beginning of man; and that after the waters had [a]receded from off the face of this [b]land it became a choice land above all other lands, a chosen land of the Lord; wherefore the Lord would have that all men should [c]serve him who dwell upon the face thereof;

3 And that it was the place of the [a]New Jerusalem, which should [b]come down out of heaven, and the holy sanctuary of the Lord.

4 Behold, Ether saw the days of Christ, and he spake concerning a [a]New Jerusalem upon this land.

5 And he spake also concerning the house of Israel, and the [a]Jerusalem from whence [b]Lehi should come—after it should be destroyed it should be built up again, a [c]holy city unto the Lord; wherefore, it could not be a new Jerusalem for it had been in a time of old; but it should be built up again, and become a holy city of the Lord; and it should be built unto the house of Israel—

6 And that a [a]New Jerusalem should be built up upon this land, unto the remnant of the seed of [b]Joseph, for which things there has been a [c]type.

7 For as Joseph brought his father down into the land of [a]Egypt, even so he died there; wherefore, the Lord brought a remnant of the seed of Joseph out of the land of Jerusalem, that he might be merciful unto the seed of Joseph that they should [b]perish not, even as he was merciful unto the father of Joseph that he should perish not.

8 Wherefore, the remnant of the house of Joseph shall be built upon this [a]land; and it shall be a land of their inheritance; and they shall build up a holy [b]city unto the Lord, like unto the Jerusalem of old; and they shall [c]no more be confounded, until the end come when the earth shall pass away.

9 And there shall be a [a]new heaven and a new earth; and they shall be like unto the old save the old have passed away, and all things have become new.

10 And then cometh the New Jerusalem; and blessed are they who dwell therein, for it is they whose garments are [a]white through the blood of the Lamb; and they are they who are numbered among the remnant of the seed of Joseph, who were of the house of Israel.

11 And then also cometh the [a]Jerusalem of old; and the inhabitants thereof, blessed are they, for

---

41*b* 3 Ne. 11:32 (32, 36).
13 2*a* Gen. 7:19 (11–24); 8:3.
b TG Earth, Dividing of.
c Ether 2:8.
3*a* 3 Ne. 20:22; 21:23 (23–24). TG Jerusalem, New.
b Rev. 3:12; 21:2.
4*a* TG Zion.
5*a* TG Jerusalem.
b 1 Ne. 1:18 (18–20); 2:2.
c Joel 2:18; Rev. 21:10 (10–27); 3 Ne. 20:46 (29–36, 46).
6*a* D&C 42:9; 45:66 (66–67); 84:2 (2–5); A of F 1:10.
b Ezek. 48:5 (4–5); D&C 28:8. TG Israel, Joseph, People of.
c Alma 46:24 (24–26). TG Symbolism.
7*a* Gen. 46:6 (2–7); 47:6.
b 2 Ne. 3:5 (5–24).
8*a* TG Promised Lands.
b Rev. 21:10 (10–27).
c Moro. 10:31.
9*a* Heb. 8:13; 2 Pet. 3:13 (10–13); Rev. 21:1; 3 Ne. 12:47 (46–47); 15:3 (2–10); D&C 101:25 (23–25).
10*a* Rev. 7:14.
11*a* TG Israel, Gathering of; Israel, Land of; Jerusalem.

they have been washed in the blood
of the Lamb; and they are they who
were scattered and gathered in from
the four quarters of the earth, and
from the [b]north countries, and are
partakers of the fulfilling of the
covenant which God made with
their father, [c]Abraham.
12 And when these things come,
bringeth to pass the scripture which
saith, there are they who were [a]first,
who shall be last; and there are they
who were last, who shall be first.
13 And I was about to write more,
but I am forbidden; but great and
marvelous were the prophecies of
Ether; but they esteemed him as
naught, and cast him out; and he
[a]hid himself in the cavity of a rock
by day, and by night he went forth
viewing the things which should
come upon the people.
14 And as he dwelt in the cavity
of a rock he made the [a]remainder
of this record, viewing the destructions which came upon the people,
by night.
15 And it came to pass that in that
same year in which he was cast out
from among the people there began
to be a great war among the people,
for there were many who rose up,
who were mighty men, and sought
to destroy Coriantumr by their secret plans of wickedness, of which
hath been spoken.
16 And now Coriantumr, having
studied, himself, in all the arts
of war and all the cunning of the
world, wherefore he gave battle unto
them who sought to destroy him.
17 But he repented not, neither his
[a]fair sons nor daughters; neither the
fair sons and daughters of Cohor;
neither the fair sons and daughters
of Corihor; and in fine, there were
none of the fair sons and daughters
upon the face of the whole earth
who repented of their sins.
18 Wherefore, it came to pass that
in the first year that Ether dwelt
in the cavity of a rock, there were
many people who were slain by the
sword of those [a]secret combinations,
fighting against Coriantumr that
they might obtain the kingdom.
19 And it came to pass that the
sons of Coriantumr fought much
and bled much.
20 And in the second year the word
of the Lord came to Ether, that he
should go and [a]prophesy unto [b]Cori-
antumr that, if he would repent,
and all his household, the Lord
would give unto him his kingdom
and spare the people—
21 Otherwise they should be
destroyed, and all his household
save it were himself. And he should
only live to see the fulfilling of the
prophecies which had been spoken
concerning [a]another people receiving the land for their inheritance;
and Coriantumr should receive
a burial by them; and every soul
should be destroyed save it were
[b]Coriantumr.
22 And it came to pass that Coriantumr repented not, neither his
household, neither the people; and
the wars ceased not; and they sought
to [a]kill Ether, but he fled from
before them and hid again in the
cavity of the rock.
23 And it came to pass that there
arose up Shared, and he also gave
battle unto Coriantumr; and he did
beat him, insomuch that in the third
year he did bring him into captivity.
24 And the sons of Coriantumr, in
the fourth year, did beat Shared,
and did obtain the kingdom again
unto their father.
25 Now there began to be a war

11*b* D&C 133:26 (26–35).
TG Israel, Ten Lost Tribes of.
c Isa. 27:6.
12*a* Mark 10:31; Luke 13:30; 1 Ne. 13:42; Jacob 5:63; D&C 18:26 (26–27); 90:9.
13*a* 1 Kgs. 17:3 (1–16); 1 Ne. 3:27; Mosiah 17:4 (1–4).
14*a* Ether 15:33 (13, 33).
17*a* Morm. 6:19 (16–22).
18*a* Ether 8:9 (9–26).
20*a* Ether 15:1.
b Omni 1:21; Ether 12:1 (1–2).
21*a* Ether 11:21.
b Ether 14:24; 15:29 (29–32).
22*a* Prov. 29:10.

upon all the face of the land, [a]every man with his band fighting for that which he desired.
26 And there were robbers, and in fine, all manner of wickedness upon all the face of the land.
27 And it came to pass that Coriantumr was exceedingly angry with Shared, and he went against him with his armies to battle; and they did meet in great anger, and they did meet in the valley of Gilgal; and the battle became exceedingly sore.
28 And it came to pass that Shared fought against him for the space of three days. And it came to pass that Coriantumr beat him, and did pursue him until he came to the plains of Heshlon.
29 And it came to pass that Shared gave him battle again upon the plains; and behold, he did beat Coriantumr, and drove him back again to the valley of Gilgal.
30 And Coriantumr gave Shared battle again in the valley of Gilgal, in which he beat Shared and slew him.
31 And Shared wounded Coriantumr in his thigh, that he did not go to battle again for the space of two years, in which time all the people upon the face of the land were shedding blood, and there was none to restrain them.

CHAPTER 14

The iniquity of the people brings a curse upon the land—Coriantumr engages in warfare against Gilead, then Lib, and then Shiz—Blood and carnage cover the land.

AND now there began to be a great [a]curse upon all the land because of the iniquity of the people, in which, if a man should lay his tool or his sword upon his shelf, or upon the place whither he would keep it, behold, upon the morrow, he could not find it, so great was the curse upon the land.
2 Wherefore every man did cleave unto that which was his own, with his hands, and would not borrow neither would he lend; and every man kept the hilt of his sword in his right hand, in the [a]defence of his property and his own life and of his wives and children.
3 And now, after the space of two years, and after the death of Shared, behold, there arose the brother of Shared and he gave battle unto Coriantumr, in which Coriantumr did beat him and did pursue him to the wilderness of Akish.
4 And it came to pass that the brother of Shared did give battle unto him in the wilderness of Akish; and the battle became exceedingly sore, and many thousands fell by the sword.
5 And it came to pass that Coriantumr did lay siege to the wilderness; and the brother of Shared did march forth out of the wilderness by night, and slew a part of the army of Coriantumr, as they were drunken.
6 And he came forth to the land of [a]Moron, and placed himself upon the throne of Coriantumr.
7 And it came to pass that Coriantumr dwelt with his army in the wilderness for the space of two years, in which he did receive great strength to his army.
8 Now the brother of Shared, whose name was Gilead, also received great strength to his army, because of secret combinations.
9 And it came to pass that his high priest murdered him as he sat upon his throne.
10 And it came to pass that one of the secret combinations murdered him in a secret pass, and obtained unto himself the kingdom; and his name was Lib; and Lib was a man of great stature, more than any other man among all the people.
11 And it came to pass that in the first year of Lib, Coriantumr came up unto the land of Moron, and gave battle unto Lib.

25*a* TG Covet; Selfishness.
14 1*a* Hel. 12:18; 13:18 (17–23); Morm. 1:18 (17–19); 2:10 (10–14).
2*a* Morm. 2:23.
6*a* Ether 7:5.

12 And it came to pass that he fought with Lib, in which Lib did smite upon his arm that he was wounded; nevertheless, the army of Coriantumr did press forward upon Lib, that he fled to the borders upon the seashore.
13 And it came to pass that Coriantumr pursued him; and Lib gave battle unto him upon the seashore.
14 And it came to pass that Lib did smite the army of Coriantumr, that they fled again to the wilderness of Akish.
15 And it came to pass that Lib did pursue him until he came to the plains of Agosh. And Coriantumr had taken all the people with him as he fled before Lib in that quarter of the land whither he fled.
16 And when he had come to the plains of Agosh he gave battle unto Lib, and he smote upon him until he died; nevertheless, the brother of Lib did come against Coriantumr in the stead thereof, and the battle became exceedingly sore, in the which Coriantumr fled again before the army of the brother of Lib.
17 Now the name of the brother of Lib was called Shiz. And it came to pass that Shiz pursued after Coriantumr, and he did overthrow many cities, and he did slay both women and children, and he did burn the cities.
18 And there went a fear of Shiz throughout all the land; yea, a cry went forth throughout the land—Who can stand before the army of Shiz? Behold, he sweepeth the earth before him!
19 And it came to pass that the people began to flock together in armies, throughout all the face of the land.
20 And they were divided; and a part of them fled to the army of Shiz, and a part of them fled to the army of Coriantumr.
21 And so great and lasting had been the war, and so long had been the scene of bloodshed and carnage, that the whole face of the land was covered with the [a]bodies of the [b]dead.
22 And so swift and speedy was the war that there was none left to bury the dead, but they did march forth from the shedding of [a]blood to the shedding of blood, leaving the bodies of both men, women, and children strewed upon the face of the land, to become a prey to the [b]worms of the flesh.
23 And the [a]scent thereof went forth upon the face of the land, even upon all the face of the land; wherefore the people became troubled by day and by night, because of the scent thereof.
24 Nevertheless, Shiz did [a]not cease to pursue Coriantumr; for he had sworn to avenge himself upon Coriantumr of the blood of his brother, who had been slain, and the word of the Lord which came to Ether that Coriantumr should not fall by the sword.
25 And thus we see that the Lord did visit them in the fulness of his [a]wrath, and their wickedness and abominations had prepared a way for their everlasting destruction.
26 And it came to pass that Shiz did pursue Coriantumr eastward, even to the borders by the seashore, and there he gave battle unto Shiz for the space of three days.
27 And so terrible was the destruction among the armies of Shiz that the people began to be frightened, and began to flee before the armies of Coriantumr; and they fled to the land of Corihor, and swept off the inhabitants before them, all them that would not join them.
28 And they pitched their tents in the valley of Corihor; and Coriantumr pitched his tents in the valley of Shurr. Now the valley of Shurr was near the hill Comnor;

21*a* Ether 11:6.
b Ezek. 35:8.
22*a* Hosea 4:2 (1–3).
b Isa. 14:11 (9–11).
23*a* Alma 16:11 (9–11).
24*a* Ether 13:21.
25*a* TG God, Indignation of.

wherefore, Coriantumr did gather
his armies together upon the hill
Comnor, and did sound a trumpet
unto the armies of Shiz to invite
them forth to battle.
29 And it came to pass that they
came forth, but were driven again;
and they came the second time, and
they were driven again the second
time. And it came to pass that they
came again the third time, and the
battle became exceedingly sore.
30 And it came to pass that Shiz
smote upon Coriantumr that he
gave him many deep wounds; and
Coriantumr, having lost his blood,
fainted, and was carried away as
though he were dead.
31 Now the loss of men, women
and children on both sides was so
great that Shiz commanded his people that they should not pursue the
armies of Coriantumr; wherefore,
they returned to their camp.

CHAPTER 15

Millions of the Jaredites are slain in battle—Shiz and Coriantumr assemble all the people to mortal combat—The Spirit of the Lord ceases to strive with them—The Jaredite nation is utterly destroyed—Only Coriantumr remains.

And it came to pass when Coriantumr had recovered of his wounds,
he began to remember the [a]words
which Ether had spoken unto him.
2 He saw that there had been
slain by the sword already nearly
[a]two millions of his people, and he
began to sorrow in his heart; yea,
there had been slain two millions
of mighty men, and also their wives
and their children.
3 He began to repent of the evil
which he had done; he began to
remember the words which had
been spoken by the mouth of all
the prophets, and he saw them that
they were fulfilled thus far, every
whit; and his soul [a]mourned and
refused to be [b]comforted.
4 And it came to pass that he wrote
an epistle unto Shiz, desiring him
that he would spare the people, and
he would give up the kingdom for
the sake of the lives of the people.
5 And it came to pass that when
Shiz had received his epistle he
wrote an epistle unto Coriantumr,
that if he would give himself up,
that he might slay him with his own
sword, that he would spare the lives
of the people.
6 And it came to pass that the
people repented not of their iniquity; and the people of Coriantumr
were stirred up to anger against the
people of Shiz; and the people of
Shiz were stirred up to anger against
the people of Coriantumr; wherefore, the people of Shiz did give battle unto the people of Coriantumr.
7 And when Coriantumr saw that
he was about to fall he fled again
before the people of Shiz.
8 And it came to pass that he came
to the waters of Ripliancum, which,
by interpretation, is large, or to
exceed all; wherefore, when they
came to these waters they pitched
their tents; and Shiz also pitched
his tents near unto them; and therefore on the morrow they did come
to battle.
9 And it came to pass that they
fought an exceedingly sore battle,
in which Coriantumr was wounded
again, and he fainted with the loss
of blood.
10 And it came to pass that the
armies of Coriantumr did press
upon the armies of Shiz that they
beat them, that they caused them
to flee before them; and they did
flee southward, and did pitch their
tents in a place which was called
Ogath.
11 And it came to pass that the
army of Coriantumr did pitch their
tents by the hill Ramah; and it was
that same hill where my father
Mormon did [a]hide up the records
unto the Lord, which were sacred.

15 1*a* Ether 13:20 (20–21).
2*a* Ether 1:43.
3*a* TG Mourning.
b Gen. 37:35; Moses 7:44. TG Comfort.
11*a* Morm. 6:6.

12 And it came to pass that they
did gather together all the people
upon all the face of the land, who
had not been slain, save it was Ether.
13 And it came to pass that Ether
did [a]behold all the doings of the
people; and he beheld that the people who were for Coriantumr were
gathered together to the army of
Coriantumr; and the people who
were for Shiz were gathered together to the army of Shiz.
14 Wherefore, they were for the
space of four years gathering together the people, that they might
get all who were upon the face of
the land, and that they might receive all the strength which it was
possible that they could receive.
15 And it came to pass that when
they were all gathered together, every one to the army which he would,
with their wives and their children—
both men, women and children being armed with [a]weapons of war,
having shields, and [b]breastplates,
and head-plates, and being clothed
after the manner of war—they did
march forth one against another to
battle; and they fought all that day,
and conquered not.
16 And it came to pass that when
it was night they were weary, and
retired to their camps; and after they
had retired to their camps they took
up a howling and a [a]lamentation for
the loss of the slain of their people;
and so great were their cries, their
howlings and lamentations, that
they did rend the air exceedingly.
17 And it came to pass that on the
morrow they did go again to battle, and great and terrible was that
day; nevertheless, they conquered
not, and when the night came again
they did rend the air with their
cries, and their howlings, and their
mournings, for the loss of the slain
of their people.
18 And it came to pass that Coriantumr wrote again an epistle unto
Shiz, desiring that he would not
come again to battle, but that he
would take the kingdom, and spare
the lives of the people.
19 But behold, the [a]Spirit of the
Lord had ceased striving with them,
and [b]Satan had full power over
the [c]hearts of the people; for they
were given up unto the hardness
of their hearts, and the blindness of
their minds that they might be destroyed; wherefore they went again
to battle.
20 And it came to pass that they
fought all that day, and when the
night came they slept upon their
swords.
21 And on the morrow they fought
even until the night came.
22 And when the night came they
were [a]drunken with anger, even as a
man who is drunken with wine; and
they slept again upon their swords.
23 And on the morrow they fought
again; and when the night came they
had all fallen by the sword save it
were fifty and two of the people of
Coriantumr, and sixty and nine of
the people of Shiz.
24 And it came to pass that they
slept upon their swords that night,
and on the morrow they fought
again, and they contended in their
might with their swords and with
their shields, all that day.
25 And when the night came there
were thirty and two of the people
of Shiz, and twenty and seven of
the people of Coriantumr.
26 And it came to pass that they
ate and slept, and prepared for
death on the morrow. And they
were large and mighty men as to
the strength of men.
27 And it came to pass that they
fought for the space of three hours,
and they fainted with the loss of
blood.
28 And it came to pass that when

13*a* Ether 13:14.
15*a* Ether 10:27.
b Mosiah 8:10.
16*a* TG Mourning.
19*a* TG God, Spirit of; Holy Ghost, Loss of.
b TG Devil.
c TG Hardheartedness.
22*a* Moro. 9:23.

the men of Coriantumr had received
sufficient strength that they could
walk, they were about to flee for
their lives; but behold, Shiz arose,
and also his men, and he swore in
his wrath that he would slay Coriantumr or he would perish by the
sword.
29 Wherefore, he did pursue them,
and on the morrow he did overtake
them; and they fought again with
the sword. And it came to pass that
when they had [a]all fallen by the
sword, save it were Coriantumr and
Shiz, behold Shiz had fainted with
the loss of blood.
30 And it came to pass that when
Coriantumr had leaned upon his
sword, that he rested a little, he
smote off the head of Shiz.
31 And it came to pass that after
he had smitten off the head of Shiz,
that Shiz raised up on his hands and
[a]fell; and after that he had strug-
gled for breath, he died.
32 And it came to pass that
[a]Coriantumr fell to the earth, and
became as if he had no life.
33 And the Lord spake unto Ether,
and said unto him: Go forth. And
he went forth, and beheld that the
words of the Lord had all been fulfilled; and he [a]finished his [b]record;
(and the [c]hundredth part I have
not written) and he hid them in a
manner that the people of Limhi
did find them.
34 Now the last words which are
written by [a]Ether are these: Whether
the Lord will that I be translated,
or that I suffer the will of the Lord
in the flesh, it mattereth not, if it
so be that I am [b]saved in the kingdom of God. Amen.

THE BOOK OF MORONI

CHAPTER 1

Moroni writes for the benefit of the Lamanites—The Nephites who will not deny Christ are put to death. About A.D. 401–21.

NOW I, Moroni, after having
made an end of abridging
the account of the people of
Jared, I had supposed [a]not to have
written more, but I have not as yet
perished; and I make not myself
known to the Lamanites lest they
should destroy me.
2 For behold, their [a]wars are exceedingly fierce among themselves;
and because of their [b]hatred they
[c]put to death every Nephite that
will not deny the Christ.
3 And I, Moroni, will not [a]deny
the Christ; wherefore, I wander
whithersoever I can for the safety
of mine own life.
4 Wherefore, I write a few more
things, contrary to that which I
had supposed; for I had supposed
not to have written any more; but
I write a few more things, that perhaps they may be of [a]worth unto
my brethren, the Lamanites, in some
future day, according to the will of
the Lord.

CHAPTER 2

Jesus gave the twelve Nephite disciples power to confer the gift of the Holy Ghost. About A.D. 401–21.

29a Ether 13:21.
31a Judg. 5:27 (26–27).
32a Omni 1:21 (20–22).
33a Ether 13:14.
b Mosiah 8:9; 21:27; 28:11; Alma 37:21 (21–31); Ether 1:2 (1–5).
c 3 Ne. 26:6; Ether 3:17.
34a Ether 1:6; 11:23; 12:2.
b Mosiah 13:9.

[MORONI]

1 1a Morm. 8:5; Moro. 10:1 (1–2).
2a 1 Ne. 12:21 (20–23).
b TG Hate.
c Alma 45:14.
3a Matt. 10:33 (32–33); 3 Ne. 29:5.
4a 2 Ne. 3:12 (11–12, 19).

THE words of Christ, which he spake
unto his [a]disciples, the twelve whom
he had chosen, as he laid his hands
upon them—
2 And he called them by name,
saying: Ye shall [a]call on the Father
in my name, in mighty prayer; and
after ye have done this ye shall have
[b]power that to him upon whom ye
shall lay your [c]hands, [d]ye shall give
the Holy Ghost; and in my name
shall ye give it, for thus do mine
apostles.
3 Now Christ spake these words
unto them at the time of his first
appearing; and the multitude heard
it not, but the disciples heard it;
and on as many as they [a]laid their
hands, fell the Holy Ghost.

CHAPTER 3

Elders ordain priests and teachers by the laying on of hands. About A.D. 401–21.

THE manner which the disciples,
who were called the [a]elders of
the church, [b]ordained [c]priests and
teachers—
2 After they had prayed unto the
Father in the name of Christ, they
[a]laid their hands upon them, and
said:
3 In the name of Jesus Christ I
ordain you to be a priest (or if he
be a [a]teacher, I ordain you to be a
teacher) to preach repentance and
[b]remission of sins through Jesus
Christ, by the endurance of faith
on his name to the end. Amen.
4 And after this manner did they
[a]ordain priests and teachers, according to the [b]gifts and callings of God
unto men; and they ordained them
by the [c]power of the Holy Ghost,
which was in them.

CHAPTER 4

How elders and priests administer the sacramental bread is explained. About A.D. 401–21.

THE [a]manner of their [b]elders and
priests administering the flesh and
blood of Christ unto the church;
and they administered it [c]accord-
ing to the commandments of Christ;
wherefore we know the manner to
be true; and the elder or priest did
minister it—
2 And they did kneel down with
the [a]church, and pray to the Father
in the name of Christ, saying:
3 O God, the Eternal Father, we
ask thee in the name of thy Son,
Jesus Christ, to bless and [a]sanctify
this [b]bread to the souls of all those
who partake of it; that they may
eat in [c]remembrance of the body
of thy Son, and witness unto thee,
O God, the Eternal Father, that
they are willing to take upon them
the [d]name of thy Son, and always
remember him, and keep his commandments which he hath given
them, that they may always have
his [e]Spirit to be with them. Amen.

CHAPTER 5

The mode of administering the sacramental wine is set forth. About A.D. 401–21.

THE [a]manner of administering the
wine—Behold, they took the cup,
and said:
2 O God, the Eternal Father, we

---

2 1*a* 3 Ne. 13:25; 15:11.
2*a* Gen. 4:26; Ether 4:15.
b Matt. 10:1. TG Priesthood, Melchizedek.
c TG Hands, Laying on of.
d 3 Ne. 18:37.
3*a* Acts 19:6.
3 1*a* Alma 6:1. TG Elder.
b TG Church Organization.
c Mosiah 6:3.
2*a* TG Hands, Laying on of.
3*a* TG Teacher.
b TG Remission of Sins.
4*a* D&C 18:32; 20:39 (39, 60). TG Priesthood; Priesthood, History of.
b TG God, Gifts of.
c 1 Ne. 13:37; Moro. 6:9.
4 1*a* 3 Ne. 18:5 (1–7).
b TG Elder.
c D&C 20:76.
2*a* TG Church.
3*a* 1 Sam. 21:4.
b TG Sacrament.
c Luke 22:19; 3 Ne. 18:7; 20:8.
d TG Jesus Christ, Taking the Name of.
e TG God, Spirit of.
5 1*a* 3 Ne. 18:11 (8–11); D&C 20:78.

ask thee, in the name of thy Son, Jesus Christ, to bless and sanctify this [a]wine to the souls of all those who drink of it, that they may do it in [b]remembrance of the [c]blood of thy Son, which was shed for them; that they may witness unto thee, O God, the Eternal Father, that they do always remember him, that they may have his [d]Spirit to be with them. Amen.

CHAPTER 6

Repentant persons are baptized and fellowshipped—Church members who repent are forgiven—Meetings are conducted by the power of the Holy Ghost. About A.D. *401–21.*

AND now I speak concerning baptism. Behold, elders, priests, and teachers were baptized; and they were not baptized save they brought forth [a]fruit meet that they were [b]worthy of it.

2 Neither did they receive any unto baptism save they came forth with a [a]broken [b]heart and a contrite spirit, and witnessed unto the church that they truly repented of all their sins.

3 And none were received unto baptism save they [a]took upon them the name of Christ, having a determination to serve him to the end.

4 And after they had been received unto baptism, and were wrought upon and [a]cleansed by the power of the Holy Ghost, they were numbered among the people of the [b]church of Christ; and their [c]names were taken, that they might be remembered and nourished by the good word of God, to keep them in the right way, to keep them continually [d]watchful unto prayer, [e]relying alone upon the merits of Christ, who was the author and the finisher of their faith.

5 And the [a]church did meet together [b]oft, to [c]fast and to pray, and to speak one with another concerning the welfare of their souls.

6 And they did [a]meet together oft to partake of bread and wine, in [b]remembrance of the Lord Jesus.

7 And they were strict to observe that there should be [a]no iniquity among them; and whoso was found to commit iniquity, and [b]three witnesses of the church did condemn them before the [c]elders, and if they repented not, and [d]confessed not, their names were [e]blotted out, and they were not [f]numbered among the people of Christ.

8 But [a]as oft as they repented and sought forgiveness, with real [b]intent, they were [c]forgiven.

9 And their meetings were [a]conducted by the church after the manner of the workings of the Spirit, and by the [b]power of the Holy Ghost; for as the power of the Holy Ghost led them whether to preach, or to exhort, or to pray, or to supplicate, or to sing, even so it was done.

2*a* TG Sacrament.
b Luke 22:20; 1 Cor. 11:25.
c D&C 27:2 (2–4).
d TG Spirituality.

6 1*a* TG Baptism, Qualifications for.
b TG Worthiness.
2*a* TG Poor in Spirit.
b TG Contrite Heart.
3*a* 2 Ne. 9:23. TG Jesus Christ, Taking the Name of.
4*a* TG Purification.
b TG Jesus Christ, Head of the Church.
c D&C 20:82; 47:1 (1–4).
d D&C 20:53. TG Watch.
e 2 Ne. 31:19; D&C 3:20.
5*a* Acts 1:14 (13–14). TG Church.
b 3 Ne. 24:16.
c 4 Ne. 1:12; D&C 88:76.
6*a* TG Assembly for Worship; Meetings.
b TG Sacrament.
7*a* D&C 20:54.
b D&C 42:80 (80–81). TG Witness.
c Ex. 4:29; Josh. 20:4; Alma 6:1. TG Elder.
d TG Confession.
e Ex. 32:33; D&C 20:83. TG Excommunication.
f TG Book of Life.
8*a* Mosiah 26:30 (30–31).
b TG Sincere.
c TG Forgive.
9*a* D&C 20:45; 46:2.
b 1 Ne. 13:37; Moro. 3:4. TG Holy Ghost, Gifts of; Teaching with the Spirit.

CHAPTER 7

An invitation is given to enter into the rest of the Lord—Pray with real intent—The Spirit of Christ enables men to know good from evil—Satan persuades men to deny Christ and do evil—The prophets manifest the coming of Christ—By faith, miracles are wrought and angels minister—Men should hope for eternal life and cleave unto charity. About A.D. *401–21.*

AND now I, Moroni, write a few of
the words of my father Mormon,
which he spake concerning [a]faith,
hope, and charity; for after this
manner did he speak unto the people, as he taught them in the [b]syna-
gogue which they had built for the
place of worship.
2 And now I, Mormon, speak unto
you, my beloved brethren; and it
is by the [a]grace of God the Father,
and our Lord Jesus Christ, and his
holy will, because of the gift of his
[b]calling unto me, that I am permitted to speak unto you at this time.
3 Wherefore, I would speak unto
you that are of the [a]church, that are
the [b]peaceable followers of Christ,
and that have obtained a sufficient
[c]hope by which ye can enter into
the [d]rest of the Lord, from this time
henceforth until ye shall rest with
him in heaven.
4 And now my brethren, I judge
these things of you because of your
peaceable [a]walk with the children
of men.
5 For I remember the word of God
which saith by their [a]works ye shall
know them; for if their works be
good, then they are good also.
6 For behold, God hath said a man
being [a]evil cannot do that which is
good; for if he [b]offereth a gift, or
[c]prayeth unto God, except he shall
do it with real [d]intent it profiteth
him nothing.
7 For behold, it is not counted unto
him for righteousness.
8 For behold, if a man being [a]evil
giveth a gift, he doeth it [b]grudgingly;
wherefore it is counted unto him
the same as if he had retained the
gift; wherefore he is counted evil
before God.
9 And likewise also is it counted
evil unto a man, if he shall pray
and not with [a]real intent of heart;
yea, and it profiteth him nothing,
for God receiveth none such.
10 Wherefore, a man being evil
cannot do that which is good; neither will he give a good gift.
11 For behold, a bitter [a]fountain
cannot bring forth good water; neither can a good fountain bring forth
bitter water; wherefore, a man being
a servant of the devil cannot follow
Christ; and if he [b]follow Christ he
cannot be a [c]servant of the devil.
12 Wherefore, all things which
are [a]good cometh of God; and that
which is [b]evil cometh of the devil;
for the devil is an enemy unto God,
and fighteth against him continually, and inviteth and enticeth

7 1*a* 1 Cor. 13:13 (1–13); Ether 12:3 (3–37); Moro. 8:14; 10:20 (20–23).
b Alma 16:13; 3 Ne. 18:32.
2*a* TG Grace.
b 3 Ne. 5:13. TG Called of God.
3*a* TG Jesus Christ, Head of the Church.
b Acts 13:16; Rom. 16:20.
c Alma 7:16; Ether 12:4; D&C 138:14.
d TG Rest.
4*a* 1 Jn. 2:6; D&C 19:23.
5*a* 3 Ne. 14:20 (15–20).
6*a* Matt. 7:16 (15–18).
b Lev. 17:8 (8–9); D&C 132:9.
c Prov. 28:9; Alma 34:28. TG Prayer.
d Lev. 19:5. TG Hypocrisy; Motivations; Sincere.
8*a* Prov. 15:8.
b 1 Chr. 29:9; D&C 64:34.
9*a* James 1:6 (6–7); 5:16; Moro. 10:4. TG Sincere.
11*a* Prov. 13:14; James 3:11.
b Matt. 6:24; 8:19; 2 Ne. 31:10 (10–13); D&C 56:2.
c TG Servant.
12*a* Gen. 1:31; James 1:17 (17–21); 1 Jn. 4:1 (1–6); 3 Jn. 1:11 (1–14); Ether 4:12; D&C 59:17 (16–20); Moses 2:31.
b Isa. 45:7; 2 Cor. 4:4. TG Evil.

to [c]sin, and to do that which is evil
continually.
13 But behold, that which is of God
inviteth and enticeth to do [a]good
continually; wherefore, every thing
which inviteth and [b]enticeth to do
[c]good, and to love God, and to serve
him, is [d]inspired of God.
14 Wherefore, take heed, my beloved brethren, that ye do not judge
that which is [a]evil to be of God,
or that which is good and of God to
be of the devil.
15 For behold, my brethren, it is
given unto you to [a]judge, that ye
may know good from evil; and the
way to judge is as plain, that ye may
know with a perfect knowledge, as
the daylight is from the dark night.
16 For behold, the [a]Spirit of Christ
is given to every [b]man, that he may
[c]know good from evil; wherefore,
I show unto you the way to judge;
for every thing which inviteth to
do good, and to persuade to believe
in Christ, is sent forth by the power
and gift of Christ; wherefore ye may
know with a perfect knowledge it
is of God.
17 But whatsoever thing persuadeth men to do [a]evil, and believe not
in Christ, and deny him, and serve
not God, then ye may know with
a perfect knowledge it is of the
devil; for after this manner doth
the devil work, for he persuadeth
no man to do good, no, not one; neither do his angels; neither do they
who subject themselves unto him.
18 And now, my brethren, seeing
that ye know the [a]light by which
ye may judge, which light is the
light of Christ, see that ye do not
judge wrongfully; for with that
same [b]judgment which ye judge ye
shall also be judged.
19 Wherefore, I beseech of you,
brethren, that ye should search
diligently in the [a]light of Christ
that ye may know good from evil;
and if ye will lay hold upon every
good thing, and condemn it not, ye
certainly will be a [b]child of Christ.
20 And now, my brethren, how
is it possible that ye can lay hold
upon every good thing?
21 And now I come to that faith,
of which I said I would speak; and
I will tell you the way whereby ye
may lay hold on every good thing.
22 For behold, God [a]knowing all
things, being from [b]everlasting to
everlasting, behold, he sent [c]angels
to minister unto the children of
men, to make manifest concerning the coming of Christ; and in
Christ there should come every
good thing.
23 And God also declared unto
prophets, by his own mouth, that
Christ should come.
24 And behold, there were divers
ways that he did manifest things
unto the children of men, which
were good; and all things which are
good cometh of Christ; otherwise
men were [a]fallen, and there could
no good thing come unto them.

12*c* Alma 5:40 (39–42); Hel. 6:30. TG Sin.
13*a* D&C 35:12; 84:47 (47–51).
b 2 Ne. 33:4; Ether 8:26.
c TG Benevolence.
d TG Inspiration.
14*a* Isa. 5:20; 2 Ne. 15:20; D&C 64:16; 121:16.
15*a* Ezek. 44:24. TG Discernment, Spiritual.
16*a* TG Conscience; God, Spirit of; Light of Christ.
b TG Mortality.
c Gen. 3:5; Amos 5:14 (14–15); Matt. 12:33 (33–37); 2 Ne. 2:5 (5, 18, 26); Mosiah 16:3; Alma 29:5; Hel. 14:31; Ether 4:12 (11–12).
17*a* TG Sin.
18*a* Mosiah 16:9; Ether 3:14; D&C 50:24; 88:13 (7–13). TG Light of Christ.
b Luke 6:37.
19*a* D&C 84:45; 88:7 (6–13).
b Mosiah 15:10; 27:25. TG Sons and Daughters of God.
22*a* TG God, Foreknowledge of; God, Omniscience of.
b 2 Ne. 19:6; 26:12; Mosiah 3:5; Alma 11:39 (38–39, 44); Moro. 8:18. TG God, Eternal Nature of.
c Acts 10:3 (3, 22); 2 Ne. 10:3; 11:3; Jacob 7:5.
24*a* 2 Ne. 2:5.

25 Wherefore, by the ministering
of [a]angels, and by every word which
proceeded forth out of the mouth
of God, men began to exercise faith
in Christ; and thus by faith, they
did lay hold upon every good thing;
and thus it was until the coming
of Christ.
26 And after that he came men also
were [a]saved by faith in his name;
and by faith, they become the [b]sons
of God. And as surely as Christ liveth he spake these words unto our
fathers, saying: [c]Whatsoever thing
ye shall ask the Father in my name,
which is good, in faith believing that
ye shall receive, behold, it shall be
done unto you.
27 Wherefore, my beloved brethren, have [a]miracles ceased because
Christ hath ascended into heaven,
and hath sat down on the right hand
of God, to [b]claim of the Father his
rights of mercy which he hath upon
the children of men?
28 For he hath answered the ends
of the law, and he claimeth all those
who have faith in him; and they who
have faith in him will [a]cleave unto
every good thing; wherefore he [b]ad-
vocateth the cause of the children
of men; and he dwelleth eternally
in the heavens.
29 And because he hath done this,
my beloved brethren, have miracles ceased? Behold I say unto you,
Nay; neither have [a]angels ceased to
minister unto the children of men.
30 For behold, they are subject
unto him, to minister according to
the word of his command, showing
themselves unto them of strong
faith and a firm mind in every form
of [a]godliness.
31 And the office of their ministry is to call men unto repentance,
and to fulfil and to do the work of
the covenants of the Father, which
he hath made unto the children of
men, to prepare the way among the
children of men, by declaring the
word of Christ unto the [a]chosen
vessels of the Lord, that they may
bear testimony of him.
32 And by so doing, the Lord God
prepareth the way that the [a]residue
of men may have [b]faith in Christ,
that the Holy Ghost may have place
in their hearts, according to the
power thereof; and after this manner bringeth to pass the Father, the
covenants which he hath made unto
the children of men.
33 And Christ hath said: [a]If ye
will have [b]faith in me ye shall have
power to do whatsoever thing is
[c]expedient in me.
34 And he hath said: [a]Repent all
ye ends of the earth, and come unto
me, and be baptized in my name,
and have faith in me, that ye may
be saved.
35 And now, my beloved brethren,
if this be the case that these things
are true which I have spoken unto
you, and God will show unto you,
with [a]power and great glory at the
last [b]day, that they are true, and if
they are true has the day of miracles ceased?
36 Or have angels ceased to appear
unto the children of men? Or has
he [a]withheld the power of the Holy
Ghost from them? Or will he, so

25*a* Alma 12:29 (28–30);
Moses 5:58.
26*a* D&C 3:20.
b TG Sons and Daughters of God.
c 3 Ne. 18:20.
TG Prayer.
27*a* TG Miracle.
b Isa. 53:12 (11–12);
2 Ne. 2:9.
28*a* TG Motivations.
b 1 Jn. 2:1;
2 Ne. 2:9;
Mosiah 14:12; 15:8;
3 Ne. 18:35.
TG Jesus Christ, Relationships with the Father.
29*a* Judg. 13:3;
Luke 1:26;
Acts 5:19 (19–20).
TG Angels;
Miracle.
30*a* TG Godliness.
31*a* D&C 20:10.
32*a* Acts 15:17;
Moses 7:28.
b Acts 16:5;
D&C 46:14.
33*a* Moro. 10:23.
b Gal. 2:16.
TG Faith.
c D&C 88:64 (64–65).
34*a* 3 Ne. 27:20;
Ether 4:18.
35*a* 2 Ne. 33:11;
Ether 5:4 (4–6).
b Morm. 9:15;
D&C 35:8.
36*a* 1 Ne. 10:17 (17–19);
Moro. 10:7 (4–5, 7, 19).

long as time shall last, or the earth
shall stand, or there shall be one man
upon the face thereof to be saved?
37 Behold I say unto you, Nay;
for it is by faith that [a]miracles are
wrought; and it is by faith that angels appear and minister unto men;
wherefore, if these things have
ceased wo be unto the children of
men, for it is because of [b]unbelief,
and all is vain.
38 For no man can be saved, according to the words of Christ, save
they shall have faith in his name;
wherefore, if these things have
ceased, then has faith ceased also;
and awful is the state of man, for
they are as though there had been
no redemption made.
39 But behold, my beloved brethren, I judge better things of you, for
I judge that ye have faith in Christ
because of your meekness; for if ye
have not faith in him then ye are
not [a]fit to be numbered among the
people of his church.
40 And again, my beloved brethren,
I would speak unto you concerning
[a]hope. How is it that ye can attain
unto faith, save ye shall have hope?
41 And what is it that ye shall
[a]hope for? Behold I say unto you
that ye shall have [b]hope through the
atonement of Christ and the power
of his resurrection, to be raised
unto life [c]eternal, and this because
of your faith in him according to
the promise.
42 Wherefore, if a man have [a]faith
he [b]must needs have hope; for without faith there cannot be any hope.
43 And again, behold I say unto
you that he cannot have faith and
hope, save he shall be [a]meek, and
lowly of heart.
44 If so, his [a]faith and hope is vain,
for none is [b]acceptable before God,
save the [c]meek and lowly in heart;
and if a man be meek and lowly in
heart, and [d]confesses by the power
of the Holy Ghost that Jesus is the
Christ, he must needs have charity; for if he have not charity he is
nothing; wherefore he must needs
have charity.
45 And [a]charity suffereth long, and
is [b]kind, and [c]envieth not, and is not
puffed up, seeketh not her own, is
not easily [d]provoked, thinketh no
evil, and rejoiceth not in iniquity
but rejoiceth in the truth, beareth
all things, believeth all things, hop-
eth all things, endureth all things.
46 Wherefore, my beloved brethren, if ye have not charity, ye are
nothing, for charity never faileth.
Wherefore, cleave unto charity,
which is the greatest of all, for all
things must fail—
47 But [a]charity is the pure [b]love
of Christ, and it endureth [c]forever;
and whoso is found possessed of
it at the last day, it shall be well
with him.
48 Wherefore, my beloved brethren, [a]pray unto the Father with all
the energy of heart, that ye may be
filled with this love, which he hath
bestowed upon all who are true
[b]followers of his Son, Jesus Christ;
that ye may become the sons of
God; that when he shall appear we

37*a* Matt. 13:58; Morm. 8:26; 9:20; Ether 12:12 (12–18).
b Moro. 10:19 (19–27).
39*a* TG Worthiness.
40*a* Heb. 11:1; Ether 12:4. TG Hope.
41*a* D&C 138:14.
b Zech. 9:12 (11–12); Titus 1:2; Jacob 2:19; Alma 46:39.
c TG Eternal Life.
42*a* TG Faith.
b Moro. 10:20.
43*a* TG Humility.
44*a* 1 Cor. 13:13 (1–13); Alma 7:24; Ether 12:31 (28–35).
b Lev. 10:19.
c TG Meek.
d Luke 12:8 (8–9). TG Holy Ghost, Gifts of; Testimony.
45*a* 1 Cor. 13:4 (1–13).
b TG Kindness.
c TG Envy.
d TG Provoking.
47*a* Rom. 13:10; 2 Ne. 26:30. TG Charity.
b Josh. 22:5; Ether 12:34; Moro. 7:48. TG Love.
c TG Eternity.
48*a* TG Communication; Prayer.
b TG Jesus Christ, Exemplar.

shall [c]be like him, for we shall see
him as he is; that we may have this
hope; that we may be [d]purified even
as he is pure. Amen.

CHAPTER 8

The baptism of little children is an evil abomination—Little children are alive in Christ because of the Atonement—Faith, repentance, meekness and lowliness of heart, receiving the Holy Ghost, and enduring to the end lead to salvation. About A.D. 401–21.

AN epistle of my [a]father Mormon,
written to me, Moroni; and it was
written unto me soon after my calling to the ministry. And on this
wise did he write unto me, saying:
2 My beloved son, Moroni, I rejoice
exceedingly that your Lord Jesus
Christ hath been mindful of you,
and hath called you to his ministry,
and to his holy work.
3 I am mindful of you always in
my prayers, continually praying
unto God the Father in the name
of his Holy Child, Jesus, that he,
through his infinite [a]goodness and
[b]grace, will keep you through the
endurance of faith on his name to
the end.
4 And now, my son, I speak unto
you concerning that which grieveth me exceedingly; for it grieveth
me that there should [a]disputations
rise among you.
5 For, if I have learned the truth,
there have been disputations among
you concerning the baptism of your
little children.
6 And now, my son, I desire that
ye should labor diligently, that this
gross error should be removed from
among you; for, for this intent I have
written this epistle.
7 For immediately after I had
learned these things of you I inquired of the Lord concerning the
matter. And the [a]word of the Lord
came to me by the power of the
Holy Ghost, saying:
8 [a]Listen to the words of Christ,
your Redeemer, your Lord and
your God. Behold, I came into the
world not to call the righteous but
sinners to repentance; the [b]whole
need no physician, but they that are
sick; wherefore, little [c]children are
[d]whole, for they are not capable
of committing [e]sin; wherefore the
curse of [f]Adam is taken from them
in me, that it hath no power over
them; and the law of [g]circumcision
is done away in me.
9 And after this manner did the
Holy Ghost manifest the word of
God unto me; wherefore, my beloved son, I know that it is solemn
[a]mockery before God, that ye should
baptize little children.
10 Behold I say unto you that this
thing shall ye teach—repentance
and baptism unto those who are
[a]accountable and capable of committing sin; yea, teach parents that
they must repent and be baptized,
and humble themselves as their
little [b]children, and they shall all
be saved with their little children.
11 And their little [a]children need
no repentance, neither baptism. Behold, baptism is unto repentance to
the fulfilling the commandments
unto the [b]remission of sins.
12 But little [a]children are alive in
Christ, even from the foundation of
the world; if not so, God is a partial

48*c* 1 Jn. 3:2 (1–3); 3 Ne. 27:27.
d 3 Ne. 19:28 (28–29). TG Cleanliness; Purity.
8 1*a* W of M 1:1.
3*a* Ex. 34:6 (5–7); Mosiah 4:11.
b TG Grace.
4*a* TG Disputations.
7*a* TG Word of the Lord.
8*a* D&C 15:1.
b Mark 2:17.
c Mark 10:14 (13–16). TG Conceived in Sin.
d Mosiah 3:16; D&C 29:46; 74:7.
e TG Sin.
f Mosiah 3:16; Morm. 9:12.
g Gen. 17:11 (10–27); Acts 15:24. TG Circumcision.
9*a* 2 Ne. 31:13.
10*a* TG Accountability.
b TG Family, Children, Responsibilities toward; Family, Love within.
11*a* TG Baptism, Qualifications for; Children.
b TG Remission of Sins.
12*a* D&C 29:46; 93:38.

God, and also a changeable God,
and a [b]respecter to persons; for
how many little children have died
without baptism!
13 Wherefore, if little children
could not be saved without baptism, these must have gone to an
endless hell.
14 Behold I say unto you, that he
that supposeth that little children
need baptism is in the gall of bitterness and in the bonds of iniquity;
for he hath neither [a]faith, hope,
nor charity; wherefore, should he
be cut off while in the thought, he
must go down to hell.
15 For awful is the wickedness to
suppose that God saveth one child
because of baptism, and the other
must perish because he hath no
baptism.
16 Wo be unto them that shall
pervert the ways of the Lord after
this manner, for they shall perish
except they repent. Behold, I speak
with boldness, having [a]authority
from God; and I fear not what man
can do; for [b]perfect [c]love [d]casteth
out all fear.
17 And I am filled with [a]charity,
which is everlasting love; wherefore, all children are alike unto
me; wherefore, I love little children
with a perfect love; and they are all
alike and [b]partakers of salvation.
18 For I know that God is not a
partial God, neither a changeable
being; but he is [a]unchangeable from
[b]all eternity to all eternity.
19 Little [a]children cannot repent;
wherefore, it is awful wickedness to
deny the pure mercies of God unto
them, for they are all alive in him
because of his [b]mercy.
20 And he that saith that little
children need baptism denieth
the mercies of Christ, and setteth
at naught the [a]atonement of him
and the power of his redemption.
21 Wo unto such, for they are in
danger of death, [a]hell, and an [b]end-
less torment. I speak it boldly; God
hath commanded me. Listen unto
them and give heed, or they stand
against you at the [c]judgment-seat
of Christ.
22 For behold that all little children are [a]alive in Christ, and also all
they that are without the [b]law. For
the power of [c]redemption cometh on
all them that have [d]no law; wherefore, he that is not condemned, or
he that is under no condemnation,
cannot repent; and unto such baptism availeth nothing—
23 But it is mockery before God,
denying the mercies of Christ, and
the power of his Holy Spirit, and
putting trust in [a]dead works.
24 Behold, my son, this thing
ought not to be; for [a]repentance is
unto them that are under condemnation and under the curse of a
broken law.
25 And the first fruits of [a]repen-
tance is [b]baptism; and baptism
cometh by faith unto the fulfilling
the commandments; and the fulfilling the commandments bringeth
[c]remission of sins;
26 And the remission of sins
bringeth [a]meekness, and lowliness
of heart; and because of meekness
and lowliness of heart cometh the

12*b* Eph. 6:9;
D&C 38:16.
14*a* 1 Cor. 13:13 (1–13);
Ether 12:3 (3–37);
Moro. 7:1; 10:20 (20–23).
16*a* TG Authority.
b TG Perfection.
c TG Love.
d 1 Jn. 4:18.
17*a* TG Charity.
b Mosiah 3:16 (16–19).
18*a* Alma 7:20;
Morm. 9:9.
TG God, Perfection of.
b Moro. 7:22.
19*a* Luke 18:16 (15–17).
b TG God, Mercy of.
20*a* TG Jesus Christ,
Atonement through;
Salvation, Plan of.
21*a* TG Hell.
b Jacob 6:10;
Mosiah 28:3;
D&C 19:12 (10–12).
c TG Jesus Christ, Judge.
22*a* TG Salvation of Little
Children.
b Acts 17:30.
c TG Redemption.
d TG Accountability.
23*a* D&C 22:2.
24*a* TG Repent.
25*a* TG Baptism,
Qualifications for.
b Moses 6:60.
c D&C 76:52.
TG Remission of Sins.
26*a* TG Meek.

visitation of the [b]Holy Ghost, which
[c]Comforter [d]filleth with hope and
perfect [e]love, which love endureth
by [f]diligence unto [g]prayer, until the
end shall come, when all the [h]saints
shall dwell with God.
27 Behold, my son, I will write
unto you again if I go not out soon
against the Lamanites. Behold, the
[a]pride of this nation, or the people
of the Nephites, hath proven their
destruction except they should
repent.
28 Pray for them, my son, that
repentance may come unto them.
But behold, I fear lest the Spirit
hath [a]ceased [b]striving with them;
and in this part of the land they
are also seeking to put down all
power and authority which cometh
from God; and they are [c]denying
the Holy Ghost.
29 And after rejecting so great a
knowledge, my son, they must perish soon, unto the fulfilling of the
prophecies which were spoken by
the prophets, as well as the words
of our Savior himself.
30 Farewell, my son, until I shall
write unto you, or shall meet you
again. Amen.

The second epistle of Mormon to his son Moroni.

Comprising chapter 9.

CHAPTER 9

Both the Nephites and the Lamanites are depraved and degenerate—They torture and murder each other—Mormon prays that grace and goodness may rest upon Moroni forever. About A.D. 401.

MY beloved son, I write unto you
again that ye may know that I am
yet alive; but I write somewhat of
that which is grievous.
2 For behold, I have had a sore battle with the Lamanites, in which we
did not conquer; and Archeantus has
fallen by the sword, and also Luram
and Emron; yea, and we have lost
a great number of our choice men.
3 And now behold, my son, I fear
lest the Lamanites shall destroy this
people; for they do not repent, and
Satan stirreth them up continually
to [a]anger one with another.
4 Behold, I am laboring with them
continually; and when I speak the
word of God with [a]sharpness they
tremble and anger against me; and
when I use no sharpness they [b]harden their hearts against it; wherefore, I fear lest the Spirit of the Lord
hath ceased [c]striving with them.
5 For so exceedingly do they anger
that it seemeth me that they have
no fear of death; and they have lost
their love, one towards another; and
they [a]thirst after blood and revenge
continually.
6 And now, my beloved son, notwithstanding their hardness, let us
labor [a]diligently; for if we should
cease to [b]labor, we should be brought
under condemnation; for we have a
labor to perform whilst in this tabernacle of clay, that we may conquer
the enemy of all righteousness, and
rest our souls in the kingdom of God.
7 And now I write somewhat concerning the sufferings of this people.

26*b* TG Holy Ghost, Baptism of.
c TG Holy Ghost, Comforter; Holy Ghost, Mission of.
d 1 Ne. 11:22 (22–25). TG Hope.
e 1 Pet. 1:22.
f TG Diligence; Perseverance.
g TG Prayer.
h TG Saints.
27*a* D&C 38:39. TG Pride.
28*a* TG Holy Ghost, Loss of.
b Morm. 5:16; Moro. 9:4.
c Alma 39:6. TG Holy Ghost, Unpardonable Sin against.
9 3*a* TG Anger.
4*a* 2 Ne. 1:26 (26–27); W of M 1:17; D&C 121:43 (41–43).
b TG Hardheartedness.
c Moro. 8:28; D&C 1:33.
5*a* Morm. 4:11 (11–12).
6*a* TG Dedication; Diligence; Perseverance.
b 1 Sam. 8:9; 2 Cor. 5:9; Jacob 1:19; Enos 1:20. TG Duty; Priesthood, Magnifying Callings within.

For according to the knowledge
which I have received from Amoron,
behold, the Lamanites have many
prisoners, which they took from the
tower of Sherrizah; and there were
men, women, and children.
8 And the husbands and fathers
of those women and children they
have slain; and they feed the women
upon the [a]flesh of their husbands,
and the children upon the flesh of
their fathers; and no water, save a
little, do they give unto them.
9 And notwithstanding this great
[a]abomination of the Lamanites, it
doth not exceed that of our people
in Moriantum. For behold, many of
the daughters of the Lamanites have
they taken prisoners; and after [b]de-
priving them of that which was most
dear and precious above all things,
which is [c]chastity and [d]virtue—
10 And after they had done this
thing, they did murder them in a
most [a]cruel manner, torturing their
bodies even unto death; and after
they have done this, they devour
their flesh like unto wild beasts,
because of the hardness of their
hearts; and they do it for a token of
bravery.
11 O my beloved son, how can a
people like this, that are without
civilization—
12 (And only a few years have
passed away, and they were a civil
and a delightsome people)
13 But O my son, how can a people like this, whose [a]delight is in
so much abomination—
14 How can we expect that God
will [a]stay his hand in judgment
against us?
15 Behold, my heart cries: Wo
unto this people. Come out in judgment, O God, and hide their sins,
and wickedness, and abominations
from before thy face!
16 And again, my son, there are
many [a]widows and their daughters
who remain in Sherrizah; and that
part of the provisions which the
Lamanites did not carry away, behold, the army of Zenephi has carried away, and left them to wander
whithersoever they can for food;
and many old women do faint by
the way and die.
17 And the army which is with
me is weak; and the armies of the
Lamanites are betwixt Sherrizah
and me; and as many as have fled
to the army of [a]Aaron have fallen
victims to their awful brutality.
18 O the depravity of my people! They are without [a]order and
without mercy. Behold, I am but a
man, and I have but the [b]strength
of a man, and I cannot any longer
enforce my commands.
19 And they have become strong
in their perversion; and they are
alike brutal, sparing none, neither
old nor young; and they delight in
everything save that which is good;
and the suffering of our women and
our children upon all the face of
this land doth exceed everything;
yea, tongue cannot tell, neither can
it be written.
20 And now, my son, I dwell no
longer upon this horrible scene.
Behold, thou knowest the wickedness of this people; thou knowest
that they are without principle,
and past feeling; and their wickedness doth [a]exceed that of the
Lamanites.
21 Behold, my son, I cannot rec-
ommend them unto God lest he
should smite me.
22 But behold, my son, I recom-
mend thee unto God, and I trust in
Christ that thou wilt be saved; and
I [a]pray unto God that he will [b]spare
thy life, to witness the return of his

8*a* Lev. 26:29; 1 Ne. 21:26.
9*a* TG Body, Sanctity of.
b TG Sensuality.
c TG Chastity.
d TG Virtue.
10*a* TG Cruelty.
13*a* 2 Ne. 9:9 (8–9); Jacob 3:11.
14*a* 2 Sam. 24:16; Alma 10:23.
16*a* Mosiah 21:10 (10, 17). TG Widows.
17*a* Morm. 2:9.
18*a* TG Order.
b TG Strength.
20*a* Hel. 6:34 (18–35).
22*a* W of M 1:8.
b Morm. 8:3.

people unto him, or their utter destruction; for I know that they must perish except they [c]repent and return unto him.

23 And if they perish it will be like unto the [a]Jaredites, because of the wilfulness of their hearts, [b]seeking for blood and [c]revenge.

24 And if it so be that they perish, we know that many of our brethren have [a]deserted over unto the Lamanites, and many more will also desert over unto them; wherefore, write somewhat a few things, if thou art spared and I shall perish and not see thee; but I trust that I may see thee soon; for I have sacred records that I would [b]deliver up unto thee.

25 My son, be faithful in Christ; and may not the things which I have written grieve thee, to weigh thee down unto [a]death; but may Christ lift thee up, and may his sufferings and death, and the showing his body unto our fathers, and his mercy and [b]long-suffering, and the hope of his glory and of eternal life, rest in your [c]mind forever.

26 And may the grace of God the Father, whose throne is high in the heavens, and our Lord Jesus Christ, who sitteth on the [a]right hand of his power, until all things shall become subject unto him, be, and abide with you forever. Amen.

CHAPTER 10

A testimony of the Book of Mormon comes by the power of the Holy Ghost—The gifts of the Spirit are dispensed to the faithful—Spiritual gifts always accompany faith—Moroni's words speak from the dust—Come unto Christ, be perfected in Him, and sanctify your souls. About A.D. *421.*

Now I, Moroni, write somewhat as seemeth me good; and I write unto my brethren, the [a]Lamanites; and I would that they should know that more than [b]four hundred and twenty years have passed away since the sign was given of the coming of Christ.

2 And I [a]seal up [b]these records, after I have spoken a few words by way of exhortation unto you.

3 Behold, I would exhort you that when ye shall read these things, if it be wisdom in God that ye should read them, that ye would remember how [a]merciful the Lord hath been unto the children of men, from the creation of Adam even down until the time that ye shall receive these things, and [b]ponder it in your [c]hearts.

4 And when ye shall receive these things, I would exhort you that ye would [a]ask God, the Eternal Father, in the name of Christ, if these things are not [b]true; and if ye shall ask with a [c]sincere heart, with [d]real intent, having [e]faith in Christ, he will [f]manifest the [g]truth of it unto you, by the power of the Holy Ghost.

5 And by the power of the Holy Ghost ye may [a]know the [b]truth of all things.

6 And whatsoever thing is good is

22*c* 1 Sam. 7:3; Hel. 13:11; 3 Ne. 10:6 (5–7); 24:7.
23*a* Jacob 5:44.
b Morm. 4:11 (11–12).
c Ether 15:22 (15–31).
24*a* Alma 45:14.
b Morm. 6:6; 8:1.
25*a* TG Jesus Christ, Death of.
b TG Forbear.
c TG Mind.
26*a* TG Jesus Christ, Relationships with the Father.
10 1*a* D&C 10:48.
b Morm. 8:5; Moro. 1:1.
2*a* Morm. 5:12; 8:4 (4, 13–14). TG Scriptures, Preservation of; Seal.
b Morm. 6:6.
3*a* Gen. 19:16.
b Deut. 11:18. TG Meditation; Study.
c Deut. 6:6.
4*a* TG Prayer.
b 1 Ne. 13:39; 14:30; Mosiah 1:6; Alma 3:12; Ether 4:11 (6–11); 5:3 (1–4). TG Book of Mormon.
c TG Honesty; Sincere.
d James 1:5 (5–7); Moro. 7:9.
e TG Faith.
f TG Revelation.
g Ps. 145:18. TG Guidance, Divine; Truth.
5*a* D&C 35:19. TG Discernment, Spiritual; Holy Ghost, Source of Testimony.
b John 8:32.

just and true; wherefore, nothing
that is good denieth the Christ, but
acknowledgeth that he is.
7 And ye may [a]know that he is, by
the power of the Holy Ghost; wherefore I would exhort you that ye deny
not the power of God; for he worketh
by power, [b]according to the faith
of the children of men, the same
today and tomorrow, and forever.
8 And again, I exhort you, my
brethren, that ye deny not the
[a]gifts of God, for they are many;
and they come from the same God.
And there are [b]different ways that
these gifts are administered; but it
is the same God who worketh all in
all; and they are given by the manifestations of the [c]Spirit of God unto
men, to profit them.
9 [a]For behold, to one is given by
the Spirit of God, that he may [b]teach
the word of wisdom;
10 And to another, that he may
[a]teach the word of [b]knowledge by
the same Spirit;
11 And to another, exceedingly
great [a]faith; and to another, the
gifts of [b]healing by the same Spirit;
12 And again, to another, that he
may work mighty [a]miracles;
13 And again, to another, that he
may prophesy concerning all things;
14 And again, to another, the beholding of angels and ministering
spirits;
15 And again, to another, all kinds
of tongues;
16 And again, to another, the interpretation of [a]languages and of
divers kinds of tongues.
17 And all these gifts come by the
Spirit of Christ; and they come unto
every man severally, according as
he will.
18 And I would exhort you, my
beloved brethren, that ye remember that [a]every good [b]gift cometh
of Christ.
19 And I would exhort you, my
beloved brethren, that ye remember that he is the [a]same yesterday,
today, and forever, and that all
these gifts of which I have spoken,
which are spiritual, never will be
done away, even as long as the world
shall stand, only according to the
[b]unbelief of the children of men.
20 Wherefore, there must be [a]faith;
and if there must be faith there must
also be hope; and if there must be
hope there must also be charity.
21 And except ye have [a]charity
ye can in nowise be saved in the
kingdom of God; neither can ye be
saved in the kingdom of God if ye
have not faith; neither can ye if
ye have no hope.
22 And if ye have no hope ye must
needs be in [a]despair; and despair
cometh because of iniquity.
23 And Christ truly said unto our
fathers: [a]If ye have faith ye can do
all things which are expedient unto
me.
24 And now I speak unto all the
ends of the earth—that if the day
cometh that the power and gifts of
God shall be done away among you,
it shall be [a]because of [b]unbelief.
25 And wo be unto the children
of men if this be the case; for there
shall be [a]none that doeth good
among you, no not one. For if there

7*a* TG Testimony.
b 1 Ne. 10:17 (17–19); Moro. 7:36.
8*a* TG God, Gifts of; Holy Ghost, Gifts of.
b D&C 46:15.
c TG God, Spirit of.
9*a* 1 Cor. 12:8 (8–11); D&C 46:12 (8–30).
b Ex. 35:34; D&C 38:23; 88:77 (77–79, 118); 107:85 (85–89).
10*a* TG Education.
b 1 Cor. 12:8. TG Learn.
11*a* TG Faith.
b TG Heal.
12*a* TG Miracle.
16*a* TG Language.
18*a* James 1:17.
b TG Talents.
19*a* Heb. 13:8.
b Moro. 7:37. TG Doubt.
20*a* 1 Cor. 13:13 (1–13); Ether 12:3 (3–37); Moro. 7:1, 42 (42–44); 8:14.
21*a* TG Charity.
22*a* TG Despair.
23*a* Moro. 7:33.
24*a* Moro. 7:37.
b TG Doubt; Unbelief.
25*a* Ps. 14:3; Rom. 3:12.

be one among you that doeth good,
he shall work by the power and
gifts of God.
26 And wo unto them who shall
do these things away and die, for
they [a]die in their [b]sins, and they
cannot be saved in the kingdom
of God; and I speak it according to
the words of Christ; and I lie not.
27 And I exhort you to remember
these things; for the time speedily
cometh that ye shall know that I
lie not, for ye shall see me at the
bar of God; and the Lord God will
say unto you: Did I not declare my
[a]words unto you, which were written by this man, like as one [b]cry-
ing from the dead, yea, even as one
speaking out of the [c]dust?
28 I declare these things unto the
fulfilling of the prophecies. And
behold, they shall proceed forth
out of the mouth of the everlasting
God; and his word shall [a]hiss forth
from generation to generation.
29 And God shall show unto you,
that that which I have written is
[a]true.
30 And again I would exhort you
that ye would [a]come unto Christ,
and lay hold upon every good [b]gift,
and [c]touch not the evil gift, nor the
[d]unclean thing.
31 And [a]awake, and arise from the
dust, O Jerusalem; yea, and put on
thy beautiful garments, O daughter of [b]Zion; and [c]strengthen thy
[d]stakes and enlarge thy borders forever, that thou mayest [e]no more be
confounded, that the covenants of
the Eternal Father which he hath
made unto thee, O house of Israel,
may be fulfilled.
32 Yea, [a]come unto Christ, and be
[b]perfected in him, and [c]deny yourselves of all ungodliness; and if ye
shall deny yourselves of all ungodliness, and [d]love God with all your
might, mind and strength, then is
his grace sufficient for you, that
by his grace ye may be [e]perfect in
Christ; and if by the grace of God
ye are perfect in Christ, ye can in
nowise deny the power of God.
33 And again, if ye by the grace of
God are perfect in Christ, and deny
not his power, then are ye [a]sancti-
fied in Christ by the grace of God,
through the shedding of the [b]blood
of Christ, which is in the covenant
of the Father unto the remission of
your [c]sins, that ye become [d]holy,
without spot.
34 And now I bid unto all, farewell.
I soon go to [a]rest in the [b]paradise
of God, until my [c]spirit and body
shall again [d]reunite, and I am
brought forth triumphant through
the [e]air, to meet you before the [f]pleas-
ing bar of the great [g]Jehovah, the
Eternal [h]Judge of both quick and
dead. Amen.

26*a* Ezek. 18:26; 1 Ne. 15:33 (32–33); Mosiah 15:26.
b John 8:21 (21–24).
27*a* Isa. 51:16; 2 Ne. 33:10 (10–11); D&C 1:24.
b 2 Ne. 3:19 (19–20); 27:13; 33:13 (13–15); Morm. 9:30.
c Isa. 29:4.
28*a* 2 Ne. 29:2.
29*a* TG Book of Mormon.
30*a* 1 Ne. 6:4; Morm. 9:27; Ether 5:5.
b TG Talents.
c 2 Ne. 18:19.
d TG Uncleanness.
31*a* Isa. 52:1 (1–2). TG Israel, Restoration of.
b TG Zion.
c Isa. 54:2. TG Priesthood, Power of.
d TG Stake.
e Ether 13:8.
32*a* Rev. 22:17 (17–21); Jacob 1:7; Omni 1:26. TG Teachable.
b Gal. 3:24; Philip. 3:15 (14–15). TG Man, New, Spiritually Reborn; Worthiness.
c Rom. 12:1 (1–3). TG Perseverance.
d Deut. 11:1; Mosiah 2:4; D&C 20:19; 59:5 (5–6). TG Commitment; Dedication.
e Rom. 6:6 (1–7). TG Perfection.
33*a* TG Sanctification.
b TG Jesus Christ, Atonement through.
c Ex. 34:7.
d TG Holiness.
34*a* TG Rest.
b TG Paradise.
c TG Spirit Body.
d TG Resurrection.
e 1 Thes. 4:17.
f Jacob 6:13.
g TG Jesus Christ, Jehovah.
h TG Jesus Christ, Judge.

THE END